Forde Abbey Gardens, Dorset © Carole Drake

172

High Glanau Manor, Gwent © Val Corbett

680

Knitson Old Farmhouse, Dorset © Louise Jolley

175

Contents

D1387465

ngs gardens open for charity

The National Gardens Scheme
A company limited by guarantee. Registered in England & Wales.
Charity No. 1112664. Company No. 5631421

Registered & Head Office: Hatchlands Park, East Clandon,
Guildford, Surrey, GU4 7RT

T 01483 211535
Web www.ngs.org.uk

© The National Gardens Scheme 2016

Published by Constable, an imprint of Little, Brown Book Group,
Carmelite House, 50 Victoria Embankment, London EC4Y 0DZ
An Hachette UK Company
www.hachette.co.uk
www.littlebrown.co.uk

Front cover image: Cerney House, Gloucestershire
Photographer: Val Corbett

When I talk to people about the National Gardens Scheme and explain what it does, the two things that they are fascinated by are the sheer number of gardens that open and the scale of the charitable donations.

This year some 3,800 gardens will open in support of the Scheme, starting in early February to show often breath-taking carpets of snowdrops and continuing right through to the end of October with dramatic displays of Autumn colour. In the middle is a mid-Summer peak when anything from 300 to 400 gardens will open every weekend. This is an amazing feat of organization that no other garden-opening operation can match.

Given the volume of gardens opening, it is equally impressive that the standards remain uncompromised. Quality has always been a watchword of the National Gardens Scheme throughout its long life and as it approaches the landmark of its 90th anniversary in 2017, this is something I know we will all be celebrating. There is a particular magic in arriving to visit a garden about which you previously knew nothing, somewhere with no public reputation, and being bowled over by what you discover once you are through the gate.

Of course, the enjoyment offered to visitors is only half the story. The very fact that the National Gardens Scheme is the largest single benefactor of Macmillan Cancer Support, of which I am also Patron, illustrates emphatically the scale of the Scheme's contribution to nursing and caring in this country as a result of its annual donations.

The annual total of more than £2.5 million that is currently being donated is made up of thousands of contributions from gardens large and small. It is the fundraising part of a remarkable story that I hope many more people will hear about and, as a result, perhaps visit a garden and support this unique organization.

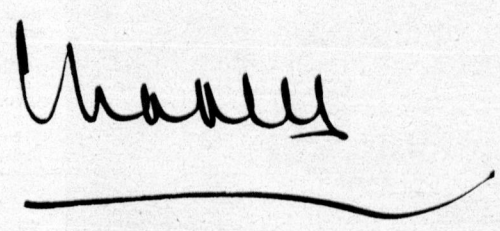

Who's Who

Patron
HRH The Prince of Wales

President
Joe Swift (retiring)

Vice-Presidents
Elizabeth Anton
Mrs Angela Azis
Ann Budden
Fred Carr
Daphne Foulsham MBE
Carolyn Hardy OBE VMH
Nicholas Payne OBE
Penny Snell
Michael Toynbee DL
Ann Trevor-Jones MBE

Ambassadors
Emma Bridgewater CBE
Alan Gray

Chairman
A Martin McMillan OBE

Deputy Chairman
Heather Skinner

Hon Treasurer
Andrew Ratcliffe

Trustees
Miranda Allhusen
Peter Clay
Susan Copeland
Rosamund Davies
Biddy Marshall
Colin Olle
Sue Phipps
Patrick Ramsay
Sir Richard Thompson KCVO
Rupert Tyler

Chief Executive
George Plumptre

Chairman's Message

I am delighted to report that 2015 was a record year for the National Gardens Scheme, despite the weather not being as continuously good as it was in 2014.

As the country's biggest charitable benefactor to the nursing and caring sectors we are now beginning to increase the public's awareness of our work which hopefully will further grow our audience of visitors to even greater numbers and in turn enable us to be able to increase the grants to our family of charitable causes.

This year again, our guide lists numerous potential days out visiting our lovely gardens – the great majority of which open exclusively to support the NGS, for which we are immensely grateful. Most gardens offer gorgeous teas so you can really indulge yourselves, knowing that in doing so you are directly supporting our beneficiaries.

Thank you to Investec Wealth & Investment, our core sponsor and to you, all garden owners and visitors. Enjoy.

Martin McMillan, OBE

Above: Martin and Pat McMillan at Chelsea Flower Show 2015 © Marcus Harpur

How to use your *Gardens to Visit 2016*

This book lists all gardens opening for the NGS between January 2016 and early 2017. It is divided up into county sections, each including a calendar of opening dates and details of each garden, listed alphabetically.

There are three simple ways to find gardens to visit:

1 If you are looking for a specific garden, you can look it up in the index at the back, or if you know which county it is in, you can go straight to the relevant county section.

2 If you want to find out more about gardens near you or in a specific location, go to the relevant county map (at the front of each section) and look for the numbered markers. Use those numbers to look up further information in the county listings.

3 If you are looking to see what is open near you on a specific date, go straight to the relevant county. There is a calendar of opening dates after each county introduction page.

Images and longer descriptions of over 3,800 gardens that will open this year on behalf of the National Gardens Scheme can be found by visiting: **www.ngs.org.uk**

County name
Gardens in England are listed first, followed
by gardens in Wales.

Directions
A simple set of directions to each garden.
Most gardens also list postcodes for use with
computer or satellite navigation systems.

Admission price
The admission price applies to all visitors
unless exceptions are noted e.g. child free

Group opening information
Showing gardens that open together on
the same day or days.

Description
A short description of each garden covers
the main features. This is written by the
garden owner.

Symbols explained

NEW Gardens opening for the first
time this year or re-opening after a
long break.

◆ Garden also opens on non-NGS
days. (Gardens which carry this
symbol contribute to the NGS either
by opening on a specific day(s) and/or
by giving a guaranteed contribution.)

♿ Wheelchair access to at least the
main features of the garden.

🐕 Dogs on short leads welcome.

❀ Plants usually for sale.

NCH Plant Heritage National Plant
Collection.

🛏 Gardens that offer
accommodation.

☕ Refreshments are available,
normally at a charge.

D Garden designed by a Fellow,
Member or Pre-registered Member of
The Society of Garden Designers.

🚌 Garden accessible to coaches.
Coach sizes vary so please contact
garden owner or County Organiser
in advance to check details.

Group Visits Group Organisers may
contact the County Organiser or a
garden owner direct to organise a
group visit to a particular county or
garden. See the front of each county
section for County Organiser contact
details, or visit www.ngs.org.uk

Children must be accompanied by
an adult

Photography is at the discretion of
the garden owner; please check first.
Photographs must not be used for
sale or reproduction without prior
permission of the owner.

Donation To indicates that a
proportion of the money collected will
be given to the nominated charity.

**Toilets are not usually available at
private gardens**

**If you cannot find the information
you require from a garden or
County Organiser, call the NGS
office on 01483 211535**

" Investec wishes
everyone involved with the
National Gardens Scheme
a successful 2016. "

Jonathan Wragg
Chief Executive, Investec Wealth & Investment

Wealth & Investment. Tending to your future

We focus on developing strong relationships with our clients and providing the highest standards of personal service. Across a network of 15 offices, over 50,000 clients in the UK entrust us with over £26bn* of their wealth. For a fresh perspective on your wealth, call us today.

Please bear in mind that the value of investments and the income derived from them can go down as well as up and that you may not get back the amount that you have invested.

For more information on how we have supported The National Gardens Scheme please visit **investecwin.co.uk/ngs**

Opening Gardens to Raise £millions for Nursing and Caring

The National Gardens Scheme is one of the most significant charitable funders of nursing and caring in the UK and the money is all raised by private individuals opening their gardens

In 1927, the NGS's first year, 600 gardens opened, they all charged one shilling and they raised a total of £8,000. Last year, 2015, 3,800 gardens opened and raised more than £3 million.

Funds are donated to our beneficiaries annually. How much we are able to give away is driven by the number of visitors that go to the gardens. So by visiting a garden that opens on behalf of the National Gardens Scheme you can really make a difference and help raise much needed money.

We pride ourselves on the quality of our gardens. At the same time, the variety is breathtaking: from village openings to roof gardens, tiny cottage gardens to rolling acres, allotments to barges, you will find gardens to inform and inspire. And you will want to visit more.

Since our foundation we have donated well over £40 million to

NGS beneficiaries past and present. **Above:** a Queen's Nurse administering to children in 1949 **Below:** the new NGS Macmillan Wellbeing Centre that will be opened in Chesterfield in 2016

our beneficiaries and currently donate in excess of £2.5 million every year. The physical and mental health benefits of visiting gardens and gardening, are very real and form an increasingly significant link between NGS and its beneficiaries.

It is integral to our charitable heritage to actively develop partnerships with our beneficiaries. Working together with them for the maximum benefit for all of our audiences and to provide the lead on the link between gardens and people's wellbeing is a major priority for us all.

The National Gardens Scheme's commitment to nursing and caring remains constant and we are working increasingly closely with our beneficiaries to maximise the amounts we are able to give and the effect that the funds have.

Qni The Queen's Nursing Institute

The Queen's Nursing Institute founded the National Gardens Scheme in the 1920s, to raise money to support district nursing and the two charities have developed strong ties and a shared heritage ever since. As the Scheme grew through the post-war years it continued to be run directly as part of the Queen's Nursing Institute until it was set up as an independent charity in 1980.

Today the Queen's Nursing Institute works to improve nursing services for patients in their own homes and communities. We believe that skilled and compassionate nursing should be available to everyone, where and when they need it. We achieve this through our network of Queen's Nurses who are experts in delivering care, benefiting the patients and the communities they serve.

It was a trustee of The Queen's Nursing Institute, Elsie Wagge, whose idea it was to open gardens for charity back in 1927. The idea was so successful it grew year on year and became the National Gardens Scheme.

To this day the NGS remains the QNI's biggest and most important funder, enabling us to improve nurse education and supporting nurses to deliver excellent patient care in people's homes and communities around the country.

We are passionate about the value of garden visiting to improve the physical and mental health of patients, families and carers, at all stages of life. Our Queen's Nurses are champions of excellent patient care and are also regular visitors to NGS gardens themselves.

Dr Crystal Oldman, Chief Executive

NFU Mutual
HOME INSURANCE

30% OFF
HOME INSURANCE
IF YOU HAVEN'T CLAIMED IN 4 YEARS

And if you come to claim,
there are no forms and
no quibbles.

You won't find us on comparison sites.
For a home insurance quote call us on

0800 197 1283

nfumutual.co.uk

WE ARE MACMILLAN. CANCER SUPPORT

The NGS is Macmillan's largest single donor having donated an incredible £15.2 million since the partnership first took root in 1985. Since then, the NGS has funded 147 Macmillan professional posts, this and the NGS's funding of Macmillan services has helped Macmillan ensure that no one has to face cancer alone.

There are 2.5 million people living with cancer in the UK today, and as more people live longer with their cancer, this number is set to grow to 4 million by 2030. At Macmillan we want to make sure we can provide support to everyone who needs it, to help people affected by cancer feel more in control of their lives.

We are extremely proud of our longstanding partnership with the National Gardens Scheme which has gone from strength to strength over the last 30 years. In this time they have raised a fantastic £15.2 million. This has been achieved with the support of the amazing NGS garden owners and volunteers, who have given their time and passion to make a difference to the lives of people affected by cancer.

We are delighted to be in partnership with the NGS and recognise the outstanding contribution that the NGS has made to Macmillan over the years. I hope that you enjoy reading Gardens to Visit 2016 and take pleasure in these stunning gardens around the country.

Lynda Thomas,
Chief Executive

Marie Curie

Care and support
through terminal illness

Marie Curie was founded in 1948 and today provides a lifeline for people living with any terminal illness and for their families. We offer expert care, guidance and support to help them get the most from the time they have left. Marie Curie nurses work day and night supporting people in their own homes, while their hospices offer the reassurance of specialist round-the-clock care and support both for people who stay and for others who visit on a day basis.

Marie Curie nurses are one of the most recognised and respected of all nursing groups in the UK and their addition to the group of charities supported annually by the National Gardens Scheme was a significant milestone for both charities.

The National Gardens Scheme (NGS) is Marie Curie's biggest corporate supporter, donating more than £6.9 million to the charity since 1997. We're proud to be working with them on such a successful partnership and their support has helped Marie Curie to provide more care to people with a terminal illness and their families.

'We often hear how much enjoyment our patients, their families and our staff get from the gardens around them, both at home and in our hospices. Being outside or looking out of the window onto a colourful garden can bring comfort and peace to people at the end of their lives and their loved ones. I hope people continue to visit the stunning NGS gardens and help raise money for Marie Curie to care for more people living with a terminal illness.'

Dr Jane Collins,
Chief Executive

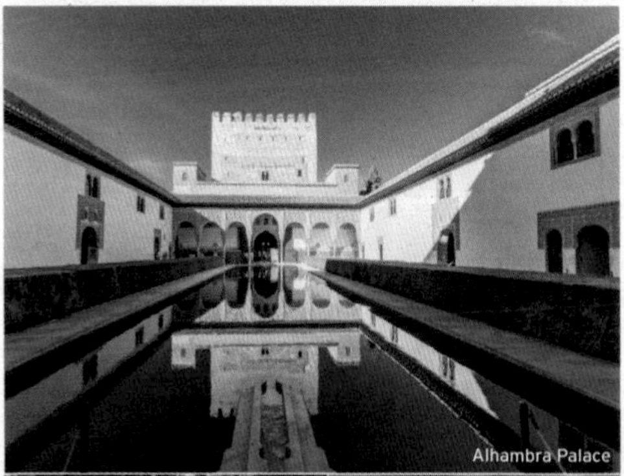
Alhambra Palace

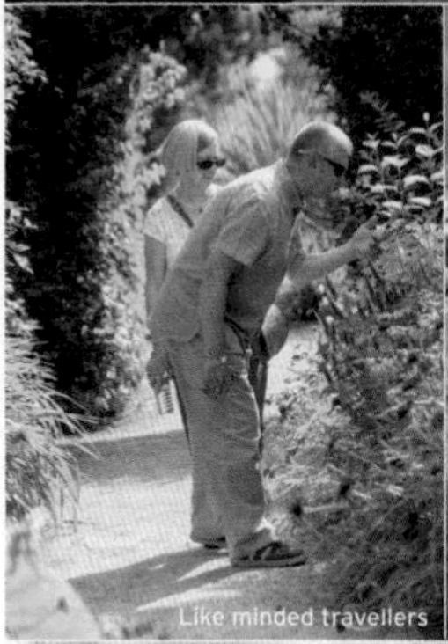
Like minded travellers

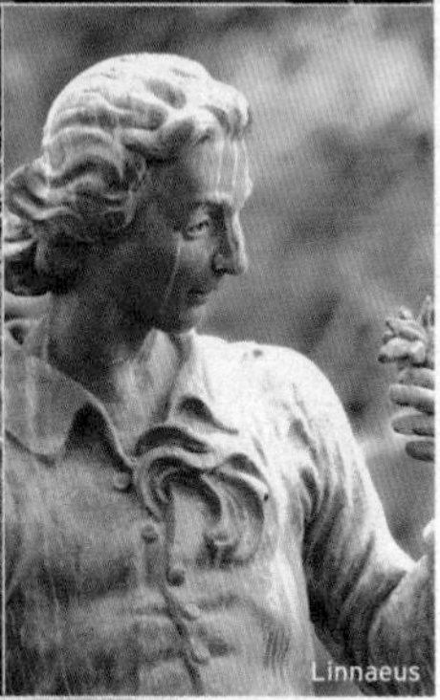
Linnaeus

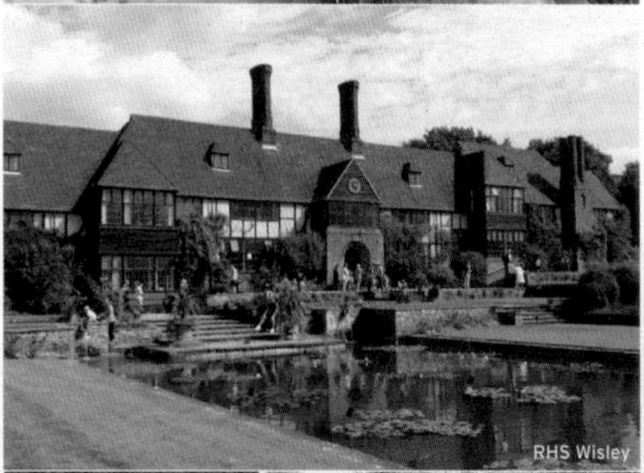
RHS Wisley

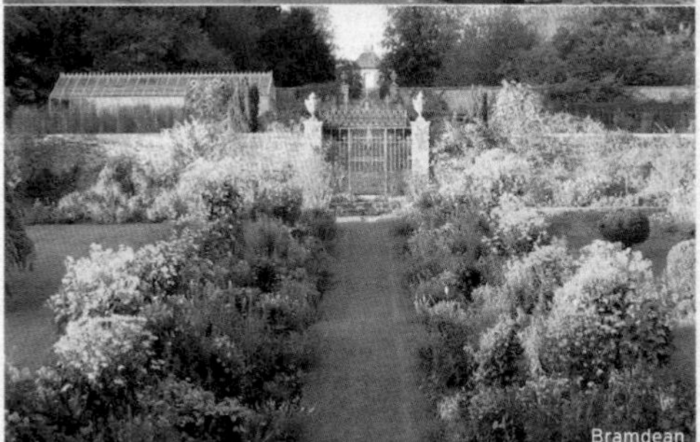
Bramdean

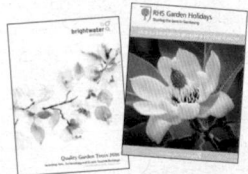

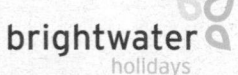

hospice UK

Hospice UK believes hospice care should be available to all those who need it. Every single person matters, throughout their life and right up until the moment they die. Hospice UK supports more than 200 hospices across the UK, so that they can deliver the highest quality care to 360,000 children, young people, adults and their families every year.

The NGS has raised over £3.5 million for hospice care since 1996 and is the largest single benefactor of Hospice UK. Their annual funding supports all of our vital projects and directly helps us to support individual hospices all over the country. As the challenge to improve end of life care for all grows and the part that hospices can play in the improvement becomes more crucial, the constant support of such a significant benefactor makes a vital contribution.

We are very grateful for the incredible generosity of the NGS and the fantastic volunteers who open up their gardens to the public. Thanks to the many people who take time to visit the gardens, the NGS are able to generate important funds for hospice care.

Gardens provide a peaceful location for everyone and horticulture has long been a feature of hospices. They are important in promoting patient wellbeing so it is wonderful that so many people support our work in this way.

The vital funding NGS donate will help enable hospices to continue to provide the best possible end of life care to patients and their families.

The Rt. Hon. Lord Howard of Lympne, CH, QC
Chair, Hospice UK

The National Gardens Scheme first funded carers in 1996 when it began annual support for Crossroads Care. In 2012 Crossroads Care merged with Princess Royal Trust for Carers to form Carers Trust which the NGS has funded ever since.

Carers Trust works to improve support, services and recognition for anyone living with the challenges of caring, unpaid, for a family member or friend who is ill, frail, disabled or has mental health or addiction problems.

The photograph above shows HRH The Princess Royal, Patron of Carers Trust, visiting an NGS garden in Gloucestershire in July 2015.

There are seven million unpaid carers in the UK caring for family members or friends who couldn't cope without their help. Carers often suffer from stress and isolation as a result of their caring role.

The NGS's donation contributes towards our core activities, including working with our network of local carers' centres and services to support carers locally, reaching carers via our dedicated online services, providing essential grants, raising greater awareness of carer's important role in society and influencing change.

Carers Trust offer a range of support to help carers manage their stress, and this includes facilitating access to breaks and activities, such as gardening. Indeed, some of our support services have gardens which give carers the chance to get outdoors and have some time for themselves. Many carers tell us that having a break from their caring role, even for one hour, can help enormously.

'NGS is one of our largest single donors and we can't thank them enough for their generous donations. A big thank you also to the garden owners and people who visit gardens for supporting Carers Trust.'

Gail Scott-Spicer,
Chief Executive

PERENNIAL
GARDENERS' ROYAL BENEVOLENT SOCIETY
Helping Horticulturists In Need Since 1839

As the single largest supporter of Perennial, the NGS has made a massive difference to the lives of thousands of current, former and retired horticulturists, and their families. We are indebted to those who open their gardens for the NGS, and those who visit them.

They help fund our nationwide team of trained professional Caseworkers and Debt Advisers, who travel the length and breadth of the UK, dealing with problems such as debt, homelessness, illness, poverty, disability and workplace accidents. Our free and confidential services can be life changing, and they help their clients for as long as they need us, sometimes for years.

By showing and sharing the beauty of gardens, NGS garden owners and visitors are helping to keep Britain beautiful, and play their part to ensure that gardeners and horticulturists across the country can count on Perennial for many years to come.

Richard Capewell, Chief Executive

Perennial combines two charities which have been supported annually by the National Gardens Scheme since 1986, the Gardeners' Royal Benevolent Society and the Royal Fund for Gardeners' Children. Through Perennial, the National Gardens Scheme helps horticulturalists who are facing difficulties. The NGS donation is invaluable to the charity's on-going work to help individuals and families.

The annual donation to Perennial for gardeners' children also enables on-going support for families when one or both parents have died, and for children who are disadvantaged by other circumstances.

Perennial owns two outstanding gardens, York Gate in Yorkshire and Fullers Mill in Suffolk, both of which open in support of NGS.

COBRA

The UK's largest range of lawnmowers

Create a lawn that is the envy of your neighbours with a new lawnmower from Cobra. At the heart of these powerful, stylish mowers is a choice of either electric, cordless or petrol engines powered by Briggs & Stratton, Honda and Subaru.

Cobra have over 45 lawnmowers in their range including rear roller, 4 wheeled and professional models and are sure to have a lawnmower to suit your specific gardening needs.

Promo prices start from just £84.99 inc VAT

COBRA
For a Great British striped lawn

COBRA PRO

LI-ION 40v Lithium-ion

For your nearest dealer visit: **www.cobragarden.co.uk** or call: **0115 986 6646**   *Promotional prices only at participating dealers*

Celebrating 'Capability' Brown – England's Greatest Gardener

Ceryl Evans, Director of the Capability Brown Festival 2016, explains why it's a great time to visit a Brown landscape

This year marks the 300th anniversary of the birth of Lancelot 'Capability' Brown, a designer associated with more than 250 landscapes across England and Wales.

We're celebrating Brown as the 'father of landscape architecture,' a man who changed the face of the nation with his naturalistic style, rolling vistas and serpentine waterways.

Brown's name will hopefully be familiar, as it is one that is closely linked to the NGS. A number of his surviving landscapes have been supporting the scheme since its inception in 1927, and this is why the NGS is a key part of our Festival, acting as one of our valued national partners.

But if Brown's still a mystery, don't worry. Our Festival is running throughout 2016, celebrating Brown as an artist and a landscape designer, with a huge range of events, openings and exhibitions taking place around the country.

The Festival is the largest of its kind to date, managed by the Landscape Institute and funded by the Heritage Lottery Fund. We have two key aims. The first is to open up as many Brown landscapes to as many people as possible – an area where the NGS is playing a key role. We really want to encourage new visitors, people who may never ordinarily think of visiting a Brown site, to go along, learn about, and enjoy the landscapes.

Left: © Portrait of Lancelot 'Capability' Brown, c.1770–75, Cosway, Richard (1742–1821). Private Collection /Bridgeman Images
Opposite: Southill Park, Bedfordshire, with Brown's lake in the distance

Below: The Manor House, Fenstanton, owned by Brown from 1767

The second is to discover more about Brown's work, and how his designs were created. Brown was known to ask workmen to move hills, and occasionally even entire villages, to make way for his designs, often putting in vast lakes covering acres upon acres of land. All of this was achieved with the limited tools available in the 18th century, and doubtless a lot of blood, sweat and tears! We're building up a body of new research on Brown and his sites, and making sure this is available and shared, leaving a legacy that will reach beyond 2016 and the life of our Festival.

Our activities will peak between Easter and October this year, with a special focus in August, Brown's birth month. This description is deliberately vague as we know when and where he was baptised – August 30 1716 in St Wilfrid's Church, Kirkharle, Northumberland – but not exactly when he was born.

We're really excited about 2016, proud to be working with the NGS, and very thankful to all those opening up their Brown landscapes for this very special year. Please do use the NGS Gardens to Visit 2016, or see the interactive map at www.capabilitybrown.org.

The NGS brings a unique quality to our portfolio in that a few places opening to support the NGS are never accessible to visitors at other times; such as Packington Hall, Southill Park, and Brown's own home at the Manor House, Fenstanton – all illustrated here.

Below: Packington Hall, Warwickshire, an important early Brown landscape

heritage lottery fund
LOTTERY FUNDED

Griffin Glasshouses

Griffin Glasshouses is proud to support the National Gardens Scheme. Griffin Glasshouses creates beautiful bespoke glasshouses, greenhouses and orangeries for discerning gardeners, featuring the National Gardens Scheme (NGS) Collection. This exclusive collection includes five popular designs which can be personalised with a range of accessories and finished in any colour. Griffin's glasshouses are individually designed, offering many gardener-friendly features, virtually no maintenance and with a lifetime structural guarantee.

GRIFFIN GLASSHOUSES
GLASSHOUSES OF DISTINCTION

Quality Garden Tours

Brightwater Holidays are delighted to continue partnering with the National Gardens Scheme to offer exclusive holidays based on stunning NGS gardens. For each place booked on these tours Brightwater will make a donation to the NGS. For any other Brightwater holiday, booked through the NGS, Brightwater will again make a donation to the NGS. For full details contact Brightwater Holidays 01334 657155 or ngs@brightwaterholidays.com

brightwater
holidays

Buy a Woodmansterne greeting card and spread the word

Woodmansterne's greeting cards have been bringing awareness of the NGS brand to the High Street since 2006 and helping to contribute to the wonderful work of the charities the NGS supports. Look out for the ever-changing photography being added every year. Ever popular are favourite themes such as making fun in the garden, relaxing, admiring flowers and cheeky garden animals. A range of small square cards are the latest innovation. Cards are available from all good independent card and gift shops, garden centres and WHSmith, Waitrose, and John Lewis.

Woodmansterne
Top-notch British greeting cards
for thoughts that count

The NGS Posh Shed

The Posh Shed Company is the latest member of our partnership scheme and has designed and built the very first NGS Posh Shed. The cost is £4,995 which includes delivery and installation as well as a contribution to the NGS. The NGS Posh Shed has a 8ft by 7ft footprint which includes the veranda, and is constructed from FSC certified tanalised timber that has been pressure treated. It also comes with a two year guarantee for complete peace of mind. The Posh Shed Company produces a standard range of sheds, as well creating bespoke, one-off creations. For more information visit www.theposhshedcompany.co.uk

THE
POSHSHED®
COMPANY

Geographical area map

The areas shown on this map are specific to the organisation of The National Gardens Scheme. The Gardens of Wales, listed by area, follow the Gardens of England.

BEDFORDSHIRE

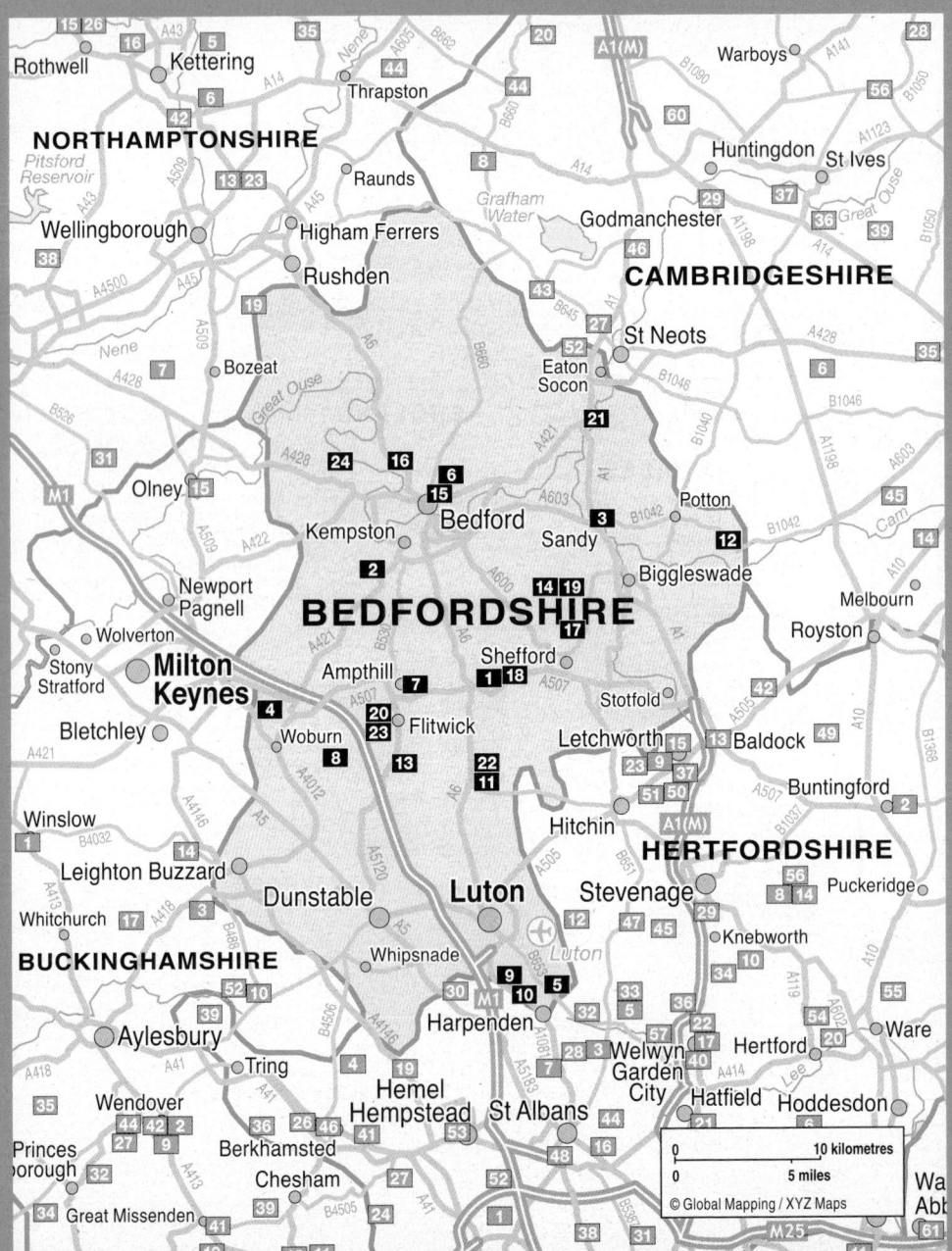

Bedfordshire

Bedfordshire may be one of England's smallest counties, but it has a lot to be proud of.

The county town of Bedford was named the most generous town in the UK by JustGiving in 2014. Bedford can also boast of having one of the finest riverside settings in the country, with stunning panoramic views of the River Great Ouse from the restored Castle Mound – the last remnant of Bedford Castle which was destroyed in 1224.

The county of Bedfordshire is steeped in history; many kings and queens held court and hunted in its forests over the centuries.

The impressive country house of Luton Hoo (now a luxury spa hotel) has enjoyed many famous visitors over the years, including Samuel Johnson in 1771 and Winston Churchill.

The grounds of Luton Hoo and the Luton Hoo Walled Garden, which was designed by Capability Brown and established by Lord Bute in the late 1760s, are open for the NGS today.

Bedfordshire offers a variety of stunning NGS gardens, perfect for those seeking a special day out.

Bedfordshire Volunteers

County Organiser
Position Vacant
For details please contact
Susan Copeland
01799 550553
susan.copeland@ngs.org.uk

County Treasurer
Colin Davies
01525 712721
colin.davies@which.net

Publicity
Position Vacant
For details please contact
Doug Copeland
01799 550553
dougcopeland@btinternet.com

Facebook
Richard Hall
RichH17@aol.com

Newsletter
Kate Gardner
07725 307803
kgardner287@gmail.com

Assistant County Organisers
Geoff & Davina Barrett
01908 585329
geoffanddean@gmail.com

Victoria Diggle
01767 627247
victoria@diggledesign.com

Position Vacant
For details please contact
Susan Copeland
01799 550553
susan.copeland@ngs.org.uk

Left: Linden Lodge

Opening Dates

All entries subject to change.
For latest information check www.ngs.org.uk

January

Sunday 31
7 King's Arms Garden

March

Monday 28
13 The Old Vicarage

April

Sunday 24
19 The Swiss Garden

Saturday 30
16 Secret Garden

May

Sunday 8
4 Flaxbourne Farm

Sunday 22
12 The Old Rectory
14 Old Warden Village Gardens

June

Festival Weekend

Sunday 5
12 The Old Rectory
17 Southill Park

Saturday 11
20 NEW Townsend Farmhouse
23 NEW West Oak

Sunday 12
5 The Hyde Walled Garden
13 The Old Vicarage

Saturday 18
6 NEW 192 Kimbolton Road

Sunday 19
11 The Manor House, Barton-le-Clay
24 Park End Thatch
22 Wayside Cottage

Sunday 26
18 Speeds Dairy Farmhouse

July

Sunday 3
5 The Hyde Walled Garden

Sunday 10
2 22 Elmsdale Road

Sunday 24
9 Luton Hoo Hotel Golf & Spa

Saturday 30
21 Walnut Cottage

Sunday 31
3 The Firs
4 Flaxbourne Farm
8 NEW Linden Lodge
21 Walnut Cottage

August

Wednesday 3
10 Luton Hoo Walled Garden

Saturday 6
15 1a St Augustine's Road

September

Sunday 4
1 Dragons Glen

October

Sunday 30
7 King's Arms Garden

Gardens open to the public

7 King's Arms Garden
10 Luton Hoo Walled Garden

Also open by arrangement

1 Dragons Glen
2 22 Elmsdale Road
3 The Firs
6 NEW 192 Kimbolton Road
12 The Old Rectory
24 Park End Thatch
21 Walnut Cottage

Herbaceous borders, waterfall and wildlife pond create distinct spaces . . .

The Gardens

1 DRAGONS GLEN

17 Great Lane, Clophill, Bedford MK45 4BQ. Kate Gardner, 07725 307803, kgardner287@gmail.com. *Great Lane is situated approx halfway along the high st almost opp the Village Primary School. The house is approx. 500m up the lane on the L.* **Sun 4 Sept (2-5). Adm £4, chd free. Home-made teas. Gluten and dairy free as standard. Visits also by arrangement June to Aug.**
This contemporary garden takes full advantage of the sloped landscape and dry conditions of its Greensand Ridge location to great effect. Dry woodland, herbaceous borders, waterfall and wildlife pond create distinct spaces that are linked together by the oriental influences that run throughout the garden. Featured on BBC Gardeners World. Partial wheelchair access due to steep slopes and steps around the garden.
❀ ☕

2 22 ELMSDALE ROAD

Wootton, Bedford MK43 9JN. Roy & Dianne Richards, 07733 222495, roy.richards60@ntlworld.com. *4m from J13 M1. Join old A421 towards Bedford, follow signs to Wootton. Turn R at The Cock PH follow Rd to Elmsdale Rd on R.* **Sun 10 July (1-6). Adm £4, chd free. Home-made teas. Visits also by arrangement May to Sept for groups 8+.**
Topiary garden greets visitors before they enter a genuine Japanese Feng Shui garden incl bonsai every plant is strictly Japanese, large Koi pond with bridge and Tea House. The garden was created from scratch by the owners and has many interesting features. Japanese lanterns and a large collection of Japanese plants and bonsai. From China the Kneeling Archer terracotta soldier. Partial wheelchair access. The Garden is on 2 levels and has gravel type paths but some of the garden can be viewed from the lower level.
♿ 🚫 🚌 ☕

3 THE FIRS

33 Bedford Road, Sandy SG19 1EP. Mr & Mrs D Sutton, 01767 227589, d.sutton7@ntlworld.com. *7m E of Bedford. On B1042 between Sandy town centre & A1. On-road parking.* **Sun 31 July (2-5.30). Adm £3.50, chd free. Home-made teas, cakes and jams. Visits also by arrangement May to Sept, light refreshments for groups of 10+ by request.**
¼-acre town garden surrounding a Victorian Gentlemans residence. Designed and created from scratch since 2000 this garden has many individual features that could be incl into anyone's garden. The garden is productive in fruit, flowers, vegetables and features modern sculpture and railway memorabilia. Money raised from the refreshments will go to the Need Project, providing food parcels in Bedfordshire. Some gravel paths.
♿ ❀ ☕

Townsend Farmhouse

4 ▶ FLAXBOURNE FARM
Salford Road, Aspley Guise
MK17 8HZ. Geoff & Davina Barrett,
01908 585329,
geoffanddean@gmail.com. *5m W of
Ampthill. 1m S of J13 of M1.Turn R in
village centre, 1m over railway line.*
Sun 8 May, Sun 31 July (2-5.30).
Adm £5, chd free. Home-made
teas.
A beautiful, entertaining and fun
garden of 3 acres, lovingly developed
with numerous water features, a
windmill, modern arches and bridges,
a small moated castle, lily pond,
herbaceous borders and a Greek
temple ruin. A recently established
jungle garden complete with a three
way bridge, planted up with
Japanese acers, tree fernes, hostas,
gunneras and large bamboos. An
orchard garden with oriental features
with a flyover walkway, an
inspirational woodland setting. Crow's
nest, crocodiles, tree house with zip
wire for children. Huge Roman arched
stone gateway. An ideal garden for

coach tours. Conducted tours, tea
and coffee available on request.
Featured in The Daily Telegraph.
Wheelchair access is available to all
the main parts of the garden.
♿ 👚 ⊛ 🚐 ☕

GREYWALLS
See Northamptonshire

**5 ▶ THE HYDE WALLED
GARDEN**
East Hyde, Luton LU2 9PS. D J J
Hambro Will Trust. *2m S of Luton.
M1 exit/10a Exit to A1061 towards
Harpenden take 2nd on L signed East
Hyde. From A1 exit J4 follow A3057
N to r'about 1st L to B653 follow
road to Wheathampstead/Luton to
East Hyde.* Sun 12 June, Sun 3 July
(2-5). Adm £4.50, chd free. Home-
made teas.
Walled garden adjoins the grounds of
The Hyde (not open). Extends to
approx 1 acre and features rose
garden, seasonal beds and
herbaceous borders, imaginatively

interspersed with hidden areas of
formal lawn. An interesting group of
Victorian greenhouses, coldframes
and cucumber house are serviced
from the potting shed in the
adjoining vegetable garden. Gravel
paths.
♿ ⊛ ☕

**6 ▶ NEW ▶ 192 KIMBOLTON
ROAD**
Bedford MK41 8DP. Tricia
Atkinson, 01234 406926,
triciaatkinson@outlook.com. *On
B660 between Brickhill Drive & Avon
Drive nr pedestrian crossing.* Sat 18
June (11-4). Adm £3.50, chd free.
Visits also by arrangement May &
June.
A third of acre cottage garden.
Grape vine, vegetable and soft fruit
patch and orchard. Garden incl over
60 roses. Wheelchair access with
care. Some gravel.
♿ ⊛

7 ♦ KING'S ARMS GARDEN

Ampthill MK45 2PP. Ampthill Town Council, 01525 755648, bryden.k@ntlworld.com. *8m S of Bedford. Free parking in town centre. Entrance opp Old Market Place, down King's Arms Yard.* For NGS: Sun 31 Jan, Sun 30 Oct (2-4). Adm £2, chd free. Light refreshments. For other opening times and information, please phone or email. Small woodland garden of about 1½ acres created by plantsman the late William Nourish. Trees, shrubs, bulbs and many interesting collections throughout the yr. Maintained since 1987 by 'The Friends of the Garden' on behalf of Ampthill Town Council. See us on Facebook Kings Arms Garden. Wheelchair access to most of the garden.

♿ ❀ ☕

8 NEW LINDEN LODGE

1 Tyrells End, Eversholt, Milton Keynes MK17 9DS. Daniel Iddon. *Next door to village hall.* Sun 31 July (11-3). Adm £3, chd free. Home-made teas in village hall. Linden Lodge was built as the gatehouse to the Linden Estate. It was acquired by the Duke of Bedford when he bought the estate around 1890. The main house was soon demolished, but the Duke kept Linden Lodge. The garden borders represent a varied truly amazing hydrangea collection built up over the last ten years with a pond and allotment.

9 LUTON HOO HOTEL GOLF & SPA

The Mansion House, Luton Hoo, Luton LU1 3TQ. Luton Hoo Hotel Golf & Spa, 01582 734437, www.lutonhoo.co.uk. *Approx 1m from J10 M1, take London Rd A1081 signed Harpenden for approx ½ m - entrance on L for Luton Hoo Hotel Golf & Spa.* Sun 24 July (10-4). Adm £5, chd free. Light refreshments. The gardens and parkland designed by Capability Brown are of national historic significance and lie in a conservation area. Main features - lakes, woodland and pleasure grounds, Victorian grass tennis court and late C19 sunken rockery. Italianate garden with herbaceous borders and topiary garden. Gravel paths.

♿ 🚪 ☕

10 ♦ LUTON HOO WALLED GARDEN

Luton Hoo Estate, Luton LU1 4LF. Exors of N H Phillips, 01582 721443, office@lutonhooestate.co.uk, www.lutonhooestate.co.uk. *Take A1081. Turn at West Hyde Road (signed for Newmill End). After approx 100 metres turn L through black gates. Follow red signs to Walled Garden.* For NGS: Wed 3 Aug (11-3). Adm £3, chd free. Light refreshments. For other opening times and information, please phone, email or visit garden website. The 5 acre Luton Hoo Walled Garden was designed by Capability Brown and established by Lord Bute in the late 1760s. Successive owners of the estate adapted the garden to match changing horticultural fashions, only for it to fall into decline in the 1980s. The garden is now being restored. Guided tours. Illustrated talks. Exhibition of old tools. Children's trail. Disabled parking next to Walled Garden Entrance. A hard path goes through and around the garden.

♿ 🚪 ❀ 🚌 ☕

WE ARE MACMILLAN. CANCER SUPPORT

In 2016 the Chesterfield Royal NGS Macmillan Cancer Unit will open

11 THE MANOR HOUSE, BARTON-LE-CLAY

87 Manor Road, Barton-le-Clay MK45 4NR. Mrs Veronica Pilcher. *Off A6 between Bedford & Luton. Take old A6 (Bedford Rd) through Barton-le-Clay Village (not the by-pass) and Manor Rd is off Bedford Rd. Parking in paddock.* Sun 19 June (2-5). Combined adm with Wayside Cottage £5, chd free. Home-made teas. The garden was beautifully

landscaped during the 1930s and much interest is created by picturesque stream which incorporates a series of waterfalls and ponds. Colourful streamside planting incl an abundance of arum lilies. Sunken garden with lily pond and a magnificent wisteria thrives at the rear of the house. Children under supervision as there is a water hazard. Partial wheelchair access, 2ft wide bridges.

♿ 🚪 ❀ ☕

12 THE OLD RECTORY

Church Lane, Wrestlingworth, Sandy SG19 2EU. Mrs Josephine Hoy, 01767 631204, hoyjosephine@hotmail.co.uk. *5m E of Sandy, 5m NE of Biggleswade. Wrestlingworth is situated on B1042. 5m from Sandy & 6m from Biggleswade.* Sun 22 May, Sun 5 June (2-6). Adm £4, chd free. Home-made teas. Visits also by arrangement May & June groups are welcome with prior appointment. 4 acre garden full of colour and interest. The owner has a free style of gardening sensitive to wildlife. Beds overflowing with tulips, alliums, bearded iris, peonies, poppies, geraniums and much more. Beautiful mature trees and many more planted in the last 30 years. Incl a large selection of betulas. Gravel gardens, box hedging, woodland garden and wild flower meadows. Wheelchair access maybe limited on grass paths.

♿ 🚪 ❀ 🚌 ☕

13 THE OLD VICARAGE

Church Road, Westoning MK45 5JW. Ann & Colin Davies. *2m S of Flitwick. Off A5120, 2m N of M1 J12. ¼ m up Church Rd, next to church.* Mon 28 Mar, Sun 12 June (2-5.30). Adm £4, chd free. Cream teas in C14 church next door. A traditional 2-acre vicarage garden on sandy soil with box and laurel hedges, a formal lawn and many mature shrubs and trees. Following recent tree clearance the colour co-ordinated herbaceous beds have been expanded. There is also an enlarged cornfield meadow, an English rose garden, pond, rockery and small vegetable garden. There should be a good show of hellebores and daffodils in spring. Wheelchair access generally good.

♿ ❀ ☕

GROUP OPENING

14 OLD WARDEN VILLAGE GARDENS
Old Warden, Biggleswade
SG18 9HB. *3m W of Biggleswade.*
Parking in the village hall car park opp
the Hare and Hounds PH, at Orchard
Grange, or on the cricket field. **Sun**
22 May (2-5). Combined adm £6,
chd free. Home-made teas in the
Village Hall and at Laundry Farm.
Donation to St Leonard's, Old
Warden.

NEW LAUNDRY FARM
Julie Janes

THE OLD VICARAGE
Michael & Sue Scott

ORCHARD GRANGE
Robert & Victoria Diggle

SWISS COTTAGE
Paul Quenby

28 THE VILLAGE
Bob Parr

30 THE VILLAGE
Shirley Benjamin

31 THE VILLAGE
Mike & Penny Prior

NEW WARREN LODGE
Sylvia Cooper

Old Warden, with its picturesque
cottages, medieval church, neat holly
hedges and charming pub, is one of
the prettiest villages in Bedfordshire.
Many of the houses were built by the
3rd Lord Ongley in the early C19 in
the cottage-ornée style. Further
attractive buildings were added by
the Shuttleworth family. This year 8
gardens will be opening. The largest
is that at Orchard Grange, which has
a walled kitchen garden, formal areas,
and a wild flower orchard. The Old
Vicarage has an established garden
with year-round interest. In late Spring
there are plenty of seats from which
to enjoy the camellias and hellebores,
a large wisteria, early perennials and
colourful bulbs and containers set off
by striped lawns and mature trees.
Swiss Cottage and the other village
gardens all have wonderful cottage
planting with some lovely topiary,
elaborate bedding schemes and
other surprises. Most gardens are
accessible to wheelchairs but there
are some steps, banks and gravel
paths.

24 PARK END THATCH
58 Park Road, Stevington,
Bedford MK43 7QG. Susan Young
01234 826430
info@susanyoungdesign.co.uk
www.susanyoungdesign.co.uk. *5m*
NW of Bedford. Off A428, through
Bromham. **Sun 19 June (12-5).**
Adm £4, chd free. Light
refreshments. Visits also by
arrangement.
¹/₂-acre cottage garden set within old
orchard and designed by the owner,
Professional Gardeners' Guild
Member and Society of Garden
Designers Pre-Registered Member.
Sunny borders of flowering shrubs
with herbaceous planting. Fragrant
roses and climber covered pergola.
Winding grass paths shaded by trees.
Trellis border featuring colour and
texture. Garden cultivated to be
drought tolerant. Wildlife friendly. Fruit
production and herbs. Small plant
nursery. View of Stevington windmill.
Featured in Garden News - Garden of
The Week and 'Stevington - The
Natural History of a Bedfordshire
Parish'. Outside WC, regret cannot
be accessed by wheelchair. Main
path is gravel on a slight slope, grass
paths. Most of garden is accessible
by wheelchair.

15 1A ST AUGUSTINE'S ROAD
Bedford MK40 2NB. Chris Damp.
St. Augustine's Rd on L off Kimbolton
Rd as you leave the centre of
Bedford. **Sat 6 Aug (12-4.30). Adm**
£2.50, chd free. Tea.
A small but colourful suburban
garden, comprising mainly of flower
beds and a few vegetables. Path
from street is level.

16 SECRET GARDEN
4 George Street, Clapham, Bedford
MK41 6AZ. Graham Bolton. *3m N*
of Bedford (not the bypass). Clapham
Village High St. R into Mount Pleasant
Rd then L into George St. 1st white
Bungalow on R. **Sat 30 Apr (2-5.30).**
Adm £2.50, chd free. Light
refreshments.
Alpine lovers can see a wide variety of
alpines in two small scree gardens,
front and back of bungalow plus pans,
tubs with dwarf Salix, rhododendron,
daphne's. Dwarf acers conifers and
pines hellebores epimediums. Two
small mixed borders of herbaceous
salvias, lavenders and potentillas. Two
small greenhouses and cold frames
with plants for sale. Partial wheelchair
access. No access at the rear of
property due to narrow gravel paths
but garden can be viewed from the
patio.

West Oak

17 SOUTHILL PARK

Southill, nr Biggleswade SG18 9LL. Mr & Mrs Charles Whitbread. *3m W of Biggleswade. In the village of Southill. 3m from A1 junction at Biggleswade.* **Sun 5 June (2-5). Adm £4, chd free. Cream teas.**

Large garden, with mature trees and flowering shrubs, herbaceous borders, rose garden and wild garden. Large conservatory with tropical plants. The parkland was designed by Lancelot 'Capability' Brown in 1777.

18 SPEEDS DAIRY FARMHOUSE

Beadlow, Shefford SG17 5PL. Martin & Sarah Hind. *Take the turning opp Beadlow Manor Golf Club off A507, you will find our Farmhouse at the end of a dead end road on the sharp bend. Signed with a blue sign saying Sandy Smith & Shefford.* **Sun 26 June (2.30-5). Adm £4, chd free. Home-made teas.**

The front garden is laid mainly to mature trees, a pond that was completed in 2015 and fruit trees. The back garden was landscaped 5 years ago and comprises of a gravel path meandering through borders with a mixture of shrubs and perennials. At the bottom of the rear garden is a vegetable patch and wooden framed greenhouse. Access via a gravel driveway.

19 THE SWISS GARDEN

Old Warden Aerodrome, Old Warden, Biggleswade SG18 9ER. Shuttleworth Trust in Partnership with Central Beds Council, www.shuttleworth.org/the-swiss-garden/. *2m W of Biggleswade. Signed from A1 & A600.* **Sun 24 Apr (9.30-5). Adm £8, chd free. The Shuttleworth Restaurant - open all day.**

This enchanting garden was created in the 'Swiss Picturesque' style for the 3rd Lord Ongley in the early C19 and reopened in July 2014 after a major HLF-funded restoration. Serpentine paths lead to cleverly contrived vistas, many of which focus on the thatched Swiss Cottage. Beautiful wrought-iron bridges, ponds, sweeping lawns and the magnificent Pulhamite-lined Grotto Fernery have all been given a new lease of life by this landmark restoration. Annual Plant Fair to coincide with NGS opening. The pathways in the Swiss Garden are firm and even, with minimal gradients, and most are suitable for access by wheelchair users.

Garden has been developed over nearly 30 years by the present owners from a completely bare plot . . .

20 NEW TOWNSEND FARMHOUSE

Rectory Road, Steppingley, Bedford MK45 5AT. Mrs Indi Jackson. *In Steppingley Village. Follow directions to Steppingley village and follow yellow signs from the village centre.* **Sat 11 June (2-5). Combined adm with West Oak £5, chd free. Home-made teas.**

A medium sized country garden with tree lined driveway, herbaceous borders, flowering shrubs, box hedging, natural pond, vegetable beds and pretty courtyard. Although wheel chairs are welcome, the gravelled driveway and gravelled paths around the garden may be difficult to negotiate.

21 WALNUT COTTAGE

8 Great North Road, Chawston MK44 3BD. D G Parker, 07784 792975. *2m S of St Neots. Between Wyboston & Blackcat r'about on S-bound lane of A1. Turn off at McDonalds, at end of filling station forecourt turn L. Off rd parking.* **Sat 30, Sun 31 July (2-6). Adm £4, chd free. Home-made teas. Visits also by arrangement Feb to Nov refreshments on request.**

Once a land settlement. 4 acre smallholding. 1 acre cottage garden. Over 2000 species give year round interest. Bulbs, herbaceous, water, bog plants, ferns, grasses, shrubs, trees, coppiced paulownias. Rare, exotic and unusual plants abound. Large pond, level grass paths. 1 acre young trees and shrubs. 2500sq metre glasshouse growing Chinese vegetable. 1½ -acre picnic and party zone. Level grass paths.

22 WAYSIDE COTTAGE

74 Manor Road, Barton-le-Clay MK45 4NR. Nigel Barrett. *1m off A6. Take old A6 (Bedford Rd) through Barton-le-Clay Village (not the by-pass), Manor Rd is off Bedford Rd. Parking in paddock at the Manor House.* **Sun 19 June (2-5). Combined adm with The Manor House, Barton-le-Clay £5, chd free. Home-made teas at The Manor House.**

The garden is sited on a ½ -acre plot. Developed over 50yrs it has mature trees, shrubs and flower borders. A well-stocked pond with fountain and waterfalls. A variety of attractive outbuildings nestle within the old walled garden for a tranquil scene with plenty of hidden corners.

23 NEW WEST OAK

50 Rectory Road, Steppingley, Bedford MK45 5AT. John & Sally Eilbeck. *Steppingley Village. Follow signs to Steppingley from A507 r'about between Ampthill & Flitwick, pick up yellow signs from centre of village.* **Sat 11 June (2-5). Combined adm with Townsend Farmhouse £5, chd free. Home-made teas at Townsend Farmhouse opp West Oak.**

An informal garden of approx ¾ acre with open countryside on two sides. It consists of lawns and shrubs with perennial planting.There is a herb garden, greenhouse, vegetable gardens with soft fruit, and small orchard with chickens. The garden has been developed over nearly 30 years by the present owners from a completely bare plot. The garden is approached across a gravel drive and there are some steps.

The Manor House, Barton-le-Clay

Find a garden near you – download our free iOS **APP**

BERKSHIRE

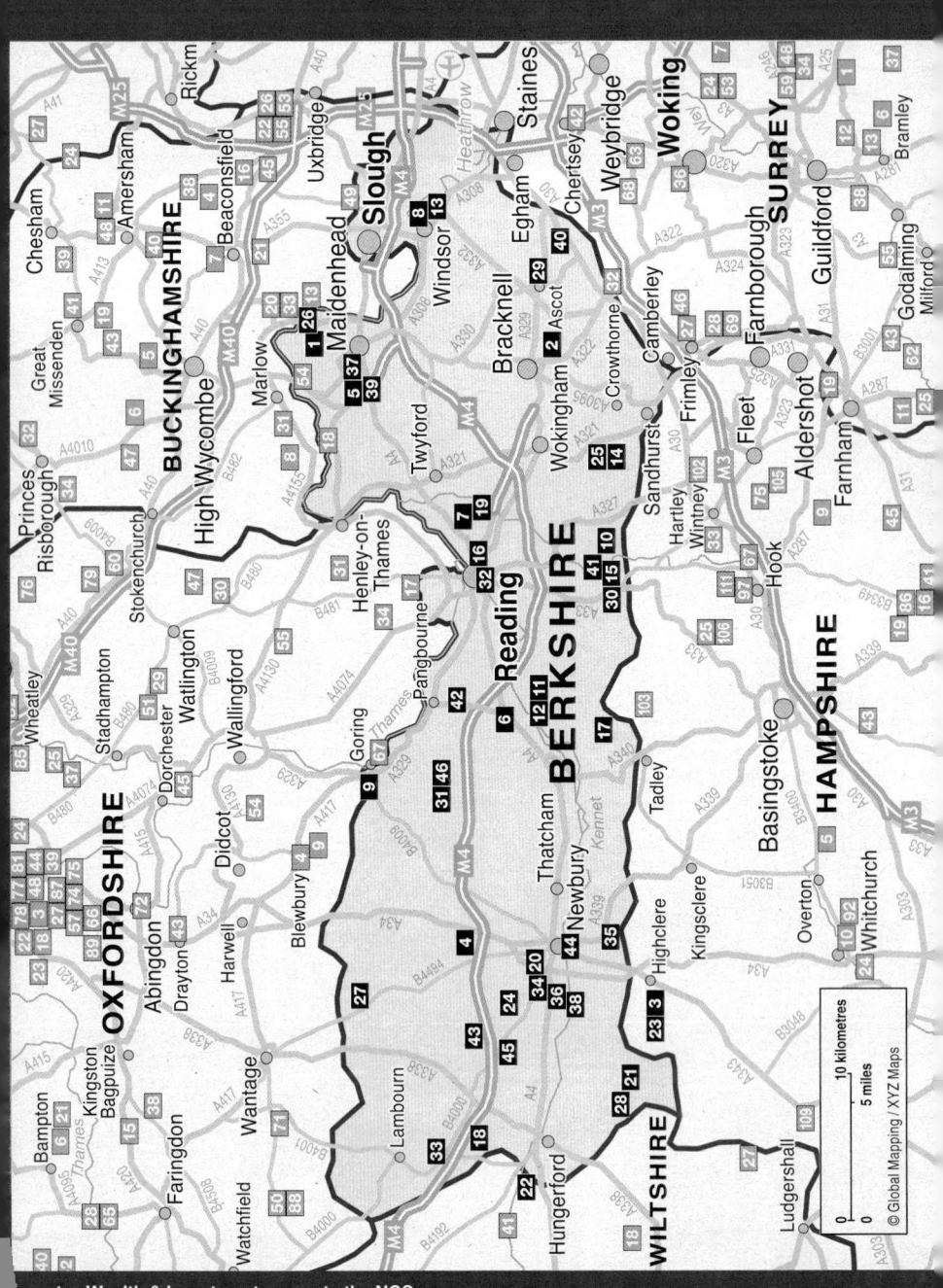

Berkshire

The Royal County of Berkshire offers a wonderful mix of natural beauty and historic landmarks that are reflected in the portfolio of gardens opening for the NGS.

The Thames flows right through the county, passing picturesque towns and villages, many of which have beautiful gardens opening in 2016.

Private gardens at famous places such as Windsor Castle and Eton College provide rare opportunities for NGS visitors to enjoy gardens not normally open to the public. All are generously opened to raise funds for the nursing and caring charities we support.

If you are organising a group visit, please see our gardens open 'by arrangement', or if you would like someone locally to give a talk about the NGS, contact Angela at angela.oconnell@icloud.com.

Our gardens come in every shape, size and style - from small urban gardens in Bracknell to large country estates such as Rooksnest near Lambourn. We also offer new and returning gardens such as St Timothee at Pinkneys Green and Hunters Lodge in Padworth Common, both of which have lovely ponds encouraging wildlife in natural settings.

Some gardens may capture your interest due to their designers or their historic setting, while most have evolved thanks to the efforts of their enthusiastic owners. We think they all offer moments of inspiration and look forward to welcoming you at a garden soon.

Berkshire Volunteers

County Organiser
Heather Skinner
01189 737197
heatheraskinner@aol.com

County Treasurer
Hugh Priestley
01189 744349 Fri – Mon
hughpriestley@aol.com

Publicity
Heather Skinner
(as above)

Booklet Co-ordinator
Heather Skinner
(as above)

Assistant County Organisers
Gill Cheetham
01344 423440
gillcheetham@btopenworld.com

Ron Cummings
01488 608124
ron@roncummings.co.uk

Cathie Davies
07718 589347
cathieldavies@gmail.com

Carolyn Foster
01628 624635
candrfoster@btinternet.com

Angela O'Connell
01252 668645
angela.oconnell@icloud.com

Graham O'Connell
01252 668645
graham.oconnell22@gmail.com

Nikki Sketch
07768 934030
Nikki@sketch.cc

Yvonne Sonsino
07557 133140
yvonnesonsino@gmail.com

Charlotte Stacey
07785 308109
charlotte_stacey@hotmail.co.uk

Left: Rooksnest

Opening Dates

All entries subject to change.
For latest information check www.ngs.org.uk

February

Snowdrop Festival

Wednesday 10
43 Welford Park
Sunday 21
25 Oak Cottage

March

Saturday 19
39 Stubbings House
Sunday 20
39 Stubbings House

April

Saturday 23
3 Canje Grove
Sunday 24
1 2 Belle Vue Cottages
3 Canje Grove
23 **NEW** Malverleys
26 Odney Club
27 The Old Rectory Farnborough
Wednesday 27
18 Inholmes
33 Rooksnest

Saturday 30
2 Bracknell Gardens
39 Stubbings House

May

Sunday 1
39 Stubbings House
Monday 2
39 Stubbings House
Sunday 8
14 Glenmere
25 Oak Cottage
Sunday 15
17 Hunters Lodge
35 Sandleford Place
Saturday 21
32 The RISC Roof Garden, Reading
Sunday 22
27 The Old Rectory Farnborough
Sunday 29
34 Rookwood Farm House
36 Springfield Cottage
Tuesday 31
40 Sunningdale Park

June

Festival Weekend

Saturday 4
9 **NEW** Fairway

Sunday 5
9 **NEW** Fairway
37 **NEW** St Timothee
38 Stockcross House
Tuesday 7
13 Frogmore House Garden
Saturday 11
8 Eton College Gardens
Sunday 12
4 Chieveley Manor
7 **NEW** Estoril
15 Handpost
16 The Harris Garden
27 The Old Rectory Farnborough
Sunday 19
21 Kirby House
28 The Old Rectory Inkpen
34 Rookwood Farm House
36 Springfield Cottage
42 The Tithe Barn
Wednesday 22
18 Inholmes
33 Rooksnest
Sunday 26
31 Pyt House
35 Sandleford Place
41 Swallowfield Horticultural Society
46 Willow Tree Cottage

July

Saturday 2
32 The RISC Roof Garden, Reading

Sunday 3
44 West Mills Allotments & Island Cottage
Tuesday 12
45 Wickham House
Saturday 16
20 Jannaways
Sunday 17
10 Farley Hill Place Gardens
22 Littlecote House Hotel
Sunday 24
23 **NEW** Malverleys
Sunday 31
5 Deepwood Stud Farm
22 Littlecote House Hotel

August

Monday 1
5 Deepwood Stud Farm
Saturday 6
32 The RISC Roof Garden, Reading
Sunday 14
22 Littlecote House Hotel

February 2017

Sunday 19
25 Oak Cottage

Gardens open to the public

6 Englefield House
43 Welford Park

By arrangement only

11 Field Farm Cottage
19 Ivydene
24 The Mill House, Boxford
29 Old Waterfield
30 The Priory

Also open by arrangement

2 Devonia, Bracknell Gardens
4 Chieveley Manor
10 Farley Hill Place Gardens
14 Glenmere
33 Rooksnest
35 Sandleford Place
39 Stubbings House
40 Sunningdale Park
44 Island Cottage
45 Wickham House

Canje Grove

The Gardens

1 2 BELLE VUE COTTAGES
The Pound, Cookham SL6 9QF. Liz & William Wells. $3\frac{1}{2}$ N of Maidenhead. On B4447 in Cookham. Car parking is difficult, use NT car park on Cookham Moor, or around Cookham train station, or street parking. **Sun 24 Apr (2-6). Adm £2.50, chd free. Also open Odney Club (10 mins walk).**
This small, stunning modern garden shows just what can be achieved within a narrow space. Cleverly designed and planted, a curving walkway weaves through arbours bordered by lush exotic and native evergreen planting, punctured by dabs of intense colour. Sorry, garden is not suitable for children, wheelchairs, or dogs.

GROUP OPENING

2 BRACKNELL GARDENS
The Parks Community Centre, 8-10 Nicholson Park, Bracknell RG12 9NF. 1m S of Bracknell. Follow the NGS signs from all major routes to The Parks Community Centre for parking, tickets & map, WC, teas & plants. You can walk to most gardens. Optional street parking, but tricky at individual gardens. **Sat 30 Apr (2-5). Combined adm £5, chd free. Home-made teas in The Parks Community Centre.**

DEVONIA
Andrew Radgick
Visits also by arrangement May to Aug for groups of 6+.
aradgick@btinternet.com
01344 862683

NEW GLENWOOD ALLOTMENTS
Gill Cheetham

NEW 24 LYSANDER DRIVE
Adam Atkinson-Young

10 SHAFTESBURY CLOSE
Gill Cheetham

Three interesting town gardens, all completely different, and lovely local allotments. Devonia is a plantsman's garden designed for all seasons with areas showcasing different conditions. 24 Lysander Drive is a young, modern square garden, densely planted with architectural shrubs, grasses and small trees. 10 Shaftesbury Close is a woodland garden, planted to reflect the challenges that pine trees offer.

Glenwood Allotments have enthusiastic owners who plant a wide variety of vegetables for all year cropping.
✿ ☕

3 CANJE GROVE
Church Road, Woolton Hill, Newbury RG20 9XQ. Yvonne & Simon Sonsino. 12 mins S of M4 J13, follow A34 to Winchester. A34 exit for Highclere & Wash Common A343. At end of slip road go R on A343. Approx $\frac{1}{2}$ m turn R at Xrds. Take 3rd L onto Church Rd with NGS signs. Street parking. **Sat 23, Sun 24 Apr (2-5). Adm £3.50, chd free. Home-made teas.**
An artist and flower arrangers garden of just over $\frac{1}{3}$ acre. The garden features multiple colour and plant themed rooms, ranging from cool shady impact planting, courtyard styling near the house/art studio, raised ponds, a wooden Shepherd's hut, a small orchard, rose hedges, peonies, topiary and picket fences, to a gated vegetable garden at the rear complete with hens. Art studio open with botanical art and calligraphy.
☕

4 CHIEVELEY MANOR
Chieveley, Nr Newbury RG20 8UT. Mr & Mrs CJ Spence, 01635 248208, spence@chieveleymanor.fsworld. co.uk. 5m N of Newbury. Take A34 N, pass under M4, then L to Chieveley. After $\frac{1}{2}$ m L up Manor Lane. **Sun 12 June (2-5). Adm £5, chd free. Home-made teas. Visits also by arrangement June & July for groups of 20 max.** Donation to St Mary's Church, Chieveley.
Large garden surrounding listed house (not open) in the heart of Chieveley village. Attractive setting with fine views over stud farm. Walled garden containing lovely borders, shrubs and rose garden evolving every year. Box parterre filled with alliums, white geraniums and lavender. Many viticella clematis growing through shrubs.
♿ ✿ ☕

5 DEEPWOOD STUD FARM
Henley Road, Stubbings, Nr Maidenhead SL6 6QW. Mr & Mrs E Goodwin. 2m W of Maidenhead. M4 J8/9 take A404M N. 2nd exit for A4 to Maidenhead. L at 1st r'about on A4130 Henley, approx 1m on R.

Sun 31 July, Mon 1 Aug (2-5). Adm £4, chd free. Home-made teas on lawn or in conservatory.
4 acres of formal and informal gardens within a stud farm, so great roses! Small lake with Monet style bridge and 3 further water features. Several neo-classical follies and statues. Walled garden with windows cut in to admire the views and horses. Woodland walk and enough hanging baskets to decorate a pub! Partial wheelchair access.
♿ ☕

6 ◆ ENGLEFIELD HOUSE
Englefield, Reading RG7 5EN. Mr & Mrs Richard Benyon, 01189 302221, www.englefieldestate.co.uk. 6m W of Reading. M4 J12. Take A4 towards Theale. 2nd r'about take A340 to Pangbourne. After $\frac{1}{6}$ m entrance on L. **For opening times and information, please phone or visit garden website.**
The 12 acre garden descends dramatically from the hill above the historic house through woodland where mature native trees mix with Victorian conifers. Drifts of spring and summer planting are followed by striking autumn colour. Stone balustrades enclose the lower terrace, with wide lawns, roses, mixed borders and topiary. Open every Mon from April-Sept (10-6) and Oct-March (10-4). Group bookings by arrangement from March-Oct with option of refreshments and tour with gardener.
🚌

7 NEW ESTORIL
9 Old Bath Road, Sonning, Reading RG4 6SZ. Fiona & Jonathan Hill. Just off A4 between Charvil & Woodley. Turn into Old Bath Rd close to pedestrian crossing, follow road around to the R, Estoril is 5th house on L. **Sun 12 June (2-5). Adm £3.50, chd free. Home-made teas.**
An attractive $\frac{1}{4}$ acre family garden with a contemporary feel that has been lovingly developed by the owner over the last 10 yrs. The beautifully planted mixed borders are filled with a wide variety of shrubs, perennials, grasses and bulbs. There are 2 mature willow trees with examples of planting for dry shade, a pretty summerhouse, wildlife pond and a small vegetable garden and greenhouse.
🐶 ☕

8 ETON COLLEGE GARDENS

Eton SL4 6DB. Eton College. *¹/₂ m N of Windsor. Parking signed off B3022, Slough Rd, entering Eton. Walk across fields to entry. Cars with disabled badges will be directed closer. Tickets & maps sold at entrance to Head Master's garden.* **Sat 11 June (2-5). Adm £5, chd free. Home-made teas.**

A rare chance to visit a group of central College gardens surrounded by historic school buildings, incl Luxmoore's garden on an island in the Thames reached across two attractive bridges. Also an opportunity to explore the fascinating Eton College Natural History Museum and a small group of other private gardens. Wheelchair access limited to 3 central gardens and over grass to Luxmoores (with no access to the Museum or further gardens in Eton town).

 🐕 🌼 ☕

9 NEW FAIRWAY

Rectory Road, Streatley, Reading RG8 9QA. Marcus & Emma Francis. *1¹/₂ m from Goring & Streatley Station. From Streatley centre take A329 N, fork L on A417 towards Wantage, then L onto Rectory Rd. Fairway is on L before Golf Club.* **Sat 4, Sun 5 June (2-5). Adm £4, chd free. Home-made teas.**

Remarkable ¹/₂ acre hillside garden. Infinity lawn at front with far-reaching views over the North Wessex Downs and Chilterns, and back garden (created by removing 3000 tonnes of chalk) planted in cottage style with an element of formality. Perennial wild flower scheme being established and top garden with fruit trees and more views of the surrounding countryside. No wheelchair access, entrance is fairly steep.

🐕 🌼 ☕

10 FARLEY HILL PLACE GARDENS

Church Road, Farley Hill, Reading RG7 1TZ. Tony & Margaret Finch, 01189 762544, tony.finch67@btinternet.com. *From M4 J11, take A33 S to Basingstoke. At T-lights turn L for Spencers Wood, B3349. Go 2m turn L, through Swallowfield towards Farley Hill. Garden ¹/₂ m on R.* **Sun 17 July (2-5). Adm £4.50, chd free. Visits also by arrangement Mar to Oct for groups of 15+. Please mention NGS.**

A 4 acre, C18 cottage garden. 1¹/₂ acre walled garden with yr-round interest and colour. Well stocked herbaceous borders, large productive vegetable areas with new herb garden, dahlia and cutting flower beds. Victorian glasshouse recently renovated and small nursery. Plants, lovely cut flowers and produce for sale. Partial wheelchair access.

🌼 🚌 ☕

11 FIELD FARM COTTAGE

Sulhamstead Hill, Sulhamstead RG7 4DA. Mrs Anne Froom, 01189 302735, anne.froom@knowall.it, www.bandbwestberkshire.co.uk. *From A4 take lane by The Spring Inn for 1m. Garden is on L, 150yds past 2 LH turns.* **Visits by arrangement May to Oct for groups of 10+. Refreshments on request. Adm £4, chd free.**

A pretty ³/₄ acre cottage garden planted with a wide variety of herbaceous perennials, set in a series of garden rooms. Lovely borders spill over the lawn and there is a large pond which is fed by a natural spring. Wild garden, small white garden and a variety of trees planted by the owner. Small vegetable garden and greenhouse.

🛏 ☕

12 FOLLY FARM

Sulhamstead Hill, Sulhamstead RG7 4DG. *7m SW of Reading. From A4 between Reading & Newbury (2m W of M4 J12) take road marked Sulhamstead at The Spring Inn. Restricted car parking.* **Thur 21, Fri 22 July. Adm £25. Pre-booking essential, please phone 01483 211535 for information & booking. Private Tours for groups of 12 only. Tea & home-made pastries. All adm to the NGS, and matched by an identical donation from the Garden Owners.**

Gardens laid out in 1912 by Sir Edwin Lutyens and Gertrude Jekyll. Garden designs evolved during culmination of their partnership and considered one of their most complex. Extensively restored and replanted by current owners assisted by Dan Pearson. Recently reopened for private group visits which include 1¹/₂ hour guided tour and refreshments. Please note paths are uneven and there are many sets of steps between areas of the garden. Sorry no dogs.

🄳 ☕

13 ◆ FROGMORE HOUSE GARDEN

Windsor SL4 1LB. Her Majesty The Queen. *1m SE of Windsor. Entrance via Park St gate into Long Walk.* **For NGS Tue 7 June. For advance tickets, please visit www.ngs.org.uk or phone 01483 211535 for information & booking. Light refreshments. Picnics welcome.**

The private royal garden at Frogmore House on the Crown Estate at Windsor. This landscaped garden set in 30 acres with notable trees, lawns, flowering shrubs and C18 lake, is rich in history. It is largely the creation of Queen Charlotte, who in the 1790s introduced over 4,000 trees and shrubs to create a model picturesque landscape. The historic plantings, incl tulip trees and redwoods, along with Queen Victoria's Tea House, remain key features of the garden today. Please note the Royal Mausoleum is closed due to long term restoration. Last entry 4pm. To book optional garden history tours (approx 45 mins) with limited availability, please visit www.ngs.org.uk or phone NGS 01483 211535. Tickets for entrance and to visit the House are also available on the day but cash payment only.

🚌 ☕

14 GLENMERE

246 Nine Mile Ride, Finchampstead RG40 3PA. Heather Bradly & John Kenney, 01189 733274. *2¹/₂ m S of Wokingham. On B3430, ¹/₄ m E of California Crossroads r'about.* **Sun 8 May 2-5). Combined adm with Oak Cottage £4.50, chd free. Home-made teas at Oak Cottage. Visits also by arrangement for 12 max. Teas on request.**

Delightful Japanese style garden with waiting arbour, raked gravel area, teahouse, Torii gate, dry stream bed with bridge and pond. Vegetable garden, greenhouse and soft fruit area.

🌼 ☕

15 HANDPOST
**Basingstoke Road, Swallowfield,
Reading RG7 1PU. Faith Ramsay,**
www.mycountrygarden.co.uk. *From
M4 J11, take A33 S. At 1st T-lights
turn L on B3349 Basingstoke Rd.
Follow road for 2¾ m, garden on L.*
**Sun 12 June (2-5). Adm £4, chd
free. Home-made teas.**
4 acre designer's garden with many
areas of interest. Features incl two
lovely long borders attractively and
densely planted in six colour sections,
a formal rose garden, old orchard
with a grass meadow, pretty pond
and peaceful wooded area. Large
variety of plants, trees and a
productive fruit and vegetable patch.
⊗ D 🍵

Art studio open with botanical art and calligraphy . . .

16 THE HARRIS GARDEN
**Whiteknights, Pepper Lane,
Reading RG6 6AS. The University
of Reading,**
www.friendsoftheharrisgarden.org.
uk. *1½ m S of Reading. Off A327
Shinfield Rd. From Pepper Lane
entrance to campus, turn R to car
park.* **Sun 12 June (2-5). Adm £3,
chd free. Tea.**
Described as 'a real gem', the Harris
Garden at the Whiteknights campus
of Reading University is a 12 acre
haven of peace and tranquillity.
Planting provides yr-round interest
including notable trees, stream, pond
and herbaceous borders. With lots to
enjoy it is an important amenity for
University visitors, as well as for
teaching and research. National Plant
Heritage collection of Digitalis.
& ⊗ NPC 🍵

17 HUNTERS LODGE
**Rectory Road, Padworth Common,
Nr Reading RG7 4JB. John & Carol
West.** *Between Reading & Newbury.
From A4 take Padworth Lane at the
Holiday Inn. Keep straight for 2m.
From Tadley take Burghfield Rd & turn
L into Rectory Rd. From Burghfield,
turn R into Rectory Rd.* **Sun 15 May
(2-5.30). Adm £4, chd free. Tea.**
The 2 acre garden has evolved over
30 yrs from woodland and fields
adjoining Padworth Common
designated Local Nature Reserve. An

attractive feature is a large natural
pond, home to busy ducks with a
waterfall and bridges, surrounded by
mature oaks and rhododendrons. In
contrast, there is a small wild area, a
wisteria walk, sunken garden, and
several mixed shrub and herbaceous
borders. Gravel drive and slope to
pond area.
& 🍵

18 INHOLMES
Woodlands St Mary RG17 7SY. *3m
SE Lambourn. M4 J14, take A338 N,
take 1st L onto B4000 towards
Lambourn. After 1½ m Inholmes
signed on L.* **Wed 27 Apr, Wed 22
June (11-4). Adm £4.50, chd free.
Light refreshments. Combined
adm with Rooksnest £6.50, chd
free.**
Set in 10 acres with wonderful views
over parkland. A wide variety of
different areas to enjoy such as a
walled garden, many spring bulbs,
inspirational herbaceous borders and
rose beds. Walks to the lake and
through the meadow. Most areas
accessible by wheelchair over grass,
gravel and paving. Assistance
available.
& 🚌 🍵

19 IVYDENE
**283 Loddon Bridge Road,
Woodley, Reading RG5 4BE. Janet
& Bill Bonney, 01189 697591,**
billabonney@aol.com. *3½ m E of
Reading. Loddon Bridge Rd is main
road through Woodley. Garden
approx 100yds S of Just Tiles
r'about. Parking in adjacent roads.*
**Visits by arrangement June to
Sept for groups of 10-25. Adm £4,
chd free. Home-made teas.**
Small urban gardeners' garden with
mature tree fern walkway and many
unusual hostas, ornamental grasses
and plants. Overflowing herbaceous
borders and rose bed, using mainly
patio roses. New and developing are
the vertical garden and the Heuchera
Tapestry bed. The garden also
features stained glass and ceramic
art to complete the picture. Owner is
a previous BBC Gardener of the Year
finalist. Featured in Garden News and
Garden of the Week.
🐾 ⊗ ☕ 🍵

20 JANNAWAYS
**Bagnor, Newbury RG20 8AH. Mr &
Mrs Sharples.** *3m W of Newbury.
From M4 J13, S on A34. Take A4 exit
towards Newbury. 1st L to Station
Rd. Turn L to Lambourn Rd. 1st R to

Bagnor, past Watermill Theatre, then
follow NGS signs.* **Sat 16 July
(2-5.30). Adm £5, chd free. Teas &
biscuits included.**
This 5 acre garden encompasses a
lake naturally fed by springs. A
circular walk from formal beds near
the house, leads along a woodland
path, crossing a weir to wild flowers
and specimen trees. A pitch perfect
lawn, fish pond, pagodas and many
hidden gems provide visitors with a
rich panoply of vistas round every
corner. Children's jungle gym.
🐾 🍵

21 KIRBY HOUSE
**Upper Green, Inkpen RG17 9ED.
Mr & Mrs R Astor.** *5m SE of
Hungerford. A4 to Kintbury. At Xrds
by Corner Stores take Inkpen Rd.
Follow road into Inkpen. Pass
common on L. Just past Crown &
Garter PH, turn L (to Combe &
Faccombe), at T-junction turn L,
house on R.* **Sun 19 June (2-5).
Adm £4, chd free. Combined adm
with The Old Rectory Inkpen £6,
chd free.**
7 acres in beautiful setting with views
of S Berkshire Downs and historical
Combe Gibbet, across lawn with ha-
ha and parkland. C18 Queen Anne
House (not open). Formal rose
borders, double herbaceous border,
colour themed border between yew
buttress hedges. Lily pond garden
and terraces laid out by Harold Peto.
Reflecting pond with fountain, lake,
walled garden and contemporary
sculptures. Some uneven paths.

**22 LITTLECOTE HOUSE
HOTEL**
**Hungerford RG17 0SU. Warner
Leisure Hotels, 01488 682509,**
www.warnerleisurehotels.co.uk.
*2m W of Hungerford. From A4 turn R
onto B4192 signed Swindon. After
1½ m exit L & follow signs.* **Sun 17,
Sun 31 July, Sun 14 Aug (12-4).
Adm £4. Light refreshments in
Kennet Bar.**
Beautiful setting around Grade I listed
house with views of the Kennet Valley
over lawns and parkland. Formal
areas incl herbaceous borders, rose
and herb garden, clipped yew, box
hedging, and fruit trees. Don't miss
the stumpery and the courtyard with
large planters. Attractive selection of
hanging baskets. Sorry, no children.
Plants for sale and also garden gifts in
Potting Shed Shop. Gravel paths,
some slopes.
& ⊗ 🚌 🛏 🍵

Estoril

greenhouse, island beds and eclectic planting. Small vegetable patch with fruit trees. Main paths offer partial wheelchair access, but others are chipped bark and unsuitable.

26 ODNEY CLUB
Odney Lane, Cookham SL6 9SR. John Lewis Partnership. *3m N of Maidenhead. Off A4094 S of Cookham Bridge. Signs to car park in grounds.* **Sun 24 Apr (2-6). Adm £4.50, chd free. Light refreshments. Also open 2 Belle Vue Cottages (10 mins walk).** *Donation to Thames Valley Adventure Playground.*

This 120 acre site is beside the Thames with lovely riverside walks. A favourite with Stanley Spencer who featured our magnolia in his work. Magnificent wisteria, specimen trees, herbaceous borders, side gardens, spring bedding and ornamental lake. The John Lewis Partnership Heritage Centre will be open, showcasing the textile archive and items illustrating the history of John Lewis and Waitrose. Some gravel paths. Dogs on leads please.

THE OLD MILL
See Wiltshire

27 THE OLD RECTORY FARNBOROUGH
Wantage, Oxon OX12 8NX. Mr & Mrs Michael Todhunter, 01488 638298. *4m SE of Wantage. Take B4494 Wantage-Newbury road, after 4m turn E at sign for Farnborough. Approx 1m to village, Old Rectory on L.* **Sun 24 Apr, Sun 22 May, Sun 12 June (2-5.30). Adm £5, chd free. Home-made teas.** *Donation to Farnborough PCC.*

In a series of immaculately tended garden rooms, incl herbaceous borders, arboretum, boules, roses, vegetable and new bog garden, there is an explosion of rare and interesting plants, beautifully combined for colour and texture. With stunning views across the countryside, it is the perfect setting for the 1749 rectory (not open), once home of John Betjeman, in memory of whom John Piper created a window in the local church. Awarded Finest Parsonage in England by Country Life and The Rectory Society. Plants and home-made preserves for sale. Some steep slopes and gravel paths.

---

23 NEW MALVERLEYS
East End, Newbury RG20 0AA. *A34 S of Newbury, exit signed for Highclere. Follow A343 for ¹/₂ m, turn R to Woolton Hill. Pass school & turn L to East End. After 1m R at village green, then after 100 metres, R onto Fullers Lane.* **Sun 24 Apr, Sun 24 July (2-5). Adm £10, chd free. Pre-booking essential, please visit www.ngs.org.uk or phone 01483 211535 for information & booking. Tea & cake and tour with Head Gardener included. Ticket availability is limited so please book early to avoid disappointment.**

10 acres of dynamic gardens which have been developed over the last 5 yrs to include magnificent mixed borders and a series of contrasting yew hedged rooms, hosting flame borders, a cool garden and a pond garden. A vegetable garden with striking fruit cages sit within a walled garden, also encompassing a white garden. Meadows open out to views over the parkland. Will feature in Gardens Illustrated (Summer 2016).

24 THE MILL HOUSE, BOXFORD
Boxford, Newbury RG20 8DP. Mrs Heather Luff, 01488 608385, H4luff@gmail.com. *5m W of Newbury. Take B4000 to Stockcross for 2m, then turn R signed Boxford.*

At T-junction turn R & then L. Over bridge, The Mill House is 1st on L. **Visits by arrangement Apr to Sept for groups of 4-20. Adm £5.50, chd free. Home-made teas.**
Very attractive large mature garden surrounding Grade II listed Mill House (not open) with R Lambourn running through. Herbaceous borders, rose garden, espalier fruit trees, lawns and vegetables. Good spring colour with daffodils, tulips and alliums. Riverside walk overlooking water meadows. Lovely autumn garden with sedum, echinacea and clipped box.

25 OAK COTTAGE
99B Kiln Ride, Finchampstead, Wokingham RG40 3PD. Ms Liz Ince, www.facebook.com/oakcottagegarden. *2¹/₂ m S of Wokingham. Off B3430 Nine Mile Ride between A321 Sandhurst Rd & B3016 Finchampstead Rd.* **Sun 21 Feb (2-4.30). Adm £3.50, chd free. Light refreshments. Sun 8 May (2-5). Combined adm with Glenmere £4.50, chd free. Home-made teas. 2017: Sun 19 Feb.**
¹/₄ acre garden with woodland feel. Mature trees underplanted with snowdrops and other spring flowering bulbs. Several unusual winter flowering plants incl an Edgeworthia chrysantha, Chrysosplenium macrophyllum and many hellebores. Pine pergola with various climbers,

28 THE OLD RECTORY INKPEN

Lower Green, Inkpen RG17 9DS. Mrs C McKeon. *4m SE of Hungerford. From centre of Kintbury at the Xrds, take Inkpen Rd. After ¹/₂ m turn R, then go approx 3m (passing Crown & Garter PH, then Inkpen Village Hall on L). Nr St Michaels Church, follow car park signs.* **Sun 19 June (2-5). Adm £3.50, chd free. Tea. Combined adm with Kirby House £6, chd free.**

On a gentle hillside with lovely countryside views, the Old Rectory offers a peaceful setting for this pretty 2 acre garden. Enjoy strolling through the formal and walled gardens, herbaceous borders, pleached lime walk and wild flower meadow (some slopes).

29 OLD WATERFIELD

Winkfield Road, Ascot SL5 7LJ. Hugh & Catherine Stevenson, catherine.stevenson@oldwaterfield. com. *6m SW of Windsor to E of Ascot Racecourse. On E side of A330 midway between A329 & A332.* **Visits by arrangement Feb to Sept for groups of 10-25. Light refreshments on request. Adm £4, chd free.**

Set in 4 acres between Ascot Heath and Windsor Great Park, the original cottage garden has been developed and extended over the past few years. Herbaceous borders, meadow with specimen trees, large productive vegetable garden, orchard, and mixed hedging. Winter bed with dogwoods and snowdrops at its best in late February.

30 THE PRIORY

Beech Hill RG7 2BJ. Mr & Mrs C Carter, 01189 883146, tita@getcarter.org.uk. *5m S of Reading. M4 J11, A33 S to Basingstoke. At T-lights, L to Spencers Wood. After 1¹/₂ m turn R for Beech Hill. After approx 1¹/₂ m, L into Wood Lane, R down Priory Drive.* **Visits by arrangement June to Aug for groups of 10+. Teas on request. Adm £4.50, chd free.**

Extensive gardens in grounds of former C12 French Priory (not open), rebuilt 1648. The mature gardens are in a very attractive setting beside the R Loddon. Large formal walled garden with espalier fruit trees, lawns, mixed and replanted herbaceous borders, vegetables and roses. Woodland, fine trees, lake and Italian style water garden.

31 PYT HOUSE

Ashampstead RG8 8RA. Hans & Virginia von Celsing, www.Vvcgardendesign.com. *4m W of Pangbourne. From Yattendon head towards Reading. Road forks L into a beech wood towards Ashampstead. Keep L & join lower road. ¹/₂ m turn L just before houses.* **Sun 26 June (2-5). Combined adm with Willow Tree Cottage £5, chd free. Home-made teas.**

A 4 acre garden planted over the last 9 yrs by designer owner, around C18 house (not open). Mature trees, yew, hornbeam and beech hedges, pleached limes, modern perennial borders, pond, orchard and vegetable garden. New iris beds. Broadly organic, a haven for bees and butterflies, and we also have chickens.

An explosion of rare and interesting plants, beautifully combined for colour and texture . . .

32 THE RISC ROOF GARDEN, READING

35-39 London Street, Reading RG1 4PS. Reading International Solidarity Centre, www.risc.org.uk/gardens. *Central Reading. 5 mins walk from Oracle Shopping Centre. 10 mins from station. Park in Queens Rd or Oracle car parks. Disabled parking at rear of building.* **Sat 21 May, Sat 2 July, Sat 6 Aug (12-4). Adm £3.50, chd free. Light refreshments at RISC Global Cafe.** *Donation to RISC.*

Small edible roof forest garden developed to demonstrate sustainability and our dependence on plants. All plants in the garden have an economic use for food, clothing, medicine etc, and come from all over the world. Demonstration of renewable energy, water harvesting and irrigation systems. Garden accessed by external staircase. Regular tours of garden. Featured in The New Kitchen Garden by Mark Diacono.

33 ROOKSNEST

Ermin Street, Lambourn Woodlands RG17 7SB. Dame Theresa Sackler, 01488 71678, garden@rooksnest.net. *2m S of Lambourn on B4000. From M4 J14, take A338 Wantage Rd, turn 1st L onto B4000 (Ermin St) to Lambourn. Rooksnest signed after 3m.* **Wed 27 Apr, Wed 22 June (11-4). Adm £4.50, chd free. Light refreshments. Combined adm with Inholmes £6.50, chd free. Visits also by arrangement Apr to July for groups of 15+.**

Approx 10 acre exceptionally fine traditional English garden. Rose and herbaceous garden, pond garden, herb garden, vegetables and glasshouses. Many specimen trees and fine shrubs, orchard and terraces renovated and recently replanted. Garden mostly designed by Arabella Lennox-Boyd since 1980. Light refreshments incl teas, coffees, home-made cakes and light lunches. Plants sale at June opening only. Mostly grass, gravel and some paved areas. Happy to provide assistance to wheelchair users.

34 ROOKWOOD FARM HOUSE

Stockcross RG20 8JX. The Hon Rupert & Charlotte Digby, 01488 608676, charlotte@rookwoodfarmhouse.co. uk, www.rookwoodfarmhouse.co.uk. *3m W of Newbury. M4 J13, A34(S). After 3m exit for A4(W) to Hungerford. At 2nd r'about take B4000 towards Stockcross, after approx ³/₄ m turn R into Rookwood.* **Sun 29 May, Sun 19 June (1-5). Combined adm with Springfield Cottage £5, chd free. Home-made cakes & teas.**

This exciting valley garden, a work in progress, has elements all visitors can enjoy. A rose covered pergola, fabulous tulips, giant alliums, a kitchen garden featuring a parterre of raised beds, as well as bog gardens and colour themed herbaceous planting, all make Rookwood well worth a visit. Gravel paths, some steep slopes.

35 SANDLEFORD PLACE

Newtown, Newbury RG20 9AY.
Mel Gatward, 01635 40726,
melgatward@btinternet.com. *1¹/₂ m S of Newbury on A339. House on NW side of Swan r'about at Newtown on A339 1¹/₂ m S of Newbury.* **Sun 15 May (2-5.30); Sun 26 June (2-6). Adm £6, chd free. Cream teas. Visits also by arrangement Mar to Oct.**
A plantswoman's 4 acres, more exuberant than manicured with R Enborne flowing through. Various areas of shrub and mixed borders create a romantic, naturalistic effect. Wonderful old walled garden. Long herbaceous border flanks wild flower meadow. Yr-round interest from early carpets of snowdrops and daffodils, crocus covered lawn, to autumn berries and leaf colour. A garden for all seasons. Featured in Country Homes & Interiors (March 2015). Wheelchair access to most areas. Guide dogs only.

36 SPRINGFIELD COTTAGE

Stockcross RG20 8LJ. Anne & Ron Cummings. *3m W of Newbury. M4 J13, A34(S). After 3m exit for A4(W) to Hungerford. At 2nd r'about take B4000 towards Stockcross, after approx ³/₄ m you will find us on the L. Car park at Rookwood Farm House (150yds away).* **Sun 29 May, Sun 19 June (1-5). Combined adm with Rookwood Farm House £5, chd free. Home-made cakes & teas at Rookwood Farm House.**
Pretty cottage garden attached to a C16 listed thatched property (not open) and terraced on three levels. Lovingly designed and created by the owner over the last 8 yrs with mixed shrub and herbaceous borders, rose garden and lawns with seating areas, small pond and laburnum arbour.

37 NEW ST TIMOTHEE

Darlings Lane, Maidenhead SL6 6PA. Sarah & Sal Pajwani. *1m N of Maidenhead. M4 J8/9 to A404M. 2nd exit onto A4 to Maidenhead. L at 1st r'about to A4130 Henley Rd. After ¹/₂ m turn R onto Pinkneys Drive. At Pinkneys Arms PH, turn L into Lee Lane, follow NGS signs.* **Sun 5 June (11-5). Adm £4, chd free. Home-made teas.**
A recently created 2 acre garden adjacent to Pinkneys Green. Deep, gently flowing, colour themed borders planted for yr-round interest with a

wide range of attractive grasses and perennials. Other features incl a box parterre, wildlife pond, rose terrace and wild areas all set around established trees and a 1930s family home (not open).

Infinity lawn at front with far-reaching views over the North Wessex Downs and Chilterns . . .

---

38 STOCKCROSS HOUSE

Church Road, Stockcross, Newbury RG20 8LP. Susan & Edward Vandyk. *3m W of Newbury. M4 J13, A34(S). After 3m exit A4(W) to Hungerford. At 2nd r'about take B4000, 1m to Stockcross, 2nd L into Church Rd.* **Sun 5 June (11-4.30). Adm £5, chd free. Refreshments & light lunches.**
A lovely 2 acre garden set around a Grade II listed former vicarage (not open) with an emphasis on plant partnerships, colour combinations and naturalistic planting. Long wisteria and clematis covered pergola, reflecting pool with folly, cascade with pond and duck house, rich variety of roses, vegetable and cutting garden. Sculptural elements by local artists. Partial wheelchair access with some gravelled areas.

39 STUBBINGS HOUSE

Henley Road, Maidenhead SL6 6QL. Mr & Mrs D Good, 01628 825454, info@stubbingsgroup.com, www.stubbingsnursery.co.uk. *2m W of Maidenhead. From A4130 Henley Rd follow signed private access road opp Stubbings Church. See website for further directions.* **Sat 19 Mar (10-4.30); Sun 20 Mar (10-4); Sat 30 Apr (10-4.30); Sun 1 May (10-4); Mon 2 May (10-4.30). Adm £3.50, chd free. Light refreshments in Nursery Café. Visits also by arrangement Apr to Sept for groups of 10-20.**
Parkland garden accessed via adjacent retail nursery. Set around

C18 house (not open), home to Queen Wilhelmina of Netherlands in WW2. Large lawn with ha-ha and woodland walks. Notable trees incl historic cedars and araucaria. March brings an abundance of daffodils and in May a 60 metre wall of wisteria. Attractions incl a C18 icehouse and access to adjacent NT woodland. A level site with firm gravel paths for wheelchair access.

40 SUNNINGDALE PARK

Larch Avenue, Ascot SL5 0QE. De Vere Venues, 01252 668645, graham.oconnell22@gmail.com, www.deverevenues.co.uk/en/venues/sunningdale-park. *6m S of Windsor. On A30 at Sunningdale take Broomhall Lane. After ¹/₂ m, R into Larch Ave. From A329 turn into Silwood Rd towards Sunningdale.* **Tue 31 May (2-5). Adm £5, chd free. Home-made teas. Visits also by arrangement in May (Mon 23 to Fri 27 only), with a guided history tour for groups of 10+.**
Over 20 acres of beautifully landscaped gardens in Capability Brown style. Terrace garden and Victorian rockery designed by Pulham incl cave and water features. Lake area with paved walks, extensive lawns with specimen trees, flower beds, many rhododendrons and azaleas. Lovely 1m woodland walk. Grade II listed building (not open). Free garden history tour at 3pm.

GROUP OPENING

41 SWALLOWFIELD HORTICULTURAL SOCIETY

The Street, Swallowfield RG7 1QY. *5m S of Reading. M4 J11 & A33/B3349 signed Swallowfield NGS Opening. Tickets & map from Doctors Surgery car park, The Street, RG7 1QY.* **Sun 26 June (11-5). Combined adm £6, chd free. Light lunches at Brambles & tea, coffee & cakes at Hornbeams.**

APRIL COTTAGE
Linda & Bill Kirkpatrick

5 BEEHIVE COTTAGES
Ray Tormey

BRAMBLES
Sarah & Martyn Dadds

GREENWINGS
Liz & Ray Jones

NEW ▶ LAMBS FARMHOUSE
Eva Koskuba

LODDON LOWER FARM
Mr & Mrs J Bayliss

NORKETT COTTAGE
Jenny Spencer

PRIMROSE COTTAGE
Hilda & Eddie Phillips

THREE GABLES
Sue & Keith Steptoe

WESSEX HOUSE
Val Payne

Swallowfield is a real village enhanced by a C12 church, nestled amongst rural countryside by the Whitewater, Blackwater and Loddon rivers which creates an abundance of wildlife and lovely views. We are proud to offer a variety of beautiful well stocked gardens of all shapes and sizes, incl a model train at Wessex House. Some gardens are within walking distance of each other, but transport is required to see the gardens that are not in the village centre.

42 ▶ THE TITHE BARN
Tidmarsh RG8 8ER. Fran Wakefield. *1m S of Pangbourne, off A340. In Tidmarsh, turn by side of Greyhound PH, over bridge, R into Mill Corner field for car park. Short walk over field to garden.* **Sun 19 June (2-5). Adm £3.50, chd free. Home-made teas at adjacent Norman church.**
This is a delightful 1/4 acre village garden within high brick walls around The Tithe Barn (not open) dating from 1760. Formally laid out with parterres of box and yew. There are roses, hostas, delphiniums and lavender as well as interesting vintage pots and containers. Working beehives. Winner of the English Garden magazine Gardener's Garden competition.

43 ▶ ◆ WELFORD PARK
Welford, Newbury RG20 8HU. Mrs J H Puxley, www.welfordpark.co.uk. *6m NW of Newbury. M4 J13, A34(S). After 3m exit for A4(W) to Hungerford. At 2nd r'about take B4000, after 4m turn R signed Welford. Entrance on Newbury-Lambourn road.* **For NGS: Wed 10 Feb (11-4). Adm £6, chd free. Light refreshments. For other opening times and information, please visit garden website.**

One of the finest natural snowdrop woodlands in the country, approx 4 acres, along with a wonderful display of hellebores throughout the garden and winter flowering shrubs. This is an NGS 1927 pioneer garden on the R Lambourn set around Queen Anne House (not open). Also the stunning setting for BBC Great British Bake Off 2014 & 2015. Dogs welcome on leads. Coach parties please book in advance.

PERENNIAL
GARDENERS' ROYAL BENEVOLENT SOCIETY

NGS support is vital to Perennial for our work

GROUP OPENING

44 ▶ WEST MILLS ALLOTMENTS & ISLAND COTTAGE
West Mills, Newbury RG14 5HT. *In centre of Newbury nr the canal. Park in town centre car parks. Walk either side of St Nicholas Church or between Cote Restaurant & Holland & Barrett to canal. 100yds to Swing Bridge & follow signs. Limited side road parking.* **Sun 3 July (2-5). Combined adm £4.50, chd free. Home-made teas at Island Cottage (weather permitting).**

ISLAND COTTAGE
Karen & Roger Swaffield
Visits also by arrangement Apr to Sept for small groups.
karen.swaffield@btinternet.com

WEST MILLS ALLOTMENTS
Newbury Town Council (local contact Jo Dobson)

Allotments and small town garden in the centre of Newbury. You are welcome to visit a small selection of allotments on our 120 plot site and the opportunity to talk to some of the plot holders about their methods. A variety of fruit, vegetables and flowers to see, some in greenhouses and polytunnels. Island Cottage is a small town garden set between a backwater of the R Kennet and the Kennet and Avon Canal. You will find

interesting combinations of colour and texture to look at rather than walk through, although you can do that too! A deck overlooks a sluiceway towards a lawn and border. Started from scratch in 2005, and mostly again after the floods of 2014. Featues incl a studio with a small art display of local artists at Island Cottage and plants for sale at both sites.

45 ▶ WICKHAM HOUSE
Wickham, Newbury RG20 8HD. Mr & Mrs James D'Arcy, philippa@darcy3.com, www.wickhamhouse.com. *7m NW of Newbury or 6m NE of Hungerford. From M4 J14, take A338(N) signed Wantage. Approx 3/4 m turn R onto B4000 for Wickham & Shefford Woodlands.Through Wickham village, entrance 100yds on R. Or take the B4000 from Newbury, to Wickham village.* **Tue 12 July (11-4). Adm £5, chd free. Home-made teas & home cooked gammon rolls. Visits also by arrangement June to Sept for groups of 20+.**
In a beautiful country house setting, this exceptional 1/2 acre walled garden was created from scratch in 2008. Designed by Robin Templar-Williams, the different rooms have distinct themes and colour schemes. Delightful arched clematis and rose walkway. Wide variety of trees, planting, pots brimming with colour and places to sit and enjoy the views. Separate cutting and vegetable garden. Featured in The English Garden magazine (Aug 2015). Gravel paths.

46 ▶ WILLOW TREE COTTAGE
Ashampstead RG8 8RA. Katy & David Weston. *4m W of Pangbourne. From Yattendon head towards Reading. L fork in beech wood to Ashampstead, keep L, join lower road, 1/2 m turn L before houses.* **Sun 26 June (2-5). Combined adm with Pyt House £5, chd free. Home-made teas at Pyt House.**
Small pretty cottage garden surrounding the house that was originally built for the gardener of Pyt House. Substantially redesigned and replanted in recent yrs. Perennial borders, vegetable garden, pond with ducks and chickens.

BUCKINGHAMSHIRE

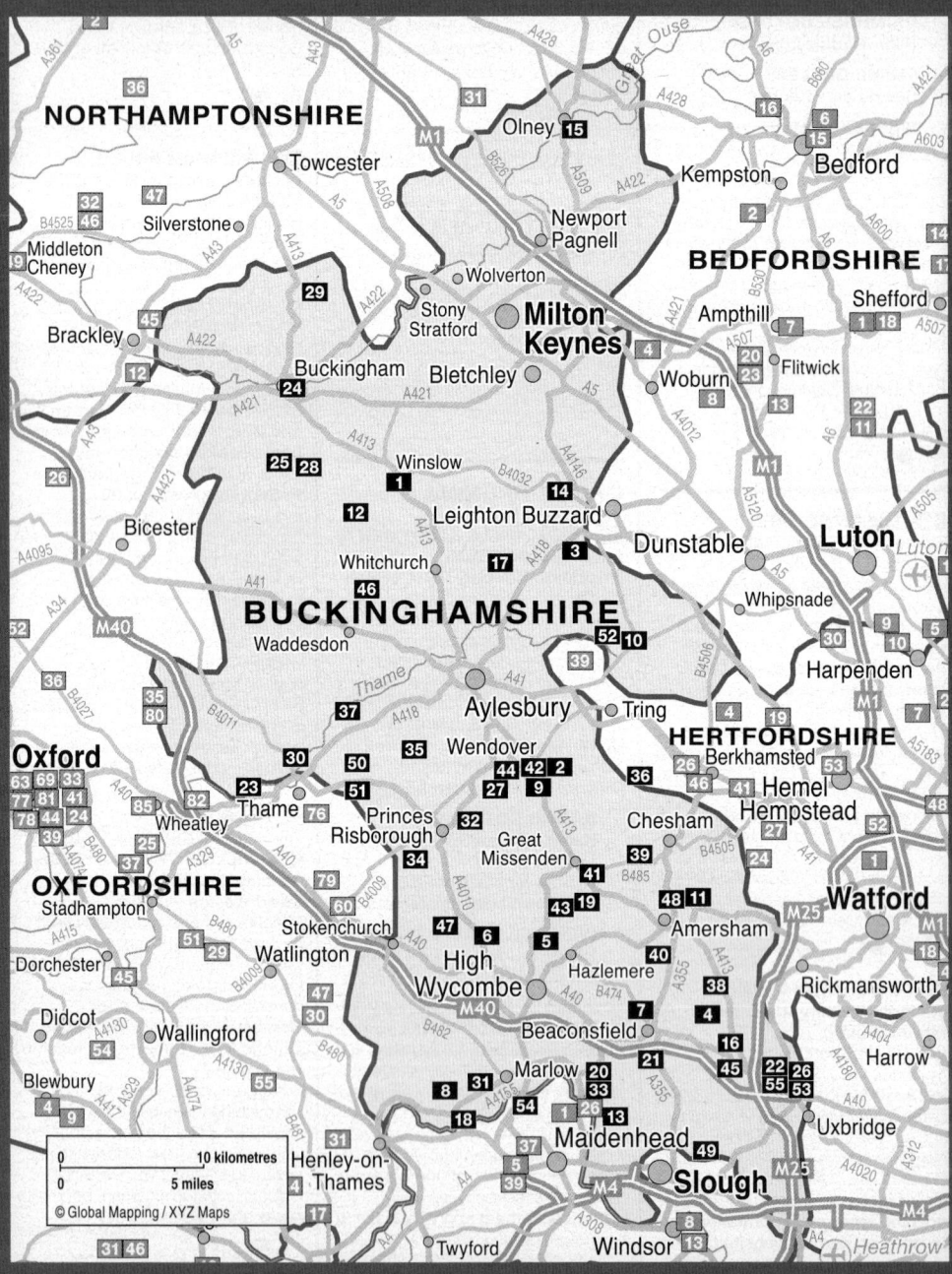

Buckinghamshire

Buckinghamshire has a beautiful varied landscape; edged by the River Thames to the south, crossed by the Chiltern Hills, and with the Vale of Aylesbury stretching to the north.

Many of our group openings can be found in villages of thatched or brick and flint cottages. We boast many historical gardens including Ascott, Stoke Poges Memorial Gardens (Grade 1 listed), Cliveden and Cowper and Newton Museum Gardens.

So many Buckinghamshire gardens have been used as locations for films and television, with the Pinewood Studios nearby and excellent proximity to London.

Visitors looking for a really interesting afternoon out are encouraged to visit the Cheddington Combined School Sensory Garden, which was created in 2007 by a Year 5 class based on the senses of sight, sound, taste and smell.

The Cheddington Allotments are also well worth a visit, and offer fine vegetable plots, soft fruit trees and beautiful wide views of the Chilterns.

Buckinghamshire Volunteers

County Organiser
Maggie Bateson
01494 866265
maggiebateson@gmail.com

County Treasurer
Tim Hart
01494 837328
tim.hart@virgin.net

Publicity
Sandra Wetherall
01494 862264
sandracwetherall@gmail.com

Booklet Co-ordinator
Maggie Bateson
(as above)

Assistant County Organisers
Janice Cross
01494 728291
gwendalice@aol.com

Judy Hart
01494 837328
judy.hart@virgin.net

Margaret Higgins
01844 347072
jhiggins816@btinternet.com

Mhairi Sharpley
01494 782870
mhairisharpley@btinternet.com

Below Cliveden

Opening Dates

All entries subject to change.
For latest information check www.ngs.org.uk

February

Snowdrop Festival

Sunday 21
46 Quainton Gardens

March

Sunday 6
33 Magnolia House
Sunday 13
55 Wind in the Willows
Sunday 20
11 Chesham Bois House
Sunday 27
41 Overstroud Cottage

April

Sunday 10
48 Rivendell
Sunday 17
26 NEW Hills House
Saturday 23
13 Cliveden
Sunday 24
30 Long Crendon Gardens
52 Westend House

May

Sunday 1
14 NEW Close Cottage
41 Overstroud Cottage

Monday 2
3 Ascott
50 Turn End
Sunday 8
11 Chesham Bois House
44 The Plough
Sunday 15
19 Fressingwood
Tuesday 17
47 Red Kites
Sunday 22
34 The Manor House
41 Overstroud Cottage
49 Stoke Poges Memorial Gardens
Sunday 29
39 The Old Sun House
Monday 30
37 Nether Winchendon House
44 The Plough

June

Festival Weekend

Sunday 5
1 Abbots House
8 Burrow Farm
12 The Claydons
22 Higher Denham Gardens
45 Ponders
53 The White House
Wednesday 8
40 Orchard House
Saturday 11
15 Cowper & Newton Museum Gardens
Sunday 12
7 18 Brownswood Road
15 Cowper & Newton Museum Gardens

17 Cublington Gardens
Sunday 19
10 Cheddington Gardens
25 Hillesden House
26 NEW Hills House
29 Lillingstone Lovell Gardens
Thursday 23
31 Lords Wood
Saturday 25
42 11 The Paddocks
Sunday 26
6 Bradenham Manor
41 Overstroud Cottage
42 11 The Paddocks
51 Tythrop Park
Wednesday 29
20 Grange Drive Wooburn

July

Saturday 2
42 11 The Paddocks
Sunday 3
23 Hill House
32 Lowthorpe House
42 11 The Paddocks
Tuesday 5
47 Red Kites
Wednesday 6
20 Grange Drive Wooburn
Sunday 10
8 Burrow Farm
11 Chesham Bois House

August

Wednesday 10
18 Danesfield House
Monday 29
3 Ascott

September

Thursday 15
31 Lords Wood

October

Saturday 15
2 Acer Corner
Sunday 16
2 Acer Corner

Gardens open to the public

3 Ascott
13 Cliveden
15 Cowper & Newton Museum Gardens
37 Nether Winchendon House
49 Stoke Poges Memorial Gardens

By arrangement only

4 Beech House
5 NEW Boss Lane House
9 Cedar House
16 Craiglea House
21 Hall Barn
24 Hill House, Buckingham
27 Homelands
28 NEW Kingsbridge
35 Moat Farm
38 North Down
43 NEW Peterley Corner Cottage
54 Whitewalls

Also open by arrangement

1 Abbots House
2 Acer Corner
8 Burrow Farm
11 Chesham Bois House
14 NEW Close Cottage
17 Larkspur House, Cublington Gardens
25 Hillesden House
31 Lords Wood
33 Magnolia House
41 Overstroud Cottage
42 11 The Paddocks
44 The Plough
45 Ponders
47 Red Kites
55 Wind in the Willows

Cedar House

The Gardens

1 ABBOTS HOUSE

10 Church Street, Winslow MK18 3AN. Mrs Jane Rennie, 01296 712326, jane@renniemail.com. *9m N of Aylesbury. A413 into Winslow. From town centre take Horn St & R into Church St, L fork at top. Entrance 20 metres on L. Parking in town centre & adjacent streets.* **Sun 5 June (12.30-5). Adm £3, chd free. Home-made teas. Visits also by arrangement Apr to Aug for groups of 20 max.**
Garden on different levels divided into four; courtyard near house with arbour, pond with waterfall and pots, woodland garden with rose gazebo, and swimming pool garden with grasses. Walled Victorian kitchen garden with glasshouses, potager, fruit pergola, wall trained fruit, many Mediterranean plants and recent meadow planting. Featured in the Buckingham & Winslow Advertiser 2015. Partial wheelchair access, garden levels accessed by steps only.

2 ACER CORNER

10 Manor Road, Wendover HP22 6HQ. Jo Naiman, 07958 319234, jo@acercorner.com, www.acercorner.com. *3m S of Aylesbury. Follow A413 into Wendover. L at clock tower r'about into Aylesbury Rd. R at next r'about into Wharf Rd, continue past schools on L, garden on R.* **Sat 15, Sun 16 Oct (2-5). Adm £2.50, chd free. Home-made teas. Visits also by arrangement July to Oct.** *Donation to South Bucks Jewish Community Charity.*
Garden designer's garden with Japanese influence and large collection of Japanese maples. The enclosed front garden is Japanese in style. Back garden is divided into three areas; patio area surrounded by roses; densely planted area with many acers and roses; and the corner which includes a productive greenhouse and interesting planting. Featured in the RHS The Garden magazine (Nov 2015).

3 ◆ ASCOTT

Ascott, Wing, Leighton Buzzard LU7 0PR. Sir Evelyn de Rothschild, National Trust, 01296 688242, joshv@ascottestate.co.uk, www.nationaltrust.org.uk/ascott. *2m SW of Leighton Buzzard, 8m NE of Aylesbury. Via A418. Buses: 150 Aylesbury - Milton Keynes, 100 Aylesbury & Milton Keynes.* **For NGS: Mon 2 May, Mon 29 Aug (2-6). Adm £5, chd £2.50. Tea. (NT members are required to pay to enter the gardens on NGS days). For other opening times and information, please phone, email or visit garden website.**
Combining Victorian formality with early C20 natural style and recent plantings to lead it into the C21, with a recently completed garden designed by Jacques and Peter Wirtz who designed the gardens at Alnwick Castle, and also a Richard Long Sculpture. Terraced lawns with specimen and ornamental trees, panoramic views to the Chilterns. Naturalised bulbs, mirror image herbaceous borders, impressive topiary incl box and yew sundial. Entry into Ascott House is free to NT members, non-members will be required to pay. Outdoor wheelchairs available from car park. Indoor wheelchairs available in the house. Mobility buggy, prior booking advised.

4 BEECH HOUSE

Long Wood Drive, Jordans, Beaconsfield HP9 2SS. Sue & Ray Edwards, raybcm@tiscali.co.uk. *From A40, L to Seer Green & Jordans for approx 1m. Turn into Jordans Way on L. Longwood Drive 1st L. From A413 turn into Chalfont St Giles. Straight ahead until L signed Jordans. 1st L Jordans Way.* **Visits by arrangement Mar to Nov for groups of 2-30. Adm £3, chd free.**
2 acre plantsman's garden built up over the last 28 yrs, with a wide range of plants aimed at providing yr-round interest. Many shrubs, roses, grasses, ferns, perennials and trees planted for their ornamental bark and autumnal foliage. A particular feature is the meadow in the back garden with numerous bulbs and wild flowers in spring and early summer. Wheelchair access dependent upon weather conditions.

Stoke Poges Memorial Gardens

5 NEW BOSS LANE HOUSE
Boss Lane, Hughenden Valley, High Wycombe HP14 4LQ. Jacqui Martin-Lof, 07785 771761, talk2jacqui@icloud.com. *3m N of High Wycombe, 2m SW of Great Kingshill. From the centre of High Wycombe, nr Eden Centre, follow A4128 for 3m to r'about, take 1st exit to next r'about, take 2nd exit & then immed turn R into Boss Lane. Follow NGS signs & continue up Boss Lane for 300 metres & house on R. Parking signposted.* **Visits by arrangement only Sun 17 April, Sun 29 May, Sun 5 June, 2-5.30pm. Pre-booking essential due to limited parking. Adm £4, chd free. Home-made teas.**
A quintessentially English garden set in just over 1 acre around a C16, Grade II listed historical brick and flint house (not open). Informal and generous planting within a formal layout. The yew topiaries, clematis and wisteria clad obelisks give yr-round structure. Colourful herbaceous perennials; peonies, hellebores and stunning views from the top terrace knot garden. Plants, wooden obelisks and plant stands for sale. Sadly no disabled access; steps and uneven paving.

6 BRADENHAM MANOR
Bradenham, High Wycombe HP14 4HF. National Trust & Grant Thornton UK, www.nationaltrust.org.uk. *2½ m NW of High Wycombe, 5m S of Princes Risborough. On A4010, turn by Red Lion PH, car park signed on village green.* **Sun 26 June (12.30-4). Adm £3.50, chd free. Home-made teas in the cricket pavillion on the village green.**
C17 yew trees line a unique wilderness garden cut into a steep hill, offering stunning views of the Chilterns and a haven for wildlife. NT restoration reinstated Victorian parterres, summer borders, and rejuvenated 100 yr old orchard. New guardians are in the process of restoring the Walled Garden, cut flower borders, the Gardeners Cottage Garden, and a Secret Garden overlooking a Medieval church. Share our plans and progress in our second yr, chat with our beekeeper and try Bradenham Manors' own apple juice in the orchard.

7 18 BROWNSWOOD ROAD
Beaconsfield HP9 2NU. John & Bernadette Thompson. *From New Town turn R into Ledborough Lane, L into Sandleswood Rd, 2nd R into Brownswood Rd.* **Sun 12 June (2-6). Adm £3.50, chd free. Home-made teas & gluten free options.**
A plant filled garden designed by Barbara Hunt. A harmonious arrangement of arcs and circles introduces a rhythm that leads through the garden. Sweeping box curves, gravel beds, brick edging and lush planting. A restrained use of purples and reds dazzle against a grey and green background.

8 BURROW FARM
Hambleden RG9 6LT. David Palmer, 01491 571256. *1m SE of Hambleden. On A4155 between Henley & Marlow, turn N at Mill End. After 300yds, R onto Rotten Row. After ½ m, Burrow Farm entrance on R.* **Sun 5 June, Sun 10 July (1-5). Adm £5, chd free. Home-made teas. Visits also by arrangement May to July for groups of 25 max.**
Burrow Farm and the adjacent cottages (not open) are part Tudor and part Elizabethan, set in the Chilterns above Hambleden Valley where it meets the Thames. Views of pasture and woodlands across the ha-ha greatly enhance the setting. Special features are the parterre, arboretum and C15 barn, where home-made teas will be served.

9 CEDAR HOUSE
Bacombe Lane, Wendover HP22 6EQ. Sarah Nicholson, 01296 622131, jeremynicholson@btinternet.com. *5m SE Aylesbury. From Gt Missenden take A413 into Wendover. Take 1st L before row of cottages, house at top of lane.* **Visits by arrangement May to Sept for groups of 10+. Adm £3.50, chd free.**
A chalk garden in the Chiltern Hills with a steep sloping lawn leading to a natural swimming pond with aquatic plants. Wild flowers with native orchids. Shaped borders hold a great variety of trees, shrubs and perennials. A lodge greenhouse and a good collection of half hardy plants in pots. Steep, sloping lawn.

GROUP OPENING

10 CHEDDINGTON GARDENS
Leighton Buzzard LU7 0RQ, www.cheddington.org.uk. *7m E of Aylesbury, 5m S of Leighton Buzzard, 5m W of Dunstable. Turn off B489 at Pitstone. Turn off B488 at Cheddington Station. ¾ m walk from train station to village, approx 15 mins.* **Sun 19 June (1.30-5.30). Combined adm £5, chd free. Home-made teas in Methodist hall by the green & village hall adjacent to allotments.** *Donation to Methodist Church, St Giles Church & Village School.*

> **CHEDDINGTON ALLOTMENTS**
> Cheddington Parish Council
>
> **CHEDDINGTON COMBINED SCHOOL SENSORY GARDEN**
> Cheddington Combined School
>
> **NEW 87 CHURCH HILL**
> Pat Garrett
>
> **NEW THE CORNER HOUSE**
> Charles Storr
>
> **NEW 8 MENTMORE ROAD**
> Mr & Mrs Evans
>
> **THE OLD POST OFFICE**
> Alan & Wendy Tipple
>
> **THE OLD READING ROOM**
> Mrs Kim Goldhagen
>
> **NEW SPRINGBRAE**
> Pier Thomas
>
> **THE VICARAGE**
> Revd Gill Rowell

Celebrating our 25th consecutive year of Cheddington Gardens! Mentioned in Domesday Book, Cheddington is a friendly, active, award-winning village, situated in the Vale of Aylesbury at the northern end of the Chilterns. 2016 we have nine gardens to view, varying in size, aspect and content, each reflecting their owners' style and passions. The School was the first in the UK to join a NGS Group. Cheddington has St Giles Church which dates back to C12, the present buildings are C14/C15 (open) and located just a short walk from the allotments, through the old orchards or by car to Church Path. Cheddington is home to the world's first branch railway line (closed 1964) along with the infamous Great Train Robbery of 1963. Partial wheelchair access.

11 CHESHAM BOIS HOUSE

85 Bois Lane, Chesham Bois HP6 6DF. Julia Plaistowe, 01494 726476, julia.plaistowe@yahoo.co.uk, cheshamboishouse.co.uk. *1m N of Amersham-on-the-Hill. Follow Sycamore Rd (main shopping centre road of Amersham) which becomes Bois Lane. Do not use SatNav once in lane as you will be led astray.* **Sun 20 Mar (2-5); Sun 8 May (2-5.30); Sun 10 July (11.30-5.30). Adm £4, chd free. Home-made teas. Visits also by arrangement Mar to Sept.**
3 acre plantswoman's garden with primroses, daffodils and hellebores in early spring. Interesting for most of the yr with lovely herbaceous borders, rill with small ornamental canal, walled garden, old orchard with wildlife pond, and handsome trees of which some are topiaried. It is a peaceful oasis. During the Sunday openings, the nearby 800 yr old church will be open. Featured in Country Life magazine as 'Garden of the Week' (March 2015). Gravel at front of the house.

GROUP OPENING

12 THE CLAYDONS

East Claydon MK18 2ND. *1½ m SW Winslow. In Winslow turn R off High St, follow NT signs to Claydon House. The Old Rectory, Middle Claydon is close to the entrance to Claydon House (NT).* **Sun 5 June (2-6). Combined adm £5, chd free. Home-made teas in the village hall.**

CLAYDON COTTAGE
Mr & Mrs Tony Evans

INGLENOOKS
Mr & Mrs David Polhill

THE OLD RECTORY
Mrs Jane Meisl

THE OLD VICARAGE
Nigel & Esther Turnbull

Three small villages originally part of the Claydon Estate with typical N Buckinghamshire cottages and two C13 churches. Inglenooks is an informal cottage garden with different areas of interest, many roses, surrounding C17 timber framed thatched cottage (not open). The Old Vicarage, a large garden on clay with mixed borders, scented garden, dell, shrub roses, vegetables and a natural clay pond. Small meadow area and planting to encourage wildlife. Access via gravel drive. Claydon Cottage has many quirky features and surprises. The Old Rectory is a large garden with a wild flower meadow, herbaceous borders, a woodland walk and cloud hedging. Partial wheelchair access.

13 ◆ CLIVEDEN

Taplow, Maidenhead SL6 0JA. National Trust, 01628 605069, www.nationaltrust.org.uk/cliveden. *2m N of Taplow. Leave M4 at J7, take A4 towards Maidenhead or M40 at J4, take A404 S & follow brown tourism signs.* **For NGS: Sat 23 Apr (10-5). Adm £11, chd £5.50. For other opening times and information, please phone or visit garden website.**
Set high above the R Thames, discover a garden that delights throughout the seasons with a colourful planting scheme for the famous parterre, impressive floral displays, distinctive topiary and an outstanding sculpture collection. Garden highlights incl spring and summer floral displays on the parterre and in the long garden, autumn colour in the water garden and a new rose garden. Features incl a children's storybook themed play area, yew tree maze, woodland play trail and a shop. Step free route map available from information centre. Wheelchairs available to borrow.

14 NEW CLOSE COTTAGE

Church Lane, Soulbury, Leighton Buzzard LU7 0BU. Rachel Belsham & Daniel Storey, belshamstorey@btinternet.com. *Approx 3m NW of Leighton Buzzard. In centre of village, next to field below church, on narrow country lane leading uphill from The Boot PH. Parking in field below church, access from the High Rd.* **Sun 1 May (1.30-5.30). Adm £4.50, chd free. Light refreshments. Visits also by arrangement Apr to Aug.**
The 3 acre garden at Close Cottage is 14 yrs old and encompasses a formal terraced garden, orchard and paddock. The garden is laid to lawn and planted with a wide variety of shrubs, bulbs and perennials. The orchard incl an avenue of cherry trees, various fruit trees, a wild flower meadow, woodland area, vegetable beds and a cutting garden. The garden is terraced, with broad steps and ramps to negotiate. Wheelchairs will require assistance due to steep incline.

Children's storybook themed play area . . .

15 ◆ COWPER & NEWTON MUSEUM GARDENS

Market Place, Olney MK46 4AJ. Mrs E Knight, 01234 711516, www.cowperandnewtonmuseum.org.uk. *5m N of Newport Pagnell. 12m S of Wellingborough. On A509. Please park in public car park in East St.* **For NGS: Sat 11, Sun 12 June (10.30-4.30). Adm £3, chd free. Home-made teas. For other opening times and information, please phone or visit garden website.**
The Flower Garden of C18 poet William Cowper, who said 'Gardening was, of all employments, that in which I succeeded best', has plants introduced prior to his death in 1800, many mentioned in his writings. The Summer House Garden, with Cowper's 'verse manufactory', now a Victorian Kitchen Garden, has new and heritage vegetables organically grown, also a herb border and medicinal plant bed. Features incl lacemaking demonstrations and local artists painting live art.

© Marianne Majerus

Chesham Bois House

 CRAIGLEA HOUSE

Austenwood Lane, Chalfont St Peter, Gerrards Cross SL9 9DA. Jeff & Sue Medlock, 01753 884852, suemedlock@msn.com, www.craigleahouse.com. *6m SE Amersham. From Gerrards Cross take B416 to Amersham. Take L fork after ¹/₂ m into Austenwood Lane, garden is ¹/₃ m on R. Park at St Joseph's Church or Priory Rd.* **Visits by arrangement May to Sept for groups of 8+. Home-made teas on request. Adm £4, chd free.** Delightful 1 acre garden complements the Arts and Crafts House which it surrounds. The planting ranges from the formal rose garden, lawns, herbaceous borders and pergola, to the natural planting around wildlife ponds, and fruit trees. Garden contains a wide range of plants, incl many hostas, a small vegetable and cutting garden and many seats affording lovely views of garden.

GROUP OPENING

17 CUBLINGTON GARDENS

Cublington, Leighton Buzzard LU7 0LF. *5m SE Winslow, 5m NE Aylesbury. From Aylesbury take A413 Buckingham Rd. After 4m, at Whitchurch, turn R to Cublington.* **Sun 12 June (2-5.30).**

Combined adm £4, chd free. Home-made teas at the village hall, an old Victorian school.

CEDAR COTTAGE, 4 THE WALLED GARDENS
April Curnow

LARKSPUR HOUSE
Mr & Mrs S Jenkins
Visits also by arrangement June & July for groups of 16 max.
gstmusketeers3@aol.com
01296 682615

NEW ▶ MIMOSA COTTAGE, 2 THE WALLED GARDEN
Cathy & Paul

1 STEWKLEY ROAD
Tom & Helen Gadsby

A group of diverse gardens in this attractive Buckinghamshire village listed as a conservation area. Larkspur House is a beautifully maintained modern garden with hostas and alliums being firm favourites. It has a large, newly planted orchard and wild flower meadow. 1 Stewkley Road has a strong focus on home grown food with an idyllic organic kitchen garden, small orchard and courtyard garden. The cottages of The Walled Gardens that are accessed via a private tree lined drive, demonstrate how small gardens can be full of interest and accommodate the lifestyle of the owners. New for 2016 Mimosa Cottage, 2 The Walled Garden has its

own beach hut! Partial wheelchair access to some gardens.

---

18 DANESFIELD HOUSE

Henley Road, Marlow SL7 2EY. Danesfield House Hotel, 01628 891010, www.danesfieldhouse.co.uk. *3m from Marlow. On the A4155 between Marlow & Henley-on-Thames. Signed on the LH-side Danesfield House Hotel and Spa.* **Wed 10 Aug (10.30-4.30). Adm £4, chd free. Pre-booking essential for lunch and afternoon tea.** The gardens at Danesfield were completed in 1901 by Robert Hudson, the Sunlight Soap magnate who built the house. Since the house opened as a hotel in 1991, the gardens have been admired by several thousand guests each yr. However, in 2009 it was discovered that the gardens contained outstanding examples of pulhamite in both the formal gardens and the waterfall areas. The 100 yr old topiary is also outstanding. Part of the grounds incl an Iron Age fort. Guided tours welcome on NGS open days. There will be two tours offered by our Head Gardener at 10.30am and 1.30pm. Pre-booking essential. Restricted wheelchair access to the gardens due to gravel paths.

19 FRESSINGWOOD
Hare Lane, Little Kingshill, Great Missenden HP16 0EF. John & Maggie Bateson. *1m S of Gt Missenden, 4m W of Amersham. From the A413 at Chiltern Hospital, turn L signed Gt & Lt Kingshill. Take 1st L into Nags Head Lane. Turn R under railway bridge, then L into New Rd & continue to Hare Lane.* **Sun 15 May (2-5.30). Adm £3.50, chd free. Home-made teas.**
Thoughtfully designed garden with yr-round colour and many interesting features. Shrubbery with ferns, grasses and hellebores. Small formal garden, herb garden, pergolas with roses and clematis. Topiary and landscaped terrace. Newly developed area incorporating water with grasses. Herbaceous borders and bonsai collection.

An impressive collection of majestic specimen trees . . .

GROUP OPENING

20 GRANGE DRIVE WOOBURN
Wooburn Green HP10 0QD. *On A4094, 2m SW of A40, between Bourne End & Wooburn. From Wooburn Church, direction Maidenhead, Grange Drive is on L before r'about. From Bourne End, L at 2 mini-r'abouts, then 1st R.* **Wed 29 June, Wed 6 July (2-5). Combined adm £3.50, chd free. Home-made teas.**

MAGNOLIA HOUSE
Alan & Elaine Ford
(See separate entry)

THE SHADES
Pauline & Maurice Kirkpatrick

2 diverse gardens in a private tree lined drive which formed the entrance to a country house now demolished. Magnolia House is a ¹/₂ acre garden with many mature trees incl

magnificent copper beech and magnolia reaching the rooftop, a small cactus bed, fernery, stream leading to pond and greenhouses with 2 small aviaries. Front garden now has natural pond and bees. The Shades drive is approached through mature trees and beds of herbaceous plants and 60 various roses. A natural well is surrounded by shrubs and acers. The garden was developed in 2010 to incl a natural stone lawn terrace and changes made to the existing flower beds. A green slate water feature with alpine plants completes the garden. Child friendly. Partial wheelchair access.

21 HALL BARN
Windsor End, Beaconsfield HP9 2SG. The Hon Mrs Farncombe, jenefer@farncombe01.demon.co.uk. *¹/₂ m S of Beaconsfield. Lodge gate 300yds S of St Mary & All Saints' Church in Old Town centre. Please do not use SatNavs.* **Visits by arrangement Feb to Sept. Teas and tour on request for groups of 10+ only. Adm £4, chd free.**
Historical landscaped garden laid out between 1680-1730 for the poet Edmund Waller and his descendants. Features 300 yr old cloud formation yew hedges, formal lakes and vistas ending with classical buildings and statues. Wooded walks around the grove offer respite from the heat on sunny days. One of the original NGS garden openings of 1927. Gravel paths.

GROUP OPENING

22 HIGHER DENHAM GARDENS
Higher Denham UB9 5EA. *6m E of Beaconsfield. Turn off the A412 about ¹/₂ m N of junction with A40 into Old Rectory Lane. After 1m enter Higher Denham straight ahead. Tickets for all gardens available at the community hall.* **Sun 5 June (1-5). Combined adm £5, chd free. Tea in community hall.** *Donation to Higher Denham Community CIO.*

9 LOWER ROAD
Ms Patricia Davidson

19 MIDDLE ROAD
Sonia Harris

SHILLONG
Mrs Pauline Flack

WIND IN THE WILLOWS
Ron James
(See separate entry)

4 gardens, incl 1 new last yr, in the delightful chalk stream Misbourne Valley. Wind in the Willows has over 350 shrubs and trees, informal woodland and wild gardens incl riverside and bog plantings and a collection of 80 hostas and 12 striped roses in 3 acres. 'Really different' and 'stunning' are typical visitor comments. 19 Middle Road has a terrace overlooking a garden crowded with as many plants as possible with some fruit bushes and vegetables. The garden in Lower Road is a medium size garden backing onto the river and recently professionally redesigned and highly praised by visitors last yr. Compare the design with the outcome and see how existing shrubs and trees have been integrated into the now maturing design. Shillong, reopening in 2016, is a long plantswoman's garden of rooms each with a different style and many interesting plants. The owner of Wind in the Willows will lead optional guided tours of the garden starting at 2pm and 4pm. Tours last approx 1 hour. Partial wheelchair access to some gardens.

23 HILL HOUSE
Mill Road, Shabbington, Aylesbury HP18 9HQ. Professor Richard Mayou. *2m from Thame between Oxford & Aylesbury. From A418 Wheatley to Thame/Aylesbury road, follow sign to Shabbington. Hill House is on the L 300yds beyond The Old Fisherman & next to the church. Parking in roads.* **Sun 3 July (2-5). Adm £4, chd free. Home-made teas.**
Garden created over 24 yrs around a C18 and C19 vicarage next to C11 church. 1 acre with 10 compartments incl parterre, herbaceous border, new perennial garden, pool garden, creatively planted pots and orchard. Walk around 1¹/₂ acre field with views of church, house and countryside. Home-made teas and exhibition of village photographs in St Mary Magdalene Church (next door).

24 ▶ HILL HOUSE, BUCKINGHAM

Castle Street, Buckingham MK18 1BS. Leonie & Peter Thorogood, 07860 714758, leonie@pjtassociates.com. *By parish church in Buckingham town centre. Signed Tingewick Road Industry off bypass.* **Visits by arrangement June to Sept. Home-made teas on request. Adm £3, chd free.**

¹/₃ acre town garden on old castle walls by parish church in Buckingham conservation area. Aiming for ease of maintenance, yr-round interest and colour, incl good roses, hostas and herbaceous, a gardener's garden. Slight slopes to some areas of the garden.

25 ▶ HILLESDEN HOUSE

Church End, Hillesden MK18 4DB. Mr & Mrs R M Faccenda, 01296 730451, suefaccenda@aol.com. *3m S of Buckingham through Gawcott. Next to church in Hillesden.* **Sun 19 June (2-5). Adm £5, chd free. Light refreshments. Visits also by arrangement June to Aug for groups of 20+.**

By superb church Cathedral in the Fields. Carp lakes, fountains and waterfalls with mature trees. Rose, alpine and herbaceous borders, 5 acres of formal gardens with 80 acres of deer park and parkland. Wild flower areas and extensive lakes developed by the owner. Lovely walks and plenty of wildlife. Also a newly created woodland and vegetable garden. An orchard was planted in 2015. No wheelchair access to lakes.

26 ▶ NEW ▶ HILLS HOUSE

Village Road, Denham, Uxbridge UB9 5BH. Mr & Mrs B Savory. *Turn off M40 J1A towards London. Turn L at T-lights, stay in middle lane, turn L at r'about & stay in RH lane. Follow sign Village Only & follow road ¹/₄ m. Turn L over bridge, next to St Mary's Church.* **Sun 17 Apr, Sun 19 June (2-5). Adm £4, chd free. Home-made teas.**

A C16 3 acre garden in Denham Village with an impressive collection of majestic specimen trees, walled garden and designated shrub borders. A large rose garden and perennial border frame a sunken buxus parterre, and annual display of baskets that flow to an orchard on long gravel paths. Walk through serene areas and woodland plantings, with a spring display of bulbs underneath mature trees. No wheelchair access to sunken parterre area. Gravel paths.

27 ▶ HOMELANDS

Springs Lane, Ellesborough, Aylesbury HP17 0XD. Jean & Tony Young, 01296 622306, young@ellesborough.fsnet.co.uk. *6m SE of Aylesbury. On the B4010 between Wendover & Princes Risborough. Springs Lane is between village hall at Butlers Cross & the church. Narrow lane with an uneven surface.* **Visits by arrangement May to Aug. Adm £3.50, chd free. Light refreshments.**

Secluded ³/₄ acre garden on difficult chalk, adjoining open countryside. Designed to be enjoyed from many seating positions. Progress from semi formal to wild flower meadow and wildlife pond. Deep borders with all season interest and gravel beds with exotic late summer and autumn planting.

A natural stream containing bog plants meanders through the woodland garden . . .

---

28 ▶ NEW ▶ KINGSBRIDGE

Steeple Claydon MK18 2EJ. Mr & Mrs T Aldous, 01296 730224. *3m S of Buckingham. Halfway between Padbury & Steeple Claydon. Xrds with sign to Kingsbridge Only.* **Visits by arrangement for groups of 8+. Adm £5, chd free. Home-made teas.**

A stunning 6 acre garden, the product of 26 yrs of dedication by current owners. The main lawn is enclosed by softly curving herbaceous borders leading past clipped yews, a semicircle of pleached hornbeams and out across the ha-ha to countryside beyond. Interestingly planted throughout with many shrubs and roses. A natural stream containing bog plants meanders through the woodland garden.

GROUP OPENING

29 ▶ LILLINGSTONE LOVELL GARDENS

Lillingstone Lovell, Buckingham MK18 5BD. *5m E Buckingham. From Old Gaol in centre of Buckingham take A413 towards Towcester for 5m. Turn R on a bend when you see signs to Lillingstone Lovell. Parking may be limited with some walking involved.* **Sun 19 June (1-6). Combined adm £3.50, chd free. Home-made teas.**

9 BROOKSIDE 🛏
Mrs Jane Scott
01280 860014
jane@thatchedholidaycottage.co.uk

GLEBE FARM 🛏
Mr David Hilliard
01280 860384
thehilliards@talk21.com

Two lovely gardens in the pretty conservation village of Lillingstone Lovell. The enthusiastic keen gardeners have an abundance of colourful planting and creative ideas. Beds of perennials, ponds, vegetables, sculptural elements and everything you would expect from true cottage gardens. Enjoy delicious home-made cakes and a cup of tea at both gardens. Partial wheelchair access with some steps and narrow pathways.

GROUP OPENING

30 ▶ LONG CRENDON GARDENS

Long Crendon HP18 9AN. *2m N of Thame. Long Crendon Village is situated on the B4011 Thame-Bicester road. Maps showing the location of the gardens will be available on the day.* **Sun 24 Apr (2-6). Combined adm £6, chd free. Home-made teas at Church House, High St. *Donation to Long Crendon Day Centre & Community Library.***

BAKER'S CLOSE
Mr & Mrs Peter Vaines

BARRY'S CLOSE
Mr & Mrs Richard Salmon

48 CHILTON ROAD
Mr & Mrs M Charnock

COP CLOSE
Sandra & Tony Phipkin

25 ELM TREES
Carol & Mike Price

MANOR HOUSE
Mr & Mrs West

MULBERRY HOUSE
Ken Pandolfi & James
Anderson

TOMPSONS FARM
Mr & Mrs T Moynihan

8 gardens to visit, 4 along the High St. Tompsons Farm a large woodland garden with mature trees and lawns sweeping down to a lake; Mulberry House a restored, old vicarage garden which incl a formal knot garden, a wooded walkway, pond and Zen style area; Manor House a large garden with views towards the Chilterns, 2 ornamental lakes, with a large variety of spring bulbs and shrubs; Cop Close, 1¹/₃ acre garden has a bog garden, vegetable and cutting garden and many varieties of daffodil and spring bulbs. Along the Bicester Rd, 2 large gardens; Baker's Close partly walled with terraced lawns, rockery, shrubs and a wild area, a spring planting of thousands of daffodils, narcissi and tulips; Barry's Close has a collection of spring flowering trees forming a backdrop to borders, pools and a water garden. Then 2 cottage gardens; 25 Elm Trees with a terrace, small orchard area, wildlife pond, rockery and deep borders; and 48 Chilton Road with spring bulbs, shrubs, perennial borders and a summerhouse area. Partial wheelchair access to some gardens.

& ⚘ ☕

---

31 ▶ LORDS WOOD
Frieth Road, Marlow Common SL7 2QS. Mr & Mrs Messum, millie-messum@messums.com. 1¹/₂ m NW Marlow. From Marlow turn off the A4155 at Platts Garage into Oxford Rd, towards Frieth for 1¹/₂ m. Garden is 100yds past the Marlow Common turn, on the L, opp Valley View Stables. **Thur 23 June, Thur 15 Sept (11-4.30). Adm £4, chd free. Home-made teas. Visits also by arrangement June to Sept for groups of 15+.**
Lords Wood was built in 1899 and

has been the Messums family home since 1974. The 5 acres of garden feature extensive borders in widely varying styles. From vegetable, flower and herb gardens, to large water gardens and rockery, orchard, woodland, and meadow with fantastic views over the Chilterns. We are always bringing new ideas to Lords Wood, you will find something different to enjoy with every visit. Partial wheelchair access; gravel paths and steep slopes.

& ☕

Carers Trust improves support, services and recognition for unpaid carers

---

32 ▶ LOWTHORPE HOUSE
Crowbrook Road, Askett, Princes Risborough HP27 9LS. Margaret & John Higgins. *100 metres down Crowbrook Rd (north end) on LH-side.* **Sun 3 July (2-5.30). Adm £3, chd free. Home-made teas.**
Set in the conservation area of Askett, the garden has been extensively altered and replanted by the current owners since 2012. A south facing garden with features incl herbaceous border, shrub border, roses, fruit cage, and ferns. Wheelchair access to all areas over grass and a gravel drive.

& ⚘ ☕

---

33 ▶ MAGNOLIA HOUSE
Wooburn HP10 0QD. Alan & Elaine Ford, 01628 525818, lanforddesigns@gmail.com, https://sites.google.com/site/lanforddesigns/. *On A4094 2m SW of A40 between Bourne End & Wooburn. From Wooburn Church, direction Maidenhead, Grange Drive*

is on L before r'about. From Bourne End, L at 2 mini-r'abouts, then 1st R. **Sun 6 Mar (11-2). Adm £3, chd free. Light refreshments. Opening with Grange Drive Wooburn on Wed 29 June, Wed 6 July. Visits also by arrangement Feb to Sept.**
¹/₂ acre, many mature trees incl magnificent copper beech and large magnolia. Wollemi pine, cactus, fernery, stream, 2 ponds, 2 greenhouses. 2 small aviaries, beehives, 10,000 snowdrops and hellebores in spring. Collection of over 60 different hostas. Child friendly. Stay in our self-catering accommodation and enjoy the garden. It is constantly being updated and new features added. Partial wheelchair access. Small well behaved dogs allowed by arrangement.

& ⊛ ⊨ ☕

---

34 ▶ THE MANOR HOUSE
Church End, Bledlow, Nr Princes Risborough HP27 9PB. The Lord Carrington. *9m NW of High Wycombe, 3m SW of Princes Risborough. ¹/₂ m off B4009 in middle of Bledlow Village. SatNav directions HP27 9PA.* **Sun 22 May (2-5). Adm £5, chd free. Light refreshments.**
Paved garden, parterres, shrub borders, old roses and walled kitchen garden. Water garden with paths, bridges and walkways fed by 14 chalk springs. Plus 2 acres of landscaped planting with sculptures. Partial wheelchair access as there is stepped access or sloped grass to enter the gardens.

& ☕

---

35 ▶ MOAT FARM
Water Lane, Ford, Aylesbury HP17 8XD. Mr & Mrs P Bergqvist, 01296 748560, patricia@quintadelarosa.com. *Turn up Water Lane by Dinton Hermit in the middle of Ford Village, after approx 200yds, turn L over cattle grid between beech hedges into Moat Farm.* **Visits by arrangement May to Aug. Adm £4, chd free. Home-made teas.**
A country garden with herbaceous borders, roses, hostas, trees and water. A moat that flows through the garden and a blind moat through the arboretum. Small walled garden and some vegetables.

& ☕

---

37 ◆ NETHER WINCHENDON HOUSE
Nether Winchendon, Thame, Aylesbury HP18 0DY. Mr Robert Spencer Bernard, 01844 290101, Contactus@netherwinchendon house.com, www.netherwinchendonhouse. com. *6m SW of Aylesbury, 6m from Thame. Approx 4m from Thame on A418, turn 1st L to Cuddington, turn L at Xrds, downhill turn R & R again to parking by house.* **For NGS: Mon 30 May (2-5.30). Adm £4, chd free. Home-made teas at the church (2.30-5). For other opening times and information, please phone, email or visit garden website.**
Nether Winchendon House is set in 7 acres of garden with fine and rare trees and surrounded by parkland. A Founder Garden (1927). Medieval and Tudor house set in stunning landscape. The South Lawn runs down to the R Thame. Picturesque village with interesting church. Conducted tours of the house (additional adm, not to NGS).

&. 🛇 🚐 🛏 ☕

38 NORTH DOWN
Dodds Lane, Chalfont St Giles HP8 4EL. Merida Saunders, 01494 872928. *4m SE of Amersham, 4m NE of Beaconsfield. Opp the green in centre of village, at Costa turn into UpCorner onto Silver Hill. At top of hill fork R into Dodds Lane. North Down is 7th on L.* **Visits by arrangement May to Aug for groups of 4-35. Adm £3.50, chd free. Light refreshments.**
A passion for gardening is evident in this plantswomans lovely ³/₄ acre garden which has evolved over the yrs with scenic effect in mind. Colourful and interesting throughout the yr. Large grassed areas with island beds of mixed perennials, shrubs and some unusual plants. Variety of rhododendrons, azaleas, acers, clematis and a huge Kiftsgate rose. Displays of sempervivum varieties, alpines, grasses and ferns. Small patio and water feature, greenhouse and an Italianate front patio to owner's design.

🏵 ☕

39 THE OLD SUN HOUSE
Pednor, Chesham HP5 2SZ. Mr & Mrs M Sharpley. *3m E of Gt Missenden, 2m W of Chesham. From Gt Missenden take B485 to Chesham, 1st L & follow signs approx 2m. From Chesham Church St*

(B485) follow signs approx 1¹/₂ m. **Sun 29 May (2-5.30). Adm £4, chd free. Home-made teas.**
5 acre garden on a Chiltern ridge giving superb views over organic farmland. Mature native trees surround the garden with inner planting of unusual trees and shrubs. Large ornamental pond with water loving marginal plants. Other features incl herbaceous beds, vegetable and herb garden, woodland walk, pheasants and chickens. A natural garden in harmony with its setting. Gravel drive.

&. 🛇 🏵 ☕

> A tremendous variety of colour in a small area . . .

40 ORCHARD HOUSE
Tower Road, Coleshill, Amersham HP7 0LB. Mr & Mrs Douglas Livesey. *From Amersham Old Town take the A355 to Beaconsfield. Appox ³/₄ m along this road at top of hill, take the 1st R into Tower Rd. Parking in cricket club grounds.* **Wed 8 June (2-5). Adm £4.50, chd free. Home-made teas in the barn.**
The 5 acre garden is made up of two wooded areas with eco hedges for wildlife. Two ponds with wild flower planting, large avenues of silver birches, a bog garden with board walk running through, and a wild flower meadow. There is a raised garden area with numerous raised beds used as a cutting garden for flowers and some vegetables. Bees. Rear garden lawn slopes down.

&. 🛇 ☕

41 OVERSTROUD COTTAGE
The Dell, Frith Hill, Gt Missenden HP16 9QE. Mr & Mrs Jonathan Brooke, 01494 862701, susie@jandsbrooke.co.uk. *¹/₂ m E Gt Missenden. Turn E off A413 at Gt Missenden onto B485 Frith Hill to Chesham Rd. White Gothic cottage set back in lay-by 100yds uphill on L.*

Parking on R at church. **Suns 27 Mar, 1, 22 May, 26 June (2-5). Adm £3, chd free. Cream teas at parish church. Visits also by arrangement Apr to July for groups of 15+.**
Artistic chalk garden on two levels. Collection of C17/C18 plants including auriculas, bulbs, hellebores, pulmonarias, geraniums, herbs, succulents and peonies. Many antique, species and rambling roses. Potager and lily pond. Cottage was once C17 fever house for Missenden Abbey. Features incl a garden studio with painting exhibition (share of flower painting proceeds to NGS).

🏵 ☕

42 11 THE PADDOCKS
Wendover HP22 6HE. Mr & Mrs E Rye, 01296 623870, pam.rye@talktalk.net. *5m from Aylesbury on A413. From Aylesbury turn L at mini-r'about onto Wharf Rd. From Gt Missenden turn L at the Clock Tower, then R at mini-r'about onto Wharf Rd.* **Sat 25, Sun 26 June, Sat 2, Sun 3 July (2-5). Adm £2.50, chd free. Visits also by arrangement June & July for groups of 30 max.** *Donation to Bonnie People in South Africa.*
Small peaceful garden with mixed borders of colourful herbaceous perennials, a special show of David Austin roses and a large variety of spectacular named Blackmore and Langdon delphiniums. A tremendous variety of colour in a small area. The White Garden with a peaceful arbour, The Magic of Moonlight created for the BBC. Featured in Garden Answers magazine (July 2015). Most of the garden can be viewed from the lawn.

&. 🏵

43 NEW PETERLEY CORNER COTTAGE
Perks Lane, Prestwood, Great Missenden HP16 0JH. Dawn Philipps, 01494 862198, dawn.philipps@googlemail.com. *Turn in to Perks Lane from the Wycombe Road, Peterley Corner Cottage is the 3rd house on the L.* **Visits by arrangement May to Aug for groups of 10+. Tea.**
A 3 acre mature garden, incl an acre of wild flower meadow. Surrounded by tall hedges and a wood, the garden has evolved over the last 30 yrs. There are many specimen trees and mature roses incl a Paul's

Baker's Close, Long Crendon Gardens

© Fiona McLeod

Himalaya Musk and a Kiftsgate. A large herbaceous border runs alongside the formal lawns with other borders like heathers and shrubs. The most recent addition is a potager.

 ♿ ☕

44 ▶ THE PLOUGH
Chalkshire Road, Terrick, Aylesbury HP17 0TJ. John & Sue Stewart, 01296 612477, johngooldstewart@gmail.com. *2m W of Wendover. Entrance to garden & car park signed off B4009 Nash Lee Rd. 200yds E of Terrick r'about. Access to garden from field car park.* **Sun 8, Mon 30 May (1-5). Adm £3.50, chd free. Home-made teas. Visits also by arrangement May to**

Sept for groups of 12+.
Formal garden with open views to the Chiltern countryside. Designed as a series of outdoor rooms around a listed former C18 inn, incl border, parterre, vegetable and fruit gardens, and a newly planted orchard. Delicious home-made teas and jams for sale made with fruits from the garden.

 ♿ ⊕ ☕

45 ▶ PONDERS
Hedgerley Lane, Gerrards Cross SL9 8SY. Mr & Mrs R Willans, 01753 480460, cristina.willans@mela.co.uk. *1½ m S of Gerrards Cross. From T-lights at Gerrards Cross main Xrd, turn into*

Windsor Rd. At next T-lights, turn R into Hedgerley Lane. Continue for ½ m, Ponders is on RH-side. **Sun 5 June (2-5.30). Adm £4, chd free. Home-made teas. Visits also by arrangement June & July.**
The 11 acre garden at Ponders was originally the kitchen garden for nearby Bulstrode Manor. Many original features remain incl extensive walls with impressive wrought iron gates, a long pear archway and a vineyard. Today the gardens incl a rose garden, long borders, rockery, woodlands with wide selection of mature trees, meadows, orchard, soft fruit and productive vegetable gardens. Steps to some areas.

 ♿ ⊕ ☕

GROUP OPENING

46 QUAINTON GARDENS
Quainton HP22 4AY. *7m W of Aylesbury, 2m N of Waddesdon A41. Nr Waddesdon turn off A41.* **Sun 21 Feb (12-4). Combined adm £4, chd free. Tea at Thorngumbald.**

CAPRICORNER
Mrs Davis

MILL VIEW
Jane & Nigel Jackson
www.millviewquainton.com

THORNGUMBALD
Jane Lydall

THE VINE
Mr & Mrs D A Campbell

The village lies at foot of Quainton Hills with fine views over Vale of Aylesbury to Chiltern Hills. There is a C14 church with outstanding monuments, a C19 working windmill milling Quainton flour (open Sundays am), and a steam railway centre. Heavy clay but well watered from the hills. The gardens are varied in their styles and content and also incl part of the allotments. No wheelchair access at The Vine or rear garden at Mill View.

♿ 🐶 ⊛ 🚐 ☕

47 RED KITES
46 Haw Lane, Bledlow Ridge HP14 4JJ. Mag & Les Terry, 01494 481474, les.terry@lineone.net. *4m S of Princes Risborough. Off A4010 halfway between Princes Risborough & West Wycombe. At Hearing Dogs sign in Saunderton turn into Haw Lane, then ³/₄ m on L.* **Tue 17 May, Tue 5 July (2-5). Adm £3.50, chd free. Home-made teas. Visits also by arrangement May to Sept for groups of 15+.**
Much loved Chiltern hillside garden with terracing, slopes and superb views. The 1½ acres are planted for yr-round interest and lovingly maintained with mixed and herbaceous borders, wild flower orchard, established pond, vegetable garden, managed woodland area and hidden garden. Wide use of climbers and clematis throughout.

48 RIVENDELL
13 The Leys, Amersham HP6 5NP. Janice & Mike Cross. *Off A416. Take A416 N towards Chesham. The Leys is on L ½ m after Boot & Slipper PH. Park at Beacon School, 100yds N.* **Sun 10 Apr (2-5). Adm £3, chd free. Home-made teas.**
S-facing garden featuring a series of different areas, incl a raised woodland bed under mature trees, bog garden, gravel area with grasses and pond, fruit and vegetable garden, bug hotel, herbaceous beds containing a wide variety of shrubs, bulbs and perennials which surround a circular lawn with a rose and clematis arbour.

⊛ ☕

Red Kites

49 ◆ STOKE POGES MEMORIAL GARDENS

Church Lane, Stoke Poges, Slough SL2 4NZ. South Bucks District Council, 01753 523744, memorial.gardens@southbucks. gov.uk, http://www.southbucks.gov.uk/ stokepogesmemorialgardens. *1m N of Slough, 4m S of Gerrards Cross, follow signs to Stoke Poges & then to Memorial Gardens. The car park for the Memorial Gardens is opp the gardens entrance. Disabled visitor parking in the gardens.* **For NGS: Sun 22 May (2-5). Adm £4, chd free. Home-made teas. For other opening times and information, please phone, email or visit garden website.**
Unique 20 acre Grade I registered garden constructed 1934-9. Rock and water gardens, sunken colonnade, rose garden, 500 individual gated gardens. Spring garden with bulbs, wisteria and rhododendrons. Guided tours on the hour. Guide dogs only.

50 TURN END

Townside, Haddenham, Aylesbury HP17 8BG. Peter Aldington, www.turnend.org.uk. *3m NE of Thame, 5m SW of Aylesbury. Turn off A418 to Haddenham. Turn at Rising Sun to Townside. Please park at a distance with consideration for neighbours.* **Mon 2 May (2-5.30). Adm £4, chd free. Home-made teas.**
Intriguing series of garden rooms enveloping architect's own post war 2* listed house (not open). Sunken gardens, raised beds, formal box garden, richly planted borders, curving lawn and glades framed by ancient walls and mature trees. Spring bulbs, irises, wisteria, roses and climbers. Courtyards with pools, secluded seating and Victorian Coach House. Open studios with displays and demonstrations by creative artists.

51 TYTHROP PARK

Kingsey HP17 8LT. Nick & Chrissie Wheeler. *2m E of Thame, 4m NW of Princes Risborough. Via A4129, at T-junction in Kingsey turn towards Haddenham, take L turn on bend. Parking in field on L.* **Sun 26 June (2-5.30). Adm £6, chd free. Home-made teas.** *Donation to St Nicholas Church, Kingsey.*

10 acres of gardens surrounding C17 Grade I listed manor house. In the past 7 yrs the grounds at Tythrop have undergone some major changes and now blend traditional styles with more contemporary planting. Features incl large intricate parterre, deep mixed borders, water features, large greenhouse, kitchen and cut flower garden, wild flower meadow, many old trees and shrubs.

52 WESTEND HOUSE

Cheddington, Leighton Buzzard LU7 0RP. His Honour Judge & Mrs Richard Foster, www.westendhousecheddington. co.uk. *5m N of Tring. From double mini-r'about in Cheddington take turn to Long Marston. Take 1st L & Westend House is on your R.* **Sun 24 Apr (2-5). Adm £3.50, chd free. Home-made teas.**
2 acre garden restored and developed during the last 11 yrs featuring herbaceous and shrub borders, formal rose garden with swags, wild flowers, natural pond and stream recently planted, potager with vegetables and flowers for picking. More spring bulbs planted for 2016. Wood and metal sculptures. Rare breed hens, sheep and pigs. Wildlife pond with dragonflies, butterflies and much more. Home-made cakes and tea served in bone china, with waitress service. Some bespoke sculptures and seasonal vegetables for sale. Wheelchair access to wild flower garden and one side of the pond.

53 THE WHITE HOUSE

Village Road, Denham Village UB9 5BE. Mr & Mrs P G Courtenay-Luck. *3m NW of Uxbridge, 7m E of Beaconsfield. Signed from A40 or A412. Parking in village road. The White House is in centre of village.* **Sun 5 June (2-5). Adm £5, chd free. Cream teas.**
Well established 6 acre formal garden in picturesque setting. Mature trees and hedges with R Misbourne meandering through lawns. Shrubberies, flower beds, rockery, rose garden and orchard. Large walled garden with Italian garden and developing laburnum walk. Herb garden, vegetable plot and Victorian greenhouses. Gravel entrance and path to gardens.

54 WHITEWALLS

Quarry Wood Road, Marlow SL7 1RE. Mr W H Williams, 01628 482573. *½ m S Marlow. From Marlow crossover bridge. 1st L, 3rd house on L with white garden wall.* **Visits by arrangement Apr to Sept. Adm £2.50, chd free.**
Thames side garden approx ½ acre with spectacular view of weir. Large water lily pond, interesting planting of trees, shrubs, herbaceous perennials and bedding, and a large conservatory. Many chairs to sit by river and view weir.

55 WIND IN THE WILLOWS

Moorhouse Farm Lane, Off Lower Road, Higher Denham UB9 5EN. Ron James, 07740 177038, r.james@company-doc.co.uk. *Moorhouse Farm Lane, off Lower Rd, Higher Denham. Take lane next to the community centre & Wind in the Willows is the 1st house on L.* **Sun 13 Mar (2-5). Adm £4.50, chd free. Tea. Opening with Higher Denham Gardens on Sun 5 June. Visits also by arrangement Feb to Sept for groups of 10+.**
3 acre wildlife friendly, yr-round garden, comprising informal woodland and wild gardens, separated by streams lined by iris and primulas. Over 350 shrubs and trees, many variegated or uncommon, marginal and bog plantings incl a collection of 80 hostas. 'Stunning' was the word most often used by visitors last year. 'Best private garden I have visited in 20 yrs of NGS visits' said another. Although unlikely to be seen on busy open days, 65 species of bird and 13 species of butterfly have been seen in and over the garden, which is also home to the now endangered water vole (Water Rat in the book Wind in the Willows), frogs and toads. Featured as a case study in the water garden section of Carol Klein's new book 'Making a Garden'. Gravel paths and spongy lawns.

CAMBRIDGESHIRE

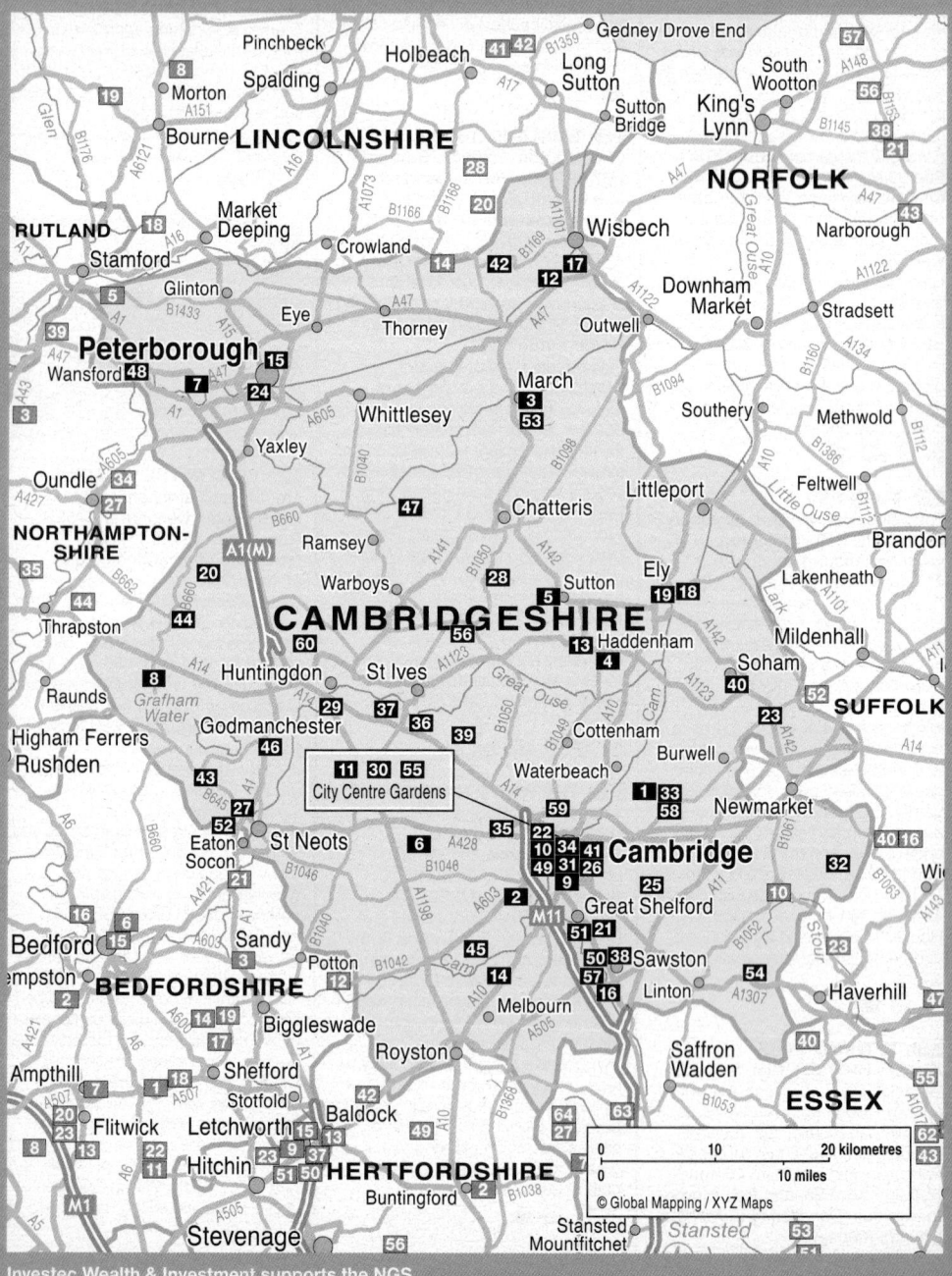

Cambridgeshire

The low-lying flat lands of Cambridgeshire offer many diverse and interesting gardens.

The Cambridge University gardens are well worth a visit, and people interested in urban gardens can find plenty in the city of Cambridge - these smaller gardens are ideal for giving inspiration for back garden planting and design.

Ely has a delightful group of gardens in this historic Cathedral City, and Peterborough has a fascinating collection of town gardens. The National Trust property of Anglesey Abbey is also well worth a visit.

The whole county embraces many delightful gardens, from former rectory gardens to very small urban gardens. There are many surprises waiting to be discovered in Cambridgeshire, and our generous garden owners invite you to come and take a closer look.

Cambridgeshire Volunteers

County Organiser
George Stevenson
01733 262698
ChrisGeorge1a@aol.com

County Treasurer
Nicholas Kyberd
01954 200568
n.kyberd@ntlworld.com

Publicity
Angie Jones
01733 222367
janda.salix@gmail.com

Booklet Coordinator
Robert Marshall
01733 555978
robfmarshall@btinternet.com

Assistant County Organisers
Pam Bullivant
01353 667355
pbu1@hotmail.co.uk

Patsy Glazebrook
01799 541180
glazebrc@doctors.org.uk

Nicholas Kyberd
(as above)

Mike Tuplin
01353 612029
miketuplin@yahoo.co.uk

Annette White
01638 730876
annette323@btinternet.com

Left: Norfolk Terrace Garden © Howard Rice

Opening Dates

All entries subject to change.
For latest information check www.ngs.org.uk
Extended openings are shown at the begining of the month

January
49 **Robinson College (Daily)**

February
49 **Robinson College (Daily)**

Snowdrop Festival
Sunday 28
48 6 Robins Wood

March
49 **Robinson College (Daily)**
Sunday 27
40 Netherhall Manor

April
49 **Robinson College (daily until Apr 15)**
Sunday 3
32 Kirtling Tower
Sunday 10
2 Barton Gardens
10 Churchill College
22 Fitzwilliam College
32 Kirtling Tower
55 Trinity College, Fellows' Garden
Sunday 17
30 NEW Jesus College
Sunday 24
14 Docwra's Manor

May
Sunday 1
34 Lucy Cavendish College
40 Netherhall Manor
Sunday 8
33 21 Lode Road
Sunday 15
20 NEW Ferrar House
Sunday 29
4 NEW Bell Gables
5 NEW The Burystead

13 College Farm
16 Duxford Gardens
29 Island Hall
47 Ramsey Forty Foot
Monday 30
4 NEW Bell Gables

June
49 **Robinson College (daily from June 13)**

Festival Weekend
Saturday 4
12 Clear View
45 NEW Orwell Gardens
56 Twin Tarns
Sunday 5
2 Barton Gardens
6 Cambourne Gardens
8 Catworth, Molesworth & Brington Gardens
12 Clear View
35 Madingley Hall
42 The Old Rectory
54 Streetly End Gardens
56 Twin Tarns
Saturday 11
52 Staploe Gardens
Sunday 12
18 Ely Gardens 1
38 Mary Challis Garden
51 Stapleford Gardens
52 Staploe Gardens
Thursday 16
7 Castor House (Evening)
Saturday 18
25 NEW Fulbourn Gardens
36 The Manor House
Sunday 19
25 NEW Fulbourn Gardens
36 The Manor House
57 Whittlesford Gardens
Monday 20
1 Anglesey Abbey, Gardens & Lode Mill
Saturday 25
3 45 Beaver Lodge
53 Steeple View
Sunday 26
3 45 Beaver Lodge
32 Kirtling Tower
53 Steeple View

July
49 **Robinson College (Daily)**

Saturday 2
26 NEW 10 Gwydir Street
41 Norfolk Terrace Garden
Sunday 3
11 Clare College Fellows' Garden
26 NEW 10 Gwydir Street
41 Norfolk Terrace Garden
50 Sawston Gardens
60 Wytchwood
Saturday 9
21 6 Finch's Close
Sunday 10
21 6 Finch's Close
23 NEW Fordham Abbey
Sunday 17
20 NEW Ferrar House
31 King's College Fellows' Garden
33 21 Lode Road
Saturday 23
21 6 Finch's Close
Sunday 24
21 6 Finch's Close
Sunday 31
44 NEW Old Weston Garden Farm

August
49 **Robinson College (Daily)**
Sunday 7
17 Elgood's Brewery Gardens
19 Ely Gardens 2
40 Netherhall Manor
Sunday 14
7 Castor House
40 Netherhall Manor
Saturday 20
3 45 Beaver Lodge
Sunday 21
3 45 Beaver Lodge
Sunday 28
9 Chaucer Road Gardens
15 289 Dogsthorpe Road (Evening)
Monday 29
9 Chaucer Road Gardens
15 289 Dogsthorpe Road

September
49 **Robinson College (Daily)**

October
49 **Robinson College (Daily)**

November
49 **Robinson College (Daily)**

December
49 **Robinson College (Daily)**

Gardens open to the public
1 Anglesey Abbey, Gardens & Lode Mill
14 Docwra's Manor
17 Elgood's Brewery Gardens
20 NEW Ferrar House
37 The Manor, Hemingford Grey

By arrangement only
24 39 Foster Road
27 109 High Street
28 Horseshoe Farm
39 5 Moat Way
43 The Old Vicarage
46 23a Perry Road
58 Wild Rose Cottage
59 The Windmill

Also open by arrangement
3 45 Beaver Lodge
6 14 Miller Way, Cambourne Gardens
8 32 High Street, Catworth, Molesworth & Brington Gardens
12 Clear View
13 College Farm
15 289 Dogsthorpe Road
18 12 & 26 Chapel Street, Ely Gardens 1
23 NEW Fordham Abbey
42 The Old Rectory
45 NEW 57 Cakebreade Cottage, Orwell Gardens
45 NEW Meadowbank, Orwell Gardens
48 6 Robins Wood
53 Steeple View
54 Clover Cottage, Streetly End Gardens
56 Twin Tarns

The Gardens

1 ♦ ANGLESEY ABBEY, GARDENS & LODE MILL
Quy Road, Lode, Cambridge
CB25 9EJ. National Trust,
01223 810080,
www.nationaltrust.org.uk/anglesey
abbey. *6m NE of Cambridge. From
A14 J35, on B1102 through Stow-
cum-Quy.* For NGS: Mon 20 June
(10-5.30). Adm £7.95, chd free.
**For other opening times and
information, please phone or visit
garden website.**
Anglesey is one of England's great
gardens, with captivating views,
vibrant colour and delicious fragrance
for every season. Delight in the
sweeping avenues, classical statuary
and beautiful flower borders. June
favourites incl the colourful
herbaceous borders, rose garden and
wildlife rich wild flower meadows.
Take a tour with a garden guide and
be inspired by the seasonal
highlights. Large proportion of
gardens fully accessible for
wheelchair users with hard surfaced
paths.

GROUP OPENING

2 BARTON GARDENS
High Street, Barton, Cambridge
CB23 7BG. *3¹/₂ m SW of Cambridge.
Barton is on A603 Cambridge to
Sandy Rd, ¹/₂ m for J12 M11.* Sun 10
Apr, Sun 5 June (2-5). Combined
adm £5, chd free. Home-made
teas in Barton Village Hall.

NEW THE COTTAGES
Irene Ng.
Open on Sun 10 Apr

FARM COTTAGE
Dr R M Belbin.
Open on all dates

GLEBE HOUSE
David & Sue Rapley.
Open on Sun 5 June

114 HIGH STREET
Meta & Hugh Greenfield.
Open on all dates

31 NEW ROAD
Dr & Mrs D Macdonald.
Open on Sun 5 June

THE SIX HOUSES
Perennial.
Open on all dates

Clare College Fellow's Garden

Varied group of large and small
gardens reflecting different
approaches to gardening. Farm
Cottage: landscaped cottage garden
with herbaceous beds and themed
woodland walk. 114 High Street:
small cottage garden with an unusual
layout comprising several areas incl
vegetables, fruit and a secret garden.
31 New Road: large, wildlife friendly
cottage garden with a good show of
spring flowers, mature shrubs, trees
and a kitchen garden. The Six
Houses: recently renovated gardens,
incl winter and dry gardens, lovely
spring bulbs and a small wood. The
White Horse Inn(118 High Street)
serves meals. Some gardens have
gravel paths.

---

3 45 BEAVER LODGE
Henson Road, March PE15 8BA.
Mr & Mrs Maria & Paul Nielsen
Bom, 01354 656185,
beaverbom@gmail.com. *A141 to
Wisbech rd into March, turn L into
Westwood Ave, follow rd leading to
Henson Rd, turn R. Property opp
school playground.* Sat 25, Sun 26
June, Sat 20, Sun 21 Aug
(10.30-4). Adm £3, chd free.
Home-made teas. **Visits also by
arrangement June to Oct small
groups welcome.**
A delightful town garden divided into
several rooms. A pergola leads to an
ornamental pond with koi carp,
surrounded by borders with a large
variety of plants and ornamental
trees. Fern area with ornamental
waterfall. The whole garden has an
Oriental theme with bonsais and
statues. Also a corner with a fountain

that has a Mediterranean feel.
Featured in Fenland Citizen and
Cambridgeshire Times.

4 NEW BELL GABLES
Church Lane, Wilburton, Ely
CB6 3RQ. Shona Mckay & William
Bertram. *Church Lane is off A1123
between Stretham & Haddenham
behind the parish church in
Wilburton.* Sun 29 May (11-5). Tea
in St Peter's Church opp house
(Sun only) 2-5, also open The
Burystead and College Farm (Sun
only). Mon 30 May (11-5). Adm £3,
chd free.
Approx one acre of garden with a
large natural pond with moorhen,
grass snakes and other pond life. A
small walled garden and formal fruit
and flower parterre. Level access
drive but with gravel finish with a
concrete ramp down to the lawn.

5 NEW THE BURYSTEAD
Bury Lane, Sutton, Ely CB6 2BB.
Sarah Cleverdon & Stephen
Tebboth. *6m W of Ely. Drive through
Sutton towards Earith. Turn R, signed
'Sutton Gault' & 'Anchor Inn', Bury
Lane. Our house is 1st on L, approx
300 metres.* Sun 29 May (1-5).
Combined adm with College Farm
£5, chd free. Tea. Also open Bell
Gables.
¹/₂ -acre walled courtyard garden of
formal design, set against a backdrop
of a recently restored C16 thatched
barn. Mature planting in former
farmyard. Semi-mature orchard and
sculpture at front of house. Aso a
cottage garden at back of house.

Marie
Curie

The NGS is Marie
Curie's largest
single donor

GROUP OPENING

6 CAMBOURNE GARDENS
Great Cambourne CB23 6AH. *8m W of Cambridge on A428. From A428: take Cambourne junction into Great Cambourne. From B1198, enter village at Lower Cambourne and drive through to Great Cambourne. Follow NGS signs via either route to start at any garden.* **Sun 5 June (11-5). Combined adm £5, chd free. Tea and cakes at 128 Greenhaze Lane and 5 Mayfield Way.**

14 GRANARY WAY
Mrs Jackie Hutchinson

128 GREENHAZE LANE
Fran & John Panrucker

22 JEAVONS LANE
Mr Sheppard

5 MAYFIELD WAY
Debbie & Mike Perry

14 MILLER WAY
Geoff Warmington
Visits also by arrangement in June.
01954 710152

43 MONKFIELD LANE
Tony & Penny Miles

NEW **4 THE MALTINGS**
Pam & Len Thornton

A unique and inspiring modern group, all created from new build in just a few years. This selection of seven, including a new entry for 2016, demonstrates how imagination and gardening skill can be combined in a short time to create great effects from unpromising and awkward beginnings. The grouping includes a garden inspired by the French Riviera complete with a miniature meadow, a foliage garden, and many other beautiful borders showing their owners' creativity and love of growing fine plants well. Cambourne is one of

Cambridgeshire's newest communities, and this grouping showcases the happy, vibrant place it has become. No garden is more than 15 years old, and most are much younger.

7 CASTOR HOUSE
Peterborough Road, Castor, Peterborough PE5 7AX. Ian & Claire Winfrey, www.castorhousegardens.co.uk. *4m W of Peterborough. House on main Peterborough rd in Castor. Parking in paddock off Water Lane.* **Evening opening Thur 16 June (6-9). Wine. Sun 14 Aug (2-5). Home-made teas. Adm £5, chd free.** 12 acres of gardens and woodland on a slope, terraced and redesigned 2010. Italianate spring fed ponds and stream gardens. Potager with greenhouse and exotic borders. Annual meadow and willow arbour. Woodland garden. Peony and prunus walk. Rose and cottage gardens, 'Hot' double border. Stumpery. Year round interest. Late C17 house (closed). Drinks 16 June, homemade teas Aug 14. No dogs. Coaches welcome. For more information and openings by appt please see garden website.

GROUP OPENING

8 CATWORTH, MOLESWORTH & BRINGTON GARDENS
Huntingdon PE28 0PF. *10m W of Huntingdon. A14 W for Catworth, Molesworth & Brington exit at J16 onto B660.* **Sun 5 June (2-6). Combined adm £4, chd free. Home-made teas at Molesworth House and Yew Tree Cottage.**

32 HIGH STREET
Colin Small
Visits also by arrangement in June evenings & Weekends
sheila.small@btinternet.com
01832 710269

MOLESWORTH HOUSE
John Prentis

YEW TREE COTTAGE
Christine & Don Eggleston

3 varied gardens showing the best of planting, design and creativity. 32 High Street is a long narrow garden with many rare plants including ferns, herbaceous borders, woodland area and wildlife pond. Molesworth House is an old rectory garden with everything that you'd both expect and hope for, given its Victorian past. There are surprising corners to this traditional take on a happy and relaxed garden. Yew Tree Cottage, informal garden approx 1 acre, complements the C17 building (not open) and comprises flower beds, lawns, vegetable patch, boggy area, copses and orchard. Plants in pots and hanging baskets. Partial wheelchair access.

GROUP OPENING

9 CHAUCER ROAD GARDENS
Cambridge CB2 7EB. *1m S of Cambridge. Off Trumpington Rd (A1309), nr Brooklands Ave junction. Parking available at MRC Psychology Dept on Chaucer Rd.* **Sun 28, Mon 29 Aug (2-5). Combined adm £5, chd free. Home-made teas at Upwater Lodge.**

16 CHAUCER ROAD
Mrs V Albutt

UPWATER LODGE
Mr & Mrs George Pearson

16 Chaucer Road ½-acre garden, divided by arches and hedges into separate areas, each with its own character. Front rose garden. Unusual hawthorn and late summer borders. Blackberries and apple trees. Wildlife area with new sculpture. Waterproof footwear advised. Upwater Lodge is an Edwardian academic's house with 6 acres of grounds. It has mature trees, fine lawns, old wisterias, and colourful borders. There is a small, pretty potager with vegetables and autumn fruits, and a well maintained grass tennis court. A network of paths through a wooded area lead down to a dyke, water meadows and a small flock of rare breed sheep. Enjoy a walk by the river and watch the punts go by. Buy homemade teas and sit in the garden or take them down to enjoy a lazy afternoon with ducks, geese, swans and heron on the riverbank. Cakes made with garden fruit where possible. Swings and climbing ropes. Stalls selling plants, cards, prints and fabric crafts. Some gravel areas and grassy paths with fairly gentle slopes.

10 CHURCHILL COLLEGE

Storey's Way, Cambridge CB3 0DS. University of Cambridge, www.chu.cam.ac.uk. *1m from M11 J13. 1m NW of Cambridge city centre. Turn into Storeys Way from Madingley Rd (A1303), or from Huntingdon Rd (A1307). Parking on site.* Sun 10 Apr (2-5). Combined adm with Fitzwilliam College £5, chd free. Home-made teas.

42-acre site designed in 1960s for foliage and form, to provide year round interest in peaceful and relaxing surrounds with courtyards, large open spaces and specimen trees. 10m x 5m orchid house, herbaceous plantings. Beautiful grouping of Prunus Tai Haku (great white cherry) trees forming striking canopy and drifts of naturalised bulbs in grass around the site. The planting provides a setting for the impressive collection of modern sculpture. Orchid house, Sculptures. The greenhouse is restricted in size.

11 CLARE COLLEGE FELLOWS' GARDEN

Trinity Lane, Cambridge CB2 1TL. The Master & Fellows, www.clare.cam.ac.uk. *Central to city. From Queens Rd or city centre via Senate House Passage, Old Court & Clare Bridge.* Sun 3 July (2-6). Adm £4, chd free. Home-made teas.

2 acres. One of the most famous gardens on the Cambridge Backs. Herbaceous borders; sunken pond garden, fine specimen trees and tropical garden. Featured on BBC Gardeners World. Gravel paths.

12 CLEAR VIEW

Cross Lane, Wisbech St Mary PE13 4TX. Margaret & Graham Rickard, 01945 410724, magsrick@hotmail.com. *3m SW of Wisbech. Approach village via Barton Rd from Wisbech. Leverington Common into Station Rd, or Sandbank & from Guyhirn. Yellow signs at most junctions.* Sat 4, Sun 5 June (10-5). Adm £3.50, chd free. Home-made teas, all cakes are home-made. Visits also by arrangement May to July please telephone a week before your intended arrival.

Approx 1½ -acre with lake incorporating large wildlife area, and wildlife meadow. Secluded cottage garden with many old fashioned plants, herbaceous border, gravel garden with raised bed and pond. Allotments and small orchard. Plenty of secluded seating. Were interviewed by BBC Radio Cambridge as part of a gardening programme. Gravel paths in cottage garden are too narrow but it can be viewed from the picket fencing and the grass.

Peaceful garden of a Retreat House with beautiful uninterrupted views across meadows and farm land . . .

13 COLLEGE FARM

Station Road, Haddenham, Ely CB6 3XD. Mr & Mrs J & S Waller, 0777 9302777, jeremyprimavera@aol.com, www.primaveragallery.co.uk. *From Stretham & Wilburton, at the Xrds in Haddenham, turn R, then past the church. Exactly at the bottom of the hill, turn L down narrow drive, with a mill wheel on R of the drive.* Sun 29 May (1-5). Combined adm with The Burystead £5, chd free. Also open Bell Gables. Visits also by arrangement June & July.

40 acres around an intact Victorian farm. New walk overlooking Sutton, and other walks across ponds and through meadows. Roses, wild flowers, water plants, foxgloves and sculpture add colour and shape. Splendid fen views, lovely water features and ancient pasture land with interesting wild flowers, original farm buildings and abundant wildlife - in its midst a beautiful gallery (Primavera) full of extraordinary paintings, and contemporary artwork and craft. Wow factor is the sculpture. Wheelchair access is only possible around the garden near the house, but not through the gallery, farm, milking parlour, and many of the walks.

14 ◆ DOCWRA'S MANOR

2 Meldreth Road, Shepreth, Royston SG8 6PS. Mrs Faith Raven, 01763 260677, www.docwrasmanorgarden.co.uk. *8m S of Cambridge. ½ m W of A10. Garden is opp the War Memorial in Shepreth. King's Cross-Cambridge train take 5 min walk.* For NGS: Sun 24 Apr (2-5). Adm £5, chd free. Teas. For other opening times and information, please phone or visit garden website.

2½ acres of choice plants in a series of enclosed gardens. Tulips and Judas trees. Opened for the NGS for more than 40yrs. The garden is featured in great detail in a book published 2013 'The Gardens of England' edited by George Plumptre. Wheelchair access to most parts of the garden, gravel paths.

15 289 DOGSTHORPE ROAD

Peterborough PE1 3PA. Michael & Julie Reid, 01733 553784, julie@juliereid.co.uk, https://www.facebook.com/AnArtistsGarden?ref=stream. *1m N of city centre. A47 Paston turn. Exit r'about South. Down Fulbridge rd to end & turn L into St Paul's Rd. Turn R at end down Dogsthorpe Rd. Garden 600 metres on R.* Evening opening Sun 28 Aug (5.30-9). Adm £5, chd free. Wine. Mon 29 Aug (12-6). Adm £3, chd free. Home-made teas. Wine and light snacks incl 29 Aug. 'pop-up' tea shop, sweet and savoury selection available all day. Visits also by arrangement July & Aug evenings & weekends only. Don't be shy.

A 'peaceful' urban garden designed by Fine Artist, Julie Reid. Divided into rooms using layers and texture from brave use of trees, shrubs and year round perennial planting including ferns, bamboos and Acers. Subtle structural and sculptural additions including our new water features and Japanese inspired garden. Social and intimate seating areas allow guests and gardeners to relax and enjoy. Open Artists Studio and Fine Art Exhibition. 'Pop-up tea shop.

45 Beaver Lodge

GROUP OPENING

16 DUXFORD GARDENS
Cambridge CB22 4PT. *M11 leave at J10, A505. 1/2 m signed Duxford. St Peter's St gardens close to Londis shop. The Biggen is a cul de sac off Hinxton Rd, which starts at the trianglular War Memorial at end of St Peter's St. The entrance to Mill Lane is opp The John Barleycorn PH. Garden is at the end of Mill Lane with white gates and white sign Parking at Temple Farm House.* Sun 29 May (2-6). Combined adm £5, chd free. Tea at United Reformed Church, Chapel Street, short walk from all the open gardens.

2 THE BIGGEN
Mr & Mrs Derek & Judy Chamberlain

6 THE BIGGEN
Mrs Bettye Reynolds

BUSTLERS COTTAGE
John & Jenny Marks

31 ST PETER'S STREET
Mr David Baker

TEMPLE FARMHOUSE
Peter & Jenny Shaw

These gardens are an extremely interesting mix, ranging from very large to very small. The gardens are all examples of what can be easily grown in Duxford. 2 The Biggen

created in 9yrs from an overgrown plot of greenery, has mixed borders, small stumpery and alpine area. 6 The Biggen a 1/4 acre plants women's garden with unusual perennials, charming places to sit and enjoy. 31 St Peter's Street the garden slopes down to a rockery and circular stone steps leading to a secluded patio. Bustlers Cottage is a traditional Cambridgeshire cottage garden extending over 1 acre with old roses, herbaceous borders, vegetables and an old fig tree. Temple Farmhouse the R Cam flows gently through the 3½ acre rural garden with majestic trees, informal flowerbeds, vegetable garden enclosed with mature box hedges. Plants for sale at Bustlers Cottage.

&♿ ✿ ☕

17 ◆ ELGOOD'S BREWERY GARDENS
North Brink, Wisbech PE13 1LW. Elgood & Sons Ltd, 01945 583160, info@elgoods-brewery.co.uk, www.elgoods-brewery.co.uk. *1m W of town centre. Leave A47 towards Wisbech Centre. Cross river to North Brink. Follow river & brown signs to brewery & car park beyond.* For NGS: Sun 7 Aug (11.30-4.30). Adm £4, chd free. Light refreshments. **For other opening times and information, please phone, email or visit garden website.**

Approx 4 acres of peaceful garden featuring 250yr old specimen trees providing a framework to lawns, lake, rockery, herb garden, dipping pool and maze. Wheelchair access to Visitor Centre and most areas of the garden.

♿ ✿ 🚐 ☕

GROUP OPENING

18 ELY GARDENS 1
Ely CB7 4DW. *14m N of Cambridge. Parking at Barton Rd car park, Tower Road or the Grange Council Offices. (Disabled parking only at Deanery.). Map given at first garden visited.* Sun 12 June (2-6). Combined adm £5, chd free. Home-made teas at 42 Cambridge Road.

THE BISHOPS HOUSE
The Bishop of Ely

42 CAMBRIDGE ROAD
Mr & Mrs J & C Switsur

12 & 26 CHAPEL STREET
Ken & Linda Ellis
Visits also by arrangement May to Sept please call for details of garden.
ken.ellis1@yahoo.com
01353 664219

NEW THE DEANERY
Very Rev & Mrs Mark Bonney

A delightful and varied group of gardens in an historic Cathedral city. The Bishop's house and the Deanery are monastic buildings. The former garden adjoins Ely Cathedral and has mixed planting with a formal rose garden, wisteria and more. Close by, The Deanery, with lawns, an orchard, lavender hedge, developing borders and shrubs, is a secluded walled garden with views over the Dean's meadow and towards the Cathedral.12 & 26 Chapel Street: the former a small town garden reflecting the owners eclectic outlook, from alpine to herbaceous, all linked with a model railway! The latter a surprisingly long garden with shrubs and developing areas of herbaceous planting. An oasis of peace in the city. 42 Cambridge Road is a secluded town garden with interesting herbaceous borders, roses, shrubs and trees. A vegetable garden with raised beds. Wheelchair access to areas of most gardens. Disabled parking for Deanery.

♿ ✿ ☕

GROUP OPENING

19 ELY GARDENS 2
Barton Road, Ely CB7 4DX. *A10 from Cambridge (14m). Parking at Barton Rd car park.* Sun 7 Aug (2-5). Combined adm £4, chd free. Home-made teas. Refreshments at Bishop Woodford House.

BISHOP WOODFORD HOUSE
Miss Michelle Collins

12 & 26 CHAPEL STREET
Ken & Linda Ellis
(see Ely Gardens 1)

32B DOWNHAM ROAD
Mrs P Carrott

Bishop Woodford House is a garden for all seasons and in August has well stocked, colourful borders. Downham Road is a modern bungalow, surrounded by a deceptively spacious garden with paving and interesting planting. The gardens are within walking distance of the Cathedral, park and river. They are mature gardens and close attention has been given to colour combinations with a succession of planting. August brings the beginning of Autumn colour with dahlias and rudbeckias. Gardens are level and accessible.

Wild flower
meadow and lily
pond with
footbridge . . .

20 NEW ◆ FERRAR HOUSE
Little Gidding, Huntingdon PE28 5RJ. Mr Andrew Good, 01832 293383, info@ferrarhouse.co.uk, www.ferrarhouse.co.uk. *Take Mill Rd from Great Gidding (turn at Fox & Hounds) then after 1m turn R down single track lane. Car Park at Ferrar House.* For NGS: Sun 15 May, Sun 17 July (10-5). Adm £3, chd free. Light refreshments. For other opening times and information, please phone, email or visit garden website.

A peaceful garden of a Retreat House with beautiful uninterrupted views across meadows and farm land. Adjacent to the historic Church of St John's it was here that a small religious community was formed in the C17. The poet T. S. Eliot visited in 1936 and it inspired the 4th of his Quartets named Little Gidding. Lawn and walled flower beds with a walled vegetable garden. WC accessible at Ferrar House.

21 6 FINCH'S CLOSE
Stapleford, Cambridge CB22 5BL. Prof & Mrs S Sutton. *4m S of Cambridge. From the London Road (A1301) turn into Bury Road (by the Rose PH), then turn 2nd L into Bar Lane and 3rd L into Finch's Close.* Sat 9, Sun 10, Sat 23, Sun 24 July (1-6). Adm £3, chd free. Home-made teas.

A small patio leads to the productive vegetable garden, greenhouse and mini orchard. The borders around the lawn and wildlife pond are well-stocked with shrubs and mature trees while gentle musical chimes can be heard in the breeze. Featured in edition of Cambridge magazine. Limited access on gravel paths but large lawn area.

22 FITZWILLIAM COLLEGE
Storey's Way, Cambridge CB3 0DG. Master & Fellows, www.fitz.cam.ac.uk. *1m NW of Cambridge city centre. Turn into Storey's Way from Madingley Rd (A1303) or from Huntingdon Rd (A1307). Free parking.* Sun 10 Apr (2-5). Combined adm with Churchill College £5, chd free. On-site cafe for drinks and snacks.

Traditional topiary, borders, woodland walk, lawns from the Edwardian period and specimen trees are complemented by modern planting and wild meadow. The avenue of limes, underplanted with spring bulbs, leads to The Grove, the 1813 house once belonging to the Darwin Family (not open). Some ramped pathways.

23 NEW FORDHAM ABBEY
Newmarket Road, Fordham, Ely CB7 5LL. Dojima Sake Brewery UK & Co, 01638-721695, contact@fordhamabbey.co.uk, www.fordhamabbey.co.uk. *Approx 6m from Newmarket. Fordham Abbey is situated on the edge of the village on Newmarket Rd.* Sun 10 July (2-6). Adm £4, chd free. Home-made teas. Visits also by arrangement June to Sept.

This delightful Grade II* listed Georgian house (not open) is set behind extensive mature trees on the edge of the village of Fordham. The gardens, being restored, are laid to lawn with borders containing mature shrubs, perennials and roses. Two walled gardens both of which have mature fruit trees, one with a kitchen garden. There is a wild flower meadow and lily pond with footbridge.

24 39 FOSTER ROAD
Campaign Ave, Sugar Way, Woodston PE2 9RS. Robert Marshall & Richard Handscombe, 01733 555978, robfmarshall@btinternet.com. *1m SW of Peterborough City Centre. A605 Oundle Rd, N into Sugar Way. Cross r'about, L at 2nd r'about to Campaign Ave. R at next r'about on C. Ave. 2nd R to Foster Rd. L into cul-de-sac. Continue until very end.* Visits by arrangement Feb to Sept weekends & weekdays possible, groups very welcome. Adm £4, chd free incl tea/coffee and biscuits. Light refreshments in garden pergola or indoor lounge, weather depending.

Plantsman's garden in small, new estate plot. Mixed borders; woodland/shade; 'vestibule' garden; exotics and ferns; espaliered fruit; pergola; patio; pond; parterre; many pots; octagonal greenhouse; seating and sculpture. Uncommon snowdrops, over 200 hostas, plus daphnes, acers and other choice/unusual cultivars. Trees and hedges create enclosure and intimacy. 4 x British Shorthair cats. Compact 'town garden' conceals many design ideas to maximise planting - without grass to cut. See how trees (x12) and hedges can be used in a small garden. Large collection, approaching 250 cultivars, of Hostas. Uncommon and some very rare snowdrops. Featured in Garden News, Mail on Saturday, Nene Living. All viewings accompanied by garden owner(s). Main garden and WC accessible by wheelchair.

GROUP OPENING

25 NEW FULBOURN GARDENS

Fulbourn, Cambridge CB21 5BZ. *3¹/₂ m SE of Cambridge. Take Fulbourn junction off A11, turn onto Balsham Rd. No 8 is on L nearly opp PH. For 2 Home End, turn R past the PH. Parking at Fulbourn Social Club on R opp 2 Home End.* Sat 18, Sun 19 June (11-5). Combined adm £5, chd free. Light refreshments at 8 Balsham Road.

NEW 8 BALSHAM ROAD
Phil & Amanda Wharrier

NEW 2 HOME END
Mrs Polly Butt

At 2 Home End, the garden is surrounded by high flint walls, with mature trees and borders well stocked with herbaceous plants, roses and bulbs. There is a large formal pond with a pergola on one side and a rockery on the other. On the patio area you can sit and enjoy the view. The upper garden has a large greenhouse, established fruit trees, vegetable beds, and wild flower area. At 8 Balsham Road a large Koi Carp pond is the focal point of the lower section of the garden. Raised borders surround this area planted with a variety of shrubs and cottage garden flowers. There is a vegetable garden and a chicken run to the right hand side. Brick steps and a ramp lead up to the lawned area which contains mature trees and has a path running around it.

An artist's garden with attention to form and colour combination . . .

26 NEW 10 GWYDIR STREET
Cambridge CB1 2LL. Mrs Rosemary Catling. *A603 East Rd, R into St Matthews St, L into Norfolk Terrace then R at junction with Gwydir St.* Sat 2, Sun 3 July (11-5). Combined adm with Norfolk Terrace Garden £4, chd free. Light refreshments at Norfolk Terrace. L shaped town garden, paved with some raised beds. The formal structure is informally planted with perennials, shrubs and small trees. Many in pots. There is a sitting area under a mature fig tree and small pond. An artist's garden with attention to form and colour combination. Unusual plants and shrubs. Wheelchair access down narrow side passage.

27 109 HIGH STREET
Hail Weston PE19 5JS. Dawn Isaac, 01480 477003, dawn@dawn-isaac.com, www.dawn-isaac.com. *1m W of St Neots. Take 1st R signed Hail Weston & follow High St round. 109 is opp church & village hall.* Visits by arrangement Apr to Oct. Set in ¹/₃ acre, this space has been designed to show that a practical family garden can still be beautiful. There is a large lawn with a sunken trampoline surrounded by mixed borders, ornamental vegetable garden, children's play area and greenhouse. Featured in House Beautiful - profile of the garden.

28 HORSESHOE FARM
Chatteris Road, Somersham, Huntingdon PE28 3DR. Neil & Claire Callan, 01354 693546, nccallan@yahoo.co.uk. *9m NE of St Ives, Cambs. Easy access from the A14. Situated on E side of B1050, 4m N of Somersham Village. Parking for 8 cars in the drive.* Visits by arrangement Apr to Sept groups up to 25. Adm £4, chd free. Home-made teas.
This ³/₄ acre plant-lovers' garden not only has lots of spring interest, but has a large pond with summer-house and decking, bog garden, alpine troughs, more than 25 varieties of irises, mixed rainbow island beds, water features, a small hazel woodland area, wildlife meadow and lookout tower, for wide fenland views and bird watching. Featured in WI Life magazine.

29 ISLAND HALL
Godmanchester PE29 2BA. Mr Christopher & Lady Linda Vane Percy, www.islandhall.com. *1m S of Huntingdon (A1). 15m NW of Cambridge (A14). In centre of Godmanchester next to free car park.* Sun 29 May (11-4.30). Adm £4, chd free. Home-made teas.
3-acre grounds. Mid C18 mansion (not open). Tranquil riverside setting with mature trees. Chinese bridge over Saxon mill race to an embowered island with wild flowers. Garden restored in 1983 to mid C18 formal design, with box hedging, clipped hornbeams, parterres, topiary and good vistas over borrowed landscape, punctuated with C18 wrought iron and stone urns. The ornamental island has been replanted with Princeton elms (ulmus americana).

30 NEW JESUS COLLEGE
Jesus Lane, Cambridge CB5 8BL. Mr Paul Stearn. *Entrance via Victoria Ave, via entry phone system. Exit via Jesus Lane Gate. Automatic opening on approach. Disabled parking.* Sun 17 Apr (1-5). Adm £4, chd free. Light refreshments.
27 acre site comprising of C12 chapel C15 - 21st additions. Established garden's (Fellows garden open). Many specimen trees, award winning woodland walk, flower borders. Mini arboretum, sculptures. Fine spring colour. Home-made cakes etc will be available for donations. Wheelchair access to most areas, sloped pathways. WC.

31 KING'S COLLEGE FELLOWS' GARDEN
Queen's Road, Cambridge CB2 1ST. Provost & Scholars of King's College. *In Cambridge, the Backs. Entry by gate at junction of Queen's Rd & West Rd. Parking at Lion Yard 10mins walk, or some pay & display places in West Rd & Queen's Rd.* Sun 17 July (2-6). Adm £3.50, chd free. Cream teas.
Fine example of a Victorian garden with rare specimen trees. With a small woodland walk and a kitchen/allotment garden created in 2011 and I new rose pergola and herbaceous border created in 2013. Gravel paths.

32 ▶ **KIRTLING TOWER**
Newmarket Road, Kirtling,
Newmarket CB8 9PA. The Lord &
Lady Fairhaven. *6m SE of
Newmarket. From Newmarket head
towards village of Saxon Street,
through village to Kirtling, turn L at
war memorial, entrance is signed on L. Sun 3, Sun
10 Apr, Sun 26 June (11-4). Adm
£5, chd free. Light refreshments.
Selection of hot & cold food,
sandwiches & cakes, tea & coffee.*
Surrounded by a moat, formal
gardens and parkland. In the spring
swathes of daffodils, narcissi, crocus,
muscari, chionodoxa and tulips.
Closer to the house vast lawn areas,
Secret and Cutting Gardens. In the
summer the Walled Garden has
superb herbaceous borders with
anthemis, hemerocalis, geraniums
and delphiniums. The Victorian
Garden is filled with peonies. Views of
surrounding countryside. Display of
stonemasonry from Lady Fairhaven's
stone yard. Collection of Classic Cars
on display. Many of the paths and
routes around the garden are grass -
they are accessible by wheelchairs,
but can be hard work if wet.

Visit a garden and
support hospice
care in your
community

33 ▶ **21 LODE ROAD**
Lode, Cambridgeshire CB25 9ER.
Mr Richard P Ayres. *2m from Quy
junction on the A14, follow signs for
Lode. Sun 8 May, Sun 17 July (12-
5). Adm £4, chd free. Home-made
teas.*
Small garden, designed by the owner
(retired head gardener at Anglesey
Abbey NT) adjoining C15 thatched
cottage (not open). Planted with bold
groups of herbaceous plants
complementing a fine lawn and
creating an element of mystery and
delight.

34 ▶ **LUCY CAVENDISH
COLLEGE**
Lady Margaret Road, Cambridge
CB3 0BU. Lucy Cavendish College.
*1m NW of Gt St Mary. College
situated on corner of Lady Margaret
Rd & Madingley Rd (A1303). Entrance
off Lady Margaret Rd. Sun 1 May
(2-5). Adm £3.50, chd free.*
The gardens of 4 late Victorian
houses have been combined and
developed over past 25yrs into an
informal 3 acre garden. Fine mature
trees shade densely planted borders.
An Anglo Saxon herb garden is
situated in one corner. The garden
provides a rich wildlife habitat.

35 ▶ **MADINGLEY HALL**
Cambridge CB23 8AQ. University
of Cambridge, 01223 746222,
reservations@madingleyhall.co.uk,
www.madingleyhall.co.uk. *4m W of
Cambridge. 1m from M11 J13. Sun
5 June (2.30-5.30). Adm £5, chd
free. Home-made teas at St Mary
Magdalene Church adjacent to
Madingley Hall Drive.*
C16 Hall (not open) set in 8 acres of
attractive grounds landscaped by
Capability Brown. Features incl
landscaped walled garden with hazel
walk, alpine bed, medicinal border
and rose pergola. Meadow, topiary,
mature trees and wide variety of
hardy plants. St Mary Magdalene
Church open throughout the event.

36 ▶ **THE MANOR HOUSE**
Chequer Street, Fenstanton,
Huntingdon PE28 9JQ. Lynda
Symonds & Nigel Ferrier. *10m NW
of Cambridge. Opp chapel and
village green, 500 metres E of King
William IV PH. Sat 18, Sun 19 June
(1.30-5.30). Adm £3.50, chd free.
Light refreshments.*
Formal garden with parterre,
pleached limes and interesting
cottage borders set in just over ⅓
acre surrounding The Manor House,
once the home of Capability Brown
as featured on C4 Alan Titchmarsh's
television programme.

37 ▶ ◆ **THE MANOR,
HEMINGFORD GREY**
Hemingford Grey PE28 9BN. Mrs D
S Boston, 01480 463134,
diana_boston@hotmail.com,
www.greenknowe.co.uk. *4m E of
Huntingdon. Off A14. Entrance to*
garden by small gate off river
towpath. Limited parking on verge
halfway up drive, parking near house
for disabled. Otherwise park in village.
**For opening times and information,
please phone, email or visit garden
website.**
Garden designed and planted by
author Lucy Boston, surrounds C12
manor house on which Green Knowe
books based (house open by appt).
4 acres with topiary; over 200 old
roses, extensive collection of irises
incl Cedric Morris varieties and
herbaceous borders with mainly
scented plants. Meadow with mown
paths. Enclosed by river, moat and
wilderness. Late May splendid show
of Irises followed by the old roses.
Care is taken with the planting to start
the year with a large variety of
snowdrops and to extend the
flowering season right through to the
first frosts. The garden is interesting
even in winter with the topiary.
Featured in Country Life 'The Luck of
the Iris' by George Plumptre. Gravel
paths but wheel chairs are
encouraged to go on the lawns.

38 ▶ **MARY CHALLIS GARDEN**
High Street, Sawston, Cambridge
CB22 3BG. A M Challis Trust Ltd.
*7m SE of Cambridge. Entrance via
lane between 60 High St & 66 High
St (Billsons Opticians). Sun 12 June
(2-5). Adm £3, chd free. Home-
made teas.*
Given to Sawston in 2006 this 2 acre
garden is being restored by
volunteers: formal flower garden,
vegetable beds with vine house,
meadow and woodland, with
concern for the flora and fauna -
and the village children. Paths and
lawns should be accessible from carpark.

39 ▶ **5 MOAT WAY**
Swavesey CB24 4TR. Mr & Mrs N
Kyberd, 01954 200568,
n.kyberd@ntlworld.com. *Off A14,
2m beyond Bar Hill. Look for School
Lane/Fen Drayton Rd, at mini r'about
turn into Moat Way, no.5 is approx
100 metres on L. Visits by
arrangement June to Aug. Adm
£3, chd free.*
Colourful garden filled with collection
of trees, shrubs and perennials. Large
patio area displaying many specimen
foliage plants in planters, incl pines,
hostas and acers.

40 ▶ NETHERHALL MANOR
Tanners Lane, Soham CB7 5AB.
Timothy Clark. *6m Ely, 6m
Newmarket. Enter Soham from
Newmarket, Tanners Lane 2nd R
100yds after cemetery. Enter Soham
from Ely, Tanners Lane 2nd L after
War Memorial.* Sun 27 Mar, Sun 1
May, Sun 7, Sun 14 Aug (2-5). Adm
£2, chd free. Home-made teas.
An elegant garden 'touched with
antiquity' Good Gardens Guide. An
unusual garden appealing to those
with an historical interest in the
individual collections of genera and
plant groups: March - old primroses,
daffodils and Victorian double
flowered hyacinths. May - old English
tulips. Crown Imperials. Aug -
Victorian pelargonium, heliotrope,
calceolaria, dahlias. Author of
Margery Fish's Country Gardening
and Mary McMurtrie's Country
Garden Flowers. Historic Plants
1500-1900. Double flowered
Hyacinths,. Tudor type primroses.
Victorian Pelargoniums. The only bed
of English tulips on display in the
country. Author's books for sale. Flat
garden with two optional steps.
Lawns.

41 ▶ NORFOLK TERRACE GARDEN
38 Norfolk Terrace, Cambridge
CB1 2NG. John Tordoff & Maurice
Reeve. *Central Cambridge. A603
East Rd turn R into St Matthews St to
Norfolk St, L into Blossom St &
Norfolk Terrace is at the end.* Sat 2,
Sun 3 July (11-5). Combined adm
with 10 Gwydir Street £4, chd
free. Light refreshments.
A small, paved courtyard garden in
Moroccan style. Masses of colour in
raised beds and pots, backed by
oriental arches. An ornamental pool
done in patterned tiles offers the
soothing splash of water. The owners'
previous, London garden, was named
by BBC Gardeners' World as 'Best
Small Garden in Britain'. There will
also be a displays of recent paintings
by John Tordoff and handmade
books by Maurice Reeve.

42 ▶ THE OLD RECTORY
312 Main Road, Parson Drove,
Wisbech PE13 4LF. Helen Roberts,
01945 700415,
yogahelen@talk21.com. *SW of
Wisbech. From Peterborough on A47
follow signs to Parson Drove L after
Thorney Toll. From Wisbech follow
the B1166 through Levrington
Common.* Sun 5 June (11-4). Adm
£3.50, chd free. Home-made teas.
**Visits also by arrangement Mar to
Aug.**
Walled Georgian cottage garden of 1
acre, opening into wild flower
meadow and paddocks. Long
herbaceous border, 2 ponds and
unusual weeping ash tree. Terraced
areas and outdoor kitchen! No hills
but lovely open Fen views.

> Hens range freely in
> the orchard . . .

43 ▶ THE OLD VICARAGE
Causeway, Great Staughton, St
Neots PE19 5BF. Mr & Mrs Richard
Edmunds, 01480860397,
elizabeth.edmunds4@btinternet.com. *5m off A1, 8m from St Neots.
Take the B645 to Great Staughton.*
Visits by arrangement May to
Sept groups of 10+, do tea and a
garden visit. Just let us know in
advance. Adm £4, chd free. Teas
in the kitchen or out in the area of
the garden by the summer
houses. A nice place to have a
picnic.
A good Old Vicarage garden,
redesigned in 2008/9 to enhance
original plan. A Natural Swimming
Pond which has pretty rockery
planting with ferns and a man made
waterway running into it over rocks.
Also, a Wendy house on a platform
with swings and slide off it. Some
gravel paths easily negotiable by
wheelchair.

44 ▶ NEW ▶ OLD WESTON GARDEN FARM
High Street, Old Weston,
Huntingdon PE28 5LA. Sylvia &
John Younger,
www.oldwestongardenfarm.weebly
.com. *Coming from Old Weston
Village, with PH on R take next R into
High St (a country rd), go past the
chicken farm on R, we are within 500
meters.* Sun 31 July (1-4.30). Adm
£4, chd free. Home-made teas.
An interesting 9 acre smallholding.
The 2 acre Kitchen Garden has been
laid out in an intricate 'Potager'
design mixing flowers for cutting
(available as 'Pick Your Own') and
companion planting among the wide
range of fruit, vegetables and herbs.
Hens range freely in the orchard,
turkeys and geese are raised for
Christmas along with rare-breed pigs.
Grass paths throughout which can be
uneven and bumpy for wheelchairs.

GROUP OPENING

45 ▶ NEW ▶ ORWELL GARDENS
Orwell, Royston SG8 5QN. *8m SW
of Cambridge. Meadowbank 34 High
Street is between the village hall &
thatched wall. For 57 Cakebreade
Cottage, Town Green Road, park at
recreation ground & walk up gravel
drive opp.* Sat 4 June (12-5).
Combined adm £3.50, chd free.
Home-made teas at Meadowbank
only.

NEW ▶ 57 CAKEBREADE
COTTAGE
Mrs Verity Tilleard-Haines
Visits also by arrangement May
to July.
verity_haines@yahoo.com
01223 208605 or 07805 857550

NEW ▶ MEADOWBANK
Sue and Paddy Ward
Visits also by arrangement May
to Sept.
Sue.paddy@btinternet.com
01223 208852 or 07969 554069

Two very different country gardens.
Cakebreade Cottage c1600 is a small
intimate cottage garden on an old
orchard footprint, and is a charming
informal organic secluded garden
planted mostly within the last three
years. Containing a large range of
herbaceous plants in soft colours.
Climbing roses, fruit trees, herbs and
a small meadow area surrounded by
some mature trees. Meadowbank is a
large 2 acre garden with lovely views
across the fields, and has been
mostly replanted within the last 6
years on a mature site. Rose garden,
herbaceous borders and herb
garden, vegetable patch, extensive
wildflower meadow, stream with bog
plants, and a newly planted grove of
trees. Art studio open at Cakebreade
Cottage with art work for sale.
Cakebreade Cottage uneven lawn
area, side access. Meadowbank
access for wheelchairs down the right
side of the house.

46 23A PERRY ROAD

Buckden, St. Neots PE19 5XG. **David & Valerie Bunnage,** 01480 810553, **d.bunnage@btinternet.com.** *5m S of Huntingdon on A1. From A1 Buckden r'about take B661, Perry Rd approx 300yds on L.* Visits by arrangement Apr to Oct. Adm £3.50, chd free.

Approx 1 acre garden consisting of many garden designs incl Japanese interlinked by gravel paths. Large selection of acers, pines, rare and unusual shrubs. Also interesting features, a quirky garden. Plantsmans garden for all seasons new wildlife pond with small stumpery and woodland plus small seaside garden with beach hut. WC. Coaches welcome.

GROUP OPENING

47 RAMSEY FORTY FOOT

Ramsey PE26 2YA. *3m N of Ramsey. From Ramsey (B1096) travel through Ramsey Forty Foot, just before bridge over drain, turn into Hollow Rd at The George PH, First Cottage 300yds on R, next door to The Elms.* Sun 29 May (2-6). Combined adm £3, chd free. Tea.

THE ELMS
Mr R Shotbolt

THE WILLOWS
Jane & Andrew Sills

Two interesting and contrasting gardens in the village of Ramsey Forty Foot. The Elms is a 1½ -acre informal garden with ancient water-filled clay pits teeming with wildlife and backed by massive elms. Large collection of shrubs, perennials, bog and aquatic plants. Woodland and arid plantings. The Willows is a cottage garden with riverside location filled with old roses, herbaceous beds; shrubs, ferns, pond and vegetable garden. Some wheelchair access.

48 6 ROBINS WOOD

Wansford, Peterborough PE8 6JQ. **Carole & Forbes Smith,** 01780 783094, **caroleannsmith@tiscali.co.uk.** *7m W of Peterborough on A1/A47 junction. From A47 turn towards Wansford. At Xrds by church turn W onto Old Leicester Rd. Approx 500yds turn R into Robins Field, follow on to Robins Wood.* Sun 28 Feb (11-4). Adm £3, chd free. Home-made teas. Visits also by arrangement Jan to Apr.

Small woodland garden with a collection of 300+ varieties of snowdrops. Various hellebore and corydalis followed by other spring woodland plants and bulbs. Small alpine plant house. Still creating beds in any spare corner to accommodate new varieties.

The Queen's Nursing Institute

The NGS is The QNI's largest single donor

49 ROBINSON COLLEGE

Grange Road, Cambridge CB3 9AN. Warden and Fellows, 01223 339100, http://www.robinson.cam.ac.uk/about-robinson/gardens/national-gardens-scheme. *Garden at main Robinson College site, report to Porters' Lodge. There is only on-street parking.* Every Mon to Fri 1 Jan to 15 Apr (10-4). Every Sat and Sun 2 Jan to 17 Apr (2-4). Every Mon to Fri 13 June to 31 Dec (10-4). Every Sat and Sun 18 June to 31 Dec (2-4). Adm £4, chd free.

10 original Edwardian gardens are linked to central wild woodland water garden focusing on Bin Brook with small wealth at heart of site. This gives a feeling of park and informal woodland, while at the same time keeping the sense of older more formal gardens beyond. Central area has a wide lawn running down to the lake framed by many mature stately trees with much of the original planting intact. More recent planting incl herbaceous borders and commemorative trees. Please report to Porters' Lodge on arrival to pay for entry and guidebook. No picnics. Children must be accompanied at all times. NB from time to time some parts, or occasionally all, of Robinson College gardens may be closed for safety reasons involving work by contractors and our maintenance staff. Please report to Porters' Lodge on arrival for information. Ask at Porters' Lodge for wheelchair access.

GROUP OPENING

50 SAWSTON GARDENS

Sawston, Cambridge CB22 3HY. *5m SE of Cambridge. Halfway between Saffron Walden & Cambridge on A1301.* Sun 3 July (1-6). Combined adm £5, chd free. Cream teas at Sweet Tea cafe, High St.

BROOK HOUSE
Mr & Mrs Ian & Mia Devereux

DRIFT HOUSE
Mr Alan & Mrs Jean Osborne

11 MILL LANE
Tim & Rosie Phillips

35 MILL LANE
Doreen Butler

22 ST MARY'S ROAD
Ann & Mike Redshaw

VINE COTTAGE
Dr & Mrs Tim Wreghitt

6 delightful gardens. Brook House has many lovely recently designed and planted features set in 1½ acres. One of the many highlights is a stunning large walled garden not to be missed. Drift House has ⅓ acre mature mixed planting, lawns, fish pond, kitchen garden and a cloud-pruned Juniper tree. 35 Mill Lane has colourful massed annual and perennial floral displays and fascinating water features. Find immaculate lush lawns, delightful mature mixed borders and large fruit cage at 11 Mill Lane. 22 St Mary's Road has views over SSS1 meadows, wildlife friendly planting and charming colour-themed contemporary borders. Vine Cottage's large mature garden has an intriguing secret Japanese courtyard. Many other features to be found something for everyone. Great value six gardens for £5. Enjoy a cream tea at 'Sweet Tea', or take up the discounts on offer for garden visitors at the Jade Fountain Chinese restaurant. With such a variety of gardens, clearly wheelchair access is variable.

GROUP OPENING

51 STAPLEFORD GARDENS
Stapleford, Cambridge CB22 5DG.
*4m S of Cambridge on A1301. In
London Road next to Church Street.
Parking available on site.* Sun 12
June (2-6). Combined adm £5, chd
free. Home-made teas. at 6
Finch's Close and 59-61 London
Road. Jam & Chutney sale at 59-
61 London Road.

59-61 LONDON ROAD
Dr & Mrs S Jones

57 LONDON ROAD
Mrs M Spriggs

5 PRIAMS WAY
Tony Smith

Contrasting gardens showing a range
of size, planting and atmosphere in
this village just S of Cambridge. The
London Road and Priam's Way
gardens form an interlocking series of
garden rooms incl herbaceous beds,
kitchen garden, pit and summer
houses with sculptures set around.
Priam's Way small mature borders
with a wide variety of plants and
shrubs.

Climbing roses, fruit
trees, herbs and a
small meadow . . .

GROUP OPENING

52 STAPLOE GARDENS
Staploe, St. Neots PE19 5JA. *Great
North Rd in western part of St Neots.
At r'about just N of the Coop store,
exit westwards on Duloe Rd. Follow
this under the A1, through the village
of Duloe & on to Staploe.* Sat 11,
Sun 12 June (1-5). Combined adm
£3.50, chd free. Home-made teas.

FALLING WATER HOUSE
Caroline Kent

OLD FARM COTTAGE
Sir Graham & Lady Fry

Old Farm Cottage: flower garden
surrounding thatched house (not
open), with 3 acres of orchard,

grassland, young woodland and
pond maintained for wildlife. Falling
Water House: a mature woodland
garden, partly reclaimed from
farmland 10yrs ago, it is constructed
around several century old trees incl
three Wellingtonia. Kitchen garden
potager, courtyard and herbaceous
borders, planted to attract bees and
wildlife, through which meandering
paths have created hidden vistas. Old
Farm Cottage has rough ground and
one steep slope.

53 STEEPLE VIEW
20 Steeple View, March PE15 9QH.
Mr & Mrs Allan & April Hammond,
01354 659629,
allan@darcy143.plus.com. *1m S of
March town centre. Steeple View is a
turning off Knights End Rd which is
situated off A141 March bypass.
Limited parking at garden. Therefore
please park in the rd leading up to St
Wendreda's Church.* Sat 25, Sun 26
June (10-5). Adm £3, chd free.
Light refreshments. **Visits also by
arrangement June to Sept approx
10 or negotiable. Refreshments
incl in adm.**
Enter the main garden through a neat
pebbled side walkway. The garden
overlooks meadows and comprises
of a mixture of well stocked beds and
borders. An elegant pergola
accessed via a bridge over the main
pond stretches the full length of the
garden. Bog garden and wildlife
pond. Exit via a small orchard with
small selection of fruit trees and
cottage garden. Cottage garden
(separated from main garden),
contains a hobbit house and many
animal (ornaments) for children.
Featured in Cambs Times. Narrow
pebbled path not suitable for
wheelchair access.

GROUP OPENING

54 STREETLY END
GARDENS
West Wickham CB21 4RP. *3m from
Haverhill & 3m from Linton. On A1307
between Linton & Haverhill. Turn N at
Horseheath towards West Wickham,
from Horseheath turn L at triangle of
grass & trees, well signed.* Sun 5
June (12-5). Combined adm £3.50,
chd free. Home-made teas at
Chequer Cottage.

CHEQUER COTTAGE
Mr & Mrs D Sills
01223 891522
stay@chequercottage.com
www.chequercottage.com

CLOVER COTTAGE
Mr Paul & Mrs Shirley Shadford
Visits also by arrangement May
to July adm incl tea or coffee &
biscuits.
shirleyshadford@live.co.uk
01223 893122

Find arches of roses and clematis at
Clover Cottage and many varieties of
hardy geraniums, and raised
fruit/vegetable beds. Delightful pond
and borders of English roses,
climbers and herbaceous plants. Also
ferns and shade plants and views
over open countryside from
summerhouse in sunken garden. At
Chequer Cottage enjoy mixed
cottage and contemporary planting of
Monet style rose arch, perennial beds
with many iris, delphiniums, roses.
Unusual trees, pond, bog garden, art
studio. Long vegetable garden,
interesting walls, paths and rockery.
In walled garden evergreen shrubs,
damp shade and hot dry borders. Art
studio open, art work and home-
made teas for sale at Chequer
Cottage. Plants for sale at Clover
Cottage. NO WHEELCHAIRS, NO
PUSHCHAIRS & NO DOG ACCESS
TO GARDENS AT ALL.

55 TRINITY COLLEGE,
FELLOWS' GARDEN
Queens Road, Cambridge
CB3 9AQ. Master and Fellows' of
Trinity College, 01223 338530,
gardens@trin.cam.ac.uk,
www.trin.cam.ac.uk/about/
gardens. *Short walk from city Centre.
At the Northampton St/Madingley Rd
end of Queens Rd close to Garrett
Hostel Lane.* Sun 10 Apr (1-4). Adm
£3.50, chd free. Home-made teas.
Special dietary requirements are
available on request.
Interesting historic garden of about 8
acres with impressive specimen trees,
mixed borders, drifts of spring bulbs,
and informal lawns with notable
influences throughout from Fellows
over the years. Across the gently
flowing Bin Brook to Burrell's Field
you will find some modern planting
styles and plants nestled amongst the
accommodation blocks in smaller
intimate gardens. Members of the
Gardening staff will be on hand to

answer any queries. The teas and cakes are provided, and served, by a local Girl Guide unit. Some gravel paths.

56 TWIN TARNS

6 Pinfold Lane, Somersham PE28 3EQ. Michael & Frances Robinson, 01487 843376, mikerobinson987@btinternet.com. *Easy access from the A14. 4m NE of St Ives. Turn onto Church St. Pinfold Lane is next to the church. Please park on Church Street as access is narrow and limited.* **Sat 4, Sun 5 June (1-5). Adm £4, chd free. Cream teas. Visits also by arrangement June to Sept any size group.**
One-acre wildlife garden with formal borders, kitchen garden and ponds, large rockery, mini woodland, wild flower meadow (June/July). Topiary, rose walk, willow sculptures. Character oak bridge and tree-house. Adjacent to C13 village church. Featured in Gardeners' World, Cambridgeshire Journal, Garden News, Love Your Garden, and Landscape.

GROUP OPENING

57 WHITTLESFORD GARDENS

Whittlesford CB22 4NR. *7m S of Cambridge. 1m NE of J10 M11 & A505. Parking nr church.* **Sun 19 June (2-6). Combined adm £4.50, chd free. Home-made teas at the church.**

THE GUILDHALL
Professor Peter Spufford

MARKINGS FARM
Mr & Mrs A Jennings

5 PARSONAGE COURT
Mrs L Button

11 SCOTTS GARDENS
Mr & Mrs M Walker

WHITBY COTTAGE
Mrs Laura Latham

Find a variety of country, formal, modern and wildlife friendly gardens here. Whitby Cottage is a small claybat walled pretty cottage garden with interesting water features and large koi carp. Markings Farm is a lovely old fashioned country garden with a variety of shrubs and perennials, and a fabulous vegetable patch. Parsonage Court has an

arched walkway, shrubs, raised fish pond and delightful seating area around an old tree. 11 Scotts Gardens is a shady small walled cottage garden with a variety of shrubs and large perennials. A knot garden, large fig tree and a lovely water feature can be found at the 16th century timber framed Guildhall (house not open).

58 WILD ROSE COTTAGE

Church Walk, Lode, Cambridge CB25 9EX. Mrs Joy Martin, 01223 811132, joymartin123@outlook.com. *From A14 take the rd towards Burwell turn L in to Lode & park on L. Walk straight on between cottages to the archway of Wild Rose Cottage.* **Visits by arrangement Mar to Oct please email or phone. Adm £4, chd free.**
A real cottage garden overflowing with plants. Gardens within gardens of abundant vegetation, roses climbing through trees, laburnum tunnel, a daffodil spiral which becomes a daisy spiral in the summer. Circular vegetable garden and wildlife pond. Described by one visitor as a garden to write poetry in! It is a truly wild and loved garden where flowers in the vegetable circle are not pulled up! Chickens ducks and dog, circular vegetable garden, wild life pond, and wild romantic garden! Lots of little path ways!

59 THE WINDMILL

Cambridge Road, Impington CB24 9NU. Pippa & Steve Temple, 07775 446443, mill.impington@ntlworld.com, www.impingtonmill.org. *2½ m N of Cambridge. Off A14 at J32, B1049 to Histon, L into Cambridge Rd at T-lights, follow Cambridge Rd round to R, the Windmill is approx 400yds on L.* **Visits by arrangement Apr to Sept. Adm £4, chd free. Light refreshments. by arrangement.**
A previously romantic wilderness of 1½ acres surrounding windmill, now filled with bulbs, perennial beds, pergolas, bog gardens, grass bed and herb bank. Secret paths and wild areas with thuggish roses maintain the romance. Millstone seating area in smouldering borders contrasts with the pastel colours of the remainder of the garden. Also 'Pond Life' seat, 'Tree God' and amazing compost area! The Windmill - an C18 smock

on C19 tower on C17 base on C16 foundations - is being restored. Featured in Daily Mail, local press and radio.

60 WYTCHWOOD

7 Owl End, Great Stukeley, Huntingdon PE28 4AQ. Mr David Cox. *2m N of Huntingdon on B1043. Parking available at Great Stukeley Village Hall in Owl End.* **Sun 3 July (1.30-5.30). Adm £3.50, chd free. Home-made and cream teas and cakes.**
A 2 acre garden with borders of perennials, annuals and shrubs, lawns, fish pond and a larger wildlife pond. The garden includes 1 acre for wildlife with grasses set among rowan, birch, maple and field maple trees, foxgloves, ferns and bulbs. Roses are a special feature in June. Enjoy home made and cream teas, plenty of seats. Short gravel drive at the garden entrance.

The Six Houses, Barton Gardens

© Howard Rice

74

CHESHIRE & WIRRAL

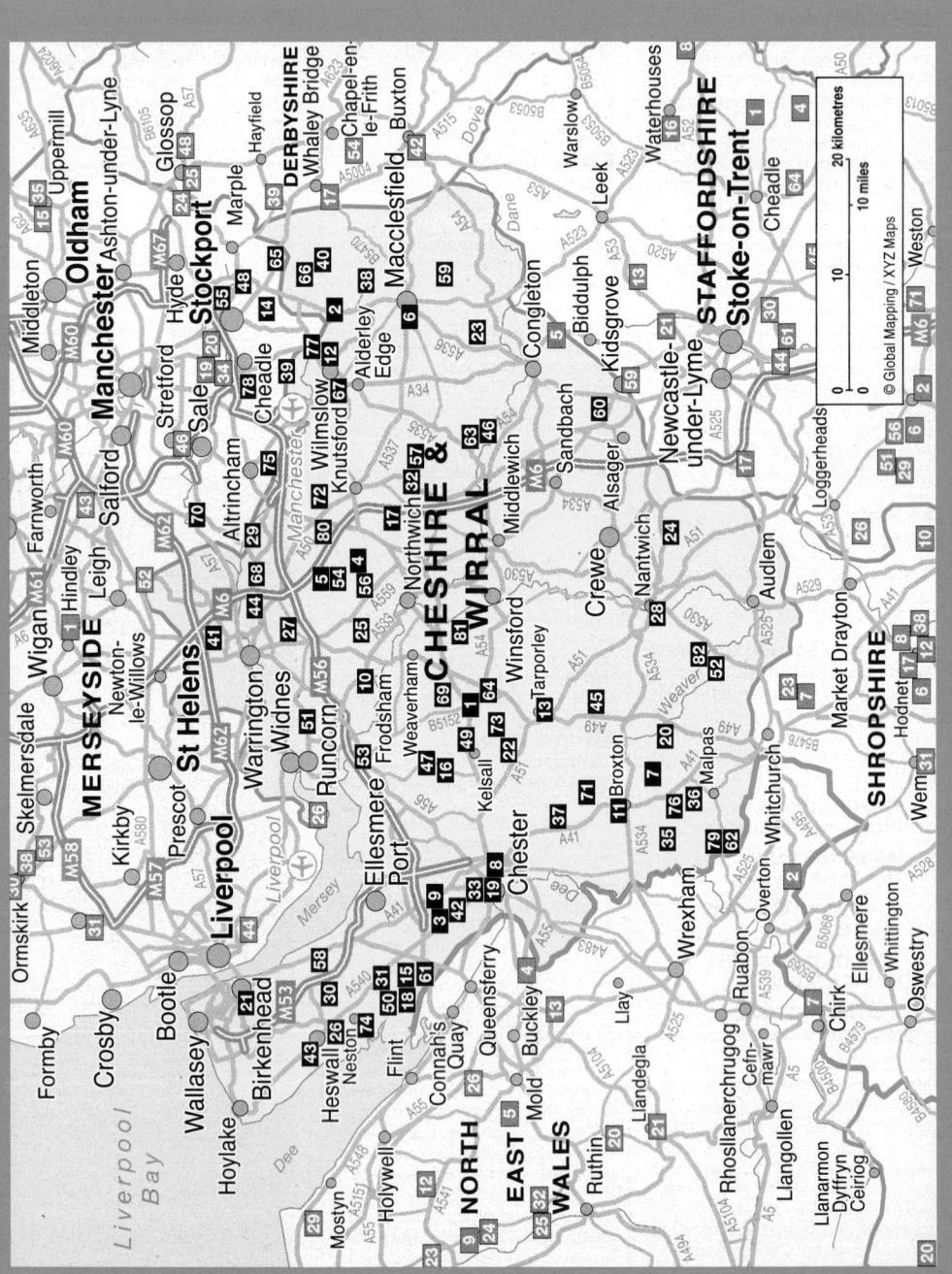

Investec Wealth & Investment supports the NGS

Cheshire & Wirral

The NGS 'county' of Cheshire and Wirral comprises what are now the four administrative regions of West Cheshire and Chester, East Cheshire, Warrington and Wirral, together with gardens in the south of Greater Manchester, Trafford and Stockport.

The perception of the area is that of a fertile county dominated by the Cheshire Plain, but to the extreme west it enjoys a mild maritime climate, with gardens often sitting on sandstone and sandy soils and enjoying mildly acidic conditions.

A large sandstone ridge also rises out of the landscape, running some 30-odd miles from north to south. Many gardens grow ericaceous-loving plants, although in some areas, the slightly acidic soil is quite clayey. But the soil is rarely too extreme to prevent the growing of a wide range of plants, both woody and herbaceous.

As one travels east and the region rises up the foothills of the Pennine range, the seasons become somewhat harsher, with spring starting a few weeks later than in the coastal region.

As well as being home to one of the RHS's major shows, the region's gardens include two NGS 'founder' gardens in Arley Hall and Peover Hall, as well as the University of Liverpool Botanic Garden at Ness.

Cheshire & Wirral Volunteers

County Organiser
John Hinde
01513 530032
john.hinde@maylands.com

County Treasurer
Andrew Collin
01513 393614
andrewcollin@btinternet.com

Social Media
Janet Bashforth
01925 349895
janbash43@sky.com

Graham Beech
01625 402946
gb.ngs@talktalk.net

Publicity
Linda Enderby
07949 496747
lmaenderby@outlook.com

Booklet Co-ordinator
John Hinde
(as above)

Assistant County Organisers
Sue Bryant
01619 283819
suewestlakebryant@btinternet.com

Jean Davies
01606 892383
mrsjeandavies@gmail.com

Sandra Fairclough
01513 424645
sandra.fairclough@tiscali.co.uk

Juliet Hill
01829 732804
t.hill573@btinternet.com

Romy Holmes
01829 732053
romy@holmes-email.co.uk

Left: Peover Hall Gardens

Opening Dates

All entries subject to change.
For latest information check www.ngs.org.uk

February

Snowdrop Festival

Sunday 28
17 Bucklow Farm
29 Dunham Massey

March

Monday 28
4 All Fours Farm

April

Sunday 3
56 Parm Place

Saturday 16
58 Poulton Hall

Sunday 17
58 Poulton Hall

Sunday 24
15 Briarfield
45 Long Acre

May

Sunday 1
49 Mount Pleasant

Monday 2
4 All Fours Farm
31 NEW Framley
49 Mount Pleasant

Saturday 7
36 Hannets Cottage

Sunday 8
1 Abbeywood Gardens
36 Hannets Cottage
73 Tirley Garth Gardens

Wednesday 11
72 Tatton Park

Thursday 12
20 Cholmondeley Castle Garden

Saturday 14
43 Inglewood

Sunday 15
43 Inglewood
50 Ness Botanic Gardens
69 Stonyford Cottage
73 Tirley Garth Gardens

Sunday 22
28 Dorfold Hall
29 Dunham Massey
70 Sycamore Cottage

73 Tirley Garth Gardens

Sunday 29
21 28 Christchurch Road
47 Manley Knoll
71 Tattenhall Hall

June

Friday 3
80 NEW Winterbottom House (Evening)

Festival Weekend

Saturday 4
16 Brooklands
37 Hatton House Gardens
53 The Old Cottage
54 The Old Parsonage
57 Peover Hall Gardens

Sunday 5
2 Adlington Hall
4 All Fours Farm
16 Brooklands
32 Free Green Farm
37 Hatton House Gardens
51 Norton Priory Museum & Gardens
53 The Old Cottage
54 The Old Parsonage
57 Peover Hall Gardens

Saturday 11
19 Chester Cathedral

Sunday 12
17 Bucklow Farm

Wednesday 15
52 Oakfield Villa
72 Tatton Park
82 Wren's Nest

Saturday 18
6 Ashmead
68 10 Statham Avenue
79 The White Cottage

Sunday 19
6 Ashmead
45 Long Acre
59 Ridgehill
64 Sandymere
68 10 Statham Avenue
79 The White Cottage

Orchard and meadow with hens . . .

Wednesday 22
74 NEW Twin Gates

Thursday 23
74 NEW Twin Gates

Saturday 25
8 150 Barrel Well Hill
10 Bluebell Cottage Gardens
36 Hannets Cottage

Sunday 26
4 All Fours Farm
8 150 Barrel Well Hill
10 Bluebell Cottage Gardens
18 Burton Village Gardens
36 Hannets Cottage
56 Parm Place
77 Well House

July

Saturday 2
3 Adswood
22 Clemley House
33 NEW 51 Garth Drive
42 Home Farm House
62 The Rowans

Sunday 3
3 Adswood
42 Home Farm House
48 218 Marple Road
62 The Rowans
70 Sycamore Cottage

Wednesday 6
33 NEW 51 Garth Drive

Saturday 9
38 18 Highfield Road
63 NEW Rowley House
67 68 South Oak Lane

Sunday 10
38 18 Highfield Road
63 NEW Rowley House
67 68 South Oak Lane

Saturday 16
75 NEW 8a Warwick Drive

Sunday 17
75 NEW 8a Warwick Drive

Saturday 23
27 Dingle Farm

Sunday 24
27 Dingle Farm
30 Fieldcrest
78 West Drive Gardens

Thursday 28
24 NEW 5 Cobbs Lane

Saturday 30
27 Dingle Farm
65 21 Scafell Close
66 NEW Smithy House

Sunday 31
27 Dingle Farm

39 73 Hill Top Avenue
65 21 Scafell Close
69 Stonyford Cottage

August

Wednesday 3
24 NEW 5 Cobbs Lane

Saturday 6
23 NEW Clover Bank Organic Farm
27 Dingle Farm

Sunday 7
5 Arley Hall & Gardens
23 NEW Clover Bank Organic Farm
25 Cogshall Grange
27 Dingle Farm
48 218 Marple Road

Saturday 13
9 NEW The Birches
36 Hannets Cottage
44 Laskey Farm

Sunday 14
1 Abbeywood Gardens
9 NEW The Birches
36 Hannets Cottage
44 Laskey Farm
80 NEW Winterbottom House

Sunday 28
71 Tattenhall Hall

September

Saturday 3
49 Mount Pleasant
55 39 Osborne Street

Sunday 4
49 Mount Pleasant
55 39 Osborne Street

Sunday 18
29 Dunham Massey

October

Sunday 2
46 The Lovell Quinta Arboretum

February 2017

Sunday 26
17 Bucklow Farm

Gardens open to the public

1 Abbeywood Gardens
2 Adlington Hall
5 Arley Hall & Gardens
10 Bluebell Cottage Gardens
20 Cholmondeley Castle Garden
29 Dunham Massey

The Gardens

1 ◆ **ABBEYWOOD GARDENS**
Chester Road, Delamere, Northwich CW8 2HS. The Rowlinson Family, 01606 889477, info@abbeywoodestate. co.uk. www.abbeywoodestate. co.uk. *11m E of Chester. On the A556 facing Delamere Church.* **For NGS: Sun 8 May, Sun 14 Aug (10-5). Adm £5, chd free. Light refreshments.** For other opening times and information, please phone, email or visit garden website.
Superb setting near Delamere Forest. Total area 45 acres incl mature woodland, new woodland and new arboretum all with connecting pathways. Approx 4½ acres of gardens surrounding large Edwardian House. Vegetable garden, exotic garden, chapel garden, pool garden, woodland garden, lawned area with beds. Restaurant in garden.

2 ◆ **ADLINGTON HALL**
Mill Lane, Macclesfield SK10 4LF. Mrs Camilla Legh, 01625 827595, enquiries@adlingtonhall.com, www.adlingtonhall.com. *4m N of Macclesfield, situated between Wilmslow & Prestbury. Well signed off A523 at Adlington.* **For NGS: Sun 5 June (2-5). Adm £6, chd free. Home-made teas.** For other opening times and information, please phone, email or visit garden website.
Adlington Hall and Gardens consists of a formal garden area with the Rose Garden and Yew maze. Beyond the South Front sits the Wilderness, a woodland with follies and a river winding through it. The trees and features date back centuries with some rare specimens having been planted by various members of the Legh family. There is often an abundance of wildlife within this area too. Recently restored Shell Cottage and T'Ing House. Bee friendly garden in the rose garden. Partial wheelchair access.

3 **ADSWOOD**
Townfield Lane, Mollington CH1 6LB. Ken & Helen Black, 01244 851327, keneblack@outlook.com. *3m N of Chester. From Wirral take A540 towards Chester. Cross A55 at r'about, past Wheatsheaf PH, turn L into Overwood Lane. At T junction turn R into Townfield Lane. Parking will be signed.* **Sat 2, Sun 3 July (1-5). Combined adm with Home Farm House £5, chd free. Home-made teas at our partner garden, Home Farm. Visits also by arrangement May to Aug groups of 8 + preferred.**
Cottage garden with side borders and island beds packed with a wide range of bulbs, perennials, climbers and traditional roses. The garden has been designed to be walked around and is home to over 100 varieties of clematis. There is a raised ornamental fish pond and several seating areas including garden pavilion. New features for 2016. There is only one 3 inch step down on to lawn. Help to negotiate this is always available.

8a Warwick Drive

4 ALL FOURS FARM
Colliers Lane, Aston by Budworth, Northwich CW9 6NF. Mrs Hazel Evans, 01565 733286. *M6 J19, take A556 towards Northwich. Turn immed R, past The Windmill PH. Turn R after approx 1m, follow rd, garden on L after approx 2m. We're happy to allow direct access for drop off and collection for those with limited mobility.* Mon 28 Mar, Mon 2 May, Sun 5, Sun 26 June (10-4). Adm £4, chd free. Home-made teas. **Visits also by arrangement Apr to July parties of 16 or more by arrangement. Please contact Hazel.**
A traditional and well established country garden with a wide range of roses, hardy shrubs, bulbs, perennials and annuals. You will also find a small vegetable garden, pond and greenhouse as well as vintage machinery and original features from its days as a working farm. The majority of the garden is accessible by wheelchair.

5 ◆ ARLEY HALL & GARDENS
Northwich CW9 6NA. The Viscount Ashbrook, www.arleyhallandgardens.com. *5m from Knutsford, Warrington & Northwich. Well signed from M6 J19 & 20, & M56 J9 & 10.* **For NGS: Sun 7 Aug (11-5). Adm £8.50, chd £3.50. For other opening times and information, please visit garden website.**
One of Britain's finest gardens, Arley has been lovingly created by the same family over 500yrs and is famous for its herbaceous border, avenue of ilex columns, walled garden, pleached lime avenue and Victorian Rootree. A garden of great atmosphere, interest and vitality throughout the seasons. Specialist nursery adjacent. Executive Vice President of the RHS Jim Gardiner has visited hundreds of gardens in the UK, Jim shared his top gardens to visit in 2015, selected for the tremendous breadth of plants on show and how they are displayed - Arley is on the list.

6 ASHMEAD
2 Bramhall Way, off Gritstone Drive, Macclesfield SK10 3SH. Peter & Penelope McDermott. *1m W of Macclesfield. Turn onto Pavilion Way, off Victoria Rd, then immediate L onto Gritstone Drive. Bramhall Way first on R.* **Sat 18, Sun 19 June (1-5). Adm £3.50, chd free. Home-made teas.**
¹/₈ acre suburban cottage garden, featuring plant packed mixed borders, rock gardens, kitchen garden, island beds, water feature, pond. The garden demonstrates how small spaces can be planted to maximum effect to create all round interest. Extensive range of plants favoured for colours, texture and scent. Pots used in a creative way to extend and enhance borders.

7 BANK HOUSE
Goldford Lane, Bickerton SY14 8LL. Dr & Mrs M A Voisey, 01829 782287, voisey598@btinternet.com. *4m NE of Malpas. 11m S of Chester on A41 turn L at Broxton r'about to Nantwich on A534. Take 5th R (1³/₄ m) to Bickerton. Take 2nd R into Goldford Lane. Bank House is approx 1m on L. Field parking.* **Visits by arrangement Apr to June, groups 10 - 40. Adm £5, chd free. Home-made teas.**
1³/₄ -acre garden at the foot of Bickerton Hill, in area of outstanding beauty, with extensive views to the East and South. Sheltered, terraced borders stocked with a wide range of shrubs, trees and herbaceous plants; established wild garden, Millennium garden with water features and productive vegetable garden. Unfenced swimming pool and ponds. Parts of garden too steep for chairs.

8 150 BARREL WELL HILL
Boughton, Chester CH3 5BR. Dr & Mrs John Browne. *On riverside ³/₄ m E of Chester off A5115. No parking at garden. Preferred access via Chester Boats, on the hour from the Groves, central Chester. Cost £3.50 one way. Or bus to St Pauls Church. Public car park adjacent to Bill Smiths Motors.* **Sat 25, Sun 26 June (11-5). Adm £4, chd £2. Home-made teas.**
Spectacular terraced garden with views over the R Dee to the Meadows and Clwyd Hills. Uniquely, preferred method of arrival is by leisurely river cruiser from Chester. Informal cottage style garden on historic site by the Martyrs Memorial. Lawns running down to the river, prolific shrub and flower beds, productive vegetable patch and soft and hard fruit areas, springs, stream and lily pond. River cruisers leave the centre of Chester regularly and arrangements have been made that they will drop off and pick up garden visitors on their way up river. Not suitable for wheelchairs or children under eight due to steps and unprotected drop into river.

9 NEW THE BIRCHES
Grove Road, Mollington, Chester CH1 6LG. Martin Bentley & Colin Williams. *Lea by Backford, nr Chester. 3m N of Chester. From the A540 Parkgate Rd turn onto Coal Pit Lane & follow around until it becomes Grove Rd. Pass riding stables on R, gardens approx ¹/₄ m further on R.* **Sat 13, Sun 14 Aug (10-6). Adm £3.50, chd £2. Home-made teas in Pemberley House front garden-next door adjoining.**
¹/₂ acre of gardens comprising of: Front night garden of pale/white herbaceous/mixed planting. Rear split into 4 areas 1, Koi and wildlife pond with herbaceous planting 2. Grasses/shrubs and fernery 3. Orchard and meadow with hens. 4, Vegetable and fruit trees and wildlife stream. Tea and locally baked cakes-traditional and modern cupcakes. Level garden with lawn or pathways to most areas.

10 ◆ BLUEBELL COTTAGE GARDENS
Lodge Lane, Dutton WA4 4HP. Sue & Dave Beesley, 01928 713718, info@bluebellcottage.co.uk, www.bluebellcottage.co.uk. *5m NW of Northwich. From M56 (J10) take A49 to Whitchurch. After 3m turn R at T-lights towards Runcorn/Dutton on A533. Then 1st L. Signed with brown tourism signs from*

A533. **For NGS: Sat 25, Sun 26 June (10-5). Adm £4, chd free. Home-made teas. For other opening times and information, please phone, email or visit garden website.**
South facing country garden wrapped around a cottage on a quiet rural lane in the heart of Cheshire. Packed with thousands of rare and familiar hardy herbaceous perennials, shrubs and trees. Unusual plants available at adjacent nursery. The opening dates coincide with the peak of flowering in the herbaceous borders. Featured in House and Garden magazine. Some gravel paths. Wheelchair access to 90% of garden. WC is not fully wheelchair accessible.

11 BOLESWORTH CASTLE
Tattenhall CH3 9HQ. Mrs Anthony Barbour, 01829 782210, dcb@bolesworth.com. *8m S of Chester on A41.* **Enter by Lodge on A41. Visits by arrangement Apr & May, groups of 10+. Light Refreshments by arrangement. Adm £5, chd free.**
Rock Walk above castle with one of the finest collections of rhododendrons, camellias and acers in any private garden in the NW. Set on a steep hillside accessed by a gently rising woodland walk and overlooking spectacular view of the Cheshire plain. Formal lawns beside and below castle with well stocked shrub borders. Regret no wheelchair access.

12 BOLLIN HOUSE
Hollies Lane, Wilmslow SK9 2BW. Angela Ferguson & Gerry Lemon, 07828 207492, fergusonang@doctors.org.uk. *Hollies Lane is off Adlington Rd 2nd exit on R coming from Wilmslow. Proceed to turning circle at end of lane, take 2nd exit off to Bollin House.* **Visits by arrangement May to July, groups 8-25. Adm £4, chd free. Tea. If more than 10 cars please phone.**
There are two components to this garden, the formal garden and the wild flower meadow. The garden contains richly planted, deep, herbaceous borders with a wide plant variety. Also an orchard, wild flower area and vegetable garden. The meadow contains both cornfield annuals and perennial wild flower areas which are easily accessible with

meandering mown paths. Ramps to gravel lined paths to most of the garden. Some narrow paths through borders. Mown pathways in the meadow.

> Always changing, Liz can't resist a new plant . . . !

13 BOWMERE COTTAGE
Bowmere Road, Tarporley CW6 0BS. Romy & Tom Holmes, 01829 732053, romy@bowmerecottage.co.uk. *10m E of Chester. From Tarporley High St (old A49) take Eaton Rd signed Eaton. After 100 metres take R fork into Bowmere Rd, Garden 100 metres on LH-side.* **Visits by arrangement June & July. Adm £4, chd free. Home-made teas.**
Mature 1-acre country style garden around a Grade II listed house (not open). Mixed shrub and herbaceous borders, pergolas, 2 plant filled courtyard gardens and small kitchen garden. Shrub and rambling roses, clematis, hardy geraniums and a wide and colourful range of plants make this a very traditional English garden. Cobbled drive and courtyard. Gravel paths.

14 167 BRAMHALL MOOR LANE
Hazel Grove, Stockport SK7 5BB. David & Angela Brannan, 0161 483 2704, mail@angela8brannan-99.co.uk. *4m S of Stockport. From Bramhall take A5102. Turn R at Bramhall Hall up Bridge Lane A5143 at r'about take 2nd exit Bramhall Moor Lane. From A6 take rd opp Sainsbury's.* **Visits by arrangement May to July, groups of approx 10. Adm £3, chd free. Home-made teas.**
The overall garden has a theme of light and dark. The front garden is a formal garden with box hedging and Indian bean trees with a background

of shrubs chosen for texture and foliage. The back garden has colourful informal herbaceous borders packed with a variety of plants and standard trees and a small nursery and vegetable plot at the side. Unusual trees in containers, small nursery.

15 BRIARFIELD
The Rake, Burton, Neston CH64 5TL. Liz Carter, 0151 336 2304, carter.burton@btinternet.com.net. *9m NW of Chester. Turn off A540 at Willaston-Burton Xrds T-lights & follow rd for 1m to Burton village centre.* **Sun 24 Apr (2-5). Adm £4, chd free. Home-made teas in St Nicholas' Church, close to the garden. Opening with Burton Village Gardens on Sun 26 June. Visits also by arrangement Apr to Sept.**
Tucked under the S-facing side of Burton Wood the garden is home to many specialist and unusual plants, some available in plant sale. This 2-acre garden is on two sites, a couple of minutes along an unmade lane. Shrubs, colourful herbaceous, bulbs, alpines and water features compete for attention as you wander through four distinctly different gardens. Always changing, Liz can't resist a new plant! Rare and unusual plants sold (65% to NGS) in Neston Market each Friday morning.

16 BROOKLANDS
Smithy Lane, Mouldsworth CH3 8AR. Barbara & Brian Russell-Moore, 01928 740413, ngsmouldsworth@aol.co.uk. *1½ m N of Tarvin. 5½ m S of Frodsham. Smithy Lane is off B5393 via A54 Tarvin/Kelsall rd or the A56 Frodsham/Helsby rd.* **Sat 4, Sun 5 June (2-5). Adm £4, chd free. Home-made teas and cakes using eggs from our own hens. Visits also by arrangement May to July for groups of 10+.**
Lovely country style, ¾ -acre garden with backdrop of mature trees and shrubs. The planting is based around azaleas, rhododendrons, mixed shrub and herbaceous borders. Small vegetable garden, supported by a greenhouse and 4 hens providing eggs for all the afternoon tea cakes!! Featured in Amateur Gardening and Cheshire Life.

Abbeywood Gardens

18 BURTON VILLAGE GARDENS

Neston CH64 5SJ. *9m NW of Chester. Turn off A540 at Willaston-Burton Xrds T-lights & follow rd for 1m to Burton. Maps given to visitors. Buy your ticket at first garden.* **Sun 26 June (11-5). Combined adm £5, chd free. Home-made teas in the centre of the village.**

BRIARFIELD
Liz Carter
(See separate entry)
Visits also by arrangement Apr to Sept.
carter.burton@btinternet.com.net
0151 336 2304

◆ **BURTON MANOR WALLED GARDEN**
Burton Manor Gardens Ltd
0151 345 1107
www.burtonmanorgardens.org.uk
LYNWOOD
Pauline Wright
Visits also by arrangement May to July.
0151 336 2311

Burton is a medieval village built on sandstone overlooking the Dee estuary, approx 1m from Ness Gardens. Three gardens are open, each with its own unique character. Lynwood, a half-acre plantswoman's garden, has a superb view across the Dee to the Clwydian hills. Set on an extensive sandstone outcrop enclosing a sunken pond, the garden is divided into 'rooms', each with its own collection of colourful herbaceous plants. Briarfield's sheltered site, nestling under the south side of Burton Wood (NT), is home to many specialist and unusual plants, some available in the plant sale at the house. The intricate layout of the 1½ acre main Briarfield garden invites exploration not only for its huge variety of plants but also for the imaginative display of ceramic sculptures. Period planting with a splendid vegetable garden surrounds the restored Edwardian glasshouse in Burton Manor's walled garden. All gardens have a plant sale. Well signed car parks. Maps available.

17 BUCKLOW FARM

Pinfold Lane, Plumley, Knutsford WA16 9RP. Dawn & Peter Freeman. *2m S of Knutsford. M6 J19, A556 Chester. L at 2nd set of T-lights. In 1¼ m, L at concealed Xrds. 1st R. From Knutsford A5033, L at Sudlow Lane. becomes Pinfold Lane.* **Sun 28 Feb (1-3). Adm £3, chd free. Light refreshments. Sun 12 June (2-5). Adm £4, chd free. Cream teas. 2017: Sun 26 Feb.** *Donation to Knutsford Methodist Church.*
Country garden with shrubs, perennial borders, rambling roses, herb garden, vegetable patch, wildlife pond/water feature and alpines. Landscaped and planted over the last 30yrs with recorded changes. Free range hens. Carpet of snowdrops and spring bulbs. Leaf, stem and berries to show colour in autumn and winter. Cobbled yard from car park, but wheelchairs can be dropped off near gate.

19 CHESTER CATHEDRAL
Chester CH1 2HU. Dean of Chester Cathedral. *Centre of Chester. Admission at SW entrance on St Werburgh St, Chester.* **Sat 11 June (1-4). Adm £3, chd free.**
Cloister Garth 2004, haven of peace and tranquillity surrounded by ancient architecture, sculpture fountain and exotic plants. 2012 Jubilee Garden with abundance of herbaceous and rare trees, fern border and new developments in Abbey Street, Abbey Square and Cathedral Green. Gardens designed by botanist and maintained by volunteers. Open day followed by (horticultural) Choral Evensong at 4.15pm in iconic C14 quire, sung by Cathedral Nave Choir. The Bishop's and Deanery Gardens will also be open. Additional attractions at the cathedral include tour of the tower and galleries and falconry display.

♿ ☕

20 ◆ CHOLMONDELEY CASTLE GARDEN
Cholmondeley, nr Malpas SY14 8AH. 01829 720383, www.cholmondeleycastle.com. *4m NE of Malpas. Signed from A41 Chester-Whitchurch rd & A49 Whitchurch-Tarporley rd.* **For NGS: Thur 12 May (11-4.30). Adm £7, chd £4. Light lunches & home-made teas. For other opening times and information, please phone or visit garden website.**
Over 20 acres of romantically landscaped gardens with fine views and eye-catching water features, but still manages to retain its intimacy. Beautiful mature trees form a background to spring bulbs, exotic plants in season incl magnolias, rhododendrons, azaleas and camellias and many other, particularly *Davidia Involucrata* which will be in flower in late May. Magnificent magnolias. One of the finest features of the gardens are its trees, many of which are rare and unusual and Cholmondeley Gardens is home to over 35 county champion trees. Partial wheelchair access.

♿ 🚲 ✿ 🚐 ☕

21 28 CHRISTCHURCH ROAD
Oxton CH43 5SF. Tom & Ruth Foster. *1m SW of Birkenhead. At M53 J3 take A552 to Birkenhead. Cross junction at T-lights after Sainsbury's. At next T-lights bear L. Take 2nd L. Christchurch R is after*

church. **Sun 29 May (1-5). Adm £4, chd free. Home-made teas.**
Grade II listed Victorian Folly with crenellated towers forms a unique feature in this ¼-acre plot. The garden is on different levels with many seating areas, terraced banks, planted sandstone walls, water features, herbaceous borders, lawns, trees (many acers) and a Japanese style garden. All areas are connected by a series of tunnels, pathways and steps.

🚲 ☕

> Wild rose and soft fruit hedging and fruit trees, large wild flower areas . . .

22 CLEMLEY HOUSE
Well Lane, Duddon Common, Tarporley CW6 0HG. Sue & Tom Makin, 077906 10586 / 01829 781737, s_makingardens@yahoo.co.uk. *8m S.E of Chester, 3m W of Tarporley. A51 from Chester towards Tarporley. 1m after Tarvin turnoff, at bus shelter, turn L into Willington Rd. After community centre, 2nd L into Well Lane. Third house.* **Sat 2 July (1-5). Adm £4, chd free. Home-made teas. Home grown organic fruits used in jams & cakes. Visits also by arrangement June & July for groups of 10+. Individuals please contact us to join groups.**
2 acre organic, wildlife friendly, gold award winning cottage garden. Features orchard, wildlife ponds, wildflower meadow, fruit and vegetables areas, badger sett, rose pergola, gazebo, summer house, barn owl and many other nest boxes, gravel and shade gardens, shepherd's hut and poly tunnel. Year round interest. Its development features regularly in the N.W. Cottage Garden Society newsletter. 'Frogwatch' charity volunteers transport migrating amphibians to the safety of these ponds when they are found on the roads in early spring.

Featured in Cheshire Life, Cottage Gardener, Cheshire Wildlife Trust Magazine. Gravel paths may be difficult to use but most areas are flat and comprise grass paths or lawn.

♿ 🚲 ✿ ☕

23 NEW CLOVER BANK ORGANIC FARM
Shellow Lane, North Rode, Congleton CW12 2NX. Brian & Jane Clarkson. *Approx 4m S Macclesfield, 4m N Congleton. From Macclesfield A523 turn R before Bosley T-lights, Bullgate Lane, Cloverbank entrance signed on R. From Congleton A536 turn R into Shellow Lane, Cloverbank entrance signed on L. NB satnav takes you to 400yds west of garden entrance.* **Sat 6, Sun 7 Aug (11-4). Adm £5, chd free. Tea.**
Began in 2010, garden complements stunning modern house above large pond with bridge and surrounding plantings of roses. dahlias, herbaceous, raised vegetable beds, marginal and wetland planting, woodland, Remembrance Garden, wild rose and soft fruit hedging and fruit trees, large wild flower areas. Spectacular views to Pennines. A 'must see' garden. Winner of the Cheshire Farm Garden Competition, finalist in the Daily Mail National Garden Competition. Mainly gravel paths, some grass areas may be difficult to manage.

♿ ☕

24 NEW 5 COBBS LANE
Hough, Crewe CW2 5JN. David & Linda Race. *4m S of Crewe. M6 J16 follow A500 & Newcastle Rd 5m. Turn L into Cobbs Lane. From the W; A51 Nantwich bypass to A500 r'about 3rd exit Newcastle Rd continue 3m passing White Hart PH, R into Cobbs Lane.* **Thur 28 July, Wed 3 Aug (11-5). Adm £5, chd free. Home-made teas.**
A plant person's ⅔ acre garden with island beds, wide cottage style herbaceous borders with bark paths running through for access. A large variety of hardy and some unusual perennials, shrubs, grasses and trees, with places to sit and enjoy the surroundings. A water feature runs to a small pond; island beds have interesting features. This is a wildlife friendly garden containing a woodland area. Finalists in the Daily Mail National Garden Competition.

🚲 ✿ ☕

25 COGSHALL GRANGE

Hall Lane, Antrobus, Northwich CW9 6BJ. Anthony & Margaret Preston. *3m NW of Northwich. Take A559 Northwich to Warrington. Turn into Wheatsheaf Lane or Well Lane. Head S on Sandiway Lane to grass triangle & then R into Hall Lane.* **Sun 7 Aug (11-5). Adm £6, chd free. Light refreshments.**
Set in the historic landscape of a late Georgian country house this is a contemporary garden, designed by the internationally renowned garden designer, Tom Stuart-Smith. The gardens contain a mixture of both informal and formal elements, modern herbaceous plantings, a walled garden, wild flower meadows, an orchard and woodland borders with views to parkland and the surrounding countryside.

27 DINGLE FARM

Dingle Lane, Appleton, Warrington WA4 3HR. Robert Bilton, www.dinglefarmonline.co.uk. *2m N from M56 J10. A49 towards Warrington, R at T-lights onto Stretton Rd, 1m turn L at The Thorn PH, after 1m turn L into Dingle Lane. Plenty of parking.* **Every Sat and Sun 23 July to 7 Aug (10-5). Adm £3, chd free. Light refreshments.**
The garden features include a large pond, an array of ornamental grasses, wild flower meadows, orchard, vegetable patch, newly planted woodland area and manicured lawns. The garden is overlooked by Dingle Farm and accessed through the Tea Rooms, lunches and cream teas served all day, Art Studio & Gift Shop set in the beautiful Cheshire countryside. Woodland walks adjacent to the site. Dingle Farm Tea Rooms were rated number 15 in the country by Sunday Times Magazine 'The UK's top twenty Tea Rooms'.

28 DORFOLD HALL

Nantwich CW5 8LD. The Roundell Family, www.dorfoldhall.com. *1m W of Nantwich. On A534 between Nantwich & Acton.* **Sun 22 May (2-5.30). Adm £6, chd £2.50. Tea.**
18-acre garden surrounding C17 house (not open) with formal approach; lawns and herbaceous borders; spectacular spring woodland garden with rhododendrons, azaleas, magnolias and bulbs.

29 ♦ DUNHAM MASSEY

Altrincham WA14 4SJ. National Trust, 0161 941 1025, www.nationaltrust.org.uk/dunham massey. *3m SW of Altrincham. Off A56; M6 exit J19; M56 exit J7. Foot: close to Trans-Pennine Trail & Bridgewater Canal. Bus: Nos 38 & 5.* **For NGS: Sun 28 Feb, Sun 22 May, Sun 18 Sept (11-5.30). Adm £8.80, chd £4.40. For other opening times and information, please phone or visit garden website.**
Enjoy the elegance of this vibrant Edwardian garden. Richly planted borders packed with colour and texture, sweeping lawns, majestic trees and shady woodland all await your discovery. Explore the largest Winter Garden in Britain and marvel at the colourful, scent-filled Rose Garden. Water features. C18 Orangery, rare Victorian Bark House. Visitors to the garden, incl NT members, should collect ticket from Visitor Reception at Visitor Centre.

30 ♦ FIELDCREST

Thornton Common Road, Thornton Hough, Wirral CH63 0LT. Paul & Christine Davies, 0151 334 8878, chris@fieldcrest.co.uk, www.fieldcrestgarden.co.uk. *5m S of Birkenhead, 4m SE of Heswall. Exit J4 M53, follow B5151 Clatterbridge/Willaston for 1m. Follow tourist sign for Merebrook House, turning L at r'about signed Raby Mere & Wirral RFC. Garden ½ m on R.* **For NGS: Sun 24 July (1-5). Adm £4, chd free. Home-made teas served in garden room. For other opening times and information, please phone, email or visit garden website.**
Country garden in 1⅓ acres, planted for year round colour and interest. Cottage garden, main garden and other 'rooms'. Kitchen garden specialising in herb and cut flower. Wildlife borders with Country lane

walk, wild flower area with young fruit trees and new water features. Wide variety of summer perennials. Colour themed 'Chocolate' border and new 'White Garden'. Winner Britains Best Lawn. Featured on BBC Northwest Tonight, Mail on Sunday, Telegraph and many local papers. Gravel in drive area and some paths.

31 NEW FRAMLEY

Hadlow Road, Willaston, Neston CH64 2US. Mrs Sally Reader, 07770 981640, sllyreader@yahoo.co.uk. *½ m S of Willaston village centre. From Willaston Green, proceed along Hadlow Rd, crossing the Wirral Way. Framley is the next house on R.* **Mon 2 May (10-2.30). Adm £4, chd free. Home-made teas. Visits also by arrangement May to July.**
This 5 acre garden holds many hidden gems. Comprising extensive mature wooded areas, underplanted with a variety of interesting and unusual woodland plants - all at their very best in spring. A selection of deep seasonal borders surround a mystical sunken garden, planted to suit its challenging conditions. Wide lawns and sandstone paths invite you to discover what lies around every corner. Please phone ahead for parking instructions for wheelchair users - access around much of the garden although the woodland paths may be challenging.

32 FREE GREEN FARM

Free Green Lane, Lower Peover WA16 9QX. Sir Philip & Lady Haworth. *3m S of Knutsford. Near A50 between Knutsford & Holmes Chapel. Off Free Green Lane.* **Sun 5 June (2-5.30). Adm £5, chd free. Home-made teas.**
2-acre garden with pleached limes, herbaceous borders, ponds, parterre, garden of the senses, British woodland with fernery, quasi jungle area with Saracenia and Banana. Topiary. Assortment of trees, and ten different forms of hedging. Ponds and underplanted woodland. Wheelchair access not easy in the wood.

33 NEW 51 GARTH DRIVE

Chester CH2 2AF. Mrs Heather Redhead, 01244 370227, redheadh@aol.com. *Bache railway station with parking is 10 min walk away. Bus stop on Liverpool Rd close*

to its junction with Lumley Rd, buses from Wirral & Chester. At the far end of Garth Drive. Limited parking in Garth Dr. **Sat 2, Wed 6 July (10-4.30). Adm £3, chd free. Home-made teas. Visits also by arrangement May to Aug refreshments by prior arrangement.**
A suburban garden a mile from Chester city centre packed with a variety of herbaceous borders, a pond, and productive areas which is set over several levels. Not suitable for wheelchairs.

35 ▶ GRAFTON LODGE
Stretton, Tilston, Malpas SY14 7JE. Simon Carter & Derren Gilhooley, 01829 250670, simoncar@aol.com, graftonlodge.tumblr.com. *For Sat Nav please use SY14 7JA NOT 7JE. 12m S of Chester. A41 S from Chester toward Wrexham on A534 at Broxton r'about. Pass Carden Park hotel - turn L at Cock o' Barton PH to Stretton & Tilston.* **Visits by arrangement June & July for groups of 6 min, no upper limit. Adm £4, chd free. Tea.**
Vibrantly colourful garden of 2 acres crammed with herbaceous plants, shrubs and roses. There are lawns, natural and formal ponds, specimen trees, mixed hedges and garden rooms incl cottage garden, rose circle, large pergola with sprawling roses and climbers, herbaceous beds, perfumed gazebo, roof terrace with far reaching views. Instagram @graftonlodgegarden. Wheelchair access bring your car right up to the garden, all on one level, and so fairly easy for a wheelchair user except in very wet conditions.

36 ▶ HANNETS COTTAGE
Tilston Road, Kidnal, Malpas SY14 7DH. Doris Bamforth, 01948 860979, deabamforth@aol.com. *Approx 1m NW of Malpas town centre. From Malpas town centre up High St towards Tilston. You are now on Tilston Rd. Continue for ³/₄ m. Do not use sat-nav.* **Sat 7, Sun 8 May, Sat 25, Sun 26 June, Sat 13, Sun 14 Aug (12-5.30). Adm £4, chd free. Cream teas. Visits also by arrangement May to Aug, groups of 10 - 30. Cream teas.**
This ¹/₂ acre cottage garden surrounds a typical Cheshire, grade 2 listed, cottage (not open). Different rooms for sun and shade lovers will

show you how to create interest and movement. Unusual plants (plus good plant stall), various water features, cosy seats and lovely views will make your visit to this quirky and much loved garden one to remember. Partial wheelchair access.

> Sandstone paths invite you to discover what lies around every corner . . .

37 ▶ HATTON HOUSE GARDENS
Hatton Heath, Chester CH3 9AP. Judy Halewood, basebotanics@hotmail.com. *4m SE of Chester. From Chester on A41 2km past The Black Dog PH. From Whitchurch on A41 7km past the Broxton r'about.* **Sat 4, Sun 5 June (11-4). Adm £5, chd free. Home-made teas. Great tea coffee and homemade cakes/sandwiches. Visits also by arrangement Apr to July for groups of 5+.**
Approx 8 acres of beautifully landscaped gardens both formal and natural. Pathways leading through extensive herbaceous borders and rose garden give way to lawns, azalea rock gardens, waterfalls and wild flowers. The 2 acre lake is rich in wildlife and flanked by woodland, wild flowers, bulbs, bridges and follies. All of the gardens are wheelchair friendly apart from the Sunken Garden.

38 ▶ 18 HIGHFIELD ROAD
Bollington, Macclesfield SK10 5LR. Mrs Melita Turner. *3m N of Macclesfield. A523 to Stockport. Turn R at B5090 r'about signed Bollington. Pass under viaduct. Take next R (by Library) up Hurst Lane. Turn R into Highfield Rd. Property on L. Park on wider road just past it.* **Sat 9, Sun 10 July (10.30-4). Adm £3, chd free. Home-made teas.**
This small terraced garden packed with plants was designed by Melita and has evolved over the past 9yrs. This plantswoman is a plantaholic

and RHS Certificate holder. An attempt has been made to combine formality through structural planting with a more casual look influenced by the style of Christopher Lloyd. Steep step on to top tier at front. Steps up to higher tiers at rear.

39 ▶ 73 HILL TOP AVENUE
Cheadle Hulme SK8 7HZ. Mrs Land, 0161 486 0055. *4m S of Stockport. Turn off A34 (new bypass) at r'about signed Cheadle Hulme (B5094). Take 2nd turn L into Gillbent Rd, signed Cheadle Hulme Sports Centre. Go to end, small r'about, turn R into Church Rd. 2nd rd on L is Hill Top Ave. From Stockport or Bramhall turn R or L into Church Rd by The Church Inn. Hill Top Ave is 1st rd on R.* **Sun 31 July (2-6). Adm £3.50, chd free. Light refreshments. Visits also by arrangement May to Aug, 5+.** *Donation to Arthritis Research UK.*
¹/₆ -acre plantswoman's garden. Well stocked with a wide range of sun-loving herbaceous plants, shrub and climbing roses, many clematis varieties, pond and damp area, shade-loving woodland plants and some unusual trees and shrubs, in an originally designed, long narrow garden.

40 ▶ HILLSIDE COTTAGE
Shrigley Road, Pott Shrigley SK10 5SG. Anne & Phil Geoghegan, 01625 572214, annegeoghegan@btinternet.com. *6m N of Macclesfield. On A523 at Legh Arms T-lights turn to Pott Shrigley. Take 3rd. L after approx 1¹/₂ m. After 1m at Green Close Methodist Church turn R to garden.* **Visits by arrangement July & Aug groups of 10+. Adm £6, chd free. Home-made teas.**
A ¹/₄ -acre garden with panoramic views over the treetops. Packed with colourful perennials, roses, clematis, shrubs and small trees. Landscaped on several discreet levels with various places to sit and enjoy the garden incl a summerhouse, conservatory and rose covered arbour. Small walled patio with a water feature and container planting. Tea, coffee and home-made cakes or wine with nibbles for evening visits incl in adm. Featured in Garden News 'Garden of the Week'. Partial wheelchair access.

41 HOLLY MERE

4 Radley Lane, Houghton Green, Warrington WA2 0SY. Angela & Graham Harrop, 01925 826230, angelaharrop@hotmail.com. *2m N of Warrington. M6 J22 to Newton. 250yds L into Highfield Lane. At T-junction L into Middleton Lane. 1st R into Delph Lane. Over M62, R into Mill Lane. Park at 'The Plough' (WA2 0SU). 50 metre walk into Radley Lane.* **Visits by arrangement June to Aug. Adm £3.50, chd free. Home-made teas.**
¹/₂ acre garden. Some specimen trees and shrubs. Wide borders of interesting herbaceous perennials (some colour themed), roses and grasses, around extensive lawns. Many AGM plants. Several seating areas. Small kitchen garden.

42 HOME FARM HOUSE

Townfield Lane, Mollington, Nr Chester CH1 6NJ. Christine & Roger Jones, 01244 851842, chrisjones@hotmail.co.uk. *3m NW of Chester heading towards the Wirral on A540. From the A540 take turning into Mollington Village opp Crabwall Manor Hotel and follow ngs signs for parking. From the field car park a short walk brings you to Home Farm House.* **Sat 2, Sun 3 July (1-5). Combined adm with Adswood £5, chd free. Home-made teas. Visits also by arrangement May to July with Adswood, for groups of 8+.**
C17 farm house and small walled garden provides the setting for your afternoon tea and cake. Many changes since last year. 2 new mixed borders offer a totally different look to the garden while favourites such as the established wisteria and climbing roses give a wow factor should you wish to view by arrangement earlier in the year, with Adswood. Gravel driveway, the garden is on two levels with steps in between. Wheelchairs have access to both levels through the use of two different entrances.

43 INGLEWOOD

4 Birchmere, Heswall CH60 6TN. Colin & Sandra Fairclough, www.inglewood-birchmere.blogspot.co.uk. *6m S of Birkenhead. From A540 Devon Doorway/Clegg Arms r'about go through Heswall. ¹/₄ m after Tesco, R into Quarry Rd East, 2nd L into Tower Rd North & L into Birchmere.* **Sat 14, Sun 15 May (1.30-4.30). Adm £4,**

chd free. **Home-made teas.**
Beautiful ¹/₂ acre garden with stream, large koi pond, 'beach' with grasses, wildlife pond and bog area. Brimming with shrubs, bulbs, acers, conifers, rhododendrons, herbaceous plants and new hosta border. Interesting features including hand cart, antique mangle, wood carvings, bug hotel and Indian dog gates leading to a secret garden. Lots of seating to enjoy refreshments.

> Recently planted contemporary garden, which is a work in progress . . .

44 LASKEY FARM

Laskey Lane, Thelwall, Warrington WA4 2TF. Howard & Wendy Platt, 07740 804825, wendy.platt1@gmail.com, www.laskeyfarm.com. *3m From M6/M56. From M56/M6 follow directions to Lymm. At T-junction turn L onto Booths Lane in Warrington direction. Turn R onto Lymm Rd. Turn R onto Laskey Lane.* **Sat 13, Sun 14 Aug (11-5). Adm £5, chd free. Home-made teas. Visits also by arrangement June to Aug groups of 12+.**
1¹/₂ acre garden packed with late summer colour incl herbaceous and rose borders, vegetable area and parterre. Greenhouse contains pelargonium and tropical plants. Interconnected pools for wildlife, fish and terrapins form an unusual water garden. Maze created in 2014 featuring prairie style planting - new for 2016 a designer tree house and Lymm Artists will stage an exhibition of their work. Most areas of the garden may be accessed by wheelchair.

45 LONG ACRE

Wyche Lane, Bunbury CW6 9PS. Margaret & Michael Bourne, 01829 260944, mjbourne249@tiscali.co.uk. *3¹/₂ m SE of Tarporley. In Bunbury village, turn into Wyche Lane by Nags Head*

PH car park, garden 400yds on L. Disabled parking in lane adjacent to garden. **Sun 24 Apr, Sun 19 June (2-5). Adm £4, chd free. Home-made teas. Visits also by arrangement Apr to June groups of 10+. Donation to St Boniface Church Flower Fund.**
Plantswoman's garden of approx 1 acre with unusual plants and trees, pool gardens, exotic conservatory, herbaceous, specialise in proteas, S African bulbs and clivia. Spring garden with camellias, magnolias, bulbs. Wheelchair access to most areas.

46 ◆ THE LOVELL QUINTA ARBORETUM

Swettenham CW12 2LD. Tatton Garden Society, 01477 537698, www.tattongardensociety.co.uk. *4m NW of Congleton. Turn off A54 N 2m W of Congleton or turn E off A535 at Twemlow Green, NE of Holmes Chapel. Follow signs to Swettenham. Park at Swettenham Arms PH.* **For NGS: Sun 2 Oct (12.30-4). Adm £5, chd free. For other opening times and information, please phone or visit garden website.**
The 28-acre arboretum has been established since 1960s and contains around 2,500 trees and shrubs of over 800 species, some very rare. Incl National Collections of Pinus and Fraxinus, large collection of oak, a collection of hebes and autumn flowering shrubs. A lake and way-marked walks. Care required but wheelchairs can access much of the arboretum on the mown paths.

47 MANLEY KNOLL

Manley Road, Manley WA6 9DX. Mr & Mrs James Timpson, 07766 520113, roisin@timpson.com, www.manleyknoll.com. *3m N of Tarvin. On B5393, via Ashton & Mouldsworth. 3m S of Frodsham, via Alvanley.* **Sun 29 May (12-5). Adm £4, chd free. Home-made teas. Visits also by arrangement May to July.**
Arts and Crafts garden created early 1900s. Covering 6 acres, divided into different rooms encompassing parterres, clipped yew hedging and ornamental ponds. Banks of rhododendron and azaleas frame a far-reaching view of the Cheshire Plain. Also a magical quarry/folly garden with waterfall.

Manley Knoll

48 ▶ 218 MARPLE ROAD
Offerton, Stockport SK2 5HE. Barry
& Pat Hadfield. *3¹/₂ m E of Stockport
leave M60 J27 at the r'about take 5th
exit onto A626 signed for Marple,
follow the A626, parking on L at
Offerton Sand & Gravel. Disabled
parking at house.* **Sun 3 July, Sun 7
Aug (11-4.30). Adm £4, chd free.**
This secret south facing garden
approx 1 acre, full of herbaceous
plants, vegetable plot, plant growing
area, topiary, unfenced ponds/water
features, fun areas/features,
developed from paddock to garden
over 20yrs by current owners,there
will be a fun quiz for children.
Wheelchair access to most areas.

&♿ ✿ ☕

49 ▶ ◆ MOUNT PLEASANT
Yeld Lane, Kelsall CW6 0TB. Dave
Darlington & Louise Worthington,
01829 751592,
louisedarlington@btinternet.com,
www.mountpleasantgardens.co.uk.
*8m E of Chester. Off A54 at T-lights
into Kelsall. Turn into Yeld Lane opp
Farmers Arms PH, 200yds on L. Do
not follow SatNav directions.* **For
NGS: Sun 1, Mon 2 May, Sat 3,
Sun 4 Sept (12-5). Adm £5, chd £1.
Tea. For other opening times and
information, please phone, email or
visit garden website.**
10 acres of landscaped garden and
woodland started in 1994 with
impressive views over the Cheshire
countryside. Steeply terraced in
places. Specimen trees,
rhododendrons, azaleas, conifers,
mixed and herbaceous borders; 4
ponds, formal and wildlife. Vegetable
garden, stumpery with tree ferns,
sculptures, wild flower meadow and
Japanese garden. Bog garden,
tropical garden. September Sculpture
Exhibition. Please ring prior to visit for
wheelchair access.

✿ 🚐 ☕

**50 ▶ ◆ NESS BOTANIC
GARDENS**
Neston Road, Ness, Neston
CH64 4AY. The University of
Liverpool, 0845 030 4063,
nessgdns@liverpool.ac.uk,
www.nessgardens.org.uk. *10 NW*
of Chester. Off A540. M53 J4, follow
signs M56 & A5117 (signed N Wales).
Turn onto A540 follow signs for
Hoylake. Ness Gardens is signed
locally.* **For NGS: Sun 15 May
(10-5). Adm £7.50, chd £3.50. For
other opening times and
information, please phone, email or
visit garden website.**
Looking out over the dramatic Dee
Estuary from a lofty perch of the
Wirral peninsula, Ness Botanic
Gardens boasts 64 spectacular
acres of landscaped and natural
gardens overflowing with
horticultural treasures. With a
delightfully peaceful atmosphere, a
wide array of events taking place,
plus a cafe and gorgeous open
spaces it's a great fun-filled day out
for all. National Collection of Sorbus.
Herbaceous borders, Rock Garden,
Mediterranean Bank, Potager and
WilderNESS conservation area.
Mobility scooters and wheelchairs
are available free but advance
booking is recommended.

&♿ ✿ 🚐 **NPC** ☕

51 ◆ NORTON PRIORY MUSEUM & GARDENS

Tudor Road, Manor Park, Runcorn WA7 1SX. Norton Priory Museum Trust, 01928 569895, info@nortonpriory.org, www.nortonpriory.org. *2m SE of Runcorn. If using Sat-Nav try WA7 1BD and follow the brown Norton Priory signs.* **For NGS: Sun 5 June (10-5). Adm £3.50, chd £2.70. For other opening times and information, please phone, email or visit garden website.**
Beautiful 2½ -acre Georgian Walled Garden, with fruit trees, herb garden, colour borders and rose walk. Home to the National Collection of Tree Quince (Cydonia Oblonga) and surrounded by historic pear orchard and wildflower meadow. Tea room and plant sales in the courtyard. Museum re-opening summer 2016. Garden paths are gravel but there is level access to the whole garden site.

 **NPC**

52 OAKFIELD VILLA

Nantwich Road, Wrenbury, Nantwich CW5 8EL. Carolyn & Jack Kennedy, 01270 781106. *6m S of Nantwich & 6m N of Whitchurch. Garden on main rd through village next to Dairy Farm. Parking in field between Oak Villas & School 1min walk to garden.* **Wed 15 June (10.30-5). Combined adm with Wren's Nest £5, chd free. Tea. Visits also by arrangement July & Aug 20 max, teas by arrangement.**
Romantic S-facing garden of densely planted borders and creative planting in containers, incl climbing roses, clematis and hydrangeas. Divided by screens into rooms, the garden incl a small fishpond and water feature. Pergola clothed in beautiful climbers provides relaxed sheltered seating area. Small front garden, mainly hydrangeas and clematis. 50+ clematis and many hydrangeas. Some gravelled areas.

53 THE OLD COTTAGE

44 High Street, Frodsham WA6 7HE. John & Lesley Corfield, 07591 609311, corfield@rock44.plus.com. *DO NOT FOLLOW SATNAV - no parking at garden. On A56 close to Frodsham town centre. Follow signs from town centre to railway car park, garden signed from there (short walk). Or park in town centre and follow signs uphill N to cottage.* **Sat 4, Sun 5 June (1-6). Adm £4, chd free. Home-made teas. Visits also by arrangement June to Aug.**
At the rear of the Grade II listed C16 cottage (not open) are ²/₃ acre, organic and wildlife friendly garden featuring many aspects that support various forms of wildlife. Steps lead up to a large vegetable and herb garden, with further mixed planting in herbaceous borders. Wildlife pond and bog garden. Further areas of fruit trees and shady woodland borders. Extensive views over Mersey estuary. Partial wheelchair access - please ring for details.

Our aim is to give nature a home and create a place of beauty . . .

54 THE OLD PARSONAGE

Arley Green, Via Arley Hall and Gardens CW9 6LZ. The Viscount & Viscountess Ashbrook, 01565 777277, ashbrook@arleyhallandgardens. com, www.arleyhallandgardens.com. *5m NNE of Northwich. 3m NNE of Great Budworth. M6 J19 & 20 & M56 J10. Follow signs to Arley Hall & Gardens. From Arley Hall notices to Old Parsonage which lies across park at Arley Green.* **Sat 4, Sun 5 June (2-5.30). Adm £4.50, chd free. Cream teas. Visits also by arrangement May & June, groups of 10+.** *Donation to Save The Children Fund.*
2-acre garden in attractive and secretive rural setting in secluded part of Arley Estate, with ancient yew hedges, herbaceous and mixed borders, shrub roses, climbers, leading to woodland garden and unfenced pond with gunnera and water plants. Rhododendrons, azaleas, meconopsis, cardiocrinum, some interesting and unusual trees.

Used as set by Disney for film 'Evermoor'. Wheelchair access over mown grass. Some slopes and bumps.

55 39 OSBORNE STREET

Bredbury, Stockport SK6 2DA. Geoff & Heather Hoyle, www.youtube.com/user/ Dahliaholic. *1½ m E of Stockport, just off B6104. Follow signs for Lower Bredbury/Bredbury Hall. Leave M60 J27 (from S & W) or J25 (from N & E). Osborne St is adjacent to pelican crossing on B6104.* **Sat 3, Sun 4 Sept (1-5). Adm £4, chd free. Light refreshments. Teas, coffees, and cakes.**
This dahliaholic's garden contains over 350 dahlias in 150+ varieties, mostly of exhibition standard. Shapely lawns are surrounded by deep flower beds that are crammed with dahlias of all shapes, sizes and colours, and complemented by climbers, soft perennials and bedding plants. An absolute riot of early autumn colour. The garden comprises two separate areas, both crammed with very colourful flowers. The dahlias range in height from 18 inches to 8 feet tall, and are in a wide variety of shapes and colours. They are interspersed with salvias, fuchsias, argyranthemums, and bedding plants. The garden is on YouTube: search for Dahliaholic.

56 PARM PLACE

High Street, Great Budworth CW9 6HF. Peter & Jane Fairclough, 01606 891131, janefair@btinternet.com. *3m N of Northwich. Great Budworth on E side of A559 between Northwich & Warrington, 4m from J10 M56, also 4m from J19 M6. Parm Place is W of village on S side of High St.* **Sun 3 Apr, Sun 26 June (1-5). Adm £4, chd free. Home-made teas. Visits also by arrangement Apr to Aug for groups 10 to 40.** *Donation to Great Ormond Street Hospital.*
Well-stocked ½ -acre plantswoman's garden with stunning views towards S Cheshire. Curving lawns, parterre, shrubs, colour co-ordinated herbaceous borders, roses, water features, rockery, gravel bed with some grasses. Fruit and vegetable plots. In spring large collection of bulbs and flowers, camellias, hellebores and blossom.

57 ◆ **PEOVER HALL GARDENS**
Over Peover, Knutsford
WA16 9HW. Randle Brooks,
01565 830395,
bookings@peoverhall.com,
www.peoverhall.com. *4m S of
Knutsford. A50/Holmes Chapel
Rd/Whipping Stocks PH turn onto
Stocks Lane. Approx 0.9m turn onto
Grotto Lane. 1/4 m turn onto Goostrey
Lane. Main entrance on bend.* For
NGS: Sat 4, Sun 5 June (2-5). Adm
£5, chd free. Home-made teas in
Park House Tea Room &
Paddock. For other opening times
and information, please phone,
email or visit garden website.
The gardens to Peover Hall are set in
15 acres and feature a number of
'garden rooms' filled with clipped
box, topiary, roses, a lily pond, a
walled garden, Romanesque loggia,
C19 dell, rhododendrons and
pleached limes. There are Grade I
listed Carolean Stables which are of
significant architectural importance.
Partial wheelchair access to
garden.

58 **POULTON HALL**
Poulton Lancelyn, Bebington
CH63 9LN. The Lancelyn Green
Family, www.poultonhall.co.uk. *2m
S of Bebington. From M53, J4
towards Bebington; at T-lights R
along Poulton Rd; house 1m on R.*
Sat 16, Sun 17 Apr (1.30-4.30).
Adm £4, chd free. Home-made
teas.
3 acres; lawns fronting house, wild
flower meadow. Surprise approach to
walled garden, with reminders of
Roger Lancelyn Green's retellings,
Excalibur, Robin Hood and
Jabberwocky. Scented sundial
garden for the visually impaired.
Memorial sculpture for Richard
Lancelyn Green by Sue Sharples.
Rose, nursery rhyme, witch, herb and
oriental gardens and new Memories
Reading room. There are often choirs
or orchestral music in the garden.
Level gravel paths. Separate access
(not across parking field) for
wheelchairs.

59 **RIDGEHILL**
Ridge Hill, Sutton, Macclesfield
SK11 0LU. Mr & Mrs Martin
McMillan, Pat@normanshall.co.uk.
*2m SE of Macclesfield. From
Macclesfield take A523 to Leek. After
Silk Rd look for T-lights signed
Langley, Wincle & Sutton. Turn L into
Byron's Lane, under canal bridge, 1st
L to Langley at junction Church
House PH. Ridge Hill Rd is opp turn
up Ridge Hill Rd, garden on R.* Sun
19 June (10-4.30). Adm £6, chd
free. Home-made teas. Pimms &
wine by donation. Visits also by
arrangement May to Aug 12+.
4 acre garden set in the hills above
Macclesfield overlooking the Cheshire
plain. Herbaceous borders, old Rose
garden, shrubbery with
rhododendron, azaleas, water
features, topiary, A Victorian
greenhouse set in a small walled
garden with fruit/vegetables/flowers
all organically grown now in its 3rd
year. Teas/coffee, cold drinks, home
made cakes, plants, raffle. Cheshire
youth brass band. Featured in The
Cheshire Magazine and local paper.
Wheelchair access only to front of
house along the drive Coffee/teas
served in that area.

60 ◆ **RODE HALL**
Church Lane, Scholar Green
ST7 3QP. Sir Richard & Lady Baker
Wilbraham, 01270 873237,
enquiries@rodehall.co.uk,
www.rodehall.co.uk. *5m SW of
Congleton. Between Scholar Green
(A34) & Rode Heath (A50).* For
opening times and information,
please phone, email or visit garden
website.
Nesfield's terrace and rose garden
with view over Humphry Repton's
landscape is a feature of Rode
gardens, as is the woodland garden
with terraced rock garden and grotto.
Other attractions incl the walk to the
lake with a view of Birthday Island
complete with heronry, restored ice
house, working 2 acre walled kitchen
garden and Italian garden. Fine
display of snowdrops in Feb. Daily for
Snowdrop Walks 30 Jan - 6 March
11-4. Closed Mons. Summer: Weds
and Bank Hol Mons 11-5. Partial
wheelchair access, some steep areas
with gravel and woodchip paths,
access to WC, kitchen garden and
tearooms.

61 **ROSEWOOD**
Old Hall Lane, Puddington, Neston
CH64 5SP. Mr & Mrs C E J Brabin,
0151 353 1193,
angela.brabin@btinternet.com. *8m
N of Chester. From A540 turn down
Puddington Lane, 1 1/2 m. Park by
village green. Walk 30yds to Old Hall
Lane, turn L through archway into
garden.* Visits by arrangement
individuals, medium or large
groups. Adm £3, chd free. Home-
made teas.
All yr garden; thousands of
snowdrops in Feb, Camellias in
autumn, winter and spring.
Rhododendrons in April/May and
unusual flowering trees from March to
June. Autumn Cyclamen in quantity
from Aug to Nov. Perhaps the
greatest delight to owners is a large
Cornus capitata, flowering in June.
Bees kept in the garden. Honey
sometimes available.

NGS donations
help support
over
200 hospices
across
the country

62 **THE ROWANS**
Oldcastle Lane, Threapwood, nr
Malpas SY14 7AY. Paul Philpotts &
Alan Bourne, 01948 770522,
alanandpaul@btinternet.com. *3m
SW of Malpas. Leave Malpas on
B5069 for Wrexham, after 3m, take
1st L after Threapwood Shop/PO into
Chapel Lane, L into Oldcastle Lane,
garden 1st Bungalow on R.* Sat 2,
Sun 3 July (1-5.30). Adm £4, chd
free. Tea.
This 1-acre multi-award winning
garden, has an Italianate theme.
Divided into numerous formal and
natural areas, in which to sit and
enjoy the views and feature statuary.
Many mature and unusual trees,
several ponds, herbaceous borders,
vegetable plots, greenhouse,
extensive Hosta collection and a
tranquil secret garden. Something of
interest for every visitor and an
exquisite sanctuary.

Hatton House Gardens

63 NEW ROWLEY HOUSE
Forty Acre Lane, Kermincham, Crewe CW4 8DX. Tim & Juliet Foden. *3m ENE from Holmes Chapel. J18 M6 to Holmes Chapel, take A535 Macclesfield Rd, 1½ m turn R towards Swettenham at Twemlow, by Yellow Broom restaurant into Forty Acre Lane, Rowley House ½ m on L.* Sat 9, Sun 10 July (1.30-4.30). Adm £5, chd free. Home-made teas.

Our aim is to give nature a home and create a place of beauty. There is a formal courtyard garden and informal gardens featuring rare trees, and colourful herbaceous borders, a pond with swamp cypress and woodland walk with maples, rhododendrons, ferns and shade loving plants. Beyond the garden there are wild flower meadows, more unusual trees, natural ponds and wood with its ancient oaks.

64 SANDYMERE
Middlewich Road, Cotebrook CW6 9EH. John & Alex Timpson, 07900 567944, rme2000@aol.com. *5m N of Tarporley. On A54 approx 300yds W of T-lights at Xrds of A49/A54.* Sun 19 June (2-5.30). Adm £6, chd free. Home-made teas. Visits also by arrangement Mar to June for groups of 10+.

16 landscaped acres of beautiful Cheshire countryside with terraces, walled garden, extensive woodland walks and an amazing hosta garden. Turn each corner and you find another gem with lots of different water features including a new rill built in 2014, which links the main lawn to the hostas. Partial wheelchair access.

65 21 SCAFELL CLOSE
High Lane, Stockport SK6 8JA. Lesley & Dean Stafford, 01663 763015, lesley.stafford@live.co.uk. *High Lane is on A6 SE of Stockport towards Buxton From A6 take Russel Ave then Kirkfell Drive.Scafell Close on R.* Sat 30, Sun 31 July (1-4.30). Adm £3, chd free. Cream teas. Visits also by arrangement July & Aug groups one per day, wander round at your leisure.

⅓ acre landscaped suburban garden. Colour themed annuals border the lawn featuring the Kinder Ram statue in a heather garden, passing into vegetables, soft fruits and fruit trees. Returning perennial pathway leads to the fishpond and secret terraced garden with modern water feature and patio planting. Finally visit the blue front garden. Featured in Amateur Gardening. Partial wheelchair access.

66 NEW SMITHY HOUSE
209 Coppice Road, Poynton, Stockport SK12 1SW. Mrs M Spencer, 01625 874617. *1m E of Poynton centre. At double r'about in Poynton centre, turn into Park Lane. 500yds take R fork into Coppice Rd. L at Bridal shop to parking. 2 min walk to garden. Disabled visitors ring for parking at house.* Sat 30 July (11-5). Adm £3, chd free. Visits also by arrangement Apr & May evening visits incl wine, adm £5. 20 max.

Deceptively large plot with mature trees, vibrant herbaceous borders, small shade garden, with ferns, hostas etc. Cottage style greenhouse garden and summerhouse. Large vegetable plot surrounded by some wild areas and unfenced water. Stone driveway to most areas.

67 68 SOUTH OAK LANE
Wilmslow SK9 6AT. Caroline & David Melliar-Smith, 01625 528147, caroline.ms@btinternet.com. *¾ m SW of Wilmslow. From M56 (J6) take A538 (Wilmslow) R into Buckingham Rd. From centre of Wilmslow turn R onto B5086, 1st R into Gravel Ln, 4th R into South Oak Lane.* Sat 9, Sun 10 July (11-4.30). Adm £3.50, chd free. Visits also by arrangement June to Aug, group 30 max.

With year-round colour, scent and interest, this attractive, narrow, hedged cottage garden has evolved over the years into 5 natural 'rooms'. These Hardy Plant Society members passion for plants, is reflected in the variety of shrubs, trees, flower borders and pond, creating havens for wildlife. Share this garden with its' varied history from the 1890's. Some rare and unusual hardy and shade loving plants. Featured in the Wilmslow Guardian.

68 ▶ 10 STATHAM AVENUE

Lymm WA13 9NH. Mike & Gail Porter. *Approx 1m from J20 M6 /M56 interchange. Take the B5158 signed Lymm. Take A56 Booth's Hill Rd, towards Warrington, turn R on to Bars Bank Lane, after passing under the Bridgewater canal turn R (50m) onto Statham Ave. No 10 is 100 metres on R.* Sat 18, Sun 19 June (11-5). Adm £4, chd free. Home-made teas, cakes and Gail's famous meringues with fresh fruit.

Described as peaceful, Monet pastel colours in June. Beautifully structured ¼ acre south facing plot, carefully terraced and planted as it rises to the Bridgewater towpath. Hazel arch opens to formal clay paved courtyard with cordoned peach trees. Working greenhouse. Rose pillars lead to established herbaceous beds, quiet shaded areas, bordered by azaleas and rhododendrons. Interesting outhouses. Featured in Amateur Gardener. Short gravel driveway and some steps to access the rear garden. The rear garden is sloping.

69 ▶ ◆ STONYFORD COTTAGE

Stonyford Lane, Oakmere CW8 2TF. Janet & Tony Overland, 01606 888970, info@stonyfordcottagegardens.co. uk, www.stonyfordcottagegardens.co. uk. *5m SW of Northwich. From Northwich take A556 towards Chester. ¾ m past A49 junction turn R into Stonyford Lane. Entrance ½ m on L.* For NGS: Sun 15 May, Sun 31 July (11.30-4.30). Adm £4.50, chd free. Light refreshments. For other opening times and information, please phone, email or visit garden website.

Set around a tranquil pool this Monet style landscape has a wealth of moisture loving plants, incl iris and candelabra primulas. Drier areas feature unusual perennials and rarer trees and shrubs. Woodland paths meander through shade and bog plantings, along boarded walks, across wild natural areas with views over the pool to the cottage gardens. Unusual plants available at the adjacent nursery. Open Tues - Sun & BH Mons Apr - Oct 10-5pm. Cottage Tea Room, Lunches and cream teas available. Plant Nursery. Some gravel paths.

In June, peaonies and roses come to the fore . . .

70 ▶ SYCAMORE COTTAGE

Manchester Road, Carrington, Manchester M31 4AY. Mrs C Newton, cottonandrose@gmail.com. *From M60 J8 take Carrington turn (A6144) through 2 sets of lights. Garden approx 1m after 2nd set of lights on R. From M6 J20 follow signs for Partington/Carrington garden approx 1m on L.* Sun 22 May, Sun 3 July (12-5). Adm £3.50, chd free. Light refreshments. Visits also by arrangement June to Aug for groups of 10+.

Approx ⅕ acre cottage garden split into distinct areas, with woodland banking, natural spring, well and ponds. Also features decking with two seating areas and summer house. Garden featured on Cupranols TV advert.

71 ▶ TATTENHALL HALL

High Street, Tattenhall CH3 9PX. Jen & Nick Benefield, Chris Evered & Jannie Hollins, 01829 770654, janniehollins@gmail.com. *8m S of Chester on A41. Turn L to Tattenhall, through village, turn R at Letters PH, past war memorial on L through Sandstone pillared gates. Park on rd or in village car park.* Sun 29 May,

Sun 28 Aug (2-5.30). Adm £4.50, chd free. Home-made teas. Visits also by arrangement Mar to Sept, limited parking facilities.

Plant enthusiasts garden around Jacobean house (not open). 4½ acres, wild flower meadows, interesting trees, large pond, stream, walled garden, colour themed borders, succession planting, spinney walk with shade plants, yew terrace overlooking meadow, views to hills. Glasshouse and vegetable garden. Wildlife friendly sometimes untidy garden, interest throughout the year, continuing to develop. Gravel paths, cobbles and some steps.

72 ▶ ◆ TATTON PARK

Knutsford WA16 6QN. National Trust, leased to Cheshire East Council, 01625 374400, www.tattonpark.org.uk. *2½ m N of Knutsford. Well signed on M56 J7 & from M6 J19.* For NGS: Wed 11 May, Wed 15 June (10-6). Adm £6, chd £4. For other opening times and information, please phone or visit garden website.

Features incl orangery by Wyatt, fernery by Paxton, restored Japanese garden, Italian and rose gardens. Greek monument and African hut. Hybrid azaleas and rhododendrons; swamp cypresses, tree ferns, tall redwoods, bamboos and pines. Fully restored productive walled gardens. Wheelcair access apart from rose garden and Japanese garden.

73 ▶ TIRLEY GARTH GARDENS

Mallows Way, Willington, Tarporley CW6 0RQ. Tirley Garth. *2m N of Tarporley. 2m S of Kelsall. Entrance 500yds from centre of Utkinton. At N of Tarporley take Utkinton rd.* Sun 8, Sun 15, Sun 22 May (1-5). Adm £5, chd free. Home-made teas.

40-acre garden, terraced and landscaped, designed by Thomas Mawson (considered the leading exponent of garden design in early C20), it is the only Grade II* Arts and Crafts garden in Cheshire that remains complete and in excellent condition. The gardens are an important example of an early C20 garden laid out in both formal and informal styles. By early May the garden is bursting into flower with almost 3000 Rhododendron and Azalea many 100 years old. Exhibition by local Artists.

74 NEW TWIN GATES
3 Earle Drive, Parkgate, Neston
CH64 6RY. John Hinde & Lilian
Baker. *Approx 1/2 m N of Neston
town centre. From Neston centre
(Tesco/Brown Horse PH), N towards
Neston Methodist Church, At church
(Brewers Arms on L), take L fork into
Park St. Latter continues becoming
Leighton Rd. Continue for approx 1/2
turn L into Earle Drive.* **Wed 22, Thur
23 June (1.30-5). Adm £3, chd
free. Tea.**
Garden developed over last 3 to 4
years and now beginning to mature.
Mixed herbaceous and shrub
borders, with some choice small
trees. In June, peaonies and roses
come to the fore.

75 NEW 8A WARWICK DRIVE
Hale, Altrincham WA15 9EA. Mr &
Mrs Chris & Gill Turner. *M56 J6,
take A538 to Altrincham. Turn L at
2nd T-lights into Park Rd. Take 2nd R
into Bower Rd & turn L immed into
Warwick Drive. Garden is 200yds on
L, on corner of Lindop Rd.* **Sat 16,
Sun 17 July (2-5). Adm £3, chd
free. Home-made teas.**
Small suburban garden designed by
a plantaholic flower-arranger to give
year-round interest with camellias,
rhododendrons and hostas. Highlight
of front garden is extensive
herbaceous border, plant-packed to
provide colour from Apr-Oct. Other
features incl colour-themed borders,
short woodland walk, raised beds
and small pond, protected by mature
trees. Many ideas to maximise
available space!

77 WELL HOUSE
Dean Row Road, Wilmslow
SK9 2BU. Steven & Jill Kimber. *2m
N of Wilmslow. On Dean Row Rd (B
5358), at junction with Adlington Rd
(A5102). Park at the Unicorn PH 300
yds, from the house. Next to Shell
garage. Less able visitors can drop
off at house limited space.* **Sun 26
June (10.30-4.30). Adm £4, chd
free. Home-made teas.**
Familiar to many gardening friends
this happily maturing 3 acre garden,
tended with a gentle hand offers; a
shady woodland, formal borders and
imaginative landscaping. Featuring
lush herbaceous planting, wild
flowers are a particular passion. Both
naturalised and planted they are
managed, cultivated and encouraged
wherever possible. Especially within

the meadow which now boasts many
wild orchids.

76 THE WELL HOUSE
Wet Lane, Tilston, Malpas
SY14 7DP. Mrs S H French-
Greenslade, 01829 250332. *3m NW
of Malpas. On A41, 1st R after
Broxton r'about, L on Malpas Rd
through Tilston. House on L.* **Visits
by arrangement Feb to Sept, not
Aug. Feb for snowdrops. Adm £5,
chd free. Refreshments by prior
arrangement.**
1-acre cottage garden, bridge over
natural stream, spring bulbs,
perennials, herbs and shrubs. Triple
ponds. Adjoining 3/4 -acre field made
into wild flower meadow; first seeding
late 2003. Large bog area of
kingcups and ragged robin. February
for snowdrop walk.

Suburban garden
designed by a
plantaholic flower-
arranger to give
year-round
interest . . .

78 WEST DRIVE GARDENS
6, 9 West Drive, Gatley, Cheadle
SK8 4JJ. Mr & Mrs D J Gane,
Thelma Bishop & John Needham.
*4m N of Wilmslow on B5166. From
J5 (M56) drive past airpt. to B5166
(Styal Rd).L to Gatley. Go over T-lights
at Heald Green. West Drive. last turn
on R before Gatley(approx.1 1/2 m
from T-lights).* **Sun 24 July (10.30-5).
Combined adm £5, chd free.
Home-made teas. and WC at
No 6.**
Cul-de-sac, do not park beyond
notice. Here are two gardens of very
different character, reflecting their
owner's gardening style. Although
suburban, they are surrounded by
mature trees and have a secluded
feel. Rich variety of planting incl.
ferns, hostas and herbaceous
borders. with phlox, hydrangeas and
clematis (hopefully) at their best. Wild

life pond at no.6. High-quality plant
stall, no.9 Home-mde teas, no.6.
Access to top of gardens giving
general overview, with shallow step
leading onto gravel at no.6 and
several steps and narrow paths at
no.9.

79 THE WHITE COTTAGE
Threapwood, Malpas, Cheshire
SY14 7AL. Chris & Carol Bennion.
*3m SW of Malpas. From Malpas take
Wrexham Rd B5069 W for 3m. From
Bangor on Dee take B5069 E to
Threapwood. Car Park in field opp
shop & garage.* **Sat 18, Sun 19 June
(1-5). Adm £4, chd free. Tea.**
Lots to see and experience in this
pretty half acre cottage garden
containing a varied mixture of mature
trees, hedging, shrubs, herbaceous
plants and bulbs. Open spaces and
secluded areas merge to provide new
interest at every corner. Flower beds
meander along the drive with roses,
astrantias, geraniums, foxgloves,
violas and other summer flowering
plants. There is a long gravel drive.
Narrow pathways and steps surround
the cottage.

**80 NEW WINTERBOTTOM
HOUSE**
Winterbottom Lane, Mere,
Knutsford WA16 0QQ.
Neil & Verona Stott,
thestotts@btinternet.com. *Half Way
between Mere T-lights & High Legh.
Signed off A50. From A50 opp Kilton
Inn turn into Hoo Green Lane, in 1/2 m
bear L down Winterbottom Lane
(narrow lane - take care!).
Winterbottom House at end. Follow
signs for ample parking with
wheelchair access.* **Evening
opening Fri 3 June (6-9). Adm £7,
chd free. Wine. Sun 14 Aug (1-5).
Adm £5, chd free. Home-made
teas. A glass of wine on the 3rd.
Visits also by arrangement May to
Sept 10 -20.**
A large garden developed over many
years with two distinct areas. One
mainly trees, grasses and woodland
planting with natural koi pond leading
to vegetable garden and greenhouse.
The other more formal area with lots
of herbaceous borders and shrubs to
give year round interest. This area incl
period summer house, ornamental rill
and extensive lawns with plenty of
seating areas. Some gravel paths but
no steps.

81 ▶ WOOD END COTTAGE
Grange Lane, Whitegate,
Northwich CW8 2BQ. Mr & Mrs M
R Everett, 01606 888236,
woodendct@supanet.com. *4m SW
of Northwich. Turn S off A556
(Northwich bypass) at Sandiway PO
T-lights; after 1³/₄ m, turn L to
Whitegate village; opp school follow
Grange Lane for 300yds.* **Visits by
arrangement May to July. Adm £4,
chd free. Home-made teas.**
Plantsman's ¹/₂ acre garden in
attractive setting, sloping to a natural
stream bordered by shade and
moisture-loving plants. Background
of mature trees. Well stocked
herbaceous borders, trellis with roses
and clematis, magnificent
delphiniums, many phlox and choice
perennials. Interesting shrubs and
flowering trees. Vegetable garden.

❀ 🚐 ☕

82 ▶ WREN'S NEST
Wrenbury Heath Road, Wrenbury,
Nantwich CW5 8EQ. Sue & Dave
Clarke, 07855 398803,
wrenburysue@gmail.com. *Nantwich
12m from M6 J16. From Nantwich
signs for A530 to Whitchurch,
reaching Sound school turn 1st R
Wrenbury Heath Rd, across the Xrds
and bungalow is on L, telegraph pole
right outside.* **Wed 15 June
(10.30-5). Combined adm with**
Oakfield Villa £5. Tea at Oakfield
Villa. **Visits also by arrangement
May to July phone or email.
Refreshments on request.**
Set in a semi-rural area, this
bungalow has a Cottage Garden
Style of lush planting and is 80ft x
45ft. The garden is packed with
unusual and traditional perennials and
shrubs incl over 100 hardy
geraniums, campanulas, crocosmias,
hostas, iris, geums, herbs and pots
and alpine troughs. Plants for sale.
National Collection of Hardy
Geraniums sylvaticum and renardii
types.

❀ **NPC**

150 Barrel Well Hill

Follow NGS Twitter 🐦 @NGSOpenGardens

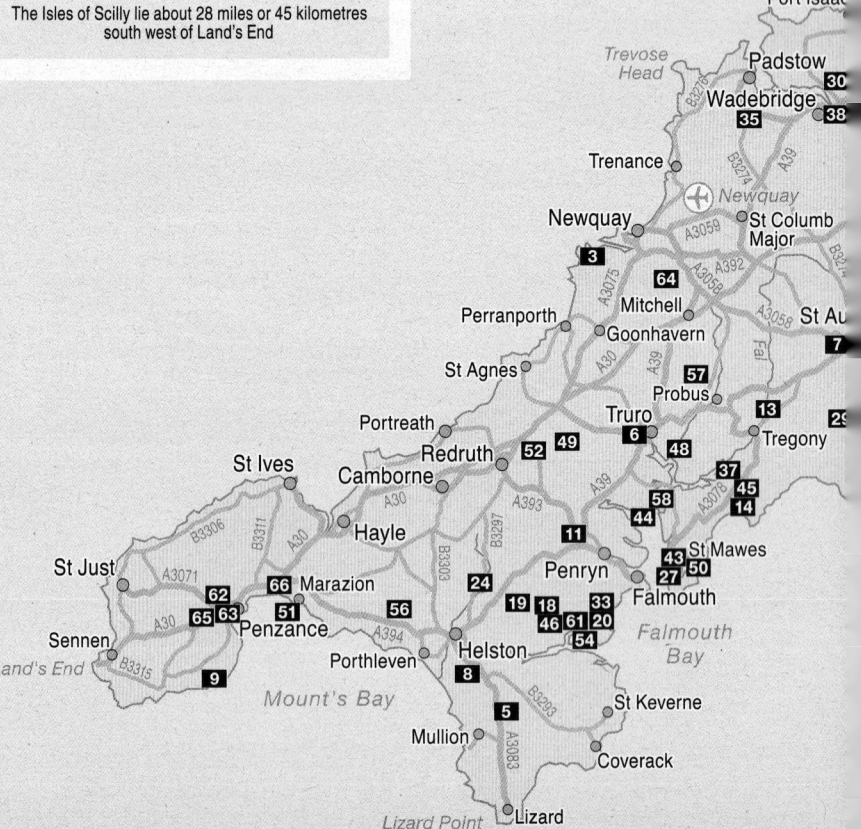

ISLES OF SCILLY

Tresco
St Martin's
Bryher
Hugh Town
St Mary's
St Agnes

The Isles of Scilly lie about 28 miles or 45 kilometres
south west of Land's End

Cornwall

Cornwall has some of the most beautiful natural landscapes to be found anywhere in the world.

Here, you will discover some of the country's most extraordinary gardens, a spectacular coastline, internationally famous surfing beaches, windswept moors and countless historic sites. Cornish gardens reflect this huge variety of environments particularly well.

A host of National Collections of magnolias, camellias, rhododendrons and azaleas, as well as exotic Mediterranean semitropical plants and an abundance of other plants flourish in our acid soils and mild climate.

Surrounded by the warm currents of the Gulf Stream, with our warm damp air in summer and mild moist winters, germination continues all year.

Cornwall boasts an impressive variety of NGS gardens. These range from coastal-protected positions to exposed cliff-top sites, moorland water gardens, Japanese gardens and the world famous tropical biomes of the Eden Project.

Cornwall Volunteers

County Organiser
Bryan Coode
01726 882488
bhcoode@btconnect.com

County Treasurer
Andrew Flint
01726 879336
flints@elizaholidays.co.uk

Publicity
Sue Bradbury
01326 567184
sue@suebradburypr.com

Nutty Lim
01726 815247
christianne.gf.lim@gmail.com

Booklet Co-ordinator
Peter Stanley
01326 565868
stanley.m2@sky.com

Assistant County Organisers
Ginnie Clotworthy
01208 872612
giles.clotworthy@btopenworld.com

William Croggon
01872 530499
wrcroggon@btinternet.com

Sarah Gordon
01579 362076
sar.gordon@virgin.net

Katie Nichols
01872 275786
katherinemlambert@gmail.com

Alison O'Connor
01726 882460
tregoose@tregoose.co.uk

Marion Stanley
01326 565868
stanley.m2@sky.com

Ian Wright
07884 425899
ian.wright@nationaltrust.org.uk

Left: Bosvigo House © Marcus Harpur

Opening Dates

All entries subject to change.
For latest information check www.ngs.org.uk

Extended openings are shown at the begining of the month

February

Snowdrop Festival

Saturday 6
41 Pinetum Park & Pine Lodge Gardens

Sunday 7
57 Tregoose

Sunday 14
10 Coombegate Cottage
22 Hidden Valley Gardens

Monday 15
22 Hidden Valley Gardens

Tuesday 16
22 Hidden Valley Gardens

Wednesday 17
22 Hidden Valley Gardens

Thursday 18
22 Hidden Valley Gardens

Friday 19
22 Hidden Valley Gardens

Saturday 20
22 Hidden Valley Gardens

Sunday 21
10 Coombegate Cottage
22 Hidden Valley Gardens

Sunday 28
10 Coombegate Cottage

March

Sunday 6
10 Coombegate Cottage

Sunday 13
10 Coombegate Cottage
25 Ince Castle

Sunday 20
63 NEW Trereife Park

Sunday 27
25 Ince Castle

Monday 28
33 NEW Meudon Hotel

April

Saturday 9
65 Trewidden Garden

Sunday 10
18 Ethnevas Cottage
25 Ince Castle

Tuesday 12
39 Pencarrow

Sunday 17
8 Carminowe Valley Garden
16 NEW East Down Barn
44 Polgwynne
48 Riverside Cottage

Saturday 23
60 NEW Trenarren House

Sunday 24
25 Ince Castle
52 Scorrier House
60 NEW Trenarren House

Saturday 30
9 Chygurno

May

Sunday 1
9 Chygurno

Monday 2
9 Chygurno
34 Moyclare

Wednesday 4
5 Bonython Manor

Sunday 8
4 Boconnoc
25 Ince Castle
27 Lamorran House

Thursday 12
50 NEW Rosteague Manor
53 South Lea

Sunday 15
18 Ethnevas Cottage
40 Penheale Manor
55 Trebartha

Friday 20
59 Trematon Castle

Saturday 21
42 Pinsla Garden & Nursery

Sunday 22
32 NEW Mary Newman's Garden
42 Pinsla Garden & Nursery

Sunday 29
30 Lower Amble Gardens

June

Festival Weekend

Saturday 4
22 Hidden Valley Gardens

Sunday 5
18 Ethnevas Cottage
22 Hidden Valley Gardens
46 Potager Garden
51 St Michael's Mount

Sunday 12
13 Creed House & Creed Lodge
24 The Homestead Woodland Garden & Tearoom

Saturday 18
21 Half Acre
49 Roseland House

Sunday 19
3 Arundell
8 Carminowe Valley Garden
21 Half Acre
49 Roseland House

Friday 24
15 NEW Dye Cottage
47 NEW Readymoney Gardens

Saturday 25
2 NEW Anvil Cottage
15 NEW Dye Cottage
68 NEW Windmills

Sunday 26
2 NEW Anvil Cottage
15 NEW Dye Cottage
53 South Lea
68 NEW Windmills

Crugsillick Manor

© Rosalind Simon

Share your day out on �'and 📧

The Gardens

1 NEW ♦ **ANTONY**
Torpoint PL11 2QA. National Trust, 01752 812191, antony@nationaltrust.org.uk, www.nationaltrust.org.uk/antony. *6m W of Plymouth via Torpoint car ferry, 2m NW of Torpoint. Follow brown signs on A374 from Torpoint or from A38 at Trerulefoot.* **For opening times and information, please phone, email or visit garden website.**
Still the home of the Carew Pole family after hundreds of years, the Humphry Repton inspired landscape garden offers sweeping views to the R Lynher and incl formal garden with topiary, knot garden, summer garden and contemporary sculptures. National Collection of Hemerocallis

(daylilies). Beautiful early C18 house has fine collections of paintings, furniture and textiles. House and garden used by Tim Burton in his 2010 film adaptation of Alice in Wonderland. Access map guide available at reception. Level access to parts of the garden and to reception/shop, tea-room and ground floor of house.

 NPC

2 NEW **ANVIL COTTAGE**
South Hill PL17 7LP. Geoff and Barbara Clemerson. *3m NW of Callington. Head N on A388 from Callington centre. After ½ m L onto South Hill Rd (signed South Hill), straight on for 3m. Gardens on R just before St Sampson's Church.* **Sat 25, Sun 26 June (1.30-5). Combined adm with Windmills £5, chd free. Cream teas.**

Essentially a plantsman's garden. Winding paths take you through a series of themed rooms housing some both familiar and rare and unusual plants. Higher up, a wild flower garden leads through a formal rose garden to a raised viewpoint with spectacular views of SE of Bodmin Moor. Very limited wheechair access due to steps.

A wild flower garden leads through a formal rose garden . . .

3 **ARUNDELL**
West Pentire, Crantock TR8 5SE.
Brenda & David Eyles, 01637
831916, david@davideyles.com.
*1m W of Crantock. From A3075 take
signs to Crantock. At junction in
village keep straight on to West
Pentire (1m). Park in field (signed) or
public car parks at W Pentire.* **Sun 19
June, Sun 17 July (1-5). Adm £5,
chd free. Home-made teas. Visits
also by arrangement May to Aug
on Thursdays.**
A garden where no garden should be!
- on windswept NT headland
between 2 fantastic beaches. 1 acre
packed with design and plant interest
round old farm cottage. Front:
cottage garden. Side: Mediterranean
courtyard. Rear: rockery and
shrubbery leading to stumpery and
fernery and on to stream and pond,
Cornish Corner, herbaceous borders,
Beth Chatto dry garden, small
pinetum and jungle garden. Featured
on Gardeners' World Coast and in
Cornwall Today and Cornish Life
magazines. Wheelchair access from
public car park with entrance via rear
gate. 14 shallow steps in centre of
garden useable with care.

NGS support
helps us to
champion
community
nurses

4 ♦ **BOCONNOC**
Lostwithiel PL22 0RG. Anthony
Fortescue, 01208 872507,
info@boconnoc.com,
www.boconnoc.com. *Lostwithiel,
Cornwall. Off A390 between Liskeard
& Lostwithiel. From East Taphouse
follow signs to Boconnoc. (SatNav
does not work well in this area).* **For
NGS: Sun 8 May (2-5). Adm £4.50,
chd free. Cream teas in Stable
Yard. For other opening times and
information, please phone, email or
visit garden website.**
20 acre gardens surrounded by

parkland and woods with magnificent
trees, flowering shrubs and stunning
views. The gardens are set amongst
mature trees which provide the
backcloth for exotic spring flowering
shrubs, woodland plants, with newly-
planted magnolias and a fine
collection of hydrangeas. Bathhouse
built in 1804, woodland gardens,
obelisk built in 1771, house dating
from Domesday, deer park, C15
church. Featured in Country Life,
Country & Townhouse and more.

5 ♦ **BONYTHON MANOR**
Cury Cross Lanes, Helston
TR12 7BA. Mr & Mrs Richard
Nathan, 01326 240550,
www.bonythonmanor.co.uk. *5m S
of Helston. On main A3083 Helston
to Lizard Rd. Turn L at Cury Cross
Lanes (Wheel Inn). Entrance 300yds
on R.* **For NGS: Wed 4 May
(2-4.30). Adm £7, chd free. Home-
made teas. For other opening
times and information, please
phone or visit garden website.**
Magnificent 20-acre colour garden
incl sweeping hydrangea drive to
Georgian manor (not open).
Herbaceous walled garden, potager
with vegetables and picking flowers;
3 lakes in valley planted with
ornamental grasses, perennials and
South African flowers. A 'must see'
for all seasons colour.

6 ♦ **BOSVIGO HOUSE**
Bosvigo Lane, Truro TR1 3NH.
Wendy Perry, 01872 275774,
www.bosvigo.com/. *Truro City
Centre. At Highertown, nr Sainsbury
r'about, turn down Dobbs Lane. After
500yds, entrance to house is on L,
after sharp LH-bend.* **For NGS: Sun
10 July (2-5.30). Adm £5, chd free.
Home-made teas at the Servants
Hall. For other opening times and
information, please phone or visit
garden website.**
Created by artist owner, the 2 acre
garden surrounding the Georgian
house has been designed to create
dazzling displays of vivid colour and
plant harmonies. Each garden room
is designed with a different palette of
colour. For the opening in July the
Vean garden and walled garden will
be looking their best. Featured
regularly on television and in
magazines. Very limited wheelchair
access.

7 **NEW** **BROOKVALE**
Gover Valley, St. Austell PL25 5RA.
Leslie and Myrna Baker. *Gover
Valley. 1m from the town, close to the
Gover Viaduct.* **Sat 30 July (2-6).
Adm £4, chd free. Cream teas.**
An all year round garden created by
the current owners over the past 30
years. Both sun and shade plantings
with significant herbaceous borders
and an extensive rockery.

8 **CARMINOWE VALLEY
GARDEN**
Tangies, Gunwalloe TR12 7PU. Mr
& Mrs Peter Stanley, 01326 565868,
stanley.m2@sky.com,
www.carminowevalleygarden.co.uk.
*3m SW of Helston. A3083 Helston-
Lizard rd. R opp main gate to
Culdrose. 1m downhill, garden on R.*
**Sun 17 Apr, Sun 19 June (12-5).
Adm £4, chd free. Home-made
teas. Visits also by arrangement
Apr to Sept.**
Overlooking the beautiful Carminowe
Valley towards Loe Pool this
abundant garden combines native
oak woodland, babbling brook and
large natural pond with more formal
areas. Wild flower meadow, mown
pathways, shrubberies, orchard,
nectar beds, cutting garden, kitchen
garden, summerhouse. Enclosed
cottage garden, tulips in spring and
roses early summer provide huge
contrast. Featured in Cornwall Today.
Gravel paths, slopes.

9 ♦ **CHYGURNO**
Lamorna TR19 6XH. Dr & Mrs
Robert Moule, 01736 732153,
rmoule010@btinternet.com. *4m S
of Penzance. Off B3315. Follow signs
for The Lamorna Cove Hotel. Garden
is at top of hill, past Hotel on L.* **For
NGS: Sat 30 Apr, Sun 1, Mon 2
May, Sat 23, Sun 24 July (2-5).
Adm £5, chd free. For other
opening times and information,
please phone or email.**
Beautiful, unique, 3-acre cliffside
garden overlooking Lamorna Cove.
Planting started in 1998, mainly S-
hemisphere shrubs and exotics with
hydrangeas, camellias and
rhododendrons. Woodland area with
tree ferns set against large granite
outcrops. Garden terraced with steep
steps and paths. Plenty of benches
so you can take a rest and enjoy the
wonderful views.

The Lost Gardens of Heligan

10 ▶ COOMBEGATE COTTAGE

St Ive, Liskeard PL14 3LZ. Michael Stephens, 01579 383520, miketheplantsman@gmail.com. *4m E of Liskeard. From A390 at St Ive take turning signed Blunts. After 100 metres turn L & continue to bottom of hill.* **Every Sun 14 Feb to 13 Mar (1-4). Adm £3.50, chd free. Home-made teas in village hall. Visits also by arrangement Feb & Mar.**

Banish the winter blues! Be entranced by how colourful, fragrant and interesting a garden can be in winter and early spring. See what use has been made of a beautiful 1 acre steep valley site. All the winter favourites including drifts of snowdrops. Also more unusual seasonal plants, many available in the excellent plant sale. Open unless ice/snow - phone to check if in doubt. Featured in Garden Answers.

11 ▶ COSAWES BARTON

Ponsanooth, nr Truro TR3 7EJ. Louise Bishop, 01872 864026, info@cosawesbarton.co.uk www.cosawesbarton.co.uk. *8¹/₂ m W of Truro. A39 Truro - Falmouth rd.*

At Treluswell r'about take A393 Redruth/Ponsanooth rd. After Burnt House 1st L. ³/₄ m nr 30mph sign, house on R. **Sun 11 Sept (2-5). Adm £4, chd free. Light refreshments.**

An idyllic spot. Gardens surround C18 farmhouse, cottage and courtyard. Inner courtyard garden, a formal, very well-established area and extensive wooded walks covering 14 acres. There are gorgeous views over the Kennal Valley and to the North beyond.

12 ▶ ◆ COTEHELE

Saltash PL12 6TA. National Trust, 01579 351346, www.nationaltrust.org.uk. *2m E of St Dominick. 4m from Gunnislake. (Turn at St Ann's Chapel); 8m SW of Tavistock; 14m from Plymouth via Tamar Bridge.* **For opening times and information, please phone or visit garden website.**

Formal garden, orchards and meadow. Terrace garden falling to sheltered valley with ponds, stream and unusual shrubs. Historic collection of daffodils. Fine Tudor house (one of the least altered in the country); armour, tapestries, furniture. Gravel paths, some steep slopes in Valley Garden.

13 ▶ CREED HOUSE & CREED LODGE

Creed, Grampound, Truro TR2 4SL. The Croggon family, 01872 530372, www.creedhouse.co.uk. *9m W of Truro. From the centre of Grampound on A390, take rd signed to Creed. After 1m turn L opp Creed Church, garden is on L.* **Sun 12 June (11-5). Adm £4.50, chd free. Home-made teas.**

5-acre landscaped Georgian rectory garden; tranquil rural setting; spacious lawns. Tree collection; rhododendrons; sunken cobbled yard and formal walled rose garden. Trickle stream to ponds and bog. Natural woodland walk together with recently planted small garden around a new house. Herbaceous beds, shrubs and large terrace with rose bed below. if fine bring your lunch picnic and a rug. Dogs welcome on leads.

14 NEW CRUGSILLICK MANOR
Ruan High Lanes, Truro TR2 5LJ. Mrs Alison Agnew, 01872 501972, alisonagnew@icloud.com. *On Roseland Peninsula. Turn off A390 Truro-St Austell rd onto A3078 towards St Mawes. Approx 5m after Tregony turn 1st L after Ruan High Lanes towards Veryan, garden is 200yds on R.* **Sun 17 July (11-5). Adm £4, chd free. Home-made teas.**
2 acre garden, substantially re-landscaped and planted - mostly over last 3 yrs. To the side of the C17/C18 house, wooded bank drops down to walled kitchen garden and hot garden. In front, sweeping yew hedges and paths define oval lawns and broad mixed borders. On a lower terrace, the focus is a large pond and the planting is predominantly exotic flowering trees and shrubs. Partial wheelchair access. Garden is on several levels connected by fairly steep sloping gravel paths.

15 NEW DYE COTTAGE
St Neot PL14 6NG. Sue & Brian Williams. *Opp The London Inn in centre of St Neot village. Turn off A38 to St Neot. Street parking.* **Fri 24, Sat 25, Sun 26 June (2-5.30). Adm £3.50, chd free. Home-made teas.**
¹/₃ acre cottage garden, designed and completely maintained by the owners over the past 23 years. Many seating areas - down by the river, in courtyard garden, fire pit corner, and on rose terrace. Wisteria walk, potting shed, greenhouse, summerhouse, office (once the tree house!), fruit cage, mature borders, and roses everywhere. Sorry, unsuitable for wheelchairs as steps down from road.

16 NEW EAST DOWN BARN
Menheniot, Liskeard PL14 3QU. David & Shelley Lockett, 07803 159662. *S side of village near cricket ground. Turn off A38 at Hayloft Restaurant/railway station junction and head towards Menheniot village. Follow NGS signs from sharp L hand bend as you enter village.* **Sun 17 Apr (1-5). Adm £3, chd free. Home-made teas. Visits also by arrangement Apr & May.**
Garden laid down in 1986 with the conversion of the Barn into a home and covers almost ¹/₂ acre of East sloping land with stream running

North - South acting as the Easterly boundary. 3 terraces before garden starts to level out at stream. Garden won awards in the early years under the stewardship of the original owners. Steep slopes.

> The planting is predominantly exotic flowering trees and shrubs . . .

17 ◆ EDEN PROJECT
Bodelva PL24 2SG. The Eden Trust, 01726 811911, www.edenproject.com. *4m E of St Austell. Brown signs from A30 & A390.* **For opening times and information, please phone or visit garden website.**
Described as 8th wonder of the world, the Eden Project is a global garden for the C21. Discover the story of plants that have changed the world and which could change your future. The Eden Project is an exciting attraction where you can explore your relationship with nature, learn new things and get inspiration about the world around you. Yr-round programme of talks, events and workshops. Wheelchairs available - booking of powered wheelchairs is essential; please call 01726 818895 in advance.

18 ETHNEVAS COTTAGE
Constantine, Falmouth TR11 5PY. Lyn Watson, 01326 340076. *6m SW of Falmouth. Nearest main rds A39, A394. Follow signs to Constantine. At lower village sign, at bottom of winding hill, turn off on private lane. Garden ³/₄ m up hill.* **Sun 10 Apr, Sun 15 May, Sun 5 June (12.30-4). Adm £4, chd free. Home-made teas.**
Isolated granite cottage in 2 acres. Intimate flower and vegetable garden. Bridge over stream to large pond and

primrose path through semi-wild bog area. Hillside with grass paths among native and exotic trees. Many camellias and rhododendrons. Mixed shrubs and herbaceous beds, wild flower glade, spring bulbs. A garden of discovery of hidden delights.

19 THE 'GARTEN' GARDEN
Lower Trecuilliacks, Constantine, Falmouth TR11 5QW. Dr Sara Gadd, 07814 885141, sara@gartendesign.co.uk, www.gardendesignincornwall.co.uk. *1¹/₂ m N of Gweek, 1m NW of Constantine. From Falmouth or Helston take turning to Gweek off A394 at Edgecumb. 2nd L after 1¹/₂ m. Only property on R. From Constantine follow signs to Brill, then to Rame. L after 1m to Seworgan. Garden on L.* **Sun 3 July (1.30-4.30). Adm £4.50, chd free. Cream teas. Visits also by arrangement May to Oct, Garden Design studio talks available.**
Ecologically, organically and artistically executed. Lovingly developed by Drs Sara Gadd & Daro Montag. Embracing ecosystems; home, children, plants, food, wildlife. Enchanting mix of natural materials and feature plantings in their low carbon life. Hot terrace near fern glades.Creative use of wood and granite, thriving vegetable garden. Honest yet magical. gARTen design studio open new 2016, cedar shingle cabin by copse. Featured in Country Homes and Interiors. Partial wheelchair access, uneven ground/boggy areas.

20 ◆ GLENDURGAN
Mawnan Smith, Falmouth TR11 5JZ. National Trust, 01326 252020, www.nationaltrust.org.uk/ glendurgan. *5m SW of Falmouth. Follow rd out of Mawnan Smith to Helford Passage. Brown signs to Glendurgan.* **For opening times and information, please phone or visit garden website.**
Three valleys of natural beauty and amazing plants. Discover lush tender plantings in the jungle-like lower valley and spiky arid plants basking on sunny upper slopes. Wander down to hamlet of Durgan on R Helford. Banks of wild flowers teeming with wildlife - and 180 yr-old maze!

21 HALF ACRE

Mount Pleasant, Boscastle PL35 0BJ. Carole Vincent, www.carolevincent.org. *5m N of Camelford. Park at doctors' surgery at top of village (clearly signed). Limited parking for disabled at garden.* **Sat 18, Sun 19 June (1.30-5.30). Adm £4, chd free. Home-made teas.**
Old stone cottage with 2 studios overlooking cliffs and sea, set in 1½ acres of gardens - cottage, small wood and Blue Circle garden (RHS Chelsea 2001) constructed in colour concrete. Owner has a national reputation for her sculpture in concrete, and sculptures all around occupy small spaces or command a view. Mid-June should see the flowering of the roses and echiums. Studio open. Painting exhibition.

22 ◆ HIDDEN VALLEY GARDENS

Treesmill, Par PL24 2TU. Tricia Howard, 01208 873225, hiddenvalleygardens@yahoo.co.uk, www.hiddenvalleygardens.co.uk. *2m SW of Lostwithiel. Yellow sign directions on A390 between Lostwithiel (2m) & St Austell (5m), directing onto B3269 towards Fowey, followed by a R turn. From Fowey, take B3269 and turn L at yellow sign.* **For NGS: Daily Sun 14 Feb to Sun 21 Feb (2-4). Sat 4, Sun 5 June (10-6). Cream teas and home-made cakes in Tea Hut for June openings. Adm £4.50, chd free. For other opening times and information, please phone, email or visit garden website.**
Award-winning 3-acre colourful garden in hidden valley with nursery. Cottage-style planting with herbaceous beds and borders, grasses, ferns and fruit. Gazebo with country views. Iris fairy well and vegetable potager. June opening for special displays of early herbaceous plants incl iris, columbines, geraniums and many other colourful flowers. Children's quiz. Dogs on lead. In Feb Tricia has a collection of some 70+ named snowdrops as well as hellebores and early flowering daffodils. Dogs on leads welcome. Feb entry incl tea/coffee. Special drop off parking for wheelchair access directly into garden area. Mainly accessible. Some gentle sloping ground.

23 HIGHCROFT GARDENS

Cargreen, Saltash PL12 6PA. Mr & Mrs B J Richards, 01752 848048, gardens@bjrichardsflowers.co.uk, www.bjrichardsflowers.com. *5m NW of Saltash. 5m from Callington on A388 take Landulph Cargreen turning. 2m on, turn L at Landulph Xrds. Park at Methodist Church.* **Sun 7, Sun 21 Aug (1.30-5). Adm £4, chd free. Cream teas in Methodist Church. Visits also by arrangement July & Aug for garden clubs and groups of 10+.**
3-acre garden in beautiful Tamar Valley. Japanese-style garden, hot border, pastel border, grasses, arboretum with hemerocallis and new blue borders. Prairie planting containing 2,500 plants of herbaceous and grasses. Buddleia and shrub rose bank. Pond. All at their best in July, Aug and Sept. Collection of hydrangeas and agapanthus.

Mature borders, and roses everywhere . . .

24 ◆ THE HOMESTEAD WOODLAND GARDEN & TEAROOM

Crelly, Trenear, Wendron TR13 0EU. Shirley Williams & Chris Tredinnick, 01326 562808, homesteadholidays@btconnect.com, www.the-homestead-woodland-garden.com. *3m N of Helston. From Helston B3297 towards Redruth, 3m. Entrance 3rd on R 200 metres past Crelly/Bodilly sign & bus shelter.* **For NGS: Sun 12 June, Sun 11 Sept (1-4). Adm £4, chd free. Refreshments available from on site tearoom, Slice Of Cornwall. For other opening times and information, please phone, email or visit garden website.**
3 acres of divided gardens giving all-yr round interest and 3 acres of wildlife habitat and deciduous woodland with primroses in spring.

Cornish variety apple orchard where chickens, ducks and geese roam free. Vegetable garden, mature garden with pond and mixed borders. Archways, pergolas, seating, water features, hot and shady areas, walled garden, Japanese and Moroccan area. Sculptures sited throughout. Unfenced ponds, uneven paths (which may be slippery when wet) and some steps.

25 INCE CASTLE

Saltash PL12 4RA. Lord & Lady Boyd, 01752 842672, www.incecastle.co.uk. *3m SW of Saltash. From A38 at Stoketon Cross take turn signed Trematon, then Elmgate. No large coaches.* **Suns 13, 27 Mar, 10, 24 Apr, 8 May, 17 July (2-5). Adm £4, chd free. Home-made teas. Visits also by arrangement Feb to Sept for groups of 15+ please.**
Romantic garden at the end of winding lanes, surrounding C17 pink brick castle on a peninsula in R Lynher. Old apple trees with bulbs, woodland garden with fritillaries, camellias and rhododendrons. Extraordinary 1960s shell house on edge of formal garden. Partial wheelchair access.

26 ◆ KEN CARO

Bicton, Liskeard PL14 5RF. Mr & Mrs K R Willcock, 01579 362446. *5m NE of Liskeard. From A390 to Callington turn off N at St Ive. Take Pensilva Rd, follow brown tourist signs, approx 1m off main rd. Plenty of parking. (SatNav is misleading).* **For information, please phone.**
Connoisseurs' garden full of interest all yr round. Lily ponds, panoramic views, plenty of seating, picnic area, in all 10 acres. Garden started in 1970, recently rejuvenated. Woodland walk, which has one of the largest beech trees. Good collection of yellow magnolias and herbaceous plants. Over 200 camellias, large collection of ilex, day lilies with iris. Full of spring bulbs. Daily 6 Mar to Sept (10-5), adm £5, chd free. Partial wheelchair access.

27 ◆ LAMORRAN HOUSE

Upper Castle Road, St Mawes, Truro TR2 5BZ. Robert Dudley-Cooke, 01326 270800, www.lamorrangarden.co.uk. *A3078, R past garage at entrance to*

St Mawes. ³/₄ m on L. ¹/₄ m from castle if using passenger ferry service. **For NGS: Sun 8 May (11-4). Adm £7, chd free. Light refreshments. For other opening times and information, please phone or visit garden website.**
4-acre subtropical garden overlooking Falmouth bay. Designed by owner in an Italianate/Cote d'Azur style. Extensive collection of Mediterranean and subtropical plants incl large collection of palms Butia capitata/Butia yatay and tree ferns. Reflects both design and remarkable micro-climate. Beautiful collection of Japanese azaleas and tender rhododendrons. Large collection of S-hemisphere plants. Italianate garden with many water features. Champion trees.

28 ◆ LANHYDROCK HOUSE & GARDENS
Bodmin PL30 5AD. National Trust, 01208 265950, www.nationaltrust. org.uk. *2¹/₂ m SE of Bodmin. 2¹/₂ m on B3268. Stn: Bodmin Parkway 1³/₄ m walk on paths through parkland.* **For opening times and information, please phone or visit garden website.**
Large formal garden laid out in 1857. Ornamental parterres. Many fine specimens of camellias, rhododendrons and magnolias. Good summer colour with herbaceous borders and roses. Parterres with seasonal planting. Woodland walks. Lovely views. Mainly Victorian country house, though some parts date back to C17, with over 50 rooms open to the public. Formal and woodland gardens. Free garden tours most weekdays. Wheelchair access route around formal garden. Gravel paths and slopes to higher woodland garden.

29 ◆ THE LOST GARDENS OF HELIGAN
Pentewan, St Austell PL26 6EN. Heligan Gardens Ltd, www.heligan.com. *5m S of St Austell. From St Austell take B3273 signed Mevagissey, follow signs.* **For opening times and information, please visit garden website.**
Lose yourself in the mysterious world of The Lost Gardens where an exotic sub-tropical jungle, atmospheric Victorian pleasure grounds, an interactive wildlife project and the finest productive gardens in Britain all await your discovery. Wheelchair access to Northern gardens. Armchair tour shows video of unreachable areas. Wheelchairs available at reception free of charge.

carerstrust
action · help · advice

NGS funding helps us reach more unpaid carers

GROUP OPENING

30 LOWER AMBLE GARDENS
Chapel Amble, Wadebridge PL27 6EW. *3m N of Wadebridge. Take lane signed Middle & Lower Amble opp PO 1m to L turn by pond. Parking in field beyond farmhouse.* **Sun 29 May (2-6). Combined adm £5, chd free. Tea at Millpond Cottage. Picnic site at Lower Amble Farmhouse wood.**

> **NEW LOWER AMBLE COTTAGE**
> Mr & Mrs C Burr

> **LOWER AMBLE FARMHOUSE**
> Mr & Mrs Laurence Grand

> **MILLPOND COTTAGE**
> Sheilagh Lees

> **NEW ROUND HOUSE**
> Mr & Mrs Nick Eshelby

Peaceful hamlet with wide valley and moorland views, developed from mill farm buildings of early 1800s. Lower Amble Cottage: 1-acre garden of 12 years' development, with lawns, mixed beds, sculptures, small pond and trees. Lower Amble Farmhouse: 1-acre garden divided into varied spaces, plus 4 acres of deciduous woodland, pond and wild flower orchard. Millpond Cottage: large 20-yr-old garden with orchard, pond, vegetable garden and mixed herbaceous borders with many roses,

geraniums and interesting perennials. The Roundhouse: sunny, sheltered garden with leat running through pond and on to Mill Barn; with patios and palm trees, it has a Mediterranean feel. Disabled parking in Millpond Cottage drive or access through side gate.

---

31 NEW MANATON
Dunheved Road, Launceston PL15 9JE. Peter & Cecilia Hodgson. *Follow signs for Leisure Centre along Dunheved Rd. At college end of rd take sharp L bend & immed after this take another L turning into Windmill Hill. Entrance to car parking approx 400yds on L.* **Sun 14 Aug (2-5). Adm £4, chd free. Cream teas.**
4 acre garden created over 50 yrs. Fine selection of unusual mature trees and shrubs. Separate areas bounded mainly by old yew hedges with herbaceous and other flower borders planted for colour from Aug onwards; informal woodland area; large productive vegetable and fruit gardens.

32 NEW MARY NEWMAN'S GARDEN
Culver Road, Saltash PL12 4DT. Tamar Protection Society, 01579 370884, sjpage@cornwall.gov.uk, www.tamarprotectionsociety. *200yds down from railway station. Lower end of Culver Rd near to Waterside of Saltash, ¹/₄ m from Saltash Fore St. Plenty of parking in adj streets.* **Sun 22 May, Sun 3 July, Sun 7 Aug (12-4). Adm by donation. Home-made teas.**
Mary Newman's is a delightful Elizabethan cottage and garden - reputedly the home of Sir Francis Drake's first wife, Mary Newman. The garden is laid out in authentic Elizabethan style, showcasing the plants and herbs vital to a household of the period, and has the feeling of being a very secret garden which is a shelter from the humdrum of the busy world we live in. Plants for sale cultivated with love. Also open April to Sept Wed, Thurs, Sat, Sun (12-4) by donation in aid of Tamar Protection Society. Featured in Evening Herald. Ramp can be requested at reception for main access. Wheelchair access to ground floor of cottage.

33 NEW MEUDON HOTEL
Maenporth Road, Mawnan Smith,
Falmouth TR11 5HT. Tessa Rabett,
www.meudon.co.uk. *Follow signs
for Mabe, then Mawnan Smith.* **Mon
28 Mar (2-5). Adm £6, chd free.
Cream teas. Bar drinks, snacks,
home-made cakes.**
Meudon has 9 acres of sub-tropical
valley garden created by the Fox
family in 1800. Wealthy Quakers and
shipping agents, their 'Packet' ships
provided transport for Meudon's
wonderful collection of rare and
exotic trees and shrubs from around
the world. Terraces, pathways,
meander down to Bream Cove
(private beach). Formal garden,
herbaceous borders, indigenous
plants, and sunken pond area.
Brazilian Gunnera manicata,
Japanese banana trees Musa basjoo,
Wollemia pine, Beschorneria
yuccoides. Restaurant. Featured in
the Telegraph as one of the top 10
English country hotel gardens.
Wheelchair access limited to upper
terrace and ponds (although they
take a little longer to get to).
♿ 🐫 🛏 ☕

Small cliffs and stone hedges smothered with alpines . . .

34 ◆ MOYCLARE
Lodge Hill, Liskeard PL14 4EH.
Elizabeth & Philip Henslowe,
01579 343114,
elizabethhenslowe@btinternet.com,
www.moyclare.co.uk. *1m S of
Liskeard centre. Approx 300yds S of
Liskeard railway stn on St Keyne-
Duloe rd (B3254).* **For NGS: Mon 2
May (2-5). Adm £3.50, chd free.
Home-made teas. For other
opening times and information,
please phone, email or visit garden
website.**
Gardened by one family for over
80yrs; mature trees, shrubs and
plants (many unusual, many
variegated). Once most televised
Cornish garden. Now revived and
rejuvenated and still a plantsman's
delight, full of character. Camellia,

brachyglottis and astrantia (all Moira
Reid) and cytisus Moyclare Pink
originated here. Meandering paths
through fascinating shrubberies,
herbacious borders and sunny
corners. Wellstocked pond. Wildlife
habitat area. Quite a lot of the garden
can be enjoyed by wheelchair users.
♿ ⭐ 🐫 ☕

35 NANFENTEN
Little Petherick, Wadebridge
PL27 7QT. Trevor & Jackie Bould,
01841 540480,
nanfentensgarden@hotmail.co.uk,
www.nanfentensgarden.com. *3m
W of Wadebridge, A389 to Little
Petherick. Turn into lane next to white
cottage almost opp church,
Nanfenten 150 metres on L. Limited
parking, larger groups please use
village hall car park.* **Visits by
arrangement May to Aug, single
visitors or groups all welcome.
Adm £3.50, chd free.**
$2/3$ -acre plantsman's garden on side
of valley. Views of Petherick Creek to
Padstow. Cottage-style planting on
difficult terrain; a surprise round every
corner with beautiful views. Many
beautiful roses. Steep sloping aspect
to rear garden with wide variety of
shrubs and plants. Unusual sloping
water feature; pergola and
summerhouse. Many seating areas.
Cream teas at The Mill House (B&B).
🐫 ☕

36 THE OLD RECTORY
Trevalga, Boscastle PL35 0EA.
Jacqueline M A Jarvis, 01840
250512,
jacqueline@jacquelinejarvis.co.uk.
*Coastal rd between Tintagel &
Boscastle. At Trevalga Xrds turn
inland away from hamlet. Garden
$1/2$ m up narrow, steep hill. Limited
parking.* **Visits by arrangement
May to Aug. Adm £4, chd free.
Tea, coffee and biscuits.**
On N Cornish coast, a challenging,
exposed, NW-facing garden with
panoramic sea views, $1/2$ m inland,
elevation 500ft. 'From Field to
Garden' a 29 yr project by artist
owner. Informal incl woodland,
perennial borders, sunken and walled
areas. Lookout at front of garden (4
step spiral stair access) with stunning
views across circa 50m of coastline -
Hartland Point to Pentire Point.
Featured in Cornish Guardian &
Amateur Gardening. Gravel drive and
partial wheelchair access to garden.
♿ ☕

37 PARC-LAMP
Ruan Lanihorne, Truro TR2 5NX.
Kathleen Ward, 01872 501530.
*$2^{1}/_2$ m W of Tregony. Truro to
Tregony: A390 E to St Austell. Turn R
on A3078 to St Mawes Rd. In
Tregony cross bridge then 1st R to
Ruan Lanihorne. Garden 1st L after
bend. Next to award winning The
Kings Head PH.* **Visits by
arrangement June to Oct, max 12.
Adm £4, chd free. Tea.**
Small, intensively-planted, terraced
Mediterranean style garden with
travertine paving and gravelled areas.
The sheltered site has a micro-climate
which allows many unusual tender
trees and plants to thrive. Enjoy the
garden from various seating places.
Entry is by steep steps. Featured in
Cornwall Life.
☕

38 NEW PENCARN
Gonvena, Wadebridge PL27 6DL.
Mr Trevor Wiltshire, 01208 814631 /
07796 184506,
trevordwiltshire@gmail.com,
www.pencarn.org.uk. *Central
Wadebridge. Follow Gonvena Hill
(B3314) past Wadebridge
comprehensive school; shortly
afterwards (at postbox in wall) turn R
towards Gonvena and St Giles.
Follow lane right down, last house at
bottom on R.* **Visits by
arrangement May to Aug 11am -
5pm. Adm £4.50, chd free. Tea.**
Sited on a tree-covered, SW-facing
hillside, a 1-acre plantsman's garden
par excellence (owner worked at RHS
Wisley). Mediterranean-themed
section, two large ponds and rock
garden. Plant collections and unusual
plants abound: in raised beds, small
cliffs and stone hedges smothered
with alpines. 3 greenhouses in a
productive vegetable garden. Sitting
areas, and decks over ponds. All
except vegetable garden accessible
to wheelchair users.
♿ 🐫 ⭐ ☕

39 ◆ PENCARROW
Washaway, Bodmin PL30 3AG.
Molesworth-St Aubyn family, 01208
841369, info@pencarrow.co.uk,
www.pencarrow.co.uk. *4m NW of
Bodmin. Signed off A389 & B3266.*
**For NGS: Tue 12 Apr (10-5.30).
Adm £5.75, chd £2.50. Cream
teas. For other opening times and
information, please phone, email or
visit garden website.**
50 acres of tranquil, family-owned
Grade II* listed gardens. Superb

specimen conifers, azaleas, magnolias and camellias galore. 700 varieties of rhododendron give a blaze of spring colour; blue hydrangeas line the mile-long carriage drive throughout the summer. Discover the Iron Age hill fort, lake, Italian gardens and granite rockery. Free parking, dogs welcome, café and children's play area. Gravel paths, some steep slopes.

40 PENHEALE MANOR
Egloskerry, Launceston PL15 8RX. Mr & Mrs James Colville. *Penheale Manor SX26 88; 3¹/₂ m NW of Launceston. Take rd from St Stephen's, Launceston, to Egloskerry. From centre of village to Penheale entrance is ¹/₂ m on R.* **Sun 15 May (2-5). Adm £6, chd £2. Tea.**
Listed walled gardens surround C17 Jacobean manor house and incl impressive yew hedges, with enclosures and surprises, herbaceous borders and rose gardens. In addition there are beautiful woodland areas with streams, pools and ponds. Wheelchair users will be given help and guidance.

41 ◆ PINETUM PARK & PINE LODGE GARDENS
Holmbush, St Austell PL25 3RQ. Mr Chang Li, 01726 73500, office@pinetumpark.com, www.pinetumpark.com. *1m East of St Austell. On A390 between Holmbush & St Blazey at junction of A391.* **For NGS: Sat 6 Feb (10-6). Adm £7.50, chd free. Delicious assortment of hot food, cream teas and sandwiches are available. For other opening times and information, please phone, email or visit garden website.**
Hidden gem on S coast of Cornwall and a must visit for garden lovers. From serious plant hunters interested in rare plants to those seeking a tranquil day out, the 30 acre park has colour for all seasons. Discover 6000 plants, trees and flowers with 23 champion trees. Pinetum Park has 10 individual gardens to explore throughout every season. Gardens easily accessible but with no wheelchair access to Japanese garden.

Arundell

42 ◆ PINSLA GARDEN & NURSERY
Cardinham PL30 4AY. Mark & Claire Woodbine, 01208 821339, cwoodbine@btinternet.com, www.pinslagarden.net. *3¹/₂ m E of Bodmin. From A30 or Bodmin take A38 towards Plymouth, 1st L to Cardinham & Fletchers Bridge, 2m on R.* **For NGS: Sat 21, Sun 22 May, Sat 6, Sun 7 Aug (9-5). Adm £3.50, chd free. Home-made teas. For other opening times and information, please phone, email or visit garden website.**
Romantic 1¹/₂ -acre artist's garden set in tranquil woodland. Naturalistic cottage garden planting surrounds our C18 fairytale cottage. Imaginative design, intense colour and scent, bees and butterflies. Unusual shade plants, acers and ferns. Fantastic range of plants and statues on display and for sale. Friendly advice in nursery. Wheelchair access limited as some paths are narrow and bumpy.

43 NEW POLDARIAN
12 Carrick Way, St. Mawes, Truro TR2 5BB. Brian & Valerie Willis. *12 Carrick Way, St.Mawes. From A390 St.Austell to Truro, turn onto A3078 to St.Mawes. Leave water tower and disused garage on R and ignore road to St.Mawes Castle on R. Continue*

¹/₄ m until yellow NGS signs. Parking by direction. **Sat 9, Sun 10 July (10.30-4.30). Adm £5, chd free. Tea, coffee, soft drinks, cream teas, home-made cakes.**
Well-structured ³/₄ acre terraced plantsman's garden of trees, shrubs and perennials with yr-round colour and harmony and lovely sea and harbour views. Sorry, no wheelchair access; some steps to terraces.

44 POLGWYNNE
Feock TR3 6SG. Amanda & Graham Piercy. *5m SW of Truro. Take A39 out of Truro signed Falmouth. At Playing Place turn L onto B3289. After 2m look for NGS signs.* **Sun 17 Apr (2-5). Adm £4, chd free. Home-made teas.**
Wonderful 4-acre garden looking out over the sea. Walled formal and cottage gardens, terraced lawns, formal pond and woodland. Vegetable and picking gardens, with greenhouses whose mechanisms were described in The Journal of the RHS in 1852. Many unusual plants and what is believed to be the largest female Ginkgo biloba in Britain. Check out our Facebook page - Polgwynne Garden. Partial wheelchair access, gravel paths, some slopes.

45 ◆ POPPY COTTAGE GARDEN
Ruan High Lanes, Truro TR2 5JR.
Tina & David Primmer,
01872 501411,
poppycottagegarden@btinternet.com,
www.poppycottagegarden.co.uk.
On Roseland Peninsula. Turn off A390 Truro - St Austell rd onto A3078 to St Mawes. Garden 4m out of Tregony. **For NGS: Sun 17 July (11-5). Adm £4, chd free. Home-made teas. Also open Crugsillick Manor.** For other opening times and information, please phone, email or visit garden website.
Situated on the beautiful Roseland peninsula, this 1-acre garden is a plantsman's paradise. Planted for yr-round interest and divided into rooms, its intense planting of shrubs and herbaceous underplanted with bulbs provides colourful and intriguing surprises around every corner. Small orchard with ornamental ducks and chickens.

& 🐕 ⊗ 🚐 ☕

NGS & Perennial;
giving support
where it
is needed

46 ◆ POTAGER GARDEN
High Cross, Constantine, Falmouth TR11 5RF. Mr Mark Harris, 01326 341258,
enquiries@potagergarden.org,
www.potagergarden.org. *5m SW of Falmouth. From Falmouth, follow signs to Constantine. From Helston, drive through Constantine and continue towards Famouth.* **For NGS: Sun 5 June (3-7). Adm by donation. Light refreshments.** For other opening times and information, please phone, email or visit garden website.
Potager has emerged from the bramble choked wilderness of an abandoned plant nursery. With mature trees which were once

nursery stock and lush herbaceous planting interspersed with fruit and vegetables Potager Garden aims to demonstrate the beauty of productive organic gardening. There are games to play, hammocks to laze in and boule and badminton to enjoy.

& 🐕 ⊗ ☕

47 NEW READYMONEY GARDENS
St Catherines Cove, Fowey PL23 1JH. Mr Darren Hawkes.
Parking available at Readymoney car park with a short (5-10min) walk along a footpath to Readymoney Cove. **Fridays 24 June, 29 July, 26 Aug, 30 Sept (10.30-5). Adm £4, chd free. Light refreshments.**
Steeply sloping garden with stunning views across Readymoney beach and out to the Fowey estuary. The garden is very much a work in progress with some areas still to be planted but others 4 years into maturity. Grasses and perennials with a young collection of shrubs and trees. Steep paths and steep steps, regret no wheelchair access.

Ⓓ ☕

48 ◆ RIVERSIDE COTTAGE
St. Clement, Truro TR1 1SZ. Billa & Nick Jeans, 01872 263830,
billajeans@gmail.com. *1½ m SE of Truro. From Trafalgar r'about on A39 in Truro, follow signs for St Clement, up St Clement Hill. R at top of hill, continue to car park by river.* **Sun 17 Apr (2-5). Adm £3.50, chd free. Cream teas. Visits also by arrangement Apr to June.**
Small garden on beautiful St Clement Estuary. Small Victorian orchard and nut walk with wild flower areas, borders and vegetable patch. Steep paths and steps but plenty of seats. Walk through to C13 St Clement Church and 'living churchyard'. Featured in Cornish Life.

🐕 ⊗ ☕

49 ◆ ROSELAND HOUSE
Chacewater TR4 8QB. Mr & Mrs Pridham, 01872 560451,
charlie@roselandhouse.co.uk,
www.roselandhouse.co.uk. *4m W of Truro. At Truro end of main st. Park in village car park (100yds) or on surrounding rds.* **For NGS: Sat 18, Sun 19 June, Sat 30, Sun 31 July (1-5). Adm £4, chd free. Home-made teas.** For other opening times and information, please phone, email or visit garden website.

The 1-acre garden is a mass of rambling roses and clematis. Ponds and borders alike are filled with plants, many rarely seen in gardens. National Collection of clematis viticella cvs can be seen in garden and display tunnel, along with a huge range of other climbing plants. Some slopes.

& 🐕 ⊗ **NPC** ☕

50 NEW ROSTEAGUE MANOR
Portscatho, Truro TR2 5EF. Mrs Jay Milton. *Roseland Peninsula. Head for St Gerrans Church in Gerrans (not Portscatho village) and turn down Treloan Lane (opp church/Royal Standard PH on L). Continue for ½ m, entrance/parking will be signed.* **Sun 8 May (2-5). Adm £4, chd free. Home-made teas.**
Rosteague is an ancient Manor house, fronted by lawns and flowerbeds, surrounded by its own farmland which rolls down to the sea. The C17 French garden is its crowning glory: 4 large geometrical parterres of intricate box hedging and topiary nestling inside protective high stone walls. For wheelchair access to French Garden turn R onto 1st path on inner driveway and through double blue doors.

& 🐕 ☕

51 ◆ ST MICHAEL'S MOUNT
Marazion TR17 0HS. James & Mary St Levan, 01736 710507,
mail@stmichaelsmount.co.uk,
www.stmichaelsmount.co.uk.
2½ m E of Penzance. ⅛ m from shore at Marazion by Causeway; otherwise by motor boat. **For NGS: Sun 5 June (10.30-5). Adm £6, chd £3.** For other opening times and information, please phone, email or visit garden website.
Infuse your senses with colour and scent in the unique sub-tropical gardens basking in the mild climate and salty breeze. Clinging to granite slopes the terraced beds tier steeply to the ocean's edge, boasting tender exotics from places such as Mexico, the Canary Islands and South Africa. The laundry lawn, mackerel bank, pill box, gun emplacement, tiered terraces, the well, tortoise lawn. Walled gardens, seagull seat. The garden lawn can be accessed with wheelchairs although further exploration is limited due to steps and steepness.

⊗ 🚐 ☕

52 SCORRIER HOUSE
Scorrier, Redruth TR16 5AU.
Richard & Caroline Williams,
www.scorrierhouse.co.uk. 2½ m E
of Redruth. Signed from B3207 and
Redruth Truro rd B3287. **Sun 24 Apr
(2-5). Adm £5, chd free. Home-
made teas.**
Scorrier House and gardens have
been in the Williams family for 7
generations. The gardens are set in
parkland with a new conservatory,
formal garden with herbaceous
borders and walled garden with
camellias, magnolias and rare trees,
some collected by the famous plant
collector William Lobb. Unfenced
swimming pool.

53 SOUTH LEA
Pillaton, Nr Saltash PL12 6QS. Viv
& Tony Laurillard, 01579 350629,
tony@laurillard.eclipse.co.uk. 4m S
of Callington. Signed from r'bouts on
A388 at St Mellion and Hatt, or on
A38 at Landrake. In middle of village
opp Weary Friar PH. Roadside
parking. Please do not park in PH
carpark. **Sun 8 May, Sun 26 June
(1-5). Adm £4, chd free. Home-
made teas. Visits also by
arrangement Apr to July for
groups of 15+, eg gardening clubs
or coach parties, please phone to
discuss arrangements.**
Cottage style garden, about 0.3 acre,
arranged with separate spaces. First
an area of landscaped dry planting
and a small pond. Outside the front
door the theme is tropical with
various palms, yuccas, agave and
cannas. S-facing rear garden with
views across the R Lynher valley, and
sun terraces with plenty of seating.
Sloping and level lawns and
herbaceous borders filled in spring
with bulbs, flowering shrubs and
clematis and, in June, are a riot of
perennial colour. Fair sized pond and
small shady woodland area. Due to
steps there is only wheelchair access
only to the front dry garden and rear
terrace, from which most of the rest
of garden can be viewed.

54 ◆ TREBAH
Mawnan Smith TR11 5JZ. Trebah
Garden Trust, 01326 252200,
mail@trebah-garden.co.uk,
www.trebah-garden.co.uk. 4m SW
of Falmouth. Follow tourist signs from
Hillhead r'about on A39 approach to
Falmouth or Treliever Cross r'about
on junction of A39-A394. Parking for
coaches. **For opening times and
information, please phone, email or
visit garden website.**
26-acre S-facing ravine garden,
planted in 1830s. Extensive collection
rare/mature trees/shrubs incl glades;
huge tree ferns 100yrs old,
subtropical exotics. Hydrangea
collection covers 2½ acres. Water
garden, waterfalls, rock pool stocked
with mature koi carp. Enchanted
garden for plantsman/artist/family.
Play area/trails for children. Use of
private beach. Steep paths in places.
2 motorised vehicles available, please
book in advance.

Tree ferns and stunning spring flower banks . . .

55 TREBARTHA
Trebartha, nr Launceston
PL15 7PD. The Latham Family. 6m
SW of Launceston. North Hill, SW of
Launceston nr junction of B3254 &
B3257. No coaches. **Sun 15 May,
Sun 9 Oct (2-5). Adm £5, chd free.
Home-made teas.**
Landscape gardens featuring ponds,
streams, cascades, rocks and
woodlands, including fine American
trees; bluebells in spring; ornamental
walled garden; and private garden at
Lemarne (best seen in autumn). Allow
at least 1 hour for a circular walk.
Some steep and rough paths, which
can be slippery when wet. Stout
footwear advised. Interesting garden
project in progress.

56 TREGONNING
Carleen, Breage, Helston
TR13 9QU. Andrew & Kathryn
Eaton, 01736 761840,
alfeaton@aol.com. 1m S of
Godolphin Cross. From Xrds in centre
of Godolphin Cross head S towards
Carleen. In ½ m at fork signed
Breage 1¼ turn R up narrow lane
marked no through road. After ½ m
parking on L opp Tregonning Farm.
**Sat 3, Sun 4 Sept (1-4). Adm £3.50,
chd free. Home-made teas. Visits
also by arrangement Apr to Sept
for groups eg clubs.**
Located 300ft up NE side of
Tregonning Hill this small (less than 1
acre) developing garden will hopefully
inspire those thinking of making a
garden from nothing more than a
pond and copse of trees (in 2009).
With the ever present challenge of
storm force winds, garden offers yr
round interest and a self-sufficient
vegetable and soft fruit paddock.
Sculpted grass meadow, with
panoramic views from Carn Brea to
Helston. Cottage garden, spring
garden and water features. Featured
in Cornwall Today and Cornwall Life.

57 TREGOOSE
Grampound TR2 4DB. Mr & Mrs
Anthony O'Connor, 01726 882460,
tregoose@tregoose.co.uk. 7m E of
Truro, 1m W of Grampound. Off
A390. Lane entrance is 100yds W of
New Stables Xrds & ½ m E of
Trewithen r'about. Half way between
Probus and Grampound. **Sun 7 Feb
(1-5). Adm £4, chd free. Home-
made teas.**
2-acre garden. Woodland area with
early spring shrubs underplanted with
snowdrops, erythroniums, hellebores
and small narcissus cultivars.
Summer and autumn flowering areas
incl walled garden overtopped by
Acacia baileyana purpurea, scarlet
blue and yellow border and potager
full of herbs and cutting beds with
arches covered with gourds, roses
and honeysuckle. Snowdrop
collection. Most of the summer
flowering area can take a wheelchair.

58 ◆ TRELISSICK
Feock, Truro TR3 6QL. National
Trust, 01872 862090,
www.nationaltrust.org.uk/trelissick.
4m S of Truro. From A39 Truro to
Falmouth, turn onto B3289 at Playing
Place. Follow signs to Trelissick &
King Harry Ferry. **For opening times
and information, please phone or
visit garden website.**
Woodland garden with fantastic views
out to water on 3 sides. Contrasts
between light and shade and
inspiration from gardening in a variety
of woodland environments. Mixed
borders designed for long term
interest with a mixture of popular
hardy favourites and tender exotics
with foliage interest. With the house
now open and the terrace boasting
one of Cornwall's finest views. Partial
wheelchair access, map provided.
Wheelchairs and mobility vehicles
available, ring to book in advance.

Glendurgan

59 ◆ **TREMATON CASTLE**
Castle Hill, Trematon, Saltash
PL12 4QW. Bannerman,
info@bannermandesign.com,
www.bannermandesign.com/
trematon. *2m SW of Saltash. Lanes
surrounding the castle are very
narrow, please approach from
Trematon and Trehan.* **For NGS: Fri
20 May (11-5). Adm £7, chd free.
Tea. For other opening times and
information, please email or visit
garden website.**
Property of Duchy of Cornwall since
the Conquest, Trematon is a perfect
miniature motte and bailey castle. On
R Lynher estuary, '... one of the
superb views of Cornwall.... all the
more romantic for being still a private
residence' (John Betjeman). Julian
and Isabel Bannerman have begun to
create a garden playing on its pre-
Raphaelite glories, wild flowers,
orchard, woodland, scented borders,
seaside and exotic planting. Featured
in World of Interiors & Gardens
Illustrated. Trematon Castle Gardens
regret that the terrain in the gardens
is not suitable for wheelchair users,
pea gravel throughout.

60 NEW **TRENARREN HOUSE**
Trenarren, St. Austell PL26 6BH. Mr
& Mrs Michelle & Dan Cohen. *3m
from St Austell at Black Head. Take
Porthpean rd from St Austell pass the
Golf Club next L signed Trenarren.
1m on park under trees. Trenarren
House on R through large black
gates.* **Sat 23, Sun 24 Apr
(1.30-5.30). Adm £5, chd free.
Cream teas.**
At the head of a steep valley this 3
acre garden offers wonderful sea
views, woodland walks
rhododendrons, camellias,
magnolias, tree ferns and stunning
spring flower banks. Once the garden
of A L Rowse it is now being
rejuvenated to include a small
orchard, ponds and a flat croquet
lawn with sweeping views across to
Mevagissey. The setting means it is
sadly unsuitable for wheelchair users.

61 **TRENARTH**
High Cross, Constantine TR11 5JN.
Lucie Nottingham, 01326 340444,
lmnottingham@btinternet.com,
www.trenarthgardens.com. *6m SW
of Falmouth. Main rd A39/A394 Truro
to Helston, follow Constantine signs.
High X garage turn L for Mawnan,
30yds on R down dead end lane,
Trenarth is 1/2 m at end.* **Sun 31 July
(2-5). Adm £4, chd free. Home-
made teas. Visits also by
arrangement Mar to Oct, garden
clubs and groups especially
welcome, tour and teas provided.**
4-acres round C17 farmhouse in
peaceful pastoral setting. Yr-round
interest. Emphasis on tender, unusual
plants, structure and form. C16
courtyard, listed garden walls, yew
rooms, vegetable garden, traditional
potting shed, orchard, new woodland
area with children's interest, palm and
gravel garden. Circular walk down
ancient green lane via animal pond to
Trenarth Bridge, returning through
woods. Abundant wildlife. Bees in
tree bole, lesser horseshoe bat
colony, swallows, wild flowers and
butterflies. Free dierama plant for all
visitors in July. Family friendly,
children's play area, the Wolery, and
plenty of room to run, jump and
climb. Featured in WI national
magazine.

62 ♦ **TRENGWAINTON**
Madron, Penzance TR20 8RZ.
National Trust, 01736 363148,
trengwainton@nationaltrust.org.uk,
www.nationaltrust.org.uk/
trengwainton. *2m NW of Penzance.*
½ m W of Heamoor. On Penzance-
Morvah rd (B3312), ½ m off St Just
rd (A3071). Signed from A30 **For**
opening times and information,
please phone, email or visit garden
website.
Glorious spring displays of magnolias,
rhododendrons, azaleas and
camellias; walled kitchen garden built
to dimensions of Noahs Ark and
breathtaking views across Mounts
Bay. Lose yourself amongst winding,
wooded paths, picnic by the stream
or simply find a quiet corner to sit
within Trengwainton's peaceful
25 acres. WW2 Dig for Victory
allotment, complete with
reproduction Anderson shelter.
Tiny 2nd hand bookshop and gallery
now open in old head gardeners
cottage. Seasonal themed activities
and things to see. Wheelchairs
available, booking essential. Gravel
paths and slope, assistance may be
needed.

63 **NEW** **TREREIFE PARK**
Penzance TR20 8TJ. Mr &
Mrs T Le Grice, 01736 362750,
trereifepark@btconnect.com,
www.trereifepark.co.uk. *2m W of*
Penzance on A30 on Lands End rd.
Garden and house signed R through
estate gates. **Sun 20 Mar, Sun 3**
July (1-5). Adm £6, chd free.
Home-made teas.
Mature gardens undergoing
restoration in the historic setting of
Trereife Park. Established garden
camellia, rhododendron, azalea walk
under mature beech trees. Modern
parterre, sculptural yew hedge,
S-facing walled terrace with wisteria
and magnolia. New hot border with
unusual Mediterranean planting.
Medlar collection around events lawn
and old kitchen garden awaiting
restoration.

64 ♦ **TRERICE**
Kestle Mill, Newquay TR8 4PG.
National Trust, 01637 875404,
www.nationaltrust.org.uk/trerice.
3m SE of Newquay. From Newquay
via A392 & A3058; turn R at Kestle
Mill (NT signs) or signed from A30 at
Summercourt via A3058. **For**
opening times and information,

please phone or visit garden
website.
Small intimate romantic house and
garden set in unspoilt countryside.
The garden has interest throughout
the year incl spring flowering bulbs,
summer annuals, borders, cut
flowers, herbs and fruit. The
magnificent newly planted Knot
Garden was opened in 2014. Due to
historic nature of property only partial
wheelchair access.

65 ♦ **TREWIDDEN GARDEN**
Buryas Bridge, Penzance
TR20 8TT. Mr Alverne Bolitho -
Richard Morton, Head Gardener,
01736 351979/363021,
contact@trewiddengarden.co.uk,
www.trewiddengarden.co.uk. *2m*
W of Penzance. Entry on A30 just
before Buryas Bridge. SatNav TR19
6AU. **For NGS: Sat 9 Apr**
(10.30-5.30). Adm £6.50, chd free.
Cream teas. For other opening
times and information, please
phone, email or visit garden
website.
Historic Victorian garden with
magnolias, camellias and magnificent
tree ferns planted within ancient tin
workings. Tender, rare and unusual
exotic plantings create a riot of colour
thoughout the season. Water
features, specimen trees and
artefacts from Cornwall's tin industry
provide a wide range of interest for
all.

66 **NEW** ♦ **VARFELL FARM**
Long Rock, Penzance TR20 8AQ.
Mr M Mann, 01736 339276,
mike.mann@national-dahlia-
collection.co.uk, www.national-
dahlia-collection.co.uk. *3m N of*
Penzance. Turn off A30 near the Long
Rock r'about, signed Varfell. **For**
opening times and information,
please phone, email or visit garden
website.
National Dahlia Collection growing in
2 acre field of riotous colour which
delights the eye. All types of Dahlias
are exhibited from dainty pompoms
to huge decoratives amounting to
1600 named varieties bred and
grown here. It is displayed in ordered
rows, fully labelled for identification in
mail order sales. We are open to the
public free of charge from August to
mid October. Come and see the
extraordinary show.
NPC

67 **WAYE COTTAGE**
Lerryn, nr Lostwithiel PL22 0QQ.
Malcolm & Jennifer Bell, 01208
872119. *4m S of Lostwithiel. Village*
parking, garden 10min, level stroll
along riverbank/stepping stones.
Visits by arrangement Apr to Sept
with garden clubs at reduced
rate. Adm £4, chd free. Home-
made teas.
Never immaculate but abundantly-
planted, this 1-acre cottage garden
has a large and interesting collection
of plants, some rare and unusual,
together with delightful bonsai
theatre. Wander along the
meandering paths, sit on the many
benches and enjoy stunning river
views. Steep and sadly only for those
sound in wind and limb. Attractive
riverside village with pub and shop
which supplies picnics to eat on
trestle tables on the village green.
Featured in Cornwall Today.

A garden full of
surprises . . .

68 **NEW** **WINDMILLS**
South Hill, Callington PL17 7LP. Mr
& Mrs Peter Tunnicliffe. *3m NW of*
Callington. Head N from Callington
A388, after about ½ m turn L onto
South Hill Rd (signed South Hill).
Straight on for 3m, the gardens are
on R just before church. **Sat 25, Sun**
26 June (1.30-5). Combined adm
with Anvil Cottage £5, chd free.
Cream teas.
Next to medieval church and on the
site of an old rectory and there are
still signs in places of that long gone
building. A garden full of surprises,
formal paths and steps lead up from
the flower beds to extensive
vegetable and soft fruit area. More
paths lead to water feature with rustic
stone bridge, past a pergola, and
down into large lawns with trees and
shrubs. Limited wheelchair access.

CUMBRIA

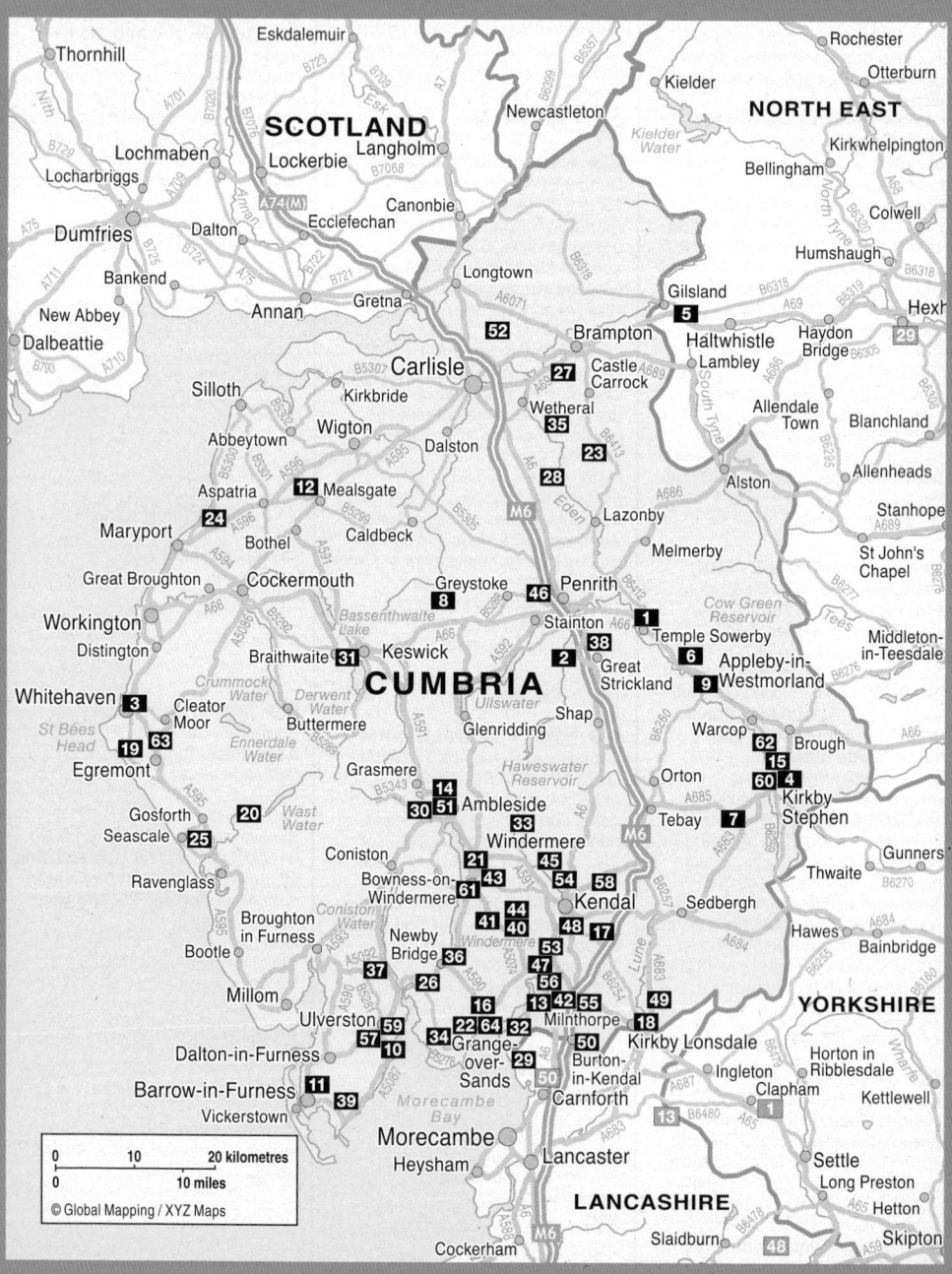

© Global Mapping / XYZ Maps

0   10   20 kilometres
0   10 miles

Cumbria

Venture into Daniel Defoe's "...County eminent only for being the wildest, most barren and frightful of any that I have passed over in England, or even in Wales itself..." and be amazed by the gardens and horticultural excellence that Cumbria can offer.

From Rydal Hall's 17C Picturesque Viewing Room, through the 19C planting of Dora's Field (Wordsworth's remembrance of his dead daughter) and the founding of the British Pteridological Society, to the 21C gardens created by Chelsea Gold Medal winners – for more than 300 years Cumberland and Westmorland (now Cumbria) have provided England with gardens and scenery second to none.

Considered by the knowledgeable to be worth the journey over 300 years ago, it is still a county to visit for gardens that encompass all gardening traditions. From real cottage gardens providing produce for the family to the set piece gardens of the great estates – all can be found in the far north west of England.

Cumbria Volunteers

County Organiser
Diane Hewitt
01539 446238
dhewitt.kinsman@gmail.com

County Treasurer
Derek Farman
01539 444893
derek@derejam.myzen.co.uk

Publicity –
Publications & Special Interest
Carole Berryman
01539 443649
Carole.Berryman@student.sac.ac.uk

Publicity – Social Media
Gráinne Jakobson
01946 813017
gmjakobson22@gmail.com

Booklet Co-ordinator
Diane Hewitt
(as above)

Assistant County Organisers

Central
Carole Berryman
(as above)

East
Sue Sharkey
07811 710248
bsjsewebank@btinternet.com

North
Alannah Rylands
01697 320413
alannah.rylands@me.com

North East
Cate Bowman
01228 573903
catebowman@icloud.com

Grace Kirby
01228 670076
gracekirby@gmail.com

South East
Linda & Alec Greening
01524 781624
lindagreening48@gmail.com

West
Gráinne Jakobson
(as above)

Left: Low Blakebank

Opening Dates

All entries subject to change.
For latest information check www.ngs.org.uk
Extended openings are shown at the begining of the month

February

Snowdrop Festival

57 Swarthmoor Hall (daily from Feb 22)
Sunday 21
55 Summerdale House

March

55 Summerdale House (every Friday & Saturday)
57 Swarthmoor Hall (daily 1 to 13 Mar)
Sunday 20
1 Acorn Bank

---

2 Askham Hall
14 Dora's Field
30 High Close Estate
31 High Moss
33 Holehird Gardens
51 Rydal Hall
Thursday 24
26 Haverthwaite Lodge
36 Lakeside Hotel & Rocky Bank

April

55 Summerdale House (every Friday & Saturday)
Sunday 10
19 NEW Fern Bank
Saturday 16
10 Conishead Priory & Buddhist Temple
Sunday 17
10 Conishead Priory & Buddhist Temple
Sunday 24
47 Orchard Cottage

May

55 Summerdale House (every Friday & Saturday)

Sunday 1
61 Windy Hall
Friday 6
8 Chapelside
Saturday 7
8 Chapelside
21 Gatesbield
Sunday 8
8 Chapelside
13 Dallam Tower
41 Low Fell West
Thursday 12
51 Rydal Hall
Saturday 21
1 Acorn Bank
37 Langholme Mill
42 Lower Rowell Farm & Cottage
Sunday 22
18 Fell Yeat
24 NEW Grow West
37 Langholme Mill
42 Lower Rowell Farm & Cottage
43 Matson Ground
Wednesday 25
38 Larch Cottage Nurseries
Friday 27
8 Chapelside

Saturday 28
8 Chapelside
Sunday 29
8 Chapelside
47 Orchard Cottage

June

55 Summerdale House (every Friday & Saturday)

Festival Weekend

Saturday 4
20 Galesyke
28 Hazel Cottage
Sunday 5
12 Crookdake Farm
20 Galesyke
28 Hazel Cottage
45 NEW Mirefoot
48 8 Oxenholme Road
61 Windy Hall
64 Yewbarrow House
Saturday 11
32 NEW Highlands
Sunday 12
2 Askham Hall
29 Hazelwood Farm
32 NEW Highlands
Tuesday 14
46 Newton Rigg College Gardens
Wednesday 15
9 Church View
Thursday 16
51 Rydal Hall
Friday 17
8 Chapelside
Saturday 18
7 The Chantry
8 Chapelside
Sunday 19
7 The Chantry
8 Chapelside
39 Leece & Dendron Village Gardens
54 Sprint Mill
55 Summerdale House
Thursday 23
26 Haverthwaite Lodge
36 Lakeside Hotel & Rocky Bank
Saturday 25
1 Acorn Bank
Sunday 26
4 Boxwood House
17 Ewebank Farm
35 Ivy House
40 Low Blakebank
44 Middle Blakebank
59 Ulverston Gardens

Braeside

© Linda Greening

July

55 **Summerdale House** (every Friday & Saturday)

Saturday 2
28 Hazel Cottage

Sunday 3
5 Braeside
6 NEW Broom Cottage
15 NEW Eden Place
22 NEW Grange Fell Allotments
27 Hayton Village Gardens
49 Park House
64 Yewbarrow House

Thursday 7
51 Rydal Hall

Friday 8
8 Chapelside

Saturday 9
8 Chapelside

Sunday 10
8 Chapelside
52 NEW Sandhouse

Thursday 14
33 Holehird Gardens

Sunday 17
58 Tenter End Barn
60 Westview

Wednesday 20
9 Church View

Sunday 24
11 NEW 6 & 8 Conyers Avenue

47 Orchard Cottage
62 Winton Park
63 Woodend House

Sunday 31
4 Boxwood House
23 Greenfield House

August

Sunday 7
18 Fell Yeat
64 Yewbarrow House

Sunday 14
3 Berriedale

Wednesday 17
9 Church View

Sunday 21
49 Park House

Thursday 25
26 Haverthwaite Lodge
34 Holker Hall Gardens
36 Lakeside Hotel & Rocky Bank

September

Saturday 3
7 The Chantry
53 Sizergh Castle

Sunday 4
7 The Chantry
41 Low Fell West
64 Yewbarrow House

Sunday 18
2 Askham Hall

Wednesday 21
9 Church View

October

Sunday 9
38 Larch Cottage Nurseries

Wednesday 12
46 Newton Rigg College Gardens

Wednesday 19
9 Church View

February 2017

Sunday 19
55 Summerdale House

Gardens open to the public

1 Acorn Bank
10 Conishead Priory & Buddhist Temple
14 Dora's Field
30 High Close Estate
33 Holehird Gardens
34 Holker Hall Gardens
51 Rydal Hall
53 Sizergh Castle
57 Swarthmoor Hall

By arrangement only

16 Eller How House
25 Hall Senna
50 Pear Tree Cottage
56 Sunnyside

Also open by arrangement

3 Berriedale
4 Boxwood House
5 Braeside
8 Chapelside
9 Church View
12 Crookdake Farm
18 Fell Yeat
22 NEW Grange Fell Allotments
26 Haverthwaite Lodge
27 Kinrara, Hayton Village Gardens
29 Hazelwood Farm
31 High Moss
32 NEW Highlands
36 Lakeside Hotel & Rocky Bank
37 Langholme Mill
41 Low Fell West
42 Lower Rowell Farm & Cottage
43 Matson Ground
44 Middle Blakebank
46 Newton Rigg College Gardens
47 Orchard Cottage
48 8 Oxenholme Road
49 Park House
54 Sprint Mill
58 Tenter End Barn
59 Wreay, Ulverston Gardens
61 Windy Hall
63 Woodend House
64 Yewbarrow House

The Gardens

1 ◆ **ACORN BANK**
Temple Sowerby CA10 1SP.
National Trust, 017683 61893,
acornbank@nationaltrust.org.uk,
www.nationaltrust.org.uk. 6m E of
Penrith. Off A66; ½ m N of Temple
Sowerby. Bus: Penrith-Appleby or
Carlisle-Darlington; alight Culgaith Rd
end. **For NGS: Sun 20 Mar, Sat 21
May, Sat 25 June (10-5). Adm
£6.75, chd £3.35. Tearoom offering
light lunches and a selection of
scones and cakes. For other
opening times and information,
please phone, email or visit garden
website.**
Sheltered and tranquil, walled
gardens contain a herb garden with
more than 250 medicinal and culinary
plants. Traditional apple orchards and
mixed borders. Beyond the walls lie
woodland walks with a wonderful

display of snowdrops, daffodils and
wild flowers in spring. Dogs welcome
on leads on woodland walks. 20
March, NGS Cumbria 'Wordsworth's
Daffodil Legacy'. 21 May and 25
June, herb garden tours with the
Gardener, 11am and 2pm, numbers
limited, additional charge. Walled
gardens accessible with grass and
firm gravel paths, woodland paths
have steep gradients and some
steps. Access map and information
available.
♿ ⚘ ☕

Beautiful views of
the Pennines and
surrounded by
pastures. A haven
for birds. . .

2 ◆ **ASKHAM HALL**
Askham, Penrith CA10 2PF.
Countess of Lonsdale,
01931 712350,
enquiries@askhamhall.co.uk,
www.askhamhall.co.uk. 5m S of
Penrith. Turn off A6 for Lowther &
Askham. **Sun 20 Mar, Sun 12 June,
Sun 18 Sept (11-4). Adm £4, chd
free. Light refreshments.** Donation
to Askham and Lowther Churches.
Askham Hall is a Pele Tower
incorporating C14, C16 and early
C18 elements in a courtyard plan.
Recently opened with luxury
accommodation, a restaurant, spa
and wedding barn. Splendid formal
garden with terraces of herbaceous
borders and topiary, dating back to
C17. Meadow area with trees and
pond, kitchen gardens and animal
trails. Combined with Summer Fair
in June.
⚘ 🚗 🛏 ☕

3 BERRIEDALE
15 Loop Road South, Whitehaven CA28 7TN. Enid & John Stanborough, 01946 695467. *From S, A595 through T-lights onto Loop Rd approx 150yds on R. From N, A595 onto Loop Rd at Pelican Garage, garden approx 1¹/₂ m on L. Whitehaven rail stn 20 mins brisk walk, mainly up hill.* Sun 14 Aug (2-5). Adm £3.50, chd free. Light refreshments. Visits also by arrangement May to Dec.
Suburban garden, surprisingly large with different areas and levels. Incl large vegetable plot (with award winning onions and leeks), pond, Japanese inspired border and many seating areas around the garden. Children love the fairy dell and mini trail. The owners raise over 1000 bedding plants which give riotous colour around the garden in mid to late summer. John shows fuchsias and has many for sale. Partial wheelchair access to most of flower garden. Vegetable garden can be accessed by separate entrance with prior notice.

♿ 🎭 ❀ 🚐 ☕

In 2015 Macmillan celebrated 30 years of partnership with the NGS

4 BOXWOOD HOUSE
Hartley, Kirkby Stephen CA17 4JH. Colin & Joyce Dirom, 01768 371306, boxwoodhouse@hotmail.co.uk. *In the centre of Hartley approx 1m from Kirkby Stephen. Exit M6 J38. Follow A685, R in Kirkby Stephen for Hartley. From A66 exit at Brough onto A685, 1st L in Kirkby St for Hartley. Kirkby Stephen Station approx. 2m. KS on Coast to Coast Walk.* Sun 26 June, Sun 31 July (11-5). Adm £3.50, chd free. Home-made teas. Visits also by arrangement June to Aug for groups of 10-30. Homemade teas incl adm.

A peaceful natural garden. Packed herbaceous borders, shrubberies, herb, hosta and heuchera beds plus the tranquil pond are all designed to be wildlife friendly. The summer house provides one of the many seating areas around the garden overlooking a productive vegetable plot and fruit trees, whilst a meadow walk leads to a stunning view of the whole garden and the fenced off chicken area. Featured in Cumberland and Westmorland garden supplement and Cumbria Life magazine.

🎭 ❀ ☕

5 BRAESIDE
Bank Top, Greenhead in Northumberland, Brampton CA8 7HA. Mrs Shelagh Potts, 016977 47443, smpotts@ymail.com. *18m E of Carlisle on A69, 18m W of Hexham, 3m W of Haltwhistle. Turn off A69 to Greenhead & Hadrian's Wall. At T-junction turn L. Go up hill thro 'No Through road' sign 400 metres. Braeside at top of hill.* Sun 3 July (1-4.30). Adm £3.50, chd free. Home-made teas. Visits also by arrangement June & July 30 max.
Cottage -style garden approx ¹/₄ acre with wonderful views towards Hadrian's Wall. Roman Army Museum and Walltown Crag minutes away. Wide Herbaceous borders with interesting and varied plants - hostas, primulas, meconopsis, grasses and ferns. Small stumpery, wild flower area, bog garden. Not suitable for wheelchairs.

❀ 🚐 🛏 ☕

6 NEW BROOM COTTAGE
Long Marton, Appleby-In-Westmorland CA16 6JP. Mr & Mrs Peter & Janet Cox, 017683 62896, peter_janet_cox@hotmail.com. *From A66 1m E of Kirkby Thore, take turn signed Long Marton. From Appleby, follow signs to Long Marton (2m), L at church. Car park at Nursery. Short walk to house with 3 disabled spaces.* Sun 3 July (2-5.30). Adm £3.50, chd free. Home-made teas.
Peaceful 2 acre wildlife garden set around C18 former farmhouse. Wildlife pond with ducks and moorhens, stream, wild copse and wildflower hay meadow with mown paths. Beautiful views of the Pennines and surrounded by pastures. A haven for birds. Large productive organic fruit and vegetable garden. Bee friendly walled herb garden, shrub

and cottage garden borders. Surfaces include tarmac, slate chippings and mown grass which may be wheelchair accessible. An area of pebbles in the walled herb garden is not.

♿ 🛏 ☕

7 THE CHANTRY
Ravenstonedale, Kirkby Stephen CA17 4NQ. Joan & John Houston. *8m E J38 M6 (Tebay), 4m W Kirkby Stephen. From A685, follow signs for Ravenstonedale, into village.* Sat 18, Sun 19 June, Sat 3, Sun 4 Sept (11-5). Adm £3.50, chd free. Home-made teas.
Set around a Victorian house, with panoramic views of the Howgill Fells (= very exposed windy site). Mostly newly established, by trial and error rather than experience. Formal areas around house contrast with informal areas, including a large wildlife pond. Various seating areas and features using reclaimed materials. Still very much 'work in progress' - 2016 plans include a new bog garden.

☕

8 CHAPELSIDE
Mungrisdale, Penrith CA11 0XR. Tricia & Robin Acland, 017687 79672. *12m W of Penrith. On A66 take minor rd N signed Mungrisdale. After 2m, sharp bends, garden on L immed after tiny church on R. Park at foot of our short drive. On C2C Reivers 71, 10 cycle routes.* Fri 6, Sat 7, Sun 8, Fri 27, Sat 28, Sun 29 May, Fri 17, Sat 18, Sun 19 June, Fri 8, Sat 9, Sun 10 July (1-5). Adm £3, chd free. Visits also by arrangement. Refreshments for groups by arrangement.
1-acre organic windy garden below fell, around C18 farmhouse and outbuildings, latter mainly open. Fine views. Tiny stream, large pond. Alpine, herbaceous, raised, gravel, damp and shade beds, bulbs in grass. Extensive range of plants, many unusual. Relaxed planting regime. Art constructions in and out, local stone used creatively. Featured in Homes and Gardens.

🎭 ❀

9 CHURCH VIEW
Bongate, Appleby-in-Westmorland CA16 6UN. Mrs H Holmes, 017683 51397, helen@holmes21.plus.com, www.engcougars.co.uk/church-view. *0.4m S of Appleby town centre. A66 N take B6542 for 2m St Michael's Church on L garden opp.*

A66 S take B6542 & continue to Royal Oak Inn, garden next door, opp church. **Wed 15 June, 20 July, 17 Aug, 21 Sept, 19 Oct (12-4). Adm £3.50, chd free. Visits also by arrangement Apr to Nov.**
A modern cottage garden with coherent layers of colour, texture and interest. From spring bulbs, through the lushness of summer roses and herbaceous plants galore, to the inherent richness of late perennials and graceful grasses well into late autumn. Plants occupy every inch of this garden for all seasons! Also vegetables in a raised bed system. Approx ²/₃ acre. Featured in Garden Answers. Partial wheelchair, main garden is on a sloping site with gravel paths.

10 ◆ CONISHEAD PRIORY & BUDDHIST TEMPLE
Ulverston LA12 9QQ. Manjushri Kadampa Meditation Centre, 01229 584029 Ext 234, visits@manjushri.com, www.manjushri.org. *2m S of Ulverston. 30 mins from M6 J36, follow A590 to Ulverston then S onto A5087 Coast Rd signed Croftlands, Bardsea & 'Coastal route to Barrow'. Rail 2 m, Bus 11, NCR 700.* **For NGS: Sat 16, Sun 17 Apr (11-5). Adm £3.60, chd free. Light refreshments. For other opening times and information, please phone, email or visit garden website.**
70 acres of gardens and woodland surrounding Temple and Romantic Gothic mansion. Temple garden an oasis of peace, wildlife and cottage gardens, arboretum. FREE map with short woodland walks to beach on Morecambe Bay. FREE simple 15 minute Guided Meditations. FREE guided tours of Temple and part of the mansion. Cafe and gift shop. Ramps to historic house and Temple.

11 NEW 6 & 8 CONYERS AVENUE
Barrow-In-Furness LA14 4JT. Kath McGrogan & Ian Mckenzie. *M6, J36, A590 to Barrow in Furness. Off Dalton Lane turn S on Dane Ave then E on Yealand Drive. Rail 1¹/₂ m, Bus 1, 6, x6, NCR 70.* **Sun 24 July (10-5). Combined adm £3, chd free. Tea.**
Two typically English gardens that have individual characters, No 6 having emphasis on structure and form with tightly clipped evergreens

and box Topiary. An elevated patio overlooks lawns and a formal pool with some statuary. No 8 greets you with two large herbaceous borders filled with a variety of perennials and old fashioned scented roses, the long borders are divided by a formal lawn. No 8 has a real ale Nano-brewery using some home-grown hops. Wheelchair access to patio areas only.

12 CROOKDAKE FARM
Aspatria, Wigton CA7 3SH. Kirk & Alannah Rylands, 016973 20413, alannah.rylands@me.com. *3m NE of Aspatria. Between A595 & A596. From A595 take B5299 at Mealsgate signed Aspatria. After 2m turn sharp R in Watch Hill signed Crookdake. House 1m on L.* **Sun 5 June (1-5). Adm £3.50, chd free. Home-made teas. Visits also by arrangement June & July 10+ Refreshments by arrangement.**
Windswept informal farmhouse (not open) garden with a careful colour combination of planting sympathetic to the landscape incl various different areas with densely planted herbaceous borders, vegetable patch, wild meadow and large pond area home to moisture-loving plants, tame hens and wild moorhens. Opening supported by old vehicle enthusiasts. All types of old vehicles encouraged to attend.

13 DALLAM TOWER
Milnthorpe LA7 7AG. Mr & Mrs R T Villiers-Smith. *7m S of Kendal. 7m N of Carnforth. Nr J36 off M6. A6 & B5282. Stn: Arnside, 4m; Lancaster, 15m.* **Sun 8 May (2-5). Adm £3.50, chd free. Cream teas.**
Large garden; natural rock garden, water garden; wood walks, lawns, shrubs. C19 cast iron orangery. Limited wheelchair access Deep gravel paths.

14 ◆ DORA'S FIELD
Rydal, Ambleside LA22 9LX. National Trust, www.nationaltrust.org.uk. *1¹/₂ m N of Ambleside. Follow A591 from Ambleside to Rydal. Dora's Field is next to St Mary's Church.* **For NGS: Sun 20 Mar (11-4). Adm by donation. Also open High Close Estate. For other opening times and information, please visit garden website.**

Named for Dora, the daughter of the poet William Wordsworth. Wordsworth planned to build a house on the land but, after her early death, he planted the area with daffodils in her memory. Now known as Dora's Field the area is renowned for its spring display of daffodils and Bluebells. 20th March; Wordsworth's Daffodil Legacy.

> Part of the garden is made over to aviaries with exotic birds, some are free - flying . . .

15 NEW EDEN PLACE
Kirkby Stephen CA17 4AP. J S Parrot Trust. *¹/₂ m N of Kirkby Stephen. A685 Kirkby Stephen to Brough.* **Sun 3 July (1-5). Adm £3.50, chd free. Home-made teas.**
3 acre garden with many large perennial borders and island beds enclosed by tall hedges. Part of the garden is made over to aviaries with exotic birds, some are free - flying. Also a lake and a woodland walk. Free-flying parrots.

16 ELLER HOW HOUSE
Lindale, Grange-Over-Sands LA11 6NA. John & Helen Churchill, 015395 32479, ellerhowhouse@hotmail.co.uk. *Off A590 above Lindale. E of the A590 on Lindale by-pass. Gateposts with large pieces limestone & avenue of trees. Rail 2.2m, Bus 530, 532, X6 NCR 70. Can send detailed directions by email.* **Visits by arrangement Jan to Oct groups 2 - 12. Adm £3.50, chd free.**
A romantic Regency house and grounds with 12 acres of steep fellside garden, designed by the architect George Webster as his family home. Wild daffodils abound in the woods and on the hillside. Eleven acres of Repton style landscaped woodland with meandering pathways, a lake with bridge and cascade, ruined folly, reposoir, sea view and rocky outcrops. Snowdrops from mid February. Daffodils from mid March. Bluebells from mid April. Autumn colours during October.

© Val Corbett

Winton Park

17 ▶ EWEBANK FARM

Old Hutton, Kendal LA8 0NS. Sue & Barry Sharkey. *3m NE of Kendal. Oxenholme Stn - B6254 - Old Hutton. 3rd turning on L. R turns at next 2 junctions. M6 take J37 A684 Sedbergh. 1st R & R again. After 3m turn L. Ewebank. From Oxenholme Station, bikes take (70)68.* **Sun 26 June (1-5). Adm £3.50, chd free. Tea.**

Relaxing, rural, flower arrangers garden, friendly hens and suggestions of music. Large lawn sloping down to a stream where curved decking follows the gentle contours of the land. Planting mostly formal with areas of shade for ferns, other moisture-loving plants and over 50 different hostas. Mixed borders, statues, topiary, orchard and espaliered apples. Visitors from an Owl Sanctuary.

18 ▶ FELL YEAT

Casterton, Kirkby Lonsdale LA6 2JW. Mrs A E Benson, 01524 271340. *1m E of Casterton Village. On the rd to Bull Pot. Leave A65 at Devils Bridge, follow A683 for 1m, take the R fork to High Casterton at golf course, straight across at two sets of Xrds, house on L, 1/4 m from no-through-rd sign.* **Sun 22 May, Sun 7 Aug (1-5). Adm £4, chd free. Home-made teas. Visits also by arrangement May to Aug groups up to 30. No coaches. Refreshments by arrangement.**

1-acre country garden with mixed planting, incl unusual trees, shrubs and some topiary. Small woodland garden and woodland glades. 2 ponds which encourage dragonflies.

Several arbours where you can sit and relax. New paved topiary garden. Many ferns in a designated area; old roses in mixed borders and a large collection of hydrangeas. A garden to explore. Metal sculptures in various areas. Adjoining nursery specialising in ferns, hostas, hydrangeas and many unusual plants. Slight rises between different areas.

19 ▶ NEW ▶ FERN BANK

High House Road, St. Bees CA27 0BZ. Chris & Charm Robson. *At the edge of the village going out towards A595. 2m from A 595 down the road signed St Bees (unsuitable for caravans & HGVs). Rail station in St Bees Village 20 mins walk.* **Sun 10 Apr (12-5). Adm £3.50, chd free. Home-made teas.**

Located in St Bees village this is a spring garden on different levels with natural planting. Nearest the house lawns and borders lead down to the 'secret' garden via a pergola clad with roses, wisteria and clematis. Hidden away are 5 ponds surrounded by trees and boardwalks. This wild area is a haven for wildlife and early in the year snowdrops, leucojum and then daffodils light up this area. The entrance level where teas are served is wheelchair accessible but because of the steep slopes the rest of the garden is not accessible.

20 ▶ GALESYKE

Wasdale CA20 1ET. Christine & Mike McKinley. *From Gosforth, follow signs to Nether Wasdale and then to Lake, approx 5m From Santon Bridge follow signs to*

Wasdale then to Lake, approx 2 1/4 m. **Sat 4, Sun 5 June (10.30-5). Adm £3, chd free. Cream teas.**
Partially landscaped garden of several acres on banks of R Irt with views of Wasdale Fells, noted for its display of rhododendrons and azaleas with planting on both sides of the river.

21 ▶ GATESBIELD

New Road, Windermere LA23 2LA. Gatesbield Quaker Housing Assoc, www.gatesbield.org.uk. *Windermere. From village take New Rd S (direction Bowness). Gatesbield is on W shortly after the Ellerthwaite Hotel. Rail 1/2 m, Bus599, NCR 6.* **Sat 7 May (2-5). Adm £3.50, chd free. Home-made teas.**

Explore the rocky dells and paths of these gardens which include some of the Rothschild collection of rhododendrons, also camellias and azaleas and many specimen trees. Gatesbield, now sheltered housing, was the home of Stanley Davies, distinguished furniture maker, and his wife, Emily. Refreshments served in Arts and Crafts House, where you can view the Stanley Davies exhibition. Some gravel paths and steep slopes. Level access to Gatesbield House.

ALLOTMENTS

22 ▶ NEW ▶ GRANGE FELL ALLOTMENTS

Fell Road, Grange-Over-Sands LA11 6HB. Mr Bruno Gouillon, 01539 532317, brunog45@hotmail.com. *Opposite Grange Fell Golf Club. Rail 1.3 m, Bus 1m X6, NCR 70.* **Sun 3 July (11-5). Adm £3, chd free. Tea. Visits also by arrangement May to Sept groups no more than 30.**

The allotments are managed by Grange Town Council. Opened in 2010, 30 plots are now rented out and offer a wide selection of gardening styles and techniques. The majority of plots grow a mixture of vegetables, fruit trees and flowers. There are a few communal areas where local fruit tree varieties have been donated by plot holders with herbaceous borders and annuals. Featured on Grange Now Bay Radio.

23 GREENFIELD HOUSE

Newbiggin, nr Cumrew, Brampton CA8 9DH. Emma & Chris Gray. *8m S of Brampton. Located between the villages of Cumrew & Croglin off B6413. Armathwaite train station, Leeds/Settle line, 5.2m.* Sun 31 July (1-5). Adm £3.50, chd free. Home-made teas.

A village garden set on the edge of the Pennines comprising of a series of garden rooms and lawn areas divided by beech and yew hedges. Contained within are richly planted shrub and herbaceous borders in colour themed planting schemes, roses, a box parterre, an orchard area with espalier apple trees and a productive vegetable garden. Approx 1 acre of gardens and grounds. The garden is mainly level, however there are some steps which make smaller parts of the garden inaccessible by wheelchair.

24 NEW GROW WEST

Allerby, Aspatria, Wigton CA7 2NL. Mrs Angela Vaughan, 01900 815 003, angela.vaughan@westhouse.org.uk, www.westhouse.org.uk/grow-west/. *Between Aspatria & Maryport. On A596 from Maryport, Sign posted as 'Community Gardens' from turn L off A596 & follow rd through village.* Sun 22 May (11-5). Adm by donation. Home-made teas.

Set in 13 acre grounds, the garden comprises of a large glass house, three large polytunnels and a net tunnel filled with fruit, vegetables and plants, 50 hens and soft fruit bushes. Our wild meadow contains one natural and two man-made ponds, filled with wildlife. Grow West is an exciting social enterprise initiative to provide work, training and skills to adults with learning disabilities. Local press coverage of the achievements of many of our students who obtained awards in woodwork! All is accessible by wheelchair apart from the Wild Meadow.

25 HALL SENNA

Hallsenna, Gosforth, Holmrook CA19 1YB. Chris & Helen Steele, 01946 725436, helen.steele5@btinternet.com. *2m SW of Gosforth. Follow main A595 either N or S. 1m S of Gosforth turn down lane opp Seven Acres Caravan Park, proceed for approx 1m.* Visits by arrangement May to Sept,

access via bridleway, no coaches. Adm £8, chd free. Home-made teas by prior arrangement.

Tucked away within the hamlet of Hallsenna close to the West Cumbrian coast this garden provides the visitor with many different aspects of gardening. The 1.3 acre site includes borders fully planted for year round colour and many delightful structures built to provide interest, and punctuate your journey through the garden. teas can be provided by prior arrangement. Partial wheelchair access due to steep slopes on entry into the garden.

26 HAVERTHWAITE LODGE

Haverthwaite LA12 8AJ. David Snowdon, 015395 39841, sheena.taylforth@lakesidehotel.co.uk. *100yds off A590 at Haverthwaite. Turn S off A590 opp Haverthwaite railway stn. Bus 6, NCR 70.* Thur 24 Mar, Thur 23 June, Thur 25 Aug (11-4). Single adm £3. Combined adm with Lakeside Hotel & Rocky Bank £6, chd free. Light refreshments at Lakeside Hotel. Visits also by arrangement Mar to Sept.

Traditional Lake District garden that has been redesigned and replanted. A wonderful display of hellebores and spring flowers. Gardens on a series of terraces leading down to the R Leven and incl: rose garden, cutting garden, dell area, rock terrace, herbaceous borders and many interesting mature shrubs. In a stunning setting the garden is surrounded by oak woodland and was once a place of C18 and C19 industry. Refreshments 20% discount from Hotel Conservatory Menu on the Open Day.

GROUP OPENING

27 HAYTON VILLAGE GARDENS

Hayton, Brampton CA8 9HR. *7m E of Carlisle. 5m east of M6 J43. ½ m S of A69, 3m east of Brampton signed to Hayton. Maps of gardens with tickets, Park on one side of road only please.* Sun 3 July (12-5). Combined adm £4, chd free. Home-made teas at Hayton Village Primary School. Usually Pimms (non alcoholic equivalent) too, by an outside fireplace under a honeysuckle laden pergola & Cava in the Conservatory at

Millbrook! *Donation to Hayton Village Primary School.*

BRACKENHOW
Susan & Jonny Tranter

THE CEDARS
Mrs Lynda Hayward

HAYTON C OF E PRIMARY SCHOOL
Hayton C of E Primary School

HOPE COTTAGE
Jonathan & Gail Cruse

KINRARA
Tim & Alison Brown
Visits also by arrangement Apr to Oct, teas may be possible for pre-arranged visits.
tim@tjbgallery.com
01228 670067 (Ashton Design)

LITTLE GARTH
Dugald Campbell

MILLBROOK
Emily & Angus Dawson

Easily accessible attractive village with a green growing one of the oldest walnut trees in the country, church and Inn (weekend meals and WCs). Not far from Hadrian's Wall, Talkin Tarn, N. Pennine fells, Eden Valley and small market town of Brampton with particular attractions such as a Philip Webb church (Burne Jones stained glass). Gardens of varied size and styles all within ½ m, mostly of old stone cottages. Smaller and larger cottage gardens, courtyards and containers, steep wooded slopes, sweeping lawns, exuberant borders, frogs, pools and poultry, colour and texture throughout. Homemade Teas at the school. Pimms in the Pergola by the fire and Cava in the Conservatory. Often an informal treasure hunt for children young and old. Gardens additional to those listed also generally open (eleven in 2015) and views into numerous others of very high standard. Varying degrees of access from full to minimal.

'secret' garden via a pergola clad with roses, wisteria and clematis . . .

28 HAZEL COTTAGE

Armathwaite CA4 9PG.
Mr D Ryland & Mr J Thexton,
david@dryland73.orangehome.
co.uk. *8m SE of Carlisle. Turn off A6
just S of High Hesket signed
Armathwaite, after 2m house facing
you at T-junction 1¼ m walk from
Armathwaite railway station.* **Sat 4,
Sun 5 June, Sat 2 July (12-5). Adm
£3.50, chd free. Home-made teas.**
Developing flower arrangers and
plantsmans garden. Extending to
approx 5 acres. Incls mature
herbaceous borders, pergola, ponds
and planting of disused railway siding
providing home to wildlife. Many
variegated and unusual plants. Varied
areas, planted for all seasons,
S-facing, some gentle slopes.

29 HAZELWOOD FARM

Hollins Lane, Silverdale, Carnforth
LA5 0UB. Glenn & Dan Shapiro,
01524 701276,
glenn@hazelwoodfarm.co.uk,
www.hazelwoodfarm.co.uk. *4m NW
of M6 J35. From Carnforth follow
signs to Silverdale, after 1m turn L
signed Silverdale, after level Xing turn
L then 1st L into Hollins Lane. Farm
on R.* **Sun 12 June (11-5). Adm £4,
chd free. Home-made teas. Visits
also by arrangement in June
groups of 20+.**
A theatre of light curtained by
backdrops of woodland. Steep paths
winding up and through natural
limestone cliff, intersected by a
tumbling rill joining ponds, provide
staging for alpine gems and drifts of
herbaceous, prairie and woodland
planting. Old and English roses, bulbs
and the National Collection of
Hepatica. Wildlife friendly garden
surrounded by NT access land. New
bird, bee and butterfly garden, rock
garden, Hepatica collection, well-
stocked plant sale. Featured on
'Gardeners' World' and in Gardeners'
World Magazine and Plant Heritage
journal. Partial wheelchair access -
lower level only.

30 ◆ HIGH CLOSE ESTATE

Loughrigg, Ambleside LA22 9HH.
National Trust, 015394 37623,
neil.winder@nationaltrust.org.uk.
*10 min NW from Ambleside.
Ambleside (A593) to Skelwith Bridge
signed for High Close, turn R & head
up hill until you see a white painted
stone sign to 'Langdale', turn L, High
Close on L.* **For NGS: Sun 20 Mar**
(11-4). Adm by donation. Also
open Dora's Field. Small cafe in
house part of the YHA. For other
opening times and information,
please phone or email.
Originally planted in 1866 by Edward
Wheatley-Balme, High Close was
designed in the fashion of the day
using many of the recently discovered
'exotic' conifers and evergreen
shrubs coming into Britain from
America. Today the garden contains a
variety of tree species many of which
are the remains of the original
Victorian plantings. Tree trail.

Secluded and
secret areas.
Courtyard garden
with water
feature . . .

31 ▶ HIGH MOSS

Portinscale, Keswick CA12 5TX.
Christine & Peter Hughes,
christine_hug25@hotmail.com. *1m
W of Keswick. Enter village off A66,
take 1st turning R through white
gates, on R of rd after ⅓ m.* **Sun 20
Mar (2-5). Adm £5, chd free. Visits
also by arrangement Apr to Oct,
Thursday only.** *Donation to
Hospice at Home.*
Lakeland Arts and Craft house (not
open) and garden (mentioned in
Pevsner). 4½ acres of formal and
informal S-facing terraced gardens.
Magnificent views of the fells. Many
fine trees and shrubs, rhododendrons
and azaleas. Spring meadow planted
with daffodils and camassia. Old
tennis court converted into
vegetable/flower parterre for the
Diamond Jubilee with rose garden
and sun dial by Joe Smith. Open as
part of Cumbria Daffodil Day. The
garden is not suitable for wheelchair
users because of the sloping ground
and steps.

32 NEW HIGHLANDS

High Knott Road, Arnside,
Carnforth LA5 0AW. Judith &
Stephen Slater, 015247 61535,
slaterhighlands@btinternet.com.
*12m J35 & J36 M6. M6. From A6
MilnthorpeT-lights take B5282 to
Arnside. Follow signs in village.* **Sat
11, Sun 12 June (10.30-5). Adm £4,
chd free. Home-made teas. Visits
also by arrangement May to Sept
for groups of 10+.**
1½ acre gently terraced garden
including 2 types of rockery. Well-
stocked herbaceous borders leading
to a tranquil woodland garden.
Raised vegetable beds and orchard
with mistletoe. Secluded and secret
areas. Courtyard garden with water
feature and beech tunnel exit.
Extensive hosta collection. Steps or
steep incline to rear garden.

33 ◆ HOLEHIRD GARDENS

Patterdale Road, Windermere
LA23 1NP. Lakeland Horticultural
Society, 015394 46008,
pr@holehirdgardens.org.uk,
www.holehirdgardens.org.uk.
*1m N of Windermere. On A592,
Windermere to Patterdale rd.* **For
NGS: Sun 20 Mar, Thur 14 July
(10-5). Adm £4, chd free. Self-
service hot drinks available. For
other opening times and
information, please phone, email or
visit garden website.**
Run by volunteers with the aim of
promoting knowledge of the
cultivation of plants particularly suited
to Lakeland conditions. One of the
best labelled gardens in the UK.
National Collections of *astilbe,
daboecia, polystichum* (ferns) and
meconopsis. Set on the fellside with
stunning views over Windermere. The
walled garden gives protection to
mixed borders whilst alpine houses
display an always colourful array of
tiny gems. Wheelchair access limited
to walled garden and beds accessible
from drive.

34 ◆ HOLKER HALL GARDENS

Cark-in-Cartmel, Grange-over-
Sands LA11 7PL. The Cavendish
Family, 015395 58328,
info@holker.co.uk,
www.holker.co.uk. *4m W of Grange-
over-Sands. 12m W of M6 (J36)
Follow brown tourist signs. Rail 1m,
NCR 700 ½ m.* **For NGS: Thur 25
Aug (11-5). Adm £8, chd free.
Light refreshments. For other
opening times and information,
please phone, email or visit garden
website.**
25 acres of romantic gardens, with
peaceful arboretum, inspirational
formal gardens, flowering meadow
and Labyrinth. Summer brings
voluptuous mixed borders and

bedding. Discover unusually large rhododendrons, magnolias and azaleas, and the National Collection of Styracaceae. Discover our latest garden feature - The Pagan Grove, designed by Kim Wilkie. Guided tour of the gardens with our experienced guide. Donation required.

 NPC

35 IVY HOUSE

Cumwhitton, Brampton CA8 9EX. **Martin Johns & Ian Forrest.** *6m E of Carlisle. At the bridge at Warwick Bridge on A69 take turning to Great Corby & Cumwhitton. Through Great Corby & woodland until you reach a T-junction Turn R.* **Sun 26 June (1-5). Adm £3.50, chd free. Home-made teas in Cumwhitton village hall.** Approx 2 acres of sloping fell-side garden with meandering paths leading to a series of 'rooms': pond, fern garden, gravel garden with assorted grasses, vegetable and herb garden. Copse with meadow leading down to beck. Trees, shrubs, bamboos and herbaceous perennials planted with emphasis on variety of texture and colour. Featured in Cumbria Life. Steep slopes.

36 LAKESIDE HOTEL & ROCKY BANK

Lake Windermere, Newby Bridge, Ulverston LA12 8AT. Mr N Talbot, 015395 39841, sheena.taylforth@lakesidehotel.co.uk, www.lakesidehotel.co.uk. *1m N of Newby Bridge. Turn N off A590 across R Leven at Newby Bridge along W side of Windermere.* **Thur 24 Mar, Thur 23 June, Thur 25 Aug (11-4). Single adm £5. Combined adm with Haverthwaite Lodge £6, chd free. Light refreshments. Visits also by arrangement Mar to Sept.** Two diverse gardens on the shores of Lake Windermere. Lakeside has been created for year round interest, packed with choice plants, incl some unusual varieties. Main garden area with herbaceous borders and foliage shrubs, scented and winter interest plants and seasonal bedding. Roof garden with lawn, espaliered local heritage apple varieties and culinary herbs. Lawn art on front lawn. Rocky Bank is a traditional garden with rock outcrops. Planted with unusual specimen alpines. Herbaceous borders, shrubs and ornamental trees. Woodland area with species rhododendrons. Working greenhouse

and polytunnels. Wild flower garden and cut flower garden. Refreshments 20% discount from Hotel Conservatory menu on the Open Day. Wheelchair access not available at Rocky Bank.

37 LANGHOLME MILL

Woodgate, Lowick Green LA12 8ES. Judith & Graham Sanderson, judith@themill.biz. *7m NW of Ulverston. West on A590. At Greenodd, N on A5902 towards Broughton. Langholme Mill is approx. 3m along this road on L as road divides.* **Sat 21, Sun 22 May (11-5). Adm £5, chd free. Home-made teas. Visits also by arrangement Apr to Oct please phone Judith on 01229 885215 to arrange.** Approx 1 acre of mature woodland garden with meandering lakeland stone paths surrounding the mill race stream which can be crossed by a variety of bridges. The garden hosts well established bamboo, rhododendrons, hostas, acers and astilbes and a large variety of country flowers. Featured in Amateur Gardening.

38 LARCH COTTAGE NURSERIES

Melkinthorpe, Penrith CA10 2DR. Peter Stott, www.larchcottage.co.uk. *From N leave M6 J40 take A6 S. From S leave M6 J39 take A6 N signed off A6.* **Wed 25 May, Sun 9 Oct (1-4). Adm £3.50, chd free.** For 2 days only Larch Cottage Nurseries are opening the new lower gardens and chapel for NGS visitors. The gardens incl lawns, flowing perennial borders, rare and unusual shrubs, small orchard and kitchen garden. A natural stream runs into a small lake - a haven for wildlife and birds. At the head of the lake

stands a chapel, designed and built by Peter for family use only. Larch Cottage has a Japanese Dry garden, ponds and Italianesque columned garden specifically for shade plants, the Italianesque tumbled down walls are draped in greenery acting as a backdrop for the borders filled with stock plants. Newly designed and constructed lower gardens and chapel. Owner Peter Stott received an Honorary Fellowship from the University of Cumbria for his services to horticulture. The gardens are accessible to wheelchair users although the paths are rocky in places.

GROUP OPENING

39 LEECE & DENDRON VILLAGE GARDENS

Cumbria LA12 0QP. *2m E of Barrow-in-Furness. J36 on M6 onto A590 to Ulverston. A5087 to Barrow. After ~8m (opp sea wall), turn R for Leece, & a further 1/2 m for Dendron. Rail, 3.5m; NCR 700.* **Sun 19 June (11-5). Combined adm £3.50, chd free. Tea in selected village gardens.**

BRIAR HOUSE
Jeff & Gill Lowden

BROW EDGE
Mrs Lynn Furzeland-Ridgway

THE DIN DRUM, DENDRON
Adrian & Julie Newnham

3 PEAR TREE COTTAGE
Jane & Rob Phizacklea

ST MARGARETS, LEECE
Lyn & Sabine Dixon

WINANDER
Mrs Enid Cockshott

Two small close villages on the Furness Peninsula 1 1/2 m from Morecambe Bay, rural but not remote, with working farms centred around a small tarn. Gardens of varying size and individual styles, all of which enjoy wonderful views. Features incl exciting and varied vegetables gardens, a willow yurt, green roof, a white garden, hay meadow with maze, mature trees, herbaceous borders, wildlife ponds and streams, bees, cottage gardens, alpines, perennials, shrubs, water features, climbers... and much much more! WC in village hall.

© Linda Greening

The Chantry

---

40 LOW BLAKEBANK

Underbarrow, Kendal LA8 8BN. Mrs Catherine Chamberlain. *Lyth Valley between Underbarrow & Crosthwaite. East off A5074 to Crosthwaite. Signed Red Scar & Broom Farm off the main rd between Crosthwaite & Underbarrow. 1st drive on R off Broom Lane.* Sun 26 June (10.30-4.30). Combined adm with Middle Blakebank £5, chd free. Home-made teas at Middle Blakebank.

Charming and secluded 3 acre garden surrounding a C17 Lakeland farmhouse (not open) and bank barn. Plenty of seating to enjoy the beautiful views of the Lyth Valley and Scout Scar. Garden under development. Mixed borders, ponds, lawned areas, topiary, small bluebell wood and vegetable garden. Uneven ground, slopes and steps.

41 LOW FELL WEST

Crosthwaite, Kendal LA8 8JG. Barbie & John Handley, 015395 68297, barbie@handleyfamily.co.uk. *4¹/₂ m S of Bowness. Off A5074, turn W just S of Damson Dene Hotel. Follow lane for ¹/₂ m.* Sun 8 May, Sun 4 Sept (10.30-5). Adm £4, chd free. Home-made teas. **Visits also by arrangement nearest access for large coaches half mile away.**

This 2 acre woodland garden in the tranquil Winster Valley has extensive views to the Pennines. The four season garden, restored since 2003, incl expanses of rock planted sympathetically with grasses, unusual trees and shrubs, climaxing for autumn colour. There are areas of plant rich meadows and native

hedges. A woodland area houses a gypsy caravan and there is direct access to Cumbria Wildlife Trust's Barkbooth Reserve of Oak woodland, blue bells and open fellside. Featured in Cumbria Life. Wheelchair access to much of the garden, but some rough paths, steep slopes.

42 LOWER ROWELL FARM & COTTAGE

Milnthorpe LA7 7LU. John & Mavis Robinson & Julie & Andy Welton, 015395 62270. *Approx 2m from Milnthorpe, 2m from Crooklands. Signed to Rowell off B6385. Garden ¹/₂ m up lane on L.* Sat 21, Sun 22 May (1-5). Adm £3.50, chd free. Home-made teas. **Visits also by arrangement Feb to Aug groups of 10+, refreshments by arrangement.**

Approx 1¹/₄ acre garden with views to Farleton Knott and Lakeland hills. Unusual trees and shrubs, plus perennial borders; architectural pruning; retro greenhouse; polytunnel with tropical plants; cottage gravel garden and vegetable plot. Fabulous display of snowdrops in spring followed by other spring flowers, with colour most of the year. Wildlife ponds and 3 friendly pet hens.

43 MATSON GROUND

Windermere LA23 2NH. Matson Ground Estate Co Ltd, 015394 47892, info@matsonground.co.uk. *²/₃ m E of Bowness. Turn N off B5284 signed Heathwaite. From E 100yds after Windermere Golf Club, from W 400yds after Windy Hall Rd. Rail 2¹/₂ m; Bus 1m, 6, 599, 755, 800; NCR 6.*

Sun 22 May (1-5). Adm £3.50, chd free. Home-made teas. **Visits also by arrangement.**

2 acre formal garden with a mix of established borders, wild flower areas and stream leading to a large pond and developing aboretum. Rose garden, rockery and topiary terrace borders; white garden. Walled kitchen garden with raised beds, fruit trees and greenhouse. The garden is constantly developing and regular visitors will see changes each year.

44 MIDDLE BLAKEBANK

Underbarrow, Kendal LA8 8HP. Mrs Hilary Crowe, 015395 68959, hfcmbb@aol.com. *Lyth Valley between Underbarrow & Crosthwaite. East off A5074 to Crosthwaite. The garden is on Broom Lane, a turning between Crosthwaite & Underbarrow signed Red Scar & Broom Farm.* Sun 26 June (10.30-4.30). Combined adm with Low Blakebank £5, chd free. Home-made teas. **Visits also by arrangement May to Sept we are happy to open for small groups.**

The garden extends to 4¹/₂ acres and overlooks the Lyth Valley with extensive views south to Morecombe Bay and east to the Howgills. We have orchards, wild flower meadow and more formal garden with a range of outbuildings. Over the last 5 years the garden has been developed with plantings that provide varying colour and texture all year. We enjoy providing home made cakes and sandwiches under cover if necessary!

45 NEW MIREFOOT

Burnside, Kendal LA8 9AB. Mark Baker & Kim Kremer. *Potter Fell Road. From A591 follow signs for Burnside. Head north on Burnside rd towards Bowston (0.5M). On entering Bowston turn 1st R and over bridge. Continue for ¹/₂ m.* Sun 5 June (11-5). Adm £3.50, chd free. Light refreshments, tea and cakes.

'A mature and relaxed 4 acre country house garden, developed to be enjoyed by the family and neighbours, including young children, pony, cats and (every gardener's nightmare), free-range pet rabbits. Extends to formal and informal areas, including rose terrace, herbaceous borders, sunken lavender garden, arboretum with many special trees, ponds with visiting heron and wild flower meadow.'. Arboretum with some unusual trees, large pond, combination of formal and informal garden areas. Wheelchair access over grass but not all areas (e.g. Sunken garden, and part of the veranda).

46 NEWTON RIGG COLLEGE GARDENS

Newton Rigg, Penrith CA11 0AH. Newton Rigg College part of Askam Bryan College, www.newtonrigg.ac.uk. *1m W of Penrith. 3m W from J40 & J41 off M6. ¹/₂ m off the B5288 W of Penrith. We have The Coast to Coast cycle route (Route 7) and a public pathway approx 500 metres from the garden entrance gates.* **Tue 14 June (3-8); Wed 12 Oct (3-6). Adm £4.50, chd free. Tea. Visits also by arrangement 15+.**
Our Educational Gardens have much of horticultural interest incl herbaceous borders, ponds, organic garden with fruit cage and display of composting techniques, woodland walk, seasonal borders, arboretums, annual Pictorial Meadows, Pleached Hornbeam Walkway and extensive range of ornamental trees and shrubs. Our new garden addition for 2016 is a Stumpery planted with ferns and shade loving plants.

47 ORCHARD COTTAGE

Hutton Lane, Levens, Kendal LA8 8PB. Shirley & Chris Band, 015395 61005, chrisband67@gmail.com. *6m S of Kendal. Turn N off A590 or A6 signed Levens. From Xrds by Methodist Church, 300 metres down Hutton Lane. Park near this Xrds. Garden access via 'The Orchard'.* **Sun 24 Apr, Sun 29 May, Sun 24 July (1-5). Adm £3.50, chd free. Visits also by arrangement Mar to Sept any from 1 to 60.**
³/₄ acre sloping garden in old orchard. Plantsperson's paradise with winding paths, diverse habitats, secret vistas, hidden places. All yr round interest and colour. Collections of ferns (100+), hellebores (70+), grasses, cottage plants, geraniums. Auricula theatres, 'imaginary' stream, bog garden. Trees support clematis, roses and honeysuckle. Wildlife friendly. Featured in 'Amateur Gardening', 'Lancashire Magazine' and 'Pteridologist - The Fern Magazine'.

48 8 OXENHOLME ROAD

Kendal LA9 7NJ. Mr & Mrs John & Frances Davenport, 01539 720934, frandav8@btinternet.com. *SE Kendal. From A65 (Burton Rd, Kendal/Kirkby Lonsdale) take B6254 (Oxenholme Rd). No.8 is 1st house on L beyond red post box.* **Sun 5 June (10-4). Adm £3.50, chd free. Light refreshments. Visits also by arrangement May to July for groups up to 25.**
Artist and potters garden of approx ¹/₂ acre of mixed planting designed for year-round interest, incl two small ponds. The garden runs all round the house with a gravel garden at the front, as well as a number of woodland plant areas. Garden essentially level, but access to WC is up steps.

Ponds with visiting heron and wild flower meadow . . .

49 PARK HOUSE

Barbon, Kirkby Lonsdale LA6 2LG. Mr & Mrs P Pattison, 015242 76346, philip@ppattison.co.uk. *2¹/₂ m N of Kirkby Lonsdale. Off A683 Kirkby Lonsdale to Sedburgh rd. Follow signs into Barbon Village.* **Sun 3 July, Sun 21 Aug (10.30-4.30). Adm £3.50, chd free. Home-made teas. Visits also by arrangement May to Sept groups of 10+.**
Romantic Manor house. Extensive vistas. Formal tranquil pond encased in yew hedging. Meadow with meandering pathways, water garden filled with bulbs and ferns. Formal lawn, gravel pathways, cottage borders with hues of soft pinks and purples, shady border, kitchen garden. An evolving garden to follow.

50 PEAR TREE COTTAGE

Dalton, Burton-in-Kendal LA6 1NN. Linda & Alec Greening, 01524 781624, lindagreening48@gmail.com, www.peartreecottagecumbria. co.uk. *5m from J35 & J36 of M6. From northern end of Burton-in-*

Kendal (A6070) turn E into Vicarage Lane & continue approx 1m. **Visits by arrangement June & July groups of 15+. Refreshments by arrangement.**
¹/₃ acre cottage garden in a delightful rural setting. A peaceful and relaxing garden, harmonising with its environment and incorporating many different planting areas, from packed herbaceous borders and rambling roses, to wildlife pond, bog garden, rock garden and gravel garden. A plantsperson's delight, incl over 200 different ferns, and many other rare and unusual plants.

51 ◆ RYDAL HALL

Ambleside LA22 9LX. Diocese of Carlisle, 01539 432050, www.rydalhall.org. *2m N of Ambleside. E from A591 at Rydal signed Rydal Hall. Bus 555, 599, X8, X55; NCR 6.* **For NGS: Sun 20 Mar, Thur 12 May, Thur 16 June, Thur 7 July (11-4). Adm by donation. For other opening times and information, please phone or visit garden website.**
Formal Italianate gardens designed by Thomas Mawson in 1911; the gardens have recently been restored to their former glory. Formal garden with fountain and croquet lawn, C17 viewing station, fine herbaceous planting, informal woodland garden, community vegetable garden, orchard and apiary. Magnificent views across Windermere and the Lakeland Fells. Open for Wordsworth's Daffodil Legacy 20th March.

52 NEW SANDHOUSE

Burnhill, Scaleby, Carlisle CA6 4LU. John Dalton & Ken Dodd. *Scaleby North Cumbria. 5m NE Carlisle. From A6071 turn at Smithfield, follow NGS signs. From M6 J44 Follow A689 Hexham, follow NGS signs.* **Sun 10 July (1-5). Adm £3.50, chd free. Home-made teas.**
A cottage garden with island beds of herbaceous perennials, foliage plants suitable for the flower arranger. Pond, hidden seating areas to surprise the visitor, and lots of nooks and crannies. John is a multiple award winner for his floral arrangements including a Chelsea GOLD, he will give a flower demonstration in the afternoon. Flower demonstration. Gravel paths.

53 ◆ SIZERGH CASTLE

Sizergh, Kendal LA8 8DZ. National Trust, 015395 60951, www.nationaltrust.org.uk. *3m S of Kendal. Approach rd leaves A590 close to & S of A590/A591 interchange.* **For NGS: Sat 3 Sept (10-5). Adm £5.45, chd £2.70. For other opening times and information, please phone or visit garden website.**

²/₃ acre limestone rock garden, largest owned by National Trust; collection of Japanese maples, dwarf conifers, hardy ferns; hot wall border with fruiting trees. Wild flower areas, herbaceous borders, 'Dutch' garden. Terraced garden and lake; kitchen garden; fruit orchard with spring bulbs. National Collections of *Asplenium scolopendrium, Cystopteris, Dryopteris, Osmunda.* National Trust members are admitted free with an opportunity to donate to the good causes the NGS supports. Non Trust members entrance fees are donated to the NGS. Featured in The Times in their 20 best Great British gardens to visit this summer.

Hidden seating areas to surprise the visitor, and lots of nooks and crannies . . .

54 SPRINT MILL

Burneside LA8 9AQ. Edward & Romola Acland, 01539 725168, edwardacland@freeuk.com. *2m N of Kendal. From Burneside follow signs to Skelsmergh for ¹/₂ m then L into drive of Sprint Mill.* **Sun 19 June (10.30-5). Adm £3, chd free. Light lunches & home-made teas all day. Visits also by arrangement Jan to Oct.**

Unorthodox organically run garden combining the wild and natural alongside provision of owners' fruit, vegetables and firewood. Idyllic riverside setting, 5 acres to explore including wooded riverbank with hand-crafted seats. Large vegetable and soft fruit area, following no-dig and permaculture principles. Hand-

tools prevail. Historic water mill with original turbine.The 3-storey building houses owner's art studio and personal museum, incl collection of many old hand tools associated with rural crafts. Green woodworking demonstrations. Goats, hens, ducks, rope swing, family-friendly. Access for wheelchairs to some parts of both garden and mill.

55 SUMMERDALE HOUSE

Nook, Lupton LA6 1PE. David & Gail Sheals, www.summerdalegardenplants.co.uk. *7m S of Kendal, 5m W of Kirkby Lonsdale. From J36 M6 take A65 towards Kirkby Lonsdale, at Nook take R turn Farleton. Location not always signed on highway. Detailed directions available on our website.* **Sun 21 Feb (11-4.30). Home-made teas. Every Fri and Sat 26 Feb to 30 July (11-4.30). Sun 19 June (11-4.30). Home-made teas. Adm £4, chd free. Refreshments on Suns only. Home-made soups & bread (Feb only). 2017: Sun 19 Feb.**

1¹/₂ -acre part-walled country garden set around C18 former vicarage. Several defined areas have been created by hedges, each with its own theme and linked by intricate cobbled pathways. Beautiful setting with fine views across to Farleton Fell. Traditional herbaceous borders, ponds, woodland and meadow planting provide year round interest. Large collections of auricula, primulas and snowdrops. Adjoining specialist nursery growing a wide range of interesting and unusual herbaceous perennials. Home made jams and chutneys for sale. Featured in House and Garden magazine.

56 SUNNYSIDE

Woodhouse Lane, Heversham, Milnthorpe LA7 7EW. Anita Gott, 015395 63249. *1¹/₂ m N of Milnthorpe. From A6 turn into Heversham, then R at church signed Crooklands. In ¹/₂ m turn L down lane.* **Visits by arrangement June to Aug groups of 15-25. Refreshments by arrangement.**

¹/₂ -acre country cottage garden with a well at the bottom, 3 greenhouses, pond and mixed borders. Large, immaculate vegetable garden. Orchard with hens. Area to attract bees and butterflies.

57 ◆ SWARTHMOOR HALL

Swarthmoor Hall Lane, Ulverston LA12 0JQ. Jane Pearson, Manager, 01229 583204, info@swarthmoorhall.co.uk, www.swarthmoorhall.co.uk. *1¹/₂ m SW of Ulverston. A590 to Ulverston. Turn off to Ulverston railway stn. Follow Brown tourist signs to Hall. Rail 0.9m.* **For NGS: Daily Mon 22 Feb to Sun 13 Mar (10.30-4.30). Adm by donation. Light refreshments at Barn Cafe. For other opening times and information, please phone, email or visit garden website.**

Wild purple crocus meadow in early spring: late February or early March depending on weather, earlier if mild winter later if cold and frosty. Also, good displays of snowdrops, daffodils and tulips.

58 TENTER END BARN

Docker, Kendal LA8 0DB. Mrs Hazel Terry, 01539 824447, hnterry@btinternet.com. *3m N Kendal. From Kendal take A685 Appleby rd. Then 2nd on R to Docker. At the junction bear L.* **Sun 17 July (11-4.30). Adm £3.50, chd free. Home-made teas. Visits also by arrangement Apr to Sept for groups of 4+.**

3 acres of cultivated and natural areas, in a secretive rural setting. A patio garden, large lawns, herbaceous borders and a small vegetable patch. Walks on the wild side around a mere and woodlands. Many birds can be seen at various feeding stations, also waterfowl on the mere. All managed by one OAP. Rather uneven around the woodland paths. Could be difficult around mere in wet weather.

GROUP OPENING

59 ULVERSTON GARDENS

Oubas Hill, Ulverston LA12 7LA. *A590 to Ulverston, parking available at Booths Supermarket. Rail Ulverston; Bus 6, 11; NCR 70, 700. Maps available at gardens.* **Sun 26 June (10.30-5). Combined adm £4, chd free. Home-made teas.**

1 GRASMERE ROAD
Wayne & Jude Evans

HAMILTON GROVE
Helen & Martin Cooper

NEW ▶ 39 MOUNTBARROW ROAD
Mrs Kathleen Wood

11 OUBAS HILL
David & Janet Parratt

14 OUBAS HILL
Pat & Barry Bentley

WREAY
Jeniffer & Maurice Snell
Visits also by arrangement in June.
01229 585542

Diverse gardens in and around Ulverston.1 Grasmere Road; small low maintenance garden packed with ideas and with a Mediterranean feel. Hamilton Grove; garden slopes down from a large terrace, through beds planted with herbaceous perennials to a, now dry, feeder stream for the Ulverston canal. A large collection of scented-leaved pelargoniums. 11 Oubas Hill; a hillside garden with flower beds around the lawn with mixed planting and small orchard. A walk leads to the summerhouse and greenhouse with various types of fruit and vegetables. The vista from the top of the garden looks towards Morecambe Bay in the distance. 14 Oubas Hill; hillside garden with steep meandering paths, densely planted beds, ponds, patio and summer house. Bees and rescue chickens. Terraced front garden with vegetable, fruit and herbaceous areas. Wreay; mature garden with dwarf conifers, rhododendrons and hidden surprises landscaped around a live model steam locomotive railway. 39 Mountbarrow Road; lovely, small random plot with flowers, vegetables and sitting areas. Working potter, 32mm and 45mm live steam railway, antique horse drawn vehicles.

🐕 ✿ ☕

60 ▶ WESTVIEW
Fletcher Hill, Kirkby Stephen CA17 4QQ. Reg & Irene Metcalfe. *Kirkby Stephen town centre, T-lights opp Antiques & Collectables. Just over 1m from local railway station.* Sun 17 July (11-5). Adm £3.50, chd free.
Tucked away behind the town centre, this secret walled cottage garden is a little haven. The main garden is filled with perennials, shrubs and large collection of hostas, with small wildlife pond. The adjacent prairie-style nursery beds are at their best in July.

🐕 ✿

61 ▶ WINDY HALL
Crook Road, Windermere LA23 3JA. Diane & David Kinsman, 015394 46238, dhewitt.kinsman@gmail.com, www.windy-hall.co.uk. *¹/₂ m S of Bowness-on-Windermere. On western end of B5284, pink house up Linthwaite Hotel driveway. Rail 2.6m; Bus 1m, 6, 599, 755, 800; NCR 6.* Sun 1 May, Sun 5 June (10-5). Adm £4.50, chd free. Home-made teas. Visits also by arrangement Apr to Sept. Guided tours & lunch for groups of 8+.
'A masterclass in gardening with nature, not against it, making the most of plants that thrive in the wet climate and acid soil'. 34 gardening years by 2 people on 4 hillside acres with 6ft of rain. Woodland with rhododendrons, camellias, magnolias, hydrangeas, bluebells and foxgloves. Extensive moss and Japanese influenced gardens, ponds, meadows, stewartias, gunneras large and small, alpine and Best gardens. And much much more. Plant Heritage Aruncus collection. Rare Hebridean sheep, exotic waterfowl and pheasants. Featured on BBC Gardeners World & Gardeners Question Time, and in Saturday Telegraph, The English Garden & Die Geheimen Gärten Von England.

✿ 🚐 NPC 🛏 ☕

62 ▶ WINTON PARK
Appleby Road, Kirkby Stephen CA17 4PG. Mr Anthony Kilvington. *2m N of Kirkby Stephen. On A685 turn L signed Gt Musgrave/Warcop (B6259). After approx 1m turn L as signed.* Sun 24 July (11-5). Adm £5, chd free. Light refreshments.
3-acre country garden bordered by the banks of the R Eden with stunning views. Many fine conifers, acers and rhododendrons, herbaceous borders, hostas, ferns, grasses and several hundred roses. Four formal ponds plus rock pool. Partial wheelchair access.

♿ ☕

63 ▶ WOODEND HOUSE
Woodend, Egremont CA22 2TA. Grainne & Richard Jakobson, 01946 813017, gmjakobson22@gmail.com. *2m S of Whitehaven. Take the A595 from Whitehaven towards Egremont. On leaving Bigrigg take 1st turn L. Go down hill, garden at bottom R opp Woodend Farm. Close to cycleways & Coast to Coast route.* Sun 24 July (11-5). Adm £3.50, chd free. Home-made teas. Visits also by arrangement Mar to Oct.
An interesting garden tucked away in a small hamlet. Meandering gravel paths lead around the garden with imaginative, colourful planting and lots of interest throughout the year. Take a look around a productive potager, shady walk, mini spring and summer meadows and a pretty summer house. The garden has some quirky features incl. scarecrows (!) and a growing collection of Vit. Clematis. Plant sale, homemade teas, mini-quiz for children. The gravel drive and paths are difficult for wheelchairs but more mobile visitors can access the main seating areas in the rear garden.

✿ 🚐 ☕

64 ▶ YEWBARROW HOUSE
Hampsfell Road, Grange-over-Sands LA11 6BE. Jonathan & Margaret Denby, 015395 32469, jonathan@bestlakesbreaks.co.uk, www.yewbarrowhouse.co.uk. *¹/₄ m from town centre. Proceed along Hampsfell Rd passing a house called Yewbarrow to brow of hill then turn L onto a lane signed 'Charney Wood/Yewbarrow Wood' & sharp L again. Rail 0.7m, Bus X6, NCR 70.* Sun 5 June, Sun 3 July, Sun 7 Aug, Sun 4 Sept (11-4). Adm £4.50, chd free. Cream teas. Visits also by arrangement May to Oct morning coffee, tea with biscuits for groups £2.50 a head. Cream teas £5 a head.
'More Cornwall than Cumbria' according to Country Life, a colourful 4 acre garden filled with exotic and rare plants, with dramatic views over the Morecambe Bay. Outstanding features include the Orangery; the Japanese garden with infinity pool, the Italian terraces and the restored Victorian kitchen garden. Dahlias, cannas and colourful exotica are a speciality. New for 2016 a woodland walk. www.youtube.com/watch?v=v--VH2cLG18

🐕 ✿ 🚐 ☕

DERBYSHIRE

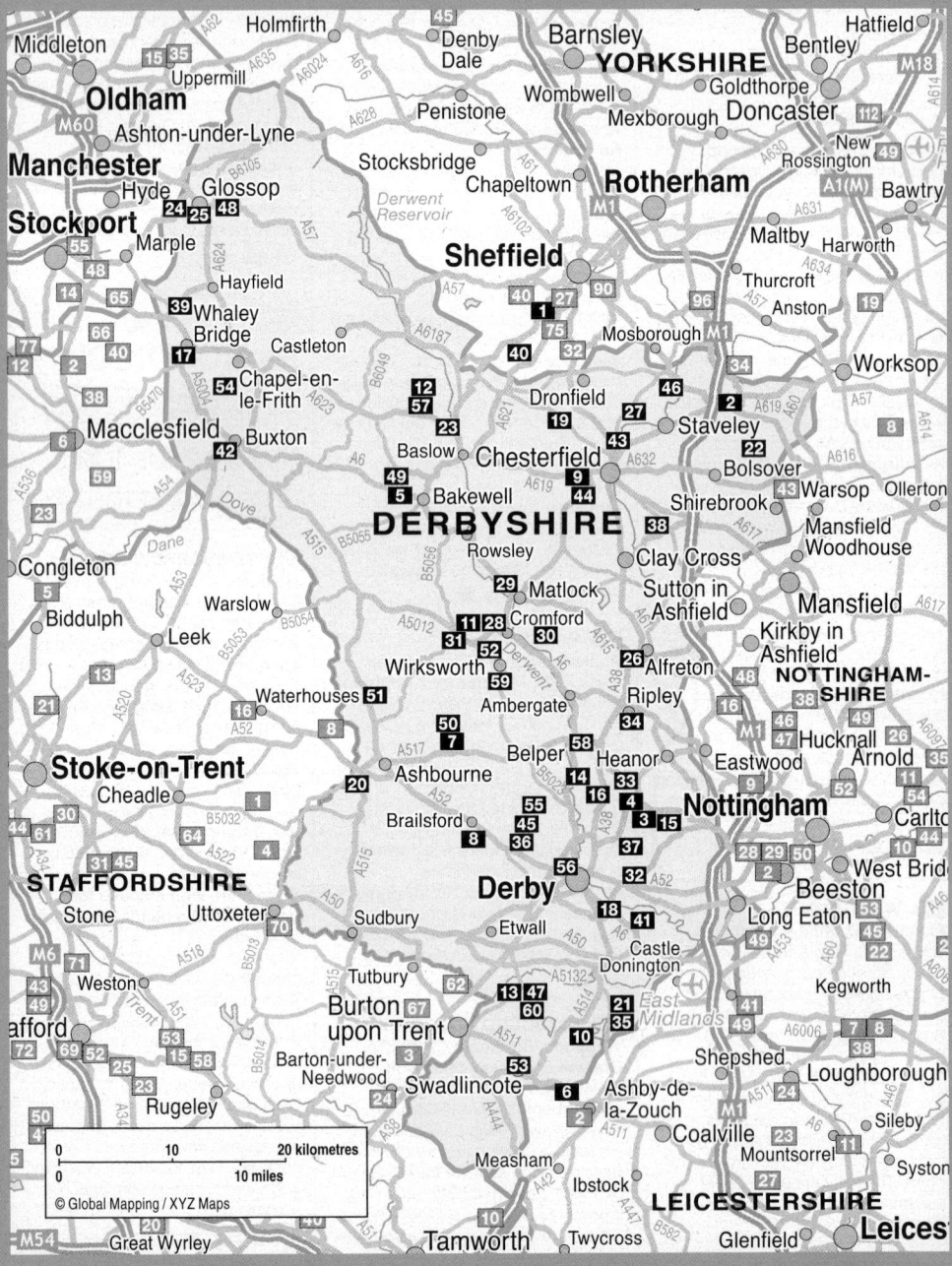

© Global Mapping / XYZ Maps

Investec Wealth & Investment supports the NGS

Derbyshire

Derbyshire is the county where the Midlands meet the North, and visitors are attracted to the rugged hills of the High Peak, the high moorlands near Sheffield and the unspoilt countryside of the Dales.

There are many stately homes in the county with world famous gardens, delightful private country gardens, and interesting small cottage and town gardens.

Some of the northern gardens have spectacular views across the Peak District; their planting reflecting the rigours of the climate and long, cold winters. In the Derbyshire Dales, stone walls give way to hedges and the countryside is hilly with many trees, good agricultural land and very pretty villages.

South of Derby the land is much flatter, the architecture has a Midlands look with red brick replacing stone and softer planting in the gardens.

The east side of Derbyshire is different again, reflecting the recent past with small pit villages, and looking towards the rolling countryside of Nottinghamshire. There are fast road links with other parts of the country via the M1 and M6, making a day trip to a Derbyshire garden a very easy choice.

Derbyshire Volunteers

County Organiser
Irene Dougan
01335 370958
irene.dougan@ngs.org.uk

County Treasurer
Robert Little
01283 702267
robert.little@ngs.org.uk

Publicity
Roger Roberts
01332 841905
roger.roberts@ngs.org.uk

Booklet Co-ordinator
Dave Darwent
01142 665881
dave.darwent@ngs.org.uk

Assistant County Organisers
Dave Darwent
(as above)

Gill & Colin Hancock
01159 301061
gillandcolin@tiscali.co.uk

Jane Lennox
01663 732381
jane@lennoxonline.net

Pauline Little
01283 702267
plittle@hotmail.co.uk

Christine Sanderson
01246 570830
christine.r.sanderson@uwclub.net

Kate & Peter Spencer
01629 822499
pandkspencer@yahoo.co.uk

Left Holme Point, Repton Village Gardens

Opening Dates

All entries subject to change.
For latest information check www.ngs.org.uk

February

Snowdrop Festival

Saturday 27
- **13** 10 Chestnut Way
- **21** The Dower House

Sunday 28
- **13** 10 Chestnut Way
- **21** The Dower House

March

Wednesday 30
- **6** Bluebell Arboretum and Nursery

April

Saturday 2
- **48** NEW 122 Sheffield Road

Sunday 3
- **14** Chevin Brae

Sunday 10
- **6** Bluebell Arboretum and Nursery

Saturday 16
- **41** Old English Walled Garden, Elvaston Castle Country Park

Saturday 23
- **21** The Dower House

Sunday 24
- **4** 334 Belper Road
- **6** Bluebell Arboretum and Nursery
- **21** The Dower House
- **59** Windward

May

Sunday 1
- **1** 12 Ansell Road
- **8** The Burrows Gardens

Monday 2
- **1** 12 Ansell Road

Saturday 7
- **48** NEW 122 Sheffield Road

Sunday 8
- **6** Bluebell Arboretum and Nursery
- **16** Coxbench Hall

Sunday 15
- **11** Cascades Gardens
- **38** Moorfields
- **43** The Paddock
- **50** Tilford House

Sunday 22
- **4** 334 Belper Road
- **23** Fir Croft
- **24** Gamesley Fold Cottage
- **32** Locko Park
- **47** NEW Repton Village Gardens

Monday 23
- **46** Renishaw Hall & Gardens

Saturday 28
- **20** Dove Cottage
- **35** Melbourne Hall Gardens
- **40** 9 Newfield Crescent
- **45** Rectory House

Sunday 29
- **1** 12 Ansell Road
- **3** NEW 228 Belper Road
- **12** Cherry Hill
- **15** 13 Chiltern Drive
- **20** Dove Cottage
- **35** Melbourne Hall Gardens
- **40** 9 Newfield Crescent
- **52** 12 Water Lane
- **54** Westgate

Monday 30
- **1** 12 Ansell Road
- **8** The Burrows Gardens
- **51** Tissington Hall
- **52** 12 Water Lane

June

Festival Weekend

Sunday 5
- **4** 334 Belper Road
- **23** Fir Croft

Saturday 11
- **10** Calke Abbey
- **29** The Holly Tree

Sunday 12
- **6** Bluebell Arboretum and Nursery
- **11** Cascades Gardens
- **29** The Holly Tree
- **37** NEW 16 Monarch Drive

Saturday 18
- **21** The Dower House
- **28** Hollies Farm Plant Centre

Sunday 19
- **1** 12 Ansell Road

- **21** The Dower House
- **23** Fir Croft
- **28** Hollies Farm Plant Centre

Wednesday 22
- **11** Cascades Gardens

Saturday 25
- **22** Elmton Gardens

Sunday 26
- **22** Elmton Gardens
- **25** High Roost
- **36** Meynell Langley Trials Garden
- **53** 13 Westfield Road
- **54** Westgate

Wednesday 29
- **50** Tilford House

Plenty of activities to keep children entertained . . .

July

Saturday 2
- **58** 26 Windmill Rise

Sunday 3
- **31** The Lilies
- **38** Moorfields
- **58** 26 Windmill Rise

Saturday 9
- **34** 2 Manvers Street
- **39** New Mills School and Sixth Form

Sunday 10
- **8** The Burrows Gardens
- **11** Cascades Gardens
- **34** 2 Manvers Street
- **39** New Mills School and Sixth Form
- **42** NEW Otterwood
- **59** Windward

Tuesday 12
- **46** Renishaw Hall & Gardens

Friday 15
- **17** Craigside

Saturday 16
- **2** Barlborough Gardens
- **17** Craigside
- **42** NEW Otterwood

Sunday 17
- **2** Barlborough Gardens
- **6** Bluebell Arboretum and Nursery
- **17** Craigside
- **18** 8 Curzon Lane
- **36** Meynell Langley Trials Garden

Saturday 23
- **57** NEW Wild in the Country

Sunday 24
- **11** Cascades Gardens
- **18** 8 Curzon Lane
- **47** NEW Repton Village Gardens

Saturday 30
- **9** Byways
- **55** Wharfedale

Sunday 31
- **6** Bluebell Arboretum and Nursery
- **9** Byways
- **49** Thornbridge Hall
- **55** Wharfedale

August

Saturday 6
- **33** 9 Main Street

Sunday 7
- **33** 9 Main Street
- **37** NEW 16 Monarch Drive
- **43** The Paddock
- **53** 13 Westfield Road
- **60** Woodend Cottage

Saturday 13
- **41** Old English Walled Garden, Elvaston Castle Country Park

Sunday 14
- **6** Bluebell Arboretum and Nursery
- **18** 8 Curzon Lane

Sunday 21
- **3** NEW 228 Belper Road
- **36** Meynell Langley Trials Garden

Sunday 28
- **6** Bluebell Arboretum and Nursery
- **47** NEW Repton Village Gardens

Monday 29
- **1** 12 Ansell Road
- **8** The Burrows Gardens
- **51** Tissington Hall

September

Sunday 4
- **31** The Lilies

The Gardens

1 12 ANSELL ROAD
Ecclesall, Sheffield S11 7PE. Dave Darwent, 01142 665881, dave@poptasticdave.co.uk, www.poptasticdave.co.uk/_/Horticulture.html. *Approx 3m SW of City Centre. Travel to Ringinglow Rd (88 bus), then Edale Rd (opp Ecclesall C of E Primary School). 3rd R - Ansell Rd. No 12 on L ¾ way down, solar panel on roof.* **Sun 1, Mon 2, Sun 29 May (12-6.30); Mon 30 May, Sun 19 June (2-8.30); Mon 29 Aug, Sat 17 Sept (10.30-4). Adm £2.50, chd free. Home-made teas. Gluten free and savoury options available. Visits also by arrangement Apr to Sept groups 20 max. No parking for large coaches.**
Established 1930s, the garden contains many original plants maintained in the original style. Traditional rustic pergola and dwarf wall greenhouse. Owner (grandson of first owner) aims to keep the garden as a living example of how interwar gardens were cultivated to provide decoration and produce. More detail online. Openings which extend to sunset will incl fairy lights and candles. Then and now pictures of the garden in 1929 and 1950's Vs present. Map of landmarks up to 55m away which can be seen from garden.
❀ ☕

GROUP OPENING

2 BARLBOROUGH GARDENS
Barlborough, Chesterfield S43 4ER. Christine Sanderson, 07956 203184, christine.r.sanderson@uwclub.net. *7m NE of Chesterfield. Off A619 midway between Chesterfield & Worksop. ½ m E M1, J30. Follow signs for Barlborough then yellow NGS signs. Parking available in village centre, parking for coaches at Royal Oak PH.* **Sat 16, Sun 17 July (1-6). Combined adm £6, chd free. Refreshments at Stone Croft and The Hollies.**

CLARENDON
Neil & Lorraine Jones

GOOSE COTTAGE
Mick & Barbara Housley

GREYSTONES BARN
Jenny & Ernie Stamp

THE HOLLIES
Vernon & Christine Sanderson

LINDWAY
Thomas & Margaret Pettinger

WOODSIDE HOUSE
Tricia & Adrian Murray-Leslie

Barlborough is an attractive historic village and a range of interesting buildings can be seen all around the village centre. The village is situated close to Renishaw Hall for possible combined visit. Map detailing location of all the gardens is issued with admission ticket, which can be purchased at any of the gardens listed. Featured in the Daily Telegraph's NGS Gardens to visit. Partial wheelchair access at The Hollies. Access to rear of Clarendon via stone slabs.
♿ 🐕 ❀ 🚐 ☕

The Dower House

© Louise Jolley

3 NEW 228 BELPER ROAD

Stanley Common, Ilkeston DE7 6FT. John Osborn, 01159 328105. *Approx 3m W of Ilkeston on A609. From Derby: Follow A608 (from the Meteor Centre). Turn R onto A609 at the Rose & Crown PH at Smalley Xrds. Garden approx 1m on L just after church. Parking on rd.* Sun 29 May, Sun 21 Aug (12.30-4). Adm £2.50, chd free. Home-made teas. **Visits also by arrangement May to Sept, groups 10 max.**
Garden borders green belt land. Current layout is about 8yrs old. Site previously dominated by old Leylandii hedge cut back to about 15ft high. This has now transformed into colourful hedge of many climbers and shrubs. Plants mostly herbaceous perennial and shrubs. Collections of hosta, tree peonies, acers, a magnificent wisteria and some unusual shrubs. Wheelchair access to patio area, steps down to main garden.

4 334 BELPER ROAD

Stanley Common DE7 6FY. Gill & Colin Hancock, 01159 301061, www.hamescovert.com. *7m N of Derby. 3m W of Ilkeston. On A609, ³/₄ m from Rose & Crown Xrds (A608). Please park in field up farm drive or Working Men's Club rear car park if wet.* Sun 24 Apr, Sun 22 May, Sun 5 June (12-5). Adm £3.50, chd free. Home-made teas. April highlight - home-made soup, bread & cakes. **Visits also by arrangement Apr to July adm £6 incl tea/coffee/cake and our personal attention.**
Relax in our constantly evolving country garden with informal planting and features. Plenty of seating to enjoy our highly recommended home-made cakes. Take a scenic walk to a 10 acre wood with glades and ¹/₂ acre lake. April:cowslips. May: laburnum tunnel and wisteria. June: wild flowers, hostas, ferns and roses. Children welcome with plenty of activities to keep them entertained. Paths round wood and lake not suitable for wheelchairs.

5 BIRCHFIELD

The Dukes Drive, Ashford in the Water, Bakewell DE45 1QQ. Brian Parker, 01629 813800 leave message. *2m NW of Bakewell. On A6 to Buxton between New Bridge & Sheepwash Bridge.* Visits by arrangement adm £3 April - Sept. £2 Oct - March. Light refreshments. Tea/coffee and selection of good quality biscuits. *Donation to Thornhill Memorial Trust.*
Beautifully situated ³/₄ acre part terraced garden with pond and a 1¹/₄ acre arboretum and wildflower meadow. An extremely varied collection of trees, shrubs, climbers, colourful perennials, bulbs, grasses and bamboos, all designed to give yr-round colour and interest. Many overgrown shrubs have been removed allowing for much new planting.

WE ARE MACMILLAN. CANCER SUPPORT

In 2016 the Chesterfield Royal NGS Macmillan Cancer Unit will open

6 ◆ BLUEBELL ARBORETUM AND NURSERY

Annwell Lane, Smisby, Ashby de la Zouch LE65 2TA. Robert & Suzette Vernon, 01530 413700, sales@bluebellnursery.com, www.bluebellnursery.com. *1m NW of Ashby-de-la-Zouch. Arboretum is clearly signed in Annwell Lane (follow brown signs), ¹/₄ m S, through village of Smisby off B5006, between Ticknall & Ashby-de-la-Zouch. Free parking.* For NGS: Wed 30 Mar, Suns 10, 24 Apr, 8 May, 12 June, 17, 31 July, 14, 28 Aug, 11, 25 Sept, Tue 25 Oct, Sat 12 Nov (10.30-4.30). Adm £5, chd free. Tea and coffee available on request.
For other opening times and information, please phone, email or visit garden website.
Beautiful 9 acre woodland garden with a large collection of rare trees and shrubs. Interest throughout the yr with spring flowers, cool leafy areas in summer and sensational autumn colour. Many information posters describing the more obscure plants. Bring wellingtons in wet weather. Adjacent specialist tree and shrub nursery. Please be aware this is not a wood full of bluebells, despite the name. The woodland garden is fully labelled and the staff can answer questions or talk at length about any of the trees or shrubs on display. Please wear sturdy, waterproof footwear during wet weather! Full wheelchair access in dry, warm weather however grass paths can become wet and inaccessible in snow or after rain.

7 BRICK KILN FARM

Hulland Ward, Ashbourne DE6 3EJ. Mrs Jan Hutchinson, 01335 370440, robert.hutchinson123@btinternet.com. *4m E of Ashbourne (A517). 1m S of Carsington Water. From Hulland Ward take Dog Lane past church 2nd L. 100yds on R. From Ashbourne A517 Bradley Corner turn L follow sign for Carsington Water 1m on L.* Visits by arrangement May to Aug (am, pm and evening visits). Adm £3.50, chd free. Home-made teas. *Donation to Great Dane Adoption Society.*
A small country garden which wraps around an old red brick farmhouse accessed through a courtyard with original well. Irregularly shaped lawn bounded by wide herbaceous borders leading to duck pond and pet's memorial garden. A description that did not disappoint - Ashbourne Telegraph. Garden can be viewed online on Peak District TV. Small holding. Cattle and horses grazing.www.youtube.com/watch?v=G-nk3hZ6Pmo. Listed in DailyTelegraph as one of the best small gardens to visit. Level garden, some uneven flagstones, gravel drive plenty of parking.

8 ◆ THE BURROWS GARDENS

Burrows Lane, Brailsford, Ashbourne DE6 3BU. Mrs N M Dalton, 01335 360745, enquiries@burrowsgardens.com, www.burrowsgardens.com. *5m SE of Ashbourne; 5m NW of Derby. A52 from Derby: turn L opp sign for Wild Park Leisure 1m before village of Brailsford. ¹/₄ m.* For NGS: Sun 1, Mon 30 May, Sun 10 July, Mon 29 Aug (11-4.30). Adm £5, chd free. Home-made teas. **For other opening times and information,** please phone, email or visit garden website.

5 acres of stunning garden set in beautiful countryside where immaculate lawns show off exotic rare plants and trees, mixing with old favourites in this outstanding garden. A huge variety of styles from temple to Cornish, Italian and English, gloriously designed and displayed. This is a must see garden. Non NGS: Open every Tues, Fri, and Sun from April - August incl. Look out for Special events such as Shakespeare productions and wine tasting. Refreshments can be provided for pre booked groups. Most of garden accessible to wheelchairs.

9 BYWAYS

7A Brookfield Avenue, Brookside, Chesterfield S40 3NX. Terry & Eileen Kelly, 01246 566376, telkel1@aol.com. *1¹/₂ m W of Chesterfield. Follow A619 from Chesterfield towards Baslow. Brookfield Av is 2nd R after Brookfield Sch. Please park on Chatsworth Rd (A619).* Sat 30, Sun 31 July (1-4.30). Adm £3, chd free. Home-made teas. Visits also by arrangement July & Aug, adm incl tea and cakes. *Donation to Ashgate Hospice.*

Previous winners of the Best Back Garden over 80sq m, Best Container Garden and Best Hanging Basket in Chesterfield in Bloom. Well established perennial borders incl helenium, monardas, phlox, penstenom, grasses, acers (30+), giving a very colourful display. Rockery and many planters containing hostas, fuchsia, ferns and roses. 5 seating areas. Featured in Garden Answers and as Garden of the Week in Garden News.

10 ◆ CALKE ABBEY

Ticknall DE73 7LE. National Trust, 01332 865587, www.nationaltrust.org.uk. *10m S of Derby. On A514 at Ticknall between Swadlincote & Melbourne.* For NGS: Sat 11 June, Sat 17 Sept (10-4.30). Adm £9.20, chd £4.60. For other opening times and information, please phone or visit garden website.

Late C18 walled gardens gradually repaired over the last 25yrs. Flower garden with summer bedding, herbaceous borders and the unique auricula theatre. Georgian orangery,

impressive collection of glasshouses and garden buildings. Ice house and repaired grotto and gardeners' tunnel. Vegetable garden growing heirloom varieties of fruit and vegetables, often on sale to visitors. Restaurant at main visitor facilities for light refreshments and locally sourced food. Electric buggy available for those with mobility problems.

11 ◆ CASCADES GARDENS

Clatterway, Bonsall, Matlock DE4 2AH. Alan & Alesia Clements, 01629 822813, cascadesgardens@gmail.com, www.derbyshiregarden.com. *5m SW of Matlock. From Cromford A6 T-lights turn towards Wirksworth. Turn R along Via Gellia, signed Buxton & Bonsall. After 1m turn R up hill towards Bonsall. Cascades on R at top of hill before village.* For NGS: Sun 15 May, Sun 12, Wed 22 June, Sun 10, Sun 24 July (1-6). Adm £4, chd free. Good range of home-made cakes. For other opening times and information, please phone, email or visit garden website.

Fascinating 4 acre garden in spectacular natural surroundings with woodland, high cliffs, stream, pond, a ruined corn mill and old lead mine. Secluded garden rooms provide peaceful views of the extensive collection of unusual plants, shrubs and trees. Featured on BBC - Escape to the Country. Gravel paths, some steep slopes.

12 CHERRY HILL

The Nook, Eyam S32 5QP. June Elizabeth Skinner, juneliza.s@btinternet.com. *6m NW of Chatsworth in Peak National Park. Off A623. In Eyam past church on R take 1st R up Hawkhill Rd. Car Park opp museum. 200yds up hill walk, entrance on bottom of The Nook. Disabled parking at Cherry Hill up drive next to house.* Sun 29 May (1-5). Adm £3.50, chd free. Home-made teas. Delicious cakes baked by my husband.

One acre naturally planted artists' garden. The S facing aspect with beautiful country views. This garden has a delightful blend of herbaceous borders, secret areas, and a geranium carpeted orchard. Sculptures hidden amongst the foliage reflect the quirky and different style, which the present owner has

brought to this garden. Artist's Studio open with a display of ceramics for sale. Garden sculptures made by the owner to be found around the garden. Special delight for children is a secret tree den.

Secret walled suburban garden, every corner brimming with plants . . .

13 10 CHESTNUT WAY

Repton DE65 6FQ. Robert & Pauline Little, 01283 702267, rlittleq@gmail.com, www.littlegarden.org.uk. *6m S of Derby. From A38, S of Derby, follow signs to Willington, then Repton. In Repton turn R at r'about. Chestnut Way is ¹/₄ m up hill, on L.* Sat 27, Sun 28 Feb (11-3). Adm £3, chd free. Home-made soup in February. Opening with Repton Village Gardens on Sun 22 May, Sun 24 July, Sun 28 Aug. Visits also by arrangement Jan to Oct for groups of 10+ (adm incl home-made tea and guided tour).

Wander through an acre of sweeping mixed borders, spring bulbs, mature trees to a stunning butterfly bed, young arboretum, established prairie. Meet a pair of passionate, practical, compost loving gardeners who gently manage this plantsman's garden. Designed and maintained by the owners. Expect a colourful display throughout the yr. Plenty of seats, conservatory if wet. Thousands of snowdrops. Excellent plant stall in Spring. Special interest in viticella clematis and organic vegetables. Level garden, good solid paths to main areas. Some grass/bark paths.

Dam Stead

displays in the mainly lawned areas. As a Residential Home for the Elderly, our Gardens are developed to inspire our residents from a number of sensory perspectives - different colours, textures and fragrances of plants, growing vegetables next to the C18 potting shed. There is also a veteran (500 - 800 yr old) Yew tree. Most of garden is lawned or block paved. Regret no wheelchair access to woodland area.

17 CRAIGSIDE
Reservoir Road, Whaley Bridge SK23 7BW. Jane & Gerard Lennox, 07939 012634, jane@lennoxonline.net, www.craigside.info. *11m SE of Stockport. 11m NNW of Buxton. Turn off A6 onto A5004 to Whaley Bridge. Turn R at train station 1st L under railway bridge onto Reservoir Rd. Park on roadside or in village. Garden is 1/2 m from village.* Fri 15 July (3-8); Sat 16, Sun 17 July (1-5). Adm £3.50, chd free. Home-made teas. Gluten free cakes also available. **Visits also by arrangement June to Aug.**

1 acre garden rising steeply from the Reservoir giving magnificent views across Todbrook reservoir into Peak District. Gravel paths, stone steps with stopping places. Many mature trees incl 500+yr old oak. Spring bulbs, summer fuchsias, herbaceous borders, alpine bed, steep mature rockery many heucheras and hydrangeas. Herbs, vegetables and fruit trees. Refreshments also available for 4 legged visitors with a selection of home-made dog biscuits! These are also edible for humans and were tested by some of the volunteers.

18 8 CURZON LANE
Alvaston, Derby DE24 8QS. John & Marian Gray, 01332 601596, maz@curzongarden.com, www.curzongarden.com. *2m SE of Derby city centre. From city centre take A6 (London Rd) towards Alvaston. Curzon Lane on L, approx 1/2 m before Alvaston shops.* Sun 17, Sun 24 July, Sun 14 Aug (1-6). Adm £2.50, chd free. Tea. **Visits also by arrangement July & Aug.**
Mature garden with lawns, borders packed full with perennials, shrubs and small trees, tropical planting and hot border. Ornamental and wildlife ponds, greenhouse with different

14 CHEVIN BRAE
Milford, Belper DE56 0QH. Dr David Moreton, 01332 843553. *1 1/2 m S of Belper. Park in Mill House PH car park. Cross A6 turn R & cont up Chevin Rd immed on L. After 300 yds follow arrow to L up Morrells Lane. After 300 yds Chevin Brae on L with silver garage.* Sun 3 Apr (1-5). Adm £2.50, chd free. Home-made teas. **Visits also by arrangement Mar to Sept. Please leave message on answer phone.**
A large garden, with swathes of daffodils in the orchard a spring feature. Extensive wild flower planting along edge of wood features aconites, snowdrops, wood anemones, fritillaries and dog tooth violets. Other parts of garden will have hellebores and early camelias. Tea and home-made pastries, many of which feature fruit and jam from the garden, served from the summer house in the middle of the orchard.

15 13 CHILTERN DRIVE
West Hallam, Ilkeston DE7 6PA. Jacqueline & Keith Holness. *Approx 7m NE of Derby. From A609, 2m W of Ilkeston, nr The Bottle Kiln, take St Wilfreds Rd. Take 1st R onto Derbyshire Av, Chiltern Drive is 3rd turning on L.* Sun 29 May (11-5). Adm £2.50, chd free. Home-made teas. Gluten free also available.

A plant lover's garden that's as pretty as a picture. A secret walled suburban garden, every corner brimming with plants, many rare and unusual. Paris, podophyllum, beesia, schefflera to name but a few and more than 30 varieties of hosta. A pretty summerhouse, two small ponds and fernery, together with over 60 different acers and some well hidden lizards!! Garden is on two levels separated by steps. Featured in Derbyshire magazine.

16 COXBENCH HALL
Alfreton Road, Coxbench, Derby DE21 5BB. Mr Brian Ballin. *4m N of Derby close to A38. After passing thru Little Eaton, turn L onto Alfreton Rd for 1m, Coxbench Hall is on L next to Fox & Hounds PH between Little Eaton & Holbrook. From A38, take Kilburn turn & go towards Little Eaton.* Sun 8 May, Sun 11 Sept (2.30-4.30). Adm £3, chd free. Tea, coffee and home-made cakes (incl diabetic and gluten free).
Formerly the ancestral home of the Meynell family, the gardens reflect the Georgian house standing in 4 1/2 acres of grounds most of which is accessible and wheelchair friendly. The garden has 2 fishponds connected by a stream, a sensory garden for the sight impaired, a short woodland walk through shrubbery, rockery, vegetable plot and seasonal

varieties of tomato, cucumber, peppers and chilies. Well stocked vegetable plot. Gravel area and large patio with container planting.

19 DAM STEAD
3 Crowhole, Barlow, Dronfield S18 7TJ. Derek & Barbara Saveall, 01142 890802, barbarasaveall@hotmail.co.uk. *Chesterfield B6051 to Barlow. Tickled Trout PH on L. Springfield Rd on L then R on unnamed rd. Last cottage on R.* **Visits by arrangement May to Sept. Adm £2.50, chd free.** Approx 1 acre with stream, weir, fragrant garden, rose tunnel, orchard garden and dam with an island. Long woodland path, alpine troughs, rockeries and mixed planting. A natural wildlife garden large summerhouse with seating inside and out. 3 village well dressings and carnival over one week mid August.

20 DOVE COTTAGE
off Watery Lane, Clifton, Ashbourne DE6 2JQ. Stephen & Anne Liverman, 01335 343545, astrantiamajor@hotmail.co.uk. *1¹/₂ m SW of Ashbourne. Enter Clifton village. Turn R at Xrds by church. After 100yds turn L, Dove Cottage 1st house on L. Always well signed on open days.* **Sat 28, Sun 29 May (11-4). Adm £4, chd free. Tea.** *Donation to British Heart Foundation.* Celebrating 30yrs of opening for NGS. ³/₄ acre cottage garden by the R Dove, has collections of new and traditional hardy plants and shrubs, notably Astrantias, alliums, geraniums, hostas, variegated and silver foliage plants. This plantsman's garden is noted for numbers of separate areas, incl a ribbon border of purple flowering plants and foliage, woodland glade planted with daffodils and shade loving plants.

21 THE DOWER HOUSE
Church Square, Melbourne DE73 8JH. William & Griselda Kerr, 01332 864756 or 07799 883777, griseldakerr@btinternet.com. *6m S of Derby. 5m W of exit 23A M1. 4m N of exit 13 M42. In Church Square, turn R at blue church service times sign, just before you pass church, gates 50 yrds ahead.* **Sat 27, Sun 28 Feb (10-3). Sat 23, Sun 24 Apr (10-4); Sat 18, Sun 19 June (10-5).**

Tea. Adm £3.50, chd free. Visits also by arrangement, please do not book more than 6 weeks in advance. Beautiful view of Melbourne Pool from balustraded terrace running length of 1831 house. Garden drops steeply by paths and steps to lawn with herbaceous border and bank of roses best in June with late summer beds good in August and September. Rose tunnel, glade, orchard, hellebores and small woodland lovely in early spring, bog planting, rockery, herb garden, other small lawns and vegetable garden. Children can search for a bronze crocodile, a stone pig and a metal bug. They might also see a huge iron sunflower hanging in a tree and a bronze girl doing cartwheels. There are many seats around the garden where visitors can sit while keeping an eye on their children as they do the searching. Featured in Derby EveningTelegraph, Derbyshire Life. Wheelchair access to most of garden.

> Currently the NGS donates around £2.5 million every year . . .

GROUP OPENING

22 ELMTON GARDENS
Elmton, Worksop S80 4LS. *2m from Creswell, 3m from Clowne, 5m from J30, M1. From M1 take A616 to Newark. Follow approx 4m. Turn R at Elmton signpost. At junction turn R.* **Sat 25, Sun 26 June (1-5). Combined adm £4, chd free. Light refreshments. Cream teas available in School Room next to church.**

ELM TREE COTTAGE
Dianne & Chris Illsley

ELMWOOD HOUSE
Ian & Liz Chapman

PINFOLD
Nikki Kirsop

Elmton is a lovely little village situated on a stretch of rare magnesian limestone in the middle of attractive

farm land. There are about 40 houses, a PH, a church and a village green. This weekend is our Well Dressing weekend. There are 3 boards to see in different locations around the village. At Spring Cottage there is a print studio offering demonstrations. Visitors welcome. In the church there will be an exhibition of local history devised by the History Group and in the Carriage House a display of local archaeology findings. Food and drink is available throughout the day at the Elm Tree PH.

23 FIR CROFT
Froggatt Road, Calver S32 3ZD. Dr S B Furness, www.alpineplantcentre.co.uk. *4m N of Bakewell. At junction of B6001 with A625 (formerly B6054), adjacent to Power Garage.* **Sun 22 May, Sun 5, Sun 19 June (2-5). Adm by donation.** Massive scree with many varieties. Plantsman's garden; rockeries; water garden and nursery; extensive collection (over 3000 varieties) of alpines; conifers; over 800 sempervivums, 500 saxifrages and 350 primulas. Many new varieties not seen anywhere else in the UK. Tufa and scree beds. 30th Anniversary of opening for NGS Large new tufa bed. Featured in BBC Great British Garden Revival.

24 GAMESLEY FOLD COTTAGE
Gamesley Fold, Glossop SK13 6JJ. Mrs G Carr, 01457 867856, gcarr@gamesleyfold.co.uk, www.gamesleyfold.co.uk. *2m W of Glossop. Off A626 Glossop - Marple Rd nr Charlesworth. Turn down lane directly opp St. Margaret's School, white cottage at bottom.* **Sun 22 May (1-4). Adm £2.50, chd free. Home-made teas. Visits also by arrangement Mar to Sept any number welcome.** Old fashioned cottage garden with rhododendrons, herbaceous borders with candelabra primulas, flowers and herbs. Vegetable garden and a water feature. Plant nursery with display garden enclosure open Sunday's 1-4pm 27 March to end August. All money raised donated to NGS. Featured in local press.

25 HIGH ROOST

27 Storthmeadow Road,
Simmondley, Glossop SK13 6UZ.
Peter & Christina Harris, 01457
863888, peter-harris9@sky.com.
*¾ m SW of Glossop. From Glossop
A57 to M/CL at 2nd r'about, up
Simmondley Ln nr top R turn. From
Marple A626 to Glossop, in Chworth
R up Town Ln past Hare & Hound PH
2nd L.* **Sun 26 June (12-4). Adm
£2.50, chd free. Light
refreshments. Visits also by
arrangement June to Aug.**
*Donation to Manchester Dogs
Home.*
Garden on terraced slopes, views
over fields and hills. Winding paths,
archways and steps explore different
garden rooms packed with plants,
designed to attract wildlife. Alpine
bed, vegetable garden, water
features, statuary, troughs and
planters. A garden which needs
exploring to discover its secrets
tucked away in hidden corners. Craft
Stall, children's garden quiz and lucky
dip. New for 2016, gravel garden with
planted beds.

26 HIGHFIELD HOUSE

Wingfield Road, Oakerthorpe,
Alfreton DE55 7AP. Paul & Ruth
Peat and Janet & Brian Costall,
01773 521342,
highfieldhouseopengardens
@hotmail.co.uk,
www.highfieldhouse.weebly.com.
*Rear of Alfreton Golf Club. A615
Alfreton-Matlock Rd.* **Visits by
arrangement in Feb, adm incl
refreshments inside by the fire!
Groups 10+. Adm £6.00, chd free.**
Lovely country garden of approx 1
acre, incorporating a shady garden,
woodland, tree house, laburnum
tunnel, orchard, parterre, herbaceous
borders and productive vegetable
garden. No general openings in 2016
whilst we undertake some major work
on our house and garden. Groups
welcome by appointment, in February
to see our Snowdrops, and come
inside for refreshments. Some steps,
slopes and gravel areas.

27 HILLSIDE

286 Handley Road, New
Whittington, Chesterfield S43 2ET.
Mr E J Lee, 01246 454960,
eric.lee5@btinternet.com. *3m N of
Chesterfield. Between B6056 &
B0652 N of village. SatNav friendly.*
Visits by arrangement Feb to
Sept, groups and individual
visitors. Adm £2.50, chd free.
Light refreshments.
⅓ acre sloping site. Herbaceous
borders, rock garden, alpines,
streams, pools, bog gardens, asiatic
primula bed, and alpine house. Acers,
bamboos, collection of approx
150 varieties of ferns, eucalypts,
euphorbias, grasses, conifers,
Himalayan bed. 1000+ plants
permanently labelled. Yr round
interest.

A garden which
needs exploring
to discover its
secrets tucked
away in hidden
corners . . .

28 HOLLIES FARM PLANT CENTRE

Uppertown, Bonsall, Matlock
DE4 2AW. Robert & Linda Wells,
01629 822734,
linda@holliesfarm.plus.com,
www.holliesfarmplantcentre.co.uk.
*From Cromford turn R off A5012 up
The Clatterway. Keep R past Fountain
Tearoom to village cross, take L up
High St, then 2nd L onto Abel Lane.
Garden straight ahead.* **Sat 18, Sun
19 June (11-4). Adm £3, chd free.
Cream teas.**
The best selection in Derbyshire with
advice and personal attention from
Robert and Linda Wells at their family
run business. Enjoy a visit to
remember in our beautiful display
garden - set within glorious Peak
District countryside. Huge variety of
hardy perennials incl the rare and
unusual. Vast selection of traditional
garden favourites. Award winning
hanging baskets. Ponds, herbaceous
borders and glorious views.

29 THE HOLLY TREE

21 Hackney Road, Hackney,
Matlock DE4 2PX. Carl
Hodgkinson. *½ m NW of Matlock,
off A6. Take A6 NW past bus stn &
1st R up Dimple Rd. At T-junction,
turn R & immed L, for Farley &
Hackney. Take 1st L onto Hackney
Rd. Continue ¾ m.* **Sat 11, Sun 12
June (11-4.30). Adm £3, chd free.
Home-made teas.**
The garden is in excess of 1½ acres
and set on a steeply sloping S facing
site, sheltering behind a high retaining
wall and incl a small arboretum, bog
garden, herbaceous borders, pond,
vegetables, fruits, apiary and
chickens. Extensively terraced with
many paths and steps and with
spectacular views across the Derwent
valley to Snitterton and Oker.

30 ◆ LEA GARDENS

Lea, Matlock DE4 5GH.
Mr & Mrs J Tye, 01629 534380,
www.leagarden.co.uk. *5m SE of
Matlock. Off A6 & A615.* **For opening
times and information, please
phone or visit garden website.**
Rare collection of rhododendrons,
azaleas, kalmias, alpines and conifers
in delightful woodland setting.
Gardens are sited on remains of
medieval quarry and cover about 4
acres. Specialised plant nursery of
rhododendrons and azaleas on site.
Open daily 1 March to 31 July (9-5).
Plant sales by appointment out of
season. Visitors welcome throughout
the yr. Coffee shop noted for home
baked cakes and light refreshments.
Gravel paths, steep slopes. Free
access for wheelchair users.

31 THE LILIES

Griffe Grange Valley, Grangemill,
Matlock DE4 4BW. Chris & Bridget
Sheppard, www.thelilies.com. *4m
N Cromford. On A5012 via Gellia Rd
4m N Cromford. 1st house on R after
junction with B5023 to Middleton.
From Grangemill 1st house on L after
Prospect Quarry (IKO Permatrack).*
**Sun 3 July, Sun 4 Sept (11.30-5).
Adm £3, chd free. Home-made
teas and light lunches.**
1 acre garden gradually restored over
the past 10yrs situated at the top of a
wooded valley, surrounded by
wildflower meadow and ash
woodland. Area adjacent to house
with seasonal planting and
containers. Mixed shrubs and
perennial borders many raised from

seed. 3 ponds, vegetable plot, barn conversion with separate cottage style garden. Natural garden with stream developed from old mill pond. Walks in large wild-flower meadow and ash woodland both SSSI's. Handspinning demonstration and natural dyeing display using materials from the garden and wool from sheep in the meadow. Light lunches served 11:30am to 2:00pm, home-made teas all day. Locally made crafts for sale. Partial wheelchair access. Steep slope from car park, limestone chippings at entrance, some boggy areas if wet.

32 LOCKO PARK
Spondon, Derby DE21 7BW. Mrs Lucy Palmer, www.lockopark.co.uk. *6m NE of Derby. From A52 Borrowash bypass, 2m N via B6001, turn to Spondon. More directions on www.lockopark.co.uk. NB. SatNav input via Locko Rd.* Sun 22 May (2-5). Adm £3, chd free. Tea, coffee, soft drinks and home-made cakes.
An original 1927 open garden for the NGS. Large garden; pleasure gardens; rose gardens designed by William Eames. House (not open) by Smith of Warwick with Victorian additions. Chapel (open) Charles II, with original ceiling. Tulip tree in the arboretum purported to be the largest in the Midlands. Large collection of rhododendron and azalea. BBC Radio Derby and Derby Telegraph. Wheelchair access to some parts of the garden is difficult so, unfortunately, not all of the garden areas are accessible.

33 9 MAIN STREET
Horsley Woodhouse DE7 6AU. Ms Alison Napier, 01332 881629, ibhillib@btinternet.com. *3m SW of Heanor. 6m N of Derby. Turn off A608 Derby to Heanor rd at Smalley, towards Belper, (A609). Garden on A609, 1m from Smalley turning.* Sat 6, Sun 7 Aug (1.30-4.30). Adm £3, chd free. Cream teas. Visits also by arrangement Apr to Sept. Refreshments by prior arrangement.
$1/3$ acre hilltop garden overlooking lovely farmland view. Terracing, borders, lawns and pergola create space for an informal layout with planting for colour effect. Features incl large wildlife pond with water

lilies, bog garden and small formal pool. Emphasis on carefully selected herbaceous perennials mixed with shrubs and old fashioned roses. Gravel garden for sun loving plants and scree garden, both developed from former drive. Plant stall has a wide collection of home grown plants and a selection of sempervivums for sale. All parts of the garden accessible to wheelchairs. Wheelchair adapted WC.

34 2 MANVERS STREET
Ripley DE5 3EQ. Mrs D Wood & Mr D Hawkins, 01773 743962, d.s.Hawkins@btinternet.com. *Ripley Town centre to Derby rd turn L opp Leisure Centre onto Heath Rd. 1st turn R onto Meadow Rd, 1st L onto Manvers St.* Sat 9, Sun 10 July (1.30-5). Adm £3, chd free. Home-made teas. Visits also by arrangement July & Aug.
Summer garden with backdrop of neighbouring trees, 10 borders bursting with colour surrounded by immaculate shaped lawn. Perennials incl 26 clematis, annuals, baskets, tubs and pots. Ornamental fish pond. Water features, arbour and summerhouse. Plenty of seating areas to take in this awe inspiring oasis.

35 ◆ MELBOURNE HALL GARDENS
Church Square, Melbourne, Derby DE73 8EN. Melbourne Gardens Charity, 01332 862502, Melbhall@globalnet.co.uk, www.melbournehallgardens.com. *6m S of Derby. At Melbourne Market Place turn into Church St, go down to Church Sq. Garden entrance across visitor centre next to Melbourne Hall tea room.* For NGS: Sat 28, Sun 29 May (1.30-5). Adm £5, chd free.
For other opening times and information, please phone, email or visit garden website.
A 17 acre historic garden with an abundance of rare trees and shrubs. Woodland and waterside planting with extensive herbaceous borders. Meconopsis, candelabra primulas, various Styrax and Cornus kousa. Other garden features incl Bakewells wrought iron arbour, a yew tunnel and fine C18 statuary and water features. 300yr old trees, waterside planting, feature hedges and herbaceous borders. Fine statuary and stonework. Featured in Derbyshire

Life, Country Images, Derbyshire magazines and the Financial Times. Gravel paths, uneven surface in places, some steep slopes.

36 ◆ MEYNELL LANGLEY TRIALS GARDEN
Lodge Lane (off Flagshaw Lane), Kirk Langley, Ashbourne DE6 4NT. Robert & Karen Walker, 01332 824358, enquiries@meynell-langley-gardens.co.uk, www.meynell-langley-gardens.co.uk. *4m W of Derby, nr Kedleston Hall. Head W out of Derby on A52. At Kirk Langley turn R onto Flagshaw Lane (signed to Kedleston Hall) then R onto Lodge Lane. Follow Meynell Langley Gdns.* For NGS: Sun 26 June, Sun 17 July, Sun 21 Aug, Sun 18 Sept, Sun 16 Oct (10.30-4.30). Adm £3, chd free.
For other opening times and information, please phone, email or visit garden website.
Formal $3/4$ acre Victorian style garden established over 20yrs, displaying and trialling new and existing varieties of bedding plants, herbaceous perennials and vegetable plants grown at the adjacent nursery. Over 180 hanging baskets and floral displays. 60 varieties of apple, pear and other fruit. Summer fruit pruning demonstrations on July NGS day and apple tasting on October NGS day. Adjacent tea rooms serving light lunches and refreshments daily. Level ground and firm grass. Full disabled access to tea rooms.

37 **NEW** **16 MONARCH DRIVE**
Oakwood, Derby DE21 2XW. Gary
& Gill Stillwell. *3m NE of Derby. Nr
A52 & A38. From A38 take A61 to
Derby, at island take 1st L to
Breadsall village. Turn R onto
Brookside Rd, at junction R & immed
L onto Lime Lane.* **Sun 12 June, Sun
7 Aug (11-5). Adm £2.50, chd free.
Light refreshments.**
A lovely plantaholic cottage style
garden, with curved lawns, island
gravel beds, small ornamental ponds.
Large collection of perennials,
displayed in curved borders. Many
grasses, acers, bamboos and palms.
3 patios with container planting.
Featured in Derby Evening Telegraph.

38 **MOORFIELDS**
257/261 Chesterfield Road, Temple
Normanton, Chesterfield S42 5DE.
Peter, Janet & Stephen Wright,
01246 852306,
peterwright100@hotmail.com. *4m
SE of Chesterfield. From Chesterfield
take A617 for 2m, turn on to B6039
through Temple Normanton, taking R
fork signed Tibshelf, B6039. Garden
¼ m on R. Limited parking.* **Sun 15
May, Sun 3 July (1-5). Adm £3, chd
free. Light refreshments. Visits
also by arrangement May to Aug
for groups 10+, afternoons or
evenings.**
Two adjacent gardens, the larger with
mature, mixed island beds and
borders, a recently extended gravel
garden to the front, a small wild
flower area, large wildlife pond,
orchard and soft fruit, and vegetable
garden. Show of late flowering tulips.
Smaller back and front gardens of
No. 257 feature herbaceous borders
and shrubs. Views across to mid
Derbyshire. Free range eggs for sale.

39 **NEW MILLS SCHOOL AND
SIXTH FORM**
Church Lane, New Mills, High Peak
SK22 4NR. Mr Craig Pickering,
07833 373593,
cpickering@newmillsschool.co.uk,
www.newmillsschool.co.uk/ngs.
html. *12m NNW of Buxton. From A6
take A6105 signed New Mills,
Hayfield. At C of E Church turn L onto
Church Lane. School on L. Parking
on site.* **Sat 9 July (10-4.30); Sun 10
July (1-5). Adm £3, chd free. Light
refreshments in School Library.
Visits also by arrangement June
to Sept for groups 10+.**
Mixed herbaceous perennials/shrub

borders, with mature trees and lawns
and gravel border situated in the semi
rural setting of the High Peak incl a
Grade II listed building with 4 themed
quads. The school was awarded a
distinction for their first garden at
Tatton RHS Flower Show 2015. Hot
and Cold Beverages and a selection
of sandwiches, cream teas and
home-made cakes available. Ramps
allow wheelchair access to most of
outside, flower beds and into Grade II
listed building and library.

*Show of late
flowering tulips . . .*

40 **9 NEWFIELD CRESCENT**
Dore, Sheffield S17 3DE. Mike &
Norma Jackson, 01142 366198,
mandnjackson@googlemail.com.
*Dore - SW Sheffield. Turn off
Causeway Head Rd on Heather Lea
Av. 2nd L into Newfield Crescent.
Parking on roadside.* **Sat 28, Sun 29
May (2-6). Adm £3, chd free. Light
refreshments. Visits also by
arrangement May to July.**
Mature, wildlife friendly garden
planted to provide all yr interest.
Upper terrace with alpines in troughs
and bowls. Lower terrace featuring
pond with cascade and connecting
stream to second pond. Bog garden,
rock gardens, lawn alpine bed, wilder
areas, mixed borders with trees,
shrubs and perennials. Featuring
azaleas, rhododendrons, camellias,
primulas. Wheelchair access without
steps to top terrace offering full view
of garden.

41 **◆ OLD ENGLISH WALLED
GARDEN, ELVASTON CASTLE
COUNTRY PARK**
Borrowash Road, Elvaston, Derby
DE72 3EP. Derbyshire County
Council, 01629 533870,
www.derbyshire.gov.uk/elvaston.
*4m E of Derby. Signed from A52 &
A50. Car parking charge applies.*
**For NGS: Sat 16 Apr, Sat 13 Aug
(12-4). Adm £2, chd free. Delicious
home-made cakes. For other
opening times and information,
please phone or visit garden
website.**

Come and discover the beauty of the
Old English walled garden at Elvaston
Castle. Take in the peaceful
atmosphere and enjoy the scents and
colours of all the varieties of trees,
shrubs and plants. Spring bulbs,
summer bedding, large herbaceous
borders. After your visit to the walled
garden take time to walk around the
wider estate featuring romantic
topiary gardens, lake, woodland and
nature reserve. Estate gardeners on
hand during the day.

42 **NEW** **OTTERWOOD**
88 St Johns Road, Buxton
SK17 6TP. Ms Simone Harch &
Mr Gary Mellor,
simoneharch@hotmail.co.uk.
*Parking on St Johns Rd & Gadley
Lane.* **Sun 10, Sat 16 July (1-5).
Adm £3, chd free. Home-made
teas. Visits also by arrangement
June & July.**
A romantic, peaceful garden featuring
summer borders, cutting and kitchen
garden, natural pond with viewing
pontoon. A haven for wildlife,
organically managed. Lovely garden
terrace for tea and cake. Winner of
Buxton in Bloom Wildlife Garden.

43 **THE PADDOCK**
12 Manknell Rd, Whittington Moor,
Chesterfield S41 8LZ. Mel & Wendy
Taylor, 01246 451001,
debijt9276@gmail.com. *2m N of
Chesterfield. Whittington Moor just off
A61 between Sheffield & Chesterfield.
Parking available at Victoria Working
Mens Club, garden signed from here.*
**Sun 15 May, Sun 7 Aug (11-5).
Adm £3.50, chd free. Cream teas.
Visits also by arrangement Apr to
Aug.**
½ acre garden incorporating small
formal garden, stream and koi filled
pond. Stone path over bridge, up
some steps, past small copse, across
the stream at the top and back down
again. Past herbaceous border
towards a pergola where cream teas
can be enjoyed.

44 **PARK HALL**
Walton Back Lane, Walton,
Chesterfield S42 7LT. Kim &
Margaret Staniforth, 01246 567412,
kim.staniforth@btinternet.com. *2m
SW of Chesterfield centre. From town
on A 619 L into Somersall Lane. On
A632 R into Acorn Ridge. Park on
field side only of Walton Back Lane.*

Visits by arrangement Apr to July for groups 20+. Adm £5.00, chd free. Home-made teas. *Donation to Bluebell Wood Childrens Hospice.*
Romantic 2 acre plantsmans garden, in a stunningly beautiful setting surrounding C17 house (not open) 4 main rooms, terraced garden, parkland area with forest trees, croquet lawn, sunken garden with arbours, pergolas, pleached hedge, topiary, statuary, roses, rhododendrons, camellias, several water features. Newly planted driveside. Two steps down to gain access to garden.

45 RECTORY HOUSE
Kedleston, Derby DE22 5JJ.
Helene Viscountess Scarsdale. *5m NW Derby. A52 from Derby turn R Kedleston sign. Drive to village turn R. Brick house standing back from rd on sharp corner.* **Sat 28 May (2-5). Adm £3.50, chd free. Home-made teas.**
The garden is next to Kedleston Park and is of C18 origin. Many established rare trees and shrubs also rhododendrons, azaleas and unusual roses. Large natural pond with amusing frog fountain. Primulas, gunneras, darmeras and lots of moisture loving plants. The winding paths go through trees and past wild flowers and grasses. New stumpery with rare plants. Delicious teas and cakes available. Soft drinks. Partial wheelchair access. Uneven paths.

46 ◆ RENISHAW HALL & GARDENS
Renishaw, Sheffield S21 3WB.
Alexandra Hayward, 01246 432310, **enquiries@renishaw-hall.co.uk, www.renishaw-hall.co.uk.** *10m from Sheffield city centre. By car: Renishaw Hall only 3m from J30 on M1, well signed from junction r'about.* **For NGS: Mon 23 May, Tue 12 July (10.30-4.30). Adm £5.50, chd free. Light refreshments at Gallery Cafe.** For other opening times and information, please phone, email or visit garden website.
Renishaw Hall and Gardens boasts 7 acres of stunning gardens created by Sir George Sitwell in 1885. The Italianate gardens feature various rooms with extravagant herbaceous borders. Rose gardens, rare trees and shrubs, National Collection of Yuccas, sculptures, woodland walks

Otterwood

and lakes create a magical and engaging garden experience. Winner of HHA Garden of the Year. Wheelchair route around garden.

GROUP OPENING

47 NEW REPTON VILLAGE GARDENS
Repton, Derby DE65 6FQ. *6m S of Derby. From A38, S of Derby, follow signs to Willington, then Repton.* **Sun 22 May, Sun 24 July, Sun 28 Aug (1.30-5.30). Combined adm £6, chd free. Home-made teas at 10 Chestnut Way.**

ASKEW COTTAGE D
Louise Hardwick.
Open on all dates
Visits also by arrangement May to Oct, groups 10+
louise.hardwick@hotmail.co.uk
01283 701608

10 CHESTNUT WAY
Robert & Pauline Little.
Open on all dates
(See separate entry)
Visits also by arrangement Jan to Oct for groups of 10+ (adm incl home-made tea and guided tour)
rlittleq@gmail.com
01283 702267

NEW HOLME POINT
Mrs Janet Holmes.
Open on all dates
Visits also by arrangement June to Sept
01283 707445

22 PINFOLD CLOSE
Mr O Jowett.
Open on Sun 22 May, Sun 28 Aug

NEW REPTON ALLOTMENTS
Mr O Jowett.
Open on Sun 28 Aug

WOODEND COTTAGE
Wendy & Stephen Longden.
Open on Sun 24 July
(See separate entry)
Visits also by arrangement July & Aug for groups 10+
wendylongden@btinternet.com
01283 703259

Repton is a thriving village dating back to Anglo Saxon times and was where Christianity was first preached in the Midlands. In the crypt of the church there are still well preserved remains of Saxon architecture. The village gardens are all quite different ranging from the very small to very large. Askew cottage is a professionally designed garden and has many structural features linked together by curving paths. 10 Chestnut Way is a plantoholic's garden often likened to a tardis - be prepared to be surprised. Holme Point is an exquisitely designed small garden, formal beds are overflowing with perennial plants, 22 Pinfold Close is the smallest garden but is packed full with a special interest in tropical plants. There is an atmospheric safari hut in the top corner. Repton allotments is a small set of allotments currently undergoing a revival - expect lots of produce in August. Woodend Cottage is an organic garden with stunning views from the grass maze. All gardens have plenty of seats. Some gardens have grass or gravel paths but most areas accessible.

48 NEW 122 SHEFFIELD ROAD

Glossop SK13 8QU. Simon Groarke. *From Glossop town centre take A57 Snake Pass for Sheffield. Cont on A57 for 1m. House on R. Park on Shirebrook Dr. From Sheffield take A57 Glossop. After long descent, house on L.* **Sat 2 Apr, Sat 7 May (10.30-4). Adm £3, chd free. Cream teas.**

A woodland garden with an array of spring bulbs and a host of bluebells in May. Pathways meander through the garden and down to the brook. Nearer the house the garden opens up to perennial borders and lawns. There are plenty of seats to sit and enjoy the garden but please note there are several steps and uneven paths. Bluebell woodland garden with a babbling brook running through. Attractive perennial borders. Camellias, azaleas and rhododendrons are focal points.

49 THORNBRIDGE HALL

Ashford in the Water DE45 1NZ. Jim & Emma Harrison, www.thornbridgehall.co.uk. *2m NW of Bakewell. From Bakewell take A6, signed Buxton. After 2m, R onto A6020. ¹/₂ m turn L, signed Thornbridge Hall.* **Sun 31 July (10-4). Adm £5, chd free. Light refreshments.**

A stunning C19, 10 acre garden, set in the heart of the Peak District overlooking rolling Derbyshire countryside. Designed to create a vision of 1000 shades of green, the garden has many distinct areas. These incl koi lake and water garden, Italian garden with statuary, grottos and temples, 100ft herbaceous border, kitchen garden, scented terrace, hot border and refurbished glasshouses. Contains statuary from Clumber Park, Sydnope Hall and Chatsworth. Tea, coffee, sandwiches, cakes and award winning ice cream available. Gravel paths, steep slopes, steps.

50 TILFORD HOUSE

Hognaston, Ashbourne DE6 1PW. Mr & Mrs P R Gardner, 01335 372001, peter.rgardner@mypostoffice.co.uk. *5m NE of Ashbourne. A517 Belper to Ashbourne. At Hulland Ward follow signs to Hognaston. Downhill (2m) to bridge. Roadside parking 100 metres.* **Sun 15 May, Wed 29 June (2-5).**

Adm £4, chd free. Home-made teas. Visits also by arrangement May to July groups of 10+. Adm £5.

A 1¹/₂ acre streamside country garden. Woodland, wildlife areas and ponds lie alongside colourful borders. Collections of primulas, hostas, iris and clematis as well as many unusual plants and trees. Raised vegetable beds and fruit trees. Relax in a magical setting to listen to the sounds of the countryside. Featured in The Derbyshire Magazine, Derby Telegraph and Ashbourne Telegraph.

Designed to create a vision of 100 shades of green . . .

51 ◆ TISSINGTON HALL

Tissington, Ashbourne DE6 1RA. Sir Richard & Lady FitzHerbert, 01335 352200, tisshall@dircon.co.uk, www.tissingtonhall.co.uk. *4m N of Ashbourne. E of A515 on Ashbourne to Buxton Rd in centre of the beautiful Estate Village of Tissington.* **For NGS: Mon 30 May, Mon 29 Aug (12-3). Adm £6, chd free. Tea. For other opening times and information, please phone, email or visit garden website.**

Large garden celebrating over 75yrs in the NGS, with stunning rose garden on west terrace, herbaceous borders and 5 acres of grounds. Refreshments available at the award winning Herberts Fine English Tearooms in village (Tel 01335 350501). Wheelchair access advice from ticket seller.

52 12 WATER LANE

Middleton, Matlock DE4 4LY. Hildegard Wiesehofer, 01629 825543, wiesehofer@btinternet.com. *Approx 2¹/₂ m SW of Matlock. 1¹/₂ m NW of Wirksworth. At A6 & B5023 intersection take rd to Wirksworth. R to Middleton. Follow NGS signs. From Ashbourne take Matlock rd & follow signs. Park on main rd. Ltd parking in Water Lane.* **Sun 29 May (11-5); Mon 30 May (11-5.30). Adm £3.50, chd free. Tea.**

Small, eclectic hillside garden on different levels, created as a series of rooms over the last 10yrs incl woodland walk, ponds, eastern garden, infinity garden and terrace with stunning panoramic views over Derbyshire and Nottinghamshire. Glorious views and short distance from High Peak Trail, Middleton Top and Engine House. Featured on BBC Look East, Derbyshire Magazine, Radio Derby, Derby Evening Telegraph. Light wheelchair access only to front terrace and conservatory only, views over some of garden possible.

53 13 WESTFIELD ROAD

Swadlincote DE11 0BG. Val & Dave Booth, 01283 221167, valerie.booth@sky.com. *5m E of Burton-on-Trent, off A511. Take A511 from Burton-on-Trent. Follow signs for Swadlincote. Turn R into Springfield Rd, take 3rd R into Westfield Rd.* **Sun 26 June, Sun 7 Aug (1-5). Adm £3, chd free. Cream teas. Visits also by arrangement June to Aug adm incl tea and cake.**

A garden on 2 levels of approx ¹/₂ an acre. (7 steps with handrail). Packed herbaceous borders designed for colour. Roses and clematis scrambling over pergolas. A passion of ours are roses with over 40 varieties. Shrubs, baskets and tubs. Greenhouses, raised bed vegetable area, fruit trees and 2 ponds. Free range chicken area. Plenty of seating.

54 WESTGATE

Combs Road, Combs, Chapel-en-le-Frith, High Peak SK23 9UP. Maurice & Chris Lomas, 07854 680170, ca-lomas@sky.com. *N of Chapel-en-le-Frith off B5470. Turn L immed before Hanging Gate PH, signed Combs Village. ³/₄ m on L by railway bridge.* **Sun 29 May, Sun 26 June (1-5). Adm £3, chd free. Home-made teas. Visits also by arrangement for groups 10+.**

Large sloping garden in quiet village with beautiful views. Features incl mixed borders and beds containing many perenials, hosta and heuchera. Large rockery. Vegetable and fruit beds. Wild flower area, grasses and fernery. Natural pond and stream with bog area. 3 formal ponds. Chicken area. Lots of places to sit and enjoy the views. Featured in Amateur Gardening.

55 WHARFEDALE
34 Broadway, Duffield, Belper DE56 4BU. Roger & Sue Roberts, 01332 841905, rogerroberts34@outlook.com, www.garden34.co.uk. *4m N of Derby. Turn onto B5023 to Wirksworth (Broadway) off A6 at T-lights midway between Belper & Derby.* Sat 30 July (11-4); Sun 31 July (10.30-5). Adm £3, chd free. Home-made teas. Visits also by arrangement July & Aug for 4-25 visitors. Admission incl beverage and cake. Adm £6.
Garden design enthusiast with over 500 varieties and rare specimens. Eclectic and replicable. 12 distinct areas incl Piet Oudolf inspired, tropical and single colour schemes. Italianate walled garden and woodland with pond and raised walkway. Japanese landscape garden with stream, moon gate and pavilion. Front cottage garden with winter shrubs and meadow planting. Stone, wire and wood sculptures. Every plant labelled. Comfortable seating around the garden. Close to Kedleston Hall and Derwent Valley World Heritage Site. Featured on BBC Derby Radio and Garden News weekly magazine.

56 26 WHEELDON AVENUE
Derby DE22 1HN. Ian Griffiths, 01332 342204, idhgriffiths@gmail.com. *1m N of Derby. 1m from city centre & approached directly off Kedleston Rd or from A6 Duffield Rd via West Bank Ave. Limited on street parking.* Visits by arrangement May to July for groups 4+. Refreshments by arrangement. Adm £3.00, chd free.
Tiny Victorian walled garden near to city centre. Lawn and herbaceous borders with newly expanded old rose collection, lupins, delphiniums and foxgloves. Small terrace with topiary, herb garden and lion fountain. Rose collection. Featured in English Home magazine and Daily Telegraph magazine. Garden on one level, lawn may be soft if wet.

57 NEW WILD IN THE COUNTRY
Hawkhill Road, Eyam, Hope Valley S32 5QQ. Mrs Gill Bagshawe. *In Eyam, follow signs to public car park. Located next to Eyam Museum & opp public car park on Hawkhill Rd.* Sat 23 July (11-4). Adm £2.50, chd free.
A rectangular plot devoted totally to growing flowers and foliage for cutting. Sweet pea, rose, larkspur, cornflower, nigella, ammi. All the florist's favourites can be found here. There is a tea room, a village PH and several cafes in the village to enjoy refreshments.

The Queen's Nursing Institute

NGS support helps us improve patient care in the community

58 26 WINDMILL RISE
Belper DE56 1GQ. Kathy Fairweather, 07779 412702. *From Belper Market Place take Chesterfield Rd towards Heage. Top of hill, 1st R Marsh Lane, 1st R Windmill Lane, 1st R Windmill Rise - limited parking only.* Sat 2, Sun 3 July (11.30-4.30). Adm £3, chd free. Delicious home baking and light lunches.
Behind a deceptively ordinary looking façade, lies a surprise. Meander along extensive pathways lined with a tapestry of texture, colour, light and shade with a lush and restful atmosphere. A plant lovers' organic garden divided into sections: woodland, Japanese, secret garden, cottage, edible, ponds, small stream with some unusual specimen trees. Interview on BBC Radio Derby and featured in Derbyshire Times, Derby Evening Telegraph and Belper News.

59 WINDWARD
62 Summer Lane, Wirksworth, Matlock DE4 4EB. Audrey & Andrew Winkler, 01629 822681, audrey.winkler@w3z.co.uk, www.grandmafrogsgarden.co.uk. *5m S of Matlock. From Wirksworth Market Place take B5023 towards Duffield. After 300yds turn R onto Summer Lane at mini r'about. Windward approx 500yds on R.* Sun 24 Apr, Sun 10 July (11-4). Adm £4, chd free. Home-made cakes, coffee, variety of herbal teas available. Visits also by arrangement Mar to Sept for groups 10+. Donation to Framework Knitters Museum.
1 acre of greenery, with pockets of colour. Wildlife friendly, furnished with many different habitats. Mature trees provide shady spots to sit and relax. The crinkle crankle Leylandii hedge and a lolly holly add a surprising touch of formality. An abundance of foliage and winding paths where you can easily lose yourself. Audrey's home-made cakes are well worth the visit. A quiet space, hidden away on the edge of a small town. Completely secluded.

60 WOODEND COTTAGE
134 Main Street, Repton DE65 6FB. Wendy & Stephen Longden, 01283 703259, wendylongden@btinternet.com. *6m S of Derby. From A38, S of Derby, follow signs to Willington, then Repton. In Repton straight on at r'about through village. Garden is 1m on R.* Sun 7 Aug (1.30-5.30). Adm £3, chd free. Home-made teas. Opening with Repton Village Gardens on Sun 24 July. Visits also by arrangement July & Aug for groups 10+.
Plant lover's garden with glorious views on a sloping 2½ acre site developed organically for yr-round interest. On lower levels herbaceous borders are arranged informally and connected via lawns, thyme bed, pond and pergolas. Mixed woodland and grassed labyrinth lead naturally into fruit, vegetable and herb potager with meadows beyond. Especially colourful in July and August. Easy and unusual perennials and grasses for sale. Why not visit St Wystan's Church Repton with its Saxon crypt, as part of your visit. Wheelchair access on lower levels only.

DEVON

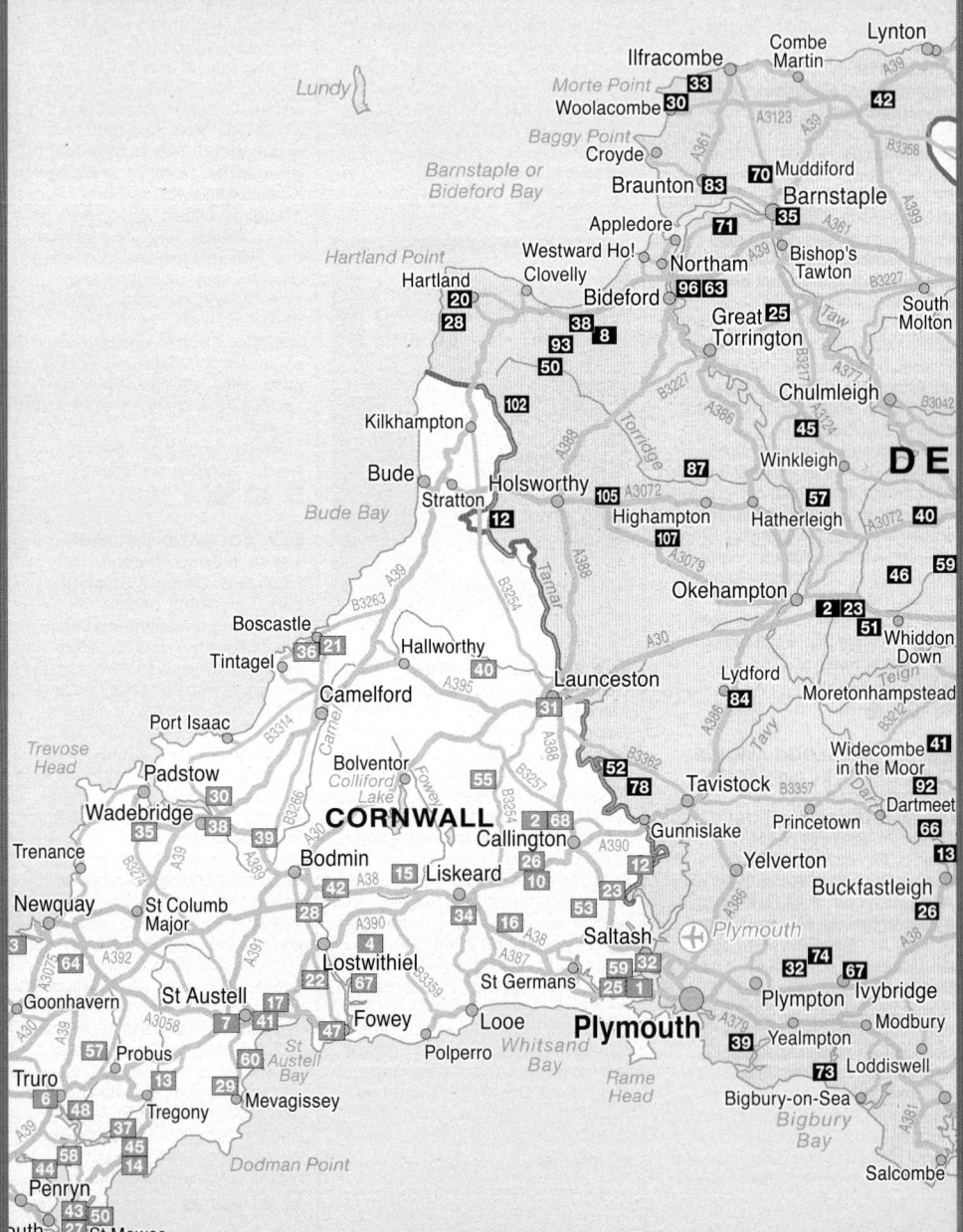

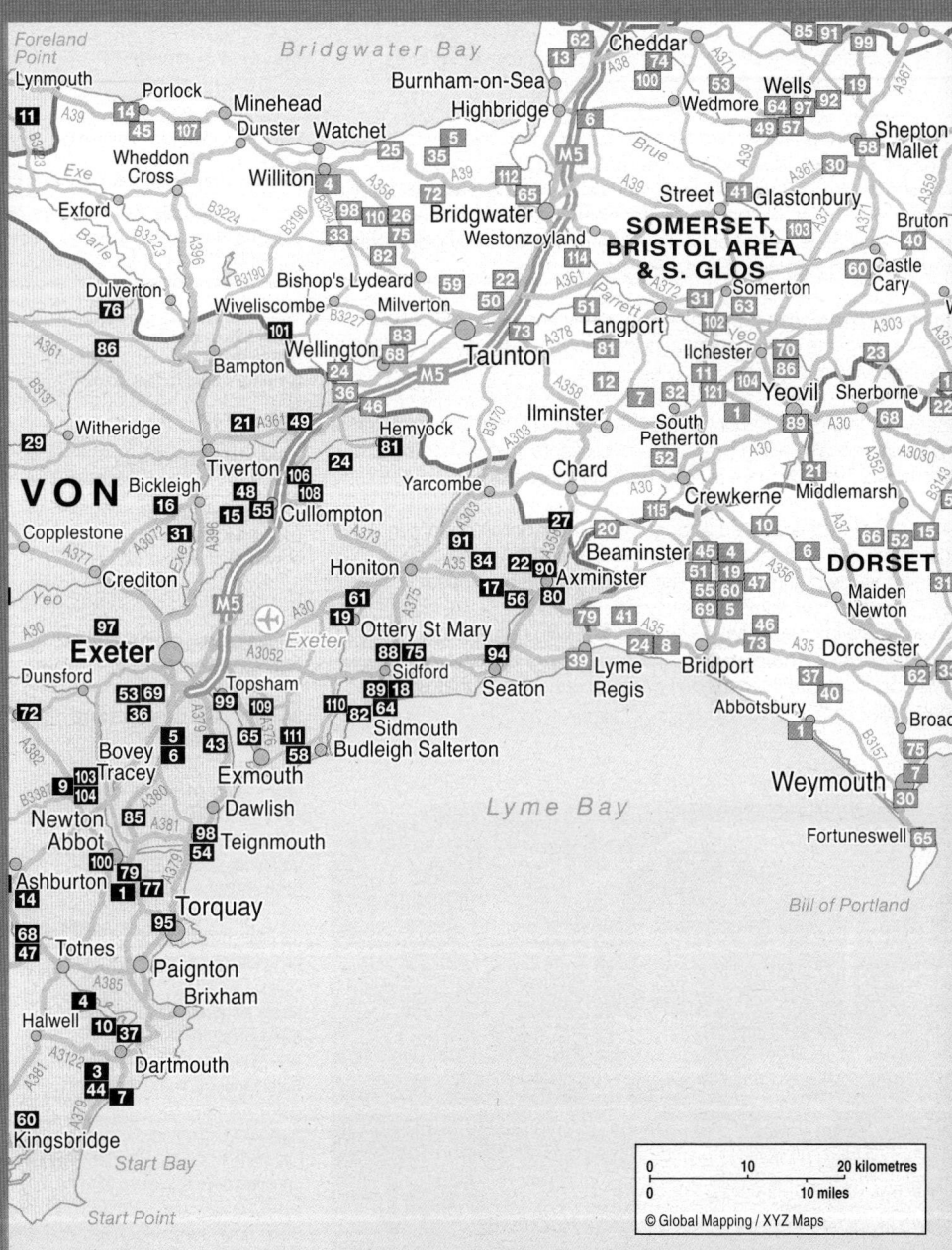

Devon

Devon is a county of great contrasts in geography and climate, and therefore also in gardening.

The rugged north coast has terraces clinging precariously to hillsides so steep that the faint-hearted would never contemplate making a garden there. But here, and on the rolling hills and deep valleys of Exmoor, despite a constant battle with the elements, NGS gardeners create remarkable results by choosing hardy plants that withstand the high winds and salty air.

In the south, in peaceful wooded estuaries and tucked into warm valleys, gardens grow bananas, palms and fruit usually associated with the Mediterranean.

Between these two terrains is a third: Dartmoor, 365 square miles of rugged moorland rising to 2000 feet, presents its own horticultural demands. Typically, here too are many NGS gardens.

In idyllic villages scattered throughout this very large county, in gardens large and small, in single manors and in village groups within thriving communities – gardeners pursue their passion.

Everywhere in Devon the NGS flourishes, with gardens on windswept cliff tops, in subtropical havens and on exposed hillsides; if you are interested in gardens you will find that Devon has it all!

Below: The School House

Devon Volunteers

**County Organisers
& Central Devon**
Edward & Miranda Allhusen
01647 440296
Miranda@allhusen.co.uk

County Treasurer
Julia Tremlett
01392 832671
jandjtremlett@hotmail.com

Publicity
Brian Mackness
01626 356004
brianmackness@clara.co.uk

Cath Pettyfer
01837 89024
cathpettyfer@gmail.com

Booklet Co-ordinator
Edward Allhusen
01647 440296
edward@allhusen.co.uk

Assistant County Organisers

East Devon
Peter Wadeley 01297 631210
wadeley@btinternet.com

Exeter
Jenny Phillips 01392 254076
jennypips25@hotmail.co.uk

Exmoor
Juliet Moss 01398 341604
julietm@onetel.com

North Devon
Jo Hynes 01805 804265
hynesjo@gmail.com

North East Devon
Jill Hall 01884 38812
jill22hall@gmail.com

Plymouth
Maria Ashurst 01752 351396
maria.ashurst@sky.com

South Devon
Sally Vincent 01803 722227
salv@hotmail.co.uk

Torbay
Christine Mackness 01626 356004
christinemack@clara.co.uk

West Devon
Sara-Jane Cumming 01822 860281
sj@broadparkdesigns.co.uk

Opening Dates

All entries subject to change.
For latest information check www.ngs.org.uk

Extended openings are shown at the begining of the month

January

43 High Garden
(every Tuesday to Friday 19 to 29 January)

February

43 High Garden
(every Tuesday to Friday)

Snowdrop Festival

Sunday 7
45 Higher Cherubeer

Saturday 13
74 NEW The Mount, Delamore

Sunday 14
74 NEW The Mount, Delamore

Friday 19
45 Higher Cherubeer

Saturday 20
74 NEW The Mount, Delamore

Sunday 21
74 NEW The Mount, Delamore

Sunday 28
29 East Worlington House

March

43 High Garden
(every Tuesday to Friday)

Sunday 6
29 East Worlington House

Sunday 20
35 Gorwell House
97 Summers Place

Friday 25
49 Holbrook Garden

Saturday 26
36 Haldon Grange
49 Holbrook Garden

Sunday 27
36 Haldon Grange
49 Holbrook Garden

Prospect House

55 Kia-Ora Farm & Gardens
108 Wood Barton

Monday 28
36 Haldon Grange
49 Holbrook Garden
55 Kia-Ora Farm & Gardens

April

43 High Garden
(every Tuesday to Friday)

Saturday 2
36 Haldon Grange
39 The Haven

Sunday 3
36 Haldon Grange
39 The Haven
41 Heathercombe
110 Yonder Hill

Saturday 9
36 Haldon Grange

Sunday 10
36 Haldon Grange
55 Kia-Ora Farm & Gardens
110 Yonder Hill

Friday 15
19 Cadhay
49 Holbrook Garden

Saturday 16
36 Haldon Grange
49 Holbrook Garden

Sunday 17
36 Haldon Grange
55 Kia-Ora Farm & Gardens
83 St Merryn
86 Shapcott Barton Estate
110 Yonder Hill

Wednesday 20
36 Haldon Grange
86 Shapcott Barton Estate

Saturday 23
36 Haldon Grange
88 Sidbury Manor

Sunday 24
2 Andrew's Corner
36 Haldon Grange
40 NEW Hayne
86 Shapcott Barton Estate
88 Sidbury Manor
110 Yonder Hill

Saturday 30
23 Cleave House
27 Dicot
36 Haldon Grange
49 Holbrook Garden

May

43 High Garden
(every Tuesday to Friday)

Sunday 1
2 Andrew's Corner
23 Cleave House
27 Dicot
36 Haldon Grange
49 Holbrook Garden
55 Kia-Ora Farm & Gardens
73 Mothecombe House
103 Whitstone Bluebells
108 Wood Barton
110 Yonder Hill

Monday 2
2 Andrew's Corner
27 Dicot
31 Fursdon
36 Haldon Grange
55 Kia-Ora Farm & Gardens
110 Yonder Hill

Saturday 7
36 Haldon Grange
57 NEW Lakesland
85 Sedgewell Coach House Gardens
87 NEW Sheepwash Gardens
102 West Down House

43 **High Garden**
(every Tuesday to
Friday)
Sunday 8
6 Bickham House
21 Chevithorne Barton
36 Haldon Grange
57 NEW Lakesland
85 Sedgewell Coach
House Gardens
87 NEW Sheepwash
Gardens
102 West Down House
105 Wick Farm Gardens
110 Yonder Hill

Wednesday 11
36 Haldon Grange

Saturday 14
13 Brocton Cottage
36 Haldon Grange
111 NEW Inner Ting Tong
Gardens
76 The Old Vicarage
85 Sedgewell Coach
House Gardens
100 NEW Torview

Sunday 15
2 Andrew's Corner
13 Brocton Cottage
35 Gorwell House
36 Haldon Grange
41 Heathercombe
44 Higher Ash Farm
111 NEW Inner Ting Tong
Gardens
55 Kia-Ora Farm &
Gardens
76 The Old Vicarage
83 St Merryn
85 Sedgewell Coach
House Gardens
100 NEW Torview
105 Wick Farm Gardens
110 Yonder Hill

Wednesday 18
36 Haldon Grange

Saturday 21
36 Haldon Grange
59 Lewis Cottage

Sunday 22
31 Fursdon
36 Haldon Grange
41 Heathercombe
44 Higher Ash Farm
59 Lewis Cottage
92 Southcombe Gardens
105 Wick Farm Gardens
110 Yonder Hill

Friday 27
49 Holbrook Garden

Saturday 28
1 Abbotskerswell
Gardens
8 Bocombe Mill Cottage

11 Brendon Gardens
23 Cleave House
26 NEW Deancombe
Farm
36 Haldon Grange
41 Heathercombe
48 NEW Hillersdon
49 Holbrook Garden
72 Moretonhampstead
Gardens

PERENNIAL
GARDENERS' ROYAL BENEVOLENT SOCIETY

NGS garden
visitors are
supporting
gardeners
across the UK

94 Springfield House
Sunday 29
1 Abbotskerswell
Gardens
2 Andrew's Corner
8 Bocombe Mill Cottage
11 Brendon Gardens
12 The Bridge Mill
23 Cleave House
26 NEW Deancombe
Farm
36 Haldon Grange
41 Heathercombe
48 NEW Hillersdon
49 Holbrook Garden
54 Jason's Garden
55 Kia-Ora Farm &
Gardens
72 Moretonhampstead
Gardens
92 Southcombe Gardens
105 Wick Farm Gardens
110 Yonder Hill

Monday 30
2 Andrew's Corner
8 Bocombe Mill
Cottage
19 Cadhay
36 Haldon Grange
48 NEW Hillersdon
55 Kia-Ora Farm &
Gardens
72 Moretonhampstead
Gardens
92 Southcombe
Gardens
105 Wick Farm Gardens
110 Yonder Hill

June

34 **Goren Farm** (every
evening 4 June to
30 June)
43 **High Garden**
(every Tuesday to
Friday)
Friday 3
53 Idestone Barton
65 The Lookout

Festival Weekend

Saturday 4
14 NEW Bullard Farm
34 Goren Farm
47 NEW Higher Velwell
Farm
53 Idestone Barton
75 The Old Dairy
92 Southcombe Gardens
107 Winsford Walled
Garden

Sunday 5
2 Andrew's Corner
14 NEW Bullard Farm
15 Burn Valley Butterleigh
Gardens
34 Goren Farm
35 Gorwell House
40 NEW Hayne
41 Heathercombe
42 Heddon Hall
45 Higher Cherubeer
47 NEW Higher Velwell
Farm
52 Hotel Endsleigh
61 Little Ash Bungalow
65 The Lookout
75 The Old Dairy
92 Southcombe Gardens
107 Winsford Walled
Garden
110 Yonder Hill

Friday 10
6 Bickham House
70 Marwood Hill Garden

Saturday 11
8 Bocombe Mill Cottage
18 Byes Reach
23 Cleave House
27 Dicot
34 Goren Farm
68 Luscombe Farm
69 Marshall Farm
71 The Mill House
106 Willand Old Village
Gardens

Sunday 12
8 Bocombe Mill Cottage
18 Byes Reach
23 Cleave House
27 Dicot

28 Docton Mill
34 Goren Farm
42 Heddon Hall
50 Hole Farm
68 Luscombe Farm
69 Marshall Farm
71 The Mill House
78 Portington
81 Regency House
92 Southcombe Gardens
106 Willand Old Village
Gardens
110 Yonder Hill

Friday 17
49 Holbrook Garden

Saturday 18
9 Bovey Tracey Gardens
10 Bramble Torre
34 Goren Farm
41 Heathercombe
49 Holbrook Garden
56 Kilmington (Shute
Road) Gardens
59 Lewis Cottage
66 Lower Spitchwick
Garden
82 Runnymede
83 St Merryn
94 Springfield House
101 Venn Cross Railway
Gardens
109 Woodbury Gardens

Sunday 19
9 Bovey Tracey Gardens
10 Bramble Torre
15 Burn Valley Butterleigh
Gardens
20 NEW Cheristow
Lavender
25 The Croft
34 Goren Farm
41 Heathercombe
46 Higher Cullaford
55 Kia-Ora Farm &
Gardens
56 Kilmington (Shute
Road) Gardens
59 Lewis Cottage
66 Lower Spitchwick
Garden
78 Portington
82 Runnymede
83 St Merryn
92 Southcombe
Gardens
101 Venn Cross Railway
Gardens
109 Woodbury Gardens
110 Yonder Hill

Monday 20
82 Runnymede

Tuesday 21
41 Heathercombe

Wednesday 22
41 Heathercombe

34 Goren Farm (every evening 4 June to 30 June)
43 High Garden (every Tuesday to Friday)

Thursday 23
41 Heathercombe

Friday 24
6 Bickham House
19 Cadhay
41 Heathercombe

Saturday 25
3 Ash Gardens
23 Cleave House
38 Harbour Lights
41 Heathercombe
98 Teignmouth Gardens

Sunday 26
3 Ash Gardens
23 Cleave House
38 Harbour Lights
41 Heathercombe
46 Higher Cullaford
92 Southcombe Gardens
98 Teignmouth Gardens
110 Yonder Hill

Tuesday 28
41 Heathercombe

Wednesday 29
41 Heathercombe

Thursday 30
41 Heathercombe

July

34 Goren Farm (every evening 1 July to 17 July)
43 High Garden (every Tuesday to Friday)

Friday 1
41 Heathercombe

Saturday 2
22 Cleave Hill
41 Heathercombe
71 The Mill House
79 NEW The Priory
96 Stone Farm

Sunday 3
22 Cleave Hill
31 Fursdon
35 Gorwell House
41 Heathercombe
71 The Mill House
79 NEW The Priory
96 Stone Farm
110 Yonder Hill

Tuesday 5
41 Heathercombe

Wednesday 6
41 Heathercombe

Thursday 7
41 Heathercombe

Friday 8
41 Heathercombe

Saturday 9
23 Cleave House
24 NEW Craddock House
41 Heathercombe
66 Lower Spitchwick Garden
84 NEW The School House
96 Stone Farm

Sunday 10
6 Bickham House
23 Cleave House
24 NEW Craddock House
41 Heathercombe
50 Hole Farm
66 Lower Spitchwick Garden
83 St Merryn
84 NEW The School House
96 Stone Farm
110 Yonder Hill

Transformed into a beautiful and productive garden . . .

Thursday 14
49 Holbrook Garden

Friday 15
49 Holbrook Garden
99 NEW Topsham Gardens

Saturday 16
23 Cleave House
49 Holbrook Garden
59 Lewis Cottage
87 NEW Sheepwash Gardens
94 Springfield House
101 Venn Cross Railway Gardens

Sunday 17
20 NEW Cheristow Lavender
23 Cleave House
25 The Croft
52 Hotel Endsleigh
59 Lewis Cottage

64 Littlecourt Cottages
86 Shapcott Barton Estate
87 NEW Sheepwash Gardens
99 NEW Topsham Gardens
101 Venn Cross Railway Gardens
110 Yonder Hill

Monday 18
64 Littlecourt Cottages (Evening)

Wednesday 20
86 Shapcott Barton Estate

Friday 22
19 Cadhay
51 NEW Hole's Meadow
90 NEW Socks Orchard

Saturday 23
90 NEW Socks Orchard

Sunday 24
51 NEW Hole's Meadow
54 Jason's Garden
55 Kia-Ora Farm & Gardens
86 Shapcott Barton Estate
110 Yonder Hill

Saturday 30
16 Burnbridge Cottage
27 Dicot

Sunday 31
16 Burnbridge Cottage
27 Dicot
95 Squirrels
110 Yonder Hill

August

43 High Garden (every Tuesday to Friday)

Wednesday 3
86 Shapcott Barton Estate

Saturday 6
84 NEW The School House
95 Squirrels
107 Winsford Walled Garden

Sunday 7
21 Chevithorne Barton
55 Kia-Ora Farm & Gardens
84 NEW The School House
95 Squirrels
104 Whitstone Farm
107 Winsford Walled Garden
110 Yonder Hill

Saturday 13
3 Ash Gardens
59 Lewis Cottage
66 Lower Spitchwick Garden

Sunday 14
3 Ash Gardens
6 Bickham House
59 Lewis Cottage
66 Lower Spitchwick Garden
81 Regency House
110 Yonder Hill

Saturday 20
76 The Old Vicarage

Sunday 21
25 The Croft
61 Little Ash Bungalow
76 The Old Vicarage
110 Yonder Hill

Friday 26
49 Holbrook Garden

Saturday 27
49 Holbrook Garden
85 Sedgewell Coach House Gardens
89 Sidmouth Gardens
101 Venn Cross Railway Gardens

Sunday 28
49 Holbrook Garden
55 Kia-Ora Farm & Gardens
85 Sedgewell Coach House Gardens
89 Sidmouth Gardens
101 Venn Cross Railway Gardens
110 Yonder Hill

Monday 29
19 Cadhay
55 Kia-Ora Farm & Gardens
89 Sidmouth Gardens
110 Yonder Hill

September

43 High Garden (every Tuesday to Friday)

Friday 2
80 Prospect House

Saturday 3
111 NEW Inner Ting Tong Gardens
72 Moretonhampstead Gardens
80 Prospect House

Sunday 4
50 Hole Farm
111 NEW Inner Ting Tong Gardens
72 Moretonhampstead Gardens
80 Prospect House
110 Yonder Hill

Join us on Facebook **f** and spread the word

43 **High Garden**
(every Tuesday to
Friday)
Saturday 10
6 Bickham House

Sunday 11
6 Bickham House
31 Fursdon
55 Kia-Ora Farm &
Gardens
110 Yonder Hill

Saturday 17
13 Brocton Cottage
91 South Wood Farm

Sunday 18
13 Brocton Cottage
91 South Wood Farm
110 Yonder Hill

Sunday 25
110 Yonder Hill

October

43 **High Garden**
(every Tuesday to
Friday)
Sunday 2
45 Higher Cherubeer

Sunday 9
44 Higher Ash Farm
81 Regency House
97 Summers Place

Sunday 16
2 Andrew's Corner
5 Bickham Cottage

November

43 **High Garden**
(every Tuesday to
Friday)

December

43 **High Garden**
(every Tuesday to
Friday from 6 to 16
December)

February 2017

Friday 10
45 Higher Cherubeer
Friday 17
45 Higher Cherubeer
Sunday 26
45 Higher Cherubeer

Gardens open to the public

7 Blackpool Gardens
17 Burrow Farm Gardens
19 Cadhay
28 Docton Mill
31 Fursdon
42 Heddon Hall
49 Holbrook Garden
52 Hotel Endsleigh
67 Lukesland
70 Marwood Hill Garden
77 Plant World
86 Shapcott Barton
Estate
107 Winsford Walled
Garden

By arrangement only

4 Avenue Cottage
30 Foamlea
32 Galen Way
37 Hamblyn's Coombe
58 Lee Ford
60 **NEW** Libertas
63 Little Webbery
93 Springfield

Also open by arrangement

1 Abbotskerswell
Gardens
1 Fairfield,
Abbotskerswell
Gardens
2 Andrew's Corner
5 Bickham Cottage
6 Bickham House
8 Bocombe Mill Cottage
11 Brendon Gardens
12 The Bridge Mill
15 Higher Burnhaies,
Burn Valley Butterleigh
Gardens
15 Shutelake, Burn Valley
Butterleigh Gardens
18 Byes Reach
20 **NEW** Cheristow
Lavender
21 Chevithorne Barton
22 Cleave Hill
25 The Croft
33 The Gate House
34 Goren Farm
35 Gorwell House

36 Haldon Grange
39 The Haven
41 Heathercombe
44 Higher Ash Farm
45 Higher Cherubeer
46 Higher Cullaford
59 Lewis Cottage
61 Little Ash Bungalow
62 Little Cumbre
66 Lower Spitchwick
Garden
71 The Mill House
72 Sutton Mead,
Moretonhampstead
Gardens
78 Portington
80 Prospect House
81 Regency House
83 St Merryn
87 **NEW** Lake
Farmhouse,
Sheepwash Gardens
87 **NEW** Musselbrook
Cottage, Sheepwash
Gardens
91 South Wood Farm
92 Southcombe Gardens
94 Springfield House
95 Squirrels
97 Summers Place
101 The Engine House,
Venn Cross Railway
Gardens
101 Venn Cross Railway
Gardens
102 West Down House
104 Whitstone Farm
105 Wick Farm Gardens
108 Wood Barton
110 Yonder Hill

The Gardens

GROUP OPENING

1 **ABBOTSKERSWELL
GARDENS**
Abbotskerswell TQ12 5PN, 01626
356004,
christinemack@clara.co.uk. *2m SW
of Newton Abbot town centre. A381
Newton Abbot/Totnes rd. Sharp L
turn from NA, R from Totnes. Field
parking at Fairfield. Maps available at
all gardens and at Church House.* Sat
28, Sun 29 May (1-5). Combined
adm £6, chd free. Home-made
teas at Church House. Teas
available from 2pm. Maps and
tickets from 1pm. Visits also by
arrangement Mar to Sept, number
of gardens available to be agreed.
Donation to Friends of St Marys.

NEW **2A MANOR CLOSE**
Ms Dorne Cornelius

ABBOTSFORD
Mrs W Grierson

**ABBOTSKERSWELL
ALLOTMENTS**
Margaret Crompton

1 ABBOTSWELL COTTAGES
Jane Taylor

BRIAR COTTAGE
Peggy & David Munden

FAIRFIELD
Christine & Brian Mackness
Visits also by arrangement Mar
to Sept other gardens also by
arrangement. Minimum group
size 10
christinemack@clara.co.uk
01626 356004

10 WILTON WAY
Mrs Margaret Crompton

37 WILTON WAY
Mrs Trish Turner

In 2016 friendly Abbotskerswell
opens another garden. 2a Manor
Close is a new property owned by an
artist, developed to show colour
themed borders, fruit trees, shrubs,
vegetables, grasses and colourful
pots. Paintings and ceramics will be
on sale. 6 other gardens have yet
more developments and, with the
allotments, show a wide range of
planting styles and innovative
landscaping. Cottage gardens,
terracing, wild flower areas, specialist
plants, vegetable production
methods. Many garden owners are
winners in the annual Village Garden
Show for produce or the garden itself.
We offer creative ideas for every type
and size of garden. Visitors are
welcome to picnic in the field or
arboretum at Fairfield. Children will
enjoy the miniature Shetland ponies,

plus finding their way through winding paths among high grasses. See You Tube Abbotskerswell Gardens 2011 for a taster. Sales of paintings, ceramics, garden produce, jams and chutneys and other creative crafts. Disabled access to 3 gardens.

2 ANDREW'S CORNER
Belstone EX20 1RD. Robin & Edwina Hill, 01837 840332, edwinarobinhill@outlook.com, www.belstonevillage.net. *3m E of Okehampton. Signed to Belstone. In village signed Skaigh. Parking restricted but cars may be left on nearby common.* Sun 24 Apr, Sun 1, Mon 2, Sun 15, Sun 29, Mon 30 May, Sun 5 June, Sun 16 Oct (2-5). Adm £4, chd free. Home-made teas. **Visits also by arrangement Feb to Nov.**
Well established, wildlife friendly, well labelled plantsman's garden in stunning high moorland setting. Variety of garden habitats incl woodland areas and pond; wide range of unusual trees, shrubs, herbaceous plants for yr-round effect with blue poppies, rhododendrons, bulbs and maples; spectacular autumn colour. Family friendly, with quiz sheet, fairy doors, playhouse, fruit, vegetables and chickens. Featured on BBC Radio Devon and in Devon Life magazine. Wheelchair access difficult when wet.

GROUP OPENING

3 ASH GARDENS
Ash, Dartmouth TQ6 0LR. *2m SW of Dartmouth. Leave A381 Totnes to Kingsbridge rd in Halwell taking A3122 for Dartmouth. Just before Sportsmans Arms turn R. At T junction turn R then 1st L. At Xrds turn R then parking 1st L.* Sat 25, Sun 26 June, Sat 13, Sun 14 Aug (2-5). Combined adm £4.50, chd free. Tea.

BAY TREE COTTAGE
Jenny Goffe

HIGHER ASH FARM
Mr Michael Gribbin & Mrs Jennifer Barwell
(See separate entry)
Visits also by arrangement Apr to Oct for 1-15
matthew.perkins18@yahoo.co.uk
07595 507516

2 delightful gardens in the tiny hamlet of Ash. The beautiful intimate little garden at Bay Tree Cottage sits in a quiet secluded valley with wonderful sunlit views across open farmland. The perfect curved lawn leads the eye to small rooms filled with surprise and clever planting. Ornamental trees punctuate the boundary and a tiny vegetable garden of raised beds overflows with produce. Higher Ash Farm has 2½ acres of established and developing garden situated around farmhouse and barn conversions. Large kitchen garden terraced into the hillside, orchard, pond, stream with bog planting and feature borders around the house offering seasonal and yr round interest.

4 AVENUE COTTAGE
Ashprington, Totnes TQ9 7UT. Mr Richard Pitts and Mr David Sykes, 01803 732769, richard.pitts@btinternet.com, www.avenuecottage.com. *3m SW of Totnes. A 381 Totnes to Kingsbridge for 1m; L for Ashprington, into village then L by PH. Garden ¼ m on R after Sharpham Estate sign.* **Visits by arrangement Mar to Oct, groups and individuals welcome. Adm £4, chd free. Tea.**

11 acres of mature and young trees and shrubs. Once part of an C18 landscape, the neglected garden has been cleared and replanted over the last 25 yrs. Good views of Sharpham House and R Dart. Azaleas and hydrangeas are a feature.

5 BICKHAM COTTAGE
Kenn, Exeter EX6 7XL. Steve Eyre, 01392 833964, bickham@live.co.uk. *6m S of Exeter. 1m off A38. Leave A38 at Kennford Services, follow signs to Kenn. 1st R in village, follow lane for ¾ m to end of no through rd.* Sun 16 Oct (2-5). Adm £3.50, chd free. Teas. **Visits also by arrangement Oct & Nov.**
Small cottage garden divided into separate areas by old stone walls and hedge banks. Front garden with mainly South African bulbs and plants. Lawn surrounded by borders with agapanthus, eucomis, crocosmia, diorama etc. Stream garden with primulas. Pond with large Koi carp. Glasshouses with National Collection of Hardy Nerines, Nerine sarniensis and cultivars, 3500 pots with in excess of 450 varieties. Featured in Gardens Illustrated, Amateur Gardener, Country Living, The English Garden and numerous other publications.

Mothecombe House

© Val Corbett

6 BICKHAM HOUSE

Kenn, Exeter EX6 7XL. John & Julia Tremlett, 01392 832671, jandjtremlett@hotmail.com. *6m S of Exeter, 1m off A38. Leave A38 at Kennford Services, follow signs to Kenn, 1st R in village, follow lane for ³/₄ m to end of no through rd.* Sun 8 May, Fri 10 June, Fri 24 June, Sun 10 July, Sun 14 Aug, Sat 10 Sept, Sun 11 Sept (2-5). Adm £5, chd free. Home-made teas. Visits also by arrangement Apr to Sept.
7 acres with colour co-ordinated borders, mature trees, lawns. Fern garden and water garden. Formal parterre with lily pond. 1 acre walled garden with profusion of vegetables and flowers. Palm tree avenue leading to summerhouse. Spring garden with cowslips, bluebells. Late summer colour with dahlias, crocosmia, agapanthus etc. Cactus and succulent greenhouse. Lakeside walk. Wide selection of plants for sales. Featured on Radio Devon and in Country Life, Sunday Telegraph.

Once an old cider orchard that had grown wild . . .

7 ◆ BLACKPOOL GARDENS

Dartmouth TQ6 0RG. Sir Geoffrey Newman, 01803 771801, beach@blackpoolsands.co.uk, www.blackpoolsands.co.uk. *3m SW of Dartmouth. From Dartmouth follow brown signs to Blackpool Sands on A379. Entry tickets, parking, toilets and refreshments available at Blackpool Sands. Sorry, no dogs permitted.* For opening times and information, please phone, email or visit garden website.
Carefully restored C19 subtropical plantsman's garden with collection of mature and newly planted tender and unusual trees, shrubs and carpet of spring flowers. Paths and steps lead gradually uphill and above the Captain's seat offering fine coastal views. Recent plantings follow the S hemisphere theme with callistemons, pittosporums, acacias and buddlejas. Open 1 Apr - 30 Sept (10-4) weather permitting.

8 BOCOMBE MILL COTTAGE

Bocombe, Parkham, Bideford EX39 5PH. Mr Chris Butler & Mr David Burrows, 01237 451293, www.bocombe.co.uk. *6m E of Clovelly, 9m SW of Bideford. From A39 just outside Horns Cross village, turn to Foxdown. At Xrds follow signs for parking.* Sat 28, Sun 29, Mon 30 May, Sat 11, Sun 12 June (12-5). Adm £4.50, chd £1. Ploughmans lunches & traditional home-made cakes & cream teas. Visits also by arrangement Mar to Sept for groups of 10+.
12 flower gardens around the house with live hermits in hermitage and grotto. 1m walk through an organic, undulating landscape with streams, 3 bog gardens, pools and 12 water features. White pergola. Japanese garden. Hillside orchard. Kitchen and soft fruit gardens. Wild meadow, wildlife haven. Garden kaleidoscope. 5 acres with garden plan incl 80 specimen trees. Goats on hillside.

GROUP OPENING

9 BOVEY TRACEY GARDENS

Bovey Tracey TQ13 9NA. *6m N of Newton Abbot. Gateway to Dartmoor. Take A382 to Bovey Tracey. Car parking at town car parks, on the road and at Parke.* Sat 18, Sun 19 June (2-6). Combined adm £5, chd free. Home-made teas at Gleam Tor. Wine at Ashwell.

ASHWELL
Tony & Jeanette Pearce

BOVEY COMMUNITY GARDEN, PARKE
NT and Bovey Tracey Climate Action www.boveycommunitygarden.org.uk

5 BRIDGE COTTAGES
Cath Valentine

GLEAM TOR
Gillian & Colin Liddy

GREEN HEDGES
Alan and Linda Jackson

PARKE VIEW
Peter & Judy Hall

2 REDWOODS
Mr & Mrs Tony Mooney

Bovey Tracey is a pretty cob and granite built town nestling in the foothills of Dartmoor beside R Bovey. Ashwell: steeply sloping Victorian walled garden, vineyard, colourful herbaceous borders, orchard with wild flowers, fruit and vegetables. At Bovey Community Garden, Parke an abundance of fruit surrounds the productive vegetable garden, solar power supplies water. Bridge Cottage: quirky garden on an historic pottery site. Structured and varied planting, plant sale. Gleam Tor: far-reaching views in all directions. Long border with colourful array of herbaceous perennials, white garden and prairie planting. Green Hedges: mature garden with Dartmoor views. Well established colourful borders incl shrubs, bulbs, perennials, vegetables and soft fruit. Parke View: 1-acre garden with meandering old stone walls leading to separate areas tucked away near the town centre. Redwoods: mature trees. Acid loving spring and summer shrubs. Moorland leat flows through unusual fernery. Limited wheelchair access at some gardens.

10 BRAMBLE TORRE

Dittisham, nr Dartmouth TQ6 0HZ. Paul & Sally Vincent, www.rainingsideways.com. *³/₄ m from Dittisham. Leave A3122 at Sportsman's Arms. Drop down into Village, at Red Lion turn L to Cornworthy. Continue ³/₄ m Bramble Torre straight ahead.* Sat 18, Sun 19 June (2-6). Adm £4, chd free. Home-made teas.
Set in 20 acres of farmland, the 3-acre garden follows a rambling stream through a steep valley: lily pond, herbaceous borders, camellias, shrubs and roses dominated by huge embothrium glowing scarlet in late spring against a sometimes blue sky! A formal herb and vegetable garden runs alongside the stream while chickens scratch in an orchard of Ditsum plums and cider apples. Well behaved dogs on leads welcome. Limited wheelchair access, parts of garden very steep and uneven. Tea area with wheelchair access and excellent garden view.

GROUP OPENING

11 BRENDON GARDENS
Brendon, Lynton EX35 6PU, 01598
741343, lalindevon@yahoo.co.uk.
*1m S of A39 North Devon coast rd
between Porlock and Lynton.* **Sat 28,
Sun 29 May (12-5). Combined adm
£4.50, chd free. Light
refreshments. Light lunches and
cream teas served at Higher
Tippacott Farm. WC available.
Visits also by arrangement May to
Sept.**

1 DEERCOMBE COTTAGES
Valerie and Stephen Exley

DOONE COTTAGE
Carole & Jason Miller

HIGHER TIPPACOTT FARM
Angela & Malcolm Percival

Stunningly beautiful part of Exmoor. 2
gardens nestling in East Lyn river
valley, 1 on heather moorland with
views. Excellent walking alongside E
Lyn river between Brendon and
Rockford, dramatic coastal path
nearby. 1 Deercombe Cottages:
delightful small garden in steeply
wooded valley, created using ditched
stone to provide a variety of levels to
display planting rich in contrasting
foliage and variety of perennials.
Featured in Amateur Gardening.
Doone Cottage: pretty garden
surrounding C17 grade 2 listed
cottage at edge of river. Terraces
containing variety of mature and
newer planting designed for yr round
colour and interest. Winding
pathways provide stunning vistas
over river. Kitchen garden. Higher
Tippacott Farm: 950ft alt overlooking
own pretty valley pasture with stream
and pond. Sunny levels of interesting
herbaceous planting, stone walls and
old barns, all blending with its
dramatic setting. Vegetable patch
with distant sea views. Chickens.
Organic. Plants, cards, books and
bric-a-brac for sale.
🐾 ⊛ ☕

12 THE BRIDGE MILL
Mill Rd, Bridgerule, Holsworthy
EX22 7EL. Rosie and Alan Beat,
01288 381341,
rosie@thebridgemill.org.uk,
www.thebridgemill.org.uk. *In
Bridgerule village on R Tamar
between Bude and Holsworthy.
Between chapel by river bridge and
church at top of hill towards*

*Holsworthy. See above website for
detailed directions.* **Sun 29 May
(11-5). Adm £3.50, chd free.
Home-made teas. Refreshments
in garden with ducks or in barn if
wet! Visits also by arrangement
May & June for groups of 15+.**
One acre organic gardens set around
mill house and restored water mill.
Small cottage garden; herb garden
with medicinal and dye plants; very
productive fruit and vegetable garden,
and a wild woodland and water
garden behind mill. The 16 acre
smallholding will be open for lake,
pond and riverside walks. Friendly
sheep, pigs and poultry! The Bridge
Mill is open for free educational visits
throughout the year to school groups.
Details on website. The mill was
restored to working order in April
2012. Featured regularly in Country
Smallholding magazine and
occasionally in local newspapers.
Wheelchair access to part of garden.
WC with access for wheelchairs.
♿ ⊛ 🚐 ☕

13 BROCTON COTTAGE
Pear Tree, Ashburton, Newton
Abbot TQ13 7QZ. Mrs Naomi
Hindley. *¼ m from A38. From A38
take Ashburton Peartree junction.
Turn R towards Princetown, then 1st
L towards Buckfastleigh. Park on
road or at Dartmoor Lodge Hotel
(lunches available). Short walk to
garden entrance.* **Sat 14, Sun 15
May, Sat 17, Sun 18 Sept (2-5).
Adm £3.50, chd free. Home-made
teas. Lunches and refreshments**

also available at the Dartmoor
Lodge Hotel.
1.3 acres recently recovered from
neglect, combining established
planting with newly developed areas.
New orchard, woodland, ponds and
productive area linked to established
herbaceous borders and shrubberies.
The woodland area being developed
was inspired by the winter garden at
Anglesea Abbey. Developed as a
single garden with views of Devon
countryside. Dogs on leads only
please.
🐾 ⊛ ☕

14 NEW ▶ BULLARD FARM
Ashburton, Newton Abbot
TQ13 7NG. S & L Middleton. *1m
from A38. Exit A38 at Peartree Cross
near Ashburton and follow signs to
Landscove, then follow NGS signs.*
**Sat 4, Sun 5 June (11-4). Adm £4,
chd free. Home-made teas. Also
open Higher Velwell Farm.**
Once an old cider orchard that had
grown wild, over the last 6 years it
has been transformed into a beautiful
and productive garden. Set over 8
acres, it makes the most of wonderful
views over rolling rural countryside.
Designed with wildlife in mind it
encompasses formal areas, prairie
planting, boardwalk water garden,
woodland trail, wildflower meadows
and terraced vegetable garden. Steps
and steep slopes although the central
path of the garden is suitable for
wheelchairs which allows great views
over the countryside and garden.
♿ 🐾 ⊛ ☕

Mardon, Moretonhampstead Gardens

South Wood Farm

Mature trees and shrubs provide the backdrop for this informal, secluded 1¼ acre garden. Reclaimed from long neglect and developed for diversity of planting and wildlife. Late summer flowerbeds attract bees and butterflies. Other moods and habitats created by copse, pond, bog garden, hedges. Mini arboretum and hillside wood can also be visited. Sloping, mostly grass site - main garden should be accessible by wheelchairs if dry.

17 ◆ BURROW FARM GARDENS
Dalwood, Axminster EX13 7ET. Mary & John Benger, 01404 831285, enquiries@burrowfarmgardens.co.uk, www.burrowfarmgardens.co.uk. *3½ m W of Axminster. From A35 turn N at Taunton Xrds then follow brown signs.* **For opening times please see below.**
Beautiful 13 acre garden with unusual trees, shrubs and herbaceous plants. Traditional summerhouse looks towards lake and ancient oak woodland with rhododendrons and azaleas. Early spring interest and superb autumn colour. The more formal Millennium garden features a rill. Anniversary Garden featuring late summer perennials and grasses. A photographer's dream. Open 1 April - 31 Oct (10 - 6). Adm £7. Café and gift shop. Various events incl spring and summer plant fair and open air theatre held at garden each year. Visit events page on Burrow Farm Gardens website for more details. Featured in Landscape Magazine and Devon Life.

GROUP OPENING

15 BURN VALLEY BUTTERLEIGH GARDENS
Butterleigh, Cullompton EX15 1PG. *Between Tiverton & Cullompton, Follow signs for Silverton from Butterleigh village. Take L fork 100yds after entrance to Pound Farm. Car park sign on L after 150yds.* Sun 5, Sun 19 June (1.30-5.30). Combined adm £5, chd free. Home-made teas.

HIGHER BURNHAIES
Richard & Virginia Holmes Visits also by arrangement Mar to Oct
01884 855748

SHUTELAKE
Jill & Nigel Hall Visits also by arrangement Mar to Sept cars/minibus only jill22hall@gmail.com
01884 38812

Higher Burnhaies is a 2½ acre site started in 1997. Situated in the beautiful Burn Valley, a plantsman's garden of herbaceous plantings with trees, shrubs, ponds and wildlife. Informal, country feel with Devon lane and wilderness walk. Vegetable garden. Live music. Cross a bridge over a babbling brook to Shutelake, a garden terraced into a hillside. Several levels blend a Mediterranean feel with natural local landscape. Borders, ponds, lake, sculptures, woodland walk. An oasis of calm. Uneven ground and steps in both gardens, not good for unsteady walkers.

16 BURNBRIDGE COTTAGE
Cadeleigh, Tiverton EX16 8RY. Kate Leevers and Martin Callaghan. *From A3072 1½ m from Bickleigh bridge, 6½ m from Crediton, follow lane behind Blue Cross centre for ¾ m. On R after stone bridge. From Cadeleigh village take lane opp PH. On L at bottom of hill.* Sat 30, Sun 31 July (2-5). Adm £3, chd free. Home-made teas. Gluten free cakes available.

18 BYES REACH
26 Coulsdon Rd, Sidmouth EX10 9JP. Lynette Talbot & Peter Endersby, 01395 578081, latalbot01@gmail.com. *Easterly on A3052. R at Sidford T-lights. In ¾ m turn L into Coulsdon Rd. On foot, enter back gate via Livonia Field bike path.* Sat 11, Sun 12 June (2-5.30). Adm £3, chd free. Home-made teas. Gluten Free cakes available. Opening with Sidmouth Gardens on Sat 27, Sun 28, Mon 29 Aug. **Visits also by arrangement May to Aug for groups of 8 to 20.**
5 yr old edible garden of approx ¼ acre. Potager style, raised beds, espalier fruit trees on arched walkway.

Designed for those with mobility problems. Colour themed herbaceous borders, herbs, ferns, hostas. Sitting areas, pond, rill, rockery, greenhouse, studio. Backing onto The Byes nature reserve and R Sid, offering an opportunity for a short walk from the garden gate. Long fruit covered archway, use of recycled materials and pond and rill. Sculptured fountain. Views into Livonia Field.

& 🐕 ✳ 🍵

19 ◆ **CADHAY**
Ottery St Mary EX11 1QT. Rupert Thistlethwayte, 01404 813511, jayne@cadhay.org.uk, www.cadhay.org.uk. *1m NW of Ottery St Mary. On B3176 between Ottery St Mary and Fairmile and follow signs for Cadhay. From E exit A30 at Iron Bridge. From W exit A30 at Patteson's Cross and follow brown signs for Cadhay.* For NGS: Fri 15 Apr (2-5). Mon 30 May, Fri 24 June, Fri 22 July, Mon 29 Aug (2-5.30). Cream teas. Adm £3, chd £1. **For other opening times and information, please phone, email or visit garden website.**
Tranquil 2-acre setting for Elizabethan manor house. 2 medieval fish ponds surrounded by rhododendrons, gunnera, hostas and flag iris. Roses, clematis, lilies and hellebores surround walled water garden. 120ft herbaceous border walk informally planted with cottage garden perennials and annuals. Walled kitchen gardens have been turned into allotments and old garden store is now tearoom. Gravel paths.

& 🚐 🍵

20 NEW **CHERISTOW LAVENDER**
Higher Cheristow, Hartland, Bideford EX39 6DA. Michelle Heard, 01237 440101, cheristow@btinternet.com, www.cheristow.co.uk. *Hartland, North Devon. Follow the brown signs from Lighthouse Cross for the Lavender Tea Rooms.* Sun 19 June, Sun 17 July (11-5.30). Adm £5, chd free. **Light refreshments at Cheristow Lavender Tearooms. Homemade cream teas, cakes and light lunches made with organic ingredients. Visits also by arrangement June & July.**
Traditional low impact beef farm with informal gardens manned entirely by volunteers who come to learn about sustainable living. A haven for wildlife

and a place to sit and embrace the calmness and birds singing in an otherwise busy world. The gardens are wild and informal with lavender, roses, wildflower plantings, shrubs and trees to encourage wildlife. Demonstrations on pruning and caring for lavender at 12noon, 2pm and 4pm on NGS open days. Coaches by appointment only. Partial wheelchair access.

& 🐕 ✳ 🚐 🍵

21 **CHEVITHORNE BARTON**
Tiverton EX16 7QB. Michael & Arabella Heathcoat Amory, pottinger985@gmail.com. *3m NE of Tiverton. Through Sampford Pev and Halberton to Tiverton, past Golf Club, turn R. R at next junction. Over bridge, L through Craze Lowman, carry on to T-junction, R then 1st L.* Sun 8 May (2-5). Sun 7 Aug (2-5). Adm £4, chd free. Cream teas on 8 May. **Visits also by arrangement May to Aug (mention NGS Yellow Book when booking).**
Terraced walled garden, summer borders and romantic woodland of rare trees and shrubs. In spring, garden features large collection of magnolias, camellias, rhododendrons and azaleas. Also incl one of only two NCCPG oak collections situated in 12 hectares of parkland and comprising over 200 different species.

🐕 ✳ 🚐 **NPC** 🍵

Embrace the calmness and birds singing in an otherwise busy world . . .

22 **CLEAVE HILL**
Membury, Axminster EX13 7AJ. Andy & Penny Pritchard, 01404 881437, penny@tonybengerlandscaping.co. uk. *4m NW of Axminster. From Membury Village, follow rd down valley. 1st R after Lea Hill B&B, last house on drive, approx 1m.* Sat 2,

Sun 3 July (11-5). Adm £4, chd free. Light lunches, cream teas and cakes. **Visits also by arrangement Jan to Nov, coach parking 1m.**
Artistic garden in pretty village situated on edge of Blackdown Hills. Cottage style garden, planted to provide all season structure, texture and colour. Designed around pretty thatched house and old stone barns. Wonderful views, attractive vegetable garden and orchard, wild flower meadow.

& 🐕 ✳ 🍵

23 **CLEAVE HOUSE**
Sticklepath EX20 2NL. Ann Bowden, www.bowdenhostas.com/pages/ National-Hosta-Collection.html. *3¹/₂ m E of Okehampton. Follow brown tourist signs for Bowden Hostas. From Okehampton, Cleave House is on L, covered with Virginia Creeper.* Sats, Suns 30 Apr, 1 May, 28, 29 May, 11, 12, 25, 26 June, 9, 10, 16, 17 July (10-4). Adm £3, chd free. Cream teas. Fantastic coffee & tea from previous owners of 'The Best Tea House in the UK'. *Donation to NCCPG.*
The National Collection of Hostas is housed in a beautifully mature garden of about ¹/₂ acre, alongside many interesting trees, shrubs and other plants. The evolving stumpery provides a focal point for ferns and tree ferns. Hostas, ferns, tree ferns and bamboos for sale with expert advice available. Tim and Ruth Penrose acquired Bowdens in 2004 from Ruth's parents. Since then they have been awarded a total of 30 RHS Gold Medals. Garden audio guide. Treasure slug hunt and craft activities for children. General knowledge quiz. Partial wheelchair access.

& 🐕 ✳ 🚐 **NPC** 🍵

24 NEW **CRADDOCK HOUSE**
Craddock, Cullompton EX15 3LJ. Carina Persey. *The hamlet of Craddock. Halfway between Uffculme and Culmstock. EX 15 3LJ.* Sat 9, Sun 10 July (2-5.30). Adm £5, chd free. Tea.
Attractive extensive garden with a small lake. House and grounds built early 1800s. Formal areas and herbaceous borders with large grasses border. Woodland area and extensive lawns and interesting water features. Large rose border with lavender and verbena.

& 🍵

25 THE CROFT
**Yarnscombe, Barnstaple
EX31 3LW. Sam & Margaret Jewell,
01769 560535.** *8m S of Barnstaple,
10m SE of Bideford, 12m W of South
Molton, 4m NE of Torrington. From
A377, turn W opp Chapelton railway
stn. Follow Yarnscombe signs, after
3m. From B3232, ¼ m N of
Huntshaw Cross TV mast, turn E and
follow Yarnscombe signs for 2m.
Parking in village hall car park.* **Sun
19 June, Sun 17 July, Sun 21 Aug
(2-6). Adm £4, chd free. Cream
teas. Visits also by arrangement
June to Aug minimum of 3 days
notice required.** *Donation to N
Devon Animal Ambulance.*
1-acre plantswoman's garden
featuring exotic Japanese garden
with tea house, koi carp pond and
cascading stream, tropical garden
with exotic shrubs and perennials,
herbaceous borders with unusual
plants and shrubs, bog garden with
collection of irises, astilbes and
moisture loving plants, duck pond.
Exotic borders, new beds around
duck pond and bog area, large
collection of rare and unusual plants.
Featured on front cover of Devon
Yellow Book 2015.

 ♿ 🐕 🚐 ☕

**WE ARE
MACMILLAN.
CANCER SUPPORT**

The NGS is
Macmillan's largest
single donor

26 NEW DEANCOMBE FARM
**Deancombe, Buckfastleigh
TQ11 0LZ. James & Deborah
Hedger.** *½ m N of A38. Leave A38 at
Dean Prior. From Exeter exit A38 at
Lower Dean (after Buckfastleigh exit)
then R under bridge, turn L and follow
NGS signs. From Plymouth exit A38
at Dean Prior then turn L and follow
NGS signs.* **Sat 28, Sun 29 May
(1.30-5.30). Adm £4, chd free.
Home-made teas. Home made
jams for sale from own fruits.**
Nestling between old walls and a
traditional Devon farm overlooked by
meadows with sheep and cattle set in
the southern foothills of Dartmoor.

Small swimming lake, waterfalls and
stream. Herbaceous beds, part
walled and terraced vegetable
garden, bog and woodland gardens,
cider orchard and stream walks
stretch over 4 acres in a naturalistic
landscape. Home composting
system. Grass paths and steep
slopes adj to deep water. Dependent
on size of wheelchair up to 50%
accessible.

 ♿ 🐕 🌸 ☕

27 DICOT
**Chardstock EX13 7DF. Mr & Mrs F
Clarkson, www.dicot.co.uk.** *5m N
of Axminster. Axminster to Chard
A358 at Tytherleigh to Chardstock. R
at George Inn, L fork to Hook, R to
Burridge, 2nd house on L.* **Sat 30
Apr, Sun 1, Mon 2 May, Sat 11,
Sun 12 June, Sat 30, Sun 31 July
(2-5.30). Adm £3.50, chd free.
Home-made teas.**
Secret garden hidden in East Devon
valley. 3 acres of unusual and exotic
plants - some rare. Rhododendrons,
azaleas and camellias in profusion.
Meandering stream, fish pool,
Japanese style garden and interesting
vegetable garden with fruit cage,
tunnel and greenhouses. Surprises
round every corner. Partial wheelchair
access.

 ♿ ☕

28 ◆ DOCTON MILL
**Lymebridge, Hartland EX39 6EA.
Lana & John Borrett, 01237
441369, doctonmill@tiscali.co.uk,
www.doctonmill.co.uk.** *8m W of
Clovelly. Follow brown tourist signs
on A39 nr Clovelly.* **For NGS: Sun 12
June (10-5). Adm £4.50, chd free.
Light refreshments. Cream teas
and light lunches available all day.
For other opening times and
information, please phone, email or
visit garden website.**
Situated in stunning valley location.
Garden surrounds original mill pond
and the microclimate created within
the wooded valley enables tender
species to flourish. Recent planting of
herbaceous, stream and summer
garden give variety through the
season. Not suitable for wheelchairs.

 🐕 🌸 ☕

29 EAST WORLINGTON
HOUSE
**East Worlington, Witheridge,
Crediton EX17 4TS. Mr & Mrs
Barnabas Hurst-Bannister.** *In centre
of East Worlington, 2m W of
Witheridge. From Witheridge Square*

*R to East Worlington. After 1½ m R at
T-junction in Drayford, over bridge
then L to Worlington. After ⅓ m L at
T-junction. Garden 200 yards on L.*
**Sun 28 Feb, Sun 6 Mar (1.30-5).
Adm £3.50, chd free.**
Thousands of crocuses. In 2 acre
garden, set in lovely position with
views down valley to Little Dart river,
these spectacular crocuses have
spread over many years through the
garden and into the neighbouring
churchyard. Cream teas in the parish
hall (in aid of its restoration fund) next
door. Dogs on leads please. Disabled
parking at house. Parking nearby.

 ♿ 🐕 🌸 ☕

30 FOAMLEA
**Chapel Hill, Mortehoe EX34 7DZ.
Beth Smith, 01271 871182,
bethmortepoint@fmail.co.uk.** *¼ m
S of Mortehoe village. A361 N from
Barnstaple. Follow B3343 to
Mortehoe car park. No parking at or
near garden. On foot L past church,
down hill, then 200yds.* **Visits by
arrangement May to Sept, max
35. Adm £5, chd £1. Home-made
teas.**
Teenage collection of plants thriving in
open cliff top site with uninterrupted
view to Morte Point (NT). Wide range
of familiar and unusual shrubs and
perennials. A maritime climate and a
gradient providing natural drainage
favour many S hemisphere plants.
Drystone walling, slate steps and
shillet paths feature throughout.
Colour-schemed areas, rockery and
mixed plantings. Featured in RHS The
Garden, SAGA magazine, ITV Love
Your Garden.

NPC ☕

31 ◆ FURSDON
**Cadbury, Thorverton, Exeter
EX5 5JS. David & Catriona
Fursdon, 01392 860860,
admin@fursdon.co.uk,
www.fursdon.co.uk.** *2m N of
Thorverton. From Tiverton S on A396.
Take A3072 at Bickleigh towards
Crediton. L after 2½ m. From Exeter
N on A396. L to Thorverton and R in
centre.* **For NGS: Mon 2, Sun 22
May, Sun 3 July, Sun 11 Sept (2-5).
Adm £4.50, chd free. Cream teas
in Coach Hall from 2pm, also
home-made cakes. For other
opening times and information,
please phone, email or visit garden
website.**
Garden surrounds Fursdon House,
home of the same family for 7
centuries. Hillside setting with

extensive views S over parkland and beyond. Sheltered by house, hedges and cob walls, there are terraces of roses, herbs and perennials in mixed traditional and contemporary planting. Woodland walk, seasonal wild flowers and pond in meadow garden. Fursdon House open for guided tours on NGS days. Some steep slopes, grass and gravel paths.

  ♿ 🎫 🛏 ☕

Small lake and ponds with river and water cascades . . .

32 ▸ GALEN WAY
Sparkwell, Plymouth PL7 5DF. Peter & Ann Tremain, 01752 837532, peteranntremain@talktalk.net. *Car parking Sparkwell Hall PL7 5DD. Follow signs approx 300yds. Limited disabled park at Galen Way.* **Visits by arrangement Apr to Sept for groups of 5 to 20. Adm £4, chd free. Cream teas. Also home made cakes and lunch if required.** Quirky garden full of surprises, developed over last 40yrs. Incl fish ponds, floating Island, water wheel, cave and sunken greenhouse. Fully organic and compost system. Vegetable garden (no dig system). Flower borders with shrubs. Various seating areas and a 'follow the sun house'! Complete walled garden. Featured in Amateur garden and PL magazines, Western Morning news and Evening Herald. Mostly wheelchair access.

  ♿ 🎫 ⊗ 🚐 ☕

33 ▸ THE GATE HOUSE
Lee EX34 8LR. Mrs H Booker, 01271 862409. *3m W of Ilfracombe. Park in Lee village car park. Take lane alongside The Grampus PH. Garden approx 30 metres past inn buildings. Open most days but wise to check by phoning between 7pm & 9pm.* **Daily Sun 1 May to Mon 12 Sept (10-3.30). Adm by donation. Visits also by arrangement May to Sept.**

Described by many visitors as a peaceful paradise, this streamside garden incl collection of over 100 rodgersia (at their best end of June), interesting herbaceous areas, patio gardens with semi-hardy exotics, many unusual mature trees and shrubs and large organic vegetable garden. Level gravel paths.

  ♿ 🎫 **NPC** ☕

34 ▸ GOREN FARM
Broadhayes, Stockland, Honiton EX14 9EN. Julian Pady, 07770 694646, gorenfarm@hotmail.com, www.goren.co.uk. *6m E of Honiton, 6m W of Axminster. Go to the Stockland television mast. 100 metres N signed from Ridge Cross.* **Evening opening Daily Sat 4 June to Sun 17 July (5-9). Sat 4, Sun 5, Sat 11, Sun 12, Sat 18, Sun 19 June (10-5). Home-made teas. Adm £3, chd free. Visits also by arrangement June & July for groups of 10+. Guided walk and talk with teas can last 3 hrs.** Wander through 50 acres of natural species rich wild flower meadows. Dozens of varieties of wild flowers and grasses. Orchids early June, butterflies July. Stunning views of Blackdown Hills. Georgian house and walled gardens, guided walks 10.30 and 2.30 on open weekends, and evenings. Picnic tables and BBQ stations around the fields. Featured in Exeter Express and Echo, East Devon Coast and Country, Coronation Meadows, Beautiful Farm Awards. Partial wheelchair access to meadows.

  ♿ 🎫 ⊗ ✿

35 ▸ GORWELL HOUSE
Goodleigh Rd, Barnstaple EX32 7JP. Dr J A Marston, 01271 323202, artavianjohn@gmail.com, www.gorwellhousegarden.co.uk. *³/₄ m E of Barnstaple centre on Bratton Fleming rd. Drive entrance between 2 lodges on L coming uphill (Bear Street) from Barnstaple centre.* **Suns 20 Mar, 15 May, 5 June, 3 July (2-6). Adm £4, chd free. Cream teas by Goodleigh W.I. Visits also by arrangement, groups of 10+ preferred.** Created mostly since 1979, this 4-acre garden overlooking the Taw estuary has a benign microclimate which allows many rare and tender plants to grow and thrive, both in the open and in walled garden. Several strategically placed follies complement the enclosures and

vistas within the garden. Opening in March especially for the magnolias. Featured in N Devon Journal, The English Garden and Devon Life magazines and on BBC Radio Devon. Recently on web-based SW1TV Summer Gardens. Mostly wheelchair access but some steep slopes.

  ♿ 🎫 ⊗ ☕

36 ▸ HALDON GRANGE
Dunchideock, Exeter EX6 7YE. Ted Phythian, 01392 832349. *5m SW of Exeter. From A30 go through Ide Village to Dunchideock 5m. Turn L to Lord Haldon, Haldon Grange is next L. From A38 (S) turn L on top of Haldon Hill follow Dunchideock signs, R at village centre to Lord Haldon.* **Sat 26, Sun 27, Mon 28 Mar, Sat 2, Sun 3, Sat 9, Sun 10, Sat 16, Sun 17, Wed 20, Sat 23, Sun 24, Sat 30 Apr, Sun 1, Mon 2, Sat 7, Sun 8, Wed 11, Sat 14, Sun 15, Wed 18, Sat 21, Sun 22, Sat 28, Sun 29, Mon 30 May (1-5). Adm £4, chd free. Home-made teas. Visits also by arrangement Apr & May, refreshments by arrangement.** 12 acre well established garden with camellias, magnolias, azaleas, various shrubs and rhododendrons; rare and mature trees; small lake and ponds with river and water cascades. 5 acre arboretum planted 2011 with wide range of trees, shrubs and a large lilac circle. Additionally a wisteria pergola with views over Exeter and Woodbury. Wheelchair access to main parts of garden.

  ♿ ⊗ ☕

37 ▸ HAMBLYN'S COOMBE
Dittisham, Dartmouth TQ6 0HE. Bridget McCrum, 01803 722228, mccrum.sculpt@waitrose.com. *3m N of Dartmouth. From A3122 L to Dittisham. In village R at Red Lion, The Level, then Rectory Lane, past River Farm to Hamblyn's Coombe.* **Visits by arrangement Mar to Nov, parking difficult for more than 20. Adm £5, chd free.** 7-acre garden with stunning views across the river to Greenway House and sloping steeply to R Dart at bottom of garden. Extensive planting of trees and shrubs with unusual design features accompanying Bridget McCrum's stone carvings and bronzes. Wild flower meadow and woods. Good rhododendrons and camellias, ferns and bamboos, acers and hydrangeas. Exceptional autumn colour.

  🎫

Woodbury Gardens

HANGRIDGE FARMHOUSE
See Somerset, Bristol & S Glos

38 ▶ HARBOUR LIGHTS
Horns Cross, Bideford EX39 5DW.
Brian & Faith Butler. *7m W of
Bideford, 3m E of Clovelly. On main
A39 between Bideford and Clovelly,
halfway between Hoops Inn and
Bucks Cross.* Sat 25, Sun 26 June
(11-6). Adm £3.50, chd free. Light
lunches, home made cakes and
cream teas, or perhaps a glass of
wine.
$1/2$ acre colourful garden with Lundy
views. A garden of wit, humour,
unusual ideas and surprises. Water
features, shrubs, herbaceous, foliage
area, grasses in an unusual setting,
fernery, bonsai and polytunnel.
Interesting time saving ideas. You will
never have seen a garden like this!
Superb conservatory for cream teas.
Free leaflet. We like our visitors to
leave with a smile! Child friendly. A
'must visit' garden. Intriguing artwork
of various kinds. Featured in West of
Morning News, Garden Questions &
Answers, Daily Mail, & Radio Devon.
🌼 🚐 ☕

HARCOMBE HOUSE
See Dorset

39 ▶ THE HAVEN
Wembury Road, Hollacombe,
Wembury, South Hams PL9 0DQ.
Mrs S Norton & Mr J Norton,
01752 862149,
suenorton1@hotmail.co.uk. *20mins
from Plymouth city centre. Use A379
Plymouth to Kingsbridge rd. At
Elburton r'about follow signs to
Wembury. Parking on roadside. Bus
stop outside, route 48 from
Plymouth.* Sat 2, Sun 3 Apr (11-5).
Adm £3.50, chd free. Cream teas.
**Visits also by arrangement Apr to
Aug.**
$1/2$ -acre sloping plantsman's garden
in the South Hams AONB. Tearoom
and seating areas. 2 ponds.
Substantial collection of large
flowering Asiatic and hybrid tree
magnolias. Large collection of
camellias including camellia reticulata.
Rare dwarf, weeping and slow
growing conifers. Daphnes, early
azaleas and rhododendrons, spring
bulbs, fritillaria and hellebores.
Magnolias, camellias. Wheelchair
access to top part of garden only.
♿ 🐕 🌳 ☕

40 ▶ NEW ▶ HAYNE
Zeal Monachorum, Crediton
EX17 6DE. Tim and Milla
Herniman, www.haynedevon.co.uk.
*Located $1/2$ m S of Zeal Monachorum.
From Zeal Monachorum, keeping
church on L, drive through village.
Continue on this road for $1/3$ m,
garden drive is 1st entrance on R.*
Sun 24 Apr, Sun 5 June (2-6). Adm
£3.50, chd free. Cream teas.
Hayne has a magical Walled Garden
brimming with mature trees, shrubs,
roses and borders. Highlights incl
beautiful tree peonies, mature wisteria
in both purple and white and rambling
wild roses in combination with a more
modern Piet Oudolf style perennial
planting which surrounds the recently
renovated grade II* farm buildings...
magic, mystery and soul by the
spadeful! Disabled WC. Wheelchair
access to walled garden through
orchard.
♿ 🐕 ☕

41 ▶ HEATHERCOMBE
Manaton, Bovey Tracey TQ13 9XE.
Claude & Margaret Pike
Woodlands Trust, 01626 354404,
gardens@pike.me.uk,
www.heathercombe.com. *7m NW
of Bovey Tracey. From Bovey Tracey
take scenic B3387 to Haytor/
Widecombe. 1.7m past Haytor Rocks
(before Widecombe hill) turn R to
Hound Tor and Manaton. 1.4m past
Hound Tor turn L at Heatree Cross to
Heathercombe.* Sun 3 Apr, Sun 15,
Sun 22, Sat 28, Sun 29 May, Sun 5
June (1.30-5.30). Adm £5, chd
free. Every Tue to Sun 18 June to
10 July (10-5.30). Adm £6, chd £2.
Home-made teas in pretty
cottage garden or conservatory if
wet. **Visits also by arrangement
Apr to Oct.** *Donation to Rowcroft
Hospice.*
Tranquil valley with tumbling streams
and quiet ponds and lake (with new
features), setting for 30 acres of
spring and summer interest -
daffodils, extensive bluebells
complementing large displays of
rhododendrons, lovely cottage
gardens, interesting herbaceous
planting, woodland walks, many
specimen trees, bog and fern
gardens, orchard and wild flower
meadow. Seats and 2m mainly level
sandy paths. From 18 June to 10 July
admission incl Heathercombe 'Edge'
sculpture trail, approx 50 sculptures
in woodland/garden settings.
Featured in Western Morning News.
♿ 🐕 ☕

42 ▶ ◆ HEDDON HALL
Parracombe EX31 4QL. Mr & Mrs
de Falbe, 07577 406238,
Jdefalbe@gmail.com. *10m NE of
Barnstaple. Follow A39 towards
Lynton around Parracombe (avoiding
village centre), then L towards village;
entrance 200 yds on L.* For NGS:
Sun 5, Sun 12 June (11-4). Adm
£5, chd free. Cream teas. **For
other opening times and
information, please phone or email.**
Stunning walled garden laid out by

Penelope Hobhouse with clipped box and cordoned apple trees, herbaceous secret garden and natural rockery leading to bog garden and 3 stew ponds. Very much a gardeners' garden, beautifully maintained, with many rare species, ferns, mature shrubs and trees all thriving in 4 acres of this sheltered Exmoor valley. Wheelchair access to walled garden only.

♿ 🌳 ✿ ☕

43 HIGH GARDEN
Chiverstone Lane, Kenton EX6 8NJ. Chris & Sharon Britton, www.highgardennurserykenton. wordpress.com. *5m S of Exeter on A379 Dawlish Rd. Leaving Kenton towards Exeter, L into Chiverstone Lane, 50yds along lane. Entrance clearly marked.* **Every Tue to Fri 19 Jan to 16 Dec (9-5). Adm by donation. Light refreshments.** *Donation to FORCE cancer care charity.*
Very interesting and wide ranging planting of trees, shrubs, climbers and perennials in relaxed but still controlled 10 yr old garden. 70 metre summer herbaceous border, colour-themed beds, grass walkways with surprises around each corner. Always something to enjoy incl winter garden. Self-service tea room open March to November. Garden attached to Plantsmans Nursery, open at same time. Suggested Donation to garden £3.50. Slightly sloping site but the few steps can be avoided.

♿ 🌳 ✿ ☕

44 HIGHER ASH FARM
Ash, Dartmouth TQ6 0LR. Mr Michael Gribbin & Mrs Jennifer Barwell, 07595 507516, matthew.perkins18@yahoo.co.uk, www.higherashfarm.com. *Leave A381 at Halwell for Dartmouth A3122. Turn R before Sportsman's Arms to Bugford. At T junction go R then next L. After 1¹/₂ m at Xrds go R, Higher Ash Farm entrance is 1st L.* **Sun 15, Sun 22 May (2-5); Sun 9 Oct (1.30-4.30). Adm £4.50, chd free. Tea. Opening with Ash Gardens on Sat 25, Sun 26 June, Sat 13, Sun 14 Aug. Visits also by arrangement Apr to Oct for 1-15.**
Evolving garden, high up in South Devon countryside. Sitting in 2.5 acres there is a large kitchen garden terraced into the hillside with adjoining orchard underplanted with a variety of daffodils. A vibrant array of azaleas and rhododendrons surround

the barns and courtyard. The farmhouse is surrounded by a mix of herbaceous borders, shrubs and lawns. Pond, stream, autumn interest.

🌳 🛋 ☕

Stunning, far reaching views north to Dartmoor . . .

45 HIGHER CHERUBEER
Dolton, Winkleigh EX19 8PP. Jo & Tom Hynes, 01805 804265, hynesjo@gmail.com, www.sites.google.com/site/cherub eergardens/the-gardens. *2m E of Dolton. From A3124 turn S towards Stafford Moor Fisheries, take 1st R, garden 500m on L.* **Sun 7, Fri 19 Feb (2-5); Sun 5 June (2.30-6); Sun 2 Oct (2-5). Adm £4, chd free.** Home-made teas. 2017: Fri 10, Fri 17, Sun 26 Feb. **Visits also by arrangement Feb to Oct for groups of 10+.**
1.5-acre country garden with gravelled courtyard, raised beds and alpine house, lawns, large herbaceous border, shady woodland beds, large kitchen garden, greenhouse, colourful collection of basketry willows. Winter opening for National Collection of cyclamen, hellebores and over 300 snowdrop varieties. Featured on BBC Spotlight and in Devon Life, Western Morning News, Telegraph. Gravel paths.

♿ ✿ 🚘 **NPC** ☕

46 HIGHER CULLAFORD
Spreyton, Crediton EX17 5AX. Dr and Mrs Kennerley, 01837 840974. *Approx ³/₄ m from centre of Spreyton, 20m W of Exeter, 10 E of Okehampton. From A30 at Whiddon Down follow signs to Spreyton. Yellow signs from A3124, the centre of the village and Spreyton parish church.* **Sun 19, Sun 26 June (2-6). Adm £3.50, chd free. Cream teas. Visits also by arrangement May to Sept.**
Traditional cottage style garden developed over past 10yrs from steep field and farmyard on northern edge

of Dartmoor National Park. Mixed borders of herbaceous plants, roses and shrubs. 30ft pergola covered with seagull rose and many varieties of clematis, raised vegetable beds and wildlife pond. Newly planted pleached hornbeam hedge. Wheelchair access limited but can drive in to garden on request.

🌳 ☕

47 NEW HIGHER VELWELL FARM
Dartington, Totnes TQ9 6AD. Tony & Jill Hulatt. *From Buckfastleigh, follow A384 to Riverford Bridge follow rd up short hill, opp school sign turn R signed Velwell and Luscombe. From Totnes, follow A384, L after Rudolf Steiner School.* **Sat 4, Sun 5 June (2-6). Adm £4, chd free. Also open Bullard Farm. Cream teas and refreshments on garden terrace.**
C17 farmhouse surrounded by hillside garden and pasture of around 13 acres with stunning, far reaching views north to Dartmoor, within sight and sound of the South Devon Railway. Steeply sloping garden with some formal beds with mature shrubs; spring-fed pond with overflow stream surrounded by mature azaleas, huge Gunnera and a variety of damp-loving plants such as astilbe.

☕

48 NEW HILLERSDON
Cullompton EX15 1LS. Mr Mike Lloyd, http://www.hillersdon.com/. *2m NW of Cullompton (M5 J28). From Fore St in Cullompton town centre (B3181) take Tiverton Rd. Continue along this road for approx 2m then follow yellow signs to Hillersdon.* **Sat 28, Sun 29, Mon 30 May (10-5). Adm £5, chd free. Light refreshments.**
After decades of neglect, the gardens at Hillersdon have been lovingly restored and developed, and this work is ongoing. Gardens and parkland now incl several ornamental lakes, new collection of rhododendrons, restored walled garden, secret garden, stumpery, formal parterres, wild flower meadow, red deer and the ancient and enigmatic chestnut walk. Gardens opening to the public for the first time. Flat formal garden areas but loose gravel on many paths. No wheelchair access to other areas (gradients and steps).

♿ ✿ **D** ☕

49 ◆ HOLBROOK GARDEN

Sampford Shrubs, Sampford Peverell EX16 7EN. Martin Hughes-Jones & Susan Proud, 01884 821164, www.holbrookgarden.com. *1m NW from M5 J27. From M5 J27 follow signs to Tiverton Parkway. At top of slip rd off A361 follow brown sign to Holbrook Garden, 1m from J27.* **For NGS: Fri 25, Sat 26, Sun 27, Mon 28 Mar, Fri 15, Sat 16, Sat 30 Apr, Sun 1, Fri 27, Sat 28, Sun 29 May, Fri 17, Sat 18 June, Thur 14, Fri 15, Sat 16 July, Fri 26, Sat 27, Sun 28 Aug (10-5). Adm £4, chd free. For other opening times and information, please phone or visit garden website.**

2 acre S-facing garden with very diverse plantings inspired by natural plant populations; the garden continually evolves - many experimental plantings - wet garden, stone garden. Perfumes, songbirds and nests everywhere in spring and early summer. Fritillaries, pulmonarias April; crocosmia, heleniums, Salvias, late perennials Aug/Sept. Productive vegetable garden and polytunnel. Coach parties by arrangement, please phone or see holbrookgarden.com. Donation to MSF UK (Medecin sans Frontieres). Narrow paths restrict access for wheelchairs and buggies.

50 HOLE FARM

Woolsery, Bideford EX39 5RF. Heather Alford. *11m SW of Bideford. Follow directions for Woolfardisworthy, signed from A39 at Bucks Cross. From village follow NGS signs from school for approx 2m.* **Suns 12 June, 10 July, 4 Sept (2-6). Adm £4, chd free. Home-made teas in converted barn.**

3 acres of exciting gardens with established waterfall, ponds, vegetable and bog garden. Terraces and features incl round house have all been created using natural stone from original farm quarry. Peaceful walks through Culm grassland and water meadows border R Torridge and host a range of wildlife. Home to a herd of pedigree native Devon cattle. Riverside walk not accessible with wheelchair.

51 NEW HOLE'S MEADOW

South Zeal, Okehampton EX20 2JS. Fi and Paul Reddaway, https://fireddaway.wordpress.com/. *4½ m from Okehampton on B3260, 4m from Whiddon Down. Signed from main street, half way between King's Arms and Oxenham Arms and opp village hall. A minute's fairly level walk along private path.* **Fri 22, Sun 24 July (11-5). Adm £3, chd free.**

2 acre secret garden offering a quirky insight into owner's love of growing many herbs. Incl 2 Plant Heritage National Plant Collections of monarda (bergamot, bee balm) and nepeta (catmint). Complemented by cutting flowers, vegetables, orchard and ornamental and coppicing trees. The collections incl over 100 forms of each, both planted in show beds and a more formal herb garden.

NPC

52 ◆ HOTEL ENDSLEIGH

Milton Abbot, Tavistock PL19 0PQ. Olga Polizzi, 01822 870000, mail@hotelendsleigh.com, www.hotelendsleigh.com/garden. *7m NW of Tavistock, midway between Tavistock and Launceston. From Tavistock, take B3362 to Launceston. 7m to Milton Abbot then 1st L, opp school. From Launceston & A30, B3362 to Tavistock. At Milton Abbot turn R opp school.* **For NGS: Sun 5 June, Sun 17 July (11.30-4.30). Adm £5, chd free. Tea in the hotel. The Hotel is also open to non residents for lunch, afternoon tea and dinner. For other opening times and information, please phone, email or visit garden website.**

200 year old Repton-designed garden in 3 parts; formal gardens around the house, picturesque dell with pleasure dairy and rockery and arboretum. Gardens were laid out in 1814 and have been carefully renovated over last 10yrs. Bordering the R Tamar, it is a hidden oasis of plants and views. Hotel was built in 1810 by Sir Jeffry Wyattville for the 6th Duchess of Bedford in the romantic cottage Orne style. Plant Nursery adjoins hotel's 108 acres. *'If ever a hotel were built in paradise, it would be like Endsleigh - I love it and envy that sublime landscape - the perfect opportunity to step back in time to a graceful age'*, Alan Titchmarsh. Partial wheelchair access.

53 IDESTONE BARTON

Dunchideock, Exeter EX2 9UE. Mr & Mrs James Studholme. *From Ide take rd to Dunchideock. After 500m fork R (signed Idestone). Take 1st L after 1m. Follow over Xrds and down steep sided S bend. Car Park signed on R.* **Fri 3, Sat 4 June (1-5). Adm £4, chd free. Home-made teas.**

Romantic 6-acre country garden in unspoilt countryside only 3m from Exeter. Built on 5 different levels, with several distinctive rooms, garden features yew-hedged kitchen garden, croquet lawn, rose terrace, orchard and arboretum. Picturesque kitchen garden. Garden still in development. No wheelchair access.

111 NEW INNER TING TONG GARDENS

Inner Ting Tong Lane, Budleigh Salterton EX9 7AP. *Parking in field in Dalditch Lane. For SatNav use EX9 7AS. Signed from B3180 Woodbury to Budleigh Salterton road. Signed from B3178, Knowle village on Newton Poppleford to Exmouth road.* **Sat 14, Sun 15 May, Sat 3, Sun 4 Sept (2-5). Combined adm £4.50, chd free. Home-made teas.**

NEW INNER TING TONG HOUSE
Richard & Catrine Waller

NEW NORTHWOODS
Sally & Ian Kellaway

The garden on acid sandy soil at Inner Ting Tong House extends to 3½ acres incl mixed woodland carpeted in wild flowers in spring, particularly primroses and bluebells. Extensive lawns and a large variety of shrubs incl azaleas, rhododendrons, pieris and hydrangeas plus several species of grasses, herbaceous plants and ground cover. Distant sea view, fountain, secret garden and small arboretum. Northwoods has a 1½ acre sloping plot with a small woodland area on north side of bungalow. Front garden consists of lawn surrounded by shrubs, trees and herbaceous borders. Rhododendrons, camellias and magnolias provide spring interest whilst hydrangeas and fuchsias extend the flowering season. If wet, wheelchair access may be difficult.

54 ▶ JASON'S GARDEN
Eastcliff Walk, Teignmouth
TQ14 8SZ. The Pope family,
www.jasonsgarden.org.uk. *Park at East Cliff car park (or anywhere else in town), follow NGS signs, walk up tarmac cliff rd with sea on R.* **Sun 29 May, Sun 24 July (10-4.30). Adm £4, chd free. Light refreshments. Quiche salad lunches, cakes and coffees, plus cold drinks.**
Magical clifftop garden with high quality landscaping with modern, stylish design. Amazing panoramic view over Lyme Bay and railway below is complemented by growing collection of sculptures. Rain water collection and compost loo add to the environmental credentials of this innovative family gathering place. Garden's underlying ethos leaves a lasting impression. Highly recommended. Combine a visit to Teignmouth during the summer holidays when there is a wonderful display of sculptures all along the sea front. Featured in BBC2 Open Garden series with Carol Klein (who said it was one of her favourite gardens!). Short steepish climb to garden (no steps).

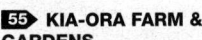

55 ▶ KIA-ORA FARM & GARDENS
Knowle Lane, Cullompton
EX15 1PZ. Mrs M B Disney, 01884 32347, rosie@kia-orafarm.co.uk, www.kia-orafarm.co.uk. *On W side of Cullompton and 6m SE of Tiverton. M5 J28, through town centre to r'about, 3rd exit R, top of Swallow Way turn L into Knowle Lane, garden beside Cullompton Rugby Club.* **Sun 27, Mon 28 Mar, Sun 10, Sun 17 Apr, Sun 1, Mon 2, Sun 15, Sun 29, Mon 30 May, Sun 19 June, Sun 24 July, Sun 7, Sun 28, Mon 29 Aug, Sun 11 Sept (2-5.30). Adm £3, chd free. Home-made teas in the garden or undercover tea barn if required for shelter or shade whatever the British weather!**
Charming, peaceful 10 acre garden with lawns, lakes and ponds. Water

features with swans, ducks and other wildlife. Mature trees, shrubs, rhododendrons, azaleas, heathers, roses, herbaceous borders and rockeries. Nursery avenue, novelty crazy golf. Lots to see and enjoy, and no afternoon would be complete without sampling a home-made Devon cream tea or a slice of one of the many tempting cakes. Kia-ora Farm will kindly donate £50 for each wedding booking.

GROUP OPENING

56 ▶ KILMINGTON (SHUTE ROAD) GARDENS
Kilmington, Axminster EX13 7ST,
www.Kilmingtonvillage.com. *1½ m W of Axminster. Signed off A35.* **Sat 18, Sun 19 June (1.30-5). Combined adm £5, chd free. Home-made teas at Breach.**

BREACH
J A Chapman & B J Lewis

SPINNEY TWO
Paul & Celia Dunsford

Set in rural E Devon in AONB yet easily accessed from A35. 2 gardens ¼ m apart. Spinney Two: ½ acre garden planted for yr-round colour, foliage and texture. Mature Oaks and Beech. Views. On gentle southerly slope. Spring bulbs, hellebores and shrubs incl azaleas, camellias, cornus, pieris, skimmias, viburnhams. Roses, acers, flowering trees, clematis and other climbers. Mixed borders and vegetable patch. Breach: set in over 3 acres with majestic woodland partially underplanted with rhododendrons and hydrangeas; also shrubberies, areas of grass, colourful beds, vegetable garden, small orchard and ponds. Bog garden developed over last 4yrs using natural springs in garden.

57 ▶ NEW LAKESLAND
Splatt, Broadwoodkelly, Winkleigh
EX19 8EQ. Diana & Bruce Tigwell. *From B3124 Winkleigh to N Tawton, through Broadwoodkelly 1m SW.* **Sat 7, Sun 8 May (11-3.30). Adm £4, chd free. Light refreshments.**
2-acre garden, winding through hay meadows, developed over last 11 yrs, with a further 4 acres of ancient bluebell and orchid wood.

Olive house, sunken garden, orchard. Vegetable area with unusual indoor and outdoor plants. Large variety of fruit. 2 large spring-fed ponds with planted wildlife islands, water lilies. Eco and wildlife-friendly.

Welcome one of the first signs of spring by wandering through swathes of thousands of unusual varieties of snowdrops . . .

58 ▶ LEE FORD
Knowle Village, Budleigh Salterton
EX9 7AJ. Mr & Mrs N Lindsay-Fynn, 01395 445894, crescent@leeford.co.uk, http://leeford.co.uk/. *3½ m E of Exmouth. For SatNav use postcode EX9 6AL.* **Visits by arrangement Apr to Sept, groups of 20+ discount, adm £5. Refreshments for groups of 10+, coffee/tea & cake, cream teas. Adm £6, chd free. Light refreshments. Numbers and special dietary requests must be pre-booked.** *Donation to Lindsay-Fynn Trust.*
Extensive, formal and woodland garden, largely developed in 1950s, but recently much extended with mass displays of camellias, rhododendrons and azaleas, incl many rare varieties. Traditional walled garden filled with fruit and vegetables, herb garden, bog garden, rose garden, hydrangea collection, greenhouses. Ornamental conservatory with collection of pot plants. Lee Ford has direct access to the Pedestrian route and National Cycle Network route 2 which follows the old railway line that linked Exmouth to Budleigh Salterton. Garden is ideal destination for cycle clubs or rambling groups. Formal gardens are lawn with gravel paths. Moderately steep slope to woodland garden on tarmac with gravel paths in woodland.

59 LEWIS COTTAGE
Spreyton, nr Crediton EX17 5AA.
Mr & Mrs M Pell and Mr R Orton,
07773 785939, rworton@mac.com,
www.lewiscottageplants.co.uk. *5m NE or Spreyton, 8m W of Crediton. From Hillerton Cross, keep Stone Cross to your R. Drive approx 1¹/₂ m, Lewis Cottage on L, proceed across cattle grid. From Crediton follow A377 to Barnstaple for 1m turn L at NGS sign.* Sats, Suns 21, 22 May, 18, 19 June, 16, 17 July, 13, 14 Aug (11-5). Adm £4, chd free. Home-made teas. **Visits also by arrangement May to Sept for groups of 20 max.**
Located on SW-facing slope in rural Mid Devon, the 4 acre garden at Lewis Cottage has evolved primarily over last 2 decades, harnessing and working with the natural landscape. Using informal planting and natural formal structures to create a garden that reflects the souls of those who garden in it, it is an incredibly personal space that is a joy to share. Spring camassia cricket pitch, newly planted rose garden and iris bed, perennial wild meadow, dew pond, woodland walks, bog garden and hornbeam rondel planted with late flowering narcissi. Featured on Pippa Quelch BBC Radio Devon show and West Country TV in Open all Flowers series http://www.itv.com/ news/ westcountry/update/2015-07-17/open-all-flowers-crediton/.
🏵 ❀ ☕

60 NEW ▶ LIBERTAS
Buckland Tout Saints, Kingsbridge TQ7 2DS. Johnny & Rosalind Spears, 01548 853653, johnny@spears.me.uk. *A381 Kingsbridge - Totnes S of Mounts turn to Buckland-tout-Saints and Hotel. Continue towards Hotel. After St Peter's Church on R, next entrance on R.* **Visits by arrangement Apr to Oct. Adm £5, chd free.**
9 acres overlooking fantastic views of S Hams. 2 large walled gardens, borders filled with flowering shrubs. Rhododendrons, camellias, roses, dahlias, hydrangeas, agapanthus etc. Sculptures. 5 acre meadow with paths and specimen trees. Woodland with natural pond. Exotic glass house and Ladies Walk. Created by present owners over last 19 yrs. Wheelchair access to walled gardens via grass paths.

61 ▶ LITTLE ASH BUNGALOW
Fenny Bridges, Honiton EX14 3BL.
Helen & Brian Brown,
01404 850941,
helenlittleash@hotmail.com,
www.facebook.com/
littleashgarden. *3m W of Honiton. Leave A30 at Iron Bridge from Honiton 1m, Patteson's Cross from Exeter ¹/₂ m and follow NGS signs.* Sun 5 June, Sun 21 Aug (12-5). Adm £4, chd free. Tea. **Visits also by arrangement June to Sept for groups of 10+.**
Country garden of 1¹/₂ acres, packed with different and unusual herbaceous perennials, trees, shrubs and bamboos. Designed for yr-round interest, wildlife and owners' pleasure. Inspirational naturalistic planting in voluptuous, colour coordinated mixed borders provides a backdrop to the view. Natural stream, pond and damp woodland area, mini wildlife meadows and developing gravel/alpine garden. Featured in Garden Answers. Grass paths.
♿ 🏵 ❀ 🚐 ☕

63 ▶ LITTLE WEBBERY
Webbery, Bideford EX39 4PS. Mr & Mrs J A Yewdall, 01271 858206, jyewdall1@gmail.com. *2m E of Bideford. From Bideford (East the Water) along Alverdiscott Rd, or from Barnstaple to Torrington on B3232. Take road to Bideford at Alverdiscott, pass through Stoney Cross.* **Visits by arrangement Apr to Oct. Adm £4, chd free. Home-made teas.**
Approx 3 acres in valley setting with pond, lake, mature trees, 2 ha-has and large mature raised border. Large walled kitchen garden with yew and box hedging incl rose garden, lawns with shrubs and rose and clematis trellises. Vegetables and greenhouse and adj traditional cottage garden. Partial wheelchair access.
♿ ☕

64 ▶ LITTLECOURT COTTAGES
Seafield Rd, Sidmouth EX10 8HF.
Geoffrey Ward & Selwyn Kussman,
www.littlecourtcottages.com.
500yds N of Sidmouth seafront off Station Rd. Take A3052 to Sidmouth. At Bowd PH take B3176 to Sidmouth. Continue towards seafront, turn R into Seafield Rd. Littlecourt is 75yds on R. Sun 17 July (2-5). Home-made teas. Evening opening Mon 18 July (6-9). Wine. Adm £4, chd free.
Oasis of calm in middle of Sidmouth.

A series of rooms for the plantaholic. Courtyard gardens behind house; in front, main lawn and water feature. Rare and tender plants everywhere. Exceptional basket colour. New features in front garden. Recent redesign of rear garden with Victorian greenhouse.
🏵 ❀ ☕

Exotic glass
house and
Ladies Walk . . .

65 ▶ THE LOOKOUT
Sowden Lane, Lympstone EX8 5HE. Will & Jackie Michelmore,
www.lympstone.org/businesses/
lookout-landscapes/. *9m SE of Exeter, 2m N of Exmouth off A376. 12mins from M5. Follow signs off A376 to Exmouth after marine camp.* Fri 3 June (2-5); Sun 5 June (2-6). Adm £4, chd free. Cream teas. Coffees, cakes & soft drinks available.
No 2 in Alan Titchmarsh's top 10 'most challenging gardens' featured in his recent Britain's Best Back Gardens series, this wildlife-friendly 2 acres sits with its toes in the Exe Estuary. Lovingly created from a derelict site to harmonise with its coastal location and maximise on far reaching views. Flotsam and jetsam sit amongst naturalistic seaside planting to give that washed up on the beach look. Giant sandpit with buckets and spades for children. Photographic display showing how the site has evolved from 1920's to present day. Love-Local pop up shop featuring nautically inspired West Country craft and gifts. Featured in The English Garden, Good Housekeeping. Limited wheelchair access to lower garden, some gravel paths, steps and slopes. Drop off area at gate. Good level access to stalls and refreshments.
♿ ❀ ☕

66 LOWER SPITCHWICK GARDEN

Poundsgate TQ13 7NU. Pauline Lee, 01364 631593, paulineleeceramics@hotmail.com. *4m NW of Ashburton. By Spitchwick Common, nr New Bridge, Dartmoor.* Sat 18, Sun 19 June, Sat 9, Sun 10 July, Sat 13, Sun 14 Aug (1-5). Adm £3.50, chd free. Light refreshments. **Visits also by arrangement May to Sept.** Beautiful valley alongside R Dart. East Lower Lodge: atmospheric woodland garden with imaginative planting in natural setting. Contains jungle area with bamboo teahouse, meandering grass pathways, lawns, borders with stream, potager and vegetable garden. Artist/designer's gallery garden showing plant inspired sculpture placed in and amongst plantings to create a 'symphony' of forms colour and texture. Visitors can buy or commission directly from the artist. Featured in Telegraph 'Living' magazine 'Artists who's gardens double as galleries'.

67 ◆ LUKESLAND

Harford, Ivybridge PL21 0JF. Mrs R Howell & Mr & Mrs J Howell, 01752 691749, lorna.lukesland@gmail.com, www.lukesland.co.uk. *10m E of Plymouth. Turn off A38 at Ivybridge. 1¹/₂ m N on Harford rd, E side of Erme valley* **Please see below for opening times.** 24 acres of flowering shrubs, wild flowers and rare trees with pinetum in Dartmoor National Park. Beautiful setting of small valley around Addicombe Brook with lakes, numerous waterfalls and pools. Extensive and impressive collections of camellias, rhododendrons, azaleas and acers; also spectacular magnolia campbellii and huge Davidia involucrata. Superb spring and autumn colour. Children's trail. Open Suns, Weds and BH (11-5) 27 March - 12 June and 9 Oct - 13 November. Adm £5, chd free. Partial wheelchair access incl tearoom and WC.

68 LUSCOMBE FARM

Colston Road, Buckfastleigh TQ11 0LP. Mr Julian David. *2¹/₂ m from A38 junction at Buckfastleigh. Follow yellow signs off A384.* Sat 11, Sun 12 June (11-5). Adm £4, chd free. Home-made teas.

Bickham House

This walled garden was designed and created by Julian and Jasmin David in the 60's. A formal garden with fastigiate yews and box hedging and topiary, loosely planted with roses, shrubs, perennials, annuals and bi-annuals. It has a magical feel and great views across the Dart Valley.

69 MARSHALL FARM

Ide, nr Exeter EX2 9TN. Jenny Tuckett. *Between Ide and Dunchideock. Drive through Ide to top of village r'about, straight on for 1¹/₂ m. Turn R onto concrete drive, parking in farmyard at rear of property.* Sat 11, Sun 12 June (1-5). Adm £3, chd free. Home-made teas. Garden approached along lane lined with home grown lime, oak and chestnut trees. A country garden created approx 1967. One acre featuring wild flower gardens, gravel beds, pond, parterre garden and a vegetable and cutting garden. Stunning views of Woodbury, Sidmouth gap and Haldon. Limited wheelchair access.

70 ◆ MARWOOD HILL GARDEN

Marwood EX31 4EB. Dr J A Snowdon, 01271 342528, info@marwoodhillgarden.co.uk, www.marwoodhillgarden.co.uk. *4m N of Barnstaple. Signed from A361 & B3230. Look out for brown signs. See website for map. New coach & car park.* **For NGS: Fri 10 June (10-4.30). Adm £6, chd free. Light refreshments. For other opening times and information, please phone, email or visit garden website.** Marwood Hill is a very special private garden covering an area of 20 acres with lakes and set in a valley tucked away in N Devon. From early spring snowdrops through to late autumn there is always a colourful surprise around every turn. National Collections of astilbe, iris ensata and tulbaghia, large collections of camellia, rhododendron and magnolia. Winner of MacLaren Cup at rhododendron and camellia show RHS Rosemoor. Featured in the Great British Garden Revival with Rachel de Thame. Winner of the Leonardslea Cup in April 2015. Partial wheelchair access.

NPC

71 **THE MILL HOUSE**
Fremington, Barnstaple EX31 3DQ.
Martin & Judy Ash, 01271 344719,
martin_s_ash@yahoo.co.uk. *3m W
of Barnstaple. Off A39, take A3125 N.
At 3rd r'about (Cedars) L on B3233.
In Fremington L at top of Church Hill
onto Higher Rd. All parking signed
100m away.* **Sat 11, Sun 12 June,
Sat 2, Sun 3 July (12-5). Adm
£3.50, chd free. Home-made teas.
Visits also by arrangement June
to Aug for groups of 10+ only.**
³/₄ acre garden, surrounding thatched
mill house and bordered by
Fremington water; the topography is
the first wow factor here. Stepped
ups and downs, ins and outs,
surprises around every corner. There
is so much on a small scale; bridges,
borders, ponds, walkways, rockery,
terracing, lawns, bog garden, quarry
garden, wild garden, a small gallery,
oh and a henge. Wandering minstrels!
Featured in Amateur Gardening.
☕

Hospice care is
there for 1 in 3
people in the UK

GROUP OPENING

72 **MORETONHAMPSTEAD
GARDENS**
Moretonhampstead TQ13 8PW.
*12m W of Exeter & N of Newton
Abbot. On E slopes of Dartmoor
National Park. Parking at both
gardens.* **Sat 28, Sun 29, Mon 30
May, Sat 3, Sun 4 Sept (2-6).
Combined adm £5, chd free.
Cream teas.**

MARDON
Graham & Mary Wilson

SUTTON MEAD
Edward & Miranda Allhusen
**Visits also by arrangement,
coach possible but 100yd walk
from main road**
miranda@allhusen.co.uk
01647 440296

2 large gardens close to moorland
town. One in a wooded valley, the
other higher up with magnificent
views of Dartmoor. Dogs on leads

welcome. Plant sale, teas are a must.
Both have mature orchards and year
round vegetable gardens. Substantial
rhododendron, azalea and tree
planting, croquet lawns, summer
colour and woodland walks through
hydrangeas and acers. Something for
all the family. Mardon: 4 acres based
on its original Edwardian design.
Long herbaceous border, rose garden
and formal granite terraces
supporting 2 borders of agapanthus.
Fernery beside stream-fed pond with
its thatched boathouse. New
arboretum with 60 specimen trees.
Sutton Mead: Paths wander through
tranquil woodland, unusual planting.
Lawns surrounding granite-lined pond
with seat at water's edge. Elsewhere
dahlias, grasses, bog garden, rill-fed
round pond, secluded seating and an
unusual concrete greenhouse. Sedum
roofed summerhouse. A garden of
variety. Limited wheelchair access.
🐕 ♿ 🚐 ☕

73 **MOTHECOMBE HOUSE**
Holbeton, Plymouth PL8 1LB. Mr &
Mrs A Mildmay-White,
www.flete.co.uk. *12m E of
Plymouth. From A379 between
Yealmpton and Modbury turn S for
Holbeton. Continue 2m to
Mothecombe.* **Sun 1 May (11-5).
Adm £5, chd free. Home-made
teas.**
Queen Anne house (not open) with
Lutyens additions and terraces set in
private estate hamlet. Walled pleasure
gardens, borders and Lutyens
courtyard. Orchard with spring bulbs,
unusual shrubs and trees, camellia
walk. Autumn garden, streams, bog
garden and pond. Bluebell woods
leading to private beach. Yr-round
interest. Sandy beach at bottom of
garden, unusual shaped large
liriodendron tulipifera. New planting of
bee friendly walled garden, featured in
Western Morning News. Gravel
paths, one slight slope.
♿ ♿ ☕

74 **NEW** **THE MOUNT,
DELAMORE**
Cornwood, Ivybridge PL21 9QP. Mr
and Mrs Gavin Dollard. *Delamore
Park PL21 9QP. Please park in car
park for Delamore Park Offices not in
village. From Ivybridge turn L at Xrds
keep PH on L, follow wall on R to
sharp R bend, turn R.* **Sat 13, Sun
14, Sat 20, Sun 21 Feb (11-3). Adm
£4, chd free. Light refreshments.**
Welcome one of the first signs of
spring by wandering through swathes

of thousands of unusual varieties of
snowdrops in this lovely wooded
Mount. Closer to the village than to
Delamore gardens (open only in May
for the Sculpture and Art Exhibition)
paths meander through a sea of
these lovely plants, some of which
are unique to Delamore and which
were sold to Covent Garden as late
as 2002. The main house and garden
open for sculpture exhibition every
day in May. Possible wheelchair
access but rough paths/woodland
tracks.
🐕 ♿ 🚐 ☕

75 **THE OLD DAIRY**
Sidbury, Sidmouth EX10 0QR.
Dame Alison Carnwath & Peter
Thomson. *¹/₂ m from Sidbury. Enter
village of Sidbury from either Honiton
or Sidford and turn into Church St
next to church. See yellow signs at
church. The Old Dairy is ³/₄ m from
church up steep hill.* **Sat 4, Sun 5
June (1-6). Adm £5, chd free.
Home-made teas. Variety of home
made cakes. Juices, teas and
coffees. Beautiful terrace to enjoy
tea or conservatory if wet.**
25 yr old garden carved out of
woodland and meadows, built on
hillside. Rhododendrons and wisteria,
bluebells and roses. Some
herbaceous around house. Small
pond and bog garden. Splendid
views over Sid Valley. The essence of
peaceful Devon countryside. Lovely
walking adj to property. Continue
from house along East Devon way to
extend your experience of glorious
East Devon. Recommended in
Sidford Herald, Western Morning
News, Express and Echo. Limited
areas for wheelchair tours but
magnificent views of course!
♿ 🐕 ♿ ☕

76 **THE OLD VICARAGE**
West Anstey, South Molton
EX36 3PE. Tuck & Juliet Moss. *9m
E of South Molton. From S Molton go
E on B3227 to Jubilee Inn. Follow
NGS signs to house. From Tiverton
r'about take A396 7m to B3227 (L) to
Jubilee Inn.* **Sat 14, Sun 15 May, Sat
20, Sun 21 Aug (12-5). Adm £4.50,
chd free. Cream teas.**
Croquet lawn leads to multi-level
garden overlooking 3 large ponds
with winding paths, climbing roses
and overviews. Brook with waterfall
flows through garden past fascinating
summerhouse built by owner.
Benched deck overhangs first pond.
Features rhododendrons, azaleas and

primulas in spring and large collection of Japanese iris in July and wonderful hydrangeas in August.

🎭 🚐 ☕

77 ◆ **PLANT WORLD**
St Marychurch Road, Newton Abbot TQ12 4SE. Ray Brown, 01803 872939, www.plant-world-gardens.co.uk. *2m SE of Newton Abbot. 1¹/₂ m from Penn Inn turn-off on A380. Follow brown tourist signs at end of A380 dual carriageway from Exeter.* **For opening times please see below.**
The 4 acres of landscape gardens with fabulous views have been called Devon's 'Little Outdoor Eden'. Representing each of the five continents, they offer an extensive collection of rare and exotic plants from around the world. Superb mature cottage garden and Mediterranean garden will delight the visitor. Attractive new viewpoint café and shop. Open 25 March - end Sept (9.30-5.00). Wheelchair access to café and nursery only.

🎭 ❀ 🚐 ☕

78 **PORTINGTON**
Lamerton PL19 8QY. Mr & Mrs I A Dingle, 01822 870364. *3m NW of Tavistock. From Tavistock take road past hospital to Lamerton. Beyond Lamerton L at Carrs garage. 1st R (signed Horsebridge), next L then L again. From Launceston turn R at Carrs garage then as above.* **Sun 12, Sun 19 June (2-5.30). Adm £3, chd free. Home-made teas. Visits also by arrangement in June, max 30.** *Donation to Plymouth & District Deaf Children's Society.*
Garden in peaceful rural setting with fine views over surrounding countryside. Mixed planting with shrubs and borders. Walk to small lake through woodland and fields, which have been designated a county wildlife site. Partial wheelchair access.

🎭 🎭 ❀ ☕

79 NEW **THE PRIORY**
Priory Road, Abbotskerswell, Newton Abbot TQ12 5PP. Priory Residents. *2m SW of Newton Abbot town centre. A381 Newton Abbot/Totnes Rd. Sharp L turn from NA. R from Totnes. At mini r'about in village centre turn L into Priory Rd.* **Sat 2, Sun 3 July (1-5). Adm £4, chd free. Home-made teas.**
The Priory is a Grade II* listed building, originally a manor house extended in Victorian times as a

home for an Augustinian order of nuns, is now a retirement complex of 43 apartments and cottages. The grounds extend to approx 5 acres and incl numerous flower borders, a wild flower meadow, an area of woodland with some interesting specimen trees, cottage gardens and lovely views. Small Mediterranean garden and area of individually owned raised beds and greenhouses. Featured in local newspapers and radio. Wheelchair access difficult when wet.

♿ 🎭 ❀ ☕

Kitchen garden with companion planting . . .

80 **PROSPECT HOUSE**
Lyme Road, Axminster EX13 5BH. Peter Wadeley, 01297 631210, wadeley@btinternet.com. *¹/₂ m uphill from centre of Axminster. Just before service station.* **Fri 2, Sat 3, Sun 4 Sept (1.30-5). Adm £4, chd free. Home-made teas. Visits also by arrangement June to Sept for groups of 6+.**
1 acre plantsman's garden hidden behind high stone walls with Axe Valley views. Well stocked borders with rare shrubs, many reckoned to be borderline tender. 200 varieties of salvia, and other late summer perennials incl rudbeckia, helenium, echinacea, helianthus, crocosmia and grasses creating a riot of colour. A gem, not to be missed. Featured in Garden News, BBC Gardens World, local press.

🎭 ❀ 🚐 ☕

81 **REGENCY HOUSE**
Hemyock EX15 3RQ. Mrs Jenny Parsons, 01823 680238, jenny.parsons@btinternet.com, www.regencyhousehemyock.co.uk. *8m N of Honiton. M5 J26. From Hemyock take Dunkeswell-Honiton rd. Entrance ¹/₂ m on R from Catherine Wheel PH and church. Disabled parking (only) at house.* **Suns 12 June, 14 Aug, 9 Oct (2-5.30). Adm £4.50, chd free. Home-made teas. Visits also by arrangement May to Sept, no coaches.**
5-acre plantsman's garden approached across private ford.

Many interesting and unusual trees and shrubs. Visitors can try their hand at identifying plants with the plant list or have a game of croquet. Plenty of space to eat your own picnic. Walled vegetable and fruit garden, lake, ponds, bog plantings and sweeping lawns. Horses, Dexter cattle and Jacob sheep. Scarecrows around the garden for June opening. Gently sloping gravel paths give wheelchair access to the walled garden, lawns, borders and terrace, where teas are served.

♿ 🎭 🛏 ☕

82 **RUNNYMEDE**
2 Orchard Close, Manor Rd, Sidmouth EX10 8RS. Veronica Wood. *12m SE of Exeter. A3052 to Sidmouth. 1st R (Bowd) onto B3176 1¹/₂ m. R into Manor Rd at Manor Pavilion Theatre, ¹/₂ m to Manor Rd Car Park (advised as disabled parking only in Orchard Close).* **Sat 18, Sun 19, Mon 20 June (2-5). Adm £3, chd free. Home-made teas.**
On western edge of Sidmouth. Beautiful tranquil garden of approx ¹/₄ acre artistically landscaped with circles, pool and rill designed by Naila Green RHS Chelsea medallist. Abundance of colourful and unusual plants. Woodland and gravel areas. Microclimate, tender plants, plentiful seating, level paths. Raised vegetable beds and greeenhouse with vines.

♿ 🎭 ❀ ☕

83 **ST MERRYN**
Higher Park Road, Braunton EX33 2LG. Dr W & Mrs Ros Bradford, 01271 813805, ros@st-merryn.co.uk. *5m W of Barnstaple. On A361, R at 30mph sign, then R into Lower Park Road, then L into Seven Acre Lane, at top of lane R into Higher Park Rd. Pink house 200 yds on R.* **Sun 17 Apr, Sun 15 May, Sat 18, Sun 19 June, Sun 10 July (2-6). Adm £4, chd free. Cream teas. Visits also by arrangement Apr to July, any small group.**
Very sheltered, peaceful, gently sloping, S-facing, artist's garden, emphasis on shape, colour, scent and yr-round interest. A garden for pleasure with swimming pool. Thatched summerhouse leading down to herbaceous borders. Winding crazy paving paths, many seating areas. Shrubs, mature trees, fish ponds, grassy knoll, gravel areas, hens. Many environmental features. Open gallery (arts & crafts).

♿ ❀ ☕

© Val Corbett

Cadhay

84 NEW THE SCHOOL HOUSE
Lydford, Okehampton EX20 4AU.
Karen Burgess,
www.sweetbabyveg.com. *9m SW
of Okehampton. From A386,
Okehampton to Tavistock rd, turn off
for Lydford at Dartmoor Inn. The
School House is just over 1/2 m away
on L and just before Primary School.*
Sat 9, Sun 10 July, Sat 6, Sun 7
Aug (11-5). Adm £5, chd free.
Light refreshments. Soup & crusty
bread, coffee, tea and cakes.
Pretty cottage garden with mixed
borders, annuals, topiary, cloud
pruning and mini pond. Kitchen
garden with companion planting,
aquilegia amongst the vegetables.
Potager with scented sweet peas
tumbling over first early potatoes and
carrots. Wildlife is at home in this
garden with insect friendly planting
and a bug hotel overlooking a wild
flower meadow.

**85 SEDGEWELL COACH
HOUSE GARDENS**
Olchard TQ12 3GU. Heather
Jansch, www.heatherjansch.com.
*4m N of Newton Abbot. 12m S of
Exeter on A380, L for Olchard,
straight ahead on private drive.* Sats,
Suns 7, 8, 14, 15 May; 27, 28 Aug

(11-5). Adm £4, chd free. Home-
made teas.
Heather Jansch, world-famous
sculptor, brings innovative use of
recycled materials to gardening. 14
acres incl stunning driftwood
sculpture, fabulous views from thrilling
woodland bluebell trail down to
timeless stream-bordered water
meadow walk, pools, herbaceous
border, medicinal herb garden.
Plentiful seating, come and picnic.
Most sculpture is on level areas near
the house. Limited disabled parking
but there is a drop off point. Sorry no
wheel chair accessible WC.

**86 ◆ SHAPCOTT BARTON
ESTATE**
(East Knowstone Manor), East
Knowstone, South Molton
EX36 4EE. Anita Allen, 01398
341664. *13m NW of Tiverton. J25
M5 take Tiverton exit. 61/2 m to
r'about take exit South Molton 10m
on A361. Turn R signed Knowstone.
Leave A361 travel 1/4 m to Roachhill
through hamlet turn L at Wiston
Cross, entrance on L 1/4 m. For NGS:*
Sun 17, Wed 20, Sun 24 Apr, Sun
17, Wed 20, Sun 24 July, Wed 3
Aug (10.30-4.30). Adm £4, chd
free. Cream teas on Suns when
fine. For other opening times and

information, please phone.
Donation to Cats Protection.
Large, ever developing garden of 200
acre estate around ancient historic
manor house. Wildlife garden.
Restored old fish ponds, stream and
woodland rich in bird life. Unusual
fruit orchard. Scented bulbs in Apr.
Flowering burst July/Aug of National
Plant Collections *Leucanthemum
superbum* (shasta daisies) and
buddleja davidii. Many butterfly plants
incl over 40 varieties of phlox. Kitchen
garden and standard orchard. Steep
slopes.

GROUP OPENING

**87 NEW SHEEPWASH
GARDENS**
Sheepwash EX21 5PE. *1.4m N of
Sheepwash. Leave Okehampton
joining A386 going N. L onto A3072
in Hatherleigh. R on sharp bend in
Highampton to Sheepwash. 1.6m
after Sheepwash sign turn L onto
farm track signed Lake Farm.* Sat 7,
Sun 8 May, Sat 16, Sun 17 July
(11-5). Combined adm £5, chd
free.

NEW LAKE FARMHOUSE
Erica Fisher
Visits also by arrangement Apr
to Sept
erica@lakefarmhouse.co.uk
01409 231582

**NEW MUSSELBROOK
COTTAGE**
Richard Coward
Visits also by arrangement Apr
to Sept
01409 231677
coward.richard@sky.com

2 gardens on opp sides of the track.
Lake Farmhouse: plenty to enjoy in
this 2 acre garden and smallholding.
Started in 2010, colour themed rose
garden, hosta border, orchard, hot
borders and raised beds, peony
borders, productive vegetable and fruit
garden, herbs, cut flower beds, giant
and unusual plant border, containers
with seasonal bedding, tender plants
and lots more. Informal, cottage style
planting, colour and interest all yr
round. Musselbrook Cottage: 1 acre
naturalistic/wildlife garden of all season
interest. Many rare/unusual plants on
sloping, sunny site. 8 ponds (koi, orfe,
rudd, dragonflies, lilies, aquatics).
Mediterranean garden, wild flower
meadow, clock golf area, oriental
features. Thousands of bulbs. Many

ericaceous plants (acers, rhododendrons, camellias, hydrangeas). Grasses, dierama. Wildlife haven. Good photographers' garden.

88 SIDBURY MANOR
Sidbury, Sidmouth EX10 0QE. Sir John & Lady Cave, www.sidburymanor.co.uk. *1m NW of Sidbury. Signed in Sidbury village off A375 between Honiton and Sidmouth.* Sat 23, Sun 24 Apr (2-5). Adm £5, chd free. Home-made teas.
Built in 1870s this Victorian manor house built by owner's family and set within East Devon AONB comes complete with 20 acres of garden incl substantial walled gardens, an extensive arboretum containing many fine trees and shrubs, a number of champion trees, and areas devoted to magnolias, rhododendrons and camellias. Partial wheelchair access.

GROUP OPENING

89 SIDMOUTH GARDENS
Sidmouth EX10 9DX. *Road plan provided at each Garden.* Sat 27, Sun 28, Mon 29 Aug (2-5.30). Combined adm £3.50, chd free. Home-made teas.

BYES REACH
Lynette Talbot & Peter Endersby
(See separate entry)
Visits also by arrangement May to Aug for groups of 8 to 20
latalbot01@gmail.com
01395 578081

ROWAN BANK
Barbara & Alan Mence

Situated on Jurassic Coast World Heritage Site, Sidmouth has fine beaches, beautiful gardens and magnificent coastal views. 2 contrasting gardens about 1m apart. Byes Reach: edible garden of ⅕ acre. Potager style, raised beds, espalier fruit trees on arched walkway, designed for those with mobility problems. Herbaceous borders, colour themed flower beds combining perennials, herbs, ferns and hostas. Pond, rockery, greenhouse and studio. Backing onto The Byes nature reserve and R Sid, offering an opportunity for a short walk from the garden gate. Rowan Bank is approx ¼ acre on a NW facing slope,

generously planted with trees, shrubs, perennials and bulbs for yr-round interest. Steps lead to wide zigzag path rising gently to woodland edge of birch and rowan, with shady bench under Mexican pine. Seats at every corner and summerhouse looking towards wooded hills. Wheelchair access at Byes Reach, regret none at Rowan Bank.

90 NEW SOCKS ORCHARD
Smallridge, Axminster EX13 7JN. Michael & Hilary Pritchard. *2m from Axminster. From Axminster on A358 L at Weycroft Mill T-lights. Pass Ridgeway Hotel on L. Continue on lane for ½ m. Park in field opp.* Fri 22, Sat 23 July (1.30-5). Adm £4, chd free. Home-made teas.
1 acre plus plantaholic's garden designed for yr round structure and colour. Many specimen trees, large collection of herbaceous plants, over 160 roses, gravel and grass borders, small orchard, vegetable patch, small pond. Steep bank inset with shrubs underplanted with wild flowers (ongoing project). Chickens and bees. Limited wheelchair access.

1 acre plus plantaholic's garden designed for year round structure and colour . . .

91 SOUTH WOOD FARM
Cotleigh, Honiton EX14 9HU. Dr Clive Potter, williamjamessmithson@gmail.com. *3m NE of Honiton. From Honiton head N on A30, take 1st R past Otter Dairy layby. Follow for 1m. Go straight over Xrds and take first L. Entrance after 1m on R.* Sat 17, Sun 18 Sept (2-5). Adm £4, chd free. Home-made teas. Visits also by arrangement Apr to Sept, guided tours of garden are available for group visits.
Large country garden surrounding listed C17 Devon farmhouse set deep

in the Blackdown Hills. Incl walled courtyard planted with late summer herbaceous and yew topiary, kitchen garden of raised beds with step over pears, fruit cages and trained fruit trees, sunken dry stream bed walk and reflecting pool, formal plum orchard, nuttery and traditional Devon cobbled yard with lean to glasshouse. Gravel pathways, cobbles and steps.

GROUP OPENING

92 SOUTHCOMBE GARDENS
Dartmoor, Widecombe-in-the-Moor TQ13 7TU, 01364 621332, amandasabin1@hotmail.com. *6m W of Bovey Tracey. B3387 from Bovey Tracey after village church take rd SW for 400yds then sharp R signed Southcombe, after 200yds pass C17 farmhouse and park on L.* Sun 22, Sun 29, Mon 30 May, Sat 4, Sun 5, Sun 12, Sun 19, Sun 26 June (2-5). Combined adm £5, chd free. Home-made teas at Southcombe Barn. Visits also by arrangement May & June (Mon - Sat incl) for groups of 10+.

SOUTHCOMBE BARN
Amanda Sabin & Stephen Hobson

SOUTHCOMBE HOUSE
Dr & Mrs J R Seale

Village famous for its Fair, Uncle Tom Cobley and its C14 church - the Cathedral of the Moor. Featured in RHS The Garden. Southcombe Barn: 4 acres, trees and drifts of flowers, abundantly wild and intensely colourful. Beautiful all yr round and busy with wildlife but this is its zenith 6 weeks of breathtaking glory. You can spend hours in it. People do. Southcombe House: 5 acres, SE-facing garden, arboretum and orchid rich restored wild flower meadow with bulbs in spring and four orchid species (early purple, southern marsh, common spotted and greater butterfly). On steep slope at 900ft above sea level with fine views to nearby tors. The teas are legendary. People starting their own wild flower meadows have used Southcombe House seed-rich fresh-cut hay to seed their newly cleared ground. Yellow rattle is then usually abundant in 1st year and orchids begin to appear in the 4th year.

93 SPRINGFIELD
Woolsery, Bideford EX39 5PZ. Ms Asta Munro, 01237 431162. *Ignore SatNav. 8m W of Bideford. 3m S of Clovelly. Turn off A39 at Buck's Cross. T-junction at school turn L past village hall. L signed Putford. 1m L.* **Visits by arrangement May to Sept, 6+ preferred but no one refused! Coach parties welcome. Adm £3.50, chd free. Tea.**
2 acre S sloping rural plot with views. Plantaholic's garden crammed with shrubs, perennials inc 100+ hardy geraniums. Paved suntrap with containers. Gravel area surrounded with herbs, aromatic, silver and pastel plants. Shade area. Small wildlife pond. Meadow with meandering paths. Kitchen garden fruit, vegetables, edible flowers. Wildlife haven incl bats. Little old fashioned 'sweetie shop' nursery.

94 SPRINGFIELD HOUSE
Seaton Road, Colyford EX24 6QW. Wendy Pountney, 01297 552481, pountneys@talktalk.net. *Colyford. Starting on A3052 coast road, at Colyford PO take Seaton Rd. House 500m on R. Ample parking in field.* **Sats 28 May, 18 June, 16 July (10-5). Adm £3.50, chd free. Home-made teas. Visits also by arrangement May to Oct for groups, max 35.**
1 acre garden of mainly fairly new planting. Numerous beds, majority of plants from cuttings and seed keeping cost to minimum, full of colour. Also vegetable garden, fruit cage and orchard with ducks and chicken. Wonderful views over R Axe and bird sanctuary, which is well worth a visit, path leads from the garden.

95 SQUIRRELS
98 Barton Road, Torquay TQ2 7NS. Graham & Carol Starkie, 01803 329241, calgra@talktalk.net. *5m S of Newton Abbot. From Newton Abbot take A380 to Torquay. After ASDA store on L, turn L at T-lights up Old Woods Hill. 1st L into Barton Rd. Bungalow 200yds on L. Also could turn by B&Q. Parking nearby.* **Sun 31 July, Sat 6 Aug (2-5). Sun 7 Aug (2-5). Adm £3.50, chd free. Teas 31 July and 6 Aug. Visits also by arrangement 25 July to 21 Aug.**
Plantsman's small town environmental garden, landscaped with small ponds and 7ft waterfall.

Interlinked through abutilons to Japanese, Italianate, tropical areas. Specialising in fruit incl peaches, figs, kiwi. Tender plants incl bananas, tree fern, brugmansia, lantanas, oleanders. Mandevilla. Collections of fuchsia, abutilons, bougainvilleas, topiary and more. Enviromental and Superclass Winners. 26 cleverly hidden rain water storage containers. Advice on free electric from solar panels and solar hot water heating and fruit pruning. 3 sculptures. Many topiary birds, animals and balls. Huge 18ft Torbay palm. 9ft geranium.15ft abutilons. Torbay in Bloom Superclass Gold Medal. Featured in local press and on radio. No wheelchair access. Mainly level paths. Conservatory for shelter and seating.

NGS support helps us to champion community nurses

96 STONE FARM
Alverdiscott Rd, Bideford EX39 4PN. Mr & Mrs Ray Auvray. *1½ m from Bideford towards Alverdiscott. From Bideford cross river using Old Bridge and turn L onto Barnstaple Rd. 2nd R onto Manteo Way and 1st L at mini r'about.* **Sat 2, Sun 3, Sat 9, Sun 10 July (2-5). Adm £3.50, chd free. Home-made teas.**
1-acre country garden with striking herbaceous borders, dry stone wall terracing, white garden, dahlia bed wild meadow area and woodland area. We also have an extensive fully organic vegetable garden with raised beds, soft fruit cage and polytunnels, together with an orchard with traditional varieties of apples, pears and nuts. Some gravel paths but wheelchair access to whole garden with some help.

97 SUMMERS PLACE
Little Bowlish, Whitestone EX4 2HS. Mr & Mrs Stafford Charles, 01647 61786. *6m NW of Exeter. From M5, A30 Okehampton. After 7m R to Tedburn St. Mary R at r'about past golf course 1st L after ½ m signed Whitestone straight ahead at Xrds follow signs. From Exeter on Whitestone rd 1 m beyond Whitestone, follow sign from Heath Cross. From Crediton follow Whitestone rd through Fordton.* **Sun 20 Mar, Sun 9 Oct (12-5). Adm £4.50, chd free. Light refreshments. Soup sandwiches and homemade teas. Visits also by arrangement Mar to Oct, 24 hrs notice required. Refreshments by arrangement.**
Rambling rustic paths and steps (some steep) lead down a shaded woodland garden; unusual trees and shrubs (profusion of spring bulbs) to ornamental orchard (berries, fruit, hip, autumn colour) with follies, sculpture, stream and ponds. Conservation as important as horticulture (wild flowers). Intimate gardens round house. Craft artists and specialist nurseries attend.

GROUP OPENING

98 TEIGNMOUTH GARDENS
Cliff Road, Teignmouth TQ14 8TW. *1m from Teignmouth town centre. From Teignmouth take A379 towards Dawlish, at top of hill L into New Rd, take 3rd L into Ferndale Rd. Grosvenor Green Gdns and 16 Ferndale Rd at bottom of hill. For other gardens park in New Rd.* **Sat 25, Sun 26 June (1-5). Combined adm £5, chd free. Home-made teas at High Tor.**

BERRY COTTAGE
Maureen Fayle

NEW 16 FERNDALE ROAD
Sue and Patrick Fischer

NEW GROSVENOR GREEN GARDENS
Michelle & Neal Fairley
www.grosvenorgreengardens.co.uk

HIGH TOR
Gill Treweek

LITTLE CLANAGE
Gill and Paul Derbyshire

NEW 20 TRIUMPH PLACE
Stuart Barker

NEW 12 WOODLAND AVENUE
Liz Mogford

4 new gardens join Teignmouth gardens in 2016. At 16 Ferndale Rd hard landscaping creates an imaginative backdrop for the colourful flower beds and small pond. At Grosvenor Green the stunning ⅓ acre plantsman's garden has a cottage garden feel. Naturalistic pond, large greenhouse and vegetable beds. 20 Triumph Place is an inspiring example of how much can be achieved in a small garden in less than 2 yrs. Every inch of space is planted with flowering shrubs and climbers. 12 Woodland Ave is a beautifully planted secluded retreat with an abundance of flowers and vegetables, featuring some of the sculptor owners work (some for sale). At Berry Cottage the artist owner has developed a wildlife haven and will display some of her stunning artwork. Little Clannage has a huge variety of trees and shrubs with superb views of the sea. High Tor has cottage garden style pollinator friendly planting with a new productive greenhouse and amazing sea views. Featured on Radio Devon The Potting Shed and in Teignmouth Post. Mostly wheelchair access, limited at Berry Cottage, 16 Ferndale, and 12 Triumph Place.

GROUP OPENING

99 NEW TOPSHAM GARDENS
Victoria Road, Topsham, Exeter EX3 0EU. *Topsham is on E side of R Exe, between Exeter and Exmouth. Regular train service running to Topsham on Exeter to Exmouth line. A map will be issued with your ticket which can be purchased from any of the gardens. Victoria Rd is off the High St in centre of Topsham.* **Fri 15, Sun 17 July (11-5). Combined adm £5, chd free. Home-made teas. Teas at Wixels.**

NEW ANCHOR HOUSE D
Sandra and Nigel Atherton

NEW 19 VICTORIA ROAD
Mr Ken Barrett

NEW WIXELS
Mary and Chris Lambert

Take a leisurely stroll through Topsham visiting three unique and beautiful gardens on the way. 19 Victoria Road is a small tropical style walled garden with a wide variety of plants including bamboo, tree ferns, bananas, palms and yuccas, a small pond and a larger one. Also a large conservatory with exotic plants. Wixels riverside garden is a very personal artist's creation from the unusual paving schemes, sculptures, large greenhouse and semi-tropical plants to the long views up and down the River Exe. Anchor House is surrounded on 3 sides by the R Exe, the garden is very tranquil and has been designed and sympathetically planted to sit in its environment, with beautiful views down the estuary towards Exmouth. Limited wheelchair access at 19 Victoria Road and not suitable for wheelchairs at Wixels.

Take a leisurely stroll through Topsham visiting three unique and beautiful gardens on the way . . .

100 NEW TORVIEW
Highweek Village, Newton Abbot TQ12 1QQ. Ms Penny Hammond. *On N of Newton Abbot accessed via A38. From Plymouth: A38 to Goodstone, A383 past Hele Park, L onto Mile End Rd. From Exeter: A38 to Drumbridges then A382 past Forches X, L signed Highweek. L at top of hill.* **Sat 14, Sun 15 May (12-5). Adm £4, chd free. Cream teas. Light refreshments.**
Run by 2 semi-retired horticulturists: formal Mediterranean front garden, with wisteria-clad Georgian house, small alpine house. Rear courtyard with tree ferns, pots/troughs, lean-to 7m conservatory with tender plants and climbers. Steps to 30x20m walled garden - flowers, vegetables and trained fruit. Shade tunnel of woodlanders. Many rare/unusual plants. Rear garden up 7 steps, pebble areas in front garden.

GROUP OPENING

101 VENN CROSS RAILWAY GARDENS
Venn Cross, Waterrow, Taunton TA4 2BE, 01398 361392, venncross@btinternet.com. *Devon/Somerset border. 4m W of Wiveliscombe, 6m E of Bampton on B3227. Easy access. Ample tarmac parking.* **Sats, Suns 18, 19 June, 16, 17 July, 27, 28 Aug (2-5.30). Combined adm £4, chd free. Home-made teas. Selection of gluten-free cakes also available. Visits also by arrangement June to Aug.**

THE ENGINE HOUSE
Kevin & Samantha Anning
Visits also by arrangement June to Aug
venncross@btinternet.com
01398 361392

STATION HOUSE
Pat & Bill Wilson

Set in beautiful countryside straddling Devon/Somerset border between Bampton and Wiveliscombe. 2 large adjoining gardens covering site of former station and goods yard on GWR line between Taunton and Barnstaple. The Engine House: approx 4 acres with colour from trees, shrubs and bulbs in spring to the wildflower meadow, bog gardens and sweeping herbaceous borders as summer progresses. Streams, ponds (incl koi), vegetable plot, hornbeam walkway and woodland paths. Railway and sculptural features add interest throughout. Station House: 2-acre sheltered garden in deep cutting. Site of old station. Steep banks featuring hostas and other plants. Deep herbaceous beds packed with flowers. Vegetable beds. Tunnel (no entry permitted) at end forming part of dell garden. Access to top of tunnel with view of garden. Woodland walk. Historic railway interest (many photographs) and garden sculptures. Wheelchair access to main areas. Some gravel paths, gentle grass slopes.

WAVERLEY
See Somerset, Bristol & South Gloucestershire

102 WEST DOWN HOUSE
Bradworthy, Holsworthy EX22 7RZ.
Richard Brookes, 01409 241400,
mail@westdownhouse.co.uk,
www.westdownhouse.co.uk. *1m
outside Bradworthy. From
Bradworthy Square take Mill Rd
(signposted Bude) past school and
down hill. At bottom of hill take R fork
(to West Down) over bridge and
follow signs to West Down House on
R after 1m.* Sat 7, Sun 8 May (10-4).
Adm £4, chd free. **Visits also by
arrangement May & June.**
Five acres of mature, beautiful
gardens dating from Victorian times
with many interesting secluded
corners and a wonderful collection of
exhibited sculptures. The varied
grounds incl woodland, shrubbery,
naturalized spring bulbs, meadow,
ephemeral pond and more formally
planted areas. We look forward to
welcoming you. Sculpture exhibition,
beautiful mature rhododendrons,
azaleas, hydrangea bushes, bluebell
wood, huge cedars and ancient trees.
Whole garden is on level ground.
Gravel drive entrance with access
around gardens on grass lawn areas.

♿ ✾ ⊨

103 WHITSTONE BLUEBELLS
Bovey Tracey, Newton Abbot
TQ13 9NA, 01626 832258,
katie@whitstonefarm.co.uk.
*Whitstone Lane. From A382 turn
towards hospital (sign opp golf
range), after 1/3 m L at swinging sign
'Private road leading to Whitstone'.
Follow NGS signs.* Sun 1 May (2-5).
Combined adm £5, chd free.
Home-made teas at Whitstone
Farm. Tea/coffee/cakes incl
gluten free option.
Stunning spring gardens each with its
own character and far reaching views
over Dartmoor. Whitstone House has
clouds of bluebells throughout
woodland walk area and at Whitstone
Farm bluebells intermingle among
camellias, azaleas, rhododendrons
and magnolias. Display of
architectural metal sculptures and
ornaments.

✾ ⊨ ☕

104 WHITSTONE FARM
Whitstone Lane, Bovey Tracey
TQ13 9NA. Katie & Alan Bunn,
01626 832258,
katie@whitstonefarm.co.uk. *1/2 m N
of Bovey Tracey. From A382 turn
towards hospital (sign opp golf
range), after 1/3 m L at swinging sign
'Private road leading to Whitstone'.*

Follow NGS signs. Sun 7 Aug (2-5).
Adm £4.50, chd free. Home-made
teas. Home made cakes and
gluten free option. **Visits also by
arrangement Apr to Sept for
group and society tours.**
Nearly 4 acres of steep hillside
garden with stunning views of Haytor
and Dartmoor. Arboretum planted 40
yrs ago, over 200 trees from all over
the world incl magnolias, camellias,
acers, alders, betula, davidias and
sorbus. Major plantings of
rhododendron and cornus. Late
summer opening for flowering
eucryphias and hydrangeas. National
Collection of Eucryphias. Beautiful yr-
round garden.

✾ **NPC** ⊨ ☕

*They show what
can be achieved
in a limited space,
yet still meet the
family's needs. . .*

105 WICK FARM GARDENS
Cookbury, Holsworthy EX22 6NU.
Martin & Jenny Sexton, 01409
253760,
cookburywick@btinternet.com. *3m
E of Holsworthy. From Holsworthy
take Hatherleigh Rd for 2m, L at Anvil
Corner, 1/4 m then R to Cookbury,
garden 1 1/2 m on L.* Suns 8, 15, 22,
29, Mon 30 May (1.30-6). Adm £4,
chd free. Cream teas. **Visits also
by arrangement in May for groups
of 10+.**
8 acre pleasure garden around
Victorian farmhouse arranged in
rooms with many attractive features.
Fernery, ornamental pond, borders,
sculptures, oriental garden with stone
bell, lake with carp. Plants in long
border to attract butterflies and bees.
Crocosmia, croquet lawn, tropical
oasis, stone henge with sacrificial
stone, arboretum with over 300 trees,
flowering cherries, rhododendrons
and azaleas. Woodland bluebell walk
1m. Some gravel paths, motor
wheelchair friendly. Woodland not
suitable for wheelchairs.

♿ 🐾 ✾ 🚐 ☕

GROUP OPENING

**106 WILLAND OLD VILLAGE
GARDENS**
Willand Old Village, Cullompton
EX15 2RH. *From J27 or J28 of M5
follow signs B3181 to Willand. Turn at
PO sign, gardens approx 200 yds,
follow yellow signs. Parking in village.*
Sat 11, Sun 12 June (2-5.30).
Combined adm £4.50, chd free.
Home-made teas.

NEW 4 BUTTERCUP ROAD
John & Sally Holmes

NEW 8 BUTTERCUP ROAD
Julie De-Anth-Lancaster

CHURCH LEA
Mrs D Anderson

HARPITT BUNGALOW
Jane & Phil Hoare

THE NEW HOUSE
Celia & Bryan Holmes

OLD JAYCROFT FARM
D Keating & M Hollings

THE VILLAGE ALLOTMENTS
c/o Mrs S. Statham

The 6 gardens, 56 allotments and
award-winning composting scheme
which make up the group opening
offer a mix from small gardens in the
recently-built housing estate to the
larger ones of the individual houses,
the oldest of which is a Grade II listed
300 year old farmhouse. They show
what can be achieved in a limited
space, while providing yr round
interest and colour. Each garden is
very different reflecting the owner's
interests and tastes. The allotment
plots demonstrate a wide range of
skills and production methods.
Gardens, village and church (open)
have good accessibility for wheelchair
users with modest slopes and few
changes of level. Allotments have
partial access. We can promise
visitors a full, interesting and varied
afternoon. Gardens, village and
church have good accessibility for
wheelchair users with modest slopes
and few changes of level. Allotments
have partial access.

♿ ✾ ☕

**107 ◆ WINSFORD WALLED
GARDEN**
Halwill Junction EX21 5XT. Dugald
and Adel Stark, 01409 221477,
dugald@dugaldstark.co.uk,

www.winsfordwalledgarden.org.uk.
*10m NW of Okehampton. On A3079
follow brown tourism signs from
centre of Halwill Junction (1m).
Straight on through Anglers Paradise.*
**For NGS: Sat 4, Sun 5 June, Sat 6,
Sun 7 Aug (10-5). Adm £5, chd
free. Tea. For other opening times
please see below.**
Historic walled gardens, redesigned
and brimming with colourful, tall and
lush planting. Large restored Victorian
glasshouses and romantic ruins.
Extensive mature bamboo grove.
Giant pergola, fruit, vegetable and
herb areas. Home of the painter,
Dugald Stark. Studio open. Garden
open May - Sept, Wed - Sun (10-5).
Owner is wheelchair bound so
access is good.

108 WOOD BARTON
Kentisbeare EX15 2AT. Mrs
Rosemary Horton, 01884 266285.
*8m SE of Tiverton, 3m E of
Cullompton. 3m from M5 J28. A373
Cullompton to Honiton. 2m L to
Bradfield/Willand, Horn Rd. After 1m
at Xrds turn R. Farm drive ¹/₂ m on L.
Bull on sign.* **Sun 27 Mar, Sun 1
May (2.30-5.30). Adm £4, chd free.
Home-made teas. Visits also by
arrangement Mar to Oct,
refreshments only by
arrangement, small coach can be
accommodated.**
Established 2-acre arboretum with
species trees on S-facing slope.
Magnolias, 2 davidia, azaleas,
camellias, rhododendrons, acers;
several ponds and water feature.
Autumn colour. New planting of
woodland trees and bluebells opp

house (this part not suitable for
wheelchairs but dogs are welcome
here). Sculptures and profiles in
bronze resin.

GROUP OPENING

109 WOODBURY GARDENS
Greenway, Woodbury, Exeter
EX5 1LW. *E of Exeter on B3179 Clyst
St George to Budleigh Salterton Rd.*
**Sat 18, Sun 19 June (1-5).
Combined adm £3.50, chd free.
Cream teas at Greenside,
between other 2 gardens, opp
village green.**

> **NEW GREENSIDE**
> Mrs Chris Lear
>
> **HAYDONS, BONFIRE LANE**
> Mr & Mrs M Jeans
>
> **TIM ANDREWS GALLERY
> AND GARDEN**
> Mr Tim Andrews

3 pretty gardens in centre of attractive
East Devon village. Tim Andrews
Gallery & Garden: compact, well
stocked garden with emphasis on
foliage planting, punctuated by
sculptures from leading Artists.
Pond/water feature and
vegetable/fruit garden. Attached
gallery with current international
exhibition will also be open. Haydons:
cottage style corner garden
landscaped into 3 different areas. S-
facing front garden with greenhouse
leading to lawned area with raised
fishpond, then shallow steps under
pergola to third enclosed garden.

Mixed planting of trees, shrubs and
herbaceous borders throughout.
Greenside: semi-walled garden,
lawns, borders of shrubs and flowers.
An ideal place for cream teas.

110 YONDER HILL
Shepherds Lane, Colaton Raleigh,
Sidmouth EX10 0LP. Judy McKay,
Eddie Stevenson, Sharon Attrell,
Bob Chambers, 07864 055532,
judy@yonderhill.me.uk,
www.yonderhill.org.uk. *4m N of
Budleigh Salterton B3178 between
Newton Poppleford and Colaton
Raleigh. Take turning signed to
Dotton and immed R into Shepherds
lane, ¹/₄ m 1st R at top of hill opp
public footpath.* **Every Sun 3 Apr to
25 Sept (1.30-4.30). Mons 2, 30
May, 29 Aug (1.30-4.30). Adm £3,
chd £1. Large choice of self-
service teas. Visits also by
arrangement Apr to Sept, picnics
welcome.**
Enjoy a warm welcome to 3¹/₂ acres
planted with love. Blazing herbaceous
borders buzzing with insects, cool
woods alive with birdsong, rustling
bamboos, delicious scents.
Eucalyptus, grasses, conifer and fern
collections. Rare plants, unusual
planting, wildlife pond, wild flower
meadow, woodland tunnels, lots of
benches. This garden will awaken
your senses and soothe your soul.
Garden attracts great variety of birds,
insects and other wildlife. Limited
wheelchair access, some slopes.
Wheelchair available, phone to book.

Sidbury Manor

DORSET

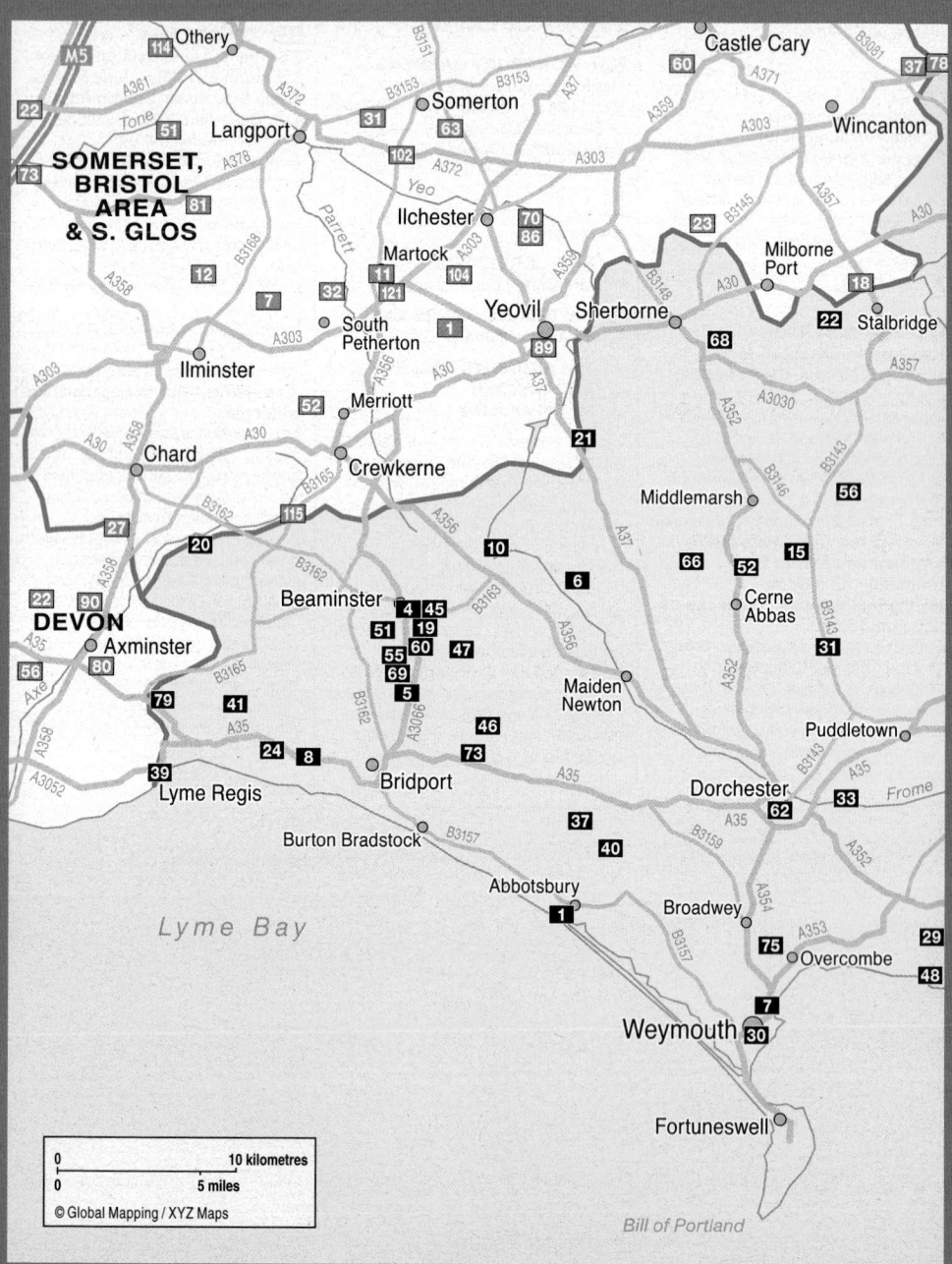

Investec Wealth & Investment supports the NGS

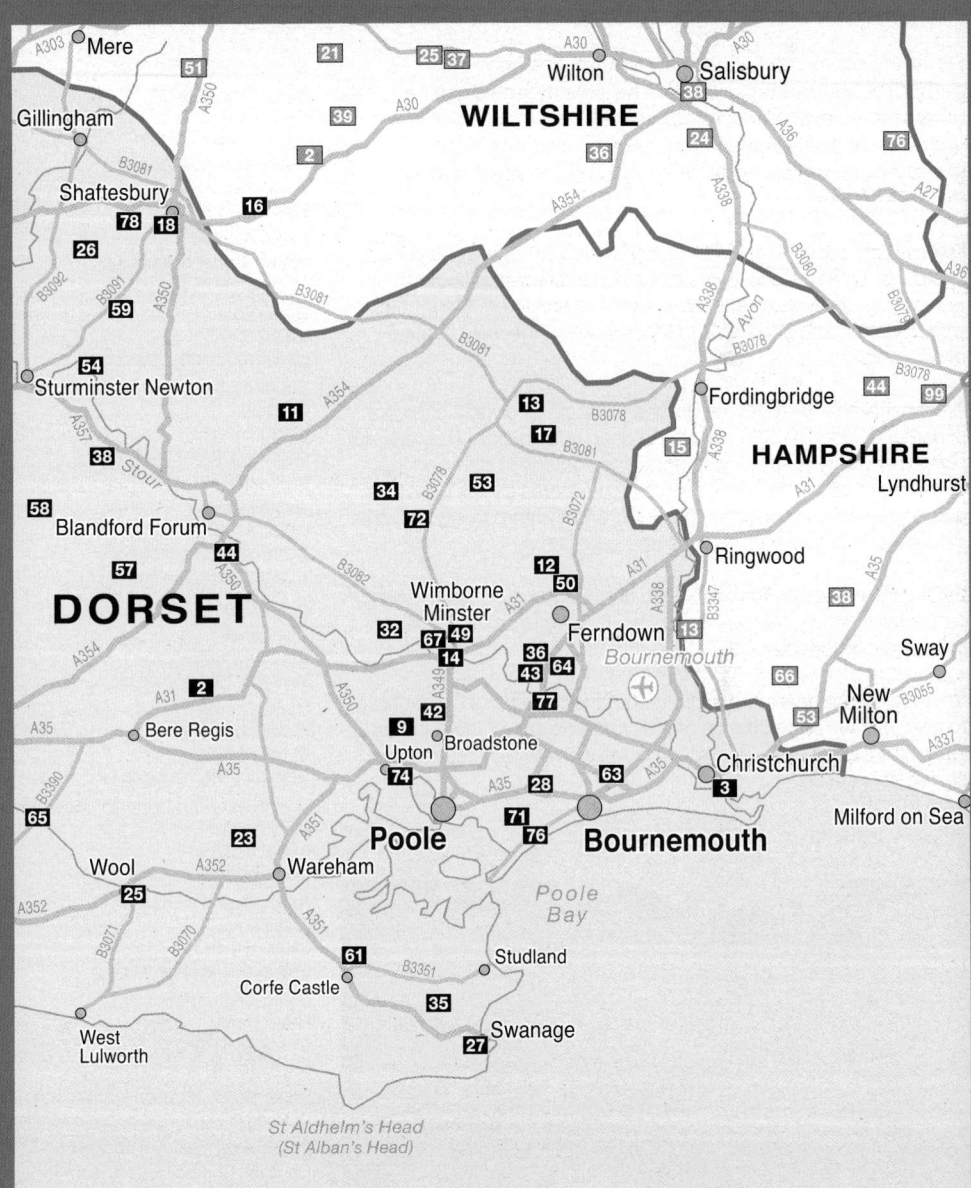

Dorset

Dorset is not on the way to anywhere. We have no cathedral and no motorways. The county has been inhabited forever and the constantly varying landscape is dotted with prehistoric earthworks and ancient monuments, bordered to the south by the magnificent Jurassic Coast.

Discover our cosy villages with their thatched cottages, churches and pubs. Small historic towns including Dorchester, Blandford, Sherborne, Shaftesbury and Weymouth are scattered throughout, with Bournemouth and Poole to the east being the main centres of population.

Amongst all this, we offer the visitor a wonderfully diverse collection of gardens, found in both towns and deep countryside. They are well planted and vary in size, topography and content. In between the larger ones are the tiniest, all beautifully presented by the generous garden owners who open for the NGS. Most of the county's loveliest gardens in their romantic settings also support us.

Each garden rewards the visitor with originality and brings joy, even on the rainiest day! They are never very far away from an excellent meal and comfortable bed.

So do come, discover and explore what the gardens of Dorset have to offer with the added bonus of that welcome cup of tea and that irresistible slice of cake, or a scone laden with clotted cream and strawberry jam!

Below: The Old Rectory, Pulham

Dorset Volunteers

County Organiser
Alison Wright
01935 83652
wright.alison68@yahoo.com

County Treasurer
Richard Smedley
01202 528286
richard@carter-coley.co.uk

Publicity
Gillian Ford
01935 83645
gillianford33@btinternet.com

Social Media
Di Reeds
07973 241028
digardengate@hotmail.co.uk

Booklet Editor
Judith Hussey
01258 474673
judithhussey@hotmail.com

Assistant County Organisers

Central East/Bournemouth
Trish Neale
01425 403565
trishneale1@yahoo.co.uk

North Central
Alexandra Davies
01747 860351
alex@theparishhouse.co.uk

North East/Ferndown/Christchurch
Mary Angus
01202 872789
mary@gladestock.co.uk

North West & Central
Annie Dove
01300 345450
anniedove1@btinternet.com

South Central/East
Helen Hardy
01929 471379
helliehardy@hotmail.co.uk

South Central/West
Di Reeds (as above)

South West
Christine Corson
01308 868203
christinekcorson@gmail.com

West Central
Alison Wright (as above)

Opening Dates

All entries subject to change.
For latest information check www.ngs.org.uk

Extended openings are shown at the begining of the month

February

Snowdrop Festival

Saturday 27
43 Manor Farm, Hampreston

Sunday 28
18 Edwardstowe
43 Manor Farm, Hampreston

March

Saturday 5
34 Kitemoor Cottage

Sunday 6
34 Kitemoor Cottage
37 Langebride House

Sunday 13
21 Frankham Farm
59 The Old Vicarage
62 Q

Sunday 20
28 22 Holt Road

Saturday 26
58 Old Smithy

Sunday 27
8 Chideock Manor
25 Herons Mead
62 Q

Monday 28
8 Chideock Manor
17 Edmondsham House
31 Ivy House Garden

April

Wednesday 6
17 Edmondsham House

Saturday 9
7 24 Carlton Road North

Sunday 10
7 24 Carlton Road North
15 Domineys Yard
25 Herons Mead
62 Q

Monday 11
7 24 Carlton Road North

Wednesday 13
17 Edmondsham House

Saturday 16
48 Marren
71 NEW 2 Spur Gate

Sunday 17
6 Broomhill
28 22 Holt Road
31 Ivy House Garden
34 Kitemoor Cottage
48 Marren
59 The Old Vicarage
71 NEW 2 Spur Gate

Wednesday 20
13 Cranborne Manor Garden
17 Edmondsham House
31 Ivy House Garden

Thursday 21
39 Little Cliff
42 17 Lower Golf Links Road

Saturday 23
39 Little Cliff
73 Uploders Place

Sunday 24
9 Corfe Barn
21 Frankham Farm
32 Kingston Lacy
42 17 Lower Golf Links Road
55 The Old Rectory, Netherbury
62 Q
73 Uploders Place

Tuesday 26
55 The Old Rectory, Netherbury

Wednesday 27
17 Edmondsham House

May

Sunday 1
25 Herons Mead
29 Holworth Farmhouse
31 Ivy House Garden
45 The Manor House, Beaminster
77 1692 Wimborne Road

Monday 2
29 Holworth Farmhouse
31 Ivy House Garden
45 The Manor House, Beaminster
56 The Old Rectory, Pulham

Sunday 8
49 Mayfield
58 Old Smithy
62 Q

Tuesday 10
5 Braddocks

Saturday 14
24 Harcombe House
66 The Secret Garden

Sunday 15
24 Harcombe House
28 22 Holt Road
66 The Secret Garden
77 1692 Wimborne Road
78 Wincombe Park
79 Wolverhollow

Monday 16
79 Wolverhollow

Tuesday 17
24 Harcombe House

Wednesday 18
49 Mayfield
78 Wincombe Park

Saturday 21
48 Marren

Sunday 22
15 Domineys Yard
44 The Manor House
48 Marren
55 The Old Rectory, Netherbury
59 The Old Vicarage
61 Puddledock Cottage
62 Q

Tuesday 24
55 The Old Rectory, Netherbury

Garden offers something for every season . . .

Wednesday 25
14 Deans Court
43 Manor Farm, Hampreston
44 The Manor House

Thursday 26
2 Anderson Manor
46 NEW Mappercombe Manor

Friday 27
35 Knitson Old Farmhouse

Saturday 28
35 Knitson Old Farmhouse

Sunday 29
29 Holworth Farmhouse
35 Knitson Old Farmhouse

Sunday 15
45 The Manor House, Beaminster
46 NEW Mappercombe Manor
49 Mayfield
69 Slape Manor

Monday 30
29 Holworth Farmhouse
35 Knitson Old Farmhouse
45 The Manor House, Beaminster

June

Wednesday 1
53 Old Down House

Festival Weekend

Saturday 4
11 Cottage Row (Evening)

Sunday 5
3 Annalal's Gallery
11 Cottage Row
21 Frankham Farm
42 17 Lower Golf Links Road
49 Mayfield
53 Old Down House
57 NEW The Old Rectory, Winterborne Stickland
77 1692 Wimborne Road

Monday 6
57 NEW The Old Rectory, Winterborne Stickland

Wednesday 8
16 NEW Donhead Hall (Evening)
53 Old Down House

Thursday 9
2 Anderson Manor
39 Little Cliff

Saturday 11
7 24 Carlton Road North
39 Little Cliff

Sunday 12
7 24 Carlton Road North
16 NEW Donhead Hall
22 Frith House
46 NEW Mappercombe Manor

Tuesday 14
5 Braddocks

Wednesday 15
4 Beaminster Gardens
49 Mayfield
65 Sculpture by the Lakes

Share your day out on 🅵 and 🅴

Saturday 18
- **8** Chideock Manor
- **18** Edwardstowe

Sunday 19
- **4** Beaminster Gardens
- **8** Chideock Manor
- **18** Edwardstowe
- **19** Farrs
- **23** Greenacres
- **28** 22 Holt Road
- **42** 17 Lower Golf Links Road
- **63** 25 Richmond Park Avenue

Tuesday 21
- **40** Littlebredy Walled Gardens

Wednesday 22
- **6** Broomhill
- **14** Deans Court

Thursday 23
- **72** Staddlestones

Saturday 25
- **45** The Manor House, Beaminster

Sunday 26
- **3** Annalal's Gallery
- **9** Corfe Barn
- **45** The Manor House, Beaminster

Tuesday 28
- **40** Littlebredy Walled Gardens
- **60** Parnham House

Thursday 30
- **60** Parnham House

July

- **27** **The Hollow (every Wednesday)**

Saturday 2
- **41** NEW Lower Abbotts Wootton Farm

Sunday 3
- **10** Corscombe House
- **29** Holworth Farmhouse
- **41** NEW Lower Abbotts Wootton Farm
- **63** 25 Richmond Park Avenue
- **64** 357 Ringwood Road

Wednesday 6
- **65** Sculpture by the Lakes

Thursday 7
- **39** Little Cliff

Saturday 9
- **13** Cranborne Manor Garden
- **39** Little Cliff

Sunday 10
- **6** Broomhill

Tuesday 12
- **5** Braddocks

Saturday 16
- **30** Holy Trinity Primary School Garden

Sunday 17
- **19** Farrs
- **26** Hilltop
- **28** 22 Holt Road
- **30** Holy Trinity Primary School Garden

- **50** Meadow Views
- **63** 25 Richmond Park Avenue

Wednesday 20
- **64** 357 Ringwood Road

Thursday 21
- **67** The Secret Garden and Serles House

Saturday 23
- **71** NEW 2 Spur Gate

Sunday 24
- **26** Hilltop
- **61** Puddledock Cottage
- **67** The Secret Garden and Serles House
- **71** NEW 2 Spur Gate

Thursday 28
- **72** Staddlestones

Sunday 31
- **3** Annalal's Gallery
- **15** Domineys Yard
- **26** Hilltop
- **43** Manor Farm, Hampreston
- **63** 25 Richmond Park Avenue
- **67** The Secret Garden and Serles House
- **76** Western Gardens

August

- **27** **The Hollow (every Wednesday)**

Wednesday 3
- **43** Manor Farm, Hampreston

Thursday 4
- **67** The Secret Garden and Serles House

Sunday 7
- **12** Cottesmore Farm
- **26** Hilltop
- **29** Holworth Farmhouse
- **50** Meadow Views
- **56** The Old Rectory, Pulham
- **67** The Secret Garden and Serles House

Saturday 13
- **24** Harcombe House
- **67** The Secret Garden and Serles House (Evening)

Sunday 14
- **12** Cottesmore Farm
- **19** Farrs
- **23** Greenacres
- **24** Harcombe House
- **26** Hilltop
- **43** Manor Farm, Hampreston
- **64** 357 Ringwood Road
- **79** Wolverhollow

Monday 15
- **79** Wolverhollow

Tuesday 16
- **24** Harcombe House

Saturday 20
- **18** Edwardstowe

Sunday 21
- **6** Broomhill
- **18** Edwardstowe
- **26** Hilltop

1692 Wimborne Road

28 22 Holt Road
67 The Secret Garden and Serles House

Thursday 25
72 Staddlestones

Sunday 28
67 The Secret Garden and Serles House
76 Western Gardens

Monday 29
67 The Secret Garden and Serles House

September

Thursday 1
67 The Secret Garden and Serles House

Saturday 3
67 The Secret Garden and Serles House

Sunday 4
67 The Secret Garden and Serles House

Friday 9
35 Knitson Old Farmhouse

Saturday 10
35 Knitson Old Farmhouse

Sunday 11
35 Knitson Old Farmhouse
67 The Secret Garden and Serles House

Sunday 18
19 Farrs
25 Herons Mead

October

Wednesday 5
17 Edmondsham House

Wednesday 12
17 Edmondsham House

Sunday 16
21 Frankham Farm

Wednesday 19
17 Edmondsham House

Gardens open to the public

1 Abbotsbury Gardens
13 Cranborne Manor Garden
17 Edmondsham House
20 Forde Abbey Gardens
26 Hilltop
32 Kingston Lacy

33 Kingston Maurward Gardens and Animal Park
36 Knoll Gardens
40 Littlebredy Walled Gardens
47 Mapperton Gardens
52 Minterne House
65 Sculpture by the Lakes
68 Sherborne Castle
74 Upton Country Park
75 NEW Upwey Wishing Well

By arrangement only

38 Lawsbrook
51 The Mill House
54 The Old Rectory, Manston

Also open by arrangement

2 Anderson Manor
3 Annalal's Gallery
5 Braddocks
6 Broomhill
8 Chideock Manor
9 Corfe Barn
11 Cottage Row

15 Domineys Yard
22 Frith House
23 Greenacres
24 Harcombe House
25 Herons Mead
27 The Hollow (formerly known as Stone Rise)
28 22 Holt Road
29 Holworth Farmhouse
31 Ivy House Garden
34 Kitemoor Cottage
35 Knitson Old Farmhouse
37 Langebride House
39 Little Cliff
44 The Manor House
48 Marren
49 Mayfield
56 The Old Rectory, Pulham
58 Old Smithy
59 The Old Vicarage
61 Puddledock Cottage
62 Q
63 25 Richmond Park Avenue
64 357 Ringwood Road
66 The Secret Garden
69 Slape Manor
71 NEW 2 Spur Gate
77 1692 Wimborne Road
79 Wolverhollow

The Gardens

1 ◆ **ABBOTSBURY GARDENS**
Abbotsbury, Weymouth DT3 4LA. Ilchester Estates, 01305 871387, www.abbotsburygardens.co.uk. *8m W of Weymouth. From B3157 Weymouth-Bridport, 200yds W of Abbotsbury village.* **For opening times and information, please phone or visit garden website.**
30 acres, started in 1760 and considerably extended in C19. Much recent replanting. The maritime micro-climate enables Mediterranean and southern hemisphere garden to grow rare and tender plants. National collection of Hoherias (flowering Aug in NZ garden). Woodland valley with ponds, stream and hillside walk to view the Jurassic Coast. Open all yr except Christmas week. Featured on Countrywise and Gardeners' World. Limited wheelchair access, some very steep paths and rolled gravel.
♿ 🐕 ⊛ 🚐 **NPC** ☕

2 **ANDERSON MANOR**
Anderson, Blandford Forum DT11 9HD. Jeremy & Rosemary Isaac, 01929 471320,

www.andersonmanor.co.uk. *3m E Bere Regis, 12m W Wimborne, 8m SW Blandford. Turn off A31 at Red Post Xrds to Anderson, follow rd around corner, entrance on R.*
Thur 26 May, Thur 9 June (2-4.30). Adm £4.50, chd free. Cream teas. Visits also by arrangement Jan to Oct, min 10.
Approx 3 acres of mature topiary, old roses and herbaceous borders surrounding Elizabethan/Jacobean manor house (Grade 1 listed, not open). Formal garden, gazebos, bowling green, walled garden, parterre and orchard. Yew and box hedges, pleached lime walk, old rose walk by R Winterborne and avenue of walnut trees. C12 church open next to house. Separate car parking via Church Lane. All gardens accessible. some gravel, mainly grass.
♿ ⊛ ☕

3 **ANNALAL'S GALLERY**
25 Millhams Street, Christchurch BH23 1DN. Anna & Lal Sims, 01202 567585, anna.sims@ntlworld.com, www.annasims.co.uk. *Town centre. Park in Saxon Square PCP - exit to Millham St via alley at side of church.*

Sun 5, Sun 26 June, Sun 31 July (2-4). Adm £3, chd free. **Visits also by arrangement May to Dec.**
Enchanting 140 yr-old cottage, home of two Royal Academy artists. 32ft x 12½ ft garden on 3 patio levels. Pencil gate leads to colourful scented Victorian walled garden. Sculptures and paintings hide among the flowers and shrubs. Not suitable for wheelchairs.

3 acres of plant-packed sloping gardens . . .

GROUP OPENING

4 ▶ BEAMINSTER GARDENS
Shadrack Street, Beaminster DT8 3BE. *6m N of Bridport, 6m S of Crewkerne on B3162. All gardens within short walk of town square or main car park (nearer parking only for disabled). In pairs, all well signed from town square. Lots of yellow arrows/balloons. Map issued with tickets.* **Wed 15 June (2-5). Sun 19 June (2-5). Combined adm £5, chd free. Also open 19 June Farrs, separate admission (£5, chd free). Home-made teas in Beaminster Church from 3pm, long gradual stairway to main Church Door and Lift for wheelchairs etc. West door open for wheelchair access.**

BARTON END
Mr & Mrs Philip Crawford

HURFORD HOUSE
Mr & Mrs Arnold Shipp

SHADRACK HOUSE
Mr & Mrs Hugh Lindsay

SHORTS ORCHARD
Mrs Sally Mallinson

4 charming town gardens, two by the river, and one a much larger town garden. All a total delight, masses of roses, unusual climbers, shrubs and swathes of perennials. Beaminster festival opens the following week June 26th. Barton End and Shorts Orchard are wheelchair friendly, Hurford House and Shadrack House have minimal wheelchair access.

& ♞ ✿ ☕

5 ▶ BRADDOCKS
Oxbridge, Bridport DT6 3TZ. Dr & Mrs Roger Newton, 01308 488441, rogernewton329@btinternet.com, www.braddocksgarden.co.uk. *3m N of Bridport. From Bridport, A3066 to Beaminster 3m, just before Melplash, L into Camesworth Lane signed Oxbridge. Single track rd, down steep hill. Garden signed.* **Tue 10 May, Tue 14 June, Tue 12 July (2-5). Adm £4.50, chd free. Home-made teas. Visits also by arrangement Apr to Oct, groups of 10+ will be offered refreshments by arrangement.**
3 acres of plant-packed sloping gardens, conceived, planted and looked after by owner. 'A feast of a garden at all times of the year'. Wild flower meadows and water. Herbaceous, underplanted shrubs and roses of all types and hues. Shady woodland garden and fine mature specimen trees. Featured in Dorset Life and Home and Garden. Steep slopes and gravel paths make the garden unsuitable for wheelchairs.
✿ ☕

Marie Curie

The NGS is Marie Curie's largest single donor

6 ▶ BROOMHILL
Rampisham DT2 0PU. Mr & Mrs D Parry, 01935 83266, carol.parry2@btopenworld.com. *11m NW of Dorchester. From Dorchester A37 Yeovil, 4m L A356 to Crewkerne, 6m R to Rampisham. From Yeovil A37 Dorchester, 7m R Evershot. From Crewkerne A356, 1½ m after Rampisham Garage L Rampisham. Follow Signs.* **Sun 17 Apr, Wed 22 June, Sun 10 July, Sun 21 Aug (2-5). Adm £4, chd free. Home-made teas. Visits also by arrangement May to Aug for groups of 8+.**
Once a farmyard now a delightful, tranquil garden set in 1½ acres. Island beds and borders are planted with shrubs, roses, masses of unusual perennials and choice annuals to give vibrancy and colour from spring to autumn. Lawns and paths lead to a less formal area with a large wildlife pond, meadow, shaded areas, bog garden and late summer border. Featured in Roger Lane's Gardens of Dorset. Gravel entrance, the rest is grass, some gentle slopes.
& ✿ ⛺ ☕

7 ▶ 24 CARLTON ROAD NORTH
Weymouth DT4 7PY. Anne Mellars and Rob Tracey. *8m S of Dorchester. A354 from Dorchester, R into Carlton Rd North. From Town Centre follow esplanade towards A354 Dorchester and L into C Rd N.* **Sat 9, Sun 10, Mon 11 Apr, Sat 11, Sun 12 June (2-5). Adm £3, chd free. Home-made teas.**
Long garden on several levels. Steps and narrow sloping paths lead to beds and borders overflowing with trees, shrubs and herbaceous plants. Unusual plants incl exotics in interesting combinations merit a second look. A garden which continues to evolve each year reflecting an interest in texture, shape, colour, wildlife and above all plants.
☕

8 ▶ CHIDEOCK MANOR
Chideock, Bridport DT6 6LF. Mr & Mrs Howard Coates, 0788 555 1795, deirdrecoates9@gmail.com. *2m W of Bridport on A35. In centre of village turn N at church. The Manor is ¼ m along this rd on R.* **Sun 27, Mon 28 Mar, Sat 18 June (2-6). Sun 19 June (2-6), also open Beaminster Gardens. Adm £5, chd free. Home-made teas. Visits also by arrangement Apr to Oct.**
6/7 acres of formal and informal gardens. Bog garden beside stream and series of ponds. Yew hedges and mature trees. Lime and crab apple walks, herbaceous borders, colourful rose and clematis arches, fernery and nuttery. Walled vegetable garden and orchard. Woodland and lakeside walks. Fine views. Separate adm amount on 19 June for Beaminster Gardens. Partial wheelchair access.
& ♞ ⛺ ☕

9 ▶ CORFE BARN
Corfe Lodge Road, Broadstone BH18 9NQ. Mr & Mrs John McDavid, 01202 694179. *1m W of Broadstone centre. From main r'about in Broadstone, W along Clarendon Rd ¾ m, N into Roman Rd, after 50yds W into Corfe Lodge Rd.* **Sun 24 Apr, Sun 26 June (2-5). Adm £2.50, chd free. Home-made teas. Visits also by arrangement Apr to July.**
Last year of opening after 26 years! Very varied garden in pleasant semi-rural environment extending to about ⅔ acre. Mixture of usual and unusual trees, shrubs and flowers on three levels in and out of the barnyard. Wildlife friendly garden (so say Dorset Wildlife Trust).
♞ ✿ ⛺ ☕

10 ▶ CORSCOMBE HOUSE
Corscombe DT2 0NU. Jim Bartos. *3½ m N of Beaminster. On A356 take southern of two signed turnings E to Corscombe, then R signed to the Church; or on A37 turn W signed to Corscombe, then L signed to the Church.* **Sun 3 July (2-5).**

Adm £4.50, chd free. Cream teas in village hall.
Strong architectural hedges define multiple rooms on different levels with yew columns, parterre and cool beds in the lower garden. Reflecting pool and hot beds in the upper garden. Wildflower meadow and orchard. Part walled vegetable garden and secret garden with Mediterranean planting and lemons in pots.

11 ♦ COTTAGE ROW

School Lane, Tarrant Gunville, nr Blandford Forum DT11 8JJ. Carolyn & Michael Pawson, 01258 830212, michaelpawson637@btinternet.com. *6m NE of Blandford Forum. From Blandford take A354 towards Salisbury, L at Tarrant Hinton. After 1½ m R in Tarrant Gunville into School Lane.* **Evening opening Sat 4 June (5-8). Wine. Sun 5 June (2-6). Cream teas. Adm £4, chd free.**
Visits also by arrangement May to Sept for groups of 6+.
Roses/clematis at best June/July, cyclamen Sept.
Maturing ½ acre partly walled garden. Formal and informal areas separated by yew hedges. Pergola, arbours, brick paths, tree house, kitchen garden and the sound of water; bees and butterflies abound in this tranquil spot. This sophisticated cottage garden reflects the owners' love of unusual plants, structure and an artist's eye for sympathetic colour also evident in new box plantings. Featured in Dorset Life.

12 ♦ COTTESMORE FARM

Newmans Lane, West Moors, Ferndown BH22 0LW. Paul & Valerie Guppy, 01202 871939. *Newmans Lane, 1m N of West Moors. Off B3072 Bournemouth to Verwood rd. Car parking in owner's field.* **Sun 7, Sun 14 Aug (2-5). Adm £4, chd free. Home-made teas.**
Gardens of over an acre, created from scratch over 17yrs. Wander through a plantsman's tropical paradise of giant gunneras, bananas, towering bamboos and over 100 palm trees, into a floral extravaganza. Large borders and sweeping island beds overflowing with phlox, heliopsis, helenium and much more combine to drown you in scent and colour.

13 ♦ CRANBORNE MANOR GARDEN

Cranborne BH21 5PP. Viscount Cranborne, 01725 517289, info@cranborne.co.uk, www.cranborne.co.uk. *10m N of Wimborne on B3078. Enter garden via Cranborne Garden Centre, on L as you enter top of village of Cranborne.* **For NGS: Wed 20 Apr, Sat 9 July (9-4). Adm £6, chd £1. Light refreshments in The Café, Cranborne Garden Centre. For other opening times and information, please phone, email or visit garden website.**
Beautiful and historic garden laid out in C17 by John Tradescant and enlarged in C20, featuring several gardens surrounded by walls and yew hedges: blue and white garden, cottage style and mount gardens, water and wild garden. Many interesting plants, with fine trees and avenues. Mostly wheelchair access.

Wander through a plantsman's tropical paradise . . .

14 ♦ DEANS COURT

Deans Court Lane, Wimborne Minster BH21 1EE. Sir William Hanham, www.deanscourt.org. *¼ m SE of Minster. Pedestrians: From Deans Court Lane, continuation of High St, over Xrds at Holmans shop (BH21 1EE). Cars: Entrance on Poole Rd, Wimborne (A349); heading S, 300m on R after Rodways r'about (BH21 1QF).* **Wed 25 May, Wed 22 June (11-5). Adm £4, chd free. Cream teas. Our Shop & Café is also open.** *Donation to Friends of Victoria Hospital.*
13 acres of peaceful, partly wild gardens in ancient setting with mature specimen trees, Saxon fish pond, herb garden and apiary beside R Allen close to town centre. Apple orchard with wild flowers. 1st Soil Association accredited kitchen garden within C18 serpentine walls.

Lunches and teas served in garden and tearoom, using estate produce (also for sale). Tours of house by owner, book upon arrival. Follow signs for parking closer to the gardens. Some paths have deeper gravel.

15 ♦ DOMINEYS YARD

Buckland Newton, Dorchester DT2 7BS. Mr & Mrs W Gueterbock, 01300 345295, cottages@domineys.com, www.domineys.com. *11m N of Dorchester, 11m S of Sherborne. 2m E A352 or take B3143. No thro' road between church & Gaggle of Geese. Enter 100yds on L.* **Sun 10 Apr, Sun 22 May, Sun 31 July (2-5.30). Adm £4.50, chd free. Home-made teas.**
Visits also by arrangement, refreshments by request.
Welcome to our 30th year of opening for the NGS and 55th year here. A varied layout, which continues to change, in attractive setting around our thatched house and other cottages. Separate naturalised arboretum. Superb soil, good micro climate. Plant diversity to enjoy throughout the year. Rare and well known trees, shrubs, herbaceous, bulbs, annuals and pots, fruit and vegetables. A place to revisit. Featured on Radio Solent and in the Blackmore Vale Magazine/associated County publications. Wheelchair access excludes arboretum.

16 NEW ♦ DONHEAD HALL

Donhead St. Mary, Shaftesbury SP7 9DS. Paul & Penny Brewer. *From A30 take turning opp sign to Tollard Royal. Follow rd for ¾ m and bear R at T-junction. Donhead Hall 50 yds on L on corner of Watery Lane, cream gates.* **Evening opening Wed 8 June (5.30-8). Wine. Sun 12 June (2-5). Home-made teas. Adm £5, chd free.**
Walled garden overlooking deer park. The house and garden are built into the side of a hill with uninterrupted views to Cranborne Chase. Martin Lane Fox designed the terracing and advised on the landscaping of the gardens which are on 4 different levels. Large mixed borders and specimen trees, kitchen garden with glasshouses. Difficult access for wheelchairs, awkward slopes and gravel paths.

17 ◆ EDMONDSHAM HOUSE

Edmondsham, Wimborne
BH21 5RE. Mrs Julia Smith, 01725
517207,
Julia.edmondsham@yahoo.co.uk.
*9m NE of Wimborne. 9m W of
Ringwood. Between Cranborne &
Verwood. Edmondsham off B3081.
Wheelchair access West front.* **For
NGS: Mon 28 Mar, Wed 6, Wed 13,
Wed 20, Wed 27 Apr, Wed 5, Wed
12, Wed 19 Oct (2-5). Adm £2.50,
chd 50p. Tea, coffee & cake 3.30-
4pm in Edmondsham House. For
other opening times and
information, please phone or email.**
6 acres of mature gardens, grounds,
views, trees and shaped hedges
surrounding C16/C18 house, giving
much to explore incl C12 church
adjacent to garden. Large Victorian
walled garden is productive and
managed organically (since 1984)
using 'no dig' vegetable beds. Wide
herbaceous borders planted for
seasonal colour. Traditional potting
shed and working areas. House also
open on NGS days.

 ♿ ❀ ☕

18 EDWARDSTOWE

50-52 Bimport, Shaftesbury
SP7 8BA. Mike & Louise
Madgwick. *Park in town's main car
park. Walk along Bimport (B3091)
500mts, Edwardstowe last house on
L.* **Sun 28 Feb (11.30-3); Sat 18,
Sun 19 June, Sat 20, Sun 21 Aug
(11-5). Adm £3.50, chd free.**
Evolving cottage garden with yr-round
interest, set behind oldest house in
Shaftesbury. Enormous magnolia tree
greets visitors, courtyard opening to
long lawns, divided by 2 colourful
borders and self-sufficient vegetable
garden. Chickens and bees complete
the scene. Seasonal plant and
produce sales. Snowdrop display 28
Feb.

 ❀

19 FARRS

Whitcombe Rd, Beaminster
DT8 3NB. Mr & Mrs John
Makepeace, 01308 862204,
info@johnmakepeacefurniture.com,
www.johnmakepeacefurniture.com.
*Southern edge of Beaminster. On
B3163. Car parking on site only for
disabled. Enter through garden door
in wall adj to Museum. Park in Square
or side streets.* **Sun 19 June (2-5),
also open Beaminster Gardens.
Sun 17 July, Sun 14 Aug, Sun 18
Sept (2-5). Adm £5, chd free. Light
refreshments.**
Enjoy several distinctive walled
gardens, rolling lawns, sculpture and
giant topiary around the house.
John's inspirational grasses garden,
Jennie's riotous potager with cleft oak
fruit cage. Glasshouse, straw bale
studio, geese in orchard. Remarkable
trees, planked and seasoning in open
sided barn. Group visits by
appointment only. On 19 June entry
ticket to Farrs does not include
Beaminster Gardens. House also
open on NGS days with selection of
furniture by John Makepeace, and
paintings, sculpture and applied arts
by living artists. Talk on design at
2.30pm each opening. Jennie
Makepeace and Neil Lucas will give
plant talks at 3.30pm (Neil on 17 July
& 18 Sept only). Some gravel paths,
alternative wheelchair route through
orchard.

 ♿ ❀ 🚐 🛏 ☕

*Spring bulbs
through to
autumn
colour . . .*

20 ◆ FORDE ABBEY GARDENS

Chard TA20 4LU. Mr & Mrs Julian
Kennard, 01460 221290,
www.fordeabbey.co.uk. *4m SE of
Chard. Signed off A30 Chard-
Crewkerne and A358 Chard-
Axminster. Also from Broadwindsor
B3164* **Please see below for
opening times.**
30 acres of fine shrubs, magnificent
specimen trees, ponds, herbaceous
borders, rockery, bog garden
containing superb collection of Asiatic
primulas, Ionic temple, working
walled kitchen garden supplying the
tearoom. Centenary fountain,
England's highest powered fountain.
Gardens open daily (10-6, last adm
4.30pm). Please ask at reception for
best wheelchair route. Wheelchairs
available to borrow/hire, advance
booking advised.

 ♿ 🎍 ❀ 🚐 ☕

21 FRANKHAM FARM

Ryme Intrinseca, Sherborne
DT9 6JT. Susan Ross, 07594
427365,
neilandsusanross@gmail.com,
www.facetbook.com/frankhamfarm
garden. *3m S of Yeovil. A37 Yeovil-
Dorchester; turn E; ¹/₄ m; drive is on
L.* **Sun 13 Mar, Sun 24 Apr, Sun 5
June, Sun 16 Oct (11.30-5). Adm
£4, chd free. Home-made teas.
Home produced pulled pork and
sausage lunches.**
3¹/₂ acre garden, created since 1960
by the late Jo Earle for yr-round
interest. This large and lovely garden
is filled with a wide variety of well
grown plants, roses, unusual labelled
shrubs and trees from around the
world. Productive vegetable garden.
Climbers cover the walls. Spring
bulbs through to autumn colour,
particularly oaks. Sorry, no dogs.
Featured, along with Abbotsbury and
Minterne, in SW1TV The Seasonal
Garden.

 ❀ 🚐 ☕

22 FRITH HOUSE

Stalbridge DT10 2SD. Mr & Mrs
Patrick Sclater, 01963 250809,
rosalynsclater@btinternet.com. *5m
E of Sherborne. Between Milborne
Port and Stalbridge. From A30 1m,
follow sign to Stalbridge. From
Stalbridge 2m and turn W by PO.*
**Sun 12 June (2-5). Adm £4, chd
free. Home-made teas. Visits also
by arrangement May to July for
groups of 10+ Mon-Fri only.**
Approached down long drive with fine
views. 4 acres of garden around
Edwardian house and self contained
hamlet. Range of mature trees, lakes
and flower borders. House terrace
edged by rose border and featuring
Lutyensesque wall fountain and game
larder. Well stocked kitchen gardens.

 ♿ ☕

23 GREENACRES

Bere Road, Coldharbour, Wareham
BH20 7PA. John & Pat Jacobs,
01929 553821. *2¹/₂ m NW of
Wareham. From r'about adj to stn
take Wareham-Bere Regis rd. House
¹/₂ m past Silent Woman Inn on R.
Plenty of off road parking.* **Sun 19
June, Sun 14 Aug (2-5.30). Adm
£3.50, chd free. Home-made teas.
Visits also by arrangement June
to Aug.**
Approx 1 acre plantswoman's garden
situated in Wareham Forest. Lawns
punctuated by colourful island beds
designed mainly for summer interest.

The Old Rectory, Netherbury

© Val Corbett

Unusual perennials, shrubs and specimen trees, spectacular flowering tulip tree. Themed areas and stone water feature with 2 ponds. Stumpery with collection of ferns and grasses. Live music. Static display of radio controlled aircraft.

 ♿ 🐕 ✿ ☕

24▶ HARCOMBE HOUSE
Pitmans Lane, Morcombelake, Bridport DT6 6EB. Jan & Martin Dixon, 01297 489229, Harcombe@hotmail.co.uk. *A35 4m W of Bridport - ignore SatNav. A35 from Bridport: R to Whitchurch just past The Artwave Gallery. Immed R, bear L into Pitmans Lane. Approx 800m, park in paddock on L.* **Sat 14, Sun 15, Tue 17 May, Sat 13, Sun 14, Tue 16 Aug (11-5). Adm £4, chd free. Home-made teas. All cakes are home-made by Jan Dixon. Visits also by arrangement Apr to Sept, groups are welcome but lane is too narrow for coaches.**
Landscaped into the hillside with wonderful views across Lyme Bay, the garden is laid out as a series of gravel paths and terraces connected by steps. Mature shrubs and perennials, many of which are unusual and visually stunning. The

garden offers something for every season. A challenge to the less mobile visitor and unsuitable for wheelchairs and buggies. Fabulous views of the Char Valley, Charmouth and Lyme Regis, with beautiful view across Lyme Bay to Teignmouth and beyond. Featured in Amateur Gardening.

☕

25▶ HERONS MEAD
East Burton Road, East Burton, Wool BH20 6HF. Ron & Angela Millington, 01929 463872, ronamillington@btinternet.com. *6m W of Wareham on A352. Approaching Wool from Wareham, turn R just before level crossing into East Burton Rd. Herons Mead ³/₄ m on L.* **Suns 27 Mar, 10 Apr, 1 May, 18 Sept (2-5). Adm £3.50, chd free. Home-made teas. Visits also by arrangement Mar to Sept for groups of 10+.**
¹/₂ acre plantlover's garden full of interest from spring (bulbs, many hellebores, pulmonaria, fritillaries) through abundant summer perennials, old roses scrambling through trees and late seasonal exuberant plants amongst swathes of tall grasses. Wildlife pond and plants to attract bees, butterflies, etc. Tiny

woodland. Cacti. Small wheelchairs can gain partial access - as far as the Teahouse!

 ♿ 🐕 ✿ ☕

26▶ ◆ HILLTOP
Woodville, Stour Provost, Gillingham SP8 5LY. Josse & Brian Emerson, 01747 838512, hilltopgardennursery@tiscali.co.uk, www.hilltopgarden.co.uk. *7m N of Sturminster Newton, 5m W of Shaftesbury. On B3092 turn E at Stour Provost Xrds, signed Woodville. After 1¹/₄ m thatched cottage on R. On A30, 4m W of Shaftesbury, turn S opp Kings Arms.* **For NGS: Every Sun 17 July to 21 Aug (2-6). Adm £3, chd free. Home-made teas. For other opening times and information, please phone, email or visit garden website.**
Summer at Hilltop is a gorgeous riot of colour and scent, the old thatched cottage barely visible amongst the flowers. Unusual annuals and perennials grow alongside the traditional and familiar, boldly combining to make a spectacular display, which attracts an abundance of wildlife. Always something new, the unique, gothic garden loo a great success. Nursery.

🐕 ✿ 🚐 ☕

27 ▶ THE HOLLOW (FORMERLY KNOWN AS STONE RISE)
25 Newton Road, Swanage
BH19 2EA. Stuart & Suzanne
Nutbeem, 07542 671091. ½ m S of
Swanage town centre. From town
follow signs to Durlston Country Park.
At top of hill turn R at red postbox
into Bon Accord Rd. 4th turn R into
Newton Rd. Every Wed 6 July to 31
Aug (2-5.30). Adm £3, chd free.
Visits also by arrangement July &
Aug.
Access down stone steps. Pause at
top of metal stairs then descend into
transformed stone quarry. Explore
densely planted beds in a relatively
confined space. Pieces of medieval
London Bridge lurk in the stonework.
'A beautiful and intriguing sunken
garden with exceptional richness and
arrangements of colour, textures and
form'. Exceptionally wide range of
plants. Featured in Amateur
Gardening.

. . . but beware
of being led
down the
garden path
by the
running hares . . . !

28 ▶ 22 HOLT ROAD
Branksome, Poole BH12 1JQ. Alan
& Sylvia Lloyd, 01202 387509,
alan.lloyd22@ntlworld.com. 2.5m W
of Bournemouth Square 3m E of
Poole Civic Centre. From Alder Rd
turn into Winston Ave, 3rd R into
Guest Ave 2nd R into Holt Rd at end
of cul de sac. Park in Holt Rd or
alternatively in Guest Ave. Sun 20
Mar (2-5). Sun 17 Apr (2-5), also
open 2 Spur Gate. Sun 15 May
(2-5), also open 1692 Wimborne
Road. Sun 19 June (2-5), also open
17 Lower Golf Links Road.
Sun 17 July (2-5), also open
25 Richmond Park Avenue. Sun
21 Aug (2-5). Adm £3.50, chd free.
Home-made teas. Visits also by
arrangement Mar to Sept for
groups of 10+.

³/₄ acre walled garden for all seasons.
Garden seating throughout the
diverse planting areas, comprising
Mediterranean courtyard garden,
wisteria pergola. Walk up slope
beside rill and bog garden to raised
bed vegetable garden. Return
through shrubbery and rockery back
to waterfall cascading into a pebble
beach. Featured in Dorset magazine.
Partial wheelchair access.

29 ▶ HOLWORTH FARMHOUSE
Holworth, Dorchester DT2 8NH.
Anthony & Philippa Bush,
01305 852242,
bushinarcadia@yahoo.co.uk,
www.inarcadia-
gardendesign.co.uk. 7m E of
Dorchester. 1m S of A352. Follow
signs to Holworth. Through farmyard
with duckpond on R. 1st L after
200yds of rough track. Ignore no
access signs. Sun 1, Mon 2, Sun
29, Mon 30 May, Sun 3 July, Sun 7
Aug (2-5). Adm £3.50, chd free.
Home-made teas. Visits also by
arrangement May to Sept, teas or
wine by arrangement.
This unusual garden is tucked away
without being isolated and has an
atmosphere of extraordinary peace
and tranquility. At no point do visitors
perceive any idea of the whole, but
have to discover, by degrees and at
every turn, its element of surprise, its
variety of features and its appreciation
of space. At all times you are invited
to look back, to look round and up.
Birds and butterflies. Beautiful
unspoilt views. Large vegetable
garden. Ponds, fish, and water
features.

**30 ▶ HOLY TRINITY PRIMARY
SCHOOL GARDEN**
Cross Rd, Weymouth DT4 9QX.
Holy Trinity C E Primary
School & Nursery,
www.holytrinityenvironmental
garden.blogspot.co.uk. 1m W of
Weymouth centre. Follow A354 from
Weymouth harbour junction by Asda.
R at top of hill into Wyke Rd. 3rd L
into Cross Rd. 200yds on R school
car park. Sat 16, Sun 17 July (1-5).
Adm £4, chd free. Home-made
teas.
An award winning wildlife garden,
started in 2008 with the donation of a
winning RHS Show Garden.
Children's raised beds, a large wildlife
pond, WWII garden with Anderson
shelter, tranquil Memory Corner,

Dorset's largest living willow
classroom, small orchard and bird
hide and composting toilet. The new
Jurassic Garden area was planted in
2015 with many ferns and dinosaurs!
Butterfly or dinosaur hunt for children.
Wheelchair access to most of garden
and WC.

31 ▶ IVY HOUSE GARDEN
Piddletrenthide DT2 7QF. Bridget
Bowen, 01300 348255,
bridgetpbowen@hotmail.com. 9m
N of Dorchester. On B3143. In middle
of Piddletrenthide village, opp
PO/village stores near Piddle Inn.
Mon 28 Mar, Sun 17, Wed 20 Apr,
Sun 1, Mon 2 May (2-5). Adm £4,
chd free. Tea. Visits also by
arrangement Apr & May for
groups of 10+.
Unusual and challenging ½ acre
garden set on steep hillside with fine
views. Wildlife friendly garden with
mixed borders, ponds, propagating
area, vegetable garden, fruit cage,
greenhouses and polytunnel,
chickens and bees, nearby allotment.
Daffodils, tulips and hellebores in
quantity for spring openings. Come
prepared for steep terrain and a warm
welcome! Run on organic lines with
plants to attract bees and other
insects. Insect-friendly plants usually
for sale. Honey and hive products
available and, weather permitting,
observation hive of honey bees in
courtyard. Beekeeper present to
answer queries! Featured in Dorset
Magazine.

32 ▶ ◆ KINGSTON LACY
Wimborne Minster BH21 4EA.
National Trust, 01202 883402,
kingstonlacy@nationaltrust.org.uk,
www.nationaltrust.org.uk/kingston-
lacy. 2½ m W of Wimborne Minster.
On Wimborne-Blandford rd B3082.
For NGS: Sun 24 Apr (10-6). Adm
£8.60, chd £4.30. Full restaurant
on site. For other opening times
and information, please phone,
email or visit garden website.
35 acres of formal garden,
incorporating parterre and sunk
garden planted with Edwardian
schemes during spring and summer.
5 acre kitchen garden and allotments,
Victorian fernery containing over 35
varieties. Rose garden, mixed
herbaceous borders, vast formal
lawns and Japanese garden restored
to Henrietta Bankes' creation of
1910. 2 National Collections:

Convallaria and Anemone nemorosa.
Deep gravel on some paths but lawns
suitable for wheelchairs. Slope to
visitor reception and South Lawn.

 ♿ ⊛ 🚐 **NPC** ☕

33 ◆ KINGSTON MAURWARD GARDENS AND ANIMAL PARK
Kingston Maurward, Dorchester
DT2 8PY. Kingston Maurward
College, 01305 215003,
events@kmc.ac.uk,
www.morekmc.com. *1m E of
Dorchester. Off A35. Follow brown
Tourist Information signs.* **For
opening times and information,
please phone, email or visit garden
website.**
35 acres of gardens laid out in C18
and C20 with 5 acre lake. Generous
terraces and gardens divided by
hedges and stone balustrades. Stone
features and interesting plants.
Elizabethan walled garden laid out as
demonstration. National Collections
of penstemons and salvias. Open
early Jan to mid Dec or dusk if earlier.
Hours will vary in winter depending on
conditions, check garden website or
call before visiting. Partial wheelchair
access only, gravel paths, steps and
steep slopes.

 ♿ 🚐 **NPC** ☕

hospiceUK

Visit a garden
and support
hospice care
in your
community

34 KITEMOOR COTTAGE
Manswood, Wimborne BH21 5BQ.
Alan and Diana Guy, 01258 840894,
diana.kitemoor@btinternet.com.
*6m N of Wimborne. From B3078 turn
to Witchampton, then from village
centre follow signs to Manswood.*
**Sat 5, Sun 6 Mar (12-4); Sun 17
Apr (2-5). Adm £3.50, chd free.
Homemade soup and roll at
lunchtime in March, home-made
teas on all open days. Visits also
by arrangement Mar to June for
groups of 15 +.**

½ acre plantsperson's garden with
glorious countryside views. Diana
(formally of Welcome Thatch) has
created a new garden full of treasures
incl large collection of hellebores.
Planted for a long season of interest.
Pond, mini meadow, naturalistic
planting and cottage garden borders.
Fruit and vegetable gardens. Plants
for sale, exquisite Holmlea hybrid
hellebores for sale in March. Partial
wheelchair access. Narrow pathways
and different levels.

 ⊛ ☕

35 KNITSON OLD FARMHOUSE
Corfe Castle, Wareham BH20 5JB.
Rachel Helfer, 01929 421681,
rjehelfer@gmail.com. *1m NW of
Swanage. 3m E of Corfe Castle.
Signed L off A351 to Knitson. Very
narrow rds for 1m. Ample parking in
yard or in adjacent field.* **Fri 27,
Sat 28, Sun 29, Mon 30 May, Fri 9,
Sat 10, Sun 11 Sept (1-5). Adm
£3.50, chd free. Cream teas.
Home-made cakes. Visits also
by arrangement Feb to Nov,
max 30.**
Mature cottage garden with
exceptional views nestled at base of
chalk downland in dry coastal
conditions. Herbaceous borders,
rockeries, climbers and shrubs.
Evolved and designed over 50yrs for
yr-round colour and interest. Large
wildlife friendly kitchen garden for self
sufficiency. Rachel is delighted to
welcome visitors and discuss
gardening. We have used a lot of
local stone in the design and have
interesting old stones and stone
baths around the garden. Uneven,
sloping paths.

 ♿ 🪑 🚐 ☕

36 ◆ KNOLL GARDENS
Hampreston, Wimborne
BH21 7ND. Mr Neil Lucas,
01202 873931,
enquiries@knollgardens.co.uk,
www.knollgardens.co.uk. *2½ m W
of Ferndown. ETB brown signs from
A31. Large car park.* **For opening
times and information, please
phone, email or visit garden
website.**
Originally a private botanic, an
exciting collection of grasses and
perennials thrive in an informal
setting of rare and unusual trees
and shrubs. Owned by the UK's
leading ornamental grass specialist,
Neil Lucas, new projects include
creating a large meadow-style

effect with naturalistic plantings in the
dragon, gravel and sunny meadow
garden areas appearing to merge as
one. Specialist nursery. Some slopes.
Various surfaces incl gravel, paving,
grass and bark.

 ♿ ⊛ 🚐 **NPC** ☕

37 LANGEBRIDE HOUSE
Long Bredy DT2 9HU. Mrs J
Greener, 01308 482257. *8m W of
Dorchester. S off A35, midway
between Dorchester and Bridport.
Well signed. 1st gateway on L in
village.* **Sun 6 Mar (2-5). Adm £4.50,
chd free. Teas at nearby Egg Cup
Tea Rooms, Vurlands Farm, Coast
Road, Swyre, DT2 9DB. 01308
897160. Visits also by
arrangement Jan to July.**
This old rectory garden has
carpets of anemones spreading
out under huge copper beech
tree on lawn. A lovely place to visit
in spring and early summer, with a
large variety of daffodils and early
spring bulbs amongst flowering
shrubs, trees and herbaceous
borders with kitchen garden.
Some steep slopes.

 ♿ 🪑 🚐 ☕

38 LAWSBROOK
Brodham Way, Shillingstone
DT11 0TE. Clive Nelson, 01258
860148, cne70bl@aol.com,
www.facebook.com/Lawsbrook.
*5m NW of Blandford. Follow signs to
Shillingstone on A357. Turn off at old
PO box, continue up Gunn Lane, 2nd
junction on R, 1st house on R
(200yds).* **Visits by arrangement
Feb to Nov, garden can
accommodate large numbers.
Adm £3, chd free. Home-made
teas. Lunches by request.**
6 acres. Over 200 trees incl the
mature and unusual. Formal borders,
wild flower and wildlife areas,
vegetable garden. Relaxed and
friendly, lovely opportunity for family
walks in all areas incl wildlife, stream,
meadow. Children and dogs
welcome. Yr-round interest incl
extensive snowdrops, hellebores and
bulbs in early spring through full
summer colour to intense autumn
hues. Large and unusual labelled tree
collection. Garden activities for all the
family. More than an acre coverage of
snowdrops in the early spring. Gravel
path at entrance, grass paths over
whole garden.

 ♿ 🪑 ⊛ 🚐 ☕

39 ▶ LITTLE CLIFF
Sidmouth Road, Lyme Regis
DT7 3EQ. Mrs Debbie Bell, 01297
444833, debbie@debbiebell.co.uk.
*Edge of Lyme Regis. Turn off A35
onto B3165 to Lyme Regis. Through
Uplyme to mini r'about by Travis
Perkins. 3rd exit on R, up to fork and
L down Sidmouth Rd following NGS
arrows from mini r'about. Garden on
R.* Thur 21, Sat 23 Apr, Thur 9, Sat
11 June, Thur 7, Sat 9 July (2-5).
Adm £3.50, chd free. **Visits also by
arrangement Apr to July, please
arrange in advance.**
South facing seaward, Little Cliff
looks out over spectacular views of
Lyme Bay. Spacious garden sloping
down hillside through series of garden
rooms where visual treats unfold.
Vibrant herbaceous borders, with hot
garden, white garden, bog garden all
intermingled with mature specimen
trees, shrubs and wall climbers.
Steep slopes. New jungle garden and
colonial pavilion in the hot garden.
Featured in Country Homes and
Interiors magazine.
❀

4 acres . . .formal
garden around
house with
wonderful arbour
and Mediterranean
feel . . .

40 ◆ LITTLEBREDY WALLED
GARDENS
Littlebredy DT2 9HL. The Walled
Garden Workshop, 01305 898055,
secretary@wgw.org.uk,
www.littlebredy.com. *8m W of
Dorchester. 10m E of Bridport.
1½ m S of A35. NGS days: park on
village green then walk 300yd. For the
less mobile (and on normal open
days) use gardens car park.* **For
NGS: Tue 21, Tue 28 June (2-7).
Adm £5, chd free. Home-made
teas. For other opening times
please see below.**
1 acre walled garden on S facing
slopes of Bride River Valley.
Herbaceous borders, riverside rose
walk, lavender beds and potager
vegetable and cut flower gardens.

Original Victorian glasshouses, one
under renovation. Gardens also open
2-5pm on Wed & Sun (see website
for other days) from Sunday April
10th to end Sept, weather permitting.
Featured in Country Living, Coast,
Dorset Magazine, Dorset Gardens
Trust, Daily Mail. Partial wheelchair
access, some steep grass slopes.
For disabled parking please follow
signs to main entrance.
& ❀ ❀ ☕

41 NEW ▶ LOWER ABBOTTS
WOOTTON FARM
Whitchurch Canonicorum, Bridport
DT6 6NL. Johnny & Clare
Trenchard. *6m W of Bridport. Well
signed from A35 at Morecombe Lake
(2m) and Bottle Inn at Marshwood on
B3165 (1.5m). Some disabled off-
road parking.* Sat 2, Sun 3 July
(2-5). Adm £4, chd free. **Home-
made teas.**
The owner is a sculptor and the
garden reflects her creative flair for
form, shape and colour. New open
gravel garden contrasts with the main
garden consisting of lawns, borders
and garden rooms which make a
perfect setting for sculptures. The
naturally edged pond provides a
tranquil moment of calm, but beware
of being led down the garden path by
the running hares! Sculpture Garden.
Partial wheelchair access.
❀ ❀ ☕

42 ▶ 17 LOWER GOLF LINKS
ROAD
Broadstone, Poole BH18 8BQ. Dr &
Mrs Nicholas Dunn. *½ m N of
Broadstone centre. Approaching from
Gravel Hill, along Dunyeats Rd, Lower
Golf Links Road is 2nd turn on R,
past the Middle School.* Thur 21,
Sun 24 Apr (2-5). Sun 5 June (2-5),
also open 1692 Wimborne Road.
Sun 19 June (2-5), also open 22
Holt Road. Adm £3.50, chd free.
Home-made teas.
Town garden of ⅔ acre, created in a
heathland suburb. Originally mainly
acid-loving plants, now, after much
clearance and soil enrichment, plants
for all seasons. Vegetable garden with
raised beds, chickens, fruit trees and
a pond as well as borders. Something
of interest all yr round, but particularly
impressive in spring and early
summer. Camellias, azaleas and
rhododendrons; Roses and pergola
leading to pond. Featured in Amateur
Gardening. Gravel drive and stone
steps. Garden on a slight slope.
❀ 🚐 ☕

43 ▶ MANOR FARM,
HAMPRESTON
Wimborne BH21 7LX. Guy & Anne
Trehane. *2½ m E of Wimborne,
2½ m W of Ferndown. From Canford
Bottom r'about on A31, take exit
B3073 Ham Lane. ½ m turn R at
Hampreston Xrds. House at bottom
of village.* Sat 27 Feb (10-12); Sun
28 Feb (12-3). Light refreshments.
Wed 25 May (11-4); Sun 31 July,
Wed 3, Sun 14 Aug (1-5). Home-
made teas. Adm £3.50, chd free.
Traditional farmhouse garden
designed and cared for by 3
generations of the Trehane family
through over 100yrs of farming and
gardening at Hampreston. Garden is
noted for its herbaceous borders and
rose beds within box and yew
hedges. Mature shrubbery, water and
bog garden. Open for hellebores in
Feb. Dorset Hardy Plant Society sales
at openings. Hellebores for sale in
Feb.
& ❀ ☕

44 ▶ THE MANOR HOUSE
Church Lane, Lower Blandford St
Mary, Blandford DT11 9ND. Mr &
Mrs Jeremy Mains, 01258 451692.
*¼ m E of Blandford. Signed off A350
to Poole from Blandford Forum Ring
Road (Tesco r'about).* Sun 22, Wed
25 May (2-5). Adm £5, chd free.
Home-made teas. **Visits also by
arrangement Apr to June.**
Traditional 3 acre walled garden
surrounding Jacobean House (not
open). Formal rose beds with mixed
herbaceous borders. Working fruit
and vegetable garden. Large and
varied shrub borders with extensive
collection of roses. Something of
interest at all times of year. Hopefully
the bearded irises will be at their best
for May opening!
& ❀ ☕

45 ▶ THE MANOR HOUSE,
BEAMINSTER
North St, Beaminster DT8 3DZ.
Christine Wood. *200yds N of town
square. Park in the square or public
car park, 5 mins walk along North St
from the Square. Limited disabled
parking on site.* Sun 1, Mon 2, Sun
29, Mon 30 May, Sat 25, Sun 26
June (11-5). Adm £5, chd free.
Home-made teas in Coach House
Garden 2 - 5pm or bring a picnic.
Set in heart of Beaminster, 16½ acres
of stunning parkland with mature
specimen trees, lake and waterfall.
Beautifully restored walled garden -
serendipity. Designed and lovingly

planted over last 7yrs. A peaceful garden with woodland walk and wild flower meadow. Featured in Dorset Life, Country Life & The English Garden. Partial wheelchair access.

46 NEW MAPPERCOMBE MANOR

Nettlecombe, Bridport DT6 3SS. Annie Crutchley. *4m NE of Bridport. From A3066 turn E signed W Milton & Powerstock. After 3m leave Powerstock on your L, bear R at Marquis of Lorne PH, entrance drive 150yds ahead.* **Thur 26, Sun 29 May, Sun 12 June (2-5). Adm £4, chd free.**

Monks' rest house with stew pond and dovecote. S-facing gardens on 4 levels with ancient monastic route. Approx 4 acres. Apart from stone work and mature trees, garden mostly replanted in last 25 yrs. Dogs on leads. Partial wheelchair access, gravel and stone paths, steps.

47 ♦ MAPPERTON GARDENS

Mapperton, Beaminster DT8 3NR. The Earl & Countess of Sandwich, 01308 862645, www.mapperton.com. *6m N of Bridport. Off A356/A3066. 2m SE of Beaminster off B3163.* **For opening times please see below.**

Terraced valley gardens surrounding Tudor/Jacobean manor house. On upper levels, walled croquet lawn, orangery and Italianate formal garden with fountains, topiary and grottos. Below, C17 summerhouse and fishponds. Lower garden with shrubs and rare trees, leading to woodland and spring gardens. Garden open 1 Mar to 31 Oct (except Sats) (11-5); café open 1 Apr to 30 Sept. Snowdrop Sundays 7 & 14 Feb 2016. Partial wheelchair access (lawn and upper levels).

48 MARREN

Holworth, Dorchester DT2 8NJ. Mr & Mrs Peter Cartwright, 01305 851503, wcartwright@tiscali.co.uk, www.wendycartwright.net. *SE of Dorchester. Don't use SatNav. Off A353 At Poxwell turn L to Ringstead. Straight on to NT Car Park at top of hill. Park before gate marked No Cars. Walk through gate, signed path, on R.* **Sat 16, Sun 17 Apr, Sat 21, Sun 22 May (2-5). Adm £4, chd free. Home-made teas. Visits also by arrangement Apr to Oct, refreshments by arrangement for groups of 10+.**

4 acres. From NT car park down steep public footpath and 64 grass steps to woodland garden with tree sculptures. Views of Weymouth Bay and Portland. More formal garden around house with wonderful arbour and Mediterranean feel. Strong structural planting. Stout footwear and strong knees recommended. Wildlife and Seaside Garden. Fedge in willow. Hornbeam house. Italianate courtyard with fountain. Hornbeam arbour on terrace. Willow arbour at the bottom. Featured in Country Homes and Interiors. Not suitable for wheelchairs but disabled access to house for tea by prior arrangement.

The Manor House

49 MAYFIELD
4 Walford Close, Wimborne Minster BH21 1PH. Mr & Mrs Terry Wheeler, 01202 849838, terry.wheeler@tesco.net. ½ m N of Wimborne Town Centre. B3078 out of Wimborne, R into Burts Hill, 1st L into Walford Close. **Sun 8, Wed 18, Sun 29 May (1.30-4.30). Sun 5 June (1.30-4.30), also open Old Down House. Wed 15 June (1.30-4.30). Adm £3, chd free. Home-made teas. Visits also by arrangement May & June for groups of 6+.** Donation to The Friends of Victoria Hospital, Wimborne.
Town garden of approx ¼ acre. Front: formal hard landscaping planted with drought-resistant shrubs and perennials. Shaded area has wide variety of hostas. Back garden contrasts with a seductive series of garden rooms containing herbaceous perennial beds separated by winding grass paths and rustic arches. Pond, vegetable beds and greenhouses containing succulents and vines. Garden access is across a pea-shingle drive. If this is manageable, wheelchairs can access the back garden provided they are no wider than 65cms.

50 MEADOW VIEWS
32 Riverside Road, West Moors, Ferndown BH22 0LQ. Sue & Norman Lynch. 2m from Ferndown towards Verwood, off B3072. From Station Rd through West Moors going N, turn L. Last house on R. Parking in rd, avoiding driveways. **Sun 17 July, Sun 7 Aug (2-5). Adm £3, chd free. Home-made teas.**
Small, informal, wildlife friendly garden overlooking Manning Brook and open farmland. Island beds showing colourful herbaceous mixed planting with additional perennials for 2016. Newly enlarged and improved fernery. Damselflies dance in the sunshine over the water whilst butterflies and bees visit their chosen blooms. Some steps and gravel paths/driveway.

51 THE MILL HOUSE
Crook Hill, Netherbury DT6 5LX. Michael & Giustina Ryan, 01308 488267, themillhouse@dsl.pipex.com. 1m S of Beaminster. Turn R off A3066 Beaminster to Bridport at signpost to Netherbury. Car park at Xrds at bottom of hill. **Visits by**

arrangement Apr to Sept, min 6, max 30. **Adm £5, chd free. Light refreshments.**
6½ acres of garden around R Brit, incl mill stream and mill pond. Extensive garden consisting of formal walled, terraced and vegetable gardens and bog-garden. Emphasis on spring bulbs, scented flowers, hardy geraniums, lilies, clematis and water irises. Wander through the wild garden planted with many rare and interesting trees incl conifers, magnolias, oak and fruit trees. Collection of Magnolias flowering March to September. Walled garden with water feature. Featured in Country Life. Partial wheelchair access.

52 ◆ MINTERNE HOUSE
Minterne Magna, Dorchester DT2 7AU. The Hon Henry & Mrs Digby, 01300 341370, enquiries@minterne.co.uk, www.minterne.co.uk. 2m N of Cerne Abbas. On A352 Dorchester-Sherborne rd. **For opening times and information, please phone, email or visit garden website.**
As seen on BBC Gardeners' World and voted one of the 10 prettiest gardens in England by The Times. Famed for their display of rhododendrons, azaleas, Japanese cherries and magnolias in April/May. Small lakes, streams and cascades offer new vistas at each turn around the 1m horseshoe shaped gardens covering 23 acres. The season ends with spectacular autumn colour. Open mid February to 9 Nov (10-6). Regret unsuitable for wheelchairs.

53 OLD DOWN HOUSE
Horton, Wimborne BH21 7HL. Dr & Mrs Colin Davidson, 07765 404248, pipdavidson59@gmail.com. 7½ m N of Wimborne. Horton Inn at junction of B3078 with Horton Rd, pick up yellow signs leading up through North Farm. No garden access from Matterley Drove. 5min walk to garden down farm track. **Wed 1 June (2-5). Sun 5 June (2-5), also open Mayfield. Wed 8 June (2-5). Adm £3.50, chd free. Home-made teas in comfortable garden room if weather inclement.**
Nestled down a farm track, this ¾ acre garden on chalk surrounds C18 farmhouse. Stunning views over Horton Tower and farmland. Cottage garden planting with formal elements,

climbing roses clothe pergola and house walls along with stunning wisteria sinensis and banksia rose. Part walled potager, well stocked. Chickens. Not suitable for wheelchairs.

54 THE OLD RECTORY, MANSTON
Manston, Sturminster Newton DT10 1EX. Andrew & Judith Hussey, 01258 474673, judithhussey2@hotmail.com. 6m S of Shaftesbury, 2½ m N of Sturminster Newton. From Shaftesbury, take B3091. On reaching Manston, past Plough Inn, L for Child Okeford on R-hand bend. Old Rectory last house on L. **Visits by arrangement May to Sept for groups of 4+. Adm £4.50, chd free. Home-made teas.**
Beautifully restored 5 acre garden. S-facing wall with 120ft herbaceous border edged by old brick path. Enclosed yew hedge flower garden. Wildflower meadow marked with mown paths and young plantation of mixed hardwoods. Well maintained walled Victorian kitchen garden. Knot garden now well established. Featured in Country Life.

55 THE OLD RECTORY, NETHERBURY
Beaminster DT6 5NB. Simon & Amanda Mehigan, www.oldrectorynetherbury.tumblr. com. 2m SW of Beaminster. Please park in Mill House field near R Brit in centre of village, walk up hill to garden. Parking available nearer house for the less able-bodied. **Sun 24, Tue 26 Apr, Sun 22, Tue 24 May (11-5). Adm £5, chd free. Home-made teas. Refreshments from 11 am.**

5 acre garden developed by present owners over last 20 yrs. Formal areas with topiary near house, naturalistic planting elsewhere. Many bulbs including fritillaries, erythroniums, tulips and wood anemones. Extensive bog garden with pond and stream planted with candelabra primroses and other moisture lovers. Flowering trees: magnolias and cornus. Hornbeam walk. Decorative vegetable garden. Featured in Country Homes and Interiors.

56 THE OLD RECTORY, PULHAM

Dorchester DT2 7EA. Mr & Mrs N Elliott, 01258 817595. *13m N of Dorchester. 8m SE of Sherborne. On B3143 turn E at Xrds in Pulham. Signed Cannings Court.* **Mon 2 May, Sun 7 Aug (2-5). Adm £5, chd free. Home-made teas. Visits also by arrangement May to Sept for groups, weekdays only.**
4 acres formal and informal gardens surround C18 rectory with splendid views. Yew hedges enclose circular herbaceous borders with late summer colour. Exuberantly planted terrace with purple and white beds. Box parterres, mature trees, pond, fernery, ha-ha, pleached hornbeam circle. 10 acres woodland walks. Flourishing and newly extended bog garden with islands; awash with primulas and irises in May. Home-made teas and cakes, interesting plants for sale. Featured in Country Life, Homes and Garden, Country Homes and Interiors, Dorset Life and ITV Spotlight Programme. Mostly wheelchair access.

57 NEW THE OLD RECTORY, WINTERBORNE STICKLAND

North Street, Winterborne Stickland, Blandford Forum DT11 0NL. Kate and Gareth Penny. *5m SW of Blandford. From Blandford (Bryanston gates) follow signs on Fairmile Rd to Winterborne Stickland, 5m. On L past PH. From A354 take Whatcombe Lane through W Clenston to W Stickland. On R opp the green.* **Sun 5, Mon 6 June (2-5). Adm £5, chd free. Home-made teas.**
2 acre garden surrounding C17 house. A 500 year old lime and superb ancient trees form the backdrop to a romantic unexpected and structured garden. Beech and yew hedges create terraced rooms

on the sloping site for vegetable, rose and swimming pool gardens. Orchard with folly. Wood with hidden tree house. Formal around the house, drifting to less structured areas. Interesting garden sculptures. Slopes and steps.

Beech and yew hedges create terraced rooms on the sloping site . . .

58 OLD SMITHY

Ibberton DT11 0EN. Carol & Clive Carsley, 01258 817361, carolcarsley@btinternet.com. *9m NW of Blandford Forum. From Blandford A357 to Sturminster Newton. After 6.5m L to Okeford Fitzpaine. Follow signs to Ibberton, 3m, park by village hall, about 5 min walk to garden.* **Sat 26 Mar, Sun 8 May (2-5). Adm £3.50, chd free. Home-made teas in Village Hall. Visits also by arrangement Feb to Sept for groups of 10+.**
Worth driving twisty narrow lanes to reach this rural 2½ acre streamside garden framing a thatched cottage. Back of beyond setting which inspired international best seller Mr Rosenblum's List. Succession of ponds. Mown paths. Spring bulbs in profusion, primula candelabras, aquilegia and hellebores. Sit beneath rustling trees. Views of Bulbarrow and church. Featured in Period Living, Dorset Life and Blackmore Vale Magazine.

59 THE OLD VICARAGE

East Orchard, Shaftesbury SP7 0BA. Miss Tina Wright, 01747 811744, tina_lon@msn.com. *4½ m S of Shaftesbury, 3½ m N of Sturminster Newton. On B3091, on 90 degree bend, next to lay-by with phone box. Park in field opp. Walk along verge, cross at 2nd open gate carefully checking in mirror.* **Sun 13 Mar (1.30-4.30); Sun 17 Apr, Sun**

22 May (2-5). **Adm £4, chd free. Home-made teas. Visits also by arrangement any size group.**
1.7 acre, award winning wildlife friendly garden. Swathes of crocus, primula and unusual snowdrops in spring. A large number of different daffodils follow, then herbaceous borders and wild flowers. Sit by the bubbling stream or gaze at beautiful reflections in the swimming pond. Dogs welcome and children can pond dip. Swing and tree platform overlooking Duncliffe woods. Teas indoors and various shelters around the garden if wet. Featured in Independent, Mail on Sunday & Dorset magazine. Not suitable for wheelchairs if very wet.

60 PARNHAM HOUSE

Beaminster DT8 3LZ. Mr & Mrs M B Treichl. *Turn R off A3066 1m S of Beaminster. Follow signs.* **Tue 28, Thur 30 June (2-5). Adm £5, chd free.**
Beautifully presented spacious gardens surrounding Elizabethan Manor House. Terraced formal gardens on S side of house with topiary features leading to a lake within a deer park setting. Walled gardens with themed borders and vegetable garden. House not open to the public. Partial wheelchair access, gravel paths and steep grass slopes.

61 PUDDLEDOCK COTTAGE

Scotland Heath, Norden, nr Corfe Castle, Wareham BH20 5DY. Ray and Ann George, 07715 749147, malcolmorgee@yahoo.co.uk. *Scotland Heath, Norden. From Wareham to Corfe Castle turn L at Norden Park and Ride, then L signed Slepe and Arne. Garden 500m on R.* **Sun 22 May, Sun 24 July (12-4). Adm £4, chd free. Tea. Visits also by arrangement Apr to Sept for any size groups.**
Puddledock Cottage was originally a quarryman's cottage. Newly renovated, it now stands at the centre of a big lovingly created garden with streams and ponds edged with nectar rich plants that attract a myriad of butterflies and bees. Shady walks snake though birch and willow, underplanted with rhododendrons and ferns. Views to Corfe Castle and Scotland Heath. Children's activities. Good wheelchair access.

62 Q

113 Bridport Road, Dorchester DT1 2NH. Heather & Chris Robinson, 01305 263088, hmrobinson45@gmail.com. *Approx 300m W of Dorset County Hospital. From Top o' Town r'about head W towards Dorset County Hospital, Q 300 metres further on.* **Sun 13 Mar (2-4.30); Sun 27 Mar, Sun 10, Sun 24 Apr, Sun 8, Sun 22 May (2-5). Adm £3, chd free. Home-made teas. Visits also by arrangement Mar to July min number 8, 40 max, 1wk notice preferred.**

Q is essentially all things to all men, a modern cottage town garden with many facets, jam packed with bulbs, shrubs, trees, climbers and bedding plants. Gazebo, statues, water, bonsai and topiary. Planting reflects the owners' many and varied interests including over 100 clematis, 1000+ spring bulbs purchased yearly. Easter Sunday celebrated for children with Easter Egg Hunt. Featured on Radio Solent and in local press. Small number of paths available for wheelchair users.

A good example of what can be achieved in a small plantaholics' garden. . .

63 **25 RICHMOND PARK AVENUE**

Bournemouth BH8 9DL. Barbara Hutchinson and Mike Roberts, 01202 531072, barbarahutchinson@tiscali.co.uk. *2½ m NE Bournemouth Town Centre. From T-lights at junction with Alma Rd and Richmond Park Rd, head N on B3063 Charminster Rd, 2nd turning on R into Richmond Park Ave.* **Sun 19 June (1-5), also open 22 Holt Road. Sun 3 July (1-5). Sun 17 July (1-5), also open 22 Holt Road. Sun 31 July (1-5). Adm £3, chd free. Home-made teas. Visits also by arrangement June & July for groups of 10+.**

Beautifully designed town garden with pergola leading to ivy canopy over raised decking. Cascading waterfall connects 2 wildlife ponds enhanced with domed acers. Circular lawn with colourful herbaceous border planted to attract bees and butterflies. Fragrant S-facing courtyard garden at front, sparkling with vibrant colour and Mediterranean planting incl Asian lilies, brugmansias and lemon tree. Partial wheelchair access.

64 **357 RINGWOOD ROAD**

Ferndown BH22 9AE. Lyn & Malcolm Ovens, 01202 896071, lynandmalc@btinternet.com, www.lynandmalc.co.uk. *¾ m S of Ferndown. On A348 towards Longham. Parking in Glenmoor Rd or other side rds. Avoid parking on main rd.* **Sun 3 July (1.30-5); Wed 20 July (2-5); Sun 14 Aug (1.30-5). Adm £3, chd free. Home-made teas. Visits also by arrangement June to Aug.**

The original Dorset His and Hers garden. Hers in cottage style with clematis, phlox, lilies, roses, monarda, encouraging butterflies and bees, providing a riot of colour and perfume into late summer. Walk through a Moorish keyhole doorway into His exotic garden with brugmansias, canna, oleander, banana, dahlia and bougainvillea. A good example of what can be achieved in a small plantaholics' garden. Ferndown Common nearby.

65 ◆ **SCULPTURE BY THE LAKES**

Pallington Lakes, Pallington, Dorchester DT2 8QU. Mrs Monique Gudgeon, 07720 637808, sbtl@me.com, www.sculpturebythelakes.co.uk. *6m E of Dorchester. ½ m E of Tincleton, see beech hedge and security gates. From other direction 0.8m from Xrds. No catering facilities but Purbeck ice cream available. No children under 14. No dogs allowed.* **For NGS: Wed 15 June, Wed 6 July (11-5). Adm £7.50. For other opening times and information, please phone, email or visit garden website.**

Recently created modern garden with inspiration taken from all over the world. Described as a modern arcadia it follows traditions of the landscape movement, but for C21. Where sculpture has been placed,

the planting palette has been kept simple, but dramatic, so that the work remains the star. Home to Monique and her husband, renowned British sculptor Simon Gudgeon, the sculpture park features over 30 of his most iconic pieces including Isis, which is also in London's Hyde Park and a dedicated gallery where some of his smaller pieces can be seen and purchased. Disabled access limited though possible to go round paths on mobility scooter or electric wheelchair if care taken.

66 **THE SECRET GARDEN**

The Friary, Hilfield, Dorchester DT2 7BE. The Society of St Francis, 01300 341345, hilfieldssf@franciscans.org.uk, www.hilfieldfriary.org.uk. *10m N of Dorchester, on A352 between Sherborne & Dorchester. 1st L after Minterne Magna, 1st turning on R signed The Friary. From Yeovil turn off A37 signed Batcombe, 3rd turning on L.* **Sat 14, Sun 15 May (2-5). Adm £4.50, chd free. Home-made teas. Visits also by arrangement May & June.**

Ongoing reclamation of neglected woodland garden. New plantings from modern day plant hunters. Mature trees, bamboo, rhododendrons, azaleas, magnolias, camellias, other choice shrubs with stream on all sides crossed by bridges, and in spring a growing collection of loderi hybrids with other choice shrubs. Stout shoes recommended for woodland garden. Friary grounds open where meadows, woods and livestock can be viewed. Friary Shop selling a variety of gifts.

67 **THE SECRET GARDEN AND SERLES HOUSE**

47 Victoria Road, Wimborne BH21 1EN. Ian Willis. *Centre of Wimborne. On B3082 W of town, very near hospital, Westfield car park 300yds. Off-road parking close by.* **Thur 21, Sun 24, Sun 31 July, Thur 4, Sun 7 Aug (2-5). Adm £3, chd free. Home-made teas. Evening opening Sat 13 Aug (6-9.30). Adm £5, chd free. Wine. Sun 21, Sun 28, Mon 29 Aug, Thur 1, Sat 3, Sun 4, Sun 11 Sept (2-5). Adm £3, chd free. Home-made teas.** *Donation to Wimborne Civic Society and NADFAS.*

Broomhill

© Roger Lane

Alan Titchmarsh described this amusingly creative garden as 'one of the best 10 private gardens in Britain'. The ingenious use of unusual plants complements the imaginative treasure trove of garden objects d'art. The enchanting house is also open. A feeling of a by gone age accompanies your tour as you step into a world of whimsical fantasy that is theatrical and unique. Oriental garden now open. New sculpture 'A flight in time' to commemorate the Queen being our longest reigning monarch, unveiled Sept 2015. Featured in Dorset Magazine and Stour and Avon Magazine. Wheelchair access to garden only. Narrow steps may prohibit wide wheelchairs.

68 ◆ **SHERBORNE CASTLE**
New Rd; Sherborne DT9 5NR. Mr E Wingfield Digby, 01935 812072, www.sherbornecastle.com. *1/2 m E of Sherborne. On New Road B3145. Follow brown signs from A30 & A352.* **For opening times and information, please phone or visit garden website.**
40+ acres. Grade I Capability Brown garden with magnificent vistas across surrounding landscape, incl lake and views to ruined castle. Herbaceous planting, notable trees, mixed ornamental planting and managed wilderness are linked together with lawn and pathways. Dry Grounds Walk. Partial wheelchair access, gravel paths, steep slopes, steps.

69 ▶ **SLAPE MANOR**
Netherbury DT6 5LH. Mr & Mrs Antony Hichens, 01308 488232, sczhichens@btinternet.com. *1m S of Beaminster.* Turn W off A3066 to Netherbury. House *1/2 m S of Netherbury on back rd to Bridport signed Waytown.* **Sun 29 May (2-5). Adm £4, chd free. Home-made teas. Visits also by arrangement for groups of 10+.**
River valley garden with spacious lawns and primula fringed streams down to lake. Walk over the stream with magnificent hostas, gunneras and horizontal cryptomeria Japonica Elegans, and around the lake. Admire the mature wellingtonias, ancient wisterias, rhododendrons and planting around the house. Mostly flat with some sloping paths and steps.

71 NEW 2 SPUR GATE
24 Spur Hill Avenue, Parkstone, Poole BH14 9PH. Mr & Mrs R J P Butler, 01202 732342, annebbutler@btinternet.com. *3m W of Bournemouth. At end of Wessex Way (A 338) take 3rd exit (Lindsay Rd). Continue to end. R at T-Lights. After next T-Lights, 2nd L into Kings Ave. Top of hill turn R into Spurhill Ave. Please park on road.* **Sat 16 Apr (1-4). Sun 17 Apr (1-4), also open 22 Holt Road. Sat 23, Sun 24 July (2-5). Adm £4, chd free. Home-made teas. Visits also by arrangement Apr to Oct for groups of 10 to 20.**
Town garden designed around modern house on steep slope. Over 7yrs this challenging site has been converted into a series of banks and terraces which progress from the formality of pool terraces to a gravel garden, Japanese area and woodland. The Teahouse offers a peaceful and sheltered destination from which to view the house set above its bank of Stipa grasses. Unfortunately, because of the steep slopes and gravel paths, this garden is not suitable for wheelchairs.

72 STADDLESTONES
14 Witchampton Mill, Witchampton, Wimborne BH21 5DE. Mrs Annette Lockwood. *5m N of Wimborne off B3078. Follow signs through village and park in the sports field, 7 min walk to garden, limited disabled parking near garden.* **Thur 23 June, Thur 28 July, Thur 25 Aug (2-5). Adm £4, chd free. Home-made teas.**

Cottage garden with colour themed borders, pleached limes and hidden gems, leading over chalk stream to shady area which has some unusual plants incl hardy orchids and arisaemas. Plenty of areas just to sit and enjoy the wildlife. Wire bird sculptures by local artist. Wheelchair access to first half of garden.

73 UPLODERS PLACE
Uploders, Bridport DT6 4PF. Mrs Venetia Ross Skinner. *3m E of Bridport. From A35 to Bridport or Dorchester take turning for Uploders on S side of main rd. R and R again under A35. At Crown Inn PH (excellent food) R, 2 bends and Private Parking notice.* **Sat 23, Sun 24 Apr (2-5). Adm £4.50, chd free.**
Old yews, cedar of Lebanon and a

Upwey Wishing Well

tulip tree form the bones of this garden created from wilderness in 1993. Trees and shrubs with unusual barks and flowers with rhododendrons and camellias. A quiet contemplative meander with the R Asker flowing through. Spring bulbs. Wheelchair access only to terrace by request.

🗙 ⊗ ☕

The Teahouse offers a peaceful and sheltered destination from which to view the house set above its bank of Stipa grasses . . .

74 ◆ UPTON COUNTRY PARK
Upton, Poole BH17 7BJ. Borough of Poole, 01202 262753, www.uptoncountrypark.com. *3m W of Poole town centre. On S side of A35/A3049. Follow brown signs.* **For further information, please phone or visit garden website.**
Over 100 acres of award winning parkland incl formal gardens, walled garden, woodland and shoreline. Maritime micro-climate offers a wonderful collection of unusual trees, vintage camellias and stunning roses. Home to Upton House, Grade II* listed Georgian mansion. Regular special events. Plant centre, art gallery and tea rooms. Free car parking and entry to park. Open 9am - 6 pm (winter) and 9am - 8pm (summer). Featured in Bournemouth Echo, Dorset Life, Hardy Plant Society and national press.

🗙 🗙 ⊗ 🚐 ☕

75 NEW ◆ UPWEY WISHING WELL
161 Church Street, Upwey DT3 5QE. Alan & Louisa Hardy, 01305 814470, info@upweywishingwell.co.uk, www.upweywishingwell.co.uk. *4m*

SW of Dorchester. Dorchester take A354 S, turn R onto B3159 signed Upwey. Parking available on street and in church car park (approx 2 min walk). **For opening times and information, please phone, email or visit garden website.**
Upwey Wishing Well is an award-winning tearoom within an acre of ornamental water gardens close to South Dorset Ridgeway. The gardens are full of hidden gems with an array of floral colour providing a back drop to the beautiful and tranquil water gardens. The ancient wishing well is said to have healing powers and King George III visited the garden around 1770 on a number of occasions. The gardens have been recently restored and returned to their former glory, although work is still ongoing. Dogs on leads welcome in tearoom and gardens. Open from 10.30am daily (closed Mondays). The gardens and café are fully wheelchair accessible and there are disabled toilet facilities.

♿ 🗙 🚐 ☕ 🍺

WATERDALE HOUSE
See Wiltshire

76 WESTERN GARDENS
(formerly 24A Western Ave), 24A Western Ave, Branksome Park, Poole BH13 7AN. Mr Peter Jackson. *3m W of Bournemouth. From S end Wessex Way (A338) take The Avenue, second exit. At T-lights turn R into Western Rd then L. At church turn R into Western Ave.* **Sun 31 July, Sun 28 Aug (2-5.30). Adm £4, chd free. Home-made teas.**
'This secluded and magical 1-acre garden captures the spirit of warmer climes and begs for repeated visits' (Gardening Which?). Created over 40 yrs it offers enormous variety with rose, herbaceous walk, courtyard and woodland gardens and exuberant foliage and flowers giving yr-round colour and interest enhanced by sculpture and topiary. Featured in Dorset Society magazine. Wheelchair access to ³/₄ garden.

♿ ☕

77 1692 WIMBORNE ROAD
Bear Cross BH11 9AL. Sue & Mike Cleall, 01202 573440. *5m NW of Bournemouth. On A341, 200yds E of Bear Cross r'about.* **Sun 1 May (2-5). Sun 15 May (2-5), also open 22 Holt Road. Sun 5 June (2-5), also open 17 Lower Golf Links Road. Adm £3, chd free. Home-made**

teas. Visits also by arrangement Apr to June for groups of 10+.
Suburban garden 120ft x 50ft. Rhododendrons, acers and azaleas are underplanted with woodland plants for spring. Tulips add colour. Man-made stream with waterfall and water feature runs through lawned area. Pond with statue. Fountain attracts wildlife. Various seating areas around garden and tea in summerhouse is a pleasant experience. Mostly flat areas.

♿ 🚐 ☕

78 WINCOMBE PARK
Shaftesbury SP7 9AB. John & Phoebe Fortescue. *2m N of Shaftesbury. A350 Shaftesbury to Warminster, past Wincombe Business Park, 1st R signed Wincombe & Donhead St Mary. ³/₄ m on R.* **Sun 15, Wed 18 May (2-5). Adm £4.50, chd free. Cream teas, homemade cakes and biscuits, tea, coffee and squash. Dairy and gluten free available.**
Extensive mature garden with sweeping panoramic views from lawn over parkland to lake and enchanting woods through which you can wander amongst bluebells. Garden is a riot of colour in spring with azaleas, rhododendrons and camellias in flower amongst shrubs and unusual trees. Beautiful walled kitchen garden. Partial wheelchair access, slopes and gravel paths.

♿ 🗙 ⊗ 🚐 ☕

79 WOLVERHOLLOW
Elsdons Lane, Monkton Wyld DT6 6DA. Mr & Mrs D Wiscombe, 01297 560610. *4m N of Lyme Regis. 4m NW of Charmouth. Monkton Wyld is signed from A35 approx 4m NW of Charmouth off dual carriageway. Wolverhollow is next to the church.* **Sun 15, Mon 16 May, Sun 14, Mon 15 Aug (11.30-4.30). Adm £3.50, chd free. Home-made teas. Visits also by arrangement.**
Over 1 acre of informal garden on different levels. Lawns lead past borders and rockeries down to shady lower garden. Numerous paths take you past a variety of uncommon shrubs and plants. Managed meadow has an abundance of primulas growing close to stream. A garden not to be missed! There is now a cabin in meadow area of garden from which vintage, retro and other lovely things can be purchased.

🗙 ⊗ ☕

ESSEX

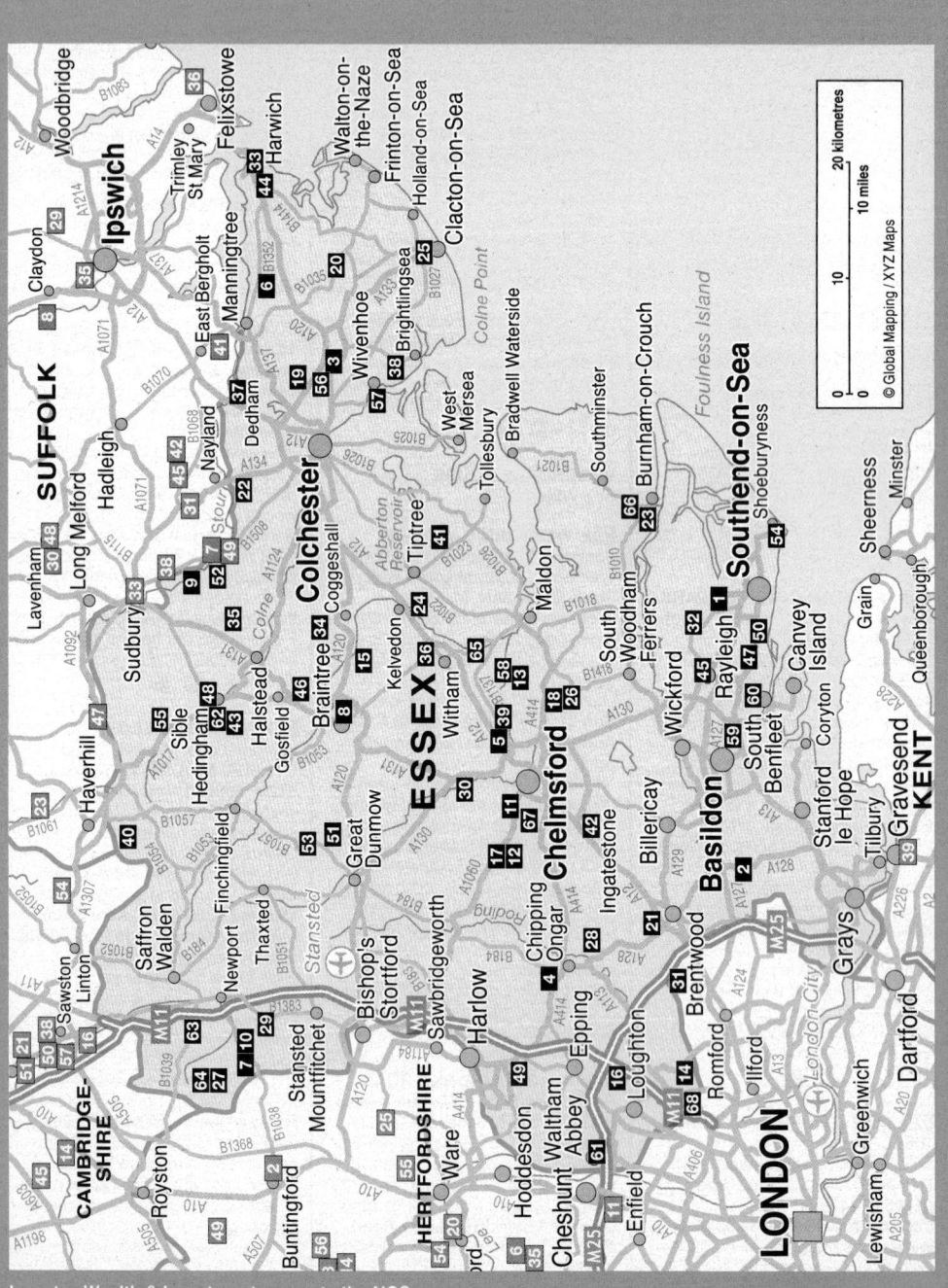

Essex

Close to London but with its own unique character, Essex is perhaps England's best kept secret – with a beautiful coastline, rolling countryside, exquisite villages and great pubs. It is a little known fact that over seventy per cent of Essex is rural.

So please come and visit our Essex gardens and gain inspiration for your own keenly cultivated patch. There are wide horizons, ancient woodlands and hamlets pierced by flint church spires.

Essex is the home of 'Constable Country', and we have a range of attractive gardens in and around that delightful picturesque area. Indeed, from the four corners of Essex we offer lots to explore, from a garden featuring the smallest thatched cottage in England within its grounds, to grand country estates. Our biggest open garden is just south of Brentwood at Barnards Farm with 60 sculptures to enjoy within 40 acres of garden and woodland.

For 2016 we have lots of exciting gardens to discover, many surrounding exquisite, 'chocolate box' thatched cottages.

So why not take the time to visit our gardens, hidden away down narrow country lanes, in attractive towns and along the estuaries of the east coast? Visitors can be assured of a warm welcome at every open garden gate.

Forget the clichés – rediscover Essex!

Essex Volunteers

County Organiser
Susan Copeland
01799 550553
susan.copeland@ngs.org.uk

County Treasurer
Richard Steers
07414 167443
steers123@aol.com

Publicity & Booklet Co-ordinator
Doug Copeland
01799 550553
dougcopeland@btinternet.com

Publicity
David Cox
01245 222165
elwylodge@gmail.com

Assistant County Organisers
Tricia Brett
01255 870415
brett.milestones@hotmail.co.uk

Avril & Roger Cole-Jones
01245 225726
randacj@gmail.com

David Cox
(as above)

Linda & Frank Jewson
01992 714047
frank.jewson@btconnect.com

Groups and Talks
Linda Holdaway
01621 782137
lindaholdaway@btinternet.com

Talks
Neil Holdaway
01621 782137
mail@neilholdaway.com

Left: April Cottage, Langley Village Gardens

Opening Dates

All entries subject to change.
For latest information check www.ngs.org.uk

Extended openings are shown at the begining of the month

February

Snowdrop Festival

Saturday 20
39 The Old Rectory

Sunday 21
39 The Old Rectory

April

15 **Feeringbury Manor (every Thursday & Friday)**

Sunday 10
42 Peacocks

Saturday 16
57 Tudor Roost

Sunday 17
57 Tudor Roost

Thursday 21
2 Barnards Farm

Sunday 24
58 Ulting Wick

Wednesday 27
18 Furzelea

Thursday 28
2 Barnards Farm

Friday 29
58 Ulting Wick

Saturday 30
51 St Helens

May

15 **Feeringbury Manor (every Thursday & Friday)**

Sunday 1
18 Furzelea
40 Parsonage House
41 Paternoster House
43 Peppers Farm
57 Tudor Roost

Monday 2
41 Paternoster House
57 Tudor Roost

Thursday 5
2 Barnards Farm

Saturday 7
19 Green Island

Sunday 8
19 Green Island
58 Ulting Wick

Monday 9
24 Kelvedon Hall

Thursday 12
2 Barnards Farm
67 Writtle College

Friday 13
58 Ulting Wick

Sunday 15
13 Elwy Lodge
42 Peacocks

Thursday 19
2 Barnards Farm

Thursday 26
2 Barnards Farm

Friday 27
11 8 Dene Court
12 Dragons

Sunday 29
9 Daws Hall
14 Fairwinds
39 The Old Rectory
53 Snares Hill Cottage

Monday 30
35 NEW 8 Mill Lane
48 Rookwoods

June

15 **Feeringbury Manor (every Thursday & Friday)**

Thursday 2
2 Barnards Farm

Friday 3
1 NEW Avalon

Festival Weekend

Saturday 4
38 Moverons

Sunday 5
1 NEW Avalon
6 Chippins
18 Furzelea
36 Miraflores
38 Moverons
47 Reprise
50 22 St Clements Drive
55 Spencers
61 Waltham Abbey Group
63 Wendens Ambo Gardens

Tuesday 7
11 8 Dene Court

Thursday 9
2 Barnards Farm
22 Horkesley Hall

Saturday 11
5 NEW Boreham Gardens
50 22 St Clements Drive (Evening)

Sunday 12
5 NEW Boreham Gardens
7 Clavering Gardens
36 Miraflores
42 Peacocks
45 Rayleigh Gardens

Tuesday 14
11 8 Dene Court

Wednesday 15
31 NEW Long House Plants

Thursday 16
2 Barnards Farm
30 NEW Little Waltham Hall
58 Ulting Wick

Saturday 18
51 St Helens

Sunday 19
4 Blake Hall
13 Elwy Lodge
23 Keeway
25 NEW 15 Kilburn Gardens
27 Langley Village Gardens
40 Parsonage House
46 Rayne Hatch Farm

Tuesday 21
11 8 Dene Court
12 Dragons

Wednesday 22
23 Keeway

Thursday 23
2 Barnards Farm

Saturday 25
2 Barnards Farm (Musical Evening)

Sunday 26
2 Barnards Farm
17 Fudlers Hall
36 Miraflores
60 37 Underhill Road
62 Washlands

Wednesday 29
62 Washlands (Evening)

Thursday 30
2 Barnards Farm

Stunning driveway, beautiful topiary shrubs . . .

July

15 **Feeringbury Manor (every Thursday & Friday)**

Friday 1
37 Monks Cottage

Sunday 3
6 Chippins
16 56 Forest Drive
28 Little Myles
47 Reprise
68 37 Turpins Lane
62 Washlands

Tuesday 5
11 8 Dene Court

Thursday 7
2 Barnards Farm

Saturday 9
57 Tudor Roost
64 Wickets (Evening)

Sunday 10
57 Tudor Roost

Wednesday 13
31 NEW Long House Plants

Thursday 14
2 Barnards Farm

Friday 15
11 8 Dene Court
12 Dragons

Saturday 16
49 69 Rundells
56 Spring Cottage
59 NEW 14 Una Road

Sunday 17
13 Elwy Lodge
17 Fudlers Hall
21 262 Hatch Road
45 Rayleigh Gardens
56 Spring Cottage
59 NEW 14 Una Road

Thursday 21
2 Barnards Farm

Friday 22
11 8 Dene Court

Sunday 24
21 262 Hatch Road
25 NEW 15 Kilburn Gardens
46 Rayne Hatch Farm
68 37 Turpins Lane
60 37 Underhill Road

Tuesday 26
11 8 Dene Court

Thursday 28
2 Barnards Farm

Saturday 30
32 262 Main Road

Peacocks

Sunday 31
47 Reprise

August

Thursday 4
2 Barnards Farm

Saturday 6
33 447 Main Road
44 NEW 10 Ramsey Road

Sunday 7
33 447 Main Road
44 NEW 10 Ramsey Road

Tuesday 9
11 8 Dene Court
12 Dragons

Thursday 11
2 Barnards Farm

Saturday 13
56 Spring Cottage
57 Tudor Roost

Sunday 14
56 Spring Cottage
57 Tudor Roost

Wednesday 17
31 NEW Long House Plants

Thursday 18
2 Barnards Farm

Saturday 20
29 NEW Little Mynchens (Evening)
32 262 Main Road

Sunday 21
25 NEW 15 Kilburn Gardens

29 NEW Little Mynchens
60 37 Underhill Road

Wednesday 24
12 Dragons

Thursday 25
2 Barnards Farm

Sunday 28
10 Deers

September

15 **Feeringbury Manor (every Thursday & Friday)**

Thursday 1
2 Barnards Farm

Sunday 4
2 Barnards Farm
16 56 Forest Drive
18 Furzelea
53 Snares Hill Cottage
68 37 Turpins Lane
61 Waltham Abbey Group

Saturday 10
38 Moverons
51 St Helens

Sunday 11
38 Moverons
55 Spencers
58 Ulting Wick

Tuesday 13
12 Dragons

Wednesday 14
31 NEW Long House Plants

Friday 16
58 Ulting Wick

October

Thursday 6
15 Feeringbury Manor

Friday 7
15 Feeringbury Manor

Saturday 15
19 Green Island

Sunday 16
19 Green Island

Gardens open to the public

3 Beth Chatto Gardens
9 Daws Hall
19 Green Island
34 Marks Hall Gardens & Arboretum
55 Spencers

By arrangement only

8 352 Coggeshall Road
20 Hannams Hall
26 Kingsteps
52 Shrubs Farm
54 South Shoebury Hall
65 Wickham Place Farm
66 Woodpeckers

Also open by arrangement

2 Barnards Farm
7 Piercewebbs, Clavering Gardens
11 8 Dene Court

12 Dragons
13 Elwy Lodge
14 Fairwinds
15 Feeringbury Manor
17 Fudlers Hall
18 Furzelea
21 262 Hatch Road
22 Horkesley Hall
31 NEW Long House Plants
36 Miraflores
37 Monks Cottage
38 Moverons
39 The Old Rectory
41 Paternoster House
42 Peacocks
43 Peppers Farm
45 1 Cherrydown, Rayleigh Gardens
45 36 London Road, Rayleigh Gardens
47 Reprise
48 Rookwoods
49 69 Rundells
51 St Helens
53 Snares Hill Cottage
56 Spring Cottage
57 Tudor Roost
68 37 Turpins Lane
58 Ulting Wick
60 37 Underhill Road
61 62 Eastbrook Road, Waltham Abbey Group
62 Washlands
67 Writtle College

Follow NGS Twitter 🇪 @NGSOpenGardens

The Gardens

1 NEW AVALON
Hall Road, Rochford SS4 1NX.
Sheila Kerr & Gary Reynolds. *3m N
of Southend on Sea, 5m E of
Rayleigh, 400yds from Rochford
Station.* Fri 3, Sun 5 June (10-4.30).
Adm £4, chd free. Home-made
teas.
A one acre plot divided into 4 areas.
Stunning driveway, beautiful topiary
shrubs. Formal Italianate garden,
interesting pergola, pond, parterre
lawns. Large rhododendrons.
Relaxing lawn area, shrub borders
and a well. Kitchen garden, fruit cage,
vegetable plot, original old
greenhouses and box hedged
borders. Enclosed area with mature
shrubs. Photographs of Avalon in the
1920/30s on display. Wheelchair
access some narrow pathways and
steps although these can be avoided.
Gravel driveway. Phone for advice
07740 355496.

2 BARNARDS FARM
Brentwood Road, West Horndon,
Brentwood CM13 3LX. Bernard &
Sylvia Holmes & The Christabella
Charitable Trust, 01277 811262,
sylvia@barnardsfarm.eu,
www.barnardsfarm.eu. *5m S of
Brentwood. On A128 1½ m S of
A127 Halfway House flyover. From
Junction continue on A128 under
the railway bridge. Garden on R just
past bridge.* Pre- booking
essential for Musical Evening Sat
25 June. adm £20 chd £10. Please
book via Barnards Farm website.
Musical Evening Opening
featuring Dixie Mix Jazz Band.
Rod Stewart's backing group on
his 2014 UK tour. Adm £20 chd
£10 incl a glass of wine
strawberries and cream.
Champagne and Wine Bar. Light
refreshments. Picnics allowed.
Sat 25 June (5-9) gates open 5pm,
concert starts 6.15pm. Every Thur
21 Apr to 1 Sept (11-4). Adm £6,
chd £2.50. Light refreshments.
Sun 26 June, Sun 4 Sept (2-5).
Adm £7.50, chd £2.50. Home-
made teas, tea, coffee, cakes,
soup and light lunches (Thurs),
home-made cakes, teas (Suns).
Visits also by arrangement May to
Sept for groups of 20 min.
Donation to St Francis Church.
So much to explore! Climb the
belvedere for the wider view or take
the train through the woodland.
Spring bulbs and blossom, summer
beds and borders, ponds, lakes and
streams, walled vegetable plot.
'Japanese garden', sculptures grand
and quirky enhance and delight.
Barnards Miniature Railway rides
(BMR). Sunday extras: Bernard's
Sculpture tour 3pm. Veteran and
vintage vehicle collection. 1920s
Cycle shop Collect loyalty points on
Thur visits and earn a free Sun or
Thur visit. Aviators welcome (PPO),
see website for details. Wheelchair
accessible WC Golf buggy tour
available.

3 ◆ BETH CHATTO GARDENS
Elmstead Market, Colchester
CO7 7DB. Mrs Beth Chatto, 01206
822007, www.bethchatto.co.uk.
*¼ E of Elmstead Market. On A133
Colchester to Clacton Rd in village of
Elmstead Market.* For opening times
and information, please phone or
visit garden website.
Internationally famous gardens,
including dry, damp and woodland
areas. The result of over fifty years of
hard work and application of the huge
body of plant knowledge possessed
by Beth Chatto and her late husband
Andrew. Visitors cannot fail to be
affected by the peace and beauty of
the garden. Large plant nursery and
modern Tea Room. Admission £6.95,
chd under 14 free. Carers free.
Disabled WC & parking.

4 BLAKE HALL
Bobbingworth CM5 0DG. Mr & Mrs
H Capel Cure,
www.blakehall.co.uk. *10m W of
Chelmsford. Just off A414 between
Four Wantz r'about in Ongar & Talbot
r'about in North Weald. Signed on
A414.* Sun 19 June (11-4). Adm £4,
chd free. Home-made teas in C17
barn.
25 acres of mature gardens within the

Elwy Lodge

historic setting of Blake Hall (not open). Arboretum with broad variety of specimen trees. Spectacular rambling roses clamber up ancient trees. Traditional formal rose garden and herbaceous border. Sweeping lawns. Some gravel paths.

GROUP OPENING

5 NEW BOREHAM GARDENS
Boreham, Chelmsford CM3 3EF. *4m NE Chelmsford. Take B1137 Boreham Village, turn into Church Rd at Lion Inn. Caynton Cottage is 50mtrs on L. Brookfield 400mtrs on R, Monalee is accessed from Brookfield.* Sat 11 June (11–5); Sun 12 June (1–5). Combined adm £5, chd free. Home-made teas at Brookfield. Cream teas.

> **NEW BROOKFIELD**
> Bob & Linda Taylor

> **NEW CAYNTON COTTAGE**
> Les & Lynn Mann

> **NEW MONALEE**
> Andrew & Debora Overington

Three stunning, inspirational and very different gardens in the lovely village of Boreham. At Brookfield, a rose covered wall backing a perennial border greets you, with a raised bed vegetable garden, perennial island beds and pond with shrub bank. A meadow, bright with buttercups, is bordered by many trees and a woodland walk, where the last rhododendrons and camellias may be seen. Roses abound and the Rambling Rector in the orchard is a delight. Since 2013 the new garden at Caynton Cottage has been designed and planted by the owners from a neglected and overgrown plot surrounding a C15 thatched cottage. It is now planted with an excellent selection of shrubs and perennials for maximum all year interest, with a small wildlife pond and dry stream. At Monalee, after the removal of several trees, the new light gained has allowed larger, colourful flower beds to flourish. Highlights are an oriental garden, raised pond, new cut flower bed, enclosed patio and summer house. Brookfield, wheelchair accessible, partial access to meadow. Caynton Cottage gravel paths throughout, Monalee narrow paths, not wheelchair friendly.

6 CHIPPINS
Heath Road, Bradfield CO11 2UZ. Kit & Ceri Leese, 01255 870730, ceriandkit1@btinternet.com. *3m E of Manningtree. On B1352, take main rd through village. Bungalow is directly opp primary school.* Sun 5 June, Sun 3 July (11–4.30). Adm £3.50, chd free. Cream teas. Delicious home made cakes also available!
Artist's garden and plantaholics paradise packed with interest. Springtime heralds irises, hostas and alliums. Stream and wildlife pond brimming with bog plants. Summer hosts an explosion of colour-abundance of tubs and hanging baskets. Wide borders feature hemerocallis with swathes of lilies, later dahlias and exotics (front bed featuring, aeonium unusual agaves, aloes and cacti). Kit is a landscape artist, pictures always on display.

GROUP OPENING

7 CLAVERING GARDENS
Clavering CB11 4PX. Mr S H Cooke. *7m N of Bishop's Stortford. On B1038. Turn W off B1383 at Newport.* Sun 12 June (2–5). Combined adm £7, chd free.

> **APRIL COTTAGE**
> Anne & Neil Harris

> **NEW CHESTNUT COTTAGE**
> Carol & Mike Wilkinson

> **DEERS**
> Mr S H Cooke
> (See separate entry)

> **PIERCEWEBBS**
> Mrs J William-Powlett
> Visits also by arrangement Mar to Oct.
> jwp@william-powlett.net

Popular village with many C16/17 timber-framed dwellings. Beautiful C14 church, village green with thatched cricket pavilion and pitch. Deers (see separate entry) for 9 acres, judged by visitors to be a very romantic garden. April Cottage, charming and thatched with well established colourful garden packed with many unusual plants, old fashioned roses, clematis, wildlife and ornamental pond. Lined damp garden with primula candelabras and astilbes. Hosta collection. All to be discovered down winding paths. Chestnut Cottage garden is on

several levels, sweeping lawns, mixed borders with stunning views over historic heart of village. Piercewebbs is formal walled garden, lawns, shrubs, topiary, trellised rose garden. Jamie Oliver was brought up in Clavering where his parents still run The Cricketers PH. At Chestnut Cottage see 'The Little House' reputedly smallest thatched cottage in England. Dogs on leads please but no dogs at Chestnut Cottage. Parking available at Fox PH. April Cottage 1m away at Sheepcote Green. Wheelchair access at Deers to main lawn flowerbeds, vegetable garden. April Cottage: some narrow paths. Very limited access at Chestnut Cottage due to slopes.

> *Three stunning, inspirational and very different gardens in the lovely village of Boreham . . .*

8 352 COGGESHALL ROAD
Braintree CM7 9EH. Sau Lin Goss, 01376 329753, Richandsally.goss@yahoo.com. *15m W of Colchester, 10m N of Chelmsford. From M11 J8 take A120 Colchester. Follow A120 to Braintree r'about (McDonalds). 1st exit into Cressing rd follow to T-lights. R into Coggeshall rd.* Visits by arrangement May to Aug 15 min. 35 max. Light refreshments.
Sau Lin was born and raised in Hong Kong and brought up on the family small holding. She loves gardening and is rarely away from the garden. 'My little heaven', she says of her garden which has themed areas, perennials, roses and many other plants. Japanese mixed border, fruit trees and shrubs. Seating and relaxing areas, fish pond with plants and wildlife. Mediterranean patio with a wide array of pots. Partial wheelchair access, ramp from patio to main garden.

9 ◆ DAWS HALL

Henny Road, Lamarsh, Bures CO8 5EX. Major Iain Grahame, 01787 269213, info@majorbooks.co.uk, www.dawshallnature.co.uk. *3m from Sudbury. 2m from Bures on Essex side of R. Stour.* For NGS: Sun 29 May (1-5). Adm £5, chd free. Cream teas (on NGS day only). For other opening times and information, please phone, email or visit garden website.

8 acres of rare, unusual trees, shrubs and a huge collection of old-fashioned roses, all labeled. Series of interlinking ponds containing a collection of native and exotic waterfowl, incl a breeding flock of Red-breasted Geese. 20 acre nature reserve incl river, stream, woodland and wild flower meadow. Thousands of spring bulbs, superb autumn colours. Observation bee hive, own honey for sale. Guided tours for groups (min 8) in aid of The Daws Hall Trust.

10 DEERS

Clavering CB11 4PX. Mr S H Cooke. *7m N of Bishop's Stortford on B1038. Turn W off B1383 (old A11) at Newport & follow signs to Clavering then Langley & 1st L to Ford End (³/₄ m).* Sun 28 Aug (2-5). Adm £5, chd free. Home-made teas. Opening with Clavering Gardens on Sun 12 June. *Donation to Clavering Jubilee Field.*

9 acres. Judged by visitors to be a romantic set of gardens. The R Stort runs through the gardens. Shrub and herbaceous borders, 3 ponds with water lilies, old roses in formal garden, pool garden, walled vegetable garden, moon gate, field and woodland walks. Plenty of seats to enjoy the tranquility of the gardens. A wildlife oasis in a farming desert. 2016 marks 25th Anniversary of our gardens being open under the Scheme as well as 50 years at Deers for the Cooke family. Dogs on leads please. Featured in Garden News 'Garden of the Week'. Wheelchair access main lawn and flower beds plus vegetable garden only.

11 8 DENE COURT

Chignall Road, Chelmsford CM1 2JQ. Mrs Sheila Chapman, 01245 266156. *W of Chelmsford (Parkway). Take A1060 Roxwell Rd for 1m. Turn R at T-lights into Chignall Rd. Dene Court 3rd exit on R. Parking in Chignall Rd.* Fri 27 May (2-5), also open Dragons, Tue 7, Tue 14 June (2-5), Tue 21 June (2-5), also open Dragons, Tue 5 July (2-5), Fri 15 July (2-5), also open Dragons, Fri 22, Tue 26 July (2-5), Tue 9 Aug (2-5), also open Dragons. Adm £3, chd free. Visits also by arrangement June to Aug.

Beautifully maintained and designed compact garden (250sq yds). Owner is well-known RHS gold medal-winning exhibitor (now retired). Circular lawn, long pergola and walls festooned with roses and climbers. Large selection of unusual clematis. Densely-planted colour coordinated perennials add interest from May to Sept in this immaculate garden.

WE ARE **MACMILLAN.** CANCER SUPPORT

In 2015 Macmillan celebrated 30 years of partnership with the NGS

12 DRAGONS

Boyton Cross, Chelmsford CM1 4LS. Mrs Margot Grice, 01245 248651, mandmdragons@tiscali.co.uk. *3m W of Chelmsford. On A1060. ¹/₂ m W of The Hare PH.* Fri 27 May, Tue 21 June, Fri 15 July, Tue 9 Aug (2-5), also open 8 Dene Court, Wed 24 Aug, Tue 13 Sept (2-5). Adm £4, chd free. Tea. Visits also by arrangement Jan to Oct.

A plantswoman's ³/₄ -acre garden, planted to encourage wildlife. Sumptuous colour-themed borders with striking plant combinations, featuring specimen plants, fernery, clematis,and grasses. Meandering paths lead to ponds, patio, scree garden and small vegetable garden. Two summerhouses, one overlooking stream and farmland. Featured in Essex Life.

13 ELWY LODGE

West Bowers Rd, Woodham Walter CM9 6RZ. David & Laura Cox, 01245 222165, elwylodge@gmail.com. *Just outside Woodham Walter village. From Chelmsford, A414 to Danbury. L at 2nd mini r'about into Little Baddow Rd. From Colchester, A12 to Hatfield Peverel, L onto B1019. Follow NGS signs.* Sun 15 May (11-5); Sun 19 June, Sun 17 July (10-5). Adm £4.50, chd free. Home-made teas. Seasonal and Special home made cakes (Suns) not to be missed. Visits also by arrangement May to July.

On entering the drive, the hidden secrets of this highly praised, peaceful garden will surprise and delight! Flowing lawns, herbaceous borders, unusual plants, trees, wildlife pond, sedum roof and a meadow area. Secluded chamomile-scented lower garden with raised vegetable. beds and fruit garden. leading to a delightful summer house with amazing views over the countryside towards the Blackwater Estuary. Sloping uneven lawn in parts. Please check wheelchair access with garden owner before visiting.

14 FAIRWINDS

Chapel Lane, Chigwell Row, Chigwell IG7 6JJ. Sue & David Coates, 07731 796467, scoates@forest.org.uk. *2m SE of Chigwell. Grange Hill Tube, turn R at exit, 10 mins walk uphill. Nr M25 J26 & N Circular, turn off Lambourne Rd signed Chigwell. Park in Lodge Close Car Park.* Sun 29 May (2-5.30). Adm £3.50, chd free. Home-made teas. Free refills of tea/coffee. Visits also by arrangement Mar to Oct refreshments only by arrangement. Groups preferred.

A gravelled front garden and three differently styled back garden areas, Places for you to sit, relax and enjoy. A rich variety of planting influenced by Beth Chatto, Penelope Hobhouse and Christopher Lloyd. Start with themed flower borders. Hidden beyond is a woodland garden; home to shade loving plants and our hens. Finally, beyond the rustic fence, lies the wildlife pond and vegetable plot. Happy hens. Happy insects in bee house, bug house, log piles and sampling the spring pollen. Newts in pond. There be dragons a plenty!! Gardeners World photo shoot with Joe Swift. Also filming for Gardeners

World wildlife dvds. Space for 2 disabled cars to park by the house. Wood chip paths in woodland area may require assistance.

15 FEERINGBURY MANOR
Coggeshall Road, Feering, Colchester CO5 9RB. Mr & Mrs Giles Coode-Adams, 01376 561946, seca@btinternet.com. *12m SW of Colchester. Between Feering & Coggeshall on Coggeshall Rd, 1m from Feering village.* Every Thur and Fri 1 Apr to 29 July (9-4). Every Thur and Fri 1 Sept to 7 Oct (9-4). Adm £5, chd free. **Visits also by arrangement.** *Donation to Firstsite.* There is always plenty to see in this 10 acre garden with two ponds and river Blackwater. Jewelled lawn in early April then spectacular tulips and blossom lead on to a huge number of different and colourful plants, many unusual, culminating in a purple explosion of michaelmas daisies in Sept. Sculpture by Ben Coode-Adams. Featured in Essex Life and Country Life. No wheelchair access to arboretum, steep slope.

&

16 56 FOREST DRIVE
Theydon Bois CM16 7EZ. John & Barbara. *2m S of Epping. J26 on M25 onto A121 to Wake Arms r'about 2nd exit B 172 into Theydon Bois. Turn L at The Bull PH 1st L into rd. Central line station 2nd on R.* Sun 3 July, Sun 4 Sept (12-5). Adm £3, chd free. Teas, coffee, available in the summerhouse.
Elegant, tranquil garden set on a sloping site, developed by us since 1996, featuring specimen trees and plants. Shaded seating areas in this surprisingly secluded natural garden allow visitors to sit and watch the birds and admire Gladys in her reflective pool. Along with a collection of historic motorcycles.

17 FUDLERS HALL
Fox Road, Mashbury, Chelmsford CM1 4TJ. Mr & Mrs A J Meacock, 01245 231335. *7m NW of Chelmsford. Chelmsford take A1060, R into Chignal Rd. 1/2 m L to Chignal St James approx 5m, 2nd R into Fox Rd signed Gt Waltham. From Gt Waltham take Barrack Lane for 2m.* Sun 26 June, Sun 17 July (2-6). Adm £4, chd free. Tea. **Visits also by arrangement June & July.** An award winning, romantic 2 acre

garden surrounding C17 farmhouse with lovely pastoral views. Old walls divide garden into many rooms, each having a different character, featuring long herbaceous borders, ropes and pergolas festooned with rambling old fashioned roses. Enjoy the vibrant hot border in late summer. Yew hedged kitchen garden. Ample seating.

&

18 FURZELEA
Bicknacre Road, Danbury CM3 4JR. Avril & Roger Cole-Jones, 01245 225726, randacj@gmail.com. *4m E of Chelmsford, 4m W of Maldon A414 to Danbury. At village centre turn S into Mayes Lane Take first R. Go past Cricketers PH, L on to Bicknacre Rd see NT carpark on L (Park in carpark) garden 50m further on R (3rd house on R).* Wed 27 Apr (2-5); Sun 1 May, Sun 5 June, Sun 4 Sept (11-5). Adm £4, chd free. Home-made teas. Renowned for the quality and variety of our home-made cakes. **Visits also by arrangement Apr to Sept, groups 15+ (not Aug).** A Victorian country house surrounded by a garden designed, created and maintained by the owners to provide maximum all year round interest. The colour coordinated borders and beds are enhanced with topiary, grasses, climbers and many unusual plants. Spring incl tulips and summer bursts into colour with roses and perennials continuing into autumn with vibrant showy dahlias and many other exotics. Opp Danbury Common (NT), short walk to Danbury Country Park and Lakes and short drive to RHS Hyde Hall. National and local publications. Very limited wheelchair access, with some steps and gravel paths and drive.

19 ◆ GREEN ISLAND
Park Road, Ardleigh CO7 7SP. Fiona Edmond, 01206 230455, fionaedmond7@aol.com, www.greenislandgardens.co.uk. *3m NE of Colchester. From Ardleigh village centre, take B1029 towards Great Bromley. Park Rd is 2nd on R after level Xing. Garden is last on L.* For NGS: Sat 7, Sun 8 May, Sat 15, Sun 16 Oct (10-5). Adm £6, chd £2. Home-made teas. Light lunches, and home made cakes. **For other opening times and information, please phone, email or visit garden website.**
'A garden for all seasons' A

plantsman's paradise with 20 acres packed with rare and unusual plants. Carved within mature woodland are huge island beds, Japanese garden, terrace, gravel garden, seaside garden, water gardens and extensive woodland plantings. Also tearoom with homemade cakes and snacks and nursery offering plants all seen growing in the gardens. Bluebells and azaleas, acers and rhododendrons in May. Water gardens, island beds all summer. Stunning Autumn colour. Featured on the front cover of the English Garden, Mon Jardin et Ma Maison and Garden Answers. Flat and easy walking /pushing wheelchairs. Ramps at entrance and tearoom. Disabled parking and toilets.

The shaded pergola seating area with a water feature . . .

20 HANNAMS HALL
Thorpe Road, Tendring CO16 9AR. Mr & Mrs W Gibbon, 01255 830292, w.gibbon331@btinternet.com. *10m E of Colchester. From A120 take B1035 at Horsley Cross, through Tendring Village (approx 3m) pass Bicycle PH on R, after 1/3m over small bridge 1st house L.* Visits by arrangement Mar to Nov 30 max. Adm £6.50, chd free. Tea. C17 house (not open) set in 6 acres of formal and informal gardens and grounds with extensive views over open countryside. Herbaceous borders and shrubberies, many interesting trees incl flowering paulownias. Lawns and mown walks through wild grass and flower meadows, woodland walks, ponds and stream. Walled vegetable potager and orchard. Lovely autumn colour. Some gravel paths.

21 262 HATCH ROAD
Pilgrims Hatch, Brentwood
CM15 9QR. **Mike & Liz Thomas,
01277 220584, mikethomas-
home@btconnect.com.** *2m N of
Brentwood town centre. On A128
N toward Ongar turn R onto
Doddinghurst Rd at mini-r'about (to
Brentwood Centre) After the Centre
turn next L into Hatch Rd. Garden 4th
on R.* **Sun 17, Sun 24 July
(11-4.30). Adm £4, chd free.
Home-made teas. Visits also by
arrangement July & Aug min
parties of ten.**
A formal frontage with lavender. An
eclectic rear garden of around an
acre divided into 'rooms' with themed
borders, several ponds, three green
houses, fruit and vegetable plots and
oriental garden. There is also a secret
white garden, spring and summer
wild flower meadows, folly and an
exotic area. There is plenty of seating
to enjoy the views and a cup of tea.

22 HORKESLEY HALL
Little Horkesley, Colchester
CO6 4DB. **Mr & Mrs Johnny Eddis,
078085 99290,
pollyeddis@hotmail.com.** *6m N of
Colchester City Centre. 2m W of
A134. Drive through Little Horkesley
Church car park & access is via low
double black gates at the far end. 10
mins from A12, 20 from Sudbury &
1hr from Newmarket.* **Thur 9 June
(10.30-4). Adm £6, chd free.
Home-made teas. Visits also by
arrangement Mar to Oct very
flexible and warm welcome
assured! Coffee, teas or light
lunch available by arrangement.**
8 acres of romantic garden
surrounding classical house (not
open) in mature parkland setting.
Stream feeds 2 lakes. Ancient,
enormous trees. Largest ginkgo tree
outside Kew. Walled garden, pear
avenue, acer walk, eucalyptus.
Blossom, spring bulbs, roses. Formal
terrace overlooking sweeping lawns
to wild woodland. A timeless, family
garden with recent and ongoing
improvements. Wonderful natural
setting, vast plane trees and stunning
tree barks. Large Victorian
glasshouse, walled garden, scented
plants and established climbers
including roses, clematis, wisteria,
hydrangea. A charming enclosed
swimming pool garden and long-
established bay and yew. Plants
sometimes for sale. Limited
wheelchair access to some areas,

gravel paths and slopes quite easy
access to tea area with lovely views
over lake and garden.

23 KEEWAY
Ferry Road, Creeksea, nr
Burnham-on-Crouch CM0 8PL.
John & Sue Ketteley. *2m W of
Burnham-on-Crouch. B1010 to
Burnham on Crouch. At town sign
take 1st R into Ferry Rd signed
Creeksea & Burnham Golf Club &
follow NGS signs.* **Sun 19, Wed 22
June (2-5). Adm £4, chd free.
Home-made teas.**
Large, mature country garden with
stunning views over the R Crouch.
Formal terraces surround the house
with steps leading to sweeping lawns,
mixed borders packed full of bulbs
and early perennials, a formal rose
and herb garden with interesting
water feature. Further afield there are
wilder areas, fields and paddocks. A
productive greenhouse, vegetable
and cutting gardens complete the
picture.

Wander through
the orchard
and say
'hello' to
Camilla the
Cow . . .

24 KELVEDON HALL
Kelvedon, Colchester CO5 9BN. **Mr
& Mrs Jack Inglis.** *Take Maldon Rd
from Kelvedon High St over A12.
After bridge turn R onto Kelvedon Rd.
Turn 1st L, single gravel road, oak
tree on corner.* **Mon 9 May (1.30-4).
Adm £5, chd free. Home-made
teas in the Modern Pool House
Walled Garden, weather
permitting.**
Varied 6 acre garden surrounding a

pretty C18 Farmhouse. A blend of
formal and informal spaces
interspersed with modern sculpture.
Pleached hornbeam and topiary
provide structure. Courtyard walled
garden juxtaposes a modern walled
pool garden, both providing season
long displays. Herbaceous borders
offset an abundance of roses around
the house. Lily covered ponds with a
new wet garden. Topiary, sculpture,
tulips and roses. Featured in Country
Homes and Interiors and Period
Living.

**25 NEW 15 KILBURN
GARDENS**
Clacton-On-Sea CO16 7HB.
Mr & Mrs Sue & Sean Daniels. *NW
of Clacton-on-Sea. From A133 at
r'about turn R onto B1027 St Johns
Rd. First L Hampstead Ave. Parking
only in Hampstead Ave. Continue on
foot 1st L then 1st R.* **Sun 19 June,
Sun 24 July, Sun 21 Aug (10-4).
Adm £3, chd free.**
A small, L shaped town garden,
densely planted with a varied mix of
shrubs and perennials. The front
garden is Mediterranean in style,
while the main garden with a lawn is
surrounded by borders of salvias,
roses, grasses, ginger plants, cannas
and heucheras. Turn into the shaded
pergola seating area with a water
feature, and then the third part of the
garden is planted for shade loving
plants.

26 KINGSTEPS
Moor Hall Lane, Danbury
CM3 4ER. **Mr David Greenwood,
01245 223883, david-
greenwood@live.com.**
*Bicknacre/Danbury. A414 from
Chelmsford Turn R at The Bell in
Danbury. L at T-junction approx 1¹⁄₂
m. R turn by post box into Moor Hall
Lane.* **Visits by arrangement May
to Sept. Adm £3.00, chd free.
Home-made teas.**
Country garden in ¹⁄₂ acre plot.
Gardens front and rear with good
selection of herbaceous plants and
shrubs, roses, fuchsias, dahlias,
begonias, bedding plants, tubs and
hanging baskets. Fish pond with Koi
carp and others. Well kept lawns and
plenty of colour, especially late
summer. Large horse chestnut tree in
rear. Many seating areas.

GROUP OPENING

27 LANGLEY VILLAGE GARDENS

Langley Upper Green, Saffron Walden CB11 4RY. *7m W of Saffron Walden 10m N of Bishops Stortford. At Newport take B1038. After 3m turn R at Clavering, signed Langley. Upper Green is 3m further on. Sheepcote Green will also be signed on day.* **Sun 19 June (11-5). Combined adm £7, chd free. Light refreshments at Village Hall on Langley Village Green. Light lunches & home-made teas.**

APRIL COTTAGE
Mr & Mrs Harris

THE CHESTNUTS
Jane & David Knight

CHURCH COTTAGE
Jago Russell & Maeve Polkinhorn

WICKETS
Susan & Doug Copeland
(See separate entry)

April Cottage, at Sheepcote Green just 2m from Langley is a charming thatched cottage, with well established and colourful garden packed with unusual plants; roses, clematis, wildlife and ornamental ponds, lined damp garden, hosta collection. The Chestnuts is a large garden with many mature trees surrounding thatched cottage on village green, new planting beds, extensive grass meadow. Church Cottage is a 1/3 acre informal cottage garden, countryside views with Interesting planting, perennials, grasses, roses, climbers and shrubs, Seating to relax and enjoy garden. June highlights incl. abundant roses. Wickets has wide, mixed borders, hundreds of roses feature, landscaped meadows, lily pond, parterre and gravel garden. Langley is highest Essex village set in rolling countryside. Gravel drive at Wickets.

28 LITTLE MYLES

Ongar Road, Stondon Massey, Brentwood CM15 0LD. Judy & Adrian Cowan, Littlemyles@gmail.com. *1½ m SE of Chipping Ongar. Off A128 at Stag PH, Marden Ash, towards Stondon Massey. Over bridge, 1st house on R*

262 Hatch Road

after S bend. 400yds Ongar side of Stondon Church. **Sun 3 July (11-4). Adm £3.50, chd £1. Home-made teas.**
Romantic, naturalistic garden full of hidden features, set in 3 acres. Full borders, meandering paths to Beach Garden, Perennial Prairie border, Exotic Jungle around elephant, monkeys and giraffe. Fountains, sculptures and tranquil benches. Hidden Asian garden, Slate garden, hornbeam pergola, ornamental vegetable patch and natural pond. Herb garden that inspired Little Myles herbal cosmetics. Crafts and handmade herbal cosmetics for sale. Explorers sheet and map for children. Featured in Essex Life. Gravel paths.

29 NEW LITTLE MYNCHENS

Brick Kiln Lane, Rickling, Saffron Walden CB11 3YH. Mr Howard Crouch. *5m N of Bishops Stortford. ¼ m from Rickling village green past copse in Brick Kiln Lane, signed Clavering & Rickling Church. Car parking in nearby farmyard.* **Evening opening Sat 20 Aug (5-8). Wine. Sun 21 Aug (2-5). Home-made teas. Adm £5, chd free.**
Wander through the orchard and say 'hello' to Camilla the Cow. Enter an artistic garden behind an historic thatched cottage to a garden featuring long, deep borders with imaginative planting. Witty artwork, sculptures, topiary and stumpery. Unique living painted trees. Natural pond and meadow with unusual features. A surprise wherever you look! Partial wheelchair access.

Share your day out on and

30 NEW **LITTLE WALTHAM HALL**

Little Waltham, Chelmsford CM3 3LJ. Mr Rupert & Lady Vanessa Watson. *On the corner of Brook Hill & Back Lane in Little Waltham. Entrance opposite the gates to Little Waltham church. Please park carefully on the street.* **Thur 16 June (2-5). Adm £5, chd free. Home-made teas.**
A four acre garden, with sweeping lawns bordered by mature shrubs, forms a fine setting for the C18 listed Hall. The walled garden, in which informal herbaceous planting complements structural formality, is of special interest. Good wheelchair access but paths are gravelled.

31 NEW **LONG HOUSE PLANTS**

Church Road, Noak Hill, Romford RM4 1LD. Tim Carter, 01708 371719, tim@longhouse-plants.co.uk, www.longhouse-plants.co.uk. *3¹/₂ m NW of J28 M25. J28 M25 take A1023 Brentwood. At 1st T-lights, turn L to South Weald after 0.8m turn L at T junction. After 1.6m turn L, over M25 after ¹/₂ m turn R into Church Rd, nursery opp church.* **Wed 15 June, Wed 13 July, Wed 17 Aug, Wed 14 Sept (11-4). Adm £5, chd £3. Home-made teas. Visits also by arrangement Feb to Oct Mon - Thur inclusive (not Bank Hol). Groups of 10+. Additional fee for conducted tours.**
A beautiful garden - yes, but one with a purpose. Long House Plants has been producing home grown plants for more than 10 years - here is a chance to see where it all begins! With wide paths and plenty of seats carefully placed to enjoy the plants and views. It has been thoughtfully designed so that the collections of plants look great together through all seasons.

32 **262 MAIN ROAD**

Hawkwell, Hockley SS5 4NW. Karen Mann. *3m NE of Rayleigh. From A127 at Rayleigh Weir take B1013 towards Hockley. Garden on L after White Hart PH & village green.* **Sat 30 July, Sat 20 Aug (1-5.30). Adm £3.50, chd free. Home-made teas.**
The garden comprises of 185 metres of island beds and borders sited on

¹/₃ acre. Some of the borders are elevated from the house resulting in steep banks which provide a different and interesting aspect. Salvia, dahlia, hedychium, brugmansia peak in the summer months.

> Wildlife is very important in our garden and we keep areas in a natural (wild) state . . .

33 **447 MAIN ROAD**

Harwich CO12 4HB. J Shrive & S McGarry. *1m out of Dovercourt town centre. Follow the signs along the A120 to Harwich. Turn R at 1st r'about, up towards church, proceed along main rd, straight over 3 mini r'abouts, on R after shops. All signed.* **Sat 6, Sun 7 Aug (11-4). Adm £3, chd free. Home-made teas. Also open 10 Ramsey Road.**
Come and view something different. No bedding plants or shrubs,unless you want to argue about the Banana plants being one. Large town garden totally redesigned in 2007 as a tropical oasis, with its own Treasure Island and treasure chest and a new Tree Fern walk and borders brimming with colour. A decking area for teas and delicious cakes! Featured in Colchester Gazette and Essex Coastal Life.

34 ◆ **MARKS HALL GARDENS & ARBORETUM**

Coggeshall CO6 1TG. Marks Hall Estate, 01376 563796, enquiries@markshall.org.uk, www.markshall.org.uk. *1¹/₂ m N of Coggeshall. Follow brown & white tourism signs from A120 Coggeshall bypass.* **For opening times current admission charges and information, please phone, email or visit garden website.**
Marks Hall Gardens and Arboretum features a tree collection from all the temperate areas of the world set in more than 200 acres of historic landscape providing interest and enjoyment throughout the year.

Highlights include: the Millennium Walk designed for structure, colour and scent on the shortest days of the year; the largest planting in Europe of Wollemi pine and the inspired combination of traditional and contemporary planting in the C18 Walled Garden. Spring snowdrop and autumn colour displays are annual highlights. Featured in Daily Mail - Weekend Magazine 'The colourful Millennium Walk is especially striking ...' The Mail on Sunday '...gem near Colchester'. Hard paths lead to all key areas of interest. Wheelchairs or staff-driven buggy available for visitors with mobility issues (booking essential).

35 NEW **8 MILL LANE**

Pebmarsh, Halstead CO9 2NW. Danny McGovern & Michael Roberts. *Half way between Sudbury and Halstead. From Braintree A120 take A131. From Colchester A1124 at White Colne village green follow sign 'Pebmarsh 3 Miles'.* **Mon 30 May (12-4). Adm £5, chd free.**
Our garden is a series of formal and informal 'rooms'. A mixture of herbaceous and shrub beds, with many beautiful trees, most of which we planted. Wildlife is very important in our garden and we keep areas in a natural (wild) state. This encourages a diverse variety of wild creatures which share the garden with us.

36 **MIRAFLORES**

5 Rowan Way, Witham CM8 2LJ. Yvonne & Danny Owen, 07976 603863, danny@dannyowen.co.uk. *ACCESS via CM8 2PS. For SATNAV house postcode is not to be used, as access is from the rear of the garden via Forest Rd & please follow yellow signs.* **Sun 5, Sun 12, Sun 26 June (2-5). Adm £3, chd free. Home-made teas. Visits also by arrangement May & June 10 min 20 max, £7 inc cream tea.**
An award-winning, medium-sized garden described by one visitor as a ''Little Bit of Heaven''. A blaze of colour with roses, clematis, pergola rose arch, triple fountain with box hedging and deep herbaceous borders. See our 'Folly', and our exuberant and cascading hanging baskets. Featured in Garden Answers and Essex Life. We have tranquil seating areas and cakes to die for, some being gluten free.

37 MONKS COTTAGE

Monks Lane, Dedham nr Colchester CO7 6DP. Nicola Baker, 01206 322210, nicola_baker@tiscali.co.uk. *6m NE of Colchester. Leave Dedham village with the church on L. Take 2nd main rd on R (Coles Oak Lane) Monks Lane is first rd on L.* Fri 1 July (11-5). Adm £3.50, chd free. Tea. **Visits also by arrangement May to July, small groups.**
¹/₂ acre cottage garden on a sloping site in the heart of Constable country. Colour-themed borders filled with bulbs, shrubs and perennials. Mature trees and pond. Highlights include roses, clematis and box-edged parterre beds. Features incl boggy area with strong foliage shapes and small woodland garden. Gin-and-tonic balcony with views of the garden. New for 2016 - rill garden and terrace garden.

38 MOVERONS

Brightlingsea CO7 0SB. Lesley & Payne Gunfield, 01206 305498, lesleyorrock@me.com, www.moverons.co.uk. *7m SE of Colchester. At old church turn R signed Moverons Farm. Follow lane & garden signs for approx 1m. Beware some SatNavs take you the wrong side of the river.* Sat 4, Sun 5 June, Sat 10, Sun 11 Sept (11-5). Adm £5, chd free. Home-made teas. **Visits also by arrangement June to Sept for groups of 10+ only.**
Beautiful tranquil 4 acre garden in touch with its surroundings and enjoying stunning estuary views. A wide variety of planting in mixed borders to suit different growing conditions and provide all year colour. Courtyard, reflection pool, large natural ponds, sculptures and barn for rainy day teas! Magnificent trees some over 300yrs old give this garden real presence.

39 THE OLD RECTORY

Church Road, Boreham CM3 3EP. Sir Jeffery & Lady Bowman, 01245 467233, bowmansuzy@btinternet.com. *4m NE of Chelmsford. Take B1137 Boreham Village, turn into Church Rd at the Lion PH. ¹/₂ m along on R opp church.* Sat 20, Sun 21 Feb (12-3). Light refreshments. Sun 29 May (2-5). Home-made teas. Adm £5, chd free. Hot soup & hot sausages in rolls (Feb). **Visits also**

by arrangement Feb to June for groups of 10+.
2¹/₂ -acre garden surrounding C15 house (not open). Ponds, stream, with bridges and primulas, small wild flower meadow and wood with interesting trees and shrubs, herbaceous borders with emphasis on complementary colours. Vegetable garden. February opening for crocus, snowdrops and cyclamen. Possibly largest gunnera in Essex. Lovely views over Chelmer/Blackwater canal. Stream, ponds, woodland garden. Stunning wisteria in May. Herbaceous borders. Refreshments soup and roll type lunch in winter. Teas or evening refreshments in summer. Featured in Country Homes and Interiors, Essex Chronicle, East Anglian Daily News. Wheelchair access, gravel drive but large part of garden accessible.

Marie Curie

Last year, NGS funded 25,000 hours of our nursing care

40 PARSONAGE HOUSE

Wiggens Green, Helions Bumpstead, Haverhill CB9 7AD. The Hon & Mrs Nigel Turner. *3m S of Haverhill. From the Xrds in the village centre go up past the Church for approx 1m. Parking on R through a five bar gate into the orchard.* Sun 1 May, Sun 19 June (2-5). Adm £4, chd free. Home-made teas. Apple juice from the orchard available on the day for sale.
C15 house (not open) surrounded by 3 acres of formal gardens with mixed borders, topiary, pond, potager and greenhouse. Further 3-acre wild flower meadow with orchids and rare trees and further 3 acre orchard of old East Anglian apple varieties in two small fields across the lane. Gravel drive and small step into WC.

41 PATERNOSTER HOUSE

Barnhall Road, Tolleshunt Knights, Maldon CM9 8HA. Julia & Michael Bradley, juliaabradley@gmail.com. *From A12 J24 (Kelvedon) Take B1023 to Tiptree through Tiptree on B1023 bottom of Factory Hill turn L to Tolleshunt Knights on Brook Rd S bend onto Barnhall Rd. Continue to 30mph sign house on R.* Sun 1, Mon 2 May (10-4). Adm £5, chd free. Light refreshments. Tea, coffee, orange juice & cakes. **Visits also by arrangement Apr to July children welcome but MUST be supervised because of deep ponds.**
Peaceful 5 acre garden rescued from a derelict state some 15 yrs ago. It has an enclosed flower garden, 2 meadows, orchards of apples, pears, stone fruit, mulberry trees and peaches. Ornamental kitchen garden with raised beds and extensive lawns with large shrubberies. Some rare and unusual shrubs (large collection of viburnums) and plants young and mature trees. 3 beautiful ponds. Some vintage tractors and machinery. Chickens, mandarin ducks, guinea fowl (The Freds), golden pheasants and semi-permanent mallards. Gravel drive. Rough grass in meadows (parking), otherwise reasonably level.

42 PEACOCKS

Main Road, Margaretting CM4 9HY. Phil Torr, 07802 472382, phil.torr@btinternet.com. *Margaretting Village Centre. From village Xrds go 75yds in the direction of Ingatestone, entrance gates will be found on L set back 50 feet from the road frontage.* Sun 10 Apr (1-4). Cream teas. Sun 15 May, Sun 12 June (2-5). Home-made teas. Adm £5, chd free. **Visits also by arrangement Mar to June adm incl refreshments.** *Donation to St Francis Hospice.*
5-acre garden surrounding Regency house with mature native and specimen trees. Restored horticultural buildings. Formal walled garden (2nd under construction), long herbaceous/mixed border. Vegetable garden. Temple of Antheia sits on the banks of a lilly lake. Large areas for wildlife incl woodland walk and orchard. Traditionally managed wildflower meadow. Sunken dell. Display of old Margaretting postcards. Artist studio, small art exhibition. Most of garden wheelchair accessible.

43 PEPPERS FARM

Forry Green, Sible Hedingham
CO9 3RP. Mrs Pam Turtle,
01787 460221,
pam@peppersfarm.entadsl.com.
*1m SW of Sible Hedingham. From S
after Gosfield L for Southey Green. L
for Forry Green. From N for Sible
Hedingham R at Sugar Loaves,
Rectory Rd. L at White Horse until
Forry Green.* Sun 1 May (2-5). Adm
£4, chd free. Light refreshments.
**Visits also by arrangement Mar to
Sept.**
1/2 acre country garden set high on
quiet rural green with farmland views.
Hedges divide informal borders
featuring flowering shrubs, fruit and
specimen trees, many grown from
seed. Beautiful alpine scree and sinks
overlook spring fed pond. In April,
May beautiful bluebells in Lowts
Wood. Stout shoes recommended.
Free standing Wisteria, and set in
Essex countryside. Partial wheelchair
access, large pond with steep sides.
Some gravel.
&. 🐕 ❀ ☕

18 PETTITS BOULEVARD, RM1
See London

44 NEW 10 RAMSEY ROAD
Harwich CO12 4RZ. Linda & David
Rogers. *Follow signs along the A120
to Harwich. Turn R at 1st r'about up
the hill to Ramsey church. Proceed*

*along Main Rd on L before first mini
r'about. All signed.* Sat 6, Sun 7 Aug
(11-4). Adm £3, chd free. Also
open 447 Main Road.
Town garden developed over the last
37 years, divided into different areas.
Pond, patio with numerous pots,
leading to colour themed borders
filled with shrubs and perennials
(hydrangeas, salvias, and
thalictrums). Features a secluded
garden with box hedging.
❀

GROUP OPENING

45 RAYLEIGH GARDENS
Rayleigh SS6 9ND. *All the group
gardens are within 1m from Rayleigh
station. From A127 take A1245
towards Chelmsford. At r'about turn
towards Rayleigh on A129, London
Rd. At Travellers Joy PH turn L
(Downhall Rd) to access 3 gardens,
the 4th is off A129 on R.* Sun 12
June, Sun 17 July (12-5).
Combined adm £5, chd free. Light
refreshments at Cherrydown
(June) and London Rd. (July)
Ploughmans at Lower Lambricks
both openings.

1 CHERRYDOWN
SS6 9ND. Richard & Gill
Thrussell
Visits also by arrangement

June to Aug for groups of
6 plus.
richardthrussell@lineone.net
01268 781057

35 LANGDON ROAD
SS6 9HY. Mrs Louise Reed

36 LONDON ROAD
SS6 9JE. Jenny & Ron Coutts
**Visits also by arrangement July
& Aug groups of 6 or more
welcome. Hot food can be
provided with prior agreement.
Price to be agreed.**
couttsier2@btinternet.com
01268 781329

2 LOWER LAMBRICKS
SS6 8DB. Linda & Alan Davison

Four diverse town gardens to delight
and inspire the visitor. Cherrydown's 3
levels burst with over 350 perennial
cultivars. Shade planting leads to a
terrace with views over raised
borders. Up steps to fruit trees, a
greenhouse, parterre herb garden
bordered with carnations,
agapanthus and annuals. London Rd
boasts hot planting, succulents, Koi
ponds to the front, with a lawn,
pergolas groaning with climbers and
baskets to the rear. Gingers,
brugmansia, shrubs and perennials
can be enjoyed from seating areas.
Lower Lambricks sloping garden is
imaginatively terraced with vertical
planting, a trained fruit arbour and
secluded seating, water features and
containers. Perennials, grasses,
greenhouse and productive area fill
this great garden. Langdon Rd is a
delightful white garden boasting over
100 roses, unusual perennials and
ferns, all crammed into a tiny plot.
Shady fernery, arches, pond and a
succession of bloom surround a
handkerchief lawn providing interest
all summer long. Wheelchair access
to 36 London Rd and partial access
to 2 Lower Lambricks.
&. ❀ ☕

46 RAYNE HATCH FARM
Rayne Hatch, Stisted, Braintree
CM77 8BY. Dr Jill Chaloner. *1m NE
Braintree. From Braintree bypass take
A131 towards Sudbury passing
through High Garrett & Three
Counties Crematorium on L take R
turn signed Stisted 2 then R at T-
junction 4th house on R.* Sun 19
June, Sun 24 July (11-4). Adm £5,
chd free. Light refreshments.
2 1/2 acre garden surrounding grade II
listed Elizabethan farmhouse lovingly

Brookfield, Boreham Gardens

created in past 14 yrs by plantaholic owner with 4 ponds providing a rich wildlife habitat. Enjoy waterside paths, ornamental bridge, well stocked herbaceous borders, woodland walk, orchard and walled garden. Fragrant arbours and ample seating throughout aid contemplation and tranquility.

47 REPRISE
5 Mornington Crescent, Hadleigh, Benfleet SS7 2HW. David & Rosemary King, 01702 557632, david.rosie@talktalk.net. *5m W of Southend-on-Sea. A13 E through Hadleigh town, Woodfield Rd L. A13 W pass Hadleigh Boundary sign, Woodfield Rd R. Follow signs.* Sun 5 June, Sun 3, Sun 31 July (2-5). Adm £3.50, chd free. Home-made teas. Visits also by arrangement June & July adm £7.50 incl cream tea.
A 250 sq-metre garden, created over 5yrs. Patio, with flower-filled containers, gives garden views. The gravel path winds through colourful perennials to a raised seating area screened by apple tree and climbers. Beyond the lawn is a pond, backed by shrubs and trees. Vegetable plot and greenhouse tucked away completes the scene. Gold Medal Winners for Best Small Garden, Castle Point in Bloom. Featured on BBC Essex (Radio).

48 ROOKWOODS
Yeldham Road, Sible Hedingham CO9 3QG. Peter & Sandra Robinson, 07770 957111, sandy1989@btinternet.com. *8m NW of Halstead. Entering Sible Hedingham from the direction of Haverhill on A1017 take 1st R just after 30mph sign.* Mon 30 May (12-5). Adm £4, chd free. Cream teas. Visits also by arrangement May to Sept, cream teas can be organised in advance.
Rookwoods is a tranquil garden. There are a mix of mature and young trees and shrubs. The herbaceous borders feature columns of tumbling roses. A few pleached hornbeam rooms lead to a young wild flower bed. All this surrounded by a Victorian red brick wall enhanced with clematis and vitis coignetiae. An ancient oak wood lies beyond a meadow of buttercups. Gravel drive.

49 69 RUNDELLS
Harlow CM18 7HD. Mr & Mrs K Naunton, 01279 303471, k_naunton@hotmail.com. *Harlow. M11 J7 A414 exit T-lights take L exit Southern Way, mini r'about 1st exit Trotters Rd leading into Commonside Rd, take 2nd L into Rundells.* Sat 16 July (2-5). Adm £2.50, chd free. Home-made tea and cakes, coffee. Visits also by arrangement June to Sept please give plenty of notice.
As featured on Alan Tichmarsh's first 'Love Your Garden' series ('The Secret Garden') 69, Rundells is a very colourful, small town garden packed with a wide variety of shrubs, perennials, herbaceous and bedding plants in over 200 assorted containers. Hard landscaping on different levels incl's summer house, various seating areas and water features. Steep steps. Access to adjacent allotment open to view. Various small secluded seating areas. The garden is next to a large allotment and this is open to view with lots of interesting features. Honey and other produce for sale (conditions permitting). Full size hot tub/jacuzzi.

The NGS is Hospice UK's largest single donor

50 22 ST CLEMENTS DRIVE
Leigh-On-Sea SS9 3BJ. Lesley & Alan Kirkman. *3m W of Southend on Sea. From A127 take R filter at Progress Road towards Leigh on Sea & follow signs along the Fairway. From A13 follow signs from Kingswoods Chase.* Sun 5 June (11-4). Adm £3.50, chd free. Light refreshments. Evening opening Sat 11 June (6.30-10). Adm £5, chd free. 11th June is a Pimms and music evening, with glass of Pimms.
Modern circular designed rear garden created for high impact and low maintenance. A rich mixture of planting incorporating semi exotics, a wide range of perennials and shrubs for all year round interest. 'Hot beds' full of colour and architectural

planting. Designed to be an extension of the house for entertaining both friends and wildlife. Featured on TV Sky 1 'Show me your garden' series. Wheelchair access would be via the sideway to the main decked area.

51 ST HELENS
High Street, Stebbing CM6 3SE. Stephen & Joan Bazlinton, 01371 856495, revbaz@care4free.net. *3m E of Great Dunmow. Leave Gt Dunmow on B1256. Take 1st L to Stebbing, at T-junction turn L into High St, garden 2nd on R.* Sat 30 Apr, Sat 18 June, Sat 10 Sept (1-5). Adm £4, chd free. Home-made teas. Visits also by arrangement Apr to Aug. *Donation to Dentaid.*
A garden of contrasts due to moist and dry conditions, laid out on a gentle Essex slope from a former willow plantation. These contours give rise to changing vistas and unanticipated areas of seclusion framed with hedging and generous planting. Walkways and paths alongside natural springs and still waters. Partial wheelchair access.

52 SHRUBS FARM
Lamarsh, Bures CO8 5EA. Mr & Mrs Robert Erith, 01787 227520, bob@shrubsfarm.co.uk, www.shrubsfarm.co.uk. *1¼ m from Bures. On rd to Lamarsh, the drive is signed to Shrubs Farm.* Visits by arrangement May to Oct groups 6 min. No max. Tours led by owner £6.
2 acres with shrub borders, lawns, roses and trees. 50 acres parkland with wild flower paths and woodland trails. Over 70 species of oak. Superb 10m views over Stour valley. Ancient coppice and pollards incl largest goat (pussy) willow (*Salix caprea*) in England. Wollemi and Norfolk pines, and banana trees. Full size black rhinoceros. Display of Bronze Age burial urns. Large grass maze Refreshments by arrangement. Guided Tour to incl park and ancient woodland. Restored C18 Essex barn is available for homemade teas £4, also wine, canapes and other refreshment all by prior arrangement. Featured in East Anglian Daily Times and Suffolk Free Press of events in barn and garden during 2015. Some ground may be boggy in wet weather.

53 SNARES HILL COTTAGE
Duck End, Stebbing CM6 3RY.
Pete & Liz Stabler, 01371 856565,
petestabler@gmail.com. *Between
Dunmow & Bardfield. On B1057 from
Great Dunmow to Great Bardfield,
1/2 m after Bran End on L.* Sun 29
May, Sun 4 Sept (10.30-4). Adm
£4, chd free. Home-made teas.
**Visits also by arrangement Apr to
Sept.**
A 'quintessential English Garden' -
Gardeners World. Our quirky 1 1/2 acre
garden has surprises round every
corner and many interesting
sculptures. A natural swimming pool
is bordered by romantic flower beds,
herb garden and Victorian folly. A bog
garden borders woods and leads to
silver birch copse, beach garden and
'Roman' temple. Natural Swimming
Pond. Classic cars. Sculptures.

54 SOUTH SHOEBURY HALL
Church Road, Shoeburyness
SS3 9DN. Mr & Mrs M Dedman,
01702 299022,
michael@shoeburyhall.co.uk. *4m E
of Southend-on-Sea. Enter Southend
on A127 to Eastern Ave A1159
signed Shoebury. R at r'about to join
A13. Proceed S to Ness Rd. R into
Church Rd. Garden on L 50 metres.*
Visits by arrangement Apr to Aug
for groups of 10 + to a coach
party. Adm £3.50, chd free. Home-
made teas.
Delightful, 1-acre established walled
garden surrounding Grade II listed
house (not open) and bee house.
New agapanthus and hydrangea
beds. April is ablaze with 3000 tulips
and fritillaria. July shows 200+
varieties of agapanthus. Unusual
trees, shrubs, rose borders, with 50yr
old plus geraniums, Mediterranean
and Southern Hemisphere planting in
dry garden. New planting for 2016 in
large beds. C11 St Andrews Church
open to visitors (by arrangement)
Garden close to sea. Featured in
many monthly periodicals and
appeared on BBC Gardeners World.
Possibly the largest show of
Agapanthus in Essex.

55 ◆ SPENCERS
Tilbury Road, Great Yeldham
CO9 4JG. Mr & Mrs Colin Bogie,
01787 238175,
lynne@spencersgarden.net,
www.spencersgarden.net. *Just N of
Gt Yeldham on Tilbury Rd. In village
centre, turn at 'Blasted Oak' (huge
oak stump). Keep L, following stream
(signed 'Tilbury Juxta Clare').
Spencers is clearly signed on L after
approx 1/4 m.* For NGS: Sun 5 June,
Sun 11 Sept (2-5). Adm £5, chd
free. Home-made teas. **For other
opening times and information,
please phone, email or visit garden
website.**
Romantic C18 walled garden laid out
by Lady Anne Spencer, overflowing
with blooms following Tom Stuart-
Smith's renovation. Huge wisteria,
armies of Lord Butler delphiniums
('Rab' lived at Spencers). Many
varieties of roses, spectacular
herbaceous borders, oldest
greenhouse in Essex. Parkland with
many specimen trees. Victorian
woodland garden.

56 SPRING COTTAGE
Chapel Lane, Elmstead Market,
Colchester CO7 7AG. Mr & Mrs
Roger & Sharon Sciachettano,
sharons4852@gmail.com. *3m from
Colchester. Overlooking village green
N of A133 through Elmstead Market.
Parking limited adjacent to cottage,
village car park nearby on S side of
A133.* Sat 16, Sun 17 July, Sat 13,
Sun 14 Aug (1-5). Adm £3, chd
free. Home-made teas. **Visits also
by arrangement June to Aug
small groups only, 10 max.**
From Acteas to Zauschenerias and
Aressima to Zebra grass we hope our
large variety of plants will please. Our
award winning garden features a
range of styles and habitats e.g.
woodland dell, stumpery,
Mediterranean area, perennial
borders and pond. Our C17 thatched
cottage and garden show case a
number of plants found at the world
famous Beth Chatto gardens 1/2 m
down the road.

57 TUDOR ROOST
18 Frere Way, Fingringhoe,
Colchester CO5 7BP. Chris & Linda
Pegden, 01206 729831,
pegdenc@gmail.com. *5m S of
Colchester. In centre of village by
Whalebone PH, follow sign to Ballast
Quay, after 1/2 m turn R into Brook
Hall Rd, then 1st L into Frere Way.*
Sat 16, Sun 17 Apr, Sun 1, Mon 2
May, Sat 9, Sun 10 July, Sat 13,
Sun 14 Aug (2-5). Adm £3.50, chd
free. Home-made teas. Large
conservatory to sit in if inclement
weather. **Visits also by
arrangement Apr to Aug 10 min,**
adm incl tea & cake.
An unexpected hidden colourful 1/4 -
acre garden. Well manicured grassy
paths wind round island beds and
ponds. Densely planted subtropical
area with architectural and exotic
plants - cannas, bananas, palms,
agapanthus, agaves and tree ferns
surround a colourful gazebo. Garden
planted to provide yr-round colour
and encourage wildlife. Many
peaceful seating areas. Within 1m of
Fingringhoe Wick Nature Reserve.
Local PH that serves meal. PLEASE
CONFIRM OPENING DATES ON
NGS WEBSITE OR TELEPHONE.
Featured in East Anglian Daily Times.
Look Magazine. Shingle drive but can
park right next to garden gate.

> Bordered by
> romantic flower
> beds, herb
> garden and
> Victorian folly . . .

68 37 TURPINS LANE
Chigwell, Woodford Green
IG8 8AZ. Fabrice Aru & Martin
Thurston 0208 5050 739
martin.thurston@talktalk.net
*Between Woodford & Epping. Tube:
Chigwell, 2m from North Circular Rd
at Woodford, follow the signs for
Chigwell (A113) through Woodford
Bridge into Manor Rd & turn L, Bus
275.* Sun 3, Sun 24 July, Sun 4
Sept (11-6). Adm £3, chd free.
**Visits also by arrangement May to
Oct, 8 max.**
An unexpected hidden, magical,
small part-walled garden showing
how much can be achieved in a small
space. An oasis of calm with densely
planted rich, lush foliage, tree ferns,
hostas, topiary and an abundance of
well maintained shrubs
complemented by a small pond and
3 water features designed for yr
round interest.

22 St Clements Drive

58 ► ULTING WICK
Crouchmans Farm Road, Maldon
CM9 6QX. Mr & Mrs B Burrough,
01245 380216,
philippa.burrough@btinternet.com,
www.ultingwickgarden.co.uk. *3m
NW of Maldon. Take turning to Ulting
off B1019 as you exit Hatfield
Peverel. Garden on R after 2m.* Sun
24 Apr (11-5). Light refreshments.
Fri 29 Apr (2-5). Cream teas. Sun 8
May (2-5). Home-made teas. Fri
13 May, Thur 16 June (2-5). Cream
teas. Sun 11 Sept (2-5). Home-
made teas. Fri 16 Sept (2-5).
Cream teas. Adm £5, chd free.
Homemade soup using
ingredients from the garden, filled
rolls & home-made teas on 24th
April. **Visits also by arrangement
Apr to Sept groups of 15+. Other
catering by arrangement.**
Donation to All Saints Ulting Church.
Listed black barns provide backdrop
for colourful and exuberant planting in
8 acres. Thousands of tulips, flowing
innovative spring planting,
herbaceous borders, pond, mature
weeping willows, kitchen garden,
dramatic late summer beds with
zingy, tender, exotic plant
combinations. Drought tolerant
perennial wild flower and annual
wildflower meadows. Woodland.

Many plants propagated in-house.
Lots of unusual plants for sale. All
Saints Church Ulting will be open in
conjunction with the garden for talks
on its history on Sun openings only.
Listed as one of the top 10 Spring
Gardens to visit in The English
Garden, Featured in East Anglian
Daily Times, Garden Style (Germany),
tulips in Country Life. Pictures in
many newspapers. Some gravel
around the house but main areas of
interest are accessible for
wheelchairs.

59 ► NEW ► 14 UNA ROAD
Bowers Gifford, Basildon
SS13 2HU. Mr & Mrs John &
Barbara Spooner. *4m E of Basildon
on B1464 between Pitsea & Saddlers
Farm r'about (A130/A13.) From
Pitsea turn L into Pound Lane. From
Southend (A127) X A130/A1245
junction. 1m turn L & follow NGS
signs.* Sat 16, Sun 17 July (11-5).
Adm £3.50, chd free. Light
refreshments.
A beautiful 1/2 acre garden featuring 2
ponds. Garden divided into 'rooms'
each with an interesting view, drawing
you on to the next room. Small
vegetable patch with greenhouse plus

a family of gnomes. Refreshments
and WC available. Winner of Bowers
Gifford in Bloom.

60 ► 37 UNDERHILL ROAD
Benfleet SS7 1EP. Mr Allan & Mrs
Diane Downey, 01268 565291,
allan.downey@yahoo.co.uk. *Approx
2m from Sadlers Farm r'about on
A13. Towards Southend, take R turn
at Tarpots Harvester continue to
South Benfleet School turn L opp, in
to Thundersley Park Rd, continue to
Underhill Rd 500yds on R.* Sun 26
June, Sun 24 July, Sun 21 Aug (1-
5). Adm £3.50, chd free. Home-
made teas. **Visits also by
arrangement June to Aug
weekdays only, min 10.**
A 1/4 acre garden offering a relaxing
visit, featuring topiary shrubs and
climbers incl campsis, clematis,
honeysuckle and jasmine. Over 40
heucheras in beds with sedums,
rudbeckias and hydrangeas. Lovely
views from all areas. Undercover
Bonsai area, many colourful baskets
and containers. Several cast iron and
stone sculptures. Patio area to enjoy
refreshments.

Vegetable patch
with greenhouse
plus a family of
gnomes . . .

GROUP OPENING

61 WALTHAM ABBEY GROUP
Waltham Abbey EN9 1LG. *8m W of Epping Town. M25, J26 to Waltham Abbey. At T-lights by McD turn R to r'about. Take 2nd exit to next r'about. Take 3rd exit (A112) to T-lights. L to Monkswood Av.* **Sun 5 June, Sun 4 Sept (11-6). Combined adm £5, chd free. Home-made teas at Silver Birches, Quendon Drive. Bacon Sandwiches made to order and homemade cakes available.**

62 EASTBROOK ROAD
Caroline Cassell.
Open on Sun 5 June
Visits also by arrangement June to Aug, vintage afternoon teas for groups of 3/4.
cvcassell@gmail.com
07973 551196

39 HALFHIDES
Chris Hamer.
Open on all dates

76 MONKSWOOD AVENUE
Cathy & Dan Gallagher.
Open on all dates

SILVER BIRCHES
Linda & Frank Jewson.
Open on all dates

Historic Waltham Abbey is near Epping Forest. The Abbey is purported to be last resting place of King Harold. Lee Valley Regional Park is nearby. Silver Birches boasts 3 lawns on 2 levels. This surprisingly secluded garden has many mixed borders packed with all year interest. Mature shrubs and trees create a short woodland walk. Crystal clear water flows through a shady area of the garden. At 39 Halfhides the garden has evolved over 45yrs. It features mixed shrubs and perennial

borders on 2 levels. Waterfall linking two ponds leads to shade garden. Alpines thrive on scree and in troughs. Beautiful autumn colour. 76 Monkswood Ave is a plantswoman's garden. Mixed borders filled with specimen trees, shrubs and perennials incl asters, dahlias and late-flowering anemones. Wildlife pond. 62 Eastbrook Rd: No Parking in Eastbrook Rd. Off Honey Lane, walking distance from Halfhides and The Glade Way approx. 7 mins. This is a small cottage garden, traditional perennial planting, topiary and circular themed hard landscaping. Reclaimed chimney pots for sale as planters. 62 Eastbrook Rd not suitable for wheelchairs.

🐾 ☕

62 WASHLANDS
Prayors Hill, Sible Hedingham CO9 3LE. Tony & Sarah Frost, 01787 460732, tony@washlands.co.uk. *¼ m NW of Sible Hedingham Church. At former Sugar Loaves PH on A1017 turn SW into Rectory Rd, R at former White Horse PH, pass St Peters Church on RH-side, ¼ m NW on Prayors Hill.* **Sun 26 June (2-5). Home-made teas. Evening opening Wed 29 June (7-9). Wine. Sun 3 July (2-5). Home-made teas. Adm £3.50, chd free. Visits also by arrangement June to Aug, groups of 10+.**
Informal, tranquil garden approx 1 acre with good views over rolling countryside. Features incl a horse pond. Wide herbaceous, shrub and woodland borders incl roses and peonies. Many young and mature trees enhance the garden. A developing retirement project. Pond has steep banks. Woodland walk unsuitable for wheelchairs.

♿ 🐕 🐾 ☕

GROUP OPENING

63 WENDENS AMBO GARDENS
Saffron Walden CB11 4UJ. *Parking at village hall nr Church, nr Crossways & Chinnel Barn all signed on day. Not all gardens are within walking distance. Map of gardens available on day.* **Sun 5 June (2-6). Combined adm £6, chd free.**

2 CHURCH PATH
Mr Rupert Fulford

3 CHURCH PATH
Ms Liz Hartley

COURTLANDS HOUSE
Dr & Mrs C Glazebrook

CROSSWAYS
Mrs Andrea Reynolds

KATIE'S MILLENNIUM WOOD
Dr Katie Petty-Saphon

NEW ▸ OLD RECTORY COTTAGE
Professor Patrick & Loretta Smith

NEW ▸ 1 SPARROWS END
Mark & Miranda Pender
www.mirandapender.com

3 Church Path, quintessential cottage garden adjacent to historic church set behind a chocolate box thatched cottage. Terraced garden with mixed shrubs, perennials, beautiful clematis and roses. Hidden vegetable garden and fruit trees. 2 Church Path, lawn and small orchard area. Access to number 3. Wonderful views of historic village. Courtlands House, low maintenance, minimalistic garden with interesting topiary, varieties of hostas, seasonal pots. Ferns and gunnera in shady areas. Crossways, 5 acre informal 'family' garden with mixed planting. Sweeping lawn and wild flowers. Wildlife areas and large pond, a haven for frogs! Specimen trees. Katie's Millenium Wood,10,000 trees planted as whips in 2000 - 2001.Remarkable height achieved in 15yrs. 1 Sparrows End, romantic garden of secret paths and hidden corners. The Old Rectory Cottage, garden has lawns, mixed borders and areas to discover behind mature trees and hedges. Wendens Ambo is a meandering historic village with a busy B road through village. Please use car parks. Beware.There is a lack of pavements in places so take great care if walking on the road. Plants at Courtlands House. Teas at Crossways. Art display at 1 Sparrows End. Village very close to Audley End House.

🐾 ☕

64 WICKETS
Langley Upper Green CB11 4RY. Susan & Doug Copeland, 01799 550553, susan.copeland2@btinternet.com. *7m W of Saffron Walden, 10m N of Bishops Stortford. At Newport take B1038 After 3m turn R at Clavering, signed Langley. Upper Green is 3m further on. At cricket green turn R. House 200m on R.* **Evening opening Sat 9 July (5.30-9). Adm £5, chd free. Wine. Musical**

interludes featuring Alex Wilkinson, local musician and singer/songwriter. Opening with Langley Village Gardens on Sun 19 June.

Peaceful country garden 'Far from the Madding Crowd'. Wide, informal mixed borders include camassia, shrub roses and alliums. Two landscaped meadows and shepherd's hut with fine pastoral views. Large lily pond sheltered by silver birch. Curvilinear design links themed planting areas. Espalier apples enclose parterre with sweet peas, delphiniums, lavender. Secluded gravel garden. Featured in Garden Answers. Gravel drive.

65▶ WICKHAM PLACE FARM
Station Road, Wickham Bishops, Witham CM8 3JB. Mrs J Wilson, 01621 891282, info@wickhamplacefarm.co.uk, www.wickhamplacefarm.co.uk. *2½ m SE of Witham. On B1018 from Witham to Maldon. After going under A12 take 3rd L (Station Rd). 1st house on L.* **Visits by arrangement for groups of 15+. Nursery by appt any day/time. Adm £5, chd free. Donation to Farleigh Hospice.**
14 acres for all seasons. 2 acre walled garden is home to climbers, shrubs, perennials and bulbs.

Renowned for enormous wisterias in May (one over 250ft long) with further flowering in July. Ponds, intricate box knot garden and lovely woodland walks with rabbit resistant plants. In September cyclamen carpet the woodland, replacing earlier bluebells. New 135m sq. herbaceous border. Note, wisterias face all aspects, extending flowering time during May. Featured on BBC TV Great British Gardens Revival with Joe Swift.

66▶ WOODPECKERS
Mangapp Chase, Burnham-on-Crouch CM0 8QQ. Neil & Linda Holdaway, & Lilian Burton, 01621 782137, lindaholdaway@btinternet.com. *1m N of Burnham-on-Crouch. B1010 to Burnham-on-Crouch. Just beyond town sign turn L into Green Lane. Turn L after ½ m. Garden 200yds on R.* **Visits by arrangement in June open for pre booked groups with refreshments by arrangement. Adm £4, chd free.**
Hedges divide and add structure to the exuberant planting in this 1½ acre country garden. Maintained for a long season of interest, the densely planted colour themed borders and mini wild flower meadows are packed full of bulbs, roses, clematis, and interesting perennials, many specifically chosen to be of particular

interest to our resident honey bees as well as butterflies and other pollinators. Featured in several UK and continental life style and gardening magazines.

67▶ WRITTLE COLLEGE
Writtle CM1 3RR. Writtle College, 01245 424200 x25758, Charlotte.Power@writtle.ac.uk, www.writtle.ac.uk. *4m W of Chelmsford. On A414, nr Writtle village, please approach the college from the direction of Writtle Village only as Chelmsford Marathon running through college grounds.* **Thur 12 May (10-3). Adm £4, chd free. Tea in The Garden Room (main campus) & The Lordship tea room (Lordship campus). Visits also by arrangement May to Oct.**
15 acres; informal lawns with naturalised bulbs and wild flowers. Large tree collection, mixed shrubs, herbaceous borders. Landscaped gardens designed and built by students. Development of 13-acre parkland. Orchard meadow started. Landscaped glasshouses and wide range of seasonal bedding. Herbaceous perennial borders. Extended naturalised bulb areas on front campus lawns. Renovated Rockery. Some gravel, however majority of areas accessible to all.

262 Main Road

GLOUCESTERSHIRE

(for South Gloucestershire see Somerset, Bristol Area & S Glos)

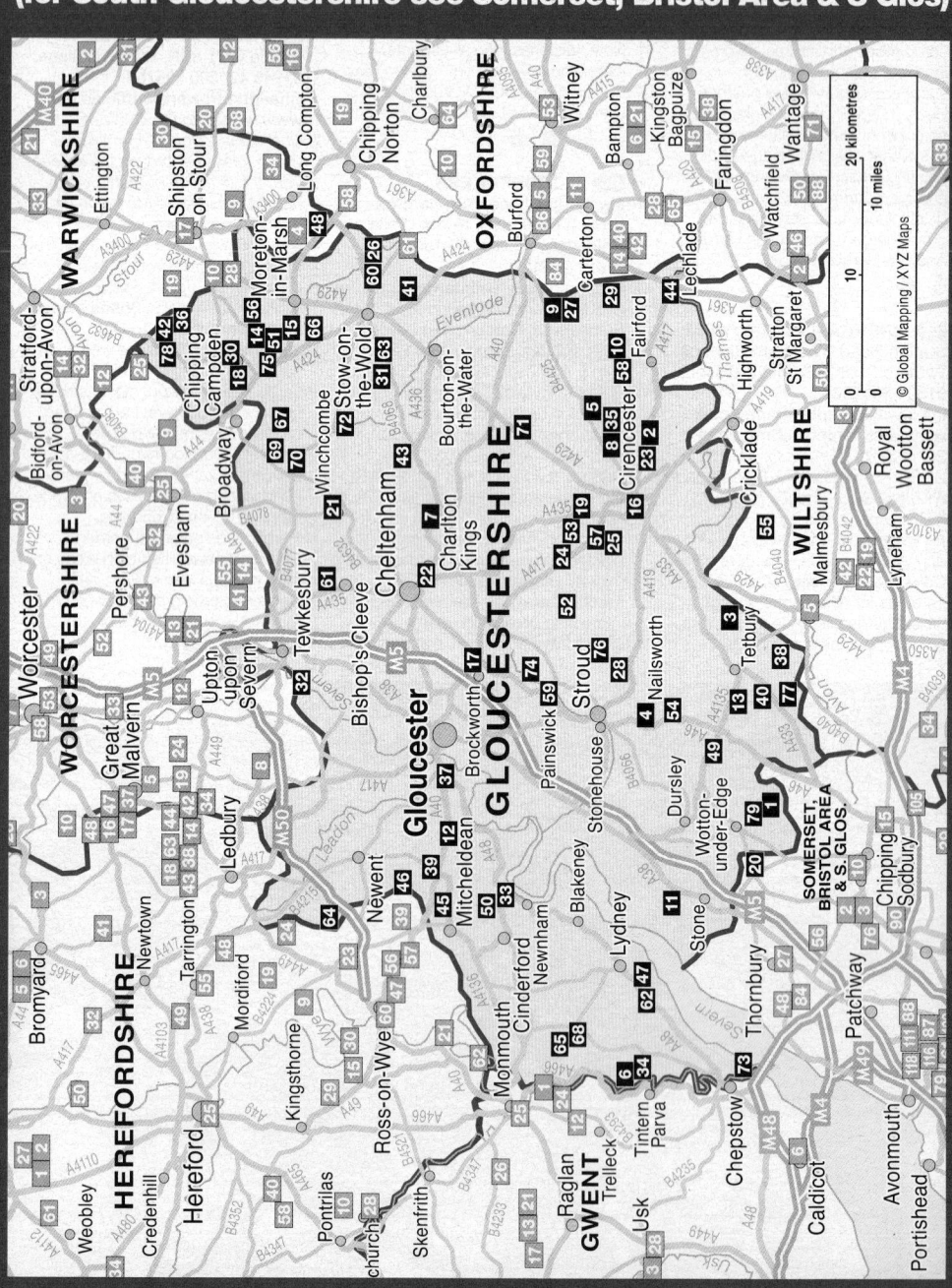

Gloucestershire

Gloucestershire is one of the most beautiful counties in England, spanning as it does a large part of the Cotswolds, as well as the Forest of Dean, and the Wye and Severn Valleys.

The Cotswolds is an expanse of gently sloping green hills, wooded valleys and ancient, picturesque towns and villages; it is designated as an Area of Outstanding Natural Beauty, and its quintessentially English charm attracts many visitors.

Like the county itself, many of the gardens which open for the NGS are quite outstanding. There are major public gardens such as Hidcote Manor Garden, as well as large private gardens such as Highnam Court and Stowell Park.

There are, however, many more modest gardens whose gates only open on an NGS open day, such as 25 Bowling Green Road with over 400 varieties of Hemerocallis. This tiny garden has opened for the NGS for over thirty five years! The National Collection of Rambling Roses is held at Moor Wood, and that of Juglans and Pterocarya at Upton Wold.

Several Cotswold villages also open their gardens, and a wonderful day can be had strolling from cottage to house, marvelling at the gardens, only to pause for the obligatory tea and cake!

Gloucestershire Volunteers

County Organiser
Norman Jeffery
01793 762805
norman.jeffery@ngs.org.uk

County Treasurer
Graham Baber
01285 650961
grayanjen@onetel.com

Publicity
Vanessa Berridge
01242 609535
vanessa.berridge@sky.com

Norman Jeffery
(as above)

Booklet Coordinator
Nick Kane
07768 478668
nick@kanes.org

Assistant County Organisers
Sue Hunt
01453 521263
suehunt2@btinternet.com

Trish Jeffery
01793 762805
trishjeffery@aol.com

Valerie Kent
01993 823294

Shirley & Gordon Sills
01242 820606
shirley.sills@ngs.org.uk

Pat Willey
01285 762946
patwilley1@gmail.com

Gareth & Sarah Williams
01531 821654
dgwilliams84@hotmail.com

Left: Littlefield Garden

Opening Dates

All entries subject to change.
For latest information check www.ngs.org.uk
Extended openings are shown at the begining of the month

February

Snowdrop Festival

Sunday 14
- **6** Barn House, Chepstow
- **74** Trench Hill

Sunday 21
- **74** Trench Hill

Monday 22
- **57** The Old Rectory, Duntisbourne Rous

March

Sunday 13
- **39** Home Farm

Sunday 27
- **13** Beverston Castle
- **52** Misarden Park
- **74** Trench Hill

Monday 28
- **13** Beverston Castle
- **74** Trench Hill

April

Saturday 2
- **68** South Lodge

Sunday 3
- **37** Highnam Court

Sunday 10
- **39** Home Farm
- **56** The Old Chequer

Monday 11
- **42** Kiftsgate Court

Tuesday 12
- **8** Barnsley House

Sunday 17
- **75** Upton Wold

Monday 18
- **57** The Old Rectory, Duntisbourne Rous

Sunday 24
- **14** Blockley Gardens
- **39** Home Farm

Saturday 30
- **68** South Lodge

May

Sunday 1
- **20** Charfield Village Gardens
- **28** Eastcombe, Bussage and Brownshill Gardens
- **37** Highnam Court
- **62** Ramblers

Monday 2
- **20** Charfield Village Gardens
- **28** Eastcombe, Bussage and Brownshill Gardens

Sunday 8
- **70** Stanway Fountain & Water Garden
- **71** Stowell Park

Wednesday 11
- **47** Lydney Park Spring Garden
- **68** South Lodge

Saturday 21
- **21** Charingworth Court

Sunday 22
- **21** Charingworth Court
- **23** The Coach House Garden
- **68** South Lodge

Saturday 28
- **40** Hookshouse Pottery
- **45** Longhope Gardens

Sunday 29
- **7** Barn House, Sandywell Park
- **40** Hookshouse Pottery
- **45** Longhope Gardens
- **51** Mill Dene Garden
- **60** Pasture Farm

Monday 30
- **7** Barn House, Sandywell Park
- **40** Hookshouse Pottery
- **60** Pasture Farm

Tuesday 31
- **40** Hookshouse Pottery

June

Wednesday 1
- **17** Brockworth Court
- **40** Hookshouse Pottery
- **46** Lower Farm House

Thursday 2
- **40** Hookshouse Pottery

Friday 3
- **40** Hookshouse Pottery

Festival Weekend

Saturday 4
- **24** Cotswold Farm
- **40** Hookshouse Pottery
- **45** Longhope Gardens

Sunday 5
- **3** Ashley Grange, Dillycot & Ox Barn
- **19** Cerney House Gardens
- **24** Cotswold Farm
- **37** Highnam Court
- **38** Hodges Barn
- **40** Hookshouse Pottery
- **45** Longhope Gardens
- **48** The Manor

Monday 6
- **38** Hodges Barn

Wednesday 8

Redesigned to reflect the local landscape and encourage wildlife . . .

- **31** Eyford House
- **63** Rockcliffe House
- **68** South Lodge
- **74** Trench Hill

Thursday 9
- **18** Campden House
- **30** Ernest Wilson Memorial Garden

Saturday 11
- **4** Atcombe Court

Sunday 12
- **14** Blockley Gardens
- **49** Matara Gardens of Wellbeing
- **78** White House

Monday 13
- **11** Berkeley Castle

Wednesday 15
- **74** Trench Hill

Thursday 16
- **18** Campden House
- **30** Ernest Wilson Memorial Garden

Saturday 18
- **12** Berrys Place Farm
- **44** Loders Gate
- **64** Rose Cottage

Sunday 19

- **10** Beech House
- **12** Berrys Place Farm
- **54** Nailsworth Gardens - off Chestnut Hill
- **58** The Old Rectory, Quenington
- **64** Rose Cottage
- **69** Stanton Village Gardens
- **71** Stowell Park
- **76** Wells Cottage

Tuesday 21
- **36** Hidcote Manor Garden (Evening)

Wednesday 22
- **12** Berrys Place Farm
- **26** Daylesford House
- **31** Eyford House
- **63** Rockcliffe House
- **74** Trench Hill

Thursday 23
- **1** Alderley Grange
- **12** Berrys Place Farm
- **79** Wortley House

Friday 24
- **67** Snowshill Manor & Garden

Saturday 25
- **68** South Lodge

Sunday 26
- **6** Barn House, Chepstow
- **13** Beverston Castle
- **33** The Gables
- **34** NEW 'Greenfields'
- **41** Icomb Gardens
- **51** Mill Dene Garden
- **52** Misarden Park
- **53** Moor Wood
- **55** NEW Oakwood Farm Plant Fair and Garden
- **72** Temple Guiting Manor

Monday 27
- **16** 25 Bowling Green Road

Wednesday 29
- **35** Herbs for Healing

July

Sunday 3
- **5** NEW Awkward Hill Cottage
- **7** Barn House, Sandywell Park
- **16** 25 Bowling Green Road
- **32** Forthampton Court
- **37** Highnam Court
- **43** Littlefield Garden
- **66** Sezincote

Monday 4
- **16** 25 Bowling Green Road

Sunday 10
16 25 Bowling Green Road
73 Three Salmons House

Monday 11
16 25 Bowling Green Road

Sunday 17
9 Barrington Downs
27 1 Drive Cottage
43 Littlefield Garden
74 Trench Hill
77 Westonbirt School Gardens

Monday 18
16 25 Bowling Green Road
57 The Old Rectory, Duntisbourne Rous

Wednesday 27
35 Herbs for Healing

August

Sunday 7
7 Barn House, Sandywell Park
37 Highnam Court

Sunday 14
15 Bourton House Garden

Monday 15
42 Kiftsgate Court

Wednesday 17
17 Brockworth Court

Sunday 21
33 The Gables
48 The Manor
70 Stanway Fountain & Water Garden

Sunday 28
5 NEW Awkward Hill Cottage (Evening)
74 Trench Hill

Wednesday 31
18 Campden House
30 Ernest Wilson Memorial Garden

September

Sunday 4
37 Highnam Court

Saturday 10
64 Rose Cottage

Sunday 11
64 Rose Cottage
74 Trench Hill

Sunday 18
22 NEW Cheltenham Town Gardens

Bourton House Garden

January 2017

Sunday 29
39 Home Farm

February 2017

Sunday 12
39 Home Farm
74 Trench Hill

Sunday 19
74 Trench Hill

Gardens open to the public

15 Bourton House Garden
19 Cerney House Gardens
23 The Coach House Garden
35 Herbs for Healing
36 Hidcote Manor Garden
42 Kiftsgate Court
47 Lydney Park Spring Garden
49 Matara Gardens of Wellbeing
51 Mill Dene Garden
52 Misarden Park
59 Painswick Rococo Garden
66 Sezincotè
67 Snowshill Manor & Garden
70 Stanway Fountain & Water Garden
77 Westonbirt School Gardens

By arrangement only

2 Ampney Brook House
25 Daglingworth House
29 Eastleach House
50 The Meeting House
61 Pear Tree Cottage
65 Scatterford

Also open by arrangement

1 Alderley Grange
3 Ashley Grange, Dillycot & Ox Barn
5 NEW Awkward Hill Cottage
6 Barn House, Chepstow
7 Barn House, Sandywell Park
8 Barnsley House
9 Barrington Downs
13 Beverston Castle
16 25 Bowling Green Road
17 Brockworth Court
20 Pemberley Lodge, Charfield Village Gardens
21 Charingworth Court
24 Cotswold Farm
28 Hawkley Cottage, Eastcombe, Bussage and Brownshill Gardens
34 NEW 'Greenfields'
38 Hodges Barn
39 Home Farm
45 Longhope Gardens
46 Lower Farm House
56 The Old Chequer
57 The Old Rectory, Duntisbourne Rous
60 Pasture Farm
62 Ramblers
68 South Lodge
74 Trench Hill
75 Upton Wold
78 White House

The Gardens

1 ALDERLEY GRANGE
Alderley GL12 7QT. The Hon Mrs Acloque, 01453 842161, milly@acloque-alderley.co.uk. *2m S of Wotton-under-Edge. Turn NW off A46 Bath to Stroud rd at Dunkirk. L signed Hawkesbury Upton & Hillesley. In Hillesley follow sign to Alderley.* **Visits by arrangement May to July for small or large groups, max 40. Adm £6, chd free. Please phone 01453 842161 or email milly@acloque-alderley.co.uk. Thur 23 June (2-4). Combined adm with Wortley House £20, chd free. Pre-booking essential, please visit www.ngs.org.uk or phone 01483 211535 for information & booking.** Originally designed by Alvilde Lees-Milne in the early 1960's, this quintessentially English garden boasts an abundance of old-fashioned roses and many aromatic and medicinal plants and herbs. Features include a pleached lime walk, fine trees and a Regency summerhouse. Some gravel paths.

 ♿ ☕

WE ARE MACMILLAN. CANCER SUPPORT

The NGS is Macmillan's largest single donor

2 AMPNEY BROOK HOUSE
Ampney Crucis, Cirencester GL7 5RT. Allan and Louise Hirst, 01285 851098, allan.hirst@clmail.co.uk. *From Cirencester go E on A417 toward Fairford. After passing the Crown of Crucis take 1st L and also immed L again onto School Lane and L again into the gated (open automatically) drive.* **Visits by arrangement Apr to Sept for groups of all sizes. Adm £5, chd free. Light refreshments to be mutually agreed prior to arrival.** Striking Grade II Cotswold country house on 4.3 acres fronting Ampney Brook. The gardens are 4yrs into a

5yr project to create a haven for wildlife with fun and stimulating spaces yr-round. Incl woodland, kitchen garden, herbaceous borders, meadows, lawns for picnicking (encouraged). No wheelchair access to kitchen garden and greenhouse.

 ♿ 🐕 ❀ ☕

GROUP OPENING

3 ASHLEY GRANGE, DILLYCOT & OX BARN
Ashley & Culkerton GL8 8SX. *Between Tetbury and Cirencester off A433. Dillycot is at Culkerton. Ashley has no signage. Park at Ox Barn. Gardens well signed.* **Sun 5 June (2-5.30). Combined adm £5, chd free. Home-made teas. Refreshments at Ashley Grange.**

 ASHLEY GRANGE
 Mr & Mrs Richard Atkinson
 Visits also by arrangement June/July.
 richard@richardatkinson.eu
 01666 577249

 DILLYCOT
 Mr & Mrs M Oates

 OX BARN
 Jo & Johnny Nettleton

Ashley Grange: Original garden was designed by the late Miss Avice Pearson and opened in 1990s through NGS. Current owners have extended the garden and added new borders. Peonies and iris borders are a feature in June. Plants and cakes for sale. Dillycot: Pottager garden with flowers, fruit and vegetables. Exuberant planting grown on biodynamic principles. Wildlife friendly planting. Featured in Gardens Illustrated. Ox Barn: Herbaceous borders full of roses and delphiniums. Orchard and well-tended vegetable garden. WCs at refreshments venue. Dillycot not accessible by wheelchair. Mostly level access at Ashley Grange and Ox Barn.

 ♿ 🐕 ❀ ☕

4 ATCOMBE COURT
South Woodchester GL5 5ER. John & Josephine Peach. *2m S of Stroud. Take turning off A46 signed S Woodchester, Frogmarsh Mill (do not use turning signed S Woodchester, The Ram).* **Sat 11 June (2-6). Adm £4, chd free. Home-made teas.** 12-acre grounds around C17 house (not open) with later Regency front.

Delightful views over valley with lakes, mature trees and paddocks. Terraced herbaceous borders, lawns, extensive shrubberies, cutting garden mostly annuals. Long peony border. Woodland walk through beechwood. Wheelchair access to some of garden.

 ❀ ☕

5 NEW AWKWARD HILL COTTAGE
Awkward Hill, Bibury GL7 5NH. Mrs Victoria Summerley, 01285 740289, v.summerley@hotmail.com, www.awkwardhill.co.uk. *Bibury, Gloucestershire. Parking very limited, so best to park in village and walk past Arlington Row up Awkward Hill, or up Hawkers Hill from Catherine Wheel PH.* **Sun 3 July (2-6). Adm £3, chd free. Home-made teas. Evening opening Sun 28 Aug (6-8.30). Adm £4.50, chd free. Wine. Visits also by arrangement June to Oct, preferably weekdays (parking is easier), groups are welcome, max 20.** A country Cotswold garden, Awkward Hilll Cottage is a work in progress. A second home for 40yrs, since 2012 it has been redesigned to reflect the local landscape and encourage wildlife. Planting is both formal and informal contributing yr round interest. Pond and waterfall. The owner, a journalist, is author of Secret Gardens of the Cotswolds and Great Gardens of London. Wonderful view over neighbouring meadow and woodland, 2 sunny terraces and plenty of places to sit and relax.

 🐕 ☕

6 BARN HOUSE, CHEPSTOW
Brockweir Common, Chepstow NP16 7PH. Mrs Kate Patel, 01291 680041, barnhousegarden@gmail.com, www.thegardenbarnhouse.com. *10m S of Monmouth & N of Chepstow, under 1 hr from Hereford, Cheltenham & Cardiff. From Chepstow A466 to Monmouth. 2m past Tintern Abbey R across Brockweir Bridge then up Mill Hill ½ m, turn L at The Rock (cottage), signed to Cold Harbour. Narrow lane, no large coaches.* **Sun 14 Feb (11-3). Adm £3.50, chd free. Light refreshments. Sun 26 June (1-5.30), combined adm with 'Greenfields' £6, chd free. Home-made teas. Visits also by arrangement Apr to Sept. Possibility of visiting Greenfields by arrangement on the same day.**

Boldly and generously planted garden of an acre. Wealth of ornamental grasses plus long, late flowering perennials. Stunning mass plantings incl 70m miscanthus hedge. Imaginatively designed contrasting areas incl tranquil sunken terrace with lush Asian grasses, hot border of potted tender perennials, orchard and exuberantly planted vegetable garden screened by bamboos. Barn House Garden is open jointly with Greenfields, a 10 minute walk from Barn House. Visitors can enjoy a great day out in the Wye Valley and visit 2 spectacular gardens. Featured in The English Garden, Amateur Gardening, Mail on Sunday, Saturday Telegraph. Filmed for Gardeners World 2016 season.

7 BARN HOUSE, SANDYWELL PARK
Whittington, Cheltenham GL54 4HF. Shirley & Gordon Sills, 01242 820606, shirleysills@btinternet.com. *4m E of Cheltenham on A40. Between Andoversford and Whittington villages on A40.* **Sun 29, Mon 30 May, Sun 3 July, Sun 7 Aug (11-5). Adm £4.50, chd free. Home-made teas. Teas on 7th Aug in aid of Somerset Court Autistic Trust. Visits also by arrangement June to Aug for groups of 10+.**
2½ -acre plantaholic's garden inside weathered walls of former Victorian kitchen garden. Designed, created and maintained by the owners as a series of exuberantly planted enclosures both formal and informal, sometimes quirky. Herbaceous, climbers, shrubs, trees, lawns, hedges, structures, vistas, water features. Fairly level site although mostly grass paths.

8 BARNSLEY HOUSE
Barnsley, Cirencester GL7 5EE. Calcot Health & Leisure Ltd, 01285 740000, reception@barnsleyhouse.com, www.barnsleyhouse.com. *4m NE of Cirencester. From Cirencester, take B4425 to Barnsley. House entrance on R as you enter village.* **Tue 12 Apr (10-4). Adm £5.50, chd free. Visits also by arrangement for groups of 10+.**
The beautiful garden at Barnsley House, created by Rosemary Verey, is one of England's finest and most famous gardens incl knot garden,

potager garden and mixed borders in Rosemary Verey's successional planting style. The House also has an extensive kitchen garden which will be open with plants and vegetables available for purchase. Narrow paths mean restricted wheelchair access but happy to provide assistance.

9 BARRINGTON DOWNS
Aldsworth, Cheltenham GL54 3PT. Sir Jeremy & Lady Morse, 01451 844382, belindamorse@btinternet.com. *2m E of Aldsworth on B4425. Entrance marked on rd.* **Sun 17 July (2-6). Combined adm with 1 Drive Cottage £5, chd free. Home-made teas. Visits also by arrangement May to Sept, appointments to be made min 2 weeks in advance.**
Barrington Downs is a charming rural garden surrounded by farmland. It has a wide selection of herbaceous plants, shrubs and borders designed to look their best in high summer. Vegetable and herb garden. Sculpture by William Pye and others. Children's play area. Regret not suitable for wheelchairs.

10 BEECH HOUSE
Victoria Road, Quenington, Cirencester GL7 5BW. Mr & Mrs A H Bradley. *8m NE of Cirencester. Garden well signed once in village.* **Sun 19 June (2-5.30). Combined adm with The Old Rectory, Quenington £5, chd free.**
Informal paddock with the R Coln boundary, planted with trees, shrubs and bulbs. Seating by river. Riverside vegetable garden. Formal planted terraces near the house, herb garden and greenhouse. Large paved terrace with views over garden, river and countryside. Limited wheelchair access - on terrace with views over the garden down to the river.

11 BERKELEY CASTLE
Berkeley GL13 9PJ. Mr & Mrs RGJ Berkeley, www.berkeley-castle.com. *Half-way between Bristol & Gloucester, 10mins from J14 of M5. Follow signs to Berkeley from A38 & B4066. Visitors' entrance is on L of Canonbury St, just before town centre.* **Mon 13 June (11-4). Adm £5, chd free.**
Unique historic garden of a keen plantsman, with far-reaching views across R Severn. Gardens contain

many rare plants which thrive in the warm micro-climate against stone walls of mediaeval castle. Woodland, historic trees and stunning terraced borders. Butterfly house with free-flying tropical butterflies. Lunches, snacks and afternoon tea available in Yurt Restaurant. Gift shop and plant sales. Used as a film location for BBC2's Wolf Hall drama. Featured in Cotswold Life. Difficult for wheelchairs due to terraced nature of gardens.

Butterfly house with free-flying tropical butterflies. . . .

12 BERRYS PLACE FARM
Bulley Lane, Churcham, Gloucester GL2 8AS. Anne Thomas, 07950 808022, g.j.thomas@btconnect.com. *6m W of Gloucester. A40 towards Ross. Turning R into Bulley Lane at Birdwood.* **Sat 18, Sun 19, Wed 22, Thur 23 June (11-5). Adm £3, chd free. Home-made teas. Ploughmans lunches, cream teas.**
Country garden, approx 1 acre, surrounded by farmland and old orchards. Lawns and large sweeping mixed herbaceous borders with over 100 roses. Formal kitchen garden and beautiful rose arbour leading to lake and summerhouse with a variety of water lilies and carp. All shared with peacocks and ducks.

13 BEVERSTON CASTLE
nr Tetbury GL8 8TU. Mrs A L Rook, 07866 452645. *2m W of Tetbury. On A4135 to Dursley between Tetbury & Calcot Xrds.* **Sun 27, Mon 28 Mar, Sun 26 June (2-5.30). Adm £4, chd free. Home-made teas. Visits also by arrangement Apr to Sept, a tour detailing history of castle and buildings may be arranged for a small fee. Max 15.**
Overlooked by romantic C12-C17 castle ruin (not open), copiously-planted paved terrace leads from C18 house (not open) across moat to sloping lawn with spring bulbs in abundance, and full herbaceous and shrub borders. Large walled kitchen garden and greenhouses. Partial wheelchair access.

Misarden Park

BLICKS HILL HOUSE
See Wiltshire

GROUP OPENING

14 BLOCKLEY GARDENS
Blockley GL56 9DB, 01386 700903,
nickplantsperson@btinternet.com.
*3m NW of Moreton-in-Marsh. Just off
the Morton-in-Marsh to Evesham Rd
A44.* **Sun 24 Apr, Sun 12 June
(2-6). Combined adm £6, chd free.
Home-made teas at Mill Dene &
St George's Hall on April 24, at St
George's Hall & The Manor House
on June 12.**

CHURCH GATES
Mrs Brenda Salmon.
Open on all dates

LANDGATE
Mrs Hilary Sutton.
Open on Sun 12 June

THE MANOR HOUSE
George & Zoe Thompson.
Open on all dates

◆ MILL DENE GARDEN
Mr & Mrs B S Dare.
Open on all dates
(See separate entry).

THE OLD CHEQUER
Mr & Mrs H Linley.
Open on Sun 12 June
(See separate entry)

PORCH HOUSE
Mr & Mrs Johnson.
Open on Sun 24 Apr

NEW ◆ 'RODNEYS'
Mr Duncan & Mrs Amelia
Stewart.
Open on Sun 12 June

SNUGBOROUGH MILL ⌂
Rupert and Mandy Williams-
Ellis.
Open on Sun 12 June
01386 701310
rupert.williams-
ellis@talk21.com

WOODRUFF
Paul & Maggie Adams.
Open on all dates

This popular historic hillside village
has a great variety of high quality,
well-stocked gardens - large and
small, old and new. Blockley Brook,
an attractive stream which flows right
through the village, graces some of
the gardens; these incl gardens of
former water mills, with millponds
attached. From some gardens there
are wonderful rural views. Shuttle
coach service provided. Children
welcome but close supervision
required. Access to some gardens
quite steep and allowances should be
made.

**15 ◆ BOURTON HOUSE
GARDEN**
Bourton-on-the-Hill GL56 9AE. Mr
& Mrs R Quintus, 01386 700754,
info@bourtonhouse.com,
www.bourtonhouse.com. *2m W of
Moreton-in-Marsh. On A44.* **For
NGS: Sun 14 Aug (10-5). Adm £6,
chd free. Home-made teas in
Grade I listed C16 Tithe Barn. For
other opening times and
information, please phone, email or
visit garden website.**
Award winning 3 acre garden
featuring imaginative topiary, wide
herbaceous borders with many rare,
unusual and exotic plants, water
features, unique shade house and
many creatively planted pots.
Fabulous at any time of year but
magnificent in summer months. Walk
in 7 acre pasture with free printed
guide to specimen trees available to
garden visitors. Featured in Secret
Gardens of The Cotswolds - A
Personal Tour of 20 Private Gardens
by Victoria Summerley. Photographs
by Hugo Ritson-Thomas. 70%
access for wheelchairs.

16 25 BOWLING GREEN ROAD
Cirencester GL7 2HD. Fr John &
Susan Beck, 01285 653778,
sjb@beck-hems.org.uk. *On NW
edge of Cirencester. Take A435 to
Spitalgate/Whiteway T-lights, turn into*

The Whiteway (Chedworth turn), then 1st L into Bowling Green Rd. **Mon 27 June (11-4); Sun 3 July (2-5); Mon 4 July (11-4); Sun 10 July (2-5); Mon 11, Mon 18 July (11-4). Adm £3, chd free. Visits also by arrangement June & July, max 35-40. Tea/coffee/biscuits can be provided for small groups by arrangement.**
Wander at will along winding walkways and billowing borders in a mini jungle of heavenly hemerocallis, gorgeous grasses, curvaceous clematis, romantic roses and hopeful hostas to glimpse friendly frogs and a graceful giraffe, rated by visitors as a wonderful hidden gem (and even as 'cool' by the young!). In 2015, the garden was visited by Sarah Wint and her NGS Yellow Daisy Bus. Garden owner received the International Service Award from the American Hemerocallis Society. Featured in Cheltenham Echo, Gloucester Citizen and other regional papers.

BRETFORTON MANOR
See Worcestershire

17 ▶ BROCKWORTH COURT
Court Road, Brockworth GL3 4QU. Tim & Bridget Wiltshire, 01452 862938, timwiltshire@hotmail.co.uk. *6m E of Gloucester. 6m W of Cheltenham. Adj St Georges Church on Court Rd. From A46 turn into Mill Lane, turn R, L, R at T junctions. From Ermin St, turn into Ermin Park, then R at r'about then L at next r'about.* **Wed 1 June, Wed 17 Aug (2-5). Adm £5, chd free. Home-made teas in tithe barn. Visits also by arrangement Apr to Sept, house tour available for groups of 10+. Light refreshments by arrangement.**
This intense yet informal tapestry style garden beautifully complements the period manor house which it surrounds. Organic, with distinct cottage-style planting areas that seamlessly blend together. Natural fish pond, with Monet bridge leading to small island with thatched Fiji house. Kitchen garden once cultivated by the monks. Historic tithe barn. Views to Crickley and Coopers Hill. Adj Norman Church (open). Featured on Gloucester radio and in Gloucester Echo and Citizen. Partial wheelchair access.

18 ▶ CAMPDEN HOUSE
Chipping Campden GL55 6UP. The Hon Philip & Mrs Smith. *Entrance on Chipping Campden to Weston Subedge Rd (Dyers Lane), approx ¼ m SW of Campden, 1¼ m drive. Do not use SatNav.* **Thur 9, Thur 16 June (2-6); Wed 31 Aug (2-5.30). Combined adm with Ernest Wilson Memorial Garden £6, chd free. Home-made teas.**
2 acres featuring mixed borders of plant and colour interest around house and C17 tithe barn (neither open). Set in fine parkland in hidden valley with lakes and ponds. Woodland walk, vegetable garden. Gravel paths, steep slopes.

19 ▶ ◆ CERNEY HOUSE GARDENS
North Cerney, Cirencester GL7 7BX. Lady Angus, 01285 831300, www.cerneygardens.com. *4m NW of Cirencester. On A435 Cheltenham rd turn L opp Bathurst Arms, follow road past church up hill, then go straight towards pillared gates on R (signed Cerney House).* **For NGS: Sun 5 June (10-5). Adm £5, chd £1. Light refreshments. A selection of tea, coffee and cakes available. For other opening times and information, please phone or visit garden website.**
Romantic walled garden filled with old-fashioned roses and herbaceous borders. Working kitchen garden, scented garden, Who's Who beds and genera borders. Spring bulbs in abundance all around the wooded grounds. Bothy, pottery, walled garden, green and white garden, koi carp pond, woodland walks, knot garden, bee garden. Limited wheelchair access available, some access difficult.

GROUP OPENING

20 ▶ CHARFIELD VILLAGE GARDENS
Charfield GL12 8TG. *3m S of Wotton-under-Edge on B4058. From M5 take J14 towards Wotton-Under-Edge. At r'about turn L for 3 of the gardens into village or take 2nd exit into Churchend Lane.* **Sun 1, Mon 2 May (2-6). Combined adm £6, chd free. Light refreshments, cakes and cream teas.**

THE PADDOCK
Joanna & Gary Davis

PEMBERLEY LODGE
Rob & Yvette Andrewartha
Visits also by arrangement prior notice required please. Groups of 10+
yvette@gryfindor.info
01454 260885

10 STATION ROAD
Mrs Sue Laing

WARNERS COURT
Barbara & Mike Adams

4 charming gardens in Charfield village. Warners Court (through village, opp Memorial Hall on L): formal garden, shrubbery, wildlife area with pool, vine house and productive vegetable garden. 10 Station Road (through village, over bridge then R into Station Rd. No 10 is on L): beautifully planted in country cottage style, full of plants, successful vegetable and fruit garden and lovely front garden. The Paddock: (through village, over bridge then R into Station Rd then R into Horsford Rd. House is on L): garden wraps round a striking modern house. Space for children to kick a ball and run around while the plant lover in the family has a dedicated charming and relaxing area plus chickens and vegetable patch. Pemberley Lodge (at r'about take 2nd exit into Churchend Lane, garden approx 600 metres on R): a modern garden, designed to provide all yr interest but low maintenance. Unusual roof garden. Light refreshments, tasty cakes and lots of parking for all gardens or the energetic can walk around the village to visit them all. Plenty of plants to buy as you visit the different gardens. Have lunch in one of three village PHs. Nearby Charfield Meadow, an Avon Wildlife Trust site and the C15 St James Church. All gardens have good wheelchair access although some areas may be inaccessible.

Monet bridge leading to small island with thatched Fiji house . . .

21 CHARINGWORTH COURT

Broadway Road, Winchcombe GL54 5JN. Susan & Richard Wakeford, 01242 603033, susanwakeford@gmail.com, www.charingworthcourtcotswolds garden.com. *8m NE of Cheltenham. 400 metres N of Winchcombe town centre car park in Bull Lane; walk down Chandos St, L onto Broadway Rd. Garden is on L or park along Broadway Rd.* **Sat 21, Sun 22 May (11-5.30). Adm £4, chd free. Home-made teas from 2pm. Visits also by arrangement May & June for small groups, day and evening.**

Artistically and lovingly created 1½ acre garden surrounding restored Georgian/Tudor house (not open). Relaxed country style with Japanese influences, large pond and walled vegetable garden. Mature copper beech trees, Cedar of Lebanon and Wellingtonia; and younger trees replacing an excess of Cupressus leylandii. Garden will be backdrop for garden sculpture selling exhibition curated by Winds of Change Gallery. Featured in Daily Telegraph, Gloucestershire Echo, Cotswold Life and in Country Homes and Interiors (2015) and on Radio Gloucestershire. Most paths are gravelled but several areas accessible without steps. Disabled Parking next to the house.

Marie Curie

The NGS is Marie Curie's largest single donor

22 NEW CHELTENHAM TOWN GARDENS

Cheltenham GL53 8HG. *Car parking at St Edwards Junior School, London Rd, Charlton Kings, Cheltenham. From here walk across main rd, then down Hamilton Street; turn R at end to Garlands, 24 Cudnall St, tel 01242 511890 (Lorraine du Feu), where map & details of all the gardens can be obtained.* **Sun 18 Sept (11-5). Combined adm £4, chd free. Home-made teas.**

A selection of small town gardens across Cheltenham incorporating many environmental features including planting for pollinators, intensive organic fruit and vegetables, wildlife ponds, wormeries and composting, rainwater harvesting, beehives and hens. No dogs except guide dogs.

23 ◆ THE COACH HOUSE GARDEN

Ampney Crucis, Cirencester GL7 5RY. Mr & Mrs Nicholas Tanner, 01285 850256, mel@thegenerousgardener.co.uk, www.thegenerousgardener.co.uk. *3m E of Cirencester. Turn into village from A417, immed before Crown of Crucis Inn. Over hump-back bridge, parking immed to R on cricket field (weather permitting) or signposted.* **For NGS: Sun 22 May (2-5). Adm £5, chd free. Home-made teas. For other opening times and information, please phone, email or visit garden website.**

Approx 1½ acres and full of structure and design. Garden is divided into rooms which incl rill garden, gravel garden, rose garden, herbaceous borders, green garden with pleached lime allee and potager. Created over last 28yrs by present owners and constantly evolving. Rare Plant Sales (in aid of James Hopkins Trust) and Garden Lecture Days (www.thegenerousgardener.co.uk). Featured in Cotswold Life. Limited wheelchair access. Ramp available to enable access to main body of garden but some other areas are reached via short flights of steps.

CONDERTON MANOR
See Worcestershire

24 COTSWOLD FARM

Duntisbourne Abbots, Cirencester GL7 7JS. Mrs Mark Birchall, 01285 821857, iona@cotswoldfarmgardens.org.uk, www.cotswoldfarmgardens.org.uk. *5m NW of Cirencester off old A417. From Cirencester L signed Duntisbourne Abbots Services, R and R underpass. Drive ahead. From Gloucester L signed Duntisbourne Abbots Services. Pass Services. Drive L.* **Sat 4, Sun 5 June (2-5). Adm £5, chd free. Cream Teas by WI. Visits also by arrangement, all dates, no limit on numbers.** *Donation to A Rocha.*

Arts and Crafts garden in lovely position overlooking quiet valley on descending levels with terrace designed by Norman Jewson in 1930s. Snowdrops named and naturalised, aconites in Feb. Winter garden, bog garden best in May, White border overflowing with texture and scent. Shrubs, trees, shrub roses. Allotments in old walled garden, 8 native orchids, hundreds of wild flowers and Roman snails. Family day out. Croquet and toys on lawn. Picnics welcome. Partial wheelchair access.

25 DAGLINGWORTH HOUSE

Daglingworth, nr Cirencester GL7 7AG. David & Henrietta Howard, 01285 885626, daglingworthhse@aol.com. *3m N of Cirencester off A417/419. House with blue gate beside church in Daglingworth.* **Visits by arrangement May to Sept for groups between 4 & 25. Adm £6.**

Walled garden, water features, temple and grotto. Classical garden of 2 acres, views and vistas with humorous contemporary twist. Attractive planting, hedges, topiary shapes, herbaceous borders. Pergolas, woodland, pool, cascade and mirror canal. Lovely Cotswold village setting beside church. Magazine articles in Cotswold Life and The Gloucester Echo.

26 DAYLESFORD HOUSE

Daylesford GL56 0YG. Lord Bamford & Lady Bamford, 01608 658888, estate.office@daylesford.co.uk. *5m W of Chipping Norton. Off A436. Between Stow-on-the-Wold & Chipping Norton.* **Wed 22 June (1-5). Adm £5, chd free. Light refreshments.**

Magnificent C18 landscape grounds created 1790 for Warren Hastings, greatly restored and enhanced by present owners. Lakeside and woodland walks within natural wild flower meadows. Large walled garden planted formally, centred around orchid, peach and working glasshouses. Trellised rose garden. Collection of citrus within period orangery. Secret garden with pavilion and formal pools. Very large garden with substantial distances to be walked. General pathways allow access however the terraine is not always easy for pushing a wheelchair.

27 1 DRIVE COTTAGE
Aldsworth GL54 3PT. Mrs & Miss
Walton. *Situated 4m from Burford,
3m from Aldsworth on A4425.* **Sun
17 July (2-6). Combined adm with
Barrington Downs £5, chd free.**
Surrounded by farmland with
perennials, shrubs and young acers.
The hot bed is full of echinaceas and
other bee and butterfly friendly plants
in July and Aug. No hard pathways,
flat grassed area.

GROUP OPENING

**28 EASTCOMBE, BUSSAGE
AND BROWNSHILL GARDENS**
Eastcombe GL6 7DS. *3m E of
Stroud. 2m N of A419 Stroud to
Cirencester rd on turning signed to
Bisley & Eastcombe. Please park
considerately in villages.* **Sun 1, Mon
2 May (2-6). Combined adm £6,
chd free.** Home-made teas at
Eastcombe Village Hall. Cream
teas/home-made cakes. *Donation
to Acorns Children's Hospice; Breast
Cancer Care; Hope for Tomorrow.*

CADSONBURY
Mr & Mrs Beswetherick

21 FARMCOTE CLOSE
Mr & Mrs Bryant

HAWKLEY COTTAGE
Helen Westendorp
Visits also by arrangement May
to Oct. Helen@tree-house.co.uk
01452 770680

**NEW HAWKLEY FARM
HOUSE**
Paul and Wendy Bates

1 HIDCOTE CLOSE
Mr & Mrs J Southall

12 HIDCOTE CLOSE
Mr & Mrs K Walker

1 THE LAURELS
Andrew & Ruth Fraser

MARYFIELD
Mrs M Brown

MIDDLEGARTH
Peter Walker

REDWOOD
Rita Collins

ROSE COTTAGE
Mrs Juliet Shipman

VATCH RISE
Peggy Abbott

YEW TREE COTTAGE
Andy & Sue Green

A group of gardens, medium and
small, set in picturesque hilltop
location. Some approachable only by
foot. (Exhibitions may be on view in
Eastcombe village hall). Glos Plant
Heritage may have a sale of plants at
Eastcombe Village Hall. There may
also be other small plant sales in
some gardens. Please visit the NGS
website www.ngs.org.uk for further
information. Wheelchair access to
some gardens.

Selection of small town gardens across Cheltenham . . .

29 EASTLEACH HOUSE
Eastleach Martin, Cirencester
GL7 3NW. Mrs David Richards,
garden@eastleachhouse.com,
www.eastleachhouse.com. *5m NE
of Fairford, 6m S of Burford. Entrance
opp church gates in Eastleach Martin.
Lodge at gate and driveway is quite
steep up to house.* **Visits by
arrangement May to July for any
size group. Refreshments at
Victoria Inn, Eastleach, must book.**
Large traditional all-yr-round garden.
Wooded hilltop position with long
views S and W. New parkland, lime
avenue and arboretum. Wild flower
walk, wildlife pond, lawns, walled and
rill gardens, with modern herbaceous
borders, yew and box hedges, iris and
paeony borders, lily ponds, formal
herb garden and topiary. Rambling
roses into trees. Gravel paths and
some steep slopes. Limited access.

**30 ERNEST WILSON
MEMORIAL GARDEN**
Leysbourne, Chipping Campden
GL55 6DL. EWMG Trust. *High St.
Chipping Campden, at Leysbourne
below church.* **Thur 9, Thur 16 June
(2-6); Wed 31 Aug (2-5.30).
Combined adm with Campden
House £6, chd free.**
The Ernest Wilson Memorial Garden
was created in 1984 in memory of
Ernest Wilson, the celebrated plant
hunter who was born in Chipping
Campden in 1876. This small tranquil
walled garden in the centre of town
features entirely plants, shrubs and
trees introduced by Ernest Wilson.

NPC

31 EYFORD HOUSE
Upper Slaughter, Cheltenham
GL54 2JN. Mrs C Heber-Percy.
*2¹/₂ m from Stow on the Wold on
B4068 Stow to Andoversford Rd.*
**Wed 8 June (11-6), home-made
teas. Wed 22 June (11-4). Adm £4,
chd free. Also open Rockcliffe
House.**
1¹/₂ -acre sloping N facing garden,
ornamental shrubs and trees. Laid
out originally by Graham Stuart
Thomas, 1976. West garden and
terrace, red border, walled kitchen
garden, two lakes with pleasant walks
and views, boots recommended! Holy
well. Walled garden now open after
reconstruction. Featured in The
Secret Gardens of the Cotswolds by
Victoria Summerely.

32 FORTHAMPTON COURT
Forthampton, Tewkesbury
GL19 4RD. John Yorke. *W of
Tewkesbury. From Tewkesbury A438
to Ledbury. After 2m turn L to
Forthampton. At Xrds go L towards
Chaceley. Go 1m turn L at Xrds.* **Sun
3 July (11-4). Adm £4.50, chd free.
Home-made teas.**
Charming and varied garden
surrounding North Gloucestershire
Medieval manor house (not open)
within sight of Tewkesbury Abbey. Incl
borders, lawns, roses and magnificent
Victorian vegetable garden.

33 THE GABLES
Riverside Lane, Broadoak,
Newnham on Severn GL14 1JE.
Bryan & Christine Bamber. *1m NE
of Newnham on Severn. Park in
White Hart PH unsurfaced car park,
to R when facing river. Please follow
the signs. Walk 250 metres along
road towards Gloucester past PH to
The Gables. Access through marked
field gate.* **Sun 26 June, Sun 21 Aug
(11-4). Adm £3.50, chd free. Light
refreshments.**
Garden was started in 2006 from a
blank canvas. Large flat garden with
formal lawns, colourful herbaceous
borders and shrubberies. Incl wild
flower meadow incorporating soft
fruits and fruit trees, an allotment-size
productive vegetable plot, greenhouse
and composting area. Disabled
parking information available at
entrance. All areas of garden visible for
wheelchair users but with limited
access.

34 **NEW** **'GREENFIELDS'**
Brockweir Common, Brockweir
NP16 7NU. Jackie Healy, 07747
186302,
greenfieldsgarden@icloud.com,
www.greenfieldsgarden.com.
*Located in the Wye valley - mid way
between Chepstow and Monmouth.
A446: from M'mouth: Thru Llandogo.
L to Brockweir, (from Chepstow, thru
Tintern. R to B'weir) over bridge, pass
PH up hill, 1st L, follow lane to fork,
take L at fork. 1st property on R.* **Sun
26 June (1-5.30). Combined adm
with Barn House, Chepstow £6,
chd free. Home-made teas. Visits
also by arrangement Apr to Sept,
groups up to 20 persons
welcome. Possibility of visiting
Barn House by arrangement on
same day.**
1.5 acre plant person's gem of a
garden set in the beautiful Wye Valley.
Many mature trees and numerous
unusual plants and shrubs, all planted
as discrete gardens within a garden.
Greenfields is the passion and work
of 'head gardener' Jackie who has a
long interest in the propagation of
plants. Open jointly with Barn House
Gardens, 10 mins from Greenfields.
Enjoy a great day out in the Wye
Valley and visit 2 spectacular
gardens. Mostly wheelchair access.
& ⊛ ☕

Enjoy a great day
out in the Wye
Valley and visit
2 spectacular
gardens . . .

35 ◆ **HERBS FOR HEALING**
Claptons Lane (behind Barnsley
House Hotel), Barnsley GL7 5EE.
Davina Wynne-Jones, 07773
687493,
davina@herbsforhealing.net,
www.herbsforhealing.net. *4m NE of
Cirencester. Coming into Barnsley
from Cirencester - turn R after
Barnsley House Hotel and R again at
dairy barn. Follow signs.* **For NGS:
Wed 29 June, Wed 27 July (10.30-
4.30). Adm £3, chd free. Teas,
herb teas and home made cakes.
For other opening times and
information, please phone, email or
visit garden website.**

Not a typical NGS garden, rural and
naturalistic. Davina, the daughter of
Rosemary Verey, has created a
unique nursery, specialising in
medicinal herbs and a tranquil
organic garden in secluded field
where visitors can enjoy the beauty of
plants and learn more about
properties and uses of medicinal
herbs. Informative tours of the garden
with Davina at 11.30 and 2.30.
Products made from the herbs are
available. Access to WC is difficult for
wheelchair users however the garden
itself is all level.
& ⊞ ⊛ ☕

36 ◆ **HIDCOTE MANOR
GARDEN**
Hidcote Bartrim, Chipping
Campden GL55 6LR. National
Trust, 01386 438333,
www.nationaltrust.org.uk/hidcote.
*4m NW of Chipping Campden. Off
B4081.* **For NGS: Evening opening
Tue 21 June (6-9). Adm £10.90,
chd £5.45. Light refreshments in
Winthrops Café. For other opening
times and information, please
phone 01386 438333 or visit
www.nationaltrust.org.uk/hidcote.**
One of England's great gardens.
10½ acre Arts and Crafts
masterpiece created by Major
Lawrence Johnston. Series of
outdoor rooms, each with a different
character, separated by walls and
hedges of many different species.
Rare trees, shrubs, outstanding
herbaceous borders, and unusual
plant species from all over the world.
Head Gardener will give short talk on
history of garden at 6.30, 7.30 & 8.30
and will be available during the
evening to answer questions (no
additional cost). Regret no
admission concessions for NT
members. Motorised buggies
available to borrow. One or two areas
not completely accessible to
wheelchairs.
& ⊛ ⇌ ☕

37 ▶ **HIGHNAM COURT**
Highnam, Gloucester GL2 8DP. Mr
and Mrs R J Head,
www.HighnamCourt.co.uk. *2m W of
Gloucester. On A40/A48 from
Gloucester.* **Sun 3 Apr, Sun 1 May,
Sun 5 June, Sun 3 July, Sun 7 Aug,
Sun 4 Sept (11-5). Adm £5, chd
free. Light refreshments in
Orangery. Tea, coffee from 11am.
Sandwiches available until
1.30pm. Cream teas served from
1.30 to 5pm.**

40 acres of Victorian landscaped
gardens surrounding magnificent
Grade I house (not open), set out by
artist Thomas Gambier Parry. Lakes,
shrubberies and listed Pulhamite
water gardens with grottos and
fernery. Exciting ornamental lakes,
and woodland areas. Extensive 1
acre rose garden and many features,
incl numerous wood carvings. Some
gravel paths and steps into
refreshment area. Disabled WC.
& ⊛ ⇌ ☕

38 ▶ **HODGES BARN**
Shipton Moyne, Tetbury GL8 8PR.
Mr & Mrs N Hornby, 01666 880202,
hornby@cernocapital.com. *3m S of
Tetbury. On Malmesbury side of
village.* **Sun 5, Mon 6 June (2-6).
Adm £5, chd free. Visits also by
arrangement for groups.**
Very unusual C15 dovecote
converted into family home. Cotswold
stone walls host climbing and
rambling roses, clematis, vines,
hydrangeas and together with yew,
rose and tapestry hedges create
formality around house. Mixed shrub
and herbaceous borders, shrub
roses, water garden, woodland
garden planted with cherries,
magnolia and spring bulbs. Some
gravel, mostly grass.
& ⊞

39 ▶ **HOME FARM**
Newent Lane, Huntley GL19 3HQ.
Mrs T Freeman, 01452 830210,
torill@ukgateway.net. *4m S of
Newent. On B4216 ½ m off A40 in
Huntley travelling towards Newent.*
**Sun 13 Mar, Sun 10, Sun 24 Apr
(11-4). Adm £4, chd free. 2017:
Sun 29 Jan, Sun 12 Feb. Visits
also by arrangement Jan to May.**
Set in elevated position with
exceptional views. 1m walk through
woods and fields to show carpets of
spring flowers. Enclosed garden with
fern border, sundial and heather bed.
White and mixed shrub borders.
Stout footwear advisable in winter.
⊞

40 ▶ **HOOKSHOUSE POTTERY**
Hookshouse Lane, Tetbury
GL8 8TZ. Lise & Christopher White,
01666 880297,
hookshouse@hotmail.co.uk,
www.hookshousepottery.co.uk.
*2½ m SW of Tetbury. Follow signs
from A433 at Hare and Hounds
Hotel, Westonbirt. Alternatively take
A4135 out of Tetbury towards Dursley*

Brockworth Court

and follow signs after ½ m on L. **Sat 28, Sun 29, Mon 30, Tue 31 May, Wed 1, Thur 2, Fri 3, Sat 4, Sun 5 June (11-6). Adm £3.50, chd free. Home-made teas.**
Garden offers a combination of dramatic open perspectives and intimate corners. Planting incl wide variety of perennials, with emphasis on colour interest throughout the seasons. Borders, shrubs, woodland glade, water garden containing treatment ponds (unfenced) and flowform cascades. Kitchen garden with raised beds, orchard. Sculptural features. Run on organic principles. Pottery showroom with hand thrown wood-fired pots incl frostproof garden pots. Art & Craft exhibition incl garden furniture and sculptures. Garden games and tree house. Featured in Gloucester Citizen, Gloucestershire Echo and Wilts and Gloucester Standard. Apart from 1 small area, garden fully accessible to wheelchairs.

GROUP OPENING

41 ICOMB GARDENS
Icomb, Stow-on-the-Wold
GL54 1JL. *3m S of Stow-on-the-Wold. Take Icomb Rd off A424 Burford-Stow Rd. After 1m turn R signed Icomb. Parking near gardens as directed by stewards. No parking*

on street. **Sun 26 June (1.30-5). Combined adm £5, chd free. Home-made teas in village hall.**

CORNER COTTAGE
Jean Hartley

GUYS FARM
Vanda Palmer

HOME FARM
Miss Ellen Fisher

ICOMB BANK
David & Susie Dugdale

THE LAWNS
Rachel & Michael Stone

LITTLE DORMERS
Vanessa & Jonathan Curry

MANOR FARM
Eleanor & Hugh Paget

2 PARK VIEW COTTAGES
David Cowdery

NEW PARK VIEW HOUSE
Mr & Mrs Ros & Steve Watson

Small pretty village with glorious views and early C13 church. Manor Farm: Well laid out large garden with unusual plants, orchard and ornamental vegetable plot and exceptional views. 2 Park View Cottages: Pretty well-stocked small front garden with courtyard at back acting as outdoor room. Guy's Farm: Peaceful cottage garden with terrace and herbaceous border. Home Farm: Extensive well-stocked cottage garden with fruit and vegetables and

lovely views. Corner Cottage: Small courtyard garden with pots and climbers. The Lawns: Cottage garden enclosed in Cotswold stone walling with mature and young trees, raised fish pond and borders with all-year round interest featuring pastel colours. Little Dormers: Terraced cottage garden with dry stone walls. Park View House: Charming cottage garden with different rooms.
2 ParkView Cottages & Little Dormers have no wheelchair access. Dogs on leads welcome except at Home Farm where only guide dogs allowed.

42 ◆ KIFTSGATE COURT
Chipping Campden GL55 6LN. Mr & Mrs J G Chambers, 01386 438777, www.kiftsgate.co.uk. *4m NE of Chipping Campden. Adj to Hidcote NT Garden. 3m NE of Chipping Campden.* **For NGS: Mon 11 Apr, Mon 15 Aug (2-6). Adm £8, chd £2.50. Home-made teas. For other opening times and information, please phone or visit garden website.**
Magnificent situation and views, many unusual plants and shrubs, tree peonies, hydrangeas, abutilons, species and old-fashioned roses incl largest rose in England, Rosa filipes Kiftsgate. Steep slopes and uneven surfaces.

43 LITTLEFIELD GARDEN
Hawling, Cheltenham GL54 5SZ. Mr & Mrs George Wilk. *From A40 Cheltenham to Oxford at Andoversford turn onto A436 towards Stow-On-The-Wold. Take 2nd signed rd to Hawling.* **Sun 3, Sun 17 July (11-5). Adm £4, chd free. Home-made teas.**
Surrounded by idyllic countryside with fine views over small valley, site of old medieval village of Hawling, Littlefield Garden was originally designed by Jane Fearnley-Whittingstall. More recently the planting in the yew walk was created by Sherborne Gardens. Rose garden, mixed borders, lily pond, wildflower meadow and lavender borders. Visitors can stroll 200yds across meadow to natural pond or have tea and relax under the pergola. Featured in Cotswold Life and on BBC Radio Gloucestershire. Mostly wheelchair access. Gravel path and paved terraces.

Imaginative
stalls offering
accessories
for your home
and garden . . .

44 LODERS GATE
Fairford Road, Downington, Lechlade GL7 3DL. Mr Jim Pymer. *¹/₂ m from centre of Lechlade off A417 to Fairford. Turn R into gravel drive 100yds past West Alcott sign. No Parking.* **Sat 18 June (10.30-4). Adm £5, chd free. Tea.**
A plant lover's haven of 1¹/₂ acres. Front garden with long deep borders of herbaceous plants, ornamental grasses and yew hedging, is repeated in walled garden to rear of house. Beyond is large garden with 2 wildlife ponds, small wooded area, greenhouse, lawns, mature trees, rose garden and long herbaceous and shrub borders.

GROUP OPENING

45 LONGHOPE GARDENS
Longhope GL17 0NA, 01452 830406, sally.j.gibson@btinternet.com. *10m W of Gloucester. 7m E of Ross on Wye. A40 take Longhope turn off to Church Rd. From A4136 follow Longhope signs and turn onto Church Rd. Parking available on Church Rd.* **Sat 28 May (12-5); Sun 29 May (2-6); Sat 4 June (12-5); Sun 5 June (2-6). Combined adm £5, chd free. Home-made teas. Visits also by arrangement May & June for groups of 10+.**

CHESSGROVE COTTAGE
Mr Peter Evans

3 CHURCH ROAD
Rev Clive & Mrs Linda Edmonds

SPRINGFIELD HOUSE
Sally & Martin Gibson

WOODBINE COTTAGE
Mrs Lucille Roughley

Small village, sited in valley, with wonderful views and splendid C12 church. 4 well planted gardens, with different planting styles. Ample parking in village or if you're feeling energetic you can walk to all gardens. Refreshments and plant sales available at some gardens. 3 Church Road: long garden divided into rooms with large collection of hardy geraniums. Springfield House: large enclosed terraced garden with wide variety of shrubs and trees mingling with sweeping borders and a wildlife pond. Woodbine Cottage: tranquil garden with traditional planting. Chessgrove Cottage: delightful garden with spectacular views and access to 12 acres of surrounding woodland.

46 LOWER FARM HOUSE
Cliffords Mesne, Newent GL18 1JT. Gareth & Sarah Williams, 01531 821654. *2m S of Newent. From Newent, follow signs to Cliffords Mesne and Birds of Prey Centre (1¹/₂ m). Approx ¹/₂ m beyond Centre, turn L at Xrds (before church).* **Wed 1 June (12-6). Adm £4, chd free. Tea. Visits also by arrangement May & June for groups of 10+.**
2 acre garden, incl woodland, stream and large natural lily pond with rockery and bog garden. Herbaceous borders, pergola walk, terrace with

ornamental fishpond, kitchen and herb garden; collections of irises, hostas and paeonies. Many interesting and unusual trees and shrubs incl magnolias and cornus. Some gravel paths.

47 ◆ LYDNEY PARK SPRING GARDEN
Lydney GL15 6BU. The Viscount Bledisloe, 01594 842844/842922, www.lydneyparkestate.co.uk. *¹/₂ m SW of Lydney. On A48 Gloucester to Chepstow rd between Lydney & Aylburton. Drive is directly off A48.* **For NGS: Wed 11 May (10-5). Adm £5, chd 50p. Light lunches. For other opening times and information, please phone or visit garden website.**
Spring garden in 8 acre woodland valley with lakes, profusion of rhododendrons, azaleas and other flowering shrubs. Formal garden; magnolias and daffodils (April). Picnics in deer park which has fine trees. Important Roman Temple site and museum.

48 THE MANOR
Little Compton, Moreton-In-Marsh GL56 0RZ. Mr R Shaw. *Next to church in Little Compton. 1m from A44 and then 2m from A3400 follow signs to Little Compton and then pick up yellow ngs signs.* **Sun 5 June, Sun 21 Aug (2-5). Adm £5, chd free. Home-made teas.**
C16 historic manor house (not open) and 4 acres of stunning gardens set in a beautiful location in village of Little Compton. Enjoy the many garden rooms, the long herbaceous borders, deer walk, Japanese garden, flower garden, arboretum and specimen trees. Garden staff on site, croquet and tennis courts available to play.

49 ◆ MATARA GARDENS OF WELLBEING
Kingscote, Tetbury GL8 8YA. Herons Mead Ltd, 01453 861050, info@matara.co.uk, www.matarawellbeing.com. *5¹/₂ m NW of Tetbury. Approx 20mins from either J18 of M4 (12m) or J13 of M5 (8.5m).* **For NGS: Sun 12 June (1-5). Adm £6, chd free. Home-made teas. You are welcome to bring your own picnics if you would like to picnic in the gardens. For other opening times**

and information, please phone, email or visit garden website.

Trees of life - enjoy the tranquil beauty of Matara's Gardens of Wellbeing and its dedication to the symbolic, spiritual and cultural role of trees. What makes us special are our Chinese scholar garden, Japanese tea garden, Shinto woodland, Celtic wishing tree, labyrinth, healing spiral, field of dreams and ornamental herb and flower gardens. Woodland walk, Chinese cloistered courtyard, barefoot trail, ponds, strolling walk, walled garden and vegetable garden. Limited wheelchair access. Some steps around house area. Some grass paths.

50 THE MEETING HOUSE

New Road, Flaxley, Newnham GL14 1JS. Chris & Sally Parsons, 01452 760733. *Off A48, close to Westbury-on-Severn. S from Westbury-on-Severn, turn R signed Flaxley. Take 2nd L. 1st house on L. Park in field. Parking for coaches 500yds away (drop off at garden).* **Visits by arrangement Apr to Sept, please leave clear message on answering machine. Adm £5, chd free.**

Cottage with 2 acres developed by owners over last 20 yrs. Hedges, lawns, herbaceous borders, organic fruit trees, soft fruit and vegetables, greenhouse, orchard with wild flowers, reed bed sewage system and summerhouse. Also open: surrounding 17 acres of wild flower meadows, old and new orchards and ponds, managed for conservation.

51 ◆ MILL DENE GARDEN

School Lane, Blockley, Moreton-in-Marsh GL56 9HU. Mr & Mrs B S Dare, 01386 700457, info@milldenegarden.co.uk, www.milldenegarden.co.uk. *3m NW of Moreton-in-Marsh. From A44 follow brown signs from Bourton-on-the-Hill to Blockley. Approx 1¼ m down hill turn L behind village gates. Limited parking. Coaches by appt.* **For NGS: Sun 29 May, Sun 26 June (2-5). Adm £9, chd under 15 £3. Tea. Opening with Blockley Gardens on Sun 24 Apr, Sun 12 June. For other opening times and information, please phone, email or visit garden website.**

50 shades of green (!) at least in this 2½ acre garden hidden in the Cotswolds. Centrepiece is water mill dating from C10 (probably), with mill pond and stream. The owners have had fun creating a varied garden, from informal woodland full of bulbs, to rose walk, cricket lawn, then herb garden looking out over hills with church as backdrop. Garden trail for children. Booklet re development of garden available £2.50. Half of garden wheelchair accessible. Please ring for reserved parking/ramps. Garden in a valley but sides have slope or step alternatives.

52 ◆ MISARDEN PARK

Miserden, Stroud GL6 7JA. Major M T N H Wills, 01285 821303, estate.office@miserdenestate.co.uk, www.misardenpark.co.uk. *6m NW of Cirencester. Follow signs off A417 or B4070 from Stroud.* **For NGS: Sun 27 Mar, Sun 26 June (2-6). Adm £6, chd free. Home-made teas on terrace. For other opening times and information, please phone, email or visit garden website.**

This lovely, unspoilt garden, positioned high on the Wolds and commanding spectacular views was created in C17 and still retains a wonderful sense of timeless peace and tranquillity. Perhaps finest features in garden are double 92metre mixed border incl roses and clematis, in different colour sections. Much of original garden is found within ancient Cotswold stone walls. Partial access for wheelchairs.

NGS donations help support over 200 hospices across the country

53 MOOR WOOD

Woodmancote GL7 7EB. Mr & Mrs Henry Robinson. *3½ m NW of Cirencester. Turn L off A435 to Cheltenham at North Cerney, signed Woodmancote 1¼ m; entrance in village on L beside lodge* with white gates. **Sun 26 June (2-6). Adm £4, chd free. Home-made teas.**

2 acres of shrub, orchard and wild flower gardens in beautiful isolated valley setting. Holder of National Collection of Rambler Roses. Not recommended for wheelchairs.

NPC

GROUP OPENING

54 NAILSWORTH GARDENS - OFF CHESTNUT HILL

Nailworth GL6 0RR. *4m S of Stroud. Parking at Prices Mill Surgery, Newmarket Road, Nailsworth.* **Sun 19 June (1-6). Combined adm £4, chd free. Tea, coffee, squash and cake.**

NEW **THE BARN**
Roger & Frances Lewis

NEW **7 CHESTNUT CLOSE**
Maureen Horscroft

FLORIS HOUSE
Elly Austin

SPRINGFIELDS
Mr Andrew Joyce

4 gardens on steep hill offering completely different designs, features and planting. Many steps.

55 NEW OAKWOOD FARM PLANT FAIR AND GARDEN

Upper Minety, Malmesbury SN16 9PY. Mr & Mrs C Gallop, 01666 860286, katiegallop@btinternet.com. *7m SE of Cirencester. Follow signs from A429 (Cotswold Water Park) or alternatively from B4040 to Minety Church.* **Sun 26 June (11-5). Adm £4, chd free. Home-made teas in aid of Macmillan Cancer Support in Gloucestershire.**

Enjoy tea and home-made refreshments on the glorious farm lawn, within a garden of many gardens, overlooking Minety Church. Specialist nurseries who know and care about plants alongside imaginative stalls offering accessories for your home and garden will be showcasing at this new event. Some gravel, mostly grass. Disabled parking available.

Temple Guiting Manor

© Andrew Lawson

56 THE OLD CHEQUER

Draycott, Moreton in Marsh GL56 9LB. Mr & Mrs H Linley, 01386 700647, g.f.linley1@btinternet.com. *3m NW of Moreton-in-Marsh. Off the Moreton-in-Marsh to Evesham Rd A44. Through Blockley. Turn R by cemetery to Draycott. Through village turn R. First house on R by large box hedge.* **Sun 10 Apr (2-5). Adm £3, chd free. Home-made teas. Opening with Blockley Gardens on Sun 12 June. Visits also by arrangement Apr & May for groups of 10+.**
Cottage garden, created by owner, set in 2 acres of old orchard with original ridge and furrow. Emphasis on spring planting but still maintaining yr-round interest. Kitchen garden/soft fruit, herbaceous, shrubs, Croquet lawn, unusual plants, alpines and dry gravel borders.

57 THE OLD RECTORY, DUNTISBOURNE ROUS

Cirencester GL7 7AP. Charles & Mary Keen, mary@keengardener.com, www.keengardener.com. *4m NW of Cirencester. From Daglingworth take rd to Duntisbournes. Or from A417 from Gloucester take Duntisbourne Leer turning, follow signs for Daglingworth.* **Mon 22 Feb, Mon 18 Apr (12-4); Mon 18 July (12-5). Adm £5, chd free. Tea in schoolroom, DIY teas or coffee with a fire in winter. Visits also by arrangement Feb to Sept for groups of 10+ and short talk from Mary Keen.**
Garden in an exceptional setting made by designer and writer Mary Keen. Subject of many articles and Telegraph column. Designed for atmosphere and all yr interest, but collections of galanthus, hellebores, auriculas and half hardies - especially dahlias - are all features in their

season. Snowdrops and auriculas for sale. Featured in Country Life. Difficult access for wheelchairs, find me for help. Parking can be arranged in the yard if booked before the day.

58 THE OLD RECTORY, QUENINGTON

Church Rd, Quenington, Cirencester GL7 5BN. Mr & Mrs David Abel Smith, www.freshairsculpture.com. *Opp St Swithins Church at bottom of village. 8m NE of Cirencester. Garden well signed once in village.* **Sun 19 June (2-5.30). Combined adm with Beech House £5, chd free. Home-made teas.**
On the banks of the mill race and the River Coln, this is an organic garden of great variety. Mature trees, large vegetable garden, herbaceous borders, shade garden, pool and bog gardens.

OVERBURY COURT
See Worcestershire

59 ◆ PAINSWICK ROCOCO GARDEN

Painswick GL6 6TH. Painswick Rococo Garden Trust, 01452 813204, info@rococogarden.org.uk, www.rococogarden.org.uk. *1/2 m N of Painswick. 1/2 m outside village on B4073, follow brown tourism signs.* For opening times and information, please phone, email or visit garden website.
Unique C18 garden from the brief Rococo period, combining contemporary buildings, vistas, ponds, kitchen garden and winding woodland walks. Anniversary maze, on site restaurant, shop and plant sales. Snowdrop display late winter. Limited wheelchair access to garden due to it being set in a valley. Disabled access to WC and restaurant.

60 PASTURE FARM

Upper Oddington, Moreton-In-Marsh GL56 0XG. Mr & Mrs John LLoyd, 01451 830203, ljmlloyd@yahoo.com. *Mid-way between Upper and Lower Oddington. Oddington lies about 3m from Stow-on-the-Wold just off A436.* **Sun 29, Mon 30 May (11-6). Adm £4, chd free. Home-made teas. Visits also by arrangement June to Oct.**

Medium sized informal country garden that has evolved over 30yrs by current owners. It has all-yr interest with mixed borders, topiary, hedging both formal and informal, orchard and wealth of garden trees. In rural setting with very large spring fed pond inhabited by collection of ducks. Large plant stalls of herbaceous, shrubs and vegetables (proceeds to Kate's Home Nursing). Public footpath across 2 small fields arrives at C11 church, St Nicholas, with doom paintings, set in ancient woodlands. Truly worth a visit. See Simon Jenkins' Book of Churches. Coaches on open days by appt only.

61 ▶ PEAR TREE COTTAGE
58 Malleson Road, Gotherington GL52 9EX. Mr & Mrs E Manders-Trett, 01242 674592, edandmary@talktalk.net. *4m N of Cheltenham. From A435, travelling N, turn R into Gotherington 1m after end of Bishop's Cleeve bypass at garage. Garden on L approx 100yds past Shutter Inn.* **Visits by arrangement Apr to June for 30 max. Adm £4, chd free.**
Mainly informal country garden of approx ¹/₂ acre with pond and gravel garden, grasses and herbaceous borders, trees and shrubs surrounding lawns. Wild garden and orchard lead to greenhouses, herb and vegetable gardens. Spring bulbs, early summer perennials and shrubs particularly colourful. Featured in Cotswold Style magazine - 'Behind the Garden Gate'. Several small steps and some narrow paths.

62 ▶ RAMBLERS
Lower Common, Aylburton, Lydney GL15 6DS. Jane & Leslie Hale, leslie.hale@virgin.net. *1¹/₂ m W of Lydney. Off A48 Gloucester to Chepstow Rd. From Lydney through Aylburton, out of de-limit turn R signed Aylburton Common, ³/₄ m along lane.* **Sun 1 May (1.30-5.30). Adm £3.50, chd free. Home-made teas. Visits also by arrangement Apr to June.**
Peaceful medium sized country garden with informal cottage planting, herbaceous borders and small pond looking through hedge windows onto wild flower meadow. Front woodland garden with shade loving plants and topiary. Large productive vegetable garden. Apple orchard.

63 ▶ ROCKCLIFFE HOUSE
Upper Slaughter, Cheltenham GL54 2JW. Mr & Mrs Simon Keswick. *2m SW of Stow-on-the-Wold. 1¹/₂ m from Lower Swell on B4068 towards Cheltenham. Leave Stow on the Wold on B4068 through Lower Swell. Continue on B4068 for 1¹/₂ m. Rockcliffe is well signed on R.* **Wed 8, Wed 22 June (11-6). Adm £5, chd free. Home-made teas.** *Donation to Kates Home Nursing.*
Large traditional English garden of 8 acres incl pink garden, white and blue garden, herbaceous border, rose terrace, large walled kitchen garden and orchard. Greenhouses and pathway of topiary birds leading up through orchard to stone dovecot. Dramatic pond surrounded by 6 large cornus contraversa variegata. Featured in several magazines. 2 wide stone steps through gate, otherwise good wheelchair access.

64 ▶ ROSE COTTAGE
Kempley, Nr Dymock GL18 2BN. Naomi Cryer. *3m from Newent towards Dymock. From Newent on B4221 take turning just after PH, on R from Gloucester direction, signed Kempley. Follow rd for approx 3m.* **Sat 18, Sun 19 June, Sat 10, Sun 11 Sept (11-5). Adm £3.50, chd free. Home-made teas.**
Open this year in June and in September. About 1 acre of flat garden, put mostly to herbaceous borders. Hot bed and long border leading to borrowed view, small parterre in orchard area, grass bed and pond. Small wild flower pasture, at its best in June. Rose garden, iris bed, hydrangea bed, over 200 dahlias, vegetable plot, nursery bed and cutting garden. Home made cakes and plants for sale. Featured in Citizen Weekend. Although quite flat, wheelchair access mostly via lawn and grass which may make wheelchair use a little difficult especially in damp weather.

65 ▶ SCATTERFORD
Newland, Coleford GL16 8NG. Sean Swallow, 01291 675483, nmklweare@tiscali.co.uk, www.seanswallow.com. *1m S of Newland and just N of Clearwell, opp junction to Coleford. From Monmouth take A466/Redbrook Rd to Redbrook. From Chepstow take B4228 turn off to Clearwell. From Coleford take*

Newland Street. **Visits by arrangement for recognised horticultural and design groups of 10+. Adm £5, chd free.**
2-acre garden set in Wye valley and Forest of Dean borders. A contemporary take on a country garden: formal pond, walled garden, sculpted terraces, courtyards, ha-ha and natural pond. Home of garden maker and consultant Sean Swallow, the garden is in harmony with the historic house and setting. Serene atmosphere and softly layered planting. Head Gardener: Kelly Weare.

A contemporary take on a country garden . . .

66 ◆ SEZINCOTE
Moreton-in-Marsh GL56 9AW. Mrs D Peake, 01386 700444, enquiries@sezincote.com, www.sezincote.co.uk. *3m SW of Moreton-in-Marsh. From Moreton-in-Marsh turn W along A44 towards Evesham; after 1¹/₂ m (just before Bourton-on-the-Hill) turn L, by stone lodge with white gate.* **For NGS: Sun 3 July (2-6). Adm £5, chd free. Home-made teas. For other opening times and information, please phone, email or visit garden website.**
Exotic oriental water garden by Repton and Daniell with lake, pools and meandering stream, banked with massed perennials. Large semi-circular orangery, formal Indian garden, fountain, temple and unusual trees of vast size in lawn and wooded park setting. House in Indian manner designed by Samuel Pepys Cockerell. Garden on slope with gravel paths, so not all areas wheelchair accessible.

67 ◆ SNOWSHILL MANOR & GARDEN

Snowshill, Broadway WR12 7JU. National Trust, 01386 842810, www.nationaltrust.org.uk. *2¹/₂ m SW of Broadway. Off A44 bypass into Broadway village.* **For NGS: Fri 24 June (11-5). Adm £6.50, chd £3.50. Light refreshments. For other opening times and information, please phone or visit garden website.**
Delightful hillside garden surrounding beautiful Cotswold manor, designed in Arts & Crafts style. Garden consists of a series of contrasting outdoor rooms. Simple, colourful plantings tumble and scramble down the terraces and around byres and ponds. Enjoy produce from kitchen garden in the Tea Room. Lunches, snacks and cream teas. Gift shop. Garden not suitable for wheelchairs as terraced with many steps. Tea Room, shop and WC are wheelchair accessible.

68 SOUTH LODGE

Church Road, Clearwell, Coleford GL16 8LG. Andrew & Jane MacBean, 01594 837769, southlodgegarden@btinternet.com, www.southlodgegarden.co.uk. *2m S of Coleford. Off B4228. Follow signs to Clearwell. Garden on L of castle driveway. Please park on rd in front of church or in village.* **Sat 2, Sat 30 Apr, Wed 11, Sun 22 May, Wed 8, Sat 25 June (1-5). Adm £3.50, chd free. Home-made teas. Visits also by arrangement Apr to June for groups of 15+.**
Peaceful country garden in 2 acres with stunning views of surrounding countryside. High walls provide a backdrop for rambling roses, clematis, and honeysuckles. Organic garden with large variety of perennials, annuals, grasses, shrubs and specimen trees with yr-round colour. Vegetable garden, wildlife and formal ponds. Rustic pergola planted with English climbing roses and willow arbour in gravel garden. Gravel paths and steep grassy slopes.

69 STANTON VILLAGE GARDENS

Stanton, nr Broadway WR12 7NE. Group Opening. *3m S of Broadway. Off B4632, between Broadway (3m) & Winchcombe (6m).* **Sun 19 June (2-6). Adm £6, chd free. Home-made teas in the Burland Hall in centre of the village & in several open gardens. Ice cream trike in centre of the village.** *Donation to local charities.*
Over 15 gardens open in this picturesque Cotswold village. Many houses border the street with long gardens behind, hidden from general view. Gardens range from large houses with colourful herbaceous borders, established trees, shrubs and formal vegetable gardens, to tiny cottage gardens packed with interest. Some also have natural water features. Popular plant stall and legendary homemade teas. Regret not all gardens suitable for wheelchair users.

70 ◆ STANWAY FOUNTAIN & WATER GARDEN

Stanway, Cheltenham GL54 5PQ. The Earl of Wemyss & March, 01386 584528, www.stanwayfountain.co.uk. *9m NE of Cheltenham. 1m E of B4632 Cheltenham to Broadway rd or B4077 Toddington to Stow-on-the-Wold rd.* **For NGS: Sun 8 May, Sun 21 Aug (2-5). Adm £7, chd free. Home-made teas. For other opening times and information, please phone or visit garden website.**
20 acres of planted landscape in early C18 formal setting. The restored canal, upper pond and 165ft high fountain have re-created one of the most interesting Baroque water gardens in Britain. Striking C16 manor with gatehouse, tithe barn and church. Britain's highest fountain at 300ft, the world's highest gravity fountain which runs at 2.45 & 4.00pm for 30 mins each time. Limited wheelchair access in garden, some flat areas, able to view fountain and some of garden. House is not wheelchair suitable.

71 STOWELL PARK

Yanworth, Northleach, Cheltenham GL54 3LE. The Lord & Lady Vestey, www.stowellpark.co.uk. *8m NE of Cirencester. Off Fosseway A429 2m SW of Northleach.* **Sun 8 May, Sun 19 June (2-5). Adm £6, chd free. Home-made teas.**
Magnificent lawned terraces with stunning views over Coln Valley. Fine collection of old-fashioned roses and herbaceous plants, with pleached lime approach to C14 house (not open). Two large walled gardens containing vegetables, fruit, cut flowers and range of greenhouses. Long rose pergola and wide, plant filled borders divided into colour sections. New water features and hazel arch at bottom of garden. Open continuously for 50yrs. Plants for sale at the May opening only.

> Wide range of plants and curiosities with an Italianate feel. . . .

72 TEMPLE GUITING MANOR

Temple Guiting, Stow on the Wold GL54 5RP. Mr & Mrs S Collins, www.templeguitingmanor.co.uk. *7m from Stow-on-the-Wold. From Stow-on-the-Wold take B4077 towards Tewkesbury. On descending hill bear L to village (signed) ¹/₂ m. Garden in centre of village on R.* **Sun 26 June (12-5). Adm £5, chd free. Home-made teas.**
Five acres of formal contemporary gardens with a kitchen garden, to a Grade I listed historic manor house (not open) in Windrush Valley. Designed by Jinny Blom, gold medal winner Chelsea Flower Show. Gravel pathways.

73 THREE SALMONS HOUSE

Beachley Road, Beachley, Chepstow NP16 7HG. Christopher & Deirdre Wilson. *2m E of Chepstow. Off A48 signed Sedbury/Beachley, through Sedbury following signs for Beachley Barracks. Reach 30mph limit, garden located 150m on L next to layby.* **Sun 10 July (2-5). Adm £3, chd £1. Home-made teas.**
Interesting garden entirely built, planned and planted by current owners behind former C19 inn. Colourful well-stocked herbaceous borders filled with wide range of plants and curiosities with an Italianate feel. Different areas incl pond, rill garden, rose bed, shady gravel garden, Italian fountain, small sunken garden, Italianate caseta and iron gazebo. Short paved ramp in garden and one step otherwise flat.

74 TRENCH HILL

Sheepscombe GL6 6TZ. Celia & Dave Hargrave, 01452 814306, celia.hargrave@btconnect.com. *1¹/₂ m E of Painswick. From Cheltenham A46 take 1st turn signed Sheepscombe and follow lane towards Sheepscombe for about 1¹/₄ m. Garden on L opp lane.* **Sun 14, Sun 21 Feb (11-5); Sun 27, Mon 28 Mar (11-6); Wed 8, Wed 15, Wed 22 June (2-6); Sun 17 July, Sun 28 Aug, Sun 11 Sept (11-6). Adm £4, chd free. Home-made teas. 2017: Sun 12, Sun 19 Feb. Visits also by arrangement Feb to Sept, not suitable for large coaches, max 42 seater.**
Approx 3 acres set in small woodland with panoramic views. Variety of herbaceous and mixed borders, rose garden, extensive vegetable plots, wild flower areas, plantings of spring bulbs with thousands of snowdrops and hellebores, woodland walk, 2 small ponds, waterfall and larger conservation pond. Interesting wooden sculptures, many within the garden. Run on organic principles. Featured in Garden Answers & Guardian Weekend magazine. Mostly wheelchair access but some steps and slopes.
&. ❀ 🚐 ☕

75 UPTON WOLD

Moreton-in-Marsh GL56 9TR. Mr & Mrs I R S Bond, 01386 700667, www.uptonwoldgarden.co.uk. *4¹/₂ m W of Moreton-in-Marsh. On A44 1m past A424 junction at Troopers Lodge Garage, on R. Look out for marker posts.* **Sun 17 Apr (11-5). Adm £10, chd free. Home-made teas. Visits also by arrangement Apr to Sept.**
Ever developing and changing garden, architecturally and imaginatively laid out around C17 house (not open) with commanding views. Yew hedges, herbaceous walk, some unusual plants and trees, vegetables, pond and woodland gardens, labyrinth. National Collections of Juglans and Pterocarya. 2 Star award from GGG.
❀ 🚐 **NPC** ☕

76 WELLS COTTAGE

Wells Road, Bisley GL6 7AG. Mr & Mrs Michael Flint, 01452 770289, flint_bisley@talktalk.net. *5m N E of Stroud. Gardens & car park well signed in Bisley village. Gardens on S edge of village at head of Toadsmoor Valley, N of A419.* **Sun 19 June (2-6). Adm £3, chd free.**
Just under 1 acre. Terraced on several levels with beautiful views over valley. Much informal planting of trees and shrubs to give colour and texture. Lawns and herbaceous borders. Collection of grasses. Formal pond area. Rambling roses on rope pergola. Vegetable garden with raised beds. No access to upper terraces for wheelchair users.
&. 🐕 ⛝

77 ◆ WESTONBIRT SCHOOL GARDENS

Tetbury GL8 8QG. Holfords of Westonbirt Trust, 01666 881373, jbaker@holfordtrust.com, www.holfordtrust.com. *3m SW of Tetbury. Opp Westonbirt Arboretum, on A433. Enter via Holford wrought iron gates to Westonbirt House.* **For NGS: Sun 17 July (11-5). Adm £5, chd free. Tea in the Great Hall, tea coffee & biscuits. For other opening times and information, please phone, email or visit garden website.**
28 acres. Former private garden of Robert Holford, founder of Westonbirt Arboretum. Formal Victorian gardens incl walled Italian garden now restored with early herbaceous borders and exotic border. Rustic walks, lake, statuary and grotto. Rare, exotic trees and shrubs. Beautiful views of Westonbirt House open with guided tours to see fascinating Victorian interior on designated days of the year. Tea, coffee and biscuits available on NGS and Open House and Garden Days. Afternoon tea with sandwiches and scones available for pre-booked private tours - groups of 10-60. Only some parts of garden accessible to wheelchairs. Ramps and lift allow access to house.
🐕 🚐 ☕

WHITCOMBE HOUSE

See Worcestershire

78 WHITE HOUSE

Chapel Lane, Mickleton, Chipping Campden GL55 6SD. Mr & Mrs James Bend, jamescadebend@gmail.com. *2m NW of Chipping Campden. Approaching Mickleton heading N on B4632, turn L into Chapel Lane by Three Ways House Hotel. After 100yds garden on L opp Butchers Arms PH.* **Sun 12 June (11-4.30). Adm £3.50, chd free. Tea. Traditional Cotswold PH opp White House with attractive beer garden where meals can be obtained. Visits also by arrangement June & July.**
An Arts & Crafts inspired cottage garden encircling the house and arranged in a series of informal rooms. Incl rose garden, holly-pop walk, sunken terrace and collection of topiary faces originally established by artist Richard Sorrell. Garden has been designed to offer peaceful sitting areas from which to enjoy the plants or simply relax in contemplation. Featured in Daily Telegraph & Gloucestershire Echo Weekend magazine.
🐕 ☕

79 WORTLEY HOUSE

Wortley, Wotton-Under-Edge GL12 7QP. Simon and Jessica Dickinson. *1m from Wotton-under-Edge. Full directions will be provided with ticket.* **Thur 23 June (3-6). Combined adm with Alderley Grange £20, chd free. Pre-booking essential, please visit www.ngs.org.uk or phone 01483 211535 for information & booking.**
This diverse garden of over 20 acres has been created through the last 30 yrs by current owners and incl walled garden, pleached lime avenues, nut walk, potager, ponds, Italian garden, shrubberies and wild flower meadows. Follies urns and statues have been strategically placed throughout to enhance extraordinary vistas, and the garden has been filled with plants, arbours, roses through trees and up walls and herbaceous borders. The stunning surrounding countryside is incorporated into the garden with views up the steep valley that are such a feature in this part of Gloucestershire. Wheelchair access to most areas of the garden, golf buggy available as well.
&. ☕

HAMPSHIRE

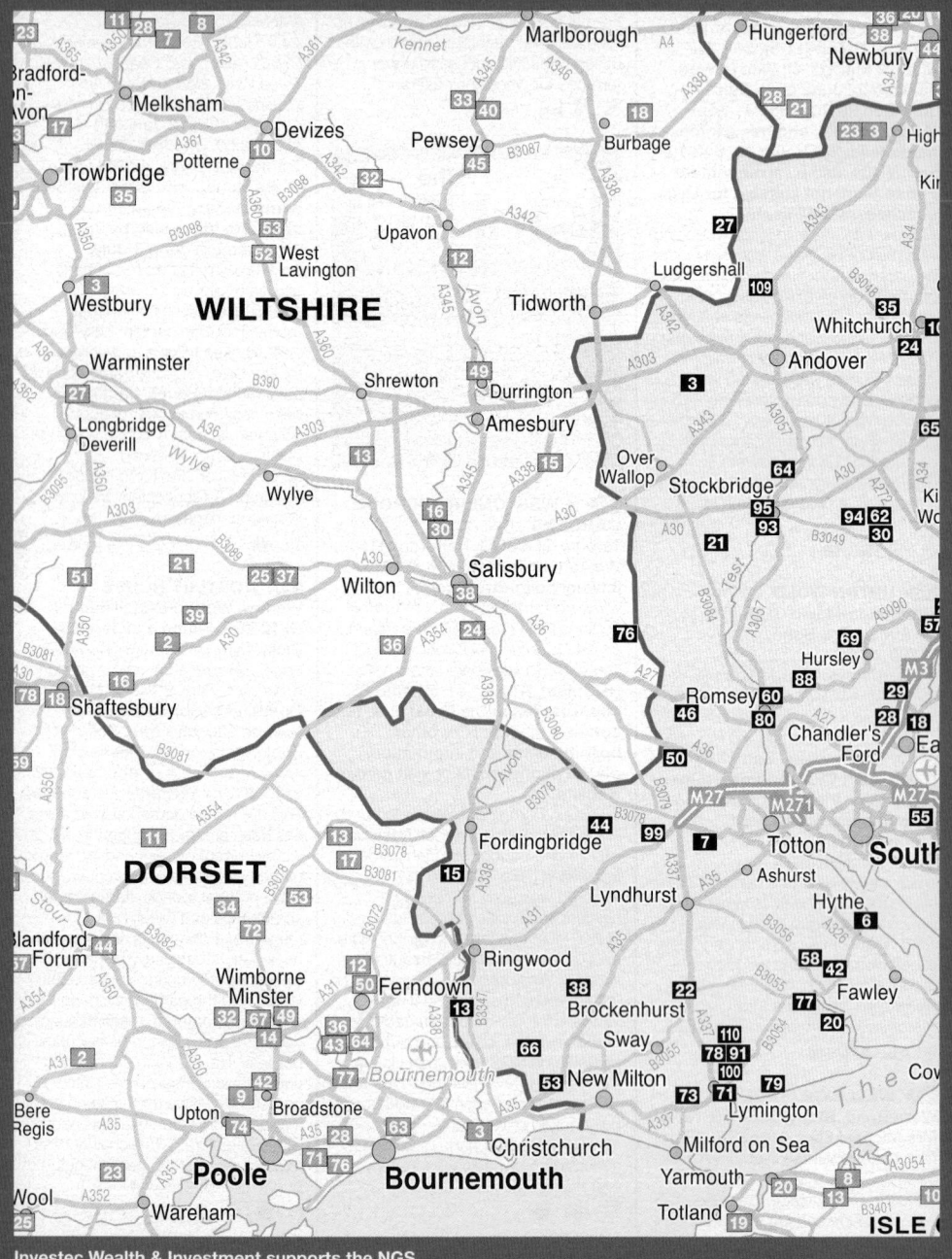

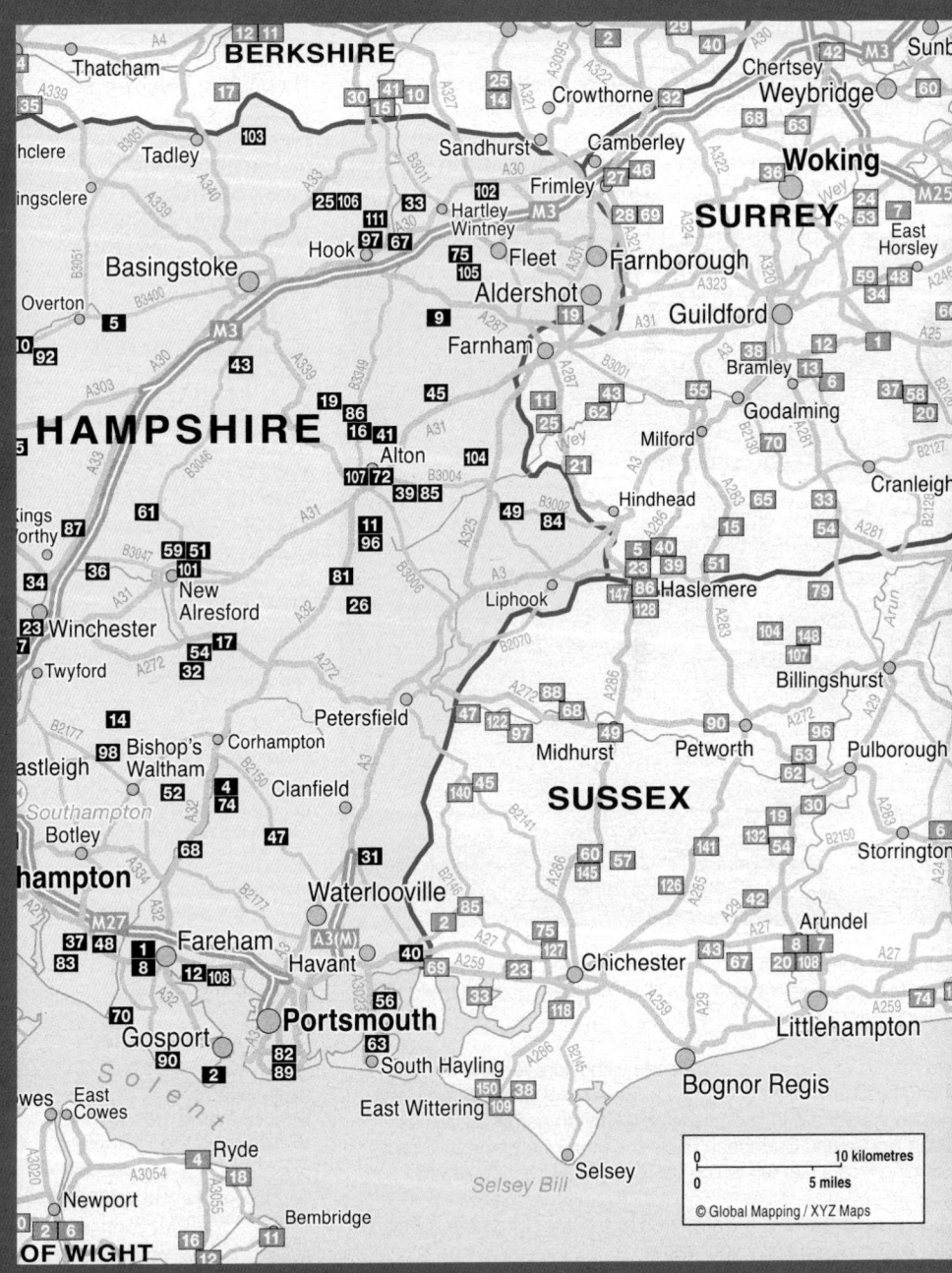

Hampshire

Hampshire is a large, diverse county. The landscape ranges from clay/gravel heath and woodland in the New Forest National Park in the south west, across famous trout rivers – the Test and Itchen – to chalk downland in the east, where you will find the South Downs National Park.

Our open gardens are spread right across the county, and offer a very diverse range of interest for both the keen gardener and the casual visitor.

We have a large number of gardens with rivers running through them, such as those in Longstock, Bere Mill, Dipley Mill and Weir House; gardens with large vegetable kitchen gardens such as Dean House and Bramdean House; and unique gardens such as Hanging Hosta Garden which has over 1300 hosta cultivars.

You will be assured of a warm welcome by all our garden owners and we hope you enjoy your visits.

Hampshire Volunteers

County Organiser
Mark Porter 01962 791054
markstephenporter@gmail.com

County Treasurer
Fred Fratter 01962 776243
fred@tanglefoot-house.demon.co.uk

Publicity
Mark Porter
(as above)

Social Media
Lorna Mann
07523 207713
lorna@meerkatmedia.net

Booklet Co-ordinator
Mark Porter
(as above)

Assistant County Organisers

Central East
Sue Alexander 01962 732043
suealex13@gmail.com

Central West
Patricia Elkington 01962 776365
elkslc@btinternet.com

East
Linda Smith 01329 833253
linda.ngs@btinternet.com

North
Cynthia Oldale 01420 520438
c.k.oldale@btinternet.com

North East
Mary Trigwell-Jones 01420 83389
mary.trigwell-jones@virgin.net

North West
Carol Pratt 01264 710305
carolacap@yahoo.co.uk

South
Barbara Sykes 02380 254521
barandhugh@aol.com

South West
Elizabeth Walker 01590 677415
elizabethwalker13@gmail.com

West
Christopher Stanford 01425 652133
stanfordsnr@gmail.com

Above: Dean House © Leigh Clapp

Opening Dates

All entries subject to change.
For latest information check www.ngs.org.uk
Extended openings are shown at the begining of the month.

February

Snowdrop Festival

Sunday 14
17 Bramdean House

Sunday 21
36 The Down House
62 Little Court

Monday 22
62 Little Court

Tuesday 23
62 Little Court

March

Saturday 19
78 Pilley Hill Cottage

Sunday 20
10 Bere Mill
78 Pilley Hill Cottage

Sunday 27
79 Pylewell Park

Monday 28
62 Little Court
91 Spinners Garden

Wednesday 30
9 Beechenwood Farm

April

9 Beechenwood Farm (every Wednesday)

Thursday 7
30 Crawley Gardens

Saturday 9
71 Moore Blatch

Sunday 10
17 Bramdean House
30 Crawley Gardens
38 Durmast House
71 Moore Blatch
98 Upham Farm

Saturday 16
78 Pilley Hill Cottage
85 Selborne

Sunday 17
75 Old Thatch & The Millennium Barn
78 Pilley Hill Cottage
85 Selborne

Sunday 24
81 Rotherfield Park
95 Terstan
97 Tylney Hall Hotel

Friday 29
16 Bluebell Wood

Saturday 30
16 Bluebell Wood
63 Littlewood

May

9 Beechenwood Farm (every Wednesday)

Sunday 1
28 The Cottage
63 Littlewood
78 Pilley Hill Cottage

Monday 2
5 Ashe Park
28 The Cottage
78 Pilley Hill Cottage
84 Sandy Slopes

Saturday 7
85 Selborne

Sunday 8
28 The Cottage
85 Selborne
87 Shroner Wood
100 Walhampton

Monday 9
28 The Cottage

Thursday 12
62 Little Court
94 Tanglefoot

Saturday 14
19 Brick Kiln Cottage
58 The House in the Wood
83 2 Sampan Close

Sunday 15
11 Berry Cottage
19 Brick Kiln Cottage
31 Crookley Pool
62 Little Court
83 2 Sampan Close
94 Tanglefoot
96 The Thatched Cottage

Saturday 21
22 21 Chestnut Road
55 Hollybrook

Sunday 22
22 21 Chestnut Road
34 The Dower House
53 Hinton Admiral
55 Hollybrook
101 Weir House

Wednesday 25
32 Dean House

Saturday 28
55 Hollybrook
60 The Island

Sunday 29
3 Amport & Monxton Gardens
11 Berry Cottage
13 NEW Bisterne Manor
37 7 Downland Close
48 Hambrooks Show Gardens
55 Hollybrook
60 The Island
68 Meon Orchard
76 Ordnance House
79 Pylewell Park
80 Romsey Gardens
96 The Thatched Cottage
103 West Silchester Hall

Monday 30
3 Amport & Monxton Gardens
11 Berry Cottage
37 7 Downland Close
80 Romsey Gardens
84 Sandy Slopes
96 The Thatched Cottage
103 West Silchester Hall

A garden trail for children . . .

June

Wednesday 1
9 Beechenwood Farm

Thursday 2
30 Crawley Gardens
31 Crookley Pool

Festival Weekend

Saturday 4
2 Alverstoke Crescent Garden
6 Atheling Villas
45 Froyle Gardens
54 Hinton Ampner
65 Lower Norton Farmhouse
109 Wildhern Gardens

Sunday 5
6 Atheling Villas
14 Blackdown House
25 The Coach House
30 Crawley Gardens
33 Dipley Mill
45 Froyle Gardens
65 Lower Norton Farmhouse
67 1 Maple Cottage
109 Wildhern Gardens

Tuesday 7
102 West Green House Gardens

Wednesday 8
4 Appletree House
9 Beechenwood Farm
67 1 Maple Cottage

Thursday 9
61 Lake House
67 1 Maple Cottage

Saturday 11
10 Bere Mill
37 7 Downland Close
39 East Worldham Gardens

Sunday 12
10 Bere Mill
17 Bramdean House
24 2 Church Cottages
29 Cranbury Park
37 7 Downland Close
39 East Worldham Gardens
61 Lake House
97 Tylney Hall Hotel

Wednesday 15
24 2 Church Cottages
35 Down Farm House
67 1 Maple Cottage

Thursday 16
67 1 Maple Cottage
93 Stockbridge Gardens

Saturday 18
22 21 Chestnut Road
35 Down Farm House
72 NEW 22 Mount Pleasant Road
107 42 Whitedown

Sunday 19
11 Berry Cottage
22 21 Chestnut Road
27 Conholt Park
40 Emsworth Gardens
64 Longstock Park
72 NEW 22 Mount Pleasant Road
89 Southsea Gardens
93 Stockbridge Gardens
96 The Thatched Cottage
107 42 Whitedown

Wednesday 22
- **4** Appletree House
- **11** Berry Cottage (Evening)
- **32** Dean House
- **96** The Thatched Cottage (Evening)

Saturday 25
- **39** East Worldham Gardens

Sunday 26
- **26** Colemore House Gardens
- **33** Dipley Mill
- **38** Durmast House
- **39** East Worldham Gardens
- **44** Fritham Lodge
- **92** NEW Spring Pond
- **95** Terstan
- **99** Waldrons

Monday 27
- **26** Colemore House Gardens

Wednesday 29
- **5** Ashe Park
- **92** NEW Spring Pond

Saturday 2
- **50** Hideaway
- **54** Hinton Ampner

Sunday 3
- **5** Ashe Park
- **8** 19 Barnwood Road
- **15** Bleak Hill Nursery & Garden
- **32** Dean House
- **50** Hideaway
- **74** Old Droxford Station
- **86** Shalden Park House
- **103** West Silchester Hall
- **106** White Gables
- **108** Wicor Primary School Community Garden

Thursday 7
- **30** Crawley Gardens

Saturday 9
- **73** Oak Tree Cottage

Sunday 10
- **11** Berry Cottage
- **30** Crawley Gardens
- **73** Oak Tree Cottage
- **96** The Thatched Cottage
- **111** 1 Wogsbarne Cottages

Monday 11
- **111** 1 Wogsbarne Cottages

Saturday 16
- **22** 21 Chestnut Road
- **82** 28 St Ronan's Avenue (Evening)

Sunday 17
- **15** Bleak Hill Nursery & Garden
- **17** Bramdean House
- **22** 21 Chestnut Road
- **27** Conholt Park
- **33** Dipley Mill
- **70** Michaelmas
- **75** Old Thatch & The Millennium Barn

Monday 18
- **70** Michaelmas

Wednesday 20
- **4** Appletree House

Saturday 23
- **12** 8 Birdwood Grove
- **39** East Worldham Gardens

Sunday 24
- **39** East Worldham Gardens

Monday 11
- **111** 1 Wogsbarne Cottages

Saturday 16
- **22** 21 Chestnut Road
- **82** 28 St Ronan's Avenue (Evening)

Sunday 17
- **15** Bleak Hill Nursery & Garden
- **17** Bramdean House
- **22** 21 Chestnut Road
- **27** Conholt Park
- **33** Dipley Mill
- **70** Michaelmas
- **75** Old Thatch & The Millennium Barn

Monday 18
- **70** Michaelmas

Wednesday 20
- **4** Appletree House

Saturday 23
- **12** 8 Birdwood Grove
- **39** East Worldham Gardens

Sunday 24
- **39** East Worldham Gardens

- **57** The Hospital of St Cross
- **95** Terstan

Tuesday 26
- **102** West Green House Gardens (Evening)

Wednesday 27
- **32** Dean House

Thursday 28
- **94** Tanglefoot

Saturday 30
- **21** The Buildings
- **42** Fairweather's Nursery
- **110** Willows

Sunday 31
- **15** Bleak Hill Nursery & Garden
- **21** The Buildings
- **42** Fairweather's Nursery
- **68** Meon Orchard
- **94** Tanglefoot
- **110** Willows

Tuesday 2
- **51** Hill House

Wednesday 3
- **41** Fairbank

The Coach House

© Nicola Stocken

Saturday 6
20 NEW Bucklers Spring
85 Selborne

Sunday 7
11 Berry Cottage
20 NEW Bucklers Spring
32 Dean House
33 Dipley Mill
51 Hill House
56 The Homestead
69 Merdon Manor
85 Selborne
96 The Thatched Cottage
103 West Silchester Hall

Monday 8
85 Selborne

Wednesday 10
109 Wildhern Gardens

Thursday 11
51 Hill House

Saturday 13
72 NEW 22 Mount Pleasant Road
107 42 Whitedown
110 Willows

Sunday 14
17 Bramdean House
72 NEW 22 Mount Pleasant Road
107 42 Whitedown
110 Willows

Wednesday 17
32 Dean House

Saturday 20
104 Wheatley House

Sunday 21
104 Wheatley House

Wednesday 24
11 Berry Cottage (Evening)
96 The Thatched Cottage (Evening)

Thursday 25
59 The Hyde

Saturday 27
59 The Hyde
60 The Island
110 Willows

Sunday 28
46 Gilberts Nursery
59 The Hyde
60 The Island
110 Willows

Monday 29
59 The Hyde

September

Saturday 3
21 The Buildings
36 The Down House

Sunday 4
11 Berry Cottage
17 Bramdean House
21 The Buildings
36 The Down House
68 Meon Orchard

75 Old Thatch & The Millennium Barn
95 Terstan

Sunday 11
31 Crookley Pool
33 Dipley Mill
43 Farleigh House
101 Weir House

Sunday 18
10 Bere Mill
108 Wicor Primary School Community Garden

October

Sunday 2
97 Tylney Hall Hotel

Sunday 16
48 Hambrooks Show Gardens

February 2017

Sunday 19
62 Little Court

Monday 20
62 Little Court

Tuesday 21
62 Little Court

Relax and enjoy tea sitting in the dappled shade of the orchard . . .

Gardens open to the public

2 Alverstoke Crescent Garden
54 Hinton Ampner
57 The Hospital of St Cross
66 Macpennys Woodland Garden & Nurseries
77 Patrick's Patch
88 Sir Harold Hillier Gardens
91 Spinners Garden
102 West Green House Gardens

By arrangement only

1 80 Abbey Road
7 Aviemore
18 6 Breamore Close
23 12 Christchurch Road
47 Hambledon House
49 Hanging Hosta Garden
52 Hill Top
90 Spindles
105 Whispers

Also open by arrangement

4 Appletree House
6 Atheling Villas
8 19 Barnwood Road
9 Beechenwood Farm
10 Bere Mill
11 Berry Cottage
12 8 Birdwood Grove
15 Bleak Hill Nursery & Garden
16 Bluebell Wood
17 Bramdean House
19 Brick Kiln Cottage
22 21 Chestnut Road
25 The Coach House
27 Conholt Park
28 The Cottage
31 Crookley Pool
34 The Dower House
36 The Down House
37 7 Downland Close
38 Durmast House
40 Emsworth Gardens
41 Fairbank
44 Fritham Lodge
50 Hideaway
51 Hill House
56 The Homestead
59 The Hyde
60 The Island
61 Lake House
62 Little Court
68 Meon Orchard
69 Merdon Manor
70 Michaelmas
76 Ordnance House
78 Pilley Hill Cottage
80 4 Mill Lane, Romsey Gardens
82 28 St Ronan's Avenue
85 Selborne
87 Shroner Wood
92 NEW Spring Pond
94 Tanglefoot
95 Terstan
96 The Thatched Cottage
101 Weir House
103 West Silchester Hall
104 Wheatley House
106 White Gables
107 42 Whitedown
110 Willows

Join us on Facebook f and spread the word

The Gardens

1 80 ABBEY ROAD

Fareham PO15 5HW. Brian & Vivienne Garford, 01329 843939, vgarford@aol.com. *1m W of Fareham. From M27 J9 take A27 E to Fareham for approx 2m. At top of hill, turn L at lights into Highlands Rd. Turn 4th R into Blackbrook Rd. Abbey Rd is 4th L.* **Visits by arrangement Apr to Sept for groups of 30 max. Light refreshments.**

Unusual small garden with large collection of herbs and plants of botanical and historical interest, many for sale. Box hedging provides structure for relaxed planting. Interesting use of containers and ideas for small gardens. Two ponds and tiny meadow for wildlife. A garden trail for children. Living willow seat, summerhouse, and trained grapevine. Areas of redesigned planting for 2016.

Waterfall cascades over rocks and magically disappears below the terrace . . .

2 ◆ ALVERSTOKE CRESCENT GARDEN

Crescent Road, Gosport PO12 2DH. Gosport Borough Council, www.alverstokecrescentgarden.co.uk. *1m S of Gosport. From A32 & Gosport follow signs for Stokes Bay. Continue alongside bay to small r'about, turn L into Anglesey Rd. Crescent Garden signed 50yds on R.* **For NGS: Sat 4 June (10-4). Adm by donation. Home-made teas. For other opening times and information, please visit garden website.**

Restored Regency ornamental garden, designed to enhance fine crescent (Thomas Ellis Owen 1828). Trees, walks and flowers lovingly maintained by community and council

partnership. Garden's of considerable local historic interest highlighted by impressive restoration and creative planting. Adjacent to St Mark's churchyard, worth seeing together. Heritage, history and horticulture, a fascinating package. Plant sale and teas. Green Flag Award.

  ♿ 🐕 ✿ ☕

GROUP OPENING

3 AMPORT & MONXTON GARDENS

Amport SP11 8AY. *3m SW of Andover. Turn off A303 signed to East Cholderton from E or Thruxton Village from W. Follow signs to Amport. Parking in field next to village green.* **Sun 29, Mon 30 May (1.30-6). Combined adm £6, chd free. Cream teas at Amport & Monxton Village Hall.**

> **AMPORT PARK MEWS**
> Amport Park Mews Ltd
>
> **BRIDGE COTTAGE**
> Jenny Van de Pette
>
> **FLEUR DE LYS**
> Ian & Jane Morrison
>
> **GAYCORREL**
> Mr & Mrs Perren
>
> **WHITE GABLES**
> Mr & Mrs D Eaglesham

Monxton and Amport are two pretty villages linked by Pill Hill Brook. Visitors have 5 gardens to enjoy. Bridge Cottage a 2 acre haven for wildlife, with the banks of the trout stream and lake planted informally with drifts of colour, a large vegetable garden, fruit cage, small mixed orchard and arboretum with specimen trees. Amport Park Mews has 11 borders arranged around a communal space surrounded by converted stable and carriage blocks in historic mews. Fleur de Lys garden is a series of rooms with glorious herbaceous borders, leading to a large orchard. Gaycorrel the ½ acre working garden of a National Vegetable Society Judge and Fellow. Vegetables, dahlias and fruit are grown for exhibition. White Gables a cottage style garden with a collection of trees, incl a young giant redwood, along with old roses and herbaceous plants. No wheelchair access to White Gables.

4 APPLETREE HOUSE

Station Road, Soberton SO32 3QU. Mrs J Dover, 01489 877333, jennie.dover@yahoo.co.uk. *10m N of Fareham. A32 to Droxford, at Xrds turn onto B2150. Turn R under bridge into Station Rd, garden 1m. Parking in lay-by 300yds or on the road.* **Wed 8, Wed 22 June, Wed 20 July (12-4). Adm £3.50, chd free. Light refreshments. Visits also by arrangement May to July. Light lunches on request.**

Designed to look larger than its 40ft x 90ft, this garden has both a shady woodland style area and also sunny areas allowing a variety of planting. Winding paths lead to different views across the garden and of the meadows beyond. Lots of ideas for the smaller garden. Large collection of over 90 clematis, mainly viticella hybrids. Winner of Best Garden by Hampshire Garden Club members 2015. Peter Maunder trophy and award, presented by Veolia.

✿ ☕

5 ASHE PARK

nr Ashe, Overton RG25 3AF. Graham & Laura Hazell. *2m E of Overton. Entrance on B3400, approx 500yds W of Deane.* **Mon 2 May, Wed 29 June, Sun 3 July (2-6). Adm £5, chd free. Home-made teas.**

Extensive new gardens within the grounds of a Georgian Country House and Estate, with further development in progress. Parkland and specimen trees, woodland and bluebell walks, large contemporary potager, lime avenue and several newly planted areas.

  ♿ 🐕 ✿ ☕

6 ATHELING VILLAS

16 Atheling Road, Hythe, Southampton SO45 6BR. Mary & Peter York, 02380 849349, athelingvillas@gmail.com. *W side of Southampton Water. At M27 J2, take A326 for Hythe & Fawley. Cross all r'abouts until Dibden r'about. L to Hythe. After Shell garage take 2nd L & immed R.* **Sat 4, Sun 5 June (2-5). Adm £3, chd free. Home-made teas in the Old Laundry. Visits also by arrangement Apr to June for groups of 10+.** *Donation to The Children's Society.*

Inspirational, imaginatively designed and comprehensively planted ⅓ acre Victorian villa garden, now in its 11th yr of opening for the NGS. Explore meandering paths set amongst structural planting and delight in the flowering trees and shrubs (many rare), bulbs and herbaceous planting of this tranquil and welcoming garden. Several seating areas throughout garden. Features incl a self-guide leaflet, children's quiz, and a display of original art by owners in the Garden Room Gallery.

7 AVIEMORE
Chinham Road, Bartley, Southampton SO40 2LF. Sandy & Alex Robinson, 02380 813651. *3m N of Lyndhurst, 7m W of Southampton. From M27 J1 go towards Lyndhurst on A337. After ³/₄ m turn L to Bartley & follow NGS signs.* **Visits by arrangement Apr to Aug for groups of 10-50. Adm £3.50, chd free. Tea.**
Richly planted, small garden in north New Forest. Our aim is to please the plant connoisseur and introduce enthusiasts to new plants and ideas for smaller plots. Every plant must play its part within a seasonal symphony of shrubs, climbers, perennials and grasses. Oak bridges criss-cross a small stream. Old alpine troughs and quirky artifacts add texture, structure and colour to this yr-round garden. No wheelchair access to some gravel and stream areas.

8 19 BARNWOOD ROAD
Fareham PO15 5LA. Jill & Michael Hill, 01329 842156, Jillhillflowers@icloud.com. *1m W of Fareham. M27 J9, A27 towards Fareham. At top of Titchfield Hill, L at T-lights, 4th R Blackbrook Rd, 4th R Meadow Bank. Barnwood Rd is off Meadow Bank. Please consider neighbours when parking.* **Sun 3 July (11-4). Adm £3.50, chd free. Home-made teas. Visits also by arrangement May to July for groups of 10-20.**
Step through the gate to an enchanting garden designed for peace with an abundance of floral colour and delightful features. Greek style courtyard leads to natural pond with bridge and bog garden, complemented by a thatched summerhouse and jetty, designed and built by owners. Secret pathways, hexagonal greenhouse and new mosaic seating area.

Whispers

9 BEECHENWOOD FARM
Hillside, Odiham RG29 1JA. Mr & Mrs M Heber-Percy, 01256 702300, beechenwood@totalise.co.uk. *5m SE of Hook. Turn S into King St from Odiham High St. Turn L after cricket ground for Hillside. Take 2nd R after 1¹/₂ m, modern house ¹/₂ m.* **Every Wed 30 Mar to 8 June (2-5). Adm £4, chd free. Home-made teas. Visits also by arrangement Mar to June.**
2 acre garden in many parts. Lawn meandering through woodland with drifts of spring bulbs. Rose pergola with steps, pots with spring bulbs and later aeoniums. Fritillary and cowslip meadow. Walled herb garden with pool and exuberant planting. Orchard incl white garden and hot border. Greenhouse and vegetable garden. Rock garden extending to grasses, ferns and bamboos. Shady walk to belvedere. 8 acre copse of native species with grassed rides. Assistance available with gravel drive, and some avoidable shallow steps.

10 BERE MILL
London Road, Whitchurch RG28 7NH. Rupert & Elizabeth Nabarro, 01256 892210, rnabarro@aol.com. *9m E of*

Andover, 12m N of Winchester. In centre of Whitchurch, take London Rd at r'about. Uphill 1m, turn R 50yds beyond The Gables on R. Drop-off point for disabled at garden. **Sun 20 Mar, Sat 11, Sun 12 June, Sun 18 Sept (1.30-5). Adm £5, chd free. Home-made teas. Visits also by arrangement Feb to Oct for groups of 15+.** *Donation to Smile Train.*
On the Upper Test with water meadows and wooded valleys, this garden offers herbaceous borders, bog and Mediterranean plants as well as a replanted orchard and two small arboretums. Features incl early bulbs, species tulips, Japanese prunus, peonies, wisteria, irises, roses, and semi-tropical planting. At heart it aims to complement the natural beauty of the site, and to incorporate elements of oriental garden design and practice. The working mill was where Portals first made paper for the Bank of England in 1716. Featured in BBC Great Garden Plant Revival and numerous glossy garden articles. Unfenced and unguarded rivers and streams. Wheelchair access unless very wet.

11 BERRY COTTAGE

Church Road, Upper Farringdon, nr Alton GU34 3EG. Mrs P Watts, 01420 588318. *3m S of Alton off A32. Turn L at Xrds, 1st L into Church Rd. Follow road past Massey's Folly, 2nd house on R opp church.* Sun 15, Sun 29, Mon 30 May, Sun 19 June (2-5.30). Evening opening Wed 22 June (5.30-8). Sun 10 July, Sun 7 Aug (2-5.30). Evening opening Wed 24 Aug (5.30-8). Combined adm with The Thatched Cottage £5, chd free. Sun 4 Sept (2-5.30). Adm £2.50, chd free. Home-made teas & wine at evening openings. Visits also by arrangement Apr to Sept for groups of 10+.

Small organic cottage garden with yr-round interest, designed and maintained by owner, surrounding C16 house (not open). Spring bulbs, roses, clematis and herbaceous borders. The borders are colour themed and contain many unusual plants. Pond and bog garden, shrubbery and small kitchen garden. Close to Massey's Folly built by the Victorian rector incl 80ft tower with unique handmade floral bricks, C11 church and some of the oldest yew trees in the county.

🚾 ⛺ ❀ 🚐 ☕

Alpacas and Jacob sheep roam the parkland . . .

12 8 BIRDWOOD GROVE

Downend, Fareham PO16 8AF. Jayne & Eddie McBride, 01329 280838, jayne.mcbride@ntlworld.com. *½ m E of Fareham. M27 J11, L lane slip to Delme r'about, L on A27 to Portchester over 2 T-lights, completely around small r'about, Birdwood Grove 1st L.* Sat 23 July (1-5). Adm £2.50, chd free. Home-made teas. Visits also by arrangement July & Aug for groups up to 25 max.

The subtropics in Fareham! This small garden is influenced by the flora of Australia and New Zealand and incl many indigenous species and plants that are widely grown 'down under'. The 4 climate zones; arid, temperate, lush fertile and a shady fernery, are all densely planted to make the most of dramatic foliage, from huge bananas to towering cordylines. Fareham in

Bloom gold award Small Plantsman's Back Garden and Best In Category for the 3rd year running! Short gravel path not suitable for mobility scooters.

🚾 🚾 ❀ ☕

13 NEW BISTERNE MANOR

Bisterne, Ringwood BH24 3BN. Mr & Mrs Hallam Mills. *2½ m S of Ringwood on B3347 Christchurch Rd, 500yds past church on L. Entrance signed Stable Family Home Trust on L (blue sign), just past lodge. Disabled parking signed near the house.* Sun 29 May (2-6). Adm £4.50, chd free. Cream teas.

Glorious rhododendrons and azaleas form a backdrop for our C19 garden which opened in the 1930s for the fledgling NGS and is now under restoration. The C16 manor house (not open) overlooks a grand parterre with box hedges and newly planted lavender. Rare tree specimens grace fine lawns leading to a boundary woodland walk with glimpses of surrounding pastures. There is a small kitchen garden. Wheelchair access to a level garden with wide gravel paths.

🚾 🚾 🚐 ☕

14 BLACKDOWN HOUSE

Blackdown Lane, Upham SO32 1HS. Mr & Mrs Tom Sweet-Escott. *5m SE of Winchester, 5m N of Bishops Waltham. 1m N of Upham, best accessed off Morestead Rd, Xrds with Longwood Dean Lane from Winchester, or through the village of Upham from Bishops Waltham.* Sun 5 June (2-5.30). Adm £4.50, chd free. Cream teas.

A 5 acre family garden with 100 metre long colourful successional herbaceous border set against a flint wall. Well established wild flower meadow with orchids and butterflies. Part-walled working kitchen garden with new summerhouse and orchard with free range hens and sunny terrace. Alpacas and Jacob sheep roam the parkland. A constantly evolving garden with new planting in 2015. Flautissimo (a flute group) will be playing in the garden. Wheelchair access with assistance, due to grass slopes.

☕

15 BLEAK HILL NURSERY & GARDEN

Braemoor, Bleak Hill, Harbridge, Ringwood BH24 3PX. Tracy & John Netherway & Judy Spratt, 01425 652983, jnetherway@btinternet.com.

2½ m S of Fordingbridge. Turn off A338 at Ibsley. Go through Harbridge Village to T-junction at top of hill, turn R for ¼ m. Sun 3, Sun 17, Sun 31 July (2-5.30). Adm £3.50, chd free. Home-made teas. Visits also by arrangement July & Aug.

Through the moongate and concealed from view are billowing borders contrasting against a seaside scene, with painted beach huts and a boat on the gravel. Herbaceous borders fill the garden with colour wrapping around a pond and small stream. Greenhouses with cacti and sarracenias. Vegetable patch and bantam chickens. Small adjacent nursery. Some gravel paths.

🚾 ❀ 🚐 ☕

16 BLUEBELL WOOD

Stancombe Lane, Bavins, New Odiham Road, Alton GU34 5SX. Mrs Jennifer Ospici, 01420 82171, bavinsbnb@hotmail.com, www.bavins.co.uk. *On the corner of Stancombe Lane & the B3349 2½ m N of Alton.* Fri 29, Sat 30 Apr (11-4). Adm £5, chd free. Light refreshments. Visits also by arrangement Mar & Apr.

Unique 100 acre ancient bluebell woodland. If you are a keen walker you will have much to explore on the long meandering paths and rides dotted with secluded seats. Those who enjoy a more leisurely pace will experience the perfume of the carpet of blue, listen to the birdsong and watch the contrasting light through the trees nearer to the entrance of the woods. Refreshments will be served in an original rustic wooden building and incl soups using natural woodland ingredients.

🚾 ❀ ☕

17 BRAMDEAN HOUSE

Bramdean, Alresford SO24 0JU. Mr & Mrs H Wakefield, 01962 771214, victoria@bramdeanhouse.com. *4m S of Alresford. In centre of village on A272. Entrance opp sign to the church.* Sun 14 Feb (2-4); Suns 10 Apr, 12 June, 17 July, 14 Aug (2-4.30); Sun 4 Sept (2-4). Adm £5, chd free. Home-made teas. Visits also by arrangement Mar to Sept.

Beautiful 5 acre garden famous for its mirror image herbaceous borders. Carpets of spring bulbs especially snowdrops. A large and unusual collection of plants and shrubs giving yr-round interest. 1 acre walled garden featuring prize-winning vegetables, fruit and flowers. Small arboretum. Trial of hardy Nerine cultivars in association with RHS. Features incl a wild flower meadow, boxwood castle, a large collection of old fashioned sweet peas. Home of the nation's tallest sunflower 'Giraffe'. Included in numerous books and Country Life.

18 6 BREAMORE CLOSE

Eastleigh SO50 4QB. Mr & Mrs R Trenchard, 02380 611230, dawndavina6@yahoo.co.uk. *1m N of Eastleigh. M3 J12, follow signs to Eastleigh. Turn R at r'about into Woodside Ave, then 1st L into Broadlands Ave (park here). Breamore Close 3rd on L.* **Visits by arrangement in July for groups of 10+.**
Delightful plant lover's garden with coloured foliage and unusual plants, giving a tapestry effect of texture and colour. Many hostas displayed in pots. The garden is laid out in distinctive planting themes with seating areas to sit and contemplate. In July several clematis scramble through roses and there are many varieties of phlox. Small gravel area.

19 BRICK KILN COTTAGE

The Avenue, Herriard, Nr Alton RG25 2PR. Barbara Jeremiah, 01256 381131, barbara@klca.co.uk. *4m NE of Alton. A339 Basingstoke to Alton, L along The Avenue, past Lasham Gliding Club on R, then past Back Lane on L & take next track on L, one field later.* **Sat 14, Sun 15 May (12-4). Adm £4, chd free. Home-made teas. Visits also by arrangement in May.**
Bluebell woodland garden with 2 acres incl treehouse, pebble garden, billabong, stumpery, ferny hollow, shepherd's hut and a traditional cottage garden filled with herbs. The garden is maintained using eco-friendly methods as a haven for wild animals, butterflies, birds and bees, in English bluebells. Families welcome to this wild garden in a former brick works, with excellent cream teas, home-made cakes, sandwiches and pots of tea. Recipient in 2015 of a Hampshire & Isle of Wight Wildlife Trust Award for a wildlife friendly garden. Featured in Hampshire Life (April 2015).

20 NEW BUCKLERS SPRING

Bucklers Hard Road, Beaulieu, Brockenhurst SO42 7XA. Miss Adrienne Page, www.bucklersspring.com. *M27 J2 (to avoid traffic in Lyndhurst) & follow brown signs to Beaulieu & follow 2m S to Bucklers Hard. Park in field leading off the Master Builder House Hotel.* **Sat 6, Sun 7 Aug (2-5.30). Adm £3, chd free. Home-made teas.**
Landscape designed garden of ¹/₂ acre with glimpses of the Beaulieu River beyond lush borders of late summer perennials bordered by gravel paths. Lawns are inset with rivers of lavender winding through ornamental grasses; circular grass mounds; and an avenue of ornamental pear trees. Additional features are a box border and a raised bed garden for cut flowers, herbs and outdoor cooking. Adjacent to the historic shipbuilding village of Bucklers Hard on the Beaulieu River, next door is the Master Builder's Hotel and The National Motor Museum is 3m away. Partial wheelchair access due to gravel driveway and paths.

21 THE BUILDINGS

Broughton, Stockbridge SO20 8BH. Dick & Gillian Pugh. *3m W of Stockbridge. Follow NGS yellow signs 2m W of Stockbridge off A30, or 6m N of Romsey off B3084.* **Sat 30, Sun 31 July, Sat 3, Sun 4 Sept (2-5). Adm £4, chd free. Home-made teas. Donation to Friends of St Mary's Broughton & St James' Bossington.**
High on the Hampshire Downs with wonderful views, our 1 acre offers modern planting in gravel, borders, and an exuberant pergola all on thin chalk soil. At its best in late summer it is often described as inspirational, the planting and layout widely admired. Many unusual plants and varieties especially in the Salvia, Clematis viticella and Pelargonium families.

22 21 CHESTNUT ROAD

Brockenhurst SO42 7RF. Iain & Mary Hayter, 01590 622009, maryiain.hayter@gmail.com, www.21-chestnut-rdgardens.co.uk. *New Forest, 4m S of Lyndhurst. At Brockenhurst turn R B3055 Grigg Lane. Limited parking, village car park nearby. Leave M27 J2, follow Heavy Lorry Route. Mainline station less*

than 10 mins walk. **Sat 21 May (11-5); Sun 22 May (1-5); Sat 18 June (11-5); Sun 19 June (1-5); Sat 16 July (11-5); Sun 17 July (1-5). Adm £3.50, chd free. Home-made teas & gluten free options. Visits also by arrangement May to Aug for groups of 10+.**
Welcome, 2016 builds on last year's projects and with maturity there promises to be lots of interest, where colourful ideas for planting in different conditions cannot fail to inspire. Plants are chosen to blend sympathetically and encourage wildlife. There are formal, relaxed and productive areas with fairies in the wild flower area. Visit Brockenhurst Village and enjoy seeing the ponies, donkeys and cattle roam freely. Visit St Nicholas Church home to New Zealand War Graves. Some gravel areas, and no wheelchair access to raised deck or some parts of the garden when wet.

> Lawns are inset with rivers of lavender winding through ornamental grasses . . .

23 12 CHRISTCHURCH ROAD

Winchester SO23 9SR. Iain & Penny Patton, 01962 854272, pjspatton@yahoo.co.uk. *S side of city. Leave centre of Winchester by Southgate St, 1st R into St James Lane, 3rd L into Christchurch Rd.* **Visits by arrangement Mar to Oct for groups of 20 max. Adm £3, chd free. Light refreshments.**
Small town garden with strong design enhanced by exuberant and vertical planting. All yr interest incl winter flowering shrubs, bulbs and hellebores. Two water features incl slate edged rill and pergolas provide structure. Small front garden designed to be viewed from the house with bulbs, roses and herbaceous planting. See www.visitwinchester.com for B&B information. Featured in Gardens Illustrated and Gardeners World. Partial wheelchair access due to small changes in levels.

24 2 CHURCH COTTAGES

Tufton, Whitchurch RG28 7RF. **Jane & John Huxford.** *N on A34 at Whitchurch exit, turn L off slip road, R at Xrds, house 2nd on R. From Whitchurch centre take Winchester Rd S. Before slip road bear R, turn R, turn R at Xrds, house 2nd on R.* **Sun 12, Wed 15 June (1.30-5). Adm £3.50, chd free. Home-made teas.**
A stone's throw from the R Test, formerly an estate cowman's cottage, the front and back is a traditional cottage garden, but there is more! Through the gate in the hedge, you'll find a nursery, greenhouses, vegetables, cutting garden and small orchard. Then a stroll through the fields to see sheep, pigs and chickens leads to an area under development to form a walk with wild flowers in the summer.

25 THE COACH HOUSE

Reading Road, Sherfield on Loddon RG27 0EX. Jane Jordan, 01256 880852, jane@janejordangardens.co.uk. *5m N of Basingstoke. Follow A33 & signs to Sherfield on Loddon. Follow signs to free car parks. Some on-road parking. Drop off only at house.* **Sun 5 June (2-5). Adm £3.50, chd free. Home-made teas. Visits also by arrangement Apr to Oct for groups of 10+.**
A hidden gem, this 510 sq-metre walled garden has been replanted extensively over the past 9 yrs. It includes a wide range of unusual plants and grasses chosen for texture and colour, roses and clematis, a formal pond, pergola and sunken brick terrace. The style is relaxed, the content stimulating and the tea fresh, so come and enjoy! A couple of low steps in garden and 3 steps down to sunken terrace.

26 COLEMORE HOUSE GARDENS

Colemore, Alton GU34 3RX. Mr & Mrs Simon de Zoete. *4m S of Alton (off A32). Approach from N on A32, turn L (Shell Lane), ¼ m S of East Tisted. Go under bridge, keep L until you see Colemore Church. Park on verge of church.* **Sun 26, Mon 27 June (2-6). Adm £5, chd free. Home-made teas.**
4 acres in lovely unspoilt countryside, featuring rooms containing many unusual plants and different aspects. A spectacular arched rose walk,

water rill, mirror pond, herbaceous and shrub borders and a new woodland walk. Many admire the lawns, new grass gardens and thatched pavilion (built by students from the Prince's Trust). A small arboretum is being planted. Change and development is ongoing, and increasing the diversity of interesting plants is a prime motivation. We propagate and sell plants, many of which can be found in the garden. Some are unusual and not readily available elsewhere.

27 CONHOLT PARK

Hungerford Lane, Andover SP11 9HA. Conholt Park Estate, 07917 796826, conholt.garden@hotmail.com. *7m N of Andover. Turn N off A342 at Weyhill Church, 5m N through Clanville. L at T-junction, Conholt ½ m on R, opp Chute Causeway. A343 to Hurstbourne Tarrant, turn R, go through Vernham Dean, L signed Conholt.* **Sun 19 June, Sun 17 July (11-5). Adm £5, chd free. Home-made teas. Visits also by arrangement May to July on weekdays only.**
10 acres surrounding Regency house (not open), with mature cedars. Rose, sensory and secret gardens. Private poppy garden (no dogs please). Glasshouses, flower cartwheel, berry wall and orchard occupy the walled garden. New herbaceous cartwheel for 2016. An Edwardian Ladies Walk. Large laurel maze with viewing platform. Visitors welcome to picnic. Deep gravel and steps, not suitable for wheelchairs.

28 THE COTTAGE

16 Lakewood Road, Chandler's Ford SO53 1ES. Hugh & Barbara Sykes, 02380 254521, barandhugh@aol.com. *2m NW of Eastleigh. Leave M3 J12, follow signs to Chandler's Ford. At King Rufus on Winchester Rd, turn R into*

Merdon Ave, then 3rd road on L. **Sun 1, Mon 2, Sun 8, Mon 9 May (2-6). Adm £3.50, chd free. Home-made teas. Visits also by arrangement Apr & May.**
³/₄ acre. Azaleas, bog garden, camellias, dogwoods, erythroniums, free-range bantams, geraniums, hostas, irises, jasmines, kitchen garden, landscaping began in 1950, maintained by owners, new planting, osmunda, ponds, quiz for children, rhododendrons, sun and shade, trilliums, unusual plants, viburnums, wildlife areas, eXuberant foliage, yr-round interest, zantedeschia. 'A lovely tranquil garden', Anne Swithinbank. Hampshire Wildlife Trust Wildlife Garden Award. Honey from our garden hives for sale.

COTTAGE IN THE TREES
See Wiltshire

29 CRANBURY PARK

Otterbourne, nr Winchester SO21 2HL. Mrs Chamberlayne-Macdonald. *3m NW of Eastleigh. Main entrance on old A33 at top of Otterbourne Hill. Entrances also in Hocombe Rd, Chandlers Ford & next to Otterbourne Church.* **Sun 12 June (2-6). Adm £4.50, chd free. Home-made teas. Donation to Rose Road Association.**
Extensive pleasure grounds laid out in late C18 and early C19 by Papworth; fountains, rose garden, specimen trees and pinetum, lakeside walk and fern walk. Family carriages and collection of prams will be on view, also photos of King George VI, Eisenhower and Montgomery reviewing Canadian troops at Cranbury before D-Day. All dogs on leads please. Disabled WC.

GROUP OPENING

30 CRAWLEY GARDENS

Crawley, Winchester SO21 2PR. F J Fratter, 01962 776243, fred@tanglefoot-house.demon.co.uk. *5m NW of Winchester. Between B3049 (Winchester - Stockbridge) & A272 (Winchester - Andover). Parking throughout village.* **Thur 7, Sun 10 Apr (2-5.30); Thur 2, Sun 5 June (2-6). Combined adm £6, chd free. Thur 7, Sun 10 July (2-6). Combined adm £7.50, chd free. Home-made teas in the village hall.**

BAY TREE HOUSE
Julia & Charles Whiteaway.
*Open on Thur 2, Sun 5 June,
Thur 7, Sun 10 July*

GABLE COTTAGE
Patrick Hendra & Ken Jones.
Open on Thur 7, Sun 10 Apr

LITTLE COURT
Mrs A R Elkington.
Open on all dates
(See separate entry)

PAIGE COTTAGE
Mr & Mrs T W Parker.
*Open on Thur 7, Sun 10 Apr, Thur
7, Sun 10 July*

TANGLEFOOT
Mr & Mrs F J Fratter.
*Open on Thur 2, Sun 5 June,
Thur 7, Sun 10 July*
(See separate entry)

Crawley is an exceptionally pretty period village nestling in chalk downland with thatched houses, C14 church and village pond with ducks. A different combination of gardens opens each month providing seasonal interest with varied character, and with traditional and contemporary approaches to landscape and planting. Most of the gardens have beautiful country views and there are other good gardens to be seen from the road. The spring gardens are Paige Cottage, Gable Cottage and the 3 acre traditional English country garden at Little Court, with carpets of spring bulbs. In summer, other gardens open. At Bay Tree House there are pleached limes, a rill and contemporary borders; while at Tanglefoot there are colour themed borders, herb wheel, exceptional kitchen garden, traditional Victorian boundary wall supporting trained fruit incl apricots; and a large wildflower meadow. Also in the summer, Little Court has a mass of colourful herbaceous planting while Paige Cottage is a typical mixed cottage garden. This year, the July openings comprise the 4 large, varied and exciting gardens. Plants from the garden for sale at Little Court and Tanglefoot.

31 ▶ CROOKLEY POOL
Blendworth Lane, Horndean PO8 0AB. Mr & Mrs Simon Privett, 02392 592662, jennyprivett@icloud.com. *5m S of Petersfield. 2m E of Waterlooville, off A3. From Horndean up Blendworth Lane entrance 200yds before church on L with white railings. Parking in field.* **Sun 15 May, Thur 2 June, Sun 11 Sept (2-5). Adm £4, chd free. Home-made teas. Visits also by arrangement Mar to Sept. Teas on request.**
Here the plants decide where to grow. Californian tree poppies elbow valerian aside to crowd round the pool. Evening primroses obstruct the way to the door and the steps to wisteria shaded terraces. Hellebores bloom under the trees. Salvias, Pandorea jasminoides, Justicia, Pachystachys lutea and passion flowers riot quietly with tomatoes in the greenhouse. Not a garden for the neat or tidy minded, although this is a plantsman's garden full of unusual plants and a lot of tender perennials. Bantams stroll throughout. Watercolour paintings of flowers found in the garden will be on display and for sale.

32 ▶ DEAN HOUSE
Kilmeston Road, Kilmeston, Alresford SO24 0NL. Mr P H R Gwyn, www.deanhousegardens.co.uk. *5m S of Alresford. Via village of Cheriton or off A272 signed at Cheriton Xrds. Follow signs for Kilmeston, through village & turn L at Dean House sign.* **Wed 25 May, Wed 22 June (10-4); Sun 3 July (12-4); Wed 27 July (10-4); Sun 7 Aug (12-4); Wed 17 Aug (10-4). Adm £6, chd free. Home-made teas & cream teas in The Orangery.**
The 7 acres have been described as 'a well-kept secret hidden behind the elegant facade of its Georgian centrepiece'. Sweeping lawns, York stone paths, gravel pathways, many young and mature trees and hedges, mixed and herbaceous borders. Rose garden, pond garden, working walled garden with glasshouses growing 125 different varieties of vegetables, which help to create a diverse and compact sliver of Eden. Over 1700 individually documented plant species and cultivars in our collection. 60 metre Laburnum and Wisteria Tunnel. Gravel paths.

Tylney Hall Hotel

© Leigh Clapp

33 DIPLEY MILL

Dipley Road, Hartley Wintney, Hook RG27 8JP. Miss Rose McMonigall, www.dipley-mill.co.uk. *2m NE of Hook. Turn E off B3349 at Mattingley (1½ m N of Hook) signed Hartley Wintney, West Green & Dipley. Dipley Mill ½ m on L just over bridge.* **Suns 5, 26 June, 17 July, 7 Aug, 11 Sept (2-5.30). Adm £6, chd free. Home-made teas.**

A romantic adventure awaits as you wander by the meandering streams surrounding this Domesday Book listed mill! Explore many magical areas, such as the rust garden, the pill box grotto and the ornamental courtyard, or just escape into wild meadows. 'One of the most beautiful gardens in Hampshire' according to Alan Titchmarsh in his TV programme Love Your Garden. Alpacas. Local fruit stalls (depending on availability). Featured in Hampshire Life (May) and on BBC Radio Solent, In the Garden with Rebecca Parker.

34 THE DOWER HOUSE

Springvale Road, Headbourne Worthy, Winchester SO23 7LD. Mrs Judith Lywood, 01962 882848, hannahlomax@thedowerhousewinchester.co.uk, www.thedowerhousewinchester.co.uk. *2m N of Winchester. Entrance is directly opp watercress beds in Springvale Rd & near The Good Life Farm Shop. Parking at main entrance to house, following path to garden.* **Sun 22 May (2.30-5.30). Adm £3.50, chd free. Home-made teas. Visits also by arrangement Mar to Sept for groups of 20-30.**

5½ acres with easy paths, numerous seats, good views, colourful perennials, shrubs and mature trees (incl large Indian bean tree and cercis Forest Pansy). Large geranium border overlooking grounds, bog garden, good pond with fish and water lilies, newly installed scented garden at entrance, small secret courtyard garden and container planting on The Dower House residents' patios.

35 DOWN FARM HOUSE

Hurstbourne Priors, Whitchurch RG28 7FB. Pat & Steve Jones. *1½ m from the centre of Whitchurch. Please do not use SatNav. From the centre of Whitchurch take the Newbury road up the hill, over railway bridge & after approx 1m turn L.*

Wed 15, Sat 18 June (1-5). Adm £3.50, chd free. Tea.

Step back in time in this 2 acre garden, created from an old walled farmyard and the surrounding land. Many of the original features are used as hard landscaping, incl organic vegetables, succulents, alpine bed created from the old concrete capped well, informal and naturalistic planting, wooded area and orchard. The garden has been created slowly over the last 30 yrs. Wheelchair access by gravel drive onto lawn.

36 THE DOWN HOUSE

Itchen Abbas SO21 1AX. Jackie & Mark Porter, 01962 791054, markstephenporter@gmail.com, www.thedownhouse.co.uk. *5m E of Winchester on B3047. 5th house on R after the Itchen Abbas village sign if coming on B3047 from Kings Worthy. 300yds on L after Plough PH if coming on B3047 from Alresford.* **Sun 21 Feb (12-4). Adm £4, chd free. Sat 3, Sun 4 Sept (1-5.30). Adm £5, chd free. Home-made teas. Visits also by arrangement in Feb for groups of 20+.**

3 acre garden laid out in rooms overlooking the Itchen Valley, adjoining the Pilgrim's Way, with walks to the river. In February come and see snowdrops, aconites and crocus, plus borders of coloured dogwood, willow stems and white birches. A garden of structure, pleached hornbeams, a rope-lined fountain garden, yew lined avenues and an ornamental potager. This autumn, come and see the vineyard. There will be 'Vine to Wine' walks and talks at 2pm and 4pm during our September 'Wine Weekend' opening, plus estate wine tasting!

37 7 DOWNLAND CLOSE

Locks Heath, nr Fareham SO31 6WB. Roy & Carolyn Dorland, 07768 107779, roydorland@hotmail.co.uk. *3m W of Fareham. M27 J9 follow A27 on Southampton Rd to Park Gate. Past Kams Palace Restaurant, L into Locks Rd, 3rd R into Meadow Ave. 2nd L into Downland Close. Please park in Locks Rd (only 2 mins from garden).* **Sun 29, Mon 30 May, Sat 11, Sun 12 June (1-5). Adm £3, chd free. Home-made teas. Visits also by arrangement May & June for groups of 15-25.**

Visit this prize-winning, beautiful, restful and inspirational 50ft x 45ft plantsman's garden, packed with ideas for the modest sized plot. Many varieties of hardy geraniums, hostas, heucheras, shrubs, ferns and other unusual perennials, weaving a tapestry of harmonious colour. Attractive water feature, plenty of seating areas and charming summerhouse. A garden to fall in love with!

38 DURMAST HOUSE

Bennetts Lane, Burley BH24 4AT. Mr & Mrs P E G Daubeney, 01425 402132, philip@daubeney.co.uk, www.durmasthouse.co.uk. *5m SE of Ringwood. Off Burley to Lyndhurst Rd, nr White Buck Hotel.* **Sun 10 Apr, Sun 26 June (2-5). Adm £4, chd free. Cream teas. Visits also by arrangement Apr to Oct, incl talk on the history and planting of the garden for groups only.** *Donation to Delhi Commonwealth Women's Assn Medical Clinic.*

Designed by Gertrude Jekyll, Durmast has contrasting hot and cool colour borders, formal rose garden edged with lavender and a long herbaceous border. Many old trees, Victorian rockery and orchard with beautiful spring bulbs. Rare azaleas: Fama, Princeps and Gloria Mundi from Ghent. Features incl new rose bowers with rare French roses, Eleanor Berkeley, Psyche and Reine Olga Wurtemberg. New Jekyll border with a blue, yellow and white scheme. Article on Durmast House Garden restoration in Hampshire Life (June 2015), entitled Back to Life: Gertrude Jekyll's designs come alive at Durmast House, Leigh Clapp. Many stone paths and some gravel paths.

GROUP OPENING

39 EAST WORLDHAM GARDENS
East Worldham, Alton GU34 3AE, 01420 83389, mary.trigwell-jones@virgin.net, www.worldham.org. *2m SE of Alton on B3004. Gardens & car parking off B3004 signed in village. Tickets & maps available at each garden.* **Sat 11, Sun 12, Sat 25, Sun 26 June, Sat 23, Sun 24 July (2-5.30). Combined adm £5, chd free. Home-made teas.**

NEW **THE COTTAGE**
Ken & Hazel Gosham.
Open on Sat 23, Sun 24 July

EAST WORLDHAM MANOR
Mrs H V Wood.
Open on Sat 11, Sun 12 June

THE OLD HOP KILN
John & Kate Denyer.
Open on Sat 25, Sun 26 June

SELBORNE
Brian & Mary Jones.
*Open on all dates
(See separate entry)*

SILVER BIRCHES
Jenny & Roger Bateman.
Open on Sat 23, Sun 24 July

East Worldham Gardens offers a different combination of gardens with varied characters and styles all with far-reaching views on each of the three openings. East Worldham Manor is a large walled Victorian garden with restored greenhouses, orchard, vegetable area and rose garden. Extensive borders feature hydrangeas, penstemons, roses, shrubs and climbing plants. Gravel paths wind through the garden. The Old Hop Kiln's terraced garden set on a hilltop, with many changes of level, has free-flowing planting that complements the hard landscaping. A series of cascades links the upper and lower levels. Selborne has a 50 yr old orchard providing dappled shade, metal and stone sculptures, conservatory and mixed borders, densely planted, features a range of hardy geraniums. The garden at Silver Birches, redesigned over the last 7 yrs has winding paths leading through shrub and herbaceous borders to fish pond with stream, rockery, summerhouse and rose garden with arbour. Garden quizzes, sandpit and bookstall at Selborne. C13 church with some modern

stained glass windows and Medieval monument of a lady. Home-made teas at East Worldham Manor & Selborne (11 & 12 June), at Selborne (25 & 26 June) and at Selborne & Three Horseshoes PH (23 & 24 July). Featured in WI Life and Tindle Group of Newspapers. Access to Old Hop Kiln is by a steep gravel track that is unsuitable for some wheelchairs.

&♿ ✿ ☕

GROUP OPENING

40 EMSWORTH GARDENS
Emsworth PO10 7PR. Lucy Watson & Mike Rogers, 07867 797622, lucywatson100@hotmail.com. *7m W of Chichester, 2m E of Havant. From Emsworth main r'about head N, under the railway bridge, under the flyover & the garden is immed on the LH-side up a slope. Parking in the recreation ground (approx 5 min walk).* **Sun 19 June (2-5.30). Combined adm £5, chd free. Home-made teas at 23 New Brighton Road. Visits also by arrangement June to Sept for groups of 12+.**

MEADOWLARK, 4 ELDERFIELD CLOSE
Miss M Morelle

23 NEW BRIGHTON ROAD
Lucy Watson & Mike Rogers

Two contrasting 'Mother and Daughter' gardens close to the centre of Emsworth. An historic fishing and sailing village on Chichester Harbour, with numerous PHs, small local museum, walks along the foreshore and a mill pond. Both gardens have a plethora of containers and both feature gravelled areas. Low maintenance but abundant flowering a priority in both. 23 New Brighton Road has several water features, a formal pond and a wildlife pond.

♞ ✿ ☕

41 FAIRBANK
Old Odiham Road, Alton GU34 4BU. Jane & Robin Lees, 01420 86665, j.lees558@btinternet.com. *1½ m N of Alton. From S, past Sixth Form College, then 1½ m beyond road junction on R. From N, turn L at Golden Pot & then 50yds turn R. Garden 1m on L before road junction.* **Wed 3 Aug (2-5). Adm £3.50, chd free. Home-made teas.**

Visits also by arrangement July to Sept for individuals or groups of 30 max.
The planting in this large garden reflects our interest in trees, shrubs and fruit. A wide variety of herbaceous plants provide colour and are placed in sweeping mixed borders that carry the eye down the long garden to the orchard and beyond. Near the house, there are rose beds and herbaceous borders, as well as a small formal pond. There is a range of acers, ferns and unusual shrubs, with 60 different varieties of fruit, along with a large vegetable garden. Please be aware of uneven ground in some areas of the garden.

&♿ 🚐 ☕

Woodland garden to explore with a wonderful feeling of sanctuary . . .

42 FAIRWEATHER'S NURSERY
Hilltop, Beaulieu, Brockenhurst SO42 7YR. Patrick & Aline Fairweather, www.fairweathers.co.uk. *1½ m NE of Beaulieu Village. Signed Beacon Gate on B3054 between Heath r'about (A326) & Beaulieu Village.* **Sat 30, Sun 31 July (11-4). Adm £3, chd free. Cream teas.**
Fairweather's holds a specialist collection of over 400 Agapanthus grown in pots and display beds, the collection should be looking at its best. Features incl; guided tours of the Nursery at 11.30am and 2.30pm, demonstrations of how to get the best from Agapanthus and companion planting, Agapanthus and a range of other traditional and new perennials for sale. Aline Fairweather's garden (adjacent to the nursery) will also be open; it has mixed shrub and perennial borders containing many unusual plants.

&♿ ♞ ✿ 🚐 **NPC** ☕

Atheling Villas

© Louise Jolley

43 FARLEIGH HOUSE
Farleigh Wallop, Basingstoke
RG25 2HT. Viscount Lymington.
*3m SE of Basingstoke. Off B3046
Basingstoke to Preston Candover
road.* Sun 11 Sept (2-5). Adm £5,
chd free. Home-made teas.
Contemporary garden of great
tranquillity designed by Georgia
Langton, surrounded by wonderful
views. 3 acre walled garden in 3
sections; ornamental potager, formal
rose garden and wild rose garden.
Greenhouse full of exotics, serpentine
yew walk, contemplative pond garden
and lake with planting for wildlife. The
grounds cover approx 10 acres and
will take about 1 hour to walk around.

44 FRITHAM LODGE
Fritham SO43 7HH. Sir Chris &
Lady Powell, 02380 812650,
chris.powell@ddblondon.com. *6m
N of Lyndhurst. 3m NW of M27 J1
(Cadnam). Follow signs to Fritham.*
Sun 26 June (2-4). Adm £4, chd
free. Cream teas. Also open
Waldrons. Visits also by
arrangement May to July.
Set in the heart of the New Forest in
18 acres with 1 acre old walled
garden round Grade II listed C17
house (not open), originally one of
Charles II hunting lodges. Parterre of
old roses, potager with wide variety of

vegetables, pergola, wisterias,
herbaceous and blue and white
mixed borders, tulips, and ponds.
Features incl a walk across hay
meadows to woodland and stream,
with ponies, donkeys, sheep and rare
breed hens. Featured in Country Life.

GROUP OPENING

45 FROYLE GARDENS
Lower Froyle, Froyle GU34 4LJ.
Ernie & Brenda Milam. *5m NE of
Alton. Access to Lower Froyle from
A31 between Alton & Farnham at
Bentley or access to Upper Froyle at
Hen & Chickens PH also on A31.
Maps given to all visitors.* Sat 4, Sun
5 June (11-5). Combined adm £5,
chd free. Home-made teas at
Froyle Village Hall or picnic at
West End House.

BRAMLINS
Mrs Anne Blunt

DAY COTTAGE
Mr Nick Whines & Ms Corinna
Furse
www.daycottage.co.uk

FORDS COTTAGE
Mr & Mrs M Carr

GLEBE COTTAGE
Barbara & Michael Starbuck

**NEW OLD BREWERY
HOUSE**
Vivienne & John Sexton

WALBURY
Ernie & Brenda Milam

NEW WEST END HOUSE
Liz & Chris Butler

You will certainly receive a warm
welcome as seven Froyle Gardens
open their gates again this yr enabling
visitors to enjoy a wide variety of
gardens. We have two new larger
gardens opening; one with a large
wildlife pond and the other has a
spectacular lake and reputedly the
best views in Froyle. The other
gardens harmonise well with the
surrounding landscape and most
have spectacular views. The gardens
themselves are diverse with rich
planting often incorporating unusual
plants. You will also see animals,
greenhouses, vegetables and wild
flower meadows as well as a gem of
a courtyard garden. The teas served
in the village hall are famous and
always delicious. If that is not enough
visit St Mary's Church, Upper Froyle
to see the large display of richly
decorated C18 church vestments
(separate donation). No wheelchair
access to Glebe Cottage and gravel
drive at Bramlins. Dogs on leads are
welcome in most gardens.

46 GILBERTS NURSERY
Dandysford Lane, Sherfield
English, nr Romsey SO51 6DT.
Nick & Helen Gilbert,
www.gilbertsdahlias.co.uk. *Midway
between Romsey & Whiteparish on
A27, in Sherfield English Village. From
Romsey 4th turn on L, just before
small petrol station on R, visible from
main road.* Sun 28 Aug (10-4). Adm
£3, chd free. Light refreshments.
This may not be a garden but do
come and be amazed by the sight of
over 300 varieties of dahlias in our
dedicated 1½ acre field. The blooms
are in all colours, shapes and sizes
and can be closely inspected from
wheelchair friendly hard grass paths.
An inspiration for all gardeners. 2015
medals awarded: Large Gold in the
New Forest Show, Gold in the
Taunton Flower Show and Gold in the
Romsey Show. Our dahlia field was
featured in the The Guardian and the
Daily Mail (2015).

MANOR HOUSE
See Wiltshire

47 HAMBLEDON HOUSE
Hambledon PO7 4RU. Capt & Mrs
David Hart Dyke, 02392 632380,
dianahartdyke@talktalk.net. *8m SW
of Petersfield, 5m NW of
Waterlooville. In village centre,
driveway leading to house in East St.
Do not go up Speltham Hill even if
advised by SatNav.* **Visits by
arrangement Apr to Oct. Teas by
prior request. Adm £5, chd free.**
3 acre partly walled plantsman's
garden for all seasons. Large borders
filled with a wide variety of unusual
shrubs and perennials with
imaginative plant combinations
culminating in a profusion of colour in
late summer. Hidden, secluded areas
reveal surprise views of garden and
village rooftops. Planting a large
central area, started in 2011, has
given the garden an exciting new
dimension. Featured in Period
Houses & Interiors and Hampshire
Life. Partial wheelchair access as
garden is on several levels.

**48 HAMBROOKS SHOW
GARDENS**
135 Southampton Road, Titchfield,
Fareham PO14 4PR. Mr Mike
Hodges. *On the old A27 opp B&Q.*
**Sun 29 May, Sun 16 Oct (10-4).
Adm by donation. Home-made
teas.**
16 individually designed showcase
gardens ranging from the traditional
to the contemporary. Each has its
own unique character, demonstrating
versatile and visionary styles. The
gardens contain different features that
incl outdoor kitchens, fireplaces,
stylish garden sofas, chandeliers,
rusty crowned obelisks, babbling
brooks, ponds and streams. Music.
Pumpkin display and children's
competition in October.

49 HANGING HOSTA GARDEN
Narra, Frensham Lane, Lindford,
Bordon GU35 0QJ. June Colley &
John Baker, 01420 489186,
hanginghostas@btinternet.com.
*Approx 1m E of Bordon. From the
A325 at Bordon take the B3002, then
B3004 to Lindford. Turn L into
Frensham Lane, 3rd house on L.*
**Visits by arrangement in July
(Mon 11 to Fri 15 & Mon 18 to Fri
22 only). Adm £3.50, chd free.**
This garden is packed with almost

2000 plants. The collection of over
1500 hosta cultivars is one of the
largest in England. Hostas are
displayed at eye level to give a
wonderful tapestry of foliage and
colour. Islamic garden, waterfall and
stream garden, cottage garden. Talks
given to garden clubs. Featured in
Country Life (2015).

NPC

> Mature plantings
> of deciduous
> azaleas and
> rhododendrons
> amidst a sea of
> bluebells . . .

50 HIDEAWAY
Hamdown Crescent, East Wellow,
Romsey SO51 6BJ. Caroline &
Colin Hart, 01794 322445,
hart.caroline@yahoo.com. *3m W of
Romsey. From M27 J2 take A36 NW
towards Salisbury. After 2m, turn R by
speed camera into Whinwhistle Rd.
Hamdown Crescent is 3rd L.* **Sat 2,
Sun 3 July (2-5.30). Adm £3.50,
chd free. Tea. Visits also by
arrangement in July for groups of
20+.**
Winding paths lead through our
peaceful 1/2 acre garden, where
diverse and unusual plants grow in
different habitats; shade, woodland,
sunny borders, grass gardens, wildlife
pond and bog gardens. Fountains
play amidst the yr-round colour and
somehow fruit and vegetables also
find a place to grow. Many plants
propagated by the owner are for sale,
as is a variety of art work.

51 HILL HOUSE
Old Alresford SO24 9DY. Mrs S
Richardson, 01962 732720,
hillhouseolda@yahoo.co.uk. *N of
Alresford. From Alresford 1m along
B3046 towards Basingstoke, then R
by church.* **Tue 2, Sun 7, Thur 11
Aug (1.30-5). Adm £4, chd free.**

**Home-made teas. Visits also by
arrangement July & Aug.**
Traditional English 2 acre garden,
established 1938, divided by yew
hedge. Large croquet lawn framing
the star of the garden, the huge
multicoloured herbaceous border.
Dahlia bed and butterfly attracting
sunken garden in lavender shades.
Prolific old fashioned kitchen garden
with hens and bantams both fluffy
and large. Small Dexter cows. Dried
flowers.

52 HILL TOP
Damson Hill, Upper Swanmore
SO32 2QR. David Green, 01489
892653, tricia1960@btinternet.com.
*1m NE of Swanmore. Junction of
Swanmore Rd & Church Rd, up
Hampton Hill, sharp L bend. After
300yds junction with Damson Hill,
house on L. Disabled parking by
house.* **Visits by arrangement May
to Sept for groups of 20+. Adm £5,
chd free.**
2 acres with extensive colourful
borders and wide lawns, this garden
has stunning views to the Isle of
Wight. The glasshouses produce
unusual fruit and vegetables from
around the world. The outdoor
vegetable plots bulge with well grown
produce, much for sale in season.
Potted specimen plants and
interesting annuals.

53 HINTON ADMIRAL
Lyndhurst Road, Hinton,
Christchurch BH23 7DY. Sir George
& Lady Meyrick. *4m NE of
Christchurch. On N side of A35, 3/4 m
E of Cat & Fiddle PH.* **Sun 22 May
(11-4.30). Adm £6, chd free.
Donation to Julia's House Childrens
Hospice.**
Magnificent 20 acre garden within a
much larger estate, now being
restored and developed. Mature
plantings of deciduous azaleas and
rhododendrons amidst a sea of
bluebells. Wandering paths lead
through rockeries and beside ponds
and a stream with many cascades.
Orchids appear in the large lawns.
The 2 walled gardens are devoted to
herbs and wild flowers and a very
large greenhouse. The terrace and
rock garden were designed by
Harold Peto. Gravel paths and some
steps.

54 ◆ HINTON AMPNER
Alresford SO24 0LA. National Trust, 01962 771305, hintonampner@nationaltrust.org.uk, www.nationaltrust.org.uk/hinton-ampner. *3¹/₂ m S of Alresford. On A272 Petersfield to Winchester road, between Bramdean & Cheriton.* **For NGS: Sat 4 June, Sat 2 July (10-5). Adm £12.50, chd £6.25. Light lunches & afternoon tea in the tearoom. For other opening times and information, please phone, email or visit garden website.**
C20 garden created by Ralph Dutton covering 14 acres. Manicured lawns and topiary combine with unusual shrubs, climbers and herbaceous plants. Vibrant dahlias alternate in spring with tulips. Rose border incorporates over 45 old and new rose varieties. Dramatic foliage planting in the Dell; orchard with spring bulbs; magnolia and philadelphus walks; restored walled garden. Wheelchair access maps available from visitor reception.

55 HOLLYBROOK
20a Chalk Hill, West End, Southampton SO18 3BZ. Michael Hook & Janet Galpin. *3m E of Southampton. Exit M27 J7 take A27 West End, Chalk Hill at T-lights by Tesco. Park on hill & side roads. Small car parks, courtesy of Swan System Wardrobes & The Master Builder PH on A27, 2 mins from Chalk Hill. Disabled parking on drive for 2 wheelchair users.* **Sat 21, Sun 22, Sat 28, Sun 29 May (2-6). Adm £2.50, chd free. Home-made teas.**
Small 25 x 12 metre town garden started in 2008. Raised beds built using railway sleepers and imaginative use of other recycled and new materials to make interesting artistic garden pieces, to complement small herbaceous border, pergola and two ponds, one with a variety of fish. Structural planting incl bamboos, grasses and hostas. Tiny vegetable patch, with a vegetable competition with friends every yr.

56 THE HOMESTEAD
Northney Road, Hayling Island PO11 0NF. Stan & Mary Pike, 02392 464888, jhomestead@aol.com, www.homesteadhayling.co.uk. *3m S of Havant. From A27 Havant & Hayling Island r'about, travel S over Langstone Bridge & turn immed L*

into Northney Rd. Car park entrance on R after Langstone Hotel. **Sun 7 Aug (2-5.30). Adm £3.50, chd free. Home-made teas. Visits also by arrangement May to Sept for groups of 10+.**
1¹/₄ acre garden surrounded by working farmland with views to Butser Hill and boats in Chichester Harbour. Trees, shrubs, colourful herbaceous borders and small walled garden with herbs, vegetables and trained fruit trees. A quiet and peaceful atmosphere with plenty of seats to enjoy the vistas within the garden and beyond. Some gravel paths.

57 ◆ THE HOSPITAL OF ST CROSS
St Cross Road, Winchester SO23 9SD. The Hospital of St Cross & Almshouse of Noble Poverty, 01962 851375, porter@hospitalofstcross.co.uk, www.hospitalofstcross.co.uk. *¹/₂ m S of Winchester. From city centre take B3335 (Southgate St & St Cross Rd) S. Turn L immed before The Bell PH. If on foot follow riverside path S from Cathedral & College, approx 20 mins.* **For NGS: Sun 24 July (2-5). Adm £4, chd free. Tea in the Hundred Men's Hall in the Outer Quadrangle. For other opening times and information, please phone, email or visit garden website.**
The Medieval Hospital of St Cross nestles in water meadows beside the R Itchen and is one of England's oldest almshouses. The tranquil, walled Master's Garden, created in the late C17 by Bishop Compton, now contains colourful herbaceous borders, old fashioned roses, interesting trees and a large fish pond. The Compton Garden has unusual plants of the type he imported when Bishop of London. There is wheelchair access but please be aware surfaces are uneven in places.

58 THE HOUSE IN THE WOOD
Beaulieu SO42 7YN. Victoria Roberts, 01590 612196, info@spinnersgarden.co.uk. *New Forest. 8m NE of Lymington. Leaving the entrance to Beaulieu Motor Museum on R (B3056), take next R signed Ipley Cross. Take 2nd gravel drive on RH-bend, approx ¹/₂ m.* **Sat 14 May (2-6). Adm £4.50, chd free. Cream teas.**

Peaceful 12 acre woodland garden with continuing progress and improvement. New areas and streams have been developed and good acers planted among mature azaleas and rhododendrons. Used in the war to train the Special Operations Executive. A magical garden to get lost in and popular with birdwatchers.

> Tractor and trailer ride to reclaimed watercress beds now a chalk lake haven for wildlife . . .

59 THE HYDE
Old Alresford SO24 9DH. Sue Alexander, 01962 732043, suealex13@gmail.com. *N of Alresford. From Alresford 1m along B3046 towards Basingstoke. House in centre of village, opp flag pole on village green.* **Thur 25, Sat 27, Sun 28, Mon 29 Aug (1.30-5). Adm £4, chd free. Home-made teas. Visits also by arrangement Aug & Sept for groups of 10+.**
Tucked behind an old field hedge, a delightful ³/₄ acre garden created by the owner to attract wildlife and reflect her passion for colour and texture. Structural trees surround flowing borders which contain an abundant mixture of perennials, half-hardies, annuals, grasses and shrubs. Wonderful ideas for late summer colour. National Collection of Patrinia. Featured in the Saturday Telegraph, Gardens to Visit (Aug 2015). Short gravel drive at entrance.

NPC

60 THE ISLAND
Greatbridge, Romsey SO51 0HP. Mr & Mrs Christopher Saunders-Davies, 01794 512100, ssd@littleroundtop.co.uk. *1m N of Romsey on A3057. Entrance alongside Greatbridge (1st bridge Xing the R Test), flanked by row of cottages on roadside.* **Sat 28, Sun 29 May, Sat 27, Sun 28 Aug (2-5). Adm £5, chd free. Home-made teas. Visits also by arrangement May to Sept for groups of 15-20 (mornings only).**

6 acres either side of the R Test. Fine display of paeonies, wisteria and spring flowering trees. Main garden has herbaceous and annual borders, fruit trees, rose pergola, lavender walk and extensive lawns. An arboretum planted in the 1930s by Sir Harold Hillier contains trees and shrubs providing interest throughout the yr.

& ⊗ ☕

61 LAKE HOUSE
Northington SO24 9TG. Lord Ashburton, 07795 364539, lukeroeder@hotmail.com. *4m N of Alresford. Off B3046. Follow English Heritage signs to The Grange, then directions.* **Thur 9, Sun 12 June (12-5). Adm £5, chd free. Home-made teas. Visits also by arrangement June to Oct for groups of 10+.**
2 large lakes in Candover Valley set off by mature woodland with waterfalls, abundant birdlife, long landscaped vistas and folly. 1½ acre walled garden with rose parterre, mixed borders, long herbaceous border, rose pergola leading to moon gate. Flowering pots, conservatory and greenhouses. Picnicking by lakes. Grass paths and slopes to some areas of the garden.

& ♞ ⊗ 🚐 ☕

62 LITTLE COURT
Crawley, Winchester SO21 2PU. Mrs A R Elkington, 01962 776365, elkslc@btinternet.com. *5m NW of Winchester. Between B3049 (Winchester - Stockbridge) & A272 (Winchester - Andover).* **Sun 21, Mon 22, Tue 23 Feb (2-5). Adm £3, chd free. Mon 28 Mar (2-5.30). Adm £4, chd free. Thur 12, Sun 15 May (2-5.30). Adm £3, chd free, also open Tanglefoot. Home-made teas in the village hall.**

2017: Sun 19, Mon 20, Tue 21 Feb. Opening with Crawley Gardens on Thur 7, Sun 10 Apr, Thur 2, Sun 5 June, Thur 7, Sun 10 July. Visits also by arrangement Feb to Sept, with teas in the garden.
In a small and pretty village, a 3 acre walled country garden which is sheltered from the wind, it is spectacular in both spring and summer, with naturalised bulbs and good snowdrops, and cowslips in the labyrinth. The large beds of perennials are in relaxing colours set off by a good lawn. It is fun for children; with treehouse and swings, but visitors of all ages love it. Comments from visitors in 2015 include; 'we enjoyed it enormously', 'a beautiful and romantic garden', 'this is my favourite garden'.

& ⊗ 🚐 ☕

63 LITTLEWOOD
West Lane, Hayling Island PO11 0JW. Mr & Mrs Steven Schrier. *3m S of Havant. From A27 Havant & Hayling Island junction, travel S for 2m, turn R into West Lane & continue 1m. House set back from road in a wood on the R.* **Sat 30 Apr, Sun 1 May (11-5). Adm £3.50, chd free. Home-made teas.**
2½ acre bluebell wood and spring flowering garden surrounded by fields and near sea, protected from sea winds by multi barrier hedge. Rhododendrons, azaleas, camellias and many other shrubs. Woodland walk to full size treehouse. Features incl pond, bog garden, house plants, summerhouse, conservatory and many places to sit outside and under cover. Dogs on leads and picnickers welcome. Close to Hayling Billy Coastal Trail. Unload wheelchairs at top of shingle drive. Garden is level throughout.

& ♞ ⊗ ☕

64 LONGSTOCK PARK
Leckford, Stockbridge SO20 6EH. Leckford Estate Ltd, part of John Lewis Partnership, www.longstockpark.co.uk. *4m S of Andover. From Leckford village on A3057 towards Andover, cross the river bridge and take 1st turning to the L signed Longstock.* **Sun 19 June (2-5). Adm £6, chd £2. Tea.**
Famous water garden with extensive collection of aquatic and bog plants set in 7 acres of woodland with rhododendrons and azaleas. A walk through the park leads to National Collections of *Buddleja* and *Clematis*

viticella; arboretum and herbaceous border. Teas at Leckford Farm Shop, at Longstock Nurseries (last orders at 3.45pm). Assistance dogs only.

& ⊗ ☕

65 LOWER NORTON FARMHOUSE
Norton, Sutton Scotney, Winchester SO21 3NE. Tom & Alison Coleman. *10m N of Winchester. From Sutton Scotney, follow Bullington Lane signed towards A303 & A34. After ¾ m turn R, signed Norton. At top of lane turn L at T-junction & follow lane for further 500 metres.* **Sat 4, Sun 5 June (2-6). Adm £4, chd free. Home-made teas.**
1 acre family garden with herbaceous borders planted in a relaxed cottage garden style, given structure by box hedging. Wildlife pond, free range call ducks, Orpington chickens and Pekin bantams. Large lawn area with wild flowers set off by water feature. Vegetable garden. Tractor and trailer ride to reclaimed watercress beds now a chalk lake haven for wildlife. Lots of interest for children. Featured in Sunday Telegraph (23 May 2015). Wheelchair access, please note gravel drive.

& ⊗ ☕

66 ◆ MACPENNYS WOODLAND GARDEN & NURSERIES
Burley Road, Bransgore, Christchurch BH23 8DB. Mr & Mrs T M Lowndes, 01425 672348, office@macpennys.co.uk, www.macpennys.co.uk. *6m S of Ringwood, 5m NE of Christchurch. From Crown PH Xrds in Bransgore take Burley Rd, following sign for Thorney Hill & Burley. Entrance ¼ m on R.* **For opening times and information, please phone, email or visit garden website.**
12 acres of nursery with 4 acre gravel pit converted into woodland garden planted with many unusual plants. Offering interest yr-round, but particularly in spring and autumn. Large nursery displaying for sale a wide selection of trees, shrubs, conifers, perennials, hedging plants, fruit trees and bushes. Tearoom offering home-made cakes, Dorset tea, New Forest ice cream, locally produced honey, jams and chutneys; using locally sourced foods wherever possible. Partial wheelchair access.

& ♞ ⊗ 🚐 ☕

67 ▶ 1 MAPLE COTTAGE

Searles Lane, off London Road (A30), Hook RG27 9EQ. John & Pat Beagley. *A30 Hartley Wintney side of Hook opp Hampshire Prestige Cars. Use Hook House parking immed on L. 1/4 m up lane entrance & parking for those with walking difficulties. Follow yellow ribbons.* **Sun 5, Wed 8, Thur 9, Wed 15, Thur 16 June (2-5). Adm £3.50, chd free. Home-made cakes, gluten free cake & biscuits.**

1/2 acre garden that has evolved over 25 yrs with views towards R Whitewater. Cottage style herbaceous borders, small courtyard garden, vegetable plots, wildlife pond with many named hostas. Features incl a tree cave for children, good selection of birds, plus the chance to purchase wood carvings for the garden and wood turning for the home. Pimms Tent on Sun 5 June only (weather permitting). Some paved paths, mainly grassed areas.

Varied topiary interplanted with stunning tulips and forget-me-nots . . .

68 ▶ MEON ORCHARD

Kingsmead, N of Wickham PO17 5AU. Doug & Linda Smith, 01329 833253, meonorchard@btinternet.com. *5m N of Fareham. From Wickham take A32 N for 1 1/2 m. Turn L at Roebuck Inn. Continue 1/2 m. Park on verge or in field N of property.* **Sun 29 May, Sun 31 July, Sun 4 Sept (2-6). Adm £4, chd free. Home-made teas. Visits also by arrangement May to Sept for groups of 20+ or minimum charge.**

1 1/2 acre garden designed and constructed by current owners. An exceptional range of rare, unusual and architectural plants incl National Collection of Eucalyptus. Dramatic foliage plants from around the world, both hardy and tender. Big bananas,

tree ferns, cannas, gingers and palms dominate in Sept, flowering shrubs in May/June and perennials in July. Streams and ponds plus an extensive range of planters complete the display. See plants you have never seen before. Visitors are welcome to explore the 20 acre meadow and 1/2 m of Meon River frontage attached to the garden. Extra big plant sale of the exotic and rare on Sun 4 Sept. Garden fully accessible by wheelchair, reserved parking.

69 ▶ MERDON MANOR

Merdon Castle Lane, Hursley, Winchester SO21 2JJ. Mr & Mrs J C Smith, 01962 775215, vronk@bluebottle.com. *5m SW of Winchester. From A3090 Winchester to Romsey road, turn R at Standon, onto Merdon Castle Lane. Proceed for 1 1/4 m. Entrance on R between 2 curving brick walls.* **Sun 7 Aug (2-6). Adm £4, chd free. Home-made teas. Visits also by arrangement May to Sept.**

5 acre country garden surrounded by panoramic views; pond with ducks, damsel flies, dragonflies and water lilies; large wisteria; roses; fruit-bearing lemon trees; extensive lawns; impressive yew hedges; small secret walled garden with fountains. Black Hebridean sheep (St. Kildas). Very tranquil and quiet.

70 ▶ MICHAELMAS

2 Old Street, Hill Head, Fareham PO14 3HU. Ros & Jack Wilson, 01329 662593, jazzjack00@gmail.com. *4 1/2 m S of Fareham. From Fareham follow signs to Stubbington, then Hill Head. Turn R into Bells Lane. After 1m pass Osborne View PH on L, next R is Old St.* **Sun 17, Mon 18 July (2-5). Adm £3, chd free. Home-made teas. Visits also by arrangement June to Aug for groups of 10-20.**

Very cheerful, colourful small garden with the wow factor. A variety of tall plants for a tall lady! Many are grown from seed or cuttings. Small vegetable garden, greenhouse, garden room, pot grown vegetables and flowers. Styled in the fashion of a country garden with a wide range of plants with the emphasis on perennials. As pictured in preface of The Gardens of England book. 1 min walk from beach, 5 mins walk from Titchfield Haven Nature Reserve.

71 ▶ MOORE BLATCH

48 High Street, Lymington SO41 9ZQ. Moore Blatch Solicitors. *Top end of Lymington High St, on S side. Follow signs for Lymington town centre & use High St car parks.* **Sat 9 Apr (9.30-1); Sun 10 Apr (2-5). Adm £3.50, chd free. Tea, coffee & cakes.**

Situated behind this elegant Georgian town house lies a surprising s-facing walled garden of 1 acre. From the raised terrace, enjoy the long vista across the croquet lawn to mature gardens beyond and then over to the Isle of Wight. Amusing and varied topiary interplanted with stunning tulips and forget-me-nots. Attractions close by incl the Lymington Saturday Market and the lively waterfront at the bottom of the High St.

72 ▶ NEW ▶ 22 MOUNT PLEASANT ROAD

Alton GU34 1NN. Phyllida McCormick. *From A31 take A339 Alton/Basingstoke. Follow signs for town centre, past Butts Green on L & garage on R. Next R is Mount Pleasant Rd car park & No 22 is on R. Spaces on road for residents only please.* **Sat 18, Sun 19 June, Sat 13, Sun 14 Aug (2-6). Combined adm with 42 Whitedown £5, chd free.**

A small garden, a few minutes' walk away from the town centre, yet quiet and peaceful. Three garden rooms are divided by arches and espalier fruit trees. There are perennials, roses and clematis, against a backdrop of mature shrubs and trees, with a covered path of clematis Viticella 'Mary Rose' in August which greets you at the gate. The final room has a wilder emphasis with several types of ferns and foxgloves, apple trees as well as a young Judas tree.

73 ▶ OAK TREE COTTAGE

Upper Common Road, Pennington, Lymington SO41 8LD. Sue Kent. *2m NW of Lymington. From N off A337, turn into Sway Rd, 1 1/2 m to Wheel Inn. Turn L into Ramley Rd & follow signs. Leave M27 J2 & follow Heavy Lorry Route to avoid traffic in Lyndhurst.* **Sat 9, Sun 10 July (2-5.30). Adm £3.50, chd free. Home-made teas.**

This 1 acre garden has a wealth of surprises, but with continuity. Using a limited palette of plants, it flows from one secluded space to another.

Designed with a gentle variation of levels and using many trees, contrasting foliage and flowers, one can become delightfully lost. Partial wheelchair access.

74 ▸ OLD DROXFORD STATION
Station Road, Soberton, Southampton SO32 3QU. Jo & Tony Williams. *12m E of Winchester, 12m SW of Petersfield. A32 N through Droxford. After ¹/₂ m turn R (opp petrol station), under bridge, turn R (before Hurdles PH), property 1st on R, park in road. Please call 01489 878271 to arrange disability parking.* **Sun 3 July (11-4). Adm £4, chd free. Home-made teas.**
A sympathetically restored railway station with wild flower garden in the former track. Established specimen trees, perennials, annuals and bulbs. Raised vegetable beds, greenhouse and a new orchard. Winston Churchill was based here before D-Day.

GROUP OPENING

75 ▸ OLD THATCH & THE MILLENNIUM BARN
Sprats Hatch Lane, Winchfield, Hook RG27 8DD. *3m W of Fleet. A287 Odiham to Farnham turn N to Dogmersfield, L by Queens Head PH & L at Barley Mow PH. From Winchfield to Dogmersfield, R after 1¹/₃ m at Barley Mow PH.* **Sun 17 Apr, Sun 17 July, Sun 4 Sept (2-6). Combined adm £4, chd free. Wine. Pimms if hot & mulled wine if cool.**

THE MILLENNIUM BARN

OLD THATCH
Jill Ede
www.old-thatch.co.uk

Two gardens in one! A small secluded haven sits under the old oak tree next to the pond, surrounded by yr-round colour and seasonal fragrance from roses and honeysuckle. You can listen to birdsong, wind chimes and the trickling of a small waterfall whilst enjoying views of Old Thatch and the cottage garden beyond. Who could resist visiting Old Thatch, a chocolate box thatched cottage, featured on film and TV, an evolving smallholding with a 5 acre garden and woodland alongside the Basingstoke Canal (unfenced). A succession of spring bulbs, a profusion of wild flowers,

80 Abbey Road

perennials and home grown annuals pollinated by our own bees and fertilised by the donkeys, who await your visit. Over 30 named clematis and rose cultivars. Lambs in April and donkey foals in summer. Children enjoy our quiz on Sundays and the tree lookout (supervised, please), Dads love the cakes and Mums enjoy the music and craft stalls. Situated on Basingstoke canal. Check www.basingstoke-canal.org.uk. Some canal boat trips will drop off and pick up on garden open days. Featured in Hampshire Life. Disabled parking for blue badge holders only. Can unload drive-on wheelchairs on-site.

76 ▸ ORDNANCE HOUSE
West Dean, Salisbury SP5 1JE. Terry & Vanessa Winters, 01794 341797, terry.winters@ordnancehouse.com, www.ordnancehouse.com. *7m W of Romsey. Park at West Dean Recreation Ground, 350yds away. Disability parking only at garden.* **Sun 29 May (12-5). Adm £3.50, chd free. Home-made teas. Visits also by arrangement June & July for groups of 10+.**
The garden changes through the seasons from its late spring and summer displays of purple and white alliums and foxgloves, to the rich

colour palette of June to August. Lavender is a signature plant and used throughout the garden. Comprises many herbaceous beds, small orchard, compact soft fruit and vegetable gardens and formal parterre. Seating areas have views of garden and countryside beyond. Televised in The Great British Garden Revival on BBC 2 and featured in Country Homes & Interiors (May 2015) and Wohn & Garten, a German magazine.

77 ▸ ◆ PATRICK'S PATCH
Fairweather's Garden Centre, High Street, Beaulieu SO42 7YB. Mr P Fairweather, 01590 612307, www.fairweathers.co.uk. *SE of New Forest at head of Beaulieu River. Leave M27 at J2 & follow signs for Beaulieu Motor Museum. Go up High St & park in Fairweather's on LH-side.* **For opening times and information, please phone or visit garden website.**
Model kitchen garden with a full range of vegetables, trained top and soft fruit and herbs. Salads in succession used as an educational project for all ages. Maintained by volunteers, primary school children and a part-time gardener. A very productive garden enclosed by walls built from New Forest heather bales and local softwood.

© Leigh Clapp

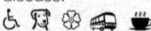
Dipley Mill

78 PILLEY HILL COTTAGE
Pilley Hill, Pilley, Lymington
SO41 5QF. Steph & Sandy Glen,
01590 677844,
stephglen@hotmail.co.uk,
www.pilleyhillcottage.com. *New
Forest. 2m N of Lymington off A337.
To avoid traffic delays in Lyndhurst
leave M27 at J2 & follow Heavy Lorry
Route.* Sat 19, Sun 20 Mar, Sat 16,
Sun 17 Apr, Sun 1, Mon 2 May
(2-5). Adm £3, chd free. Cream
teas. **Visits also by arrangement
Mar to May for groups of 20+.**
Naturalistic, wildlife friendly garden of
surprises around every corner. Enter
through the creeper covered lych
gate, to a spectacle of colour. Wild
flowers rub shoulders with perennials
among quaint objects and oak
structures. Meander through the wild
old orchard through willow walks and
oak archways, onto the shady pond
garden. Enjoy a cream tea to
complete your visit. Some visitors
with wheelchairs have managed
our garden, so please phone to
discuss.
♿ 🎉 ☘

79 PYLEWELL PARK
South Baddesley, Lymington
SO41 5SJ. Lord Teynham. *Coast
road 2m E of Lymington. From
Lymington follow signs for Car Ferry
to Isle of Wight, continue for 2m to
South Baddesley.* Sun 27 Mar, Sun
29 May (2-5). Adm £4, chd free.
Home-made teas.

A large parkland garden laid out in
1890. Enjoy a walk along the
extensive informal grass and moss
paths, bordered by fine
rhododendrons, magnolias,
embothriums and cornus. Wild
daffodils in bloom at Easter and
bluebells in May. Large lakes are
bordered by giant gunnera. Distant
views of the Isle of Wight across the
Solent. Lovely for families and dogs.
Wear suitable footwear for muddy
areas.

GROUP OPENING

80 ROMSEY GARDENS
Mill Lane, Romsey SO51 8EU. *Town
centre, all gardens within walking
distance of Romsey Abbey, clearly
signed. Car parking by King John's
Garden.* Sun 29, Mon 30 May
(11-5.30). Combined adm £6, chd
free. Home-made teas at King
John's House.

KING JOHN'S GARDEN
Friends of King John's Garden
& Test Valley Borough

4 MILL LANE
Miss J Flindall
Visits also by arrangement Mar
to Oct.
01794 513926

THE NELSON COTTAGE
Margaret Prosser

**THE OLD THATCHED
COTTAGE**
Genevieve & Derek Langford

Romsey is a small, unspoilt, historic
market town with the majestic C12
Norman Abbey as a backdrop to 4
Mill Lane, a garden described by Joe
Swift as 'the best solution for a long
thin garden with a view'. King John's
Garden, with its fascinating listed C13
house, has all period plants that were
available before 1700; it also has an
award-winning Victorian garden with
a courtyard where tea is served (no
dogs, please). The Nelson Cottage
was formally a PH; its ½ acre garden
has a variety of perennial plants and
shrubs, with a wild grass meadow
bringing the countryside into the
town. The Old Thatched Cottage
(C15) has a small garden undergoing
further development by new owners;
it features a variety of shrubs, lawn,
vegetable patch, fruit cordons,
rockery and water feature. No
wheelchair access at 4 Mill Lane.
♿ 🎉 ☘

81 ROTHERFIELD PARK
East Tisted, Alton GU34 3QE. Sir
James & Lady Scott. *4m S of Alton
on A32. Please do not use SatNav.
Entry from A32 only.* Sun 24 Apr
(2-5). Adm £5, chd free. Home-
made teas.
Take some ancient ingredients: ice
house, ha-ha, lime avenue; add a
walled garden, fruit and vegetables,
trees and hedges; set this 12 acre
plot in an early C19 park (picnic here
from noon) with views to coin clichés
about. Mix in a bluebell wood and
Kim Wilkie's modern take on an
amphitheatre by the stable block. Top
growers selling plants, incl Marcus
Dancer and Phoenix Perennial Plants.
Wheelchair access to walled garden.
♿ ☘

82 28 ST RONAN'S AVENUE
Southsea, Portsmouth PO4 0QE.
Ian Craig & Liz Jones, 02392
787331, ian.craig1@mac.com. *St
Ronan's Rd can be found off Albert
Rd, Southsea. Follow signs from
Albert Rd or Canoe Lake on seafront.
Parking in Craneswater School.*
**Evening opening Sat 16 July (5-8).
Adm £4.50, chd free. Wine.
Opening with Southsea Gardens
on Sun 19 June. Visits also by
arrangement May to Aug.**
Town garden 145ft x 25ft, 700 metres
from the sea. A mixture of tender,
exotic and dry loving plants along

with more traditional incl king protea, bananas, ferns, agaves, echeverias, echium and puya. Wild flower area and wildlife pond. Two different dry gardens showing what can be grown in sandy soil. Recycled items have been used to create sculptures.

83 2 SAMPAN CLOSE

Warsash, Southampton SO31 9BU. Amanda & Robert Bailey. *4¹/₂ m W of Fareham. M27 J9 take A27 W, L at Park Gate into Brook Lane by Esso garage. Straight over 3 r'abouts, L at 4th r'about into Schooner Way. Sampan Close, 4th on R. Please park in Schooner Way.* **Sat 14, Sun 15 May (12-4). Adm £2.50, chd free. Home-made teas.**
Sited on former strawberry fields this compact garden 50ft x 27ft was designed by the owner, an enthusiastic horticulturalist, to give yr-round interest. Inspirational design ideas for tiny plots with perennials, grasses, old roses, trough planting and raised vegetable beds. A small brick rill edges a circle of lawn. A blue, lean-to glasshouse, against a brick garden wall is an attractive feature. Fareham in Bloom gold awards for Plantsman's Front Garden and Small Plantsman's Back Garden 2015.

84 SANDY SLOPES

Honeysuckle Lane, Headley Down, Bordon GU35 8EH. Mr & Mrs R Thornton. *6m S of Farnham. From A3 exit S side of Hindhead tunnel, proceed to Grayshott, then Headley Down via B3002. From Farnham proceed S, A325 to Bordon turn L onto B3002 via Lindford & Headley to Headley Down.* **Mon 2, Mon 30 May (2-5.30). Adm £3.50, chd free. Tea.**
A plantsman's garden with a remarkable collection of mature plants from China and other parts of the world, many of these are rare and exciting. Some are naturalised and many are woodland shade lovers such as trilliums, areseamas, primulas and rare blue meconopsis, growing beneath mature rhododendrons, magnolias and rare trees. Rising terraced ground with a stream and wildlife pond. Many unusual varieties of woodland plants in season, with some for sale. Steep slopes and steps, unsuitable for pushchairs and visitors with walking difficulties.

85 SELBORNE

Caker Lane, East Worldham GU34 3AE. Brian & Mary Jones, 01420 83389, mary.trigwell-jones@virgin.net, www.worldham.org.uk. *2m SE of Alton. On B3004 at Alton end of East Worldham opp The Three Horseshoes PH (please note, not in the village of Selborne). Parking signed.* **Sat 16, Sun 17 Apr, Sat 7, Sun 8 May, Sat 6, Sun 7, Mon 8 Aug (2-5). Adm £3.50, chd free. Home-made teas. Opening with East Worldham Gardens on Sat 11, Sun 12, Sat 25, Sun 26 June, Sat 23, Sun 24 July. Visits also by arrangement Apr to Aug for individuals and groups.** *Donation to East Worldham Church Fabric Fund (Apr) & Tafara Mission Zimbabwe (Aug).*
Described as a garden of surprises this ¹/₂ acre mature garden with views across farmland features a 50 yr old orchard of named varieties. Mixed, densely planted borders contain hardy geraniums, other herbaceous plants, shrubs and climbers. Metal and stone sculptures enhance the borders. Relax and enjoy tea sitting in the dappled shade of the orchard. Summerhouses and conservatory provide shelter. Book stall, garden quizzes for children and a sandpit. Featured in Hampshire Life, WI Life, Tindle Group of Newspapers. Wheelchair access, please note some gravel paths.

Recycled items have been used to create sculptures . . .

86 SHALDEN PARK HOUSE

The Avenue, Shalden, Alton GU34 4DS. Mr & Mrs Michael Campbell. *4¹/₂ m NW of Alton. B3349 from Alton or M3 J5 onto B3349. Turn W at Golden Pot PH marked Herriard, Lasham, Shalden. Entrance ¹/₄ m on L. Disabled parking on entry.* **Sun 3 July (2-5). Adm £4, chd free. Home-made teas.**
Large 4 acre garden to stroll round with beautiful views. Herbaceous borders incl kitchen walk and rose garden, all with large scale planting

and foliage interest. Pond, arboretum, perfect kitchen garden and garden statuary.

87 SHRONER WOOD

Basingstoke Road, Martyr Worthy, Winchester SO21 1AG. John Anstruther-Gough-Calthorpe, 01962 882073. *5m N of Winchester. From S, take A33 N from Kings Worthy & after 1¹/₂ m, just before the dual carriageway begins, turn R. From N, take A33 S from M3 J7 & after 8m, at the end of the dual carriageway, turn L.* **Sun 8 May (2-5). Adm £5, chd free. Home-made teas. Visits also by arrangement Mar to May for groups of 30+.**
A 7 acre arboretum of great historical significance begun over 100 yrs ago by the Hillier family. Many fine and unusual trees and shrubs including rhododendrons, azaleas and magnolias on a carpet of bluebells and wild flowers in late spring. Extensive restoration work in recent yrs has resulted in a woodland garden to explore with a wonderful feeling of sanctuary.

88 ◆ SIR HAROLD HILLIER GARDENS

Jermyns Lane, Ampfield, Romsey SO51 0QA. Hampshire County Council, 01794 369317, info@hants.gov.uk, www.hilliergardens.org.uk. *2m NE of Romsey. Follow brown tourist signs off M3 J11, or off M27 J2, or A3057 Romsey to Andover. Disabled parking available.* **For opening times and information, please phone, email or visit garden website.**
Established by the plantsman Sir Harold Hillier, this 180 acre garden holds a unique collection of 12,000 different hardy plants from across the world. It incl the famous Winter Garden, Magnolia Avenue, Centenary Border, Himalayan Valley, Gurkha Memorial Garden, Magnolia Avenue, spring woodlands, Hydrangea Walk, fabulous autumn colour, 14 National Collections and over 400 champion trees. The Centenary Border is believed to be the longest double mixed border in the country, a feast from early summer to autumn. Celebrated Winter Garden is one of the largest in Europe. Electric scooters are available for hire (please pre-book). Disabled WC. Guide and hearing dogs only.

GROUP OPENING

89▶ SOUTHSEA GARDENS
Southsea, Portsmouth PO4 0PR.
*St Ronan's Rd can be found off
Albert Rd, Southsea. Follow signs
from Albert Rd or Canoe Lake on
seafront. Parking in Craneswater
School.* **Sun 19 June (2-6).
Combined adm £5, chd free.
Home-made teas at 28 St Ronan's
Avenue.**

27 ST RONAN'S AVENUE
Mr & Mrs S C Johns

28 ST RONAN'S AVENUE
Ian Craig & Liz Jones
(See separate entry)

85 ST RONAN'S ROAD
Mr Mike Hodges

Three town gardens conveniently
within 100 metres of each other. Each
has a distinctive style, with different
designs showing what can be
achieved in an urban setting. 85 St
Ronan's Road is a city garden with a
classical twist, featuring a Neptune
water feature in a pool of smoke. The
garden has won a national landscape
design award and has featured on TV.
There is exceptional design at 27 St
Ronan's Avenue where landscaping
has been used to create a modern
family concept with exuberant
planting. 28 St Ronan's Avenue
showcases the more traditional with a
mixture of tender, exotic and dry
loving plants incl king proteas,
bananas, ferns, agaves, echeverias
and echiums.

90▶ SPINDLES
24 Wootton Road, Lee-on-the-
Solent, Portsmouth PO13 9HB.
Peter & Angela Arnold, 02393
115181, angelliana62@gmail.com.
*6m S of Fareham. Exit A27, turn L
Gosport Rd A32. At r'about 2nd exit
Newgate Lane B3385. Through 3
r'abouts, turn L Marine Parade
B3333 onto Wootton Rd.* **Visits by
arrangement May to Aug for
groups of 6-30 (day & eve). Art
groups welcome. Adm £3, chd
free.**
A small constantly evolving garden
never boring! Traditional planting
alongside exotics and tropical,
unusual trees and shrubs, creative
use of every available space, roses
and clematis in profusion, fernery,
succulents, hostas, grasses, grapes,

blueberries, olive. Seating areas and
conservatory where home-made cake
and tea is served.

91▶ ◆ SPINNERS GARDEN
School Lane, Boldre, Lymington
SO41 5QE. Andrew & Vicky
Roberts, 07545 432090,
info@spinnersgarden.co.uk,
www.spinnersgarden.co.uk. *1½ m
N of Lymington. Follow the brown
signs off the A337 between Lymington
& Brockenhurst. Also signed off the
B3054 Beaulieu to Lymington road.
Map available on website.* **For NGS:
Mon 28 Mar (1-5). Adm £5, chd
free. Home-made teas.** For other
opening times and information,
please phone, email or visit garden
website.
Peaceful woodland garden with
azaleas, rhododendrons, magnolias,
acers and other rare shrubs
underplanted with a wide variety of
choice woodland and ground cover
plants. The garden has been extended
over the last 5 yrs and the views
opened up over the Lymington valley.
More recently, building work has been
completed on a new house in the
grounds designed to complement
the garden. Partial wheelchair
access.

92▶ NEW▶ SPRING POND
Laverstoke, Whitchurch RG28 7PD.
Mrs Carolyn Sheffield,
info@springpondgarden.co.uk,
www.springpondgarden.co.uk.
*1m S of the B3400 in Laverstoke. 8m
W of Basingstoke, 3m W of Overton.
In Laverstoke turn L opp Bombay
Sapphire brick building on B3400 to
Micheldever Station. Spring Pond is
1m along road on the L.* **Sun 26,
Wed 29 June (2-5). Adm £6, chd
free. Home-made teas.
Visits also by arrangement Mar to
Sept for groups of 10+.**
Spring Pond is full of colour
coordinated borders, with an
abundance of roses and clematis,
while hornbeam, yew and box
hedges add structure to the garden.
There is a pond with a wide variety of
marginal plants, an arboretum full of
ornamental trees, and a conservatory
with Mediterranean and tropical
plants. Hardy's Garden Plants nursery
is 1m from Spring Pond. Featured in
the Country Life.

GROUP OPENING

93▶ STOCKBRIDGE GARDENS
Stockbridge SO20 6EX. *9m W of
Winchester. On A30, at junction of
A3057 & B3049. Parking on High St.
All gardens on High St & Winton Hill.*
**Thur 16, Sun 19 June (2-5.30).
Combined adm £6, chd free. Tea
on St Peter's Church Lawn.**
Donation to St Peter's Church.

LITTLE WYKE
Mrs Mary Matthews

OLD SWAN HOUSE
Mr Herry Lawford

SHEPHERDS HOUSE
Kim & Frances Candler

TROUT COTTAGE
Mrs Sally Milligan

Stockbridge with its many listed
houses, excellent shops and
hostelries is on the famous R Test.
Four gardens are open this yr offering
a variety of styles and character.
Tucked in behind the High St, Trout
Cottage's small walled garden flowers
for almost 10 mths of the yr. Little
Wyke, also on the High St next to the
Town Hall, has a long mature town
garden with mixed borders and fruit
trees. Old Swan House, at the east
end of the High St, is a newly
designed garden offering mature fish
pond with waterlilies, long lawn facing
mirror herbaceous borders, ancient
brick walls sheltering mixed planting
and shrub roses, a gravel grass
garden and a partly mature orchard.
Shepherds House, 50yds east of the
White Hart r'about, is a s-facing,
³/₄ acre maturing garden on rising
ground with informal shrubberies,
colourful borders, terraces, lawns,
ponds, woodland glade and small
orchard.

94 ▶ TANGLEFOOT

Crawley, Winchester SO21 2QB. Mr & Mrs F J Fratter, 01962 776243, fred@tanglefoot-house.demon.co.uk. *5m NW of Winchester. Between B3049 (Winchester - Stockbridge) & A272 (Winchester - Andover). Lane beside Crawley Court (Arqiva). Parking in adjacent field.* **Thur 12, Sun 15 May (2-5.30). Adm £3, chd free, also open Little Court. Thur 28, Sun 31 July (2-5.30). Adm £4, chd free. Opening with Crawley Gardens on Thur 2, Sun 5 June, Thur 7, Sun 10 July. Visits also by arrangement May to July.**

Designed and developed by owners since 1976, Tanglefoot's ¹/₂ acre garden is a blend of influences, from Monet-inspired rose arch and small wildlife pond to Victorian boundary wall with trained fruit trees. Highlights include a raised lily pond, small wildflower meadow, herbaceous bed (a riot of colour later in the summer), herb wheel, large productive kitchen garden and unusual flowering plants. In contrast to the garden, a 2 acre field is being converted into spring and summer wildflower meadows, with mostly native trees and shrubs; already it has delighted our visitors in summer 2015. Watercolour flower paintings. Plants from the garden for sale.

  👩‍🦽 ✿ 🚌

Traditional and exotic plants mingle with sculptures . . .

95 ▶ TERSTAN

Longstock, Stockbridge SO20 6DW. Alexander & Penny Burnfield, penny.burnfield@andover.co.uk, www.pennyburnfield.wordpress.com. *¹/₂ m N of Stockbridge. From Stockbridge (A30) turn N to Longstock at bridge. Garden ¹/₂ m on R.* **Suns 24 Apr, 26 June, 24 July, 4 Sept (2-6). Adm £4, chd free. Home-made teas. Visits also by arrangement May to Sept with coach parking available.**

1 acre, intensively planted, with an artist's flair for colour and design. Relax on one of the many seats with views across the R Test to the Hampshire Downs and listen to gentle summer music. An exuberance of rare and unusual plants. Featured in several magazines. Wheelchair access, but some gravel paths and steps.

  👩‍🦽 ✿ 🚌 ☕

96 ▶ THE THATCHED COTTAGE

Church Road, Upper Farringdon, Alton GU34 3EG. Mr & Mrs David & Cally Horton, 01420 587922, dwhorton@btinternet.com. *3m S of Alton off A32. At S end of Lower Farringdon take road to Upper Farringdon. At top of hill turn L into Church Rd, follow road to cottage on R, opp church.* **Sun 15, Sun 29, Mon 30 May, Sun 19 June (2-5.30). Evening opening Wed 22 June (5.30-8). Wine. Sun 10 July, Sun 7 Aug (2-5.30). Evening opening Wed 24 Aug (5.30-8). Wine. Combined adm with Berry Cottage £5, chd free. Visits also by arrangement May to Sept for groups of 10+.**

A once neglected 1¹/₂ acre garden that has been lovingly restored over the last 5 yrs. Running south from a beautiful C16 thatched cottage the formal lawn and packed borders blend into more informal areas of perennial and shrub planting, vegetables, fruit and wild flowers surrounding a gypsy caravan. Chickens, ducks and guinea fowl. Fully accessible by wheelchair after a short gravel drive.

  👩‍🦽 ✿ ☕

97 ▶ TYLNEY HALL HOTEL

Ridge Lane, Rotherwick RG27 9AZ. Elite Hotels, 01256 764881, sales@tylneyhall.com, www.tylneyhall.co.uk. *3m NW of Hook. From M3 J5 via A287 & Newnham, M4 J11 via B3349 & Rotherwick.* **Sun 24 Apr, Sun 12 June, Sun 2 Oct (10-4). Adm £5, chd free. Light refreshments in the Chestnut Suite from 12pm.**

Large garden of 66 acres with extensive woodlands and fine vista being restored with new planting. Fine avenues of wellingtonias, rhododendrons and azaleas, Italian garden, lakes, large water and rock garden, dry stone walls originally designed with assistance of Gertrude Jekyll. Partial wheelchair access.

  👩‍🦽 ✿ 🛏 ☕

98 ▶ UPHAM FARM

Upham SO32 1JD. Penny Walker. *2m NW of Bishop's Waltham. Turn into Upham St from B2177, then ¹/₂ m on R just past post box, turn R into farmyard.* **Sun 10 Apr (12-4). Adm £3.50, chd free. Home-made teas.**

Established 1¹/₂ acre garden with mature trees and shrubs. Borders continually being added to, with planting combinations following colour themes. Recent improvements incl an extension of the hot border, a small woodland garden and renovated wild flower meadow. Together with a traditional orchard, rose garden and productive kitchen garden, Upham Farm is well worth a visit. Gravel drive and path to garden.

  👩‍🦽 ✿ ☕

99 ▶ WALDRONS

Brook, Bramshaw SO43 7HE. Major & Mrs J Robinson. *4m N of Lyndhurst. On B3079 1m W from M27 J1. 1st house L past Green Dragon PH & directly opp Bell PH.* **Sun 26 June (2-5). Adm £3, chd free. Home-made teas. Also open Fritham Lodge.**

A thick high hedge hides our 1 acre garden and C18 New Forest cottage (not open). Large mixed island beds have been created round old orchard trees with shrubs, cottage and unusual garden plants. There is a hosta and fern area, raised alpine and flower garden and raised vegetable beds. A brick based greenhouse, fruit cage and 3 large compost bins.

  👩‍🦽 ☕

100 ▶ WALHAMPTON

Beaulieu Road, Walhampton, Lymington SO41 5ZG. Walhampton School Trust Ltd. *1m E of Lymington. From Lymington follow signs to Beaulieu (B3054) for 1m & turn R into main entrance at 1st school sign 200yds after top of hill.* **Sun 8 May (2-5). Adm £4.50, chd free. Tea.** *Donation to St John's Church, Boldre.*

Glorious walks through large C18 landscape garden surrounding magnificent mansion (not open). Visitors will discover 3 lakes, serpentine canal, climbable prospect mount, period former banana house and orangery, fascinating shell grotto, glade and terrace by Peto (c1907), drives and colonnade by Mawson (c1914). Seating, guided tours with garden history. Gravel paths, some slopes.

  👩‍🦽 ☕

101 WEIR HOUSE

Abbotstone Road, Old Alresford SO24 9DG. **Mr & Mrs G Hollingbery, 07767 606729, jhollingbery@me.com.** *½ m N of Alresford. From New Alresford down Broad St (B3046), past Globe PH, take 1st L signed Abbotstone. Park in signed field.* **Sun 22 May, Sun 11 Sept (2-5). Adm £5, chd free. Home-made teas. Visits also by arrangement May to Sept for groups of 10+ (no refreshments available).**
Spectacular riverside garden with sweeping lawn backed by old walls, yew buttresses and mixed perennial beds. Contemporary vegetable garden at its height in Sept. Also incl newly designed garden around pool area, bog garden (at best in May) and wilder walkways through wooded areas. Children welcome. Wheelchair access to most of the garden.

Marie Curie

Last year, NGS funded 25,000 hours of our nursing care

102 ◆ WEST GREEN HOUSE GARDENS

Thackhams Lane, Hartley Wintney RG27 8JB. **Miss Marylyn Abbott, 01252 844611, enquiries@westgreenhouse.co.uk, www.westgreenhouse.co.uk.** *3m NE of Hook. Turn off A30 at Phoenix Green at Thackhams Lane, follow signs.* **For NGS: Tue 7 June (11-4.30). Adm £8, chd £4. Light refreshments in the Courtyard Tearooms. Evening opening Tue 26 July (8-10). Adm £10, chd £5. On Tue 26 July you can picnic by the lake or undercover and gardens will be illuminated at 9pm. For other opening times and**

information, please phone, email or visit garden website.
Within its C18 walls the magnificent Walled Garden is a tapestry of exuberantly planted lavish herbaceous borders, elaborate potager and parterres. Outside the walls an informal lake field is studded with neoclassical follies, chinoiserie bridges and cascades. A grand water staircase and Italianate fountain provide a dramatic focal point. Wheelchair access, but some of the paths around the garden are gravel.

103 WEST SILCHESTER HALL

Silchester RG7 2LX. **Mrs Jenny Jowett, 01189 700278, www.jennyjowett.com.** *8m N of Basingstoke. 9m S of Reading, off A340 (signed from centre of village).* **Sun 29, Mon 30 May, Sun 3 July, Sun 7 Aug (2-5.30). Adm £4, chd free. Home-made teas. Visits also by arrangement May to Sept for groups of 10+.**
This much loved 2 acre garden has fascinating colour combinations inspired by the artist owners' with many spectacular herbaceous borders filled with rare and unusual plants flowering over a long period. Many pots filled with half hardies, a wild garden surrounding a natural pond, banks of rhododendron, a self supporting kitchen garden with lovely views across a field of grazing cattle. Large studio with exhibition of the owners botanical, landscape and portrait paintings, cards and prints. Near Roman site. Wheelchair access to large part of the garden, gravel drive.

104 WHEATLEY HOUSE

Wheatley Lane, between Binsted & Kingsley, Bordon GU35 9PA. **Mr & Mrs Michael Adlington, 01420 23113, susannah@westcove.ie.** *4m E of Alton, 5m SW of Farnham. Take A31 to Bentley, follow sign to Bordon. After 2m, R at Jolly Farmer PH towards Binsted, 1m L & follow signs to Wheatley.* **Sat 20, Sun 21 Aug (1.30-5.30). Adm £4.50, chd free. Home-made teas. Visits also by arrangement Apr to Sept for groups of 10+. Refreshments on request.**
Situated on a rural hilltop with panoramic views over Alice Holt Forest and beyond, the owner admits to being much more of an artist than a plantswoman, but has had great

fun creating this 1½ acre garden full of interesting and unusual planting combinations. The sweeping, mixed borders, shrubberies and grasses are spectacular with colour throughout the season. The black and white border is also proving very popular with visitors, now with deep red accents. Local craft stalls, paintings, and home-made teas in Old Barn. Wheelchair access with care on lawns, good views of garden and beyond from terrace.

105 WHISPERS

Chatter Alley, Dogmersfield RG27 8SS. **Mr & Mrs John Selfe, 01252 613568.** *3m W of Fleet. Turn N to Dogmersfield off A287 Odiham to Farnham Rd. Turn L by Queen's Head PH.* **Visits by arrangement June to Aug for groups of 20+. Adm £5, chd free.**
Come and discover new plants in this 2 acre garden of manicured lawns surrounded by large borders of colourful shrubs, trees and long flowering perennials. Wild flower area, water storage system, greenhouse, kitchen garden and living sculptures. Spectacular waterfall cascades over large rock slabs and magically disappears below the terrace. A garden not to be missed. Gravel entrance.

106 WHITE GABLES

Breach Lane, Sherfield-on-Loddon RG27 0EU. **Terry & Brian Raisborough, 01256 882269, brianraisborough@aol.com.** *5m N of Basingstoke. From Basingstoke follow A33 to Reading for approx 5m. Breach Lane (unmade lane) immed on R before Sherfield-on-Loddon r'about. Parking in 2 free car parks in main village only. 150yds to garden.* **Sun 3 July (1-5). Adm £4, chd free. Home-made teas. Visits also by arrangement June to Aug for groups of 10+.**
A plantaholic's paradise! Consisting of many sections, this garden provides a host of stimulating inspirations and ideas towards visitors own garden. Large collection of exotic plants, hostas, cacti and lots more, revealing the owners passion for plants. Meandering paths take the visitor through various themed areas on a journey through a yr-round garden containing life sized statues, various arches and areas of sheer enjoyment.

107 **42 WHITEDOWN**
Alton GU34 1LU. Ms Jo Carter,
01420 542949,
jocarterartworks@yahoo.co.uk. *In
Alton, leave The Butts Green on your
L, go past stone fountain & L into
Borovere Gardens. Go down to T-
junction then L into Whitedown,
follow road round. 42 is on R. Park on
road or at Butts Green.* **Sat 18, Sun
19 June, Sat 13, Sun 14 Aug (2-6).
Combined adm with 22 Mount
Pleasant Road £5, chd free.
Home-made teas. Visits also by
arrangement June to Sept for
groups of 15 max.**
A warm welcome awaits at this small
town garden, which is a feast for the
eyes and shows what can be done
within a limited space and lots of
creativity. Garden designer Jo and her
sculptor husband Richard have
created from scratch an exuberant
and varied collection of shapes,
colours and textures, where
traditional and exotic plants mingle
with sculptures.

The banks
of the trout
stream and
lake planted
informally with
drifts of
colour . . .

108 **WICOR PRIMARY SCHOOL
COMMUNITY GARDEN**
Portchester, Fareham PO16 9DL.
Louise Bryant. *Halfway between
Portsmouth & Fareham on A27. Turn
S at Seagull PH r'about into
Cornaway Lane, 1st R into Hatherley
Drive. Entrance to school is almost
opp.* **Sun 3 July, Sun 18 Sept (12-
4). Adm £3.50, chd free. Home-
made teas.**
Beautiful school gardens tended by

pupils, staff and community
gardeners. Wander along the
Darwin's path to see the Jurassic
garden, orchard, tropical bed, wildlife
areas and allotment, plus one of the
few camera obscuras in the south of
England. The gardens are situated in
historic Portchester with views of
Portsdown Hill. The planting has been
chosen to provide nectar and habitat
for Wicor's rich wildlife. At the July
opening you will have the opportunity
to see Children's Art in the Garden.
Wheelchair access to all areas, flat
ground.

GROUP OPENING

109 **WILDHERN GARDENS**
Wildhern, Andover SP11 0JE. *From
Andover or Newbury A343. After
Enham Alamein or Hurstbourne
Tarrant turn at Xrd towards Penton
Mewsey. Wildhern is ³/₄ m on R.
Parking at village hall.* **Sat 4, Sun 5
June, Wed 10 Aug (2-5.30).
Combined adm £5, chd free.
Cream teas & home-made cakes
in the village hall (June) & at
Starlings (Aug).**

> **FINCH COTTAGE**
> Ray Curtis
>
> **OAKWOOD**
> Jean Pittfield
>
> **STARLINGS**
> Annie Bullen & Roy Wardale
>
> **WALNUT COTTAGE**
> Tym Paige-Dickins

All four gardens are within easy
walking distance of each other.
Oakwood with its enticing paths and
mature and colourful borders is
planted for yr-round interest and has
a large pond framed by unusual
plants. Interesting trees create shade
and diversity. Mixed woodland behind
the garden frames the well kept
shrubs and perennials. The
restoration of the ³/₄ acre garden at
Starlings, begun 5 yrs ago, features a
sunken gravel garden with nectar
bearing plants, many salvias and
grasses, a small winter garden, a
rose-bearing pergola and enclosed
vegetable beds shared by a tortoise.
The walled garden at Finch Cottage
contains many colourful climbers, a
terrace full of brightly planted pots,
herbaceous borders and a large and
productive vegetable enclosure.
Walnut Cottage, with wide views over
the surrounding countryside, has

mature fruit trees, a well-kept rose
bed, a superb wall trained peach tree
and well-filled beds and borders. No
wheelchair access to sunken gravel
garden at Starlings, but can be
viewed from decking.

110 **WILLOWS**
Pilley Hill, Boldre, Lymington
SO41 5QF. Elizabeth & Martin
Walker, 01590 677415,
elizabethwalker13@gmail.com,
www.willowsgarden.co.uk. *New
Forest. 2m N Lymington off A337. To
avoid traffic in Lyndhust, leave M27 at
J2 & follow Heavy Lorry Route.*
**Sat 30, Sun 31 July (2-5), also
open Fairweather's Nursery. Sat
13, Sun 14, Sat 27, Sun 28 Aug
(2-5). Adm £3.50, chd free. Cream
teas. Visits also by arrangement
July to Sept (mid July to mid Sept)
for groups of 20+.**
Willows greets you with a wow! Late
summer sizzle and vibrant exotics
with a jungly mix of bananas,
bamboos, gunnera and ferns around
the tranquil pond and bog garden.
Bold brilliant borders frame the front
lawn. Rich red crocosmias, dahlias,
zinnias, cannas and heleniums star in
succession. Sunny hot upper borders
of coleus, salvias and bedding dahlias
mingling with billowing grasses.
Specialist Plant Sale on Sun 28 Aug.
Also good plant stalls at the Saturday
market on Lymington High St and
Sunday car boot sale on A337.
Featured in Berthon Lifestyle
Magazine.

111 **1 WOGSBARNE COTTAGES**
Rotherwick RG27 9BL. Miss S & Mr
R Whistler. *2¹/₂ m N of Hook. M3 J5,
M4 J11, A30 or A33 via B3349.*
**Sun 10, Mon 11 July (2-5). Adm £3,
chd free. Home-made teas.**
Small traditional cottage garden with
a roses around the door look, much
photographed, seen on calendars,
jigsaws and in magazines. Mixed
flower beds and borders. Vegetables
grown in abundance. Ornamental
pond and alpine garden. Views over
open countryside to be enjoyed
whilst you take afternoon tea on
the lawn. The garden has been open
for the NGS for more than 30 yrs.
Small vintage motorcycle display
(weather permitting). Some gravel
paths.

HEREFORDSHIRE

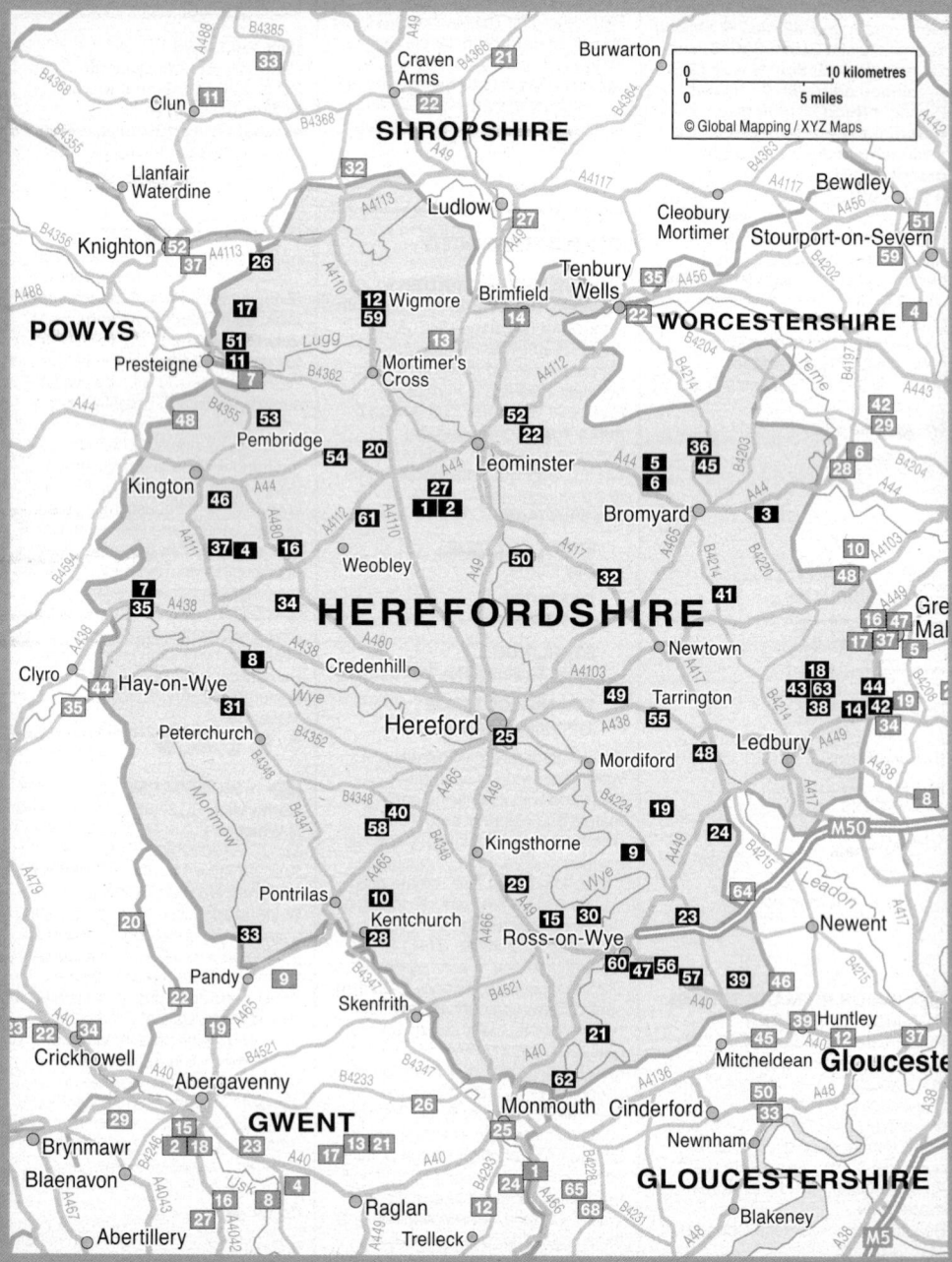

Herefordshire

Herefordshire is essentially an agricultural county, characterised by small market towns, black and white villages, fruit and hop orchards, meandering rivers, wonderful wildlife and spectacular, and often remote, countryside (a must for keen walkers).

As a major region in the Welsh Marches, Herefordshire has a long and diverse history, as indicated by the numerous prehistoric hill forts, medieval castles and ancient battle sites. Exploring the quiet country lanes can lead to many delightful surprises.

For garden enthusiasts there are many NGS gardens to visit, ranging from small village plots to informal cottage, wildlife, sculpture and grand formal gardens.

Widely contrasting in design and planting, they offer inspiration and innovative ideas to the garden visitor – and always a warm welcome. In addition, a range of excellent specialist nurseries propagate tempting collections of rare and unusual plants.

Herefordshire Volunteers

County Organiser
Rowena Gale
01568 615855
rowena.jimgale@btinternet.com

County Treasurer
Michael Robins
01531 632232
m.robins101@btinternet.com

Publicity
Sue Evans
01568 614501
s.evans.gp@btinternet.com

Booklet Coordinator
Chris Meakins
01544 370215
christine.meakins@btinternet.com

Booklet Distribution
Andrew Hallett
01981 570401
ar.hallett@gmail.com

Assistant County Organisers
David Hodgson
01531 640622
dhodgson363@btinternet.com

Sue Londesborough
01981 510148
slondesborough138@btinternet.com

Gill Mullin
01989 750593
gill@longorchard.plus.com

Penny Usher
01568 611688
pennyusher@btinternet.com

Left: Brilley Court © Val Corbett

Opening Dates

All entries subject to change.
For latest information check www.ngs.org.uk
Extended openings are shown at the begining of the month

February

Snowdrop Festival

Thursday 4
27 Ivy Croft

Thursday 11
27 Ivy Croft

Sunday 14
39 The Old Corn Mill

Thursday 18
27 Ivy Croft

Thursday 25
27 Ivy Croft

March

Sunday 6
39 The Old Corn Mill

Saturday 19
3 The Bannut
45 Ralph Court Gardens

Sunday 20
3 The Bannut
45 Ralph Court Gardens

Monday 21
36 Moors Meadow Gardens & Nursery

Sunday 27
39 The Old Corn Mill

Monday 28
39 The Old Corn Mill

April

Friday 1
52 Stockton Bury Gardens

Sunday 3
58 Whitfield

Saturday 9
45 Ralph Court Gardens

Sunday 10
12 Bury Court Farmhouse
45 Ralph Court Gardens

Saturday 16
3 The Bannut

Sunday 17
3 The Bannut
32 Lower Hope

39 The Old Corn Mill
58 Whitfield

Sunday 24
2 Aulden Farm
8 Brobury House Gardens
27 Ivy Croft

Monday 25
36 Moors Meadow Gardens & Nursery

A small coppice of white birch trees with woodland plants . . .

May

42 **Perrycroft (every Thursday & Friday)**

Sunday 1
7 Brilley Court
39 The Old Corn Mill
42 Perrycroft
62 Woodview

Friday 6
46 Rhodds Farm

Saturday 7
46 Rhodds Farm

Sunday 8
29 The Laskett Gardens
38 Old Colwall House
58 Whitfield

Monday 9
11 Bryan's Ground

Sunday 15
39 The Old Corn Mill

Saturday 21
43 Phelps Cottage Garden
50 NEW Southbourne & Pine Lodge

Sunday 22
28 Kentchurch Gardens
32 Lower Hope
35 Montpelier Cottage
43 Phelps Cottage Garden
50 NEW Southbourne & Pine Lodge

Monday 23
36 Moors Meadow Gardens & Nursery

Saturday 28
45 Ralph Court Gardens

Sunday 29
2 Aulden Farm
27 Ivy Croft
39 The Old Corn Mill
45 Ralph Court Gardens
48 NEW Sheepcote
51 Stapleton Castle Court Garden

Monday 30
2 Aulden Farm
27 Ivy Croft
39 The Old Corn Mill
51 Stapleton Castle Court Garden

Tuesday 31
15 Church Cottage
61 Windsor Cottage

June

15 **Church Cottage (every Tuesday & Wednesday)**
42 **Perrycroft (every Thursday & Friday until 24 June)**
61 **Windsor Cottage (every Tuesday & Thursday)**

Friday 3
46 Rhodds Farm

Festival Weekend

Saturday 4
5 Bredenbury, Mistletoe Lodge
6 NEW Bredenbury, The Coppice
46 Rhodds Farm
60 Wilton Castle on the Wye

Sunday 5
5 Bredenbury, Mistletoe Lodge
6 NEW Bredenbury, The Coppice
19 Croose Farm
34 Midland Farm
60 Wilton Castle on the Wye

Monday 6
37 Newport House

Tuesday 7
37 Newport House

Wednesday 8
37 Newport House

Thursday 9
37 Newport House

Friday 10
37 Newport House

Saturday 11
5 Bredenbury, Mistletoe Lodge
6 NEW Bredenbury, The Coppice
54 NEW Victoria Place
55 The Vine

Sunday 12
5 Bredenbury, Mistletoe Lodge
6 NEW Bredenbury, The Coppice
9 Brockhampton Cottage
14 Caves Folly Nurseries
19 Croose Farm
23 Grendon Court
54 NEW Victoria Place

Friday 17
21 Goodrich Gardens
25 Hereford Cathedral Gardens

Saturday 18
57 Weston Mews

Sunday 19
10 The Brooks
49 Shucknall Court
57 Weston Mews

Wednesday 22
24 Hellens (Evening)

Friday 24
13 NEW Byecroft

Saturday 25
1 Aulden Arts and Gardens
13 NEW Byecroft

Sunday 26
1 Aulden Arts and Gardens
17 Cloister Garden
20 Glan Arrow
28 Kentchurch Gardens
34 Midland Farm

Monday 27
36 Moors Meadow Gardens & Nursery

July

15 **Church Cottage (every Tuesday & Wednesday)**
42 **Windsor Cottage (every Tuesday & Thursday)**

Friday 1
46 Rhodds Farm

Saturday 2
46 Rhodds Farm

15 **Church Cottage**
(every Tuesday &
Wednesday)
42 **Windsor Cottage**
(every Tuesday &
Thursday)

Saturday 9
45 Ralph Court Gardens
47 Ross-on-Wye
Community Garden

Sunday 10
32 Lower Hope
38 Old Colwall House
45 Ralph Court Gardens
47 Ross-on-Wye
Community Garden
62 Woodview

Saturday 16
26 Hill House Farm

Sunday 17
26 Hill House Farm
62 Woodview

Monday 25
36 Moors Meadow
Gardens & Nursery

Sunday 31
16 Clarkesfield

August

61 **Windsor Cottage**
(every Tuesday &
Thursday)

Friday 5
46 Rhodds Farm

Saturday 6
44 The Picton Garden
46 Rhodds Farm

Sunday 7
2 Aulden Farm
27 Ivy Croft

Sunday 14
44 The Picton Garden

Sunday 21
44 The Picton Garden

Friday 26
21 Goodrich Gardens

Saturday 27
33 Middle Hunt House

Sunday 28
16 Clarkesfield
33 Middle Hunt House
51 Stapleton Castle Court
Garden

Monday 29
44 The Picton Garden
51 Stapleton Castle Court
Garden

September

Thursday 31
61 Windsor Cottage

Grendon Court

© Val Corbett

Saturday 3
50 **NEW** Southbourne &
Pine Lodge

Sunday 4
50 **NEW** Southbourne &
Pine Lodge

Friday 9
44 The Picton Garden

Sunday 11
10 The Brooks
38 Old Colwall House

Saturday 17
45 Ralph Court Gardens

Sunday 18
32 Lower Hope
45 Ralph Court
Gardens
59 Wigmore Gardens

Tuesday 27
44 The Picton Garden

October

Sunday 2
42 Perrycroft

Monday 3
37 Newport House

Tuesday 4
37 Newport House

Wednesday 5
37 Newport House

Thursday 6
37 Newport House

Friday 7
37 Newport House
44 The Picton Garden

Sunday 16
44 The Picton Garden

Sunday 23
8 Brobury House
Gardens

February 2017

Thursday 2
27 Ivy Croft

Thursday 9
27 Ivy Croft

Thursday 16
27 Ivy Croft

Thursday 23
27 Ivy Croft

Gardens open to the public

3 The Bannut
8 Brobury House
Gardens
11 Bryan's Ground
14 Caves Folly Nurseries
24 Hellens
25 Hereford Cathedral
Gardens
33 Middle Hunt House
36 Moors Meadow
Gardens & Nursery
44 The Picton Garden
45 Ralph Court Gardens
52 Stockton Bury
Gardens

By arrangement only

4 Batch Cottage
18 Coddington Vineyard
22 Grantsfield

30 Lawless Hill
31 Little Llanavon
40 The Old Rectory,
Thruxton
41 The Orchards
53 Upper Tan House
56 Weston Hall
63 Woofields Farm

Also open by arrangement

2 Aulden Farm
7 Brilley Court
12 Bury Court Farmhouse
13 **NEW** Byecroft
15 Church Cottage
16 Clarkesfield
17 Cloister Garden
21 Mulberry House,
Goodrich Gardens
21 Poole Cottage,
Goodrich Gardens
23 Grendon Court
27 Ivy Croft
37 Newport House
39 The Old Corn Mill
42 Perrycroft
49 Shucknall Court
51 Stapleton Castle Court
Garden
57 Weston Mews
58 Whitfield
61 Windsor Cottage
62 Woodview

Share your day out on 📘 and 🐦

The Gardens

GROUP OPENING

1 AULDEN ARTS AND GARDENS

Aulden, Leominster HR6 0JT,
www.auldenfarm.co.uk/auldenarts.
*4m SW of Leominster. From
Leominster, take Ivington/Upper Hill
rd, ³/₄ m after Ivington church turn R
signed Aulden. From A4110 signed
Ivington, take 2nd R signed Aulden.*
Sat 25 June (2-6); Sun 26 June
(11-3.30). Combined adm £6, chd
free. Home-made teas.

AULDEN FARM NPC
Alun & Jill Whitehead
(See separate entry)
Visits also by arrangement Apr
to Sept groups or individuals
web@auldenfarm.co.uk
01568 720129

HILL VIEW
Tricia & Andy Mitchell

HONEYLAKE COTTAGE
Jennie & Jack Hughes

NEW OAK HOUSE
Bob & Jane Langridge

Is gardening an art form? We are a
group of neighbours who share an
active interest in art and gardens, and
believe that gardens give ever-
changing colour and composition in
3 dimensions. Art, in a variety of
forms, will be on display. Come and
see the art, explore the gardens and
decide for yourself. Aulden Farm art
will be on display in the barn, alias the
potting shed! Hill View is about green
space and views. Besides mature
trees the emphasis has been on
hardscape and sculpture with a
minimal amount of planting. Prints,
drawings and paintings will be on
display. Honeylake Cottage has views
over the wonderful Herefordshire
countryside. The garden emphasis on
traditional cottage flowers is reflected
in some of the art work. Oak House:
²/₃ of an acre of evolving garden with
amazing views towards Upper Hill.
Currently has good bones, but is
fraying round the edges. Divided into
several areas including borders,
ponds, chickens and a working
vegetable plot. Art is photography
which will be displayed throughout
the garden.

2 AULDEN FARM

Aulden, Leominster HR6 0JT. Alun
& Jill Whitehead, 01568 720129,
web@auldenfarm.co.uk,
www.auldenfarm.co.uk. *4m SW of
Leominster. From Leominster take
Ivington/Upper Hill rd, ³/₄ m after
Ivington church turn R signed Aulden.*
*From A4110 signed Ivington, take
2nd R signed Aulden.* Sun 24 Apr,
Sun 29, Mon 30 May, Sun 7 Aug
(2-5.30). Single adm £3.50,
combined adm with Ivy Croft £6,
chd free, Home-made teas and
ice cream. Opening with Aulden
Arts and Gardens on Sat 25, Sun
26 June. Visits also by
arrangement Apr to Sept groups
or individuals.

Informal country garden surrounding
old farmhouse, 3 acres planted with
wildlife in mind. Emphasis on
structure and form, with a hint of
quirkiness, a garden to explore with
eclectic planting. Irises thrive around
a natural pond, shady beds and open
borders, seats abound, feels mature
but ever evolving. Homemade ice
cream and yummy cakes! National
Collection of Siberian Iris and plant
nursery.

3 ◆ THE BANNUT

Bringsty, Bromyard WR6 5TA.
Gareth & Tamla Bowdler, 01885
483545, thebannut@yahoo.com,
www.bannut.co.uk. *2¹/₂ m E of
Bromyard. On A44 Worcester Rd,
¹/₂ m E of entrance to National Trust,
Brockhampton.* For NGS: Sat 19,
Sun 20 Mar, Sat 16, Sun 17 Apr
(12-4). Adm £4.50, chd free.
Home-made teas. For other
opening times and information,

Church Cottage

please phone, email or visit garden website.

Traditional 3 acre garden with all year interest. Late winter colour with heathers, snowdrops and hellebores. Vivid spring colour with daffodils, tulips, camelias, azaleas, rhododendrons, wisteria and laburnum. Summer borders and hydrangea garden with 60 varieties. Wide variety of specimen trees and a unique knot garden. Tea room serving homemade cakes and refreshments. Children's treasure trail. Some garden rooms not accessible to wheelchairs.

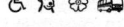

THE BARTON
See Worcestershire

Sue and Peter are retired nursery owners and hope to offer a good sales table . . .

4 BATCH COTTAGE
Almeley HR3 6PT. Jeremy & Elizabeth Russell, 01544 327469. *16m NW of Hereford. 2m off A438-A4111 to Kington, turn R at Eardisley.* Visits by arrangement Apr to Oct, groups up to 30. Adm £4, chd free. Cream teas.
Established unregimented, conservation-oriented garden of some 2½ acres with streams and large pond, set in a natural valley, surrounded by woodland and orchard. Over 360 labelled trees and shrubs, mixed borders, fern and bog beds, wild flower bank, stumpery, woodland walk. Fritillaries and spotted orchids abound in season. Partial wheelchair access- some gravel paths and steep slopes.

BIRTSMORTON COURT
See Worcestershire

5 BREDENBURY, MISTLETOE LODGE
Wacton Lane, Bromyard HR7 4TF. Jewels Williams Peplow & Mark Peplow, www.jewelsporcelain.com. *A44 between Bromyard & Leominster. At Bredenbury turn onto*

Wacton Lane between Three Pines Garage & Barneby Inn. Garden 50yds on L. Drop off for disabled, parking at Barnaby Arms. Sat 4, Sun 5, Sat 11, Sun 12 June (11-5). Single adm £3, combined adm with The Coppice £5, chd free. Home-made teas. Gluten free options available.
Small but charming, secluded garden, centred around a natural pond with lush planting. 'A tranquil hidden gem.' Complimented by a mixed media art exhibition, 'Coast and Garden.' Homemade cakes, teas and coffee to enjoy in the garden.

6 NEW BREDENBURY, THE COPPICE
Wacton Lane, Bromyard HR7 4TF. Peter & Wendy Kirk. *A44 between Bromyard & Leominster. At Bredenbury turn onto Wacton Lane between Three Pines Garage & Barneby Inn. Garden is 50 yards on left. Disabled drop off at garden. Parking at the Barneby Inn.* Sat 4, Sun 5, Sat 11, Sun 12 June (11-5). Single adm £3, combined adm with Bredenbury, Mistletoe Lodge £5, chd free. Home-made teas at Mistletoe Lodge.
In collaboration with and in contrast to Mistletoe Lodge, next door, The Coppice garden is a mature garden with some recent changes by the present owners. The garden is a mixture of perennial borders with mature Japanese acers, a fern garden, koi pond and a natural pond. In the front, a small coppice of white birch trees with woodland plants, and new rhododendron border. Suitable for wheelchairs with large wheels for some gravelled paths and grass.

BRIDGES STONE MILL
See Worcestershire

7 BRILLEY COURT
Whitney-on-Wye HR3 6JF. Mr & Mrs David Bulmer, 01497 831467, rosebulmer@hotmail.com. *6m NE of Hay-on-Wye. 5m SW of Kington. 1½ m off A438 Hereford to Brecon rd signed to Brilley.* Sun 1 May (2-6). Adm £5, chd free. Tea. Visits also by arrangement Apr to Oct for individuals and groups.
Garden created 35 years ago, 7 acres in total, wild valley stream garden with special trees, ornamental walled kitchen garden, tulips and wild flower areas. Summer roses and herbaceous. Wonderful views to the

Black Mountains. Regret no dogs. Featured in Homes & Gardens, Gardens Illustrated and Country Living. Limited wheelchair access.

8 ◆ BROBURY HOUSE GARDENS
Brobury by Bredwardine HR3 6BS. Keith & Pru Cartwright, 01981 500229, enquiries@broburyhouse.co.uk, www.broburyhouse.co.uk. *10m W of Hereford. S off A438 signed Bredwardine & Brobury. Garden 1m on L (before bridge).* For NGS: Sun 24 Apr (11-5); Sun 23 Oct (11-4). Adm £5, chd £1. Home-made teas. For other opening times and information, please phone, email or visit garden website.
9 acres of gardens, set on the banks of an exquisitely beautiful section of the R Wye, offer the visitor a delightful combination of Victorian terraces with mature specimen trees, inspiring water features, architectural planting and woodland areas. Redesign and development is ongoing. Bring a picnic, your paint brushes, binoculars and linger awhile. Wheelchair users, strong able-bodied assistant advisable.

9 BROCKHAMPTON COTTAGE
Brockhampton HR1 4TQ. Peter Clay. *8m SW of Hereford;. 5m N of Ross-on-Wye on B4224. In Brockhampton take rd signed to church, cont up hill for ½ m, after set of farm buildings, driveway on L, over cattle grid. Car park 500yds from garden.* Sun 12 June (10.30-2). Single adm £5, combined adm with Grendon Court £8, chd free,.
Created from scratch in 1999 by the owner and Tom Stuart-Smith, this beautiful hilltop garden looks S and W over miles of unspoilt countryside. On one side a woodland garden and 5 acre wild flower meadow, on the other side a Perry pear orchard and in valley below: lake, stream and arboretum. The extensive borders are planted with drifts of perennials in the modern romantic style. Allow 1hr 30 mins. Picnic parties welcome by the lake until 2pm. Visit Grendon Court (2-5) after your visit to us. Featured in Country Life, House and Garden, The English Garden magazine, Country Living and The Independent.

10 THE BROOKS

Pontrilas HR2 0BL. Marion & Clive Stainton, 01981 241161, Marion.stainton@marionet.co.uk, www.marionet.co.uk/the_brooks. *12m SW of Hereford. From the A465 Hereford to Abergavenny rd, turn L at Pontrilas onto B4347, take next R, then immediate L signed Orcop & Garway Hill. Garden 1³/₄ m on L.* Sun 19 June, Sun 11 Sept (2-5.30). Adm £4, chd free. Home-made teas.

This 2¹/₂ -acre Golden Valley garden incl part-walled enclosed vegetable garden and greenhouse (wind/solar-powered), orchard, ornamental, perennial, shade and shrub borders, wildlife pond, evolving arboretum cum coppice, and meadow with stunning views. Surrounding a stone 1684 farmhouse (not open), the garden has mature elements, but much has been created since 2006, with future development plans.

11 ◆ BRYAN'S GROUND

Letchmoor Lane, Stapleton, Presteigne LD8 2LP. David Wheeler & Simon Dorrell, 01544 260001, simondorrell@gmail.com, www.bryansground.co.uk. *12m NW of Leominster. Between Kinsham & Stapleton. At Mortimer's Cross take B4362 signed Presteigne. At Combe, follow signs. SATNAV is misleading. Coaches: please pre-book.* For NGS: Mon 9 May (2-5). Adm £6, chd £2. Home-made teas. **For other opening times and information, please phone, email or visit garden website.**
8-acre internationally renowned contemporary reinterpretation of an Arts and Crafts garden dating from 1912, conceived as series of rooms with yew and box topiary, parterres,

colour-themed flower and shrub borders, reflecting pools, potager, Edwardian greenhouse, heritage apple orchard, follies. Arboretum of 400 specimen trees and shrubs with wildlife pool beside R Lugg. Home of Hortus, garden journal. Featured in Country Life, The Oldie and Hortus. The majority of the garden is accessible by wheelchair, though there are some steps adjoining the terrace.

12 BURY COURT FARMHOUSE

Ford Street, Wigmore, Leominster HR6 9UP. Margaret & Les Barclay, 01568 770618, l.barclay2@virgin.net. *10m from Leominster, 10m from Knighton, 8m from Ludlow. On A4110 from Leominster, at Wigmore turn R just after shop & garage. Follow signs to parking and garden.* Sun 10 Apr (2-5). Adm £3.50, chd free. Home-made teas. Opening with Wigmore Gardens on Sun 18 Sept. **Visits also by arrangement Mar to Sept individual visitors and groups of any size.**
³/₄ acre garden, 'rescued' since 1997, surrounds the 1840's stone farmhouse (not open). The courtyard contains a pond, mixed borders, fruit trees and shrubs, with steps up to a terrace which leads to lawn and vegetable plot. The main garden (semi-walled) is on two levels with mixed borders, greenhouse, pond, mini-orchard with daffodils in spring, and wildlife areas. Year-round colour. Limited access only for wheelchairs (gravelled access).

13 NEW BYECROFT

Welshman's Lane, Bircher, Leominster HR6 0BP. Sue & Peter Russell, 01568 780559, peterandsuerussell@btinternet.com. *6m N of Leominster. From Leominster take B4361. Turn L at T-junction with B4362. ¹/₄ m beyond Bircher village turn R at war memorial into Welshman's Lane, signed Bircher Common.* Fri 24, Sat 25 June (12.30-5.30). Adm £4, chd free. Home-made teas. **Visits also by arrangement Apr to Nov for groups of 10+.**
Developed almost from scratch over 8 yrs, Byecroft is a compact garden stuffed full of interesting plants, many (incl all acers) grown from seed. Herbaceous borders, pergola with old roses, formal pond, lots of pots,

vegetable garden, wild flower orchard, soft fruit area. Sue and Peter are retired nursery owners and hope to offer a good sales table. Wheelchairs: most areas accessible with assistance. Some small steps.

14 ◆ CAVES FOLLY NURSERIES

Evendine Lane, Colwall WR13 6DX. Wil Leaper & Bridget Evans, 01684 540631, bridget@cavesfolly.com, www.cavesfolly.com. *1¹/₄ m NE of Ledbury. B4218. Between Malvern & Ledbury. Evendine Lane, off Colwall Green.* For NGS: Sun 12 June (2-5). Adm £3, chd free. Home-made teas. **For other opening times and information, please phone, email or visit garden website.**
Organic nursery and display gardens. Specialist growers of cottage garden plants and alpines. All plants are grown in peat free organic compost. This is not a manicured garden! It is full of drifts of colour and wild flowers and a haven for wildlife.

15 CHURCH COTTAGE

Hentland, Ross-on-Wye HR9 6LP. Sue Emms & Pete Weller, 01989 730222, sue.emms@mac.com. *6m from Ross-on-Wye. A49 from Ross. R turn to Hentland/Kynaston. At bottom of hill sharp R to St Dubricius Church. Narrow lane - please take care. Unsuitable for motor homes/caravans.* Every Tue and Wed 31 May to 27 July (2-5). Adm £3, chd free. Tea. **Visits also by arrangement June to Aug, groups welcome.**
Garden designer and plantswoman's ¹/₂ -acre evolving garden packed with plants, many unusual varieties mixed with old favourites, providing interest over a long period. Wildlife pond, rose garden, potager, mixed borders, white terrace, gravel garden. Interesting plant combinations and design ideas to inspire.

16 CLARKESFIELD

Meer, Woonton, Hereford HR3 6QP. Christopher & Marion Scott, 01544 340069, marion@meeraccountants.co.uk. *13m NW of Hereford. Follow signs to Kington (A480), turn R (signed) Meer/Broxwood. ¹/₂ m LH-side.* Sun 31 July, Sun 28 Aug (2-6). Adm £3, chd free. Cream teas. **Visits also by arrangement Apr to Sept for**

individuals and groups up to 20.
The garden has been redeveloped since 2006 by present owners. Contemporary herbaceous borders for lasting interest and colour, incorporating grasses, small formal pond and Japanese area, kitchen garden and cutting flower garden. Wildlife pond now being planted with walks through meadowland. Stunning views towards Black Mountains.

17 CLOISTER GARDEN
Pant Hall, Willey, Presteigne LD8 2LY. Malcolm Temple & Karen Roberts, 01544 260066, karml@live.co.uk, www.karenontheborders.wordpress. com. *3m N of Presteigne. Exactly 3m from Lugg Bridge at St Andrews Church in Presteigne. Follow rd from bridge, signed to Willey. Pass Stapleton Castle on R. Pant Hall on L on 3rd hill - blue house.* Sun 26 June (2-5). Adm £4, chd free. Home-made teas. **Visits also by arrangement July to Sept individuals and small groups (up to 10).**
Total 6 acres. ½ acre of lavender. borders, rose bank, terraced lawns and shrubberies leading down to a bog garden. Over a brook to a birch grove, Wave Garden and up to orchard terraces. Beyond is a new 3 acre woodland, planted between avenues and a central meadow. Behind the house is a layout for the cloister, a swimming pond and wild field - level at the top ready for an Earthwork Art project. Artist designed garden.

18 CODDINGTON VINEYARD
Coddington HR8 1JJ. Sharon & Peter Maiden, 01531 641817, sgmaiden@yahoo.co.uk, www.coddingtonvineyard.co.uk. *4m NE of Ledbury. From Ledbury to Malvern A449, follow brown signs to Coddington Vineyard.* Visits by arrangement Apr to Oct open for groups of 10 or more. Adm £4, chd free, combined with Woofields Farm, adm £7. Afternoon teas and light lunches. 5 acres incl 2-acre vineyard, listed farmhouse, threshing barn and cider mill. Garden with terraces, wild flower meadow, woodland with masses spring bulbs, pond and stream. Unusual perennials, trees and shrubs.

19 CROOSE FARM
Woolhope HR1 4RD. Mrs C Malim. *5m N of Ross-on-Wye. Woolhope signed off the B4224 Ross to Hereford rd. From Woolhope take rd opp the Church signed Sollars Hope & The Hyde. Follow garden signs.* Sun 5, Sun 12 June (2-6). Adm £5, chd free. Home-made teas.
3-acre country garden, set in middle of lovely Woolhope dome, created from original farmyard in 1987. Now well established it has as its theme a number of separate small gardens. These incl a rose garden, white garden, courtyards, knot garden, The garden is stocked with a great variety of shrubs, trees and herbaceous plants.

20 GLAN ARROW
Eardisland, Leominster HR6 9BW. Christopher & Lotty James. *5m W of Leominster on B4529. Cross bridge & immed turn sharp L up driveway. Recommend parking in car park opp the dovecote & walking up drive.* Sun 29 June (2-6). Adm £4, chd free. Home-made teas.
4-acre English riverside garden with herbaceous borders, roses, bog garden leading to small lake, white garden, herringbone ha-ha and potager.

Brockhampton Cottage

© Julia Stanley

GROUP OPENING

21 GOODRICH GARDENS
Goodrich, Ross on Wye HR9 6HX.
5m from Ross on Wye 7m from Monmouth. Close to Goodrich Castle in Wye Valley AONB. Goodrich signed from A40 or take B4234 from Ross on Wye. Park in village & follow signs to gardens. No parking close to Poole Cottage - use shuttle service or walk 10-15 minutes uphill from village. **Fri 17 June, Fri 26 Aug (11-5). Combined adm £5, chd free. Home-made teas.**

MULBERRY HOUSE
Tina & Adrian Barber
Visits also by arrangement May & June.
tinaabarber@hotmail.co.uk
01600 891372

POOLE COTTAGE D
Jo Ward-Ellison & Roy Smith
Visits also by arrangement June to Sept individuals and groups.
jo@ward-ellison.com
01600 890148

Two hidden gems of Goodrich: contrasting in terms of style and size but each making the most of their very different settings. One in village centre, the other a 10 min walk up Coppett Hill overlooking the R Wye. Mulberry House: a delightful rear garden with views out to beautiful listed village buildings. Imaginatively planted and nurtured by a plant lover with an artistic eye. Themed herbaceous borders and areas of shrub planting provide a long season of colour and interest. Roses, peonies and alliums enhance the predominately cottage garden feel. Poole Cottage: created from scratch over the past 5yrs, this 2 acre hillside garden has a predominantly naturalistic style with many grasses and later flowering perennials. Home to designer Jo Ward-Ellison, the garden continues to evolve with new plantings to extend the seasons. Some steep slopes, steps and uneven paths. Features incl a pond loved by wildlife, small orchard and kitchen garden with fabulous views.
❀ ☕

22 GRANTSFIELD
nr Kimbolton, Leominster HR6 0ET.
Mrs J G T Polley, 01568 613338.
3m NE of Leominster. A49 N from Leominster, at A4112 turn R, then

immed R (signed Hamnish), 1st L, then R at Xrds. Garden on R after ¹/₂ m. **Visits by arrangement Apr to Sept, groups 40 max. Adm £3.50, chd free. Tea.**
Large, informal country garden in contrasting styles surrounding old stone farmhouse. Wide variety of unusual plants, mature specimen trees and shrubs, old roses, climbers, herbaceous borders, superb views. 1¹/₂ -acre orchard and kitchen garden. Spring bulbs.
&. ❀ ☕

23 GRENDON COURT
Upton Bishop, Ross on Wye, Herefordshire HR9 7QP. Mark & Kate Edwards, 01971 339126, kate@grendoncourt.co.uk. *3m NE of Ross-on-Wye. M50, J3. Hereford B4224 Moody Cow PH, 1m open gate on R. From Ross. A40, B449, Xrds R Upton Bishop. 100yds on R by cream cottage.* **Sun 12 June (2-5). Single adm £4, combined adm with Brockhampton Cottage £8, chd free. Light refreshments. Visits also by arrangement June to Sept. for individuals and groups up to 50+. Can provide lunch for 50 max.**
A contemporary garden designed by Tom Stuart-Smith. Planted on 2 levels, a clever collection of mass-planted perennials and grasses of different heights, textures and colour give all-yr round interest. The upper walled garden with a sea of flowering grasses makes a highlight. Views of pond and valley walk. Visit Brockhampton Cottage (10.30-2) before you visit us (picnic in parking field). Please note that Grendon Court garden does not open until 2pm.
&. ☕

24 ◆ HELLENS
Much Marcle, Ledbury HR8 2LY.
PMMCT, 01531 660504, info@hellensmanor.com, www.hellensmanor.com. *6m from Ross-on-Wye. 4m SW of Ledbury, off A449. L at Xrds in front of The Walwyn PH. Continue past school on R & Memorial Hall on L. Drive on L 300yds past the Memorial Hall.* **For NGS: Evening opening Wed 22 June (6-9). Adm £5, chd free. Wine. For other opening times and information, please phone, email or visit garden website.**
In the grounds of Hellens house, the gardens are being gently redeveloped to enhance the ambiance of the C15-17 house. The grounds incl a rare

C17 octagonal dovecote, knot garden, physic garden. flower meadows, yew labyrinth, lawns, herb and kitchen gardens, woodlands,ponds, ancient pear and apple orchards and lovely walks to the 55 acre Hall Wood, top rated Herefordshire SSSI. In the Hellens tea room cakes, teas and coffee are available. Adm incl a glass of Hellens select wine or Hellens own apple juice. Gardens are fairly level but pathways are earth and gravel. Unfortunately, the house is not wheelchair accessible.
&. 🐕 🚐 ☕

Roses, peonies
and alliums
enhance the
predominately
cottage garden
feel . . .

25 ◆ HEREFORD CATHEDRAL GARDENS
Hereford HR1 2NG. Dean of Hereford Cathedral, 01432 374202, www.herefordcathedral.org. *Centre of Hereford. Approach rds to the Cathedral are signed. Tours leave from information desk in the cathedral building.* **For NGS: Fri 17 June (11-4). Adm £5, chd free. Tea in Cathedral's Cloister Café. For other opening times and information, please phone or visit garden website.** *Donation to Homeless Charity.*
Guided tours of historic gardens which won 2 top awards in 'It's Your Neighbourhood 2012 &13'. The tour incl: a courtyard garden; an atmospheric cloisters garden enclosed by C15 buildings; the Vicar's Choral garden; the Dean's own garden; and 2 acre Bishop's garden with free trees, vegetable and cutting garden, outdoor chapel for meditation in a floral setting, all sloping to the river Wye. Collection of plants with ecclesiastical connections in College Garden. Partial wheelchair access.
&. 🚐 ☕

HIGH VIEW
See Worcestershire

HIGHFIELD COTTAGE
See Worcestershire

26 HILL HOUSE FARM
Knighton LD7 1NA. Simon &
Caroline Gourlay, 01547 528542,
simongourlay@btinternet.com. *4m
SE of Knighton. S of A4113 via
Knighton (Llanshay Lane, 3m) or
Bucknell (Reeves Lane, 3m).* Sat 16,
Sun 17 July (2-5.30). Adm £4, chd
free. Home-made teas.
5-acre south facing hillside garden
developed over past 40 years with
magnificent views over unspoilt
countryside. Some herbaceous
around the house with extensive
lawns and mown paths surrounded
by roses, shrubs and specimen trees
leading to the half acre Oak Pool
200ft below house. Transport
available from bottom of garden if
required.

NGS support
helps us
improve
patient care
in the
community

27 IVY CROFT
Ivington Green, Leominster
HR6 0JN. Sue & Roger Norman,
01568 720344,
ivycroft@homecall.co.uk,
www.ivycroftgarden.co.uk. *3m SW
of Leominster. From Leominster take
Ryelands Rd to Ivington. Turn R at
church, garden ³/₄ m on R. From
A4110 signed Ivington, garden 1³/₄ m
on L.* Every Thur 4 Feb to 25 Feb
(9-4). Adm £3.50, chd free. Sun 24
Apr, Sun 29, Mon 30 May, Sun 7
Aug (2-5.30). Single adm £3.50,
combined adm with Aulden Farm

£6, chd free. Tea. 2017: Thurs 2, 9,
16, 23 Feb. **Visits also by
arrangement all year.**
A maturing rural garden with areas of
meadow, wood and orchard,
blending with countryside and
providing habitat for wildlife. The
cottage is surrounded by borders,
raised beds, trained pears and
containers giving all year interest.
Paths lead to the wider garden
including herbaceous borders,
vegetable garden framed with
espalier apples and seasonal pond
with willows, ferns and grasses.
Snowdrops. Partial wheelchair
access.

GROUP OPENING

28 KENTCHURCH GARDENS
Pontrilas HR2 0DB, 01981 240228,
jan@kentchurchcourt.co.uk. *12m
SW of Hereford. From Hereford A465
to Abergavanny, at Pontrilas turn L
signed Kentchurch. After 2m fork L,
after Bridge Inn. Drive opp church.*
Sun 22 May, Sun 26 June (11-5).
Combined adm £5, chd free.
Home-made teas.

KENTCHURCH COURT 🛏
Mrs Jan Lucas-Scudamore
01981 240228
jan@kentchurchcourt.co.uk
www.kentchurchcourt.co.uk

UPPER LODGE
Jo Gregory

Kentchurch Court is sited close to the
Welsh border. The large stately home
dates to C11 and has been in the
Scudamore family for over 1000yrs
The deer-park surrounding the house
dates back to the Knights
Hospitallers of Dinmore and lies at the
heart of an estate of over 5000 acres.
Historical characters associated with
the house incl Welsh hero Owain
Glendower, whose daughter married
Sir John Scudamore. The house was
modernised by John Nash in 1795.
First opened for NGS in 1927. Formal
rose garden, traditional vegetable
garden redesigned with colour, scent
and easy access. Walled garden and
herbaceous borders, rhododendrons
and wild flower walk. Deer-park and
ancient woodland. Extensive
collection of mature trees and shrubs.
Stream with habitat for spawning
trout. Upper Lodge is a tranquil and
well-established walled cottage
garden situated at the centre of the
main garden. Incl a wide variety of

herbaceous plants, bulbs and shrubs
ranging from traditional favourites to
the rare and unusual. Most of the
garden can be accessed by
wheelchairs.

29 THE LASKETT GARDENS
Much Birch, Hereford HR2 8HZ.
Sir Roy Strong,
www.thelaskettgardens.co.uk.
*Approx 7m from Hereford; 7m from
Ross. On A49, midway between
Ross-on-Wye & Hereford, turn into
Laskett Lane towards Hoarwithy. The
drive is approx 350yds on L.* Sun 8
May (10-4). Single adm £10,
combined adm with Whitfield £14,
chd free. Tea.
The Laskett Gardens are the largest
private formal gardens to be created
in England since 1945 consisting of 4
acres of stunning garden rooms incl
rose and knot garden, fountains,
statuary and topiary.Why not make a
day of it and visit both The Laskett
and Whitfield (2-5). Partial wheelchair
access.

30 LAWLESS HILL
Sellack, Ross-on-Wye HR9 6QP.
Keith Meehan & Katalin Andras,
07595 678837,
Lawlesshill@gmail.com. *4m NW of
Ross-on-Wye. Western end of M50.
On A49 to Hereford, take 2nd R,
signed Sellack. After 2m, turn R by
white house, to Sellack church. At
next church sign, turn L. Garden
halfway down lane, before church.*
Visits by arrangement Mar to Oct
individuals and small groups
welcome. Adm £5, chd free. Light
refreshments.
Modernist Japanese-influenced
garden with dramatic views over R
Wye. Collection of 'rooms' sculpted
from the steep hillside using network
of natural stone walls and huge rocks.
Among exotic and unusual plantings,
natural ponds are held within the
terracing, forming waterfalls between
them. Due to steep steps and
stepping stones open by water, the
garden is unsuitable for the less
mobile and young children. Tea and
cake in the round house and magical
views overlooking waterfall and the
river valley. Featured in Historic
Gardens of Herefordshire by Timothy
Mowl and Jane Bradney.
🛏 ☕

The Brooks

---

31 ▶ LITTLE LLANAVON
Dorstone, Hereford HR3 6AT. Jenny Chippindale, 01981 550984, jennychip@hotmail.co.uk, www.goldenvalleybandb.co.uk. *2m W of Peterchurch. In the Golden Valley, 15m W of Hereford on B4348, 1/2 m towards Peterchurch from Dorstone.* Visits by arrangement May to Sept individuals and groups. Adm £3.50, chd free. Home-made teas.
1/2 -acre S-facing cottage-style walled garden in lovely rural location. Meandering paths among shrubs in shady spring garden. Hot gravel area and herbaceous borders closely planted with select perennials and grasses, many unusual. Good late colour.

 ☕

LITTLE MALVERN COURT
See Worcestershire

32 ▶ LOWER HOPE
Lower Hope Farm, Ullingswick, Hereford HR1 3JF. Mr & Mrs Clive Richards. *5m S of Bromyard. A465 N from Hereford, after 6m turn L at Burley Gate onto A417 towards Leominster. After approx 2m turn R to Lower Hope. After 1/2 m garden on L.* Sun 17 Apr, Sun 22 May, Sun 10 July, Sun 18 Sept (2-5). Adm £5, chd £1. Tea.

5-acre garden facing S and W. Herbaceous borders, rose walks and gardens, laburnum tunnel, Mediterranean, Italian, new Japanese garden and bog gardens. Lime tree walk, lake landscaped with wild flowers, streams, ponds. Conservatories and large glasshouse with exotic species incl orchids, colourful butterflies, bougainvilleas. Prizewinning herd of pedigree Hereford cattle and Suffolk sheep.

♿ ❀ 🚌 ☕

33 ◆ MIDDLE HUNT HOUSE
Walterstone, Hereford HR2 0DY. Rupert & Antoinetta Otten, 01873 860359, rupertotten@gmail.com, Gardeninthewind.blogspot. *4m W of Pandy, 17m S of Hereford, 10m N of Abergavenny. A465 to Pandy, L towards Longtown, turn R at Clodock Church, 1m on R. Disabled parking available.* For NGS: Sat 27, Sun 28 Aug (2-5). Adm £5, chd free. Home-made teas. For other opening times and information, please phone, email or visit garden website.
A modern garden using swathes of herbaceous plants and grasses, surrounding stone built farmhouse and barns with stunning views of the Black Mountains. Special features: rose borders, hornbeam alley, formal parterre with sensory plants, fountain court with Wlliam Pye water feature,

architecturally designed greenhouse complex, vegetable gardens. Carved lettering and sculpture throughout, garden covering about 4 acres. Partial wheelchair access.

♿ ❀ ☕

34 ▶ MIDLAND FARM
Pig Street, Norton Wood HR4 7BP. Sarah & Charles Smith. *10m NW of Hereford. From Hereford take the A480 towards Kington. 1/2 m after Norton Canon turn L towards Calver Hill. At bottom of the hill turn R into Pig St, garden 1/4 m on L.* Sun 5, Sun 26 June (11-4). Adm £4, chd free. Home-made teas.
A new 1.2 acre cottage garden begun in 2008 and ongoing. Designed as a series of rooms incl flower, spring and kitchen gardens; perennials, roses and helebores a speciality.

❀ 🛏 ☕

35 ▶ MONTPELIER COTTAGE
Brilley, Whitney-on-Wye, Hereford HR3 6HF. Dr Noel Kingsbury & Ms Jo Eliot, noel.k57@virgin.net, www.noelkingsbury.com. *Between Hay-on-Wye & Kington. From A438 1/2 m E of Rhydspence Inn, take rd signed Brilley, then 0.9m. From Kington, follow rd to Brilley, then 0.6m from Brilley Church.* Sun 22 May (2-5). Adm £5, chd free. Home-made teas.

Exuberant wild-style garden created – by well-known garden writer. Approx 1 acre of garden and trial beds where English cottage style meets German parks and American prairie. Wide range of perennials, plus ponds, vegetable garden and fruit. A further 3 acres incl hay meadow habitat and unusual wild flower-rich wet meadow. Children's playground. Featured in Gardens Illustrated, Country Life, The Garden and English Garden.

36 ◆ MOORS MEADOW GARDENS & NURSERY
Collington, Bromyard HR7 4LZ. Ros Bissell, 01885 410318 / 07812041179, moorsmeadow@hotmail.co.uk, www.moorsmeadow.co.uk. *4m N of Bromyard, on B4214.* ½ *m up lane follow yellow arrows.* For NGS: Mons 21 Mar, 25 Apr, 23 May, 27 June, 25 July (11-5). Adm £6, chd £1. **For other opening times and information, please phone, email or visit garden website.**
Gaining international recognition for its phenomenal range of wildlife and rarely seen plant species, this inspirational 7-acre organic hillside garden is a 'must see'. Full of peace, secret corners and intriguing features and sculptures with fernery, grass garden, extensive shrubberies, herbaceous beds, meadow, dingle, pools and kitchen garden. Resident Artist Blacksmith. Huge range of unusual and rarely seen plants from around the world. Unique home-crafted sculptures.

37 NEWPORT HOUSE
Almeley HR3 6LL. David & Jenny Watt, 07754 234903, david.gray510@btinternet.com. *5m S of Kington. 1m from Almeley Church, on rd to Kington. From Kington take A4111 to Hereford. After 4m turn L to Almeley, continue 2m, garden on L.* Daily Mon 6 June to Fri 10 June (11-7). Daily Mon 3 Oct to Fri 7 Oct (11-5). Adm £5, chd free. Home-made teas. **Visits also by arrangement June to Oct.**
20 acres of garden, woods and lake (with walks). Formal garden set on 3 terraces with large mixed borders framed by formal hedges, in front of Georgian House (not open). 2½ -acre walled organic garden in restoration since 2009.

38 OLD COLWALL HOUSE
Old Colwall, Malvern WR13 6HF. Mr & Mrs Roland Trafford-Roberts. *3m NE of Ledbury. From Ledbury, turn L off A449 to Malvern towards Coddington. Signed from 2½ m along lane. Signed from Colwall and Bosbury.* Sun 8 May, Sun 10 July, Sun 11 Sept (2-5). Adm £5, chd free. Home-made teas.
Early C18 garden on a site owned by the Church till Henry VIII. Walled lawns and terraces on various levels. The heart is the yew walk, a rare survival from the 1700s: 100 yds long, 30ft high, cloud clipped, and with a church aisle-like quality inside. Later centuries have brought a summer house, water garden, and rock gardens. Fine trees, incl enormous veteran yew; fine views. Steep in places.

39 THE OLD CORN MILL
Aston Crews, Ross-on-Wye HR9 7LW. Mrs Jill Hunter, 01989 750059. *5m E of Ross-on-Wye. A40 Ross to Gloucester. Turn L at T-lights at Lea Xrds onto B4222 signed Newent, Garden ½ m on L. Parking for disabled down drive. DO NOT USE THE ABOVE POSTCODE IN YOUR SATNAV - try HR9 7LA.* Sun 14 Feb (1-4); Sun 6, Sun 27, Mon 28 Mar, Sun 17 Apr, Sun 1, Sun 15, Sun 29, Mon 30 May (1-5). Adm £3.50, chd free. Home-made teas. **Visits also by arrangement Feb to Oct groups up to 50. Refreshments incl in adm.**
Forget the stresses of life and experience the calm of this relaxed 2-acre country garden. Birdsong and a babbling brook, numerous places to sit and dream. Interest all year with spectacular tulips and common spotted orchids in spring. A place of peace and tranquility. Children's trail and quirky garden sculptures.

40 THE OLD RECTORY, THRUXTON
Thruxton HR2 9AX. Mr & Mrs Andrew Hallett, 01981 570401, ar.hallett@gmail.com, www.thruxtonrectory.co.uk. *6m SW of Hereford. A465 to Allensmore. At Locks (Shell) garage take B4348 towards Hay-on-Wye. After 1½ m turn L towards Abbey Dore & Cockyard. Car park 150yds on L.* Visits by arrangement May to Sept. Adm £4, chd free. Home-made teas.

With breathtaking views over Herefordshire countryside this four acre garden - two acres formal and two acres paddock with ornamental trees and shrubs, and heritage apples - has been created since 2007. Constantly changing plantsman's garden stocked with unusual perennials and roses, together with woodland borders, gazebo, vegetable parterre, glasshouse and natural pond. Many places to sit and relax. Most plants labelled. Chickens, Mr Reynard permitting. Selected for NGS entry in Country Life. Mainly level with some gravel paths.

> Birdsong and a babbling brook, numerous places to sit and dream . . .

41 THE ORCHARDS
Golden Valley, Bishops Frome, Bromyard WR6 5BN. Mr & Mrs Robert Humphries, 01885 490273, theorchards.humphries@btinternet.com. *14m E of Hereford. A4103 turn L at bottom of Fromes Hill, through Bishops Frome on B4214. Turn R immed after de-regulation signs. Follow NGS signs to car park, garden 250yds along track.* Visits by arrangement June to Sept. Adm £3, chd free. Cream teas and ploughman's lunches.
Mature 1-acre garden, with many species of trees and shrubs. The garden is laid out on various levels and intensely planted, incorporating collections of roses, clematis, fuchsias and dahlias. There are 15 water features. Many herbaceous borders, the garden overflows with annuals in pots and baskets during the summer months. Several seating areas around the garden.

PEAR TREE COTTAGE
See Worcestershire

42 PERRYCROFT

Jubilee Drive, Upper Colwall, Malvern WR13 6DN. Gillian & Mark Archer, 07858 393767, gillianarcher@live.co.uk. *Between Malvern & Ledbury. On B4232 between British Camp & Wyche cutting. Park in Gardiners Quarry pay & display car park opp, short walk to garden. No parking at house except for disabled by prior arrangement.* Sun 1 May (2-5). Every Thur and Fri 5 May to 24 June (11-4). Sun 2 Oct (2-5). Adm £5, chd free. Home-made teas. **Visits also by arrangement groups and individuals all year. Teas by prior arrangement for groups 10+.** 10-acre garden and woodland on upper slopes of Malvern Hills with magnificent views. Arts and Crafts house (not open), garden partly designed by CFA Voysey. Walled garden with mixed and herbaceous borders, yew and box hedges and topiary, dry garden, natural wild flower meadows, ponds (unfenced), bog garden, woodland walks. Some steep and uneven paths.

43 PHELPS COTTAGE GARDEN

Coddington, Ledbury HR8 1JH. David & Diane Hodgson. *From Ledbury take the Bromyard road, 1st R to T junction turn R, 1st L for Coddington. From Worcester to Colwall signed for Coddington.* Sat 21, Sun 22 May (1.30-5). Adm £3.50, chd free. Home-made teas. Plantsmans ³/₄-acre cottage garden on different levels (some steps), mixed borders, terrace, wild areas, stream and bog garden, large fruit and vegetable potager with poly tunnel. Featured on BBC Hereford and Worcester, and in Wye Valley News.

44 ◆ THE PICTON GARDEN

Old Court Nurseries, Walwyn Road, Colwall WR13 6QE. Mr & Mrs Paul Picton, 01684 540416, oldcourtnurseries@btinternet.com, www.autumnasters.co.uk. *3m W of Malvern. On B4218 (Walwyn Rd) N of Colwall Stone. Turn off A449 from Ledbury or Malvern onto the B4218 for Colwall.* For NGS: Sat 6, Sun 14, Sun 21, Mon 29 Aug, Fri 9, Tue 27 Sept, Fri 7, Sun 16 Oct (11-5). Adm £3.50, chd free. **For other opening times and information, please phone, email or visit garden website.**

1¹/₂ acres W of Malvern Hills. Interesting perennials and shrubs in Aug. In late Sept and early Oct colourful borders display the National Plant Collection of Michaelmas daisies, backed by autumn colouring trees and shrubs. Many unusual plants to be seen, incl bamboos, ferns and acers. Features raised beds and silver garden. National Plant Collection of autumn-flowering asters and an extensive nursery that has been growing them since 1906. Featured in Garden News.

 NPC

Carers Trust improves support, services and recognition for unpaid carers

45 ◆ RALPH COURT GARDENS

Edwyn Ralph, Bromyard HR7 4LU. Mr & Mrs Morgan, 01885 483225, ralphcourtgardens@aol.com, www.ralphcourtgardens.co.uk. *From Bromyard follow the Tenbury rd for approx 1m. On entering the village of Edwyn Ralph take 1st turning on R towards the church.* For NGS: Sat & Suns 19, 20 Mar, 9, 10 Apr, 28, 29 May, 9, 10 July, 17, 18 Sept (10-5). Adm £7.50, chd £5. Light refreshments. **For other opening times and information, please phone, email or visit garden website.**

12 amazing gardens set in the grounds of a gothic rectory. A family orientated garden with a twist, incorporating an Italian Piazza, an African Jungle, Dragon Pool, Alice in Wonderland and the elves in their conifer forest. These are just a few of the themes within this stunning garden. Tea room overlooks Malvern Hills. 80 seater Restaurant offering lunches, light meals and afternoon

tea. Featured on BBC 'Midlands Today'. All areas ramped for wheelchair and pushchair access. Some grass areas, without help can be challenging during wet periods.

46 RHODDS FARM

Lyonshall HR5 3LW. Richard & Cary Goode, 01544 340120, cary.goode@russianaeros.com, www.rhoddsfarm.co.uk. *1m E of Kington. From A44 take small turning S just E of Penrhos Farm, 1m E of Kington. Continue 1m garden straight ahead.* Fri & Sat 6, 7 May, 3, 4 June, 1, 2 July, 5, 6 Aug (11-5). Adm £5, chd free. Tea and cake will be available for guests to help themselves in return for a donation.

The garden began in 2005 and is still a work in progress. The site is challenging with steep banks rising to overhanging woodland but has wonderful views. Formal garden leads to new dovecote, mixed borders have interest throughout the year with the double herbaceous borders of hot colours being particularly good in summer. Woodland walks with wonderful bluebells in spring. See garden website for detailed description.

47 ROSS-ON-WYE COMMUNITY GARDEN

Old Gloucester Rd, Ross-On-Wye HR9 5AE. Haygrove Ltd, 07972 624378, tim.shelley@haygrove.co.uk. *The garden is situated halfway along Old Gloucester Rd and opp the former Walter Scott School.* Sat 9, Sun 10 July (10-4). Adm £2.50, chd free. Tea.

The Community Garden is a three and a half acre site in the centre of Ross which is run by Haygrove Ltd to grow fruit and vegetables - see our Facebook page. The project works mainly with adults with learning disabilities, mental health illnesses and those who are long term unemployed. Produce and plants are for sale as well as garden tours, demonstrations and activities for children. Awarded 'Outstanding, Level 5 ' in It's your Neighbourhood Award 2015 - The RHS and Britain in Bloom. Half of the site is accessible for those using wheelchairs.

48 **NEW** **SHEEPCOTE**
Putley, Ledbury HR8 2RD. Tim &
Julie Beaumont. *7m W of Ledbury
off the A438 Hereford to Ledbury rd.
Passenger drop off, parking 4 minute
walk.* Sun 29 May (1.30-5.30). Adm
£4, chd free. Home-made teas.
1/3 acre garden taken in hand from
2011 retaining many quality plants,
shrubs and trees from earlier
gardeners. Topiary holly, box,
hawthorn, privet and yew formalise
the varied plantings around the
croquet lawn and gravel garden; beds
with heathers, azaleas, lavender
surrounded by herbaceous perennials
and bulbs; pond in shade of ancient
apple tree; kitchen garden with raised
beds.

Wisteria screen
under an ancient
mulberry tree . . .

49 **SHUCKNALL COURT**
Hereford HR1 4BH. Mr & Mrs Henry
Moore, 01432 850230. *5m E of
Hereford. On A4103, signed
(southerly) Weston Beggard, 5m E of
Hereford towards Worcester.* Sun 19
June (11-6). Adm £5, chd free.
Cream teas. Visits also by
arrangement May to July.
Tree paeonies in May. Large collection
of species, old-fashioned and shrub
roses. Mixed borders in old walled
farmhouse garden. Wild garden,
vegetables and fruit. Partial
wheelchair access.

SHUTTIFIELD COTTAGE
See Worcestershire

50 **NEW** **SOUTHBOURNE &
PINE LODGE**
Dinmore, Hereford HR1 3JR.
Lavinia Sole & Frank Ryding. *8m N
of Hereford; 8m S of Leominster. A49
from Hereford. Turn R at bottom of
Dinmore Hill (Hereford side) signed
Dinmore, gardens 1m on L. A49
south from Leominster, L onto A417,
1st R, R at T-junction to Bodenham,
follow signs to Dinmore.* Sat 21, Sun
22 May, Sat 3, Sun 4 Sept (1.30-
5.30). Adm £5, chd free. Light
refreshments. Cold drinks and
cakes available.

2 south facing gardens of 4½ acres
opened as one with panoramic views
over Bodenham Lakes to the Black
Mountains and Malvern Hills.
Southbourne: steeply terraced with
lawns, perennial and shrub beds and
a recently re-developed woodland.
Pine Lodge: 2½ acres of wild
woodland featuring most of Britain's
native trees. Paths wind throughout
the steep site. Rather spooky.
Beware of Goblins!

51 **STAPLETON CASTLE
COURT GARDEN**
Stapleton, Presteigne LD8 2LS.
Margaret & Trefor Griffiths, 01544
267327. *2m N of Presteigne. From
Presteigne cross Lugg Bridge at
bottom of Broad St & continue to
Stapleton. Do not turn towards
Stapleton but follow signs to garden
on R.* Sun 29, Mon 30 May, Sun 28,
Mon 29 Aug (2-5.30). Adm £4, chd
free. Home-made teas. Visits also
by arrangement May to Aug for
groups up to 40, min group
charge £25.
Situated on a gentle slope overlooked
by the remains of Stapleton Castle.
The garden, developed over the past
8 yrs by an enthusiastic plantswoman, benefits from considered and
colour-themed borders. Guided tour
of the castle 2.30 and 3.30 each day.
Display of site history incl house ruins,
mill pond, mill pit and disused turbine,
etc. Enjoy a last look around the
garden before the owners move.
Wheelchairs not suitable for castle
tour.

52 **◆ STOCKTON BURY
GARDENS**
Kimbolton HR6 0HA. Raymond G
Treasure, 07880 712649,
twstocktonbury@outlook.com,
www.stocktonbury.co.uk. *2m NE of
Leominster. From Leominster to
Ludlow on A49 turn R onto A4112.
Gardens 300yds on R.* For NGS: Fri
1 Apr (12-5). Adm £6, chd £3.
Home-made teas. NO CHILDREN
UNDER 3. **For other opening times
and information, please phone,
email or visit garden website.**
Superb, sheltered 4-acre garden with
colour and interest all yr. Extensive
collection of plants, many rare and
unusual set amongst medieval
buildings. Features pigeon house,
tithe barn, grotto, cider press, pools,
ruined chapel and rill, all surrounded
by unspoilt countryside. All plants

sold are grown on site. Stockton Bury
has a garden school which features
courses from high profile speakers
such as Chris Beardshaw. Our
restaurant offers a varied and very
tasty menu. We pride ourselves in
offering great plant and gardening
advice to our visitors. Refreshments
in Tithe Barn Restaurant, open
11 - 4.30. Featured in The English
Country Garden. Partial wheelchair
access.

53 **UPPER TAN HOUSE**
Stansbatch, Leominster HR6 9LJ.
James & Caroline Weymouth,
01544 260574,
caroline.weymouth@btopenworld.
com, www.uppertanhouse.com.
*4m W of Pembridge. From A44 in
Pembridge take turn signed Shobdon
& Presteigne. After exactly 4m & at
Stansbatch Nursery turn L down hill.
Garden on L 100yds after chapel.*
Visits by arrangement May to
Sept, groups welcome. Adm £4,
chd free.
S-facing garden sloping down to
Stansbatch brook in idyllic spot. Deep
herbaceous borders with informal and
unusual planting, pond and bog
garden, formal vegetable garden
framed by yew hedges and
espaliered pears. Reed beds, wild
flower meadow with orchids in
June. Good late summer colour and
diverse wildlife. Featured in Country
Living.

54 **NEW** **VICTORIA PLACE**
East Street, Pembridge,
Leominster HR6 9HB. Philip & Judy
Rogers. *In the middle of Pembridge
midway between Leominster &
Kington on A44. The garden is
immediately opp the Kings House
Restaurant and village car park.* Sat
11 June (12-5); Sun 12 June (2-5).
Adm £3.50, chd free. Home-made
teas.
A deceptively large garden built on a
burgage plot behind a medieval hall
house in the centre of an attractive
Black and White village. Patio
gardens lead through a Wisteria
screen under an ancient mulberry tree
to lawns with herbaceous borders.
Hellebore and hosta beds thrive in
dappled shade. Wild flowers and
arbours with clematis and roses.
Pembridge is well served for
alternative refreshments with two
PHs, restaurant and two cafes.

Share your day out on and

55 THE VINE

Tarrington HR1 4EX. Richard Price.
*Between Hereford & Ledbury on
A438. Follow signs from Tarrington
Arms on A438. Park as directed.
Disabled parking only at house.* Sat
11 June (2-6). Adm £4, chd free.
Cream teas.
Mature, traditional garden in peaceful
setting with stunning views of the
surrounding countryside. Consisting
of various rooms with mixed and
herbaceous borders. Secret garden in
blue/yellow/white, croquet lawn with
C18 summer house, temple garden
with ponds, herb and nosegay
garden, vegetable/cutting/soft fruit
garden around greenhouse on the
paddock. Cornus avenues and
obelisk on paddock.

56 WESTON HALL

Weston-under-Penyard, Ross-on-
Wye HR9 7NS. Mr P & Miss L
Aldrich-Blake, 01989 562597,
aldrichblake@btinternet.com. *1m E
of Ross-on-Wye. On A40 towards
Gloucester.* Visits by arrangement
Apr to July groups only. Light
refreshments by request at
modest extra cost. Adm £4, chd
free.
6 acres surrounding Elizabethan
house (not open). Large walled
garden with herbaceous borders,
vegetables and fruit, overlooked by
Millennium folly. Lawns with both
mature and recently planted trees,
shrubs with many unusual varieties.
Ornamental ponds and lake. 4
generations in the family, but still
evolving year on year.

57 WESTON MEWS

Weston-under-Penyard HR9 7NZ.
Ann Rothwell & John Hercock,
01989 563823. *2m E of Ross-on-
Wye. Towards Gloucester on A40,
continue approx 100yds past the
Weston Cross PH & turn R into grey
brick-paved courtyard.* Sat 18, Sun
19 June (11-5). Adm £3, chd free.
Home-made teas. Wine, light
refreshments. Visits also by
arrangement May to Sept.
Walled ex-kitchen garden divided by
yew and box hedges. Traditional in
style and planting with large
herbaceous beds and borders at
different levels. Broad range of plants
incl roses. Enclosed garden with
sundial. Large vine house. Partial
wheelchair access.

58 WHITFIELD

Wormbridge HR2 9BA. Mr & Mrs
Edward Clive, 01981 570202,
tclive@whitfield-hereford.com,
www.whitfield-hereford.com. *8m
SW of Hereford. The entrance gates
are off the A465 Hereford to
Abergavenny rd, ¹/₂ m N of
Wormbridge.* Sun 3, Sun 17 Apr
(2-5). Single adm £5, chd free. Sun
8 May (2-5). Combined adm with
The Laskett Gardens £14, chd
free. Home-made teas. Visits also
by arrangement Mar to July, tour
and refreshments available for
groups 15+.
Parkland, wild flowers, ponds, walled
garden, many flowering magnolias
(species and hybrids), 1780 ginkgo
tree, 1¹/₂ m woodland walk with 1851
grove of coastal redwood trees.
Picnic parties welcome. Why not
make a day of it on May 8th and visit
both Whitfield and The Laskett (open
10-4pm). Partial access to wheelchair
users, some gravel paths and steep
slopes.

GROUP OPENING

59 WIGMORE GARDENS

Wigmore, Leominster HR6 9UP,
01568 770618,
l.barclay2@virgin.net. *10m from
Leominster, 10m from Knighton. On
A4110 from Leominster, at Wigmore
turn R just after shop & garage into
Ford St.Follow signs to parking &
gardens.* Sun 18 Sept (2-5).
Combined adm £6, chd free.
Home-made teas at Bury Court
Farmhouse.

NEW ▶ 2 BURY COURT PARK
Ivan & Cathy Jones

BURY COURT FARMHOUSE
Margaret & Les Barclay
(See separate entry)
Visits also by arrangement Mar
to Sept individual visitors and
groups of any size.
l.barclay2@virgin.net
01568 770618

The ancient village of Wigmore is
known for its C12 castle, home to the
Mortimer family and now a 'romantic
ruin', and its medieval church. The
two gardens are both within 100yds
of the parking area. Bury Court
Farmhouse has a ³/₄ -acre garden,
'rescued' since 1997, surrounding an
1840's stone farmhouse (not open).
The courtyard contains a pond,

mixed borders, fruit trees and shrubs,
with steps up to a terrace which
leads to lawn and vegetable plots.
The main garden (semi-walled) is on
2 levels with mixed borders
greenhouse, pond, mini-orchard with
daffodils in spring and wildlife area.
The garden is designed for yr-round
interest and colour. 2 Bury Court Park
is a small garden with beautiful views.
Herbaceous and evergreen shrub
borders, pond, bog garden, gravelled
areas, patio, pergola with climbers,
raised beds with companion planting,
greenhouse, arbour, paved seating
and sun areas, lawns. Specimen
trees, fruit area and watering system.

S-facing garden
sloping down
to Stansbatch
brook in idyllic
spot . . .

60 WILTON CASTLE ON THE WYE

Wilton, Ross-on-Wye HR9 6AD.
Alan & Suzie Parslow,
www.wiltoncastle.co.uk. *¹/₂ m NW
of Ross on R Wye. Signed at Wilton
r'about on M50/A40/A449 trunk rd.
Immd turn L opp garage. Castle
entrance behind Castle Lodge Hotel.
DO NOT cross bridge into Ross.* Sat
4, Sun 5 June (12-5). Adm £5, chd
£2. Home-made teas.
The romantic ruins of a restored C12
castle and C16 manor house (ruin)
form the perfect backdrop for
herbaceous borders, roses entwined
around mullion windows, an
abundance of sweetly scented old-
fashioned roses, gravel gardens and
shrubberies. The 2-acre gardens are
surrounded by a dry moat which
leads down to the R Wye with swans,
ducks, kingfishers etc. Featured in
Country Life. No disabled access into
dry moat area, or inside towers;
disabled WC.

61 WINDSOR COTTAGE
Dilwyn, Hereford HR4 8HJ. Jim & Brenda Collins, 01544 319011, jamescollins385@btinternet.com. *6m W of Leominster off A4112. Turn L off A4112 into Dilwyn. From centre of village, with PH on L, turn L. After 100y turn R. Cottage 400yds on L. Limited parking.* Every Tue and Thur 31 May to 1 Sept (2-5.30). Adm £3, chd free. Home-made teas and cakes, ground coffee, choice of teas and Gluten free available.
Visits also by arrangement June to Aug by arrangement for groups of up to 20. Adm incls home-made teas.
¹/₂ -acre wildlife friendly garden redesigned over the last 5yrs by present owners. Herbaceous borders, shrub bed, wildlife ponds, fruit and vegetables in raised beds. Extensive use of gravel beds. Wide selection of plants for all year interest including peonies, irises, hostas and clematis. Exhibition of watercolour and oil paintings. Wildlife friendly garden. Plants chosen to encourage bees, birds, and butterflies. Featured in Amateur Gardening. Gravelled drive giving access to level, lawned garden.

    ♿ 🐕 ❀ ☕

62 WOODVIEW
Great Doward, Whitchurch, Ross-on-Wye HR9 6DZ. Janet & Clive Townsend, 01600 890477, clive.townsend5@homecall.co.uk. *6m SW of Ross-on-Wye, 4m NE of Monmouth. A40 Ross/Mon At Whitchurch follow signs to Symonds Yat west, then to Doward Park campsite. Take forestry rd 1st L garden 2nd L - follow NGS signs.* Sun 1 May, Sun 10, Sun 17 July (1-6). Adm £4, chd free. Light refreshments. **Visits also by arrangement June to Sept please phone for details.**
Formal and informal gardens approx 4 acres in woodland setting. Herbaceous borders, hosta collection, mature trees, shrubs and seasonal bedding. Gently sloping lawns. Statuary and found sculpture, local limestone, rockwork and pools. Woodland garden, wild flower meadow and indigenous orchids. Collection of vintage tools and memorabilia. Croquet, clock golf and garden games.

    ♿ 🐕 ❀ ☕

63 WOOFIELDS FARM
Coddington, Ledbury HR8 1JJ. Mrs Rosemary Simcock, 01531 640583. *3m N of Ledbury. From Ledbury to Malvern rd A449, follow brown signs to Coddington Vineyard.* Visits by arrangement. Adm £4, chd free, combined with Coddington Vineyard adm £7.
2-acre garden on working farm: an eclectic mixture of planting, colour all yr round. Variety in shape and texture. Spring bulbs and shrubs. Borders planted with roses, clematis, wide range of herbaceous plants, many alstromeria, gravel garden, ornamental pond. Natural pond recently re-landscaped and planted by Peter Dowle.

    ♿ ❀ ☕

The Bannut

HERTFORDSHIRE

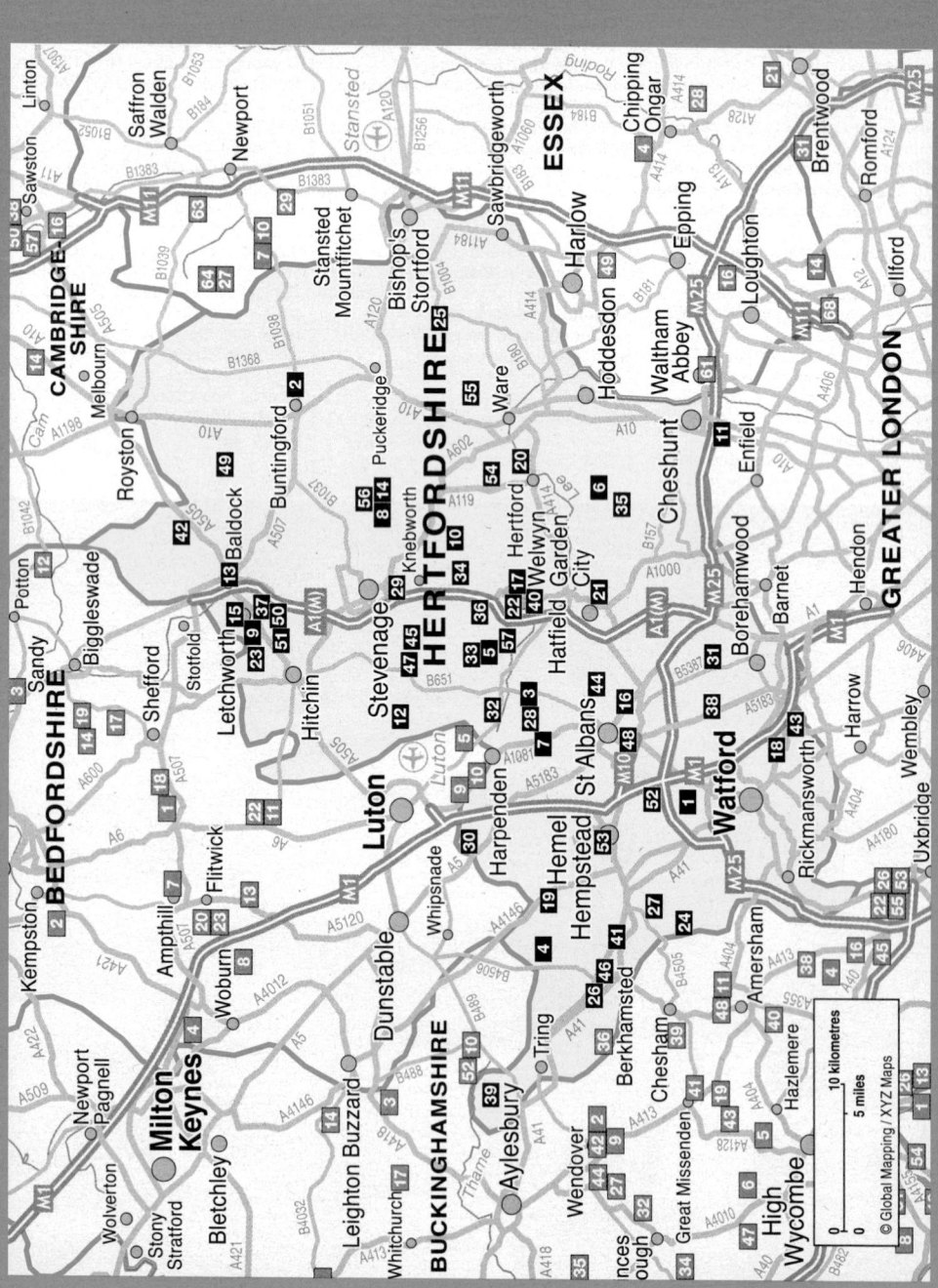

Hertfordshire

With its proximity to London, Hertfordshire became a breath of country air and a retreat for wealthy families wishing to escape the grime of the city – hence the county is peppered with large and small country estates, some of which open their garden gates for the NGS.

Hertfordshire was home for a long time to a flourishing fruit, vegetable and cut-flower trade, with produce sent up from nurseries and gardens to the London markets. There is a profusion of inviting rural areas with flower-filled country lanes and some of the best ancient woodlands carpeted with bluebells in late spring. Pretty villages sit in these rural pockets, with farmhouse and cottage gardens to visit.

Our towns, such as St Albans with its abbey, Baldock and Berkhamsted with their markets, and the garden cities of Welwyn and Letchworth all have interesting town gardens, both modern and traditional in their approach.

We have many gardens open 'by arrangement', and we are happy to arrange tours for large groups.

So next time you are heading through our county, don't just drive on – stop and visit one of our gardens to enjoy the warm welcome Hertfordshire has to offer.

Left: 42 Church Street © Chris Roper

Hertfordshire Volunteers

County Organiser
Julie Wise
01438 821509
juliewise@f2s.com

County Treasurer
Peter Barrett
01442 393508
peter.barrett@ngs.org.uk

Publicity
Julie Knight
01727 752375
jknight21@gmail.com

Chris Roper
07793 739732
chris.roper79@gmail.com

Social Media
Edwina Robarts
01279 842422
edwina.robarts@gmail.com

Booklet Coordinator
Julie Ryan
01707 874957
julieannryan@tiscali.co.uk

Group Tours
Sarah Marsh
07813 083126
sarahkmarsh@hotmail.co.uk

Assistant County Organisers
Kate de Boinville
07973 558838
katedeboinville@btconnect.com

Marion Jay
01707 334274
marion@garden84.net

Julie Loughlin
01438 871488
jloughlin11@gmail.com

Christopher Melluish
01920 462500
c.melluish@btopenworld.com

Karen Smith
01462 673133
hertsgardeningangel@googlemail.com

Opening Dates

All entries subject to change.
For latest information check www.ngs.org.uk

February

Snowdrop Festival

Saturday 13
8 Benington Lordship
Sunday 14
45 Rustling End Cottage
Saturday 20
56 Walkern Hall
Sunday 21
56 Walkern Hall
Saturday 27
39 Old Church Cottage
Sunday 28
39 Old Church Cottage

March

Saturday 5
11 Capel Manor Gardens
Saturday 19
21 Hatfield House West Garden

April

Saturday 9
56 Walkern Hall

Sunday 10
47 St Paul's Walden Bury
56 Walkern Hall
Sunday 17
2 Alswick Hall
Sunday 24
3 Amwell Cottage
Saturday 30
45 Rustling End Cottage (Evening)

May

Sunday 1
27 Huntsmoor
41 Patchwork
Monday 2
45 Rustling End Cottage
Friday 6
13 42 Church Street (Evening)
Sunday 8
37 324 Norton Way South
Sunday 15
42 Pembroke Farm
47 St Paul's Walden Bury
Sunday 22
33 The Manor House, Ayot St Lawrence
34 43 Mardley Hill
Saturday 28
36 The Mill House
Sunday 29
19 15 Gade Valley Cottages
38 45 Oakridge Avenue
Monday 30
36 The Mill House

June

Festival Weekend

Saturday 4
12 8 Chapel Road
Sunday 5
4 Ashridge House
12 8 Chapel Road
32 Mackerye End House
47 St Paul's Walden Bury
Saturday 11
5 Ayot Gardens
16 25 Cunningham Hill Road
Sunday 12
5 Ayot Gardens
16 25 Cunningham Hill Road
Friday 17
51 Serendi (Evening)
Saturday 18
30 The Lodge
40 NEW 120 Parkway
57 NEW The White Cottage (Evening)
Sunday 19
6 Bayford Musical Gardens Day
30 The Lodge
46 St Michael's Croft
51 Serendi
52 Serge Hill Gardens
55 Thundridge Hill House
57 NEW The White Cottage

Wednesday 22
23 Hitchin Lavender (Evening)
Friday 24
3 Amwell Cottage (Evening)
Saturday 25
49 Sandon Bury
Sunday 26
8 Benington Lordship
22 NEW Hill House
35 Michaels Folly
48 St Stephens Avenue Gardens
49 Sandon Bury
Wednesday 29
44 217 The Ridgeway

July

Sunday 3
24 NEW Home Farm Plants
44 217 The Ridgeway
Friday 8
54 NEW Threshing Barn (Evening)
Sunday 10
53 9 Tannsfield Drive
54 NEW Threshing Barn
Sunday 17
19 15 Gade Valley Cottages
38 45 Oakridge Avenue
50 Scudamore
Friday 22
23 Hitchin Lavender (Evening)
Sunday 24
12 8 Chapel Road
Friday 29
9 44 Broadwater Avenue (Evening)
Saturday 30
18 42 Falconer Road
Sunday 31
9 44 Broadwater Avenue
17 35 Digswell Road
18 42 Falconer Road

August

Saturday 6
18 42 Falconer Road
Sunday 7
18 42 Falconer Road
53 9 Tannsfield Drive
Sunday 14
7 Beesonend Gardens
41 Patchwork
43 Reveley Lodge

15 Gade Valley Cottages

Friday 19
20 8 Gosselin Road (Evening)

Saturday 20
34 43 Mardley Hill (Evening)

Sunday 21
20 8 Gosselin Road

Monday 22
23 Hitchin Lavender (Evening)

Sunday 28
42 Pembroke Farm

Monday 29
14 Croft Cottage
15 10 Cross Street

September

Friday 2
10 NEW 60 Bury Lane (Evening)

Sunday 4
10 NEW 60 Bury Lane
26 Hospice of St Francis
31 NEW 90 London Road
48 St Stephens Avenue Gardens

Friday 9
28 8 Kingcroft Road (Evening)

Sunday 11
28 8 Kingcroft Road

Sunday 18
27 Huntsmoor

November

Saturday 5
18 42 Falconer Road (Evening)

Gardens open to the public

4 Ashridge House
8 Benington Lordship
11 Capel Manor Gardens
21 Hatfield House West Garden
23 Hitchin Lavender
24 NEW Home Farm Plants
25 Hopleys
29 Knebworth House Gardens
42 Pembroke Farm
47 St Paul's Walden Bury

By arrangement only

1 The Abbots House

Also open by arrangement

16 25 Cunningham Hill Road
17 35 Digswell Road
18 42 Falconer Road
22 NEW Hill House
27 Huntsmoor
28 8 Kingcroft Road
41 Patchwork
48 20 St Stephens Avenue, St Stephens Avenue Gardens
53 9 Tannsfield Drive
55 Thundridge Hill House

The Gardens

1 THE ABBOTS HOUSE
10 High Street, Abbots Langley
WD5 0AR. Peter & Sue Tomson,
01923 264946,
peter.tomson@btinternet.com. *5m
NW of Watford. M25, J20, take
A4251 signed Kings Langley. R at
r'about, R at T-junction, under railway
bridge & follow yellow signs. Park in
free village car park.* **Visits by
arrangement Mar to Aug groups
of 10 - 30. Adm £4.50, chd free.**
*Donation to Friends of St Lawrence
Church.*
1³/₄ -acre garden with unusual trees,
shrubs, mixed borders with
interesting colour combinations,
scented garden, sunken garden,
pond, conservatory and a bed with
many Himalayan plants. A garden of
'rooms' with different styles and
moods. Many half-hardy plants. Oast
House. Pea shingle path.
& 👄

2 ALSWICK HALL
Hare Street Road, Buntingford
SG9 0AA. Mike & Annie Johnson,
www.alswickhall.co.uk. *1m from
Buntingford on B1038. From the S
take A10 to Buntingford, drive into
town & take B1038 E towards Hare
Street Village. Alswick Hall is 1m on
R.* **Sun 17 Apr (12-4.30). Adm £5,
chd free. Wine. Tea & cake.**
Listed Tudor House with 5 acres of
landscaped gardens set in unspoiled
farmland. Two well established natural

ponds with rockeries. Herbaceous
borders, shrubs, woodland walk and
wild flower meadow with a fantastic
selection of daffodils, tulips,
camassias and crown imperial.
Spring blossom, formal beds, orchard
and glasshouses. Licensed Bar, Hog
Roast, Teas, delicious homemade
cakes, plant stall and various other
trade stands. Good access for
disabled with lawns and wood chip
paths. Slight undulations.
& 🐕 😊 🚐 👄

Lively mix of perennials and grasses give a joyous display of texture and colour into the Autumn . . .

3 AMWELL COTTAGE
Amwell Lane, Wheathampstead
AL4 8EA. Colin & Kate Birss. *¹/₂ m S
of Wheathampstead. From St Helen's
Church, Wheathampstead turn up
Brewhouse Hill. At top L fork (Amwell*

*Lane), 300yds down lane, park in field
opp.* **Sun 24 Apr (2-5). Home-made
teas. Evening opening Fri 24 June
(6-9). Wine. Adm £3.50, chd free.**
Informal garden of approx 2¹/₂ acres
around C17 cottage. Large orchard
of mature apples, plums and pear laid
out with paths. Extensive lawns with
borders, framed by tall yew hedges
and old brick walls. A large variety of
roses, stone seats with views,
woodland pond, greenhouse,
vegetable garden with raised beds
and fire-pit area. Gravel drive.
& 🐕 😊 Ⓓ 👄

4 ◆ ASHRIDGE HOUSE
Berkhamsted HP4 1NS. Ashridge
(Bonar Law Memorial) Trust, 01442
843491, events@ashridge.hult.edu,
www.ashridgehouse.org.uk. *3m N
of Berkhamsted. A4251, 1m S of
Little Gaddesden.* **For NGS: Sun 5
June (2-6). Adm £4.50, chd £2.50.
Home-made teas. For other
opening times and information,
please phone, email or visit garden
website.**
The gardens cover 190-acres forming
part of the Grade II Registered
Landscape of Ashridge Park. Based
on designs by Humphry Repton in
1813 modified by Jeffry Wyatville.
Small secluded gardens, as well as a
large lawn area leading to avenues of
trees. 2013 marked the 200th
anniversary of Repton presenting
Ashridge with the Red Book, detailing
his designs for the estate.
& 🐕 🚐 👄

PERENNIAL
GARDENERS' ROYAL BENEVOLENT SOCIETY

NGS garden visitors
are supporting
gardeners across
the UK

GROUP OPENING

5 AYOT GARDENS
Ayot St. Lawrence, Welwyn
AL6 9BT. *4m W of Welwyn, 20 mins J4 A1M. A1(M) J6 follow signs to Welwyn, Codicote (B656) then signs to Ayot St Lawrence (Shaws Corner NT). Parking in field short walk to gardens.* **Sat 11 June (11-5); Sun 12 June (2-5). Combined adm £5, chd free. Home-made teas in nearby Palladian Church beside carpark.**

2 RUINS COTTAGE
Joe & Heather Warwick

WEST HOUSE
Alban & Susie Warwick

Set in the centre of one of the most picturesque villages in Hertfordshire and surrounded by rolling countryside with a backdrop of the 11C ruined Church, are two quintessentially English country gardens. West House part of The Old Rectory (not open) was landscaped 40 years ago and featured in Homes & Gardens 1987. Mature specimen trees, shrubs, herbaceous border, woodland and recently added old roses are a feature. 2 Ruins Cottages with entry through the adjacent ruined Church is an informal cottage garden with herbaceous border, fernery, ponds, rose garden, garden house, and tree deck with pastoral views towards the nearby Palladian Church where homemade Teas are available all day. Gardens open in conjunction with the 42nd Ayot St Lawrence Art Show held in the nearby Palladian Chuch where refreshments are also available. Lunches available at The Brocket Arms and BBQ in good weather. There are gravel paths in both gardens which may make access difficult.

⎣ ⚘ 🚐 ☕

GROUP OPENING

6 BAYFORD MUSICAL GARDENS DAY
Bayford SG13 8PX,
www.bayfordgardensday.org. *3m S of Hertford. Off B158 between Hatfield & Hertford. Car parking.* **Sun 19 June (11.30-5.30). Combined adm £10. Refreshments available in gardens, village school, village hall.**
A popular biennial event held for over 20yrs. More than a dozen gardens from large, long established formal layouts to pretty cottage gardens. 5 live bands incl jazz, steel and brass add a festive backdrop, while visitors can enjoy a variety of ploughman's lunches, cream teas and licensed bars. Stalls sell plants, local produce, cakes and ice-cream. For the more active there are a number of signed walks, complementary transport around the village is also provided and there is ample car parking. Bayford itself remains an oasis of countryside even though it is just 3m S of Hertford, and 10mins from Potters Bar. Mentioned in the Doomsday book of 1086 as Begesford, the village today is fortunate to retain much of its old world charm, incl a fine church with C15 font. Please see website for more details. All proceeds are for charitable causes; so far the open days have raised more than £250,000. People return year after year and many regard it as a great day out in the countryside. Wheelchairs are of course welcome but we would ask people to remember that garden surfaces can be difficult.

⎣ 🏠 ⚘ 🚐 ☕

GROUP OPENING

7 BEESONEND GARDENS
Harpenden AL5 2AN. *1m S of Harpenden. Take A1081 S from Harpenden, after 1m turn R into Beesonend Lane, bear R into Burywick to T-junction. Follow signs to Barlings Road & The Deerings.* **Sun 14 Aug (2-5.30). Combined adm £5, chd free. Home-made teas at 17 The Deerings.**

2 BARLINGS ROAD
Liz & Jim Machin

17 THE DEERINGS
Mr & Mrs Phillip Thompson

Set in a mature development these two gardens reflect their owners individual interests and needs. 2 Barlings Road is packed with unusual plants, shrubs and climbers to provide yr-round structure. The colourful courtyard garden with water feature and secluded shade garden add extra interest. 17 The Deerings offers specimen trees, architectural plants, ornamental grasses, herbaceous borders as well as a compact kitchen garden and herb bed.

⚘ ☕

8 ◆ BENINGTON LORDSHIP
Stevenage SG2 7BS. Mr & Mrs R Bott, 01438 869668,
garden@beningtonlordship.co.uk,
www.beningtonlordship.co.uk. *4m E of Stevenage. In Benington Village, next to church. Signs off A602.* **For NGS: Sat 13 Feb (12-4). Cream teas. Sun 26 June (12-5). Adm £5, chd free. For other opening times and information, please phone, email or visit garden website.**
7-acre garden incl historic buildings, kitchen garden, lakes, roses. Spectacular herbaceous borders, unspoilt panoramic views.

☕

9 44 BROADWATER AVENUE
Letchworth Garden City SG6 3HJ. Karen & Ian Smith. *½ m SW Letchworth town centre. A1(M) J9 signed Letchworth. Straight on at 1st three r'abouts, 4th r'about take 4th exit then R into Broadwater Ave.* **Evening opening Fri 29 July (6-9). Wine. Sun 31 July (12-5). Home-made teas. Adm £4, chd free.**
Town garden in the Letchworth Garden City conservation area that successfully combines a family garden with a plantswoman's garden. Out of the ordinary, unusual herbaceous plants and shrubs. Constantly evolving to include lots of colour and texture. Topiary underpins the whole garden. Attractive front garden designed for year- round interest.

⎣ 🏠 ☕

10 NEW 60 BURY LANE
Datchworth, Knebworth SG3 6SS. Delith & John Wringe. *5m S of Stevenage. Leave A1(M) at J6. Take B197 to Knebworth. Turn R at Woolmer Green signpost to Datchworth. Garden opposite Datchworth church. Evening*

opening Fri 2 Sept (5-7.30). Wine. Sun 4 Sept (1-4.30). Home-made teas. Adm £4.50, chd free.
¹/₂ acre Edwardian house garden with lovely views of surrounding countryside. Windy, exposed situation demands innovative planting and a lively mix of perennials and grasses give a joyous display of texture and colour into the Autumn. Contrasting shady woodland brings some calm and respite. Hard working greenhouse area for propagation of unusual varieties. Pond and gravel garden.

11 ◆ CAPEL MANOR GARDENS
Bullsmoor Lane, Enfield EN1 4RQ. Capel Manor College, 08456 122 122, www.capelmanorgardens.co.uk. *2m from Cheshunt. 3 mins from J25 of M25/A10. Nearest train station is Turkey Street, then 20 mins walk.* **For NGS: Sat 5 Mar (10-5). Adm £5.50, chd £2.50. Light refreshments. For other opening times and information, please phone or visit garden website.**
A beautiful 30-acre estate providing a colourful and scented oasis surrounding a Georgian Manor House and Victorian Stables. Be inspired by prize winning themed, model and historical gardens incl the latest additions the Old Manor House Garden and the Australian Garden (Chelsea Gold Medal winner). Jungle Gym Garden for under 5's Amazing holly maze to explore. Meercats, Shetland Ponies, Alpacas and reptile house. Wheelchair loan available and free with advanced booking.

12 8 CHAPEL ROAD
Breachwood Green, Hitchin SG4 8NU. Mr & Mrs Melvin Gore. *Midway between Hitchin Harpenden & Luton, Breachwood Green is well signed. We are just 2 doors from Red Lion PH.* **Sat 4, Sun 5 June, Sun 24 July (12-5). Adm £3, chd free. Home-made teas.**
Standing in the heart of the village surrounding a C17 cottage is an informal garden having no lawns or straight level pathways with a good selection of perennials, shrubs and alpines. With one of the largest collections of vintage garden tools and machinery on display. Featured in Hertfordshire Life.

13 42 CHURCH STREET
Baldock SG7 5AF. Leila Shafarenko. *Baldock town centre. 3m N of A1M J9 in the center of Baldock. 2m S of A1M J10. At the end of High St turn R at r'about, soon L into Sun St, continue Church St.* **Evening opening Fri 6 May (5.30-8.30). Adm £3.50, chd free. Wine.**
Secluded walled garden hidden behind a C16 house in the heart of Baldock's conservation area. Mature trees, incl a magnificent magnolia, wisteria-clad walls, wide herbaceous borders. Cottage-style planting featuring species peonies, and many varieties of thornless roses.

14 ◆ CROFT COTTAGE
9 Church Green, Benington SG2 7LH. Richard Arnold-Roberts & Julie Haire. *4m E of Stevenage. A1 J7 onto A602 to Hertford. Onto single carridgeway. Next r'about L down hill to mini r'about. Up hill through Aston. 1¹/₂ m to Xrd. Then 1¹/₂ m. Park on road opp cottage.* **Mon 29 Aug (1-5). Adm £3.50, chd free.**
C16 cottage with small, extensively planted garden divided into several areas. Many variegated and colourful-leafed shrubs and perennials. Mixed border in pastel shades. Euphorbia and hosta collection. Pool with fish, waterspout and seat. Rose and clematis shaded arbour with view over fields. Japanese maple garden with pool overlooking C13 church. Gravel paths.

15 10 CROSS STREET
Letchworth Garden City SG6 4UD. Renata & Colin Hume, www.cyclamengardens.com. *Nr town centre. From A1(M) J9 signed Letchworth, across 2 r'abouts, R at 3rd, across next 3 r'abouts L into Nevells Rd, 1st R into Cross St.* **Mon 29 Aug (2-5). Adm £3.50, chd free. Home-made teas.**
A cottage garden fronts a Letchworth Garden City exhibition cottage of 1905. The back garden contains informal planting dictated by the gently sloping plot and three formal circular lawns. Trees, shrubs, grasses and herbaceous perennials combine to create interest in the different areas. The garden also contains a lily pond, small pond for wildlife, well-stocked greenhouse and an apple walk with a selection of old varieties.

16 25 CUNNINGHAM HILL ROAD
St. Albans AL1 5BX. David & Anne Myles, annemyles@ymail.com. *1m S of St Albans City Centre. At A414 London Colney r'about turn onto London Road (City Centre). Turn R at sign 30mph.* **Sat 11, Sun 12 June (2-5.30). Adm £4, chd free. Home-made teas. Visits also by arrangement Apr to Sept for groups of 10-20.**
¹/₂ acre gardens with mature trees and shrubs, developed for all round colour. Wildlife ponds are linked to a fish pond. Wrought iron arches of roses, lonicera and clematis, are flanked by double herbaceous borders. A lawn, bordered by woodland planting beneath a beech tree, ends in a conifer and heather bed; behind which a sunny trellis separates the fruit and kitchen garden.

Delphiniums make a spectacular show in mid summer . . .

17 35 DIGSWELL ROAD
Welwyn Garden City AL8 7PB. Adrian & Clare de Baat, 01707 324074, adrian.debaat@ntlworld.com, www.adriansgarden.org. *¹/₂ m N of Welwyn Garden City centre. From the Campus r'about in city centre take N exit just past the Public Library into Digswell Rd. Over the White Bridge, 300yds on L.* **Sun 31 July (2-5.30). Adm £4, chd free. Home-made teas. Visits also by arrangement June to Oct groups of up to 20, adm incl tea & cake.**
Town garden of around a third of an acre with naturalistic planting inspired by the Dutch garden designer, Piet Oudolf. The garden has perennial borders plus a small meadow packed with herbaceous plants and grasses. The contemporary planting gives way to the exotic, incl a succulent bed and under mature trees, a lush jungle garden incl bamboos, bananas, palms and tree ferns. Grass paths and gentle slopes to all areas of the garden.

18 42 FALCONER ROAD

Bushey, Watford WD23 3AD. Mrs Suzette Fuller, 077142 94170, suzettesdesign@btconnect.com. *M1 J5 follow signs for Bushey From London A40 via Stanmore towards Watford. From Watford via Bushey Arches, through to Bushey High St turn L into Falconer Rd, opp St James church.* **Sat 30, Sun 31 July, Sat 6, Sun 7 Aug (12-6). Evening opening Sat 5 Nov (4-8). Adm £3, chd free. Light refreshments.**

Visits also by arrangement in July. Enchanting magical unusual Victorian style space. Children so very welcome. Winter viewing for fairyland lighting, for all ages, bring a torch. Bird cages and chimneys a feature, plus a walk through conservatory with orchids.

In the meadow enjoy beautiful grasses, wild flowers and ponds, plus the owners' beehives - from a distance . . .

19 15 GADE VALLEY COTTAGES

Dagnall Road, Great Gaddesden, Hemel Hempstead HP1 3BW. Bryan Trueman. *3m N of Hemel Hempstead. Follow A4146 N from Hemel Hempstead. Past Water End. Go past turning for Great Gaddesden. Gade Valley Cottages on R. Park in village hall car park.* **Sun 29 May, Sun 17 July (1.30-5). Adm £3, chd free. Home-made teas.**

165ft x 30ft sloping rural garden. Patio, lawn, borders and pond. Paths lead through a woodland area emerging by wildlife pond and sunny border. A choice of seating offers sunny rural views or quiet shady contemplation with sounds of rustling bamboos and bubbling water. Featured in Garden News.

20 8 GOSSELIN ROAD

Bengeo, Hertford SG14 3LG. Annie Godfrey & Steve Machin, www.daisyroots.com. *Take B158 from Hertford signed to Bengeo. Gosselin Rd 2nd R after White Lion PH (phone box on corner).* **Evening opening Fri 19 Aug (6-8.30). Wine. Sun 21 Aug (1-5). Adm £4, chd free.**

Owners of Daisy Roots nursery, garden acts as trial ground and show case for perennials and ornamental grasses grown there. Lawn replaced in 2010 by a wide gravel path, flanked by deep borders packed with perennials and grasses. Sunken area surrounded by plants chosen for scent. Small front garden with lots of foliage interest.

21 ◆ HATFIELD HOUSE WEST GARDEN

Hatfield AL9 5NQ. The Marquess of Salisbury, 01707 287010, www.hatfield-house.co.uk. *Opp Hatfield Stn, 21m N of London, M25 J23. 7m A1(M) J4 signed off A414 & A1000. Free parking.* **For NGS: Sat 19 Mar (11-5). Adm £6, chd free. For other opening times and information, please phone or visit garden website.**

Visitors can enjoy the spring bulbs in the lime walk, sundial garden and view the famous Old Palace garden, childhood home of Queen Elizabeth I. The adjoining woodland garden is at its best in spring with masses of naturalised daffodils and bluebells. Restaurant open. Shopping in Stable Yard.

22 NEW HILL HOUSE

Water End Lane, Ayot St. Peter, Welwyn AL6 9BB. Mr & Mrs Nic Savage, nic@savagemarketing.co.uk. *1m N of Welwyn Village & J6 of A1(M), follow the B197 towards Stanborough for approx 1m. Turn R just past the Red Lion over the bridge onto Ayot Green, take L fork towards the Sawmills & follow signs. Disabled parking will be as close as possible, at top of meadow or on gravel drive.* **Sun 26 June (2-5). Adm £4.50, chd free. Home-made teas. Visits also by arrangement Apr to Sept for groups of 10+.**

Plenty to see here - an acre of garden and four acres of meadow, with extensive views over the countryside. The garden features lawns, parterre, box hedging, mixed borders, mature shrubs and trees, terrace, pool and summer house, greenhouse, fruit cage and vegetable garden. In the meadow enjoy beautiful grasses, wild flowers and ponds, plus the owners' beehives - from a distance. (Honey on sale). Wheelchair access to all areas.

23 ◆ HITCHIN LAVENDER

Cadwell Farm, Ickleford, Hitchin SG5 3UA. Mr Tim Hunter, 01462 434343, tim@hitchinlavender.com, www.hitchinlavender.com. *2m N of Hitchin. From Hitchin take A600 N. At r'about R into Turnpike Lane. Continue into Arlsey Rd, garden on R after railway Xing.* **For NGS: Evening opening Wed 22 June, Fri 22 July, Mon 22 Aug (5-9). Adm £4.50, chd free. For other opening times and information, please phone, email or visit garden website.**

Visitors are encouraged to walk through the miles of lavender rows at Hitchin Lavender. As well as taking home some great photos you can also pick a bunch of lavender. The fields are a great spot for photographers, artists or those just wanting to take life a little slower. Entrance on 22 July and 22 Aug incl pick your own bunch of lavender - please bring your own scissors! Partial wheelchair access.

24 NEW ◆ HOME FARM PLANTS

Home Farm, Shantock Lane, Bovingdon, Hemel Hempstead HP3 0NG. Mr Graham Austin, 07773 798068, enquiries@homefarmplants.com, www.homefarmplants.co.uk. *Approx 4m SW of Hemel Hempstead. From Bovingdon, take the B4505 towards Chesham, then turn L onto the Ley Hill Road. Turn L down Shantock Hall Lane. Follow to T-junction, turn R into Shantock Lane, then follow signs.* **For NGS: Sun 3 July (2-5). Adm £4, chd free. Home-made teas. For other opening times and information, please phone, email or visit garden website.**

Family run Nursery set in lovely rural location. Specialising in Elatum delphiniums growing over 60 named cultivars. The Delphiniums growing make a spectacular sight in mid summer. At 3pm talk from nurseryman Graham Austin Getting

Serge Hill. Serge Hill Gardens

the Best from your delphiniums. Also seed from award winning delphiniums for sale THIS DAY ONLY. PYO cut flowers also available. PYO seasonal cut flowers grown on the nursery (weather dependent). Partial wheelchair access over grass.

25 ◆ HOPLEYS
High Street, Much Hadham SG10 6BU. Aubrey & Jan Barker, 01279 842509, www.hopleys.co.uk. *5m W of Bishop's Stortford. On B1004. M11 (J8) 7m or A10 (Puckeridge) 5m via A120. 50yds N of Bull PH in centre of Much Hadham.* **For opening times and information, please phone or visit garden website.**
4 acres laid out in informal style with island beds. The garden has become a useful collection of stock plants and trial ground for many new plants collected over the years, and features a wide selection of trees, shrubs, perennials and grasses. The nursery production area is hidden by an avenue of fastigiate hornbeams.

26 HOSPICE OF ST FRANCIS
Spring Garden Lane, Berkhamsted HP4 3GW. Hospice of St Francis. *1½ m W of Berkhamsted town centre. Leave A41 at A416 Chesham exit. Follow signs for Berkhamsted,* *When rd bends R go straight on into Shootersway, signed Northchurch, for 1¼ m.* **Sun 4 Sept (2-5). Adm £4, chd free. Tea.**
The hospice was built in 2006 on seven acres of previously damaged land and designed to resemble a farmhouse, barns and outbuildings. The garden has pergolas, paved terraces, lawns, ponds, and flower and shrub beds visible and accessible from patients' bedrooms; a peaceful oriental healing garden; and a sensory garden with views across to Ashridge. It is bounded by native woodland. Most of the woodland is not suitable for wheelchairs.

27 HUNTSMOOR
Stoney Lane, Bovingdon, Hemel Hempstead HP3 0DP. Mr Brian Bradnock & Ms Jane Meir, 01442 832014, b.bradnock@btinternet.com. *Between Bovingdon & Hemel Hempstead. Do not follow SatNav directions along Stoney Lane. Huge pot holes and ruts in lane. Approach from Bushfield Rd.* **Sun 1 May, Sun 18 Sept (2-5). Adm £5, chd free. Home-made teas. Gluten free provided. Visits also by arrangement for groups of 10+.**
Rose garden, rhododendron border, arboretum, Koi pond, nature pond, shrub and herbaceous borders. Also has a 'cave', and lots of places to sit. Full access to garden including easy access to WC.

28 8 KINGCROFT ROAD
Southdown, Harpenden AL5 1EJ. Zia Allaway, 07770 780 231, zia.allaway@ntlworld.com, www.ziaallaway.com. *1½ m S of Harpenden town centre. From Harpenden take the St Albans Rd A1081 S. At 1st r'about turn L onto Southdown Rd. Continue straight over 3 r'abouts to Grove Rd.* **Evening opening Fri 9 Sept (5-8). Wine. Sun 11 Sept (2-6). Home-made teas. Adm £3.50, chd free. Visits also by arrangement Apr to Sept for small groups.**
Beautiful mature town garden designed by garden writer and designer in a contemporary informal style, with small pond and pebbled beach area, gravel garden, a wide range of summer bulbs, herbaceous perennials and shrubs, mature trees, shady borders, greenhouse, and inspirational container displays. A small courtyard features flower-filled window boxes and vegetables in raised beds. Featured on the Wildlife Special of Alan Titchmarsh's Love Your Garden TV series.

29 ◆ KNEBWORTH HOUSE GARDENS

Knebworth SG1 2AX. The Hon Henry Lytton Cobbold, 01438 812661, info@knebworthhouse.com, www.knebworthhouse.com. *28m N of London. Direct access from A1(M) J7 at Stevenage.* **For opening times and information, please phone, email or visit garden website.**
Knebworth's magnificent gardens were laid out by Lutyens in 1910. Lutyens' pollarded lime avenues, Gertrude Jekyll's herb garden, the restored maze, yew hedges, roses and herbaceous borders are key features of the formal gardens with peaceful woodland walks beyond. Gold garden, green garden, brick garden and walled kitchen garden. Delicious afternoon teas are served in the Garden Terrace Tea Room. Plants for sale in the Gift shop. RHS Partner Garden. Free tours of the Gardens on Wednesday afternoons in July. Ideal for a gardening group visit, and garden tours can be arranged. Maze and Dinosaur trail for children.

A flowing route takes visitors on a journey through the garden . . .

30 THE LODGE

Luton Road, Markyate, St Albans AL3 8QA. Jan & John Paul. *2m N of M1 J9. Turn off A5 to Luton on B4540. The garden is between the villages of Markyate & Slip End.* **Sat 18, Sun 19 June (11-5). Adm £4, chd free. Tea, coffee or squash and homemade cakes.**
The garden, of nearly 3 acres, has evolved over 47yrs, partly through our own efforts and partly through nature growing plants wherever it chooses. The garden, mainly informal with a series of rooms, with small wooded area, a wild flower meadow and remains of an orchard full of common spotted orchids and other lovely wild flowers all of which arrived by themselves. Come and see for yourself. Main entrance gravel. Garden mostly flat.

31 NEW 90 LONDON ROAD

Shenley, Radlett WD7 9DX. Mr & Mrs Guy & Nicky Beaton. *3m from Elstree/Borehamwood. A1 exit B'hamwood follow signs to town then Shenley. Past White Horse PH on L then past King WilliamIV PH on R. No 90 tucked behind Methodist church. From M25 Jct22 Radlett, Shenley B3578 park on road.* **Sun 4 Sept (12-6). Adm £3, chd free. Home-made teas.**
A newly extended garden once a jungle with self-seeded trees and brambles. Designed by Hudson De Maeijer Landscapes & Gardens, now divided into 4 different gardens by clipped laurel and beech. A flowing route takes visitors on a journey through the garden. A graceful water pool, fruit trees and wild flowers, late flowering borders attractive in September and Hazel copse with a tapestry of hostas, hellebores and ferns.

32 MACKERYE END HOUSE

Mackerye End, Harpenden AL5 5DR. Mr & Mrs G Penn. *3m E of Harpenden. A1 J4 follow signs Wheathampstead. then turn R Marshalls Heath Lane. M1 J10 follow Lower Luton Road B653. Turn L Marshalls Heath Lane. Follow signs.* **Sun 5 June (12-5). Adm £5, chd free. Home-made teas.**
C16 (Grade 1 listed) Manor House (not open) set in 15 acres of formal gardens, parkland and woodland, front garden set in framework of formal yew hedges. Victorian walled garden with extensive box hedging and box maze, cutting garden, kitchen garden and lily pond. Courtyard garden with extensive yew and box borders. West garden enclosed by pergola walk of old English roses. Walled garden access by gravel paths.

33 THE MANOR HOUSE, AYOT ST LAWRENCE

Welwyn AL6 9BP. Rob & Sara Lucas. *4m W of Welwyn. 20 mins J4 A1M. Take B653 Wheathampstead. Turn into Codicote Rd follow signs to Shaws Corner. Parking in field, short walk to garden.* **Sun 22 May (11-5). Adm £5, chd free. Home-made teas.**
A 6-acre garden set in mature landscape around Elizabethan Manor House (not open). 1-acre walled garden incl glasshouses, fruit and vegetables, double herbaceous borders, rose and herb beds. Herbaceous perennial island beds, topiary specimens. Parterre and temple pond garden surround the house. Gates and water features by Arc Angel. Garden designed by Julie Toll. Home-made cakes and tea/coffee.

34 43 MARDLEY HILL

Welwyn AL6 0TT. Kerrie & Pete, www.agardenlessordinary.blogspot .co.uk. *5m N of Welwyn Garden City. On B197 between Welwyn & Woolmer Green, on crest of Mardley Hill by bus stop for Arriva 300/301.* **Sun 22 May (1-5). Home-made teas. Evening opening Sat 20 Aug (6-9). Wine. Adm £3, chd free.**
An unexpected garden transformed by plantaholics since 2009 and packed with unusual plants and inspiring combinations. Seating areas offer different perspectives on the design and plant composition. From a small bridge see the man-made stream cascade to the pond. For sale: cakes, teas and very large plant selection. NEW August evening opening for late summer's jewel colours, wine and fairy lights.

35 MICHAELS FOLLY

Henderson Place, Epping Green, Hertford SG1 38NE. Fabrizia Verrecchia, Tessa Verrecchia & Tim Metcalfe, www.bitzia.co.uk. *4m SW of Hertford. A414 follow signs to Berkhamsted. L at war memorial to Epping Green. Turn R into Henderson Place. Garden 100yds on L.* **Sun 26 June (2-5.30). Adm £3.50, chd free. Home-made teas.**
Something different! Forget your busy life and enter this atmospheric naturalistic garden. Meander the woodland walk and visit the earth labyrinth. Sit and reflect by the large natural pond and enjoy the abundant organic kitchen garden. Interesting structures abound a straw bale studio for yoga and dance and a Mongolian Yurt where tea will be served. Artist Tessa Verrechia's stained glass studio will be open with her art work for sale. www.fusingglass.co.uk.

36 THE MILL HOUSE

**31 Mill Lane, Welwyn AL6 9EU.
Sarah & Ian.** *Old Welwyn. J6 A1M
approx ³/₄ m to garden, follow yellow
arrows to Welwyn Village.* **Sat 28,
Mon 30 May (2-5.30). Adm £4, chd
free. Home-made teas.**
Listed millhouse with semi-walled
garden bordered by a bridged
millstream and mill race. This
romantic spring garden has ancient
apple trees underplanted with an
abundant display of alliums,
camassias and foxgloves. These set
off a garden full of perennial promise,
within which nestles a stylish
summerhouse, a hidden parterre and
productive potager. Featured in The
English Garden April edition.

♿ ✿ ☕

37 324 NORTON WAY SOUTH

**Letchworth Garden City SG6 1TA.
Roger & Jill Thomson.** *Just off the
A505, E of town centre. From the
A1M leave at J9 (A505) to
Letchworth. At 2nd r'about turn L to
Hitchin, still on A505. At T-lights turn
R into Norton Way South.* **Sun 8 May
(11-5). Adm £3.50, chd free.
Home-made teas. Serving
ploughman's lunches from 12
noon to 2pm then teas thereafter.**
¹/₅ acre organic garden of a
sympathetically extended Garden City
house (1906). Features include an
informal knot garden, a bespoke
David Harber armillary sphere as focal
point of a lawn surrounded by a
rockery, scree garden, borders,
summerhouse and pond with Koi
carp. Mature trees, shrubs and
seasonal planting in beds and
containers, alpine troughs,
sculptures, greenhouse and kitchen
garden. Wheelchair access to most
areas of the garden.

♿ ✿ ☕

38 45 OAKRIDGE AVENUE

**Radlett WD7 8EW. Mr & Mrs
Vaughan, 01923 854650,
ekvaughan@btinternet.com.** *1m N
of Radlett off A5183, Watling St.
From S, through Radlett Village last
turning on L Follow yellow arrows.*
**Sun 29 May, Sun 17 July (2-5).
Adm £4, chd free. Cream teas.**
The garden has been redesigned and
replanted over the past 10 years and
backs on to a working farm. The
planting has been carefully chosen to
combine the use of colour with
prominence given to dark foliage. The
garden is in two halves, looping to the
end with soft fruit and vegetables,

divided by sleepers and dominated
by a huge foxglove tree. Plants for
sale are propagated from the garden.
Gravel driveway.

♿ ✿ ☕

**WE ARE
MACMILLAN.
CANCER SUPPORT**

The NGS
is Macmillan's
largest single
donor

39 OLD CHURCH COTTAGE

**Chapel Lane, Long Marston, Tring
HP23 4QT. Dr John & Margaret
Noakes.** *A41 to Aylesbury take Tring
exit. On outskirts of Tring take B488
towards Ivinghoe. At 1st r'about go
on to Long Marston. Park at village
hall, disabled parking & drop off only
at house.* **Sat 27, Sun 28 Feb
(11.30-3). Adm £5, chd free.
Mulled wine and muffins.**
Small garden around a 400yr old
thatched cottage adjoining a disused
churchyard with ancient yews and
Norman tower being the remnant of a
Chapel of Ease. Many species and
varieties of snowdrops together with
cyclamen, crocuses,irises and other
early spring bulbs. Garden is at the
end of a very narrow country lane
hence request to park at Village Hall.
Ancient listed buildings in a
conservation zone. Garden laid out
with raised beds with many unusual
snowdrops.

40 NEW 120 PARKWAY

**Welwyn Garden City AL8 6HN. Mr
Peter Jenkins.** *¹/₂ m S from Welwyn
Garden City town centre (or from
John Lewis). From town centre take
Parkway until dual carriageway
merges; 120 is on R. From A1(M): J4,
take A6129 N to r'about, turn R into
Stanborough Rd & L into Parkway at
next r'about; 120 is on L.* **Sat 18
June (2-5.30). Adm £3.50, chd
free. Light refreshments. Home
made teas, cakes and Pimm's.**
Donation to Herts Society for the

Blind & Herts Action on Disability.
An established garden, lovingly
developed over 30 yrs, set against a
backdrop of mature trees. The
garden has a wide range of shrubs,
perennials and small trees, incl some
unusual and interesting varieties,
providing year round interest. Other
features incl rose beds, many
attractive climbers, a wild area, small
pond and rockery. Two small steps
with ramps in access route to garden.
Wheelchair access to most areas.

♿ ♯ ✿ ☕

41 PATCHWORK

**22 Hall Park Gate, Berkhamsted
HP4 2NJ. Jean & Peter Block,
01442 864731.** *3m W of Hemel
Hempstead. Entering E side of
Berkhamsted on A4251, turn L
200yds after 40mph sign.* **Sun 1
May, Sun 14 Aug (2-5). Adm £3,
chd free. Light refreshments.
Visits also by arrangement Mar to
Oct, groups of 10 to 50.**
¹/₄ -acre garden with lots of year-
round colour, interest and perfume,
particularly on opening days. Sloping
site containing rockeries, 2 small
ponds, herbaceous border, island
beds with bulbs in Spring and dahlias
in Summer, roses, fuchsias, patio
pots and tubs galore - all set against
a background of trees and shrubs of
varying colours. Seating and cover
from the elements. Not suitable for
wheelchairs, as side entrance is
narrow, and there are many steps
and levels.

♯ ✿ ☕

42 ♦ PEMBROKE FARM

**Slip End, Ashwell, Baldock
SG7 6SQ. Krysia Selwyn-Gotha,
01462 743100,
www.pembrokefarmgarden.co.uk.**
*¹/₂ m S of Ashwell. Turn off A505 (The
Ashwell turn opp the Wallington &
Rushden junction.) Go Under a
railway bridge & past a cottage on R,
after 200 yards enter the white farm
gates on R. Car park close to garden
entry.* **For NGS: Sun 15 May, Sun
28 Aug (12-5). Adm £4, chd free.
Home-made teas in the courtyard.
For other opening times and
information, please phone or visit
garden website.**
A country house garden with a wildlife
walk and formal surprises. You are
invited to meander through changing
spaces creating a palimpsest of
nature and structure.

♿ ♯ ☕

35 Digswell Road

43 REVELEY LODGE

88 Elstree Road, Bushey Heath WD23 4GL. Bushey Museum Property Trust,
www.reveleylodge.org. *3½ m E of Watford & 1½ m E of Bushey Village. From A41 take A411 signed Bushey & Harrow. At mini-r'about 2nd exit into Elstree Rd. Garden ½ m on L. Disabled parking only onsite.* **Sun 14 Aug (2-6). Adm £4, chd free.**
2½ -acre garden surrounding a Victorian house bequeathed to Bushey Museum in 2003 and in process of re-planting and renovation. Featuring colourful annual, tender perennial and medicinal planting in beds surrounding a mulberry tree. Conservatory, lean-to greenhouse, vegetable garden and beehive. Analemmatic (human) sundial constructed in stone believed unique to Hertfordshire. Partial wheelchair access.

44 217 THE RIDGEWAY

Marshalswick, St. Albans AL4 9XG. Kathy & Keith Caddy. *1½ m NE of St Albans city centre. A1081 towards Harpenden. B561 towards Sandridge. At 0.7m R at T-lights. At 0.6m L at 2nd r'about to The Ridgeway. Garden is 0.2m on R*
behind the green. **Wed 29 June, Sun 3 July (2-6). Adm £4, chd free. Home-made teas.**
²/₃ acre divided into different areas full of colour and interest. Sunken central patio with pond and fountain. Summer house surrounded by gravel garden. Box hedge parterre, many flower beds with acers, shrubs and perennials. Patio with hanging baskets and pots. Greenhouse, rose arches, water features and ponds. Garden begun from scratch 19 years ago.

45 RUSTLING END COTTAGE

Rustling End, Codicote SG4 8TD. Julie & Tim Wise,
www.rustlingend.com. *1m N of Codicote. From B656 turn L into '3 Houses Lane' then R to Rustling End. House 2nd on L.* **Sun 14 Feb (12.30-4.30). Light refreshments. Evening opening Sat 30 Apr (5.30-7.30). Wine. Mon 2 May (2-5.30). Home-made teas. Adm £4.50, chd free. Mulled Wine & Muffins at winter opening.**
Meander through our wild flower meadow to a cottage garden with contemporary planting. Behind lumpy hedges explore a simple box parterre, topiary, reflecting pool and abundant

planting. Deep borders feature blue Camassia in late spring. Our terrace hosts drought tolerant planting. Hens in residence. Come to our first winter opening to see the bones and structure of the garden in this season also showing those flowers brave enough to emerge. The garden also hosts many wild birds at our feeders. Busy Bee handmade cards for sale. Featured in Gardens Illustrated, Country Homes & Interiors & Hertfordshire Life magazines.

46 ST MICHAEL'S CROFT

Woodcock Hill, Durrants Lane, Berkhamsted HP4 3TR. Sue & Alan O'Neill.
www.stmichaelscroft.co.uk. *1¼ m W of Berkhamsted town centre. Leave A41 signed A416 Chesham. Follow sign to Berkhamsted, after 500 metres straight on to Shootersway. 1m on turn R into Durrants Lane. Garden 1st on L.* **Sun 19 June (1.30-5). Adm £4, chd free. Home-made teas.**
1-acre S-facing garden with variety of densely planted borders surrounded by mature trees. Rhododendrons, azaleas, hostas, ferns, alliums, palms and bananas. Water features and waterfall from lock gate. Pergolas

with clematis and climbers, vegetable beds, 2 greenhouses. Playhouse. Working beehives. Seating and cover. Home produced honey and plants for sale. Easy access for wheelchairs.

47 ◆ ST PAUL'S WALDEN BURY

Whitwell, Hitchin SG4 8BP. Simon & Caroline Bowes Lyon, www.stpaulswaldenbury.co.uk. *5m S of Hitchin. On B651; ¹/₂ m N of Whitwell village. From London leave A1(M) J6 for Welwyn (not Welwyn Garden City). Pick up signs to Codicote, then Whitwell.* **For NGS: Sun 10 Apr, Sun 15 May, Sun 5 June (2-7). Adm £5, chd £1. For other opening times and information, please visit garden website.**

Spectacular formal woodland garden, Grade 1 listed, laid out 1720. Long rides lined with clipped beech hedges lead to temples, statues, lake and a terraced theatre. Seasonal displays of snowdrops, daffodils, cowslips, irises, magnolias, rhododendrons, lilies. Wild flowers are encouraged. This was the childhood home of the late Queen Mother. Children welcome. 5th June, Open Garden combined with Open Farm Sunday with free tours of the farm. Featured in Country Life, and 'Die Geheimen Garten von England' (The Secret Gardens of England) by Howcroft and Majerus, published Deutsche Verlag-Anstalt. Wheelchair access to part of the garden. Steep grass slopes in places.

GROUP OPENING

48 ST STEPHENS AVENUE GARDENS

St Albans AL3 4AD. *1m S of St Albans City Centre. From A414 take A5183 Watling St. At double mini-r'about by St Stephens Church/King Harry PH take B4630 Watford Rd. St Stephens Ave is 1st R.* **Sun 26 June, Sun 4 Sept (2-6). Combined adm £5, chd free.** Home-made teas at No 20. Accessible WC, gluten free cake provided.

20 ST STEPHENS AVENUE

Heather & Peter Osborne Visits also by arrangement Mar to Oct for groups of 10+. heather.osborne20@btinternet.com
01727 856354

30 ST STEPHENS AVENUE

Carol & Roger Harlow

Two gardens of similar size and the same aspect, developed in totally different ways. The plantswoman's garden at Number 20 has been designed to supply successional waves of coordinated colour. Varied habitats include cool shade, hot and dry, and lush pondside displays. Paths weave through the carefully maintained borders packed with unusual plants. Specimen trees and fences clothed with climbers contribute to the peaceful seclusion. Recent additions include a gravel bed of ornamental grasses and late summer perennials. Seating throughout the garden gives different views, a conservatory provides shelter. Number 30 has a southwest facing gravelled front garden that has a Mediterranean feel. Herbaceous plants, such as sea hollies and achilleas, thrive in the poor, dry soil. Clipped box, beech and hornbeam in the back garden provide a cool backdrop for the strong colours of the herbaceous planting. A gate beneath a beech arch frames the view to the park beyond. Plants for sale at June opening only. Compost making demonstrations at number 20.

Wildlife haven which could be a setting for 'Wind in the Willows'. An idyllic and atmospheric setting . . .

---

49 ◆ SANDON BURY

Sandon, Buntingford SG9 0QY. Teddy & Louise Faure Walker. *5m N of Buntingford. A10 N of Buntingford. L at Buckland. Follow signs to Sandon. A1 N of Stevenage, A505 towards Royston. R after 2¹/₂ m to Sandon. Disabled Parking WC at Village Hall Church and Garden easy access.* **Sat 25, Sun 26 June (2-5). Adm £4.50, chd free. Home-made**

teas at Sandon Village Hall.
1640 Manor House in 2 acre garden. The highest point in Hertfordshire with views over countryside. Large herbaceous borders, walled vegetable garden, parterre, dovehouse, mature trees. Recently restored 1250 Saxon Barn one of the oldest in Europe. C13 church, village hall Teas WC, easy parking. Wheelchair access to garden, barn up sloping gravel path.

50 ◆ SCUDAMORE

1 Baldock Road, Letchworth Garden City SG6 3LB. Michael & Sheryl Hann. *Opp Spring Rd, between Muddy Lane & Letchworth Lane. J9 A1. Follow directions to Letchworth. Turn L to Hitchin A505. After 1m House on L opp corner shop. Parking in Muddy Lane & Spring Rd.* **Sun 17 July (11-5). Adm £4.50, chd free. Light refreshments.** *Donation to Garden House Hospice.*

¹/₂ acre garden surrounding early C17 cottages that were converted and extended in 1920s to form current house (not open). Family garden of mature trees, mixed herbaceous borders with shrubs, pond and stream, wet bed, wild garden and orchard/vegetable area. Many sculptures add interest to the garden.

51 ◆ SERENDI

22 Hitchin Road, Letchworth Garden City SG6 3LT. Valerie & Ian Aitken. *1m from city centre. A1(M) J9 signed Letchworth on A505. At 2nd r'about turn L to Hitchin on A505. Straight over T-lights. Garden 1m on R.* **Evening opening Fri 17 June (6-9). Wine. Sun 19 June (2-5). Home-made teas. Adm £4, chd free.**

¹/₃ acre plot comprising several different areas. Front garden - wisteria, mature shrubs, roses and exuberant cottage style planting. An 'S' loop of lavender, alliums and verbena bonariensis. A 'back yard' of hosts and acres, memento wall and gravel area. Shrubs, topiary, roses, magnolia, aeoniums and succulents plus a formal contemporary knot garden and greenhouse. Featured in Garden News extended article ('Garden of the Week') scheduled for publication late May/June with photography by Neil Hepworth. Gravel entrance driveway.

GROUP OPENING

52 SERGE HILL GARDENS
Serge Hill Lane, Bedmond, Watford WD5 0RT. ½ m E of Bedmond. Go to Bedmond & take Serge Hill Lane, where you will be directed past the lodge & down the drive. **Sun 19 June (2-5). Combined adm £7, chd free. Home-made teas at Serge Hill.**

THE BARN
Sue & Tom Stuart-Smith

SERGE HILL D
Kate Stuart-Smith

Two very diverse gardens. At its entrance the Barn has an enclosed courtyard, with tanks of water, herbaceous perennials and shrubs tolerant of generally dry conditions. To the N there are views over the 5-acre wild flower meadow, and the West Garden is a series of different gardens overflowing with bulbs, herbaceous perennials and shrubs. Serge Hill is originally a Queen Anne House (not open), beautifully remodelled by Busby (architect of Brighton and Hove) in 1811. It has wonderful views over the ha-ha to the park; a walled vegetable garden with a large greenhouse, roses, shrubs and perennials leading to a long mixed border. At the front of the house there is an outside stage used for family plays, and a ship.

53 9 TANNSFIELD DRIVE
Hemel Hempstead HP2 5LG. Peter & Gaynor Barrett, 01442 393508, tterrabjp@ntlworld.com, www.peteslittlepatch.co.uk. Approx 1m NE of Hemel Hempstead town centre & 2m W of J8 on M1. From J8 cross r'about to A414 Hemel Hempstead. Under ftbridge, cross r'dabout then 1st R across dual c'way to Leverstock Green Rd. Straight on to High St Green. L into Ellingham Rd then follow signs. **Sun 10 July, Sun 7 Aug (1.30-5). Adm £3, chd free. Home-made teas.**
Visits also by arrangement June to Sept, groups 4 min 10 max are very welcome. Tea/coffee available by arrangement. Adm £4, chd free.
This small, town garden is decorated with over 450 plants creating a welcoming oasis of calm. The owners love to experiment with the garden planting scheme which ensures the look of the garden alters from year to year. Narrow paths divide, leading the visitor on a discovery of the garden's many features. The sound of water is ever-present. Water features, metal sculptures, wall art and mirrors run throughout the garden. As a time and cost saving experiment all hanging baskets are planted with hardy perennials most of which are normally used for ground cover.

Stream where you may see ducks and moorhens scooting along . . .

54 NEW THRESHING BARN
Bullsmill Lane, Waterford, Hertford SG14 2RF. Ms Nicola Sussams. 2kms N of Hertford. Leave Hertford on A119. After the hamlet of Waterford turn R into Bullsmill Lane. Take 1st turning on R just before the railway bridge. Park on the grass verge on L. **Evening opening Fri 8 July (6-9). Wine. Sun 10 July (2-5.30). Home-made teas. Adm £4, chd free. Evening: wine and elderflower cordial. Afternoon: tea, squash (for children) and cakes.**
The Threshing Barn is a conversion dating back to the 1890s. The Barn is in the peaceful rural setting of Waterford with a nature reserve in close proximity to the property with open views across the Beane flood plain. The river side garden is a mix of perennial and herbaceous borders leading down to the stream where you may see ducks and moorhens scooting along. Wheelchair access into the garden but not across the bridge into the meadow.

55 THUNDRIDGE HILL HOUSE
Cold Christmas Lane, Ware SG12 0UE. Christopher & Susie Melluish, 01920 462500, c.melluish@btopenworld.com. 2m NE of Ware. ¾ m from The Sow & Pigs PH off the A10 down Cold Christmas Lane, crossing new bypass. **Sun 19 June (2-5.30). Adm £4.50, chd free. Cream teas. Visits also by arrangement May to Sept for groups of ten+.**

Well-established garden of approx 2½ acres; good variety of plants, shrubs and roses, attractive hedges. We are at present creating an unusual yellow-only bed. Several delightful places to sit. Wonderful views in and out of the garden especially down to the Rib Valley. 'A most popular garden to visit'.

56 WALKERN HALL
Walkern, Stevenage SG2 7JA. Mrs Kate de Boinville, 07973 558838, katedeboinville@btconnect.com. 4m E of Stevenage. Turn L at War Memorial as you leave Walkern, heading for Benington (immed after small bridge). Garden 1m up hill on R. **Sat 20, Sun 21 Feb, Sat 9, Sun 10 Apr (12-4.30). Adm £4.50, chd free. Home-made teas. Warming homemade soup.**
Walkern Hall is essentially a winter woodland garden. Set in 8 acres, the carpet of snowdrops and aconites is a constant source of wonder in Jan/Feb. This medieval hunting park is known more for its established trees such as the tulip trees and a magnificent London plane tree which dominates the garden. Following on in March and April is a stunning display of daffodils. There is wheelchair access but no WC.

57 NEW THE WHITE COTTAGE
Waterend Lane, Wheathampstead, St. Albans AL4 8EP. Sally Trendell. 2m E of Wheathampstead. Approx 10mins from J5 A1M Take B653 to Wheathampstead. Soon after Crooked Chimney PH turn R into Waterend Lane garden 300yds on L. Parking in field opp. **Evening opening Sat 18 June (4-9). Wine. Sun 19 June (2-6). Cream teas. Adm £4, chd free. Sat Teas 4pm til 6pm.**
Sally spent 2 decades creating her previous NGS garden at 2 Ruins Cottage. After just 2 years taming this neglected overgrown cottage garden it's still in an early stage of development. Riverside retreat in rural position nestling adjacent to a ford. The R Lea widens and forms the boundary of this wildlife haven which could be a setting for 'Wind in the Willows'. An idyllic and atmospheric setting. Piano recital Saturday opening at 7.30pm. Picnickers welcome all weekend.

43 Mardley Hill

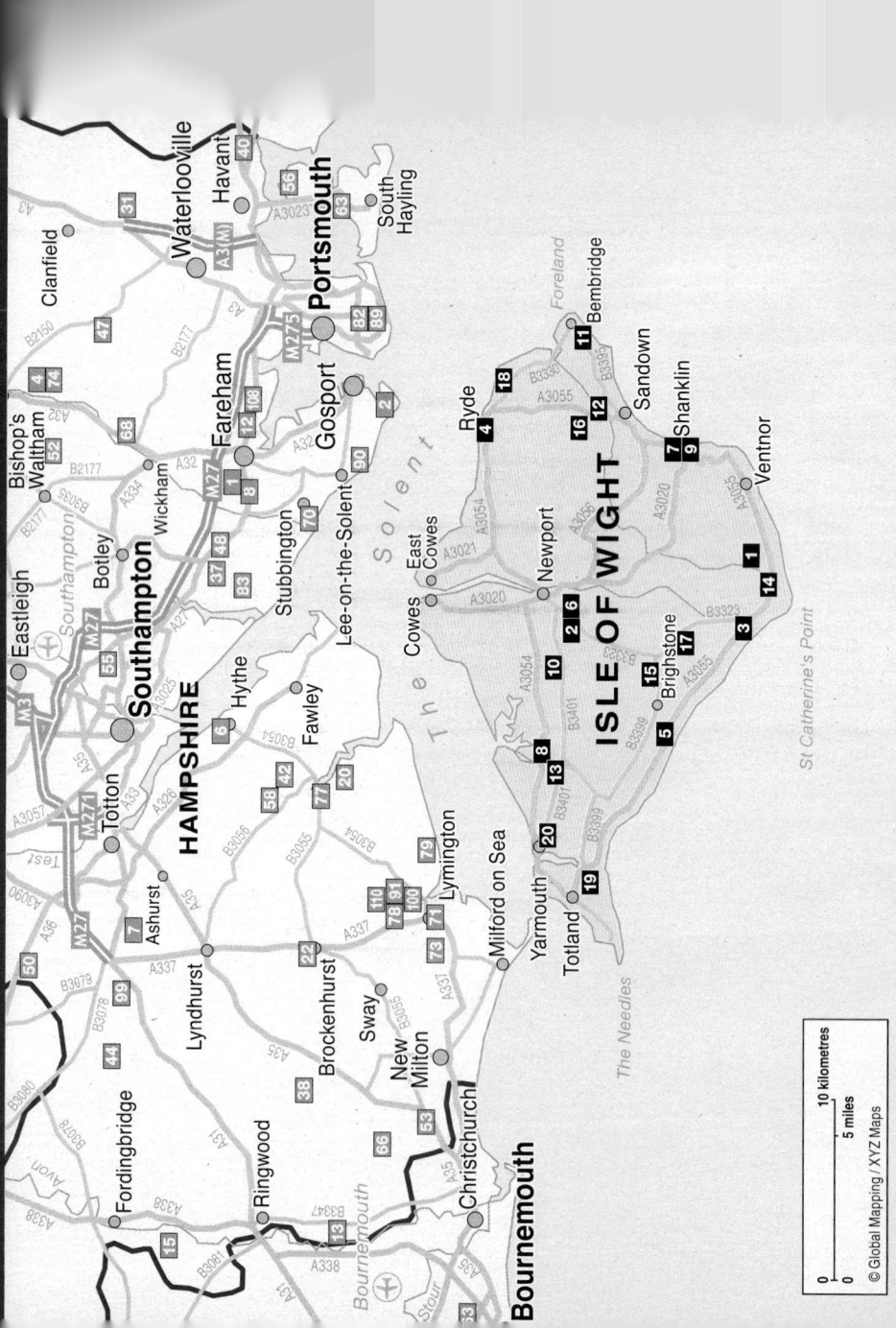

Isle of Wight

The island is a very special place to those who live and work here and to those who visit and keep returning. We have a range of natural features, from a dramatic coastline of cliffs and tiny coves to long sandy beaches.

Inland, the grasslands and rolling chalk downlands contrast with the shady forests and woodlands. Amongst all of this beauty nestle the picturesque villages and hamlets, many with gardens open for the NGS. Most of our towns are on the coast and many of the gardens have wonderful sea views.

The one thing that makes our gardens so special is our climate. The moderating influence of the sea keeps hard frosts at bay, and the range of plants that can be grown is therefore greatly extended. Conservatory plants are planted outdoors and flourish. Pictures taken of many island gardens fool people into thinking that they are holiday snaps of the Mediterranean and the Canaries.

Our gardens are very varied and our small enthusiastic group of garden owners are proud of their gardens, whether they are small town gardens or large manor gardens, and they love to share them for the NGS.

Below: Salterns Cottage, Seaview Gardens © Heather Edwards

Isle of Wight Volunteers

County Organiser
Jennie Fradgley
01983 730805
jenniemf805@yahoo.co.uk

County Treasurer
Jennie Fradgley
(as above)

Publicity
Jennie Fradgley
(as above)

Booklet Co-ordinator
Jennie Fradgley
(as above)

Assistant County Organisers
Mike Eastwood
01983 721060
mike@aristia.co.uk

Louise Ness
01983 551701
louiseness@gmail.com

Sally Parker
01983 612495
sallyparkeriow@btinternet.com

Opening Dates

All entries subject to change.
For latest information check www.ngs.org.uk

February

Snowdrop Festival

Sunday 21
6 Clatterford House

March

Sunday 20
6 Clatterford House
Sunday 27
6 Clatterford House

May

Saturday 7
3 The Beeches

Sunday 8
15 Northcourt Manor Gardens
Sunday 15
12 Morton Manor
Sunday 22
2 Badminton
Saturday 28
19 Sunny Patch
Sunday 29
10 Meadowsweet
19 Sunny Patch

June

Festival Weekend

Sunday 5
20 Thorley Manor
Saturday 11
17 The Old Rectory
Sunday 12
16 Nunwell House
Saturday 18
11 Mill Farm

---

14 Niton Gardens
Sunday 19
5 Brighstone Village Gardens
14 Niton Gardens
Saturday 25
1 Ashknowle House
Sunday 26
1 Ashknowle House

July

Sunday 3
18 NEW Seaview Gardens
Saturday 9
4 Blenheim House
Sunday 10
4 Blenheim House
Sunday 24
6 Clatterford House

August

Tuesday 2
7 NEW The Clifton
9 NEW The Havelock

Wednesday 3
7 NEW The Clifton
9 NEW The Havelock
Sunday 21
8 Crab Cottage
Sunday 28
12 Morton Manor

Gardens open to the public

16 Nunwell House

By arrangement only

13 Ningwood Manor

Also open by arrangement

4 Blenheim House
8 Crab Cottage
15 Northcourt Manor Gardens
17 The Old Rectory
19 Sunny Patch

The Gardens

1 ASHKNOWLE HOUSE
Ashknowle Lane, Whitwell, Ventnor PO38 2PP. Mr & Mrs K Fradgley.
4m W of Ventnor. Take the Whitwell Rd from Ventnor or Godshill. Turn into unmade lane next to Old Rectory. Field parking & disabled parking at house. **Sat 25, Sun 26 June (12.30-4.30). Adm £4, chd free. Home-made teas.**
A variety of features to explore in the grounds of this Victorian house. Informative woodland walks, borders, wildlife pond and other water features. Ongoing development of ornamental areas. The well maintained kitchen garden is highly productive and boasts a wide range of fruit and vegetables grown in cages, tunnels, glasshouses and raised beds. Young productive orchard incl protected cropping. Display and DVD of red squirrel antics.

2 BADMINTON
Clatterford Shute, Carisbrooke, Newport PO30 1PD. Mr & Mrs G S Montrose, 01983 526143.
1½ m SW of Newport. Free parking in Carisbrooke Castle car park. Garden signed approx 200yds. Parking for disabled can be arranged,

please phone prior to opening. **Sun 22 May (2-5). Adm £3.50, chd free. Home-made teas.**
1 acre garden on sheltered south and west facing site with good vistas. Planted for yr-round interest with many different shrubs, trees and perennials to give variety, structure and colour. Natural stream with bridges and waterfall. Pond being developed alongside kitchen garden.

3 THE BEECHES
Chale Street, Chale, Ventnor PO38 2HE. Mr & Mrs Andrew & Anne Davidson, 01983 551876.
Turn off A3055 at Chale onto B3399. Entrance between Old Rectory & bus stop, in gap in stone wall. On entry turn up the gravel drive towards our house which is two storey, tile hung. **Sat 7 May (10-5). Adm £3, chd free. Light refreshments.**
The garden is laid out mainly to shrubs and border plants designed for colour and texture. A haven of peace with extensive 270 degree views of the countryside incl the south west coast of the island down to The Needles and Dorset beyond. Features incl a grassland meadow and a deep pond home to fish and wildlife (children to be supervised because of deep water). This winter's main project is to improve and reseed

the wild flower meadow. The garden is not easy for wheelchairs due to gravel driveway and some steps, however can be accommodated with prior arrangement.

4 BLENHEIM HOUSE
9 Spencer Road (use Market St entrance), Ryde PO33 2NY. David Rosewarne & Magie Gray, 01983 614675, david65rosewarne@gmail.com.
Market St entrance behind Ryde Town Hall/Theatre. **Sat 9, Sun 10 July (11-4). Adm £3, chd free. Home-made teas. Visits also by arrangement May to Sept.**

A garden developed over 11 yrs, exploring the decorative qualities and long term effects of pattern making, colour and texture. This terraced 116ft x 30ft sloping site is centred on a twisting red brick path that both reveals and hides interesting and contrasting areas of planting, creating intimate and secluded spaces that belie it's town centre location.

GROUP OPENING

5 BRIGHSTONE VILLAGE GARDENS

Brighstone PO30 4BP. *7m from both Newport & Freshwater. Follow signs for Brighstone from Military Rd or from the B3399. Tickets to all gardens available at both village stores.* **Sun 19 June (11-4). Combined adm £4.50, chd free. Home-made teas at the Brighstone Scout Hut.**

KIPLINGS
David & Margaret Williamson

LITTLE ORCHARD
Elaine & Tom Boyer

RED GABLES
Mr & Mrs Peter & Shirley Cornelius

STONERIDGE
Mrs Sheila Easby & Mrs Sandra Dickie

TRALEE
Mr & Mrs Mike & Joan Kirby

Brighstone is an attractive large village with an interesting C12 church. A collection of very varied village gardens will be on show, including gardens established on challenging sites. The gardens vary in size and setting and are full of bright ideas as well as traditional planting and design. The gardens are within a fairly concise area of the village and so walking distances are comfortable. Partial wheelchair access.

6 CLATTERFORD HOUSE

Clatterford Shute, Carisbrooke PO30 1PD. Sylvia & David Hughes, 01983 537338, sylvia.clare@btinternet.com, www.mindfullyalive.org/gallery. *1¹/₂ m SW of Newport. On-site parking available for small groups of up to 10 cars.* **Suns 21 Feb, 20, 27 Mar, 24 July (2-4.30). Adm £3.50, chd free. Home-made teas.**

Morton Manor

© Heather Edwards

Developing garden, reclaimed in the year 2000 from derelict and overgrown property. Fantastic views enhance the naturalistic planting, managed for wildlife conservation using organic principles. Winter garden, bulbs and summer plantings worth seeing. No wheelchair access and not suitable for motorised chairs.

7 NEW THE CLIFTON

1 Queens Road, Shanklin PO37 6AN. Mr David Beeson, 01983 863015, reception@thecliftonshanklin.co.uk. *Follow signs to Shanklin on the A3055, at Arthurs Hill T-lights take Queens Rd.* **Tue 2, Wed 3 Aug (11-3). Combined adm with The Havelock £3.50, chd free. Light refreshments.**
From the hotel entrance through to the lovely frontage there is a riot of colour. Herbaceous ground hugging and cascading perennials adorn and many unusual shrubs enrich the display with their colour shape and form. Annual plantings enrich the whole effect in this small but lovely garden.

8 CRAB COTTAGE

Mill Road, Shalfleet PO30 4NE. Mr & Mrs Peter Scott, mencia@btinternet.com. *4¹/₂ m E of Yarmouth. Turn past New Inn into Mill Rd. Please park before going through NT gates. Entrance 1st on L, less than 5 mins walk.* **Sun 21 Aug (11.30-5). Adm £3.50, chd free.**

Home-made teas. Visits also by arrangement May to Aug.
1¹/₄ acres on gravelly soil. Part glorious views across croquet lawn over Newtown Creek and Solent leading to wild flower meadow, woodland walk and hidden waterlily pond. Part walled garden protected from westerlies, with mixed borders, leading to terraced sunken garden with ornamental pool and pavilion; planted with exotics, tender shrubs and herbaceous perennials. Gravel and uneven grass paths.

9 NEW THE HAVELOCK

2 Queens Road, Shanklin PO37 6AN. Mr & Mrs David Bunney, 01983 862747, info@havelockshanklin.co.uk. *Located in the heart of Shanklin. From Newport take the A3056 to Shanklin. Turn R onto the A3055 & follow signs to Ventnor via Queens Rd. The hotel is 500 metres on the R.* **Tue 2, Wed 3 Aug (11-3). Combined adm with The Clifton £3.50, chd free. Cream teas.**
Swimming pool garden with cabbage palms and scarlet geraniums. Small patio garden with pots containing summer flowering lilies. Essential bed display with palm, New Zealand flax and Bishop of Landalff dalias. Main formal garden with lawn edged by lavender and cape daisies, with island bed with small monkey puzzle tree. Hanging baskets, pots of cabbage trees and summer bedding plants.

Share your day out on and

10 MEADOWSWEET
5 Great Park Cottages, off Betty-Haunt Lane, Carisbrooke PO30 4HR. Gunda Cross. *4m SW of Newport. From A3054 Newport/Yarmouth road, turn L at Xrd Porchfield/Calbourne, over bridge into 1st lane on R. Parking along one side, on grass verge, past house.* **Sun 29 May (11.30-4.30). Adm £3.50, chd free. Home-made teas.**
From windswept barren 2 acre cattle field to developing tranquil country garden. Natural, mainly native planting and wild flowers. Cottagey front garden, herb garden, orchard, fruit cage and large pond. The good life and a haven for wildlife! Flat level garden with grass paths.
&♿ ❀ ☕

This garden is a celebration of fun, fantasy and life, so look closely to appreciate its diversity . . .

11 MILL FARM
Mill Road, Bembridge PO35 5PD. Peter, Alice & Kirsty Summerhayes. *Follow brown signs to Bembridge Windmill, go through NT gate, past windmill to the R. Limited parking on roadside.* **Sat 18 June (12-4). Adm £3, chd free. Light refreshments.**
Delightful informal cottage garden surrounding C17 farmhouse (not open) in windswept location with wonderful views. The garden is set out in a number of areas incl a gravel garden, vegetable patch and orchard. Gravel drive.
♿ ❀ ☕

12 MORTON MANOR
Morton Manor Road, Brading, Sandown PO36 0EP. Mr & Mrs G Godliman. *Off A3055 5m S of Ryde, just out of Brading. At Yar Bridge T-lights turn into lower Adgestone Rd. Take next L into Morton Manor Rd.* **Sun 15 May, Sun 28 Aug (11-4). Adm £4, chd free. Home-made teas.**

A colourful garden of great plant variety. Mature trees incl many acers with a wide variety of leaf colour. Early in the season a display of rhododendrons, azaleas and camellias. Ponds, sweeping lawns, roses set on a sunny terrace and much more to see in this extensive garden surrounding a picturesque C16 manor house (not open).
 🏵 ☕

13 NINGWOOD MANOR
Station Road, Ningwood, Nr Newport PO30 4NJ. Nicholas & Claire Oulton, 01983 761352, claireoulton@gmail.com. *Nr Shalfleet. From Newport, turn L opp the Horse & Groom PH. Ningwood Manor is 300-400yds on the L. Please use 2nd set of gates.* **Visits by arrangement June to Sept. Adm £4, chd free. Light refreshments.**
A 3 acre, landscape designed country garden with a walled courtyard garden, croquet lawn garden, white garden and kitchen garden. Much new planting has taken place over the last few yrs. The owners have several new garden projects underway, so the garden is a work in progress. Features incl a vegetable garden with raised beds and a small summerhouse, part of which is alleged to be Georgian.
♿ ☕

GROUP OPENING

14 NITON GARDENS
Niton PO38 2AZ. *5m W of Ventnor. Parking at football ground (Blackgang Rd), in village and Allotment Rd car park. Tickets & maps from the library in the heart of the village.* **Sat 18, Sun 19 June (11.30-4.30). Combined adm £5, chd free. Home-made teas at selected gardens on route.**

> **NEW HOLLY BANK**
> Mr & Mrs Brian Anderson
>
> **KINGS MANOR FARM**
> Ian & Catherine Hoare
>
> **LUCERNE**
> Peter & Elizabeth Marsden
>
> **NEW PUCKASTER CORNER**
> Mr & Mrs Ian McCallum
>
> **NEW SOUTHCLIFF**
> Mr & Mrs Martin & Eleanor Bowen

> **NEW SPRING COTTAGE**
> Mr & Mrs Neil White
>
> **SPRINGMEAD**
> Mr & Mrs John Hill
>
> **NEW TALSA**
> Frances Pritchard
>
> **NEW TILLINGTON VILLA**
> Paul & Catherine Miller
>
> **NEW WINFRITH**
> Mrs Janet Tedman
>
> **WYNCROFT**
> Helen Freeston

Niton is a delightful village with a busy community spirit, blessed with lovely churches, two PHs (one of which was renowned for smuggling), PO and shops, lovely walks and bridleways, school, football and cricket pitches and recreation ground. The gardens of this walk are very varied in both style and size and are full of colour, fragrance and interest; from cottage and country gardens to vegetable plot and havens for wildlife. The gardens are situated both in the heart of the village and the undercliff. We do hope you will enjoy them all.
🏵 ☕

15 NORTHCOURT MANOR GARDENS
Main Road, Shorwell PO30 3JG. Mr & Mrs J Harrison, 01983 740415, john@northcourt.info, www.northcourt.info. *4m SW of Newport. On entering Shorwell from Newport, entrance at bottom of hill on R. If entering from other directions head through village in direction of Newport. Garden on the L, on bend after passing the PO.* **Sun 8 May (12.30-5). Adm £5, chd free. Home-made teas. Visits also by arrangement Apr to Sept. Teas or light lunch for groups.**
15 acre garden surrounding large C17 manor house (not open), incl walled kitchen garden, chalk stream, terraces, magnolias and camellias. Boardwalk along jungle garden. A large variety of plants enjoying the different microclimates. There are roses, primulas by the stream and hardy geraniums in profusion. Picturesque wooded valley around the stone manor house. Bathhouse and snail mount leading to terraces. 1 acre walled garden being restored. Last yr the house celebrated its 400th yr anniversary. Wheelchair access on main paths only.
♿ 🏵 ❀ 🛏 ☕

16 ◆ NUNWELL HOUSE

West Lane, Brading PO36 0JQ. Mr & Mrs S Bonsey, 01983 407240, www.nunwellhouse.co.uk. *3m S of Ryde. Signed off A3055 into Coach Lane.* **For NGS: Sun 12 June (1-4.30). Adm £4, chd £1. Home-made teas. For other opening times and information, please phone or visit garden website.**

5 acres of beautifully set formal and shrub gardens and old fashioned shrub roses prominent. Exceptional Solent views from the terraces. Small arboretum and walled garden with herbaceous borders. House (not open) developed over 5 centuries and full of architectural interest.

17 THE OLD RECTORY

Kingston Road, Kingston PO38 2JZ. Derek & Louise Ness, www.theoldrectorykingston.co.uk. *8m S of Newport. Entering Shorwell from Carisbrooke, take L turn at mini r'about towards Chale (B3399). Follow road, house 2nd on L, after Kingston sign. Park in adjacent field.* **Sat 11 June (1-5). Adm £4, chd free. Home-made teas. Visits also by arrangement May to July. Refreshments by prior request for small groups only.**

Constantly evolving romantic country garden surrounding the late Georgian Rectory (not open). Areas of interest incl the walled kitchen garden, orchard, formal and wildlife ponds, a wonderfully scented collection of old and English roses and a ³/₄ acre perennial wild flower meadow. Bearded irises feature heavily as well; to see these at their best, visit by arrangement late May to early June. Featured in LandScape magazine (June 2015). Partial wheelchair access, some gravel and grass paths.

GROUP OPENING

18 NEW SEAVIEW GARDENS

Duver Road, Seaview PO34 5AJ. *Along E coast of Ryde. Follow signs for Seaview from Ryde or Brading along A3055. Parking in village or Duver Rd. Tickets & map available at each garden.* **Sun 3 July (11-5). Combined adm £4.50, chd free. Home-made teas at Northbank Hotel, Circular Road.**

HIGH VISTA
Mrs Linda Bush

NEW RED CROSS COTTAGE
Mr & Mrs Stephen Jones

SALTERNS COTTAGE
Susan & Noël Dobbs

NEW 10 SPITHEAD CLOSE
Mr Peter Muspratt

Enjoy a variety of garden styles set in the popular village resort of Seaview. Colourful borders of herbaceous perennials and annual bedding, trees, shrubs and climbers, grasses and water features. Raised vegetable beds, glasshouses and potager. Vine covered pergolas to sit and imagine the Mediterranean, plus sunny patios with a touch of the exotic.

19 SUNNY PATCH

Victoria Road, Freshwater PO40 9PP. Mrs Eileen Pryer, 01983 752974, freshair33@hotmail.com. *Halfway between Freshwater Village & Freshwater Bay. Down Afton Rd, L at garage up Stroud Rd. Keep L, just up from Parish Hall on same side. Parking in road outside house.* **Sat 28 May (10-4.30); Sun 29 May (9.30-4). Adm £3.50, chd free. Home-made teas. Visits also by arrangement Mar to Sept, mainly at weekends and advanced notice only.**

A garden of an eccentric plantaholic and sculpture collector. This large and constantly evolving area has been created over 30 yrs to accommodate and reflect the owners passion. Seasonal interest is sustained and nurtured through an extensive and interesting collection of trees, shrubs, perennials and bulbs including some rare specimens. Features incl a fairy wood, 2 ponds and a variety of seated areas from which to view the landscape. This garden is a celebration of fun, fantasy and life, so look closely to appreciate its diversity. There are no paths and numerous yrs of moles has made the ground very uneven.

20 THORLEY MANOR

Thorley, Yarmouth PO41 0SJ. Mr & Mrs Anthony Blest. *1m E of Yarmouth. From Bouldnor take Wilmingham Lane. House ¹/₂ m on L.* **Sun 5 June (2-5). Adm £3.50, chd free. Home-made teas.**

Delightful informal gardens of over 3 acres surrounding manor house (not open). Garden set out in a number of walled rooms incl herb garden, colourful perennial and self seeding borders, sweeping lawn and shrub borders, plus unusual island croquet lawn. Venue renowned for excellent home-made teas and the eccentric head gardener.

Northcourt Manor Gardens

© Heather Edwards

KENT

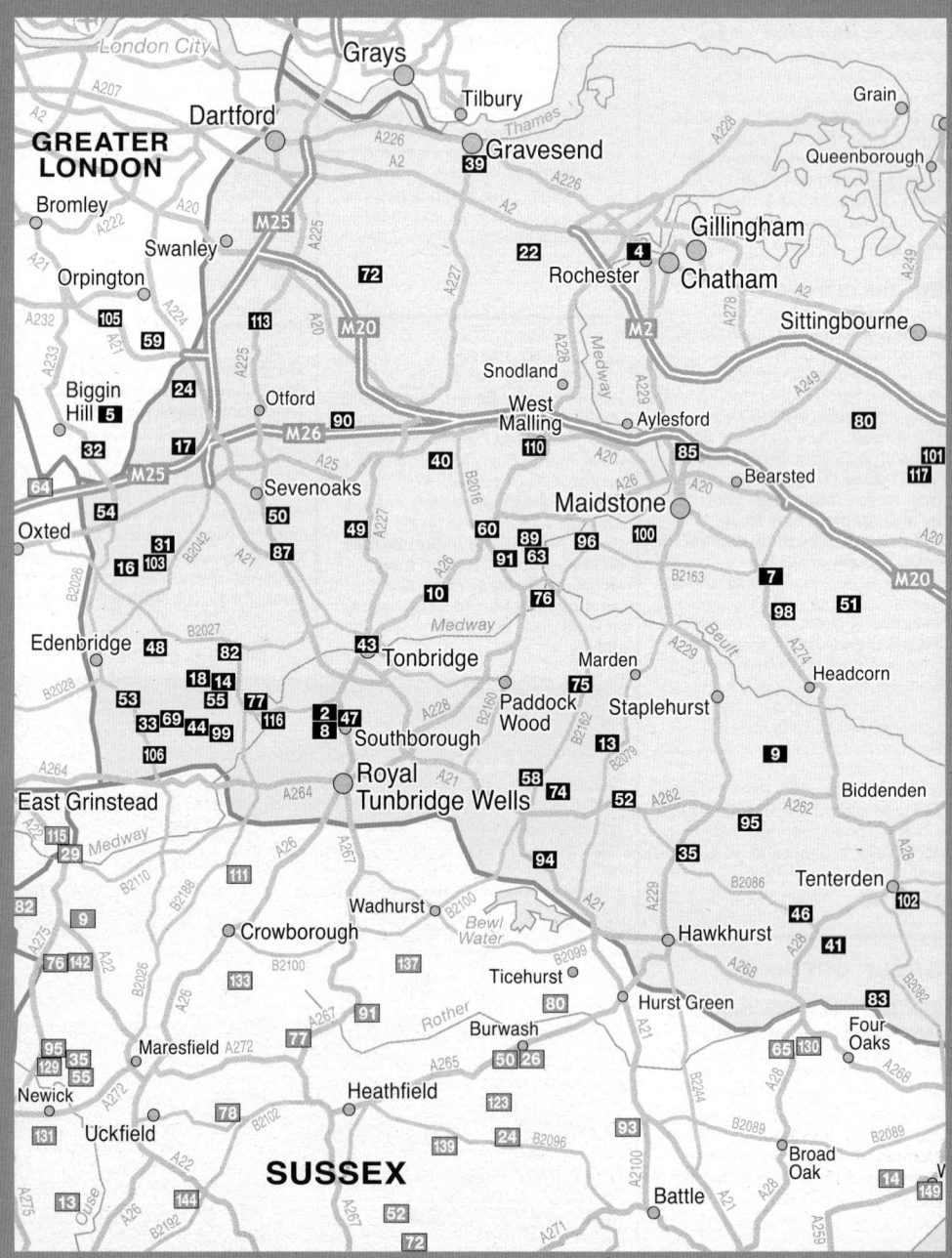

London City
Grays
Tilbury
Grain
A2
A207
Dartford
Thames
A226
A228
Queenborough
Gravesend
GREATER
LONDON
39
A2
A226
Bromley
A222
A2
Gillingham
A20
M25
A225
22
Sittingbourne
Swanley
72
Rochester
4
Chatham
A249
Orpington
A21
A224
Snodland
M2
A278
A228
105
113
A20
West
Malling
Medway
A229
A249
59
A227
Biggin
Hill 5
Otford
90
Aylesford
80
24
M26
110
Bearsted
85
101
32
17
A25
40
Maidstone
100
117
64
M25
54
Sevenoaks
B2016
A26
A20
M20
Oxted
50
49
60
89
96
A20
31
87
91 63
B2163
7
16 103
A21
10
76
98
51
A274
M20
Edenbridge
B2027
43 Tonbridge
Marden
A229
Beult
Headcorn
48
82
75
33 69 44 99
18 14
55
77
116
2 47
8
Paddock
Wood
Staplehurst
9
53
A228
13
Biddenden
106
Southborough
A264
East Grinstead
A264
Royal
Tunbridge Wells
A21
58
74
52
A262
95
A262
115
29 Medway
111
94
35
Tenterden
A28
102
82
9
Wadhurst
Bewl
Water
Hawkhurst
46
76 142
Crowborough
B2099
Hurst Green
41
133
Ticehurst
80
83
91
Rother
Burwash
A21
65 130
Four
Oaks
95
35
77
Maresfield A272
50 26
129 55
A265
Newick
Heathfield
123
131
Uckfield
78
24
93
Broad
Oak
13
144
SUSSEX
139
52
14
Battle
149
72

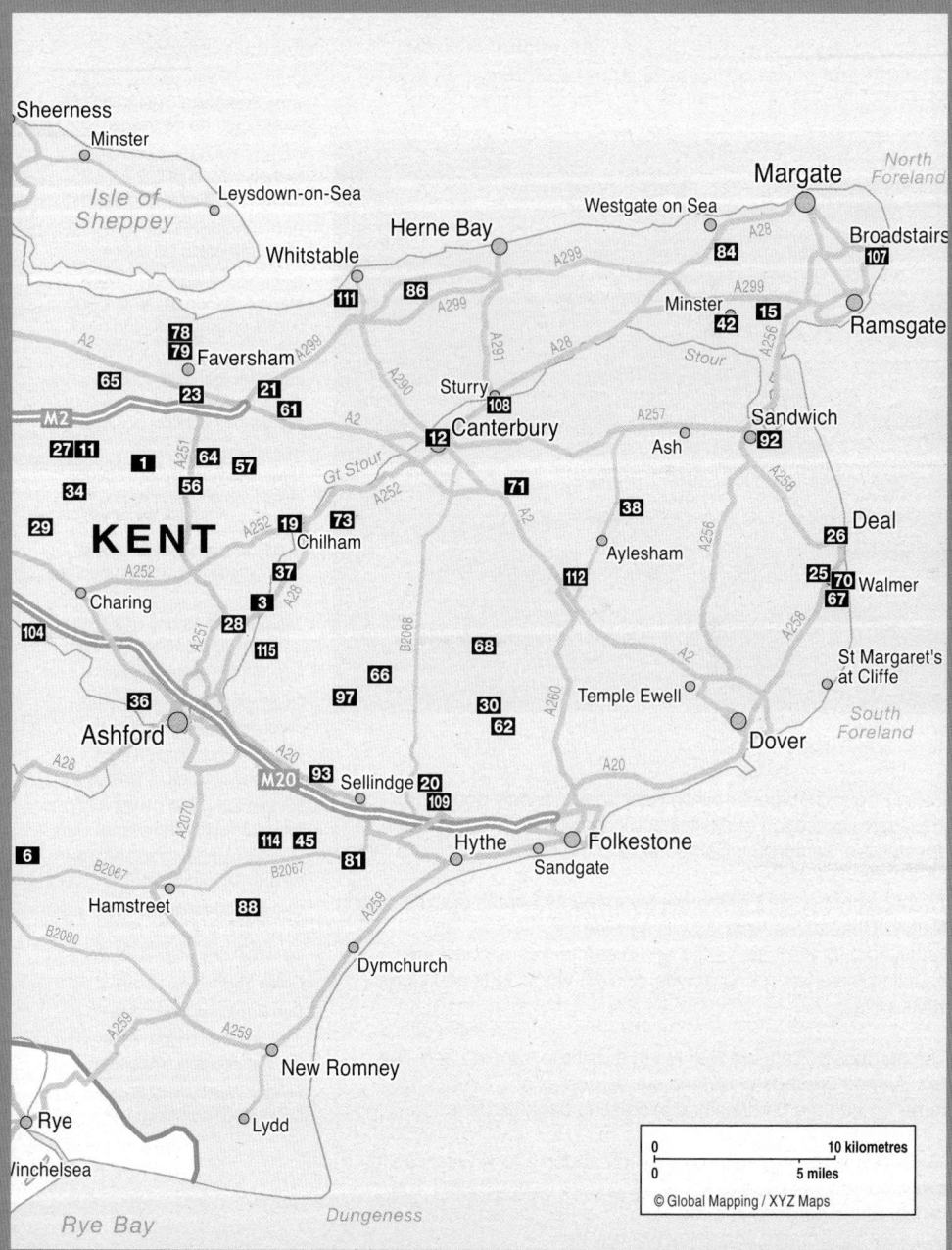

Sheerness
Minster
Isle of
Sheppey
Leysdown-on-Sea
Whitstable
Herne Bay
Margate
North
Foreland
Westgate on Sea
Broadstairs
107
84
15
Minster
42
Ramsgate
111
86
A299
A299
A28
A299
78
79 Faversham
A299
Sturry
108
Sandwich
92
65
21
Canterbury
A257
Ash
23
61
12
A2
27 **11**
1
64 **57**
71
38
Deal
26
34
56
29
KENT
19 **73**
Chilham
Aylesham
25 **70** Walmer
67
112
37
Charing
3
28
St Margaret's
at Cliffe
104
115
68
South
Foreland
36
66
Temple Ewell
97
30
62
Dover
Ashford
93 Sellindge **20**
109
6
114 **45**
81
Hythe
Folkestone
Sandgate
Hamstreet
88
Dymchurch
New Romney
Rye
Lydd
Winchelsea
Rye Bay
Dungeness

0			10 kilometres
0		5 miles	

© Global Mapping / XYZ Maps

Kent

Famously known as 'The Garden of England', Kent is a county full of natural beauty, special landscapes and historical interest.

Above: Chapel House

Being England's oldest county, Kent unsurprisingly boasts an impressive collection of castles and historic sites, notably the spectacular Canterbury Cathedral, and the medieval Ightham Mote.

Twenty eight per cent of the county forms two Areas of Outstanding Natural Beauty: the Kent Downs and the High Weald. The landscapes of Kent are varied and breathtaking, and include haunting marshes, rolling downs, ancient woodlands and iconic white cliffs.

The gardens of Kent are well worth a visit too, ranging from the landscaped grounds of historic stately homes and castles, to romantic cottage gardens and interesting back gardens.

Never has a county been so close to London and yet feels so far away, so why not escape to the peace of a Kent garden? The variety of the gardens and the warmth of the garden owners will ensure a memorable and enjoyable day out.

Kent Volunteers

County Organiser
Jane Streatfeild 01342 850362
jane@hoath-house.freeserve.co.uk

County Treasurer (Acting)
Nicholas Ward 01732 810525
hookwood1@yahoo.co.uk

Publicity (Radio)
Jane Streatfeild (as above)

Booklet Advertising
Marylyn Bacon 01797 270300
ngsbacon@ramsdenfarm.co.uk

Booklet Co-ordinator
Ingrid Morgan Hitchcock
01892 528341
ingrid@morganhitchcock.co.uk

Booklet Distribution
Diana Morrish 01892 723905
diana.morrish@hotmail.co.uk

Group Tours
Sue Robinson 01622 729568
suerobinson.timbers@gmail.com

Assistant County Organisers
Jacqueline Anthony 01892 518879
jacquelineanthony7@gmail.com

Marylyn Bacon (as above)

Clare Barham 01580 241386
clarebarham@holepark.com

Mary Bruce 01795 531124
mary.bruce@churchmans.co.uk

Bridget Langstaff 01634 842721
bridget.langstaff@btinternet.com

Virginia Latham 01303 862881
lathamvj@gmail.com

Caroline Loder-Symonds
01227 831203
caroline@dennehill.co.uk

Diana Morrish (as above)

Sue Robinson (as above)

Julia Stanton 01227 700421
familystanton@hotmail.com

Felicity Ward 01732 810525
hookwood1@yahoo.co.uk

Opening Dates

All entries subject to change.
For latest information check www.ngs.org.uk

February

Snowdrop Festival

Sunday 7
51 Knowle Hill Farm

Monday 8
44 Hoath House

Tuesday 9
44 Hoath House

Sunday 14
23 Copton Ash

Sunday 21
51 Knowle Hill Farm
60 Mere House

Wednesday 24
116 Yew Tree Cottage

Thursday 25
10 Broadview Gardens

Sunday 28
60 Mere House
116 Yew Tree Cottage

March

Sunday 6
36 Godinton House & Gardens

Monday 7
44 Hoath House

Tuesday 8
44 Hoath House

Wednesday 9
44 Hoath House
116 Yew Tree Cottage

Thursday 10
44 Hoath House

Sunday 13
61 Mount Ephraim
116 Yew Tree Cottage

Saturday 19
99 Stonewall Park

Sunday 20
36 Godinton House & Gardens
38 Goodnestone Park Gardens
40 Great Comp Garden
58 Marle Place

Wednesday 23
116 Yew Tree Cottage

Saturday 26
42 Haven

Sunday 27
42 Haven

Monday 28
22 Cobham Hall
42 Haven
60 Mere House

Wednesday 30
92 The Secret Gardens of Sandwich at The Salutation

The NGS: Macmillan Cancer Support's largest ever benefactor. . .

April

Sunday 3
37 Godmersham Park
57 Luton House
76 Parsonage Oasts

Sunday 10
23 Copton Ash
46 Hole Park
60 Mere House
116 Yew Tree Cottage

Wednesday 13
116 Yew Tree Cottage

Sunday 17
3 Bilting House
25 34 Cross Road
56 Lords
67 NEW The Old Bakehouse

Wednesday 20
27 Doddington Place

Thursday 21
66 Oak Cottage

Saturday 23
42 Haven
66 Oak Cottage
69 Old Buckhurst
108 Watergate House

Sunday 24
6 Boldshaves
23 Copton Ash
34 Frith Old Farmhouse
42 Haven
69 Old Buckhurst
95 Sissinghurst Castle Garden

116 Yew Tree Cottage

Tuesday 26
87 Riverhill Himalayan Gardens

Wednesday 27
41 Great Maytham Hall
69 Old Buckhurst
116 Yew Tree Cottage

Saturday 30
11 Calico House
69 Old Buckhurst

May

Sunday 1
83 Potmans Heath House
85 11 Raymer Road
93 Sandown

Monday 2
9 1 Brickwall Cottages
93 Sandown

Wednesday 4
46 Hole Park

Sunday 8
52 Ladham House
57 Luton House
69 Old Buckhurst
99 Stonewall Park
116 Yew Tree Cottage

Wednesday 11
16 Chartwell
116 Yew Tree Cottage

Saturday 14
69 Old Buckhurst

Sunday 15
3 Bilting House
7 Boughton Monchelsea Place
23 Copton Ash
27 Doddington Place
29 Eagleswood
34 Frith Old Farmhouse
79 Pheasant Farm
82 3 Post Office Cottages
91 St Michael's Gardens
101 Torry Hill

Tuesday 17
94 Scotney Castle

Saturday 21
69 Old Buckhurst

Sunday 22
73 The Orangery
75 Orchard House, Spenny Lane
103 Toys Hill Gardens
116 Yew Tree Cottage

Wednesday 25
41 Great Maytham Hall
116 Yew Tree Cottage

Saturday 28
12 Canterbury Cathedral Gardens
42 Haven

Sunday 29
12 Canterbury Cathedral Gardens
33 Falconhurst
34 Frith Old Farmhouse
42 Haven
59 12 The Meadows
68 Old Bladbean Stud
93 Sandown

Monday 30
29 Eagleswood
42 Haven
93 Sandown

June

Festival Weekend

Saturday 4
11 Calico House
21 The Coach House
38 Goodnestone Park Gardens
45 Hogben House
69 Old Buckhurst
88 NEW Rock Cottage
114 Wyckhurst

Sunday 5
17 Chevening
21 The Coach House
45 Hogben House
63 Nettlestead Place
80 Placketts Hole
88 NEW Rock Cottage
91 St Michael's Gardens
96 Smiths Hall
104 Tram Hatch
105 223 Tubbenden Lane
110 West Malling Early Summer Gardens
114 Wyckhurst

Monday 6
65 Norton Court

Tuesday 7
65 Norton Court

Wednesday 8
116 Yew Tree Cottage

Saturday 11
4 Bishopscourt
15 NEW Chapel House
30 Elham Gardens
45 Hogben House
78 Pheasant Barn
79 Pheasant Farm
108 Watergate House
114 Wyckhurst

Sunday 12
4 Bishopscourt
14 NEW 9 Chantlers Cottages
15 NEW Chapel House
30 Elham Gardens
37 Godmersham Park

Sunday 12
45 Hogben House
78 Pheasant Barn
79 Pheasant Farm
82 3 Post Office Cottages
90 St Clere
93 Sandown
101 Torry Hill
102 Townland
111 **NEW** Whitstable Gardens
114 Wyckhurst
116 Yew Tree Cottage
117 **NEW** Yokes Court

Wednesday 15
31 Emmetts Garden
46 Hole Park
106 Upper Pryors

Thursday 16
61 Mount Ephraim

Friday 17
33 Falconhurst

Saturday 18
24 **NEW** Cromlix

Sunday 19
7 Boughton Monchelsea Place
24 **NEW** Cromlix
25 34 Cross Road
33 Falconhurst
67 **NEW** The Old Bakehouse
68 Old Bladbean Stud
83 Potmans Heath House
113 The World Garden at Lullingstone Castle
115 Wye Gardens

Wednesday 22
13 Capel Manor Estate Gardens
116 Yew Tree Cottage

Thursday 23
92 The Secret Gardens of Sandwich at The Salutation
95 Sissinghurst Castle Garden (Evening)

Friday 24
36 Godinton House & Gardens

Saturday 25
42 Haven
71 The Old Palace
112 Womenswold Gardens

Sunday 26
13 Capel Manor Estate Gardens
18 Chiddingstone Castle
42 Haven
43 37 The Haydens
68 Old Bladbean Stud
71 The Old Palace
93 Sandown
112 Womenswold Gardens

116 Yew Tree Cottage

Wednesday 29
41 Great Maytham Hall
87 Riverhill Himalayan Gardens
89 Rock Farm

Planting is
romantic
rather than
manicured . . .

July

Friday 1
33 Falconhurst

Saturday 2
1 Belmont

Sunday 3
1 Belmont
22 Cobham Hall
26 **NEW** Deal Gardens
35 Goddards Green
51 Knowle Hill Farm
58 Marle Place
74 Orchard End
78 Pheasant Barn
89 Rock Farm
104 Tram Hatch

Tuesday 5
50 Knole

Friday 8
33 Falconhurst

Saturday 9
32 Eureka
54 Little Gables
64 **NEW** 6 Newhouse Farm Cottages

Sunday 10
32 Eureka
54 Little Gables
56 Lords
64 **NEW** 6 Newhouse Farm Cottages
68 Old Bladbean Stud
84 Quex Gardens
102 Townland
116 Yew Tree Cottage

Wednesday 13
8 Boundes End
69 Old Buckhurst
116 Yew Tree Cottage

Saturday 16
39 Gravesend Gardens Group

Sunday 17
2 Bidborough Gardens
8 Boundes End
39 Gravesend Gardens Group
101 Torry Hill

Saturday 23
42 Haven
69 Old Buckhurst
74 Orchard End

Sunday 24
42 Haven
68 Old Bladbean Stud
74 Orchard End
85 11 Raymer Road
93 Sandown
96 Smiths Hall
116 Yew Tree Cottage

Tuesday 26
5 The Blacksmiths Arms

Wednesday 27
27 Doddington Place
41 Great Maytham Hall
116 Yew Tree Cottage

Friday 29
33 Falconhurst

Saturday 30
73 The Orangery

Sunday 31
73 The Orangery

August

Friday 5
33 Falconhurst

Saturday 6
32 Eureka

Sunday 7
32 Eureka
53 Leydens
68 Old Bladbean Stud
69 Old Buckhurst

Wednesday 10
49 Ightham Mote
116 Yew Tree Cottage

Thursday 11
5 The Blacksmiths Arms

Sunday 14
70 **NEW** Old Church House
104 Tram Hatch
116 Yew Tree Cottage

Monday 15
81 Port Lympne, The Aspinall Foundation

Thursday 18
66 Oak Cottage

Saturday 20
5 The Blacksmiths Arms
19 Chilham Castle
48 **NEW** How Green Nursery
66 Oak Cottage

107 The Watch House

Sunday 21
48 **NEW** How Green Nursery
68 Old Bladbean Stud
75 Orchard House, Spenny Lane
107 The Watch House

Wednesday 24
41 Great Maytham Hall

Saturday 27
42 Haven

Sunday 28
32 Eureka
42 Haven
55 Long Meadow
82 3 Post Office Cottages
93 Sandown

Monday 29
32 Eureka
42 Haven
93 Sandown

Wednesday 31
70 **NEW** Old Church House

September

Saturday 3
4 Bishopscourt

Sunday 4
4 Bishopscourt
70 **NEW** Old Church House

Friday 9
77 Penshurst Place & Gardens

Saturday 10
69 Old Buckhurst
88 **NEW** Rock Cottage

Sunday 11
6 Boldshaves
69 Old Buckhurst
88 **NEW** Rock Cottage

Tuesday 20
92 The Secret Gardens of Sandwich at The Salutation

Saturday 24
42 Haven

Sunday 25
27 Doddington Place
42 Haven
61 Mount Ephraim

October

Sunday 2
38 Goodnestone Park Gardens
63 Nettlestead Place

Sunday 9
46 Hole Park

The Gardens

1 ◆ BELMONT

Belmont Park, Throwley, Faversham ME13 0HH. Harris (Belmont) Charity, 01795 890202, Administrator@belmont-house.org, www.belmont-house.org. *4½ m SW of Faversham. A251 Faversham-Ashford. At Badlesmere, brown tourist signs to Belmont.* **For NGS: Sat 2, Sun 3 July (12-5.30). Adm £4, chd free. For other opening times and information, please phone, email or visit garden website.**

Belmont house is surrounded by large formal lawns that are landscaped with fine specimen trees, a pinetum and a walled garden containing long borders, wisteria and large rose border. There is a second walled kitchen garden, restored in 2000 (to a design by Arabella Lennox Boyd), featuring lawns, hop arbours, pleached fruit, vegetables and flowers. During the season (April-September) the tea room is open on Wednesdays from 12pm for light lunches and afternoon teas. At the weekend tea and home-made cake is available between 1-5pm. Out of season the tea room is open on a self service basis and welcomes visitors.

♿ 🐕 🌸 🚐 ☕

2 BIDBOROUGH GARDENS

Bidborough, Tunbridge Wells TN4 0XB. *3m N of Tunbridge Wells, between Tonbridge & Tunbridge Wells W off A26. Take B2176 Bidborough Ridge signed to Penshurst. Take 1st L into Darnley Drive, then 1st R into St Lawrence Ave.* **Sun 17 July (2-5). Combined adm £5, chd free. Home-made teas.** *Donation to Hospice in the Weald.*

The Bidborough gardens (collect garden list from Boundes End) are in a small village at the heart of which are The Kentish Hare PH (book in advance), the church, village store and primary school. It is a thriving community with many clubs incl a very active Garden Association! In the surrounding countryside there are several local walks. The gardens are owner designed. Enjoy a variety of formal and informal features in front and main gardens, raised beds, a pebble bed, terraces and pergolas. There are specimen trees, interesting plants and plenty of places to sit and enjoy the peaceful surroundings. Partial wheelchair access, some steps to other gardens.

♿ 🐕 🌸 ☕

Little Gables

© Leigh Clapp

Join us on Facebook 🔲 and spread the word

3 BILTING HOUSE
nr Ashford TN25 4HA. Mr John Erle-Drax, 07764 580011, jdrax@marlboroughfineart.com. *5m NE of Ashford. A28, 9m S from Canterbury. Wye 1¹/₂ m.* **Sun 17 Apr, Sun 15 May (2-6). Adm £5, chd free. Home-made teas. Visits also by arrangement Apr to June for groups 10+.**
6 acre garden with ha-ha set in beautiful part of Stour Valley. Wide variety of rhododendrons, azaleas and ornamental shrubs. Woodland walk with spring bulbs. Mature arboretum with recent planting of specimen trees. Rose garden and herbaceous borders. Conservatory.

&♿ ✿ 🚐 ☕

4 BISHOPSCOURT
24 St Margaret's Street, Rochester ME1 1TS. Mrs Bridget Langstaff, 07816 828439, bridget.langstaff@btinternet.com. *Central Rochester, nr castle & cathedral. On St Margaret's St at junction with Vines Lane. Rochester train station 10 mins walk. Disabled parking only at garden but many car parks within 5-7 mins walk.* **Sat 11, Sun 12 June, Sat 3, Sun 4 Sept (1-5). Adm £3, chd free. Good range of delicious home-made cakes, served in tea tent.**
The residence of the Bishop of Rochester, this 1 acre historic walled garden is a peaceful oasis in the heart of Rochester with views of the castle from a raised lookout. Mature trees, lawns, yew hedges, rose garden, gravel garden, sculptures, fountain, wild flowers and mixed borders with perennials. Greenhouse and small vegetable garden. Featured in Amateur Gardener magazine. Child friendly. Most of garden is accessible by wheelchair. WC incl disabled.

&♿ 🐕 ✿ ☕

5 THE BLACKSMITHS ARMS
Cudham Lane South, Cudham, Sevenoaks TN14 7QB. Joyce Cole, 01959 572678, mail@theblacksmithsarms.co.uk. *Leave M25 at J4. At Hewitts r'about take 3rd exit onto A21. At Pratts Bottom r'about take 2nd exit onto A21. At r'about take 1st exit onto Cudham Lane North & follow for 4m.* **Tue 26 July, Thur 11, Sat 20 Aug (1-5). Adm by donation. Light refreshments. Visits also by arrangement July & Aug.**
Exceptionally pretty and colourful summer garden set in the grounds of

a C17 inn. Unusual varieties of summer bedding plants and annuals, mostly grown and cared for by the landlady. Decking and seating areas surrounded by spectacular hanging baskets and patio displays. Open lawn area with deep colour coordinated beds. We also are proud of our small natural area to attract and sustain wildlife. Partial wheelchair access inside PH.

&♿ 🐕 🚐 ☕

WE ARE MACMILLAN. CANCER SUPPORT

The NGS has funded 147 Macmillan professional posts

6 BOLDSHAVES
Woodchurch, nr Ashford TN26 3RA. Mr & Mrs Peregrine Massey, 01233 860302, masseypd@hotmail.co.uk, www.boldshaves.co.uk. *Between Woodchurch & High Halden off Redbrook St. From A28 towards Ashford turn R in High Halden at village green; 2nd R on to Redbrook St, then R down unmarked lane after ¹/₂ m to brick entrance to Boldshaves at bottom of hill.* **Sun 24 Apr, Sun 11 Sept (2-6). Adm £5, chd free. Home-made teas in C18 Barn.** *Donation to Kent Minds.*
7 acre garden, partly terraced, S facing, with ornamental trees and shrubs, walled garden, Italian Garden, Diamond Jubilee Garden, Camellia Dell, herbaceous borders (incl flame bed, red borders and new rainbow border), bluebell walks in April, woodland and ponds. **For details of other opening times see garden website www.boldshaves.co.uk.** Grass paths.

&♿ ✿ 🛏 ☕

7 BOUGHTON MONCHELSEA PLACE
Church Hill, Boughton Monchelsea, Maidstone ME17 4BU. Mr & Mrs Dominic Kendrick, 01622 743120, info@boughtonplace.co.uk,

www.boughtonplace.co.uk. *4m SE of Maidstone. From Maidstone follow A229 (Hastings Rd) S for 3¹/₂ m to major T-lights at Linton Xrds, turn L onto B2163, house 1m on R; or take junction 8 off M20 & follow Leeds Castle signs to B2163, house 5¹/₂ m on L.* **Sun 15 May, Sun 19 June (2-5.30). Adm £5, chd £1. Home-made teas.**
150 acre estate mainly park and woodland, spectacular views over own deer park and the Weald. Grade I manor house (not open). Courtyard herb garden, intimate walled gardens, box hedges, herbaceous borders, orchard. Planting is romantic rather than manicured. Do not miss St Peter's Church next door. Traditional greenhouse and kitchen garden. For other opening times and information please phone or see garden website. Regret, no dogs. Featured in The Kent Messenger.

☕

8 BOUNDES END
2 St Lawrence Avenue, Bidborough, Tunbridge Wells TN4 0XB. Carole & Mike Marks, 01892 542233, carole.marks@btinternet.com, www.boundesendgarden.co.uk. *Between Tonbridge & Tunbridge Wells off A26. Take B2176 Bidborough Ridge signed to Penshurst. Take 1st L into Darnley Drive, then 1st R into St Lawrence Ave.* **Wed 13 July (2-5). Adm £3, chd free. Sun 17 July (2-5). Adm £5, chd free. Home-made teas. Visits also by arrangement June to Aug, groups 20 max.** *Donation to Hospice in the Weald.*
Garden, designed by owners, on an unusually shaped ¹/₃ acre plot formed from 2 triangles of land. Front garden features raised beds, and the main garden divided into a formal area with terrace, pebble bed and 2 pergolas, an informal area in woodland setting with interesting features and specimen trees. Plenty of places to sit and enjoy the garden. Some uneven ground in lower garden.

&♿ 🐕 ✿ ☕

9 1 BRICKWALL COTTAGES
Frittenden, Cranbrook TN17 2DH. Mrs Sue Martin, 01580 852425, sue.martin@talktalk.net, www.geumcollection.co.uk. *6m NW of Tenterden. E of A229 between Cranbrook & Staplehurst & W of A274 between Biddenden & Headcorn. Park in village & walk*

along footpath opp school. **Mon 2 May (11-4). Adm £4, chd free. Home-made teas. Visits also by arrangement May & June, 30 max.** Although less than ¼ acre, the garden gives the impression of being much larger as it is made up of several rooms all intensively planted with a wide range of hardy perennials, bulbs and shrubs, with over 100 geums which comprise the National Collection planted throughout the garden. Pergolas provide supports for climbing plants and there is a small formal pond. The garden has been featured in a number of magazines incl The Garden, Gardens Illustrated, Country Life, The English Garden, Kent Life and House Beautiful. Some paths are narrow and wheelchairs may not be able to reach far end of garden.

♿ 🐕 🐾 🚐 **NPC** ☕

10 ◆ **BROADVIEW GARDENS**
Hadlow TN11 0AL. Hadlow College, 01732 853211, www.broadviewgardens.co.uk. *On A26, 2½ m NE of Tonbridge on L, 200 metres before village of Hadlow, enter through main Hadlow College entrance.* **For NGS: Thur 25 Feb (11-4.30). Adm £3, chd free. For other opening times and information, please phone or visit garden website.**
10 acres of ornamental planting in attractive landscape setting; 100m double mixed border, island beds with mixed plantings, lakes and water gardens; series of demonstration gardens incl Italian, Oriental and Hampton Court show gardens. National Collections of Anemone japonica and Helleborus. Wheelchair access difficult when wet due to grass paths.

♿ 🐾 🚐 **NPC** ☕

11 **CALICO HOUSE**
The Street, Newnham, Sittingbourne ME9 0LN. Graham Lloyd-Brunt. *Garden located in middle of village on rd that runs through Newnham from A2 to A20. Roadside parking only.* **Sat 30 Apr, Sat 4 June (2-5). Adm £5, chd free.**
The contemporary garden created at Calico House between 2008 and 2013 is set within a traditional English garden framework of topiary yew hedges and terraced lawns dating from the 1920s. Themed flower borders are at their best May to August set against the garden's strong structural backdrop.

Timbers
© Nicola Stocken

GROUP OPENING

12 **CANTERBURY CATHEDRAL GARDENS**
Canterbury CT1 2EP, 01227 762862, events@canterbury-cathedral.org, www.canterbury-cathedral.org. *Canterbury Cathedral Precincts.* **Enter precincts via main Christchurch gate.** No access for cars, use park & ride or public car parks. **Sat 28 May (11-5); Sun 29 May (2-5). Combined adm £5, chd free. Please note** on Sat, in addition to £5 adm, precinct charges apply. On Sun there are no precinct charges. Home-made teas on Green Court.

ARCHDEACONRY

THE DEANERY
The Dean

15 THE PRECINCTS
Canon Papadapulos

19 THE PRECINCTS
Canon Irvine

22 THE PRECINCTS
Canon Clare Edwards

A wonderful opportunity to visit and enjoy 5 Canonical gardens within the historic precincts of Canterbury Cathedral: The Deanery Garden with wonderful roses, wildflower planting and orchard, unusual Medlar Tree, vegetable garden and wild fowl enclosure; the Archdeaconry incl the ancient Mulberry Tree, contrasting traditional and modern planting and a Japanese influence; the three further Precinct gardens, varied in style, offer sweeping herbaceous banks, delightful enclosed spaces, and areas planted to attract and support birds, insects and wildlife. All the gardens now incl vegetable plots personal to each house. Step back in time and see the herb garden, which show the use of herbs for medicinal purposes in the Middle Ages. The walled Memorial Garden has wonderful Wisteria, formal roses, mixed borders and the stone war memorial at its centre, and hidden Bastion Chapel in the city wall. Gardeners' plant stall and home-made refreshments. Dover Beekeepers Association, up close and personal opportunity with Birds of Prey and unique access to Bastion Chapel. Classic cars on Green Court. Wheelchair access to all gardens. Archdeaconry has separate entrance for people who require a flat entrance.

♿ 🐾 🛏 ☕

GROUP OPENING

13 CAPEL MANOR ESTATE GARDENS

Grovehurst Lane, Horsmonden TN12 8BG. *Approx 8m SE of Tonbridge, 10 m E of Tunbridge Wells. From Horsmonden village, follow yellow NGS signs towards Goudhurst, leaving the Gun & Spitroast PH on R.* **Wed 22, Sun 26 June (12-5). Combined adm £5, chd free. Home-made teas in The Courtyard.**

CHURCH VIEW
Mr & Mrs H Tangen

THE COURTYARD
Mr & Mrs Iain Stewart

The two gardens form a substantial part of the former Capel Manor estate built for the Austen family (relatives of the renowned Jane Austen). The Courtyard gardens cover several acres of formal gardens and woodland incl a stunning Mediterranean courtyard garden using tranquil coloured planting with a fountain at its centre. Church View is a lovely 1 acre S facing sloping garden with spectacular countryside views. Both gardens have had substantial work done since the last opening in June 2014. Amazing tearoom situated in The Courtyard with plenty of seating and delicious selection of cakes and scones. Church View featured in Period Homes and Interiors. Most of the gardens can be seen by wheelchair users but some gravel paths and steep slopes may prove difficult to negotiate.

  ♿ ❀ ☕

14 NEW 9 CHANTLERS COTTAGES

Wellers Town Road, Chiddingstone, Edenbridge TN8 7BD. Jim French. *5m SE of Edenbridge via B2027. ¾ m from Chiddingstone Village on L. Garden a short walk along unmade rd following footpath sign, parking at top of this unmade rd.* **Sun 12 June (11-5). Adm £3, chd free. Also open 3 Post Office Cottages.**
Country cottage garden surrounded by an old hedge consisting of oak, hawthorn and damsons. The garden has shrubs, perennials, annuals and vegetables with a selection of fruit and ornamental trees all mixed in together. Natural pond with woodland

surround and only a light hand being laid on nature.

15 NEW CHAPEL HOUSE

Thorne Hill, Ramsgate CT12 5DS. Andrew Montgomery. *4m W of Ramsgate. From Canterbury take A253 towards Ramsgate, from Sandwich take A256 towards Ramsgate. At Sevenscore r'about take slip rd turn R, Cottington Rd, follow Thorne Farm signs.* **Sat 11, Sun 12 June (2-5). Adm £5. Regret, no children. Tea.**
A small, formal garden surrounding a converted C13 chapel (not open). Apple trees, roses, lavender and cranesbills enclosed by old brick and flint walls. A vegetable garden, small courtyard with fountain and an orchard walk leading to a Rotunda. Because of unfenced ponds and a working farm, unsuitable for children. Uneven paving and steps may cause difficulties.

  ♿ ❀ ☕

16 ◆ CHARTWELL

Mapleton Road, Westerham TN16 1PS. National Trust, 01732 868381, chartwell@nationaltrust.org.uk, www.nationaltrust.org.uk. *4m N of Edenbridge, 2m S of Westerham. Fork L off B2026 after 1½ m. For NGS:* **Wed 11 May (10-4). Adm £6.70, chd free. For other opening times and information, please phone, email or visit garden website.**
Informal gardens on hillside with glorious views over Weald of Kent. Water garden and lakes together with red brick wall built by Sir Winston Churchill, former owner of Chartwell. Lady Churchill's rose garden. Avenue

of golden roses runs down the centre of a must see productive kitchen garden. Hard paths to Lady Churchill's rose garden and the terrace. Some steep slopes and steps.

  ♿ 🐕 ❀ 🚌 ☕

17 CHEVENING

Nr Sevenoaks TN14 6HG. The Board of Trustees of the Chevening Estate, www.cheveninghouse.com. *4m NW of Sevenoaks. Turn N off A25 at Sundridge T-lights on to B2211; at Chevening Xrds 1½ m turn L.* **Sun 5 June (2-5). Adm £5, chd £2. Home-made teas.**
27 acres with lawns, woodland, lake, maze and parterre. Gentle slopes, gravel paths throughout.

  ♿ 🐕 ❀ ☕

18 ◆ CHIDDINGSTONE CASTLE

Hill Hoath Road, Chiddingstone, Edenbridge TN8 7AD. Trustees of the Denys Eyre Bower Bequest, 01892 870347, events@chiddingstonecastle.org. uk, www.chiddingstonecastle.org.uk. *From B2027 in village of Bough Beech follow signs to Castle via Mill Lane. Entrance is on Hill Hoath Rd.* **For NGS: Sun 26 June (1-5). Adm £4.50, chd free. Cream teas. For other opening times and information, please phone, email or visit garden website.**
Chiddingstone Castle, a historic garden, is surrounded by 35 acres of unspoilt informal gardens incl a large fishing lake, waterfall and woodland. During spring the East Meadow is a riot of daffodils and cherry trees blossom in the Japanese Earthquake Memorial Orchard. Beautiful views from the North Lawn, and the South Lawn leads to the restored Grade II* Victorian Orangery. Chiddingstone Castle's history can be traced to C16. It now houses the remarkable collections of the late antiquarian, Denys Eyre Bower - featuring Japanese, Egyptian and Buddhist artefacts. A new grass maze garden, The Fields of Eternity, links to the Egyptian antiquities within the house. Tea rooms serving cream teas and gift shop also open. The path to village across lake suitable for wheelchairs, although steep in places. All other paths are either grass or gravel.

  ♿ 🐕 ❀ 🚌 ☕

19 ◆ **CHILHAM CASTLE**
Canterbury CT4 8DB. Mr & Mrs Wheeler, 01227 733100, chilhamcastleinfo@gmail.com, www.chilham-castle.co.uk. *6m SW of Canterbury, 7m NE of Ashford, centre of Chilham Village. Follow NGS signs from A28 or A252 up to Chilham village square & through main gates of Chilham Castle.* **For NGS: Sat 20 Aug (10.30-5). Adm £5, chd free. Light refreshments. For other opening times and information, please phone, email or visit garden website.**
The garden surrounds Jacobean house 1616 (not open). C17 terraces with herbaceous borders. Topiary frames the magnificent views with lake walk below. Extensive kitchen and cutting garden beyond spring bulb filled Quiet Garden. Established trees and ha-ha lead onto park. May 21-22nd, celebrations for 400th anniversary of completion of Chilham Castle. Partial wheelchair access.

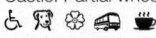

20 **CHURCHFIELD**
Pilgrims Way, Postling, Hythe CT21 4EY. Mr & Mrs C Clark, 01303 863558, coulclark@hotmail.com. *2m NW of Hythe. From M20 J11 turn S onto A20. 1st L after ½ m on bend take rd signed Lyminge. 1st L into Postling.* **Visits by arrangement Apr to Sept in conjunction with West Court Lodge. Groups max 35. Adm £5.00, chd free. Home-made teas.**
At the base of the Downs, springs rising in this garden form the source of the East Stour. Two large areas are home to wildfowl and fish and the banks have been planted with drifts of primula and large leaved herbaceous. The rest of the 5 acre garden is a Kent cobnut platt and vegetable garden, large grass areas and naturally planted borders with an area under development as a prairie garden. Postling Church open for visitors. Areas around water may be slippery. Children must be carefully supervised.

21 **THE COACH HOUSE**
Kemsdale Road, Hernhill, Faversham ME13 9JP. Alison & Philip West, 07801 824867, alison.west@kemsdale.plus.com. *3m E of Faversham. At J7 of M2 take A299, signed Margate. After 600 metres take 1st exit signed Hernhill, take 1st L over dual carriageway to T-junction, turn R & follow yellow NGS signs.* **Sat 4, Sun 5 June (12-6). Adm £3.50, chd free. Cream teas. Visits also by arrangement May to Aug.**
The ½ acre garden has views over surrounding fruit producing farmland. Sloping terraced site, and island beds with yr-round interest, a pond room, herbaceous borders containing bulbs, shrubs, and perennials, and a developing tropical bed. The different areas are connected by flowing curved paths. Unusual planting on light sandy soil where wildlife is encouraged. Most of garden accessible to wheelchairs. Seating available in all areas.

22 ◆ **COBHAM HALL**
Cobham DA12 3BL. Mr D Standen (Bursar), 01474 823371, www.cobhamhall.com. *3m W of Rochester, 8m E of M25 J2. Ignore SatNav directions to Lodge Lane. Entrance drive is off Brewers Rd, 50 metres E from Cobham/Shorne A2 junction.* **For NGS: Mon 28 Mar, Sun 3 July (2-5). Adm £2.50, chd free. Home-made teas in the Gilt Hall. For other opening times and information, please phone or visit garden website.**
1584 brick mansion (open for tours) and parkland of historical importance, now a boarding and day school for girls. Some herbaceous borders, formal parterres, drifts of daffodils, C17 garden walls, yew hedges and lime avenue. Humphry Repton designed 50 hectares of park, most garden follies restored in 2009. Combined with tours to the Darnley Mausoleum. Film location for BBC's Bleak House series and films by MGM and Universal. ITV serial The Great Fire. CBBC filmed serial 1 & 2 of Hetty Feather. Gravel and slab paths through gardens. Land uneven, many slopes. Stairs and steps in Main Hall. Please call in advance to ensure assistance.

23 ◆ **COPTON ASH**
105 Ashford Road, Faversham ME13 8XW. Drs Tim & Gillian Ingram, 01795 535919, coptonash@yahoo.co.uk, www.coptonash.plus.com. *½ m S of A2, Faversham. On A251 Faversham to Ashford rd. Opp E bound J6 with M2.* **Sun 14 Feb (12-4); Sun 10, Sun 24 Apr, Sun 15 May (12-5). Adm £3.50, chd free.**
Home-made teas. Home-made soup (Feb). **2017: Sun 12 Feb. Visits also by arrangement Feb to Sept.**
Garden grown out of a love and fascination with plants from an early age. Contains very wide collection incl many rarities and newly introduced species raised from wild seed. Special interest in woodland flowers, snowdrops and hellebores with flowering trees and shrubs of spring. Wide range of drought tolerant plants. Raised beds with choice alpines and bulbs. Small alpine nursery. Gravel drive and some narrow grass paths.

During spring the East Meadow is a riot of daffodils . . .

24 **NEW** **CROMLIX**
Otford Lane, Halstead, Sevenoaks TN14 7EB. The Kitchener family. *5m NW of Sevenoaks, 3m from M25 J4. Exit M25 at J4 for A21/A224. After ½ m, 1st exit at r'bout for Badgers Mount A224. At next r'bout 3rd exit to Shoreham Lane, past Cock Inn, turn L at Xrds to Otford Ln. Field entrance to garden 400yds on L.* **Sat 18, Sun 19 June (1-5). Adm £5, chd free. Home-made teas.** *Donation to West Kent Cruse Bereavement Care.*
13 acre grounds, of which 7 acres are a botanist's garden with some unusual plants. Colourful herbaceous borders, scented garden, croquet and tennis lawns contrast with informal wooded walks opening up varied vistas. Laid out in the 1960s with specimen trees incl Giant Redwood and further enhanced since 2010; many bamboos. Wisteria covers tree tops and shaded areas accommodate c.400 ferns.

The Blacksmiths Arms

© Leigh Clapp

trees, studio and a greenhouse. Designed for hospitality and entertaining. The Landmark Community Garden: The emphasis is on useful native plants, self seeding, edible annuals, fruiting perennials and useful foliage. Approx 130 different plants in the garden, all labelled. Gleaners: Down a pretty alleyway there is a secret garden. A colourful courtyard leading into a vibrant cottage garden with a summer house. Partial wheelchair access at 53 Sandown Rd and 20 West Lea. No access at Gleaners.

 🏵️ ☕

27 ◆ DODDINGTON PLACE
Church Lane, Doddington, Sittingbourne ME9 0BB. Mr & Mrs Richard Oldfield, 01795 886101, www.doddingtonplacegardens.co.uk. *6m SE of Sittingbourne. From A20 turn N opp Lenham or from A2 turn S at Teynham or Ospringe (Faversham), all 4m.* **For NGS: Wed 20 Apr, Sun 15 May, Wed 27 July, Sun 25 Sept (11-5). Adm £6, chd £2. Home-made teas. For other opening times and information, please phone or visit garden website.**
10 acre garden, landscaped with wide views; trees and cloud clipped yew hedges; woodland garden with azaleas and rhododendrons; Edwardian rock garden recently renovated (not wheelchair accessible); formal garden with mixed borders. New gothic folly. Wheelchair access possible to majority of gardens except Rock Garden.

28 DOWNS COURT
Church Lane, Boughton Aluph, Ashford TN25 4EU. Mr & Mrs Bay Green, 07984 558945, bay@baygee.com. *4m NE of Ashford. From A28 Ashford or Canterbury, after Wye Xrds take next turn NW to Boughton Aluph Church. Fork R at pillar box, garden only drive on R.* **Visits by arrangement May to July. Adm £5.00, chd free. Coaches welcome, no size restriction. Light refreshments.**
3 acre downland garden on alkaline soil with fine trees, mature yew and box hedges, mixed borders with many unusual plants. Shrub roses and rose arch pathway, small parterre. Sweeping lawns and lovely views over surrounding countryside.

25 34 CROSS ROAD
Walmer CT14 9LB. Mr Peter Jacob & Mrs Margaret Wilson. *A258 Dover to Deal. In Upper Walmer turn L into Station Rd. Under railway bridge, Cross Rd is 2nd R. N.B. Do not approach from Ringwould as SatNav suggests.* **Sun 17 Apr, Sun 19 June (11-5). Adm £3.50, chd free. Also open The Old Bakehouse.**
An exciting and lovely garden combining great artistic sensibility with an extensive and fascinating variety of plants. ¹/₃ acre plantsman's garden. Collection of daphnes, hardy geraniums, herbaceous beds, unusual trees, shrubs and alpines. Home-made teas at The Old Bakehouse.

🏵️

GROUP OPENING

26 NEW DEAL GARDENS
Deal CT14 6EB. Lyn & Peter Buller. *A258 to Deal. Signs from all town car parks, maps & tickets at all gardens.* **Sun 3 July (10-4). Combined adm £5, chd free. Home-made teas at 20 West Lea and 53 Sandown Road.**

NEW GLEANERS
The High Street
Lyn Freeman & Barry Popple

NEW THE LANDMARK GARDEN
The High Street
Imogen Jenkins on behalf of the DWCA
www.facebook.com/thelandmarkgarden

NEW 53 SANDOWN ROAD
Robin Green & Ralph Cade

NEW 20 WEST LEA
Jan Ware

NEW 88 WEST STREET
Lyn & Peter Buller

Start your tour from any town car park (there will be signs from here). Tickets and maps available at all the gardens. 20 West Lea: Small, beach inspired garden packed full of interest through creative use of space and colourful planting, and a small beach house. 88 West Street: Small cottage garden, with beds packed full of perennials, shrubs, grasses, clematis and roses. Shade garden and sunken pot ponds. Finalist Kent Life Garden of the Year. 53 Sandown Road: Three rooms incl decked terrace with pots, courtyard with water feature and olive

29 **EAGLESWOOD**
Slade Road, Warren Street,
Lenham ME17 2EG. Mike & Edith
Darvill, 01622 858702,
mike.darvill@btinternet.com. *Going
E on A20 nr Lenham, L into
Hubbards Hill for approx 1m then 2nd
L into Slade Rd. Garden 150yds on
R. Coaches permitted.* **Sun 15, Mon
30 May (11-5). Adm £3.50, chd
free. Light refreshments. Visits
also by arrangement May to Oct.**
*Donation to Demelza House
Hospice.*
2 acre plantsman's garden situated
high on N Downs, developed over the
past 28yrs. Wide range of trees and
shrubs (many unusual), herbaceous
material and woodland plants grown
to give yr-round interest, particularly in
spring and for autumn colour. Some
gravel areas. Grass paths may be
slippery when wet.

30 **ELHAM GARDENS**
Elham CT4 6TU. *10m S of
Canterbury, 6m N of Hythe. Enter
Elham from Lyminge (off A20) or
Barham (off A2). Car parking as
directed on entering village. Tickets &
maps from gazebo on main rd opp
Browns estate agents.* **Sat 11, Sun
12 June (1-5). Combined adm £5,
chd free. Home-made teas at the
Old Vicarage.**
Elham boasts a thriving community of
amateur gardeners, many of whom
will open their gardens in this idyllic
setting. Wide range of styles of
garden all within easy walking
distance of each other. Owners on
hand to ensure you make the most of
your visit to the picturesque Elham
valley. Old market town in middle of
Elham Valley. Unspoilt countryside.
Special offer - Ploughman's Lunch
just £5 at The King's Arms, in village
square.

31 **♦ EMMETTS GARDEN**
Ide Hill, Sevenoaks TN14 6BA.
National Trust, 01732 750367,
emmetts@nationaltrust.org.uk,
www.nationaltrust.org.uk. *5m SW
of Sevenoaks. 1¹/₂ m S of A25 on
Sundridge-Ide Hill Rd. 1¹/₂ m N of Ide
Hill off B2042.* **For NGS: Wed 15
June (10-4). Adm £8, chd free.**
**For other opening times and
information, please phone, email or
visit garden website.**
5 acre hillside garden, with the
highest tree top in Kent, noted for its
fine collection of rare trees and

flowering shrubs. The garden is
particularly fine in spring, while a rose
garden, rock garden and extensive
planting of acers for autumn colour
extend the interest throughout the
season. Hard paths to the Old
Stables for light refreshments and
WC. Some steep slopes. Volunteer
driven buggy available for lifts up
steepest hill.

Garden grown out
of a love and
fascination with
plants . . .

32 **EUREKA**
Buckhurst Road, Westerham Hill
TN16 2HR. Gordon & Suzanne
Wright. *Off A233, 1¹/₂ m N of
Westerham, 1m S from centre of
Biggin Hill. 5m from J5 & J6 of M25.
Parking at Westerham Heights
Garden Centre at top of Westerham
Hill on A233, 200yds from garden.
Disabled parking at house.* **Sat 9,
Sun 10 July, Sat 6, Sun 7, Sun 28,
Mon 29 Aug (1.30-5). Adm £4, chd
free. Home-made teas.**
1 acre garden with a riot of colourful
displays in perennial borders and the
cartwheel centre beds, 50 hanging
baskets, 150 tubs and troughs, plus
plenty of sculptures and garden art.
Many quirky surprises, chickens, lots
of seating, and stairs to a viewing
platform. Child friendly. Garden art
incl a 12ft red dragon, a horse's head
carved out of a 200yr old yew tree
stump and 10ft dragonfly on a reed.
Featured in Amateur Gardening
magazine. Partial wheelchair access.

33 **FALCONHURST**
Cowden Pound Road, Markbeech,
Edenbridge TN8 5NR. Mr & Mrs
Charles Talbot,
www.falconhurst.co.uk. *3m SE of
Edenbridge. B2026 at Queens Arms
PH turn E to Markbeech. 2nd drive on
R before Markbeech village. Parking
1st L in paddock if dry.* **Sun 29 May,
Fri 17, Sun 19 June, Fri 1, Fri 8, Fri
29 July, Fri 5 Aug (1.30-5). Adm £5,
chd free. Home-made teas
Sundays only.**
4 acre garden with fabulous views
devised and cared for by the same
family for 160yrs. Deep mixed

borders with old roses, peonies,
shrubs and a wide variety of
herbaceous and annual plants; ruin
garden; walled garden; interesting
mature trees and shrubs; kitchen
garden; wild flower meadows with
woodland and pond walks.
Woodland pigs; orchard chickens;
lambs in the paddocks.

34 **FRITH OLD FARMHOUSE**
Frith Road, Otterden, Faversham
ME13 0DD. Drs Gillian & Peter
Regan, 01795 890556,
peter.regan@cantab.net. *¹/₂ m off
Lenham to Faversham rd. From A20
E of Lenham turn up Hubbards Hill,
follow signs to Eastling. After 4m turn
L into Frith Rd. From A2 in Faversham
turn S towards Brogdale & cont,
turning R 1¹/₂ m beyond Eastling.* **Sun
24 Apr, Sun 15, Sun 29 May (11-5).
Adm £4, chd free. Tea. Visits also
by arrangement Apr to Oct
groups up to 50; please contact
owners in advance.**
A riot of plants growing together as if
in the wild, developed over 30yrs. No
neat edges or formal beds, but a very
wide range of unusual and interesting
plants, together with trees and shrubs
chosen for yr-round appeal. Special
interest in bulbs and woodland
plants. Visitor comments - 'a plethora
of plants', 'inspirational', 'a hidden
gem'. Limited parking. Featured in
Kent Life and RHS The Garden.

35 **GODDARDS GREEN**
Angley Road, Cranbrook
TN17 3LR. John & Linde Wotton,
01580 715507,
jpwotton@gmail.com,
www.goddardsgreen.btck.co.uk. *¹/₂ m SW of Cranbrook. On W of
Angley Rd. (A229) at junction with
High St, opp War Memorial.* **Sun 3
July (12.30-4.30). Adm £5, chd
free. Home-made teas. Visits also
by arrangement Apr to Sept
coaches welcome, but no coach
parking on site.**
Garden of about 2 acres, surrounding
beautiful 500yr old clothier's hall (not
open), laid out in 1920s and
redesigned over past 23yrs to
combine traditional and modern
planting schemes. Fountain, rill and
water garden, borders with bulbs,
herbaceous plants, flowering shrubs,
trees and exotics, birch grove, grass
border, pond, kitchen garden and
mature mixed orchard.

36 ◆ **GODINTON HOUSE & GARDENS**

Godinton Lane, Ashford TN23 3BP. Godinton House Preservation Trust, 01233 643854, info@godintonhouse.co.uk, www.godintonhouse.co.uk. *1¹/₂ m W of Ashford. M20 J9 to Ashford. Take A20 towards Charing & Lenham, then follow brown tourist signs.* **For NGS: Sun 6, Sun 20 Mar (1-6); Fri 24 June (1-8). Adm £5, chd free. Home-made teas. For other opening times and information, please phone, email or visit garden website.**

12 acres complement the magnificent Jacobean house. Terraced lawns lead through herbaceous borders, rose garden and formal lily pond to intimate Italian garden and large walled garden with delphiniums, potager, cut flowers and iris border. March/April the wild garden is a mass of daffodils, fritillaries, other spring flowers. Large collection of Bearded Iris flowering late May. Delphinium Festival (17-26 June). Garden sculpture show (23 July-14 Aug). Macmillan Coffee Morning (Sept). Garden workshop and courses throughout the yr. Featured in Daily Telegraph. Partial wheelchair access to ground floor of house and most of gardens.

37 **GODMERSHAM PARK**

Godmersham CT4 7DT. Mrs Fiona Sunley, 01227 730293. *5m NE of Ashford. Off A28, midway between Canterbury & Ashford.* **Sun 3 Apr, Sun 12 June (1-5). Adm £5, chd free. Home-made teas. Visits also by arrangement Mar to Sept, min 12, max 50.** *Donation to Godmersham Church.*

24 acres restored wilderness and formal gardens set around C18 mansion (not open). Topiary, rose garden, herbaceous borders, walled kitchen garden and recently restored Italian garden. Superb daffodils in spring and roses in June. Historical association with Jane Austen. Also visit the Heritage Centre. Deep gravel paths.

38 ◆ **GOODNESTONE PARK GARDENS**

Wingham, Canterbury CT3 1PL. Francis Plumptre, 01304 840107, www.goodnestoneparkgardens.co. uk. *6m SE of Canterbury. Village lies S of B2046 from A2 to Wingham.*

Brown tourist signs off B2046. **For NGS: Sun 20 Mar (12-5); Sat 4 June (11-5); Sun 2 Oct (12-5). Adm £7, chd £2. Delicious home-made cakes, cream teas and light lunches. For other opening times and information, please phone or visit garden website.**

One of Kent's outstanding gardens and the favourite of many visitors. 14 acres around C18 house (not open) and with views over cricket ground and parkland. Something special yr-round from snowdrops and spring bulbs to the famous walled garden with old fashioned roses and kitchen garden. Outstanding trees and woodland garden with cornus collection and hydrangeas later. 2 arboretums, contemporary gravel garden. Picnics welcome. Featured in The Lady magazine and Country Life.

Owners will be on hand to make sure you make the most of your visit . . .

GROUP OPENING

39 **GRAVESEND GARDENS GROUP**

Gravesend DA12 1JZ. *Approx ¹/₂ m from Gravesend town centre. From A2 take A227 towards Gravesend. At T-lights with Cross Lane turn R then L at next T-lights following yellow NGS signs. Park in Sandy Bank Rd or Leith Park Rd.* **Sat 16, Sun 17 July (12-5). Combined adm £4, chd free. Home-made teas.**

58A PARROCK ROAD
Mr Barry Bowen

68 SOUTH HILL ROAD
Judith Hathrill

Enjoy two lovely gardens, very different in character, close to Windmill Hill which has extensive

views over the Thames estuary. 58A Parrock Road is a beautiful, well established town garden, approx 120ft x 40ft, nurtured by owner for 54yrs. There is a stream running down to a pond, luscious planting along the rocky banks, fascinating water features, mature trees and shrubs, magnificent display of hostas and succulents. 68 South Hill Road is an award winning wildlife garden, showing that wildlife friendly gardens need not be wild. Flowers, herbs and vegetables in the raised beds. Ferns, grasses, perennials and shrubs in the borders and fruit and vegetables grown in containers on the terrace. Tender vegetables thrive in the greenhouse, two ponds planted with native species and wildflowers. Jazz Trio at 58A Parrock Road.

40 ◆ **GREAT COMP GARDEN**

Comp Lane, Platt, nr Borough Green, Sevenoaks TN15 8QS. Great Comp Charitable Trust, 01732 885094, office@greatcompgarden.co.uk, www.greatcompgarden.co.uk. *7m E of Sevenoaks. 2m from Borough Green Station. Accessible from M20 & M26 motorways. A20 at Wrotham Heath, take Seven Mile Lane, B2016; at 1st Xrds turn R; garden on L ¹/₂ m.* **For NGS: Sun 20 Mar, Sun 30 Oct (11-5). Adm £8, chd £3. Light refreshments at The Old Dairy Tearooms. For other opening times and information, please phone, email or visit garden website.**

Skilfully designed 7 acre garden of exceptional beauty. Spacious setting of well maintained lawns and paths lead visitors through plantsman's collection of trees, shrubs, heathers and herbaceous plants. Good autumn colour. Early C17 house (not open). Magnolias, hellebores and snowflakes (leucojum), hamamellis and winter flowering heathers are a great feature in the spring. A great variety of perennials in summer incl salvias, dahlias and crocosmias. Tearoom open daily for morning coffee, home-made lunches and afternoon teas. Garden Curator, William Dyson, awarded Silver Gilt at RHS Chelsea and Gold at RHS Hampton Court for his Salvias. Great Comp Garden is home to the Dyson Salvia collection. Most of garden accessible to wheelchair users. Disabled WC.

41 GREAT MAYTHAM HALL
Maytham Road, Rolvenden, Tenterden TN17 4NE. The Sunley Group, 01580 241346, gmh@greatmaythamhall.co.uk. *3m from Tenterden. Maytham Rd off A28 at Rolvenden Church, ½ m from village on R. Designated parking for visitors.* Wed 27 Apr, Wed 25 May, Wed 29 June, Wed 27 July, Wed 24 Aug (1-4.30). Adm £5, chd free.
Lutyens designed gardens famous for having inspired Frances Hodgson Burnett to write The Secret Garden (pre Lutyens). Parkland, woodland with bluebells. Walled garden with herbaceous beds and rose pergola. Pond garden with mixed shrubbery and herbaceous borders. Interesting specimen trees. Large lawned area, rose terrace with far reaching views.

42 HAVEN
22 Station Road, Minster, Ramsgate CT12 4BZ. Robin Roose-Beresford, 01843 822594, robin.roose@hotmail.co.uk. *Off A299 Ramsgate Rd, take Minster exit from Manston r'bout, straight rd, R fork at church is Station Rd.* Sat 26, Sun 27, Mon 28 Mar, Sat 23, Sun 24 Apr, Sat 28, Sun 29, Mon 30 May, Sat 25, Sun 26 June, Sat 23, Sun 24 July, Sat 27, Sun 28, Mon 29 Aug, Sat 24, Sun 25 Sept, Sat 22, Sun 23 Oct (10-4). Adm £4, chd free. Visits also by arrangement Mar to Oct.
A 300ft garden, designed in the Glade style, which is similar to Forest gardening but more open and with greater use of exotic and unusual trees, shrubs and perennials, with wildlife in mind, devised and maintained by the owner, densely planted in a natural style with meandering stepping stone paths. Two ponds (one for wildlife, one for fish with water lillies), gravel garden, rock garden, bog areas, fernery, Japanese garden, hostas and many exotic, rare and unusual trees, shrubs and plants incl tree ferns and bamboos and yr-round colour. Gold award from Kent Wildlife Trust, runner up Kent Life, Garden of the Year.

43 37 THE HAYDENS
Tonbridge TN9 1NS. Angie Boakes. *N Tonbridge, off Yardley Park Rd (between Shipbourne Rd & Hadlow Rd). Please park on Yardley Park Rd by green & follow signs. Limited disabled parking on rd.* Sun 26 June

(1-5). Adm £3, chd £2. Home-made teas.
A small modern garden redesigned by the current owner in 2014 after trying to grow a peony on a N facing wall! Split into sections which mirror the house, the borders (separated by a slate path) feature roses, cornus, birches, salvia, perennials and grasses plus a small area of planting from a Chelsea Show Garden. Hopefully it will give visitors ideas for typical modern house sized gardens. Winner of Kent Life Amateur Gardener Award. Slate paths.

44 HOATH HOUSE
Chiddingstone Hoath, Edenbridge TN8 7DB. Mr & Mrs Richard Streatfeild, 01342 850362, jane@hoath-house.freeserve.co.uk. *4m SE of Edenbridge via B2026. At Queens Arms PH turn E to Markbeech. Approx 1m E of Markbeech.* Mon 8, Tue 9 Feb (11-4). Daily Mon 7 Mar to Thur 10 Mar (11-4). Adm £5, chd free. Visits also by arrangement.
Mediaeval/Tudor family house (not open) surrounded by mature and unusual young trees, gravel garden in former stable yard, knot garden, shaded garden, herbaceous borders, yew hedges. Massed daffodils, single snowdrops; drive edged with doubles from great grandmother's garden, growing collection of special snowdrops. Home-made teas/soup in this enchanting garden with stunning views over rural Kent. Wheelchair access to many snowdrop views via rough gravel drive.

45 HOGBEN HOUSE
Church Lane, Aldington, Ashford TN25 7EG. Margaret & Rod Gibbs. *From A20 heading towards Sellindge, past sign for Aldington, take next turning on R immed after KOS business centre, Church Lane. Hogben House is 6th property on R.* Sat 4, Sun 5, Sat 11, Sun 12 June (10-4.30). Adm £4, chd free. Home-made teas. Also open Wyckhurst.
Pretty period cottage (not open) situated in the old part of Aldington, with typical cottage garden plantings, herbaceous borders of roses, perennials, shrubs and ornamental trees to the front garden and vegetable garden and orchard to the side and rear. Small water feature and

hand crafted gypsy type caravan in orchard. Wheelchair access to most areas of garden.

46 ◆ HOLE PARK
Benenden Road, Rolvenden, Cranbrook TN17 4JB. Mr & Mrs E G Barham, 01580 241344, www.holepark.com. *4m SW of Tenterden. Midway between Rolvenden & Benenden on B2086. Follow brown tourist signs from Rolvenden.* For NGS: Sun 10 Apr, Wed 4 May, Wed 15 June, Sun 9 Oct (11-6). Adm £7, chd £1. Home-made teas. For other opening times and information, please phone or visit garden website.
Hole Park is proud to stand amongst the group of gardens which first opened in 1927 soon after it was laid out by my great grandfather. Our 15 acre garden is surrounded by parkland with beautiful views and contains fine yew hedges, large lawns with specimen trees, walled gardens, pools and mixed borders combined with bulbs, rhododendrons and azaleas. Massed bluebells in woodland walk, standard wisterias, orchids in flower meadow and glorious autumn colours make this a garden for all seasons. Light lunches available on all openings. Good wheelchair access throughout but beware of steep inclines. Wheelchairs are available for free hire and may be reserved.

47 HONNINGTON FARM GARDENS

Vauxhall Lane, Southborough, Tunbridge Wells TN4 0XD. Mrs Ann Tyler, 01892 536990, ann.honnington@btinternet.com, www.honningtonfarmgardens.co. uk. *Between Tonbridge & Tunbridge Wells. A21 to A26. Large coaches must only access Vauxhall Lane from A26 & use Equestrian Centre car park. Ring for additional directions.* **Visits by arrangement Mar to Oct, groups 20+. Coach 60 seater max. Adm £5.00, chd free. Light refreshments.**

6 acre garden, with natural pool in wild flower meadow and extensive gravel garden. Rose walkways, rockery, lakes and water features. Heavy clay soil enriched yearly producing a wide range of habitats, incl water and bog gardens, primrose and bluebell walks. Wildlife promotion a priority. Wonderful views and herbaceous beds. Glass houses and large vegetable garden. Newly renovated Kent Barn which holds 60 for teas/lunches by prior arrangement. Steep slopes and gravel drives. Disabled WC.

48 NEW HOW GREEN NURSERY

How Green Lane, Hever TN8 7PS. Simon Sutcliffe, 01732 700382, plants@howgreennursery.co.uk, www.howgreennursery.co.uk. *How Green Nursery is 3m from the town of Edenbridge. 1m from Hever Castle.* Sat 20, Sun 21 Aug (10-5). Adm £3, chd free. Home-made teas.

We are a family run trade nursery and supply garden centres, landscapers, designers and local authorities. In recent years, we have grown for the Chelsea Flower Show. We grow an extensive range of perennials, grasses, ferns, alpines, herbs, vegetable plants, patio plants and a small range of shrubs and topiary. We specialise in brand new and desirable introductions. Refreshments will also be available in our summer house and nursery garden. Nursery talk and tour at 11am and 3pm on both Saturday and Sunday. Most of site accessible for wheelchair users, some greenhouse paths very narrow.

49 ◆ IGHTHAM MOTE

Ivy Hatch, Sevenoaks TN15 0NT. National Trust, 01732 810378, ighthammote@nationaltrust.org.uk, www.nationaltrust.org.uk. *6m E of Sevenoaks. Off A25, 2¹/₂ m S of Ightham. Buses from train stns Sevenoaks or Borough Green to Ivy Hatch & Ightham Mote on weekdays.* For NGS: Wed 10 Aug (10-5). Adm £12.50, chd £6.30. Light refreshments in The Mote Cafe. **For other opening times and information, please phone, email or visit garden website.**

14 acre garden and moated medieval manor c1320, first opened for NGS in 1927. North lake and pleasure gardens, ornamental pond and cascade created in early C18. Orchard, enclosed formal vegetable and cutting gardens all contribute to the sense of tranquillity. Wheelchairs available from visitor reception and shop. Ask for a wheeled access guide at visitor reception.

50 ◆ KNOLE

Knole, Sevenoaks TN15 0RP. Lord Sackville, 01732 462100, knole@nationaltrust.org.uk, www.nationaltrust.org.uk. *1¹/₂ m SE of Sevenoaks. Leave M25 at J5 (A21). Park entrance S of Sevenoaks town centre off A225 Tonbridge Rd (opp St Nicholas church). For SatNav use TN13 1HU.* For NGS: Tue 5 July (11-4). Adm £8.50, chd £4.25. Light refreshments. **For other opening times and information, please phone, email or visit garden website.**

Lord Sackville's 26 acre private walled garden includes features which transport you back centuries to horticultural fashions long forgotten. Lose yourself in the C16 wilderness garden and enjoy little seen views of the house. Last entry at 3.30pm. Knole's garden is accessed via the beautiful Orangery space off Green Court. Refreshments are available in the Bookshop Café or from the Outdoor Café in the park. Wheelchair access possible but difficult in poor weather. Assistance dogs are allowed in the garden.

51 KNOWLE HILL FARM

Ulcombe, Maidstone ME17 1ES. The Hon Andrew & Mrs Cairns, 01622 850240, elizabeth.cairns@btinternet.com, www.knowlehillfarmgarden.co.uk. *7m SE of Maidstone. From M20 J8 follow A20 towards Lenham for 2m. Turn R to Ulcombe. After 1¹/₂ m, L at Xrds, after ¹/₂ m 2nd R into Windmill Hill. Past Pepper Box PH, ¹/₂ m 1st L to Knowle Hill.* Sun 7, Sun 21 Feb (11-3). Light refreshments. Sun 3 July (2-6). Home-made teas. Adm £5, chd free. 2017: Sat 4, Sun 5 Feb. **Visits also by arrangement Feb to Sept access for 25-30 seater coaches.**

2 acre garden, created over 30yrs, on S facing slope of N Downs with spectacular views. Snowdrops: Mediterranean and tender plants, roses, agapanthus, verbenas, salvias and grasses, flourish on the light soil. Many unusual plants. Evolving topiary. Lavender ribbons are magnets for bees. Pool and rill enclosed in small walled garden planted mainly with white flowers. New green garden taking shape. Featured in Country Living. Some steep slopes.

Contemporary cottage garden with a gorgeous mix of traditional and modern planting . . .

52 LADHAM HOUSE

Goudhurst TN17 1DB. Mr Guy Johnson. *8m E of Tunbridge Wells. On NE of village, off A262. Through village towards Cranbrook, turn L at The Goudhurst Inn. 2nd R into Ladham Rd, main gates approx 500yds on L.* Sun 8 May (2-5). Adm £5, chd £1. Tea.

Large garden and parkland with rhododendrons, camellias, azaleas and magnolias. Spectacular twin borders, a rose garden and an arboretum containing some fine specimens. Also, an Edwardian sunken rockery, woodland walk, ha-ha and vegetable garden.

53 LEYDENS

Hartfield Road, Edenbridge TN8 5NH. Roger Platts, www.rogerplatts.com. *1m S of Edenbridge. On B2026 towards Hartfield (use Nursery entrance & car park).* Sun 7 Aug (12-5). Adm £4.50, chd free. Tea.

Small private garden of garden designer, nursery owner and author who created NGS Garden at Chelsea in 2002, winning Gold and Best in

Show, and in 2010 Gold and People's Choice for the M&G Garden and Gold in 2013. A wide range of shrubs and perennials incl late summer flowering perennial border adjoining wild flower hay meadow. Kitchen garden. Plants clearly labelled and fact sheet available.

54 ▶ LITTLE GABLES
Holcombe Close, Westerham
TN16 1HA. Mrs Elizabeth James.
Centre of Westerham. Off E side of London Rd A233, 200yds from The Green. Please park in public car park. No parking available at house. **Sat 9, Sun 10 July (2-5). Adm £4, chd free.**
³/₄ acre plant lover's garden extensively planted with a wide range of trees, shrubs, perennials etc, incl many rare ones. Collection of climbing and bush roses. Large pond with fish, water lilies and bog garden. Fruit and vegetable garden. Large greenhouse.

55 ▶ LONG MEADOW
1 Bourne Row, Wellers Town Road, Chiddingstone TN8 7BQ. Ian & Jo Peel, 01892 870705. *5m SE of Edenbridge via B2027. 1m S of Chiddingstone Village. Garden on L, parking on R after Wellers Town sign.* **Sun 28 Aug (11-4). Adm £3, chd free. Home-made teas.** **Visits also by arrangement July & Aug groups 12 max.**
A contemporary cottage garden of ¹/₃ of an acre that wraps around the house with a pond and wonderful countryside views. A gorgeous mix of traditional and modern varieties of late summer perennials and grasses. The colour palette is kept simple but the planting is dense and many plants are designed to peak at the end of summer with shades of pink, purple, copper and bronze. Featured in Period Homes & Interiors and Kent Life.

56 ▶ LORDS
Sheldwich, Faversham ME13 0NJ.
John Sell CBE, 01795 536900,
john@sellwade.co.uk. *4m S of Faversham. From A2 or M2 take A251 towards Ashford. ¹/₂ m S of Sheldwich church find entrance lane on R adjacent to wood. (3¹/₂ m N of Challock Xrds).* **Sun 17 Apr (2-5). Sun 10 July (2-5). Also open 6 Newhouse Farm Cottages. Adm £5, chd free. Home-made teas.**

Visits also by arrangement Apr to July adm incl refreshment.
C18 walled garden and greenhouse. A herb terrace overlooks a citrus standing. Flowery mead beneath medlar and quince trees. Across a grass tennis court a cherry orchard grazed by Jacob sheep. A shady fernery, lawns, ponds and wild area. Old specimen trees include sweet chestnut, planes, copper beech, yew hedges and 120ft tulip tree. Daffodils, primroses, cowslips, tulips, fritillaries in spring. Tea and home-made cake on regular openings. Refreshments by arrangement for by appointment openings. Some gravel paths.

57 ▶ LUTON HOUSE
Selling ME13 9RQ. Sir John & Lady Swire, 07866 601230,
w.stokes266@btinternet.com. *4m SE of Faversham. From A2 (M2) or A251 make for White Lion, entrance 30yds E on same side of rd.* **Sun 3 Apr, Sun 8 May (2-5). Adm £4, chd free. Visits also by arrangement Mar to Oct.**
6 acres; C19 landscaped garden; ornamental ponds; trees underplanted with azaleas, camellias, woodland plants, hellebores, spring bulbs, magnolias, cherries, daphnes, halesias, maples, Judas trees and cyclamen. Depending on the weather, those interested in camellias, early trees and bulbs may like to visit in late Mar/early April. Partial wheelchair access.

58 ▶ ♦ MARLE PLACE
Marle Place Road, Brenchley
TN12 7HS. Mrs Lindel Williams,
01892 722304,
lindelwilliams@googlemail.com,
www.marleplace.co.uk. *8m SE of Tonbridge. At Forstal Farm r'about N of Lamberhurst bypass on A21 take B2162 Horsmonden direction approx 3m. From Brenchley follow brown & white tourism signs 1¹/₂ m.* **For NGS: Sun 20 Mar (11-5). Adm £8.50, chd £4. Sun 3 July (11-5). Combined adm with Orchard End £9, chd free. Home-made teas. For other opening times and information, please phone, email or visit garden website.**
In March dancing daffodils. Victorian gazebo, plantsman's shrub borders, walled scented garden, Edwardian rockery, herbaceous borders, bog and kitchen gardens. Garden sculptures. Arboretum, woodland walks, mosaic terrace, artist's studio. Gallery with contemporary art. Autumn colour. Restored Victorian 40ft greenhouse with orchids. C17 listed house (not open) Guided tour at 2 pm. Cart-bay Café offering light lunches and scrumptious teas (closes at 4pm). All produce from the garden or locally sourced. Ramps in place for stepped areas. Access incl some sloping lawns and gravel paths. Wheelchair users enter free of charge.

St Michael's Cottage, St Michael's Gardens

© Leigh Clapp

59 12 THE MEADOWS

Chelsfield, Orpington BR6 6HS. Mr & Mrs Roger & Jean Pemberton. *3m from J4 on M25. Exit M25 at J4. At r'about 1st exit for A224, next r'about 3rd exit - A224, ½ m, take 2nd L, Warren Rd. Bear L into Windsor Drive. 1st L The Meadway, follow signs to garden.* **Sun 29 May (11-5.30). Adm £4, chd free.**
Front garden Mediterranean style gravel with sun loving plants. Rear ³/₄ acre garden in 2 parts. Semi formal area with two ponds, one Koi and one natural (lots of Spring interest). Mature bamboos, acers, grasses etc and semi wooded area, children's path with 13ft high giraffe, Sumatran tigers and lots of points of interest. Designated children's area. Only children allowed access! Wheelchair access to all parts except small stepped area at very bottom of garden.

60 MERE HOUSE

Mereworth ME18 5NB. Mr & Mrs Andrew Wells, www.mere-house.co.uk. *7m E of Tonbridge. From A26 turn N on to B2016 & then R into Mereworth village. 3¹/₂ m S of M20/M26 junction, take A20, then B2016 to Mereworth.* **Sun 21, Sun 28 Feb, Mon 28 Mar, Sun 10 Apr, Sun 23 Oct (2-5). Adm £4, chd free. Home-made teas. 2017: Sun 19, Sun 26 Feb.**
C18 landscape surrounding 6 acre garden, completely replanted since 1958, bounded to S by lake created 1780. Increasing areas of snowdrops and daffodils in spring. Extensive lawns set off herbaceous borders, ornamental shrubs and trees with yr-round foliage contrast and striking autumn colour. Major tree planting since 1987 storm; woodland, park and lake walks can be enjoyed beyond the garden. Featured in DailyTelegraph's Garden to Visit.

61 ◆ MOUNT EPHRAIM

Hernhill, Faversham ME13 9TX. Mr & Mrs E S Dawes & Mr W Dawes, 01227 751496 or 07516 664151, info@mountephraim.co.uk, www.mountephraimgardens.co.uk. *3m E of Faversham. From end of M2, then A299 take slip rd 1st L to Hernhill, signed to gardens.* **For NGS: Sun 13 Mar, Thur 16 June, Sun 25 Sept (11-5). Adm £7, chd £2.50. Light refreshments in Topiary Tea Rooms. For other**

opening times and information, please phone, email or visit garden website.
Herbaceous border, topiary, daffodils and rhododendrons, rose terraces leading to small lake. Rock garden with pools, water garden, young arboretum. Rose garden with arches and pergola planted to celebrate the Millennium. Magnificent trees. Grass maze. Superb views over fruit farms to Swale estuary. Village craft centre. Cream teas, home-made teas, light refreshments, wine available. Appeared in What's On for coverage of occasional special events. Partial wheelchair access; top part manageable, but whole ten acres could not be described as easy. Disabled WC. Full access to tea room.

The NGS is The QNI's largest single donor

62 MOUNTS COURT FARMHOUSE

Acrise, Folkestone CT18 8LQ. Graham & Geraldine Fish, 01303 840598, geraldine_fish@btinternet.com. *6m NW of Folkestone. From A260 Folkestone to Canterbury rd, turn L at Densole opp Black Horse Inn, 1³/₄ m towards Elham & Lyminge, on N side.* **Visits by arrangement May to Sept, groups 8+. Adm £5.00, chd free.**
Developed from a 1¹/₂ acre horse paddock over 30yrs in surroundings designated as an Area of Outstanding Natural Beauty at a height of 150 metres. Variety of trees, shrubs, grasses and herbaceous plants. Wide winding paths flow through deep, densely planted mixed borders varying from cottage to woodland in character, with an eye to foliage pattern and changing colour mixes. Pond and bog garden.

63 NETTLESTEAD PLACE

Nettlestead ME18 5HA. Mr & Mrs Roy Tucker, www.nettlesteadplace.co.uk. *6m W/SW of Maidstone. Turn S off A26 onto B2015 then 1m on L, next to Nettlestead Church.* **Sun 5 June, Sun 2 Oct (2-5). Adm £5, chd free. Tea.**
C13 manor house in 10 acre plantsman's garden. Large formal rose garden. Large herbaceous garden of island beds with rose and clematis walkway leading to garden of China roses. Fine collection of trees and shrubs; sunken pond garden, terraces, bamboos, glen garden, acer lawn. Young pinetum adjacent to garden. Sculptures. Wonderful open country views. Gravel paths, partial access: sunken pond garden. New large steep bank and lower area in development.

64 NEW 6 NEWHOUSE FARM COTTAGES

Newhouse Lane, Sheldwich, Faversham ME13 9QS. Ms Kylie O'Brien. *Newhouse Lane is on L off A251, just before Sheldwich (from the Faversham direction). House among small cluster of houses, opp big white house.* **Sat 9 July (11-5). Sun 10 July (11-5). Also open Lords. Adm £3, chd free. Home-made teas.**
¹/₂ acre country garden on the edge of Lees Court estate. Est 10yrs ago with classic drought resistant, prairie style and wildlife friendly plantings (gaura, stipas, salvias and artemesias). Terrace garden with yew topiary, wildlife pond and rugosa hedges give way to a cherry orchard surrounded by hollyhocks. Hen enthusiasts will enjoy the two flocks of rare brown and red Sussex hens. Within an AONB.

65 NORTON COURT

Teynham, Sittingbourne ME9 9JU. Tim & Sophia Steel, 07798 804544, sophia@nortoncourt.net. *Off A2 between Teynham & Faversham. L off A2 at Texaco garage into Norton Lane; next L into Provender Lane; L signed Church for car park.* **Mon 6, Tue 7 June (2-5). Adm £5, chd free. Visits also by arrangement May to Sept, min 10, max 30. Conducted tours.**
10 acre garden within parkland setting. Mature trees, topiary, wide lawns and clipped yew hedges. Orchard with mown paths through

wild flowers. Walled garden with mixed borders and climbing roses. Pine tree walk. Formal box and lavender parterre. Tree house in the Sequoia. Church open, adjacent to garden. Flat ground except for 2 steps where ramp is provided.

66 OAK COTTAGE
Elmsted, Ashford TN25 5JT. **Martin & Rachael Castle.** *6m NW of Hythe. From Stone St (B2068) turn W opp the Stelling Minnis turning. Follow signs to Elmsted. Turn L at Elmsted village sign. Limited parking at house. Further parking at Church (7mins walk).* **Thur 21, Sat 23 Apr, Thur 18, Sat 20 Aug (11-4). Adm £3.50, chd free. Home-made teas.**
Get off the beaten track and discover this beautiful ½ acre cottage garden in the heart of the Kent countryside. This plantsman's garden is filled with unusual and interesting perennials, incl a wide range of salvias. There is a small specialist nursery packed with herbaceous perennials. For our April opening a large auricula collection will be showcased in a range of traditional theatres.

67 NEW THE OLD BAKEHOUSE
340 Dover Road, Walmer, Deal CT14 7NX. **Sue Evans.** *On A258 Dover to Deal rd. Opp Thompson Bell PH.* **Sun 17 Apr, Sun 19 June (10-4). Adm £2.50, chd free. Home-made teas. Also open 34 Cross Road.**
Tucked away behind this Georgian cottage in Walmer village is a walled garden full of interest and variety. This is a garden that draws you in and leads you through a Wisteria dominated courtyard to a variety of spaces with their own themes and artistic features. This garden demonstrates what can be done with a small space and a lot of imagination. A delight, full of pleasant surprises. Hot drinks, home-made cakes and snacks served throughout the day.

68 OLD BLADBEAN STUD
Bladbean, Canterbury CT4 6NA. **Carol Bruce,** oldbladbeanstud@sky.com, www.oldbladbeanstud.co.uk. *6m S of Canterbury. From B2068, follow signs into Stelling Minnis, turn R onto Bossingham Rd, then follow yellow NGS signs through single track lanes.*

Suns 29 May, 19, 26 June, 10, 24 July, 7, 21 Aug (2-6). Adm £6, chd free. Cream teas.
5 interlinked gardens all designed and created from scratch by the garden owner on 3 acres of rough grassland between 2003 and 2011. Romantic walled rose garden with over 90 labelled old fashioned rose varieties, tranquil yellow and white garden, square garden with blended pastels borders and Victorian style greenhouse, 300ft long colour schemed symmetrical double borders. An experimental self sufficiency project comprises a wind turbine, rain water collection, solar panels and a ground source heat pump, an organic fruit and vegetable garden. The gardens are maintained entirely by the owner and were designed to be managed as an ornamental ecosystem with a large number of perennial species encouraged to set seed, and with staking, irrigation, mulching and chemical use kept an absolute minimum. Each garden has a different season of interest - please see the garden website for more information. Featured in Country Life, The English Garden Magazine and Period Living Magazine.

Perfect harmony of vistas, contrasts and proportions. Everything that makes an English garden the envy of the world . . .

69 OLD BUCKHURST
Markbeech, Edenbridge TN8 5PH. **Mr & Mrs J Gladstone,** 01342 850825. *4m SE of Edenbridge. B2026, at Queens Arms PH turn E to Markbeech. In approx 1½ m, 1st house on R after leaving Markbeech. Parking in paddock if dry. Last entry 4.30pm.* **Sat 23, Sun 24, Wed 27, Sat 30 Apr (11-5). Sun 8 May (11-5). Also open Stonewall Park. Sat 14, Sat 21 May, Sat 4 June, Wed 13, Sat 23 July (11-5). Sun 7 Aug (11-5). Also open Leydens. Sat 10, Sun 11 Sept (11-5). Adm £4, chd free.**

1 acre partly walled cottage garden around C15 Grade II listed farmhouse with catslip roof (not open). Comments from Visitors' Book: 'perfect harmony of vistas, contrasts and proportions. Everything that makes an English garden the envy of the world'. 'The design and planting is sublime, a garden I doubt anyone could forget'. Stefan Buczacki in Garden News said - 'My favourite cottage garden is Old Buckhurst in Kent'. Mixed borders with roses, clematis, wisteria, poppies, iris, peonies, lavender, July/Aug a wide range of day lilies.

70 NEW OLD CHURCH HOUSE
26a Church Street, Walmer, Deal CT14 7RT. **Christine & Mark Symons.** *A258 Dover to Deal. In Upper Walmer turn on to Church St.* **Sun 14, Wed 31 Aug, Sun 4 Sept (1-6). Adm £3.50, chd free. Home-made teas at 28 Church Street.**
Delightful small garden packed with a wide variety of interesting plants. Gravelled front garden and several areas on different levels divided by pergola, paths and steps, each with their own character. Perennials, shrubs and trees, bamboos and palms, with pond area. Numerous Salvia and waving grasses in late summer.

71 THE OLD PALACE
Old Palace Road, Bekesbourne, Canterbury CT4 5ES. **Mrs Nicky Fry,** 01227 830319, nicolafry@cscope.co.uk. *2m S of Canterbury. A2 towards Dover take Bridge/Bekesbourne exit. Turn R into School Lane, in 500 yds turn R into Old Palace Rd. Parking for small coaches only.* **Sat 25, Sun 26 June (1-5). Adm £5, chd free. Home-made teas. Visits also by arrangement May to July.**
The site of Thomas Cranmer's Old Palace and home of Ian Fleming. 4 acre garden created by present owner with many interesting features. A natural pond, planted to encourage wildlife. 100yr old Scots pines, other specimen trees incl large flowering tulip tree. Walled potager with rose pergola and espaliered fruit trees. New laburnum and allium walkway and herbaceous border planted in 2013.

© Leigh Clapp

1 Brickwall Cottages

resident landscape designer. Divided into rooms with linking vistas. Incl hot borders, white garden, exotics, oak and glass summerhouse amongst magnolias. Dramatic changes in level. Formal pool with damp garden, ornamental vegetable potager. Wildlife orchards and woodland walks.

72 THE OLD RECTORY

Valley Road, Fawkham, Longfield DA3 8LX. Karin & Christopher Proudfoot, 01474 707513, keproudfoot@firenet.uk.net. *1m S of Longfield. Midway between A2 & A20, on Valley Rd 1½ m N of Fawkham Green, 0.3m S of Fawkham church, opp sign for Gay Dawn Farm/Corinthian Sports Club. Parking on drive only. Not suitable for coaches.* **Visits by arrangement in Feb for individuals and groups, 20 max. Adm £4.00, chd free. Home-made teas. Visits by arrangement also available Feb 2017.**
1½ acres with impressive display of long established naturalised snowdrops and winter aconites; over 70 named snowdrops added recently. Garden developed around the snowdrops over 30yrs, incl hellebores, pulmonarias and other early bulbs and flowers, with foliage perennials, shrubs and trees, also natural woodland. Gentle slope, gravel drive, some narrow paths.

73 THE ORANGERY

Mystole, Chartham, Canterbury CT4 7DB. Rex Stickland & Anne Prasse, 01227 738348, rex@mystole.fsnet.co.uk. *5m SW of Canterbury. Turn off A28 through Shalmsford Street. In 1½ m at Xrds turn R downhill. Cont, ignoring rds on L & R. Ignore drive on L - Mystole*

House only. At sharp bend in 600yds turn L into private drive. **Sun 22 May (1-6); Sat 30, Sun 31 July (1-5). Adm £4.50, chd free. Home-made teas. Visitors also welcome by arrangement Apr to Sept.**
1½ acre gardens around C18 orangery, now a house (not open). Front gardens, established well stocked herbaceous border and large walled garden with a wide variety of shrubs and mixed borders. Splendid views from terraces over ha-ha and paddocks to the lovely Chartham Downs. Water features and very interesting collection of modern sculptures set in natural surroundings. Ramps to garden.

74 ORCHARD END

Cock Lane, Spelmonden Road, Horsmonden TN12 8EQ. Mr Hugh Nye, 01892 723118, hughnye@aol.com. *8m E of Tunbridge Wells. From A21 going S turn L at r'bout onto B2162 to Horsmonden. After 2m turn R onto Spelmonden Rd. After ½ m turn R into Cock Lane. Garden on R.* **Sun 3 July (11-5). Combined adm with Marle Place £9, chd free. Sat 23, Sun 24 July (11-5). Adm £4, chd free. Home-made teas. Visits also by arrangement, groups 40 max.** *Donation to The Amyloidosis Foundation.*
Contemporary classical garden within a 4 acre site. Made over 15yrs by

75 ORCHARD HOUSE, SPENNY LANE

Claygate, Marden, Tonbridge TN12 9PJ. Mr & Mrs Lerwill, 01892 730662, jeanette@lerwill.com. *Just off B2162 between Collier St & Horsmonden. Spenny Lane is adjacent to White Hart PH. Orchard House is 1st house on R about 400m from PH.* **Sun 22 May, Sun 21 Aug (11-4). Adm £4, chd free. Home-made teas.**
A relatively new garden created within the last 10yrs. Gravel garden with potted tender perennials, cottage garden and herbaceous borders. Potager with vegetables, fruit and flowers for cutting. Bee friendly borders. Hornbeam avenue underplanted with camassia. Small nursery on site specialising in herbaceous perennials and ornamental grasses. Featured in The English Garden, Kent Life and Period Homes and Interiors. Access for wheelchairs but some pathways are gravel, grassed areas uneven in places.

76 PARSONAGE OASTS

Hampstead Lane, Yalding ME18 6HG. Edward & Jennifer Raikes, 01622 814272, jmraikes@parsonageoasts.plus. com. *6m SW of Maidstone. On B2162 between Yalding village & stn, turn off at Anchor PH over canal bridge, cont 150yds up lane. House & car park on L.* **Sun 3 Apr (2-4.30). Adm £4, chd free. Home-made teas. Visits also by arrangement Apr to Aug.**
Our garden has a lovely position on the bank of the R Medway. Typical Oast House (not open) often featured on calendars and picture books of Kent. 70yr old garden now looked after by grandchildren of its creator. ¾ acre garden with walls, daffodils, crown imperials, shrubs, clipped box and a spectacular magnolia. Small woodland on river bank. Unfenced river bank. Gravel paths.

77 ◆ **PENSHURST PLACE & GARDENS**
Penshurst TN11 8DG. Lord & Lady De L'Isle, 01892 870307, www.penshurstplace.com. *6m NW of Tunbridge Wells. SW of Tonbridge on B2176, signed from A26 N of Tunbridge Wells.* **For NGS: Fri 9 Sept (10.30-6). Adm £8.50, chd £6. Cream teas. For other opening times and information, please phone or visit garden website.**
11 acres of garden dating back to C14; garden divided into series of rooms by over a mile of yew hedge; profusion of spring bulbs; formal rose garden; famous peony border. Woodland trail and arboretum. Yr-round interest. Toy museum.
♿ ❀ ☕

78 **PHEASANT BARN**
Church Road, Oare ME13 0QB. Paul & Su Vaight, 01795 591654, paul.vaight@btinternet.com. *2m NW of Faversham. Entering Oare from Faversham, turn R at Three Mariners PH towards Harty Ferry. Garden 400yds on R, before church. Parking on roadside.* **Sat 11, Sun 12 June (1-5). Combined adm with Pheasant Farm £8, chd free. Home-made teas Pheasant Barn (Sat 11) and Pheasant Farm (Sun 12). Sun 3 July. Visits also by arrangement Apr to July.**
Series of smallish gardens around award winning converted farm buildings in beautiful situation overlooking Oare Creek. Main area is nectar rich planting in formal design with a contemporary twist inspired by local landscape. Also vegetable garden, parterre, water features, wild flower meadow and labyrinth. July optimum for wild flowers. Spring blossom. Kent Wildlife Trust Oare Marshes Bird Reserve within 1m. Two village inns serving lunches/dinners.
🐕 ☕

79 **PHEASANT FARM**
Church Road, Oare, Faversham ME13 0QB. Jonathan & Lucie Neame, 01795 535366, neamelucie@gmail.com. *2m NW of Faversham. Enter Oare from Faversham. R at Three Mariners PH towards Harty Ferry. Garden 450yds on R, beyond Pheasant Barn, before church. Parking on roadside & as directed.* **Sun 15 May (12-5). Adm £4, chd free. Home-made teas. Sat 11, Sun 12 June (1-5). Combined adm with Pheasant Farm £8, chd free. Home-made**

teas Pheasant Barn (Sat 11) and Pheasant Farm (Sun 12). **Visits also by arrangement May & June, groups of 10-30 welcome.**
Redesigned in 2008, a walled garden surrounding C17 farmhouse with outstanding views over Oare marshes and creek. Main garden with shrubs and herbaceous plants. Infinity lawn overlooking creek. Circular walk through orchard and adjoining churchyard. Two local Public Houses serving lunches. Wheelchair access in main garden only.
♿ ☕

80 **PLACKETTS HOLE**
Bicknor, nr Sittingbourne ME9 8BA. Allison & David Wainman, 01622 884258, allison@kwes.org.uk. *5m S of Sittingbourne. W of B2163. Bicknor is signed from Hollingbourne Hill & from A249 at Stockbury Valley. Placketts Hole is midway between Bicknor & Deans Hill.* **Sun 5 June (2-6.30). Adm £5, chd free. Light refreshments. Visits also by arrangement May to July, groups 2-20 welcome.**
Mature 3 acre garden in Kent Downland valley incl herbaceous borders, rose and formal herb garden, small, walled kitchen garden and informal pond intersected by walls, hedges and paths. Many unusual plants, trees and shrubs and small wildflower calcareous meadow. Most of garden accessible by wheelchair.
♿ ❀ ☕

81 **PORT LYMPNE, THE ASPINALL FOUNDATION**
Aldington Road, Lympne, Hythe CT21 4PD. The Aspinall Foundation, 08448 424647, info@aspinallfoundation.org. *Follow signs from M20, J11, to Port Lympne Reserve. Park in Main customer car park.* **Mon 15 Aug (10-3). Adm £6, chd free. Howletts/Port Lympne passport holders half price. Home-made teas.**
Port Lympne Mansion Hotel. 15 acres of beautiful landscaped grounds cut out of the old sea cliffs overlooking Romney Marsh and out to the English Channel. Features incl formal ponds, chessboard and striped gardens with an outdoor staircase - Italian inspired. Lunch available at the Mansion Hotel 12noon - 2.30pm. Full afternoon tea also available. Partial wheelchair access. Historical site with steps and terraces.
♿ ❀ 🚌 🛏 ☕

82 **3 POST OFFICE COTTAGES**
Chiddingstone Causeway, Tonbridge TN11 8JP. Julie & Graham Jones-Ellis. *Approx 6m W of Tonbridge & approx 6m E of Edenbridge. On B2027 Clinton Lane into Chiddingstone Causeway same side as PO, garden is end of terrace cottage with hedge & small gravel driveway.* **Sun 15 May (12-5.30). Sun 12 June (12-5.30). Also open 9 Chantlers Cottages. Sun 28 Aug (12-5.30). Also open Long Meadow. Adm £3.50, chd free. Home-made teas.**
Small but charming cottage garden, with large selection of clematis and over 30 varieties of roses. Herbaceous borders filled with colour in May and June, with roses in their second flush in late August along with late flowering perennials. Several seating areas and small water features.
🐕 ❀ ☕

83 **POTMANS HEATH HOUSE**
Wittersham TN30 7PU. Dr Alan & Dr Wilma Lloyd Smith, 01797 270221, potmansheath@gmail.com. *1½ m W of Wittersham. Between Wittersham & Rolvenden, 1m from junction with B2082. 200yds E of bridge over Potmans Heath Channel.* **Sun 1 May, Sun 19 June (2-6). Adm £5, chd free. Home-made teas. Visits also by arrangement Mar to Oct groups 20 max welcome. Refreshments on request.**
Large compartmentalised country garden. Our specialities are widespread naturalised bulbs and spectacular blossom in spring, followed by a variety of climbing roses and mixed borders in summer. Part walled vegetable garden, greenhouses. Specimen trees, some unusual. Orchards. Adjoining parkland with duck ponds. Rich variety of garden birds. Wheelchair users welcome. Some awkward slopes but generally good.
♿ 🐕 ☕

84 ◆ QUEX GARDENS

Quex Park, Birchington CT7 0BH. Powell-Cotton Museum, 01843 842168, enquiries@quexmuseum.org, www.quexpark.co.uk/museum/quex-gardens/. *3m W of Margate. Follow signs for Quex Park on approach from A299 then A28 towards Margate, turn R into B2048 Park Lane. Quex Park is on L.* **For NGS: Sun 10 July (10-5). Adm £4, chd £3. Cream teas. For other opening times and information, please phone, email or visit garden website.**

10 acres of woodland and gardens with fine specimen trees unusual on Thanet, spring bulbs, wisteria, shrub borders, old figs and mulberries, herbaceous borders. Victorian walled garden with cucumber house, long glasshouses, cactus house, fruiting trees. Peacocks, dovecote, woodland walk, wildlife pond, children's maze, croquet lawn, picnic grove, lawns and fountains. Head Gardener will be available on NGS open days to give tours and answer questions. Mama Feelgoods Boutique Café serving morning coffee, lunch or afternoon tea. Quex Barn farmers market selling local produce and serving breakfasts to evening meals. Picnic sites available. Garden almost entirely flat with tarmac paths. Sunken garden has sloping lawns to the central pond.

Traditional cottage garden so it cannot be seen all at once . . .

85 11 RAYMER ROAD

Penenden Heath, Maidstone ME14 2JQ. Mrs Barbara Badham. *1m from J6 M20. At M20, J6 at Running Horse r'about take Penenden Heath exit along Sandling Lane towards Bearsted. At T-lights turn into Downsview Rd & follow yellow NGS signs.* **Sun 1 May, Sun 24 July (11-4). Adm £3.50, chd free. Home-made teas.**

Inspirational small garden with lovely views of the Downs, divided into different areas and intensely planted for yr-round interest. Cottage garden border, oriental themed pond, secret woodland garden plus a selection of ferns and hostas arranged under the canopy of a strawberry tree. Organic fruit and vegetables in raised beds and containers, minarette fruit trees underplanted with wild flowers.

86 43 THE RIDINGS

Chestfield, Whitstable CT5 3QE. David & Sylvie Sayers, 01227 500775, sylviebuat-menard@hotmail.com. *Nr Whitstable. From M2 heading E cont onto A299. In 3m take A2990. From r'about on A2990 at Chestfield, turn onto Chestfield Rd, 5th turning on L onto Polo Way which leads into The Ridings.* **Visits by arrangement Apr to Sept for groups 8+. Coach 25 seater max. Adm £3.50, chd free. Light refreshments.**

Delightful small garden brimming with interesting plants both in the front and behind the house. Many different areas. Dry gravel garden in front, raised beds with alpines and bulbs and borders with many unusual perennials and shrubs.

87 ◆ RIVERHILL HIMALAYAN GARDENS

Riverhill, Sevenoaks TN15 0RR. The Rogers Family, 01732 459777, sarah@riverhillgardens.co.uk, www.riverhillgardens.co.uk. *2m S of Sevenoaks on A225. Leave A21 at A225 & follow signs for Riverhill Himalayan Gardens.* **For NGS: Tue 26 Apr, Wed 29 June (10.30-5). Adm £7.75, chd £5.75. Light refreshments. For other opening times and information, please phone, email or visit garden website.**

Beautiful hillside garden, privately owned by the Rogers family since 1840. Extensive views across the Weald of Kent. Spectacular rhododendrons, azaleas and fine specimen trees. Bluebell and natural woodland walks. Rose Garden. Walled Garden has extensive new planting, terracing and water feature. Children's adventure playground, den building trail, hedge maze and Yeti Spotting. Cafe serving freshly ground coffee, speciality teas, light lunches, home-made cream teas, cakes, gluten free cakes and soya milk.

Wheelchair access to Walled Garden only. Good access to café, shop and tea terrace (no disabled WC).

88 NEW ROCK COTTAGE

New Church Road, Bilsington, Ashford TN25 7LA. Bill & Penny Sisley. *6¹/₂ m SE of Ashford. From M20, J10 take A2070 to Hastings. Join B2067 to Hamstreet, turn L on B2067 towards Bilsington. Proceed 2¹/₂ m, at White Horse PH turn R, onto New Church Rd.* **Sat 4, Sun 5 June, Sat 10, Sun 11 Sept (10-6). Adm £4.50, chd free. Tea.**

Tranquil 2 acre garden, created by the owners over the last 30yrs. A surprise around every corner with a series of garden rooms and a mixture of styles. Large collection of clematis and rambling roses. Topiary garden, lime walk, wild flower meadow, living willow and native hedges, wildlife pond, fruit orchard and trained fruit. Specimen trees and shrubs, Mediterranean garden. Partial wheelchair access.

89 ROCK FARM

Gibbs Hill, Nettlestead ME18 5HT. Mrs S E Corfe, 01622 812244. *6m SW of Maidstone. Turn S off A26 onto B2015, then 1m S of Wateringbury turn R up Gibbs Hill.* **Wed 29 June, Sun 3 July (11-6). Adm £4, chd free. Visits also by arrangement May to Sept.** *Donation to Nettlestead Church.*

2 acre garden set around old Kentish farmhouse (not open) in beautiful setting; created with emphasis on yr-round interest and ease of maintenance. Plantsman's collection of shrubs, trees and perennials for alkaline soil; extensive herbaceous border, vegetable area, bog garden and plantings around two large natural ponds. Steep paths.

90 ◆ ST CLERE

Kemsing, Sevenoaks TN15 6NL. Mr & Mrs Simon & Eliza Ecclestone, www.stclere.com. *6m NE of Sevenoaks. 1m E of Seal on A25, turn L signed Heaverham. In Heaverham turn R signed Wrotham. In 75yds straight ahead marked private rd; 1st L to house.* **Sun 12 June (2-5). Adm £5. Home-made teas in Garden Room.**

4 acre garden, full of interest. Formal terraces surrounding C17 mansion (not open), with beautiful views of the

Kent countryside. Herbaceous and shrub borders, productive kitchen and herb gardens, lawns and rare trees. Garden tours with Head Gardener at 2.30pm and 3.45pm (£1 per person). Some gravel paths and small steps.

GROUP OPENING

91 ST MICHAEL'S GARDENS
Roydon Hall Road, East Peckham TN12 5NH. *5m NE of Tonbridge, 5m SW of Maidstone. Turn off A228 between Mereworth & Paddock Wood into Roydon Hall Rd. Gardens ¹/₂ m up hill on L.* **Sun 15 May, Sun 5 June (2-4.30). Combined adm £5, chd free. Home-made teas.** *Donation to Friends of St Michael's Church, Roydon.*

ST MICHAEL'S COTTAGE
Mr Peter & Mrs Pauline Fox

ST MICHAEL'S HOUSE
The Magan family

A Victorian house and cottage garden come together to provide colour, scent and inspiration in April and June in this rural village. The year unfolds at the grey stone old vicarage with a lovely display of tulips in spring, followed by irises, then a mass of roses from red hot to old soft colours, all complemented by yew topiary hedges and wonderful views from the meadow. The traditional cottage garden, with a wildlife area, was designed so it cannot be seen all at once. Explore and enjoy the collection of lavenders, hostas, clematis, ferns, heathers and heucheras. Southdown sheep and lambs, Carp lake. Partial wheelchair access to St Michael's Cottage.

92 ◆ THE SECRET GARDENS OF SANDWICH AT THE SALUTATION
Knightrider Street, Sandwich CT13 9EW. Mr & Mrs Dominic Parker, 01304 619919, enquiries@the-salutation.com, www.the-secretgardens.co.uk. *In the heart of Sandwich. Turn L at Bell Hotel & into Quayside car park. Entrance in far R corner of car park.* **For NGS: Wed 30 Mar, Thur 23 June, Tue 20 Sept (10-5). Adm £7, chd free. Light refreshments. For other opening times and**

information, please phone, email or visit garden website.
3¹/₂ acres of ornamental and formal gardens designed by Sir Edwin Lutyens and Gertrude Jekyll in 1911 surrounding Grade I listed house. Designated historic park and garden, lake. White, yellow, spring, woodland, rose, kitchen, vegetable and herbaceous gardens. Designed to provide yr-round changing colour. Unusual plants for sale. Tea Rooms open offering cream teas and light lunches. Gardens, tearoom and shop are wheelchair friendly.

93 SANDOWN
Plain Road, Smeeth, nr Ashford TN25 6QX. Malcolm & Pamela Woodcock, 01303-813478, pmw@woodcock.mail1.co.uk. *4m SE of Ashford. Exit J10 onto A20, take 2nd L signed Smeeth, turn R Woolpack Hill, past garage on L, past next L, garden on L. From A20 in Sellindge at Church, turn R carry on 1m. Park in layby on hill.* **Sun 1, Mon 2, Sun 22, Mon 30 May, Sun 12, Sun 26 June, Sun 24 July, Sun 28, Mon 29 Aug (1-5). Adm £3.50. Cream teas. Visits also by arrangement May to Aug groups 20 max.**
Our small compact Japanese style garden and Koi pond has visitor book comments such as: inspirational, just like Japan, stunning a hidden gem. There is a Japanese arbour, tea house/veranda, waterfall and stream. Acers, bamboos, ilex crenata (Cloud Trees), ginkgo, fatsia japonica, akebia quinata, clerodendrum trichotomum, pinus mugos, wisterias, hostas and mind your own business for ground cover. WC available. Regret no small children owing to deep pond. Featured in local Parish magazines and mentioned on Radio Kent.

94 ◆ SCOTNEY CASTLE
Lamberhurst TN3 8JN. National Trust, 01892 893820, scotneycastle@nationaltrust.org.uk, www.nationaltrust.org.uk. *6m SE of Tunbridge Wells. On A21 London - Hastings, brown tourist signs. Bus: (Mon to Sat) Tunbridge Wells - Wadhurst, alight Lamberhurst Green.* **For NGS: Tue 17 May (10-5). Adm £14.30, chd £7.20. Light refreshments. For other opening times and information, please phone, email or visit garden website.**

The medieval moated Old Scotney Castle lies in a peaceful wooded valley. In the 19th century its owner Edward Hussey III set about building a new house, partially demolishing the Old Castle to create a romantic folly, the centrepiece of his picturesque landscape. From the terraces of the new house, sweeps of rhododendron and azaleas cascade down the slope in summer, mirrored in the moat. In the house three generations have made their mark, adding possessions and character to the homely Victorian mansion which enjoys far reaching views out across the estate. Wheelchairs available for loan.

Lose yourself in the numerous themed rooms . . .

95 ◆ SISSINGHURST CASTLE GARDEN
Sissinghurst TN17 2AB. National Trust, 01580 710700, sissinghurst@nationaltrust.org.uk, www.nationaltrust.org.uk. *On A262 1m E of Sissinghurst. Bus: Arriva Maidstone-Hastings, alight Sissinghurst 1¹/₄ m. Approx 30 mins walk from village.* **For NGS: Sun 24 Apr (11-5.30). Adm £12.90, chd £6.25. Evening opening Thur 23 June (6.30-9). Adm £20, chd £10. Pre-booking essential, please visit www.ngs.org.uk or phone 01483 211535 for information & booking. For other opening times and information, please phone, email or visit garden website.**
Garden created by Vita Sackville-West and Sir Harold Nicolson. Spring garden, herb garden, cottage garden, white garden, rose garden. Tudor building and tower, partly open to public. Moat. Vegetable garden and estate walks. Free welcome talks and estate walks leaflets. Cafe, restaurant and shop open from 10am-5.30pm daily, closed Christmas Eve and Christmas Day. Some areas unsuitable for wheelchair access due to narrow paths and steps.

96 ▸ SMITHS HALL

**Lower Road, West Farleigh
ME15 0PE. Mr S Norman,**
www.smithshall.com. *3m W of
Maidstone. A26 towards Tonbridge,
turn L into Teston Lane B2163. At T-
junction turn R onto Lower Rd
B2010. Opp Tickled Trout PH.* Sun 5
June, Sun 24 July (11-5). Adm £5,
chd free. Home-made teas.
Donation to Free Me.
Delightful 3 acre gardens surrounding
a beautiful 1719 Queen Anne House
(not open). Lose yourself in numerous
themed rooms: sunken water garden,
iris beds, scented old fashioned rose
walk, formal rose garden, intense wild
flowers, peonies, deep herbaceous
borders and specimen trees. Walk 9
acres of park and woodland with
great variety of young native and
American trees and fine views of the
Medway valley. Cakes, quiche, jams
and preserves available. Gravel paths.

97 ▸ SOUTH HILL FARM

**Tamley Lane, Hastingleigh, Ashford
TN25 5HL. Sir Charles Jessel,
01233 750325,
sircjj@btinternet.com.** *4¹/₂ m E of
Ashford. Turn off A28 to Wye,
through village & ascend Wye Downs.
2m turn R at Xrds, Brabourne &
South Hill, then 1st L. From Stone St
(B2068) turn W opp Stelling Minnis,
follow signs to Hastingleigh. Cont
towards Wye, turn L at Xrds marked
Brabourne & South Hill, then 1st L.*
Visits by arrangement June to
Aug. Adm incl tea and guided
tour. Groups min 4, max 30. Adm
£4.50, chd free.
2 acres high up on N Downs, C17/18
house (not open). Old walls, ha-ha,
formal water garden; old and new
roses, unusual shrubs, perennials and
coloured foliage plants.

98 ▸ SPRING PLATT

**Boyton Court Road, Sutton
Valence, Maidstone ME17 3BY. Mr
& Mrs John Millen, 01622 843383,
carolyn.millen@virginmedia.com,
www.kentsnowdrops.com.** *5m SE
of Maidstone. From A274 nr Sutton
Valence follow yellow NGS signs.
Limited parking.* Visits by
arrangement in Feb 2016 & 2017,
limited parking but large groups
by coach welcome. Adm £4.00,
chd free. Light refreshments.
1 acre garden under continual
development with panoramic views of
the Weald. Over 500 varieties of
snowdrop grown in tiered display
beds with spring flowers in borders.
An extensive collection of alpine
plants in a large greenhouse.
Vegetable garden and water feature
under construction. Home-made
soup and home-made bread
tea/coffee and cake. Garden on a
steep slope and many steps.

99 ▸ STONEWALL PARK

**Chiddingstone Hoath, nr
Edenbridge TN8 7DG. The Fleming
Family.** *4m SE of Edenbridge. via
B2026. Halfway between Markbeech
& Penshurst.* Sat 19 Mar, Sun 8 May
(2-5). Adm £5, chd free. Home-
made teas. *Donation to Sarah
Matheson Trust & St Mary's Church,
Chiddingstone.*
Romantic woodland garden in historic
setting featuring species
rhododendrons, magnolias, azaleas,
bluebells, a range of interesting trees
and shrubs, sandstone outcrops,
wandering paths and lakes. Historic
parkland with cricket ground, sea of
wild daffodils in March.

Sweeps of
rhododendrons and
azaleas cascade
down the slope in
summer . . .

100 ▸ TIMBERS

**Dean Street, East Farleigh, nr
Maidstone ME15 0HS. Mrs Sue
Robinson, 01622 729568,
suerobinson.timbers@gmail.com,
www.timbersgardenkent.co.uk.** *2m
S of Maidstone. From Maidstone take
B2010 to East Farleigh. After Tesco's
on R follow Dean St for ¹/₂ m. Timbers
on L behind 8ft beech hedge. Parking
through gates. Access for 54 seater
coaches.* Visits by arrangement
Apr to July day and evening
openings. Adm £5.00, chd free.
Home-made teas.
5 acre garden stocked with unusual
hardy plants, annuals and shrubs,
designed with flower arranger's eye.
Formal areas (parterre, pergola)
herbaceous, vegetables, lawns and
mature specimen trees surrounded
by 100yr old Kentish cobnut plat, wild
flower meadows and woodland. Rock
pool with waterfalls. Valley views.
Plant list. Newly designed walled
garden. Kent Wildlife Trust Gold
Award. Featured in Garden News
Magazine. Most of garden is flat,
some steep slopes to rear.

101 ▸ TORRY HILL

**Frinsted/Milstead, Sittingbourne
ME9 0SP. Lady Kingsdown,
01795 830258,
lady.kingsdown@btinternet.com.**
*5m S of Sittingbourne. From M20 J8
take A20 (Lenham). At r'about by
Mercure Hotel turn L Hollingbourne
(B2163). Turn R at Xrds at top of hill
(Ringlestone Rd). Thereafter Frinsted-
Doddington (not suitable for
coaches), then Torry Hill/NGS signs.
From M2 J5 take A249 towards
Maidstone, then 1st L (Bredgar),
Lagain (follow Bredgar signs), R at
War Memorial, 1st L (Milstead), Torry
Hill/NGS signs from Milstead. Please
use entrance marked D (on red
background) for disabled parking.*
Sun 15 May, Sun 12 June, Sun 17
July (2-5). Adm £4, chd free.
Home-made teas. Visits also by
arrangement May to July
weekdays only. Tea/coffee and
biscuits available. *Donation to St
Dunstan's Church (May/June),
Parkinsons UK (July).*
8 acres; large lawns, specimen trees,
flowering cherries, rhododendrons,
azaleas and naturalised daffodils;
walled gardens with lawns, shrubs,
herbaceous borders, rose garden incl
shrub roses, wild flower areas and
vegetables. Extensive views to
Medway and Thames estuaries.
Some shallow steps. No wheelchair
access to rose garden but can be
viewed from pathway.

102 ▸ TOWNLAND

**Sixfields, Tenterden TN30 6EX.
Alan & Lindy Bates, 01580 764505,
alanandlindybates@yahoo.co.uk.**
*Just off Tenterden High St. Park in
Bridewell Lane car park (Sunday free).
From centre of Tenterden High St,
walk down Jackson's Lane next to
Webbs Ironmongers. Follow lane to
end (400m). Phone for disabled
parking.* Sun 12 June, Sun 10 July
(2-5.30). Adm £5, chd free. Home-
made teas. Visits also by
arrangement June & July for
groups 10+. *Donation to Pilgrims
Hospice and ShelterBox.*
A 1 acre family garden in a unique
position. Mixed borders, with a wide

range of shrubs and flowers providing a riot of colour throughout the yr, flow into the more naturalistic planting which is adjacent to meadow areas and fruit trees. A gravel garden, rose arbour and intensive fruit and vegetable areas complete the experience. Small area redesigned this yr due to encroaching development. Wide range of plants. Listed in Kent Life as one of the top 25 gardens to visit in Kent.

GROUP OPENING

103 TOYS HILL GARDENS
Scords Lane, Toys Hill, Westerham TN16 1QE. Mrs Jeremy Seddon. *4m from J5 of M25 & 8m from J6. In Brasted (on A25) turn into Chart Lane signed Toys Hill. Turn E at Xrds in Toys Hill into Scords Lane. Parking adjacent to Meadow House.* **Sun 22 May (1.30-5). Combined adm £5, chd free. Home-made teas.**

THE MEADOW HOUSE
Mrs Jeremy Seddon

OLD FARM COTTAGE
The Lady Nolan

THE RUSHES
Mr & Mrs Howard Jarvis

Three gardens (a short walk apart) brimming with colourful acid loving plants, waterbirds and livestock, surrounded by farmland with truly exceptional panoramic views to the South, bordering 450 acres of NT woodland and a short distance from Emmetts NT garden.

104 TRAM HATCH
Charing Heath, Ashford TN27 0BN. Mrs P Scrivens, www.tramhatchgardens.co.uk. *10m NW of Ashford. A20 turn towards Charing Railway Stn on Pluckley Rd, over motorway then 1st R signed Barnfield to end, turn L carry on past Barnfield, Tram Hatch ahead.* **Sun 5 June, Sun 3 July, Sun 14 Aug (1-5.30). Adm £5, chd free. Home-made teas.**
Meander your way off the beaten track to a mature, extensive garden changing through the seasons. You will enjoy a garden laid out in rooms - what surprises are round the corner? Large selection of trees, vegetable, rose and gravel gardens, colourful containers. The R Stour and the

The Meadow House, Toys Hill Gardens
© Leigh Clapp

Angel of the South enhance your visit. Please come and enjoy, then relax in our new garden room for tea. The garden is totally flat, apart from a very small area which can be viewed from the lane.

105 223 TUBBENDEN LANE
Orpington BR6 9NN. Jo & Disha Sehmi, dsehmi@live.co.uk. *1m SW of Orpington. Off A21 into Tubbenden Lane. Turn 1st R into Beechcroft Rd, entrance is through garage between 1A & 3 Beechcroft Rd.* **Sun 5 June (2-5). Adm £5, chd free. Home-made teas.**
A small plantsman's garden with lots of interest created by exotic planting. The emphasis is on foliage provided by ferns, bamboos and hostas. These are set off by topiary, sculpture and water features.

106 UPPER PRYORS
Butterwell Hill, Cowden TN8 7HB. Mr & Mrs S G Smith. *4½ m SE of Edenbridge. From B2026 Edenbridge-Hartfield, turn R at Cowden Xrds & take 1st drive on R.* **Wed 15 June (12-6). Adm £5, chd free. Home-made teas.**
10 acres of English country garden

surrounding C16 house - a garden of many parts; colourful profusion, interesting planting arrangements, immaculate lawns, mature woodland, water and a terrace on which to appreciate the view, and tea!

107 THE WATCH HOUSE
7 Thanet Road, Broadstairs CT10 1LF. Dan Cooper & Alex Dawson, www.frustratedgardener.com. *Off Broadstairs High St on narrow side rd. At Broadstairs station, cont along High St (A255) towards sea front. Turn L between Lloyds Bank & Estate Agent then immed turn R.* **Sat 20, Sun 21 Aug (12-4). Adm £3, chd free. Light refreshments.**
Adjoining an historic fishermen's cottage in the town centre, this tiny garden measures just 20ft x 30ft. Sheltered, and enjoying a unique microclimate, the garden is home to an array of exotic and unusual plants and trees. A constantly changing display of tender plants in containers demonstrates how yr-round interest can be achieved in the smallest of spaces. Within a few mins walk of Viking Bay, The Dickens Museum and Bleak House.

108 WATERGATE HOUSE

King Street, Fordwich, Canterbury CT2 0DB. Fiona Cadwallader, 01227 710470, fiona@cadwallader.co.uk, www.cadwallader.co.uk. *2m E of Canterbury. From Canterbury A257 direction, Sandwich, 1m L to Fordwich. 1m L on Moat Lane, direct to Watergate House bottom of High St. Follow parking instructions.* **Sat 23 Apr, Sat 11 June (2-6). Adm £4, chd free. Home-made teas. Visits also by arrangement Apr to Aug for groups 10+.**
Magical walled garden by the R Stour: Defined areas of formal, spring, woodland, vegetable and secret garden reveal themselves in a naturally harmonious flow, each with its own colour combinations. Ancient walls provide the garden's basic structure, while a green oak pergola echoes a monastic cloister. The garden is mainly on one level with one raised walkway under pergola.

109 WEST COURT LODGE

Postling Court, The Street, Postling, nr Hythe CT21 4EX. Mr & Mrs John Pattrick, 01303 863285, malliet@hotmail.co.uk. *2m NW of Hythe. From M20 J11 turn S onto A20. Immed 1st L. After ½ m on bend take rd signed Lyminge. 1st L into Postling.* **Visits by arrangement Apr to Sept in conjunction with Churchfield. Groups 35 max. Adm £5.00, chd free. Home-made teas in Village Hall or garden.**
S facing 1 acre walled garden at the foot of the N Downs, designed in 2 parts: main lawn with large sunny borders and a romantic woodland glade planted with shadow loving plants and spring bulbs, small wildlife pond. Lovely C11 church will be open next to the gardens.

GROUP OPENING

110 WEST MALLING EARLY SUMMER GARDENS

West Malling ME19 6LW. *On A20, nr J4 of M20. Park in West Malling for Brome House, Town Hill Cottage and Went House where maps, directions to 1 & 2 New Barns Cottages, & combined tickets available.* **Sun 5 June (12-5). Combined adm £6, chd free. Home-made teas at New Barns Cottages.** *Donation to St Mary's Church, W Malling.*

BROME HOUSE
John Pfeil & Shirley Briggs

NEW BARNS COTTAGES
Mr & Mrs Anthony Drake

TOWN HILL COTTAGE
Mr & Mrs P Cosier

WENT HOUSE
Alan & Mary Gibbins

West Malling is an attractive small market town with some fine buildings. Enjoy four lovely gardens that are entirely different from each other and cannot be seen from the road. Brome House has colour themed herbaceous borders, specimen trees and an ornamental vegetable garden. Went House is a Queen Anne house surrounded by a secret garden with a stream, specimen trees, old roses, mixed borders, attractive large kitchen garden, fountain and parterre. Town Hill Cottage is a part walled garden with mature and interesting planting. New Barns Cottages have serpentine paths leading through woodland to roomed gardens: tea and cakes in the courtyard garden of the cottages. Town Hill Cottage garden and New Barns Cottages are difficult to access but the other gardens have wheelchair access.

5-acre garden designed with a flower arranger's eye . . .

GROUP OPENING

111 NEW WHITSTABLE GARDENS

Whitstable CT5 4LT. *Off A299, or A290. Drive down Borstal Hill, L by garage into Joy Lane to collect map of participating gardens.* **Sun 12 June (10-5). Combined adm £6, chd free. Home-made teas at Stream Walk Community Gardens.**

NEW 87 ALBERT STREET
Paul Carey & Phil Gomm

NEW 6 ALEXANDRA ROAD
Andrew Mawson & Sarah Rees

NEW 56 ARGYLE ROAD
Emma Burnham & Mel Green

NEW CAPLE HOUSE
Efua Thomas

NEW 19 JOY LANE
Francine Raymond
www.kitchen-garden-hens.co.uk

NEW STREAM WALK FOOTPATH
Stream Walk Community Gardens

NEW 34 VICTORIA STREET
Caroline Burgess

Enjoy a day of eclectic gardens by the sea. 7 people are showing off their gardens, but many others, marked with yellow balloons, are there to admire from the street or sea front. From fishermen's yards to formal gardens, the residents of Whitstable are making the most of our quirky plots, enjoying our mild climate and the range of plants we can grow. Drop in and admire wildlife (19 Joy Lane), edible (Caple House) and experimental gardens (6 Alexandra Rd), and those starting from scratch (56 Argyle Rd & 34 Victoria St). We're maximising our space, be it tiny (87 Albert St), on a busy road or in deep shade. We garden on heavy Kent clay and are prone to northerly winds. Stream Walk is the heart of our gardening community, where residents can learn new skills, buy surplus produce and enjoy communal celebrations - the ideal spot for those without outside space of their own. By opening, we're hoping to encourage those new to gardening with our ingenuity and style, rather than rolling acres. Combined adm £6 per adult or £10 for 2.

112 WOMENSWOLD GARDENS

Womenswold, Canterbury CT4 6HE. Mrs Maggie McKenzie. *6m S of Canterbury, midway between Canterbury & Dover. Take B2046 for Wingham at Barham Xover. Turn 1st R, following signs.* **Sat 25, Sun 26 June (1-5.30). Adm £5, chd free. Home-made teas.**
A diverse variety of cottage gardens in an idyllic situation in an unspoilt hamlet, mostly surrounding C13 Church. These incl a cottage garden with a number of old climbing and shrub roses and clematis, a vegetable bed and beehives; a traditional thatched cottage garden; colourful

garden with ponds and other interesting features with many unusual plants; a garden with a large display of perennials, inc kniphofias and hemerocallis; a 2 acre plantsman's garden with a vegetable garden and orchard, large greenhouse with cacti and tropical plants. Easy walking distance to gardens. North Downs Way runs through village. Many unusual plants for sale. Teas in lovely restful garden with home-made cakes. Produce stall; Church open. Most gardens have good wheelchair access although some areas may be inaccessible.

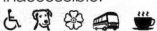

113 ◆ THE WORLD GARDEN AT LULLINGSTONE CASTLE
Eynsford DA4 0JA. Guy Hart Dyke, 01322 862114, www.lullingstonecastle.co.uk. *1m from Eynsford. Over Ford Bridge in Eynsford Village. Follow signs to Roman Villa. Keep Roman Villa immed on R then follow Private Rd to Gatehouse.* **For NGS: Sun 19 June (12-5). Adm £8, chd free. For other opening times and information, please phone or visit garden website.**
Interactive world map of plants laid out as a map of the world within a walled garden. The oceans are your pathways as you navigate the world in 1 acre. You can see Ayers Rock and walk alongside the Andes whilst reading tales of intrepid plant hunters. Discover the origins of some 6,000 different plants - you'll be amazed where they come from! Plant Hunters Nursery and Lullingstone World Garden seeds for sale. Wheelchairs available upon request.

114 WYCKHURST
Mill Road, Aldington, Ashford TN25 7AJ. Mr & Mrs Chris Older, 01233 720395, cdo@rmfarms.co.uk. *4m SE of Ashford. From M20 J10 take A20 2m E to Aldington turning; turn R at Xrds & proceed 1½ m to Aldington Village Hall. Turn R & immed L by Walnut Tree Inn down Forge Hill. After ¼ m turn R into Mill Rd.* **Sat 4, Sun 5, Sat 11, Sun 12 June (12-6). Adm £4.50, chd free. Home-made teas on terrace. Lunchtime soup & rolls. Also open Hogben House. Visits also by arrangement in June.**
C16 Kent Cottage (not open) nestles in romantic seclusion at the end of a drive. This enchanting garden is a

mixture of small mixed herbaceous borders, roses and unusual topiary incl a wildflower meadow. There is plenty of seating round the lawns to enjoy the garden, teas and the extensive views across Romney Marsh towards the sea. Shepherds Hut, small water feature and meadow to stroll in. Some gentle slopes which limit wheelchair access to some small areas.

GROUP OPENING

115 WYE GARDENS
Wye TN25 5BJ. *3m NE of Ashford. From A28 take turning signed Wye. Bus: Ashford to Canterbury via Wye. Train: Wye. Collect map of gardens at Church.* **Sun 19 June (2-6). Combined adm £5, chd free. Home-made teas at Wye Church.**

3 BRAMBLE CLOSE
Dr M Copland

CUMBERLAND COURT [D]
Mr & Mrs F Huntington

SPRING GROVE FARM HOUSE
Heather Van den Bergh

YEW TREES
Elizabeth Coulson

Start at the centre of an historic village to visit 4 unusual gardens. 3 Bramble Close is a unique experience, a very wild garden with meadow, pond and ditches, mown paths, hedges. Research carried out on the effects of wildlife. A water feature and unusual artefacts complement an exciting courtyard garden at Cumberland Court, once an asphalt car park now densely planted with a wide range of unusual plants, pots and secret garden. Mature shrub pruning of particular interest. 250 species of botanical interest (labelled) flourish at Spring Grove Farm House a country garden full of colour and interest with stream, lily pond and gravel garden. Yew Trees is a traditional garden divided into 3 distinct, secluded areas with lawns, naturalised wildlife area, pond, mature trees, wide borders planted with shrubs, grasses and herbaceous perennials and enclosed potager. Wye Gardens opening coincides with Stour Music Festival.

116 YEW TREE COTTAGE
Penshurst TN11 8AD. Mrs Pam Tuppen, 01892 870689. *4m SW of Tonbridge. From A26 Tonbridge to Tunbridge Wells, join B2176 Bidborough to Penshurst rd. 2m W of Bidborough, 1m before Penshurst. Please phone for further directions. Unsuitable for coaches.* **Wed 24, Sun 28 Feb, Wed 9, Sun 13, Wed 23 Mar, Sun 10, Wed 13, Sun 24, Wed 27 Apr, Sun 8, Wed 11, Sun 22, Wed 25 May, Wed 8, Sun 12, Wed 22, Sun 26 June, Sun 10, Wed 13, Sun 24, Wed 27 July, Wed 10, Sun 14 Aug (12-5). Adm £2.50, chd free. Light refreshments.**
Small, romantic cottage garden with steep hillside entrance. Lots of seats and secret corners, many unusual plants - hellebores, spring bulbs, old roses, many special perennials. Small pond; something to see in all seasons. Created and maintained by owner, a natural garden full of plants. Featured in Kent Life, Garden of the Month.

117 NEW YOKES COURT
Coal Pit Lane, Frinsted, Sittingbourne ME9 0ST. Mr & Mrs John Leigh Pemberton. *2.4m from Doddington. Turn off Old Lenham Rd towards Hollingbourne. Take 1st L at Torry Hill Chestnut Fencing, then 1sr L towards Torry Hill. Take 1st L into Coal Pit Lane.* **Sun 12 June (2-5). Adm £3, chd free. Also open Torry Hill.**
3 acre garden surrounded by countryside. Herbaceous borders set in open lawns. Rose walk, serpentine walk through wild flowers. Walled vegetable garden. Refreshments available at Torry Hill.

LANCASHIRE

Merseyside, Greater Manchester and Isle of Man

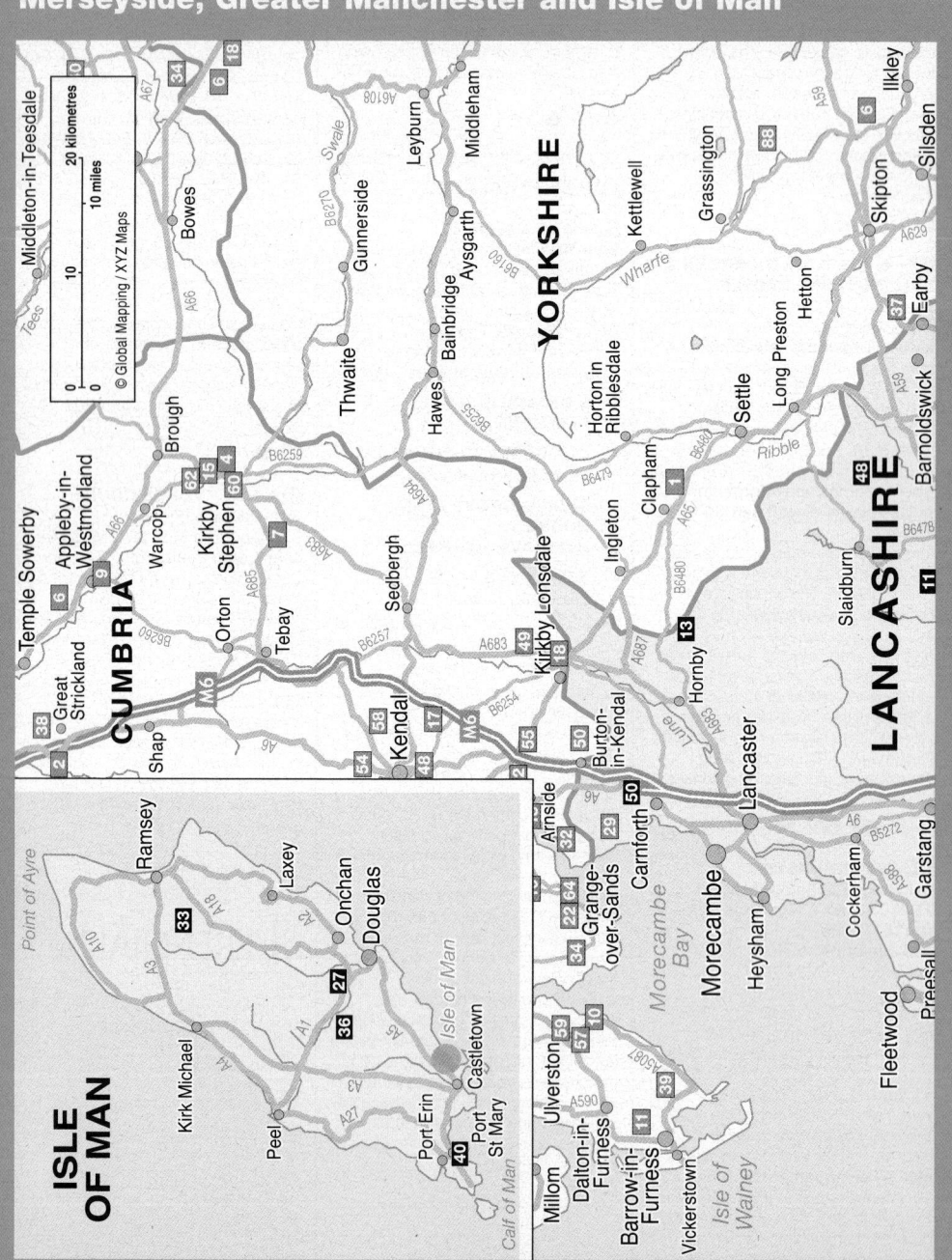

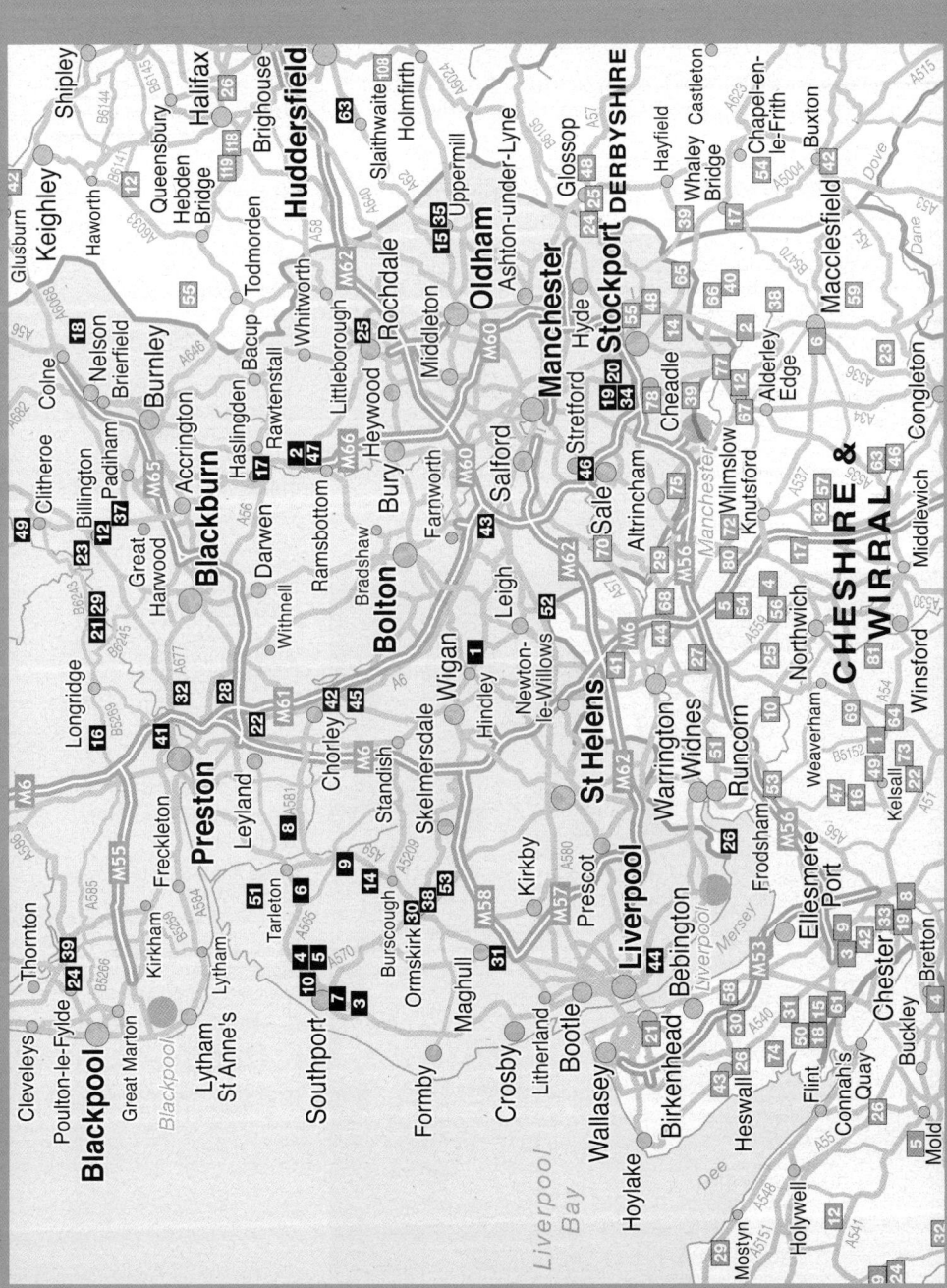

Lancashire, Merseyside, Greater Manchester & Isle of Man

You can always be sure of a really warm red-rose welcome when you visit any of Lancashire's beautiful gardens.

From the tiniest of cottage gardens to spectacular views of Pendle Hill – there is something to delight every taste in all parts of the county.

From Chorley Cakes to Eccles Cakes, from Lemon Drizzle to Victoria Sponge, we have delicacies to tempt every palate. Add a few choice plants to the mix and you can have a fantastic day out for under £10.

Where else can you get such value for money in such beautiful settings, and at the same time support your favourite charities?

We will tell you where – since 2014 the Isle of Man has joined with Lancashire in inviting islanders and holiday-makers alike to visit an increasing number of their fantastic gardens.

Left: 4 Brocklebank Road © Howard Walker

Lancashire, Merseyside, Greater Manchester & Isle of Man Volunteers

County Organiser
Margaret Fletcher
01704 567742
margaret.fletcher@ngs.org.uk

County Treasurer
Geoff Fletcher
01704 567742
geoffwfletcher@hotmail.co.uk

Publicity
Lynn Kelly
01704 563740
lynn-kelly@hotmail.co.uk

Christine Ruth
01517 274877
caruthchris@aol.com

Booklet Co-ordinator
Brenda Doldon
01704 834253
doldon@btinternet.com

Assistant County Organisers
Anne & Jim Britt
01614 458100
annebritt@btinternet.com

Peter & Sandra Curl
01704 893713
peter.curl@btinternet.com

Brenda Doldon
(as above)

Carole Ann & Stephen Powers
01254 824903
powers@carolepower6.orangehome.co.uk

Eric & Sharon Rawcliffe
01253 883275
ericrawk@talktalk.net

Isle of Man
Caroline Couch
01624 832266
carolinecouch@manx.net

Opening Dates

All entries subject to change.
For latest information check www.ngs.org.uk

February

Snowdrop Festival

Sunday 14
52 Weeping Ash Garden
Sunday 21
52 Weeping Ash Garden
Sunday 28
52 Weeping Ash Garden

March

Sunday 6
52 Weeping Ash Garden

April

Sunday 3
43 The Secret Valley
Saturday 16
16 Dale House Gardens
Sunday 17
2 Arevinti
16 Dale House Gardens
52 Weeping Ash Garden

May

Sunday 1
43 The Secret Valley
Monday 2
42 The Ridges
Sunday 8
7 Birkdale Village Gardens
20 3 The Drive
34 Moor Cottage
Sunday 15
14 79 Crabtree Lane
Sunday 22
50 Warton Gardens

Currently the NGS donates around £2.5 million every year . . .

June

Sunday 29
8 Bretherton Gardens
13 Clearbeck House
49 Waddow Lodge Garden
Monday 30
13 Clearbeck House

June

Festival Weekend

Saturday 4
6 Becconsall
15 5 Crib Lane
32 Mill Barn
35 Moordale Paddock
Sunday 5
6 Becconsall
7 Birkdale Village Gardens
15 5 Crib Lane
22 17 Glenmore
32 Mill Barn
35 Moordale Paddock
43 The Secret Valley
Saturday 11
18 Dent Hall
31 Maghull Gardens
32 Mill Barn
Sunday 12
9 NEW 90 Brick Kiln Lane
12 Casa Lago
14 79 Crabtree Lane
18 Dent Hall
31 Maghull Gardens
32 Mill Barn
Saturday 18
50 Warton Gardens
Sunday 19
19 Didsbury Village Gardens
24 Green Farm Cottage
50 Warton Gardens
Saturday 25
16 Dale House Gardens
21 Dutton Hall
53 NEW Edge Hill University
23 Great Mitton Hall
26 Hale Village Gardens
28 NEW Jack Green Cottage
30 72 Ludlow Drive
38 NEW 1 Pinfold Road
Sunday 26
1 40 Acreswood Avenue
13 Clearbeck House
16 Dale House Gardens
21 Dutton Hall
53 NEW Edge Hill University

July

Saturday 2
6 Becconsall
Sunday 3
6 Becconsall
11 Browsholme Hall
13 Clearbeck House
14 79 Crabtree Lane
37 NEW 8 Park Head
43 The Secret Valley
Sunday 10
7 Birkdale Village Gardens
8 Bretherton Gardens
47 The Stubbins Gardens
Tuesday 12
3 23 Ashton Road (Evening)
Saturday 16
4 NEW 12 Bankfield Lane
5 8 Bankfield Lane
46 Southlands
Sunday 17
4 NEW 12 Bankfield Lane
5 8 Bankfield Lane
41 Ribbleton Library
46 Southlands
Saturday 23
17 NEW 23 Dalesford
45 Silver Birches
Sunday 24
17 NEW 23 Dalesford
39 NEW Pool Foot Barn
45 Silver Birches
Sunday 31
8 Bretherton Gardens
44 Sefton Park Gardens
49 Waddow Lodge Garden

August

Saturday 6
25 NEW The Growth Project
Sunday 7
43 The Secret Valley
Monday 29
42 The Ridges

September

Sunday 4
8 Bretherton Gardens
43 The Secret Valley

July

Sunday 11
52 Weeping Ash Garden

February 2017

Sunday 12
52 Weeping Ash Garden
Sunday 19
52 Weeping Ash Garden
Sunday 26
52 Weeping Ash Garden

Isle of Man Gardens

June

Sunday 19
27 NEW Hospice Isle of Man
Saturday 25
36 NEW Old Vicarage
Sunday 26
36 NEW Old Vicarage

July

Sunday 17
40 Red Roofs

September

Monday 12
33 NEW Milntown

Gardens open to the public

11 Browsholme Hall
13 Clearbeck House
42 The Ridges

By arrangement only

10 4 Brocklebank Road
29 Lower Dutton Farm
48 Varley Farm

Also open by arrangement

2 Arevinti
4 NEW 12 Bankfield Lane
7 71 Dunbar Crescent, Birkdale Village Gardens
7 22 Hartley Crescent, Birkdale Village Gardens
7 14 Saxon Road, Birkdale Village Gardens
8 Hazel Cottage, Bretherton Gardens

Share your day out on 𝐟 and 𝐄

8 Owl Barn, Bretherton Gardens
12 Casa Lago
14 79 Crabtree Lane
16 Dale House Gardens
18 Dent Hall
19 38 Willoughby Avenue,

Didsbury Village Gardens
20 3 The Drive
24 Green Farm Cottage
28 **NEW** Jack Green Cottage
32 Mill Barn

34 Moor Cottage
36 **NEW** Old Vicarage
40 Red Roofs
41 Ribbleton Library
43 The Secret Valley
45 Silver Birches
46 Southlands

50 111 Main Street, Warton Gardens
51 Wedgwood

The Gardens

1 40 ACRESWOOD AVENUE

Hindley Green, Wigan WN2 4NJ. Angie Barker, www.angiebarker.co.uk. *4m E of Wigan. Take A577 from Wigan to Manchester, L at Victoria Hotel, at T-junction L for parking on former Dray King car park. Walk back to T-junction & take 1st L.* Sun 26 June (11-4). Adm £3.50, chd free. Tea. This small garden in the middle of a modern housing estate, has been created from scratch over the last 9 years. It uses planting to bring privacy to an overlooked space and has a mix of contemporary and cottage garden styles. It features a formal decked pond area and small wildlife pond and manages to squeeze in a small vegetable plot.

PERENNIAL
GARDENERS' ROYAL BENEVOLENT SOCIETY

NGS & Perennial;
over 30 years of
caring for
horticulturists

2 AREVINTI

1 School Court. BL0 0SD. Lavinia Tod, 01706 822474, vinnie.tod@hotmail.com. *4m N of Bury. Exit at J1 turn R onto A56 signed Ramsbottom continue straight until yellow signs.* Sun 17 Apr (12-5). Adm £3, chd free. Home-made teas. Opening with The Stubbins Gardens on Sun 10 July. Visits also by arrangement Apr to Sept.
A garden of 2 rooms a courtyard topiary garden with flower filled tubs

and water feature leading to a curvicular garden with lawn and raised pond, fountains, flower covered archway and interesting planting. From here through our lych gate to our churchyard garden with herbaceous borders. We also have a garden room filled with flowers shaded by a vine and thornless blackberry. Local history folders available. Featured in Amateur Gardener. Garden room has wheelchair access.

3 23 ASHTON ROAD

PR8 4QE. John & Jennifer Mawdsley. *³⁄₄ m S from village along Liverpool Rd, turn R into Sandon Rd (church on corner) 2nd L Ashton Rd.* Evening opening Tue 12 July (7-9). Adm £3.50, chd free. Wine. Opening with Birkdale Village Gardens on Sun 8 May, Sun 5 June.
A lawn in the front garden shows off a collection of ferns, alpine plants and formal bedding of fuchsias. A well established long back garden with circular lawn and pergola hiding other areas including water feature and vegetable/fruit area.

5 8 BANKFIELD LANE

Churchtown, Southport PR9 7NJ. Alan & Gill Swift. *2¹⁄₂ m N of Southport. Turn R at T-lights on A565 in Churchtown, 1st L at r'about past Hesketh Arms PH & Botanic Gardens main entrance on L. Garden is 200yds on R.* Sat 16, Sun 17 July (11-5). Combined adm with 12 Bankfield Lane £4, chd free, Home-made teas. *Donation to Southport Spinal Unit.*
Open aspect to rear of garden, double herbaceous borders, small vegetable garden, greenhouse, chickens coup, two raised patio areas. Front garden has trees, shrubs and roses. Restricted parking on Bankfield Lane. Parking available at rear of Botanic Gardens on Veralum Road. A short walk through Botanic Gardens to Bankfield Lane via main

or side gate. Wheelchair access to most areas.

4 **NEW** 12 BANKFIELD LANE

Churchtown, Southport PR9 7NJ. Alan & Eileen Brannigan, 07570 799593, abrannigan@sky.com. *2¹⁄₂ m N of Southport. Turn R at T-lights on A565 in Churchtown 1st L at r'about, then past Hesketh Arms PH & Botanic Gardens main entrance on L. Garden is 220yds on R.* Sat 16, Sun 17 July (11-5). Combined adm with 8 Bankfield Lane £4, chd free. Light refreshments. Visits also by arrangement May to July for groups of 10 to 20. *Donation to Southport Spinal Injuries Unit.*
This attractive walled garden has been lovingly landscaped by current owners over 30yrs and is continually evolving. It has a well stocked pond with waterfalls, a stone bed, alpine troughs, mixed borders with magnolias, and rhododendrons. Open aspect to rear. Greenhouse and patio areas. The front garden has a newly planted stone bed and mixed borders. Level paths but entrance gate to rear garden too narrow for wheelchairs.

6 BECCONSALL

Hunters Lane, Tarleton Moss, Tarleton, Preston PR4 6JL. John & Elizabeth Caunce. *11m S of Preston. Situated off A565. Take A59 to Tarleton then A565 towards Southport. After 2m rd goes down to one lane. Turn R, & back on other side of rd. Hunters Lane ¹⁄₂ m on L. Parking in nearby field.* Sat 4, Sun 5 June, Sat 2, Sun 3 July (11-5). Adm £3.50, chd free. Home-made teas.
1 acre sympathetically combining different areas lawn, rill, arboretum, herbaceous border, wild flower area and raised vegetable beds. Music in the afternoon. Wheelchair access to most of the garden.

GROUP OPENING

BIRKDALE VILLAGE GARDENS
Birkdale, Southport PR8 2AX. *1m S of Southport. Off A565 Southport to Liverpool rd. 4th on L after r'about, opp St James Church. Maps available at each location.* Sun 8 May, Sun 5 June, Sun 10 July (11-5). Combined adm £4.50, chd free. Home-made teas at Saxon Rd and Quiet Garden. Bacon sandwiches at 22 Hartley Crescent. *Donation to Southport Lifeboat & Birkdale Civic Society.*

23 ASHTON ROAD
John & Jennifer Mawdsley.
Open on Sun 8 May, Sun 5 June
(See separate entry)

71 DUNBAR CRESCENT
Mrs Kimberley Gittins.
Open on all dates
Visits also by arrangement, refreshments may be incl for groups.
kgo611@ymail.com
01704 579325

22 HARTLEY CRESCENT
Sandra & Keith Birks.
Open on Sun 5 June, Sun 10 July
Visits also by arrangement June to Aug groups of 10+.
sandie.b@talktalk.net
01704 567182

THE QUIET GARDEN
St Peter's Church.
Open on Sun 8 May, Sun 5 June

14 SAXON ROAD
Margaret & Geoff Fletcher.
Open on all dates
Visits also by arrangement May to July for groups of 10+.
geoffwfletcher@hotmail.co.uk
01704 567742

66 SHAWS ROAD
Vivienne Rimmer.
Open on all dates

An established group of gardens surrounding the NW in Bloom award winning Victorian village of Birkdale, some within easy walking distance, others reached by a short car journey. Some gardens opening on all 3 dates, others less. Gardens feature a plantswoman's garden in cottage garden style, a walled garden with an array of tender plants amongst informal island beds and a developing family garden with pond, mini orchard and use of reclaimed materials. An impressive example of a Quiet

Garden with labyrinth and hut for peaceful contemplation. Finally a garden of different rooms with inspirational fruit and vegetable plot, returning this year after major hard landscaping incl new pond and decking area, a delightful L shaped garden. Wheelchair access to some gardens.

GROUP OPENING

BRETHERTON GARDENS
South Road, Bretherton, Leyland PR26 9AD. *8m SW of Preston. Between Southport & Preston, from A59, take B5247 towards Chorley for 1m. Gardens signed from South Rd (B5247).* Sun 29 May, Sun 10, Sun 31 July, Sun 4 Sept (12-5). Combined adm £5, chd free. Home-made teas at Bretherton Congregational Church. Light lunches (10 July only).

GLYNWOOD HOUSE
Terry & Sue Riding

HAZEL COTTAGE
John & Kris Jolley
Visits also by arrangement Apr to Oct.
jolley@johnjolley.plus.com
01772 600896

OWL BARN
Richard & Barbara Farbon
Visits also by arrangement May to Sept small groups only (less than 10).
farbons@btinternet.com
01772 600750

PEAR TREE COTTAGE
John & Gwenifer Jackson

Four contrasting gardens spaced across attractive village with conservation area. Glynwood House has ¾-acre mixed borders, pond with drystone-wall water feature, woodland walk, patio garden with pergola and raised beds, all in a peaceful location with spectacular open aspects. Pear Tree Cottage garden blends seamlessly into its rural setting with informal displays of ornamental and edible crops, water and mature trees, against a backdrop of open views to the West Pennine Moors. Owl Barn has a working kitchen garden and mixed borders with exuberant planting to complement an historic C18 listed building (not open). Hazel Cottage garden has evolved from a Victorian subsistence plot to encompass a

series of themed spaces packed with plants to engage the senses and the mind. Live music at Glynwood. Home-made preserves for sale at Pear Tree Cottage. Visited by BBC Radio Lancashire's 'Lancashire Outdoors' programme. Narrow and uneven paths in some areas.

This attractive walled garden has been lovingly landscaped . . .

NEW 90 BRICK KILN LANE
Rufford, Ormskirk L40 1SZ. Mrs Jacky Soper. *From M6 J27, follow signs for Parbold then Rufford. Turn L onto the A59. Turn R at Hesketh Arms PH. Turn 3rd L.* Sun 12 June (11-4.30). Adm £3, chd free. Also open 79 Crabtree Lane.
A small cottage garden, with a variety of different garden rooms containing shrubs, perennials, alpines, climbers, cobbled courtyard and a small pond. Wheelchair access limited: due to narrow paths and large step down to cobbled courtyard.

4 BROCKLEBANK ROAD
Southport PR9 9LP. Alan & Heather Sidebotham, 01704 543389, alansidebotham@yahoo.co.uk. *1¼ m N of Southport. Off A565 Southport to Preston Rd, opp North entrance to Hesketh Park.* Visits by arrangement May to Aug, groups of 8+. Adm £3.00, chd free. Home-made teas.
A walled garden incorporating a church folly. Landscaped with reclaimed materials from historic sites in the Southport area. There are several water features, an extensive herbaceous border and various areas of differing planting, thus creating a garden with much interest.

Didsbury Village Gardens

'outstanding' ' just like sitting in a Chelsea show garden' 'lovely people, lovely cakes'.

♿ ❖ ☕

13 ♦ **CLEARBECK HOUSE**
Mewith Lane, Higher Tatham via Lancaster LA2 8PJ. Peter & Bronwen Osborne, 01524 261029, bronwenmo@gmail.com, www.clearbeckgarden.org.uk. *13m NE of Lancaster. Signed from Wray (M6 J34, A683, B6480) & Low Bentham.* For NGS: Sun 29, Mon 30 May, Sun 26 June, Sun 3 July (11-5). Adm £4, chd free. Light refreshments. For other opening times and information, please phone, email or visit garden website.
'A surprise round every corner' is the most common response as visitors encounter fountains, streams, ponds, sculptures, boathouses and follies: Rapunzel's tower, temple, turf maze, giant fish made of CDs, walk-through pyramid. 2-acre wildlife lake attracts many species of insects and birds. Planting incl herbaceous borders, grasses, bog plants and many roses. Vegetable and fruit garden. Painting studio open. Children- friendly incl quiz. Artists and photographers welcome by arrangement. Featured in Lancashire Life. Many grass paths, some sloped.

♿ 🏻 ❖ 🚐 ☕

14 **79 CRABTREE LANE**
Burscough L40 0RW. Sandra & Peter Curl, 01704 893713, peter.curl@btinternet.com. *3m NE of Ormskirk. A59 Preston - Liverpool Rd. From N before bridge R into Redcat Lane signed for Martin Mere. From S over 2nd bridge L into Redcat Lane after ³/₄ m L into Crabtree Lane.* Sun 15 May (11-4). Sun 12 June (11-4), also open 90 Brick Kiln Lane. Sun 3 July (11-4). Adm £3.50, chd free. Home-made teas. Visits also by arrangement May to July.
³/₄ acre garden that over recent yrs has been changed and replanted but still has many established and contrasting hidden areas. Patio surrounded by shrubs and alpine bed. Colour themed herbaceous and island beds with shrubs. Rose garden, fish pond surrounded by a large rockery and a koi pond with waterfall, recently rebuilt and shallow area for wildlife. Spring and woodland garden, gravel garden with tender Mediterranean planting and late

11 ♦ **BROWSHOLME HALL**
Clitheroe Road, Cow Ark, Clitheroe BB7 3DE. Mr & Mrs R Parker, 01254 827160, cturner@browsholme.com, www.browsholme.com. *5m NW of Clitheroe. From Clitheroe, leave on B6243 via Eidisford Bridge,R to Bashall Eaves. From Whalley turn L to Great Mitton, then to Bashall Eaves. From Longridge follow signs to Trough of Bowland.* For NGS: Sun 3 July (10.30-4). Adm £3.50, chd free. Light refreshments in the Tithe Barn (licensed). For other opening times and information, please phone, email or visit garden website.
Historic garden and parkland in the setting of a 500 year old grade 1 listed Hall (open). Evidence remains of the C17 garden with magnificent yew walk and 'wilderness' undergoing restoration.The parkland setting is in the style of Capability Brown with C18 origins of lakes, woodland views and a ha-ha; while the immediate garden area reflects the later Edwardian period. Garden nursery stalls, guided walks, demonstrations and tours of historic house (separate charge). Gravel paths and lawns. Car park 300 yds.

♿ 🏻 ❖ 🚐 ☕

12 ♦ **CASA LAGO**
1 Woodlands Park, Whalley BB7 9UG. Carole Ann & Stephen Powers, 01254 824903, powers@carolepowers6.orangeho me.co.uk. *2¹/₂ m S of Clitheroe. From M6 J31, take A59 to Clitheroe. 9m take 2nd exit at r'about for Whalley. After 2m reach village & follow yellow signs. Parking in village car parks or nearby.* Sun 12 June (1-5). Adm £3, chd free. Home-made teas. Visits also by arrangement May to Sept.
Casa Lago has koi ponds, bonsai trees, acers, bamboos, hosta collection, grasses, bananas, succulent garden, black limestone wall, oak pergolas, and secluded havens encased in glass. A raised decked area surrounded by a pebbled beach with box insets and an alpine display. 2015 Visitor comments include 'exquisite'

summer hot bed. Hosta and fern walk. A derelict, dry stone bothy and stone potting shed. Featured in Lancashire Life & Ormskirk Champion. Flat grass paths.

15 5 CRIB LANE
Dobcross, Oldham OL3 5AF. Helen Campbell. *5m E of Oldham. From Dobcross village-head towards Delph on Platt Lane. Crib Lane is opp Dobcross Band Club - go straight up the lane, there is limited parking across from a double green garage door.* Sat 4, Sun 5 June (12.30-4.30). Combined adm with Moordale Paddock £3.50, chd free. Light refreshments.
A well loved and well used family garden which is challenging as on a high stony hillside and encompasses hens, a site for annual bonfires, some small wildlife ponds, vegetable garden, a poly tunnel and areas that are always being re thought and dug up and changed depending on time and aged bodies aches and pains! Plant sale by the National Trust.

16 DALE HOUSE GARDENS
off Church Lane, Goosnargh, Preston PR3 2BE. Caroline & Tom Luke, 01772 862464, tomlukebudgerigars@hotmail.com. *2¹/₂ m E of Broughton. M6 J32 signed Garstang Broughton, T-lights R at Whittingham Lane, 2¹/₂ m to Whittingham at PO turn L into Church Lane garden between nos 17 & 19.* Sat 16, Sun 17 Apr, Sat 25, Sun 26 June (10-4). Adm £3.50, chd free. Home-made teas. **Visits also by arrangement Apr to June.** *Donation to St Francis Church.*
¹/₂ -acre tastefully landscaped gardens comprising of limestone rockeries, well stocked herbaceous borders, raised alpine beds, well stocked koi pond, lawn areas, greenhouse and polytunnel, patio areas, specialising in alpines rare shrubs and trees, large collection unusual bulbs. All year round interest. Large indoor budgerigar aviary. 300+ budgies to view. Gravel path, lawn areas.

17 NEW 23 DALESFORD
Haslingden, Rossendale BB4 6QH. Jefferson & Susan Conway. *10m N of Bury. N bound M66/A56 exit A56 Blackburn/Clitheroe. After approx 30yds exit again A680 Haslingden.*

Keep on A680. After 2 r'bouts look for yellow signs. Dalesford is cul-de-sac on the L. Sat 23, Sun 24 July (12-4.30). Adm £3, chd free. Light refreshments. *Donation to RNLI and Rochdale Hedgehog Rescue.*
A garden with humour and personality. Inspired by our travels. Features inc Chinese Garden, American Indian Plain, sculptures, 'a gold mine', wildlife ponds and herbaceous borders, outdoor chess and vegetable beds. ³/₄ acre hillside plot with views to Musbury Tor from the Mediterranean Garden. Strong footwear recommended. Several steps. Sorry not suitable for wheelchairs. Rochdale Hedgehog Rescue will be bringing a hedgehog and birds of prey (NOT being flown).

18 DENT HALL
Colne Road, Trawden, Colne BB8 8NX. Mr Chris Whitaker-Webb, 01282 861892, denthall@tiscali.co.uk. *Turn L at end of M65. Follow A6068 for 2m; after 3rd r'about turn R down B6250. After 1¹/₂ m, in front of church, turn R, signed Carry Bridge. Parking 200yds in village 5 mins walk on public footpaths.* Sat 11, Sun 12 June (12-5). Adm £3.50, chd free. Cream teas. **Visits also by arrangement June to Sept for groups of 10+.** *Donation to Pendleside Hospice.*
Nestled in the oldest part of Trawden villlage and rolling Lancashire countryside, this mature and evolving country garden surrounds a 400 year old grade II listed hall (not open); featuring a parterre, lawns, herbaceous borders, shrubbery, wildlife pond with bridge to seating area and a hidden summerhouse in a woodland area. Plentiful seating throughout. Some uneven paths and gradients.

GROUP OPENING

19 DIDSBURY VILLAGE GARDENS
South Manchester M20 3GZ. *5m S of Manchester. From M60 J5 follow signs to Northenden. Turn R at T-lights onto Barlow Moor Rd to Didsbury. From M56 follow A34 to Didsbury.* Sun 19 June (12-5). Combined adm £6, chd free. Home-made teas at Moor Cottage & 68 Brooklawn Drive.

68 BROOKLAWN DRIVE
Anne & Jim Britt

3 THE DRIVE
Peter Clare & Sarah Keedy
(See separate entry)
Visits also by arrangement Mar to Oct, on rd parking available.
peter_clare@ntlworld.com.
07710 321913

GROVE COTTAGE, 8 GRENFELL ROAD
Mrs Susan Kaberry

MOOR COTTAGE
William Godfrey
(See separate entry)
Visits also by arrangement May to Sept for groups only.
info@manlangschool.co.uk
0161 448 8372

2 PARKFIELD ROAD SOUTH
Conrad & Kate Jacobson, Mary Butterworth

38 WILLOUGHBY AVENUE
Mr Simon Hickey
Visits also by arrangement.
0161 478 5589

Didsbury is an attractive South Manchester suburb which retains its village atmosphere. There are interesting shops, cafes and restaurants, well worth a visit in themselves! This year we have 6 gardens. The gardens demonstrate a variety of beautiful spaces- one is a large family garden divided into several enchanting areas incl pretty courtyard and Jewel garden, another is an expertly planted shade garden with many rarities, whilst another reflects the charm of the cottage garden ethos with rose covered pergola, old fashioned perennials and tranquil raised pool. Our smaller gardens show beautifully how suburban plots, with limited space, can be packed full of interesting features and a range of planting styles. Dogs allowed at some gardens. Wheelchair access to some gardens.

A garden with humour and personality. Inspired by our travels . . .

20 3 THE DRIVE

Didsbury, Manchester M20 6HZ.
Peter Clare & Sarah Keedy, 07710
321913, peter_clare@ntlworld.com.
*From M60 J5 follow signs to
Northenden. Turn R at T-lights onto
Barlow Moor Rd to Didsbury. From
M56. A tiny road off Fog Lane with an
old gatehouse on the corner. No 3 is
the first gap in the hedge on L. Close
to Burnage Railway Stn & local bus
services.* Sun 8 May (12-5).
Combined adm with Moor
Cottage £5, chd free. Opening
with Didsbury Village Gardens on
Sun 19 June. Visits also by
arrangement Mar to Oct, on rd
parking available.
Secluded part woodland garden with
winding paths from ponds and
waterfalls to pergolas and ferneries.
Stone steps lead to different levels
and hidden views emerge from old
seats tucked into leafy corners. There
is a mix of formality and informality
with subtle use of colour and a wide
range of shade planting and foliage
for spring, summer and autumn.
Partial wheelchair access, gravel
paths and drive.

*Afternoon tea is
served in the
Victorian style
ornate 'Woodland
Green'
woodworking
station . . .*

21 DUTTON HALL

Gallows Lane, Ribchester
PR3 3XX. Mr & Mrs A H Penny,
www.duttonhall.co.uk. *2m NE of
Ribchester. Signed from B6243 &
B6245 also directions on website.*
Sat 25, Sun 26 June (1-5). Adm £5,
chd free. Home-made teas.
Formal garden at front with backdrop
of C17 house (not open). 2 acres at
rear which incl large collection of old
fashioned roses, water feature, wild
orchid meadow and viewing
platforms with extensive views over
the Ribble Valley. Visitors requested to
keep to mown paths in meadow
areas. Also Orangery collection of
Pemberton roses. Analemmatic

sundial orchid meadow interesting
collection of plants. Home-made teas
provided by St John's Church.
Disabled access difficult due to
different levels and steps.

53 NEW EDGE HILL UNIVERSITY

Ormskirk L39 4QP. 1m SE of
Ormskirk. *From M58 J3 to
Southport turn R at 3rd t-lights onto
the campus. Car parking available
near the main visitor entrance.*
Sat 25 June, Sun 26 June (11-4).
Combined adm with 72 Ludlow
Drive and 1 Pinfold Road £3.50,
chd free. Tea.
Edge Hill University boasts a vibrant
campus community in 160 acres. A
variety of landscapes can be found
alongside award winning buildings
which reflect almost 130 years of
history and innovation. The campus
has been awarded the prestigious
'green flag' award for the 4th year.
The main features include 3 lakes,
waterfalls, extensive rock garden,
allotment, wild flower meadows and
even a beach. Meet the resident duck
population or follow the sculpture trail
and discover over a dozen beautiful
pieces integrated into the natural
environment.

22 17 GLENMORE

Clayton-le-Woods, Chorley
PR6 7TA. Mr & Mrs P Hothersall.
*1m E of J28 M6 Leyland, take B5256
towards Chorley, turn R into
Glenmore at crest of hill, after
thatched cottage on R.* Sun 5 June
(11-5). Adm £3, chd free. Light
refreshments.
This *1/3* acre corner on the fringe of
Cuerden Valley Park is home to a
constantly evolving garden
incorporating lawns, shrubs, colourful
borders and peaceful seating areas
for sun and shade, amidst a
borrowed backdrop of surrounding
trees. Features incl a fabulous
wisteria, pond, terraced family dining
area and a quirky collection of frogs.

23 GREAT MITTON HALL

Mitton Road, Mitton, nr Clitheroe
BB7 9PQ. Jean & Ken Kay. *2m W of
Whalley. Take Mitton Rd out of
Whalley pass Mitton Hall on L,
Aspinall Arms on R over bridge. Hall
is on R next to Hillcrest tearooms.*
Sat 25, Sun 26 June (1-5). Adm
£3.50, chd free. Light

refreshments. *Donation to Help for
Heroes.*
Overlooked by C12 Allhallows
Church, with stunning views to the
river and Pendle Hill the terraced
gardens with herbaceous borders,
lawn, topiary and raised lily pond,
sympathetically surround the
medieval hall (not open). Chickens,
fruit and vegetables, summer house
and seating add to the overall
experience. Stalls on village green at
side of Hall.

24 GREEN FARM COTTAGE

42 Lower Green, Poulton-le-Fylde
FY6 7EJ. Eric & Sharon Rawcliffe,
ericrawk@talktalk.net. *500yds from
Poulton-le-Fylde Village. M55 J3
follow A585 Fleetwood. T- lights turn
L. Next lights bear L A586. Poulton
2nd set of lights turn R Lower Green.
Cottage on L.* Sun 19 June (10-5).
Adm £3, chd free. Light
refreshments. Visits also by
arrangement May to July, groups
of 6+.
1/2 acre well established formal
cottage gardens. Feature koi pond,
paths leading to different areas. Lots
of climbers and rose beds. Packed
with plants of all kinds. Many shrubs
and trees. Themed colour borders.
Well laid out lawns. Said by visitors to
be 'a real hidden jewel'.

25 NEW THE GROWTH PROJECT

Kellett Street Allotments, Rochdale
OL16 2JU. Karen Hayday. *From
A627M. R A58 L Entwistle Rd R
Kellett St.* Sat 6 Aug (11.30-4). Adm
£3, chd free. Home-made teas.
*Donation to The Growth Project
(Rochdale & District Mind).*
With parking and guides to give
horticultural advice and over an acre
of organic unusual vegetable
varieties, the Project incl wildlife pond,
insect hotels, formal flower and wild
flower borders and a potager. Visit
the hand built straw house, stroll
down the pergola walk and under the
handcrafted arches. Afternoon tea is
served in the Victorian style ornate
'Woodland Green' woodworking
station. The Growth Project is a
partnership between Hourglass and
Rochdale and District mind. Featured
on Rochdale on line. Awarded level 5
outstanding from NW in Bloom. No
disabled WC, ground can be uneven.

GROUP OPENING

26 HALE VILLAGE GARDENS

Liverpool L24 4BA. *6m S of M62 J6. Take A5300, A562 towards Liverpool, then A561, L for Hale opp the RSPCA. From S L'pool head for the airport then follow signs for Hale. The 82a bus route passes through the village.* Sat 25, Sun 26 June (2-5). Combined adm £4, chd free. Tea.

37 CHURCH ROAD
Betty Henson

66 CHURCH ROAD
Liz Kelly-Hines & David Hines

Neighbouring gardens in the delightful village of Hale, set in rural S Merseyside between Widnes and Liverpool Airport. Church Road is also home to the cottage, sculpture and grave of the famous Childe of Hale.

HAZELWOOD FARM
See Cumbria

27 NEW HOSPICE ISLE OF MAN

Strang, Douglas IM4 4RP. Hospice Isle of Man, www.hospice.org.im. *2m NW of Douglas. Follow directions to the Nobles Hospital. Turn R at the 'Private patients' sign and follow road around. Hospice is on the R.* Sun 19 June (12-4). Adm £3, chd free. Cream teas.

The Hospice garden was designed by Diarmuid Gavin in 2007 themed on the landscape and hills of the Isle of Man, and featuring Tynwald Hill. Since then there have been a number of additions including the Jackie Corkill Garden and the Eva Rose Sensory Garden for children. The Hospice's many volunteers have planted hundreds of bulbs and in Spring and Summer the garden looks especially beautiful. All areas of the Hospice garden are accessible by meandering pathways which are suitable for wheelchair bound visitors.

28 NEW JACK GREEN COTTAGE

Mill House Lane, Brindle, Chorley PR6 8NS. Aurelia & Peter McCann, 07985 054616. *5m N Chorley. From Chorley A6 turn R at r'about on B5256 Westwood Rd then L at r'about on B5256 Sandy Lane through Brindle for 2m, then L on Hill House Lane for ³/₄ m. Turn L on Oram Rd for 200yd.* Sat 25, Sun 26 June (11-4). Adm £4, chd free. Light refreshments. Visits also by arrangement Apr to Sept for groups of 15+.

This 2.7 acre garden has been developed in the last 5 years by a young family and it is still 'work in progress'. With long borders of cottage style plants, Japanese garden, herb garden, small parterre, orchard, fruit cage and vegetable plots, there is a surprise around every corner. Chicken pen, secluded BBQ area and children's play area. Not all areas are suitable for wheelchair use.

29 LOWER DUTTON FARM

Gallows Lane, Ribchester PR3 3XX. Mr R Robinson, 01254 878405. *1¹/₂ m NE of Ribchester. Leave M6 J31. Take A59 towards Clitheroe, turn L at T-lights towards Ribchester. Signed from B6243 & B6245. Ample car parking in adjacent field.* Visits by arrangement July & Aug. Light refreshments. Wine.

Traditional long Lancashire farmhouse and barn (not open), with 1¹/₂ acre garden. Formal gardens nr house with mixed herbaceous beds, wild flower beds and shrubs, sweeping lawns leading to wildlife area and established large pond and small woodland with mix of trees and plants. Lawns may be difficult in very wet weather.

30 72 LUDLOW DRIVE

Ormskirk L39 1LF. Marian & Brian Jones. *¹/₂ m W of Ormskirk. Take Southport Rd (A570) turn R onto Heskin Lane then 1st R onto Ludlow Drive.* Sat 25, Sun 26 June (11-4). Combined adm with Edge Hill University and 1 Pinfold Road £3.50, chd free. Home-made teas.

Plantswoman's small corner house garden with well stocked colourful herbaceous and shrub borders. The garden also features a gravel garden with sun loving plants, raised beds with some unusual shade loving plants, modern and old roses and many clematis. There are also alpine troughs and a raised fish pond. The owners are beekeepers and will have observation hive on show. Wheelchair access to front garden but limited access to rear garden.

GROUP OPENING

31 MAGHULL GARDENS

Maghull, Liverpool L31 7DR. *7m N of Liverpool. End of M57/M58/A59 take A59 towards O/skirk after 1¹/₂ m take next slip rd on L, L at bridge onto Liverpool Rd Sth, L Balmoral Rd, R Buckingham Rd.* Sat 11, Sun 12 June (12-5). Combined adm £2.50, chd free. Home-made teas. *Donation to Woodlands Hospice.*

136 BUCKINGHAM ROAD
Debbie & Mark Jackson

MAGHULL STATION
Merseyrail

One garden and an award winning station. 136 Buckingham Road is a small suburban garden owned by a plantaholic. The garden is brimming with roses, cottage garden plants, containers and hanging baskets full of colour and a small pond stocked with fish. The garden is planted to attract birds, butterflies and bees. Plenty of seating. Maghull Station: Named The Best Small Station of the year 2013. Filled with herbaceous plants, shrubs, rockery, hanging baskets, troughs and large planters tumbling with a wide variety of bedding plants - a wonderful sight for commuters arriving in Maghull.

32 MILL BARN

Goosefoot Close, Samlesbury, Preston PR5 0SS. Chris Mortimer, 01254 853300, chris@millbarn.net, www.millbarn.net. *6m E of Preston. From M6 J31 2¹/₂ m on A59/A677 B/burn. Turn S. Nabs Head Lane, then Goosefoot Lane.* Sat 4, Sun 5, Sat 11, Sun 12 June (1-5). Adm £4, chd free. Home-made teas. Visits also by arrangement May to July min group donation £40 or £4 per head.

The unique and quirky garden at Mill Barn is a delight: or rather a series of delights. Along the R Darwin, through the tiny secret grotto, past the suspension bridge and view of the fairytale tower, visitors can a stroll past folly, sculptures, lily pond, and lawns, enjoy the naturally planted flowerbeds, then enter the secret garden and through it the pathways of the wooded hillside beyond. A garden developed on the site of old mills gives a fascinating layout which evolves at many levels. Partial wheelchair access, visitors have not been disappointed in the past.

33 NEW MILNTOWN
Lezayre Road, Ramsey, Isle of Man
IM7 2AB. Milntown, 01624 812321,
milntown@manx.net,
www.milntown.org. ½ m W of
Ramsey on A3. 15 minute easy walk
from Ramsey train station. Bus stop
by gate. Car & coach park. **Mon 12
Sept (10-5). Adm £3.50, chd £1.
Light refreshments at The
Milntown Cafe.**
15 acres of gardens and woodland in
a historical setting. Walled gardens,
kitchen garden, herbaceous borders
bursting with summer colour,
rhododendrons, camellias and
magnolias in spring. Many unusual
and interesting plant collections
growing in a unique microclimate. Mill
pond and waterwheel, woodland
walks with sculptures, fishpond,
grass labyrinth, seating throughout.
Nursery and plant sales. Wheelchair
access to most parts of the gardens.
Two disability scooters available for
free use on request.

34 MOOR COTTAGE
Grange Lane, Didsbury,
Manchester M20 6RW. William
Godfrey, 0161 448 8372,
info@manlangschool.co.uk. 5m
S of Manchester. Off Wilmslow Rd,
behind Shell Petrol Station. Easy
access by public transport: Metro
tram train (East Didsbury) & bus. **Sun
8 May (12-5). Combined adm with
3 The Drive £5, chd free. Home-
made teas. Opening with
Didsbury Village Gardens on Sun
19 June. Visits also by
arrangement May to Sept for
groups only.**
Moor Cottage is a delightful walled
garden hidden from the street. It
opens up into a series of flower-filled
rooms packed with choice planting
combinations. Lawn and yew
hedging create firm structure and
design. A small kitchen garden with
chickens is adjacent. Level access
but gravel drive.

35 MOORDALE PADDOCK
Huddersfield Road, Diggle,
Oldham OL3 5NT. Mrs H Barnes.
5m E of Oldham. The garden is
located up driveway beside 109
Huddersfield Rd, Diggle. Garden on R
as you go up drive. NB Parking is
available on Huddersfield Rd only.
**Sat 4, Sun 5 June (12.30-4.30).
Combined adm with 5 Crib Lane**

£3.50, chd free. Light
refreshments.
The mature gardens are to the front
and rear of the large stone built house
and consist of deep beds containing
a wide range of herbaceous
perennials, roses and shrubs and a
shade bed at the rear planted with
hostas. There is also a wide range of
container planting. There are ponds
front and rear and a vegetable plot at
the top of the garden with
greenhouse. The garden is on a
slope.

36 NEW OLD VICARAGE
Vicarage Road, Braddan IM4 2AB.
Mrs Mandy Jones, 07624 330176,
Mandydkjones@btinternet.com. 1m
E of Douglas. From Douglas take Peel
Rd. L at Braddan church, R at mini
island, cross 2nd, garden 200m on R.
From Cooil Rd A24 take A6 through
Business park. L at island junction
Stephensons Way then 100m on L.
**Sat 25, Sun 26 June (1-5). Adm £3,
chd free. Light refreshments.
Visits also by arrangement Mar to
Oct.**
A mature garden, including
established shrubbery, herbaceous
borders, a croquet lawn and many
protected trees, some dating back to
the construction of The Old Vicarage
in 1848. Almost entirely walled, the
garden borrows views from local
farmland and distantly to the sea, and
there is a shady woodland to the
side. The current guardians nurture
what has been planted over many
years by former owners. Limited
wheelchair access as there is a lot of
gravel, woodchip and leaves, but
gateways are wide.

37 NEW 8 PARK HEAD
Portfield Bar, Whalley, Clitheroe
BB7 9FB. Phil & Barbara Walton.
1m S of Whalley. Take exit from A59
onto A671 At 2nd T-lights follow
A680 towards Accrington Parkhead is
1st L after these lights. **Sun 3 July
(1-5). Adm £3, chd free. Light
refreshments.**
Field to wildlife garden in 10yrs.
Terrace with far reaching views.
Exuberant planting of
perennials/shrubs surround the house
incl over 100 pots whilst kitchen
garden salads fruit and vegetable
squeeze among them! Summer
house leads along dry river bed to
natural pond and bog garden -
newts, frogs and an abundance of

aquatic life. Grass pathways lead
through wild flower meadows to
woodland stream.

> Summer house
> leads along dry river
> bed to natural pond
> and bog garden -
> newts, frogs and an
> abundance of
> aquatic life . . .

38 NEW 1 PINFOLD ROAD
Ormskirk L39 4AB. Linda Murray.
¼ m E of Ormskirk. Take A577
(Wigan Rd) from Ormskirk & turn R
after 0.25 m into Pinfold Rd just
before the Ormskirk Hospital
buildings. **Sat 25, Sun 26 June
(11-4). Combined adm with
72 Ludlow Drive and Edge Hill
University £3.50, chd free.**
Delightful small garden composed of
two separate but linked rooms; a
courtyard with water feature and two
garden beds with trellises. The linked
area has two garden beds, filled with
a diverse range of plants, one in
particular designed to attract wildlife.
Gardens framed by pleached
hornbeams, a yew hedge and
architectural fence. Over 50 different
species of plants, some of them
unusual. The original garden was a
tiny and difficult space behind a new
build house, with the ground sloping
in many directions. Part of the parking
space was taken into the garden, and
a clever design and build provided
four light, level and protected medium
sized garden beds. The garden
contains some steps.

39 NEW POOL FOOT BARN
Poolfoot Lane, Little Singleton,
Poulton-Le-Fylde FY6 8LY. Mrs
Amanda Ackroyd. Blackpool 6m.
2m from Jct3 M55 off A585 to
Fleetwood. Poolfoot Lane is opp the
Shell Garage at the 5 lanes end T-
lights. Park on lane, one side only.
**Sun 24 July (10-6). Adm £4, chd
free. Home-made teas. Donation
to World Horse Welfare, Penny
Farm, Blackpool.**

Our 2 acre garden has several distinct areas including a cottage garden, kitchen garden, greenhouse, small pond, butterfly bed, shrub borders, hot summer beds and an area for moisture loving plants. In addition the terrace by the duck pond has alpine beds and is surrounded by perennial borders. Behind the breeze house is a copse leading to a wild flower area and field with Shetlands. Local Art club exhibition. A cobbled yard under restoration.

40 RED ROOFS
Fistard, Port St Mary IM9 5PG. Maggie Wright, 01624 833050, maggiewright@manx.net. *1/4 m from the centre of Port St Mary. Drive through PSM & then follow 1 way system into Park Rd. Continue up the hill on Fistard Rd, until it narrows & bears L. Garden on R.* Sun 17 July (11-4). Adm £2, chd free. Home-made teas. Visits also by arrangement May to Sept no min, 25 Max.
A coastal garden on varying levels on 3 sides of the property, each area having its own planting style, main season of interest and colour palette. Lots of evergreen shrubs, roses, perennials and herbs supplemented with bulbs, annuals and container planting to provide year round interest. Plant house, cutting garden and vegetable plot. Some semi-wild areas. Winner of Port St Mary in Bloom. Home-made cakes and scones; tea, coffee and soft drinks available.

41 RIBBLETON LIBRARY
Ribbleton Hall Drive, Ribbleton, Preston PR2 6EE. Friends of Ribbleton Library Gardening Club, 07813 890177, friendsofribbletonlibrary@gmail.com, www.friendsofribbletonlibrary.com. *E of Preston. M6 J31 Tickled Trout, follow A59 to Preston, R at 1st r'about Hesketh Arms along Blackpool Rd A5085, R at 2nd set of T- lights - Ribbleton Ave. Ribbleton Hall Dr is on R.* Sun 17 July (1-4). Adm £3, chd free. Light refreshments. Visits also by arrangement June to Aug.
This haven in a busy urban area is a community garden created and maintained by a group of volunteers - Friends of Ribbleton Library Gardening Club. We have a pleasant garden which contains flowers, fruit

and vegetable growing areas and large eco friendly bottle greenhouse. There are well used seating areas for library users and the wider community to enjoy the garden's tranquility. The Bottle Greenhouse was featured on BBC Radio Lancashire, and in The Lancashire Evening Post & Home Farmer Magazine. The garden is all on a flat level. The library building can be accessed via a ramp.

42 ◆ THE RIDGES
Weavers Brow (cont. of Cowling Rd), Limbrick, Chorley PR6 9EB. Mr & Mrs J M Barlow, 01257 279981, barbara@barlowridges.co.uk, www.bedbreakfast-gardenvisits.com. *2m SE of Chorley town centre. From M6 J27, M61 J8. Follow signs for Chorley A6 then signs for Cowling & Rivington. Passing Morrison's up Brooke St, mini r'about 2nd exit.* For NGS: Mon 2 May, Mon 29 Aug (11-5). Adm £4, chd free. Home-made teas. For other opening times and information, please phone, email or visit garden website.
3 acres, incl old walled orchard garden, cottage-style herbaceous borders, and perfumed rambling roses through the trees Arch leads to formal lawn, surrounded by natural woodland, shrub borders and trees with contrasting foliage. Woodland walks and dell. Natural looking stream, wildlife ponds. Walled water

feature with Italian influence, and walled herb garden. Classical music played. Home made cakes, baked and served by ladies of St James Church, Chorley. Some gravel paths and woodland walks not accessible.

43 THE SECRET VALLEY
The Reach, off Hopefold Drive, Worsley, Manchester M28 3PN. Sally Berry, 07999 422731, sallyuk@gmail.com, www.thesecretvalley.com. *7 1/2 m from central Manchester. 1 1/2 m from J13 M60. Straight over r'about onto Walkden Rd, at 1st T-lights turn R onto A580, Take 1st L onto Old Clough Lane, turn L at T-junction onto A6. Park on A6 please. No parking on The Reach.* Suns 3 Apr, 1 May, 5 June, 3 July, 7 Aug, 4 Sept (11-5). Adm £5, chd free. Light refreshments. Visits also by arrangement Apr to Sept.
Large 2 acre water garden with ponds, streams, waterfalls, islands and lake. High variety of trees, plants and climbers. It is a haven for waterfowl and local wildlife (incl swans, ducks, geese, coots, moorhens, grebes, herons and kingfishers). Adjoining gardens include an exotic planting scheme and high production allotment with extended chicken run. Large daffodil display in Mar/Apr. Plenty of seating for picnics.

2 Church Hill Avenue, Warton Gardens

GROUP OPENING

44 **SEFTON PARK GARDENS**
Sefton Drive, Sefton Park,
Liverpool L8 3SD. *1m S of Liverpool
city centre. From end of M62 take
A5058 Queens Drive ring rd S
through Allerton to Sefton Park.
Parking roadside in Sefton Park.*
Sun 31 July (12-5). Combined adm
£5, chd free. Home-made teas.

BUCKINGHAM HOUSE
Val Covey & Roni Stephen

**THE COMMUNITY ORCHARD
AND WILDLIFE GARDEN**
The Society of Friends
www.tann.org.uk

NEW **6 CROXTETH GROVE**
Stuart Speeden

**FERN GROVE COMMUNITY
GARDEN**
Liverpool City Council

NEW **NEW LAND**
Family Refugee Support
Project
www.familyrefugeesupport
project.org.uk

PARKMOUNT
Jeremy Nicholls

SEFTON PARK ALLOTMENTS
Sefton Park Allotments Society

SEFTON VILLA ⌂
Patricia Williams
0151 281 3687
seftonvilla@live.co.uk

YORK HOUSE GARDENS
Jean Niblock & Your Housing

A varied group showing a range of
gardening possible within the city,
from the long colour themed
herbaceous borders at Parkmount to
the 6 acres of vegetables and flowers
of the allotments. A Family Refugee
Support Project joins the group this
year with raised bed gardens tended
by families from as far afield as
Mongolia, Nigeria, Syria and Pakistan.
And a new small private city garden
can be seen, along with two
inspirational tower block gardens with
roses, herbaceous borders and
colourful containers tended by
residents. Surprises and rare and
unusual plants at Park Mount with
special plants for sale and
refreshments. The small walled
garden at Sefton Villa is secluded and
tranquil, with rare plants and an
enclosed Japanese garden. And
there are two local community

projects to see - a garden with bee
hives, and an orchard under
development in a former Quaker
Burial Ground. Beekeeping
demonstration at Fern Grove
Community Garden at 2pm.
Children's activities also at Fern
Grove. Buckingham House awarded
Best Communal Garden 2015 in
Liverpool City Garden Competition.
Wheelchair access at York House,
Buckingham House and wheelchair
access WC at Sefton Park allotments.
♿ ✿ ☕

45 **SILVER BIRCHES**
Rawlinson Lane, Heath Charnock,
Chorley PR7 4DE. Margaret & John
Hobbiss, 01257 480411. *2¹/₂ m S of
Chorley. From the A6 turn into Wigan
Lane (A5106). After 0.4m turn L into
Rawlinson Lane. Silver Birches is
0.2m on L. Disabled parking only next
to the house.* Sat 23, Sun 24 July
(1-6). Adm £4, chd free. Home-
made teas. **Visits also by
arrangement in July.** *Donation to
St George's Church, Chorley.*
The garden has evolved from a family
garden into one with a variety of
features. There are herbaceous
borders, sunken shaded dell, an
African hut, lawns, 2 ponds,
polytunnel, vegetable plot and
orchard. The embankment of a
disused railway has been turned into
rockeries with a wood of native trees.
There are paths for exploring which
lead to the nearby Leeds-Liverpool
canal. Wheelchair access is possible
to many areas of the garden.
♿ 🐕 ✿ ☕

46 **SOUTHLANDS**
12 Sandy Lane, Stretford M32 9DA.
Maureen Sawyer & Duncan
Watmough, 0161 283 9425,
moe@southlands12.com,
www.southlands12.com. *3m S of
Manchester. Sandy Lane (B5213) is
situated off A5181 (A56) ¹/₄ m from
M60 J7.* Sat 16, Sun 17 July (1-
5.30). Adm £3.50, chd free. Home-
made teas. Cake-away service
(take a slice of your favourite
cake home). **Visits also by
arrangement June to Aug guided
tours for groups over 10.**
Artist's multi-award winning,
inspirational s facing garden unfolding
into a series of beautiful garden
'rooms' each with its own theme incl
courtyard, Mediterranean, ornamental
and woodland garden. Organic
kitchen garden with large glasshouse

containing vines and tomatoes.
Extensive herbaceous borders,
stunning containers of exotics,
succulents and annuals, 2 ponds and
water feature. Featured in Garden
Answers magazine.
✿ ☕

GROUP OPENING

47 **THE STUBBINS GARDENS**
Ramsbottom, Bury BL0 0SD,
01706 822474,
vinnie.tod@hotmail.com. *4m N of
Bury. Exit at J1 M66 turn R onto A56
signed Ramsbottom, continue
straight until yellow NGS signs.*
Sun 10 July (12-5). Combined adm
£4, chd free. Home-made teas at
1 School Court.

AREVINTI
Lavinia Tod
(See separate entry)
Visits also by arrangement Apr
to Sept.
vinnie.tod@hotmail.com
01706 822474

155 BOLTON ROAD NORTH
David Ireland

1 EAST VIEW
Robert Townsend

NUTWOOD
Sheila Sherris

4 SCHOOL COURT
Barbara Morris

A fine opportunity to see 5 different
examples of how to make small
gardens into attractive areas. Water
features, mixed planting, unusual
ornamentation, mirror, statuary and
much more besides. Nutwood a
traditional garden with lawn, clematis,
sweet peas, delphiniums, lupins.
Variety of hanging baskets, troughs
and containers. Arevinti has 3 gardens
rooms- court yard garden with topiary,
curvicular garden with lawns raised
pond interesting planting lych gate to
church yard garden with herbaceous
borders. Tea and cakes served here in
our flower filled garden room shaded
with vine and thornless blackberry.
4 School Court,a walled garden with
colour coordinated planting described
as artist meets cottage garden.
155 Bolton Rd North a well designed
shaded garden on an usual plot with
collection of hostas and ferns and
state of the art oak greenhouse 1 East
St situated in the narrow streets of old
Stubbins unusual plants in this tropical
garden with Japanese section. The

area is rich in history.On the hillside stands a tower in memory of Robert Peel. Woods rivers and waterfalls can be enjoyed on walks. Across the road in Chatterton is the site of the Luddite riots. The pretty Church is open to the public. Partial wheelchair access in 3 gardens.

Marie Curie

The NGS is Marie Curie's largest single donor

48 VARLEY FARM

Anna Lane, Forest Becks, Bolton-by-Bowland, Clitheroe BB7 4NZ. Mr & Mrs B Farmer, 07887 638436, varleyforestbecks@btinternet.com. *7m N of Clitheroe. A59 off at Sawley follow Settle 2nd L after Copy Nook onto Settle Rd turn L at rd sign on L. Follow lane 1m to a sharp R hand bend garden on L.* **Visits by arrangement July & Aug for groups of 10+. Adm £5, chd free. Adm incl home-made teas.** 1½ -acre garden that's been developing from 2004. Varley Farm is 700ft above sea level with views across the Forest of Bowland and Pendle. Herbaceous lawned cottage garden, flagged herb garden and walled gravel garden, steps to orchard and organic kitchen garden. Stream and pond area planted in 2009 still maturing with a grassed walk through natural meadow and wild flower meadow.

49 WADDOW LODGE GARDEN

Clitheroe Road, Waddington, Clitheroe BB7 3HQ. Liz & Peter Foley, www.gardentalks.co.uk. *1½ m N of Clitheroe. From M6 J31 take A59 (Preston-Skipton). A671 to Clitheroe then B6478. 1st house on L in village. Parking available on rd before entering village; blue badges in drive parking area on gravel.* **Sun 29 May, Sun 31 July (1-5). Adm £4, chd free. Home-made teas.** Inspirational 2-acre organic garden

for all seasons surrounding Georgian house (not open) with views to Pendle and Bowland. An enthusiast's collection of many unusual plants with herbaceous borders, large island beds, shrubs, heathers, rhododendrons, small mature wooded area, old fashioned and hybrid roses. Extensive kitchen garden of vegetables and soft fruit, interesting heritage apple orchard, herbs, alpines and greenhouse, wildlife meadow and bog garden. Colourful containers. Some gravel/bark paths, otherwise level surfaces.

GROUP OPENING

50 WARTON GARDENS

Warton LA5 9PJ. *1½ m N of Carnforth. From M6 J35 take A601M NW for 1m, then N on A6 for 0.7m turn L signed Warton Old Rectory. Warton Village 1m down Borwick Lane. From Carnforth pass train stn and follow signs Warton & Silverdale.* **Sun 22 May (10-5); Sat 18 June (1-7); Sun 19 June (10-5). Combined adm £4, chd free. Home-made teas at 111 Main Street.**

2 CHURCH HILL AVENUE
Mr & Mrs J Street

111 MAIN STREET
Mr & Mrs J Spendlove
Visits also by arrangement June to Sept gardening groups (up to 20), are welcome by prior arrangement claire@lavenderandlime.co.uk

TUDOR HOUSE
Mr & Mrs T Singleton

The 3 gardens are spread across the village and offer a wide variety of planting and design ideas incl cottage charm, unusual herbaceous and more formal approaches. Visitors to the gardens will be able to park in the village or the public car park which is situated up Crag Rd in the centre of the village. Warton has 2 PHs and WCs. Warton is the birthplace of the medieval ancestors of George Washington, of which the family coat of arms can be seen in St Oswald's Church. The ruins of the Old Rectory (English Heritage) is the oldest surviving building in the village. Ascent of Warton Crag (AONB), provides panoramic views across Morecambe Bay to the Lakeland hills beyond. During the 22nd May

opening, 3 local makers/designers will be displaying and selling garden related products. On Saturday 18th June, between 5pm and 7pm, gardens will be offering a glass of wine (at extra charge).

51 WEDGWOOD

Shore Road, Hesketh Bank, Preston PR4 6XP. Denis & Susan Watson, 01772 816509, heskethbank@aol.com, www.wedgwoodgarden.com. *10m SW of Preston & 8m E of Southport. From Preston: A59. Turn R at Coe Lane, Tarleton T-lights. Turn R onto Hesketh Lane for 2½ m continue onto Shore Rd,. Garden is 1½ m on L. Park on Rd. Yellow NGS sign in hedge.* **Sun 26 June (11-5). Adm £3.50, chd free. Home-made teas. Visits also by arrangement June & July.** 1-acre country garden containing gravel garden with pots, formal pond, 2 lawns surrounded by extensive herbaceous borders in sun or shade, with mature trees, 50ft square glasshouse, 50ft x 30ft sheltered patio, leading to 90ft square parterre with colour themed beds, archways, pergolas and rose covered gazebo, wild flower meadow, fruit trees. Featured in Lancashire Life 10 top gardens. Wood chip paths in parterre.

52 WEEPING ASH GARDEN

Bents Garden & Home, Warrington Road, Glazebury WA3 5NS. John Bent, www.bents.co.uk. *15m W of Manchester. Located next to Bents Garden & Home, just off the East Lancs Rd A580 at Greyhound r'about near Leigh. Follow brown 'Garden Centre' signs.* **Sun 14, 21, 28 Feb (12-4). Sun 6 Mar, Sun 17 Apr, Sun 11 Sept (12-4). Adm £3, chd free. 2017: Sun 12, 19, 26 Feb.** Created by retired nurseryman and photographer John Bent, Weeping Ash is a garden of all-yr interest with beautiful display of early snowdrops. Broad sweeps of colour lend elegance to this beautiful garden. In addition on 11 September Bent's Community Allotments will be open to visitors (opp Bent's nursery). Weeping Ash Garden is located immed adjacent to Bents Garden & Home with its award winning Fresh Approach Restaurant and children's adventure play area. Partial wheelchair access and weather dependent.

LEICESTERSHIRE & RUTLAND

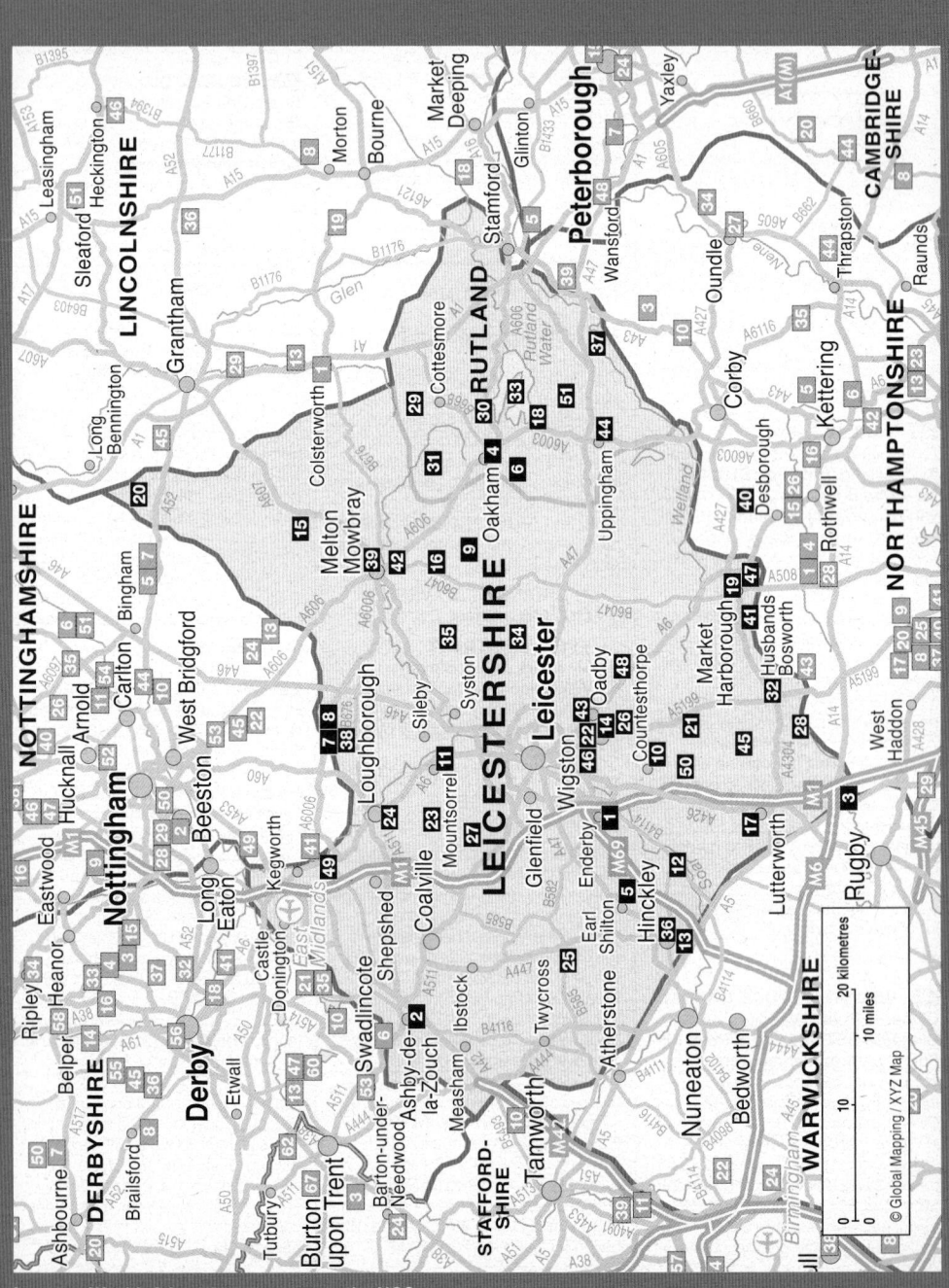

Leicestershire & Rutland

Leicestershire is very much in the centre of England, and has a diverse landscape and wide range of settlements.

Our open gardens are of corresponding variety. From compact Victorian terraces with inspirational planting, large country houses with broad vistas, an arboretum with four national champion trees, to an allotment with over 100 plots. Most gardens welcome groups, sell plants and offer tea and cake.

Confident in the knowledge that your donation goes to wonderful causes, you can look for inspiration for your own garden or plot, or simply take pleasure looking at beautiful gardens.

'Much in Little' is Rutland's motto. They say small is beautiful and never were truer words said.

Rutland is rural England at its best. Honey-coloured stone cottages make up pretty villages nestling amongst rolling hills; the passion for horticulture is everywhere you look, from stunning gardens to the hanging baskets and patio boxes showing off seasonal blooms in our two attractive market towns of Oakham and Uppingham.

There's so much to see in and around Rutland whatever the time of year, including many wonderful NGS gardens.

Left: The Old Hall

Leicestershire & Rutland Volunteers

Leicestershire

County Organiser
Colin Olle
01858 575791
colin.olle@ngs.org.uk

County Treasurer
Martin Shave
01455 556633
martinshave@kilworthaccountancy.co.uk

Publicity
Janet Currie
01509 212191
janet.currie@me.com

Assistant County Organisers
Mary Hayward
01162 884018
mary.hayward@ngs.org.uk

Verena Olle
01858 575791
colin.olle@ngs.org.uk

Pamela Shave
01858 575481
pamelashave@btconnect.com

David & Beryl Wyrko
01664 840385

Rutland

County Organiser
Rose Dejardin
01572 737788
rosedejardin@btopenworld.com

County Treasurer
David Wood
01572 737465
rdavidwood@easynet.co.uk

Publicity
Jane Alexander-Orr
01572 737368
janealexanderorr@hotmail.com

Leicestershire & Rutland

Booklet Co-ordinator
Mary Hayward
01162 884018
mary.hayward@ngs.org.uk

Opening Dates

All entries subject to change.
For latest information check www.ngs.org.uk

Extended openings are shown at the begining of the month

February

Snowdrop Festival

Sunday 28
- **13** 6 Denis Road

March

Sunday 6
- **48** Westview

April

- **23** Long Close (every Wednesday to Sunday)

Sunday 3
- **18** Gunthorpe Hall
- **35** Parkside

May

Sunday 1
- **4** Barleythorpe Gardens
- **42** Tresillian House
- **48** Westview

Monday 2
- **23** Long Close
- **48** Westview

Sunday 8
- **9** Burrough Gardens
- **19** Hammond Arboretum

Sunday 15
- **31** The Old Vicarage, Whissendine
- **47** NEW Westbrooke House

Friday 20
- **41** Thorpe Lubenham Hall

Sunday 22
- **26** Mill House
- **30** The Old Vicarage, Burley
- **49** Whatton Gardens

Saturday 28
- **15** Goadby Marwood Hall

Monday 30
- **23** Long Close
- **27** Newtown Linford Gardens

June

- **23** Long Close (every Wednesday to Sunday)

Wednesday 1
- **40** Stoke Albany House

Festival Weekend

Saturday 4
- **44** Uppingham Gardens

Sunday 5
- **10** Countesthorpe Gardens
- **28** Oak Tree House

Wednesday 8
- **40** Stoke Albany House

Saturday 11
- **24** Loughborough Gardens
- **34** The Paddocks

Sunday 12
- **7** 88 Brook Street
- **8** 109 Brook Street
- **12** Dairy Cottage
- **24** Loughborough Gardens
- **29** The Old Hall
- **34** The Paddocks
- **36** NEW 60 Princess Road

Wednesday 15
- **40** Stoke Albany House

Sunday 19
- **2** Ashby-de-la-Zouch Gardens
- **10** Countesthorpe Gardens
- **16** NEW Great Dalby
- **45** Walton Gardens
- **51** Wing Gardens

Wednesday 22
- **40** Stoke Albany House
- **45** Walton Gardens

Saturday 25
- **14** 28 Gladstone Street

Sunday 26
- **14** 28 Gladstone Street
- **21** NEW Homestead Farmhouse
- **25** Market Bosworth Gardens

Wednesday 29
- **40** Stoke Albany House

July

- **23** Long Close (every Wednesday to Sunday to 17 July)

Sunday 3
- **33** Orchard House, Hambleton
- **42** Tresillian House
- **47** NEW Westbrooke House

Wednesday 6
- **40** Stoke Albany House

Sunday 10
- **17** Green Wicket Farm
- **26** Mill House

Wednesday 13
- **17** Green Wicket Farm

Saturday 16
- **14** 28 Gladstone Street

Sunday 17
- **14** 28 Gladstone Street
- **37** NEW Redhill Lodge
- **50** Willoughby Gardens

Sunday 24
- **32** Orchard House
- **39** 119 Scalford Road

August

Sunday 7
- **22** Knighton Sensory
- **43** University Botanic Garden

Sunday 14
- **6** Braunston Gardens

Sunday 21
- **1** 12 Alexander Avenue

Sunday 28
- **3** Avon House
- **42** Tresillian House

September

- **23** Long Close (every Wednesday to Sunday)

Sunday 4
- **48** Westview

Saturday 10
- **28** Oak Tree House

Sunday 11
- **28** Oak Tree House
- **46** Washbrook Allotments

October

- **23** Long Close (every Wednesday to Sunday to 5th October)

Sunday 23
- **42** Tresillian House

Gardens open to the public

- **49** Whatton Gardens

By arrangement only

- **5** Barracca
- **11** 7 The Crescent
- **20** The Homestead
- **38** Ridgewold Farm

Also open by arrangement

- **3** Avon House
- **7** 88 Brook Street
- **8** 109 Brook Street
- **10** 2 Elliots Yard, Countesthorpe Gardens
- **10** NEW 29 Peatling Road, Countesthorpe Gardens
- **12** Dairy Cottage
- **15** Goadby Marwood Hall
- **17** Green Wicket Farm
- **18** Gunthorpe Hall
- **22** Knighton Sensory
- **23** Long Close
- **24** 134 Herrick Road, Loughborough Gardens
- **26** Mill House
- **28** Oak Tree House
- **30** The Old Vicarage, Burley
- **32** Orchard House
- **34** The Paddocks
- **35** Parkside
- **37** NEW Redhill Lodge
- **39** 119 Scalford Road
- **40** Stoke Albany House
- **42** Tresillian House
- **45** Orchards, Walton Gardens
- **45** Toad Hall, Walton Gardens
- **48** Westview
- **50** Farmway, Willoughby Gardens

Our garden is an extension of the house, a place to potter, relax and enjoy . . .

The Gardens

1 12 ALEXANDER AVENUE

Enderby, Leicester LE19 4NA. Mr &
Mrs J Beeson. *4m S of Leicester.
From M1 J21 take A5460 to Fosse
Park, turn R on B4114. Turn R to
Enderby at next r'about, straight on
to church then follow yellow NGS
signs.* **Sun 21 Aug (11-5). Adm £2,
chd free. Home-made teas.**
Our small town garden has been
carefully designed to make full use of
the space available and to provide
interest all yr-round. We have
dispensed with the lawn giving us
space to create different areas in the
garden, incl a pond, and to
accommodate a wide variety of
plants chosen for colour and to
attract wildlife. Our garden is an
extension of the house, a place to
potter, relax and enjoy. Some gravel
areas.

GROUP OPENING

2 ASHBY-DE-LA-ZOUCH GARDENS

Ashby-De-La-Zouch LE65 2FA. *10
mins walk from town centre. 1m from
A42 J12. At bottom of Ashby High St,
turn L, follow rd past Royal Hotel,
under bridge, then follow signs. From
M42, N, J12, 1m past golf course,
then R after carwash into Avenue Rd.*
**Sun 19 June (11-6). Combined
adm £3, chd free. Home-made
teas.**

7 AVENUE ROAD
Mrs Jane Sheffield

27 AVENUE ROAD
Annie & Steve Mills

72 TAMWORTH ROAD
Mike & Jane Plackett

Set in the historic market town in the
heart of The National Forest, three
gardens in close walking distance are
opening for the second time to NGS
visitors. All set behind Victorian town
houses, are three very different
approaches to similar spaces.
72 Tamworth Rd - A relatively new
garden bordered by a wall and a
hedge which we've tried to make
seem less narrow with the use of
circular lawns. Plenty of seating areas
for enjoying the view! Featured in The
Gardener's World magazine.
7 Avenue Rd - With a high Jungle
feel, as the seasons pass, it has
herbaceous plants, shrubs and trees
with an emphasis on texture. Planting
and water features encourage wildlife.
27 Avenue Rd - A constantly evolving
plant addicts garden with many
unusual specimen plants. A 15ft
curved rose tunnel is at the core of
the garden. Christopher Lloyd
inspiration evident in the late summer
planting. Choice perennials, annuals
and exotic plants for sale from my
private nursery. Featured in Amateur
Gardening.

3 AVON HOUSE

4 Rugby Road, Catthorpe,
Lutterworth LE17 6DA. David &
Julia King, 01788 860346,
avonhouse4@btinternet.com. *3m
NE Rugby. 3m S Lutterworth. 1m SW
M1 J19, A14, M6 Junctions. ¹/₂ m NE
A5. Ongoing rd works at Catthorpe
Interchange, please check directions
closer to date. Parking at Manor Farm
Shop.* **Sun 28 Aug (11-5.30). Adm
£2.50, chd free. Light
refreshments at Manor Farm
shop. Visits also by arrangement
June to Sept, refreshments by
request.**
A surprising ¹/₂ acre garden in the
heart of the village. Large vegetable
plot, mixed borders of late season
interest, fruit trees, hens, bees and
garden ponds all tucked away behind
a country cottage. Some gravelled
areas and uneven ground.

Stoke Albany House

GROUP OPENING

4 BARLEYTHORPE GARDENS

Barleythorpe, nr Oakham
LE15 7EQ. *1m from Oakham on A6006 towards Melton Mowbray. Car park in Pasture Lane 1st L in Barleythorpe by post box. Please park in field on L not on lane.* **Sun 1 May (2-5). Combined adm £5, chd free. Home-made teas at Dairy Cottage.** *Donation to East Midlands Immediate Care Scheme.*

BARLEYTHORPE HOUSE
Richard Turner

DAIRY COTTAGE
Mr & Mrs W Smith

THE LODGE
Dr & Mrs T J Gray

Visit 3 beautiful gardens in this Rutland village. Dairy Cottage (opp car park) is a cottage style garden at rear with interesting and unusual shrubs and spring bulbs. Paved/walled garden to front (with pond) and lime hedge. Orchard with spring bulbs and unusual shrubs and trees. The Lodge (next door) has colourful mixed borders and spring bulbs surrounding a formal lawn within a walled garden, a vegetable garden to the rear is separated from the lawn and adjacent sitting area by a small stretch of gravel path. Follow path alongside Dairy Cottage, turn left into Manor Lane for Barleythorpe House - offering both water and woodland. Flowering shrubs, mature large weeping trees, a small lake with interesting marginal planting and a woodland walk.

♿ 🎉 ❀ ☕

5 BARRACCA

Ivydene Close, Earl Shilton
LE9 7NR. Mr & Mrs John & Sue Osborn, 01455 842609, susan.osborn1@btinternet.com, www.barraccagardens.co.uk. *10m W of Leicester. From A47 after entering Earl Shilton, Ivydene Close is 4th on L from Leicester side of A47.* **Visits by arrangement May to July for groups 10+. Smaller groups considered. Adm £6, chd free. Adm incl tea/coffee and home-made cakes.**
1 acre garden with lots of different areas, silver birch walk, wildlife pond with seating, apple tree garden, Mediterranean planted area and lawns surrounded with herbaceous

plants and shrubs. Patio area with climbing roses and wisteria. There is also a utility garden with greenhouse, vegetables in beds, herbs and perennial flower beds, lawn and fruit cage. Part of the old gardens owned by the Cotton family who used to open approx 9 acres to the public in the 1920's. Partial wheelchair access.

♿ 🚌 ☕

WE ARE MACMILLAN. CANCER SUPPORT

The NGS is Macmillan's largest single donor

GROUP OPENING

6 BRAUNSTON GARDENS

Braunston, nr Oakham LE15 8QS. *Quaintree Hall is located in Braunston, 2m S of Oakham. Hill Top Farm is ½ m out of Oakham in the direction of Braunston.* **Sun 14 Aug (2-6). Combined adm £5, chd free. Home-made teas at Hill Top Farm.**

HILL TOP FARM 🛌
Jane & William Cross.
01572 755744
janecross@btconnect.com
www.cross-in-rutland.co.uk

QUAINTREE HALL
Mrs Caroline Lomas.

Two large gardens belonging to keen gardening friends with different styles. Hill Top Farm - Fabulous views of the surrounding countryside from this aptly named property. The terrace surrounding the house is host to containers and beds packed with sun loving plants. Paths invite the visitor to stroll amongst borders of interesting shrubs and perennials, over treed lawns and through wildflowers areas. A woodland area with hazel walk has recently been extended with plantings of oak and fir and a new wildlife pond. Quaintree Hall in Braunston - An established garden surrounding the medieval hall house (not open) incl a formal box parterre to the front of the house, a woodland walk, formal walled garden with yew hedges, a small picking

garden and a terraced courtyard garden with conservatory. A wide selection of interesting plants can be enjoyed here, each carefully selected for its specific site by the knowledgeable garden owner. Featured in Rutland Pride magazine. Some gravel and steps.

♿ 🎉 ❀ ☕

7 88 BROOK STREET

Wymeswold LE12 6TU. Adrian & Ita Cooke, 01509 880155, itacooke@btinternet.com. *4m NE of Loughborough. From A6006 Wymeswold turn S by church onto Stockwell, then E along Brook St. Roadside parking on Brook St.* **Sun 12 June (11-5). Combined adm with 109 Brook Street £4, chd free. Visits also by arrangement May & June (combined visits to incl 109 Brook Street possible).**
The ½ acre garden is set on a hillside, which provides lovely views across the village, and comprises 3 distinct areas: firstly, a cottage style garden; then a water garden with a stream and champagne pond; and finally at the top there is a vegetable plot, small orchard and wildflower meadow. The ponds are a breeding ground for great crested newts, common newts, frogs and toads.

🎉 ❀ ☕

8 109 BROOK STREET

Wymeswold LE12 6TT. Maggie & Steve Johnson, 01509 880866, sameuk@tiscali.co.uk. *4m NE of Loughborough. From A6006 Wymeswold turn S onto Stockwell, then E along Brook St. Roadside parking along Brook St. Steep drive with limited disabled parking at house.* **Sun 12 June (11-5). Combined adm with 88 Brook Street £4, chd free. Light refreshments. Visits also by arrangement May & June for groups 10+. Min 2 weeks notice please. (Combined visits to incl 88 Brook Street possible).**
S facing ¾ acre gently sloping garden with views to open country. Mature garden much improved. Patio with roses and clematis, wildlife and fish ponds, mixed borders, vegetable garden, orchard, hot garden and woodland garden. Something for everyone. Demonstration of rain water harvesting on limited budget. Some gravel paths.

♿ 🎉 ❀ ☕

GROUP OPENING

9 BURROUGH GARDENS

Burrough on the Hill, Nr Melton Mowbray LE14 2QZ. *Close to B6047. 10 mins from A606. 20 mins from Melton Mowbray.* **Sun 8 May (2-5). Combined adm £5, chd free. Home-made teas at Burrough Hall.**

BURROUGH HALL
Richard & Alice Cunningham

BURROUGH HOUSE
Roger & Sam Weatherby

2 large gardens, both with magnificent views over High Leicestershire. Burrough House, in the middle of the village, has an extensive garden surrounding a former stone farmhouse with stunning views over the surrounding countryside. The current owners are adding to the former established garden to create a series of vistas and spaces and maximise the views in and out of the garden with the use of clipped hedges and avenues. Burrough Hall, outside the village between Somerby and Burrough, was built in 1867 as a classic Leicestershire hunting lodge. The garden, framed by mature trees and shrubs, was extensively redesigned by garden designer George Carter in 2007. This family garden, which continues to develop for the enjoyment of all generations, consists of extensive lawns, mixed borders, a vegetable garden and woodland walks. There will be a small collection of vintage and classic cars on display at Burrough Hall.

GROUP OPENING

10 COUNTESTHORPE GARDENS

Countesthorpe, Leicester LE8 5RG. *5m S Leicester. From r'bout in centre of village follow yellow NGS arrows.* **Sun 5, Sun 19 June (11-5). Combined adm £5, chd free. Home-made teas.**

2 ELLIOTS YARD
Sue Hobson
Visits also by arrangement May & June, groups 15 max.
martinandsuehobson@btinternet.com
01162 788070

4 PACKMAN GREEN
Roger Whitmore & Shirley Jackson

NEW 29 PEATLING ROAD
Jane & Mike Thompson
Visits also by arrangement May & June, groups 20 max
P_jane_thompson@hotmail.com
01162 770584

All gardens are close to the village centre, but about 400yds apart. Elliots Yard is a small sheltered garden planted with an emphasis on variegated and contrasting foliage, interspersed with some seasonal flowers. A water feature and small pond add additional interest. 4 Packman Green is a small town house garden packed with hardy perennials and surrounded by climbing roses, clematis, honeysuckle and jasmine, making it an enclosed peaceful haven filled with colour and scent. The Peatling Rd garden is ¹/₃ acre, with mixed cottage garden flowers, shrubs, vegetables and a water feature. With the additional interest of a bonsai collection and summer house.

11 7 THE CRESCENT
Rothley LE7 7RW. Mrs Fiona Dunkley, 01162 376301, fiona.dunkley@btinternet.com. *Off Montsorrel Lane, Rothley. Parking on Montsorrel Lane.* **Visits by arrangement May to Aug for groups, min 10, max 30. Adm £2, chd free. Home-made teas.**
Small, well designed garden with interesting and unusual plants. Good display of alliums in spring. Many diverse grasses and bamboos combined with verbena bonariensis create a very special effect in late summer and autumn.

12 DAIRY COTTAGE
15 Sharnford Road, Sapcote LE9 4JN. Mrs Norah Robinson-Smith, 01455 272398, nrobinsons@yahoo.co.uk. *9m SW of Leicester. Sharnford Rd joins Leicester Rd in Sapcote to B4114 Coventry Rd. Follow NGS signs at both ends.* **Sun 12 June (1-5). Adm £3, chd free. Home-made teas. Visits also by arrangement May to July.**
From a walled garden with colourful mixed borders to a potager approached along a woodland path, this mature cottage garden combines extensive perennial planting with many unusual shrubs and specimen trees. More than 100 clematis and climbing roses are trained up pergolas, arches and into trees 50ft high, so don't forget to look up!

13 6 DENIS ROAD
Burbage LE10 2LR. Mr & Mrs D A Dawkins. *13m SW of Leicester. From M69 J1 take B4109 signed Hinckley. First L after 2nd r'about. Follow yellow signs.* **Sun 28 Feb (11-4). Adm £2.50, chd free. Light refreshments.**
Small garden open for snowdrops, spring bulbs and hellebores.

> Garden developed as a contemporary take on a traditional English cottage . . .

14 28 GLADSTONE STREET
Wigston Magna LE18 1AE. Chris & Janet Huscroft, 01162 886014, chris.huscroft@tiscali.co.uk. *4m S of Leicester. Off Wigston by-pass (A5199) follow signs off r'about.* **Sat 25, Sun 26 June, Sat 16, Sun 17 July (11-5). Adm £2.50, chd free. Cream teas.**
Our small town garden is divided into rooms and bisected by a pond with a bridge. It is brimming with unusual hardy perennials, incl collections of ferns and hostas. David Austin roses chosen for their scent feature throughout, incl a 30' rose arch. An unusual shade house with rare plants, incl hardy orchids and arisaema's. Some replanting in 2015. Come and see the difference! Frameworks Knitters Museum nearby - open Suns.

The Old Vicarage, Burley

15 **GOADBY MARWOOD HALL**
Goadby Marwood LE14 4LN. Mr & Mrs Westropp, 01664 464202. *4m NW of Melton Mowbray. Between Waltham-on-the-Wolds & Eastwell, 8m S of Grantham.* **Sat 28 May (11-4). Adm £3.50, chd free. Home-made teas in Village Hall. Visits also by arrangement Mar to Oct, plenty of parking space.**
Redesigned in 2000 by the owner based on C18 plans. A chain of 5 lakes (covering 10 acres) and several ironstone walled gardens all interconnected. Lakeside woodland walk. Planting for yr-round interest. Landscaper trained under plantswoman Rosemary Verey at Barnsley House. Beautiful C13 church open. Featured in Good Gardens of England guide and on Castles in the Country, BBC 2. Gravel paths and lawns.

GROUP OPENING

16 **NEW** **GREAT DALBY**
Melton Mowbray LE14 2EY. Jane West. *3m S of Melton Mowbray on B6047. On arrival in village, from any direction, follow NGS signs.* **Sun 19 June (11-5). Combined adm £5,** chd free. Home-made teas at Crossfell House.

NEW **CROSSFELL HOUSE**
Jane & Ian West

NEW **RAMBLER COTTAGE**
Peter & Robina Mitchell

Two very different gardens. Crossfell House has a formal garden with a terraced herbaceous border, rockery, and shrubs, together with two acres of meadows containing wild grasses and flowers. Rambler Cottage is a country garden of $^2/_3$ acre with mixed borders, a small orchard, potager, patio garden herbaceous borders, greenhouse, potting shed, a vegetable garden and a wildlife pond with great crested newts. Wheelchair access at Crossfell House only.

17 **GREEN WICKET FARM**
Ullesthorpe Road, Bitteswell, Lutterworth LE17 4LR. Mrs Anna Smith, 01455 552646, greenfarmbitt@hotmail.com. *2m NW of Lutterworth J20 M1. From Lutterworth follow signs through Bitteswell towards Ullesthorpe. Garden situated behind Bitteswell Cricket Club. Field parking available subject to weather conditions.*
Sun 10, Wed 13 July (2-5). Adm £3, chd free. Home-made teas. Visits also by arrangement May to Sept for groups min 10, max 30.
Created in 2008 on a working farm. Clay soil and very exposed but beginning to look established. Many unusual hardy plants along with a lot of old favourites have been used to provide a long season of colour and interest. Anemone nemorosa, Pacific coast iris, sedums and salvias are of particular interest. Formal ponds and water feature. Some gravel paths.

18 **GUNTHORPE HALL**
Gunthorpe, Oakham LE15 8BE. Tim Haywood, tim.haywood@gam.com. *A6003 between Oakham & Uppingham; 1m from Oakham, up drive between lodges. Proceed over railway bridge to gardens, 600 yards ahead. Please follow the signs for parking.* **Sun 3 Apr (2-5). Adm £4, chd free. Light refreshments. Visits also by arrangement May to Sept (visits subject to major works completion).**
Large garden in a country setting with extensive views across the Rutland landscape. A great deal of recent re-design have transformed this garden.

The new spring bulbs and shrubs are notable features. More recent works have been undertaken on the kitchen garden and around the (former) stable yard.

19 HAMMOND ARBORETUM
Burnmill Road, Market Harborough LE16 7JG. The Robert Smyth Academy. *15m S of Leicester on A6. From High St, follow signs to The Robert Smyth Academy via Bowden Lane to Burnmill Rd. Park in 1st entrance on L.* **Sun 8 May (2-4.30). Adm £4, chd free. Home-made teas.**
A site of just under 2½ acres containing an unusual collection of trees and shrubs, many from Francis Hammond's original planting dating from 1913 to 1936 whilst headmaster of the school. Species from America, China and Japan with malus and philadelphus walks and a moat. Proud owners of 4 champion trees identified by national specialist. Guided walks and walk plans available. Some steep slopes.

20 THE HOMESTEAD
Normanton-by-Bottesford NG13 0EP. John & Shirley Palmer, 01949 842745. *8m W of Grantham. From A52, turn N in Bottesford, signed Normanton; last house on R. From A1, 1st house on L.* **Visits by arrangement Feb to June. Adm £2.50, chd free. Light refreshments.**
¾ acre informal plant lover's garden. Vegetable garden, small orchard, shaded area, hellebores, growing collection (over 100) of snowdrops and some single peonies and salvias. Collections of hostas and sempervivums. National Collection of heliotropes. A garden where plants (incl vegetables) come first to produce a peaceful and relaxed overall effect.

21 NEW HOMESTEAD FARMHOUSE
St Peters Road, Arnesby LE8 5WJ. Alison Platts. *On L of St Peter's Rd. Thatched brick house on village green.* **Sun 26 June (12-4.30). Adm £3, chd free. Tea in village church.** *Donation to Parkinsons UK.*
This small walled garden was part of the original farmyard. It has been developed as a contemporary take on a traditional English cottage

garden. Although there is a strong underlying design element there is an informality in the way the mixed herbaceous borders have been planted. Raised vegetable beds, fruit trees and a rill add further interest. There are a number of view points with seats.

Since our foundation we have donated more than £45 million to charity . . .

22 KNIGHTON SENSORY
Knighton Park, Leicester LE2 3YQ. Mike Chalk, kpgc@hotmail.co.uk, www.knightonparkgardeningclub. com. *Off A563 (Outer Ring Rd) S of Leicester. From Palmerston Blvd, turn into South Kingsmead Rd then 1st L into Woodbank Rd. Park entrance at end of rd. Enter park, follow path to R, garden then on R.* **Sun 7 Aug (1-5). Adm by donation. Tea. Visits also by arrangement May to Aug for groups 10 - 20.**
This ¼ acre community garden stands in a secluded corner of Knighton Park away from the bustle of the city. It is a feast for all the senses incl shrubs, some traditional bedding, herbaceous borders, bog garden with bridge, dry riverbed with wild flowers and wildlife area, Separate area contains raised beds for edibles. Awarded outstanding by the It's Your Neighbourhood Scheme.

23 LONG CLOSE
60 Main St, Woodhouse Eaves LE12 8RZ. John Oakland, 01509 890376, longclosegardens@btinternet.com, www.longclose.org.uk. *4m S of Loughborough. Nr M1 J23. From A6, W in Quorn.* **Every Wed to Sun 1 Apr to 17 July (10.30-4.30). Mon 2, Mon 30 May (10.30-4.30). Every Wed to Sun 1 Sept to 9 Oct (10.30-4.30). Adm £4, chd 50p. Visits also by arrangement Apr to Oct, groups min 15. Tea/coffee & biscuits for booked groups.**
5 acres spring bulbs, rhododendrons, azaleas, camellias, magnolias, many rare shrubs, mature trees, lily ponds;

terraced lawns, herbaceous borders, potager in walled kitchen garden, wildflower meadow walk. Winter, spring, summer and autumn colour, a garden for all seasons. 100yr old wildflower meadows open May to 15th July.

GROUP OPENING

24 LOUGHBOROUGH GARDENS
Loughborough LE11 2BU, www.thesecateur.com. *1m SW Loughborough. From M1 J23 take A512 Ashby Rd to Loughborough. At r'about R onto A6004 Epinal Way. At Beacon Rd r'about L, Herrick Rd 1st on R.* **Sat 11 June (12-5); Sun 12 June (11-5). Combined adm £3, chd free. Tea.**

94 HERRICK ROAD
Marion Smith

134 HERRICK ROAD
Janet Currie
Visits also by arrangement June to Sept
janet.currie@me.com
01509 212191

47 PARKLANDS DRIVE
Lynda & Alan Burton

This side of Loughborough is a quiet leafy area with a mix of Victorian and mid century homes. The gardens in this group contain plenty of horticultural and creative interest. 134 Herrick Road is a garden designed for tranquility, wildlife and produce brimming with texture, colour and creative flair. The excellent Secret Craft Fair held during the open gardens weekend provides additional delight and surprises for visitors. 94 Herrick Road is a traditional old fashioned English garden with mainly perennial planting, an interest in hardy geraniums and Heucheras, and home to two active and productive beehives. 47 Parklands Drive has mixed borders with a wide variety of shrubs, herbaceous perennials and bulbs, planted to attract and support wildlife as well as creating an attractive place to sit and relax. Herrick Road Honey will also be on sale. Loughborough NGS Open Gardens weekend is part of a gardens and arts trail across Loughborough in 2016.

GROUP OPENING

25 MARKET BOSWORTH GARDENS

Market Bosworth CV13 0LE. *13m W of Leicester; 8m N of Hinckley. 1m off A447 Coalville to Hinckley Rd, 3m off A444. Burton to Nuneaton Rd.* Sun 26 June (1-6). Combined adm £5, chd free. Light refreshments at 13 Spinney Hill & 15 York Close. *Donation to Bosworth in Bloom.*

> **GLEBE FARM HOUSE**
> Mr Peter Ellis & Ms Ginny Broad
>
> **4 LANCASTER AVENUE**
> Mr Peter Bailiss
>
> **26 NORTHUMBERLAND AVENUE**
> Mrs Kathy Boot
>
> **30 PARK STREET**
> Lesley Best
>
> **4 PRIORY ROAD**
> Mrs Margaret Barrett
>
> **5 PRIORY ROAD**
> David & Linda Chevell
>
> **RAINBOW COTTAGE**
> Mr David Harrison
>
> **13 SPINNEY HILL**
> Mrs J Buckell
>
> **3 WARWICK CLOSE**
> Mrs Margaret Birch
>
> **6 WARWICK CLOSE**
> Mrs Betty Zuger
>
> **15 YORK CLOSE**
> Mrs G M Clinton

Market Bosworth is an attractive market town, with an enviable record for the quality of its regular entry in the annual East Midlands in Bloom competition. There are a number of gardens open, some for the first time, and all within walking distance of the Market Square. The gardens show various planting styles and different approaches to small and intimate spaces in the historic town centre, as well as larger plots in more recent developments. Tickets and descriptive maps obtainable in the Market Place, with refreshments available there and at two of the gardens. Plants will be on sale at a number of gardens. A proportion of the proceeds from the Gardens Open Day will be used to support Bosworth in Bloom, the voluntary group responsible for the town's floral displays; see

www.bosworthinbloom.co.uk. Farmers' Market in town centre (9-2) local produce, hot and cold food.

26 MILL HOUSE

118 Welford Road, Wigston LE18 3SN. Mr & Mrs P Measures, 01162 885409, petemeasures@hotmail.co.uk. *4m S of Leicester. From Leicester to Wigston Magna follow A5199 Welford Rd S towards Kilby, up hill past Mercers Newsagents, 100yds on L.* Sun 22 May, Sun 10 July (12-5). Adm £2.50, chd free. Home-made teas. Visits also by arrangement May to July, flexible times for groups 3 - 25.

Walled town garden with an extensive plant variety, many rare and unusual. A plant lovers garden, with interesting designs incorporated in the borders, rockery and scree. It is full of surprises with memorabilia and bygones a reminder of our past. Good variety of reasonably priced plants for sale.

GROUP OPENING

27 NEWTOWN LINFORD GARDENS

86 - 114 Main Street, Newtown Linford, Leicester LE6 0AF. *6m NW Leicester. 2½ m from M1 J22. ½ m W of main Bradgate Park Entrance.* Mon 30 May (11-5). Combined adm £5, chd free. Home-made teas at Meadow Cottage, 98 Main Street.

> **APPLETREE COTTAGE**
> Katherine Duffy Anthony
>
> **BANK COTTAGE**
> Jan Croft
>
> **DELL COTTAGE**
> Maureen Sutton
>
> **DINGLE HOUSE**
> Mr & Mrs R Howard
>
> **LINCROFT**
> Stan Clarke
>
> NEW **MEADOW COTTAGE**
> Michael & Rosemarie Upstone
>
> **WOODLANDS**
> Mary Husseini

Newtown Linford is a historic village bordering Bradgate Park and is part of Charnwood Forest. Through the village runs the R Lin, and four adjacent properties have banks from where you can see brown trout or the occasional kingfisher. All of the neighbours share a passion for their very different gardens. Appletree Cottage has a charming enclosed garden surrounding C17 thatched cottage, interesting paths leading to lawns, borders, sun terrace and small lily pond. Bank Cottage is set on different levels and is a typical cottage garden providing yr-round colour but prettiest in spring. Dell Cottage is a small sheltered garden where azaleas and rhododendrons grow well. The R Lin runs through Woodlands where grow many varied shrubs and spring flowers around the mature trees. Dingle House has a small garden on many levels with yr-round colour. Lincroft is noted for spectacular rhododendrons and azaleas. You will enjoy tea and cake at Meadow Cottage. Not to be missed. Stall offering vintage garden tools for sale.

28 OAK TREE HOUSE

North Road, South Kilworth LE17 6DU. Pam & Martin Shave, 01858 575481, pamelashave@btconnect.com. *15m S of Leicester. From M1 J20, take A4304 towards Market Harborough. At North Kilworth turn R, signed South Kilworth. Garden on after approx 1m.* Sun 5 June (11-5); Sat 10 Sept (1-5); Sun 11 Sept (11-5). Adm £3, chd free. Home-made teas. Visits also by arrangement May to Sept.

⅔ acre garden. Beautiful country garden full of colour, formal design, softened by cottage style planting. Stone circle and sculpture. Large herbaceous borders, vegetable plots, pond, greenhouse, shady area, grass border. Extensive collections in pots, including perennial violas. Trees chosen for attractive bark. Nearly 40 types of clematis and many more roses. Dramatic arched pergola. Gravel drive.

29 ▶ THE OLD HALL

Main Street, Market Overton
LE15 7PL. Mr & Mrs Timothy Hart,
01572 767145,
stefa@hambleton.co.uk. *6m N of Oakham. Beyond Cottesmore from Oakham; 5m from A1 via Thistleton. 10m E from Melton Mowbray via Wymondham.* **Sun 12 June (2-6). Adm £4.50, chd free. Teas and coffees served with Hambleton Bakery cakes.**

Set on a southerly ridge overlooking Catmose Vale, the garden is now on 4 levels. Stone walls and yew hedges divide the garden into enclosed areas with herbaceous borders, shrubs, and young and mature trees. In 2006 the lower part of garden was planted with new shrubs to create a walk with mown paths. There are interesting plants flowering most of the time. Neil Hewertson has been involved in the gardens design since 1990s. Partial wheelchair access. Gravel and mown paths. Return to house is steep.

30 ▶ THE OLD VICARAGE, BURLEY

Church Road, Burley, Nr Oakham
LE15 7SU. Jonathan & Sandra
Blaza, 01572 770588,
sandra.blaza@btinternet.com,
www.theoldvicarageburley.com.
1m NE of Oakham. In Burley just off B668 between Oakham & Cottesmore. Church Rd is opp village green. **Sun 22 May (1.30-5). Adm £4.50, chd free. Home-made teas. Visits also by arrangement May & June for groups 10+.**

Country garden, planted for yr round interest, incl a walled garden (with vine house) producing fruit, herbs, vegetables and cut flowers. Formal lawns and borders, lime walk, rose gardens and a rill through an avenue of standard wisteria. Wildlife garden with pond, 2 orchards and mixed woodland. Featured in Period Living magazine. Some gravel and steps between terraces.

31 ▶ THE OLD VICARAGE, WHISSENDINE

2, Station Road, Whissendine
LE15 7HG. Prof Peter & Dr Sarah
Furness,
www.pathology.plus.com/Garden.
Station Rd. Garden situated up hill from St Andrew's church in Whissendine. 1st gate on L in Station Rd. **Sun 15 May (2-5). Adm £4, chd free. Home-made teas in St**

Andrew's Church, Whissendine.
$2/3$ acre packed with variety. Terrace with topiary, a formal fountain courtyard and raised beds backed by small gothic orangery burgeoning with tender plants. Herbaceous borders surround main lawn. Wisteria tunnel leads to new raised vegetable beds and large ornate greenhouse, four beehives, Gothic hen house plus six rare breed hens. Hidden white walk, unusual plants and much, much more! Teas served in the Lady Chapel of the Church and outside if clement. Access to the church can be gained from the garden or from Main Street. Featured in Rutland Life and The GGG. Partial wheelchair access due to gravel paths, slopes and steps.

32 ▶ ORCHARD HOUSE

14 Mowsley Rd, Husbands
Bosworth LE17 6LR. David & Ros
Dunmore, d.dunmore@yahoo.com.
6m W of Market Harborough. A4304 from Market Harborough enter village. Mowsley Rd is 3rd R. A4304 from Lutterworth/ M1, enter village. Mowsley Rd is 3rd L. **Sun 24 July (12-4). Adm £3, chd free. Home-made teas. Visits also by arrangement June to Aug for groups 20 max, afternoon or evenings.** *Donation to Rainbows children's hospice.*

A hidden gem. Small enclosed cottage garden with elements of surprise around each corner. Five garden rooms shaded by mature trees and linked by Victorian gravel paths. Patio area with summer planting, small pond and other water features. Alpine bed and varied use of container planting. Wheelchair access to main features of the garden. Some gravel paths.

33 ▶ ORCHARD HOUSE, HAMBLETON

Lyndon Road, Hambleton, Nr
Oakham LE15 8TJ. Richard & Celia
Foulkes. *Next to Rutland Water, 400 yds from centre of Hambleton. Enter village, turn R at church, down hill, only house at bottom on R.* **Sun 3 July (2-5). Adm £3.50, chd free. Home-made teas.**

Beautifully situated partly bordering Rutland Water. Series of garden rooms incl formal, Japanese and vegetable gardens; newly planted orchard; and large informal garden with rose pergola and copses.

34 ▶ THE PADDOCKS

Main Street, Hungarton LE7 9JY.
Michael & Helen Martin, 01162
595230. *8m E of Leicester. Follow NGS signs.* **Sat 11, Sun 12 June (12-5). Adm £4, chd free. Light refreshments at Village Hall. Visits also by arrangement May to Aug for groups 20+.**

2 acre garden with mature and specimen trees, rhododendrons, azaleas, magnolia grandiflora, wisterias. Two lily ponds and stream. Three lawn areas surrounded by herbaceous and shrub borders. Woodland walk. Pergola with clematis and roses, hosta collection and two rockeries. Large well established semi permanent plant stall in aid of local charities. Featured on Radio Leicester and in Leicester Mercury. Partial wheelchair access due to steep slopes at rear of garden. Flat terrace by main lawn provides good viewing area.

> From the banks of the river you can see brown trout or the occasional kingfisher. . . .

35 ▶ PARKSIDE

6 Park Hill, Gaddesby LE7 4WH.
Mr & Mrs D Wyrko, 01664 840385.
8m NE of Leicester. From A607 Rearsby bypass turn off for Gaddesby. L at Cheney Arms. Garden 400yds on R. **Sun 3 Apr (11-5). Adm £3, chd free. Home-made teas. Visits also by arrangement Apr to Sept, adm £5 incl tea and cake for groups 30 max.**

Woodland garden of approx $1\frac{1}{4}$ acres containing many spring flowers and bulbs. Vegetable garden with cordon fruit trees and soft fruit. Greenhouse, cold frame and pond with bog garden and other features. Informal mixed borders planted to encourage wildlife, to provide a family friendly environment and offering all yr-round interest.

36 NEW **60 PRINCESS ROAD**
Hinckley LE10 1EB. Cynthia Lines.
*From J1 M69 take B4109. Under rail
bridge, turn R at T-lights. Take 4th L
then 1st L.* **Sun 12 June (11-5).
Adm £2.50, chd free. Home-made
teas.**
A town garden on a corner plot with
surprises round every corner. The front
garden is small with mixed planting for
yr round interest. The rear garden has
many nooks and crannies. There are
cordon trained minarette fruit trees, a
rose pergola, wildlife friendly pond with
water lilies, bog garden, sunken patio
and a summerhouse which looks over
the lawn.

37 NEW **REDHILL LODGE**
Seaton Road, Barrowden, Oakham
LE15 8EN. Richard & Susan Moffitt,
01572 748653,
s.moffitt@yahoo.co.uk. *Redhill
Lodge is 1m from village of
Barrowden along Seaton Rd.* **Sun 17
July (12-6). Adm £4, chd free.
Light refreshments. Visits also by
arrangement May to Oct.**
Still evolving bold contemporary
design with formal lawns, grass
amphitheatre and turf viewing mound,
herbaceous borders and cutting
garden. Praire style planting showing
vibrant colour in late summer. Also
natural swimming pond surrounded
by Japanese style planting, bog
garden and meadow area.

38 **RIDGEWOLD FARM**
Burton Lane, Wymeswold
LE12 6UN. Robert & Ann Waterfall,
01509 881689,
robert.waterfall@yahoo.co.uk. *5m
SE of Loughborough. Off Burton
Lane between A6006 & B676. Ample
car & coach parking.* **Visits by
arrangement May to July for
groups 10 - 50 max. Adm incl
home-made teas. Adm £5.50, chd
free.**
2½ acre rural garden in the Leics
Wolds. Conducted tours of garden
and working farm, start at the
sweeping drive of specimen trees.
Beech, laurel and saxon hedges
divide different areas. Lawn, rill, water
feature, summer house, shrubs, rose
fence, clematis arch, wisteria, ivy
tunnel, rose garden, herbaceous,
orchard, vegetable patch. Birch
avenue gives view of the village.
Woodland walk. Wildlife pond.

ROSEBRIAR
See Northamptonshire

39 **119 SCALFORD ROAD**
Melton Mowbray LE13 1JZ.
Richard & Hilary Lawrence, 01664
562821, randh1954@me.com. *½ m
N of Melton Mowbray. Take Scalford
Rd from town centre past Cattle
Market. Garden 100yds after 1st
turning on L (The Crescent).* **Sun 24
July (11-5). Adm £2.50, chd free.
Home-made teas. Gluten-free
available! Visits also by
arrangement June to Aug for
groups 10 - 25 max.**
Larger than average town garden
which has evolved over the last
25yrs. Mixed borders with traditional
and exotic plants, enhanced by
container planting particularly
begonias. Vegetable parterre and
greenhouse. Various seating areas for
viewing different aspects of the
garden. Water features incl ponds.
Partial wheelchair access. Gravelled
drive, ramp provided up to lawn but
paths not accessible.

40 **STOKE ALBANY HOUSE**
Desborough Road, Stoke Albany
LE16 8PT. Mr & Mrs A M Vinton,
del.jones7@googlemail.com,
www.stokealbanyhouse.co.uk. *4m
E of Market Harborough. Via A427 to
Corby, turn to Stoke Albany, R at the
White Horse (B669) garden ½ m on
L.* **Weds 1, 8, 15, 22, 29 June, Wed
6 July (2-4.30). Adm £4.50, chd
free. Visits also by arrangement
for groups 10+ (Weds preferably).**
*Donation to Marie Curie Cancer
Care.*
4 acre country house garden; fine
trees and shrubs with wide
herbaceous borders and sweeping
striped lawn. Good display of bulbs in
spring, roses June and July. Walled
grey garden; nepeta walk arched with
roses, parterre with box and roses.
Mediterranean garden. Heated
greenhouse, potager with topiary,
water feature garden and sculptures.

SULBY GARDENS
See Northamptonshire

41 **THORPE LUBENHAM HALL**
Farndon Road, Lubenham
LE16 9TR. Sir Bruce & Lady
MacPhail. *2m W of Market
Harborough. From Market
Harborough take 3rd L off main rd,
down Rushes Lane, past church on*
*L, under old railway bridge & straight
on up private drive.* **Fri 20 May
(10.30-4). Adm £3.50, chd free.
Cream teas.**
15 acres of formal and informal
garden surrounded by parkland and
arable. Many mature trees. Traditional
herbaceous borders and various
water features. Walled pool garden
with raised beds. Ancient moat area
along driveway. Gravel paths, some
steep slopes and steps.

Parts left
uncultivated
with wild cowslips
and grasses . . .

42 **TRESILLIAN HOUSE**
67 Dalby Road, Melton Mowbray
LE13 0BQ. Mrs Alison Blythe,
01664 481997,
studentsint@aol.com,
www.studentsint.com. *Melton
Mowbray. Situated on B6047 Dalby
Rd (Melton to Gt Dalby) going S.
Parking on site. NB: We are not
actually in Great Dalby but in the
south of Melton Mowbray.* **Sun 1
May, Sun 3 July, Sun 28 Aug
(11-4.30). Cream teas. Sun 23 Oct
(11-4). Light refreshments. Adm
£2.50, chd free. Visits also by
arrangement Apr to Oct, groups
30 max.**
¾ acre garden re-established by new
owner between 2009 and 2012.
Beautiful blue cedar trees, excellent
specimen tulip tree. Parts of garden
original, others reinstated with variety
of plants and bushes. Original bog
garden and natural pond reinstated
2015. Koi pond added 2015.
Vegetable plot. Parts left uncultivated
with wild cowslips and grasses. Quiet
oasis. Ploughmans lunches available.
Soup offered on cold days. Stew and
dumplings in October. Slate paths,
steep in places but manageable.

Westbrooke House

43 UNIVERSITY BOTANIC GARDEN

'The Knoll' entrance, Glebe Road, Oadby LE2 2LD. University of Leicester, www.le.ac.uk/botanicgarden. *2m SE of Leicester off A6. On outskirts of city opp race course.* **Sun 7 Aug (10-4). Adm by donation. Light refreshments.**

16 acre garden, whose formal planting centres around a restored Edwardian garden. Plantings originate from around the world and incl an arboretum, a herb garden, woodland and herbaceous borders, rock gardens, a water garden, special collections of skimmia, aubretia and hardy fuchsia, and a series of glasshouses displaying temperate and tropical plants, alpines and succulents. Open daily. Please phone or see garden website.

GROUP OPENING

44 UPPINGHAM GARDENS

Uppingham LE15 9TT. *6m S of Oakham. 7m N of Corby. 5m SW of Rutland Water. On A47 halfway between Leicester & Peterborough. Car parking in market town centre, along Stockerston Rd and in Uppingham School sports centre car park. WC in Market Square.* **Sat 4 June (2-5). Combined adm £5, chd free. Home-made teas in Church Hall, Market Place.**

HILLSIDE
Mr & Mrs Lawrence Fenelon.

THE ORCHARD
Doug & Margaret Stacey.

NEW UPPINGHAM SCHOOL

From the Sports Centre enter the new School Western Quad with its dramatic paving, planting and sculptures. On exiting onto Stockerston Rd, diagonally to the R is Hillside, a 1 acre S facing garden with spring fed pond, recently redesigned to provide terrace and patio, orchard, vegetable garden and woodland walk through mature trees. Continue to explore the beautifully maintained gardens of Uppingham School incl new planting to the fronts of the school houses on the approach to the town centre and, via an imposing stone arch, the main School Quad surrounded by its dramatic buildings. At the other end of town is The Orchard, another S facing garden taking advantage of the stream which runs through the lower reaches of the town. With its view out over the stream to sheep pastures beyond, the garden is full of interesting trees, shrubs, bulbs and perennials. Picturesque town centre and Uppingham School historic buildings with new Science Centre nationally recognised in the 2015 Royal Institute of British Architects Awards (RIBA) as making a significant contribution to the country's architecture. Wheelchair access at Hillside and Uppingham School. Some gravel paths on Headmasters' Lawn.

GROUP OPENING

45 WALTON GARDENS
Walton LE17 5RG. *4m NE of Lutterworth. M1 J20, via Lutterworth follow signs for Kimcote & Walton, or from Leicester take A5199. After Shearsby turn R signed Bruntingthorpe. Follow signs.* Sun 19, Wed 22 June (11-5). Combined adm £4, chd free. Cream teas at The Dog and Gun (proceeds to NGS).

THE MEADOWS
Mr & Mrs Falkner

THE OLD HALL
Mr & Mrs Field

ORCHARDS
Mr & Mrs G Cousins
Visits also by arrangement in June for groups 10+
01455 556958

NEW RAINBOW COTTAGE
Linda & Terry Allcott

RYLANDS FARMHOUSE
Mark & Sonya Raybould

SANDYLAND
Martin & Linda Goddard

TOAD HALL
Sue Beardmore
Visits also by arrangement in June groups 10+
01455 204353

Small village set in beautiful south Leicestershire countryside with traditional country PH. The seven gardens at Walton are in such contrasting sizes and styles that, together, they make the perfect garden visit. There is a 1½ acre garden featuring some lovely trees and open views, a plants man's garden filled with gorgeous rare plants; a Modernist garden where all the leaves are green (no variegated, gold or purple foliage) featuring the extensive use of grasses and a lovely view across the surrounding landscape; a walled garden with a unique water feature and a traditional garden with a small working pottery. There are also two delightful cottage gardens, one of which has an interesting green roof garden and the other usually combines planting with a bit of theatre to raise a smile. Some wood chip and cobbled paths that can be accessed by wheelchairs but may prove difficult.

ALLOTMENTS

46 WASHBROOK ALLOTMENTS
Welford Road, Leicester LE2 6FP. Sharon Maher. *Approx 2½ m S of Leicester, 1½ m N of Wigston. Regret no onsite parking. Welford Rd difficult to park on. Please use nearby side rds & Pendlebury Drive (LE2 6GY).* Sun 11 Sept (11-3). Adm £3, chd free. Tea.
Our allotment gardens have been described as a hidden oasis off the main Welford Road. There are over 100 whole and half plots growing a wide variety of fruit and vegetables. We have a fledgling wildflower meadow, a composting toilet and a shop. Keep a look out for the remains of Anderson Shelters, and see how woodchip is put to good use. Circular route around the site is uneven in places but is suitable for wheelchairs.

47 NEW WESTBROOKE HOUSE
52 Scotland Road, Little Bowden LE16 8AX. Bryan & Joanne Drew. *½ m S Market Harborough. From Northampton Rd follow NGS arrows.* Sun 15 May, Sun 3 July (11-5). Adm £5, chd free. Home-made teas.
Westbrooke House is a late Victorian property built in 1887. The gardens comprise 6 acres in total and are approached through a tree lined driveway of mature limes and wellingtonias. Key features are walled flower garden, walled kitchen garden, pond area, spring garden, lawns, woodland paths and a meadow with a wild flower area, ha-ha and Hornbeam avenue.

Oak Tree House

48 WESTVIEW

1 St Thomas's Road, Great Glen LE8 9EH. Gill & John Hadland, 01162 592170, gill@hadland.wanadoo.co.uk. *7m S of Leicester. Take either r'about from A6 into village centre (War Memorial) then follow NGS signs. Please park in Oaks Rd.* **Sun 6 Mar (12-4); Sun 1, Mon 2 May, Sun 4 Sept (12-5). Adm £2, chd free. Home-made teas. Visits also by arrangement Feb to Sept for groups 20 max.** Organically managed small walled cottage style garden with yr-round interest. Interesting and unusual plants, many grown from seed. Formal box parterre herb garden, courtyard, herbaceous borders, small wildlife pond, greenhouse, beehives, vegetable and fruit area. Auricula display. Handmade sculptures and artefacts made from recycled materials on display. Collection of Galanthus (snowdrops). Featured as Garden of the Week in Garden News.

Each garden planted in traditional cottage style but with the distinctive touch of their individual owner . . .

49 ◆ WHATTON GARDENS

Long Whatton, Kegworth LE12 5BG. Lord & Lady Crawshaw, 01509 842225, whattonhouse@gmail.com, www.whattonhouseandgardens.co. uk. *4m NE of Loughborough. On A6 between Hathern & Kegworth; 2¹/₂ m SE of M1J24.* **For NGS: Sun 22 May (10.30-5). Adm £4, chd free. Home-made teas. For other opening times and information, please phone, email or visit garden website.** Often described by visitors as a hidden gem, this 15 acre C19 Country House garden is a relaxing experience for all the family. Listen to the birds, and enjoy walking through the many fine trees, spring bulbs and shrubs, large herbaceous border, traditional rose garden, ornamental

ponds and lawns. Open daily (excl Sat) March to Oct. Available for group bookings. Closed Sat 30 July - Sat 6 Aug (2016 only). Gravel paths.

GROUP OPENING

50 WILLOUGHBY GARDENS

Willoughby Waterleys LE8 6UD. *9m S of Leicester. Follow yellow NGS rd arrows.* **Sun 17 July (11-5). Combined adm £4, chd free. Tea in Village Hall.**

1 CHURCH FARM LANE
Kathleen & Peter Bowers

2 CHURCH FARM LANE
Valerie & Peter Connelly

FARMWAY
Eileen Spencer
Visits also by arrangement July & Aug, 25 max
eileenfarmway9@msn.com
01162 478321

HIGH MEADOW
Phil & Eva Day

JOHN'S WOOD
John & Jill Harris

KAPALUA
Richard & Linda Love

3 ORCHARD ROAD
Diane & Roger Brearley

Willoughby Waterleys lies in the South Leicestershire countryside. The Norman Church will be open, hosting a film of the local bird population filmed by a local resident. 7 gardens are open. John's Wood is a 1¹/₂ acre nature reserve planted to encourage wildlife. 1 Church Farm Lane is a well stocked garden with lawn, trees and shrubs, roses and climbers. 2 Church Farm Lane has been professionally designed with many interesting features. Farmway is a plant lovers garden with many unusual plants in colour themed borders. High Meadow has been evolving over 5yrs. Incl mixed planting and ornamental vegetable garden. Kapalua has interesting planting design incorporating open views of countryside. 3 Orchard Road is a small garden packed with interest. Lawncare advice clinic 2-4pm. Willoughby embroidery on display in village hall. Wildlife film in the church.

GROUP OPENING

51 WING GARDENS

Wing, Oakham LE15 8SA. *2m S of Rutland Water. Off A6003 between Oakham & Uppingham.* **Sun 19 June (11-5). Combined adm £5, chd free. Home-made teas in Wing Village Hall.**

AUTUMN HOUSE
Jane & Jeremy Wood.

16 CHURCH STREET
Mr & Mrs Mick & Mary Rodgers.

DOVE COTTAGE
Mr & Mrs David & Alison Seviour.

GREYSTONES
Mr & Mrs Alisdair & Jane Alexander-Orr.

HOME CLOSE
Joanne Beaver.

NEW 33 MORCOTT ROAD
Angela Harding.

TOWNSEND HOUSE
David & Jeffy Wood.

NEW WING HOUSE
Stewart & Judith Campbell.

8 very different gardens in pretty stone village of Wing with medieval church and turf maze. For map and directions start visit at Townsend House opposite Village Hall. Each planted in traditional cottage garden style but with the distinctive touch of their individual owners, the larger with mature trees and lawns, and all with mixed borders of shrubs, perennials and grasses, roses, fruit trees and vegetable and herb gardens. Sizes range from the 2 largest, ¹/₂ acre gardens, Wing House and Autumn House, through medium sized cottage gdns at Dove Cottage, Greystones and Townsend House, to the very small at Home Close, 16 Church St and 33 Morcott Rd. The 2 latter, both with stunning views over the Rutland countryside from sitting areas, along with Dove Cottage all have Open Studios displaying work by the garden owners. Partial wheelchair access to some gardens.

LINCOLNSHIRE

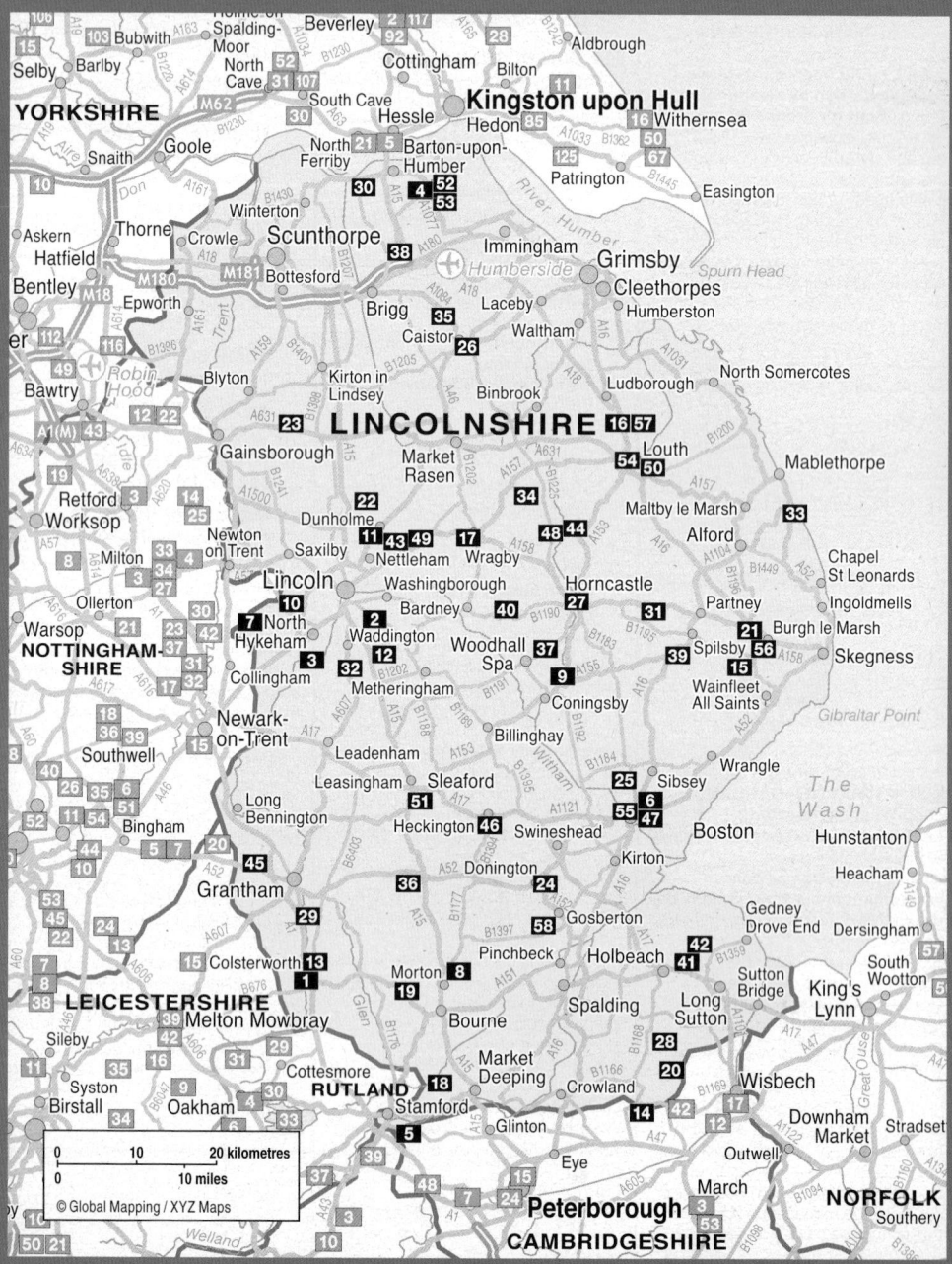

Lincolnshire

Lincolnshire is a county shaped by a rich tapestry of fascinating heritage, passionate people and intriguing traditions; a mix of city, coast and countryside.

The city of Lincoln is dominated by the iconic towers of Lincoln Cathedral. The eastern seaboard contains windswept golden sands and lonely nature reserves. The Lincolnshire Wolds is a nationally important landscape of rolling chalk hills and areas of sandstone and clay, which underlie this attractive landscape.

To the south is the historic, religious and architectural heritage of The Vales, with river walks, the fine Georgian buildings of Stamford and historic Burghley House. In the east the unique Fens landscape thrives on an endless network of waterways inhabited by an abundance of wildlife.

Beautiful gardens of all types, sizes and designs are cared for and shared by their welcoming owners. Often located in delightful villages, a visit to them will entail driving through quiet roads often bordered by verges of wild flowers.

Lincolnshire is rural England at its very best. Local heritage, beautiful countryside walks, aviation history and it is the home of the Red Arrows.

Lincolnshire Volunteers

County Organiser
Sally Grant
01205 750486
sallygrant50@btinternet.com

County Treasurer
Helen Boothman
01652 628424
boothmanhelen@gmail.com

Publicity
Margaret Mann
01476 585905
marg_mann2000@yahoo.com

Erica McGarrigle
01476 585909
ericamcg@hotmail.co.uk

Assistant County Organisers
Lynne Barnes
01529 497462
lynnebarnes14@googlemail.com

Helen Boothman
(as above)

Tricia Elliot
01427 788517
triciaelliott921@btinternet.com

Stephanie Lee
01507 442151
marigoldlee@btinternet.com

Sylvia Ravenhall
01507 526014
sylvan@btinternet.com

Creina Roberts
01529 497104
creina.roberts@mypostoffice.co.uk

Left: Mill Farm

Opening Dates

All entries subject to change.
For latest information check www.ngs.org.uk

February

Snowdrop Festival

Saturday 13
29 Little Ponton Hall

Sunday 14
29 Little Ponton Hall

Saturday 20
2 Ashfield House

Sunday 21
2 Ashfield House

Saturday 27
8 21 Chapel Street

Sunday 28
8 21 Chapel Street

March

Friday 25
13 Easton Walled Gardens

April

Sunday 3
57 Woodlands

Saturday 9
5 Burghley House Private South Gardens

Sunday 10
5 Burghley House Private South Gardens
8 21 Chapel Street
15 Firsby Manor
19 Grimsthorpe Castle
45 NEW Sedgebrook Manor

Sunday 17
39 The Old Rectory

Saturday 23
18 Greatford Mill

Sunday 24
17 Goltho House

May

Sunday 1
16 NEW Fotherby Gardens

Saturday 7
33 Marigold Cottage

Sunday 8
11 Dunholme Lodge
33 Marigold Cottage

Sunday 15
41 The Old Vicarage
42 Old White House
44 Pear Tree Cottage
47 NEW 66 Spilsby Road

Sunday 22
25 Holly House
39 The Old Rectory

Saturday 28
33 Marigold Cottage

Sunday 29
15 Firsby Manor
31 Manor House
33 Marigold Cottage

Spectacular spring bulbs in park like setting . . .

June

Festival Weekend

Sunday 5
57 Woodlands

Wednesday 8
19 Grimsthorpe Castle

Sunday 12
4 The Barn
20 Guanock House
22 Hackthorn Hall
27 Horncastle Gardens
52 NEW 8 Westcote Farm
53 3 Westcote Farm House

Sunday 19
3 Aubourn Hall
23 Hall Farm
30 Manor Farm
46 Shangrila
51 NEW West Syke

Saturday 25
33 Marigold Cottage

Sunday 26
7 45 Chapel Lane
9 Courtlands
24 The Hawthorns
32 March House
33 Marigold Cottage
56 Willow Cottage

July

Saturday 2
34 2 Mill Cottage
35 Mill Farm

Sunday 3
14 NEW Fenleigh
16 NEW Fotherby Gardens
35 Mill Farm
54 NEW 48 Westgate

Sunday 10
11 Dunholme Lodge

Wednesday 13
50 68 Watts Lane

Sunday 17
12 East Mere House
44 Pear Tree Cottage
48 NEW The Stables

Saturday 23
33 Marigold Cottage

Sunday 24
33 Marigold Cottage
58 NEW Yew Tree Farm

Sunday 31
50 68 Watts Lane

August

Sunday 7
21 Gunby Hall & Gardens
32 March House
50 68 Watts Lane
57 Woodlands

Sunday 14
6 NEW Butterfly Hospice
50 68 Watts Lane
55 NEW Willoughby Road Allotments

Sunday 21
1 Ashcroft House
38 Old Quarry Lodge
50 68 Watts Lane

Saturday 27
33 Marigold Cottage

Sunday 28
31 Manor House
33 Marigold Cottage
50 68 Watts Lane

September

Sunday 4
16 NEW Fotherby Gardens
23 Hall Farm
54 NEW 48 Westgate

Saturday 17
28 NEW Inley Drove Farm

Sunday 18
28 NEW Inley Drove Farm

Wednesday 21
10 Doddington Hall Gardens

Sunday 25
8 21 Chapel Street

17 Goltho House

October

Sunday 23
2 Ashfield House

February 2017

Saturday 25
8 21 Chapel Street

Sunday 26
8 21 Chapel Street

Gardens open to the public

5 Burghley House Private South Gardens
10 Doddington Hall Gardens
13 Easton Walled Gardens
17 Goltho House
19 Grimsthorpe Castle
21 Gunby Hall & Gardens
23 Hall Farm

By arrangement only

26 Hope House
36 The Moat
37 Nova Lodge
40 NEW The Old Rectory
43 Overbeck
49 Thornham

Also open by arrangement

8 21 Chapel Street
9 Courtlands
15 Firsby Manor
16 Nut Tree Farm, Fotherby Gardens
16 Shepherds Hey, Fotherby Gardens
24 The Hawthorns
25 Holly House
27 15 Elmhirst Road, Horncastle Gardens
31 Manor House
32 March House
33 Marigold Cottage
35 Mill Farm
38 Old Quarry Lodge
39 The Old Rectory
41 The Old Vicarage
44 Pear Tree Cottage
48 NEW The Stables
50 68 Watts Lane
56 Willow Cottage
57 Woodlands
58 NEW Yew Tree Farm

The Gardens

1 ASHCROFT HOUSE

45 Newton Way, Woolsthorpe by Colsterworth, Grantham NG33 5NP. Lucienne Bennett. *7m from Grantham, 400 metres from Woolsthorpe Manor (NT). No parking in Newton Way. Plenty of parking along Woolsthorpe Rd or at Woolsthorpe Manor (if visiting property). There are 4 dedicated disabled parking spaces.* **Sun 21 Aug (12-5). Adm £3, chd free. Home-made cakes incl gluten free.**
Back garden created in 2012 from part of a pony paddock on a filled in ironstone quarry. Sloping ground necessitated terracing and having natural springs running down one side, and boggy ground in deep shade at the bottom of the plot meant that this small garden needed careful planning.

2 ASHFIELD HOUSE

Lincoln Road, Branston, Lincoln LN4 1NS. John & Judi Tinsley, 07977 505682, jmt@ashtreedevelopments.co.uk. *3m S of Lincoln. From Branston off B1188 Lincoln Rd on L; 1m from Branston Hall Hotel signed Ashfield Farms.* **Sat 20, Sun 21 Feb, Sun 23 Oct (11-4). Adm £4, chd free. Light refreshments.**
10 acre garden constructed around a planting of trees and shrubs. This yr we have decided to open the garden in February to give visitors the opportunity to see the wonderful masses of snowdrops and aconites all through the grounds and maybe some of the early flowering cherries. Sweeping lawns with massed plantings of spring bulbs. In the autumn the colours can be amazing. Fairly level garden. Grass paths.

3 AUBOURN HALL

Harmston Road, Aubourn, nr Lincoln LN5 9DZ. Mr & Mrs Christopher Nevile, www.aubournhall.co.uk. *7m SW of Lincoln. Signed off A607 at Harmston & off A46 at Thorpe on the Hill.* **Sun 19 June (2-5). Adm £4.50, chd free. Home-made teas.**
Approx 8 acres. Lawns, mature trees, shrubs, roses, mixed borders, new rose garden, new large prairie and topiary garden, spring bulbs and ponds. C11 church adjoining. Access to garden is fairly flat and smooth. Depending on weather some areas may be inaccessible to wheelchairs. Parking in field not on tarmac.

4 THE BARN

6 Westcote Farm, Wold Road, Barrow-upon-Humber DN19 7DY. Lesley & Ian Pepperdine. *Outskirts of Barrow upon Humber, 3m S of Humber Bridge. From A15 follow B1206 towards Barrow upon Humber. Indicate L turn at 30 mph sign on entering village, lane down to Westcote Farm is on immed L.* **Sun 12 June (11-5). Combined adm with 3 Westcote Farm House £3.50, chd free. Home-made teas.**
An open space garden set in approx 1 acre of land with orchard, formal yew hedging, mature trees, topiary, herbaceous border, shrubbery and vegetable area. Garden room to shelter if weather is inclement. Wheelchair and scooter access over lawn and most hard surfaces.

5 ◆ BURGHLEY HOUSE PRIVATE SOUTH GARDENS

Stamford PE9 3JY. Burghley House Preservation Trust, 01780 752451, burghley@burghley.co.uk, www.burghley.co.uk. *1m E of Stamford. From Stamford follow signs to Burghley via B1443.* **For NGS: Sat 9, Sun 10 Apr (11-4). Adm £3.50, chd £2. Light refreshments in The Orangery Restaurant. For other opening times and information, please phone, email or visit garden website.**
On 9th and 10th April the Private South Gardens at Burghley House will open for the NGS with spectacular spring bulbs in park like setting with magnificent trees and the opportunity to enjoy Capability Brown's famous lake and summerhouse. Entry to the Private South Gardens via orangery. The Garden of Surprises, Sculpture Garden and house are open as normal. (Regular adm prices apply). Food Fair. Gravel paths.

6 NEW BUTTERFLY HOSPICE

Rowan Way, Boston PE21 9DH. Steve Doughty. *From Spilsby Rd, Hospital Ln, R into Linden Way then R again into Rowan Way.* **Sun 14 Aug (11-4). Adm £3, chd free. Cream teas.**
Set in 4 acres the gardens surround the Butterfly Hospice. A mixture of traditional beds, orchard and large wildflower meadow. Willow arbours, pathways and disabled access greenhouse with raised beds are other parts of the peaceful and relaxing gardens which form part of the care provided to inpatients by the hospice. Tea/coffee available, cream teas by booked ticket. Mentioned in article as part of Boston in Bloom.

Yew Tree Farm

7 45 CHAPEL LANE

North Scarle, Lincoln LN6 9EX. **Michael & Anna Peacock.** *12m SW of Lincoln; 9m NW Newark. From A46 follow signs to Whisby & Eagle. On entering Eagle take 1st R, cont for approx 1m take 1st L. Cont to Xrds in centre of N Scarle. Turn R into Chapel Lane. Garden last on L.* **Sun 26 June (1-5). Adm £2.50, chd free. Home-made teas.**
This is a good example of a garden designed by the owners to provide a cottage style feel to a relatively modern village property. The ³/₄ acre garden was started from a blank canvas in 2011. Three offset circular lawns are edged with bee friendly hardy perennials, lavenders, roses, shrubs and fruit trees. Gravel area with low rockery. Small orchard to front. Pretty gazebo. Some features made from recycled materials. Single cobble path may prove difficult to wheelchair users.

8 21 CHAPEL STREET

Hacconby, Bourne PE10 0UL. **Cliff & Joan Curtis and Sharon White,** 01778 570314, cliffordcurtis@btinternet.com. *3m N of Bourne. A15, turn E at Xrds into Hacconby, L at village green.* **Sat 27 Feb (11-4). Adm £3, chd free. Sun 28 Feb (11-4). Adm £3. Sun 10 Apr, Sun 25 Sept (11-4). Adm £3, chd free. Home-made teas, hot soup (Feb). 2017: Sat 25, Sun 26 Feb. Visits also by arrangement Jan to Oct.**
A cottage garden behind a 300yr old cottage. Snowdrops, primroses, hellebores and many different spring flowering bulbs. Colour with bulbs and herbaceous plants through the yr, autumn with asters, dahlias, salvias and many of the autumn flowering yellow daises. Featured in Garden News. Part gravel and part grass paths.

9 COURTLANDS

Tattershall Road, Kirkby-on-Bain, Woodhall Spa LN10 6YN. **Peter & Jill Hilton,** 01526 353115, peter@courtlandshilton.co.uk. *Kirkby on Bain. Garden located on S edge of village, on rd leading to Recycling Centre, gravel pits & Coningsby.* **Sun 26 June (2-5). Adm £3, chd free. Home-made teas. Visits also by arrangement May to Sept for groups 10+.**
Enjoy the peace and quiet of this lovely 3¹/₂ acre garden and paddock. A flat established garden with large trees (60 mature Scots Pines), open lawn, herbaceous borders, island beds, folly area, water feature, Japanese garden, tree house, and a large vegetable garden with raised beds. Featured in Lincolnshire Pride. Full wheelchair access to garden but regret no accessible WC.

Marie Curie

Last year, NGS funded 25,000 hours of our nursing care

10 ◆ DODDINGTON HALL GARDENS

Doddington, Lincoln LN6 4RU. **Claire & James Birch,** 01522 812510, info@doddingtonhall.com, www.doddingtonhall.com. *5m W of Lincoln. Signed clearly from A46 Lincoln bypass & A57, 3m.* **For NGS: Wed 21 Sept (11-4). Adm £6.50, chd £3.50. For other opening times and information, please phone, email or visit garden website.**
5 acres of romantic walled and wild gardens. Naturalised spring bulbs and scented shrubs from Feb to May. Spectacular iris display late May/early June in box edged parterres of West Garden. Sumptuous herbaceous borders throughout summer; ancient chestnut trees; turf maze; Temple of the Winds. Fully productive, walled kitchen garden. Wheelchair access possible via gravel paths. Ramps also in use. Access map available from Gatehouse Shop.

11 ◆ DUNHOLME LODGE

Dunholme, Lincoln LN2 3QA. **Hugh & Lesley Wykes.** *4m NE of Lincoln. Turn off A46 towards Welton at Hand Car Wash garage. After ¹/₂ m turn L up long concrete rd. Garden at top.* **Sun 8 May, Sun 10 July (11-5). Adm £3.50, chd free. Home-made teas.**
3 acre garden. Spring bulb area, shrub borders, fern garden, topiary, large natural pond, wild flower area, orchard and vegetable garden. RAF Dunholme Lodge Museum and War Memorial in the grounds. Most areas wheelchair accessible but some loose stone and gravel.

12 EAST MERE HOUSE

Bracebridge Heath, Lincoln LN4 2JB. **Mr James Dean.** *Turn off A15 to Bardney & Mere on B1178. After 1m turn R on LH bend. Garden 100yds on R.* **Sun 17 July (11.30-5). Adm £3, chd free. Home-made cakes, biscuits incl gluten free.**
2 acre formal country garden, recently redesigned by Angel Collins, surrounding a stone farmhouse. Box edged borders planted with grasses, perennials and seasonal bedding. Lawns, ornamental trees, crab apple avenue and small rose garden. Parterre planted with rosemary, lavender, santolina and alliums. Large kitchen garden with raised vegetable beds and young fruit trees on the farm yard walls. Wildflower meadow.

13 ◆ EASTON WALLED GARDENS

Easton NG33 5AP. **Sir Fred & Lady Cholmeley,** 01476 530063, info@eastonwalledgardens.co.uk, www.eastonwalledgardens.co.uk. *7m S of Grantham. 1m off A1. Follow village signposts via B6403.* **For NGS: Fri 25 Mar (11-4). Adm £7, chd £3. Light refreshments. For other opening times and information, please phone, email or visit garden website.**
12 acres of 400yr old forgotten gardens undergoing extensive renovation. Set in parkland with dramatic views. C16 garden with Victorian embellishments. Italianate terraces; yew tunnel; snowdrops and cut flower garden. David Austin roses, meadows and sweet pea collections. Cottage and vegetable gardens. Please wear sensible shoes suitable for country walking. Childrens' Trail. Regret no wheelchair access to lower gardens but tearoom, shop and upper gardens all accessible.

14 NEW FENLEIGH

Inkerson Fen, Throckenholt, Spalding PE12 0QY. **Jeff & Barbara Stalker.** *2m from Gedney Hill. Turn R on to B1166 take next R into Common Rd following NGS signs* approx 1m. From Parson Drove on B1166 turn L into Common Rd following NGS signs approx 3m. **Sun 3 July (10-5). Adm £3, chd free. Light refreshments.**

Set in 4 acres incl two acre paddock. Quirky areas for easy maintenance. A fish pond dominates the garden surrounded with planting. Seating and two permanent gazebo's if the weather is inclement. Patio with pots and raised beds and BBQ area containing ferns and acers. Small wooded area, poly tunnels and corners of the garden for wildlife. Large grass area for family fun and games.

15 ▸ FIRSBY MANOR
Firsby, Spilsby PE23 5QJ. **David & Gill Boldy, 01754 830386, gillboldy@gmail.com.** 5m E of Spilsby. From Spilsby take B1195 to Wainfleet all Saints. In Firsby, turn R into Fendyke Rd. Firsby Manor is 0.8m along lane on L. **Sun 10 Apr, Sun 29 May (1-4.30). Adm £2.50, chd free. Home-made teas. Visits also by arrangement Feb to July.**
Firsby Manor is a garden of 3 acres surrounding a Georgian farmhouse. It has been developed by the current owners over two decades and has been designed to provide interest throughout the yr, although it is at its most lovely in late spring and early summer. A visit in April offers a great opportunity to see many different daffodil cultivars. Most of garden accessible by wheelchair, but no disabled WC.

🌾 ❀ ☕

GROUP OPENING

16 ▸ NEW FOTHERBY GARDENS
Peppin Lane, Fotherby, Louth LN11 0UW. 2m N of Louth on A16 signed Fotherby. Please park on R verge opp allotments & walk to gardens. Free taxi service between Woodlands & Nut Tree Farm. No parking at gardens. Please do not park beyond designated area. **Sun 1 May, Sun 3 July (11-5). Combined adm £4, chd free. Sun 4 Sept (11-5). Combined adm £5, chd free. Home-made teas at Woodlands.**

NUT TREE FARM
Tim & Judith Hunter.
Open on Sun 1 May, Sun 4 Sept

Visits also by arrangement June to Sept
01507 602208
nuttreefarm@hotmail.com

SHEPHERDS HEY
Barbara Chester.
Open on Sun 3 July, Sun 4 Sept
Visits also by arrangement June to Sept
barbaraandrogerchester@talktalk.net
01507 605016

WOODLANDS NPC
Ann & Bob Armstrong.
Open on all dates
(See separate entry)
Visits also by arrangement Feb to Oct
annbobarmstrong@btinternet.com
01507 603586

Start your visit at Shepherds Hey (July & Sept), a small garden packed with unusual and interesting perennials. Its open frontage gives a warm welcome, with a small pond, terraced border and steep bank side to a small stream. The rear garden, with colour themed borders, takes advantage of the panoramic views over open countryside. Recently featured in Lincolnshire Life. 350yds along Peppin Lane is Woodlands, a lovely mature woodland garden with many unusual plants set against a backdrop of an ever changing tapestry of greenery. A peaceful garden where wildlife can thrive and the front garden is a crevice area for alpine plants. There is a Plant Heritage collection of Codonopsis, and the nursery, featured in RHS Plantfinder, gives visitors the opportunity to purchase plants seen in the garden. An award winning professional artist's studio/gallery is also open. The garden was featured in Lincolnshire Pride magazine. Complete your visit at Nut Tree Farm (May & Sept). The garden, est in 2007, is over an acre and enjoys stunning views of Lincolnshire Wolds. A sweeping herbaceous border frames the lawn and a double wall, planted with seasonal annuals, surrounds the house. From the raised terrace a rill runs to the large pond. As well as a raised bed brick vegetable garden, there is a prize winning flock of Hampshire Down sheep in fields surrounding part of garden. Locally made honey for sale.

🌾 ❀ ☕

17 ▸ ◆ GOLTHO HOUSE
Lincoln Road, Goltho, Wragby, Market Rasen LN8 5NF. **Mr & Mrs S Hollingworth, 01673 857768, bookings@golthogardens.com, www.golthogardens.com.** 10m E of Lincoln. On A158, 1m before Wragby. Garden on L (not in Goltho Village). **For NGS: Sun 24 Apr, Sun 25 Sept (10-4). Adm £5, chd free. Light refreshments. For other opening times and information, please phone, email or visit garden website.**
4¹/₂ acre garden started in 1998 but looking established with long grass walk flanked by abundantly planted herbaceous borders forming a focal point. Paths and walkway span out to other features incl nut walk, prairie border, wildflower meadow, rose garden and large pond area. Snowdrops, hellebores and shrubs for winter interest.

♿ ❀ 🚐 🛏 ☕

> Large grass area for family fun and games . . .

18 ▸ GREATFORD MILL
Greatford PE9 4QA. **Mr & Mrs D Lygo.** 4m E of Stamford. At T-junction in village nr Hare & Hounds PH, take route to Carlby & Braceborough. Garden is 2nd on L. **Sat 23 Apr (2-4.30). Adm £4, chd free. Home-made teas.**
Lovely ¹/₂ acre village garden with special spring interest overlooking St Thomas's church. Situated on the R Glen, original water wheel and open, unfenced mill pond. Informal planting of shrubs, Japanese Maples, herbaceous borders around lawn and formal parterre garden of fruit/vegetables. Large decking with seating area and prairie planting. Duck race and waterwheel. Featured in Garden Answers magazine, Rutland Pride and Garden News. Some gravel paths.

♿ ❀ ☕

Easton Walled Gardens

19 ◆ GRIMSTHORPE CASTLE

Grimsthorpe, Bourne PE10 0LZ. Grimsthorpe & Drummond Castle Trust, 01778 591205, ray@grimsthorpe.co.uk, www.grimsthorpe.co.uk. *3m NW of Bourne. 8m E of A1 on A151 from Colsterworth junction. Main entrance indicated by brown tourist sign.* **For NGS: Sun 10 Apr, Wed 8 June (11-5). Adm £6, chd £2.50. Light refreshments. For other opening times and information, please phone, email or visit garden website.**

15 acres of formal and woodland gardens incl bulbs and wildflowers. Formal gardens encompass fine topiary, roses, herbaceous borders and unusual ornamental kitchen garden. Home-made lunches, afternoon tea and cakes. Gift shop, cycle hire and adventure playground, historic house, park trails. Gravel paths.

20 GUANOCK HOUSE

Guanock Gate, Sutton St Edmund PE12 0LW. Mr & Mrs Michael Coleman. *16m SE of Spalding. From village church turn R, cross rd, then L Guanock Gate. Garden at end of rd on R.* **Sun 12 June (1.30-5). Adm £3, chd free. Home-made teas.**

5 acre garden designed by Arne Maynard. Herbaceous border, knot garden, rose garden and lime walk. Orchard, walled kitchen garden, Italian garden. Guanock House is a C16 manor house built in the flat fens of S Lincolnshire. Plant stall. Partial wheelchair access. Garden on different levels.

21 ◆ GUNBY HALL & GARDENS

Spilsby PE23 5SS. National Trust, 01754 890102, gunbyhall@nationaltrust.org.uk, www.nationaltrust.org.uk. *2¹/₂ m NW of Burgh-le-Marsh. 7m W of Skegness. Signed off Gunby r'about.* **For NGS: Sun 7 Aug (11-5). Adm £6, chd £3. Light refreshments in Gunby tea-room. For other opening times and information, please phone, email or visit garden website.**

8 acres of formal and walled gardens; old roses, herbaceous borders; herb garden; kitchen garden with fruit trees and vegetables. Greenhouses, carp pond and sweeping lawns. Tennyson's Haunt of Ancient Peace. House built by Sir William Massingberd in 1700. Wheelchair access in gardens but not hall.

22 HACKTHORN HALL

Hackthorn, Lincoln LN2 3PQ. Mr & Mrs William Cracroft-Eley, 01673 860423, office@hackthorn.com, www.hackthorn.com. *6m N of Lincoln. Follow signs to Hackthorn. Approx 1m off A15 N of Lincoln.* **Sun 12 June (1-5). Adm £3.50, chd free. Home-made teas at Hackthorn Hall Gardens.**

Formal and woodland garden, productive and ornamental walled gardens surrounding Hackthorn Hall and church extending to approx 15 acres. Parts of the formal gardens designed by Bunny Guinness. The walled garden boasts a magnificent Black Hamburg vine, believed to be second in size to the vine at Hampton Court. Partial wheelchair access, gravel paths, grass drives.

23 ◆ HALL FARM

Harpswell, Gainsborough DN21 5UU. Pam & Mark Tatam, 01427 668412, pamtatam@gmail.com, www.hall-farm.co.uk. *7m E of Gainsborough. On A631, 1¹/₂ m W of Caenby Corner.* **For NGS: Sun 19 June, Sun 4 Sept (10-5). Adm £3.50, chd free. Light refreshments. For other opening times and information, please phone, email or visit garden website.**

The 3 acre garden encompasses formal and informal areas, incl a parterre, a sunken garden, a courtyard with rill, a walled Mediterranean garden, double herbaceous borders for late summer, lawns, pond, giant chess set, and a flower and grass meadow. It is a short walk to the medieval moat, which surrounds an acre of wild semi woodland garden currently under development. Free seed collecting on Sun 4 Sept. Most of garden suitable for wheelchairs.

24 THE HAWTHORNS

Bicker Road, Donington PE11 4XP. Colin & Janet Johnson, 01775 822808, colinj04@hotmail.com, www.thehawthornsrarebreeds.co.uk. *¹/₂ m NW of Donington. Bicker Rd is directly off A52 opp Church Rd. Parking available in Church Rd or village centre car park.* **Sun 26 June (11-4). Adm £3.50, chd free. Visits also by arrangement for groups 12+.**

Traditional garden with extensive herbaceous borders, pond, large old English rose garden, vegetable and fruit areas with feature greenhouse. Cider orchard and area housing rare breed animals incl pigs, sheep and chickens. Home produced honey avaliable.

25 **HOLLY HOUSE**
Fishtoft Drove, Frithville, Boston
PE22 7ES. Sally & David Grant,
01205 750486,
sallygrant50@btinternet.com. *3m N
of Boston. 1m S of Frithville.
Unclassified rd. On W side of West
Fen Drain. Marked on good maps*.
**Sun 22 May (12-5). Adm £3.50,
chd free. Home-made teas. Visits
also by arrangement May & June
for groups 10+. Adm incl
refreshments £5.**
Approx 1 acre informal mixed
borders, steps leading down to pond
with cascade and stream. Small
woodland area. Quiet garden with
water feature. Extra 2$^1/_2$ acres
devoted to wildlife, especially bumble
bees and butterflies. Partial
wheelchair access with some steep
slopes and steps.

♿ 🏫 ☘ 🚐 ☕

26 **HOPE HOUSE**
15 Horsemarket, Caistor LN7 6UP.
Sue Neave, 07940 567079,
hopehousegardens@aol.com,
www.hopehousegardens.co.uk. *Off
A46 Between Lincoln & Grimsby.
Centre of town.* **Visits by
arrangement May to Sept, groups
welcome. Adm £3.50, chd free.
Light refreshments.**
A country garden in an attractive
historic town in the heart of the
Lincolnshire Wolds. Small walled
garden attached to an interesting
Georgian house. Roses, perennials,
shrubs, trees, fruit and a small raised
vegetable area. Wildlife pond and
formal water trough in the dining area.
Yr-round colour and interest in a
tranquil space created by its garden
designer owner. Caistor Arts and
Heritage Centre (opp) organise walks
around the historic town and local
areas of interest and provide
information on the history of Caistor
and the area. Cafe and Library.
Featured on Love Your Garden, Alan
Titchmarsh. Various magazine
coverage incl Garden News.

🏫 ☘ 🛋 ☕

GROUP OPENING

27 **HORNCASTLE GARDENS**
Horncastle LN9 5AS. *Take A158
from Lincoln. Just inside 40mph turn
L into Accommodation Rd. Gardens
signed from here. Roadside parking
only. Please park sensibly.* **Sun 12
June (11-4.30). Combined adm
£5, chd free. Home-made cakes**
incl gluten free at 15 Elmhirst
Road.

NEW **23 ACCOMMODATION
ROAD**
Mr & Mrs D Chapman

40 ACCOMMODATION ROAD
Eddie & Marie Aldridge

15 ELMHIRST ROAD
Sylvia Ravenhall
**Visits also by arrangement
June & July daytime or evening
visits, individuals or groups**
sylvan@btinternet.com
01507 526014

30 ELMHIRST ROAD
Andy & Yvonne Mathieson

The market town of Horncastle some
20m to the E of Lincoln on the A158
is often called The Gateway to the
Wolds. These 4 very different gardens
are within easy walking distance of
each other. New for 2016 is 23
Accommodation Rd a garden planted
with a variety of perennials, iris,
alpines, auriculas and fruit plus
fishpond and seating. 40
Accommodation Rd is packed with
perennials and climbers in a garden
wrapped around three sides of a
bungalow. 15 Elmhirst Rd is a long
and narrow town garden, with
winding gravel paths and shallow
steps around secret corners. It is
planted with perennials, shrubs,
climbers, small trees and lawn. Many
hostas are grown in pots and in the
ground. There are plenty of seats. 30
Elmhirst Rd contains colourful
planting, raised vegetable beds, small
greenhouse and fruit. The quirky
handmade features raise a smile on
most faces. Some gravel paths and
shallow steps in all gardens.

☘ ☕

28 **NEW** **INLEY DROVE FARM**
Inley Drove, Sutton St James,
Spalding PE12 0LX.
Francis & Maisie Pryor,
https://pryorfrancis.wordpress.
com/. *Just off rd from Sutton St
James to Sutton St Edmund. 2m S of
Sutton St James. Look for yellow
NGS signs on double bend.* **Sat 17,
Sun 18 Sept (11-5). Adm £4, chd
free. Home-made teas.**
Over 3 acres of Fenland garden and
meadow plus 6$^1/_2$ acre wood
developed over 20yrs. Garden
planted for colour, scent and wildlife.
Double mixed borders and less
formal flower gardens all framed by
hornbeam hedges. Unusual shrubs

and trees, incl fine stand of Black
Poplars, vegetable garden, woodland
walks and orchard. Some gravel and
a few steps but mostly flat grass.

♿ ☘ ☕

29 **LITTLE PONTON HALL**
Grantham NG33 5BS. In the
Memory of Mrs Rosemary
McCorquodale,
www.littlepontonhallgardens.org.
uk. *2m S of Grantham. $^1/_2$ m E of A1
at S end of Grantham bypass.
Disabled parking.* **Sat 13, Sun 14
Feb (11-4). Adm £5, chd free. Light
refreshments.**
3 to 4 acre garden. Massed
snowdrops and aconites in Feb.
Stream, spring blossom and
hellebores, bulbs and river walk.
Spacious lawns with cedar tree over
200yrs old. Formal walled kitchen
garden and listed dovecote, with herb
garden. Victorian greenhouses with
many plants from exotic locations.
Featured in Country Life magazine.
Wheelchair access on hard surfaces,
unsuitable on grass. Disabled WC.

♿ 🏫 ☘ 🚐 ☕

> The garden has
> been designed to
> offer a place to
> relax and enjoy
> the view . . .

30 **MANOR FARM**
Horkstow Road, South Ferriby,
Barton-upon-Humber DN18 6HS.
Geoff & Angela Wells. *3m from
Barton-upon-Humber on A1077, turn
L onto B1204, opp Village Hall.* **Sun
19 June (11-5.30). Adm £3, chd
free. Home-made teas.**
A traditional farmhouse set within
approx 1 acre with mature
shrubberies, herbaceous borders,
gravel garden and pergola walk.
Many old trees with preservation
orders. New rose garden planted
2013. Wildlife pond set within a
paddock. New white garden and
fernery in progress.

♿ 🏫 ☘ 🚐 ☕

31 ▸ MANOR HOUSE

Manor Road, Hagworthingham, Spilsby PE23 4LN. Gill Maxim & David O'Connor, 01507 588530, vcagillmaxim@aol.com. *5m E of Horncastle. S of A158 in Hagworthingham, turn into Bond Hayes Lane downhill, becomes Manor Rd. Please follow signs down gravel track to parking area.* **Sun 29 May, Sun 28 Aug (2-5). Adm £3, chd free. Home-made teas. Visits also by arrangement June to Sept.** 2 acre garden on S facing slope, partly terraced and well protected by established trees and shrubs. Redeveloped over 10yrs with natural and formal ponds. Shrub roses, laburnum walk, hosta border, gravel bed and other areas mainly planted with hardy perennials, trees and shrubs.

32 ▸ MARCH HOUSE

3 Harmston Park Avenue, Harmston, Lincoln LN5 9GF. Asif & Barbara Kamal, 01522 722554, bkamal@btinternet.com. *7m S of Lincoln. In village of Harmston, off Church Ln.* **Sun 26 June, Sun 7 Aug (1-5). Adm £3, chd free. Light refreshments. Visits also by arrangement June to Sept, groups 10+ daytime or evening visits.** The unexpected garden. Beautifully designed, lush with many unusual plants. Bird friendly with a large pond teeming with wildlife. An oasis, verdant with semi tropical colours. Very atmospheric and described by a visitor as a 'piece of paradise'. Featured in Garden Answers. Gravel paths and some uneven surfaces.

33 ▸ MARIGOLD COTTAGE

Hotchin Road, Sutton-on-Sea LN12 2NP. Stephanie Lee & John Raby, 01507 442151, marigoldlee@btinternet.com, www.marigoldcottage.webs.com. *16m N of Skegness on A52. 7m E of Alford on A1111. 3m S of Mablethorpe on A52. Turn off A52 on High St at Cornerhouse Cafe. Follow rd past playing field on R. Rd turns away from the dunes. House 2nd on L.* **Sat 7, Sun 8, Sat 28, Sun 29 May, Sat 25, Sun 26 June, Sat 23, Sun 24 July, Sat 27, Sun 28 Aug (2-5). Adm £3, chd free. Home-made teas. Visits also by arrangement May to Sept for groups.**

Slide open the Japanese gate to find secret paths, lanterns, a circular window in a curved wall, water lilies in pots and a gravel garden, vegetable garden and propagation area. Take the long drive to see the sea. Back in the garden, find a seat, enjoy the birds and bees. We face the challenges of heavy clay and salt ladened winds but look for unusual plants not the humdrum for these conditions. Most of garden accessible to wheelchairs along flat, paved paths.

34 ▸ 2 MILL COTTAGE

Barkwith Road, South Willingham, Market Rasen LN8 6NN. Mrs Jo Rouston, 01673 858656, jo@rouston-gardens.co.uk. *5m E of Wragby. On A157 turn R at PH in East Barkwith then immed L to South Willingham. Cottage 1m on L. Please email or phone for more directions.* **Sat 2 July (12-5). Adm £3, chd free. Home-made teas.** A garden of several defined spaces, packed with interesting features, unusual plants and well placed seating areas, created by garden designer Jo Rouston. Original engine shed, a working well, raised beds using local rock with small pond. Clipped box, alpines, roses, summerhouses and water feature. Box and lavender hedge to greenhouse and herb garden. Late season bed. Woven metal and turf tree seat. Featured in Garden Answers. Partial wheelchair access. Gravel at far end of garden. Steps down to main greenhouse.

35 ▸ MILL FARM

Caistor Road, Grasby, Caistor DN38 6AQ. Mike & Helen Boothman, 01652 628424, boothmanhelen@gmail.com, www.millfarmgarden.co.uk. *3m NW of Caistor on A1084. Between Brigg & Caistor. From Cross Keys PH towards Caistor for approx 200yds.* **Sat 2, Sun 3 July (11-4). Adm £3, chd free. Home-made teas. Visits also by arrangement May to Sept.** Over 3 acres of garden with many diverse areas. The frontage is formal with shrubs and trees. The rear a plantsman haven. There is a peony and rose garden, wildlife ponds, specimen trees, vegetable area, an old windmill adapted into a fernery, alpine house and a shade house with a variety of shade loving plants. There

are a number of herbaceous beds with many different grasses and hardy perennials. Small nursery on site with home grown plants available.

36 ▸ THE MOAT

Newton NG34 0ED. Mr & Mrs Mike Barnes, 01529 497462, lynnebarnes14@googlemail.com. *Off A52 halfway between Grantham & Boston. In Newton village, opp church. Please park sensibly in village.* **Visits by arrangement May to Sept. Adm £4.00, chd free. Home-made teas. For evening visits wine and canapés.** Delightful 3 acre country garden established 14yrs. Created to blend with its country surroundings and featuring large island beds planted with a variety of unusual perennials. Natural pond and ha-ha, again imaginatively planted. Topiary, courtyard and orchard. Small vegetable garden. Garden on slope but accessible to wheelchair users.

> Enjoy afternoon tea with a few friends on the terrace . . .

37 ▸ NOVA LODGE

150 Horncastle Road, Roughton Moor, Woodhall Spa LN10 6UX. Leo Boshier, 01526 354940, moxons555@btinternet.com. *On B1191. Approx 2m E of centre of Woodhall Spa on Horncastle Rd. Roadside parking.* **Visits by arrangement June & July for groups 10+. Adm £3.00, chd free. Home-made teas.** $^2/_3$ acre traditional garden set within mature trees started 2009. Herbaceous borders and beds, rare and unusual perennials. Shrub beds with grasses and ferns, large collection of hostas and heucheras, area for vegetables, fruit and herbs. Summerhouse, greenhouses, lawns and ponds. Central arbour with climbing roses and clematis.

38 OLD QUARRY LODGE
15 Barnetby Lane, Elsham, nr
Brigg DN20 0RB. Mel & Tina
Welton, 01652 680309,
melwelton60@hotmail.com. *6m S of
Humber Bridge. Leave M180 at J5.
Take 1st exit L passing petrol station
into Elsham village. Old Quarry Lodge
is 1st house on R on entering village.*
Sun 21 Aug (10.30-5). **Adm £4, chd
free. Light refreshments** at Village
Hall, Elsham. **Visits also by
arrangement Apr to Sept, groups
10+.**
Approx ¹/₂ acre sloping garden with
formal and informal features.
Abundant borders and island beds
with architectural focal points,
Mediterranean influence in parts.
Highly imaginative garden with
exciting mixture of the flamboyant
and the quintessentially English.
Garden is always packed with yr
round interest. Featured in several
garden magazines. Gravel drive,
sloping site.

39 THE OLD RECTORY
East Keal, Spilsby PE23 4AT. Mrs
Ruth Ward, 01790 752477,
rfjward@btinternet.com. *2m SW of
Spilsby. Off A16. Turn into Church
Lane by PO.* **Sun 17 Apr, Sun 22
May** (2-5). **Adm £3.50, chd free.
Home-made teas. Visits also by
arrangement Mar to Sept,
refreshments on request.**
Beautifully situated, with fine views,
rambling cottage garden on different
levels falling naturally into separate
areas, with changing effects and
atmosphere. Steps, paths and vistas
to lead you on, with seats well placed
for appreciating special views or
relaxing and enjoying the peace.
Dry border, vegetable garden,
orchard, woodland walk, wildflower
meadow.

40 NEW THE OLD RECTORY
Main Street, Bucknall, Woodhall
Spa LN10 5DT. Elizabeth Pittel,
01526 388205,
lizziepi@hotmail.com. *Property next
to Church on main st in Bucknall.
Roadside parking available.* **Visits by
arrangement May & June, groups
10 +. Adm £5.00, chd free. Home-
made teas. Adm incl tea and cake.**
1710 Grade 2 listed Old Rectory.
mixed herbaceous borders, formal
water feature, natural pond. Walled
potage. Meadow with mown paths.
Woodland area with hellebores.

Wheelchair access to most of garden,
some gravelled areas.

41 THE OLD VICARAGE
Low Road, Holbeach Hurn
PE12 8JN. Mrs Liz Dixon-Spain,
01406 424148,
lizdixonspain@gmail.com. *2m NE of
Holbeach. Turn off A17 N to
Holbeach Hurn, past post box in
middle of village, 1st R into Low Rd.
Old Vicarage on R approx 400yds.*
Sun 15 May (1-5). **Combined adm
with Old White House £5, chd
free. Home-made teas** at Old
White House. **Visits also by
arrangement Mar to Sept.**
2 acres of garden with 150yr old tulip,
plane and beech trees: borders of
shrubs, roses, herbaceous plants.
Shrub roses and herb garden in old
paddock area, surrounded by informal
areas with pond and bog garden, wild
flowers, grasses and bulbs. Small fruit
and vegetable gardens. Kids love
exploring winding paths through the
wilder areas. Garden is managed
environmentally. Gravel drive, some
paths, mostly grass access.

42 OLD WHITE HOUSE
Holbeach Hurn PE12 8JP. Mr & Mrs
A Worth. *2m N of Holbeach. Turn off
A17 N to Holbeach Hurn, follow signs
to village, cont through, turn R after
Rose & Crown PH at Baileys Lane.*
Sun 15 May (1-5). **Combined adm
with The Old Vicarage £5, chd
free. Home-made teas.**
1¹/₂ acres of mature garden, featuring
herbaceous borders, roses, patterned
garden, herb garden and walled
kitchen garden. Large catalpa, tulip
tree that flowers, ginko and other
specimen trees. Flat surfaces, some
steps but wheelchair access to all
areas without using steps.

43 OVERBECK
46 Main Street, Scothern LN2 2UW.
John & Joyce Good, 01673 862200,
jandjgood@btinternet.com. *4m E of
Lincoln. Scothern signed from A46 at
Dunholme & A158 at Sudbrooke.
Overbeck is at E end of Main St.*
**Visits by arrangement May to
Aug, daytime and evenings. Adm
£3.00, chd free. Light
refreshments.**
Situated in an attractive village this
approx ²/₃ acre garden is a haven for
wildlife. Long herbaceous borders
and colour themed island beds with

some unusual perennials. Hosta
border, gravel bed with grasses,
fernery, trees, numerous shrubs,
small stumpery, climbers, a
developing parterre and large prolific
vegetable and fruit area.

44 PEAR TREE COTTAGE
Butt Lane, Goulceby, Louth
LN11 9UP. Jill Mowbray & Miranda
Manning Press, 01507 343201,
chirpy@theraggedrobin.co.uk,
www.theraggedrobin.co.uk. *6m N
of Horncastle & 8m SW of Louth. 2m
off A153 between Louth &
Horncastle. 2m off Caistor High St
(B1225). Please note: This is a small
rural village, please park
considerately.* **Sun 15 May** (11-4).
Adm £3, chd free. Sun 17 July
(11-4). **Combined adm with
The Stables £5, chd free. Home-
made teas. Visits also by
arrangement May to Aug for
groups 15+.**
Situated in the heart of the Wolds, the
garden which surrounds the house on
three sides, is an oasis of bright
colour within the delightful village of
Goulceby. The balance of perennials
and annuals ensure a vibrant display
throughout the seasons. Productive
fruit and vegetable plots and
greenhouses lie alongside the
borders which only serves to add to
the verdant atmosphere within the
garden. Visit The Three Horseshoes
PH (www.the3horseshoes.com) and
Workshop in the Wolds
(www.workshopinthewolds.co.uk).
Featured in Garden News. Wheelchair
access via front gate with access on
grass paths only.

45 NEW SEDGEBROOK
MANOR
Church Lane, Sedgebrook,
Grantham NG32 2EU. Hon James
& Lady Caroline Ogilvy. *2m E of
Grantham on A52. In Sedgebrook
village by church.* **Sun 10 Apr** (1-5).
**Adm £4, chd free. Home-made
teas.**
Yew and box topiary surround this
charming Manor House (not open).
Massed spring bulbs. Croquet lawn,
herbaceous border and summer
house. Bridge over small pond and
two larger ponds. Ancient mulberry
tree. Tennis court, vegetable patch,
woodland area with chickens.
Swimming pool in enclosed garden.
Wheelchair access to most areas.

46 SHANGRILA

Little Hale Road, Great Hale, Sleaford NG34 9LH. Marilyn Cooke & John Knight. *On B1394 between Heckington & Helpringham.* **Sun 19 June (11-5). Adm £4, chd free. Home-made teas.**
Approx 3 acre garden with sweeping lawns long herbaceous borders, colour themed island beds, hosta collection, lavender bed with seating area, topiary, acers, small raised vegetable area, 3 ponds and new exotic borders. Wheelchair access to all areas.

47 NEW 66 SPILSBY ROAD

Boston PE21 9NS. Rosemary & Adrian Isaac. *From Boston town take A16 towards Spilsby. On L after Trinity Church. Parking on Spilsby Rd.* **Sun 15 May (11-4). Adm £3, chd free. Cream teas.**
1¹/₃ acre with mature trees, moat, tudor garden house, summer house and orangery, lawns and herbaceous borders. Children's Tudor garden house, gatehouse and courtyard. Wide paths.

48 NEW THE STABLES

Ranby, Market Rasen LN8 5LN. Russ & Chris Hibbins, 01507 343581, russhibbins@btinternet.com. *SW corner of Lincolnshire Wolds - between Horncastle & Market Rasen. On A158, halfway between Wragby & Horncastle, is Baumber. Here, turn N on B1225 (direction Caistor & Belmont tv mast) for 3m. Garden well signed. From N follow B1225.* **Sun 17 July (12-4.30). Combined adm with Pear Tree Cottage £5, chd free. Home-made teas. Visits also by arrangement June to Sept, groups 10+ welcome.**
The garden approaches ¹/₂ acre and has been developed over last 15yrs as a place to sit, relax and look at a variety of trees, shrubs and plants (some not so common), together with statuary and sculptures. S facing and extremely fertile, well drained soil helps most plants to quickly become established. The many seats around the garden are intended for use! Some covered seating and tables if needed. Wonderfully rural setting, in a quiet hamlet, the garden is not really visible from the road and often surprises people who see it for the first time. Features a much admired foxglove gate. Local press coverage.

For wheelchair users there is a slightly different entry to the garden, along a flat gravel drive, with no steps.

49 THORNHAM

Northing Lane, Scothern, Lincoln LN2 2WL. Janis Mason, 07525 052834. *4m E of Lincoln. Scothern is signed from A46 at Dunholme & A158 at Sudbrooke. Thornham is a 150 metre walk up Northing Lane, which is opp Overbeck at E end of Main St.* **Visits by arrangement June to Sept for small groups. Adm £2.50, chd free. Tea/coffee and biscuits.**
Medium sized, densely planted, naturalistic, perennial garden. Many hardy plants, some unusual. Plantaholic gardener aims to have something in flower yr-round. Gravel pathways lead through the flower beds as there is no lawn.

Developed into lush, colourful, exotic plant packed haven . . .

50 68 WATTS LANE

Louth LN11 9DG. Jenny & Rodger Grasham, 07977 318145, sallysing@hotmail.co.uk, www.facebook.com/thesecretgardenoflouth. *¹/₂ m S of Louth town centre. Watts Lane off Newmarket (on B1200). Turn by pedestrian lights & Co-op Some SatNavs unreliable. Try LN119DJ for Mount Pleasant Av, this leads on to Watts Lane.* **Wed 13, Sun 31 July (11-4). Every Sun 7 Aug to 28 Aug (11-4). Adm £2.50, chd free. Home-made teas. Visits also by arrangement July to Sept, refreshments on request when booking.**
Blank canvas of ¹/₅ acre in early 90s. Developed into lush, colourful, exotic plant packed haven. A whole new world on entering from street. Exotic borders, raised island, long hot border, ponds, stumpery, developing prairie style border. Conservatory, grapevine. Intimate seating areas along garden's journey. Facebook page - The Secret Garden of Louth. Children, find where the frogs are hiding! Many butterflies and bees but how many different types? Feed the

fish. Featured in Period Ideas magazine. Grass pathways, main garden area accessible. Wheelchairs not permitted on bridge over pond, both sides can be reached via pathways.

51 NEW WEST SYKE

38 Electric Station Road, Sleaford NG34 7QJ. Ada Trethewey. *From A17, A15 & A153 take bypass exit at r'about to Sleaford Town centre. At HSBC & Lloyds Bank turn R into Westgate. Turn R, 38 at end of rd. Ample parking.* **Sun 19 June (12-5). Adm £3, chd free. Cream teas.**
Over 1 acre, comprising bog gardens, rockeries, 3 large ponds, wildflower meadow, lawns and cottage garden planting. Rambling roses a feature. Designed for wildlife habitats; sustainable principles and a wealth of native species. Garden evolved over 30yrs. Lawned paths. WC wheelchair accessible.

52 NEW 8 WESTCOTE FARM

Wold Road, Barrow-upon-Humber DN19 7DY. Joe & Lindy Mansley. *On outskirts of Barrow-upon-Humber, 3m from Humber Bridge. From A15 follow B1206 towards Barrow-upon-Humber, indicate L turn at 30 mph sign then L down lane signed Westcote Farm.* **Sun 12 June (11-5). Combined adm with The Barn £3.50, chd free.**
Joe and Lindy are new but enthusiastic about gardening. We are learning from our neighbours 3 and 6 Westcote Farm whose gardens are adjacent either side. Herbaceous boarder created in 2015 along with newly built pergola. Plans for further boarders and lavender hedging currently being developed. All areas accessible.

53 3 WESTCOTE FARM HOUSE

Wold Road, Barrow-upon-Humber DN19 7DY. Gary & Ali Baugh. *On outskirts of Barrow-upon-Humber, 3m from Humber Bridge. From A15 follow B1206 towards Barrow-upon-Humber, indicate L turn at 30 mph sign then L down lane signed Westcote Farm.* **Sun 12 June (11-5). Adm £3.50, chd free. Home-made teas. Also open 8 Westcote Farm.**
The garden has been designed to offer a place to relax and enjoy the surrounding countryside. Yew hedges

are used to give a formal but contemporary feel throughout the garden giving unity and seclusion to each individual area. Large drifts of herbaceous plants add a new dimension during the summer months. Trees and shrubs form the backbone of the garden. Wheelchair and scooter access over lawn and most hard surfaces.

54 NEW 48 WESTGATE
Louth LN11 9YD. Kenneth Harvey. *Approx 100 yrds before The Wheatsheaf PH, nr to Church.* Sun 3 July, Sun 4 Sept (11-4). Adm £3.50, chd free. Tea.
Large town garden of about 1½ acres that crosses the R Ludd. Hidden away behind the high Georgian facades of Louth is a good example of a town garden of trees, herbaceous borders, two small ponds, a fern and white garden and formal vegetable parterre. Wonderful views of Louth church spire. The garden was originally planted in the late 1950s, but has been remodelled over the last 5yrs.

ALLOTMENTS

55 NEW WILLOUGHBY ROAD ALLOTMENTS
Willoughby Road, Boston PE21 9HN. Willoughby Road Allotments Association. *Entrance adjacent to 109 Willoughby Rd.* Sun 14 Aug (11-4). Adm £3, chd free. Light refreshments.
Set in 5 acres the allotments comprise 60 plots growing fine vegetables, fruit, flowers and herbs. There is a small orchard and wildflower area and a community space adjacent. Grass paths run along the site. Several plots will be open to walk round. There will be a seed and plant stall. Featured as part of Boston in Bloom with a large mural being unveiled on the new community plot.

56 WILLOW COTTAGE
Gravel Pit Lane, Burgh-le-Marsh PE24 5DW. Bob & Karen Ward, 01754 811450, robertward055@aol.com, www.willowcottagecl.webs.com. *6m W of Skegness. S of Gunby*

Dunholme Lodge

r'about on A158, take 1st R signed Bratoft & Burgh-le-Marsh. 1st R again onto Bratoft Lane. L at T-junction, parking on R 25yds. Sun 26 June (2-5). Adm £3, chd free. Home-made teas. Visits also by arrangement May to July.
Ever changing colourful borders, shaded glades by tranquil ponds, pleasant woodland walk, new prairie planting, and so much more to explore. Enjoy home-made afternoon tea with a few friends at your favourite spot on the terrace overlooking the quintessential English cottage garden. Open on some sunny Sunday afternoons 2 to 5 pm, ring ahead and check! Woodland walk and Victorian glasshouse. Featured in Lincolnshire Today magazine. Partial wheelchair access. For assistance please phone ahead of visit.

57 WOODLANDS
Peppin Lane, Fotherby, Louth LN11 0UW. Ann & Bob Armstrong, 01507 603586, annbobarmstrong@btinternet.com, www.woodlandsplants.co.uk. *2m N of Louth on A16 signed Fotherby. Please park on R verge opp allotments & walk approx 350 yds to garden. No parking at garden. Please do not drive beyond designated area.* Sun 3 Apr, Sun 5 June, Sun 7 Aug (11-5). Adm £3, chd free. Home-made teas. Opening with Fotherby Gardens on Sun 1 May, Sun 3 July, Sun 4 Sept. Visits also by arrangement Feb to Oct.
A lovely mature woodland garden with many unusual plants set against a backdrop of an ever changing tapestry of greenery. A peaceful garden where wildlife is given a chance to thrive. The front garden has been developed into a crevice area for alpine plants. The nursery, featured in RHS Plantfinder, gives visitors the opportunity to purchase plants seen in the garden. Award winning professional artist's studio/gallery open to visitors. Specialist collection of Codonopsis for which Plant Heritage status has been granted. Featured in Lincolnshire Pride magazine.

58 NEW YEW TREE FARM
Westhorpe Road, Gosberton, Spalding PE11 4EP. Robert & Claire Bailey-Scott, 01775 840821, rbaileyscott@aol.com. *Nr Spalding. Enter the village of Gosberton. Turn into Westhorpe Rd, opp The Bell Inn, cont for approx. 1½ m. Property is 3rd on R after bridge.* Sun 24 July (11-5). Adm £4, chd free. Home-made teas. Visits also by arrangement June & July for groups 10+.
A lovely country garden, 1½ acres. Large herbaceous and mixed borders surround the well kept lawns. Large wildlife pond with 2 bog gardens, woodland garden and shaded borders containing many unusual plants. A mulberry tree forms the centre piece of 1 lawn. Stunning annual flower meadow has real wow factor. 2 magnificent yew trees, organic vegetable plot and orchard, under planted with a wildflower meadow. Gravel driveway, some gravel paths.

LONDON

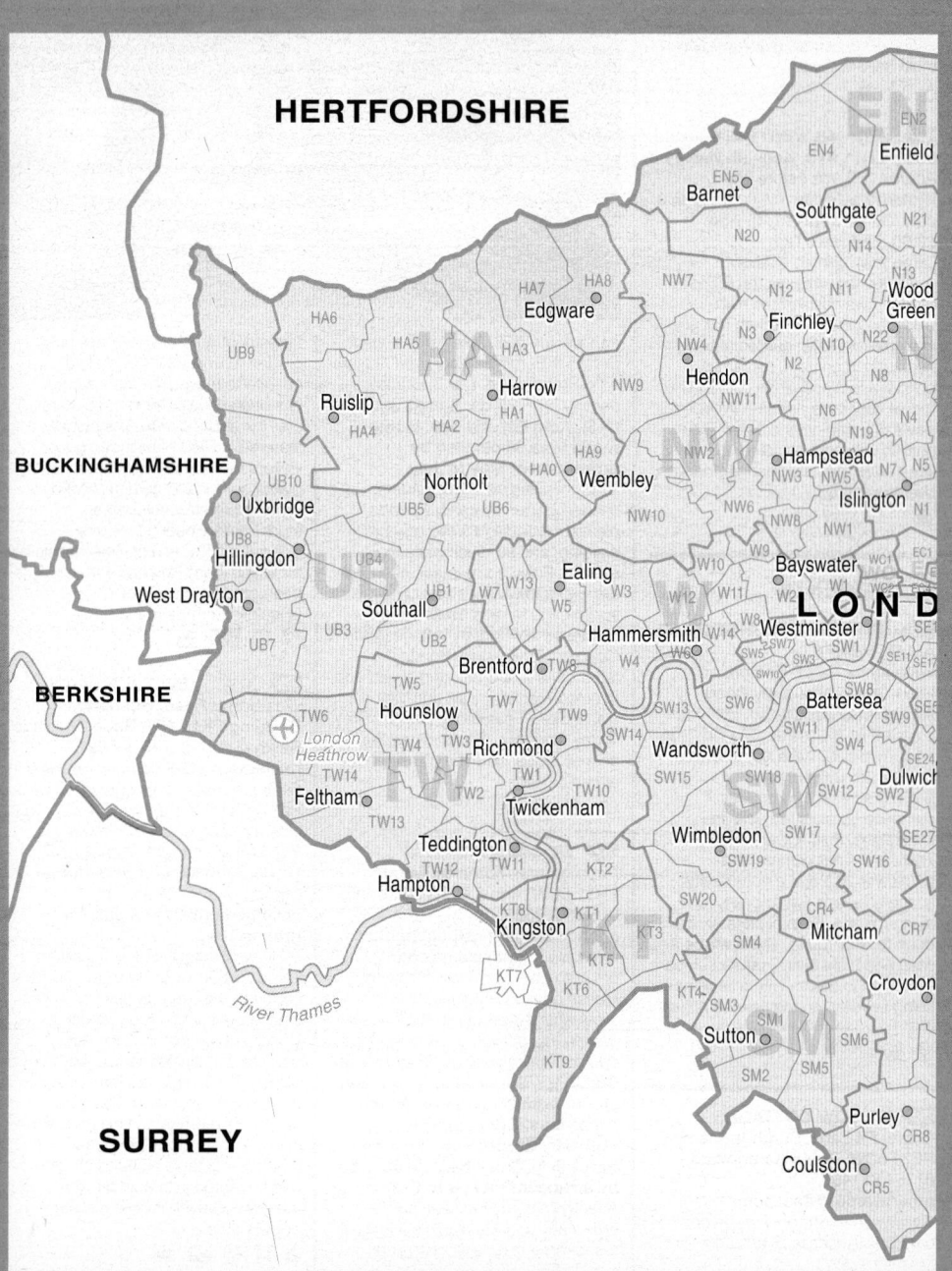

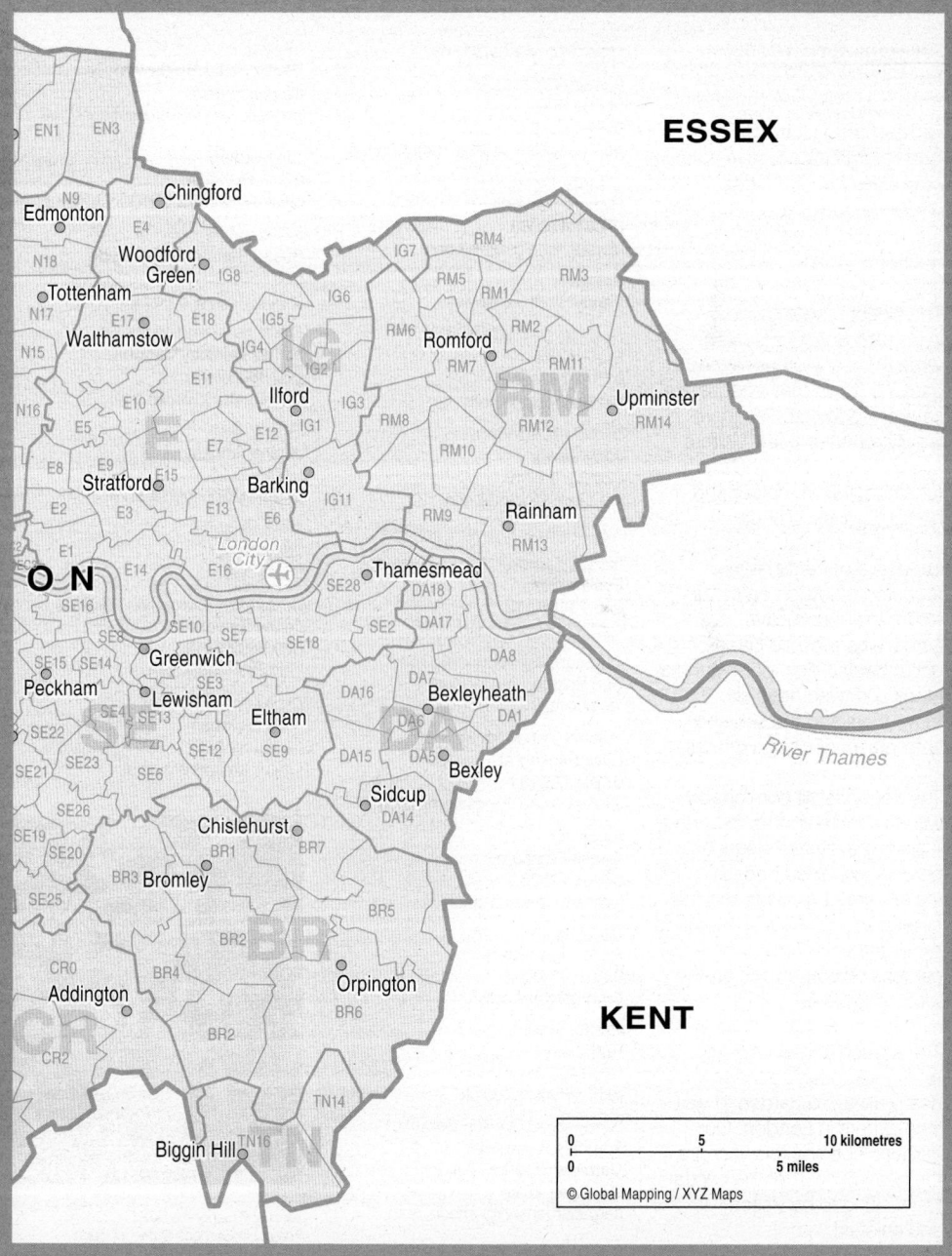

ESSEX

EN1 EN3

N9 Chingford

Edmonton

E4

N18 Woodford
Green IG8

Tottenham

N17 E17 E18 IG5

Walthamstow IG4

N15

N16 E11 IG2

E10 E12 Ilford IG3

E5 E7 IG1

E9 E15

E8 E13 Stratford

E2 E6 Barking

E1 E3

E14 E16

London
City

SE16

SE28 Thamesmead

SE8 SE10 SE7 SE18 SE2

SE15 SE14 SE3 Greenwich

Peckham SE4 SE13 Lewisham

SE22 SE5 Eltham

SE21 SE23 SE6 SE9

SE26

SE19 SE20

SE25 BR3 Bromley

BR1 BR7

BR5

BR2

CR0 BR4

Addington Orpington

BR6

CR2 BR2

TN14

Biggin Hill TN16

IG7 RM4

RM5 RM1

IG6 RM3

RM6 RM2

Romford RM11

RM7

RM8 Upminster

RM12 RM14

RM10

IG11 RM9 Rainham

RM13

DA18

DA17

DA8

DA7

DA16 Bexleyheath

DA6 DA1

DA15 DA5 Bexley

Sidcup

DA14

Chislehurst

KENT

River Thames

| 0 | | 5 | | 10 kilometres |
| 0 | | | 5 miles | |

© Global Mapping / XYZ Maps

Investec Wealth & Investment supports the NGS

London

From the tiniest to the largest, London gardens offer exceptional diversity. Hidden behind historic houses in Spitalfields are exquisite tiny gardens, while on Kingston Hill there are 9 acres of landscaped gardens.

The oldest private garden in London boasts 5 acres, while the many other historic gardens within these pages are smaller – some so tiny there is only room for a few visitors at a time – but nonetheless full of innovation, colour and horticultural excellence.

London allotments have attracted television cameras to film their productive acres, where exotic Cape gooseberries, figs, prizewinning roses and even bees all thrive thanks to the skill and enthusiasm of city gardeners.

The traditional sit comfortably with the contemporary in London – offering a feast of elegant borders, pleached hedges, topiary, gravel gardens and the cooling sound of water – while to excite the adventurous there are gardens on barges and green roofs to explore.

The season stretches from April to October, so there is nearly always a garden to visit somewhere in London. Our gardens opening this year are the beating heart of the capital just waiting to be visited and enjoyed.

London Volunteers

County Organiser
Penny Snell
01932 864532
pennysnellflowers@btinternet.com

County Treasurer
Richard Raworth
07831 476088
raworthrichard@gmail.com

Publicity
Penny Snell (as above)

Booklet Co-ordinator
Sue Phipps
07771 767196
sue@suephipps.com

Booklet Distributor
Joey Clover
020 8870 8740
joeyclover@hotmail.com

Assistant County Organisers

Central London
Eveline Carn
020 7388 1113
evelinecbcarn@icloud.com

Clapham & surrounding area
Sue Phipps
(as above)

Dulwich & surrounding area
Clive Pankhurst
07941 536934
alternative.ramblings@gmail.com

E London
Teresa Farnham
07761 476651
farnhamz@yahoo.co.uk

Hackney
Philip Lightowlers
020 8533 0052
plighto@gmail.com

Hampstead
Ruth Levy
020 7435 4124
ruthlevy@tiscali.co.uk

Hampstead Garden Suburb, Finchley & Barnet
Caroline Broome
020 8444 2329
carosgarden@virginmedia.com

Islington
Penelope Darby Brown
020 7226 6880
pendarbybrown@blueyonder.co.uk

Gill Evansky
020 7359 2484
gevansky@gmail.com

NW London
Susan Bennett & Earl Hyde
020 8883 8540
suebearlh@yahoo.co.uk

Outer NW London
James Duncan Mattoon
020 8830 7410
jamesmattoon@msn.com

SE London
Janine Wookey
07711 279636
j.wookey@btinternet.com

SW London
Joey Clover
(as above)

W London, Barnes & Chiswick
Jenny Raworth
020 8892 3713
jraworth@gmail.com

Outer W London
Julia Hickman
020 8339 0931
julia.hickman@virgin.net

Above: 7 Canonbie Road, Forest Hill Gardens © Jacqui Hurst

London gardens listed by postcode

Inner London postcodes

E & EC London

Spitalfields Gardens E1
70 Bushwood E11
17 Greenstone Mews E11
37 Harold Road E11
12 Western Road E13
Richard House Children's Hospice E16
87 St Johns Road E17
46 Cheyne Avenue E18
5 Brodie Road E4
Homerton Gardens E5
Lower Clapton Gardens E5
42 Latimer Road E7
London Fields Gardens E8
53 Mapledene Road E8
17a Navarino Road E8
12 Bushberry Road E9
The Charterhouse EC1
The Inner and Middle Temple Gardens EC4

N & NW London

37 Alwyne Road N1
Arlington Square Gardens N1
Barnsbury Group N1
Canonbury House N1
4 Canonbury Place N1
De Beauvoir Gardens N1
41 Ecclesbourne Road N1
King Henry's Walk Garden N1
Malvern Terrace Gardens N1
North Bridge House Senior School N1
5 Northampton Park N1
20 St Mary's Grove N1
19 Hillfield Park N10
Princes Avenue Gardens N10
5 St Regis Close N10
25 Springfield Avenue N10
14 Tetherdown N10
27 Wood Vale N10
33 Wood Vale N10
21 Woodland Rise N10
94 Brownlow Road N11
Golf Course Allotments N11
The Rose Garden at Golf Course Allotments N11
5 Russell Road N13
15 Norcott Road N16

77 Handsworth Road N17
159 Higham Road N17
36 Ashley Road N19
79 Church Lane N2
91 Vicar's Moor Lane N21
Alexandra Park Road Gardens N22
23 Imperial Road N22
Railway Cottages N22
31 Church Crescent N3
Gordon Road Allotments N3
31 Hendon Avenue N3
18 Park Crescent N3
32 Highbury Place N5
Olden Garden Community Project N5
7 The Grove N6
2 Millfield Place N6
3 The Park N6
44 Southwood Lane N6
Southwood Lodge N6
10 Woodside Avenue N6
9 Furlong Road N7
33 Huddleston Road N7
1a Hungerford Road N7
62 Hungerford Road N7
11 Park Avenue North N8
12 Warner Road N8
69 Gloucester Crescent NW1
70 Gloucester Crescent NW1
The Holme NW1
4 Park Village East (Tower Lodge Gardens) NW1
Royal College of Physicians Medicinal Garden NW1
4 Asmuns Hill NW11
48 Erskine Hill NW11
74 Willifield Way NW11
86 Willifield Way NW11
121 Anson Road NW2
20 Exeter Road NW2
27 Menelik Road NW2
93 Tanfield Avenue NW2
208 Walm Lane, The Garden Flat NW2

The NGS: Macmillan Cancer Support's largest ever benefactor . . .

Fenton House NW3
27 Nassington Road NW3
Copthall Group NW7
Highwood Ash NW7
116 Hamilton Terrace NW8
2 Hillside Close NW8

S, SE & SW London

Garden Barge Square at Downings Roads Moorings SE1
Lambeth Palace SE1
41 Southbrook Road SE12
28 Granville Park SE13
Choumert Square SE15
122 Court Lane SE21
Dulwich Village Two Gardens SE21
4 Cornflower Terrace SE22
49 Jennings Road SE22
55 Jennings Road SE22
9 The Gardens SE22
174 Peckham Rye SE22
45 Underhill Road SE22
86 Underhill Road SE22
Forest Hill Gardens SE23
5 Burbage Road SE24
South London Botanical Institute SE24
Stoney Hill House SE26
49 Lee Road SE3
8 Calais Street SE5
35 Camberwell Grove SE5
81 Camberwell Grove SE5
24 Grove Park SE5
Cadogan Place South Garden SW1
Eccleston Square SW1
Fern Cottage SW12
28 Old Devonshire Road SW12
61 Arthur Road SW19
97 Arthur Road SW19
Eaton Square Garden SW1W
11 Ernle Road SW20
Paddock Allotments & Leisure Gardens SW20
Chelsea Physic Garden SW3
51 The Chase SW4
Clapham Manor Street Gardens SW4
4 Macaulay Road SW4
Trinity Hospice SW4
The Hurlingham Club SW6
50 Viceroy Rd SW8

W London

57 St Quintin Avenue W10
Arundel & Ladbroke Gardens W11
12 Lansdowne Road W11
49 Loftus Road W12

41 Mill Hill Road W3
65 Mill Hill Road W3
Zen Garden W3
Chiswick Mall Gardens W4
The Orchard W4
36 Park Road W4
56 Park Road W4
All Seasons W5
60 Ranelagh Road W5
38 York Road W5
27 St Peters Square W6
1 York Close W7
Edwardes Square W8
7 Upper Phillimore Gardens W8
57 Tonbridge House WC1H
The Cottage WC1N
14 Doughty Street WC1N
61 Doughty Street WC1N

Outer London postcodes

174 Ravensbourne Avenue BR2
22 Kelsey Way BR3
109 Addington Road BR4
White Cottage BR5
2 Springhurst Close CR0
Whitgift School CR2
Elm Court Gardens EN4
West Lodge Park EN4
190 Barnet Road EN5
Blue Hills EN5
13 Greenhill Park EN5
96 Station Road EN5
31 Arlington Drive HA4
4 Ormonde Road HA6
Treetops HA6
7 Woodbines Avenue KT1
9 Imber Park Road KT10
The Watergardens KT2
The Circle Garden KT3
Hampton Court Palace KT8
6 Manor Road KT8
61 Wolsey Road KT8
239a Hook Road KT9
18 Pettits Boulevard RM1
7 St George's Road TW1
Ormeley Lodge TW10
Petersham House TW10
St Michael's Convent TW10
Stokes House TW10
Hampton Hill Gardens TW12
20 Beechwood Avenue TW9
Kew Green Gardens TW9
Marksbury Avenue Gardens TW9
Trumpeters House & Sarah's Garden TW9
29 West Park Road TW9
31 West Park Road TW9
34 Ridding Lane UB6
L'Escala WD6

Opening Dates

All entries subject to change.
For latest information check www.ngs.org.uk

February

Saturday 13
NEW▶ 44 Southwood Lane, N6
Saturday 20
NEW▶ 44 Southwood Lane, N6

April

Friday 1
Chelsea Physic Garden, SW3
Sunday 10
5 Burbage Road, SE24
7 The Grove, N6
NEW▶ Richard House Children's Hospice, E16
Trinity Hospice, SW4
Saturday 16
11 Ernle Road, SW20
Sunday 17
Cadogan Place South Garden, SW1
4 Canonbury Place, N1
NEW▶ Eaton Square Garden, SW1W
Edwardes Square, W8
11 Ernle Road, SW20
Lower Clapton Gardens, E5
17a Navarino Road, E8
20 St Mary's Grove, N1
South London Botanical Institute, SE24
Sunday 24
51 The Chase, SW4
Olden Garden Community Project, N5
St Michael's Convent, TW10
Southwood Lodge, N6
7 Upper Phillimore Gardens, W8
Wednesday 27
51 The Chase, SW4 (Evening)

May

Sunday 1
2 Millfield Place, N6
5 St Regis Close, N10
21 Woodland Rise, N10
Thursday 5
27 Wood Vale, N10 (Evening)

Sunday 8
Arundel & Ladbroke Gardens, W11
Eccleston Square, SW1
Malvern Terrace Gardens, N1
The Orchard, W4
27 St Peters Square, W6
45 Underhill Road, SE22
86 Underhill Road, SE22
NEW▶ 50 Viceroy Rd, SW8
The Watergardens, KT2
Sunday 15
20 Beechwood Avenue, TW9 (Evening)
Forest Hill Gardens, SE23
Highwood Ash, NW7
West Lodge Park, EN4
33 Wood Vale, N10
Saturday 21
The Hurlingham Club, SW6

Since our foundation we have donated more than £45 million to charity . . .

Sunday 22
109 Addington Road, BR4
190 Barnet Road, EN5
NEW▶ Canonbury House, N1
Kew Green Gardens, TW9
NEW▶ North Bridge House Senior School, N1
NEW▶ 4 Ormonde Road, HA6
Princes Avenue Gardens, N10
Stoney Hill House, SE26
Trinity Hospice, SW4
Whitgift School, CR2
Tuesday 24
Lambeth Palace, SE1 (Evening)
Wednesday 25
12 Lansdowne Road, W11
Thursday 26
4 Park Village East (Tower Lodge Gardens), NW1 (Evening)

Saturday 28
1 York Close, W7 (Evening)
Sunday 29
36 Ashley Road, N19
Chiswick Mall Gardens, W4
Garden Barge Square at Downings Roads Moorings, SE1
13 Greenhill Park, EN5
King Henry's Walk Garden, N1
174 Peckham Rye, SE22
208 Walm Lane, The Garden Flat, NW2
1 York Close, W7
Monday 30
36 Ashley Road, N19

June

Gardens Festival

Saturday 4
The Circle Garden, KT3
Hampton Hill Gardens, TW12
NEW▶ 34 Ridding Lane, UB6 (Evening)
7 St George's Road, TW1 (Evening)
12 Western Road, E13
Zen Garden, W3
Sunday 5
37 Alwyne Road, N1
NEW▶ 31 Arlington Drive, HA4
Barnsbury Group, N1
Blue Hills, EN5
35 Camberwell Grove, SE5
Choumert Square, SE15
The Circle Garden, KT3
4 Cornflower Terrace, SE22
NEW▶ 41 Ecclesbourne Road, N1
11 Ernle Road, SW20 (Evening)
NEW▶ L'Escala
NEW▶ Fern Cottage, SW12
69 Gloucester Crescent, NW1
70 Gloucester Crescent, NW1
Hampton Hill Gardens, TW12
Homerton Gardens, E5
Kew Green Gardens, TW9 (Evening)
27 Nassington Road, NW3
28 Old Devonshire Road, SW12
11 Park Avenue North, N8
4 Park Village East (Tower Lodge Gardens), NW1
NEW▶ 34 Ridding Lane, UB6

Royal College of Physicians Medicinal Garden, NW1
96 Station Road, EN5
Stokes House, TW10
91 Vicar's Moor Lane, N21
White Cottage, BR5
Zen Garden, W3
Tuesday 7
The Charterhouse, EC1 (Evening)
Wednesday 8
NEW▶ Fern Cottage, SW12 (Evening)
239a Hook Road, KT9 (Evening)
28 Old Devonshire Road, SW12 (Evening)
Friday 10
NEW▶ Marksbury Avenue Gardens, TW9 (Evening)
Saturday 11
18 Pettits Boulevard, RM1
41 Southbrook Road, SE12
Spitalfields Gardens, E1
Sunday 12
Arlington Square Gardens, N1
81 Camberwell Grove, SE5
79 Church Lane, N2
Clapham Manor Street Gardens, SW4
Copthall Group, NW7
122 Court Lane, SE21
De Beauvoir Gardens, N1
28 Granville Park, SE13
7 The Grove, N6
77 Handsworth Road, N17
159 Higham Road, N17
1a Hungerford Road, N7
62 Hungerford Road, N7
22 Kelsey Way, BR3
NEW▶ 49 Lee Road, SE3
Lower Clapton Gardens, E5
18 Pettits Boulevard, RM1
41 Southbrook Road, SE12
Southwood Lodge, N6
NEW▶ 25 Springfield Avenue, N10
Trumpeters House & Sarah's Garden, TW9
12 Warner Road, N8
Tuesday 14
Fenton House, NW3 (Evening)
49 Loftus Road, W12 (Evening)
Wednesday 15
239a Hook Road, KT9 (Evening)
2 Millfield Place, N6 (Evening)
Saturday 18
7 St George's Road, TW1 (Evening)
Zen Garden, W3

Sunday 19
61 Arthur Road, SW19
97 Arthur Road, SW19
20 Beechwood Avenue,
    TW9 (Evening)
5 Brodie Road, E4
Dulwich Village Two
    Gardens, SE21
9 Furlong Road, N7
32 Highbury Place, N5
6 Manor Road, KT8
15 Norcott Road, N16
Ormeley Lodge, TW10
3 The Park, N6
18 Park Crescent, N3
5 St Regis Close, N10
2 Springhurst Close, CR0
NEW 29 West Park Road,
    TW9
31 West Park Road, TW9
74 Willifield Way, NW11
61 Wolsey Road, KT8
Zen Garden, W3

Tuesday 21
Lambeth Palace, SE1
    (Evening)

Wednesday 22
The Inner and Middle
    Temple Gardens, EC4
61 Wolsey Road, KT8
    (Evening)

Saturday 25
The Holme, NW1
5 Northampton Park, N1
Paddock Allotments &
    Leisure Gardens, SW20
7 Woodbines Avenue, KT1
    (Evening)

Sunday 26
109 Addington Road, BR4
The Holme, NW1
NEW 9 Imber Park Road,
    KT10
London Fields Gardens, E8
The Rose Garden at Golf
    Course Allotments, N11
208 Walm Lane, The
    Garden Flat, NW2

Thursday 30
Hampton Court Palace,
    KT8 (Evening)

July

Saturday 2
NEW 33 Huddleston
    Road, N7

Sunday 3
121 Anson Road, NW2
116 Hamilton Terrace, NW8
    (Evening)
2 Hillside Close, NW8
NEW 33 Huddleston
    Road, N7
Railway Cottages, N22

14 Tetherdown, N10

Thursday 7
27 Wood Vale, N10
    (Evening)

Saturday 9
All Seasons, W5

Sunday 10
All Seasons, W5
NEW The Cottage, WC1N
NEW 14 Doughty Street,
    WC1N
NEW 61 Doughty Street,
    WC1N
27 Menelik Road, NW2
NEW 57 Tonbridge
    House, WC1H

Wednesday 13
20 Exeter Road, NW2
    (Evening)

Friday 15
41 Mill Hill Road, W3
    (Evening)
65 Mill Hill Road, W3
    (Evening)

Saturday 16
190 Barnet Road, EN5
The Circle Garden, KT3
42 Latimer Road, E7
18 Pettits Boulevard, RM1

Sunday 17
12 Bushberry Road, E9
NEW 70 Bushwood,
    E11
Elm Court Gardens, EN4
116 Hamilton Terrace, NW8
    (Evening)

19 Hillfield Park, N10
42 Latimer Road, E7
17a Navarino Road, E8
18 Park Crescent, N3
18 Pettits Boulevard, RM1
60 Ranelagh Road, W5
NEW 172 Ravensbourne
    Avenue, BR2
NEW 174 Ravensbourne
    Avenue, BR2
87 St Johns Road, E17
57 St Quintin Avenue, W10
5 St Regis Close, N10

Wednesday 20
9 The Gardens, SE22
    (Evening)

Friday 22
NEW 55 Jennings Road
    (Evening)

Sunday 24
4 Asmuns Hill, NW11
NEW 31 Hendon Avenue,
    N3
NEW 49 Jennings Road
NEW 55 Jennings Road
NEW 36 Park Road, W4
NEW 56 Park Road, W4
87 St Johns Road, E17
Treetops, HA6
86 Willifield Way, NW11
NEW 38 York Road, W5

Wednesday 27
NEW 50 Viceroy Rd, SW8
    (Evening)

Thursday 28
Hampton Court Palace,
    KT8 (Evening)

Sunday 31
79 Church Lane, N2
NEW 37 Harold Road,
    E11
57 St Quintin Avenue, W10
93 Tanfield Avenue, NW2

August

Saturday 6
The Holme, NW1

Sunday 7
Alexandra Park Road
    Gardens, N22
31 Church Crescent, N3
69 Gloucester Crescent,
    NW1
70 Gloucester Crescent,
    NW1
The Holme, NW1
NEW 10 Woodside
    Avenue, N6

Sunday 14
94 Brownlow Road, N11
46 Cheyne Avenue, E18
17 Greenstone Mews, E11
41 Mill Hill Road, W3
65 Mill Hill Road, W3
5 Russell Road, N13
33 Wood Vale, N10

Sunday 21
5 Brodie Road, E4

Thursday 25
Hampton Court Palace,
    KT8 (Evening)

Sunday 28
190 Barnet Road, EN5

16 Eyot Gardens, Chiswick Mall Gardens

Join us on Facebook ⓕ and spread the word

4 Park Village East, Tower Lodge Gardens

© Marianne Majerus

September

Sunday 4
8 Calais Street, SE5
Golf Course Allotments, N11
Gordon Road Allotments, N3
24 Grove Park, SE5
Trinity Hospice, SW4
Thursday 8
4 Macaulay Road, SW4 (Evening)
Sunday 25
Petersham House, TW10

October

Sunday 2
23 Imperial Road, N22
Sunday 9
The Watergardens, KT2
Sunday 23
West Lodge Park, EN4

Gardens open to the public

Chelsea Physic Garden, SW3
Fenton House, NW3
Hampton Court Palace, KT8

By arrangement only

48 Erskine Hill, NW11
53 Mapledene Road, E8

Also open by arrangement

Arundel & Ladbroke Gardens, W11
36 Ashley Road, N19
4 Asmuns Hill, NW11
190 Barnet Road, EN5
1 Battlebridge Court, Barnsbury Group, N1

94 Brownlow Road, N11
Cadogan Place South Garden, SW1
35 Camberwell Grove, SE5
46 Cheyne Avenue, E18
Field House, Chiswick Mall Gardens, W4
21 Northchurch Terrace, De Beauvoir Gardens, N1
3 Elm Court, Elm Court Gardens, EN4
27 Horniman Drive, Forest Hill Gardens, SE23
70 Gloucester Crescent, NW1
7 The Grove, N6
116 Hamilton Terrace, NW8
Highwood Ash, NW7
2 Hillside Close, NW8
1a Hungerford Road, N7
49 Loftus Road, W12
8 Almack Road, Lower Clapton Gardens, E5
41 Mill Hill Road, W3

65 Mill Hill Road, W3
2 Millfield Place, N6
NEW 4 Ormonde Road, HA6
3 The Park, N6
4 Park Village East (Tower Lodge Gardens), NW1
2 Dorset Road, Railway Cottages, N22
7 St George's Road, TW1
57 St Quintin Avenue, W10
5 St Regis Close, N10
41 Southbrook Road, SE12
Southwood Lodge, N6
Stokes House, TW10
93 Tanfield Avenue, NW2
West Lodge Park, EN4
White Cottage, BR5
86 Willifield Way, NW11
33 Wood Vale, N10
21 Woodland Rise, N10

The Gardens

109 ADDINGTON ROAD, BR4

Coney Hall, West Wickham BR4 9BG. Mrs Sheila Chivers. *A2022 Bromley to Croydon rd, between Glebe Way & Corkscrew Hill/Layhams Rd r'abouts. Please park on main rd.* **Sun 22 May, Sun 26 June (1.30-5.30). Adm £3.50, chd free. Home-made teas.** An Informal garden. Winding paths lead you past hot sunny borders, cool shady areas with contrasting foliage plants, a bog garden and ponds with water lilies. There are shady seating areas surrounded by colourful borders, an apple tree with woodland planting. Hanging baskets and various containers adding extra colour and interest throughout the garden.

GROUP OPENING

ALEXANDRA PARK ROAD GARDENS, N22

Nos 272, 279, 289 & 300, Alexandra Park Road, London N22 7BG. *Tube: Bounds Green or Wood Green, then bus 10 mins. Train: Alexandra Park. Buses: 184, W3. Alight at junction of Alexandra Park Rd & Palace Gates Rd.* **Sun 7 Aug (2-6). Combined adm £4.50, chd free. Home-made teas at No 272.**

272 ALEXANDRA PARK ROAD
Clive Boutle & Kate Tattersall

289 ALEXANDRA PARK ROAD
Julie Littlejohn

300 ALEXANDRA PARK ROAD
Paul Cox & Bee Peak

On the site of the original Alexandra Park estate are three front gardens and a back garden to enjoy: the surprisingly long rear garden of a 1920s house backing onto deer enclosure, and four exuberant contrasting front gardens. The back garden retains many pre war features incl an Anderson Shelter, rock garden, crazy paving and venerable trees as well as a tree house, greenhouse and wildlife friendly eclectic planting. The front gardens all provide colour and interest for the community and are inspiring examples of how much can be

achieved in a very small space. There is a profusion of colour in pots, while tall plants hide a secret hidden from the street. One steeply sloping front garden has a semi tropical theme, with a rill running through a riverbed rockery, disappearing under the path and dropping into a pool surrounded by beautiful stones, another is a modern re-creation of a cottage country garden. Winner of Gardens that make you Smile, Haringey in Bloom Best Front Garden and London Green Corners Award.

> The garden continues to develop, visitors return to see what's new and to enjoy the good home-made cakes . . .

ALL SEASONS, W5

97 Grange Road, Ealing W5 3PH. Dr Benjamin & Mrs Maria Royappa. *Tube: Ealing Broadway/South Ealing/Ealing Common: 10-15 mins walk.* **Sat 9 July (1-6); Sun 10 July (12.30-6). Adm £3, chd free. Tea.** Garden designed, built and planted by owners, with new interesting planting, features incl ponds, pergolas, Japanese gardens, tropical house for orchids, exotics and aviaries. Several recycled features, composting and rain water harvesting, orchard, kiwi, grape vines, architectural and unusual plants incl ferns, bamboos, conifers and cacti. Partial wheelchair access.

37 ALWYNE ROAD, N1

London N1 2HW. Mr & Mrs J Lambert. *Buses: 38, 56, 73, 341 on Essex Rd; 4, 19, 30, 43 on Upper St, alight at Town Hall; 271 on Canonbury Rd, A1. Tube: Highbury &*

Islington. **Sun 5 June (2-5). Adm £4, chd free. Home-made teas. Also open 41 Ecclesbourne Road.** *Donation to The Friends of the Rose Bowl.* The New River curves around the garden, freeing it from the constraints of the usual London rectangle and allowing differing degrees of formality - topiary, roses along the river, an urban meadow next to the conservatory, a secluded spot where the life of the river is part of the charm. The garden continues to develop, visitors return to see what's new and to enjoy the good home-made cakes. Shelter if it rains. Wheelchair access only with own assistant for 3 shallow entrance steps.

⑤ 121 ANSON ROAD, NW2

London NW2 4AH. Helen Marcus. *Cricklewood. Tube: Willesden Grn or Kilburn, Thameslink: Cricklewood, Buses: 226, (Dawson Rd stop) 16, 32, 189, 245, 260, 266, 316 to Cricklewood Bdy.* **Sun 3 July (2-5.30). Adm £3, chd free.** Two gardens in one. Country style garden brimming with colour screened by mature trees and shrubs giving a sense of seclusion. Densely planted borders, shrubs, perennials, clematis, old fashioned roses, cottage garden and unusual plants. Up 2 shallow steps into a surprise secret garden with vegetable beds, fruit trees; trellis with roses and clematis, and wild flowers. Arches, urns, and statues used throughout to create unexpected vistas and focal points. Featured in Ham & High.

NEW ▶ 31 ARLINGTON DRIVE, HA4

Ruislip HA4 7RJ. John & Yasuko O'Gorman. *Tube: Ruislip. Then bus H13 to Arlington Drive, or 15 mins walk up Bury St. Arlington Drive is opp Millar & Carter Steakhouse on Bury St.* **Sun 5 June (2-5). Adm £3.50, chd free. Home-made teas.** 80ft x 40ft NW facing garden, highly structured and loosely planted. To the front, wide borders and beds curve around an oval lawn. Climbing roses and clematis screen the rear section, which comprises rectangular beds and a small vegetable patch. Small trees, shrubs and perennials incl many varieties of acer, cornus, tree paeony, flowering cherry and hosta.

A lush town garden rich in textures, colour and forms . . .

GROUP OPENING

ARLINGTON SQUARE GARDENS, N1
London N1 7DP,
arlingtonassociation@hotmail.co.uk,
www.arlingtonassociation.org.uk.
South Islington. Off New North Rd via Arlington Ave or Linton St. Buses: 21, 76, 141, 271. **Sun 12 June (1-5.30). Combined adm £6, chd free. Home-made teas at The Vicarage, 1A Arlington Square.**

NEW 14 ARLINGTON AVENUE
Dominic Richards

26 ARLINGTON AVENUE
Mr Thomas Blaikie

21 ARLINGTON SQUARE
Ms Alison Rice

25 ARLINGTON SQUARE
Mr Michael Foley

27 ARLINGTON SQUARE
Mr Geoffrey Wheat & Rev Justin Gau

28 ARLINGTON SQUARE
Mr & Mrs H Li

NEW 39 ARLINGTON SQUARE
Hazel Fletcher

5 REES STREET
Gordon McArthur & Paul Thompson

ST JAMES' VICARAGE
John & Maria Burniston

Behind the early Victorian facades of Arlington Square are 9 town gardens that cover the full spectrum of gardening styles, from modern contemporary design to the traditional cottage garden. It is interesting to see how each garden has used the limited area available to create an inspiring and relaxing space. 2 new gardens have joined the group, one is a completely new garden, the other has evolved over decades, and whilst both are small they show how valuable outdoor space can be maximised. The other gardens in the group reflect the diverse tastes and interests of each garden owner who have got to know each other through the community gardening of Arlington Square. It is hard to believe you are moments from the bustle of the City of London. Live music. Featured in The English Garden magazine.

---

61 ARTHUR ROAD, SW19
Wimbledon SW19 7DN. Daniela McBride. *Tube: Wimbledon Park, then 8 mins walk. Mainline: Wimbledon, 18 mins walk.* **Sun 19 June (2-6). Adm £5, chd free. Home-made teas. Also open 97 Arthur Road.**
In spring, the main feature of this steeply sloping garden are the woodland walks, filled with bulbs, flowering shrubs and ferns. In early summer the focus moves to the many roses grown around the garden, then later the autumn colour is provided by trees and shrubs. Partial wheelchair access to top lawn and terrace only, steep slopes elsewhere.

&

97 ARTHUR ROAD, SW19
Wimbledon SW19 7DP. Tony & Bella Covill. *Wimbledon Park tube, then 200yds up hill on R.* **Sun 19 June (2-6). Adm £5, chd free. Light refreshments. Also open 61 Arthur Road.**
1/3 acre garden of an Edwardian house. Garden established for more than 20yrs and constantly evolving with a large variety of plants and shrubs. It has grown up around several lawns with pond and fountains. Abundance of wildlife and a bird haven. A beautiful place with much colour, foliage and texture.

ARUNDEL & LADBROKE GARDENS, W11
Kensington Park Road, Notting Hill W11 2LW. Arundel & Ladbroke Gardens Committee, 020 7460 8895, susan.lynn1@ntlworld.com, www.arundelladbrokegardens.co.uk. *Entrance on Kensington Park Rd, between Ladbroke & Arundel Gardens. Tube: Notting Hill Gate, Buses: 23, 52, 452. Alight at stop for Portobello Market.* **Sun 8 May**
(1.30-6). Adm £4, chd free. Home-made teas. **Visits also by arrangement Apr to Oct.**
A private square, of mid Victorian design, planted as a woodland garden: massed rhododendrons, camellias, some crinodendron and flowering dogwoods, a glade of spring bulbs among birch, dogwood, cercis and amelanchier; Australasian plants, such as prostanthera, corokia, correa and dicksonias, as well as acers, clerodendron, lindera and a stachyurus chinensis for foliage interest. Wheelchair access possible but 2 steps and gravel paths to negotiate.

&

36 ASHLEY ROAD, N19
London N19 3AF. Alan Swann & Ahmed Farooqui, 020 7281 4586. *Crouch Hill. Underground: Archway or Finsbury Park Overground: Crouch Hill Buses: 210 from Archway to Hornsey Rise. W7 from Finsbury Park to Heathville Rd. Car: Free parking in Ashley Rd.* **Sun 29 May (2-6.30); Mon 30 May (2-6). Adm £3.50, chd free. Home-made teas. Visits also by arrangement June to Oct. Groups 10 max.**
A lush town garden rich in textures, colour and forms. At its best in late spring as Japanese maple cultivars display great variety of shape and colour whilst ferns unfurl fresh, vibrant fronds over a tumbling stream and alpines and clematis burst into flower on the rockeries and pergola. New for 2016: a cascade of new ponds, fern columns and some experimental vertical plantings. The garden has a number of micro habitats incl a fernery, bog garden, stream and pond plantings, rockeries, alpines and shade plantings. Young ferns and garden developed aquilegias for sale. Featured in Natureza, Brazil's leading garden magazine and Ham & High.

4 ASMUNS HILL, NW11
Hampstead Garden Suburb NW11 6ET. Peter & Yvonne Oliver, 020 8455 8741, yvonne.oliver17@gmail.com. *Close to Finchley Rd & N Circular. Tube: Golders Green, then buses 82, 102 or 460 to Temple Fortune, then 2 mins walk along Hampstead Way, Asmuns Hill 2nd on L.* **Sun 24 July (2-6). Adm £3.50, chd free. Also open 86 Willifield Way. Visits also by arrangement June to Aug, groups 20 max.**

Arts and Crafts cottage garden in the Artisan's Quarter of Hampstead Garden Suburb. Many clematis in front and back gardens; Heleniums, crocosmias, salvias, echinacea and grasses as well as other bee friendly plants. Pond, patio, shade area. Succulents and acers. Sculptures and Objets Trouvés. Garden visited by HRH Prince Edward Earl of Wessex. Awarded First Prize - London Gardens Society, Small Back Garden.

190 BARNET ROAD, EN5
Arkley, Barnet EN5 3LF. Hilde & Lionel Wainstein, 020 8441 4041, hildewainstein@hotmail.co.uk. *1m S of A1, 2m N of High Barnet tube. Garden is located on corner of A411, Barnet Rd & Meadowbanks cul-de-sac. Nearest tube: High Barnet, then 107 bus, Glebe Lane stop. Plenty of unrestricted roadside parking.* Sun 22 May, Sat 16 July (2-6). Home-made teas. Sun 28 Aug (2-6). Adm £3.50, chd free. **Visits also by arrangement May to Sept.**
Garden designer's walled garden, approx 90ft x 36ft. Modern, asymmetric design thickly planted in flowing, natural drifts around trees, shrubs and central pond; a changing array of interesting containers and found objects. Handmade beaten copper trellis divides the space into contrasting areas. The garden continues to evolve as new planted areas are expanded. Lawn is still contracting! Selection of home-made cakes worthy of Mary Berry! Refreshments May and July only. Wide range of interesting plants for sale, incl akebia, all propagated from the garden. Featured as Garden of the Week in Garden News magazine. Single steps within garden.

GROUP OPENING

BARNSBURY GROUP, N1
London N1 1BE. *Barnsbury N1. Tube: King's Cross, Caledonian Rd or Angel. Overground: Caledonian Rd & Barnsbury. Buses: 17, 91, 259 to Caledonian Rd.* Sun 5 June (2-6). Combined adm £8, chd free. Home-made teas at 36 Thornhill Square.

BARNSBURY WOOD,
Crescent Street
London Borough of Islington

1 BATTLEBRIDGE COURT
Mike Jackson
Visits also by arrangement Mar to Sept. Groups 20 max
michaeljackson215@me.com

44 HEMINGFORD ROAD
Peter Willis & Haremi Kudo

36 THORNHILL SQUARE
Anna & Christopher McKane

Walk through Islington's historic Georgian squares and terraces to these four contrasting gardens, all within walking distance of the vibrant development at King's Cross. Barnsbury Wood is London's smallest nature reserve and Islington's hidden secret, a tranquil oasis of wild flowers and massive trees just minutes from Caledonian Road. The three gardens have extensive collections of unusual plants; specimen trees, shrubs and perennials and a pond at 44 Hemingford Road; old and new roses and many herbaceous perennials at 36 Thornhill Square, a 120ft long garden with a country atmosphere. There is also a bonsai collection. 1 Battlebridge Court is a small plantsman's garden making optimum use of sun and shade beside the canal basin, together with four contrasting beds in front of the block of flats. All the gardens have evolved over many yrs, to incl plants to suit their particular growing conditions, and show what can be achieved while surmounting the difficulties of dry walls and shade.

20 BEECHWOOD AVENUE, TW9
Kew, Richmond TW9 4DE.
Dr Laura de Beden, lauradebeden@hotmail.com, www.lauradebeden.co.uk. *Within walking distance of Kew Gardens Tube Station.* Evening opening Sun 15 May, Sun 19 June (5.30-7.30). Adm £5, chd free. Drinks and nibbles.
Delightful town garden, minutes away from Royal Botanic Gardens and Kew Retail Park. 'Follow your Bliss' Joseph Campbell's words guided the creation of this place by the designer owner. Topiary, pots, sculpture, surprises, and good humour are all on offer. A decidedly minimalist layout offsets exquisite favourite planting combinations. Writing shed holds pride of place as the main idea production centre.

BLUE HILLS, EN5
Windmill Lane, Barnet EN5 3HX.
Anne Bickel, 020 8440 7626. *1m S of A1, 2m N of High Barnet tube. A411 Barnet Rd. Ample parking. Tube High Barnet, 107 bus to Glebe Lane stop. Walk same direction along Barnet Rd. R into Windmill Lane. Blue Hills top L.* Sun 5 June (2-6). Adm £4.50, chd free. Cream teas.
3 acres of beautiful mature garden with large, mature trees and shrubs. Swimming pool, thatched summer house and small thatched house. Very large pond with island, weeping willow and three bridges. Large fountain. Fish pond. Waterfall with rockery, winding round to bog pond and onto very large island pond. Beautiful bronzes, urns and baskets. A wonderful garden to stroll around in, sit and enjoy your tea and cakes. Limited wheelchair access to lawned areas due to uneven surfaces.

5 BRODIE ROAD, E4
Chingford, London E4 7HF. Mr & Mrs N Booth. *From Chingford train station, any bus to Chingford Green (Co-op), turn L at Prezzo, 2nd R (Scholars Rd), then 1st L.* Sun 19 June, Sun 21 Aug (2-5). Adm £3, chd free. Home-made teas.
A constantly evolving garden with new plantings annually obtained from specialist nurseries. The gardener's love of butterflies has moulded the planting style over the years, with two wide herbaceous borders packed with stunning colour from heleniums, rudbeckia, hydrangeas and dahlias. The borders are intersected by a narrow path leading to clematis and rose covered arches.

Share your day out on 📘 and 🐦

94 BROWNLOW ROAD, N11
Bounds Green N11 2BS. Spencer Viner, www.northeleven.co.uk. *Close to N Circular. Tube: Bounds Green then 5 mins walk, direction N Circular. Corner of Elvendon Rd & Brownlow Rd.* Sun 14 Aug (2-6). Adm £2.50, chd free. Tea. Also open 5 Russell Road. **Visits also by arrangement July to Sept, groups min 6, max 12.**
A small courtyard for meditation. The conception of this garden by a designer has the ability to transport the visitor to a different, foreign place of imagination and tranquillity, far away from the suburbs. Features incl reclaimed materials, trees, water, pergola, pleached limes, seating and a strong theme of pared back simplicity. Design and horticultural advice.

5 BURBAGE ROAD, SE24
Herne Hill SE24 9HJ. Crawford & Rosemary Lindsay, 020 7274 5610, rl@rosemarylindsay.com, www.rosemarylindsay.com. *Nr junction with Half Moon Lane. Herne Hill & N Dulwich mainline stns, 5 mins walk. Buses: 3, 37, 40, 68, 196, 468.* Sun 10 Apr (2-5). Adm £3.50, chd free. Home-made teas.
The garden of a member of The Society of Botanical Artists. 150ft x 40ft with large and varied range of plants. Herb garden, herbaceous borders for sun and shade, climbing plants, pots, terraces, lawns. Gravel areas to reduce watering. See our website for what the papers say. Very popular and extensive plant sale.

12 BUSHBERRY ROAD, E9
Hackney E9 5SX. Molly St Hilaire. *Overground stn: Homerton, then 5 mins walk. Buses: 26, 30, 488, alight last stop in Cassland Rd.* Sun 17 July (2-6). Adm £3, chd free. Tea.
Petite courtyard garden with water feature. Rambling roses, jasmine, vine and clematis cover the overarching pergola. Small but beautifully formed... a pure joy to see.

NEW 70 BUSHWOOD, E11
London E11 3BW. Mr & Mrs Duncan. *6 mins walk from Leytonstone tube station or from Leytonstone bus station. Parking available outside house. Entrance via side entrance in Woodville Rd.* Sun 17 July (2-5.30). Adm £3.50, chd

free. Selection of delicious home-made cakes and brownies.
Victorian S facing garden which was redesigned 10yrs ago to use the space as creatively as possible to provide yr-round colour and shape, using both planting and moveable pots. Huge fatsia japonicas fill borders, with colour provided by agapantha and fuchsias. Two seating areas in the garden to sit and relax and absorb the shapes and textures.

CADOGAN PLACE SOUTH GARDEN, SW1
Sloane Street, London SW1X 9PE. The Cadogan Estate, 07890 452992, Ric.Glenn@cadogan.co.uk. *Entrance to garden opp 97 Sloane St.* Sun 17 Apr (10-4). Combined adm with Eaton Square Garden £6, chd free. Light refreshments. **Visits also by arrangement Apr to June with head gardener tours by request.**
Many surprises and unusual trees and shrubs are hidden behind the railings of this large London square. The first square to be developed by architect Henry Holland for Lord Cadogan at the end of C18, it was then called the London Botanic Garden. Mulberry trees planted for silk production at end of C17. Cherry trees, magnolias and bulbs are outstanding in spring, when the fern garden is unfurling. Award winning Hans Sloane Garden exhibited at the Chelsea Flower Show. Pond. Spring walk on East side of garden. Feel free to bring a picnic to enjoy in the garden.

8 CALAIS STREET, SE5
Myatts Fields, Camberwell SE5 9LP. Mr Patrick de Nangle. *N side of Myatts Fields. Buses 36, 185, 436 along Camberwell New Rd. Alight at Flodden Rd, walk to r'about, turn R on to Calais Rd. Nearest tube: Oval. Stn: Denmark Hill.* Sun 4 Sept (1-5.30). Adm £4, chd free. Home-made teas.
An unexpected primeval grove lies behind a traditional Victorian facade offering a host of delights. The dramatic heart of this surprising and totally original garden consists of a grove of 45 tall tree ferns clustered on a carpet of lush, low level ground cover and surrounded by a host of exotic and dramatic large leaved plants. A labour of love - and watering! Featured in Garden News,

the Mail, Independent - Anna Pavord, Garden Answers, Salt of the Earth magazine.

35 CAMBERWELL GROVE, SE5
London SE5 8JA. Lynette Hemmant & Juri Gabriel, 020 7703 6186, juri@jurigabriel.com. *Backing onto St Giles Church, Camberwell Church St. From Camberwell Green go down Camberwell Church St. Turn R into Camberwell Grove.* Sun 5 June (12-6). Adm £3.50, chd free. Fruit juice/biscuits available. **Visits also by arrangement May to July, min charge £70. Max group size 25.** *Donation to St Giles Church.*
Plant packed 120ft x 20ft garden with charming backdrop of St Giles Church. Evolved over 30yrs into a romantic country style garden brimming with colour and overflowing with pots. In June, spectacular roses stretch the full length of the garden, both on the artist's studio and festooning an old iron staircase. Artist's studio open. Lynette (who has earned her living by pen and brush throughout her life) has painted the garden obsessively for the past 20yrs; see her (lynettehemmant.com) and NGS websites.

Selection of home-made cakes worthy of Mary Berry . . .

81 CAMBERWELL GROVE, SE5
London SE5 8JE. Jane & Alex Maitland Hudson. *5 mins from Denmark Hill mainline & Overground stn. Buses: 12, 36, 68, 148, 171, 185, 436. Entrance at rear, please follow yellow NGS signs.* Sun 12 June (2-6). Adm £3, chd free. Home-made teas.
A large Japanese maple and a tall trachycarpus palm shade York stone paving and borders filled with

West Lodge Park

herbaceous perennials, roses, clematis and shade loving ground cover. There is a pond and bog garden. Pots are a feature of the garden bringing colour and diversity. A W facing garden room filled with scented leaf geraniums catches the afternoon sun, and small greenhouse allows propagation. Plants propagated in the garden for sale. Our home-made cakes are delicious.

NEW ▶ CANONBURY HOUSE, N1

Canonbury Place, London N1 2NQ. *Mr & Mrs Gavin Ralston. Junction of Canonbury Place & Alwyne Villas, next to Canonbury Tower. Tube & Overground: Highbury & Islington. Buses to Canonbury Sq. Entrance by side gate opp 1 Canonbury Place.* **Sun 22 May (2-6). Combined adm with North Bridge House Senior School £5, chd free. Home-made teas.**
Large secluded garden next to historic Canonbury Tower and 500yr old mulberry. Magnificent mature trees, woodland planting, clipped box lining lawn. Sheltered herbaceous border. Fountain and well stocked pond; hidden children's play area. Wheelchair entry via shallow ramp to patio area from which garden can be viewed.

4 CANONBURY PLACE, N1

London N1 2NQ. *Mr & Mrs Jeffrey Tobias. Highbury & Islington Tube & Overground. Buses: 271 to Canonbury Square. Located in old part of Canonbury Place, off Alwyne Villas, in a cul de sac.* **Sun 17 Apr (2-6). Adm £3.50, chd free. Home-made teas. Also open 20 St Mary's Grove.**
A paved, 100ft garden behind a 1780 house. Spectacular mature trees enclosed in a walled garden. Mostly pots and also interesting shrubs and climbers. Daffodlils, tulips and bluebells abound for this springtime opening. Artisan pastries and sourdough bread available.

CAPEL MANOR GARDENS
See Hertfordshire

THE CHARTERHOUSE, EC1

Charterhouse Square, London EC1M 6AN. *The Governors of Sutton's Hospital,* www.thecharterhouse.org. *Buses: 4, 55. Tube: Barbican. Turn L out of stn, L into Carthusian St & into square. Entrance through car park.* **Evening opening Tue 7 June (6-9). Adm £5, chd free. Wine. Evening to incl BBQ (additional charge).**
Enclosed courtyard gardens within the grounds of historic Charterhouse, which dates back to 1347. English country garden style featuring roses, herbaceous borders, ancient mulberry trees and small pond. Various garden herbs found here are still used in the kitchen today. In addition, two other areas are being opened for the NGS. Pensioners Court, which is partly maintained by the private tenants and Master's Garden, the old burial ground which now consists of lawns, borders and wildlife garden planted to camouflage a war time air raid shelter. A private garden for the Brothers of Charterhouse, not usually open to the public. (Buildings not open).

51 THE CHASE, SW4

London SW4 0NP. *Mr Charles Rutherfoord & Mr Rupert Tyler,* 020 7627 0182, mail@charlesrutherfoord.net, www.charlesrutherfoord.net. *Off Clapham Common Northside. Tube: Clapham Common. Buses: 137, 452.* **Sun 24 Apr (12-5); Evening opening Wed 27 Apr (6-8). Adm £4, chd free. Light refreshments.**
Member of the Society of Garden Designers, Charles has created the garden over 30yrs. In 2015 the main garden was remodelled, to much acclaim. Spectacular in spring, when 2000 tulips bloom among irises and tree peonies. Scented front garden. Rupert's geodetic dome shelters seedlings, succulents and subtropicals.

Marie Curie

Patients and families can enjoy beautiful gardens at our hospices

◆ **CHELSEA PHYSIC GARDEN, SW3**

66 Royal Hospital Road, London SW3 4HS. Chelsea Physic Garden Company, 020 7352 5646, www.chelseaphysicgarden.co.uk. *Tube: Sloane Square (10 mins). Bus: 170. Parking: Battersea Park (charged). Entrance in Swan Walk.* For NGS: Fri 1 Apr (11-6). Adm £10.50, chd £6.95. Lunches and afternoon tea at Tangerine Dream Cafe. For other opening times and information, please phone or visit garden website.
Come and explore London's oldest botanic garden situated in the heart of Chelsea. With a unique living collection of around 5000 plants this walled garden is a celebration of the importance of plants and their beauty. Highlights of the garden incl Europe's oldest pond rockery, the Garden of Edible and Useful plants, the Garden of Medicinal Plants and the World Woodland Garden. Tours available. Wheelchair access is via 66 Royal Hospital Rd.

46 CHEYNE AVENUE, E18

South Woodford, London E18 2DR. Helen Auty, 020 8530 1343 or 07944 375874, helenauty20@hotmail.co.uk. *Nearest tube S Woodford. Short walk. From station take Clarendon Rd. Cross High Rd into Broadwalk, 3rd on L Bushey Ave. 1st R Cheyne Ave.* Sun 14 Aug (12-5). Adm £4, chd free. Light refreshments. Visits also by arrangement Apr to Oct.
On site of Lord Cheyne's original market garden, typical suburban garden with lawn and borders of shrubs, climbers and perennials - greenhouse and productive fruit and vegetable garden. Featured in Guardian Gazette, Wanstead and Woodford and South Woodford Village Gazette.

GROUP OPENING

CHISWICK MALL GARDENS, W4

Chiswick W6 9TN. *Car: Towards Hogarth r'about, A4 (W) turn Eyot Grds S. Tube: Stamford Brook or Turnham Green. Buses: 27, 190, 267 & 391 to Young's Corner. From Chiswick High Rd or Kings St S under A4 to river.* Sun 29 May (2-6). Combined adm £6, chd free. Home-made teas at 16 Eyot Gardens.

> **16 EYOT GARDENS**
> Ms Dianne Farris

> **FIELD HOUSE**
> Rupert King
> Visits also by arrangement May to Sept
> kingrupert@hotmail.com

> NEW ▶ **6 ST PETERS WHARF**
> Barbara Brown

> **SWAN HOUSE**
> Mr & Mrs George Nissen

This peaceful riverside setting offers four unique gardens. An informal walled garden with herbaceous borders, fruit trees and a small vegetable garden. An Eastern style water garden with exotic planting. A communal garden for seven artists with beautiful river frontage. And lastly an end of terrace inner city garden with wisteria, Canary Bird Rosa, and two lovingly maintained lawns.

CHOUMERT SQUARE, SE15

London SE15 4RE. The Residents. *Off Choumert Grove. Trains from London Bridge, Clapham Junction to Peckham Rye; buses (12, 36, 37, 63, 78, 171, 312, 345). Car park 2 mins.* Sun 5 June (1-6). Adm £4, chd free. Light refreshments. *Donation to St Christopher's Hospice.*
About 46 mini gardens with maxi planting in Shangri-la situation that the media has described as a Floral Canyon, which leads to small communal secret garden. The popular open gardens will combine this yr with our own take on a village fete with home produce stalls, arts, crafts and music.

31 CHURCH CRESCENT, N3

Finchley Church End, London N3 1BE. Gerald & Margaret Levin. *7 min walk from Finchley Central Underground (Northern Line, High Barnet branch). Buses nearby incl 82, 460, 125, 326, 143 and 382. No parking restrictions on Sun.* Sun 7 Aug (2-6). Adm £3.50, chd free. Home-made teas.
120ft x 30ft E facing garden designed and built by us with no straight lines, three season interest and a wildlife pond as the focal point. A sunny terrace with tubs, three beds around the pond with interesting shrubs and perennials, and a more challenging shadier area with trees, shrubs and ferns. Recent removal of a large birch has given us many new planting opportunities. Home-made jams and marmalade for sale. Featured in Ham & High. Partial wheelchair access. Two shallow steps from public footpath into garden, one within garden. Level access to refreshments in conservatory.

79 CHURCH LANE, N2

London N2 0TH. Caro & David Broome, 020 8444 2329, carosgarden@virginmedia.com. *Tube: E Finchley, then East End Rd for ³/₄ m, R into Church Lane. Buses: 143 to Five Bells PH, 3 min walk; 263 to E Finchley Library, 5 min walk.* Sun 12 June, Sun 31 July (2-6). Adm £3.50, chd free. Mouth watering selection of home-made cakes incl gluten free.
Constantly evolving, a garden writer's garden with a twist. Enter through a plant filled open air catatorium, into the patio garden beyond, packed full of shrubs, roses and unusual perennials to create a colour coordinated palette, with curved rill, hidden water features and quirky ornamentals! Rustic archway leads to secluded ferny glen, home to a secret hideaway. New front garden for 2016. Locally propagated perennials ideal for London clay soils. Ever popular raffle, children's treasure hunt and always something new to see. Columnist for Garden News - Over The Fence. As seen on BBC1 The One Show and ITV Love Your Garden. Awarded London Gardens Society Gold Certificate.

THE CIRCLE GARDEN, KT3

33 Cambridge Avenue, New Malden KT3 4LD. Vincent & Heidi Johnson-Paul-McDonnell, www.thecirclegarden.com. *1¼ m N of A3 Malden junction. Bus: 213. 10 mins walk from New Malden railway station; A3 signposted for Kingston; 213 bus stop located a short distance from end of rd; our house is pink!* Sat 4 June (2-5); Sun 5 June (3-6); Sat 16 July (2-5). Adm £3.50, chd free. Tea.

A welcoming front garden with cottage style planting leading to an unexpected rear garden with intriguing vistas where you will find herbaceous and annuals in mixed borders. Relax in the Japanese area, stroll through the potager and chat to our suburban hens. An ever evolving garden with plans for further developments.

GROUP OPENING

CLAPHAM MANOR STREET GARDENS, SW4

Clapham Old Town SW4 6DZ. *Tube: Clapham Common. Off Clapham High St.* Sun 12 June (2-5). Combined adm £6, chd free. Home-made teas.

40 CLAPHAM MANOR STREET
Mrs Nina Murdoch

44 CLAPHAM MANOR STREET
Mrs Annette Marchini

Two creatively inspired secret, romantic walled gardens. No.40 is a large garden divided by trained arches of apple trees. It contains a cobbled courtyard, a stream, ferns and ivy garden, 2 ponds and many climbers. No.44 has the emphasis on lush green planting with white flowers, creating a soft, organic counterpoint to the contemporary extension.

GROUP OPENING

COPTHALL GROUP, NW7

Mill Hill, London NW7 2NB. *Short bus ride (221) from Edgware tube or Mill Hill East. Free parking vouchers available if restrictions are in force.* Sun 12 June (2-5.30). Combined adm £4.50, chd free. Home-made teas at 2 Copthall Drive.

2 COPTHALL DRIVE
Mrs Janet Jomain

13 COPTHALL GARDENS
Mrs Lise Marshfield

Two small town gardens enthusiastically gardened by their plantaholic owners. 13 Copthall Gardens is a mature leafy garden in a quiet cul-de-sac. Emphasis on form and texture. Clipped shrubs, topiary, perennials and roses. Small pond, portal to third dimension. Traditional Finnish swing seat. 2 Copthall Drive is a small east facing town garden with more than 60 roses and many clematis, alliums, hydrangeas and a wildlife pond. A small but productive fruit and vegetable patch incl nectarines and kiwi fruit, and in the greenhouse there may be a pineapple nearly ready to pick.

4 CORNFLOWER TERRACE, SE22

East Dulwich SE22 0HH. Clare Dryhurst. *5 mins walk from 63 bus stop at bottom of Forest Hill Rd. Turn into Dunstans Rd, then 2nd on L. Mainline: Peckham Rye or Honor Oak Park.* Sun 5 June (2-5.30). Adm £3.50, chd free. Tea. Also open Choumert Square.

Still defying size limits, now featuring wrought iron trellises to use every available inch. A pretty, secluded and tiny courtyard cottage garden, only 26ft x 9ft in a quiet street in the heart of artistic East Dulwich. Around a sunken patio with a bench and solar fountain are clustered climbers, roses, ferns, annuals and herbs in raised beds and pots backed by a charming painted garden shed. Added mirrors to iron trellises this year. If your space is small, come and exchange ideas.

NEW THE COTTAGE, WC1N

Henrietta Mews, London WC1N 1PH. Ray Cheeseborough. *Tube: King's Cross & Russell Square. Entry via side gate from St George's Gardens at Wakefield St/Handel St entrance.* Sun 10 July (2-6). Adm £3.50, chd free. Light refreshments. Also open 57 Tonbridge House.

This small garden beside a 250yr old cottage is surrounded on three sides by what the Japanese call borrowed landscape of very mature plane, sycamore, lime and cherry trees. As garden designers, texture, leaf form, colour and plant association are of utmost importance. Paved areas are second hand natural York stone, hand cut and dressed to shape. Plant selection reflects the often deep shade.

122 COURT LANE, SE21

Dulwich SE21 7EA. Jean & Charles Cary-Elwes. *Buses P4, 12, 40, 176, 185 (to Dulwich Library) 37. Mainline; North Dulwich then 16 mins walk. Ample free parking.* Sun 12 June (2-5.30). Adm £5, chd free. Tea.

Generously proportioned, mature garden with unusual and marginally tender shrubs which thrive in the hands of a keen propagator. Agapanthus, a signature plant followed by oleander, and a splendid clerodendron. Backing onto Dulwich Park it has a countryside feel - a true family garden with sandpit and hammock mingling with a hardworking greenhouse and a super wormery, which will be demonstrated. Jazz band, cakes and tea, children's trail, plant sales and wormery demonstration. Wheelchair access to terrace only but good view of garden.

6 Manor Road

See more images at nationalgardensscheme

© Matthew Bruce

The Chase

GROUP OPENING

DE BEAUVOIR GARDENS, N1
London N1 4HU. *Highbury &
Islington tube then 30 or 277 bus;
Angel tube then 38, 56 or 73 bus;
Bank then 21, 76 or 141 bus. 10
mins walk from Dalston Overground
stations. Street parking available.* **Sun
12 June (11-3). Combined adm £5,
chd free. Home-made teas at 158
Culford Road.**

158 CULFORD ROAD
Gillian Blachford

**21 NORTHCHURCH
TERRACE**
Nancy Korman
Visits also by arrangement May
to July
nancylkorman@hotmail.co.uk
020 7249 4919

**NEW ▶ 24 NORTHCHURCH
TERRACE**
Sue Pedder

Three gardens to explore in De
Beauvoir, a leafy enclave of Victorian
villas near to Islington and Dalston.
The area boasts some of Hackney's
keenest gardeners and a thriving
gardening club. New this yr is 24
Northchurch Terrace which boasts 7
arches of Dublin Bay roses and
shaped trees such as olive,
pittosporum and feijoa. The walled
garden at 21 Northchurch Terrace
has a formal feel, with deep
herbaceous borders, pond, fruit trees,

pergola, patio pots and herb beds.
158 Culford Road is a long narrow
garden with a romantic feel and a
path winding through full borders with
shrubs, small trees, perennials and
many unusual plants.

**NEW ▶ 14 DOUGHTY STREET,
WC1N**
London WC1N 2PL. Gillian Darley
& Michael Horowitz QC. *Off Guilford
St or Theobalds Rd. Tube: Chancery
Lane or Russell Sq. Buses: 19, 38,
55. Garden S of Guilford St on W side
of Doughty St with brown LCC
plaque to Sidney Smith on house.*
**Sun 10 July (2-6). Adm £3.50, chd
free. Also open 61 Doughty Street.
Home-made teas at 61 Doughty
Street.**
Small paved rear garden with a
wilderness feel, surprisingly since the
house opens directly off the street.
Medlar tree, vine, plants jostling for
space and pots, standing on boards
over a redundant pond, add extra
interest. Pleasing disorder best
describes it. Access via house, small
entrance step. Paved surfaces, not
much room for manoeuvre.

**NEW ▶ 61 DOUGHTY STREET,
WC1N**
London WC1N 2JY. Bill Thomas &
Teresa Borsuk. *Between Guilford St
& Theobald's Rd. Tube: Chancery
Lane or Russell Sq. Buses: 19, 38,
55.* **Sun 10 July (2-6). Adm £3.50,**

chd free. Home-made teas. Also
open 14 Doughty Street.
Demolition of offices left a space 40ft
wide by 65ft deep at its longest. An
acer, two magnolias, viburnum and
silk tree flourish, with wisteria,
passion flower, akebia (quinata and
trifoliate), clematis, jasmine,
honeysuckles, Parthenocissus.
Holboelia. Hellebores, two tree
peonies, actinidia kolomikta and
schizophragma integrifolium. Two
ponds and a rill. A space to relax and
entertain.

GROUP OPENING

**DULWICH VILLAGE TWO
GARDENS, SE21**
London SE21 7BJ. *Rail: N Dulwich
or W Dulwich then 10 -15 mins walk.
Tube: Brixton then P4 bus, alight
Dulwich Picture Gallery stop. Street
parking.* **Sun 19 June (2-5).
Combined adm £5, chd free.
Home-made teas at 103 Dulwich
Village.** *Donation to Macmillan
Cancer Care.*

103 DULWICH VILLAGE
Mr & Mrs N Annesley

105 DULWICH VILLAGE
Mr & Mrs A Rutherford

2 Georgian houses with large
gardens, 3 mins walk from Dulwich
Picture Gallery and Dulwich Park. 103
Dulwich Village is a country garden in

London with a long herbaceous border, lawn, pond, roses and fruit and vegetable gardens. 105 Dulwich Village is a very pretty garden with many unusual plants, lots of old fashioned roses, fish pond and water garden. Amazing collection of plants for sale. Music played by wind players from Dulwich Symphony Orchestra and others throughout the afternoon. A destination opening!

NEW ▶ EATON SQUARE GARDEN, SW1W

London SW1W 9BD. The Grosvenor Estate, www.grosvenorlondon.com. *Easy walk from Victoria Station or Sloane Sq. Many bus routes passing close to square incl C1, C2, 16, 38, 52 and 73.* **Sun 17 Apr (10-4). Combined adm with Cadogan Place South Garden £6, chd free. Light refreshments.**

Thomas Cubitt laid out the 6 formal gardens flanking either side of the Kings Road in 1826 in what was the main approach to Buckingham Palace. Eaton Square Gardens today combines well manicured lawns, shady pathways and mixed borders with quiet seating and contemporary sculptures. The fabulously preserved regency buildings form a fine backdrop, complimented by the square's mature London planes. Winner London in Bloom - Small Park of the Year. This is a level access site with paths suitable for wheelchairs running the perimeter of the garden and a hard landscaped central area.

NEW ▶ 41 ECCLESBOURNE ROAD, N1

London N1 3AF. Steve Bell & Sandie Macrae. *Tube: Highbury & Islington 12 mins walk or 271 bus to Ecclesbourne Rd. Or Angel tube 15 mins walk or bus 73, 38, 56, 341, 476 to Northchurch Rd. Cross Essex Rd, down Halliford Rd, R on Ecclesbourne Rd.* **Sun 5 June (1.30-7). Adm £3.50, chd free. Home-made teas. Also open 37 Alwyne Road.**

A delightful, interesting and surprising artists' Mediterranean garden complemented by new contemporary architecture. This garden has a hoggin surface with trees and pots on two levels. Many edible plants incl a mature fig tree, young olive and almond trees and a prolific vine. There

is a birch, a handkerchief tree, herbs, trailing clematis, roses, and unbelievably, a hand gilded bay.

ECCLESTON SQUARE, SW1

London SW1V 1NP. Roger Phillips & the Residents, roger.phillips@rogersroses.com, www.rogerstreesandshrubs.com. *Off Belgrave Rd nr Victoria Stn, parking allowed on Suns.* **Sun 8 May (2-5). Adm £4, chd free. Home-made teas.**

Planned by Cubitt in 1828, the 3 acre square is subdivided into mini gardens with camellias, iris, ferns and containers. Dramatic collection of tender climbing roses and 20 different forms of tree peonies. National Collection of ceanothus incl more than 70 species and cultivars. Notable important additions of tender plants being grown and tested. World collection of ceanothus, tea roses and tree peonies.

  NPC

A delightful, interesting and surprising artists' Mediterranean garden . . .

EDWARDES SQUARE, W8

South Edwardes Square, Kensington W8 6HL. Edwardes Square Garden Committee. *Tube: Kensington High St & Earls Court. Buses: 9, 10, 27, 28, 31, 49 & 74 to Odeon Cinema. Entrance in South Edwardes Square.* **Sun 17 Apr (12-5). Adm £4, chd free. Cream teas.**

One of London's prettiest secluded garden squares. 3½ acres laid out differently from other squares, with serpentine paths by Agostino Agliothe, Italian artist and decorator who lived at no.15 from 1814-1820, and a beautiful Grecian temple which is traditionally the home of the head gardener. Romantic rose tunnel winds through the middle of the garden. Good displays of bulbs and blossom.

Tea and home-made cakes, Pimms if sunny. Childrens play area. WC. Good wheelchair access.

GROUP OPENING

ELM COURT GARDENS, EN4

Oakhurst Avenue, East Barnet EN4 8HA. *200 yds from Oakleigh Pk Stn on rail line to Welwyn Garden City. M25 J24, then A111 to Cockfosters & A110 down Cat Hill to East Barnet Village.* **Sun 17 July (2-6). Combined adm £4.50, chd free. Home-made teas.**

3 ELM COURT
Mike & Alyne Lidgley
Visits also by arrangement July to Sept no min, max 20
bearcat@talktalk.net
020 8361 2642

4 ELM COURT
Simon Moor & Jayne Evans

Two, larger than average, contrasting gardens. Front gardens - one a formal parterre, one natural, with gravel, grasses, conifers and reclaimed materials. Back gardens: No3 with hot planting, full size and miniature topiary, annuals, perennials, shrubs, baskets, interesting containers, two water features, themed pink, blue, spiky and heuchera beds, a ball bed, greenhouse, sheds that bear close scrutiny, 2 rockeries, alpine display and home grown bonsai. No4 is long and shady, with curving lawns, a gravel area with containers full of colour, a white bed, a rockery and the whole emphasis is on attracting pollinators - blue, pink, purple and yellow shrubs and perennials. Jayne is a successful artist and has her studio in the garden. A developing garden, still evolving, and gradually triumphing over poor soil, overhanging trees and lack of water. A new stumpery, full of ferns, is loving the shade, and many new perennials are now in place. Plant creche: plants purchased delivered locally; raffle prizes are high quality; great cakes, jolly helpers and gazebos for sun or rain make this worth the journey. A third neighbour provides a tranquil landscaped haven for visitors to relax with their refreshments. 4 Elm Court featured as Garden of the Week in Garden News.

11 ERNLE ROAD, SW20
Wimbledon, London SW20 0HH.
Theresa-Mary Morton. *¼ m from
Wimbledon Village, 200yds from
Crooked Billet PH. Exit A3 at A238 to
Wimbledon, turning L at Copse Hill.
Mainline: Wimbledon or Raynes Park.
Tube: Wimbledon; Bus: 200 to
Christchurch then 100yds walk.* Sat
16, Sun 17 Apr (2.30-6). Adm
£3.50, chd free. Home-made teas.
Evening opening Sun 5 June
(6-8.30). Adm £6, chd free. Wine.
Established suburban garden of
¼ acre on sandy acid soil, spatially
organised into separate sections: oak
pergola framing the main vista,
hidden parterre, woodland, pool, yew
circle, flower garden and
summerhouse. Featured in Country
Life Magazine. Beaten gravel paths,
one step up to main garden.

48 ERSKINE HILL, NW11
Hampstead Garden Suburb,
London NW11 6HG. Marjorie &
David Harris, 020 8455 6507,
marjorieharris@btinternet.com. *1m
N of Golders Green. Nr A406 & A1.
Tube: Golders Green. H2 Hail & Ride
bus from Golders Green to garden, or
82, 460, 102 buses to Temple
Fortune (10 mins walk).* Visits by
arrangement May to Sept no min,
max 20. Adm £5.00, chd free.
Light refreshments. Adm incl tea
and cake.
Bird friendly organic garden, wrapped
around Arts and Crafts artisan's
cottage. Perennials, shrubs, roses,
clematis, old apple tree and new
containerised vegetable plot. Terrace
with well planted pots. Intriguing brick
paved area with four raised beds.
Greenhouse. Nest box, miniature long
grass areas, organic and pesticide
free. Visited by LGS patron, HRH
Prince Edward. Winner of Suburb in
Bloom. Featured in Hampstead and
Highgate Express. Some single steps
and narrow paths. Rail to lawn.

20 EXETER ROAD, NW2
London NW2 4SP. Theo & Renee
Laub. *Mapesbury. Nearest tube
Kilburn few mins walk.* Evening
opening Wed 13 July (6.30-8.30).
Adm £20, chd free. Pre-booking
essential, please visit
www.ngs.org.uk or phone 01483
211535 for information & booking.
Wine and canapes. Talk by
professional garden designer
owner.

Garden designer's very new garden
started from scratch 2½ yrs ago.
Large garden by London standards,
with many interesting features and
unusual plants, sculpture and pots.
No lawn, good collection of
interesting plants - many perennials
grown from seed. Water feature and
living wall behind it.

◆ **FENTON HOUSE, NW3**
Hampstead Grove, Hampstead
NW3 6SP. National Trust,
www.nationaltrust.org.uk. *300yds
from Hampstead tube. Entrances:
Top of Holly Hill & Hampstead Grove.*
For NGS: Evening opening Tue 14
June (6.30-8.30). Adm £10, chd
free. Pre-booking essential,
please visit www.ngs.org.uk or
phone 01483 211535 for
information & booking. Wine. For
other opening times and
information, please visit garden
website.
Join the Gardener in Charge for a
special evening tour. Andrew Darragh
who brings over 10yrs experience
from Kew to Fenton House will
explore this timeless 1½ acre walled
garden. Laid out over 3 levels, and
featuring formal walks and areas, a
small sunken rose garden, a 300yr
old orchard and a kitchen garden,
Andrew will present the garden and
his plans for its future development.

NEW ▶ **FERN COTTAGE, SW12**
Pickets Street, London SW12 8QB.
Guy Dimond. *Nr top of short hill that
is Pickets St, on L as you walk uphill.*
Sun 5 June (2-6). Adm £3.50, chd
free. Home-made teas. Evening
opening Wed 8 June (6-8.30). Adm

£4.50, chd free. Wine. Also open
28 Old Devonshire Road.
Fern Cottage is a mid Victorian
terraced house with a small front and
side garden (52 sq m) that has been
extensively renovated and redesigned
by the current owners. The
herbaceous borders have a
contemporary and varied look that
mixes modern influences and some
unusual plants in a cottage garden
space that complements the Victorian
exterior of the house. Wheelchair
access via the house with little
assistance.

GROUP OPENING

FOREST HILL GARDENS, SE23
London SE23 3BP. *Off S Circular
(A205) behind Horniman Museum &
Gardens. Station: Forest Hill, 10 mins
walk. Buses: 176, 185, 312, P4.* Sun
15 May (1-6). Combined adm £7,
chd free. Home-made teas.
*Donation to St Christopher's
Hospice and Marsha Phoenix
Trust.*

> **7 CANONBIE ROAD**
> Mrs June Wismayer
>
> **THE COACH HOUSE, 3 THE
> HERMITAGE**
> Pat Rae
>
> **HILLTOP, 28 HORNIMAN
> DRIVE**
> Frankie Locke
>
> **27 HORNIMAN DRIVE**
> Rose Agnew
> Visits also by arrangement Mar
> to Sept, groups welcome
> roseandgraham@talktalk.net
> 020 8699 7710
>
> **53 RINGMORE RISE**
> Valerie Ward
>
> **25 WESTWOOD PARK**
> Beth & Steph Falkingham-
> Blackwell

Six gardeners a gardening in very
different ways on the highest hill in SE
London. Spectacular views over city
and Downs. The gardens are all
within a short walk of each other but
yellow ballooned taxi service on hand
(for a donation). Marvel at Great
Dixter inspired planting, jasmine
arches and topiary in the hidden
sanctuary of a true plantswoman's
garden. Delight in the double Black
Dragon wisteria draped over an
artist's studio in a C18 courtyard filled
with sculptures and plants. Feed the

resident robins! Stumble on the stories in an eclectic and charming garden for children and chickens and even adults! Enjoy an embroidery of a garden with vibrant colours, peaceful harmony and truly breathtaking views well beyond the town. Unwind with delicious cakes amid billowing pastel hues of the tea lady's garden - inspired by Beth Chatto and Mary Berry! Wander in a bee lover's organic flower and fruit haven with vintage summerhouse, gravelled terraces and billowing grasses. Central pay point at 28 Horniman Gardens. Great views everywhere. Plants for sale at 25 Westwood Park, 27 Horniman Drive and 7 Canonbie Rd.

9 FURLONG ROAD, N7
Islington, London N7 8LS. Nigel Watts & Tanuja Pandit. *Tube & Overground: Highbury & Islington, 3 mins walk along Holloway Rd, 2nd L. Furlong Rd joins Holloway Rd & Liverpool Rd. Buses: 43, 271, 393.* Sun 19 June (2-6). Adm £2, chd free. Home-made teas. Also open 32 Highbury Place.
Award winning small garden designed by Karen Fitzsimon which makes clever use of an awkwardly shaped plot. Curved lines are used to complement a modern extension. Raised beds contain a mix of tender and hardy plants to give an exotic feel and incl loquat, banana, palm, cycad and tree fern. Contrasting traditional front garden. Featured in Small Family Gardens and Modern Family Gardens by Caroline Tilston.

GARDEN BARGE SQUARE AT DOWNINGS ROADS MOORINGS, SE1
31 Mill Street, London SE1 2AX. Mr Nick Lacey. *Close to Tower Bridge & Design Museum. Mill St off Jamaica Rd, between London Bridge & Bermondsey stns, Tower Hill also nearby. Buses: 47, 188, 381, RV1.* Sun 29 May (2-5). Adm £4, chd free. Tea. *Donation to RNLI.*
Series of 7 floating barge gardens connected by walkways and bridges. Gardens have an eclectic range of plants for yr-round seasonal interest. Marine environment: suitable shoes and care needed. Small children must be closely supervised.

9 THE GARDENS, SE22
East Dulwich, London SE22 9QD. Nigel Watts. *Off Peckham Rye, Dulwich side. Stations: Peckham Rye & Honor Oak, both on Overground. Buses: 12, 37, 63,197, 363. Free parking in square.* Evening opening Wed 20 July (6.30-8.30). Adm £20. Pre-booking essential, please visit www.ngs.org.uk or phone 01483 211535 for information & booking. Wine and canapés incl. Talk by owner. Max 25 people.
A surprising garden within a garden with exuberant plants in vibrant colours, incl exotics, all within 40ft x 20ft designed to peak in high summer. Prairie planting features some spectacular grasses as well as veronicastrum and persicaria. Plants deliberately designed to provide good foliage are an important feature adding another dimension. Kentish fruit juice, art cards and paintings.

69 GLOUCESTER CRESCENT, NW1
London NW1 7EG. Sandra Clapham. *Between Regent's Park & Camden Town tube station. Tube: Camden Town 2 mins, Mornington Crescent 10 mins. Metered parking in Oval Rd.* Sun 5 June (2-5.30). Also open Royal College of Physicians Medicinal Garden. Sun 7 Aug (2-5.30). Combined adm with 70 Gloucester Crescent £4, chd free.
One of four fascinating gardens in NW1 open on the same day for the Garden Festival Weekend in June, and with an extra date in August. An ingenious and welcoming cottage garden, a treat behind front wall and gate. Roses, perennials, annuals, a bed of tomatoes, and a 17yr old vine, trained up and along the balcony, plus the odd self seeder, such as Verbascum blattaria.

70 GLOUCESTER CRESCENT, NW1
London NW1 7EG. Lucy Gent, 020 7485 6906, gent.lucy@gmail.com. *Between Regent's Park & Camden Town tube station. Tube: Camden Town 2 mins, Mornington Crescent 10 mins. Metered parking in Oval Rd.* Sun 5 June (2-5.30). Also open 4 Park Village East (Tower Lodge Gardens). Sun 7 Aug (2-5.30). Combined adm with 69 Gloucester Crescent £4, chd free. Visits also by arrangement Mar to Oct.

One of four fascinating gardens in NW1 opening on the same day for the Garden Festival Weekend. Here is an oasis in Camden's urban density, where resourceful planting outflanks challenges of space and shade. An August opening features pomegranates and shows how wonderful the month can be in a town garden.

> Picturesque corners and quirky sheds – a visit feels like being in the countryside . . .

ALLOTMENTS

GOLF COURSE ALLOTMENTS, N11
Winton Avenue, London N11 2AR. GCAA/Haringey, www.golfcourseallotments.co.uk. *Junction of Winton Av & Blake Rd. Tube: Bounds Green. Buses: 102, 184, 299 to Sunshine Garden Centre, Durnsford Rd. Through park to Bidwell Gdns. Straight on up Winton Ave. No cars on site.* Sun 4 Sept (1-4.30). Adm £3.50, chd free. Light refreshments.
Large, long established allotment with over 200 plots, some organic. Maintained by culturally diverse community growing wide variety of fruit, vegetables and flowers. Picturesque corners and quirky sheds - a visit feels like being in the countryside. Autumn Flower and Produce Show on Sun 4 Sep features prize winning horticultural and domestic exhibits and beehives. Tours of best plots. Fresh allotment produce, chutneys, jams, honey, cakes and light refreshments for sale. Wheelchair access to main paths only. Gravel and some uneven surfaces. WC incl disabled.

ALLOTMENTS

GORDON ROAD ALLOTMENTS, N3

Gordon Road, London N3 1EL. Judy Woollett, www.finchleyhorticulturalsociety. org.uk. *Finchley Central. 10 mins walk from Finchley Central tube. 326 bus. Parking in Gordon Rd & adjacent st. No parking on site.* Sun 4 Sept (1.30-5.30). Adm £3.50, chd free. Home-made teas.

Founded in 1940 to promote the interests of gardeners throughout Finchley with over 70 plots. Allotments comprise a mixture of traditional plots and raised beds for those with physical disabilities and for children from local schools. Also a wildlife area with slow worms and an area set aside for bee hives. Tours of best plots. Seasonal vegetables on sale incl perennial flowers. Winner of Barnet Federation of Allotment Holders - Best Allotment Site. Wheelchair access on main paths only. Disabled WC.

28 GRANVILLE PARK, SE13

London SE13 7EA. Joanna Herald, joannaherald.com. *On street parking, Suns & eves. 10 mins walk up hill (N) towards Blackheath from Lewisham mainline & DLR stns.* Sun 12 June (1.30-5.30). Adm £4, chd free. Light refreshments. Pimms and soft drinks. Also open 49 Lee Road.

Garden designer's relaxing and softly contoured family garden divides neatly into three sections. A wildlife friendly pool garden; carefully mixed herbaceous and shrub plantings interspersed with bulbs encompassing circular lawns and gravel garden. A sunken terrace with pots provides a suntrap seating area. 100ft x 35ft. Narrow but level side access to the garden.

13 GREENHILL PARK, EN5

Barnet EN5 1HQ. Sally & Andy Fry. *1m S of High Barnet. ½ m S of High Barnet tube stn. Take 1st L after Odeon Cinema, Weaver PH on corner. Buses: 34, 84, 234, 263, 326.* Sun 29 May (2-5). Adm £3, chd free. Home-made teas.

An oasis in suburbia of approx ¼ acre. Colourful herbaceous borders, wildlife pond, summerhouse in which to relax, Victorian plant house and shady fern garden. Series of rustic arches link main garden to path through wildlife friendly secret garden, incorporating tree fern collection, stumpery and Shepherd's hut. Japanese themed area and hidden courtyard vegetable garden with rare breed chickens.

Planting designed to produce fruit, fragrance and lovely memories . . .

17 GREENSTONE MEWS, E11

Wanstead, London E11 2RS. Mr & Mrs S Farnham. *Wanstead. Tube: Snaresbrook or Wanstead, 5 mins walk. Bus: 101, 308, W12, W14 to Wanstead High St.* Sun 14 Aug (12-4.30). Adm £5, chd free. Tea. Also open 46 Cheyne Avenue.

Slate paved garden (20ft x 17ft). Height provided by a mature strawberry tree. A buried bath used as a fishpond is surrounded by climbers clothing fences underplanted with herbs, vegetables, shrubs and perennials grown from cuttings. Plants for sale grown from cuttings. Ideas aplenty for small space gardening. Entry incl cup of tea and biscuits. Home-made cakes and books for sale. Book and plant sale. Wheelchair access through garage. Limited turning space.

7 THE GROVE, N6

Highgate Village, London N6 6JU. Mr Thomas Lyttelton, 07713 638161. *The Grove is between Highgate West Hill & Hampstead Lane. Tube: Archway or Highgate. Buses: 143, 210, 214 and 271.* Sun 10 Apr (2-5.30). Sun 12 June (2-5.30). Also open Southwood Lodge. Adm £3.50, chd free. Home-made teas. Visits also by arrangement Mar to Oct. Refreshments by arrangement. *Donation to The Harington Scheme.* ½ acre designed for yr-round interest making a tapestry of greens and yellows. A wild garden with mature trees giving a woodland feel. Brilliant for hide and seek and young explorers. Water garden, vistas, 19 paths, some leading to sunny clearings. Exceptional camellias and magnolia in the spring. The garden has been open for the NGS for 59 consecutive yrs! Wheelchair access to main lawn only; many very narrow paths.

24 GROVE PARK, SE5

Camberwell SE5 8LH. Clive Pankhurst, www.alternative-planting.blogspot.com. *Chadwick Rd end of Grove Park. Stns: Peckham Rye or Denmark Hill, both 10 mins walk. Easy bus from Oval (185) or Elephant and Castle (176, 40). Good street parking.* Sun 4 Sept (2-5.30). Adm £3.50, chd free. Home-made teas.

An exotic garden full of the exuberance of late summer inspired by travel in Southeast Asia. A lush jungle of big leafed plants, bold colours and shapes incl bananas, dahlias and towering Paulownias. Huge hidden garden gives unexpected size with ponds, sunken terrace, productive area. Lawn and lots of hidden corners give spaces to sit and enjoy. Renowned for delicious home-made cake. Featured on BBC Gardeners World and Instant Gardener and in the Independent.

116 HAMILTON TERRACE, NW8

London NW8 9UT. Mr & Mrs I B Kathuria, 020 7625 6909, gkathuria@hotmail.co.uk. *Tube: Maida Vale (5 mins) or St.Johns Wood (10 mins) Buses: 16, 98 to Maida Vale, 139, 189 to Abbey Rd. Free parking on Sundays.* Evening opening Sun 3 July (4-8). Also open 2 Hillside Close. Evening opening Sun 17 July (4-8). Adm £5, chd free. Wine. Visits also by arrangement May to July for groups 10+. *Donation to St. Mark's Church.*

Lush front garden full of dramatic foliage with a water feature and tree ferns. Large back garden of different levels with Yorkshire stone paving, many large terracotta pots and containers, water feature and lawn. Wide variety of perennials and flowering shrubs, many unusual and subtropical plants, succulents, acers, ferns, climbers, roses, fuchsias and prizewinning hostas. A great example of container gardening and varied foliage.

◆ HAMPTON COURT PALACE, KT8

East Molesey KT8 9AU. Historic Royal Palaces, 0844 482 7777, hamptoncourt@hrp.org.uk, www.hrp.org.uk. *Follow brown tourist signs on all major routes. Junction of A308 with A309 at foot of Hampton Court Bridge.* For NGS: Evening opening Thur 30 June, Thur 28 July, Thur 25 Aug (6.30-8). Adm £12, chd free. Pre-booking essential, please visit www.ngs.org.uk or phone 01483 211535 for information & booking. Wine. For other opening times and information, please phone, email or visit garden website.

Take the opportunity to join 3 special NGS private tours, after the wonderful historic gardens have closed to the public. 30th June - 2016 Year of the Royal Garden - Walk around the palace gardens and learn about the summer planting schemes. 28th July - Kings, Queens and Gardeners - Listen to some of the history of the palace gardens and their creators as you walk around. 25th August - Statues, Views & Vistas - explore the gardens learning about some of their key features. 2016 at Hampton Court Palace has been designated the 'The Year of the Royal Garden' with specialist talks, come and learn about the history of these royal gardens and find out what goes into creating and maintaining them. Some un-bound gravel paths.

GROUP OPENING

HAMPTON HILL GARDENS, TW12

Hampton Hill TW12 1DW. *3m from Twickenham. 4m from Kingston-upon-Thames. Between A312 (Uxbridge Rd & A313 (Park Rd). Bus: 285 from Kingston stops on Uxbridge Rd. Stn: Fulwell 15 mins walk.* Sat 4, Sun 5 June (2-5). Combined adm £5, chd free. Home-made teas at 30 St James's Road.

18 CRANMER ROAD
Bernard Wigginton

30 ST JAMES'S ROAD
Jean Burman

NEW ▶ WAYSIDE
Mr Steve Croft

3 gardens of diverse interest in an attractive West London suburb. With the backdrop of St James's Church spire, 18 Cranmer Rd is a colourful garden with herbaceous and exotic borders and a WW2 air raid shelter transformed as rockery and water garden with azaleas, helianthemums and foliage plants. The SE facing garden at 30 St James's Rd is subdivided into 5 rooms. Decking with seating leads to ponds surrounded by grasses and shrubs and an African themed thatched exterior sitting room. 25 St James's Rd is a large urban garden divided into several areas, the entire garden is planted to attract wildlife with 2 wildlife ponds, mixed herbaceous borders, water feature, urns and pots. Partial wheelchair access.

---

77 HANDSWORTH ROAD, N17
London N17 6DB. Serge Charles. *Seven Sisters/Turnpike Lane 15 mins walk from either station or take W4 bus from T Lane, alight Broadwater Lodge stop. 230 bus first stop Philip Lane L into Handsworth Rd. Free parking.* Sun 12 June (2-6). Adm £2.50, chd free. Also open 159 Higham Road.

Narrow front garden is home to

bamboos, roses and clematis which screen a secret knot garden of box. Container planted trees incl olive, mimosa and myrtle. Shady path, planted with a wide range of rare and unusual ferns and shade tolerant plants leads to a tiny back garden where the bamboos reach 25ft underplanted with tree ferns. Many other interesting plants and features inc sculptures. Refreshments available at 159 Higham Rd.

NEW ▶ 37 HAROLD ROAD, E11
London E11 4QX. Dr Matthew Jones Chesters. *Tube: Leytonstone exit L from subway 5 mins walk. Overground: Leytonstone High Rd 5 mins walk. Buses: 257 & W 14. Parking at station or limited on street.* Sun 31 July (1-5). Adm £3.50, chd free. Home-made teas.

50ft x 60ft pretty corner garden arranged around 7 fruit trees. Fragrant climbers, woodland plants and shade tolerant fruit along north wall. Fastigiate trees protect raised vegetable beds and herb rockery. Long lawn bordered by roses and perennials on the other. Patio with raised pond, palms and rhubarb. Planting designed to produce fruit, fragrance and lovely memories. Plant list and garden plan available.

The Watergardens

NEW **31 HENDON AVENUE, N3**
London N3 1UJ. Sandra
Tomaszewska. *15 mins walk from
Finchley Central Tube. Buses: 326 &
143. Car: 5 mins from A1 via Hendon
Ln. No parking restrictions on Sun.*
Sun 24 July (2-6). Adm £4, chd
free. Home-made teas.
An extensive garden with mature
trees, shrubs and perennials divided
into areas. Herbaceous beds in semi
shade, a raised triangular bed with
lavender, agapanthus and roses. Two
arches, draped with grapevines,
wisteria, kiwi and clematis, guide you
into a tranquil, white garden and a
wildlife pond, lead to tropical and
Mediterranean beds with olive, bean
and fig trees, palms, bamboos and
cannas.

**NGS support helps
us to champion
community nurses**

159 HIGHAM ROAD, N17
Downhills Park, Tottenham N17
6NX. Jess Kitley & Sally Gray. *Tube:
Turnpike Lane then 15 mins walk/W4
alight Higham Rd or Seven Sisters
then 41 bus alight Philip Lane, walk
up through Downhills Park. Buses
341, 230,41,W4. Free parking on
Higham Rd.* Sun 12 June (2-6).
Adm £3.50, chd free. Home-made
teas. Also open 77 Handsworth
Road.
This 80ft x 30ft garden demonstrates
a unity of design and materials,
incorporating sculptural elements
amongst dense planting with shrubs,
perennials and grasses. Areas to sit,
contemplate and enjoy as birds, bees
and butterflies abound. A natural
wildlife pond dug into clay harnesses
natural springs, mitigating constant
flooding. Backing on to woodland,
big skies...and this is Tottenham!

32 HIGHBURY PLACE, N5
London N5 1QP. Michael &
Caroline Kuhn. *Highbury & Islington
Tube; Overground & National Rail.
Buses: 4, 19, 30, 43, 271, 393 to*

*Highbury Corner. 3 mins walk up
Highbury Place which is opp stn.* Sun
19 June (2-6). Adm £3.50, chd
free. Teas.
This 80ft long garden lies behind a
C18 terrace house. An upper York
stone terrace leads down to a larger
terrace surrounded by overfilled beds
of cottage garden style planting.
Further steps lead to a lawn by a rill
and an end terrace. A large willow
tree dominates the garden which also
has amerlanchiers and fruit trees as
well as dwarf acers, a winter flowering
cherry, lemon trees and a magnolia.

HIGHWOOD ASH, NW7
Highwood Hill, Mill Hill NW7 4EX.
Mr & Mrs R Gluckstein, 020 8959
1183, pennygluckstein@gmail.com.
*Totteridge & Whetstone on Northern
line, then bus 251 stops outside -
Rising Sun/Mill Hill stop. By car:
House on A5109 from Apex Corner
to Whetstone. Garden located opp
The Rising Sun PH.* Sun 15 May
(2-5.30). Adm £4.50, chd free. Tea.
Visits also by arrangement May to
Sept, guided tours on request.
Created over the last 50yrs, this 3¼
acre garden features rolling lawns,
two large interconnecting ponds with
koi, herbaceous and shrub borders
and a modern gravel garden. A
garden for all seasons with many
interesting plants and sculptures.
Partial access for wheelchairs, lowest
parts too steep.

19 HILLFIELD PARK, N10
Muswell Hill N10 3QT. Zaki & Ruth
Elia. *Off Muswell Hill Broadway,
corner HSBC Bank. Buses: W7, 43,
102, 144, 134, 234. Tube: Highgate,
E Finchley, Finsbury Park.* Sun 17
July (2-6). Adm £3.50, chd free.
Also open 5 St Regis Close.
An orientalist garden in Edwardian
Muswell Hill. Created by
owner/designer, inspired by the
original British Raj features within the
house. Three tiled terraces with
ceramic containers unfold around a
traditional fountain. A bespoke
Eastern style shed crowns the top
terrace, while dramatic planting by
Declan Buckley cocoons visitors in
lush seclusion. Refreshments
available at 5 St Regis Close.
Featured on ITV's Love Your Garden.

2 HILLSIDE CLOSE, NW8
Off Carlton Hill, St. John's Wood,
London NW8 0EF. Kris & Barry

Musikant, 020 7624 3836,
krismusi@aol.com. *Nr to Maida Vale
end of Carlton Hill, look for large black
entrance gates. Parking in Carlton
Hill. Tube: Maida Vale (8mins); St.
John's Wood (15mins).* Buses: 16,
98, 139, 189. Sun 3 July (11.30-5).
Adm £5, chd free. Home-made
teas. Also open 116 Hamilton
Terrace. Visits also by
arrangement Mar to Aug, groups
6 min.
Set in a secluded cul de sac with
attractively planted flowerbeds, the
house has four gardens. To the front
is a small parterre. To the rear a
walled courtyard with fruit trees and
raised vegetable beds. From here,
water flows from a trough along a
52ft rill and drops into a wildlife pond
which is situated in a country style
lawned garden with herbaceous
beds, shrubs and wild flowers.

THE HOLME, NW1
Inner Circle, Regents Park
NW1 4NT. Lessee of The Crown
Commission. *In centre of Regents
Park on The Inner Circle. Within 10
mins walk from Great Portland St or
Baker St Underground Stations, opp
Regents Park Rose Garden Cafe.* Sat
25, Sun 26 June, Sat 6, Sun 7 Aug
(2.30-5.30). Adm £5, chd free.
4 acre garden filled with interesting
and unusual plants. Sweeping
lakeside lawns intersected by islands
of herbaceous beds. Extensive rock
garden with waterfall, stream and
pool. Formal flower garden with
unusual annual and half hardy plants,
sunken lawn, fountain pool and
arbour. Gravel paths and some steps
which gardeners will help wheelchair
users to negotiate.

GROUP OPENING

HOMERTON GARDENS, E5
London E5 0DS. *Gardens close to
Homerton High St. Nearest station
Homerton Overground. Nearest
buses 236, 488, 276 or W15.* Sun 5
June (2-6). Combined adm £4, chd
free. Tea at 79 Glyn Rd.

   79 GLYN RD
   Ms Pat Hornsby

   80 RODING ROAD
   Ms Joan Wadge

These are small family gardens used
to relax and enjoy. Both combine

mixed established borders with seating areas. Roding Road has a paved area surrounded by borders. The aim is to combine texture with colour and smell depending on the mood of the owner. Glyn Road has a lawn and makes the most of its fencing for climbers.

Areas to sit, contemplate and enjoy as birds, bees and butterflies abound . . .

239A HOOK ROAD, KT9

Chessington KT9 1EQ. Mr & Mrs D St Romaine, www.gardenphotolibrary.com. *4m S of Kingston. A3 from London, turn L at Hook underpass onto A243. Gdn 300yds on L. Parking opp in Park or on rd, no restrictions at night. Buses K4, 71, 465 from Kingston & Surbiton to North Star PH.* **Evening opening Wed 8, Wed 15 June (7-9.30). Adm £5, chd free. Wine.**
Garden photographer's garden. A garden of two halves - Contemporary flower garden based on 3 circles. A gravel garden and dining area, a circular lawn surrounded by deep colour themed borders, pond and L shaped rose tunnel. And a traditional potager with 20 varieties of fruit and 50+ varieties of vegetables and herbs in small beds amongst many climbing roses and ornamental flowers. Images by Derek St Romaine. Featured in many publications over the years.

NEW 33 HUDDLESTON ROAD, N7

London N7 0AD. Gilly Hatch & Tom Gretton. *5 mins from Tufnell Park Tube. Tube: Tufnell Park. Buses: 4, 134, 390 to Tufnell Park. Follow Tufnell Park Rd to 3rd rd on L.* **Sat 2, Sun 3 July (2-6). Adm £3.50, chd free. Home-made teas.**
The rambunctious front garden weaves together perennials, grasses and ferns, while the back garden

makes a big impression in a small space. After 40yrs, the lawn is now a wide curving path, a deep sunny bed on one side, mixing shrubs and perennials in an ever changing blaze of colour, on the other, a screen of varied greens and textures. This flowery passage leads to a secluded sitting area. Exhibition of paintings and handmade prints by Gilly Hatch, with 10% of sales going to the NGS.

1A HUNGERFORD ROAD, N7

London N7 9LA. David Matzdorf, davidmatzdorf@blueyonder.co.uk, www.growingontheedge.net. *Between Camden Town & Holloway. Tube: Caledonian Rd. Buses: 17, 29, 91, 253, 259, 274, 390 & 393.* **Sun 12 June (12-6). Adm £2, chd free. Also open 62 Hungerford Road.**
Visits also by arrangement Apr to Oct. *Donation to Terrence Higgins Trust.*
Unique eco house with walled, lush front garden in modern exotic style, densely planted with palms, acacia, bamboo, ginger lilies, bananas, ferns, yuccas, abutilons and unusual understorey plants. Floriferous and ambitious green roof resembling Mediterranean or Mexican hillside, planted with yuccas, dasylirions, agaves, aloes, flowering shrubs, euphorbias, grasses, alpines, sedums and aromatic herbs. Sole access to roof is via built in ladder. Garden and roof each 50ft x 18ft.

62 HUNGERFORD ROAD, N7

London N7 9LP. John Gilbert & Lynne Berry. *Between Camden Town & Holloway. Tube: Caledonian Rd, 6 mins walk. Buses: 29 & 253 to Hillmarton Rd stop in Camden Rd. Also 17, 91, 259, 393 to Hillmarton Rd. 10 to York Way.* **Sun 12 June (2-6). Adm £2.50, chd free. Also open 1a Hungerford Road.**
Densely planted mature town garden at rear of Victorian terrace house which has been designed to maximise space for planting and create several different sitting areas, views and moods. NW facing with considerable shade, it is arranged in a series of paved rooms with a good range of perennials, shrubs and trees. Professional garden designer's own garden.

THE HURLINGHAM CLUB, SW6

Ranelagh Gardens, London SW6 3PR. The Members of the Hurlingham Club, www.hurlinghamclub.org.uk. *Main*

gate at E end of Ranelagh Gardens. Tube: Putney Bridge (110yds). NB: No onsite parking. Meter parking on local streets & restricted parking on Sats (9-5). **Sat 21 May (10-5). Adm £5, chd free. Light refreshments in the Napier Servery in the East Wing.**
Rare opportunity to visit this 42 acre jewel with many mature trees, 2 acre lake with water fowl, expansive lawns and a river walk. Capability Brown and Humphry Repton were involved with landscaping. The gardens are renowned for their roses, herbaceous and lakeside borders, shrubberies and stunning bedding displays. The riverbank is a haven for wildlife with native trees, shrubs and wild flowers. Garden Tours at 11am and 2pm - ticketed event, tickets available at entrance.

NEW 9 IMBER PARK ROAD, KT10

Esher KT10 8JB. Jane & John McNicholas. *1/2 m from centre of Esher. From the A307, turn into Station Rd which becomes Ember Lane. Go past Esher train station on R. Take 3rd rd on R into Imber Park Rd.* **Sun 26 June (1-5). Adm £3.50, chd free. Home-made teas.**
An established cottage style garden, designed and maintained by the owners who are passionate about gardening and plants. The garden is south facing, with well stocked, colourful herbaceous borders containing a wide variety of perennials, evergreen and deciduous shrubs, a winding lawn area and a small garden retreat.

23 IMPERIAL ROAD, N22

London N22 N22 8DE. Kate Gadsby, 07958 901679, kate@kategadsby.co.uk. *Off Bounds Green Rd between Bounds Green Tube & Wood Green Tube. 5 mins from Alexandra Palace mainline.* **Sun 2 Oct (12.30-4.30). Adm £2.50, chd free. Tea.**
Tiny back garden overflowing with interesting and unusual plants where an inventive and inspiring approach to planting, has created a surprising number of perspectives. An early October opening to show how many varieties of aster can be fitted into a very small space. Semi covered deck allows enjoyment in sun and rain.

THE INNER AND MIDDLE TEMPLE GARDENS, EC4

Crown Office Row, Inner Temple, London EC4Y 7HL. The Honourable Societies of the Inner and Middle Temples, www.innertemple.org.uk /www.middletemple.org.uk. *Entrance: Main Garden Gate on Crown Office Row, access via Tudor Street gate or Middle Temple Lane gate.* Wed 22 June (11.30-3). Adm £50. Pre-booking essential, please visit www.ngs.org.uk or phone 01483 211535 for information & booking. Inner Temple Garden is a haven of tranquillity and beauty with a sweeping lawns, unusual trees and charming woodland areas. The well known herbaceous border shows off inspiring plant combinations from early spring through to autumn. The award winning gardens of Middle Temple are comprised of a series of courtyards and one larger formal garden. Each courtyard has its own character and continues to offer peaceful respite from the bustle of central London as they have for centuries. **Adm incl conducted tour of the gardens by Head Gardeners and lunch in the Middle Hall, one of the finest examples of an Elizabethan hall in the country.** Please advise in advance if wheelchair access is required.

NEW ▶ **49 JENNINGS ROAD**

London SE22 9JU. Phil King & Graham Clayton. *Train: North or East Dulwich 15 mins walk. Buses:*

40, 185 & 176 along Lordship Lane, off alight Heber Rd stop. Sun 24 July (1.30-6.30). Adm £3.50, chd free. Home-made teas.

There's a definite artistic flare to this very tiny but carefully crafted tropical garden where bamboos abound and *Dickonsonia Antarctica* wave their giant fronds, with the whole all interwoven with brightly coloured perennials for vibrant splashes of colour. Interesting and unusual ferns and ground covering plants thrive in the shady undergrowth and succulents and herbs grow in the sunniest spots. The lush tropical theme is carried into the house with unusual plants, figs and feathery South African shrubs growing indoors as giant house plants.

NEW ▶ **55 JENNINGS ROAD**

London SE22 9JU. Ms Antonia Schofield. *Train: North or East Dulwich 15 mins walk. Buses: 40, 185 & 176 along Lordship Lane, off alight Heber Rd stop.* **Evening opening Fri 22 July (5.30-9). Adm £5, chd free. Wine.** Sun 24 July (1.30-5.30). Adm £3.50, chd free. Home-made teas.

A garden designer with a passion for plants, especially large leafed architectural ones, has used her small garden to experiment with unusual plants giving a tropical effect. The very sunny S facing garden has been packed with giant plants to create a little tropical paradise and when visitors come round they say they feel like they are on holiday. Favourite plants are tetrapanax, a real showstopper with leaves nearly a

metre wide, *Paulownia tomentosa* coppiced to grow enormous foliage; hardy palm *Trachycarpus fortuneii* and fig trees grown for their large scented leaves and their delicious fruit. Flowering plants include ginger and canna lilies, eucomis and crocosmia to add intense pops of colour with jasmine and *Pittosporum tobira* for their heavenly scent.

22 KELSEY WAY, BR3

Beckenham BR3 3LL. Janet & Steve Wright. *From Beckenham town centre, take Kelsey Park Rd, R into Manor Way. Kelsey Way is turning off this. Bus: 367 Sunday service to Village Way stop.* Sun 12 June (2-5). Adm £3.50, chd free. Tea.

Multiple award winning garden. Colourful herbaceous borders with many tropical plants incl bananas, colocasias, alocasias, cannas and several different varieties of brugmansias. Displays of potted plants and a conservatory with a magnificent bougainvillea. Extensive and varied vegetable garden with a large fruit cage.

GROUP OPENING

KEW GREEN GARDENS, TW9

Kew TW9 3AH. *NW side of Kew Green. Tube: Kew Gardens. Mainline stn: Kew Bridge. Buses: 65, 391. Entrance via riverside.* Sun 22 May (2-6). Combined adm £6, chd free. Tea at church on the green. Evening opening Sun 5 June (6-8). Combined adm £8, chd free. Wine.

65 KEW GREEN
Giles & Angela Dixon.
Open on Sun 22 May

69 KEW GREEN
John & Virginia Godfrey.
Open on all dates

71 KEW GREEN
Mr & Mrs Jan Pethick.
Open on all dates

73 KEW GREEN
Sir Donald & Lady Elizabeth Insall.
Open on all dates

Four long gardens behind a row of C18 houses on the Green, close to the Royal Botanic Gardens. These gardens feature the profusely planted

5 Brodie Road

and traditional borders of a mature English country garden, and contrast formal gardens, terraces and lawns, laid out around tall old trees, with wilder areas and woodland and wild flower planting. One has an unusual architect designed summerhouse, while another offers the surprise of a modern planting of espaliered miniature fruit trees.

KING HENRY'S WALK GARDEN, N1

11c King Henry's Walk, London N1 4NX. Friends of King Henry's Walk Garden, www.khwgarden.org.uk. *Buses incl: 21, 30, 38, 56, 141, 277. Behind adventure playground on KHW, off Balls Pond Rd.* Sun 29 May (2-5.30). Adm £3.50, chd free. Home-made teas. *Donation to Friends of KHW Garden.*
Vibrant ornamental planting welcomes the visitor to this hidden oasis and leads you into a verdant community garden with secluded woodland area, beehives, wildlife pond, wall trained fruit trees, and plots used by local residents to grow their own fruit and vegetables. Live music. Disabled WC.

A surprising and generous oasis of calm in a busy city . . .

LAMBETH PALACE, SE1

Lambeth Palace Rd, London SE1 7JU. The Church Commissioners, www.archbishopofcanterbury.org. *Entrance via Main Gatehouse facing Lambeth Bridge. Station: Waterloo. Tube: Westminster, Lambeth North & Vauxhall all 10 mins walk. Buses: 3, C10, 77, 344, 507.* Evening opening Tue 24 May, Tue 21 June (5.30-8). Adm £6, chd free. Wine.
Lambeth Palace has one of the oldest and largest private gardens in London. It has been occupied by

Archbishops of Canterbury since 1197. Formal courtyard boasts historic White Marseilles fig planted in 1556. Parkland style garden features mature trees, woodland and native planting, orchard and pond. There is a formal rose terrace, summer gravel border, scented chapel garden and active beehives. Ramped path to rose terrace, disabled WC.

12 LANSDOWNE ROAD, W11

London W11 3LW. The Lady Amabel Lindsay. *Tube: Holland Park. Buses: 12, 88, GL 711, 715 to Holland Park, 4 mins walk up Lansdowne Rd.* Wed 25 May (2-6). Adm £4, chd free. Tea.
A country garden in the heart of London. An old mulberry tree, billowing borders, rambling Rosa banksiae, a greenhouse of climbing geraniums and a terrace filled with tender perennials. Featured in Great Gardens of London by Victoria Summerley (photos by Hugo Rittson Thomas and Marianne Majerus). Partial wheelchair access.

42 LATIMER ROAD, E7

Forest Gate E7 0LQ. Janet Daniels. *8 mins walk from Forest Gate or Wanstead Park stn. From Forest Gate cross to Sebert Rd, then 3rd rd on L.* Sat 16, Sun 17 July (11-4.30). Adm £3.50, chd free. Tea.
Passionate plant collector's garden 90ft x 15ft. An abundance of baskets, climbers, shrubs and fruit trees. Raised koi carp pond. Step down to large secret garden containing exuberant borders, wildlife pond with gunnera, small green oasis lawn with arbour. Unusual and exotic plants, herb ladders and other quirky features. Wildlife friendly. Summerhouse full of collectables, dinky toys and collection of old wooden tools.

NEW 49 LEE ROAD, SE3

Blackheath, London SE3 9RT. Jane Glynn & Colin Kingsnorth. *5 mins walk from Blackheath mainline stn. Turn R up hill to mini r'about. Take lst rd past Blackheath Halls, 5 mins downhill on Lee Rd, on L. Buses: 202, 89, 54 or 108 to Blackheath.* Sun 12 June (1.30-5.30). Adm £4.50, chd free. Home-made teas. Also open 28 Granville Park.
A surprising and generous oasis of calm in a busy city. This is a new and

emerging garden that its artist owner is enthusiastically finding new treats for visitors to enjoy. Benches are set beneath rambling roses overlooking formal lawns with flowerbeds. Wander along winding paths through silver birches and grasses to find a treehouse clad with roses and clematis. And try to remember you are still in London.

NEW L'ESCALE, WD6

Barnet Lane, Elstree WD6 3QZ. Graham & Jacqueline Colover. *Rail: Elstree & Borehamwood, L over bridge, 2nd L Deacons Hill Rd, R Barnet Lane. Tube: Stanmore then bus 616 or Edgeware, bus 107 to East PH stop Elstree Village, walk along Barnet Lane from t-lights. Car: Barnet Lane A411 runs between A1 & A5183; SatNav reliable.* Sun 5 June (2-6). Adm £4, chd free. Home-made teas. Also open Blue Hills.
Gentle hillside garden on clay soil, featuring live steam gauge 1 model railway, complete with life size station, weaving through deep borders abundant with drifts of perennials and shrubs. Enter through densely planted terraces with steps leading down to railway garden, wild flower garden and wildlife ponds. Plantswoman's joy, the garden has developed over the last 2yrs as a celebration of life. Enjoy home-made teas on the main terrace overlooking the gardens and beyond. Children must be closely supervised at all times.

49 LOFTUS ROAD, W12

London W12 7EH. Emma Plunket, emma@plunketgardens.com, www.plunketgardens.com. *Shepherds Bush or Shepherds Bush Market tube or train or bus to Uxbridge Rd. Free street parking.* Evening opening Tue 14 June (5.30-8). Adm £4, chd free. Wine. Visits also by arrangement May to Sept.
Professional garden designer, Emma Plunket, opens her acclaimed walled garden. Richly planted, it is the ultimate hard working city garden with all year structure and colour; fruit, vegetables and herbs. Set against a backdrop of trees, it is unexpectedly open and peaceful. Garden plan, plant list and advice.

GROUP OPENING

LONDON FIELDS GARDENS, E8

Hackney, London E8 3LS. *On W side of London Fields park. Short walk from Haggerston stn, London Overground; or London Fields stn (from Liverpool St) or tube to Bethnal Green or Angel then bus towards Hackney.* **Sun 26 June (2-5). Combined adm £5, chd free. Light refreshments at 84 Lavender Grove.**

84 LAVENDER GROVE
Anne Pauleau

84 MIDDLETON ROAD
Penny Fowler

Two gardens in London Fields, an area which takes its name from fields on the London side of the old village of Hackney. They are unexpected havens from the city's hustle and bustle, with an exciting range and variety of colours, scents and design. This yr we have a courtyard garden, a scented cottage garden and a very unusual, long and secret garden where sculptures mingle with vegetation. Children's quiz. 84 Lavender Grove featured in GP Magazine.

GROUP OPENING

LOWER CLAPTON GARDENS, E5

Hackney, London E5 0RL. *10 mins walk from Hackney Central or Hackney Downs stns. Buses 38, 55, 106, 253, 254 or 425, alight Lower Clapton Rd.* **Sun 17 Apr (2-5). Combined adm £4, chd free. Sun 12 June (2-6). Combined adm £6, chd free. Tea at 16, 68 and 70b Powerscroft Rd.**

8 ALMACK ROAD
Philip Lightowlers.
Open on all dates
Visits also by arrangement Apr to July
plighto@gmail.com
07910 850276

16 POWERSCROFT ROAD
Elizabeth Welch.
Open on all dates

68B POWERSCROFT ROAD
Molly & Paul Jason.
Open on Sun 12 June

70 POWERSCROFT ROAD.
Mr David Lake.
Open on Sun 12 June

99 POWERSCROFT ROAD
Rose Greenwood.
Open on Sun 12 June

Lower Clapton is an area of mid Victorian terraces sloping down to the R Lea. This group of gardens reflect their owner's tastes and interests. On Powerscroft Rd we have 3 S facing gardens featuring a gravel garden, a raised pond, space for meditation and mixed borders. No. 99 has a high level patio looking out across the garden to a thatched gazebo. No. 8 Almack Rd is a long thin garden with two different rooms, one incl a classic blue agave named Audrey.

4 MACAULAY ROAD, SW4
Clapham SW4 0QX. Mrs Diana Ross. *Clapham Common Tube. Buses 88, 87, 77, 77A, 137, 137A, 37, 35, 345, 452 from tube cross Common towards large church ahead on R. Macaulay Rd opp. Free parking on The Chase.* **Evening opening Thur 8 Sept (6.30-8.30). Adm £20, chd free. Pre-booking essential, please visit www.ngs.org.uk or phone 01483 211535 for information & booking. Talk by owner. Wine and canapes.**
A garden writer's inspirational prize winning garden, well lit for evening viewing from the conservatory and of interest at all seasons. Divided into rooms, the garden features a jungle, a grotto full of frogs, papyrus grass and

ferns, pots wherever there's space and deep flowerbeds containing late flowering grasses. Flowering in autumn Eucryphia, Clerodendron, Luma apiculata and hips on Rosa Glauca. Before and after photographs, taken over the yrs, on display.

MALVERN TERRACE GARDENS, N1
London N1 1HR. *Malvern Terrace is off Thornhill Rd (nr The Albion PH) between Hemingford Rd & Liverpool Rd.* **Sun 8 May (2.30-5.30). Combined adm £3.50, chd free. Home-made teas.**
Group of unique 1830s terrace houses built on the site of Thomas Oldfield's dairy and cricket field. Cottage style front gardens in cobbled cul-de-sac - a peaceful oasis in the heart of London. Music.

6 MANOR ROAD, KT8
East Molesey KT8 9JX. Ann & Peter Pope. *10 mins walk from Hampton Court stn.* **Sun 19 June (2-6). Combined adm with 61 Wolsey Road £5, chd free. Home-made teas.**
A charming country garden with softly planted borders of roses, lavenders and sages. Perennial and annual flowers provide a nectar rich mix for bees throughout most of the yr. Rambling rose and sweet pea arches intermingle with clematis. Hand tame robins visit this wildlife friendly garden daily. Under glass is an 80yr old grapevine originally a cutting from the Great Vine at Hampton Court.

53 MAPLEDENE ROAD, E8
London E8 3JW. Tigger Cullinan, 020 7249 3754, tiggerine8@blueyonder.co.uk. *7 mins walk from 242, 149, 38, 30 buses or Haggerston Overground stn. Also 10 mins through London Fields from buses using Mare St, Hackney.* **Visits by arrangement May to July, groups 15 max. Adm by donation.**
90ft x 15ft N facing garden, divided in 3, crammed with plants, chosen for their contrasting leaves and colour combinations. Gardening with 8 neighbours means fences and walls smothered in roses, clematis and other climbers - not an empty inch. Great profusion and variety of plants, colour coordinated.

GROUP OPENING

NEW MARKSBURY AVENUE GARDENS, TW9
Richmond TW9 4JE. *Approx 10 mins walk from Kew Gardens tube. Exit westbound platform to North Rd. Take 3rd L into Atwood Ave. Marksbury Ave is 3rd R. Buses 190, 419 or R68.* **Evening opening Fri 10 June (6-8). Combined adm £7.50, chd free. Wine.**

NEW 26 MARKSBURY AVENUE
Sue Frisby

NEW 59 MARKSBURY AVENUE
Clarissa Fletcher

NEW 61 MARKSBURY AVENUE
Siobhan McCammon

Three neighbouring gardens reflecting the enthusiasm and knowledge of their owners. One features many New Zealand natives and a variety of fruit trees incl figs, apricots and vines. A trampoline is cleverly screened by black stemmed bamboo and copper beech. There is calming water and a camomile lawn. Another garden has evolved over 11yrs and features separate areas not all visible from the house. There is a continuing process of experimenting with plants. The group provides variety and charm for the visitors.

Discover a cloud pruned tree in the oriental corner from your seat in the tea house . . .

THE MEADOWS
See Kent

27 MENELIK ROAD, NW2
West Hampstead NW2 3RJ. C Klemera. *E of Shoot up Hill. From Kilburn tube, buses 16, 32,189, 316, 332 to Mill Lane on Shoot up Hill, then Minster Rd/Menelik Rd at end. From W Hampstead tube, C11 bus to Menelik Rd.* **Sun 10 July (2-5.30). Adm £4, chd free. Tea.**
A garden full of surprises and humour. A 30yr old Trachycarpus overlooks many exotic plants of strong shape, texture and colour. Discover a cloud pruned tree in the oriental corner from your seat in the tea house. Topiary pops up in the lush colourful borders and the piazza is secluded by bay trees and a banana, often in flower. Paths will lead you on a magical journey through plants from around the world.

41 MILL HILL ROAD, W3
London W3 8JE. Marcia Hurst, 020 8992 2632 or 07989 581940, marcia.hurst@sudbury-house.co.uk. *Tube: Acton Town, turn R, Mill Hill Rd on R off Gunnersbury Lane.* **Evening opening Fri 15 July (7-9). Wine. Sun 14 Aug (2-6). Home-made teas. Combined adm with 65 Mill Hill Road £5, chd free. Visits also by arrangement July to Sept no min, max 20.**
120ft x 40ft garden. A surprisingly large and sunny garden, with lavender and hornbeam hedges, herbaceous planting and climbers, incl unusual and rare plants as the owner is a compulsive plantaholic. Good in July and August, with many salvias and clematis. Lots of space to sit and enjoy the garden. Some of the plants growing in the garden are for sale in pots. Featured in the Weekend Mail magazine and Weekend Mail online.

65 MILL HILL ROAD, W3
London W3 8JF. Anna Dargavel, 07802 241965, annadargavel@mac.com. *Tube: Acton Town, turn R, Mill Hill Rd on R off Gunnersbury Lane.* **Evening opening Fri 15 July (7-9). Wine. Sun 14 Aug (2-6). Home-made teas. Combined adm with 41 Mill Hill Road £5, chd free. Visits also by arrangement May to Sept, max 12.**

Garden designer's own garden. A secluded and tranquil space, paved, with changes of level and borders. Sunny and shady areas, topiary, fruit trees and interesting planting combine to provide a wildlife haven. A pond and organic principles are used to promote a green environment and give a stylish walk to a studio at the end. Featured in Daily Mail - Meet the Neighbours - focusing on 3 gardeners in one street.

2 MILLFIELD PLACE, N6
Highgate, London N6 6JP. c/o Peter Lloyd, 020 8348 6487, daisydogone@aol.com. *Off Highgate West Hill, E side of Hampstead Heath. Buses: C2, C11 or 214 to Parliament Hill Fields. North London Line to Gospel Oak.* **Sun 1 May (2-6). Adm £4.50, chd free.** Home-made teas. **Evening opening Wed 15 June (5.30-9). Adm £5, chd free. Wine. Visits also by arrangement May to Aug.**
1½ acre spring and summer garden with camellias, rhododendrons, many flowering shrubs and unusual plants. Spring bulbs, herbaceous borders, spacious lawns, small pond and extensive views over Hampstead Heath. Partial wheelchair access with separate entrance, assistance available, please ask at gate.

27 NASSINGTON ROAD, NW3
Hampstead. NW3 2TX. Lucy Scott-Moncrieff. *From Hampstead Heath rail stn & bus stops at South End Green, go up South Hill Pk, then Parliament Hill, R into Nassington Rd.* **Sun 5 June (2-6). Adm £5, chd free. Home-made teas.**
Double width town garden planted for colour and to support wildlife. Spectacular ancient wisteria, prolific roses; herbs and unusual fruit and vegetables in with the flowers. The main feature is a large eco pond, designed for swimming, with colourful planting in and out of the water. Pots and planters, arches, bowers, view of allotments and very peaceful location give a rural feel in the city. Pond dipping for newts and mini beasts all afternoon. Live music from the Secret Life Sax Quartet from 4:30 to 5:30pm. Cakes incl lemon drizzle made with lemons from the garden; teas incl rose hips from the garden but also real tea and wine.

17A NAVARINO ROAD, E8

London E8 1AD. Ben Nel & Darren Henderson. *Buses 30, 38, 242 or 277 alight Graham Rd. Short walk from Hackney Central or London Fields stns on Overground lines.* Sun 17 Apr, Sun 17 July (2-5). Adm £3, chd free. Selection of teas and cakes.

Established Italian and Japanese water garden. Features a square pond with Corinthian fountain, topiary yew border, lilies and Mediterranean trees. Leading to Japanese garden with pond, bridge and stream cutting the Soleirolia soleirolii landscape, with acer, cypress, ferns and bamboo, overlooked by a beautiful Japanese Tea House. Garden featured on BBC Great British Garden Revival.

15 NORCOTT ROAD, N16

Stoke Newington N16 7BJ. Amanda & John Welch. *Buses: 67, 73, 76, 106, 149, 243, 393, 476, 488. Clapton & Rectory Rd mainline stns. One way system: by car approach from Brooke Rd which crosses Norcott Rd, garden in S half of Norcott Rd.* Sun 19 June (2-6). Adm £3.50, chd free. Home-made teas.

Opening again after a year's break, this is a large (for London) walled garden. Developed by the present owners over the past 35yrs, it is a cottage style garden with a pond, ancient fruit trees and an abundance of herbaceous plants. We will be having our plant sale as usual, fewer plants this time but all choice specimens.

NEW NORTH BRIDGE HOUSE SENIOR SCHOOL, N1

Canonbury Place, London N1 2NQ. Cognita Schools. *Tube & Overground: Highbury & Islington. 100 metres from Canonbury Sq, almost directly opp The Canonbury PH.* Sun 22 May (2-6). Combined adm with Canonbury House £5, chd free. Light refreshments.

Part of a Grade II listed building dating from C16, the front garden is surrounded by a variety of mature trees, several of which are over 200yrs old.

5 NORTHAMPTON PARK, N1

Islington N1 2PP. Andrew Bernhardt & Anne Brogan. *Backing on to St Paul's Shrubbery. 5 mins*

walk from Canonbury stn, 10 mins from Highbury & Islington Tube (Victoria Line) Bus: 30, 277, 341, 476. Sat 25 June (2-6). Adm £4, chd free. Strawberries and cream, Prosecco and teas.

Early Victorian S facing walled garden, (1840's) saved from neglect and developed over the last 22yrs. Arches, palms, box and yew hedging frame the cool North European blues, whites and greys moving to splashes of red/orange Mediterranean influence. The contrast of the cool garden shielded by a small park creates a sense of seclusion from its inner London setting.

> Planting chosen to be texturally diverse whilst retaining a strong complementary theme . . .

28 OLD DEVONSHIRE ROAD, SW12

London SW12 9RB. Georgina Ivor, 020 8673 7179, georgina@balhambandb.co.uk, www.balhambandb.co.uk/page3.htm. *Off Balham High Rd/A24. Balham Northern Line tube & mainline rail: 5 mins walk. Buses 155, 249, 355 stop on Balham High Rd.* Sun 5 June (2-5.30). Adm £3.50, chd free. Home-made teas. Evening opening Wed 8 June (6-8.30). Adm £4.50, chd free. Wine. Also open Fern Cottage. *Donation to Trinity Hospice.*

Walk past the Mediterranean style front garden to a tranquil oasis at the back. A cool eucalyptus reaches for the house tops whilst a well established pear tree looks down on a walled garden full to bursting with planting both familiar and surprising. On the balustraded wooden balcony there are herbs in troughs and a vibrant orange trumpet vine.

OLDEN GARDEN COMMUNITY PROJECT, N5

Islington N5 1NH. London Borough of Islington. *Opp 22 Whistler St &*

Drayton Pk train station. Sun 24 Apr (2-5). Adm £3.50, chd free. Home-made teas.

Olden Garden Community Project is a 2 acre oasis of beauty and retreat from the busy streets surrounding it. A top terrace of beautiful herbaceous borders, lawn and patio. On the lower slopes there is an orchard, a meadow, vegetable beds and a greenhouse. In springtime, there is blossom, daffodils and bluebells. There is also a peaceful path through the woodland. Wheelchair access to all areas of top terrace. Disabled WC.

THE ORCHARD, W4

40A Hazledene Road, Chiswick, London W4 3JB. Vivien Cantor. *10 mins walk from Chiswick mainline & Gunnersbury tube. Off Fauconberg Rd. Close to junction of A4 & Sutton Court Rd,.* Sun 8 May (2-5.30). Adm £4, chd free. Home-made teas.

Informal, romantic 1/4 acre garden with mature flowering trees, shrubs and imaginative planting in flowing herbaceous borders. Climbers, fern planting and water features with ponds, a bridge and waterfall in this ever evolving garden. Featured in Garden News.

ORMELEY LODGE, TW10

Ham Gate Avenue, Richmond TW10 5HB. Lady Annabel Goldsmith. *From Richmond Pk exit at Ham Gate into Ham Gate Ave, 1st house on R. From Richmond A307, after 1 1/2 m, past New Inn on R at T-lights turn L into Ham Gate Ave.* Sun 19 June (3-6). Adm £4, chd free. Tea.

Large walled garden in delightful rural setting on Ham Common. Wide herbaceous borders and box hedges. Walk through to orchard with wild flowers. Vegetable garden, knot garden, aviary and chickens. Trellised tennis court with roses and climbers. A number of historic stone family dog memorials. Dogs not permitted.

NEW 4 ORMONDE ROAD, HA6

Moor Park, Northwood HA6 2EL. Hasruty & Yogesh Patel, Hasruty@gmail.com. *Approx 5m from J17 & 18, M25; 6 1/2 m from J5, M1. From Batchworth Lane take Wolsey Rd exit at mini r'about. Ormonde Rd is 2nd turning on L. Ample parking on Ormonde Rd & surrounding rds.* Sun 22 May (2-5).

Adm £4.50, chd free. **Home-made teas. Visits also by arrangement in May.**
Beautifully planted frontage entices visitors to large S facing rear family garden. A calm oasis enclosed by mature trees. A rare variegated flowering Tulip Tree provides dappled shelter alongside magnolias incl Yellow River, Wieseneri and diverse acers. Lavender hues of phlox foam around generous beds surrounding the spacious raised patio.

ALLOTMENTS

PADDOCK ALLOTMENTS & LEISURE GARDENS, SW20
51 Heath Drive, Raynes Park SW20 9BE. **Paddock Horticultural Society.** *Bus 57, 131, 200 to Raynes Pk station then 10 min walk or bus 163. 152 to Bushley Rd 7 min walk; 413, 5 min walk from Cannon Hill Lane. Street parking.* Sat 25 June (12-5). Adm £3.50, chd free. Home-made teas.
An allotment site not to be missed, over 150 plots set in 5½ acres. Our tenants come from diverse communities growing a wide range of flowers, fruits and vegetables, some plots are purely organic others resemble English country gardens. Plants, jams and produce for sale. Display of arts and crafts by members of the Paddock Hobby Club. Paved and grass paths, mainly level.

3 THE PARK, N6
off Southwood Lane, London N6 4EU. **Mr & Mrs G Schrager, 020 8348 3314, buntyschrager@gmail.com.** *3 mins from Highgate tube, up Southwood Lane. The Park is 1st on R. Buses: 43, 134, 143, 263.* Sun 19 June (2.30-5.30). Adm £4, chd free. Home-made teas. **Visits also by arrangement Apr to July, small groups welcome.**
Established large garden with informal planting for colour, scent and bees. Pond with fish, frogs and tadpoles. Tree peonies, Crinodendron hookerianum and Paulownia. Plants, tea and home-made jam for sale. Children particularly welcome - a treasure hunt with prizes!

11 PARK AVENUE NORTH, N8
Crouch End, London N8 7RU. **Mr Steven Buckley & Ms Liz Roberts.** *Tube: Finsbury Park & Turnpike Lane, nearest bus stop W3, 144, W7.* Sun 5 June (11.30-6). Adm £3.50, chd free. Home-made teas.
An exotic 250ft T-shaped garden, threaded through an old orchard and rose garden. Dramatic, mainly spiky, foliage dominates, with the focus on palms, agaves, dasylirions, aeoniums, bananas, tree ferns, nolinas, cycads, bamboos, yuccas, cacti and many species of succulents. Aloes are a highlight. Rocks and terracotta pots lend a Mediterranean accent.

18 PARK CRESCENT, N3
Finchley N3 2NJ. **Rosie Daniels.** *Tube: Finchley Central. Buses: 82 to Victoria Park, also 125, 460, 626, 683.* Sun 19 June, Sun 17 July (2-6). Adm £3.50, chd free. Home-made teas.
Constantly evolving, charming small garden designed and densely planted by owner. Roses and clematis in June and salvias, rudbeckia, helenium and some new grasses in July. Small

pond, tub water feature and bird haven. Stepped terrace with lots of pots. New glass installations and sculptures by owner. Hidden seating with view through garden. Secluded, peaceful, restorative. Children's treasure hunt. Awarded London Gardens Society Silver Gilt Certificate.

NEW ▶ 36 PARK ROAD, W4
London W4 3HH. **Meyrick & Louise Chapman.** *Adjacent to Chiswick House. Chiswick BR: 6 mins walk up Park Rd. District Line: Turnham Green 15 mins walk. Buses: E3 & 272 alight Chesterfield Rd then 4 mins walk. Free Street parking.* Sun 24 July (2-6). **Combined adm with 56 Park Road £6.50, chd free.** Cream teas.
City garden with distinct structure and formality based on a series of rooms within hedging. Designed to create a flavour to each room; one hot, one cool and one dark using perennials, roses, hostas and ferns against a repeated background of yew, azalea and camellia. Green wall and reflective pool.

Arundel and Ladbroke Gardens

NEW **56 PARK ROAD, W4**
London W4 3HH. Richard & Diane Treganowan. *Adjacent to Chiswick House. Chiswick BR: 6 mins walk up Park Rd. District Line: Turnham Green 15 mins walk. Buses: E3 & 272 alight Chesterfield Rd then 4 mins walk. Free street parking.* Sun 24 July (2-6). Combined adm with 36 Park Road £6.50, chd free. Cream teas at 36 Park Rd.
Distinctly and unexpectedly atmospheric, largely sub tropical planted with rare and unusual hardy exotics and large leaved perennials. Planting chosen to be texturally diverse whilst retaining a strong complementary theme. Interesting collection of ferns and palms set amongst gnarled and mature tree stumps. The garden was designed and planted by owners. Full plant list available.

4 PARK VILLAGE EAST (TOWER LODGE GARDENS), NW1
Regents Park, London NW1 7PX. Eveline Carn, 07831 136069, evelinecbcarn@icloud.com. *Tube: Camden Town or Mornington Crescent 7 mins. Bus: C2 or 274 3 mins. Opp The York & Albany, just off junction of Parkway/Prince Albert Rd.* Evening opening Thur 26 May (6-8.30). Adm £6, chd free. Wine. Sun 5 June (2.30-6). Adm £5, chd free. Home-made teas. Also open Royal College of Physicians Medicinal Garden. Visits also by arrangement May to July with home-made teas, or wine and nibbles, for groups 5+.
One of four fascinating gardens in NW1 open on the same day for the Garden Festival Weekend. This is an unexpectedly large garden hidden behind a John Nash house, screened by trees and descending over three terraces with stepped ponds to what used to be the Regents Canal. A

garden of shapes, textures and many shades of foliage set in strong landscape architecture. Tree hung swing. Featured in Die Geheimen Gäten von England (The Secret Gardens of England) by Heidi Howcroft with photos by Marianne Majerus. Also featured in Danish magazine Søndag with text and photographs by Hanne Gabel Christensen.

174 PECKHAM RYE, SE22
London SE22 9QA. Mr & Mrs Ian Bland. *Stn: Peckham Rye. Buses: 12, 37, 63, 197, 363. Overlooks Peckham Rye Common from Dulwich side.* Sun 29 May (2.30-5.30). Adm £3.50, chd free. Home-made teas. *Donation to St Christopher's Hospice.*
Visitors call our garden an oasis of calm in Peckham. Every yr the garden changes and matures. It is densely planted with a wide variety of contrasting foliage. Unusual plants are combined with old favourites. It remains easy care and child friendly. Garden originally designed by Judith Sharpe. Our ever popular plant sale and famed cakes will be available again. Easy access via side alley into a flat garden.

PETERSHAM HOUSE, TW10
Petersham Road, Petersham, Richmond TW10 7AA. Francesco & Gael Boglione, www.petershamnurseries.com. *Stn: Richmond, then 65 bus to Dysart PH. Entry to garden off Petersham Rd, through nursery. Parking very limited on Church Lane.* Sun 25 Sept (11-4). Adm £4, chd free.
Broad lawn with large topiary, generously planted double borders. Productive vegetable garden with chickens. Adjoins Petersham Nurseries with extensive plant sales, shop and café serving lunch, tea and cake.

18 PETTITS BOULEVARD, RM1
Rise Park, Romford RM1 4PL. Peter & Lynn Nutley. *From M25 take A12 towards London, at Pettits Lane junction turn R, then R again into Pettits Boulevard.* Sat 11, Sun 12 June, Sat 16, Sun 17 July (1-5.30). Adm £3, chd free. Home-made teas.
A garden 80ft x 23ft on three levels with an ornamental pond, patio area

with shrubs and perennials, many in pots. A large eucalyptus tree leads to a woodland themed garden with many ferns and hostas. There are agricultural implements and garden ornaments giving a unique and quirky feel to the garden. There are also tranquil seating areas situated throughout. Agricultural implements on show. Partial wheelchair access.

GROUP OPENING

PRINCES AVENUE GARDENS, N10
Muswell Hill N10 3LS. *Buses: 43 & 134 from Highgate tube; also W7, 102, 144, 234, 299. Princes Ave opp M&S in Muswell Hill Broadway, or John Baird PH in Fortis Green.* Sun 22 May (2-6). Combined adm £4, chd free. Home-made teas.

> **15 PRINCES AVENUE**
> Eliot & Emma Glover
>
> **28 PRINCES AVENUE**
> Ian & Viv Roberts

In a beautiful Edwardian avenue in the heart of Muswell Hill Conservation Area, two very different gardens reflect the diverse life styles of their owners. The large S facing family garden at No 15 has been designed for entertaining and yr-round interest. White, blue and blush pink themed beds with alliums and a wide variety of perennials and shrubs frame an exceptional lawn. A Wendy house, hidden wooden castle and small vegetable patch provide delight for children of all ages. The charming annexe garden at No 17 has a superb hosta and fern display. No 28 is a well established traditional garden reflecting the charm typical of the era. Mature trees, shrubs, mixed borders and woodland garden creating an oasis of calm just off the bustling Broadway.

GROUP OPENING

RAILWAY COTTAGES, N22
Dorset Road, Alexandra Palace N22 7SL. *Tube: Wood Green, 10 mins walk. Overground: Alexandra Palace, 3 mins. Buses W3, 184. 3 mins. Free parking in local streets on Suns.* Sun 3 July (2-5.30). Combined adm £4, chd free. Home-made teas at 2 Dorset Rd.

2 DORSET ROAD
Jane Stevens
Visits also by arrangement July & Aug for groups 4+
janestevens_london@yahoo.co.uk

4 DORSET ROAD
Mark Longworth

14 DORSET ROAD
Cathy Brogan

22 DORSET ROAD
Mike & Noreen Ainger

24A DORSET ROAD
Eddie & Jane Wessman

A row of historical railway cottages, tucked away from the bustle of Wood Green nr Alexandra Palace, takes the visitor back in time. No. 4 is a pretty secluded woodland garden, (accessed through the rear of No. 2), sets off sculptor owner's figurative and abstract work among acers, sambucus nigra, species shrubs and old fruit trees. Within the pretty surroundings sits the owner's working studio. Three front gardens at Nos. 14, 22 and 24a, one nurtured by the grandson of the original railway worker occupant, show a variety of planting, incl aromatic shrubs, herbs, jasmine, flax, fig, fuchsia and vines. A modern raised bed vegetable garden is a new addition this yr. The tranquil country style garden at No. 2 Dorset Rd flanks 3 sides of the house. Hawthorn topiary (by the original owner) and clipped box hedges contrast with climbing roses, clematis, honeysuckle, abutilon and cottage plants. Trees incl mulberry, quince, fig, apple and a mature willow creating an opportunity for an interesting shady corner. There is an emphasis on scented flowers that attract bees and butterflies and the traditional medicinal plants found in cottage gardens. 2 Dorset Road featured in Amateur Gardening magazine.

60 RANELAGH ROAD, W5
Ealing W5 5RP. Mr Antony Watkins & Mr Christopher Hutchings. *South Ealing Tube - 10 mins; Ealing Broadway tube - 20 mins. Off Ealing Common - Uxbridge Rd. Entry to garden via Baillies Walk.* **Sun 17 July (2-5). Adm £4, chd free. Tea.**
Palms, bamboos and sub tropical planting throughout a 50ft S facing garden with a flow of bright flowers, such as salvias, tithonias, cleome, abutilons to name some. Walk around the sunken path and stop off in the seating areas.

NEW 172 RAVENSBOURNE AVENUE
Bromley BR2 0AY. John & Christine Parris. *Train: Shortlands & Ravensbourne. Parking in Ravensbourne Av & adj rds.* **Sun 17 July (1.30-5.30). Combined adm with 174 Ravensbourne Avenue £6, chd free. Home-made teas.**
Rectangular terraced garden with a specious feel. Steps leading down to the lawn are lined with pots of giant lilies. There is an exotic feel with fantastic fuchsias, tall cannas in between taller palms. The arresting focal point in the garden is the large pond with multi coloured gigantic carp. No surprises to know that Christine does the flowers, John does the fish!

Exuberant displays of Old English roses and vigorous climbers with unusual herbaceous perennials . . .

NEW 174 RAVENSBOURNE AVENUE, BR2
Bromley BR2 0AY. Carmel & Patricia Zammit. *Train Stations: Shortlands & Ravensbourne. Parking in Ravensbourne Ave & adjacent rds.* **Sun 17 July (1.30-5.30). Combined adm with 172 Ravensbourne Avenue £6, chd free. Home-made teas.**
This vibrantly planted garden sits on two levels. At the top is a raised patio with colourful pots and a Hosta Theatre. Steps lead down to the lower area packed with colour, shape and form. It is divided by a wooden pergola swathed in Clematis Polish Spirit and Rosa New Dawn creating dramatic height and colour. A shaded area beyond the pergola is a perfect spot to sit quietly. Water feature, delicious home-made teas.

NEW RICHARD HOUSE CHILDREN'S HOSPICE, E16
Richard House Drive, Beckton E16 3RG, www.richardhouse.org.uk. *DLR to Royal Albert, follow footpath, cross Royal Albert Way, 1st L Stansfeld Way 2nd L Richard House Drive. Car: postcode for SatNav not reliable, enter Richard House Drive.* **Sun 10 Apr (2-5). Adm £3, chd free. Tea in Hospice dining hall.**
A series of individual areas around the hospice designed for children, young people, their families and others' enjoyment. Drought tolerant area with silver leaved plants (Save the Water) transferred from Chelsea Flower Show in 2001. Also one of a few sensory gardens in East London incl grassy mounds (Telly Tubby). Bulbs in spring. Shrubs and a mature fig tree. Small interesting woodland walk. Level grounds, with wheelchair accessible woodland path and other ramps as necessary.

NEW 34 RIDDING LANE, UB6
Greenford UB6 0JY. Jane Milton. *11m from central London. 3 mins walk from Sudbury Hill tube Station on Piccadilly Line. N Circ A4060 to Hanger Lane then, A40 W, follow signs for A4127/Harrow/Sudbury/ Greenford, onto A4090 Whitton Ave E. 1st L.* **Evening opening Sat 4 June (6-8). Adm £6, chd free. Sun 5 June (2-5). Adm £4, chd free. Pimms (Sat eve), home-made teas (Sun).**
Small garden with well placed plants, creating clever focal points. Even on a wet Monday morning, the garden has colour and sparkle. Coloured leaved heucheras give virtually yr-round impact, a mini hedge grown from black bamboo, architectural plants, a dramatic arch and some superb edible gems incl a fruiting Kiwi plant. Resident shy hedgehog. Winner QVC Garden Inspirations. Wheelchair access to garden via side access path, 2 steps to undercover raised area at top.

The Inner and Middle Temple Gardens

ALLOTMENTS

THE ROSE GARDEN AT GOLF COURSE ALLOTMENTS, N11

Winton Avenue, London N11 2AR. GCAA Mr George Dunnion, www.gcaa.pwp.blueyonder.co.uk. *Tube: Bounds Green, 1km Buses: 102,184 299 to Sunshine Garden Centre Durnsford Rd.* **Sun 26 June (1-5.30). Adm £3.50, chd free. Home-made teas in main allotment chalet.**
Not just roses! Lots of rare and unusual plants in the huge exotic border. Odd veggies like Fat Baby Achocha,Yacon, and Cucamelons. Annuals and perennials rub shoulders with the roses. Specialist Alpine bed. Australasian border with plants the dinosaurs munched on. A Taverna, willow seat and rose covered arbour. Owners will share their extensive knowledge with visitors. As seen on Gardener's World.

ROYAL COLLEGE OF PHYSICIANS MEDICINAL GARDEN, NW1

11 St Andrews Place, London NW1 4LE. Royal College of Physicians of London, 020 7034 4901, henry.oakeley@rcplondon.ac.uk, www.rcplondon.ac.uk/museum-and-garden/garden. *Tubes: Great Portland St & Regent's Park. Garden is one block N of station exits, on Outer Circle opp SE corner of Regent's Park.* **Sun 5 June (10-4.30). Adm £4, chd free. Tea. Also open 70 Gloucester Crescent.**
One of four beautiful and unusual gardens in NW1 opening on Sunday June 5th as part of the NGS Festival weekend. 1100 different plants used in medicines around the world throughout history; plants named after physicians and plants which make modern medicines. All are labelled and arranged by continent except for the plants from the College's Pharmacopoeia of 1618. http://garden.rcplondon.ac.uk. Guided tours all day, explaining the uses of the plants, their histories and stories about them. Books about the plants in the medicinal garden will be on sale. Featured in Great Gardens of London by Victoria Summerley (photos by Hugo Rittson Thomas and Marianne Majerus). Wheelchair ramps at steps.

5 RUSSELL ROAD, N13

Bowes Park, Bowes Park N13 4RS. Angela Kreeger. *Close to N Circular Rd & Green Lanes. Tube: Bounds Green, 10 mins walk. Mainline: Bowes Park, 3 mins walk. Numerous bus routes. Off Whittington Rd.* **Sun 14 Aug (2-6). Adm £3, chd free. Home-made teas. Also open 94 Brownlow Road.**
A poem for the eyes. Billowing, overflowing, balanced by flat lawn.
Airy, dreamy planting in small woodland, a pebble garden marks the border. Not manicured. Simple, unfussy with a contemporary feel, calm, quiet and peaceful. Autumn is rusty, loose and soft. Golden in sunlight. Small bespoke greenhouse reminiscent of Dungeness and Hastings. Front garden vegetable bed. Garden extensively revised in 2015.

7 ST GEORGE'S ROAD, TW1

St Margarets, Twickenham TW1 1QS. Richard & Jenny Raworth, 020 8892 3713, jraworth@gmail.com, www.raworthgarden.com. *1½ m SW of Richmond. Off A316 between Twickenham Bridge & St Margarets r'about.* **Evening opening Sat 4, Sat 18 June (6-8). Adm £6, chd free. Visits also by arrangement May to July for groups 10+.**
Exuberant displays of Old English roses and vigorous climbers with unusual herbaceous perennials. Massed scented crambe cordifolia. Pond with bridge converted into child safe lush bog garden and waterfall. Large N facing luxuriant conservatory with rare plants and climbers. Pelargoniums a speciality. Sunken garden and knot garden. Pergola covered with climbing roses and clematis. Water feature and fernery. Clarinet Quartet. Featured in Great Gardens of London, Summerley/ Majerus.

87 ST JOHNS ROAD, E17

London E17 4JH. Andrew Bliss. *15 mins walk from W'stow tube/overground or 212/275 bus. Ring bell at petrol station. 10 mins walk from Wood St overground. Very close to N Circular.* **Sun 17, Sun 24 July (1-5). Adm £3.50, chd free. Home-made teas.**
My garden epitomises what can be achieved with imagination, design and colour consideration in a small typical terraced outdoor area. The reoccurring circular theme, whether horizontal or vertical maintains continuity and together with overplanting creates a most beautiful and relaxing space. Seeing is believing, come and enjoy it!!!! Featured in Amateur Gardening magazine and on RHS gardening podcast, The Joys and Challenges of Opening for the NGS.

20 ST MARY'S GROVE, N1

London N1 2NT. Mrs B Capel.
Canonbury, Islington. Highbury & Islington Tube & Overground. Buses: 4, 19, 30, 277 to St Paul's Rd. 271 to Canonbury Square. **Sun 17 Apr (2-6). Adm £3, chd free. Also open 4 Canonbury Place.**
Come and discover this delightful, small paved garden with sweet smelling spring flowers and shrubs - coronilla, tree peony, sarcococca, camellias, lilac. Don't miss the auricula theatre with a variety of little potted favourites. Teas available at 4 Canonbury Place.

ST MICHAEL'S CONVENT, TW10

56 Ham Common, Ham, Richmond TW10 7JH. Community of the Sisters of the Church. *2m S of Richmond. On Ham Common nr A307 between Richmond & Kingston or 65 bus, alight at Ham Gate Avenue.* **Sun 24 Apr (2-4). Adm £3, chd free. Tea.**
4 acre organic garden comprises walled vegetable garden, orchards, vine house, ancient mulberry tree, extensive borders, meditation and Bible gardens. Some gravel paths.

27 ST PETERS SQUARE, W6

London W6 9NW. Oliver Leigh Wood. *Tube to Stamford Brook exit station & turn S down Goldhawk Rd. At T-lights cont ahead into British Grove. Entrance to garden at 50 British Grove 100 yds on L.* **Sun 8 May (2-6.30). Adm £4, chd free. Home-made teas.**
This long, secret space, is a plantsman's eclectic semi tamed wilderness. Created over the last 9yrs it contains lots of camellias, magnolias and fruit trees. Much of the hard landscaping is from skips and the whole garden is full of other people's unconsidered trifles of fancy incl a folly and summer house.

57 ST QUINTIN AVENUE, W10

London W10 6NZ. Mr H Groffman, 020 8969 8292. *1m from Ladbroke Grove or White City tube. Buses: 7, 70, 220 all to North Pole Rd. Free parking on Sundays.* **Sun 17, Sun 31 July (2-6). Adm £3.50, chd free. Home-made teas. Visits also by arrangement July & Aug, refreshments available on request.**
30ft x 40ft walled garden; wide selection of plant material incl evergreen and deciduous shrubs for foliage effects. Patio area mainly furnished with bedding material, colour themed. Focal points throughout. Refurbished with new plantings and special features. Garden theme this year is 90th birthday and longest reigning status of H.M. The Queen. Also celebrating 30yrs of opening for NGS. Awarded 1st Prize Brighter Kensington and Chelsea Scheme (back garden) and Bronze Medal London Garden Society (window boxes).

5 ST REGIS CLOSE, N10

Alexandra Park Road, Muswell Hill, London N10 2DE. Ms S Bennett & Mr E Hyde, 020 8883 8540, suebearlh@yahoo.co.uk. *Tube: Bounds Green then 102 or 299 bus, or E. Finchley take 102. Alight St Andrews Church. 134 or 43 bus stop at end of Alexandra Pk Rd, follow arrows.* **Sun 1 May, Sun 19 June, Sun 17 July (2-6.30). Adm £3.50, chd free. Home-made teas. Visits also by arrangement Apr to Oct for groups 10+. Home-made teas/light refreshments.**
Cornucopia of sensual delight. Artist's garden famous for architectural features and delicious cakes. Baroque temple, pagodas, oriental raku tiled mirrored wall conceals plant nursery. American Gothic shed overlooks Liberace Terrace and stairway to heaven. Maureen Lipman's favourite garden, combines colour, humour and trompe l'oeil with wildlife friendly ponds, waterfalls, weeping willow and lawns. Imaginative container planting, abundant borders, creating an inspirational and re-energising experience. Open studio with ceramics and prints. Home grown plants. Featured in Garden News and Woman's Weekly gardening section and on ITV's Britains Best Back Gardens. Wheelchair access to all parts of garden unless waterlogged.

SOUTH LONDON BOTANICAL INSTITUTE, SE24

323 Norwood Road, London SE24 9AQ. South London Botanical Institute, www.slbi.org.uk. *Mainline stn: Tulse Hill. Buses: 68, 196, 322 & 468 stop at junction of Norwood & Romola Rds.* **Sun 17 Apr (2-5). Adm £3, chd free. Home-made teas.**
Donation to South London Botanical Institute.
London's smallest botanical garden, densely planted with 500 labeled species grown in a formal layout of themed borders. Wildflowers flourish beside medicinal herbs. Carnivorous, scented, native and woodland plants are featured, growing among rare trees and shrubs. Spring highlights incl our new moss trail, unusual bulbs and flowering trees. The fascinating SLBI building is also open. Unusual plants for sale. Featured in Country Living - Country in the City.

Artist's garden famous for architectural features and delicious cakes . . .

41 SOUTHBROOK ROAD, SE12

Lee, London SE12 8LJ. Barbara & Marek Polanski, 020 8333 2176, polanski101@yahoo.co.uk. *Situated at Southbrook Rd off S Circular, off Burnt Ash Rd. Train: Lee & Hither Green, both 10 mins walk. Bus: P273, 202.* **Sat 11, Sun 12 June (2-5.30). Adm £3.50, chd free. Home-made teas. Visits also by arrangement May to Aug (2-5.30).**
Developed over 14yrs, this large garden has a formal layout, with wide mixed herbaceous borders full of colour and interest, surrounded by mature trees, framing sunny lawns, a central box parterre and an Indian pergola. Ancient pear trees festooned in June with clouds of white Kiftsgate and Rambling Rector roses. Discover fishes and damselflies in 2 lily ponds. Many places to sit and relax. Enjoy refreshments in a small classical garden building with interior wall paintings, almost hidden by roses climbing way up into the trees, the fountains and the fishes and damselflies, and the Indian Gazebo in the box parterre. Featured on Show me your Garden. Articles in Garden News, Bises and Garden Answers. Side access available for standard wheelchairs.

NEW **44 SOUTHWOOD LANE, N6**

London N6 5EB. Stuart Bull & Sue Vinson, 020 8340 1097, Stuart.cholm1@gmail.com. *Tube: Highgate, then 6 mins walk up Southwood Lane. 4 mins walk from Highgate Village. Buses: 143, 210, 214, 271.* **Sat 13, Sat 20 Feb. Adm £4. Home-made teas.**
Limited stair access, hence visits to this garden are by appointment only. Please call or email prior to visiting. A rare and unusual Hellebore treat in a narrow town garden, behind a terraced Georgian house. Large well shaped flowers in a wide range of colours, standards, doubles, anemone, picotees, bicolours, all originally displayed. The earliest harbingers that spring will follow winter. Free sheet of breeding tips. Featured in Ham & High.

SOUTHWOOD LODGE, N6

33 Kingsley Place, Highgate N6 5EA. Mr & Mrs C Whittington, 020 8348 2785, suewhittington@hotmail.co.uk. *Tube: Highgate then 6 mins walk up Southwood Lane. 4 min walk from Highgate Village along Southwood Lane. Buses: 143, 210, 214, 271.* **Sun 24 Apr (2-5.30). Sun 12 June (2-5.30). Also open 7 The Grove. Adm £4, chd free. Home-made teas. Visits also by arrangement Apr to July, lunches (for 10+) or teas (any number) by request.**
Plantsman's garden hidden behind C18 house (not open), laid out last century on steeply sloping site. Ponds, waterfall, frogs, toads, newts. Many topiary shapes formed from self sown yew trees. New sculpture carved from three trunks of a massive conifer which became unstable in a storm. Working greenhouse, good for tea on rainy days! Many unusual plants inc rare pelargoniums propagated for sale. Garden featured in First Ladies of Gardening by Heidi Howcroft and Marianne Majerus. Toffee hunt for children.

GROUP OPENING

SPITALFIELDS GARDENS, E1

London E1 6QH. *10 mins walk from Aldgate E Tube & 5 mins walk from Liverpool St stn. Overground: Shoreditch High St - 3 mins walk.* **Sat**

11 June (10-4). Combined adm £15, chd free. Home-made teas at Town House, 5 Fournier St.

34 ELDER STREET

7 FOURNIER STREET
John Nicolson

20 FOURNIER STREET
Ms Charlie de Wet

29 FOURNIER STREET
Juliette Larthe

31 FOURNIER STREET
Rodney Archer

THE FUTURE LABORATORY
26 Elder Street

34 HANBURY STREET
Mr Philip Vracas

21 PRINCELET STREET
Marianne & Nicholas Morse

NEW **SOCIETY FOR THE PROTECTION OF ANCIENT BUILDINGS**
37 Spital Square. Alison McClary

21 WILKES STREET
Rupert Wheeler

Ten hidden treasures behind some of the finest merchants and weavers houses in Spitalfields. Opening its courtyard for the first time is the Society for the Protection of Ancient Buildings (SPAB). The other nearby gardens incl two in Elder Street, one in Wilkes Street, one in Princelet Street, one in Hanbury Street and four in Fournier Street. These gardens give the visitor an insight into the variety of ways people have adapted different spaces to complement the houses. Featured in Country Life.

NEW **25 SPRINGFIELD AVENUE, N10**

London N10 3SU. Nigel Rag & Heather Hampson. *From main r'about at Muswell Hill (bus waiting zone) take steep rd towards Crouch End (named Muswell Hill). Springfield Av 1st L off hill.* **Sun 12 June (2-5.30). Adm £3.50, chd free. Home-made teas.**
We relandscaped our sloping town garden in 2013, transforming it's plain incline to an area of 5 individual terraces. Each layer has a distinctive feel, mixing an aura of spirituality with a country atmosphere. The mature trees of Alexander Palace's The Grove lend the garden a spectacular backdrop and together with water

features, pot and chimney planting, summerhouse and decking, make it unique.

2 SPRINGHURST CLOSE, CR0

Shirley Church Road, Croydon CR0 5AT. Ben & Peckham Carroll. *2m S of Croydon. Off A2022 from Selsdon. Off A232 from Croydon. Close opp The Addington Golf Club. Tramline 3 to Addington Village. East Croydon Station.* **Sun 19 June (2-5.30). Adm £3.50, chd free. Home-made teas.**
A garden of surprises which invites you to explore terrace beds of specimen grasses, topiary, perennials and an elegant water feature surrounded by a collection of hostas. Planting is in a soft colour palette designed to attract bees and wildlife with a new collection of black plants. Vegetable garden, bug hotel, fernery, woodland hydrangea walk add interest and variety to 1/2 acre woodland garden. All cakes home-made. Extensive plant sale. Mainly level with grass paths but a few steps.

96 STATION ROAD, EN5

New Barnet, London EN5 1QE. Graham Wright, 07984 476807. *12 mins walk from High Barnet Tube (Northern Line) or 10 mins walk from New Barnet Railway Station. Bus routes 107 & 384. No parking restrictions.* **Sun 5 June (2-6). Adm £3.50, chd free. Home-made teas.**
A hidden exotic garden full of drama and surprises. The garden began life back in 1999. It was an unused space covered in a thick blanket of ivy. Once the dreaded ivy had been removed the owner started the hard landscaping, although during the early days he had no idea which plants to keep. 10yrs ago a fellow gardener set him on the road to

creating an exotic garden, inspired by several visits to the Palm House at Kew. You will find exotic plants from all over the world within the garden, as well as a tropical tree house and tea house. A wooden foot bridge over a pond, home to giant koi carp, leads you through a glade of tree ferns, one of which is possibly the tallest to be found in a domestic London garden. Glass conservatory packed with yet more plants. Probably the tallest tree ferns in a domestic garden in London.

STOKES HOUSE, TW10
Ham Street, Ham, Richmond TW10 7HR. Peter & Rachel Lipscomb, 020 8940 2403, rlipscomb@virginmedia.com. *2m S of Richmond off A307. ¼ m from A307. Trains & tube to Richmond & train to Kingston which link with 65 bus to Ham Common.* Sun 5 June (2-5). Adm £4, chd free. Home-made teas. **Visits also by arrangement. Garden groups and clubs most welcome.**
Originally an orchard, this ½ acre walled country garden is abundant with roses, clematis and perennials. There are mature trees incl ancient mulberries and wisteria. The yew hedging, pergola and box hedges allow for different planting schemes throughout the yr. Supervised children are welcome to play on the slide and swing. Georgian house, herbaceous borders, brick garden, wild garden, large compost area and interesting trees. Many plants for sale. Wheelchair access via double doors from street with 2 wide steps. Unfortunately no access for larger motorised chairs.

STONEY HILL HOUSE, SE26
Rock Hill, London SE26 6SW. Cinzia & Adam Greaves. *Off Sydenham Hill. Train: Sydenham, Gipsy Hill or Sydenham Hill (closest) stations. Buses: To Crystal Palace, 202 or 363 along Sydenham Hill. House at end of cul-de-sac on L coming from Sydenham Hill.* Sun 22 May (2-6). Adm £4, chd free. All cakes home-made and delicious! Generous mugs of tea with free refills available.
Garden and woodland of approx 1 acre providing a secluded secret green oasis in the city. Paths meander through mature rhododendron, oak, yew and holly trees, offset by pieces of

contemporary sculpture. The garden is on a slope and a number of viewpoints set at different heights provide varied perspectives. The planting in the top part of the garden is fluid and flows seamlessly into the woodland. We hope to have a living sculpture carved into an oak tree damaged in high winds. There will also be a saxophone quartet playing throughout the afternoon. Shallow, wide steps at entrance to garden with grass slope alongside. Wheelchair access possible if these can be negotiated.

93 TANFIELD AVENUE, NW2
Dudden Hill, London NW2 7SB. Mr James Duncan Mattoon, 020 8830 7410. *Dudden Hill - Neasden. Nearest station: Neasden - Jubilee line then 10 mins walk; or various bus routes to Neasden Parade or Tanfield Av.* Sun 31 July (2-6). Adm £4, chd free. Home-made teas. **Visits also by arrangement May to Sept, groups 20 max.**
Professional plantsman's petite hillside paradise! Arid/tropical deck with panoramic views of Wembley and Harrow, descends through Mediterranean screes and warm sunny slopes, to subtropical oasis packed with many rare and exotic plants e.g. Hedychium, Plumbago, Punica, Tetrapanax. To rear, jungle shade terrace and secret summer house offer cool respite on sunny days. Stunning panoramic views. Previous garden was Tropical Kensal Rise (Doyle Gardens) featured on BBC2 Open Gardens and in Sunday Telegraph. Jim Carter and Imelda Staunton say 'A beautiful and surprising garden; an absolute delight that will inspire any gardener!'. Featured in Garden News Magazine.

14 TETHERDOWN, N10
London N10 1NB. Laura Washburn Hutton & Ian Pollock. *Opp entrance to Fortismere Secondary school.* Sun 3 July (2-6). Adm £3.50, chd free. Home-made teas in Tea Room.
The theme is based on circles using a variety of materials. Ornamental plants accompany espaliered fruit trees, soft fruit, step overs and masses of herbs. One of the owners is a food writer, so the edible aspect of the garden is important. The scheme is meant to attract bees and butterflies, be scented and have movement. An example of what can

be done in a small space with eastern exposure.

NEW ▶ 57 TONBRIDGE HOUSE, WC1H
Tonbridge Street, London WC1H 9PG. Sue Heiser. *S of Euston Road. Tube: King's Cross Stn. St Pancras Stn & Russell Sq. Behind Camden Town Hall off Judd St. Turn into Bidborough St which becomes Tonbridge St. Side entrance to garden.* Sun 10 July (2-6). Adm £3.50, chd free. Home-made teas. Also open The Cottage.
Unexpected oasis off the Euston Road, overlooked on all sides by tall buildings. Mixed informal planting, with seating, rockery, pergola and shady areas. Mature magnolia, Canadian maple, holly and some long established shrubs and perennials incl ferns, hostas and heuchera. Small vegetable beds and herbs. Evolved over 30yrs on a low budget with plenty of help from friends. Wheelchair access from street and throughout garden.

> A beautiful and surprising garden; an absolute delight that will inspire any gardener . . .

TREETOPS, HA6
Sandy Lane, Northwood HA6 3ES. Mrs Carole Kitchner. *Opp Northwood HQ. Tube: Northwood, 10 mins walk. Bus 8 stops at bottom of lane. Parking in lane.* Sun 24 July (2-6). Adm £4, chd free. Home-made teas.
Nestling in quiet lane in Northwood conservation area, sloping garden with long terrace and large pots. Rose covered pergola, water feature, small lawn, wide variety unusual shrubs incl magnolia grandiflora, paulownias, trochodendron. Peaking in high summer, heleniums, agapanthus, lobelias, eryngiums, crocosmias present a vibrant vision - well worth a visit! Mentioned in an article by Robin Lane Fox in The Financial Times.

TRINITY HOSPICE, SW4

30 Clapham Common North Side, London SW4 0RN. Trinity Hospice, www.trinityhospice.org.uk. *Tube: Clapham Common. Buses: 35, 37, 345,137 stop outside.* Sun 10 Apr, Sun 22 May, Sun 4 Sept (11-5). Adm £2.50, chd free. Light refreshments. Picnics welcome. Trinity's beautiful, award winning gardens play an important therapeutic role in the life and function of Trinity Hospice. Over the years, many people have enjoyed our gardens and today they continue to be enjoyed by patients, families and visitors alike. Set over nearly 2 acres, they offer space for quiet contemplation, family fun and make a great backdrop for events. Ramps and pathways.

♿ 🏠 ☕

TRUMPETERS HOUSE & SARAH'S GARDEN, TW9

Richmond TW9 1PD. Baron & Baroness Van Dedem. *Richmond riverside. 5 mins walk from Lordship Station via Richmond Green in Trumpeter's Yard. Parking on Richmond Green & Old Deer Park car park only.* Sun 12 June (2-5). Adm £5, chd free. Home-made teas. The 2 acre garden is on the original site of Richmond Palace. Long lawns stretch from the house to banks of the River Thames. There are clipped yews, a box parterre and many unusual shrubs and trees, a rose garden and oval pond with carp. The ancient Tudor walls are covered with roses and climbers. Discover Sarah's secret garden behind the high walls. Wheelchair access on grass and gravel.

☕

45 UNDERHILL ROAD, SE22

London SE22 0QZ. Nicola Bees. *Approx 200 metres from Lordship Lane. Train: Forest Hill 20 mins walk. Bus: Routes P13, P4, 63, 176, 185, 197, 363. Car: Off A205 nr junction with Lordship Lane. Free parking.* Sun 8 May (2-6). Combined adm with 86 Underhill Road £6, chd free. Home-made teas. An intermittently loved and neglected Victorian garden brought back to its former glory. A majestic cedar tree stands sentry over the garden. The eclectic and informal planting incl a few unusual plants and the wildlife pond is a haven for frogs and newts. A corner summer house provides a tranquil retreat at the bottom of the

garden. Teas served in our conservatory tea room come rain or shine. Three deep steps into the garden. Gravel paths.

 ☕

86 UNDERHILL ROAD, SE22

East Dulwich SE22 0QU. Claire & Rob Goldie. *Between Langton Rise & Melford Rd. Stn: Forest Hill. Buses: P13, 363, 63, 176, 185 & P4.* Sun 8 May (2-6). Combined adm with 45 Underhill Road £6, chd free. Home-made teas. A generous family space bursting with colour. Mixed beds of medicinal, fragrant and edible planting. Secluded seating set among water barrels and bamboo. See if you can spot our friendly newts and then enjoy tea and cake in the spacious garden room built on tyres.

 ☕

> A majestic cedar tree stands sentry over the garden . . .

7 UPPER PHILLIMORE GARDENS, W8

Kensington, London W8 7HF. Mr & Mrs B Ritchie. *From Kensington High St turn into Phillimore Gdns or Campden Hill Rd; entrance at rear in Duchess of Bedford Walk.* Sun 24 Apr (2.30-6.30). Adm £3.50, chd free. Light refreshments. Well planned mature garden on different levels creating areas of varied character and mood. Pergola with Italian fountain and fishpond, lawn with border plants leading to the sunken garden with rockery. Also groundcover, mature trees (making a secluded haven in central London), flowering shrubs and a fine display of spring bulbs. Plenty of seating to relax and enjoy a cup of tea!

🏠 ♿ ☕

91 VICAR'S MOOR LANE, N21

Winchmore Hill N21 1BL. Mr David & Dr Malkanthie Anthonisz. *Tube: Southgate then W9 to Winchmore Hill*

Green then short walk. *Train: Winchmore Hill then short walk via Wades Hill.* Sun 5 June (2-6). Adm £3.50, chd free. Home-made teas. Established characterful garden. Paths wind through species acers, clematis, climbers shrubs, perennials planted for colour and form. Waterfall and stream flows under raised pergola, viewing platform to home bred koi carp pond. Exotic elements, and art abound in this much loved evolving paradise. Summerhouse, terraces, sunken garden provide tranquil, comfortable places to sit and contemplate. Featured on Sky TV.

☕

NEW ► 50 VICEROY ROAD, SW8

London SW8 2EZ. Mr & Mrs Peter Marston. *Stockwell tube 9 mins. Bus: 2, 77, 87, 88, 196.* Sun 8 May (2-6). Adm £3, chd free. Tea. Evening opening Wed 27 July (5.30-8). Adm £5.50, chd free. Wine. A Stockwell gem - small intensely planted walled garden around pretty early C19 corner house. Principal garden massed with tender plants beneath a canopy of trees - a palm, cordylines, clipped arbutus, mature tree fern at the centre of a tufa mound with serpentine box hedges fronting beds of topiary, curious climbers and interesting perennials. Terrace is lined with pots of bulbs during spring.

☕

208 WALM LANE, THE GARDEN FLAT, NW2

London NW2 3BP. Miranda & Chris Mason, www.thegardennw2.co.uk. *Tube: Kilburn. Garden at junction of Exeter Rd & Walm Lane. Buses: 16, 32, 189, 226, 245, 260, 266, 316 to Cricklewood Broadway, then consult A-Z.* Sun 29 May, Sun 26 June (2-6). Adm £3.50, chd free. Home-made teas. Tranquil oasis of green. Meandering lawn with island beds, curved and deeply planted borders of perennials, scented roses and flowering shrubs. An ornamental fishpond with fountain. Shaded mini woodland area of tall trees underplanted with rhododendrons, ferns, hostas and lily of the valley with winding path from oriental inspired summerhouse to secluded circular seating area. Live music and raffle prizes. Featured as Garden of the Week in Garden News.

♿ 🏠 ☕

12 WARNER ROAD, N8

London N8 7HD. Linnette Ralph. *Nr Alexandra Palace, between Crouch End & Muswell Hill. Turning off Priory Rd. Tube to Finsbury Park then W3 bus to Hornsey Fire Station. Buses W7 & 144.* Sun 12 June (2-6). Adm £3.50, chd free. Home-made teas.
A garden divided into three distinct areas: secluded courtyard area, circular lawn surrounded by mixed planting and a kitchen garden with raised beds, potting shed and a second seating area. Established climbers clothe the tall fences promoting a feeling of seclusion and peace throughout the garden. Featured in House Beautiful to show what can be done with a typical narrow, terraced house garden.

THE WATERGARDENS, KT2

Warren Road, Kingston-upon-Thames KT2 7LF. The Residents' Association. *1m E of Kingston. From Kingston take A308 (Kingston Hill) towards London; after approx ¹/₂ m turn R into Warren Rd.* Sun 8 May, Sun 9 Oct (2-4.30). Adm £5, chd free.
Japanese landscaped garden originally part of Coombe Wood Nursery, planted by the Veitch family in the 1860s. Approx 9 acres with ponds, streams and waterfalls. Many rare trees which, in spring and autumn, provide stunning colour. For the tree lover this is a must see garden. Gardens attractive to wildlife.

WEST LODGE PARK, EN4

Cockfosters Road, Hadley Wood EN4 0PY. Beales Hotels, 020 8216 3904, headoffice@bealeshotels.co.uk, www.bealeshotels.co.uk/westlodg epark/gardens/. *2m S of Potters Bar. On A111. J24 from M25 signed Cockfosters.* Sun 15 May (2-5); Sun 23 Oct (1-4). Adm £5, chd free. Full range of refreshments available. Visits also by arrangement.
Open for the NGS for over 25yrs, the 35 acre Beale Arboretum consists of over 800 varieties of trees and shrubs, incl National Collection of Hornbeam cultivars (Carpinus betulus) and 2 planned collections (Taxodium and Catalpa). Network of paths through good selection of conifers, oaks, maples and mountain ash - all specimens labelled. Beehives and 2 ponds. Stunning collection within the M25. Guided tours

available. Breakfasts, morning coffee/biscuits, restaurant lunches, light lunches, dinner all served in the hotel. Please see website.

NPC

NEW▶ 29 WEST PARK ROAD, TW9

Kew Gardens, Richmond TW9 4DA. Silvia & Francesca Doria. *Exit Kew Gardens; 4th house (end of terrace) on L on West Park Rd. Garden entrance to R of house.* Sun 19 June (2-6). Combined adm with 31 West Park Road £5, chd free.
Landscaped garden in the Edwardian style, with rose arches and traditional Portland stone and brick paving floor layout. The garden was designed and implemented by Roger Lang of Mike Bayon Garden Design in September 2014.

31 WEST PARK ROAD, TW9

Kew, Richmond TW9 4DA. Anna Anderson. *Within Walking distance of Kew Gardens station.* Sun 19 June (2-6). Combined adm with 29 West Park Road £5, chd free.
Modern botanical garden with an oriental twist. Emphasis on foliage and an eclectic mix of plants, reflecting pool and rotating willow screens which provide varying views or privacy. Dry bed, shady beds, mature trees and a private paved dining area with dappled light and shade.

12 WESTERN ROAD, E13

Plaistow E13 9JF. Elaine Fieldhouse. *Stn: Upton Park, 3mins walk. Buses: 58, 104, 330, 376.* Sat 4 June (12-5). Adm £3.50, chd free. Home-made teas.
Urban oasis, 85ft garden designed and planted by owners. Relying heavily on evergreen, ferns, foliage and herbaceous planting. Rear of garden leads directly onto a 110ft allotment - part allotment, part extension of the garden - featuring topiary, medlar tree, mulberry tree, 2 ponds, small fruit trees, raised beds and small iris collection.

12 Warner Road

© Nicola Stocken

Cadogan Place South Garden

© Rhowena MaccCuish

WHITE COTTAGE, BR5
Crockenhill Road, Kevington
BR5 4ER. John Fuller & Alida
Burdett, 01689 875134,
alidaburdett@aol.com. *Kevingtom.*
Crockenhill Rd is B258. Garden at
junction with Waldens Rd. Sun 5
June (1-5). Adm £5, chd free. Tea.
Visits also by arrangement May to
July.
Traditional box, clipped hedging and
reclaimed materials give structure to
this informal garden surrounding a
Victorian gardener's cottage. Colour
themed beds contain grasses,
perennials, shrubs and fruit trees.
There is a small but productive
vegetable garden, a pond, rare
chickens and bees. Wildlife
promotion is a priority. Plenty of
places to sit and enjoy the garden.
Produce for sale. Majority of garden
accessible by wheelchair.

WHITGIFT SCHOOL, CR2
Haling Park, South Croydon
CR2 6YT. Sophie Tatzkow,
www.whitgift.co.uk. *Train: South*
Croydon then 5 mins walk. Buses:
119, 197, 312, 466. School entrance
on Nottingham Rd. Sun 22 May
(1-5). Adm £3.50, chd free. Tea.
Whitgift Gardens are a series of
fascinating, well maintained gardens
in a number of original styles within
the extensive grounds of Whitgift, all
of which help to provide a stimulating
environment for students. Head
Gardener, Sophie Tatzkow, is on a
mission to make sure there isn't
another school garden as excellent as
this to be found in the UK. Wildlife
and birds (wallabies, flamingos,
peacocks in an enclosed area) are a
feature of the School grounds. Most
garden areas accessible by
wheelchair. The Andrew Quadrangle
can be accessed, but non accessible
steps within the garden.

74 WILLIFIELD WAY, NW11
London NW11 6YJ. David
Weinberg, 020 8201 9052,
davidwayne@hotmail.co.uk. *From*
Golders Green Tube, H2 bus or
82,102,460 to Temple Fortune. Walk
up Hampstead Way, turn L at The
Orchard, walk through to Willifield
Way. Sun 19 June (1.30-6). Adm
£3.50, chd free. Cream teas.

A very peaceful English country
garden packed with herbaceous
borders and perfumed rose beds with
wonderful containers to the patio area
with a beautiful handmade lead
fountain. A haven of tranquillity to be
enjoyed. A large variety of herbacious
plants together with highly perfumed
roses to the side and back flower
beds together with a central white
rose flower bed edged with box
hedging with the side flower beds
packed with heracious plants to give
an old English cottage garden style.
Wheelchair access to patio area only.

86 WILLIFIELD WAY, NW11
Hampstead Garden Suburb
NW11 6YJ. Diane Berger, 020 8455
0455, dianeberger@hotmail.co.uk.
1m N of Golders Green. Tube:
Golders Green, then H2 bus to
Willifield Way. Buses 82, 102, 460 to
Temple Fortune, walk along
Hampstead Way, turn L at The
Orchard. Sun 24 July (2-6). Adm
£3.50, chd free. Home-made teas.
Also open 4 Asmuns Hill. Visits
also by arrangement June to Sept
for groups 10+.
Beautiful, cottage garden with yr
round interest set behind listed Arts
and Crafts cottage. Wildlife pond,
gazebo, pergola, private decked area,
spectacular colour themed
herbaceous borders all encased by
host of mature trees, shrubs and
perennials. A plant enthusiasts
delight. Visited by HRH Prince
Edward Earl of Wessex. Winner of the
London Garden Society Large Back
Garden Trophy. Wheelchair access on
front lawn. Back garden has very
narrow and uneven pathways.

61 WOLSEY ROAD, KT8
East Molesey KT8 9EW. Jan & Ken
Heath. *Short walk from Hampton*
Court station. Sun 19 June (2-6).
Combined adm with 6 Manor
Road £5, chd free. Home-made
teas. Evening opening Wed 22
June (7.30-10.30). Adm £5, chd
free. Wine.
Romantic, secluded and peaceful
garden of two halves designed and
maintained by the owners. Part is
shaded by two large copper beech
trees with woodland planting. The
second reached through a beech
arch has cottage garden planting,
pond and wooden obelisks covered
with roses and sweet peas. Beautiful
octagonal gazebo overlooks pond

plus a new oak framed summerhouse designed and built by the owners. Most of garden wheelchair accessible.

27 WOOD VALE, N10
Muswell Hill N10 3DJ. Mr & Mrs A W Dallman. *Muswell Hill 1m. A1 to Woodman PH; signed Muswell Hill. From Highgate tube, take Muswell Hill Rd, sharp R into Wood Lane leading to Wood Vale.* **Evening opening Thur 5 May, Thur 7 July (6-9). Adm £5, chd free. Wine.**
One of London's most popular gardens. Winner of London Gardens Society - Best Large Garden. An unexpected adventure unfolds through herbaceous borders, winding paths with water features, to lawn with orchard, vegetable garden and greenhouses. This year, we are opening on two evenings, so come along and join us for a glass of wine or soft drink in our ³⁄₄ acre garden.

33 WOOD VALE, N10
Highgate N10 3DJ. Mona Abboud, 020 8883 4955, monaabboud@hotmail.com, www.monasgarden.co.uk. *Tube: Highgate, 10 mins walk. Buses: W3, W7 to top of Park Rd.* **Sun 15 May, Sun 14 Aug (2-5.30). Adm £3, chd free. Soft drinks and biscuits. Visits also by arrangement May to Aug, groups 20 max.**
The garden opens with a view of a Sedum roof atop a greenhouse. Emphasis is on texture, shapes, contrasting foliage, colour of unusual Mediterranean, Australasian and exotic plants. Formal planting surrounds a centrepiece fountain followed by a meandering path flanked by shrubs, trees and two 30m mixed borders of perennials and grasses. The garden widens onto raised beds, small rockery, bog area and Corokia hedge. Winner - Best Back Garden, London Garden Society. Featured in Hampstead and Highgate Express.

7 WOODBINES AVENUE, KT1
Kingston-upon-Thames KT1 2AZ. Mr Tony Sharples & Mr Paul Cuthbert. *Take K2, K3, 71 or 281 bus. From Surbiton, bus stop outside Waitrose & exit bus Kingston University Stop. From Kingston, walk or get the bus from Eden Street (opp Heals).* **Evening opening Sat 25**

June (6.30-9). Adm £5.50, chd free. Wine.
We have created a winding path through our 70ft garden with trees, evergreen structure, perennial flowers and grasses. We have used deep borders to create depth, variety, texture and interest around the garden. We like to create a garden party so feel welcome to stay as long as you like.

Modern botanical garden with an oriental twist . . .

21 WOODLAND RISE, N10
London N10 3UP. Ian Potts & Jill Pack, 020 8442 1151, jill.pack@gmail.com. *Close to Highgate Wood. Tube: Highgate,10-15 mins walk. Bus 43 or 134 to Cranley Gardens stop. Off Muswell Hill Rd.* **Sun 1 May (2-6). Adm £3.50, chd free. Home-made teas. Also open 5 St Regis Close. Visits also by arrangement Apr to Aug.**
A verdant N facing terraced garden; the garden is particularly spectacular in spring with a mature tree peony, wisteria brachybotrys Shiro kapitan, ceanothus and paeonia mlokosewitschii, as well as the blossom of a malus transitoria tree. Featured in the Ham & High.

NEW ▶ 10 WOODSIDE AVENUE, N6
London N6 4SS. Sheila & Anthony Rabin. *¹⁄₂ m from East Finchley underground station.* **Sun 7 Aug (2-6). Adm £3.50, chd free. Home-made teas.**
An attractive densely planted suburban garden created from scratch 3yrs ago. Large herbaceous perennial borders give colour from April to October. A good contrast with shade loving area and terraced patio with alpine planting. Wheelchair access.

1 YORK CLOSE, W7
Hanwell W7 3JB. Tony Hulme & Eddy Fergusson. *By rd only, entrance to York Close via Church Rd. Nearest station Hanwell mainline. Buses E3, 195, 207.* **Evening opening Sat 28 May (5-8). Adm £4.50, chd free. Wine. Sun 29 May (2-5). Adm £3, chd free.**
Tiny quirky, prize winning garden extensively planted with eclectic mix incl hosta collection, many unusual and tropical plants. Plantaholics paradise. Many surprises in this unique and very personal garden. Featured in Gardening Which!

NEW ▶ 38 YORK ROAD, W5
Ealing W5 4SG. Nick & Elena Gough. *Northfields & South Ealing Tube - 5 mins. Buses: E3, 65. 5 mins. Free parking in local streets. Off Northfield Av & South Ealing Rd.* **Sun 24 July (2-6). Adm £4, chd free. Tea.**
A hidden oasis full of surprises and built on several different levels. This walled corner garden was restored in under 10 months by its present owners, having been acquired in 2014. There are a number of beautiful and diverse areas within it, incl a cottage garden border, a woodland dell path, circular sun terrace, large pond with waterfall and a sunken garden. Winner Best Improved and Best Large Garden, Ealing in Bloom Awards.

ZEN GARDEN, W3
55 Carbery Avenue, Acton, London W3 9AB. Three Wheels Shin Buddhist Temple, 020 8248 2542, threewheels@threewheels.co.uk, www.threewheels.co.uk. *Tube: Acton Town 5 mins walk, 200yds off A406.* **Sat 4, Sun 5, Sat 18, Sun 19 June (2-5). Adm £3, chd free. Home-made teas.**
Pure Japanese Zen garden (so no flowers) with 12 large and small rocks of various colours and textures set in islands of moss and surrounded by a sea of grey granite gravel raked in a stylised wave pattern. Garden surrounded by trees and bushes outside a cob wall. Oak framed wattle and daub shelter with Norfolk reed thatched roof. Japanese tea ceremony demonstration and talks by designer/creator of the garden. Buddha Room open to visitors.

NORFOLK

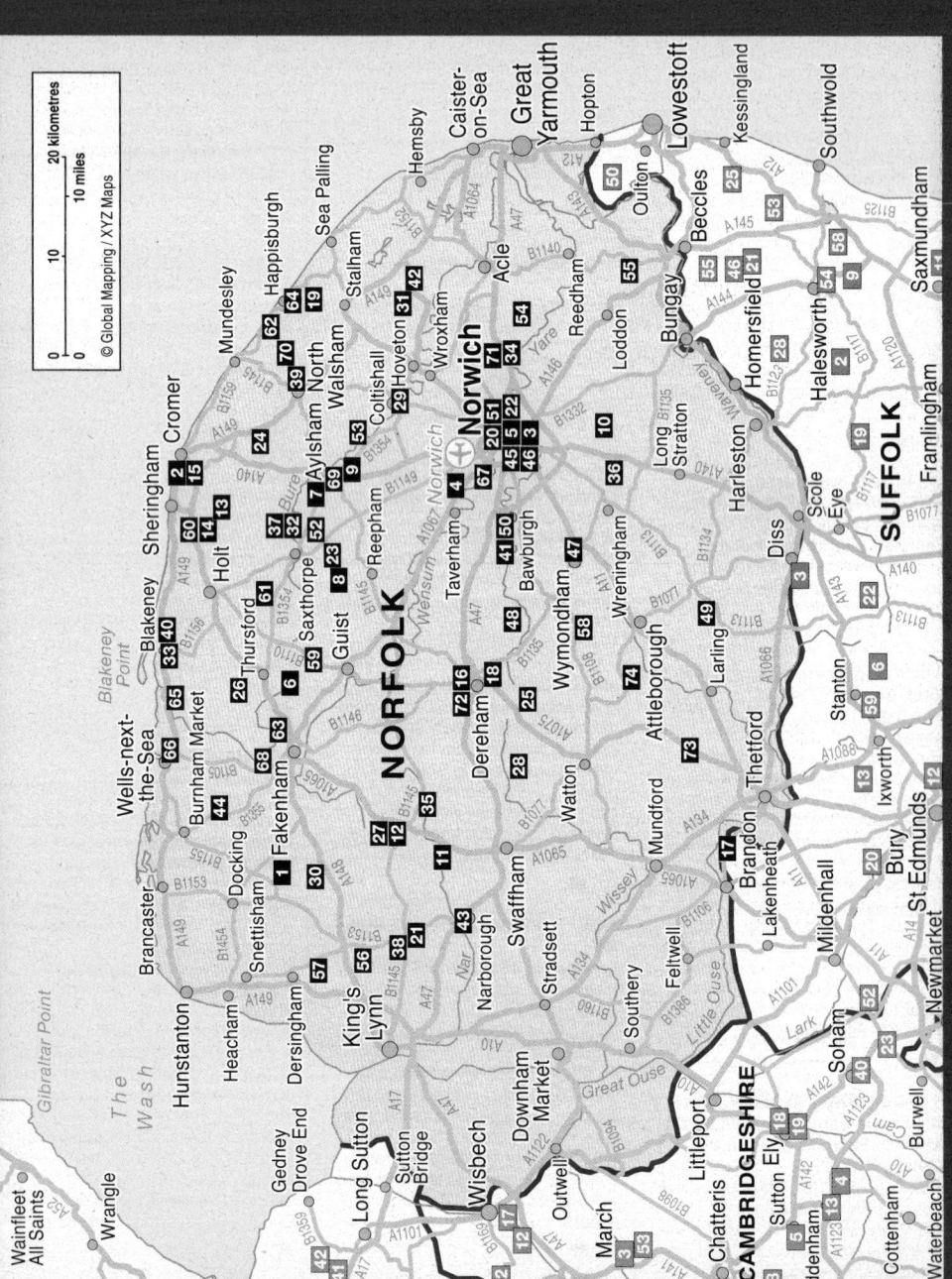

Norfolk

Norfolk is a large low-lying county, predominantly agricultural with a relatively small population.

Visitors come because they are attracted to the tranquillity of the countryside, the medieval churches, the coastal area and the large network of rivers and waterways of the Norfolk Broads.

Gardens vary in size from large historic parks and smaller manor houses, to cottages and courtyards, and are situated throughout the county. Some are old and traditional, whilst others are modern or naturalistic.

Norfolk NGS is honoured to have the support of Her Majesty the Queen at Sandringham, and is grateful to our many garden owners who include not only the descendants of our first Prime Minister, Robert Walpole at Houghton Hall and Mannington Hall, but also the Bishop of Norwich. We are also fortunate to have the beautiful gardens at East Ruston Old Vicarage, home to NGS Ambassador Alan Gray.

'Oh! Rare and beautiful Norfolk,' said the landscape painter John Sell Cotman. We think so too and feel sure you will also enjoy Norfolk's beautiful gardens.

Norfolk Volunteers

County Organisers
Fiona Black
01692 650247
fiona.black@ngs.org.uk

Julia Stafford Allen
01760 755334
julia.staffordallen@ngs.org.uk

County Treasurer
Neil Foster
01328 701288
neilfoster@lexhamestate.co.uk

Publicity
Graham Watts
01362 690065
grahamwatts@dsl.pipex.com

Booklet Co-ordinator
Julia Stafford Allen
(as above)

Assistant County Organisers
Isabel Cator
01603 270748
isabel@markcator.co.uk

Jennifer Dyer
01263 761811
jandrdyer@btinternet.com

Sue Guest
01362 858317
guest63@btinternet.com

Stephanie Powell
01328 730113
stephaniepowell@creake.com

Left: Lexham Hall

Opening Dates

All entries subject to change.
For latest information check www.ngs.org.uk

February

Snowdrop Festival

Saturday 20
29 Horstead House
Sunday 21
1 Bagthorpe Hall
Tuesday 23
7 Blickling Estate

March

Thursday 3
14 Chestnut Farm
Sunday 6
14 Chestnut Farm
55 Raveningham Hall

April

Sunday 3
17 Desert World Gardens
26 Hindringham Hall
Saturday 9
19 East Ruston Old Vicarage
Sunday 10
37 Mannington Hall
Sunday 24
14 Chestnut Farm
71 16 Witton Lane

May

Sunday 1
34 Lake House
54 Plovers Hill
73 Wretham Lodge
Monday 2
34 Lake House
54 Plovers Hill
70 Witton Hall
73 Wretham Lodge
Saturday 14
40 The Merchants House
Sunday 15
9 Bolwick Hall
28 Holme Hale Hall
Thursday 19
60 Sheringham Park
Sunday 22
31 How Hill Farm
35 Lexham Hall

48 The Old Rectory, Brandon Parva
Tuesday 24
61 Stody Lodge
Sunday 29
65 Warborough House
Monday 30
14 Chestnut Farm

June

Festival Weekend

Saturday 4
39 NEW Marshgate House
Sunday 5
21 Gayton Hall
32 NEW Itteringham Village Gardens
38 Manor Farmhouse, Gayton
39 NEW Marshgate House
Tuesday 7
13 Chaucer Barn
Wednesday 8
43 Narborough Hall
Thursday 9
60 Sheringham Park
Sunday 12
2 NEW Banville Barn
15 NEW Congham Farm,
25 High House Gardens
44 North Creake Gardens
72 Wood Hill
Wednesday 15
25 High House Gardens
Saturday 18
33 Kettle Hill
47 167 Norwich Road
49 NEW The Old Rectory, Banham
Sunday 19
46 NEW Norwich Gardens
47 167 Norwich Road
63 Thorpland Hall
68 West Barsham Hall
Thursday 23
37 Mannington Hall (Evening)
Saturday 25
3 The Bear Shop
4 9 Bellomonte Crescent
Sunday 26
3 The Bear Shop
28 Holme Hale Hall
64 Walcott House

66 Wells-Next-The-Sea Gardens

July

Sunday 3
17 Desert World Gardens
20 68 Elm Grove Lane
67 NEW 4 Wensum Crescent
Tuesday 5
41 4 Mill Road
50 The Old Smithy
Saturday 9
8 Blickling Lodge
Sunday 10
9 Bolwick Hall
Saturday 16
6 NEW Black Horse Cottage
Sunday 17
6 NEW Black Horse Cottage
Sunday 24
16 Dale Farm
69 West Lodge
Sunday 31
10 Brick Kiln House
11 NEW Castle Acre Gardens

August

Saturday 6
36 NEW The Long Barn
Sunday 7
45 North Lodge
56 Rectory Cottage
Wednesday 10
24 NEW Gunton Park
Sunday 14
20 68 Elm Grove Lane
22 NEW 38 Gorse Road
45 North Lodge
51 NEW 33 Orchard Close
59 Severals Grange
67 NEW 4 Wensum Crescent
Sunday 21
42 The Mowle
53 NEW Oxnead Hall
74 NEW Yeoman's Cottage
Saturday 27
62 Suil Na Mara
Sunday 28
62 Suil Na Mara

September

Sunday 4
5 Bishop's House

12 NEW Chapel Cottage
27 NEW 7 Holly Close
Sunday 11
25 High House Gardens
Wednesday 14
25 High House Gardens

October

Saturday 8
19 East Ruston Old Vicarage

Gardens open to the public

7 Blickling Estate
19 East Ruston Old Vicarage
26 Hindringham Hall
30 Houghton Hall Walled Garden
37 Mannington Hall
43 Narborough Hall
55 Raveningham Hall
57 Sandringham Gardens
59 Severals Grange
60 Sheringham Park
61 Stody Lodge

By arrangement only

18 Dunbheagan
23 The Grange, Heydon
58 Sea Mere

Also open by arrangement

5 Bishop's House
8 Blickling Lodge
10 Brick Kiln House
14 Chestnut Farm
16 Dale Farm
17 Desert World Gardens
21 Gayton Hall
28 Holme Hale Hall
34 Lake House
42 The Mowle
47 167 Norwich Road
54 Plovers Hill
56 Rectory Cottage
62 Suil Na Mara
66 Norfolk House, Wells-Next-The-Sea Gardens
68 West Barsham Hall
69 West Lodge
73 Wretham Lodge

The Gardens

1 BAGTHORPE HALL

Bagthorpe, Bircham PE31 6QY. Mr
& Mrs D Morton, 01485 578528,
dgmorton@hotmail.com. *3¹/₂ m N of
East Rudham, off A148. At King's
Lynn take A148 to Fakenham. At East
Rudham (approx 12m) turn L opp
The Crown, 3¹/₂ m into hamlet of
Bagthorpe. Farm buildings on L,
wood on R, white gates set back
from rd, at top of drive.* **Sun 21 Feb
(11-4). Adm £4, chd free. Home-
made teas. Home-made soups
made with vegetables from the
farm.**
Snowdrops carpeting woodland walk,
walled garden and main garden.
Some access for wheelchairs in the
garden, but not the woodland walk.

2 NEW BANVILLE BARN

Banville Lane, East Runton,
Cromer NR27 9RN. Mr & Mrs
Icarus Hines. *2m W of Cromer on
A149. In E Runton turn L opp Fishing
Boat PH & follow rd under 2 railway
bridges. Turn R at pond onto Top
Common. Rd bears L, garden is on
R.* **Sun 12 June (11-5). Combined
adm with Congham Farm £5, chd
free. Barbecue available 12 noon
to 3pm. Hot and cold drinks
available.**
South and west facing peaceful
garden of approx ¹/₃ acre. Developed
over 10 years from scratch with
unspoilt views over fields and
National Trust land. Features box and
yew topiary, herbaceous borders and
kitchen garden.

3 THE BEAR SHOP

Elm Hill, Norwich NR3 1HN. Robert
Stone. *Norwich City Centre. From St
Andrews, L to Princes St, then L to
Elm Hill. Garden at side of shop
through large wooden gate & along
alleyway.* **Sat 25, Sun 26 June (11-
4.30). Adm £3, chd free. Home-
made teas.**
Considered to be based on a design
by Gertrude Jekyll, a small terraced
garden behind a C15 house in the
historic Cathedral Quarter of Norwich.
Enjoy the tranquillity of the riverside.
Wheel chair access is limited to the
upper level of the garden.

Yeoman's Cottage

4 9 BELLOMONTE CRESCENT

Drayton, Norwich NR8 6EJ. Wendy
& Chris Fitch. *5m N of Norwich. Turn
off A1067 at Drayton Xds. Drive past
front of Red Lion PH towards church.
Access through gate back of
churchyard or continue 1st exit
r'about to School Rd, 1st L turn to
Bellomonte Cres.* **Sat 25 June
(11-4.30). Adm £3, chd free.
Home-made teas.**
On approx ¹/₄ acre plot, the garden
has deep borders of traditional
shrubs and perennials mixed with
exotic mediterranean plants. A large
deck overlooks main lawn with
planted pergolas. Borrowed
landscape with views of Drayton
church gives interest and privacy.
Terraced upper garden with fruit and
vegetables and secluded courtyard
area. Home-made cakes. No
wheelchair access to upper levels.

5 BISHOP'S HOUSE

Bishopgate, Norwich NR3 1SB.
The Bishop of Norwich,
01603 614172,
bishops.chaplain@dioceseof
norwich.org,
www.dioceseofnorwich.org/
gardens. *City centre. Located in the
city centre near the Law Courts & The
Adam & Eve PH.* **Sun 4 Sept (1-5).
Adm £3, chd free. Home-made
teas. Visits also by arrangement.**

4-acre walled garden dating back to
the C12. Extensive lawns with
specimen trees. Borders with many
rare and unusual shrubs. Spectacular
herbaceous borders flanked by yew
hedges. Rose beds, meadow
labyrinth, kitchen garden, woodland
walk and long border with hostas and
bamboo walk. Popular plant sales.
Gravel paths and some slopes.

6 NEW BLACK HORSE COTTAGE

The Green, Hickling, Norwich
NR12 0YA. Mrs Yvonne Pugh. *3m E
of Stalham. Turn E off A149 at
Catfield, turn L onto Heath Road,
1¹/₂ m to centre of Hickling village.
Next to The Greyhound Inn (Good
food!).* **Sat 16, Sun 17 July (12-5).
Adm £4, chd free. Home-made
teas.**
Thatched house with traditional barn
¹/₂ m from Hickling Broad.
Plantsman's garden over 2 acres
professionally redesigned. Spacious
borders and islands with diverse
range of characterful planting.
Particular emphasis on achieving full
year round interest. Wide range of
managed mature specimen trees.
Many long two-way vistas. Wide
mown walkways through large
meadow. Various sitting
opportunities!

7 ◆ **BLICKLING ESTATE**
Aylsham, Norwich NR11 6NF.
National Trust, 01263 738030,
blickling@nationaltrust.org.uk,
www.nationaltrust.org.uk/blickling.
*14m N of Norwich just off the A140.
1½ m NW of Aylsham on N side of
B1354.* **For NGS: Tue 23 Feb
(11-3). Adm £5, chd £2.50. For
other opening times and
information, please phone, email or
visit garden website.**
Four centuries of good husbandry
have made this 55 acre garden one
of the greatest in England. Norah
Lindsay, the society gardener, created
the garden you see today, which incl
C18 Orangery, Temple, secret
garden, beautiful double borders and
parterre, lake and ancient yew
hedges. The new rose garden is
taking shape. Sorry, no dogs. Garden
open every day of the year except
Christmas. Wheelchairs and powered
mobility vehicles available to borrow.
WC, gravel paths.

8 ▶ **BLICKLING LODGE**
Blickling, Norwich NR11 6PS.
Michael & Henrietta Lindsell,
078819 56646,
henrietta@lindsell.co.uk. *½ m N of
Aylsham. Leave Aylsham on old
Cromer rd towards Ingworth. Over
hump back bridge & house is on the
right.* **Sat 9 July (2-5.30). Adm
£4.50, chd free. Home-made teas.
Visits also by arrangement June
to Aug 30 min.**
Georgian house (not open) set in
17 acres of parkland including cricket
pitch, mixed border, walled kitchen
garden, yew garden, woodland/water
garden and river walk.

9 ▶ **BOLWICK HALL**
Marsham NR10 5PU. Mr & Mrs G C
Fisher. *8m N of Norwich off A140.
Heading N towards Aylsham, at
Marsham take 1st R after Plough PH,
signed 'By Road' then next R onto
private rd to front of Hall.* **Sun 15
May, Sun 10 July (1-5). Adm £5,
chd free. Home-made teas.**
Landscaped gardens and park
surrounding a late Georgian hall. The
original garden design is attributed to
Humphry Repton. The current owners
have rejuvenated the borders, planted
gravel and formal gardens and clad
the walls of the house in old roses.
Enjoy a woodland walk around the
lake as well as as stroll through the
working vegetable and fruit garden

with its double herbaceous border.
Please ask at gate for wheelchair
directions.

Hospice care is
there for 1 in 3
people in the UK

10 ▶ **BRICK KILN HOUSE**
Priory Lane, Shotesham St Mary,
Norwich NR15 1UJ. Jim & Jenny
Clarke, 01508 550232,
jennyclarke@uwclub.net. *9/10m S
of Norwich. Take A146 to Poringland,
then Shotesham Rd after church.
Priory Lane is 200 metres from
Shotesham All Saints Church on rd to
Saxlingham Nethergate.* **Sun 31 July
(11-5). Adm £5, chd free. Home-
made teas. Visits also by
arrangement Mar to Sept.**
2 acre garden with a mixture of
different types of planting and
sculpture. A large terrace, lawns and
herbaceous borders near the house.
A pergola with wisteria and clematis
through an intimate rose garden
surrounded by a 'topiaried 'yew
hedge. Mature trees and diverse
planting in a woodland garden with a
stream. Parking in field but easy
access to brick path.

GROUP OPENING

11 **NEW** ▶ **CASTLE ACRE
GARDENS**
King's Lynn PE32 2AN, 01760
755334. *4 m N of Swaffham off
A1065 Swaffham to Fakenham. Car
park and teas at Tudor Lodgings.*
**Sun 31 July (11-5). Combined adm
£6, chd free. Home-made teas at
Tudor Lodgings.**

NEW ▶ **HIGHFIELD HOUSE**
Back Lane. David & Jackie
Moss

NEW ▶ **ORMONDE HOUSE**
off Pales Green. Anthony &
Elizabeth Wright

NEW ▶ **ST OSYTH**
Newton Rd. Fred & Audrey Bett

NEW ▶ **TUDOR LODGINGS**
Gus & Julia Stafford Allen

Castle Acre is in rural North West
Norfolk situated on the R Nar. An
historic Norman village which has a
bailey gate, castle, earthworks, parish
church and priory. There is a tearoom,
PH and shop. The four delightful
gardens which vary in size, structure
and planting will provide the visitors
with much interest and inspiration.
Tudor Lodgings, a C15 house (not
open) has a 2 acre garden that
incorporates part of the Norman
earthworks and contains 18th century
dovecote, topiary, lawns and knot
garden. A productive fruit cage
dominates the vegetable garden. Wild
area with pond and Shepherd's hut.
Just up the road is Ormonde House,
a small rear walled garden facing
south that has mixed shrubs,
herbaceous, annuals and recent
planting added to existing 1960s
shrubs. The ¾ acre garden at
Highfield House was started 33 years
ago and has herbaceous borders,
vegetable patch, gravel garden and
pond. St Osyth has been a lifetime's
work for Fred and Audrey where they
have created a small bright garden
packed with colour and life. An inner
area luxuriates in exotic tropical
splendor.

12 **NEW** ▶ **CHAPEL COTTAGE**
Rougham, King's Lynn PE32 2SE.
Sarah Butler. *15m from King's Lynn,
8m from Fakenham. Rougham is
situated on B1145. Opp old school &
next to old methodist chapel. Parking
in the centre of the village.* **Sun 4
Sept (11-5). Combined adm with
7 Holly Close £3, chd free. Home-
made teas.**
A very naturalistic cottage garden
designed by owner who describes
herself as an 'ist', combining her
interest, study and work as a
naturalist, entomologist and botanist.
Divided into charming peaceful areas
that include a pond, vegetables,
shade, and herbs. Wild flower lawns,
and beehives. Plenty of seating.

13 ▶ **CHAUCER BARN**
Holt Road, Gresham NR11 8RL.
James Mermagen,
www.chaucerbarn.com. *3m S of
Sheringham. Turn off A149 nr junction
of A149 & A1082 signed
Gresham/East Beckham. Turn L at*

T-junction. 1st building in Gresham, gravel drive on L. **Tue 7 June (2-5.30). Adm £3.50, chd free. Light refreshments.**
5-acre garden created by owner over 20 years in ruins of farmyard. Uphill drive flanked by topiary leads to award winning barn conversion. Knot/herb garden leads to lawn flanked by walled herbaceous borders and pergola leading through contemporary topiary garden to stunning views over rolling hills to woodland. Woodland path leads downhill to wild flower meadow and young arboretum.

♿ ❉ 🛌 ☕

An inner area luxuriates in tropical splendor . . .

14 CHESTNUT FARM
Church Road, West Beckham NR25 6NX. Mr & Mrs John McNeil Wilson, 01263 822241, john@mcneil-wilson.freeserve.co.uk. *2¹/₂ m S of Sheringham. On A148 opp Sheringham Park entrance. Take the rd signed BY WAY TO WEST BECKHAM, about ³/₄ m to the village sign & you have arrived.* **Thur 3, Sun 6 Mar (11-4); Sun 24 Apr, Mon 30 May (11-5). Adm £5, chd free. Light refreshments, and home-made teas. Visits also by arrangement Feb to July group sizes 5 - 50. Conducted tours offered, refreshments by request.**
Mature 3 acre garden for all seasons with recent additions, created over 50yrs by enthusiastic plant lovers. Lawns, formal areas, herbaceous borders, vegetables and fruit. Woodland garden and small arboretum. Handkerchief tree, Tulip tree, Ginko etc. In Spring see 90 varieties of snowdrops with crocus, hellebores and daphnes planted in natural surroundings. There is always something new to see. Toby Winterbourn Artist Blacksmith. Featured in MacMillan Support Calendar 2016. The English Garden.

Marianne Majerus Book of Garden Designs. Wheelchair access tricky if wet.

♿ 🎲 ❉ 🚐 ☕

15 NEW CONGHAM FARM,
Banville Lane, East Runton, Cromer NR27 9RN. Mr & Mrs James Neal. *Approx 1m W of Cromer. In East Runton turnL opp Fishing Boat PH & follow rd under 2 railway bridges. Turn R at pond onto Top Common. Rd bears L, garden on R.* **Sun 12 June (11-5). Combined adm with Banville Barn £5, chd free.**
Country style garden with uninterrupted views to the NT Ingleborough Hill. Formal box hedge garden with urns, small woodland walk, masses of climbing roses. Mixed herbaceous borders with grasses, box balls etc.. Shallow pond with lotus fountain. Recently planted small orchard with apples and Japanese plum tree. Modern sculptures in steel and marble. Partial wheelchair access.

♿ 🎲 ☕

16 DALE FARM
Sandy Lane, Dereham NR19 2EA. Graham & Sally Watts, 01362 690065, grahamwatts@dsl.pipex.com. *16m W of Norwich. 12m E of Swaffham. From A47 take B1146 signed to Fakenham, turn R at T-junction, ¹/₄ m turn L into Sandy Lane (before pelican crossing).* **Sun 24 July (11-5). Adm £4.50, chd free. Home-made teas. Visits also by arrangement June & July, groups of 10+.**
2 acre plant lover's garden with a large spring fed pond. Over 900 plant varieties featured in exuberantly planted borders and waterside gardens.These incl a collection of 80 species and varieties of hydrangea. Kitchen garden, orchard, naturalistic planting areas, gravel garden and sculptures. Gravel drive and some grass paths. Wide range of plants for sale incl many rare hydrangeas.

🎲 ❉ 🚐 ☕

17 DESERT WORLD GARDENS
Thetford Road (B1107), Santon Downham IP27 0TU. Mr & Mrs Barry Gayton, 01842 765861. *4m N of Thetford. On B1107 Brandon 2m.* **Sun 3 Apr, Sun 3 July (10-5). Adm £3.50, chd free. Light refreshments. Visits also by arrangement Apr to Sept.**

1¹/₄ acres plantsman's garden, specialising in tropical and arid plants. Hardy succulents - sempervivums and plectranthus. Bamboos, herbaceous, ferns, spring/summer bulbs, primula theatre, over 70 varieties of magnolias. View from roof garden. New area of primula auriculas. National Gardeners Question Time. Radio Cambridge gardener. Glasshouses cacti/succulents 12500, viewing by appt. Large primula area incl theatre, large collection of hardy Ferns.

❉ 🚐 ☕

18 DUNBHEAGAN
Dereham Road, Westfield NR19 1QF. Jean & John Walton, 01362 696163, jandjwalton@btinternet.com. *2m S of Dereham. From Dereham take A1075 towards Shipdham. L into Westfield Rd at Vauxhall Garage. At Xrds ahead into lane, becomes Dereham Rd.* **Visits by arrangement June & July, groups no min. Adm £4, chd free. Home-made teas.**
Relax and enjoy walking among the borders and island beds, a riot of colour all Summer. Extensive collection of rare, unusual and more recognisable plants in this ever changing plantsman's garden. We aim for the WOW factor. New beds/ideas/plants for 2016. Featured in two books recently plus local press. Gravel driveway.

♿ 🎲 ❉ 🚐 ☕

19 ◆ EAST RUSTON OLD VICARAGE
East Ruston, Norwich NR12 9HN. Alan Gray & Graham Robeson, 01692 650432, erovoffice@btconnect.com, www.eastrustonoldvicarage.co.uk. *3m N of Stalham. Turn off A149 onto B1159 signed Bacton, Happisburgh. After 2m turn R 200yds N of East Ruston Church (ignore sign to East Ruston).* **For NGS: Sat 9 Apr, Sat 8 Oct (1-5.30). Adm £8.50, chd £1. Tea. For other opening times and information, please phone, email or visit garden website.**
32-acre exotic coastal garden incl traditional borders, exotic garden, desert wash, sunk garden, topiary, water features, walled and Mediterranean gardens. Many rare and unusual plants, stunning plant combinations, wild flower meadows, old-fashioned cornfield, vegetable and cutting gardens.

♿ ❉ 🚐 ☕

20 **68 ELM GROVE LANE**
Norwich NR3 3LF. Selwyn Taylor,
www.selwyntaylorgarden.co.uk.
1³/₄ m N of Norwich city centre.
Proceed from Norwich city centre to
Magdalen St, to Magdalen Rd, bear L
to St. Clements Hill turn L into
Elmgrove Lane. No.68 is at bottom
on R. **Sun 3 July, Sun 14 Aug (11-**
4). Adm £3, chd free. Home-made
teas. Selection of homemade
cakes incl gluten free.
This extended living/working space is
the owner's endeavour to redefine a
suburban garden and to provide
inspiration when viewed from his
studio window. Aesthetic values,
initially took precedent over gardening
know-how, but over 30 years a more
balanced approach has resulted in an
eclectic array of informal planting, rich
in colour and form and full of
surprises. Featured in Garden News
and Amateur Gardening.

21 **GAYTON HALL**
Gayton, Kings Lynn PE32 1PL.
Viscount & Viscountess Marsham,
01485 528432,
ciciromney@icloud.com. *6m E of*
King's Lynn. Gayton is situated on
B1145; R on B1153. R down Back St
1st entrance on L. **Sun 5 June (12-**
5). Combined adm with Manor
Farmhouse, Gayton £6, chd free.
Home-made teas. Visits also by
arrangement Mar to Oct,
conducted tours for groups
of 12 +.
This rambling 20-acre water garden,
with over 2 miles of paths, contains
lawns, lakes, streams, bridges and
woodland. In the traditional and
waterside borders are primulas,
astilbes, hostas, lysichiton and
gunneras. A variety of unusual trees
and shrubs have been planted over
the years with a magnificent display
of rambling roses in June. An
abundance of spring bulbs and also
autumn colour. Wheelchair access to
most areas, paths are gravel and
grass.

Kettle Hill

22 NEW 38 GORSE ROAD
Norwich NR7 0AY. Mrs Ruth
Boden. *½ m E of City Centre.
Proceed up Ketts Hill to Heartsease
r'about, straight across into
Plumstead Rd East, 1st turning on R
into Aerodrome Rd, 1st L Gorse Rd,
No 38 on R.* **Sun 14 Aug (11-4).
Combined adm with 33 Orchard
Close £4, chd free. Home-made
teas.**
A plantsman's cottage style garden,
including mixed borders of perennials
(some unusual), shrubs, roses and
grasses. Woodland area, small bog
garden and white garden. A curving
gravel path, between lawned area,
leading to summerhouse with a
beach themed area. One small step
into garden.

23 THE GRANGE, HEYDON
Heydon, Norwich NR11 6RH. Mrs T
Bulwer-Long, 01263 587543. *13m N
of Norwich. 7m from Holt off B1149
signed Heydon 2m, on entering
village, 1st drive on R, signed The
Grange.* **Visits by arrangement in
June, groups of no more than 15.
Adm £5, chd free.**
Heydon Grange is a predominantly
C17 Dutch style Gabled Farmhouse
(not open) in mellow rose brick. The
Garden has been extenively
rejuvinated over the last 7 years and
is semi enclosed by ancient brick
walls and yew hedges with various
topiary that was planted cica 1920.
There are a mixture of herbaceous
borders and a wide selection of shrub
and climbing roses.
&

24 NEW GUNTON PARK
Hanworth, Norwich NR11 7HL.
*Approx 6m N of Aysham full
directions issued with ticket.* **Wed 10
Aug (2-5). Adm £25. Home-made
teas.**
LIMITED PRE BOOKED TICKETS
ONLY please contact Jenny Dyer
jandrdyer@btinternet.com or 01263
761811 A guided tour of a recreated
landscape, originally laid out by
Charles Bridgeman, Humphrey
Repton and W.S. Gilpin, and a
restored garden originally laid out by
W. Teulon. Teas on the colonnade of
the only complete Robert Adam
Chapel in the country. The tour will be
on foot and by coach. Date is
provisional. Winner of The Country
Life and Saville's 'Genius of the Place'
Award.

25 HIGH HOUSE GARDENS
Blackmoor Row, Shipdham,
Thetford IP25 7PU. Mr & Mrs F
Nickerson. *6m SW of Dereham. Take
the airfield or Cranworth Rd off A1075
in Shipdham. Blackmoor Row is
signed.* **Sun 12, Wed 15 June, Sun
11, Wed 14 Sept (2-5.30). Adm £4,
chd free. Home-made teas.**
3 acre plantsman's garden with
colour-themed herbaceous borders
with extensive range of perennials.
Box-edged rose and shrub borders.
Woodland garden, pond and bog
area. Newly planted orchard and
vegetable garden. Wildlife area.
Glasshouses. Gravel paths.

Garden is of a
potager style, with
fruit trees, flowers
and vegetables
encouraging bees
and wildlife . . .

26 ◆ HINDRINGHAM HALL
Blacksmiths Lane, Hindringham
NR21 0QA. Mr & Mrs Charles
Tucker, 01328 878226,
info@hindringhamhall.org,
www.hindringhamhall.org. *7m from
Holt/Fakenham/Wells. Turn off A148
between Holt & Fakenham at
Crawfish PH. Drive into Hindringham
(2m). Turn L into Blacksmiths Lane.*
**For NGS: Sun 3 Apr (10-4). Adm
£5, chd free. Home-made teas.
For other opening times and
information, please phone, email or
visit garden website.**
Tudor Manor House surrounded with
complete C13 moat. Victorian nut
walk, formal beds and wild garden.
Surrounding the moat are thousands
of narcissi (32 varieties), a working
walled vegetable garden and stream
garden ablaze with hellebore and
primula in the spring. The garden has
something of interest throughout the
year continuing well into autumn.
included as one of the ' 10 Best
Secret Gardens in the U.K' Guardian
Travel. Only suitable for wheelchairs
able to cope with gravel paths.

27 NEW 7 HOLLY CLOSE
Rougham, King's Lynn PE32 2SJ.
Derek Barker. *15m from King's Lynn,
8m from Fakenham. Rougham is
situated on B1145. Parking in the
centre of the village. Holly close is
¼ m from the church.* **Sun 4 Sept
(11-5). Combined adm with
Chapel Cottage £3, chd free.**
The front garden demonstrates a
varied design of planting, with well
stocked borders, filled with colour
and structure, to last throughout the
season. The rear garden is of a
potager style, with fruit trees, flowers
and vegetables encouraging bees
and wildlife, following an organic
theme. The garden shows how much
can be achieved in a small plot.

28 HOLME HALE HALL
Holme Hale, Thetford IP25 7ED. Mr
& Mrs Simon Broke, 01760 440328,
simon.broke@hotmail.co.uk. *6m E
of Swaffham, 8m W of Dereham, 5m
N of Watton. 2m S of Necton off A47
main rd. 1m E of Holme Hale Village.*
**Sun 15 May, Sun 26 June (12-4).
Adm £5, chd free. Light
refreshments. Visits also by
arrangement May to Sept, coach
parties very welcome.**
Noted for its spring display of tulips
and alliums, historic wisteria plus mid
and late summer flowering. Walled
kitchen garden and front garden
designed and planted in 2000 by
Chelsea winner Arne Maynard. The
garden incorporates herbaceous
borders, trained fruit, vegetables and
traditional greenhouse. The garden is
going to be rejuvenated by Arne
Maynard in 2016. Featured in The
Gardens of Arne Maynard Book and
Country Life. Wheelchair access
available to the Front Garden, Kitchen
Garden and tearoom.
&

29 HORSTEAD HOUSE
Mill Road, Horstead, Norwich
NR12 7AU. Mr & Mrs Matthew
Fleming. *6m NE of Norwich on North
Walsham rd, B1150. Down Mill Rd
opp the Recruiting Sargeant PH.*
**Sat 20 Feb (11-4). Adm £4, chd
free. Tea.**
Millions of beautiful snowdrops carpet
the woodland setting with winter
flowering shrubs. A stunning feature
are the dogwoods growing on a small
island in R Bure, which flows through
the garden. Small walled garden.
Wheelchair access to main snowdrop
area.
&

30 ◆ **HOUGHTON HALL WALLED GARDEN**
New Houghton, King's Lynn PE31 6UE. The Cholmondeley Gardens Trust, 01485 528569, www.houghtonhall.com. *11m W of Fakenham. 13m E of King's Lynn. Signed from A148.* **For opening times and information, please phone or visit garden website.**
Superbly laid out award-winning 5 acre walled garden designed by the Bannermans. Divided by clipped yew hedges into 'garden rooms' which incl a kitchen garden with large fruit cage, walks, fountains, pergolas, magnificent double herbaceous borders, glasshouse, statues, rustic temple, croquet lawn and rose parterre containing 120 varieties. Contemporary sculptures in surrounding parkland. Plants on sale. Gravel and grass paths. Electric buggies available for use in the walled garden.

31 **HOW HILL FARM**
Ludham NR29 5PG. Mr P D S Boardman. *2m W of Ludham. On A1062; then follow signs to How Hill. Farm garden S of How Hill.* **Sun 22 May (1-5). Adm £5, chd free. Home-made teas.**
Broadland garden. 2 very different gardens around the house. 3rd garden started 1968 on green field site with 3 acre broad dug 1978 with views of Turf Fen Mill, R Ant and Reedham Marshes. Approx 12 acres incl Broad, 4 ponds, site of old Broad with 100yr old Tussock sedges 5ft tall, approx 1 acre of indigenous ferns under oak and alder. Paths through rare conifers, rhododendrons, azaleas, ornamental trees, shrubs and herbaceous plants. Collection of holly species and varieties. Various very old stone carvings used for seats, excellent vistas.

GROUP OPENING

32 **NEW** **ITTERINGHAM VILLAGE GARDENS**
The Street, Itteringham, Norwich NR11 7AU. *From Aylsham take B1354. After 3¹/₂ m tale R turn for Itteringham. From B1149 Norwich/Holt Rd take B1354 after 2m take L turn.* **Sun 5 June (12-5). Combined adm £5, chd free. Home-made teas in the village hall.**

NEW **GLEBE HOUSE**
Sandra Walker

NEW **OLD RECTORY**
Mrs Dawn Maydon

NEW **THE OLD SCHOOL**
Paul & Julie Sunter

NEW **11 THE STREET**
Geoff & Julia Thompson

NEW **WILLOWBECK COTTAGE**
Mrs Jenny Tibbs

NEW **22 WOLTERTON ROAD**
Helen Hagon

Itteringham is a peaceful conservation village, tucked away in beautiful countryside near Aylsham. The heart of the village is the wonderful community shop proudly selling some of Norfolk's most tasty local food. Wander along the street and visit 6 differently styled gardens, enjoy a babbling stream and spot a kingfisher. Interesting plant combinations with unusual herbaceous plants and perennials. Some steps and slopes so not all gardens accessible by wheelchair.

Visit 6 differently styled gardens, enjoy a babbling stream and spot a kingfisher . . .

33 **KETTLE HILL**
The Downs, Langham Road, Blakeney NR25 7PN. Mrs Winch. *Turning to garden is off Langham Rd.* **Sat 18 June (11-4.30). Adm £5, chd free. Home-made teas.**
Kettle Hill has been quietly simmering but is now back on the boil! With a new fruit garden designed by Tamara Bridge, as well as re designed and re planted coastal and walled gardens. A newly re designed and re planted coastal and walled garden. A formal parterre, long herbaceous borders, wild flower meadow and a secret garden. Stunning rose garden and grass paths through woods, a real treat for any garden lover. Excellent views across Morston to the sea, framed by lavender, roses and sky.

Gravel drive way and lawns but hard paving near the house. Ramps are situated around the garden making all except the wood accessible for wheelchairs.

34 **LAKE HOUSE**
Postwick Lane, Roman Drive, Brundall NR13 5LU. Mrs Janet Muter, 01603 712933. *5m E of Norwich. On A47; take Brundall turn at r'about. Turn R into Postwick Lane at T-junction.* **Sun 1, Mon 2 May (11-5). Combined adm with Plovers Hill £7, chd free. Home-made teas at Plovers Hill, Strumpshaw. Visits also by arrangement Feb to Nov, refreshments on request.**
In the centre of Brundall Gardens, a series of ponds descends through a wooded valley to the shore of a lake. Steep paths wind through a variety of shrubs and flowers in season, which attract many kinds of rare birds, dragonflies and mammals. Featured in Eastern Daily Press double page feature.

35 **LEXHAM HALL**
nr Litcham PE32 2QJ. Mr & Mrs Neil Foster, www.lexhamestate.co.uk. *2m W of Litcham. 6m N of Swaffham off B1145.* **Sun 22 May (11-5). Adm £5, chd free. Home-made teas.**
Fine C17/18 Hall (not open). Parkland with lake and river walks. Formal garden with terraces, yew hedges, roses and mixed borders. Traditional kitchen garden with crinkle crankle wall. A garden of all year round interest. Acid loving shrubs are the highlight in May, and rhododendrons, azaleas, camellias and magnolias dominate the 3 acre woodland garden. Fine trees. Bulbs, emerging perennials and shrubs in the walled garden borders. A reed thatched summerhouse, with 'Gothic' windows and door, designs for which were found on the ruins of two other summerhouses. A 15' wisteria clad 'Dome' is the centrepiece in the walled garden with trellis backed parallel borders.

36 **NEW** **THE LONG BARN**
Flordon Road, Newton Flotman, Norwich NR15 1QX. Mr & Mrs Mark Bedini. *6m S of Norwich along A140. Leave A140 in Newton Flotman towards Flordon. Exit Newton*

Flotman & approx 150 yards beyond 'passing place' on L, turn L into drive. Note that SatNav does not bring you to destination. **Sat 6 Aug (11-5). Adm £5, chd free. Tea.**
Herbaceous borders and woodland garden mainly created in 2014 around sympathetic barn conversion in parkland setting. Strong Mediterranean influences around outdoor pool, a walled group of olive trees and a courtyard feature.

The QNI founded the NGS

37 ◆ **MANNINGTON HALL**
Mannington, Norwich NR11 7BB.
The Lord & Lady Walpole,
01263 584175,
admin@walpoleestate.co.uk,
www.manningtongardens.co.uk.
18m NW of Norwich. 2m N of Saxthorpe via B1149 towards Holt. At Saxthorpe/Corpusty follow signs to Mannington. **For NGS: Sun 10 Apr (12-5). Evening opening Thur 23 June (6-9). Adm £6, chd free. Light refreshments. For other opening times and information, please phone, email or visit garden website.**
20 acres feature shrubs, lake, trees and roses. Heritage rose and period gardens. Borders. Sensory garden. Extensive countryside walks and trails. Moated manor house and Saxon church with C19 follies. Wild flowers and birds. Gravel paths, one steep slope.

38 ◆ **MANOR FARMHOUSE, GAYTON**
Back Street, Gayton, King's Lynn PE32 1QR. Alistair & Christa Beales. *6m E of King's Lynn. Signed from B1145 and B1153.* **Sun 5 June (12-5). Combined adm with Gayton Hall £6, chd free. Light refreshments.**
This secret, colourful, and heavily planted cottage garden was created in 2001 in an old garden destroyed by building work. Gravel garden, walled courtyard and conservatory with 40%

more garden bought from a neighbour in 2013. Over 300 pots provide extra colour and variety. The garden has evolved as the owner progresses from non-gardener to garden fanatic . . . gravel paths, ramps provided on steps.

39 **NEW** **MARSHGATE HOUSE**
24 Marshgate, North Walsham NR28 9EF. Felicity Elsmore & Simon Dodsworth, www.englishiriscompany.com.
Follow B1150 from Norwich to N.Walsham (16m). Pass under the railway bridge and go straight over the T-lights to mini r'about. Straight again. Follow yellow signs. **Sat 4, Sun 5 June (10-5). Adm £4, chd free. Light refreshments.**
Wild, Romantic/woodland/herbaceous garden on the edge of the market town of North Walsham, containing a spectacular collection of British Tall Bearded Irises hybridised by the late Bryan Dodsworth, twelve times Dykes medal winner. These irises have been awarded National Collection status by Plant Heritage in 2015. Opportunity to see an outstanding collection of British Tall Bearded Irises raised by the most celebrated British twentieth century hybridiser of Tall Beaded Irises. Featured in The Garden. Wheelchair users may enter the iris garden via the 'exit' gate.

40 **THE MERCHANTS HOUSE**
Blakeney, Holt NR25 7NT. Mr & Mrs David Marris. *Centre of Blakeney Village. Garden located N of A149 (New Road) up Little Lane in Blakeney.* **Sat 14 May (1-5). Adm £5, chd free. Home-made teas.**
2 acres of walled secret garden with terrace woodland walk, parterre, shrub borders, orchard, kitchen garden, herbaceous border and ice house. Dogs on leads. Most of the garden is suitable for wheelchairs.

41 **4 MILL ROAD**
Marlingford NR9 5HL. Mrs Jean Austen. *6m W of Norwich. A47 to B1108 Watton Rd junction, 3rd on R. Bear R past mill & garden on R after village hall, (parking) before The Bell. From Easton, signed opp Des Amis.* **Tue 5 July (10.30-4.30). Combined adm with The Old Smithy £5, chd free. Home-made teas.**
Take home ideas from this small

garden packed with unusual features. Designed as a collection of garden rooms divided by hedges, paths, arches and pleached limes. Colour-themed borders, Japanese garden, pond, vegetables and fruit. Wind sculpture. Views to the water meadows beyond. A children's trail, plenty of seats to sit, relax and enjoy the view. Music. Two small steps, ramps available.

42 **THE MOWLE**
Staithe Road, Ludham NR29 5NP.
Mrs N N Green, 01692 678213,
nivea.green@icloud.com. *5m E of Wroxham. A1062 Wroxham to Ludham 7m. Turn R by Ludham village church into Staithe Rd. Garden ¼ m from village.* **Sun 21 Aug (1.30-5.30). Adm £4.50, chd free. Home-made teas. Visits also by arrangement Mar to Oct any number from 2 to 100.**
Approx 2½ acres running down to marshes. The garden incl several varieties of catalpa. Japanese garden and enlarged wildlife pond with bog garden. A special border for gunnera as in Aug 2008 we were given full National Collection status. Boardwalk into wild area. 85% of the garden is acessable to wheelchairs.

43 ◆ **NARBOROUGH HALL**
Narborough Hall Gardens, Main Road, Narborough PE32 1TE. Dr Joanne Merrison, 01760 338827, narboroughevents@googlemail.com, www.narboroughhallgardens.com.
2m W of Swaffham off A47. Narborough located off A47 between Swaffham & King's Lynn. **For NGS: Wed 8 June (11-5). Adm £4, chd free. Light refreshments. For other opening times and information, please phone, email or visit garden website.**
A gently evolving, romantic English garden set in ancient parkland. Herbs, wild flowers and fruit are planted through out, with yew hedging, sumptuous herbaceous borders, willow sculpture and walled garden. Subtle and unusual colour schemes, much planting for wildlife, particularly in the gravel paths and the 'wild at heart' garden. Walled garden. Lake, river and woodland walks. Partial wheelchair access but with some gravel paths.

GROUP OPENING

44 NORTH CREAKE GARDENS
Fakenham NR21 9LG. *2m S of
Burnham Market & 5m NW of
Fakenham on B1355. From
Fakenham A148 W then 1st R on
B1355. The Red House 200yds N
past church. The Old Bakehouse 1st
drive on L in Wells Rd. The Old
Chapel by pond in West St & Drove
End further up West St on R.
Disabled parking in village hall car
park - follow signs.* **Sun 12 June
(1-5). Combined adm £5, chd free.
Home-made teas at Creake
House, Wells Rd opp The Old
Bakehouse.**

NEW DROVE END
78 West St. Mrs Edna Bizon

THE OLD BAKEHOUSE
Wells Rd. Mrs Richard Faire

NEW THE OLD CHAPEL
34 West St. Mrs M Yorke

THE RED HOUSE
Church St. Dr & Mrs J Stabler

4 attractive but very different small
gardens. The Old Bakehouse is an
informal garden with mixed planting,
on the bank of R Burn, designed by
owners to accommodate inherited
garden ornaments. A plaque on the
gate commemorates that this garden
was the scene of the only major
wartime incident to occur in North
Creake. The Red House garden was
created over last 30 years by the
present owners. Thickly planted with
many unusual and doubtfully hardy
plants, traditional herbaceous border,
stream, shell garden and area
specifically planted to attract
butterflies. The Old Chapel garden
has been created from an earlier
garden in the past 2 years with beds
filled with interesting herbaceous
plants, roses and bulbs, shaded by a
Salix Tortuosa. A white garden was
planted in 2015. Drove End garden is
divided into 3 sections. A small paved
classically designed garden leads
through an arch into a very pretty
garden with unusual plants with
interesting leaves. This leads on up to
a paved small garden. Plants for sale
at The Red House. Wheelchair
access to The Old Chapel partial
access to The Old Bakery. No
wheelchair access to Drove End &
The Red House. Wheelchair access
to Creake House for Teas.

45 NORTH LODGE
51 Bowthorpe Road, Norwich
NR2 3TN. Bruce Bentley & Peter
Wilson. *1¹/₂ m W of Norwich City
Centre. Turn into Bowthorpe Rd off
Dereham Rd, garden 150 metres on
L. By bus: 5, 21, 22, 23, 23A/B, 24 &
24A from City centre, Old Catton,
Heartsease, Thorpe & most of W
Norwich.* **Sun 7, Sun 14 Aug (11-5).
Adm £3.50, chd free. Home-made
teas.**
Town garden of almost ¹/₅ acre on
difficult triangular plot surrounding
Victorian Gothic Cemetery Lodge (not
open). Strong structure and attention
to internal vista with Gothic
conservatory, formal ponds and water
features, Oriental water garden,
classical temple and 80ft deep well!
Predominantly herbaceous planting.
Self-guided walk around associated
historic parkland cemetery also
available. House extension won
architectural award. Slide show of
house and garden history. Featured in
Amateur Gardening. Wheelchair
access possible, but difficult. Long
sloping gravel drive followed by short,
steep, narrow, brickweave ramp. WC
not easily wheelchair accessible.

GROUP OPENING

46 NEW NORWICH GARDENS
15 Waverley Road, Norwich
NR4 6SG. *Three town gardens, all
within easy walking distance. Along
Waverley Rd which is parallel to
Newmarket Rd, a few minutes from
end of A11. Turn R at Eaton Rd T-
lights or L if coming from the city
centre. Waverley Rd is 1st turn on R.*
**Sun 19 June (11-6). Combined
adm £5, chd free. Home-made
teas at 19 Branksome Road.**

**NEW 19 BRANKSOME
ROAD**
Sue & Chris Pike

NEW 15 WAVERLEY ROAD
Sue & Clive Lloyd

NEW 17 WAVERLEY ROAD
Sue & John Tuckett

Three gardens along the same road,
all different. Number 15 Waverley
Road is a long town garden that's
pretending it is in the country
including a miniature wild meadow
and fruit trees. Number 17 Waverley
Road has relaxed herbaceous
planting around established shrubs
and mature trees creating a

woodland feel and Bamboos and
Japanese Acers compliment rambling
roses. 19 Branksome Road has
varying shaped lawns and terraces
that radiate from the house, to make
the most of a corner plot. Interesting
mixed planting, plus vegetables, fruit
cage and greenhouse. Wheelchair
access challenging but not
impossible. There are a few steps and
gravel to negotiate at 15 and 17
Waverley Road. Branksome Road is
straightforward.

Town garden that's pretending it is in the country including a miniature wild meadow . . .

47 167 NORWICH ROAD
Wymondham NR18 0SJ. Rachel &
Richard Dylong, 07884 120685,
richarddylong@hotmail.co.uk. *³/₄ m
N of Wymondham centre. A11 to
Wymondham. Take exit, straight to
Waitrose & turn L at r'about. Garden
on R after ¹/₄ m.* **Sat 18, Sun 19
June (10-5). Adm £3, chd free.
Home-made teas. Visits also by
arrangement Apr to July.**
In our ¹/₄ -acre town garden, created
from a blank canvas 12 years ago,
meandering pathways round a
circular lawn to a secluded tropical
haven, on to a sunken pergola,
greenhouse with cacti collection and
fruit and vegetable plot. We love to
recycle and experiment.

**48 THE OLD RECTORY,
BRANDON PARVA**
Stone Lane, Brandon Parva
NR9 4DL. Mr & Mrs S Guest. *9m W
of Norwich. Leave Norwich on B1108
towards Watton, turn R at sign for
Barnham Broom. L at T-junction, stay
on rd approx 3m until L next turn to
Yaxham. L at Xrds.* **Sun 22 May
(11-5). Adm £4.50, chd free.
Home-made teas.**
4-acre, mature garden with large
collection (70) specimen trees, huge
variety of shrubs and herbaceous

plants combined to make beautiful mixed borders. The garden comprises several formal lawns and borders, woodland garden incl rhododendrons, pond garden, walled garden and pergolas covered in wisteria, roses and clematis which create long shady walkways. Croquet lawn open for visitors to play.

 ♿ 🐕 ✿ ☕

49 NEW THE OLD RECTORY, BANHAM

Church Hill, Banham, Norwich NR16 2HN. Ben & Heather Taylor. *20m SW of Norwich. From A11 at Attleborough follow signs for Banham Zoo on B1077. At Xrds with B1113 turn R. Garden is behind church.* **Sat 18 June (11-5). Adm £4, chd free. Home-made teas.**

The Old Rectory stands on a site of approximately ¾ acre. The garden was planted in the autumn of 2010 once extensive dredging of the large pond had taken place. It contains several mature trees, island beds planted with shrubs and herbaceous perennials, a rose border at the entrance to the large vegetable garden, small wild walk around the pond and a shade garden. Wheelchair access through side gate.

All paths are grass so difficult when wet.

 ♿ 🐕 ✿ ☕

50 THE OLD SMITHY

Mill Road, Marlingford, Norwich NR9 5HL. Kirsty Reader & David Eagles. *6m W of Norwich. A47 to B1108 Watton Road, take 3rd R down past mill, garden on R after village hall. Parking before the Bell. From Easton signed opp Des Amis.* **Tue 5 July (10.30-4.30). Combined adm with 4 Mill Road £5, chd free. Home-made teas at 4 Mill Road.**

A garden for the family designed by a plantsman, with unusual cottage garden perennials and shrubs. Large north facing border filled with colour for all seasons. Woodland planting, specimen trees, stumpery, vegetables and hens.

 ♿ 🐕 🚐 ☕

51 NEW 33 ORCHARD CLOSE

Norwich NR7 9NZ. Mr Mike & Mrs Jean Newstead. *½ m E of Norwich Centre. On outer ring road. Off Heartseas lane. By bus 23a 23b.* **Sun 14 Aug (11-4). Combined adm with 38 Gorse Road £4, chd free. Light refreshments.**

A small city garden with a central

pond and various colour themed borders planted with dahlias, grasses and perennials and lots of pleasant features.

 ✿ ☕

53 NEW OXNEAD HALL

Oxnead, Norwich NR10 5HP. Mr & Mrs David Aspinall. *3m from Aylsham. From Norwich take A140 to Cromer. After Aylsham turn R to Burgh-next-Aylsham. After Burgh take R turn at next Xrds signed Brampton & Buxton. After the Oxnead sign take 1st L.* **Sun 21 Aug (2-5). Adm £5, chd free. Home-made teas.**

The 14 acre gardens were laid out by the Pastons between 1580 and 1660 and are largely intact. The design consists of a series of Italianate courtyards and terraces which are embellished with statuary. The gardens are undergoing renovation with guidance from George Carter and now incl a parterre, viewing mound, water garden, lake, herbaceous borders, walled kitchen garden, and woodland. There are slopes to most parts of the garden, but some areas cannot be accessed by wheelchair.

 ♿ 🛏 ☕

15 Waverley Road, Norwich Gardens

Thorpland Hall

54 ▶ PLOVERS HILL
Buckenham Road, Strumpshaw
NR13 4NL. Jan Saunt, 01603
714587, sauntjan@gmail.com. *9m E
of Norwich. Off A47 at Brundall
continuing through to Strumpshaw
village. Turn R 300yds past The
Huntsman, then take 1st R, at T
junction R, Plovers Hill is 1st on R up
the hill.* **Sun 1 May (11-5); Mon 2
May (11-6). Combined adm with
Lake House £7, chd free. Home-
made teas. Visits also by
arrangement May to Sept.**
1-acre garden of contrasts, small C18
house (not open) with RIBA award
winning orangery. Formal lawn

hedged with yew and lesser species,
huge mulberry, gingko, liquidambar
and Japanese bitter orange,
herbaceous borders with a range of
varied plants and spring bulbs.
Kitchen garden with orchard and soft
fruits. Garden sculptures. Water
feature. Cast aluminium silver birches.
Wheelchair access to main part of
garden, some gentle steps to teas.

55 ▶ ◆ RAVENINGHAM HALL
Raveningham, Norwich NR14 6NS.
Sir & Lady Nicholas Bacon, 01508
548480,

barbara@raveningham.com,
www.raveningham.com. *14m SE of
Norwich. 4m from Beccles off B1136.*
**For NGS: Sun 6 Mar (11-4). Adm
£5, chd free. Home-made teas.
For other opening times and
information, please phone, email or
visit garden website.**
Traditional country house garden with
an interesting collection of
herbaceous plants and shrubs.
Restored Victorian conservatory and
walled kitchen garden. Newly planted
arboretum, lake and herb garden.
Contemporary sculpture.

56 ▸ RECTORY COTTAGE
St. Andrews Lane, Congham,
King's Lynn PE32 1DU. Jonathan &
Sarah Beart, 01485 600925,
Sarah.beart@btinternet.com. *3m E
of King's Lynn. From Kings Lynn take
A148 Fakenham rd. At Hillington turn
R towards Grimston. Take 2nd R turn
along Grassy Lane into Congham
village. Follow signs for parking.* **Sun
7 Aug (11-6). Adm £4.50, chd free.
Light refreshments. Visits also by
arrangement July to Sept wine
and cheese evenings a speciality!**
An established plant-lover's cottage
garden in ³/₄ acre, next to the Church.
Borders filled with colour and a wide
variety of herbaceous plants; shaded
beds; gravel garden; mature trees;
wildlife pond and shrubbery. A
tranquil garden with several sitting
areas, summerhouse, free-roaming
bantams and white doves.
Homemade refreshments. Featured
on Radio Norfolk, and in gardening
news and amateur gardening
magazines. There are a few gravel
paths. Well behaved dogs on leads
welcome.
   ♿ 🐕 ❀ ☕

**57 ◆ SANDRINGHAM
GARDENS**
Sandringham PE35 6EH. Her
Majesty The Queen, 01485 545408,
www.sandringhamestate.co.uk. *6m
NW of King's Lynn. By gracious
permission, the House, Museum &
Gardens at Sandringham will be
open.* **For opening times and
information, please phone or visit
garden website.**
60 acres of glorious gardens,
woodland and lakes, with rare plants
and trees. Colour and interest
throughout the year with sheets of
spring-flowering bulbs, avenues of
rhododendrons and azaleas, beds of
lavender and roses, and dazzling
autumn colour. Donations are given
from the Estate to various charities.
Open 26 March - 30 Oct, closed Wed
27 July. Gravel paths (not deep), long
distances - please tel or visit website
for our Accessibility Guide.
   ♿ ❀ 🚐 ☕

58 ▸ SEA MERE
Seamere Road, Hingham, Norwich
NR9 4LP. Judy Watson,
01953 850217,
judywatson@seamere.com,
www.seamere.com. *Off the B1108,
1m E of Hingham. From Norwich
B1108, 2m after Kimberley railway
crossing, turn L into Seamere Rd.*

Sea Mere drive is 2nd on L. **Visits by
arrangement Apr to Aug groups
of 10+, guided tour with garden
owner. Please mention NGS
Yellow Book when booking. Adm
£7, chd free incls refreshments in
Sea Mere Study Centre, adjacent
to house. Tea/coffee and cake or
wine and nibbles.**
The gardens border a 20 acre circular
mere with spectacular views to the
water over terraced lawns, gunnera
and a new wetland garden. Mature
trees, shrubs and perennials frame
the view. The 5 acre garden incl an
ornamental potager, formal oval
garden with herbaceous borders,
woodland garden, shrub roses in the
orchard and a bamboo glade. The
higher levels, near the house are
wheelchair accessible. WC suitable
for disabled use.
   ♿ ❀ 🚐 ☕

Designed to create
interesting views
from around the
garden . . .

59 ◆ SEVERALS GRANGE
Holt Road, Wood Norton
NR20 5BL. Jane Lister, 01362
684206, hoecroft@hotmail.co.uk,
www.hoecroft.co.uk. *8m S of Holt,
6m E of Fakenham. 2m N of Guist on
L of B1110. Guist is situated 5m SE
of Fakenham on A1067 Norwich rd.*
**For NGS: Sun 14 Aug (1-5). Adm
£3, chd free. Home-made teas.
For other opening times and
information, please phone, email or
visit garden website.**
The gardens surrounding Severals
Grange and the adjoining nursery
Hoecroft Plants are a perfect example
of how colour, shape and form can
be created by the use of foliage
plants, from large shrubs to small
alpines. Movement and lightness are
achieved by interspersing these
plants with a wide range of
ornamental grasses, which are at
their best in late summer. Extensive
range of ornamental grasses
herbaceous plants and shrubs in
various garden settings. Groups for
guided tours by appt July - Sept.
   ♿ 🐕 ❀ 🚐 🛏 ☕

60 ◆ SHERINGHAM PARK
Wood Farm Visitors Centre, Upper
Sheringham NR26 8TL. National
Trust, 01263 820550,
www.nationaltrust.org.uk/sheringh
am. *2m SW of Sheringham. Access
for cars off A148 Cromer to Holt Rd,
5m W of Cromer, 6m E of Holt, signs
in Sheringham town.* **For NGS: Thur
19 May, Thur 9 June (10-5). Adm
by donation. Light refreshments in
Courtyard Cafe. For other opening
times and information, please
phone or visit garden website.**
80 acres of species rhododendron,
azalea and magnolia. Also numerous
specimen trees incl handkerchief tree.
Viewing towers, waymarked walks,
sea and parkland views. No
admission charge to Sheringham
Park, car park charge payable, £5.20
for non NT members. Special
walkway and WCs for disabled.
1¹/₂ m route is accessible for
wheelchairs, mobility scooters
available to hire.
   ♿ 🐕 ❀ 🚐 ☕

61 ◆ STODY LODGE
Melton Constable NR24 2ER.
Mr & Mrs Charles MacNicol,
01263 863994,
enquiries@stodyestate.co.uk,
www.stodyestate.co.uk/stody-
lodge-gardens. *16m NW of
Norwich, 3m S of Holt. Off B1354.
Signed from Melton Constable on
Holt Rd. For SatNav NR24 2ER.
Gardens signed as you approach.*
**For NGS: Tue 24 May (1-5). Adm
£5, chd free. Home-made teas.
For other opening times and
information, please phone, email or
visit garden website.**
Spectacular gardens with one of the
largest concentrations of
rhododendrons and azaleas in East
Anglia. Created in the 1920s, the
gardens also feature magnolias,
camellias, a variety of ornamental and
specimen trees, late daffodils, tulips
and bluebells. Expansive lawns and
magnificent yew hedges. Woodland
walks and 2 acre Water Gardens filled
with over 2,000 vividly-coloured
azalea mollis. Homemade teas
provided by selected local and
national charities. Featured in Homes
& Gardens, The English Garden,
Country Life, and many national,
regional and local publications.
Access to most areas of the garden.
Gravel paths to water gardens, some
uneven ground.
   ♿ 🐕 ❀ 🚐 ☕

62 SUIL NA MARA
North Walsham Road, Bacton, Norwich NR12 0LG. Bill Kerr & Bev Cole, 01692 652386, billkerr1@btinternet.com. *19m N of Norwich on N Norfolk coast. Bacton. When you reach the Coastguard Station in Pollard St are the 3rd bungalow on L past it.* **Sat 27, Sun 28 Aug (11-5.30). Adm £3.50, chd free. Light refreshments. Visits also by arrangement June to Sept no min number.**
This ¼ acre exotic garden incorporates more than 240 plant varieties in an unusual mix of lush semi tropical planting meets Norfolk Coast meets Industrial and rural decay. Set in a series of garden rooms the striking architectural plants mixed with beachcombed wood, rusty metal and unusual water features all provides plenty to look at and enjoy. Often described as a 'Tardis' of a garden! Small photographic and Art Studio also on site with photos and artwork featuring the beautiful North Norfolk Coast. Sorry all paths are gravelled and are difficult for wheelchair/mobility access.

63 THORPLAND HALL
Thorpland, Fakenham NR21 0HD. Mr & Mrs N R Savory. *1m N of Fakenham bypass A148. Turn off r'about on A148 north of Morrisons superstore, signed Thorpland Rd. Additional parking for wheelchair users only.* **Sun 19 June (2-5). Adm £5, chd free. Home-made teas.**
Mature English garden in a superb setting, containing ruins of an old chapel, and surrounding a fine Tudor house (not open). The 6 acres of garden, with some recent re-planting, incl peony beds, herbaceous borders and a rose garden. The walled garden is in full working order and kept to a high standard. A small lake, and nearby restored shepherd's hut, are surrounded by interesting trees and shrubs. Gravel paths, paved areas and lawns. Some grass paths maybe a little uneven.

64 WALCOTT HOUSE
Walcott Green, Walcott, Norwich NR12 0NU. Mr Nick Collier. *3m N of Stalham. Off the Stalham to Walcott rd (B1159).* **Sun 26 June (1.30-5). Adm £4, chd free. Light refreshments.**
A garden in the making with emphasis on formal structure around the house and a traditional set of Norfolk farm buildings. These provide a series of connecting gardens which, through a south facing garden wall, lead to further gardens of clipped box, pleached hornbeam, fruit trees and roses. All set within recently planted woodland providing avenues and vistas. Small single steps to negotiate when moving between gardens in the yards.

carerstrust
action · help · advice

NGS funding helps us reach more unpaid carers

65 WARBOROUGH HOUSE
2 Wells Road, Stiffkey NR23 1QH. Mr & Mrs J Morgan. *13m N of Fakenham, 4m E of Wells-Next-The-Sea on A149 in the centre of village. Please DO NOT park in main rd as this causes congestion. Parking is available & signed at garden entrance. Coasthopper bus stop outside garden.* **Sun 29 May (1-5.30). Adm £5, chd free. Home-made teas.**
7 acre garden on a steep chalk slope, surrounding C19 house (not open) with views across the Stiffkey valley and to the coast. Woodland walks, formal terraces, shrub borders, lawns and walled garden create a garden of contrasts. Garden slopes steeply in parts. Paths are gravel, bark chip or grass. Disabled parking allows access to garden nearest the house and teas.

GROUP OPENING

66 WELLS-NEXT-THE-SEA GARDENS
Wells-Next-The-Sea NR23 1DP. *10m N of Fakenham. B1105 from Fakenham. Also off A149 King's Lynn to Cromer rd. Coasthopper/Norfolk Green Bus to 'The Buttlands' follow NGS signs 1 min from stop. Car park at Stearman's Yard behind Captain's Table PH, The Buttlands or Market Lane (close to gardens in Burnt St). Advisable to tour gardens on foot..* **Sun 26 June (11-5). Combined adm £5, chd free. Home-made teas at Caprice.**

CAPRICE
Clubbs Lane. David & Joolz Saunders

7 MARKET LANE
off Burnt St. Hazel Ashley

NORFOLK HOUSE
Burnt St. Katrina & Alan Jackson
Visits also by arrangement in June.
katrinaatwells@btinternet.com
01328 711099

OSTRICH HOUSE
Burnt St. Mr Stuart Rangeley-Wilson & Ms Janey Burland

POACHER COTTAGE
Burnt St. Roger & Barbara Oliver

Wells-next-the-Sea is a small friendly coastal town on the glorious North Norfolk Coast: popular with families, walkers and bird watchers. The harbour has shops, cafes, fish and chips, while a mile along The Run lies Wells Beach, served by a narrow gauge railway. Of the five in the group four are smaller town gardens and one is somewhat larger: all demonstrate a variety of design and planting approaches incorporating herbaceous borders, 'cottage', shrub and fruit, with two of the gardens providing different 'rooms'. The route around the five gardens takes in the Parish Church of St Nicholas, the High Street with its beautiful once-shop windows and the tree lined Georgian green square, The Buttlands. Wheelchair access at all gardens.

67 NEW 4 WENSUM CRESCENT
Lower Hellesdon, Norwich NR6 5DL. Mrs Moira Smith. *3m NW from City centre. From Norwich ring rd turn onto A1067, after 1m, turn L at T-lights - Hospital Lane. After ½ m turn R - Low Rd, take first L Wensum Valley Close, turn L - Wensum Crescent.* **Sun 3 July, Sun 14 Aug (12-5). Adm £3, chd free. Home-made teas. Also open 68 Elm Grove Lane.**

Site was completely cleared May 2013 so a relatively new garden with some interesting and unusual plants including lots of evergreens, so it looks good all year round. Designed to create interesting views from around the garden with different patio and seating areas throughout. A bespoke garden room was built on site for lazy afternoons. Most areas accessible by wheelchair.

♿ 🍕 ☂ ☕

68 WEST BARSHAM HALL
Fakenham NR21 9NP. Mr & Mrs Jeremy Soames, 01328 863519, susannasoames@gmail.com. *3m N of Fakenham. From Fakenham take A148 to Cromer then L on B1105 to Wells. After 1/2 m L again to Wells. After 1 1/2 m R The Barshams & West Barsham.* **Sun 19 June (11-5). Adm £5, chd free. Cream teas. Morning coffee and light refreshments, afternoon cream teas. Visits also by arrangement Apr to Sept groups welcome.**
Large garden with lake, approx 10 acres. Mature yew hedging and sunken garden originally laid out by Gertrude Jekyll. Swimming pool garden, shrub borders, kitchen garden with herbaceous borders, fruit cage, cutting garden and bog garden. Separate old fashioned cottage garden also open. Some slopes and gravel paths.

♿ 🍕 ☂ ☕

69 WEST LODGE
Aylsham NR11 6HB. Mr & Mrs Jonathan Hirst, jonathan.hirst@btinternet.com. *1/4 m NW of Aylsham. Off B1354 Blickling Rd out of Aylsham, turn R down Rawlinsons Lane, garden on L.* **Sun 24 July (12-5). Adm £5, chd free. Tea. Visits also by arrangement please email.**
9-acre garden with lawns, splendid mature trees, rose garden, well-stocked herbaceous borders, ornamental pond, magnificent 2 1/2 acre C19 walled kitchen garden (maintained as such). Georgian house (not open) and outbuildings incl a well-stocked tool shed (open) and greenhouses. Most of the garden is easily accessible to wheelchair users. Some recently repaired gravel areas a bit more difficult.

♿ 🍕 ☂ ☕

Lots packed into 0.4 acre: 'Hot' border; 'Pale and Interesting' border; Exotic-ish lush bed, Shady woodland 'hop'; 'Dry river bed' . . .

70 WITTON HALL
Old Hall Road, North Walsham NR28 9UF. Sally Owles. *3 1/2 m from North Walsham. From North Walsham take Happisburgh Rd or Byway to Edingthorpe Rd off North Walsham bypass. Situated nr to Bacton Woods.* **Mon 2 May (12-4). Adm £3, chd free. Light refreshments.**
A natural woodland garden. Walk past the handkerchief tree and wander through carpets of English bluebells, rhododendrons and azaleas. Walk from the garden down the field to the church. Stunning views over farmland to the sea. Sensible footwear required as deer, rabbits and badgers inhabit this garden! Witton Park laid out by Humphrey Repton. Wheelchair access difficult if wet.

♿ ☂ ☕

71 16 WITTON LANE
Little Plumstead NR13 5DL. Sally Ward & Richard Hobbs. *5m E of Norwich. Take A47 to Yarmouth, 1st exit after Postwick, turn L to Witton Green & Gt Plumstead, then 1st R into Witton Lane for 1 1/2 m. Garden on L.* **Sun 24 Apr (11-4). Adm £3, chd free. Light refreshments.**
An 'Aladdin's Cave' for the alpine and woodland plant enthusiast. Tiny garden with wide range of rare and unusual plants will be of great interest with its species tulips, daffodils, scillas, dog's tooth violets, other bulbous plants and many trilliums and wood anemones. A garden for the plant specialist. National Collection of Muscari. Plants for sale and refreshments. Featured in Gardens Illustrated and The English Garden. Not suitable for wheelchair access due to narrow gravel paths.

☂ **NPC** ☕

72 WOOD HILL
Hill Farm, Gressenhall, East Dereham NR19 2NR. Mr & Mrs John Bullard. *1m W of East Dereham. 1/2 m W of Dereham off A47 N on Draytonhall Lane, B1146, R at T junction, 1st L Rushmeadow Rd, 1m over small bridge, entrance on R.* **Sun 12 June (12-5.30). Adm £4, chd free. Home-made teas.**
The 3 acre garden is set in mature parkland, incl water features, statues/stones, lily pond, varied rose gardens, yew hedging, vegetable garden, lawns with floodlighting for mature hardwood trees. Home to one of East Anglia's oldest tulip trees, beautiful oaks and copper beech.

☂ ☕

73 WRETHAM LODGE
East Wretham IP24 1RL. Mr Gordon Alexander, 01953 498997. *6m NE of Thetford. A11 E from Thetford, L up A1075, L by village sign, R at Xrds then bear L.* **Sun 1, Mon 2 May (11-5). Adm £4, chd free. Visits also by arrangement Mar to Oct.**
In spring masses of species tulips, hellebores, fritillaries, daffodils and narcissi; bluebell walk. Walled garden, with fruit and interesting vegetable plots. Mixed borders and fine old trees. Double herbaceous borders. Wild flower meadows. Featured in Country Life and The English Garden Magazine.

♿ 🍕 ☕

74 NEW YEOMAN'S COTTAGE
Low Lane, Rockland All Saints, Attleborough NR17 1TU. Karen Roseberry & Paul Rutter. *Approx 4m from Attleborough & A11. Take B1077 from Attleborough or Watton. At Xrds in Rocklands turn South onto The Street. Garden is approx 700m on L opp village school.* **Sun 21 Aug (11-5). Adm £3, chd free. Home-made teas.**
Artist and Plantswoman's cottage garden ! Lots packed into 0.4 acre: 'Hot' border; 'Pale and Interesting' border; Exotic-ish lush bed, Shady woodland 'hop'; 'Dry river bed' gravel garden; Cutting Garden; Wildlife pond; Sculptures and 'Found Art'. Mostly wheelchair accessible but Woodland 'hop' and pond are up a small bank. 'Dry river bed' is thick gravel but can be viewed from edge.

♿ 🍕 ☂ ☕

NORTH EAST

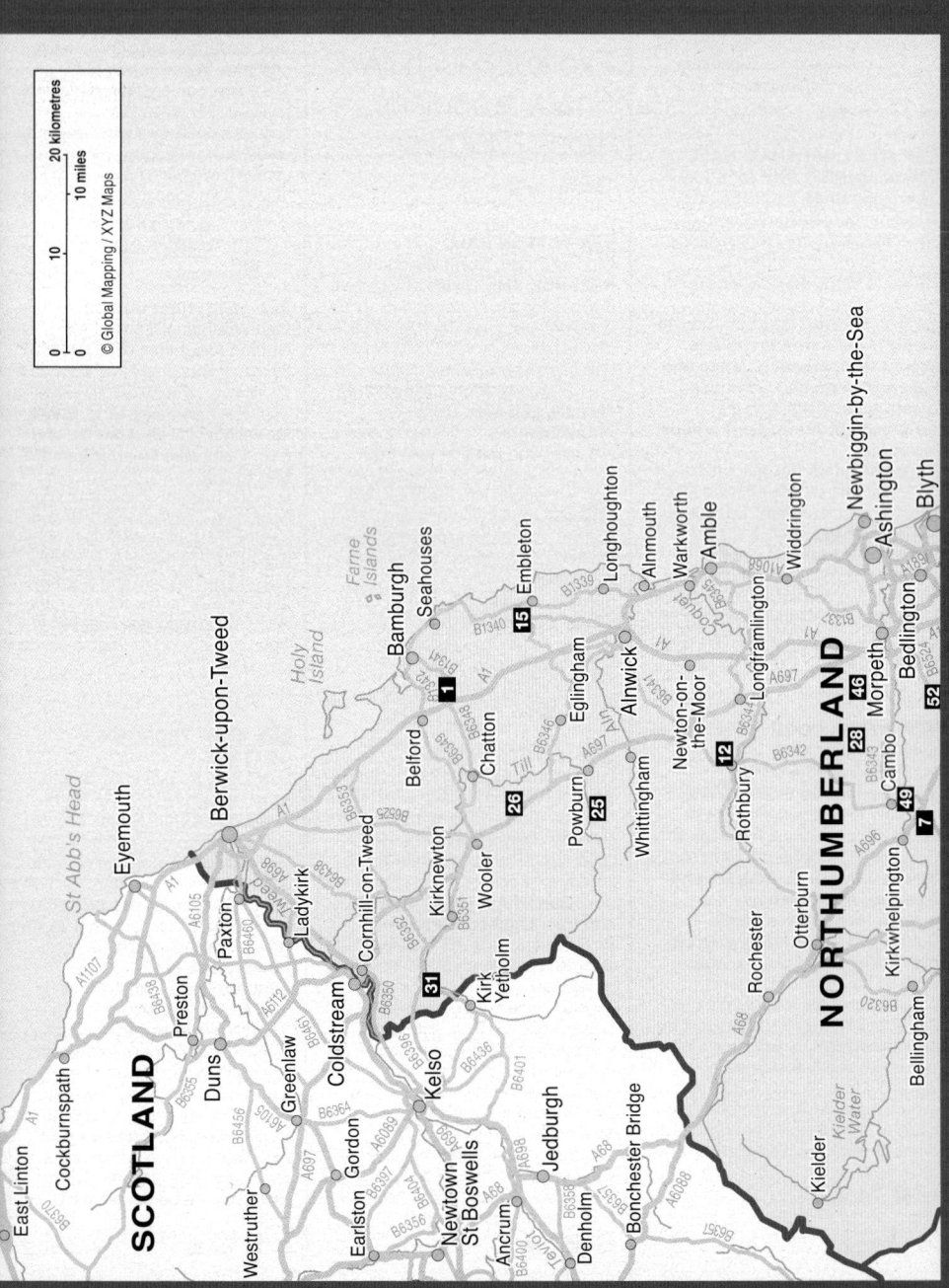

20 kilometres

10 miles

10

10

0

0

© Global Mapping / XYZ Maps

Farne Islands

Holy Island

St Abb's Head

SCOTLAND

NORTHUMBERLAND

East Linton

Cockburnspath

Eyemouth

Berwick-upon-Tweed

Preston

Duns

Greenlaw

Paxton

Ladykirk

Coldstream

Conhill-on-Tweed

Kirknewton

Wooler

Chatton

Belford

Bamburgh

Seahouses

Embleton

15

1

26

25

Eglingham

Powburn

Alnwick

Whittingham

Newton-on-the-Moor

12

Rothbury

Longhoughton

Alnmouth

Warkworth

Amble

Longframlington

Widdrington

Newbiggin-by-the-Sea

Ashington

Blyth

46

Morpeth

28

Cambo

49

7

Bedlington

52

Westruther

Earlston

Gordon

Newtown St Boswells

Kelso

Jedburgh

Bonchester Bridge

Ancrum

Denholm

Otterburn

Rochester

Kirkwhelpington

Kielder

Kielder Water

Bellingham

31

Kirk Yetholm

Investec Wealth & Investment supports the NGS

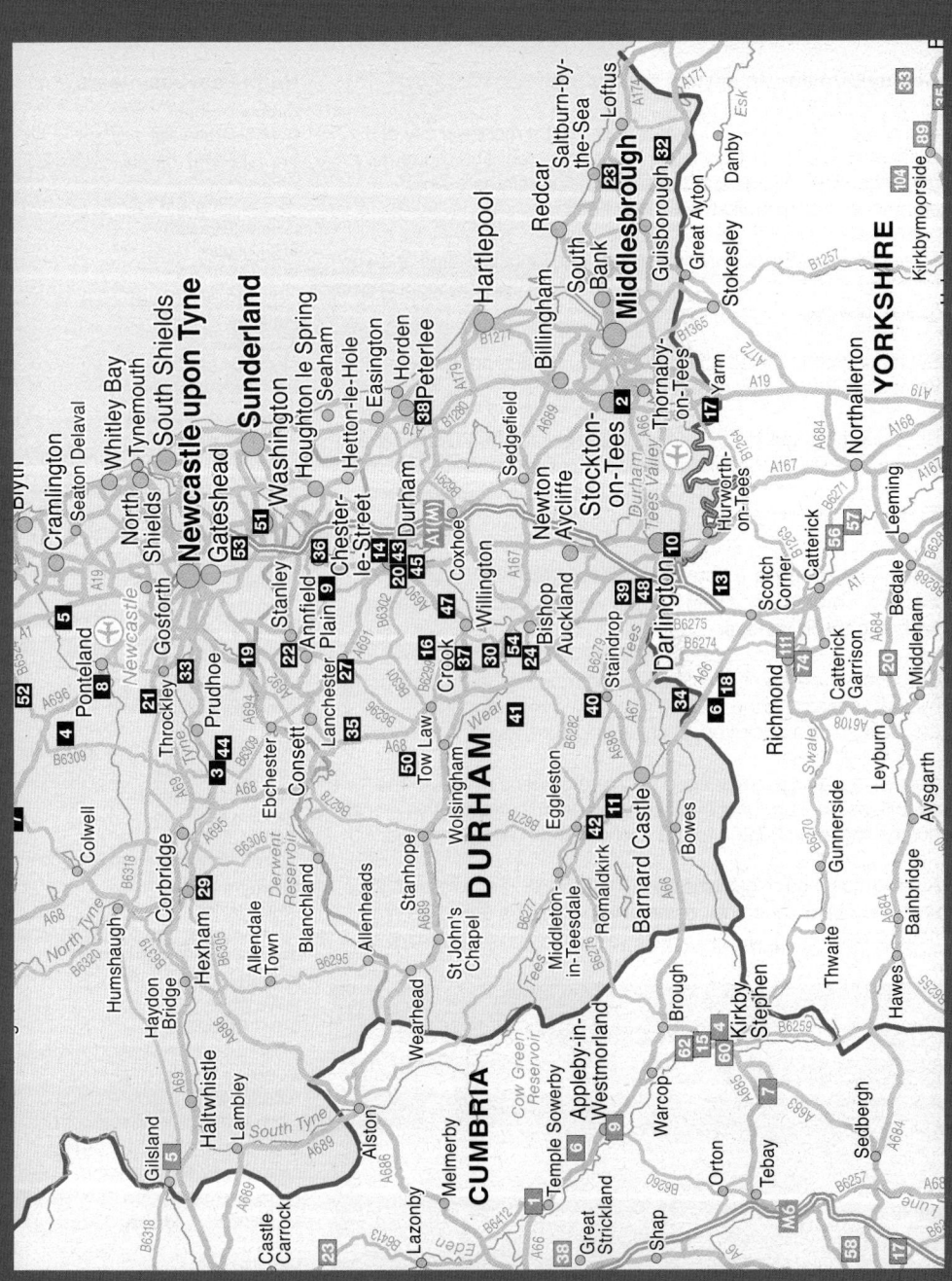

North East

County Durham: an unsung county.

At the heart of this once industrial land lies the medieval city of Durham. The city is a fascinating blend of ancient and modern, respecting the heritage and traditions of its forefathers whilst embracing changing lifestyles and culture.

This epitomises the county as a whole; old, industrial sites and coal mines have been sensitively cleared to restore the land to its original 'green' beauty.

Set amongst this varied and beautiful countryside are gardens which open their gates for the NGS.

So, stand amongst the rare and unusual plants at 14 Grays Terrace and be amazed by the spectacular view of Durham Cathedral, or visit the wonderful and imaginative hidden garden that has been created behind the working forge at Ravensworth.

Northumberland is a county rich in history with sturdy castles, stunning coastline and a wild landscape threaded with sheltered valleys.

Gardeners have learnt how to make the most of the land; terracing hillsides, enhancing the soil and often using the wonderful architecture as a backdrop, such as at Lilburn Tower.

Garden owners have managed to create gardens whatever the conditions. At Blagdon the solution has been to plant within an old quarry, and at Wallington to use a long narrow valley for shelter.

An eclectic range of gardens open for the NGS. Each reflects the style and character of their owners, with the extra attraction of home-made teas and plant sales.

North East Volunteers

County Durham
County Organiser
Alison Morgan
01913 843842
alison.morgan@ngs.org.uk

County Treasurer
Sue Douglas
07712 461002
pasm.d@btinternet.com

Publicity
Sue Walker
01325 481881
walker.sdl@gmail.com

Booklet Co-ordinator
Sheila Walke
07837 764057
sheila.walke@ngs.org.uk

Assistant County Organisers
Lynn Cameron 01915 863383
lynnanncameron@yahoo.co.uk

Gill Knights 01325 483210
Gillian.knights@ntlworld.com

Gill Naisby 01325 381324
gillnaisby@gmail.com

Mary Smith 01388 832727
mary@maryruth.plus.com

Northumberland & Tyne and Wear
County Organiser
& Booklet Coordinator
Maureen Kesteven
01914 135937
maureen@patrickkesteven.plus.com

County Treasurer
David Oakley
07941 077594
david.oakley@ngs.org.uk

Publicity
Susie White
07941 077595
susie@susie-white.co.uk

Assistant County Organisers
Patricia Fleming 01668 217009
patriciaflemingwoop@gmail.com

Natasha McEwen 07917 754155
natashamcewengd@aol.co.uk

Liz Reid 01914 165981
lizreid52@ntlworld.com

Left: The Forge

Opening Dates

All entries subject to change.
For latest information check www.ngs.org.uk

February

Snowdrop Festival

Sunday 14
9 Congburn Arboretum
Sunday 28
24 Hillside Cottages

April

Sunday 3
9 Congburn Arboretum
Sunday 24
34 The Old Vicarage

May

Sunday 1
7 NEW Capability Brown's Kirkharle Lake Courtyard
Sunday 8
49 Wallington
Sunday 15
22 Harperley Hall Farm
Sunday 22
5 Blagdon
Sunday 29
13 Croft Hall
26 Lilburn Tower

June

Festival Weekend

Sunday 5
2 Barnard Avenue Gardens
35 Oliver Ford Garden
51 Washington Old Hall
Monday 6
14 Crook Hall & Gardens
Sunday 12
10 NEW 107 Coniscliffe Road
25 Ingram House
37 Parker Towers
Wednesday 15
48 Thornton Hall Gardens
Friday 17
49 Wallington (Evening)

Coldcotes Moor Farm
© Val Corbett

Sunday 19
6 Broaches Farm
17 Forest Lane Gardens
31 Mindrum Garden
Saturday 25
15 Fallodon Hall
53 Woodlands
Sunday 26
42 Romaldkirk Gardens
46 NEW Stanton Fence
Wednesday 29
6 Broaches Farm

July

Saturday 2
50 Warrenfell
Sunday 3
11 Cotherstone Village Gardens
18 The Forge
28 NEW Longwitton hall
50 Warrenfell
52 Whalton Manor Gardens
Thursday 7
53 Woodlands
Sunday 10
4 Bichfield Tower
16 The Fold
23 NEW The Hidden Gardens of Skelton
38 Peterlee Gardens Safari
49 Wallington
Saturday 16
12 Cragside
Sunday 17
1 NEW Adderstone House

3 The Beacon
32 Moorsholm Village
43 St Margaret's Allotments
54 Woodside House
Sunday 24
29 Loughbrow House
41 Ravensford Farm
Sunday 31
33 No. 2 Ferndene
45 NEW St Cuthbert's Hospice

August

Sunday 7
47 4 Stockley Grove
Sunday 21
39 NEW Quarry End

September

Sunday 4
19 Gibside
Sunday 25
21 Halls of Heddon

October

Sunday 2
27 Lizards Farm
Sunday 9
24 Hillside Cottages

Gardens open to the public

7 NEW Capability Brown's Kirkharle Lake Courtyard

12 Cragside
14 Crook Hall & Gardens
19 Gibside
21 Halls of Heddon
31 Mindrum Garden
40 Raby Castle
49 Wallington
51 Washington Old Hall
52 Whalton Manor Gardens

By arrangement only

8 Coldcotes Moor Farm
20 14 Grays Terrace
30 10 Low Row
36 25 Park Road South
44 Skara Brae

Also open by arrangement

3 The Beacon
6 Broaches Farm
16 The Fold
18 The Forge
22 Harperley Hall Farm
24 2 Hillside Cottage, Hillside Cottages
26 Lilburn Tower
29 Loughbrow House
33 No. 2 Ferndene
41 Ravensford Farm
47 4 Stockley Grove
48 Thornton Hall Gardens
50 Warrenfell
53 Woodlands
54 Woodside House

The Gardens

① NEW ADDERSTONE HOUSE

Adderstone Mains, Belford NE70 7HS. John & Pauline Clough. *1m S of Belford off A1. Best approached from the N off A1. Adderstone Mains is 1m S of Belford, turn L off A1. From S, 0.7m N of Purdy Lodge on R but turn dangerous, continue to Belford, turn & approach from N. Ample parking.* **Sun 17 July (1-5). Adm £5, chd free. Light refreshments in the courtyard.**

A Victorian farm house, gardens, millpond and grounds of 10½ acres. Some established but many 'new projects' in development with Sean Murray (RHS Chelsea Challenge winner). Walled garden with rose arbour, mature shrubs; an orchard leads to developing sunken garden; rose walk to the formal garden, then on to the mill pond, fruit/vegetable plots and vineyard. Plant stall, teas and grape juice from vineyard.

♿ ☕

GROUP OPENING

② BARNARD AVENUE GARDENS

Stockton-On-Tees TS19 7AB. *10m E of Darlington off A66. Heading E or W from or towards Middlesbrough take slip rd marked Hartburn & Stockton W. L into Greens Lane, follow yellow signs. Off Gainford Rd & Oxbridge Rd W side of Stockton. Park in Gainford Rd.* **Sun 5 June (1.30-5). Combined adm £4, chd free. Home-made teas at Briarcroft (no 27).**

10 BARNARD AVENUE
Dennis & Jennifer Hodgson

22 BARNARD AVENUE
Laura & Peter Davison

BRIARCROFT Ⓓ
Mr Glenn Sunman

Enjoy a visit to three, small urban gardens. No. 10 is a mature secluded garden with several seating areas. Recently landscaped, it is divided into 'rooms' and backed by mature trees. There are two small ponds, a water feature, a Judas tree which is magnificent when in flower in spring and, apart from hanging baskets, no annuals. No. 22 is a quiet and relaxing suburban garden divided into three areas: a secluded sunny seating area, a larger lawned area with mixed borders and a shady section under a mature ash tree. No 27 has a wisteria covered pergola, wild flower area, willow tunnel and arbour, aerial hedge, kitchen garden and herbaceous borders. Gravel paths in some areas.

♿ ♿ ☕

In 2016
the Chesterfield
Royal NGS
Macmillan
Cancer Unit
will open

③ THE BEACON

10 Crabtree Road, Stocksfield NE43 7NX. Derek & Patricia Hodgson, 01661 842518, patandderek@btinternet.com. *12m W of Newcastle upon Tyne. From A69 follow signs into village. Station & cricket ground on L. Turn R into Cadehill Rd then 1st R into Crabtree Rd (cul de sac) Park on Cadehill.* **Sun 17 July (2-6). Adm £4, chd free. Cream teas. Visits also by arrangement groups of 10+.**

This garden illustrates how to make a cottage garden with loads of interest at different levels. Planted with acers, roses and a variety of cottage garden and formal plants. Water runs gently through it and there are tranquil places to sit and talk or just reflect. Stunning colour and plant combinations. Steep, so not wheelchair friendly but wheelchair users have negotiated the drive and enjoyed the view of the main garden.

♿ 🚙 ☕

④ BICHFIELD TOWER

Belsay, Newcastle Upon Tyne NE20 0JP. Lesley & Stewart Manners, 075114 39606, lesleymanners@gmail.com, www.bitchfieldtower.co.uk. *Private rd off B6309, 4m N of Stamfordham and SW of Belsay village.* **Sun 10 July (1-4). Adm £5, chd free. Home-made teas in the carriage house garden and building.**

6 acre maturing garden, in its 2nd year of rejuvenation, set around a Medieval Pele Tower with an impressive stone water feature, large trout lake, mature woodland, wild meadow and 2 walled gardens. Featuring this year, two stunning iron flower covered windows providing spectacular views of the surrounding countryside. There are large herbaceous borders around the garden with extensive lawns. Historic building, tennis court, woodlands fairy walk for kids, sculpture walk throughout the grounds, croquet lawn and set, trout lake, pop-up shops of local businesses.

♿ 🛏 ☕

⑤ BLAGDON

Seaton Burn NE13 6DE. Viscount Ridley, www.blagdonestate.co.uk. *5m S of Morpeth on A1. 8m N of Newcastle on A1, N on B1318, L at r'about (Holiday Inn) & follow signs to Blagdon. Entrance to parking area signed.* **Sun 22 May (1-4.30). Adm £5, chd free. Home-made teas.**

Unique 27 acre garden encompassing formal garden with Lutyens designed 'canal', Lutyens structures and walled kitchen garden. Valley with stream and various follies, quarry garden and woodland walks. Large numbers of ornamental trees and shrubs planted over many generations. National Collections of Acer, Alnus and Sorbus. Trailer rides around the estate (small additional charge) and stalls selling local produce. Partial wheelchair access.

♿ 🐕 ♿ **NPC** ☕

BRAESIDE
See Cumbria

⑥ BROACHES FARM

Dalton, Richmond DL11 7HW. Mr & Mrs Hutchinson, 01833 621369, jude1@myfwi.co.uk. *7m W of Scotch Corner. From Scotch Corner on A66 W, 7m turn L at The Rokeby Inn. After ½ m turn L to Dalton. Farm on L after 1m.* **Sun 19 June (1-5). Cream teas. Wed 29 June (2-8). Light refreshments. Adm £3, chd free. Visits also by arrangement June to Aug any number of visitors.**

In 1996 this wonderful garden was a field. It now includes 2 ponds, one with koi, stream, bog garden and wooded area. Mixed colourful borders are full of herbaceous perennials. Informal and naturalistic, this is a rural idyll. Abundant wildlife incl kingfishers, dippers, wagtails, frogs and toads. Lots of seating areas including summerhouse and gazebo.

7 NEW ◆ CAPABILITY BROWN'S KIRKHARLE LAKE COURTYARD
Kirkharle, Northumberland NE19 2PE. Kitty Anderson, 01830 540362, info@kirkharlecourtyard.net, www.kirkharlecourtyard.co.uk. *Off A696 18m N of Newcastle upon Tyne. Turn L, signed Kirkharle Courtyard, off A696 6m N of Belsay near Wallington turn off.* **For NGS: Sun 1 May (11-4). Adm by donation. Light refreshments at Kirkharle Coffee house and restaurant. For other opening times and information, please phone, email or visit garden website.**
300th ANNIVERSARY FOOD AND FLOWER FAYRE. Birthplace, and first workplace, of Lancelot 'Capability' Brown, who designed the serpentine lake, now restored, with planting, according to his original plans. Enjoy the lake, the art/craft workshops in the converted farm buildings, specialist stalls and food stalls, incl NGS Plant Stall. Featured in Titchmarsh on Capability Brown, More4.

8 COLDCOTES MOOR FARM
Ponteland, Newcastle Upon Tyne NE20 0DF. Ron & Louise Bowey, 01661 822579, info@theboweys.co.uk. *Off A696 N of Ponteland. From S, leave Ponteland on A696 towards Jedburgh, after 1m take L turn marked 'Milbourne 2m'. After 400yds turn L into drive.* **Visits by arrangement in July for groups of 10+ week commencing 11 July only. Adm £5, chd free. Home-made teas.**
The garden, landscaped grounds and woods cover around 15 acres. The wooded approach opens out to lawned areas surrounded by new ornamental and woodland shrubs and trees. A courtyard garden leads

to an ornamental walled garden, beyond which is an orchard, vegetable garden, flower garden and rose arbour. To the south the garden looks out over a lake and field walks, with woodland walk to the west. Small children's play area. Featured in WI LIfe Magazine. Most areas can be accessed though sometimes by circuitous routes or an occasional step. WC access involves three steps.

9 CONGBURN ARBORETUM
Edmondsley, Durham DH7 6DY. Mr Alan Herbert, www.congbunnurseries.co.uk. *From B6532 at Edmondsley, follow yellow NGS signs.* **Sun 14 Feb, Sun 3 Apr (10-4). Adm £3, chd free. Light refreshments in on-site cafe serving lunches and teas from 10 'til 4.**
Come and enjoy a woodland walk and find the snowdrops on St Valentine's day or come in April to see the daffodils, narcissi and hellebores. The arboretum is in the process of development and you will therefore see plenty of new planting amongst the already established trees. The site is on a hillside so please wear sturdy footwear. You can choose a longer or shorter route through the woods. The paths are steep and not suitable for wheelchairs.

10 NEW 107 CONISCLIFFE ROAD
Darlington DL3 7ET. Jill Jackson. *2m from A1 near town centre. From A1 S, L at r'about, L next r'about R onto Coniscliffe Rd. Follow signs towards Barnard Castle A167 from town centre /ring rd and this is Coniscliffe Rd. Please park in nearby streets.* **Sun 12 June (2-4). Adm £2.50, chd free. Cream teas.**
The garden is designed for a wildlife loving wheelchair user and features a pond, a patch of meadow, huge bug palace, numerous bird feeders and living brush pile. In addition vegetables shares the borders with the flowers. There are some weeds as the rule is if the bees butterflies and bugs love it, it stays. The garden owner is a wheelchair user so access is fine but it is a slope with sloped paths, not all on the flat.

GROUP GARDENS

11 COTHERSTONE VILLAGE GARDENS
Cotherstone, Barnard Castle DL12 9QW. *4m NW of Barnard Castle. On B6277 Middleton-in-Teesdale to Barnard Castle road. Gardens are spread throughout the village. Home made teas at three points in the village.* **Sun 3 July (11-4.30). Combined adm £4.50, chd free. Home-made teas in village hall and two gardens.**
Once again a warm welcome awaits you in this traditional and historic Teesdale village. The village is bounded on two sides by the Balder and Tees rivers. A variety of country gardens (& allotments) ranging from small to nearly 3 acres. Look out for some great Teesdale views as you walk between them. This year access has also kindly been made available to the ruins of Cotherstone Castle (scheduled ancient monument). Visitors can help themselves to herbs from the pick your own boxes spread throughout the village. The village is on the Teesdale Way footpath and there are many picturesque walks in and around the locality. The village hall will also host an exhibition of local arts and crafts. Cotherstone and the surrounding area is a beautiful place for walking. There are 2 PHs, cafes and a shop in the village where refreshments can also be obtained. Owing to the variety of gardens and allotments some may not be accessible for wheelchair users.

Some weeds
as the rule is
if the bees
butterflies and
bugs love it,
it stays . . .

The Beacon

12 ♦ CRAGSIDE

Rothbury NE65 7PX. National Trust, 01669 620333, www.nationaltrust.org.uk/cragside/things-to-see-and-do/garden/. *13m SW of Alnwick. (B6341); 15m NW of Morpeth (A697).* **For NGS: Sat 16 July (10-5). Adm £17.40, chd free. For other opening times and information, please phone or visit garden website.**

The Formal Garden is in the 'High Victorian' style created by the 1st Lord and Lady Armstrong. Incl orchard house, carpet bedding, ferneries, Italian terrace and Rose borders. The largest sandstone Rock Garden in Europe with its tumbling cascades. Extensive grounds of over 1000 acres famous for rhododendrons in June, large lakes and magnificent conifer landscape. The House, mainly the design of Norman Shaw, with its very fine arts and crafts interiors is worth a separate visit. Limited wheelchair access to formal garden.

♿ 🚻 🐕 🚐 ☕

13 CROFT HALL

Croft-on-Tees DL2 2TB. Mr & Mrs Trevor Chaytor Norris. *3m S of Darlington. On A167 to Northallerton, 6m from Scotch Corner. Croft Hall is 1st house on R as you enter village from Scotch Corner.* **Sun 29 May**

(2-6). **Adm £4, chd free. Home-made teas.**

A lovely lavender walk leads to a Queen Anne-fronted house (not open) surrounded by a 5-acre garden, comprising a stunning herbaceous border, large fruit and vegetable plot, two ponds and wonderful topiary arched wall. Pretty rose garden and mature box Italianate parterre are beautifully set in this garden offering peaceful, tranquil views of open countryside. Some gravel paths.

♿ 🐕 ☕

14 ♦ CROOK HALL & GARDENS

Sidegate, Durham City DH1 5SZ. Maggie Bell, 0191 384 8028, info@crookhallgardens.co.uk, www.crookhallgardens.co.uk. *Centre of Durham City. Crook Hall is short walk from Durham's Market Place. Follow the tourist info signs. Parking available at entrance.* **For NGS: Mon 6 June (10-5). Adm £7, chd £5. Cream teas. For other opening times and information, please phone, email or visit garden website.**

Described in Country Life as having 'history, romance and beauty'. Intriguing medieval manor house surrounded by 4 acres of fine gardens. Visitors can enjoy magnificent cathedral views from the 2 walled gardens. Other garden 'rooms' incl the silver and white garden. An orchard, moat pool, maze and Sleeping Giant give added interest! Refreshments in the Tea Room (main building) and the Café (entrance building). Featured on Radio 4 with John McCarthy, and Clare Balding, on Radio 4 Gardeners Question Time and in the Independent and the ' I ' as number 9 in the top ten places to visit in Britain. Wheelchair accessible and disabled WC.

♿ 🐕 🚐 🛏 ☕

15 FALLODON HALL

Alnwick NE66 3HF. Mr & Mrs Mark Bridgeman, 01665 576252, www.bruntoncottages.co.uk. *5m N of Alnwick, 2m off A1. From the A1 turn R on B6347 signed Christon Bank & Seahouses, & turn into Fallodon gates after exactly 2m, at the Xrds. Follow drive for 1m.* **Sat 25 June (2-5). Adm £4, chd free. Home-made teas in stable yard.**

Extensive, well established garden, including a 30 metre border, finishing beside a hot greenhouse and bog garden. The late C17 walls of the kitchen garden surround cutting and vegetable borders and the fruit greenhouse. The sunken garden from 1898 has been replanted by Natasha McEwen. Woodlands, pond and arboretum extend over 10 acres to explore. Renowned home-made teas in stable yard, and plant sale, predominantly of Fallodon plants. Partial wheelchair access.

16 THE FOLD
High Wooley, Stanley Crook DL15 9AP. Mr & Mrs G Young, 01388 768412, g898young@btinternet.com. *3m N of Crook. Turn R at Xrds in Brancepeth, opp turn to Castle, drive 3m along the single track rd until you reach the junction on bend with the main rd. Entrance 100yards on L.* **Sun 10 July (1.30-4.30). Adm £4, chd free. Home-made teas. Visits also by arrangement May to Sept, groups of 10+.**
Garden, approx ¹/₂ acre created over 20 years in an area that had been extensively mined. It stands at 700ft and enjoys splendid views over countryside. Herbaceous borders, alpine bed, island beds, ponds, numerous mature trees and small roof garden. Wide range of plants, mostly perennials, many grown from seed and cuttings. Emphasis on colour, harmony and texture to create all year interest. No disabled access as steep slopes and gravel paths.

'standing stone' feature and a rhododendron and azalea glade . . .

GROUP OPENING

17 FOREST LANE GARDENS
52 (The Hollies) & 48 Forest Lane, Kirklevington, Yarm TS15 9ND. Fiona & Terry Dunn, Marian & David McDonald. *200yds after village hall on R. Travelling N on A19 exit A67 to Yarm (or take Crathorne exit when heading S). At the Crown Hotel Kirklevington turn into Forest Lane & the gardens are 500yds on R.* **Sun 19 June (1-5). Combined adm £4, chd free. Home-made teas. Hot & cold drinks & cakes.**
The Hollies, informal 1 acre gardens, large island beds plus borders with shrubs and perennials with rhododendrons, wisteria, alliums, clematis and 70+ trees incl wooded wild flower area, and kitchen garden. 48 Forest Lane, superbly manicured lawns and expertly planted beds with wide variety of flowering shrubs, camellias, perennials, climbers and fruit trees. Double tiered pond, water features and lilies. The Hollies: gravel drive and paths plus shallow slopes in the garden should be ok for wheelchairs. No.48 has narrow side access only.

18 THE FORGE
Ravensworth, Richmond DL11 7EU. Mr & Mrs Peter & Enid Wilson, 01325 718242, enid.wilson@btconnect.com. *7m N of Richmond. Travel 5¹/₂ m W on A66 from Scotch Corner. Turn L to Ravensworth & follow NGS signs.* **Sun 3 July (1-5.30). Adm £3, chd free. Cream teas. Homemade cakes. Visits also by arrangement June to Sept.**
The Blacksmith's Secret Garden - the garden is hidden from view behind The Forge House, Cottage and the working Blacksmith's Forge. It has small wildlife ponds with two natural stone features and a meadow. There are a number of unusual plants i.e. Dactylorhiza Fuchsia. Featured in Northern Echo, Teesdale Mercury, Amateur Gardener. Wheelchair access across gravel path.

19 ◆ GIBSIDE
Rowlands Gill NE16 6BG. National Trust, 01207 541820, www.nationaltrust.org.uk/gibside. *6m SW of Gateshead. Follow brown signs from the A1 & take the A694 towards Rowlands Gill.* **For NGS: Sun 4 Sept (10-4.30). Adm £8.20, chd £4.10. Light refreshments in Cafe. For other opening times and information, please phone or visit garden website.**
C18 landscape garden designed by Stephen Switzer for one of the richest men in Georgian England, George Bowes, and his celebrated daughter Mary Eleanor. Inner pleasure grounds with tree-lined avenue and productive walled garden, plus miles of woodland and riverside walks in the Derwent Valley. Ongoing restoration of the gardens and woodland, one of the National Trust's most ambitious projects. Cafe offers locally-sourced produce with fruit and vegetables from the walled garden. Behind the scenes guided talks by one of the gardening team. See the walled garden come back to life as we restore it. If you have special access needs, please call us on 01207 541820 in advance of your visit.

20 14 GRAYS TERRACE
Redhills, Durham DH1 4AU. Mr Paul Beard, 0191 5972849, pauljofraeard@yahoo.co.uk. *Just off A167 on W side of Durham. ¹/₂ m S of A167 / A691 r'about, turn L into Redhills Lane. When road turns R with no entry sign, Grays Terrace is ahead. No.14 is at the very end.* **Visits by arrangement Apr.to Aug. Adm by donation.**
A steeply sloping garden of about ²/₃ acre with a superb view over Durham Cathedral, Castle and surroundings. Very informal garden; no bedding and a significant wild area. Planting is mixed with interest throughout the yr. Many unusual and rare plants. Particularly knowledgeable owner who is happy to escort groups round the garden.

21 ◆ HALLS OF HEDDON
West Heddon Nursery, Heddon-on-the-Wall, Newcastle Upon Tyne NE15 0JS. Mr David Hall, 01661 852445, www.hallsofheddon.co.uk. *Approx 5m W of Newcastle upon Tyne. Approx 1m NW of Heddon on the Wall signed off B6318 (Military Rd) at the bridge crossing the A69.* **For NGS: Sun 25 Sept (10.30-4). Adm by donation. Teas, coffees and home made cakes. For other opening times and information, please phone or visit garden website.**
Halls is a world renowned family owned nursery, full of plants set against the backdrop of an orginal heated wall garden. September sees a spectacular display of colour and foliage in its dahlia and chrysanthemum trial fields. Row upon row of brilliant hues of plants arranged to show type, colour and height. It lifts the spirits as winter approaches and makes a dahlia/chrysanthemum lover of every gardener. Introductory talks with a question and answer session will be provided throughout the day by David Hall. Harrogate Show Gold Medal Winner.

22▶ HARPERLEY HALL FARM
Harperley, Stanley DH9 9UB. Gary McDermott, 01207 233318, enquiries@harperleyhallfarm nurseries.co.uk, www.harperleyhallfarmnurseries. co.uk. *A1 leave J63 at r'about take 2nd exit A693, continue for 5m. After T-turn R Shieldrow Lane, then R Kyo Lane at end turn R Harperley Lane, garden 500yds on L.* **Sun 15 May (10-4). Adm £3, chd free. Home-made teas. Visits also by arrangement Mar to Oct, groups welcome daytime or evenings.**
An evolving garden, attached to an award winning specialist plant nursery. The garden is set within 5 acres of countryside and we grow a wide range of bog and woodland plants around a series of ponds. The garden is heavily planted with Primula 'Inverewe' and blue Himalayan poppies as well as the very rare Meconopsis punicea 'Sichuan Silk' For nursery opening times see our website. The garden is in a tranquil setting and a flock of Rainbow and other Lorikeet fly at liberty around the garden. Featured in Living North, Garden News and new plants regularly featured in the RHS Garden magazine. The majority of the garden and nursery can be accessed by wheelchair users.

&♿ ⚘ ❀ 🚐 ☕

GROUP OPENING

23▶ NEW▶ THE HIDDEN GARDENS OF SKELTON
Skelton-In-Cleveland, Saltburn-By-The-Sea TS12 2WT. Colin and Daphne Hurworth. *To Windermere Drive take A174 or A173 from Guisbrough. Parking in Health Centre.To the Ivories, head for North Skelton. Vaughan St is the High St & turn down small lane by Curly Tops Hairdressers.* **Sun 10 July (1-4). Combined adm £4, chd free. Home-made teas at The Ivories, plants for sale at 60 Windermere Drive.**

> **NEW▶ THE IVORIES, VAUGHAN STREET**
> Mr & Mrs Dave & Pauline Hutchinson

> **NEW▶ 60 WINDERMERE DRIVE**
> Daphne & Colin Hurworth

60 Windermere Drive, situated 2m inland with an elevated position and frequent strong westerly winds, this garden has been a challenge. Interestingly shaped, larger than average 'new build' garden. Divided into areas of interest, including herbaceous, ferns and hostas, dry gravel planting and late clematis. Other features are a greenhouse, a living green shed roof and newly constructed alpine bed. Parking available in the nearby Health Centre. The Ivories: Enjoy a visit to a hidden garden in the true sense of the words. When the garden was started 14 years ago it was a blank canvas. It slopes away from the house and is now terraced with mature trees, shrubs and plants, full of colour and contrast. Seating areas with water feature and gravelled areas. The summerhouse is a perfect place to relax. Handmade garden ornaments are displayed in the garden. Parking on street.

❀ ☕

The summerhouse is a perfect place to relax . . .

GROUP OPENING

24▶ HILLSIDE COTTAGES
Low Etherley, Bishop Auckland DL14 0EZ. *Off the B6282 in Low Etherley, nr Bishop Auckland. To reach the gardens walk down the track opp number 63 Low Etherley. Please park on main rd. Limited disabled parking at the cottages.* **Sun 28 Feb, Sun 9 Oct (12.30-4). Combined adm £4, chd free. Light refreshments. Soup and rolls will be available.**

> **1 HILLSIDE COTTAGE**
> Eric & Delia Ayres

> **2 HILLSIDE COTTAGE**
> Mrs M Smith
> Visits also by arrangement Feb to Nov.
> mary@maryruth.plus.com
> 01388 832727

The gardens of these two C19 cottages offer contrasting styles. At Number 1, grass paths lead you through a layout of trees and shrubs including many interesting specimens. Number 2 is based on island beds and has a cottage garden feel with a variety of perennials among the trees and shrubs and also incl a wild area, vegetables and fruit. Both gardens have ponds and water features. This year we are opening for snowdrops in spring and for autumn colour. Featured in Northern Echo and Teesdale Mercury. There are steps in both gardens.

🏡 ❀ ☕

25▶ INGRAM HOUSE
Ingram, Alnwick NE66 4LT. Adrian & Jane Levien, 01665 578906, ingramhousebookings@gmail.com, www.ingram-house.com. *7m S of Wooler. Turn R off the A697 into the Breamish Valley & Northumberland National Park.* **Sun 12 June (1.30-5). Adm £4, chd free. Home-made teas.**
In 2003 this 2 acre garden was mainly grass with mature trees and hedges. Since then, whilst the site provides the backdrop the garden has been informally landscaped. It now has a pond and stream, colourful island beds, orchard and kitchen garden. Planting is mixed and varied. It probably breaks all the rules but the overall effect of winding paths and different rooms is peaceful and relaxing. The work is ongoing, with the bottom end of the garden being landscaped and planted in 2015.

❀ 🛏 ☕

26▶ LILBURN TOWER
Alnwick NE66 4PQ. Mr & Mrs D Davidson, 01668 217291. *3m S of Wooler. On A697.* **Sun 29 May (2-6). Adm £5, chd free. Home-made teas. Visits also by arrangement Apr to Oct groups of 6+.**
10 acres of magnificent walled and formal gardens set above river; rose parterre, topiary, scented garden; Victorian conservatory, wild flower meadow. Extensive fruit and vegetable garden, large glasshouse with vines. 30 acres of woodland with walks. Giant lilies, meconopsis around pond garden. Rhododendrons and azaleas. Also ruins of Pele Tower, and C12 church. Partial wheelchair access.

&♿ ⚘ ❀ 🚐 ☕

27 LIZARDS FARM

Kitswell Road, Lanchester, Durham DH7 0RE. Mr Peter Robinson, 07713 627329, treetransplanters@tiscali.co.uk, www.northerntreetransplanters. com. *Drive full length of Kitswell Rd (signed as no through rd) & then continue straight ahead down single track to parking area.* **Sun 2 Oct (10-4). Adm £4, chd free. Light refreshments. Warming soup & bread roll, teas & cakes available all day.**

Lizards Farm: a plantation and nursery for trees. Extensive range, with unusual species inc. many maples. Glorious autumn colour. Saplings to full size trees on sale. Very knowledgeable owner available to answer queries. Tree spade demonstration can be arranged - just ask. The site has lakes, extended walks and an area dedicated to a fascinating range of chicken breeds. Wear sturdy footwear.

28 NEW LONGWITTON HALL

Longwitton, Morpeth NE61 4JJ. Michael & Louise Spriggs. *2m N of Hartburn off B6343. Entrance at east end of Longwitton village.* **Sun 3 July (12-4). Adm £5, chd free. Home-made teas.**

6 acre historic site with glorious views to the south. Sheltered, mature garden, with specimen trees and acers, currently being redeveloped with new borders. Circular rose garden, crescent shaped pool surrounded by foliage plants, 'standing stone' feature and a rhododendron and azalea glade leading to newly planted laburnum tunnel. Tree peonies and yew walk. Good wheelchair access.

29 LOUGHBROW HOUSE

Hexham NE46 1RS. Mrs K A Clark, 01434 603351, patriciaclark351@btinternet.com. *1m S of Hexham on B6306. Dipton Mill Rd. Rd signed Blanchland, ¼ m take R fork; then ¼ m at fork, lodge gates & driveway at intersection.* **Sun 24 July (2-5). Adm £4, chd free. Home-made teas. Visits also by arrangement Mar to Oct.**

Country house garden with sweeping, colour themed herbaceous borders set around large lawns. Unique Lutyens inspired rill with grass topped bridges. Part walled kitchen garden and paved courtyard. Bog garden with pond. Developing new border and rose bed. Wild flower meadow with specimen trees. Woodland quarry garden with rhododendrons, azaleas, hostas and rare trees. Home made jams and chutneys.

30 10 LOW ROW

North Bitchburn, Crook DL15 8AJ. Mrs Ann Pickering, 01388 766345, keightleyann@yahoo.co.uk. *3m NW of Bishop Auckland. From Bishop Auckland take A689 (N) to Howden-le-Wear. R up bank before petrol stn, 1st R in village at 30mph sign. Park in the village* **Visits by arrangement for individuals and groups of 20 max. Adm £2, chd free.**

Unusual, original and truly organic, rambling garden: 90% grown from seeds and cuttings. Created without commercially bought plants or expense. Environmentally friendly. A haven for wildlife! Sloping garden with a myriad of paths and extensive views over the Wear Valley. Colour yr-round from snowdrops to autumn leaves. Knowledgeable garden owner who will make your visit one to remember. Open all yr except Tuesdays. Book by phone or e-mail. Refreshment offered in adjacent PH. Featured in Weekend Guardian.

31 ◆ MINDRUM GARDEN

Mindrum, Northumberland TD12 4QN. Mr & Mrs T Fairfax, 01890 850228, tpfairfax@gmail.com, www.mindrumestate.com. *6m SW of Coldstream, 9m NW of Wooler. Off B6352, 4m N of Yetholm. 5m from Cornhill on Tweed.* **For NGS: Sun 19 June (2-5). Adm £5, chd free. Home-made teas. For other opening times and information, please phone, email or visit garden website.**

7 acres of romantic planting with old fashioned roses, violas, hardy perennials, lilies, herbs, scented shrubs, and intimate garden areas flanked by woodland and river walks. Glasshouses with vines, jasmine. Large hillside limestone rock garden with water leading to a pond, delightful stream, woodland and wonderful views across Bowmont valley. Large plant sale, mostly home grown. Featured in Country Life. Partial wheelchair access due to landscape. Disabled parking close to house. Wheelchair accessible WC available.

GROUP OPENING

32 MOORSHOLM VILLAGE

Saltburn-By-The-Sea TS12 3JF, www.moorsholminbloom.co.uk. *Moorsholm is 6m E of Guisborough on A171. Turn L at sign for Moorsholm. Village 1m from A171. Visitors proceed to centre of village where stewards will direct to car park. Guides & maps available.* **Sun 17 July (11.30-4). Combined adm £5, chd free. Home-made teas in church hall and Sports Pavilion. Cakes, scones, tea and coffee.**

A range of gardens to view including woodland gardens, cottage gardens large and small, and up to 16 allotments in a moorland village. Farming and former ironstone setting, 5m from the North Sea. 4 times winner of Northumbria in Bloom best village; winner in Britain in Bloom. The village boasts a range of heritage features and cultivated public areas, notably the 'Long Border' and wild flower areas. An interesting heritage walk takes in village allotment gardens, green lanes with wildlife habitats and conservation schemes. Victorian Churchyard, Church Hall and Quiet Garden won 'Best Grounds of a Religious Establishment' Northumbria in Bloom. Printed map and interpretation boards ensure visitors enjoy local features and natural history. Warm welcome from Moorsholm in Bloom volunteers who very much enjoyed our first entry to NGS in 2015. Depending on weather some of the green lanes could be unsuitable for wheelchairs, some open gardens have steps.

33 NO. 2 FERNDENE
2 Holburn Lane Court, Holburn Lane, Ryton NE40 3PN. Maureen Kesteven, 0191 413 5937, maureen@patrickkesteven.plus.com. *In Ryton Old Village, 8m W of Gateshead. Off B6317, on Holburn Lane in Old Ryton Village. Park in Co-op carpark on High St, cross rd and walk through Ferndene Park following yellow signs.* **Sun 31 July (1-4.30). Adm £5, chd free. Tea. Pizzas from wood fired oven and prosecco. Visits also by arrangement Apr to July groups of 10+.**
A garden, approx. ³/₄ acre, developed over the last 6yrs, surrounded by mature trees. Informal areas of herbaceous perennials, more formal box bordered area, vegetable patch, sedum roof, wildlife pond, bog and fern gardens. Willow work. Early interest - hellebores, snowdrops, daffodils, bluebells and tulips, as well as later summer flowering perennials. 1¹/₂ acre mixed broadleaf wood being restored. Pizzas cooked in wood fired oven. Jams and chutneys for sale.

34 THE OLD VICARAGE
Hutton Magna, Richmond DL11 7HJ. Mr & Mrs D M Raw. *8m SE of Barnard Castle. 6m W of Scotch Corner on A66. Turn R, signed Hutton Magna. Continue to, and through, village. Garden 200yds past village on L, on corner of T-junction.* **Sun 24 Apr (2-5.30). Adm £3, chd free. Home-made teas.**
S-facing garden, elevation 450ft. Plantings, since 1978, now maturing within original design contemporary to 1887 house (not open). Cut and topiary hedging, old orchard, rose and herbaceous borders featuring hellebores in profusion, with tulips and primulas. Large and interesting plant sale. Recent introduction of a loggery to encourage wildlife.

35 OLIVER FORD GARDEN
Longedge Lane, Rowley, Consett DH8 9HG. Bob & Bev Tridgett, www.gardensanctuaries.co.uk. *5m NW of Lanchester. Signed from A68 in Rowley. From Lanchester take rd towards Sately. Garden will be signed as you pass Woodlea Manor.* **Sun 5 June (1-5). Adm £3, chd free. Home-made teas.**
Spectacular 1¹/₂ -acre woodland garden developed and planted by 2007 BBC gardener of the year. Mini

arboretum specialising in bark that includes rare acers, stewartia, betula and prunus. Stream, wildlife pond and bog garden. Semi-shaded Japanese maple and dwarf rhododendron garden. 80 sq metre rock garden. Large insect nectar garden. Orchard and 1¹/₂ -acre upland meadow. Annual wild flower area.

Romantically planted rose covered arbours and long clematis-draped pergola walk . . .

36 25 PARK ROAD SOUTH
Chester le Street DH3 3LS. Mrs A Middleton, 0191 388 3225. *4m N of Durham. Located at S end of A167 Chester-le-St bypass rd. Precise directions provided when booking visit.* **Visits by arrangement May to July. Adm £3, chd free. Light refreshments.**
Plantswoman's garden with all-yr round interest, colour, texture and foliage. Unusual perennials, grasses, shrubs and container planting. Cool courtyard garden using foliage only. Small front gravel garden. Plants for sale.

37 PARKER TOWERS
6 Garden Place, Church Hill, Crook DL15 9DR. Clive Parker, 01388 766277, clive.m.parker@btinternet.com, www.facebook.com/parkersgarden 270615?ref=hl. *off Church Hill via access track. See entrance track opp St Cuthberts Church RC on L after row of terraces on Church Hill - if going up hill & before the barn & school.* **Sun 12 June (1-5). Adm £2.50, chd free. Home-made teas. seating in the garden and conservatory.**
Mostly woodland garden sloping down to Crook Beck with terraces incl herbaceous borders, tall perennials, wild flower grassland,

summer and spring flowering shrubs and a large collection of shade tolerant plants and bulbs. Includes rear 'potted' garden with alpine house. Most of the large feature trees are unusual and multi- featured e.g. bark, autumn colour and flowers. Has a large wooden greenhouse 10' x 6' in main garden, small summer house, water features and a gazebo. House 175+ years old large terrace with unusual headstones/gargoyles on the eaves of Shakespeare and GB Shaw? Adjacent Church Hill Allotments 100m. Plant stall, cake stall and raffle on open day. Featured on BBC Radio 4 Saturday Live. The garden is very steep and not suitable for wheelchairs.

GROUP OPENING

38 PETERLEE GARDENS SAFARI
Shotton Hall Banqueting Suites, Old Shotton, Peterlee SR8 2PH. Peterlee Town Council, 0191 518 2295. *From S-bound carriageway of A19, turn L onto slip rd signed Peterlee. At mini r'about turn L & then take the 1st turn on R into the grounds of Shotton Hall Banqueting Suites.* **Sun 10 July (10-4). Combined adm £3, chd free. Cream teas at Shotton Hall all day.**
Peterlee is opening about 12 of its prettiest gardens together with its well-managed allotments and the colourful grounds of Shotton Hall. While some of the gardens are of medium size, many are small, bijou spaces full of colour and interest. All have been ingeniously planted by imaginative owners. Because of the size of the town, visiting all the venues will take the form of a circular safari for which a vehicle will be needed. So, purchase a ticket and collect a map from Shotton Hall and start your journey wherever you wish on the well-signed route. Refreshments will be available throughout the day at Shotton Hall. Wheelchair access to most but not all gardens.

39 NEW QUARRY END
Walworth, Darlington DL2 2LY. Mr & Mrs Iain & Margaret Anderson. *Approx 5m W of Darlington on A68 or ¹/₂ m E of Piercebridge on A67 follow brown signs to Walworth Castle*

Hotel. Just up the hill from the Castle entrance, follow NGS yellow signs down private track. **Sun 21 Aug (1.30-5). Adm £3.50, chd free. Home-made teas.**
Woodland garden, about ³/₄ acre in an ancient quarry setting. Redeveloped over 15 years the garden has an C18 ice house, a wide variety of trees, shrubs and perennials, a fernery and ornamental vegetable plot. Spectacular late summer display. Recent addition of a further 1 acre naturalised woodland in adjacent quarry is under development. Extensive views over South Durham. Very limited access to new woodland area especially if wet. Main garden includes some rough steps and gravel paths.

40 ◆ RABY CASTLE
Staindrop, Darlington DL2 3AH. Lord Barnard, 01833 660202, admin@rabycastle.com, www.rabycastle.com. *12m NW of Darlington, 1m N of Staindrop. On A688, 8m NE of Barnard Castle* **For opening times and information, please phone, email or visit garden website.**
C18 walled gardens set within the grounds of Raby Castle. Designers such as Thomas White and James Paine have worked to establish the gardens, which now extend to 5 acres, displaying herbaceous borders, old yew hedges, formal rose gardens and informal heather and conifer gardens. Assistance will be needed for wheelchairs.

41 RAVENSFORD FARM
Hamsterley DL13 3NH. Jonathan & Caroline Peacock, 01388 488305, caroline@ravensfordfarm.co.uk. *7m W of Bishop Auckland. From A68 at Witton-le-Wear turn off W to Hamsterley. Go through village & turn L just before tennis courts at west end.* **Sun 24 July (2-5). Adm £4, chd free. Home-made teas. Visits also by arrangement Mar to Nov please confirm numbers for catering and parking in good time.**
This large garden, now 30 years old, surrounds an old farmhouse. It contains two ponds, an orchard and a small wood. Mid-July is possibly its peak for colour, but there is always floral interest and we grow many unusual (labelled) shrubs and trees. On NGS day we sell plants and jams

Stanton Fence

© Susie White

from the garden, we serve homemade cakes for tea, and Northumbrian pipers provide the background music. Several interesting items of garden statuary or art. Featured in Teesdale Mercury and Northern Echo and photographed for Garden News. Some gravel, so assistance will be needed for wheelchairs.

GROUP OPENING

42 ROMALDKIRK GARDENS
Teesdale DL12 9DZ. *6m NW of Barnard Castle. On B6277, 2m S of Eggleston.* **Sun 26 June (2-5.30). Combined adm £4, chd free. Home-made teas in The Reading Room, opp Rose and Crown Hotel.**
A group of 8 gardens of great variety. Most gardens are clustered around the village greens. Some are a short walk/drive to the edge of the village. Romaldkirk is an interesting, old fashioned village with a water pump, stocks and attractive church of St Romald. Some gardens are typical cottage gardens with herbaceous borders, another larger garden includes pond and grotto, one has lawns, rockery and interesting shrubs.

Another garden which is well established has an attractive design of lawns, pond, herbaceous borders, trees and shrubs. Wheelchair access to some gardens.

ALLOTMENTS

43 ST MARGARET'S ALLOTMENTS
Margery Lane, Durham DH1 4QG, 0191 386 1049, pauline@dhent.fsnet.co.uk. *From A1 take A690 to City Centre/Crook. Straight ahead at T-lights after 4th r'about. 10mins walk from bus or rail station.* **Sun 17 July (2-5). Combined adm £4, chd free.**
5 acres of 82 allotments against the spectacular backdrop of Durham Cathedral. This site has been cultivated since the Middle Ages, and was saved from development 20yrs ago, allowing a number of enthusiastic gardeners to develop plots which display a great variety of fruit, vegetables and flowers. Guided tours including unusual vegetables. Creative and fun scarecrow competition. The site has some steep and narrow paths.

© Susie White

Halls of Heddon

designed by Chelsea Gold Medal winner, Arabella Lennox-Boyd, in keeping with its rural setting. A strong underlying design unites the different areas from formal parterre and courtyard garden to orchard, wild flower meadows and woodland. Romantically planted rose covered arbours and long clematis-draped pergola walk. Nuttery, kitchen garden and greenhouse. Both Robert Iley, the garden builder, and the current gardener will be available for questions. Delightful views. Wheelchair access for those chairs that can use mown paths as well as hard paving.

🚶 🐕 ❀ ☕

47 **4 STOCKLEY GROVE**
Brancepeth DH7 8DU. Mr & Mrs Bainbridge, 079445 23551, fabb63@sky.com. *5m W of Durham City. Situated on the A690 between Durham & Crook. There is no parking available in Stockley Grove. From Durham direction turn L at village Xrds & park at castle at end of rd. Lifts to the garden will be available if required.* **Sun 7 Aug (1-5). Adm £4, chd free. Home-made teas. Visits also by arrangement May to Sept.**
A stunning ¹/₂ -acre garden with inspirational planting to provide yr-round colour and interest. Landscaped with hidden grassy paths with many unusual trees, shrubs and plants incl wildlife pond, rockery area and water features.

❀ ☕

48 **THORNTON HALL GARDENS**
Staindrop Road, Darlington DL2 2NB. Michael & Sue Manners, 07713 508222, mannersfarmsltd@msn.com, www.thorntonhallgardens.co.uk. *On B6279 Staindrop Rd. 3m W of Darlington.* **Wed 15 June (11-4). Adm £6, chd £1. Home-made teas. Light Lunches. Visits also by arrangement May to July.**
C16 Grade I listed hall (not open). 2 walled gardens with Elizabethan raised borders, separate vegetable garden. Plantsman's garden with emphasis on colour-themed borders, plant associations, form and foliage. Unusual perennials, interspersed with interesting trees and shrubs in mixed herbaceous borders, large collection of hostas, roses, clematis, and peonies. Wildlife and ornamental ponds.

🚶 ❀ 🚐 ☕

44 **SKARA BRAE**
20 Tynedale Gardens, Stocksfield NE43 7EZ. Ann Mates, 01661 843175, ann.mates@yahoo.com. *14m W of Newcastle upon Tyne. 9m E of Hexham. A1/A69 then B6309 to Stocksfield. From W, past station & cricket ground. At Quaker meeting house turn into New Ridley Rd. 2nd R is Tynedale Gardens.* **Visits by arrangement May to Aug evening visits up to 7pm welcomed during June - Aug. Adm £3.50, chd free. Tea.**
A charming, developing cottage-style garden, with established shrubs and herbaceous planting in wide borders, that is continuously being improved, on SW-facing site 150ft x 40ft. Added interest of statuary and water features, including small stream at bottom of the garden, and seating areas to sit and relax. Featured in Amateur Gardening.

🐕 ☕

45 **NEW** **ST CUTHBERT'S HOSPICE**
Park House Road, Durham DH1 3QF. Paul Marriott, CEO, www.stcuthbertshospice.com. *1m E of Durham City on A167. Turn into Park House Rd, the Hospice is on the L after bowling green car park. Parking available outside Hospice*

entrance. **Sun 31 July (11-4.30). Adm £4, chd free. Cream teas.**
5 acres of mature gardens surround this CQC Outstanding-rated Hospice. In development since 1988, the gardens are cared for by volunteers. Incl a Victorian-style greenhouse and large vegetable, fruit and cut flower area. Lawns surround smaller scale specialist planting, and areas for patients and visitors to relax. Woodland area with short and long walks, and an 'In Memory' garden with stream. Cream teas. Plants/produce for sale. Information sessions on the services offered by the Hospice which include support for the carers & loved ones of people with dementia, and information on our Everything in Place campaign, aimed at breaking the taboos surrounding death and dying. Almost all areas are accessible for wheelchairs.

🚶 ❀ ☕

46 **NEW** **STANTON FENCE**
Stanton, Morpeth NE65 8PP. Sir David & Lady Kelly. *5m NW of Morpeth. Nr Stanton on the C144 between Pigdon & Netherwitton. OS map ref NZ 13588.* **Sun 26 June (12-5). Adm £5, chd free. Light refreshments and home-made teas.** *Donation to local church.*
Contemporary 3-acre country garden

49 ◆ **WALLINGTON**
Cambo NE61 4AR. National Trust, 01670 774389, john.ellis@nationaltrust.org.uk, www.nationaltrust.org.uk/wallingto n. *12m W of Morpeth 20m NW Newcastle. From N B6343; from S via A696 from Newcastle, 6m W of Belsay, B6342 to Cambo.* **For NGS: Sun 8 May (10-5). Adm £11.80, chd £5.90. Light refreshments. Evening opening Fri 17 June (7- 10). Adm £16.80, chd £8. Wine. Sun 10 July (10-5). Adm £16.80, chd £8. Light refreshments. 10 July Light homemade refreshments in Cambo Village Hall. (School of Capability Brown). For other opening times and information, please phone, email or visit garden website.**
Walled, terraced garden with fine herbaceous and mixed borders; Edwardian conservatory; 100 acres woodland and lakes. House dates from 1688 but altered, interior greatly changed c1740; exceptional rococo plasterwork by Francini brothers. Peat free plant sales. 8 May Head Gardener's Question Time 12-4. 17 June 7-9.30. Private Garden Tour with fizz and nibbles. Booking required. 10 July incl Picturesque Cambo Village and an opportunity to take tea in the school room of Capability Brown (now the village hall). Wheelchair access limited to top terrace in Walled Garden but elsewhere possible with care and support.

  ♿ 🐕 ⊛ 🚐 ☕

50 ▶ **WARRENFELL**
2 Filter Cottages, Tunstall Reservoir, Wolsingham, Bishop Auckland DL13 3LX. Fran Toulson, 01388 528392, warrenfell@btinternet.com. *W on A689 through Wolsingham Village centre. On edge of village take R turn by Wolsingham School, signed to Tunstall Reservoir. No through Road. Garden 2m on R below dam wall.* **Sat 2, Sun 3 July (10.30-4). Adm £3, chd free. Home-made teas. Visits also by arrangement.**
A young garden, approx ¼ acre, started in 2012. A lovely location by the Waskerley river below Tunstall Reservoir. The garden visit can be combined with a walk at the reservoir. Borders with shrubs, perennials, roses and peonies. Pergola and arbour. Rock bed added in Autumn 2015. Kitchen garden with raised beds and espaliered apples and

pears. Lavender hedge around house, small wild flower area.

⊛ ☕

51 ◆ **WASHINGTON OLD HALL**
The Avenue, Washington Village NE38 7LE. National Trust, 0191 416 6879, www.nationaltrust.org.uk/washingt onoldhall. *7m SE of Newcastle upon Tyne. From A19 onto A1231 From A1 exit J64 onto A195 In both cases stay on road until you pick up brown signs to Washington Old Hall.* **For NGS: Sun 5 June (11-4). Adm by donation. Light refreshments in Friends' tearoom. For other opening times and information, please phone or visit garden website.**
The picturesque stone manor house and its gardens provide a tranquil oasis in an historic setting. It contains a formal Jacobean garden with box hedging borders around evergreens and perennials, vegetable garden, wild flower nut orchard with bee hives. Places to sit out and enjoy a picnic or afternoon tea. Delicious home made cakes. Garden lift - wheelchair users full access to the whole area. SUPER NGS PLANT SALE 11-4 AND VILLAGE GARDENS. Several private gardens will also be open. Location map and entry tickets can be purchased at the plant stall. Jams and chutneys for sale.

♿ 🐕 ⊛ 🚐 ☕

Woodland area with short and long walks, and an 'In Memory' garden with stream . . .

52 ◆ **WHALTON MANOR GARDENS**
Whalton, Morpeth NE61 3UT. Mr & Mrs T R P S Norton, 01670 775205, gardens@whaltonmanor.co.uk, www.whaltonmanor.co.uk. *5m W of Morpeth. On the B6524, the house is at E end of the village & will be signed.* **For NGS: Sun 3 July (2-5). Adm £4, chd free. Tea. For other opening times and information, please phone, email or visit garden website.**
The historic Whalton Manor, altered by Sir Edwin Lutyens in 1908, is

surrounded by 3 acres of magnificent walled gardens, designed by Lutyens with the help of Gertrude Jekyll. The gardens have been developed by the Norton family since the 1920s and incl extensive herbaceous borders, 30yd peony border, rose garden, listed summerhouses, pergolas and walls, festooned with rambling roses and clematis. Featured on the cover and an article in the' English Garden ' magazine. Partial wheelchair access, some stone steps.

♿ ⊛ 🚐 🛏 ☕

53 ▶ **WOODLANDS**
Peareth Hall Road, Gateshead NE9 7NT. Liz Reid, 07719 875750, lizreid52@ntlworld.com. *3½ m N Washington Galleries. 4m S Gateshead town centre. OnB1288 turn opp Guide Post PH (NE9 7RR) onto Peareth Hall Rd. Continue for ½ m passing 2 bus stops on L. Third drive on L past Highbury Ave.* **Sat 25 June, Thur 7 July (1.30-4.30). Adm £3, chd free. Home-made teas. Visits also by arrangement June to Aug, groups of 10+.**
Mature garden on a site of approx ⅟₇ acres- quirky, with tropical themed planting and Caribbean inspired bar. A fun garden with colour throughout the year, interesting plants, informal beds and borders, pond area and decks. Featured in Amateur Gardening and Gardening Answers, magazine, local press (Newcastle Journal),.

⊛ ☕

54 ▶ **WOODSIDE HOUSE**
Witton Park, Bishop Auckland DL14 0DU. Charles & Jean Crompton, 01388 609973, j.crompton@talktalk.net. *2m N of Bishop Auckland. from Bishop Auckland take A68 to Witton Park. In village DO NOT follow SatNav. Go down track next to St Pauls Church.* **Sun 17 July (2-5). Adm £4, chd free. Home-made teas. Visits also by arrangement Apr to Sept.**
Stunning 3-acre, mature, undulating garden full of interesting trees, shrubs and plants. Superbly landscaped with island beds, flowing herbaceous borders, an old walled garden, rhododendron beds, fernery, 3 ponds and vegetable garden. Delightful garden full of interesting and unusual features: much to fire the imagination. Winner of Bishop Auckland in Bloom. Featured in Sunday Telegraph. Partial wheelchair access.

♿ ⊛ 🚐 ☕

NORTHAMPTONSHIRE

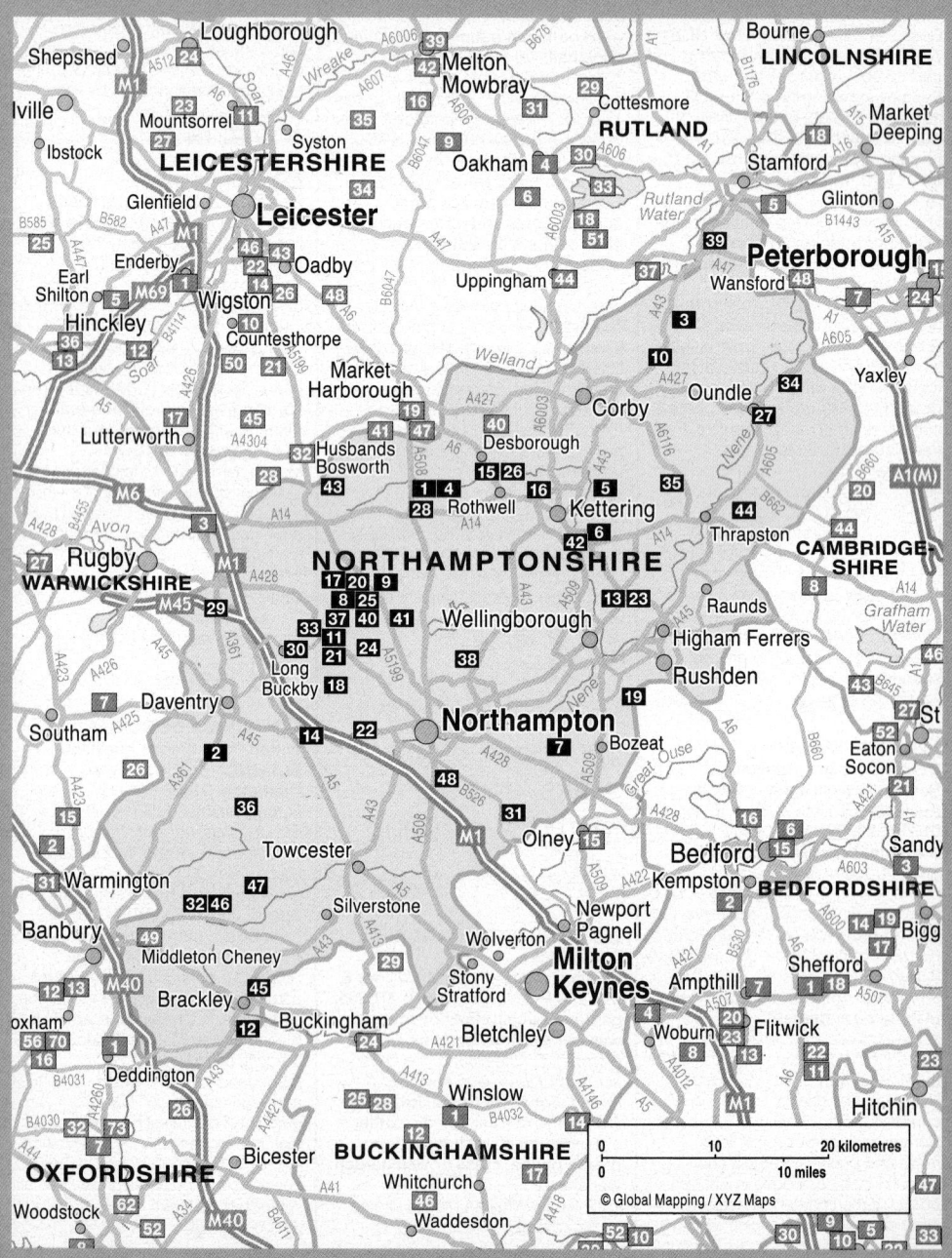

Northamptonshire

The county of Northamptonshire is famously known as the 'Rose of the Shires', but is also referred to as the 'Shire of Spires and Squires', and lies in the East Midlands area of the country bordered by eight counties.

Take a gentle stroll around charming villages with thatch and stone cottages and welcoming inns. Wander around stately homes, discovering art treasures and glorious gardens, many open for the NGS (Kelmarsh Hall, Castle Ashby, Cottesbrooke Hall and Boughton House).

Explore historic market towns such as Oundle and Brackley in search of fine footwear, antiques and curiosities. Or visit wildlife sanctuaries such as Sulby Gardens with 12 acres of interesting flora and fauna.

The serenity of our waterways will delight, and our winding country lanes and footpaths will guide you around a rural oasis, far from the pressures of modern living, where you can walk knee-deep in bluebells and snowdrops in spring at gardens such as Greywalls and Rosemount.

Our NGS year starts in February and has openings nearly every month until November, giving a glimpse of gardens through the seasons.

Below: Village Farm, Preston Capes and Little Preston Gardens

Northamptonshire Volunteers

County Organisers
David Abbott
01933 680363
d_j_abbott@btinternet.com

Gay Webster
01604 740203
gay.webster6@gmail.com

County Treasurer
Michael Heaton
01604 846032
ngs@mimomul.co.uk

Publicity
David Abbott
(as above)

Booklet Coordinators
David Abbott
(as above)

Michael Heaton
(as above)

Assistant County Organisers
Philippa Heumann
01327 860142
pmheumann@gmail.com

Geoff Sage
01788 510334
geoffsage256@btinternet.com

Opening Dates

All entries subject to change.
For latest information check www.ngs.org.uk

February

Snowdrop Festival

Sunday 28
23 67-69 High Street
27 Jericho

March

Sunday 6
5 Boughton House
19 Greywalls

Sunday 13
40 Rosemount

April

Sunday 10
14 Flore Gardens

Sunday 17
6 Briarwood
9 Cottesbrooke Hall Gardens

Sunday 24
10 Deene Park

Wednesday 27
12 Evenley Wood Garden

Thursday 28
43 Sulby Gardens

May

Sunday 1
18 Great Brington Gardens

Saturday 7
20 Guilsborough Gardens

Sunday 8
20 Guilsborough Gardens
35 The Old Rectory, Sudborough

Wednesday 18
28 Kelmarsh Hall

Sunday 22
2 Badby and Newnham Gardens
27 Jericho
48 **NEW** Old Rectory, Quinton
44 Titchmarsh House
45 Turweston Gardens

June

Thursday 2
23 67-69 High Street (Evening)

Festival Weekend

Saturday 4
39 Rosebriar

Sunday 5
13 Finedon Gardens
36 Preston Capes and Little Preston Gardens
39 Rosebriar

Thursday 9
23 67-69 High Street (Evening)

Saturday 11
44 Titchmarsh House

Sunday 12
22 Harpole Gardens
29 Kilsby Gardens
41 Spratton Gardens
47 Weedon Lois & Weston Gardens

Thursday 16
23 67-69 High Street (Evening)

Saturday 18
14 Flore Gardens

Sunday 19
14 Flore Gardens
32 Mill Hollow Barn
34 The Old Black Horse

38 Rosearie-de-la-Nymph
46 The Watermill

Thursday 23
23 67-69 High Street (Evening)
43 Sulby Gardens

Saturday 25
31 The Menagerie (Evening)

Sunday 26
1 Arthingworth Open Gardens
13 Finedon Gardens
38 Rosearie-de-la-Nymph

Thursday 30
23 67-69 High Street (Evening)
35 The Old Rectory, Sudborough

July

Saturday 2
11 East Haddon Hall
21 Haddonstone Show Gardens

Sunday 3
7 Castle Ashby Gardens
11 East Haddon Hall
21 Haddonstone Show Gardens

Sunday 10
24 Holdenby House Gardens
31 The Menagerie
37 Ravensthorpe Gardens

Sunday 17
3 Blatherwycke Estate
30 Long Buckby Gardens
33 Mill House

Sunday 31
15 Froggery Cottage
26 Hostellarie

August

Sunday 7
25 Hollowell Gardens
42 67 Stratfield Way

Thursday 25
43 Sulby Gardens

September

Sunday 4
48 **NEW** Old Rectory, Quinton

Sunday 11
8 Coton Manor Garden
35 The Old Rectory, Sudborough

The Menagerie

October

Thursday 13
43 Sulby Gardens

Sunday 30
5 Boughton House

November

Thursday 17
43 Sulby Gardens

February 2017

Sunday 26
27 Jericho

Gardens open to the public

5 Boughton House
7 Castle Ashby Gardens
8 Coton Manor Garden
9 Cottesbrooke Hall Gardens
10 Deene Park
12 Evenley Wood Garden
21 Haddonstone Show Gardens
24 Holdenby House Gardens
28 Kelmarsh Hall
35 The Old Rectory, Sudborough

By arrangement only

4 Bosworth House
16 Glendon Hall
17 Gower House

Also open by arrangement

6 Briarwood
15 Froggery Cottage
19 Greywalls
20 Dripwell House, Guilsborough Gardens
20 Four Acres, Guilsborough Gardens

22 The Close, Harpole Gardens
22 19 Manor Close, Harpole Gardens
23 67-69 High Street
26 Hostellarie
27 Jericho
29 Pytchley House, Kilsby Gardens
31 The Menagerie
33 Mill House
34 The Old Black Horse
37 Ravensthorpe Nursery, Ravensthorpe Gardens
43 Sulby Gardens
44 Titchmarsh House

The Gardens

GROUP OPENING

1 ARTHINGWORTH OPEN GARDENS
Arthingworth, nr Market Harborough LE16 8LA. *6m S of Market Harborough. From Market Harborough via A508, after 4m take L to Arthingworth. From Northampton, A508 turn R just after Kelmarsh.* Sun 26 June (2-6). Combined adm £5, chd free. Light refreshments at Bosworth House & village hall.
Arthingworth has been welcoming visitors for the NGS for more than 5 yrs. It is a village affair, with 8 to 9 gardens opening and 2 pop-up tearooms with home baked cakes. We now have some regulars who keep us on our toes and we love it. Come and enjoy the diversity, we aim to give visitors an afternoon of discovery. Our gardens have been chosen because they are all different in spirit, and tended by young and weathered gardeners. We have gardens with stunning views, traditional with herbaceous borders and vegetables, walled, and artisan. The village is looking forward to welcoming you. Wheelchair access available to some gardens.

Crafts for sale and children's quiz . . .

GROUP OPENING

2 BADBY AND NEWNHAM GARDENS
Daventry NN11 3AR. *3m S of Daventry. E side of A361. Maps provided for visitors.* Sun 22 May (2-6). Combined adm £5, chd free. Home-made teas at Badby & Newnham Churches.

THE BANKS
Newnham. Sue & Geoff Chester www.suestyles.co.uk

HILLTOP
Newnham. David & Mercy Messenger

NEW **THE OLD HOUSE**
Badby. Mr & Mrs Robert Cain

SHAKESPEARES COTTAGE
Badby. Sarah & Jocelyn Hartland-Swann

SOUTHVIEW COTTAGE
Badby. Alan & Karen Brown

TRIFIDIA
Badby. Colin & Shirley Cripps

NEW **WREN COTTAGE**
Newnham. Mr & Mrs Jim Dorkins

7 gardens within 2 beautiful villages with attractive old houses of golden coloured Hornton stone set around their village greens. In Badby, there are 4 gardens of differing styles: a wisteria-clad C18 thatched cottage with modern sculptures; a garden featuring spectacular views over Badby Wood; a newly developed elevated garden with views over the village; and a garden with pond, conservatory, glasshouses and vegetables, also featuring unusual

plants that aim for yr-round interest. The 3 gardens in Newnham comprise: a 3 acre organic garden around a C17 thatched cottage with lawns, densely planted borders, vegetable and cutting garden, with feature trees and adjacent paddocks; a traditional C17 cottage garden with landscaped water feature and a large area set aside for growing vegetables; and a garden designer's garden to wander through, with pools, herbaceous borders, vegetables and herbs developed as rooms among mature trees. Both villages are hilly.

3 BLATHERWYCKE ESTATE
Blatherwycke, Peterborough PE8 6YW. Mr George. *Blatherwycke is signed off the A43 between Stamford & Corby. Follow road through village & the gardens entrance is immed next to the large river bridge.* Sun 17 July (11-4). Adm £3.50, chd free. Home-made teas.
Blatherwycke Hall demolished in the 1940s, its grounds and gardens lost until now! In April 2011 we started the renovation of the derelict 4 acre walled kitchen garden. So far a large kitchen garden, wall trained fruit trees, extensive herbaceous borders, seasonal beds, parterre, pleaching orchard and wild flower meadows have been built, planted and sown. Also a very large arboretum is being planted. Grass and gravel paths, some slopes and steps with ramps.

4 ▶ BOSWORTH HOUSE

Oxendon Road, Arthingworth, Nr Market Harborough LE16 8LA. Mr & Mrs C E Irving-Swift, 01858 525202, irvingswift@btinternet.com. *From the phone box, when in Oxendon Rd, take the little lane with no name, 2nd to the R.* Visits by arrangement in July. On a Fri in July, visit the garden, pick and cook produce, and then have lunch (10 max). Adm £20.

Cecile offers you the chance to visit the garden, then pick produce and cook in her kitchen before eating at Bosworth House. 3 acre organic garden and paddock with fabulous panoramic views. The garden incl herbaceous borders, orchard, cottage garden with greenhouse, vegetable garden, herbs and strawberries, and little spinney. There is also a very magnificent Wellingtonia. Partial wheelchair access.

5 ▶ ◆ BOUGHTON HOUSE

Geddington, Kettering NN14 1BJ. Duke of Buccleuch & Queensberry, KBE, 01536 515731, info@boughtonhouse.co.uk, www.boughtonhouse.org.uk. *3m NE of Kettering. From A14, 2m along A43 Kettering to Stamford, turn R into Geddington, house entrance 1½ m on R.* For NGS: Sun 6 Mar, Sun 30 Oct (11-3). Adm £6, chd £3. Light refreshments in C18 Stable Block. For other opening times and information, please phone, email or visit garden website.

The Northamptonshire home of the Duke and Duchess of Buccleuch. The garden opening incl opportunities to see the historic walled kitchen garden and herbaceous border incl the newly created sensory and wildlife gardens. The wilderness woodland will open for visitors to view the spring flowers or the autumn colours. As a special treat the garden originally created by Sir David Scott (cousin of the Duke of Buccleuch) will also be open.

6 ▶ BRIARWOOD

4 Poplars Farm Road, Barton Seagrave, Kettering NN15 5AF. Elaine Christian & William Portch, 01536 522169, briarwood.garden@yahoo.co.uk, www.elainechristian-gardendesign.co.uk. *1½ m SE of Kettering Town Centre. J10 off A14*

turn onto Barton Rd (A6) towards Wicksteed Park. R into Warkton Lane, after 200 metres R into Poplars Farm Rd. Sun 17 Apr (10-4). Adm £3, chd free. Home-made teas. Visits also by arrangement Apr to Sept.

A garden in 2 parts with quirky original sculptures and many faces. Firstly a s-facing lawn and colourful borders with spring bulbs, blossom trees, summer colour, hedging, palms, climbers, lily pond, and sunny terrace. Secondly, a secret garden with summerhouse, small orchard, raised bed potager and water feature. Crafts for sale and children's quiz.

7 ▶ ◆ CASTLE ASHBY GARDENS

Castle Ashby, Northampton NN7 1LQ. Earl Compton, 07771 871766, www.castleashbygardens.co.uk. *6m E of Northampton. 1½ m N of A428, turn off between Denton & Yardley Hastings. Follow brown tourist signs (SatNav will take you to the village, look for brown signs).* For NGS: Sun 3 July (10-5.30). Adm £5.50, chd free. For other opening times and information, please phone or visit garden website.

35 acres within a 10,000 acre estate of both formal and informal gardens, incl Italian gardens with orangery and arboretum with lakes, all dating back to the 1860s, as well as a menagerie with various animals. Play area, tearooms and gift shop. Gravel paths within gardens.

8 ▶ ◆ COTON MANOR GARDEN

Coton, Northampton NN6 8RQ. Mr & Mrs Ian Pasley-Tyler, 01604 740219, www.cotonmanor.co.uk. *10m N of Northampton, 11m SE of Rugby. From A428 & A5199 follow*

tourist signs. For NGS: Sun 11 Sept (12-5.30). Adm £7, chd £2.50. Light refreshments at Stableyard Cafe. For other opening times and information, please phone or visit garden website.

10 acre garden set in peaceful countryside with old yew and holly hedges and extensive herbaceous borders, containing many unusual plants, beautiful to see in September. Other areas incl rose, water, herb and woodland gardens, our famous bluebell wood, and wild flower meadow. Adjacent specialist nursery with over 1000 plant varieties propagated from the garden. Partial wheelchair access as paths are narrow and the site is on a slope.

9 ▶ ◆ COTTESBROOKE HALL GARDENS

Cottesbrooke NN6 8PF. Mr & Mrs A R Macdonald-Buchanan, 01604 505808, www.cottesbrooke.co.uk. *10m N of Northampton. Signed from J1 on A14. Off A5199 at Creaton, A508 at Brixworth.* For NGS: Sun 17 Apr (2-5.30). Adm £6, chd £4. Home-made teas. For other opening times and information, please phone or visit garden website.

Award-winning gardens by Geoffrey Jellicoe, Dame Sylvia Crowe, James Alexander Sinclair and more recently Arne Maynard. Formal gardens and terraces surround Queen Anne house with extensive vistas onto the lake and C18 parkland containing many mature trees. Wild and woodland gardens, which are exceptional in spring, a short distance from the formal areas. Partial wheelchair access as paths are grass, stone and gravel. Access map identifies best route.

10 ▶ ◆ DEENE PARK

Corby NN17 3EW. The Trustees, 01780 450278, www.deenepark.com. *6m N of Corby. Off A43 between Stamford & Corby.* For NGS: Sun 24 Apr (12-5). Adm £6, chd £3. Light refreshments in Old Kitchen tearoom. For other opening times and information, please phone or visit garden website.

Interesting garden set in beautiful parkland. Large parterre with topiary designed by David Hicks echoing the C16 decoration on the porch stonework, long mixed borders, old

The Old Black Horse

fashioned roses, Tudor courtyard and white garden. Lake and waterside walks with rare mature trees in natural garden. Wheelchair access available to main features of garden.

11 EAST HADDON HALL
Main Street, East Haddon, Northampton NN6 8BU. Mr & Mrs John Beynon. *Located in the centre of the village near the church.* Sat 2, Sun 3 July (11-5). Combined adm with Haddonstone Show Gardens £4, chd free.
First opened for the NGS in 1928 and now restored by the present owners. 8 acres of parkland surrounding a Grade I listed Georgian house (not open) with extensive lawns, mature specimen trees and lovely views. More formal planting surrounds the house with many exuberantly planted containers.

12 ◆ EVENLEY WOOD GARDEN
Evenley, Brackley NN13 5SH. Timothy Whiteley, 07776 307849, info@evenleywoodgarden.co.uk, www.evenleywoodgarden.co.uk. *³/₄ m S of Brackley. Turn off at Evenley r'about on A43 & continue*

through village towards Mixbury before taking 1st L. For NGS: Wed 27 Apr (10.30-4.30). Adm £5, chd £1. Light refreshments in the pavilion & picnics welcome. For other opening times and information, please phone, email or visit garden website.
It doesn't matter if you are a tree lover, take a fancy to bulbs or if you are a keen gardener with a love for the natural environment. With our extensive collections of trees, shrubs and bulbs, Evenley Wood Garden is the place where you can learn something new throughout the seasons. The comprehensive list of over 3000 species of plants is increasing every yr. All paths are grass.

GROUP OPENING

13 FINEDON GARDENS
Finedon NN9 5JN. *2m NE of Wellingborough. 6m SE Kettering. All gardens individually signed from A6 & A510 junction.* Sun 5, Sun 26 June (2-6). Combined adm £3.50, chd free. Cream teas at 67-69 High Street.

67-69 HIGH STREET
Mary & Stuart Hendry
(See separate entry)

11 THRAPSTON ROAD
John & Gillian Ellson

THE VICARAGE
Revds. Richard and David Coles

All 3 gardens are very different with everything from vegetables to flowers on show. 67-69 High Street is an ever evolving ¹/₃ acre garden of a C17 cottage (not open) with mixed borders, many obelisks and containers. Planting for varied interest spring to autumn. 11 Thrapston Road is a ¹/₃ acre cottage garden with lawns and mixed borders, gravel and paved seating areas with planters and water features. Pergola, rose arches, summerhouse and treehouse. Mixed vegetable plot, and soft fruit and apple trees. Built in the 90s, The Vicarage garden has many shrubs, raised beds, sculpture and ornaments and delightful summerhouse. Large selection of home raised plants for sale at some locations (all proceeds to the NGS).

11 High Street, Spratton Gardens

GROUP OPENING

14 FLORE GARDENS

Flore, Northampton NN7 4LQ. *7m W of Northampton on A45. 2m W of M1 J16. Free car park signed from A45 where garden map provided. Coaches, please phone 01327 341225 for advice related to parking.* Sun 10 Apr (2-6); Sat 18, Sun 19 June (11-6). Combined adm £5, chd free. Home-made teas in Chapel School Room (Apr). Light lunches & teas in the Chapel School Room, & teas in the Church (June). *Donation to All Saints Church & United Reform Church, Flore.*

NEW **BEECH HILL**
Dr R B White & Dr Valerie White.
Open on Sat 18, Sun 19 June

24 BLISS LANE
John & Sally Miller.
Open on all dates

THE CROFT
John & Dorothy Boast.
Open on all dates

THE GARDEN HOUSE
Edward & Penny Aubrey-Fletcher.
Open on Sat 18, Sun 19 June

THE OLD BAKERY
John Amos & Karl Jones.
Open on all dates
www.johnnieamos.co.uk

PRIVATE GARDEN OF BLISS LANE NURSERY
Christine & Geoffrey Littlewood.
Open on all dates

ROCK SPRINGS
Tom Higginson & David Foster.
Open on all dates

RUSSELL HOUSE
Peter Pickering & Stephen George.
Open on all dates

NEW **17 THE GREEN**
Mrs Wendy Amos.
Open on Sat 18, Sun 19 June

Flore gardens have been open since 1963 as part of the Flore Flower Festival, and the partnership with the NGS started in 1992. Flore is an attractive village with views over the Upper Nene Valley. We have a varied mix of gardens, developed by friendly and enthusiastic owners. Our gardens range from the traditional to the eccentric providing yr-round interest. There is a varied selection of garden structures, incl greenhouses, gazebos and summerhouses, with seating providing opportunities to rest while enjoying the gardens. In spring there are early flowering perennials, interesting trees, shrubs, and bulbs in pots and border drifts. There is planting for all situations from shade to full sun. June gardens open in association with Flore Flower Festival. The gardens incl formal and informal designs with lots of roses, clematis and many varieties of trees, shrubs, perennials, herbs, fruit and some vegetables, with two additional gardens joining us this yr. Partial wheelchair access to most gardens, some assistance may be required.

15 FROGGERY COTTAGE
85 Breakleys Road, Desborough NN14 2PT. Mr John Lee, 01536 760002. *6m N of Kettering. 5m S of Market Harborough. Signed off A6 & A14.* Sun 31 July (11.30-5). Combined adm with Hostellarie £3, chd free. Light refreshments & gluten free cakes available. **Visits also by arrangement June to Aug for groups of 8+.**
1 acre plantsman's garden full of rare and unusual plants. NCCPG Collection of 435 varieties of penstemons incl dwarfs and species. Mediterranean and water gardens with large herbaceous borders. Artifacts on display incl old ploughs and garden implements. Workshops throughout the day.

16 GLENDON HALL
Kettering NN14 1QE. Rosie Bose, 01536 711732, rosiebose@googlemail.com. *1½ m E of Rothwell. A6003 to Corby (A14 J7) W of Kettering, turn L onto Glendon Rd signed Rothwell, Desborough, Rushton. Entrance 1½ m on L past turn for Rushton.* Visits by arrangement for groups of 25 max. Adm £3, chd free.
Mature specimen trees, topiary, box hedges, and herbaceous borders stocked with many unusual plants. Large walled kitchen gardens with glasshouse, and a shaded area well stocked with ferns. Some gravel and slopes, but wheelchair access via longer route.

17 GOWER HOUSE
Guilsborough, Northampton NN6 8PY. Ann Moss, 01604 740140, cattimoss@aol.com. *Off High St by The Witch & Sow PH, through PH car park.* Visits by arrangement Apr to July for combined visit with Dripwell House only. Adm £5. Tea.
Although Gower House garden is small, it is closely planted with specimen trees, shrubs, perennials, orchids, thyme lawn, wild flowers and alpines; some rare or unusual, with foliage colour being important. Several seating areas designed for elderly relatives incorporating recycled materials. Soft fruit and vegetable garden shared with Dripwell, is an important part of our gardening. Very steep site unsuitable for those with mobility difficulties.

GROUP OPENING

18 GREAT BRINGTON GARDENS
Northampton NN7 4JJ. *7m NW of Northampton. Off A428 Rugby Rd. From Northampton, 1st L turn past main gates of Althorp. Free parking. Programmes & maps available at car park.* Sun 1 May (11-5). Combined adm £5, chd free.

7 BEDFORD COTTAGES
Mrs Felicity Bellamy

NEW 8 BEDFORD COTTAGES
Tony & Jayne Ryan

NEW BRINGTON LODGE
Mr & Mrs James Milne

FOLLY HOUSE
Sarah & Joe Sacarello

NEW 15 HAMILTON LANE
Mr & Mrs Robin Matthews

ROSE COTTAGE
David Green & Elaine MacKenzie

THE STABLES
Mrs A George

SUNDERLAND HOUSE
Mrs Margaret Rubython

NEW YEW TREE HOUSE
Mrs Joan Heaps

Great Brington is proud of its nearly 25 yr association with the NGS and arguably one of the most successful one day scheme events in the county. This yr we offer 4 new gardens,

bringing our total to 9 opening to view. Our gardens provide superb quality and immense variety; many of the gardens continue to evolve each yr and most are designed, planted and maintained by their owners on a scale which is eminently practical and rewarding. Our particularly picturesque, predominantly stone and thatch village is well worth a day out in its own right and its configuration is perfect for the occasion; compact, self-contained, circular and virtually flat. On offer on the day, including our memorable gardens; a warm welcome, free car parking, programmes and maps, morning coffee, lunches and teas, plant stalls and a local history exhibition. Small coaches of groups up to 26 max welcome by prior arrangement only, please call 01604 770939.

Nature reserve including woodland, ponds, stream and wild flower meadows . . .

19 GREYWALLS
Farndish NN29 7HJ. Mrs P M Anderson, 01933 353495, greywalls@dbshoes.co.uk. *2½ m SE of Wellingborough. A609 from Wellingborough, B570 to Irchester, turn to Farndish by cenotaph. House adjacent to church.* Sun 6 Mar (12-3). Adm £3, chd free. Light refreshments. **Visits also by arrangement, coaches welcome.**
2 acres mature garden surrounding old vicarage (not open). Over 100 varieties of snowdrops, drifts of hardy cyclamen and hellebores. Alpine house and raised alpine beds. Water features and natural ponds with views over open countryside. Rare breed hens.

Tranquil
conservation
area with
stunning views
and setting . . .

GROUP OPENING

20 ▶ GUILSBOROUGH GARDENS
High Street, Guilsborough
NN6 8RA. *10m NW of Northampton. 10m E of Rugby. Between A5199 & A428. J1 off A14. Car parking in field on Hollowell Rd out of Guilsborough. Information & maps from village hall, next to primary school.* Sat 7, Sun 8 May (2-6). Combined adm £6, chd free. Home-made teas in the village hall.

DRIPWELL HOUSE
Mr J W Langfield & Dr C Moss
Visits also by arrangement Apr to July for combined visit with Gower House.
cattimoss@aol.com
01604 740140

FOUR ACRES
Mark & Gay Webster
Visits also by arrangement Apr to Sept for groups of 20+.
gay.webster6@gmail.com
01604 740203

THE GATE HOUSE
Mike & Sarah Edwards

GUILSBOROUGH HOUSE
Mr & Mrs John McCall

OAK DENE
Mr & Mrs R A Darker

THE OLD HOUSE
Richard & Libby Seaton Evans

THE OLD VICARAGE
John & Christine Benbow

Enjoy a warm welcome in this village with its very attractive rural setting of rolling hills and reservoirs. Seven varied village gardens, from a flower arranger's small garden surrounding a modern house, to large gardens with sweeping lawns, mature trees and beautiful views. There is plenty of room to sit and relax and picnics can be spread out in the car park field. Several of us are interested in growing fruit and vegetables, and a walled kitchen garden and a potager are an important part of our gardening. Plants both rare and unusual from our plantsmen's gardens are for sale, a true highlight here. Dripwell House has opened for the NGS since 1986, originally an individual garden and is a destination in its own right. There is thus a lot to see and visitors find that they need the whole afternoon. Wheelchair access at Four Acres, Guilsborough House, Oak Dene, The Old House and The Old Vicarage only. No dogs at Oak Dene.

&♿ 🐕 ❀ 🚐 ☕

21 ▶ ◆ HADDONSTONE SHOW GARDENS
The Forge House, Church Lane, East Haddon, Northampton NN6 8DB. Haddonstone Ltd, 01604 770711, info@haddonstone.co.uk, www.haddonstone.com. *7m NW of Northampton. Brown tourism signs from A428. Located in centre of village near church, opp school.* For NGS: Sat 2, Sun 3 July (11-5). Combined adm with East Haddon Hall £4, chd free. Home-made teas. **For other opening times and information, please phone, email or visit garden website.**
See Haddonstone's classic garden ornaments in the beautiful setting of the walled manor gardens incl planters, fountains, statues, bird baths, sundials, balustrades and follies. The garden is on different levels with roses, clematis, climbers, herbaceous borders, ornamental flowers, topiary, specimen shrubs and trees. Latest additions incl designs from the Sir John Soane's Museum. The gardens incorporate plantings used at the company's acclaimed Chelsea Flower Show exhibits. Wheelchair access to all areas of main garden from new reception area.

&♿ ❀ ☕

GROUP OPENING

22 ▶ HARPOLE GARDENS
Harpole NN7 4BX. *On A45 4m W of Northampton towards Weedon. Turn R at The Turnpike Hotel into Harpole. Village maps given to all visitors.* Sun 12 June (1-6). Combined adm £5, chd free. Home-made teas at The Close.

BRYTTEN-COLLIER HOUSE
James & Lucy Strickland

THE CLOSE
Michael Orton-Jones
Visits also by arrangement.
michael@orton-jones.com
01604 830332

NEW ▶ 14 HALL CLOSE
Marion & Charley Oliver

19 MANOR CLOSE
Caroline & Andy Kemshed
Visits also by arrangement in June, from Mon 13 June for one week only.
carolinekemshed@live.co.uk
01604 830512

MILLERS
Mrs M Still

THE OLD DAIRY
David & Di Ballard

NEW ▶ 38 UPPER HIGH STREET
Mr John Drinkwater

We welcome everyone to join in the Harpole Gardens experience. Visit us and you will delight in varied gardens of all shapes, sizes and content. Harpole is an attractive village which is renowned for its annual Scarecrow Festival (2nd weekend of Sept), well worth a visit! Amongst our various garden structures you will find a summerhouse, a treehouse, a vine-covered pergola and plenty of seating for the weary. We have herbaceous borders, luxuriant lawns, water features, including several ponds (one of which contains Koi carp). You will see mixed borders with plants for both shade and sun, mature trees, herbs, vegetables and alpines. You will be able to enjoy views over neighbouring farmland and perhaps best of all delicious home-made teas! Wheelchair access at Brytten-Collier House, The Close and The Old Dairy only.

&♿ ❀ ☕

23 ▶ 67-69 HIGH STREET
Finedon. NN9 5JN. Mary & Stuart Hendry, 01933 680414, sh_archt@hotmail.com. *6m SE Kettering. Garden signed from A6 & A510 junction.* Sun 28 Feb (11-3). Evening opening Thurs 2, 9, 16, 23, 30 June (5-8.30). Adm £3.50, chd free. Soup & roll (Feb), wine & nibbles (June). Opening with Finedon Gardens on Sun 5, Sun 26 June. **Visits also by arrangement Feb to Sept.**

Constantly evolving ⅓ acre rear garden of C17 cottage (not open). Mixed borders, many obelisks and containers, kitchen garden and herb bed, and rope border. Spring garden with snowdrops and hellebores, summer and autumn borders all giving varied interest from Feb through to Oct. Home raised plants for sale. Well behaved dogs welcome.

24 ◆ HOLDENBY HOUSE GARDENS

Holdenby House, Holdenby, Northampton NN6 8DJ. Mr & Mrs James Lowther, 01604 770074, office@holdenby.com, www.holdenby.com. *6m NW of Northampton. From A5199 or A428 between East Haddon & Spratton. Follow brown tourist signs.* For NGS: Sun 10 July (1-5). Adm £5, chd £3.50. Light refreshments. For other opening times and information, please phone, email or visit garden website.

Holdenby has an historic Grade I listed garden. The inner garden incl Rosemary Verey's renowned Elizabethan Garden and Rupert Golby's Pond Garden and long borders. There is also a delightful walled kitchen garden with original Victorian greenhouse. Away from the formal gardens the terraces of the original Elizabethan Garden are still visible, one of the best preserved examples of their kind. The estate incl gravel paths.

GROUP OPENING

25 HOLLOWELL GARDENS

Hollowell NN6 8RR. *8m N of Northampton. ½ m off A5199, turn off at Creaton. Roads are narrow & twisting, so please use car park which is clearly signed.* Sun 7 Aug (11-5). Combined adm £4, chd free. Home-made teas at village hall.

HILLVIEW
Jan & Crawford Craig

IVY COTTAGE
Rev John & Mrs Wendy Evans

ROSEMOUNT
Mr & Mrs J Leatherland
(See separate entry)

Three very different gardens in an attractive village on a very steep hillside. Styles range from the formal, with manicured lawns, to a plot with a riot of colour and chickens scratching in the vegetable garden. The garden owners are very knowledgeable and happy to give advice. No wheelchair access at Hillview, partial access at remaining two gardens. Steep hills.

Marie Curie

Patients and families can enjoy beautiful gardens at our hospices

26 ◆ HOSTELLARIE

78 Breakleys Road, Desborough NN14 2PT. Stella Freeman, stelstan78@aol.com. *6m N of Kettering. 5m S of Market Harborough. From church & war memorial turn R into Dunkirk Ave, then 3rd R. From cemetery L into Dunkirk Ave then 4th L.* Sun 31 July (11.30-5). Combined adm with Froggery Cottage £3, chd free. Light refreshments & gluten free cakes available. **Visits also by arrangement June & July for groups of 10-25.**

Over 180ft long town garden. Divided into rooms of different character; courtyard garden with a sculptural clematis providing shade, colour themed flower beds, ponds and water features, cottage gardens and gravel borders, clematis and roses, all linked by lawns and gravel paths. The collection of hostas, over 50 different varieties, are taking up more space each yr and are the pride of the garden. Featured in Amateur Gardening magazine (Sept 2015).

27 ◆ JERICHO

42 Market Place, Oundle PE8 4AJ. Stephen & Pepita Aris, 01832 275416, stephenaris@btinternet.com. *East Jericho. From the Jericho cul-de-sac at the E end of the market place, go through red door to the R of the shop, through passage, down yard.* Sun 28 Feb (12-4); Sun 22 May (12-5). Adm £3.50, chd free. Tea. 2017: Sun 26 Feb. **Visits also by arrangement Feb to Sept for individuals and groups.**

Inspired by Vita Sackville-West 60 yrs ago, the 100 metre, s-facing, walled garden is divided into a series of secret spaces. The house is clothed in wisteria, clematis and roses. A plant-led garden with massive hornbeam hedge, clipped box and lavender. A hosta courtyard. Over 50 labelled species roses, a chamomile lawn, plus a hot border. Snowdrops, crocuses and hellebores in early spring. Featured in the Peterborough Evening Telegraph.

28 ◆ KELMARSH HALL

Main Road, Kelmarsh, Northampton NN6 9LY. The Kelmarsh Trust, 01604 686543, carlacooper@kelmarsh.com, www.kelmarsh.com. *The hall is 5m S of Market Harborough & 11m N of Northampton. From A14, exit J2 & head N towards Market Harborough on the A508.* For NGS: Wed 18 May (11-5). Adm £6, chd £3.50. Light lunches, cream teas & cakes. For other opening times and information, please phone, email or visit garden website.

Kelmarsh Hall is a C18 country house, set in gardens inspired by society decorator Nancy Lancaster and surrounded by woodland and an estate of rolling Northamptonshire countryside. Hidden gems incl a newly renovated orangery, double border, sunken garden, a 30 metre long border, rose garden and at the heart of it all, a historic walled kitchen garden. Highlights incl our fritillaries, tulips, rare peonies, roses, cottage garden perennials and sweet peas. Visit late summer to see our extensive dahlia collection. Disabled parking is available close to the Visitor Centre entrance. Blue badges must be displayed and please advise staff on arrival.

GROUP OPENING

29 KILSBY GARDENS
Kilsby Village CV23 8XP. *5m SE of Rugby. 6m N of Daventry on A361. The road through village is the B4038.* Sun 12 June (1-5). Combined adm £4, chd free. Home-made teas at Kilsby Village Hall.

BOLBERRY HOUSE
Mr & Mrs Richard Linnell

GRAFTON HOUSE
Mr & Mrs Andy & Sally Tomkins

PYTCHLEY GARDENS
Kathy Jenkins & Neighbours

PYTCHLEY HOUSE
Mr & Mrs T F Clay
Visits also by arrangement May to July.
the.clays@tiscali.co.uk
01788 822373

RAINBOW'S END
Mr & Mrs J Madigan

12 RUGBY ROAD
Mr & Mrs T Hindle

Kilsby is a stone and brick village with historic interest, home of St Faith's Church dating from the C12. The village was the site of one of the first skirmishes of the Civil War in 1642, and also gave its name to Stephenson's nearby lengthy rail tunnel built in the 1830s. Six attractive gardens will be open this yr, all within easy walking distance. Do please come and see us.

Delicious home-made teas . . .

GROUP OPENING

30 LONG BUCKBY GARDENS
Northampton NN6 7RE. *8m NW of Northampton, midway between A428 & A5. Long Buckby is signed from A428 & A5. Maps available at each garden.* Sun 17 July (1.30-5.30). Combined adm with Mill House, Long Lane £5, chd free. Home-made teas at Lawn Cottage.

3 COTTON END
Roland & Georgina Wells

7 HIGH STACK
Tiny & Sheila Burt

NEW 51 HIGH STREET
Alexander & Corinne Burns

NEW LAWN COTTAGE, 36 EAST STREET
Michael & Denise Nichols

LIBRARY GARDEN
Long Buckby Library

10 LIME AVENUE
June Ford

4 SKINYARD LANE
Susie & William Mitchell

NEW WOODCOTE VILLA
Sue & Geoff Woodward

Eight gardens in the historic villages of Long Buckby and Long Buckby Wharf, most within easy walking distance of each other. Varying in size and style, from courtyard and canal side to cottage garden, some are established and others evolving. They include water features, pergolas, garden structures, chickens and pigs, but the stars are definitely the plants. Bursting with colour, visitors will find old favourites and the unusual, used in a variety of ways; trees, shrubs, perennials, annuals, fruit and vegetables. The garden map will also show places of historic interest that the visitor will pass on their way round. Our award-winning local museum will also be open. Of course there will be teas and plants for sale to complete the visit. Full or partial wheelchair access available at all gardens except 3 Cotton End & 4 Skinyard Lane.

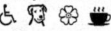

31 THE MENAGERIE
Newport Pagnell Road, Horton NN7 2BX. Hugues Decobert, hd@squarecapital.co.uk. *6m S of Northampton. 1m S of Horton. On B526, turn E at lay-by, long drive.* Evening opening Sat 25 June (5-8). Adm £20, chd free. Sun 10 July (2-5.30). Adm £6, chd free. Tea. Special evening event on Sat 25 June with Champagne and guided tour. Pre-booking essential, please phone or email Philippa Heumann 01327 860142, pmheumann@gmail.com or Gay Webster 01604 740203, gay.webster6@gmail.com. Visits also by arrangement June to Sept for groups of 20+.
Stunning garden set around C18 folly, with 2 delightful thatched arbours.

Large formal walled garden with fountain used for vegetables, fruit and cutting flowers. Recently extended exotic bog garden and native wetland area. Also rose garden, shrubberies, herbaceous borders, hornbeam allees and wild flower areas.

32 MILL HOLLOW BARN
Stockwell Lane, Sulgrave, Banbury OX17 2RS. David & Judith Thompson. *Parking in Sulgrave. Please walk down Stockwell Lane, adjacent to the village shop. The garden is at the end of the lane, next to The Watermill.* Sun 19 June (2-6). Combined adm with The Watermill £4, chd free.
7 acre garden with different levels and aspects, being developed for yr-round interest and to house a wide range of plants. Water gardens, shrubberies, herbaceous borders and gravel garden. 10 yr old arboretum with many rare and interesting trees. Water gardens with lakes, streams and bridges, and abundant wildlife. Some areas suitable for wheelchairs unless wet.

33 MILL HOUSE
East Haddon. NN6 8DU. Ken & Gill Pawson, 01604 770103, gillandken@pawsons.co.uk. *At the junction of Long Lane and the A428.* Sun 17 July (1.30-5.30). Combined adm with Long Buckby Gardens £5, chd free. Home-made teas at Lawn Cottage. Opening with Ravensthorpe Gardens on Sun 10 July. Visits also by arrangement June to Aug for groups of 40 max.
Over 1 acre in open countryside. Large fruit and vegetable plot with some old and rare varieties. Owner is Heritage Seed Library Guardian and beekeeper. Orchard, wild flower meadow, pergola, pond, grasses, hot garden, borders and shady areas. Foundations of East Haddon Windmill.

34 THE OLD BLACK HORSE
Main Street, Tansor, Peterborough PE8 5HS. Mrs Pamela Metcalf, 01832 226302, pamelametcalf@sky.com. *2m N of Oundle off A605 towards Peterborough, take L turn signed Glapthorn & Cotterstock. Follow signs to Tansor, turn R at Xrds signed Main St. Parking on roadside.* Sun 19 June (11-5). Adm £3.50, chd free.

Home-made teas. **Visits also by arrangement Apr to June for groups of 10-20.**
A cottage garden with mature trees, lawns and mixed borders. Both full sun and shady areas planted to give a natural look. Spring bulbs, flowering shrubs with colour going through the summer season. Roses climb and ramble over house, barn, arches, trees and arbours. Productive vegetable potager with greenhouse. New wild meadow with views across fields to Oundle. The garden will be featured in The Garden News magazine (Aug 2016).

48 **NEW** **OLD RECTORY, QUINTON**
Preston Deanery Road, Quinton, Northampton NN7 2ED. Alan Kennedy and Emma Wise. *M1 J15, W on A508 toward Stony Stratford. House is next to the church.* Sun 22 May, Sun 4 Sept (11-5). Adm £5, chd free.
A beautiful contemporary 3 acre rectory garden designed by multi award-winning designer, Anoushka Feiler. Taking the Old Rectory's C18 history and its religious setting as a key starting point, the main garden at the back of the house has been divided into six parts; a kitchen garden, glasshouse and flower garden, a woodland menagerie, a pleasure garden, a park and an orchard. Elements of C18 design such as formal structures, parterres, topiary, long walks, occasional seating areas and traditional craft work have been introduced however, with a distinctly C21 century twist through the inclusion of living walls, modern materials and features, new planting methods and abstract installations. Wheelchair access, but there are gravel paths.

&♿ D

35 ◆ **THE OLD RECTORY, SUDBOROUGH**
Kettering NN14 3BX. Mr & Mrs G Toller, 01832 734085, bookings@theoldrectorygardens.co.uk, www.theoldrectorygardens.co.uk. *8m NE of Kettering. Exit 12 off A14. Village just off A6116 between Thrapston & Brigstock. Free private parking in a small paddock adjacent to the house.* For NGS: Sun 8 May (12-5); Thur 30 June (12-7); Sun 11 Sept (11-5). Adm £7, chd free. Home-made teas & wine on Thur

30 June in the early eve. **For other opening times and information, please phone, email or visit garden website.**
Classic 3 acre country garden with extensive herbaceous borders and many unusual shrubs. In spring, many containers of bulbs and large plantings of tulips and daffodils, early dappled shade area. A wide variety of old roses, standard Lycianthes Rantonnetii and a walled potager designed by Rosemary Verey. Lily pond and development of woodland walk alongside Harpers Brook. Set in a tranquil conservation area with stunning views and setting. Featured in prestigious national and international publications over many yrs. Partial wheelchair access as some gravel paths. Guide dogs welcome.

GROUP OPENING

36 **PRESTON CAPES AND LITTLE PRESTON GARDENS**
Little Preston, Daventry NN11 3TF. *6m SW of Daventry. 13m NE of Banbury. 3m N of Canons Ashby. Parking for Little Preston at Old West Farm (N11 3TF), follow signs. For Preston Capes parking off High St (N11 3TB). Very limited disabled parking at The Manor House & by church, blue badge holders only.* Sun 5 June (12-5). Combined adm £5, chd free. Home-made light lunches & teas from 12pm at Old West Farm.

> **CITY COTTAGE**
> Mrs Gavin Cowen
>
> **LADYCROFT**
> Mervyn & Sophia Maddison
>
> **THE MANOR**
> Mr Graham Stanton
>
> **NORTH FARM**
> Mr & Mrs Tim Coleridge
>
> **OLD WEST FARM**
> Mr & Mrs Gerard Hoare
>
> **VILLAGE FARM**
> Trevor & Julia Clarke

A selection of differing gardens in the beautiful unspoilt south Northamptonshire ironstone villages, most with a backdrop of fantastic views of the surrounding countryside. Gardens range from small contemporary, through to classical country style with old fashioned roses and borders, to large gardens with

woodland walks and ponds. Features include attractive village with local sandstone houses and cottages, Norman church and wonderful views. Partial wheelchair access to some parts of the gardens.

&♿☕

Contemporary garden set around a 16th century watermill and mill pond . . .

GROUP OPENING

37 **RAVENSTHORPE GARDENS**
Ravensthorpe NN6 8ES. *7m NW of Northampton. Signed from A428. Mill House immed R as you turn off A428 down Long Lane, 1m from village. Wrigley Cottage is in The Hollows off Bettycroft.* Sun 10 July (1.30-5.30). Combined adm £5, chd free. Home-made teas at village hall.

> **MILL HOUSE**
> Ken & Gill Pawson
> (See separate entry)
>
> **RAVENSTHORPE NURSERY**
> Mr & Mrs Richard Wiseman
> Visits also by arrangement May to Sept.
> ravensthorpenursery@hotmail.com
> 01604 770548
>
> **WIGLEY COTTAGE**
> Mr & Mrs Dennis Patrick

Attractive village in Northamptonshire uplands near to Ravensthorpe reservoir and Top Ardles Wood Woodland Trust, which have bird watching and picnic opportunities. Three established and developing gardens set in beautiful countryside displaying a wide range of plants, many of which are available from the Nursery. Offering inspirational planting, quiet contemplation, beautiful views, water features, gardens encouraging wildlife, fruit and vegetable garden owned by a Heritage Seed Library Guardian, and flower arranger's garden. Partial wheelchair access to Wigley Cottage.

&♿☕

38 ROSEARIE-DE-LA-NYMPH

55 The Grove, Moulton, Northampton NN3 7UE. Peter Hughes, Mary Morris, Irene Kay & Jeremy Stanton. *N of Northampton town. Turn off A43 at small r'about to Overstone Rd. Follow NGS signs in village. The garden is on the Holcot Rd out of Moulton.* Sun 19, Sun 26 June (11-5). Adm £4, chd free.
We have been developing this romantic garden for about 10 yrs and now have over 1800 roses, incl English, French and Italian varieties. Many unusual water features and specimen trees. Roses, scramblers and ramblers climb into trees, over arbours and arches. We have tried to time our open days to cover the peak flowering period. Collection of 95 Japanese maples. Mostly flat, but there is a standard width doorway to negotiate.

NGS donations help support over 200 hospices across the country

39 ROSEBRIAR

83 Main Street, Collyweston PE9 3PQ. Jenny Harrison. *On A43 3½ m SW of Stamford. 3 doors from PH.* Sat 4, Sun 5 June (12-5). Adm £4, chd free. *Donation to Hearing Dogs.*
A garden situated on quite a steep slope, contains a variety of areas incl alpine and grass beds, water feature with stream and bog garden, surrounded by herbaceous and shrub borders lavishly planted with exciting combinations. All linked by gravel paths, patios and original sculptures.

40 ROSEMOUNT

18 Church Hill, Hollowell NN6 8RR. Mr & Mrs J Leatherland, 01604 740354. *10m NW of Northampton, 5m S J1 A14. Between A5199 & A428. Parking at village hall.* Sun 13 Mar (11-3). Adm £3, chd free. Light refreshments at village hall. Opening with Hollowell Gardens on Sun 7 Aug.
The Leatherlands have been developing this ½ acre garden for over 50 yrs. Both are keen and knowledgeable plantspeople, who love collecting and propagating favourite plants, many of which are for sale. March opening features their collection of over 200 different snowdrops, hellebores and unusual spring bulbs. In August the garden is full of colour and interest with unusual shrubs, herbaceous and clematis. Partial wheelchair access.

GROUP OPENING

41 SPRATTON GARDENS

Smith Street, Spratton NN6 8HP. *6½ m NNW of Northampton. On A5199 between Northampton & Welford. S from J1, A14. Car Park at Spratton Hall School with close access to gardens.* Sun 12 June (11-5). Combined adm £6, chd free. Light refreshments at St Andrew's Church, Church Road.

DALE HOUSE
Fiona & Chris Cox
01604 846458
fionacox19@aol.com

FORGE COTTAGE
Daniel & Jo Bailey

NEW **THE GRANARY**
Margo Lerin

11 HIGH STREET
Philip & Frances Roseblade

NEW **7 MANOR ROAD**
Mrs Jessica Steele

NORTHBANK HOUSE
Helen Millichamp

NEW **SPRATTON VICARAGE**
Rev Linnet Smith

NEW **STONE HOUSE**
John Forbear

NEW **2 THE WALK**
Sharon Scanlan

THREEWAYS
William Armstrong

WALTHAM COTTAGE
Norma & Allan Simons

NEW **9A YEW TREE LANE**
John Hunt

We are delighted that Spratton is continuing to open its gardens in 2016 and even more so as there will be 12 gardens, 9 of which are either completely new or returning after a break. As well as attractive cottage gardens alongside old Northampton stone houses, there are also unusual gardens, including creative design for a steep terrace; clever planting in a tiered garden; 2 showing good use of a small area; one dedicated to encouraging wildlife; a highly structured courtyard shrub garden; a newly renovated garden. Several mature gardens will be open with fruit trees and herbaceous borders, one with a 300 yr old Holm Oak and miniature Shetland ponies looking on, surrounded by beautiful views of the agricultural landscape. One of the gardens will be hosting a plant sale. Tea, cakes and rolls will be available in the Norman Church St. Andrews with additional displays of the Pocket Park, which is just a short walk away. The King's Head PH will be open, lunch reservations recommended.

42 67 STRATFIELD WAY

Kettering NN15 6GS. Mrs Paula Mantle. *5 mins off A14 (J9) Kettering. Leave J9 & turn off r'about at Park Hotel & continue along the road, next L, straight over r'about, next R, follow signs.* Sun 7 Aug (2-5). Adm £3, chd free.
After an accident in 2010 that left me injured, my garden became my soulmate. This is a pretty garden with structure and softness, work is done at a recovering pace with bursts of energy. Colour alongside gentler combinations of delicate willowy flowers. From a 3 metre fatsia to dainty alpines, climbing hydrangea, dahlias, geraniums, crocosmia, fuscia, alliums, hosta, maples and show stopping campsis.

43 SULBY GARDENS

Sulby, Northampton NN6 6EZ. Mrs Alison Lowe, 01858 880573, ecolowe@btinternet.com. *16m NW of Northampton, 2m NE of Welford off A5199. Past Wharf House Hotel take 1st R, signed Sulby. After R & L bends, turn R at sign for Sulby Hall Farm. Turn R at junction, garden is 1st L. Parking limited, no vans or buses please.* Thurs 28 Apr, 23 June, 25 Aug, 13 Oct (2-5); Thur 17 Nov (1-4). Adm £4, chd free. Home-made teas. **Visits also by arrangement for groups of 10-50.**

Unusual property, on the Leicestershire border between Welford and Husbands Bosworth, covering 12 acres comprising working Victorian kitchen garden, orchard, and C19 icehouse, plus nature reserve incl woodland, ponds, stream and wild flower meadows. Features incl April: snakeshead fritillaries, cowslips, bluebells. June: wild flower meadows in full bloom. Aug: butterflies, dragonflies, aquatic plants. Oct: Apple Day, display of apples with origin information, new season's Sulby Gardens Apple Juice for sale, and apple-themed cakes. Nov: autumn colour. Featured on the John Griff programme, BBC Radio Northampton (19 Aug 2015). NB: Children welcome but under strict supervision because of deep water.

44 **TITCHMARSH HOUSE**
Chapel Street, Titchmarsh NN14 3DA. Sir Ewan & Lady Harper, 01832 732439, ewh1939@outlook.com. *2m N of Thrapston. 6m S of Oundle. Exit A14 at junction signed A605, Titchmarsh signed as turning to E.* Sun 22 May (2-6); Sat 11 June (12-5). Adm £3, chd free. Teas at community shop on the green (May) & village fete (June). **Visits also by arrangement Apr to June.**
4½ acres extended and laid out since 1972. Special collections of magnolias, spring bulbs, iris, peonies and roses with many rare trees and shrubs. Walled ornamental vegetable garden and ancient yew hedge. Some newly planted areas. Wheelchair access to most of the garden without using steps. No dogs.

GROUP OPENING

45 **TURWESTON GARDENS**
Brackley NN13 5JY. *2m E of Brackley. A43 from M40 J10. On Brackley bypass turn R on A422 towards Buckingham, ½ m turn L signed Turweston.* Sun 22 May (2-5.30). Combined adm £5, chd free. Tea at Versions Farm.

TURWESTON HOUSE
Mr & Mrs C Allen

TURWESTON MILL
Mr Harry Leventis

VERSIONS FARM
Mrs E T Smyth-Osbourne

Charming unspoilt stone built village in a conservation area. 3 quite large beautiful gardens. The Mill with bridges over the millstream and a spectacular waterfall, wildlife pond and newly designed kitchen garden. At Versions Farm you will find a 3 acre plantsman's garden with old stonewalls, terraces, pond and small water garden and at Turweston House a 5 acre garden with borders, woodland and pond. The Farmshop at Versions selling home reared organic meat, ready meals and other foodie treats. You can also wander round the farm and coo at the piglets, chickens and lambs when you visit. Plant stall with many rare plants for sale.

46 **THE WATERMILL**
Stockwell Lane, Sulgrave OX17 2RS. Mr & Mrs A J Todd. *Parking in Sulgrave. Please walk down Stockwell Lane which is next to the village shop.* Sun 19 June (2-6). Combined adm with Mill Hollow Barn £4, chd free.
Contemporary garden set around a C16 watermill and mill pond. Extensive mixed planting in borders and gravel, with winding stream. In adjoining fields, new woodland, pathways and wild flower meadow around ponds. Designed by James Alexander Sinclair. Garden at the end of a lane, with gravelled entrance drive and also some steep slopes. Some hard surface pathways.

GROUP OPENING

47 **WEEDON LOIS & WESTON GARDENS**
Weedon Lois, Towcester NN12 8PJ. *7m W of Towcester. 7m N of Brackley. Old Barn & Hillside are on High St, Weedon Lois. Home Close, Kettle End & Vicarage Rise are off High St. Ridgeway Cottage is on Weston High St & Gardener's Cottage is off High St behind Weston Hall.* Sun 12 June (2-5.30). Combined adm £5, chd free. Tea at Tove Valley Baptist Church, Weston.

NEW **THE GARDENER'S COTTAGE**
Mrs Sitwell

HILLSIDE
Mrs Karen Wilcox

HOME CLOSE
Clyde Burbidge

LOIS WEEDON HOUSE
Lady Greenaway

OLD BARN
Mr & Mrs John Gregory

RIDGEWAY COTTAGE
Jonathan & Elizabeth Carpenter

NEW **4 VICARAGE RISE**
Ashley & Lindsey Cartwright

Two adjacent villages in south Northamptonshire with a handsome Medieval church in Weedon Lois. The extension churchyard contains the graves of the poets Dame Edith Sitwell and her brother Sir Sacheveral Sitwell who lived in Weston Hall. There are five gardens in Weedon Lois comprising a large garden with terracing, large borders and outstanding views, a plantsman's garden, an award-winning garden and a garden with lovely stone terracing. In Weston there are two charming cottage gardens and teas being provided in the local church.

Bosworth House

NOTTINGHAMSHIRE

Nottinghamshire

Nottinghamshire is best known as Robin Hood country. His legend persists and his haunt of Sherwood Forest, now a nature reserve, contains some of the oldest oaks in Europe. The Major Oak, thought to be 800 years old, still produces acorns.

Civil War battles raged throughout Nottinghamshire, and Newark's historic castle bears the scars. King Charles I surrendered to the Scots in nearby Southwell after a night at The Saracen's Head, which is still an inn today.

The Dukeries in the north of the county provide an unmatched landscape of lakes, parks and woods, so called because four dukes lived there, and their estates were contiguous. The dukes are gone, but their estates at Clumber, Thoresby and Welbeck continue to offer a pre-industrial haven in a thickly populated county.

Oaks in Sherwood, apples in Southwell (where the original Bramley tree still stands) and 100 kinds of rhubarb in the ducal kitchen garden at Clumber Park – they await your visit.

Nottinghamshire Volunteers

County Organiser
Georgina Denison
01636 821385
campden27@aol.com

County Treasurer
Donna Bemment-Morris
01636 636036
donnabm@live.co.uk

Publicity
Gillian & Trevor Frecknall
01636 702200
tfrecknall@hotmail.com

Booklet Co-ordinator
Dave Darwent
01142 665881
dave.darwent@ngs.org.uk

Assistant County Organisers
Judy Geldart
01636 823832
judygeldart@gmail.com

Beverley Perks
01636 812181
perks.family@talk21.com

Mary Thomas
01509 672056
nursery@piecemealplants.co.uk

Andrew Young
01623 863327
andrew.d.young@btinternet.com

Left: Home Farm House

Opening Dates

All entries subject to change.
For latest information check www.ngs.org.uk

February

Snowdrop Festival

Saturday 6
- **19** Hodsock Priory Gardens

Sunday 14
- **1** The Beeches
- **3** Bolham Manor

Wednesday 17
- **1** The Beeches

March

Monday 28
- **7** Cedarwood

April

Sunday 10
- **6** Capability Barn

Sunday 17
- **16** Felley Priory

Sunday 24
- **1** The Beeches
- **48** Sycamores House

May

Sunday 1
- **35** NEW The Old Hall

Monday 2
- **9** 7 Colly Gate

Sunday 8
- **4** Broadlea
- **17** Floral Media

Sunday 15
- **6** Capability Barn
- **32** Norwell Nurseries

Sunday 22
- **2** NEW Beeston & Chilwell Gardens
- **28** 6 Moor Lane
- **29** 10 Moor Lane
- **51** West Farm and Church House Gardens
- **54** Woodpeckers

Sunday 29
- **26** NEW 38 Main Street
- **38** Papplewick Hall
- **39** Park Farm

Monday 30
- **20** Holmes Villa
- **36** The Old Vicarage

June

Festival Weekend

Sunday 5
- **5** 5 Burton Lane
- **7** Cedarwood
- **18** Halam Gardens and Wildflower Meadow

Sunday 12
- **30** Normanton Hall
- **51** West Farm and Church House Gardens

Sunday 19
- **23** Hopbine Farmhouse, Ossington
- **37** NEW Ossington House
- **40** Patchings Art Centre

49 Thrumpton Hall

Friday 24
- **24** NEW Kinoulton Village Gardens (Evening)

Sunday 26
- **3** Bolham Manor
- **9** 7 Colly Gate
- **22** Home Farm House, 17 Main Street
- **24** NEW Kinoulton Village Gardens
- **28** 6 Moor Lane
- **29** 10 Moor Lane
- **31** Norwell Gardens
- **45** NEW Rose Cottage

Wednesday 29
- **31** Norwell Gardens (Evening)

July

Sunday 3
- **15** NEW Eton Avenue Growers Association
- **27** NEW The Manor House
- **33** NEW Norwood Cottage
- **53** White House

Saturday 9
- **8** Clumber Park Walled Kitchen Garden

Sunday 10
- **43** Rhubarb Farm

Sunday 17
- **36** The Old Vicarage
- **40** Patchings Art Centre

Wednesday 20
- **44** Riseholme, 125 Shelford Road (Evening)

Sunday 24
- **10** Cornerstones

Sunday 31
- **14** The Elms

August

Saturday 6
- **25** Lodge Mount

Sunday 7
- **21** The Holocaust Centre
- **34** NEW Oak Barn

Sunday 14
- **21** The Holocaust Centre
- **42** The Poplars
- **46** NEW 1 Sandy Lane
- **47** 78 Sandy Lane

Sunday 21
- **36** The Old Vicarage
- **50** University of Nottingham Gardens

Sunday 28
- **11** Dumbleside

Monday 29
- **5** 5 Burton Lane
- **7** Cedarwood

September

Sunday 4
- **15** NEW Eton Avenue Growers Association
- **47** 78 Sandy Lane
- **48** Sycamores House

Sunday 18
- **12** Ellicar Gardens
- **34** NEW Oak Barn
- **44** Riseholme, 125 Shelford Road

October

Sunday 9
- **32** Norwell Nurseries

Gardens open to the public

- **8** Clumber Park Walled Kitchen Garden
- **16** Felley Priory
- **19** Hodsock Priory Gardens
- **32** Norwell Nurseries

By arrangement only

- **13** Elm House
- **41** Piecemeal
- **52** 6 Weston Close

Also open by arrangement

- **1** The Beeches
- **5** 5 Burton Lane
- **6** Capability Barn
- **9** 7 Colly Gate
- **10** Cornerstones
- **11** Dumbleside
- **12** Ellicar Gardens
- **14** The Elms
- **20** Holmes Villa
- **22** Home Farm House, 17 Main Street
- **25** Lodge Mount
- **27** NEW The Manor House
- **34** NEW Oak Barn
- **36** The Old Vicarage
- **39** Park Farm
- **44** Riseholme, 125 Shelford Road
- **47** 78 Sandy Lane
- **48** Sycamores House
- **53** White House
- **54** Woodpeckers

7 Colly Gate

The Gardens

■1▶ THE BEECHES

The Avenue, Milton, Newark
NG22 0PW. Margaret & Jim
Swindin, 01777 870828,
james91.swindin@mypostoffice.co.
uk. *1m S A1 Markham Moor. Exit A1
at Markham Moor, take Walesby sign
into village (1m). From Main St, L up
The Avenue.* **Sun 14, Wed 17 Feb
(11-4); Sun 24 Apr (2-5). Adm £3,
chd free. Home-made teas. Visits
also by arrangement Feb to Apr,
refreshments at extra cost.**

1 acre garden full of colour and
interest to plant enthusiasts looking
for unusual and rare plants. Spring
gives some 250 named snowdrops
together with hellebores and early
daffodils. The lawn is awash with
crocus, fritillarias, anemones, narcissi
and cyclamen. Large vegetable
garden on raised beds. Lovely views
over open countryside. Newcastle
Mausoleum (adjacent) open. Featured
in Nottingham Post, Newark
Advertiser and Dutch magazine.
Some slopes and gravel paths.

GROUP OPENING

■2▶ NEW ▶ BEESTON &
CHILWELL GARDENS

Beeston, Nottingham NG9 3AE.
*J25 M1, A52 to Nottm. Turn R to
Beeston B6006 at Nurseryman
(Wollaton Rd). Follow signs. For
Audon Ave, up Wollaton Rd, through
Beeston to Tesco Xrds. Turn R, follow
rd to Christ Ch. Audon Ave on L.
Start your visit at any garden. Maps
available.* **Sun 22 May (1.30-5.30).
Combined adm £5, chd free.
Home-made teas.**

NEW ▶ 60 AUDON AVENUE
NG9 4AW Anne & Rob Mason

NEW ▶ 30 HIGHGROVE
AVENUE
NG9 4DN Sue & Malcolm
Turner

NEW ▶ 6 HOPE STREET
NG9 1DR Elaine Liquorish

Enjoy 3 contrasting gardens each
with their own appeal. 60 Audon
Avenue (The Bee Garden) - an
interesting wildlife oriented garden
featuring a range of areas, incl bee
hives (beekeeper present). Themed
borders, stumpery and dry shade
planting, pond, bug hotel, fruit and
vegetable beds and beach hut! 30
Highgrove Avenue - plant collector's
garden, yr-round colour, arranged in
different themed areas, packed with
interesting plants incl a large white
wisteria. Collections of auriculas and
species pelargoniums. Two ponds
and a rill. 6 Hope Street - a garden
filled with a wide variety of plants, incl
alpines, hostas, ferns, carnivorous
plants, agapanthus, bulbs and
shrubs. Pond, troughs, pots and a
greenhouse with many subtropical
plants. Home-made crafts.

■3▶ BOLHAM MANOR

Bolham Way, Bolham, Retford
DN22 9JG. Pam & Butch
Barnsdale. *1m from Retford. A620
Gainsborough Rd from Retford, turn
L onto Tiln Lane, signed 'A620
avoiding low bridge'. At sharp R bend
take rd ahead to Tiln then L Bolham
Way.* **Sun 14 Feb (11-3). Adm £3,
chd free. Sun 26 June (1-5). Adm
£3.50, chd free. Enjoy hot soup
(Feb) and home-made teas (June).**
This Valentine's Day visit an
interesting garden with attractive
orchard and grounds carpeted with
snowdrops. Enjoy this much loved 3
acre garden with its mature trees and
dancing ladies! Meander along the
terraced planting down to the ponds
and cave. Stroll past the herbaceous
borders, across the croquet lawn,
down mown paths into the old
orchard where Paul's Himalayan
Musk and other ramblers are there to
greet you. Wheelchair access limited
to parts of garden.

■4▶ BROADLEA

North Green, East Drayton, Retford
DN22 0LF. David & Jean Stone.
*From A1 take A57 towards Lincoln,
East Drayton is signed off A57. North
Green runs N from church. Garden
last gate on R.* **Sun 8 May (2-5).
Adm £3, chd free. Home-made
teas.**

Our aim in this 1 acre garden is to
have interest throughout the yr and
attract wildlife. There is plenty to see,
woodland walk, many perennials,
shrubs and spring bulbs. Large pond
is a haven for wildlife and a kitchen
garden together with wild bank and
dyke add attraction to the formal
vistas. Partial wheelchair access.

Park Farm

5 5 BURTON LANE

Whatton in the Vale NG13 9EQ. Ms Faulconbridge, 01949 850942, jpfaulconbridge@hotmail.co.uk. *3m E of Bingham. Follow signs to Whatton from A52 between Bingham & Elton. Garden nr Church in old part of village. Follow yellow NGS signs.* Sun 5 June, Mon 29 Aug (1.30-5). Combined adm with Cedarwood £4.50, chd free. Home-made teas. **Visits also by arrangement May to Sept.**

Modern cottage garden which is both productive and highly decorative. We garden organically and for wildlife. The garden is full of colour and scent from Spring to Autumn. Several distinct areas, incl fruit and vegetables. Large beds are filled with over 500 varieties of plants with paths through so you can wander and get close. Also features seating, gravel garden, pond, shade planting. Historic church, attractive village with walks. Featured in Nottingham Evening Post and Garden News Garden of the Week.

6 CAPABILITY BARN

Gonalston Lane, Hoveringham NG14 7JH. Malcolm & Wendy Fisher, 01159 664322, wendy.fisher111@btinternet.com, www.capabilitybarn.co.uk. *8m NE of Nottingham. A612 from Nottingham through Lowdham. Take 1st R into Gonalston Lane. 1m on L.* Sun 10 Apr, Sun 15 May (12.30-4.30). Adm £3.50, chd free. Home-made teas. **Visits also by arrangement Apr to June, adm incl refreshments.**

In early Spring see brilliant displays of daffodils, tulips and hyacinths. Fritillarias star in the wildflower meadow. Late April invites rhododendrons, azaleas and wisteria flowers and orchard apple blossom. Herbaceous borders are filled with Spring beauties - erythroniums, anemones, primulas and pulmonarias. Roses, delphiniums, lupins, hostas, vegetables/fruit will greet group visitors later. Extensive collection of dahlias and flowering begonias.

7 CEDARWOOD

Burton Lane, Whatton in the Vale NG13 9EQ. Louise Bateman. *3m E of Bingham. Cedar-clad bungalow situated in the old part of Whatton in the Vale just around the corner from*

local church. Mon 28 Mar (2-5). Adm £3, chd free. Light refreshments in Village Hall. Sun 5 June, Mon 29 Aug (1.30-5). Combined adm with 5 Burton Lane £4.50, chd free. Home-made teas.

Cedarwood is a ⅓ acre plantswoman's garden developed over the last 10yrs. It is planted for yr-round colour and plants are chosen for their attractiveness to wildlife as well as people. It incl mixed borders, a rose garden, formal pond, bog garden, raised alpine bed and new cedar alpine greenhouse. Featured in Garden News and Garden Answers. Most of the garden has gravel paths and some small steps. Plenty of seating available to rest for the less able.

&♿ ✿ ☕

8 ◆ CLUMBER PARK WALLED KITCHEN GARDEN

Clumber Park, Worksop S80 3AZ. National Trust, 01909 476592, www.nationaltrust.org.uk. *4m S of Worksop. From main car park or main entrance follow directions to Walled Kitchen Garden.* **For NGS: Sat 9 July (10-5). Adm £5, chd free. Light refreshments. For other opening times and information, please phone or visit garden website.**

Beautiful 4 acre walled kitchen garden, growing unusual and old varieties of vegetables and fruits. Herbs and flower beds, incl the magnificent 400ft double herbaceous borders. 400ft glasshouse with grapevines. Museum of gardening tools. Soft fruit garden, rose garden, National Collections of regional apples and culinary rhubarbs. Garden has been awarded National Collection status for its collection of culinary rhubarbs (over 130 varieties) and regional (Nottinghamshire, Derbyshire, Lincolnshire, Leicestershire, Yorkshire) apples (72 varieties). Gravel paths and slopes.

♿ ✿ 🚐 **NPC** ☕

9 7 COLLY GATE

Kimberley, Nottingham NG16 2PJ. Doreen Fahey, 01159 192690, dfahey456@hotmail.com. *6m W of Nottingham. From M1 J26 take A610 towards Nottingham. L at next island (B600 to Kimberley) L at Sainsbury's mini island. L at top. Park here. Garden 500yds on R.* Mon 2 May, Sun 26 June (1-5). Adm £3, chd free. Home-made teas. **Visits also**

by arrangement May to Aug for groups 6+.

Delightful garden created by a serious plant enthusiast and tucked away at the end of short narrow lane in Swingate. It greets you with an impact of unexpected colour and delights you with the variety and sensitivity of the planting. A peaceful backwater in an urban setting. Featured in Nottingham Evening Post & Advertiser. Some gravel paths.

&♿ 🎒 ✿ 🚐 ☕

10 CORNERSTONES

15 Lamcote Gardens, Radcliffe-on-Trent, Nottingham NG12 2BS. Judith & Jeff Coombes, 01158 458055, judithcoombes@gmail.com, www.cornerstonesgarden.co.uk. *4m E of Nottingham. From A52 take Radcliffe exit at RSPCA junction, then 2nd L just before hairpin bend.* Sun 24 July (1.30-5). Adm £3.50, chd free. Home-made teas. **Visits also by arrangement July & Aug for groups 15+ (mid July - mid Aug).**

Plant lovers' garden, approaching ½ acre. Flowing colour themed and specie borders, with rare, exotic and unusual plants, provide a wealth of colour and interest, whilst the unique fruit and vegetable garden generates an abundance of produce. Bananas, palms, fernery, fish pond, bog garden, lovely new summerhouse area and greenhouse. Enjoy tea and delicious home-made cake in a beautiful setting. Wheelchair access but some bark paths and unfenced ponds.

&♿ 🎒 ✿ 🚐 ☕

11 DUMBLESIDE

17 Bridle Road, Burton Joyce NG14 5FT. Mr P Bates, 01159 313725. *5m NE of Nottingham. Very narrow lane to walk up 100 yds - please park on Lambley Lane & walk if possible. Drop off if necessary for less mobile.* Sun 28 Aug (2-6). Adm

£3.50, chd free. Home-made teas. **Visits also by arrangement Feb to Nov, refreshments on request at extra cost.**

Having opened for many yrs in May, now is an opportunity to see my beautiful garden of yr round interest in Summer, with perennials in extensive borders supplemented by dahlias, castor oil plants, cannas and many interesting and colourful annuals. Cyclamen will show under the trees and colchicum emerge in newly cut meadows. Primulas in wet areas are overshadowed with tree ferns and exotic foliage. Steep slopes towards stream therefore partial access only for wheelchairs.

12 ◆ ELLICAR GARDENS

Carr Road, Gringley-on-the-Hill, Doncaster DN10 4SN. Will & Sarah Murch, 01777 817218, sarah@ellicargardens.co.uk, www.ellicargardens.co.uk. *Gringley-on-the-Hill. Approx 2m outside village of Gringley on the Hill. Turn onto Leys Lane, drive out of village, over canal, Ellicar Gardens on L on Carr Rd, opp cream house.* **Sun 18 Sept (1-5). Adm £4, chd free. Home-made teas. Visits also by arrangement Mar to Oct for groups 10+ during term time.**

This vibrant, relaxed family garden is a haven for wildlife enthusiasts, garden lovers and children. Sweeping borders with new perennials and grasses grow alongside swathes of wildflowers. Young specimen trees, shrubs, gravel garden, old roses, meadow, woodland walk, orchard, potager, winter garden, and beautiful natural swimming pool. Children love exploring the school garden and willow maze. Rare breed pets. Winner Cobra's Best Gardener's Garden, featured in English Garden, Daily Mail, Yorkshire Post, BBC2 Garden Revival, Ellicar Natural Pool Biotop international award for design. Some uneven surfaces, grass and gravel paths.

13 ◆ ELM HOUSE

Main Street, Hickling, Melton Mowbray LE14 3AJ. David & Deborah Chambers, 01664 822928, davidgeorgechambers@gmail.com. *12m E of Nottingham. 7m W of Melton Mowbray. From Nottingham take A606 E. After crossing A46 turn L at Bridgegate Lane signed Hickling. In village turn R at T-junction. Elm*

House is last on R. **Visits by arrangement Apr to Aug for groups 10+. Adm £3.00, chd free. Home-made teas.**

Large, interesting garden of over an acre with many different areas. Lovely in spring with 20 varieties of magnolia and many spring bulbs and hellebores. Herbaceous in June/July. Other features incl a railway themed summerhouse, seaside garden, small walled garden, and pond with fish. Newly formed stumpery. Best viewed mid April/early May or mid June/early July. Level garden with some gravel paths.

14 THE ELMS

Main Street, North Leverton DN22 0AR. Tim & Tracy Ward, 01427 881164, tracy@wardt2.fsnet.co.uk. *5m E of Retford, 6m SW of Gainsborough. From Retford take rd to Leverton for 5m, into North Leverton with Habblesthorpe.* **Sun 31 July (2-5). Adm £3, chd free. Home-made teas. Visits also by arrangement June to Sept.**

This garden is very different, creating an extension to the living space. Inspiration comes from Mediterranean countries, giving a holiday feel. Palms, bamboos and bananas, along with other exotics, create drama and yet make a statement true to many gardens, that of peace and calm. North Leverton Windmill may be open for visitors. Garden fully viewable but restricted wheelchair access onto decked and tiled areas.

15 NEW ETON AVENUE GROWERS ASSOCIATION

Hawton Road, Newark NG24 4QA. Mrs Gillie Wilkinson, www.etonavenuegrowers association.wordpress.com. *1m from Farndon A46 turn off. Park on Hawton Rd, walk up alleyway between 77 & 79 Hawton Rd.* **Sun 3 July, Sun 4 Sept (10.30-4). Adm £3.50, chd free. Home-made teas.**

2¹/₂ acres taken over in Feb 2009 by a community group for use by people with mental health issues. Now a peaceful haven for long term unemployed and those on ESA. Wildlife friendly, WW1 memorial gardens, Dig for Victory allotment, ponds, tunnels, compost loos, flowers, fruit and vegetables - come and join us for something different!

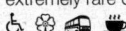

16 ◆ FELLEY PRIORY

Underwood NG16 5FJ. Ms Michelle Upchurch for the Brudenell Family, 01773 810230, michelle@felleypriory.co.uk, www.felleypriory.co.uk. *8m SW of Mansfield. Off A608 ¹/₂ m W M1 J27.* **For NGS: Sun 17 Apr (9-4). Adm £5, chd free. Light refreshments. For other opening times and information, please phone, email or visit garden website.**

Garden for all seasons with yew hedges and topiary, snowdrops, hellebores, herbaceous borders and rose garden. There are pergolas, a white garden, small arboretum and borders filled with unusual trees, shrubs, plants and bulbs. The grass edged pond is planted with primulas, bamboo, iris, roses and eucomis. Bluebell woodland walk. Orchard with extremely rare daffodils.

Eton Avenue Growers Association - come and join us for something different . . .

17 ◆ FLORAL MEDIA

Norwell Road, Caunton, Newark NG23 6AQ. Mr & Mrs Steve Routledge, 01636 636283, info@floralmedia.co.uk, www.floralmedia.co.uk. *Take Norwell Rd from Caunton. Approx ¹/₂ m from Caunton on L.* **Sun 8 May (10-4). Adm £3, chd free. Cream teas.**

A beautifully well maintained country garden. Beds overflowing with a variety of roses, shrubs and flowers. A gravel/oriental garden, wildlife pond, vegetable, herb and fruit garden. New in 2015 a contemporary purple/white garden. This garden has many different rooms for you to indulge in! A local folk group called 'The Jolly Beggars' will be playing music throughout the afternoon. Full wheelchair access incl disabled WC.

Holmes Villa

GROUP OPENING

18 ▶ HALAM GARDENS AND WILDFLOWER MEADOW
Nr Southwell NG22 8AX. *Village gardens within walking distance. Hill's Farm wildflower meadow is a short drive of ¹/₂ m towards Edingley village, turn R at brow of hill as signed.* **Sun 5 June (1-5). Combined adm £5, chd free. Home-made teas at The Old Vicarage, Halam.**

> **HILL FARM HOUSE**
> Victoria Starkey
>
> **HILL'S FARM**
> John & Margaret Hill
>
> **THE OLD VICARAGE**
> Mrs Beverley Perks
> (See separate entry)

Unusual mixture of a long standing plant lover's NGS village garden, a new small attractive cottage garden and a 6 acre wildflower meadow - part of an organic farm where the cattle are fed the herb rich pasture which is cut in July - visitors can be assured of an inspiring discussion with a farmer; passionate about the benefits of this method of farming for the environment, his Shorthorn cattle and the meat produced.

♿ 🐕 🌐 🚐 ☕

19 ◆ HODSOCK PRIORY GARDENS
Blyth, Worksop S81 0TY. Sir Andrew & Lady Buchanan, 01909 591204, info@snowdrops.co.uk, www.snowdrops.co.uk. *North Nottinghamshire. 4m N of Worksop off B6045. M1 J30 or 31 & close to A1(M). Blyth-Worksop rd approx 2m from A1M. Well signed locally. Ample free parking.* **For NGS: Sat 6 Feb (10-4). Adm £5, chd £1. Light refreshments.** For other opening times and information, please phone, email or visit garden website.
Enjoy exploring our estate and North Nottinghamshire. Visitors to the snowdrops can enjoy a leisurely walk through the surprisingly fragrant winter gardens and woods before having coffee, lunch or tea in our cafes. Aconites, irises, cornus, honeysuckles and hellebores on display. Free daily history talk by the campfire. Bacon sandwiches cooked in the wood. Wrap up warm and wear outdoors clothes and boots. See website for special offers, opening times and full details of our snowdrop events, talk and tours. Hodsock Snowdrops open daily from Sat 6th Feb to Sun 6th March (10-4). Shortbreaks available in our B&B. Recently featured in RHS The Garden magazine and listed as a Top 10 Snowdrop Garden to visit in England. Some paths difficult for wheelchairs when wet.

♿ 🌐 🚐 🛏 ☕

20 ▶ HOLMES VILLA
Holmes Lane, Walkeringham, Gainsborough DN10 4JP. Peter & Sheila Clark, 01427 890233, clarkshaulage@aol.com. *4m NW of Gainsborough. A620 from Retford or A631 from Bawtry/Gainsborough & A161 to Walkeringham then towards Misterton. Follow NGS signs for 1m. Reserved disabled parking.* **Mon 30 May (1-5). Adm £2.50, chd free. Home-made teas. Visits also by arrangement May to July.**
1³/₄ acre plantsman's interesting and inspirational garden; surprises around

every corner with places to sit and ponder, gazebos, arbours, ponds, hosta garden. Unusual perennials and shrubs for flower arranging. Lots of ideas to copy. Old tools, wildlife pond and scarecrows. A flower arranger's artistic garden. Specialist plant sale. Driftwood stall bric-a-brac.

21 ▶ THE HOLOCAUST CENTRE
Laxton, Newark NG22 0PA. Janet Mills, www.holocaustcentre.net. *Take A614 from Nottingham. At Ollerton r'about take 4th exit A6075 signed Tuxford. On leaving Boughton turn sharp R signed Laxton. Disabled parking & WC.* **Sun 7, Sun 14 Aug (10-4.30). Adm £3, chd free. Light refreshments.**
Since 1995, over 1000 highly scented Margaret Merrill roses have been planted in this poignant memorial garden. Each individual plaque reminds us that those who lost their life during the Holocaust were people with names and families not just statistics. Explore also the delightful Koi pond and see other sculptures and memorials. Visitors are welcome to view museum exhibitions (separate charge).

22 ▶ HOME FARM HOUSE, 17 MAIN STREET
Keyworth, Nottingham NG12 5AA. Graham & Pippa Tinsley, 01159 377122, Graham_Tinsley@yahoo.co.uk, www.homefarmgarden.wordpress. com. *7m S of Nottingham. Follow signs for Keyworth from A60 or A606 & head for church. Garden about 50yds down Main St. Parking at village hall or on Bunny Lane.* **Sun 26 June (1-5). Combined adm with Rose Cottage £4, chd free. Home-made teas. Visits also by arrangement June & July.**
A large garden hidden behind old farmhouse in the village centre with views over open fields. Many trees incl cedars, limes, oaks and chestnuts which, with high beech and yew hedges, create hidden places to be explored. Old orchard, ponds, turf mound, rose garden, winter garden and old garden with herbaceous borders. Pergolas with wisteria, ornamental vine and roses. Interesting and unusual perennials for sale by Piecemeal Plants (www.piecemealplants.co.uk). Wheelchair access via gravel yard.

23 ▶ HOPBINE FARMHOUSE, OSSINGTON
Hopbine Farmhouse, Main Street, Ossington NG23 6LJ. Mr & Mrs Geldart. *From A1 N take exit marked Carlton, Sutton-on-Trent, Weston etc. At T-junction turn L to Kneesall. Drive 2m to Ossington. In village turn R to Moorhouse & park in field.* **Sun 19 June (2-5). Combined adm with Ossington House £4, chd free. Home-made teas at Ossington House.**
A small but full garden with many interesting and unusual plants in a large herbaceous border facing SW. On the N side of the house, a hidden walled garden with rampant Clematis Summer Snow. Many shrub and climbing roses incl a unique x - Mary Bracegirdle. Large hostas, some in pots, herbs and an unusual Schizophragma Hydrangeoides creeping to the roof. Vegetables in raised beds. Ale House with original benches. Some narrow paths.

GROUP OPENING

24 NEW ▶ KINOULTON VILLAGE GARDENS
Nottingham NG12 3EL. *8m SE of West Bridgford. Off A46 at junction with A606. Follow rd signs into village.* **Evening opening Fri 24 June (4-8). Sun 26 June (1-5). Combined adm £5, chd free. Home-made teas at Bishops Cottage.**

> **BISHOPS COTTAGE**
> Ann Hammond

> **HALL FARM COTTAGE**
> Mrs Bel Grundy

> NEW ▶ **LANTERN COTTAGE**
> Mrs Elizabeth Evans

> NEW ▶ **LINDY EDGE**
> Mrs Jan Osbond
> lindyedge@aol.com

Bishops Cottage is a large, mature, cottage garden with mixed herbaceous borders with an emphasis on scent and colour coordination where possible. A wildlife pond and open views over the countryside. Home-made teas and plants for sale. Hall Farm Cottage is small but packed with plants and interest, and totally encircles the cottage. Archways smothered with fragrant jasmine, roses and clematis, potted lilies and exotic black/green aeoniums and stunning allium cristophii. Views over the Vale of Belvoir. Lantern Cottage has a tiny, sheltered W facing garden where flowers for all seasons are grown in sunny and shady borders as well as containers. Adjacent is The Plot where vegetables, soft fruit and flowers for cutting are grown. A florist and flower lovers' garden. Lindy Edge is an artisan garden created through imaginative planting and design with twists and turns providing surprises around every corner. Fruit and vegetables in raised beds. Plant stall and sale of original art.

A florist and flower lovers garden . . .

25 ▶ LODGE MOUNT
Town Street, South Leverton, Retford DN22 0BT. Mr A Wootton-Jones, 07427 400848, a.wj@live.co.uk. *4m E of Retford. Opp Bradley's Garage on Town Street.* **Sat 6 Aug (12-6). Adm £3, chd free. Home-made teas. Visits also by arrangement June to Sept.**
Originally a field, much of the ½ acre garden, although planned on paper for yrs, was landscaped within a few months during 2012 in order to fulfil an ambition following Helen Wootton-Jones' terminal cancer diagnosis. Following organic principles, an orchard and large vegetable and fruit plots are complemented by an area of unusual perennial edibles, and helpful plants, with a view to self sufficiency. Numerous clematis, roses, and climbers provide fragrance and a feeling of enclosure. Helen's aunt also had cancer and the garden was specifically designed to open for the NGS to raise money for cancer charities.

26 **NEW** **38 MAIN STREET**
Woodborough, Nottingham
NG14 6EA. Martin Taylor &
Deborah Bliss. *Turn off Mapperley Plains Rd at sign for Woodborough. Alternatively, follow signs to Woodborough off A6097 (Epperstone bypass). Property is between Park Av & Bank Hill.* **Sun 29 May (2-5). Adm £3, chd free. Home-made teas.**
Varied ⅓ acre. Bamboo fenced Asian species area with traditional outdoor wood fired Ofuro bath, herbaceous border, raised rhododendron bed, vegetables, greenhouse, pond area and art studio and terrace.

❀ ☕

27 **NEW** **THE MANOR HOUSE**
Church Street, East Markham,
Newark NG22 0SA. Ms Christine
Aldred, 01777 872719,
clownsca@yahoo.co.uk. *7m S of Retford. Take A1 Markham Moor r'about exit for A57 Lincoln. Turn at East Markham junction & follow signs for the church. Properties adjacent to the church.* **Sun 3 July (12-5). Combined adm with Norwood Cottage £4, chd free. Home-made teas. Visits also by arrangement Mar to Sept.**
An extensive, colour themed, scented garden on various levels. Set in lovely village next to C15 church. Planting for yr round interest, complementing the property and incl pond with koi carp, sunken garden, herbaceous border and vegetable patch. Range of seating areas to pause and enjoy the beautiful views. Varied levels. Gravel paths.

♿ 🐕 ❀ ☕

28 **6 MOOR LANE**
Bramcote, Nottingham NG9 3FH.
Carol Ward. *4m W of Nottingham. From Nottingham take A52 W. At 3rd r'about signed A6007 Ilkeston, take 5th exit (back towards Nottingham) onto A52 E. After Bramcote Leisure Centre, 1st L into Moor Lane. Roadside parking.* **Sun 22 May, Sun 26 June (1-5). Combined adm with 10 Moor Lane £4, chd free. Home-made teas.**
A beautifully designed, modern garden with sinuous curves, creative hard landscaping and stunning structural planting from statuesque bamboos and grasses to unusual shrubs and perennials. A container planted pebbled area and water features add to the delights.

❀ ☕

29 **10 MOOR LANE**
Bramcote, Nottingham NG9 3FH.
Liz Ratcliffe. *4m W of Nottingham. From Nottingham take A52 W. At 3rd r'about signed A6007 Ilkeston, take 5th exit (back towards Nottingham) onto A52 E. After Bramcote Leisure Centre, 1st L into Moor Lane. Roadside parking.* **Sun 22 May, Sun 26 June (1-5). Combined adm with 6 Moor Lane £4, chd free. Cream teas.**
A traditional, established, quintessentially romantic English garden with yr-round colour and interest from camellias and rhododendrons to rose covered rope swags. The large ornamental trees and established shrubs provide a structural backdrop to perennial planting, chosen to attract bees and butterflies. There is a raised bed vegetable plot, soft fruit area and herb bed.

❀ ☕

30 **NORMANTON HALL**
South Street, Normanton-on-Trent
NG23 6RQ. His Honour John & Mrs
Machin. *3m SE of Tuxford. Leave A1 at Sutton Carlton/Normanton-on-Trent junction. Turn L onto B1164 in Carlton. In Sutton-on-Trent turn R at Normanton sign. Go through Grassthorpe, turn L at Normanton sign.* **Sun 12 June (2-5). Adm £3, chd £1. Tea.**
3 acres with mature trees. Recently planted and developed. Swimming pool and vegetable area. Extensive herbaceous borders, enclosed parterre and 90 varieties of old roses. Fine established trees and recently planted arboretum of specimen oaks and beech. All surfaces level from car park.

♿ ❀ ☕

GROUP OPENING

31 **NORWELL GARDENS**
Newark NG23 6JX. *6m N of Newark. Halfway between Newark & Southwell. Off A1 at Cromwell turning, take Norwell Rd at bus shelter. Or off A616 take Caunton turn.* **Sun 26 June (1-5). Evening opening Wed 29 June (6.30-9). Combined adm £4.50, chd free. Home-made teas in Village Hall (26 June) and Norwell Nurseries (29 June).**

ARTISAN'S COTTAGE
Mr & Mrs B Shaw

ASH HOUSE
Mrs Fiona Mountford

ELDERBERRY COTTAGE
Nigel & Sian Marshall

NEW **JUXTA MILL**
Janet McFerran

NORTHFIELD FARM
Mr & Mrs D Adamson

NORWELL ALLOTMENT / PARISH GARDENS
Norwell Parish Council

◆ **NORWELL NURSERIES**
Andrew & Helen Ward
(See separate entry).

THE OLD FORGE
Adam & Hilary Ward

THE OLD MILL HOUSE, NORWELL
Mr & Mrs M Burgess

SOUTHVIEW COTTAGE
Margaret & Les Corbett

This is the 20th yr that Norwell has opened a range of different, very appealing gardens all making superb use of the beautiful backdrop of a quintessentially English countryside village. It incl a garden and nursery of national renown and the rare opportunity to walk around vibrant allotments with a wealth of gardeners from seasoned competition growers to plots that are substitute house gardens, bursting with both flower colour and vegetables in great variety. To top it all there are a plethora of breath taking village gardens showing the diversity that is achieved under the umbrella of a cottage garden description! The beautiful medieval church and its peaceful churchyard with grass labyrinth will be the setting for - A Journey Through Colour - this will be provided by church vestments, some flowers and objects precious to the church and its congregation.

♿ ❀ 🚐 ☕

Range of seating areas to pause and enjoy the beautiful views . . .

32 ◆ **NORWELL NURSERIES**
Woodhouse Road, Norwell
NG23 6JX. Andrew & Helen Ward,
01636 636337, wardha@aol.com,
www.norwellnurseries.co.uk. *6m N
of Newark halfway between Newark &
Southwell. Off A1 at Cromwell
turning, take rd to Norwell at bus
stop. Or from A616 take Caunton
turn.* **For NGS: Sun 15 May, Sun 9
Oct (2-5). Adm £2.50, chd free.
Home-made teas. Opening with
Norwell Gardens on Sun 26, Wed
29 June.** For other opening times
and information, please phone,
email or visit garden website.
Jewel box of over 2,500 different,
beautiful and unusual plants
sumptuously set out in a one acre
plantsman's garden incl shady garden
with orchids, woodland gems,
cottage garden borders, alpine and
scree plants. Pond with opulently
planted margins. Extensive
herbaceous borders and effervescent
colour themed beds. Innovative
Grassoretum (like an arboretum but
for grasses). New borders every yr.
Nationally renowned nursery with
over 1,000 different rare plants for
sale also open. Autumn opening
features UK's largest collection of
hardy chrysanthemums for sale.
Featured in the highly prestigious -
Best Gardens to Visit 2016. and
Country Living magazine. Grass
paths, no wheelchair access to
woodland paths.

33 **NEW** **NORWOOD
COTTAGE**
Church Street, East Markham,
Newark NG22 0SA. Anne Beeby.
*7m S of Retford. Take A1 Markham
Moor r'about exit for A57 Lincoln.
Turn at East Markham junction &
follow signs for the church. Property
adjacent the church.* **Sun 3 July
(12-5). Combined adm with The
Manor House £4, chd free. Home-
made teas at The Manor House.**
Following my move 3yrs ago the
garden is evolving to suit the cottage
and location. Situated opp both the
beautiful St John the Baptist church
and The Manor. Different areas of
interest have been created
incorporating roses, perennials, box
hedging, acers and interesting foliage
plants, trees and shrubs making for yr
round interest. In addition, visitors are
welcome to view the church. Partial
wheelchair access to parts of garden
only. Steps leading to some areas.

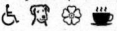

34 **NEW** **OAK BARN**
Church Street, East Markham,
Newark NG22 0SA. Simon Bennett
& Laura Holmes, 07812 146265,
she_ra@hotmail.co.uk. *From A1
Markham Moor junction take A57 to
Lincoln. Turn R at Xrds into E
Markham. L onto High St & R onto
Plantation Rd. Enter farm gates at T
junction, garden located on L.* **Sun 7
Aug, Sun 18 Sept (1-5). Adm £3,
chd free. Home-made teas. Visits
also by arrangement July to Oct,
groups 30 max.**
This small rural garden started out as
an empty plot back in 2009. Since
then I have discovered a passion for
exotic and subtropical plants. Over
time it has evolved into a densely
planted, jungle style, exotic oasis.
From the lush green foliage of
palms, tree ferns and bananas to the
vibrant underplanting of dahlias,
cannas, gingers and brugmansia, this
garden explodes into life in the
summer.

35 **NEW** **THE OLD HALL**
Church Lane, Lowdham,
Nottingham NG14 7BQ. Mr & Dr
Stewart. *Property on the R of Church
Lane, which is a turning off Ton Lane
(same side of the bypass in
Lowdham as World's End PH). The
lane is found by following the sign to
St Mary's Church.* **Sun 1 May (12-4).
Adm £3.50, chd free. Home-made
teas.**
There is a lime tree avenue leading
down to The Old Hall which is
centrally located in the garden. There
is a mound from the original Ludham
Castle to the left of the drive
surrounded on 3 sides by a moat. In
the spring the drive is lined with
daffodils. The hall itself is Wisteria
clad. There is a pergola covered in
Wisteria. There is a vegetable garden
with raised beds, and formal gardens.
Wisteria in May; Daffodils in Spring.

36 **THE OLD VICARAGE**
Halam Hill, Halam NG22 8AX. Mrs
Beverley Perks, 01636 812181,
perks.family@talk21.com. *1m W of
Southwell. Please park diagonally into
beech hedge on verge with speed
interactive sign or in village - a busy
road so no parking on roadside.* **Mon
30 May, Sun 17 July (1-5); Sun 21
Aug (12-4). Adm £3.50, chd free.
Home-made teas. Opening with
Halam Gardens and Wildflower
Meadow on Sun 5 June.** **Visits**

also by arrangement May to Aug
for groups 20+.
This beautifully designed organic,
relaxing garden on S facing hillside,
offers history, texture and colour, all
planted with an artistic eye. Swathes
of snowdrops, followed by bounteous
borders of unusual herbaceous
plants, clematis, roses, shrubs and
trees. Hidden nooks and crannies,
wildlife ponds, swimming pool
planting, kitchen garden, wildflower
meadow with glorious views - soak
up the peace and quiet. Beautiful
C12 Church open only short walk
down into the village or across field
through attractively planted
churchyard - rare C14 stained glass
window. Various local newspaper
articles over many years. Gravel drive
- undulating levels as on a hillside -
plenty of cheerful help available.

Marie
Curie

Patients and
families can enjoy
beautiful gardens
at our hospices

37 **NEW** **OSSINGTON HOUSE**
Moorhouse Road, Ossington,
Newark NG23 6LD. Georgina
Denison. *10m N of Newark, 2m off
A1. From A1 N take exit marked
Carlton, Sutton-on-Trent, Weston etc.
At T-junction turn L to Kneesall. Drive
2m to Ossington. In village turn R to
Moorhouse & park in field next to
Hopbine Farmhouse.* **Sun 19 June
(2-5). Combined adm with
Hopbine Farmhouse, Ossington
£4, chd free. Tea.**
Vicarage garden redesigned in 1960
and again in 2014. Chestnuts, lawns,
formal beds, woodland walk, poolside
planting. Orchard, kitchen garden.
Terraces, yews, grasses. Ferns,
herbaceous perennials, roses. Oaks,
antipodean freaks, clematis. Disabled
parking available in drive to Ossington
House.

Share your day out on 🅵 and 🆈

38 PAPPLEWICK HALL

Blidworth Waye, Papplewick, Nottinghamshire NG15 8FE. J R Godwin-Austen Esq, www.papplewickhall.co.uk. *7m N of Nottingham. 300 yards out N end of Papplewick village, on B683 (follow signs to Papplewick from A60 and B6011). Free parking at Hall.* Sun 29 May (2-5). Adm £3.50, chd free. *Donation to St James' Church.*

This historic, mature, 8 acre garden, mostly shaded woodland, abounds with rhododendrons, hostas, ferns, and spring bulbs. Suitable for wheelchair users, but sections of the paths are gravel.

39 PARK FARM

Crink Lane, Southwell NG25 0TJ. Ian & Vanessa Johnston, 01636 812195, v.johnston100@gmail.com. *1m SE of Southwell. From Southwell town centre go down Church St, turn R on Fiskerton Rd & 200yds up hill turn R into Crink Lane. Park Farm is on 2nd bend. Follow signs to car parking.* Sun 29 May (1-5). Adm £3.50, chd free. Home-made teas.

Visits also by arrangement May to July (guided tour 50ppp). Regret, no refreshments.

3 acre garden remarkable for its extensive variety of trees, shrubs and perennials, many rare or unusual. Long colourful herbaceous borders, roses, woodland garden, alpine/scree garden and a large wildlife pond. Spectacular views of the Minster across a wildflower meadow and ha-ha.

♿ ✿ ☕

40 PATCHINGS ART CENTRE

Oxton Road, Calverton, Nottingham NG14 6NU. Chas & Pat Wood, 01159 653479, Chas@patchingsartcentre.co.uk, www.patchingsartcentre.co.uk. *N of Nottingham city take A614 towards Ollerton. Turn R on to B6386 towards Oxton. Patchings is on L before turning to Calverton.* Sun 19 June, Sun 17 July (10.30-4). Adm £3, chd free. Home-made teas at Patchings Cafe.

Something very different, a woodland walk linked to art history and dressed to celebrate colour and textiles. Colourful wild flowers and grasses dominate the grass path walk. The two dates selected show a range of species and colour within the rolling landscape of Patchings. The walk has been extended to incl the Monet

Bridge and the lake area. Four exhibition galleries, incl the exhibitions for this yrs international painting competition organised with The Artist and Leisure Painter. Studio artists in residence. Grass paths, with some undulations and uphill sections accessible to wheelchairs with help. Please enquire for assistance.

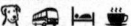

41 PIECEMEAL

123 Main Street, Sutton Bonington, Loughborough LE12 5PE. Mary Thomas, 01509 672056, nursery@piecemealplants.co.uk. *2m SE of Kegworth (M1 J24). 6m NW of Loughborough. Almost opp St Michael's Church & Sutton Bonington Hall.* **Visits by arrangement July & Aug, groups min 4, max 10. For 10+ please contact to discuss. Adm £2.75, chd free.**

Pots of pots! Tiny, sheltered walled garden housing very large collection of shrubs as well as various climbers, perennials and even a few trees, in around 400 containers as well as in small borders. Many unusual and not fully hardy. Focus on distinctive form, foliage shape and colour combination to provide interest from spring to autumn. Both garden and conservatory a jungle by midsummer! Featured in BBC Gardeners' World Magazine and as Garden of the Week in Garden News magazine.

42 THE POPLARS

60 High Street, Sutton-on-Trent, Newark NG23 6QA. Sue & Graham Goodwin-King. *7m N of Newark. Leave A1 at Sutton/Carlton/ Normanton-on-Trent junction. In Carlton turn L onto B1164. Turn R into Hemplands Lane then R into High St. 1st house on R. Limited parking.* Sun 14 Aug (1-5). Adm £3, chd free. Home-made teas.

Mature 1/2 acre garden on the site of a Victorian flower nursery, now a series of well planted areas each with its own character. A newly developed exotics courtyard. Iron balcony overlooking pond and oriental style gravel garden. Jungle with castaway's shack and lookout. Black and white garden. Woodland area. Walled potager. Fernery and hidden courtyard, Lawns, borders and charming sitting places. Some gravel paths and shallow steps, but most areas accessible.

♿ ✿ ☕

43 RHUBARB FARM

Hardwick Street, Langwith, Mansfield NG20 9DR. Community Interest Company, www.rhubarbfarm.co.uk. *On NW border of Nottinghamshire in village of Nether Langwith. From A632 in Langwith, by bridge (single file traffic) turn up steep Devonshire Drive. N.B. Turn off SatNav. Take 2nd L into Hardwick St. Rhubarb Farm at end. Parking to R of gates.* Sun 10 July (10.30-4). Adm £2.50, chd free. *Delicious cream teas and locally made cakes/biscuits.*

52 varieties of fruit and vegetables organically grown not only for sale but for therapeutic benefit. This 2 acre social enterprise provides training and volunteering opportunities to 50 ex offenders, drug and alcohol misusers, and people with mental and physical ill health and disability. Timed tours at 10.30am, 12.30pm and 2.30pm. Two 65ft polytunnels, willow domes and willow arches, 150 hens, sensory garden, watercress bed, outdoor pizza ovens, comfrey bed and comfrey fertiliser factory, composting toilet. Chance to meet and chat with volunteers who come to gain skills, confidence and training. Featured on Channel 4 Dispatches and Radio Nottingham, in Derbyshire Times, Derbyshire Life, The Mansfield Chad and Daily Mirror. Main path down site suitable for wheelchairs but a little bumpy. Not all of the site accessible, or easy for wheelchairs.

Over time it has evolved into a densely planted, jungle style, exotic oasis . . .

Oak Barn

44 RISEHOLME, 125 SHELFORD ROAD

Radcliffe on Trent NG12 1AZ. John & Elaine Walker, 01159 119867. *4m E of Nottingham. From A52 follow signs to Radcliffe. In village centre take turning for Shelford (by Co-op). Approx ¾ m on L.* Evening opening Wed 20 July (6-9). Adm £4, chd free. Wine. Sun 18 Sept (1.30-5.30). Adm £3, chd free. Home-made teas. **Visits also by arrangement May to Sept for groups 10+.**

Just under ½ acre, intensely planted plant lovers' garden. Many varieties of perennials, grasses, shrubs and trees provide colour and interest all yr. Colour themed beds, jungle area with tropical style planting, many tender perennials particularly salvias. New gravel garden with stream. Unique garden mirrors and other interesting objects complement planting. Featured on Gardeners World, in The English Garden magazine, Garden News and Garden Answers.

45 NEW ROSE COTTAGE

81 Nottingham Road, Keyworth, Nottingham NG12 5GS. Richard & Julie Fowkes. *7m S of Nottingham. Follow signs for Keyworth from A606. Garden (white cottage) on R 100yds after Sainsburys. From A60, follow Keyworth signs & turn L at church, garden is 400yds on L.* Sun 26 June (1-5). Combined adm with Home Farm House, 17 Main Street £4, chd free. Light refreshments. Small cottage garden with informal

planting and a private enclosed feel. A pebble beach, mosaics, water features, and a brick well all add unique interest. There is a decked seating area and summerhouse. A wildlife stream, installed in 2013, meanders down to a pond and bog garden. A new woodland area leads to herbs, fruit bushes and hens. Art studio will be open. Paintings and art cards designed by Julie will be on sale.

46 NEW 1 SANDY LANE

Hucknall, Nottingham NG15 7GR. Ann Bingham. *On Hucknall by-pass A611 from Nottingham 1st R then 4th L. On A611 from Mansfield or Linby 1st L then 4th R.* Sun 14 Aug (1-5). Combined adm with 78 Sandy Lane £3, chd free.

Long straight paths give good wheelchair access as needed by the lady gardener to tend her overflowing colourful borders in this delightful 120ft long garden. Secluded area at one end with raised ornamental fish pond near the house. Full wheelchair access to all areas.

47 78 SANDY LANE

Hucknall NG15 7GP. Alan & Linda Foster, 01159 534609, linda.foster78@ntlworld.com. *7m N of Nottingham, 5 mins walk from Hucknall market. On Hucknall by-pass A611 from Nottingham 1st R then 4th L. On A611 from Mansfield or Linby, 1st L then 4th R.* Sun 14 Aug (1-5). Combined adm with

1 Sandy Lane £3, chd free. Sun 4 Sept (2-5). Adm £2.50, chd free. Home-made teas. **Visits also by arrangement Aug & Sept, groups welcome.**

¼ acre long plant lovers' garden, colourful in all seasons and bursting with perennials, annuals, grasses and shrubs. Superb collection of hostas, other shade loving plants and tender plants. Lots of paths and seats. Two frog friendly ponds and at the moment one lone chicken. Interest all through the yr and borders still overflowing and awash with colour till late autumn. Grass paths, 2 small slopes.

48 SYCAMORES HOUSE

Salmon Lane, Annesley Woodhouse, Nottingham NG17 9HB. Lynne & Barrie Jackson, 01623 750466, landbjackson@gmail.com, www.sycamoreshouse.weebly.com. *From M1 J27 follow Mansfield signs to Badger Box Turn L. Turn L. Gate on L just past 'No footway for 600 yds' sign.* Sun 24 Apr, Sun 4 Sept (2-6). Adm £3, chd free. Home-made teas. **Visits also by arrangement Apr to Aug for groups 10+ from mid April.**

A grassy field in 2005, this 1⅓ acre plantsman's garden now comprises a range of growing environments incl a large, productive, organic vegetable garden, polytunnel and orchard. Visitors will discover the secret pathways and quirky ideas along with the glass garden art. All plants are

Ossington House

named to interest experienced gardeners with good ideas for the novice. Children's trail for under 5s. Refreshments under cover. Garden suitable for wheelchair users. Couple of short steep slopes. Gravel paths nr house, grass further down. Ramp available for entrance steps.

 ♿ 🐕 ✻ ☕

49 THRUMPTON HALL
Thrumpton NG11 0AX. Miranda Seymour, www.thrumptonhall.com. *7m S of Nottingham. M1 J24 take A453 towards Nottingham. Turn L to Thrumpton village & cont to Thrumpton Hall.* **Sun 19 June (2-5). Adm £3, chd free. Tea.**
2 acres incl lawns, rare trees, lakeside walks, flower borders, rose garden and box bordered sunken herb garden, all enclosed by C18 ha-ha and encircling a Jacobean house. Garden is surrounded by C18 landscaped park and is bordered by a river. Rare opportunity to visit Thrumpton Hall (separate ticket). Jacobean mansion, unique carved staircase, Great Saloon, State Bedroom, Priest's Hole.

♿ 🐕 ✻ ☕

50 UNIVERSITY OF NOTTINGHAM GARDENS
Nottingham NG7 2RD. University of Nottingham, www.nottingham.ac.uk/estates/grounds/home.aspx. *Approx 4m SW of Nottingham city centre. NGS visitors are asked to buy admission tickets in Millennium Garden in centre of University campus, signed from N & W entrances to University & within the internal road network.* **Sun 21 Aug (1.30-5). Adm £3, chd free. Light refreshments.**
University Park has many beautiful gardens incl the award winning Millennium Garden with its dazzling flower garden, timed fountains and turf maze. Also the huge Lenton Firs rock garden, the Dry Garden and the Jekyll Garden. During summer, the Walled Garden is alive with exotic plantings. In total, 300 acres of landscape and gardens. Picnic area, cafe, walking tours, accessible minibus to feature gardens within campus. Plants for sale in Millennium Garden. Some gravel paths and steep slopes.

♿ 🐕 ✻ 🚐 ☕

GROUP OPENING

51 WEST FARM AND CHURCH HOUSE GARDENS
Hoveringham NG14 7JH. *Centre of Hoveringham village. 6m NE of Nottingham. Signed from A612 Nottingham to Southwell rd, on Southwell side of Lowdham.* **Sun 22 May, Sun 12 June (1-5). Combined adm £4, chd free. Light refreshments at West Farm House.**

CHURCH HOUSE
Alex & Sue Allan

WEST FARM HOUSE
Richard & Carolyn Torr

2 contrasting gardens in the centre of Hoveringham village near St Michael's Church. West Farm House is a large cottage style garden and Church House is a small, but perfectly formed, walled garden. Both gardens host a wide range of features and plants, with specialist collections in each. Cacti and succulent collection at West Farm House. Auricula theatre and Japanese area at Church House. Gravel at both gardens. Narrow, uneven access at Church House, making it difficult for wheelchairs.

♿ 🐕 ✻ ☕

52 6 WESTON CLOSE
Woodthorpe, Nottingham NG5 4FS. Diane & Steve Harrington, 01159 857506, mrsdiharrington@gmail.com. *3m N of Nottingham. A60 Mansfield Rd. Turn R at T-lights into Woodthorpe Drive. 2nd L Grange Road. R into The Crescent. R into Weston Close. Park in The Crescent.* **Visits by arrangement June to Aug for groups 10+. Adm price incl refreshments. Adm £5.00, chd**

free. Home-made teas.
Set on a substantial slope with 3 separate areas, dense planting creates a full, varied yet relaxed display incl many scented roses, clematis and a collection of over 50 named mature hostas in the impressive colourful rear garden. Large plant sale packed with good value home propagated plants. Occasional craft stalls.

✻ ☕

53 WHITE HOUSE
39 Melton Road, Tollerton, Nottingham NG12 4EL. Joan Dean, 01159 375031, joandean4el@btinternet.com. *5m S of Nottingham. From A52 Wheatcroft island, take A606 towards Melton Mowbray. Garden is approx 1½ m on L. Parking in front of Post Office (45 Melton Rd).* **Sun 3 July (1-5). Adm £3.50, chd free. Home-made teas. Visits also by arrangement June to Aug.**
An interesting garden full of herbaceous plants, shrubs and trees. Wisteria and honeysuckle covered arches and pergola. Mirrors, statues and ornaments enhance the garden. Hidden seating area with many interesting and unusual rooms. Secluded wildlife pond, an orient inspired area along with seaside corner and a touch of the jungle. Well worth a visit.

☕

54 WOODPECKERS
35 Lambley Lane, Burton Joyce, Nottingham NG14 5BG. Lynn & Mark Carr, 01159 313237, info@woodpeckersdining.co.uk. *6m N of Nottingham. In Burton Joyce, turn off A612 (Nottingham to Southwell rd) into Lambley Ln, turn L onto private drive to access gardens. Ample parking.* **Sun 22 May (11-5). Adm £3.50, chd free. Home-made teas. Visits also by arrangement Feb to Oct (ample parking).**
4 acres of mature woodland and formal gardens with spectacular views over the Trent Valley. 500 rhododendrons and azaleas. Scented rose tunnel leading from the main lawn to the wisteria arbour. Balustrade terrace for teas. Glade with 200yr old cedars overlooking ponds, waterfalls and croquet lawn. Bog garden and sunken area below ha-ha, then onwards towards ancient well. New areas opening. Gravel and grass paths, steep slopes.

♿ 🐕 ✻ ☕

OXFORDSHIRE

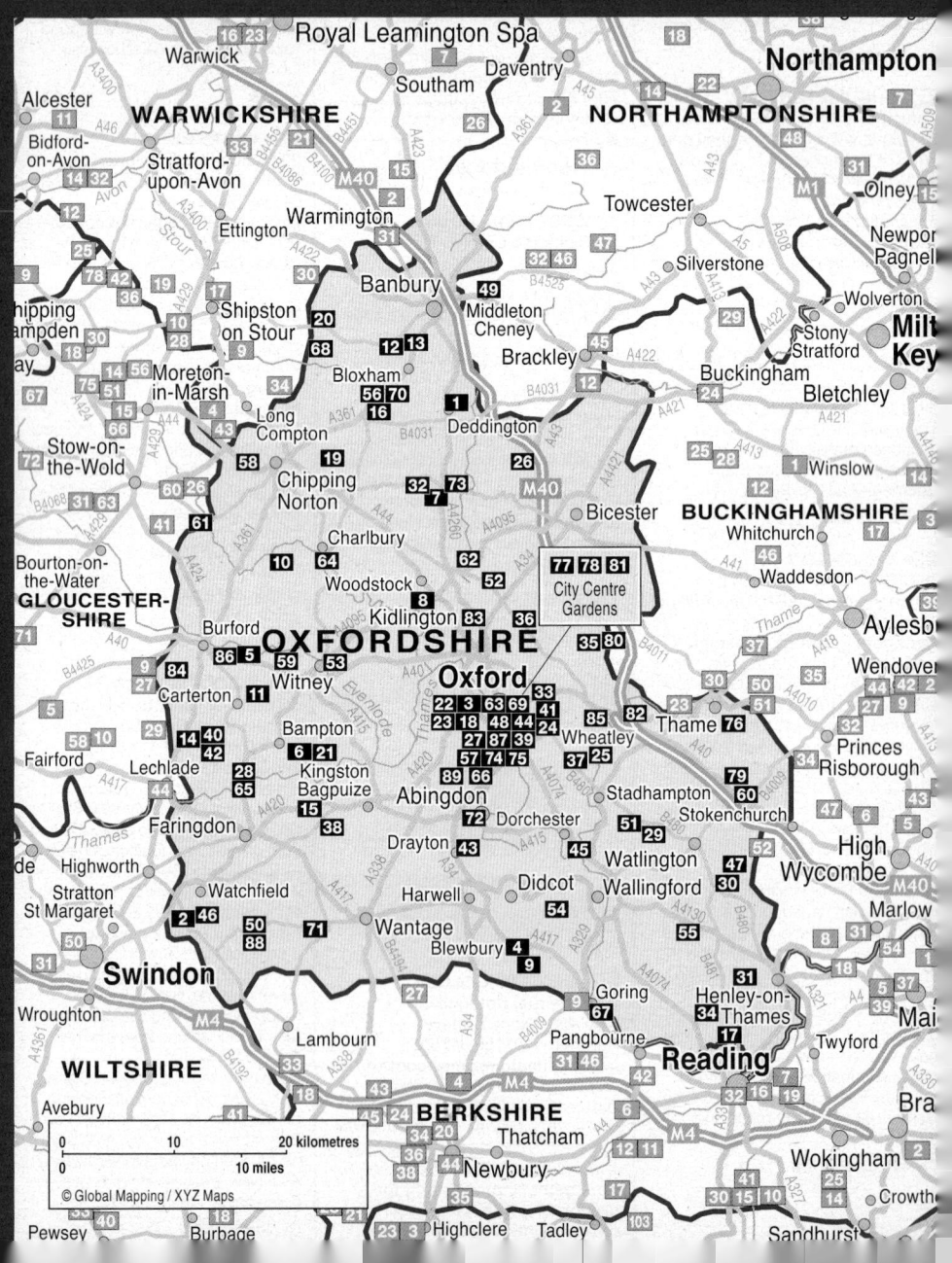

© Global Mapping / XYZ Maps

0 10 20 kilometres
0 10 miles

Oxfordshire

In Oxfordshire we tend to think of ourselves as one of the most landlocked counties, right in the centre of England and furthest from the sea.

We are surrounded by Warwickshire, Northamptonshire, Buckinghamshire, Berkshire, Wiltshire and Gloucestershire, and, like these counties, we benefit from that perfect British climate which helps us create some of the most beautiful and famous gardens in the world.

Many gardens open for Oxfordshire NGS between spring and late-autumn. Amongst these are the perfectly groomed college gardens of Oxford University, and the grounds of stately homes and palaces designed by a variety of the famous garden designers such as William Kent, Capability Brown and Harold Peto, Rosemary Verey, Tom Stuart-Smith and the Bannermans of more recent fame.

But we are also a popular tourist destination for our honey-coloured mellow Cotswold stone villages, and for the Thames which has its spring near Lechlade. More villages open as 'groups' for the NGS in Oxfordshire than in any other county, and offer tea, hospitality, advice and delight with their infinite variety of gardens.

All this enjoyment benefits the excellent causes that the NGS supports.

Oxfordshire Volunteers

County Organisers
Marina Hamilton-Baillie
01367 710486
marina_hamilton_baillie@hotmail.com

David White
01295 812679
david.white@doctors.org.uk

County Treasurer
David White
(as above)

Publicity
Priscilla Frost
01608 810578
info@oxconf.co.uk

Social Media
Lara Cowan
lara.cowan@ngs.org.uk

Booklet Co-ordinator
Catherine Pinney
01491 612638

Assistant County Organisers
Lynn Baldwin
01608 642754
elynnbaldwin@gmail.com

Lara Cowan
(as above)

Petra Hoyer Millar
01869 338156
petra.hoyermillar@ngs.org.uk

John & Joan Pumfrey
01189 722848
joanpumfrey@lineone.net

Charles & Lyn Sanders
01865 739486
sandersc4@hotmail.com

Left: 36 Bertie Road, Cumnor Village Gardens

Opening Dates

All entries subject to change.
For latest information check www.ngs.org.uk

February

Snowdrop Festival

Sunday 14
18 14 Chawley Lane
Tuesday 16
58 Old Rectory
Sunday 21
36 Hollyhocks
Sunday 28
43 Lime Close

March

Sunday 6
52 Monks Head
Sunday 20
77 Trinity College
Monday 28
40 Kencot Gardens

April

Sunday 3
15 Buckland Lakes
20 Church Farm Field
36 Hollyhocks
52 Monks Head
Sunday 10
4 Ashbrook House
44 Magdalen College
81 Wadham College
Saturday 16
2 Allsorts
46 **NEW** Maple Trees
Sunday 17
35 Hilltop Cottage
80 Upper Green
82 Waterperry Gardens

May

Sunday 1
13 Broughton Grange
57 Old Boars Hill Gardens
Monday 2
71 Sparsholt Manor
Saturday 7
63 50 Plantation Road
Sunday 8
1 Adderbury Gardens
63 50 Plantation Road

Saturday 14
63 50 Plantation Road
Sunday 15
27 Foxcombe Hall
32 The Grove
36 Hollyhocks
38 Home Farm House
43 Lime Close
63 50 Plantation Road
Sunday 22
33 Headington Gardens
64 The Priory Garden
Wednesday 25
79 Upper Chalford Farm (Evening)
84 Westwell Manor
Friday 27
59 Old Swan & Minster Mill
Sunday 29
7 Barton Abbey
58 Old Rectory
62 **NEW** Old White Barn
Monday 30
20 Church Farm Field
25 Denton House
47 Meadow Cottage

June

Festival Weekend

Sunday 5
23 **NEW** Cumnor Village Gardens
39 Iffley Gardens
73 Steeple Aston Gardens
83 Wayside
86 Whitehill Farm
Sunday 12
13 Broughton Grange
42 Langford Gardens
Tuesday 14
31 Greys Court
Wednesday 15
89 Wootton Gardens
Thursday 16
30 Greenfield Farm (Evening)
55 Nuffield Place
Friday 17
5 Asthall Manor (Evening)
Saturday 18
53 32 New Yatt Road
Sunday 19
9 Blewbury Gardens
11 Brize Norton Gardens
22 **NEW** Cumnor Hill Gardens

49 Middleton Cheney Gardens
53 32 New Yatt Road
61 The Old Vicarage, Bledington
85 Wheatley Gardens
Thursday 23
79 Upper Chalford Farm (Evening)
Friday 24
59 Old Swan & Minster Mill
Saturday 25
21 **NEW** Cote Manor House Garden
26 Field Cottage
Sunday 26
10 **NEW** Bolters Farm
26 Field Cottage
68 Sibford Gower Gardens
69 Somerville College Gardens
74 Tall Trees
75 Tanglewood
87 Whitsun Meadows

Home-made preserves for sale . . .

July

Saturday 2
8 Blenheim Palace
Sunday 3
14 Broughton Poggs & Filkins Gardens
17 Chalkhouse Green Farm
28 Friars Court
76 Thame Gardens
Thursday 7
79 Upper Chalford Farm (Evening)
Sunday 10
54 North Moreton Gardens
57 Old Boars Hill Gardens
81 Wadham College
Saturday 16
2 Allsorts
46 **NEW** Maple Trees
Saturday 23
53 32 New Yatt Road

Sunday 24
12 Broughton Castle
13 Broughton Grange
48 Merton College Oxford Fellows' Garden
53 32 New Yatt Road
Sunday 31
77 Trinity College

August

Wednesday 17
56 **NEW** The Old Bakehouse
Sunday 21
45 Manor House
65 Radcot House
Sunday 28
6 Aston Pottery
Monday 29
6 Aston Pottery

September

Sunday 4
10 **NEW** Bolters Farm
13 Broughton Grange
20 Church Farm Field
Saturday 10
67 **NEW** Rivermead
Sunday 11
4 Ashbrook House
50 **NEW** Midsummer House
66 Ridgeway
87 Whitsun Meadows
88 Woolstone Mill House
Sunday 18
82 Waterperry Gardens

October

Sunday 2
65 Radcot House

February 2017

Sunday 19
36 Hollyhocks

Gardens open to the public

8 Blenheim Palace
12 Broughton Castle
31 Greys Court
55 Nuffield Place
78 University of Oxford Botanic Garden
82 Waterperry Gardens

By arrangement only

3 Appleton Dene
16 Bush House

19 Chivel Farm
24 103 Dene Road
29 The Grange
34 Hearns House
37 Home Close
41 10 Kennett Road
51 Mill Barn
60 The Old Vicarage
70 South Newington House
72 64 Spring Road

Also open by arrangement

2 Allsorts
28 Friars Court
30 Greenfield Farm
33 40 Osler Road, Headington Gardens
36 Hollyhocks
43 Lime Close
45 Manor House
47 Meadow Cottage
52 Monks Head
57 Uplands, Old Boars Hill Gardens
58 Old Rectory
61 The Old Vicarage, Bledington
66 Ridgeway
67 NEW Rivermead
68 Carter's Yard, Sibford Gower Gardens
68 Gowers Close, Sibford Gower Gardens
73 Primrose Gardens, Steeple Aston Gardens
79 Upper Chalford Farm
80 Upper Green
83 Wayside
85 Wheatley Gardens
86 Whitehill Farm

The Gardens

GROUP OPENING

1 ADDERBURY GARDENS

Adderbury OX17 3LS. *3m S of Banbury. Adderbury is on A4260. At The Green turn into village.* **Sun 8 May (2-5.30). Combined adm £5, chd free. Home-made teas at Church House (Library), High St.** *Donation to Katharine House Hospice.*

CANALIA NPC
Mr Jeffrey Moore

THE OLD VICARAGE
Christine & Peter Job

PLACKETTS
Dr D White

Attractive Ironstone village, with gardens ranging from quite small to very large. The Old Vicarage walled front garden, large rear garden stretching from ha-ha to small lake and flood meadows. Unusual plants and trees. Japanese maple plantation. Placketts $^{1}/_{5}$ acre walled garden with sheltered gravel courtyard, main garden exposed with views. Plethora of colourful plants throughout the yr with much colour in spring. Canalia notable for remarkable collection of Mints. Restricted access at Placketts. Dogs allowed at The Old Vicarage.

2 ALLSORTS

Cleycourt Road, Shrivenham SN6 8BN. Mr & Mrs Jane-anne & Andrew Morrison, 07521 448422. *5m from Swindon. See signs from each way of the B4000 & A420 Swindon-Oxon road.* **Sat 16 Apr, Sat 16 July (10.30-4.30). Adm £3, chd free (under 12 yrs). Light refreshments. Also open Maple Trees. Visits also by arrangement Apr to Sept for groups of 8 max.**

A cottage garden with surprises. Offering varied planting areas with shrubs, climbers, herbaceous and alpine plants, along with fun topiary and a bank of wild flowers. The entrance takes you under a wisteria where we enjoy yr-round colour; some of the plants with scent and some unusual ones. We enjoy varieties of geranium, salvia, lysimachia and clematis. There is a pond with fish and wildlife. We enjoy views from our garden and are near NT villages. Assistant dogs only please. No WC available.

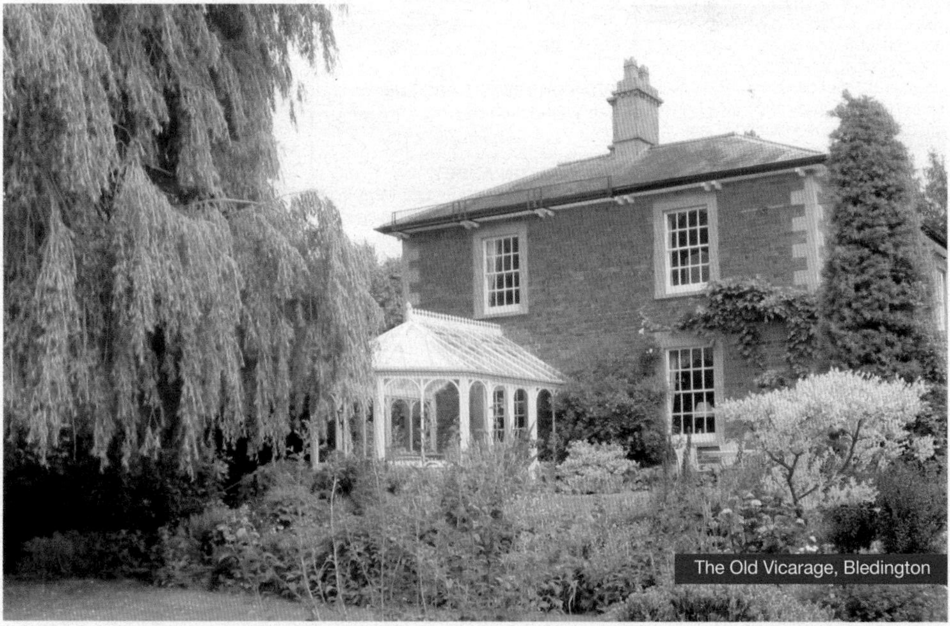

The Old Vicarage, Bledington

3 APPLETON DENE
Yarnells Hill, Botley, Oxford
OX2 9BG. Mr & Mrs A Dawson,
07701 000977, annrobe@aol.com.
*3m W of Oxford. Take W road out of
Oxford, through Botley Rd, pass
under A34, turn L into Westminster
Way, Yarnells Hill 2nd on R, park at
top of hill. Walk 200 metres.* **Visits by
arrangement May to Sept, please
phone in advance. Adm £4, chd
free. Home-made teas.**
Beautiful secluded garden set in a
hidden valley bordered by woods and
a field. The $1/4$ acre garden on a
steeply sloping site surrounds a
mature tulip tree. There is a skillfully
incorporated level lawn area
overlooked by deep borders incl a
wide variety of plants for long
seasonal interest. There will also
be some outdoor floral displays.
Featured in Garden News
magazine.

4 ASHBROOK HOUSE
Blewbury OX11 9QA. Mr & Mrs S A
Barrett. *4m SE of Didcot. Turn off
A417 in Blewbury into Westbrook St.
1st house on R. Follow yellow signs
for parking in Boham's Rd.* **Sun 10
Apr, Sun 11 Sept (2-5.30). Adm £4,
chd free. Tea.**
The garden where Kenneth Grahame
read Wind in the Willows to local
children and where he took
inspiration for his description of the
oak doors to Badger's House. Come
and see, you may catch a glimpse of
Toad and friends in this $3^1/2$ acre
chalk and water garden in a beautiful
spring line village. In spring the banks
are a mass of daffodils and in late
summer the borders are full of
unusual plants.

5 ASTHALL MANOR
Asthall, Burford OX18 4HW.
Rosanna Pearson,
www.asthallmanor.com. *3m E of
Burford. Going from Witney to
Burford on A40, turn R at r'about.
Coming from Chipping Norton, come
through Shipton-under-Wychwood &
Swinbrook.* **Evening opening Fri 17
June (6-9). Adm £7.50, chd free.
Wine.**
6 acres of dramatic planting surround
this C17 Cotswolds manor house,
once home to the Mitford family (not
open). The gardens, designed by I &
J Bannerman in 1998, offer 'a
beguiling mix of traditional and
contemporary' as described by the

Good Gardens Guide. Exuberant
scented borders, sloping box
parterres, wild flowers, gypsy
waggon, turf sculpture and hidden
lake. 'on form' an acclaimed
exhibition of contemporary stone
sculpture will be on display in the
gardens, ballroom and St Nicholas
Church next door
(onformsculpture.co.uk). Featured in
Clive Nichols English Gardens and
Secret Gardens of the Cotswolds by
Victoria Summerley (2015). Partial
wheelchair access.

6 ASTON POTTERY
Aston, Bampton OX18 2BT.
Mr Stephen Baughan,
www.astonpottery.co.uk. *On the
B4449 between Bampton &
Standlake. 4m S of Witney.* **Sun 28,
Mon 29 Aug (12-5). Adm by
donation. Light refreshments in
the café.**
4 stunning borders flowering
throughout the summer and into
autumn. Set around our pottery, gift
shop and cafe are a dense,
multilayered, traditional perennial
border. Large 72 metre double
bordered hornbeam walk with
summerhouse. 50 metre hot bank,
phlox, kniphofia and canna lilies
running 5 metre deep. New for this yr,
our seasons garden with August
offering a delight of 600 dahlias and
agapanthus. Featured in The
Telegraph.

AVON DASSETT GARDENS
See Warwickshire

7 BARTON ABBEY
Steeple Barton OX25 4QS. Mr &
Mrs P Fleming. *8m E of Chipping
Norton. On B4030, $1/2$ m from
junction of A4260 & B4030.* **Sun 29
May (2-5). Adm £5, chd free.
Home-made teas.**
15 acre garden with views from
house (not open) across sweeping
lawns and picturesque lake. Walled
garden with colourful herbaceous
borders, separated by established
yew hedges and espalier fruit,
contrasts with more informal
woodland garden paths with vistas of
specimen trees and meadows.
Working glasshouses and fine display
of fruit and vegetables.

8 ◆ BLENHEIM PALACE
Woodstock OX20 1PX.
His Grace the Duke of
Marlborough, 01993 810530,
operations@blenheimpalace.com,
www.blenheimpalace.com. *8m N of
Oxford. Bus: S3 Oxford-Chipping
Norton, alight Woodstock.* **For NGS:
Sat 2 July (9.30-6). Adm £4, chd
£2. For other opening times and
information, please phone, email or
visit garden website.**
Blenheim Gardens, originally laid out
by Henry Wise, incl the formal Water
Terraces and Italian Garden by Achille
Duchêne, Rose Garden, Arboretum,
and Cascade. The Secret Garden
offers a stunning garden paradise in
all seasons. Blenheim Lake, created
by Capability Brown and spanned by
Vanburgh's Grand Bridge, is the focal
point of over 2,000 acres of
landscaped parkland. The Pleasure
Gardens complex incl the Herb and
Lavender Garden and Butterfly
House. Other activities incl the
Marlborough Maze, adventure play
area, giant chess and draughts.
Some gravel paths, terrain can be
uneven in places, includes some
steep slopes. Dogs allowed in park
only.

GROUP OPENING

9 BLEWBURY GARDENS
Blewbury OX11 9QB. *4m SE of
Didcot. On A417. Follow yellow signs
for car parks.* **Sun 19 June (2-6).
Combined adm £5, chd free.
Home-made teas at Blewbury
Manor, all proceeds to the NGS.**

BLEWBURY MANOR
Mr & Mrs M R Blythe

BROOKS END
Jean & David Richards

GREEN BUSHES
Phil Rogers

HALL BARN
Malcolm & Deirdre Cochrane

HALL BARN CLOSE
Lindy & Richard Farrell

THE OLD MILL
Dermot & Helen Mathias

STOCKS
Norma & Richard Bird

As celebrated by Rachel de Thame in Gardener's World, 7 gardens in charming downland village. Blewbury Manor 10 acres, moat, parterre, herbaceous, mixed borders, pergola, vegetable garden, stream planting, woodland, lake, sunken gravel garden. Brooks End 1960s bungalow, colour themed beds, damp, shady border, hidden garden, small orchard, greenhouse, and vegetable garden. Green Bushes created by plant lover Rhon (dec'd 2007) around C15 cottage. Colour themed borders, ponds and poolside planting, ferns, pleached limes and roses. Hall Barn 4 acres with traditional herbaceous borders, kitchen garden, croquet lawn, C16 dovecote, thatched cob wall and chalk stream. Hall Barn Close C16 house with unusual perennials, mature shrubs, cottage garden favourites, fruit and vegetable area. The Old Mill 3 acre garden bounded by streams with unusual trees, mill pond, mixed and shrub border. Further acre with vegetable and cutting garden, orchard and wild flower field. Stocks early cruck-constructed thatched cottage surrounded by densely planted lime tolerant herbaceous perennials offering tiers of colour yr-round. Plant stall in the car park by Derry Watkins, Special Plants Nursery. Wheelchair access to some gardens.

10 NEW BOLTERS FARM
Chilson, Chipping Norton
OX7 3HU. Amanda Cooper. *Centre of Chilson Village. On arriving in Chilson, please drive past our gates (white & shabby) & park on the L by an old milking block. Our house is the last in an old row of cottages, with gravel yard & log shed.* **Sun 26 June, Sun 4 Sept (10.30-5). Adm £4, chd free. Tea.** *Donation to Hands Up Foundation.*

A cherished old cottage garden restored over the last 9 yrs. Tumbly walls and sloping lawns down to a stream with natural planting and character. Wheelchairs have to negotiate sloping deep gravel!

Established garden with an Italian theme brimming with exotic planting . . .

GROUP OPENING

11 BRIZE NORTON GARDENS
Brize Norton OX18 3LY, www.bncommunity.org/ngs. *3m SW of Witney. Brize Norton Village, S of A40, between Witney & Burford. Parking at various locations in village. Coaches welcome with plenty of parking nearby.* **Sun 19 June (2-6). Combined adm £4, chd free. Home-made teas at Elderbank Village Hall.**

BARNSTABLE HOUSE
Mr & Mrs P Butcher

CHURCH FARM HOUSE
Philip & Mary Holmes

CLUMBER
Mr & Mrs S Hawkins

NEW 3 DAUBIGNY MEAD
Mrs Denise Merriman

GRANGE FARM
Mark & Lucy Artus

MIJESHE
Mr & Mrs M Harper

95 STATION ROAD
Mr & Mrs P A Timms

STONE COTTAGE
Mr & Mrs K Humphris

Doomsday village on the edge of the Cotswold's offering a number of gardens open for your enjoyment. You can see a wide variety of planting incl ornamental trees, herbaceous borders, ornamental grasses and traditional fruit and vegetable gardens. Features incl a Mediterranean style patio, courtyard garden, water features, plus gardens where you can just sit, relax and enjoy the day. Plants will be available for sale at individual gardens. A Flower Festival will take place in the Brize Norton St Britius Church. Partial wheelchair access to some gardens.

12 ◆ BROUGHTON CASTLE
Banbury OX15 5EB. Lord Saye and Sele, 01295 276070, info@broughtoncastle.com, www.broughtoncastle.com. *2½ m SW of Banbury. On Shipston-on-Stour road (B4035).* **For NGS: Sun 24 July (2-5). Adm £5, chd free. Cream teas. For other opening times and information, please phone, email or visit garden website.**
1 acre; shrubs, herbaceous borders, walled garden, roses, climbers seen against background of C14-C16 castle surrounded by moat in open parkland. House also open (additional charge).

13 BROUGHTON GRANGE
Wykham Lane, Broughton, Banbury OX15 5DS.
Broughton Grange, www.broughtongrange.com. *¼ m out of village. From Banbury take B4035 to Broughton. Turn L at Saye & Sele Arms PH up Wykham Lane (one way). Follow road out of village for ¼ m. Entrance on R.* **Suns 1 May, 12 June, 24 July, 4 Sept (10-5). Adm £7, chd free. Light refreshments.**
An impressive 25 acres of gardens and light woodland in an attractive Oxfordshire setting. The centrepiece is a large terraced walled garden created by Tom Stuart-Smith in 2001. Vision has been used to blend the gardens into the countryside. Good early displays of bulbs followed by outstanding herbaceous planting in summer. Formal and informal areas combine to make this a special site incl newly laid arboretum with many ongoing projects.

Lime Close

GROUP OPENING

14▶ BROUGHTON POGGS & FILKINS GARDENS
Lechlade GL7 3JH,
www.filkins.org.uk. *3m N of Lechlade. 5m S of Burford. Just off A361 between Burford & Lechlade on the B4477. Map of the gardens available.* **Sun 3 July (2-6). Combined adm £5, chd free. Home-made teas in Filkins Village Hall.**

BROUGHTON HALL
Karen & Ian Jobling

BROUGHTON POGGS MILL
Charlie & Avril Payne

THE CORN BARN
Ms Alexis Thompson

FIELD COTTAGE
Peter & Sheila Gray

FILKINS ALLOTMENTS
Filkins Allotments

FILKINS HALL
Filkins Hall Residents

LITTLE PEACOCKS
Colvin & Moggridge

PEACOCK FARMHOUSE
Pauline & Peter Care

PIGEON COTTAGE
Lynne Savege

PIP COTTAGE
G B Woodin

THE TALLOT
Ms M Swann & Mr Don Stowell

TAYLOR COTTAGE
Mr & Mrs Ian & Ronnie Bailey

12 gardens in these beautiful and vibrant Cotswold stone twin villages. Scale and character vary from the grand landscape setting of Filkins Hall and the equally extensive but more intimate Broughton Hall, to the small but action packed Pigeon Cottage and The Tallot. Broughton Poggs Mill has a rushing mill stream with an exciting bridge; Pip Cottage combines topiary, box hedges and a fine rural view. In these and the other equally exciting gardens horticultural interest abounds. Features incl plant stall by professional local nursery, Swinford Museum of Cotswolds tools and artefacts, and Cotswold Woollen Weavers. Many gardens have gravel driveways, but most are suitable for wheelchair access. Most gardens welcome dogs on leads.

♿ 🐕 ❁ 🚐 ☕

15▶ BUCKLAND LAKES
Nr Faringdon SN7 8QW. **The Wellesley Family.** *3m NE of Faringdon. Buckland is midway between Oxford (14m) & Swindon (15m), just off the A420. Faringdon 3m, Witney 8m. Follow the yellow NGS signs which will lead you to driveway & car park by St Mary's Church.* **Sun 3 Apr (2-5). Adm £5, chd free. Home-made teas at Memorial Hall.** *Donation to RWMT (community bus).*

Descend down wooded path to two large secluded lakes with views over undulating historic parkland, designed by Georgian landscape architect Richard Woods. Picturesque mid C18 rustic icehouse, cascade with iron footbridge, thatched boathouse and round house, and renovated exedra. Many fine mature trees, drifts of spring bulbs and daffodils amongst shrubs. Norman church adjoins. Cotswold village. Children must be supervised due to large expanse of unfenced open water.

🐕 🚐 ☕

16 BUSH HOUSE
Wigginton Road, South Newington, Banbury OX15 4JR. Mr & Mrs John & Roberta Ainley, 01295 721207, rojoainley@btinternet.com. *In South Newington on A361 from Banbury to Chipping Norton, take 1st R to Wigginton, Bush House 1st house on the L in Wigginton Rd.* **Visits by arrangement Apr to July for individuals or groups of 40 max. Refreshments on request. Adm £5, chd free.**
Set in 8 acres over 5 yrs a 2 acre garden has emerged. Herbaceous borders partner dual level ponds and stream. The terrace leads to a walled parterre framed by roses and wisteria. The orchard is screened by rose and vine covered wrought iron trellis. Kitchen gardens, greenhouse and fruit cage provide organically grown produce. Stream and interconnecting ponds. Walled parterre and knot garden. 1000 native broadleaved trees planted 2006, 2011 and 2014. Gravel drive, a few small steps with a ramp, and two gentle grass slopes on either side of the garden.

17 CHALKHOUSE GREEN FARM
Chalkhouse Green, Kidmore End, Reading RG4 9AL. Mr & Mrs J Hall, www.chgfarm.com. *2m N of Reading, 5m SW of Henley-on-Thames. Situated between A4074 & B481. From Kidmore End take Chalkhouse Green Rd. Follow yellow signs.* **Sun 3 July (2-6). Adm £3, chd free. Cream teas.**
1 acre garden and open traditional farmstead. Herbaceous borders, herb garden, shrubs, old fashioned roses, trees incl medlar, quince and mulberries, walled ornamental kitchen garden. New cherry orchard. Rare breed farm animals incl British White cattle, Suffolk Punch horses, donkeys, Berkshire pigs, piglets, chickens, ducks and turkeys. Plant and jam stall, donkey rides, swimming in covered pool, trailer rides, farm trail, horse logging demonstration, bee display. Partial wheelchair access.

18 14 CHAWLEY LANE
Cumnor, Oxford OX2 9PX. Alice & Paul Munsey. *3m W of Oxford. From W Oxford, at top of Cumnor Hill, turn R opp Maserati garage into Chawley Lane. Garden 50 metres on R. Parking in Norreys & Bertie Rd.*

Sun 14 Feb (1.30-4). Adm £3, chd free. Home-made teas.
Plantsman's ¹/₂ acre garden with wide and interesting range of plants, many unusual. Owner has a particular interest in alpines and woodland plants. Lovely views over valley and Wytham Woods. Area of developing meadow. Well laid out vegetable garden. Extensive range of snowdrops. One slight slope and small step to WC.

Vision has been used to blend the gardens into the countryside . . .

19 CHIVEL FARM
Heythrop OX7 5TR. Mr & Mrs J D Sword, 01608 683227, rosalind.sword@btinternet.com. *4m E of Chipping Norton. Off A361 or A44.* **Visits by arrangement, with adm dependent on group size.**
Beautifully designed country garden with extensive views, designed for continuous interest that is continuously evolving. Colour schemed borders with many unusual trees, shrubs and herbaceous plants. Small formal white garden and a conservatory.

20 CHURCH FARM FIELD
Church Lane, Epwell, Banbury OX15 6LD. Mrs D V D Castle. *7¹/₂ m W of Banbury on N side of Epwell Village.* **Sun 3 Apr, Mon 30 May, Sun 4 Sept (2-6). Adm £2, chd free. Home-made teas.**
Woods, arboretum with wild flowers (planting started 1992), over 90 different trees and shrubs in 4¹/₂ acres. Paths cut through trees for access to various parts. Lawn tennis court and croquet lawns.

21 NEW COTE MANOR HOUSE GARDEN
Cote, Bampton OX18 2EG. Annabel & James Salter. *3m from Bampton towards Standlake. The postcode will take you to the middle of Cote village. Keep going straight along this road for about ¹/₂ m until you see a high wall on the RH-side.*

We are the 3rd set of gates. **Sat 25 June (11-6). Adm £5, chd free. Cream teas.**
6 acres of formal and informal gardens, including a lake, knot garden and secret garden. A moat and woodland garden containing some rare tree specimens. There is also a small vegetable and herb garden. Wheelchair access accept the cut stone path at the entrance which can be avoided.

GROUP OPENING

22 NEW CUMNOR HILL GARDENS
Hid's Copse Road, Oxford OX2 9JJ. *3m W of Oxford. Up Cumnor Hill 1m & R for No 15 & 22 Hid's Copse Rd, or L into Arnolds Way & L again for Hurst Drive. Parking on Cumnor Hill. Limited disabled parking by house.* **Sun 19 June (2-6). Combined adm £5, chd free. Home-made teas at 22 Hid's Copse Road.**

NEW 15 HID'S COPSE ROAD
James & Harriet Bretherton

NEW 22 HID'S COPSE ROAD
Donella Chapman

86 HURST RISE
Ms P Guy & Mr L Harris

Situated on the west side of Oxford 3 complementary gardens off Cumnor Hill. 86 Hurst Rise a small town garden designed and planted by the owners in 2013. A 40ft x 40ft space brimming with herbaceous perennial plants, roses, clematis, shrubs and small trees. Seasonal use of containers and hanging baskets. 15 Hid's Copse Road, a garden with dramatic use of borrowed landscape, with roses and clematis entirely clothing bordering Leylandii. A secluded, informal and mature garden which seems larger than its ¹/₂ acre. Colourful herbaceous borders, with self sown annuals, and shrubs, terrace, pots, 3 ponds, bog garden, and pergola. 22 Hid's Copse Road a more traditional garden with lawns, herbaceous beds and raised vegetable plots surrounding a 1920s Arts and Crafts house.

Hidden gardens with different plantings and peaceful places to sit . . .

GROUP OPENING

23 NEW CUMNOR VILLAGE GARDENS
Leys Road, Cumnor, Oxford OX2 9QF. *4m W of central Oxford. From A420, exit for Cumnor & follow B4017 into the village. Parking on road & side roads, behind PO, or behind village hall in Leys Rd. Additional parking in Bertie & Norreys Rd.* **Sun 5 June (2-6). Combined adm £5, chd free. Tea in United Reformed Church Hall, Leys Road.**

> **36 BERTIE ROAD** D
> Esther & Neil Whiting
>
> **NEW 10 LEYS ROAD**
> Penny & Nick Bingham
>
> **NEW 41 LEYS ROAD**
> Philip & Jennie Powell
>
> **NEW STONEHAVEN**
> Dr Dianne and Prof Keith Gull
>
> **NEW 1 THE WINNYARDS**
> Brenda & Roy Darnell

Five gardens of varying styles in attractive village setting. 10 Leys Road, long narrow cottage garden with a wide variety of shrubs and trees with many interesting and unusual perennials. 41 Leys Road, $3/4$ acre plot including C16 cottage (not open) with flower and fruit garden, orchard, large vegetable garden, mature trees and wild flowers. 1 The Winnyards, a medium sized garden planted for yr-long interest, plus a water feature, pergola and open views across a meadow. 36 Bertie Road, a small professionally designed garden, structured layout of 3 rooms, pergola, raised vegetable bed, relaxed planting style with emphasis on form and texture. Stonehaven, front garden partially gravelled, side courtyard has pots, rear garden overlooks meadows. Unusual plants, many with black or

bronze foliage, old apple trees, wildlife pond. Japanese influence. Wheelchair access to 1 The Winnyards and 36 Bertie Road and partial access to Stonehaven due to pebbles. WC facilities in United Reformed Church Hall.

⚗ ☕

---

24 103 DENE ROAD
Headington, Oxford OX3 7EQ. Mr & Mrs Steve & Mary Woolliams, 01865 764153, stevewoolliams@gmail.com. *S Headington nr Nuffield. Dene Rd accessed from The Slade from the N, or from Hollow Way·from the S. Both access roads are B4495. Garden on sharp bend.* **Visits by arrangement Apr to Sept for groups of 10 max, children very welcome. Adm £3, chd free. Home-made teas.**
A surprising eco-friendly garden with borrowed view over the Lye Valley Nature Reserve. Lawns, a wild flower meadow, pond and large kitchen garden are incl in a suburban 60ft x 120ft sloping garden. Fruit trees, soft fruit and mixed borders of shrubs, hardy perennials, grasses and bulbs, designed for seasonal colour. This garden has been noted for its wealth of wildlife incl a variety of birds and butterflies, incl the rare Brown Hairstreak butterfly. Featured in Amateur Gardening magazine, titled Me & My Eco-Friendly Garden (18 July 2015).

25 DENTON HOUSE
Denton, Oxford OX44 9JF. Mr & Mrs Luke. *In a valley between Garsington & Cuddesdon.* **Mon 30 May (2-5). Adm £5, chd free. Home-made teas.**
Large walled garden surrounds a Georgian mansion (not open), with shaded areas, walks, topiary and many interesting mature trees. Large lawns and herbaceous borders and rose beds. The windows in the wall were taken in 1864 from Brasenose College Chapel and Library. Wild garden and a further walled fruit garden.

♿ 🚌 ☕

26 FIELD COTTAGE
Fritwell Road, Fewcott, Bicester OX27 7NZ. Mrs Wendy Farha.
Follow public footpath sign turning up drive past The Old Schoolhouse. Field Cottage is at the top of this drive & through the far R gate. **Sat 25, Sun**

26 June (10.30-3). Adm £3.50, chd free. Light refreshments in wooden lodge on-site.
1 acre organic garden with perennial borders and specimen bushes and trees. Eco-friendly techniques employed to encourage a variety of wildlife and birds. Green roof primarily of sedum to counter balance the emissions from the main house heating system. Wildlife pond and wild flower bund to compliment the eco-friendly ethos. A series of woodchip and garden paths surround the garden with large lawn area for viewing borders.

♿ ⚗ ☕

27 FOXCOMBE HALL
Boars Hill, Oxford OX1 5HR. The Open University in the South, 01865 327000, south-events@open.ac.uk. *3m S of Oxford. From Oxford ring road S, follow signs for Wootton & Boars Hill. At Berkeley Rd turn R. At 1st L bend look for car park on L.* **Sun 15 May (1-5). Adm £3, chd free. Light refreshments.**
Come and explore 15 acres of beautiful garden at Foxcombe Hall, home to The Open University in the South and formerly owned by Lord Randall Berkeley. The grounds, not usually open to the public, are mostly natural woodland and incl an artificial lake, Italian garden with terrace and rockery, rhododendrons and magnolias. Partial wheelchair access, some paths very slippery when wet.

♿ 🚌 ☕

28 FRIARS COURT
Clanfield OX18 2SU. Charles Willmer, 01367 810206, charles@friarscourt.com, www.friarscourt.com. *5m N of Faringdon. On A4095 Faringdon to Witney. $1/2$ m S of Clanfield.* **Sun 3 July (2-6). Adm £4, chd free. Cream teas. Visits also by arrangement Apr to Sept for groups of 15-48.**
Approx 3 acres of formal, and informal, part-moated gardens and grounds surround the C17 Cotswold stone farmhouse (not open). Three bridges span the water and beyond the moat is a woodland walk. A level, circular path goes around the main gardens.

♿ ⚗  ☕

THE GRANARY
See Warwickshire

29 THE GRANGE

Berrick Road, Chalgrove, Oxford OX44 7RQ. Mrs Vicky Farren, 01865 400883, vickyfarren@mac.com. *12m E of Oxford & 4m from Watlington off B480.* **Visits by arrangement June to Sept. Adm £5, chd free. Light refreshments.**

10 acre plot with an evolving garden incl herbaceous borders and a prairie with many grasses inspired by the Dutch style. Lake with bridges and an island, a brook running through the garden, wild flower meadow, a further pond, arboretum, old orchard and vegetable garden. There is deep water and bridges may be slippery when wet. Grass paths.

30 GREENFIELD FARM

Christmas Common, Nr Watlington OX49 5HG. Andrew & Jane Ingram, 01491 612434, andrew@andrewbingram.com. *4m from J5 of M40, 7m from Henley. J5 M40, A40 towards Oxford for 1/2 m, turn L signed Christmas Common. 3/4 m past Fox & Hounds PH, turn L at Tree Barn sign.* **Evening opening Thur 16 June (6-8). Adm £4, chd free. Visits also by arrangement May to Sept for groups of 8+.**

10 acre wild flower meadow surrounded by woodland, established 18 yrs ago under the Countryside Stewardship Scheme. Traditional Chiltern chalkland meadow in beautiful peaceful setting with 100 species of perennial wild flowers, grasses and 5 species of orchids. 1/2 m walk from parking area to meadow. Opportunity to return via typical Chiltern beechwood. A guided tour at 6.00pm. The tour will last approx 2hrs and is 1 1/2 m long.

31 ◆ GREYS COURT

Rotherfield Greys, Henley-on-Thames RG9 4PG. National Trust, 01491 628529, www.nationaltrust.org.uk/greys-court. *2m W of Henley-on-Thames. From Nettlebed mini-r'about on A4130 take B481 & property is signed to the L after approx 3m.* **For NGS: Tue 14 June (10-5). Adm £4, chd £3. For other opening times and information, please phone or visit garden website.**

The tranquil gardens cover 9 acres and surround a Tudor house with many alterations, as well as a Donkey Wheel and Tower. They incl lawns, a maze and small arboretum. The highlights are the series of enchanting walled gardens, a colourful patchwork of interest set amid Medieval walls. Meet the gardeners and volunteers who look after the gardens. Tea, coffee, lunches and afternoon teas served in The Cowshed. Partial wheelchair access. Loose gravel paths, slopes and some cobbles in garden.

32 THE GROVE

North Street, Middle Barton, Chipping Norton OX7 7BZ. Ivor & Barbara Hill. *7m E Chipping Norton. On B4030, 2m from junction A4260 & B4030, opp Carpenters Arms PH. Parking in street.* **Sun 15 May (1.30-5). Adm £3, chd free. Home-made teas.**

Mature informal plantsman's 1/3 acre garden, planted for yr-round interest around C19 Cotswold stone cottage (not open). Numerous borders with wide variety of unusual shrubs, trees and hardy plants; several species weigela syringa viburnum and philadelphus. Pond area, well stocked greenhouse. Plant list and garden history available. Home-made preserves for sale. Wheelchair access to most of garden.

GROUP OPENING

33 HEADINGTON GARDENS

Old Headington OX3 9BT. *2m E from centre of Oxford. After T-lights in the centre of Headington heading towards Oxford take the 2nd turn on R into Osler Rd. Gardens at end of road in Old Headington.* **Sun 22 May (2-6). Combined adm £5, chd free. Tea in the cafe at Ruskin College, next door to the vegetable garden.** *Donation to Ruskin College.*

THE COACH HOUSE
Bryony & David Rowe

40 OSLER ROAD
Nicholas & Pam Coote
Visits also by arrangement May to Aug.
pamjcoote@gmail.com
07804 932748

RUSKIN COLLEGE 🛏
Ruskin College
www.headington.org.uk/crinkle crankle/history/index.html

35 ST ANDREWS ROAD
Mrs Alison Soskice

9 STOKE PLACE
Clive & Veronica Hurst

WHITE LODGE
Denis & Catharine Macksmith and Roger & Frances Little

Situated above Oxford, Headington is centred round an old village that is remarkable for its mature trees, high stone walls, narrow lanes and Norman church. The 6 gardens in Old Headington provide a rare glimpse behind the walls. 40 Osler Road is a well established garden with an Italian theme brimming with exotic planting. White Lodge provides a large park like setting for a Regency property. The Coach House combines a formal setting with hedges, lawn and flowers and a sunny courtyard on 2 levels. 35 St Andrews Road is a delightful smaller garden with pretty borders and a vegetable garden. 9 Stoke Place has a traditional lawn and mixed border on one side of the house, and a newly created formal garden on the other. The walled vegetable garden in the grounds of Ruskin College incorporates a Grade II listed Crinkle Crankle Wall designed to maximise the sunshine available to the recently planted trained fruit trees. Partial wheelchair access to most gardens due to gravel paths and steps.

34 HEARNS HOUSE

Gallowstree Common RG4 9DE.
John & Joan Pumfrey, 01189
722848, joanpumfrey@lineone.net.
*5m N of Reading, 5m W of Henley.
From A4074 turn E at Cane End.*
**Visits by arrangement May to
Sept, with introductory talk by the
owner. Adm £4, chd free. Home-
made teas.**
2 acre garden provides yr-round
interest for artists and gardeners with
pergolas, crinkle-crankle walls,
sculptures and ponds. Inspirational
indigenous and exotic planting is
designed to suit dry shade under
trees, and a hot bank. The nursery is
full of wonderful plants propagated
from the garden. An almost entirely
paved walled garden has many self-
seeding plants to give a pretty effect
with low maintenance. Groups of
gardeners and artists are welcome to
enjoy/paint inspirational hard
landscaping and planting. Grass lawn
access generally, with occasional
single steps at terrace.
  ✿ 🐾 ✿ **NPC** ☕

35 HILLTOP COTTAGE

Horton-cum-Studley, Oxford
OX33 1AU. Professor Sarah
Randolph. *Centre of village on main
road. Enter village, R up Horton Hill,
Hilltop Cottage on L at the top. 2
disabled spaces in lay-by opp, other
parking at bottom of hill.* **Sun 17 Apr
(2-5). Combined adm with Upper
Green £4, chd free. Home-made
teas at Studley Barn.**
Plantaholic's large cottage garden,
with productive vegetable plot, soft
fruit and ornamentals. Beds incl
herbaceous, shrubbery and prairie
look. Small trees incl Acer griseum,
Sorbus spp, silver-leaved shrubs.
Colour in April with shrubs and a wide
range of bulbs. Path with shallow
steps.
  ✿ ☕

36 HOLLYHOCKS

North Street, Islip, Kidlington
OX5 2SQ. Avril Hughes,
01865 377104,
ahollyhocks@btinternet.com. *3m
NE of Kidlington. From A34, exit
Bletchingdon & Islip. B4027 direction
Islip, turn L into North St.* **Sun 21 Feb
(1.30-4). Adm £3.50, chd free. Sun
3 Apr (2-6). Combined adm with
Monks Head £5, chd free. Sun 15
May (2-5.30). Adm £3.50, chd free.
Home-made teas. 2017: Sun 19
Feb. Visits also by arrangement
Feb to Sept.**

Plantswoman's small Edwardian
garden brimming with yr-round
interest, especially planted to provide
winter colour, scent and snowdrops.
Divided into areas with bulbs,
herbaceous borders, roses, clematis,
shade and woodland planting
especially Trillium, Podophyllum and
Arisaema. There are several alpine
troughs as well as lots of pots around
the house. Some steps into the
garden.
  ✿ ☕

*A cottage garden
full of scents, roses
and other floral
treats . . .*

37 HOME CLOSE

Southend, Garsington OX44 9DH.
Ms M Waud & Dr P Giangrande,
01865 361394. *3m SE of Oxford. N
of B480, opp Garsington Manor.*
**Visits by arrangement Apr to
Sept. Refreshments on request.
Adm £4, chd free.**
2 acre garden with listed house (not
open) and listed granary. Unusual
trees and shrubs planted for yr-round
effect. Terraces, walls and hedges
divide the garden and the planting
reflects a Mediterranean interest.
Vegetable garden and orchard. 1 acre
mixed tree plantation with fine views.

38 HOME FARM HOUSE

Pusey, Faringdon SN7 8QB. Mr &
Mrs Hugh Buchanan. *Take B4508
marked to Pusey from Oxford -
Swindon A420. After 1m turn L into
no through road beside 3 Georgian
cottages. Garden $1/2$ m further on R.*
**Sun 15 May (2-5). Adm £4, chd
free. Home-made teas.**
A newly formed garden in a
particularly peaceful, rural setting,
which has been created over the last
11yrs. Features incl a walled garden,
courtyard garden, seasonal shrubs,
peonies, irises and rose garden.
Partial wheelchair access. Steep
slope to rose garden and some gravel
paths.
  ✿ ☕

GROUP OPENING

39 IFFLEY GARDENS

Iffley, Oxford OX4 4EF. *2m S of
Oxford. Within Oxford's ring road, off
A4158 Iffley road from Magdalen
Bridge to Littlemore r'about to Iffley
Village. Map provided at each garden.*
**Sun 5 June (2-6). Combined adm
£5, chd free. Home-made teas in
the village hall.**

   17 ABBERBURY ROAD
   Mrs Julie Steele

   NEW ▶ 25 ABBERBURY ROAD
   Rob & Bridget Farrands

   86 CHURCH WAY
   Helen Beinart & Alex Coren

   122 CHURCH WAY
   Sir John & Lady Elliott

   6 FITZHERBERT CLOSE
   Tom & Eunice Martin

   THE MALT HOUSE
   Helen Potts

   THE THATCHED COTTAGE
   Martin & Helen Foreman

Secluded old village with renowned
Norman church, featured on cover of
Pevsner's Oxon Guide. Visit 7
gardens ranging in variety and style
from the large Malt House garden
and a thatched C17 cottage garden
to a small professionally designed
Japanese style garden, with maples
and miniature pines. Varied planting
throughout the gardens including
herbaceous borders, shade loving
plants, roses, fine specimen trees and
plants in terracing. Features incl water
features, formal gardens, small lake
and Thames riverbank. Plant Sale at
The Malt House. Wheelchair access
to some gardens only.
  ✿ ✿ ☕

GROUP OPENING

40 KENCOT GARDENS

Kencot, Lechlade GL7 3QT. *5m NE
of Lechlade. E of A361 between
Burford & Lechlade. Village maps
available.* **Mon 28 Mar (2-6).
Combined adm £4, chd free.
Home-made teas in village hall.**

   THE ALLOTMENTS
   Amelia Carter Trust

   BELHAM HAYES
   Mr Joseph Jones

   HILLVIEW HOUSE
   John & Andrea Moss

IVY NOOK
Gill & Wally Cox

KENCOT HOUSE
Tim & Katie Gardner

THE MALTINGS
Mr Ray and Jay Mathews

WELL HOUSE
Gill & Ian Morrison

Opening for 11 yrs, The Allotments have a range of vegetables, flowers and fruit. Hillview House a 2 acre garden, with lime tree drive, shrubs, borders and spring flowers. Ongoing planting of flower borders and vegetables. Ivy Nook has spring flowers, shrubs, rockery, small pond, waterfall, magnolia and fruit trees. Kencot House has 2 acres with gingko tree, shrubs, and a haven for wildlife. Clockhouse, summerhouse and carved C13 archway. The Maltings, a small cottage garden with herb wheel, pots, and mature trees. Stone steps provide background for climbing plants. Pots of herbs and flowering plants. Belham Hayes, a restored village house garden mostly laid to lawn, together with flower beds filled with spring bulbs and some mature shrubs and fruit trees, very much work in progress. Well House, a 1/3 acre garden with mature trees, hedges, wildlife pond, waterfall and small bog area. Plentiful bulbs in springtime with island beds, mixed borders providing yr-round interest, rockeries and bulb containers giving early colour. Plant and craft sale in the car park. No wheelchair access to The Allotments.

---

41 **10 KENNETT ROAD**
Headington, Oxford OX3 7BJ.
Linda & David Clover, 01865
765881, lindaclover@yahoo.co.uk.
*2m E of Oxford in Central
Headington. S of London Rd
between New High St, with Shark to
the W and Windmill Rd to the E.
Parking in Old High Street (Waitrose)
or St Leonard's Rd (off Windmill Rd).*
**Visits by arrangement for groups
of 10 max. Adm £4, chd free. Light
refreshments on request.**
Small suburban garden planted for yr-round interest. Spring snowdrops and hellebores, summer cottage garden planting, autumn colours and winter evergreens packed into a simply planned space, on a challenging sandy sub-soil, where lawns provide a focus for the surrounding deep

borders. There is also a pond and fernery, and a greenhouse with succulents, cacti and tender perennials. View of 'Untitled 1986' Headington's landmark sculpture.

GROUP OPENING

42 **LANGFORD GARDENS**
Lechlade GL7 3LF. *6m S of Burford
A361 towards Lechlade. 1 1/2 m E of
Filkins. Large free car park in village.
Maps of gardens available.* **Sun 12
June (2-6). Combined adm £5, chd
free. Home-made teas at Pember
House & village hall.**

BAKERY COTTAGE
Mr & Mrs R Robinson

THE BARN
Mr & Mrs D E Range

BAY TREE COTTAGE
Mr & Mrs R Parsons

BRIDGEWATER HOUSE
Mr & Mrs T R Redston

5 CHURCH LANE
Derek & Pat Potter

NEW **1 COOKS FARM
COTTAGES**
Mr & Mrs M Clark

CORKSCREW COTTAGE
Fiona Gilbert

COTSWOLD BUNGALOW
John & Hilary Dudley

COTSWOLD COTTAGE
Mr & Mrs Tom Marshall

NEW **THE CROWN**
Mr & Mrs D Evans

NEW **THE FORGE**
Chris King & Jum
Beyazchuman

THE GRANGE
Mr & Mrs J Johnston

KEMPS YARD
Mr & Mrs R Kemp

LIME TREE COTTAGE
Diane & Michael Schultz

LOCKEY HOUSE
Ms Sophie Hanson

LOWER FARM HOUSE
Mr & Mrs Templeman

THE OLD BAKERY
Mr & Mrs G Edwards

THE OLD SCHOOL
David Freeman

THE OLD VICARAGE
Mr & Mrs C Smith

PEMBER HOUSE
Mr & Mrs J Potter

ROSEFERN COTTAGE
Mrs D Lowden

SPRINGFIELD
Mr & Mrs M Harris

STONECROFT
Christine Apperley

WELLBANK
Sir Brian & Lady Pomeroy

WELLBANK HOUSE
Mr & Mrs Robert Hill

Langford is a charming small Cotswold village with both the important Grade I listed St Matthew's Church and a splendid PH where lunch is available. 25 gardens will be open, with a delightful mix from large formal to small cottage gardens. Ancient Cotswold stone walls provide a backdrop for many old variety roses. Our plant stall has a large range of local plants and shrubs. Live music in Pember House garden during the afternoon, as well as village teas, a church flower festival and bell ringing demonstrations add to an enjoyable day for everyone. Some gardens have gravel paths so wheelchair access may vary.

Croft House,
Middleton Cheney Gardens

43 LIME CLOSE
35 Henleys Lane, Drayton,
Abingdon OX14 4HU.
M C de Laubarede,
mail@mclgardendesign.com. *2m S
of Abingdon. Henleys Lane is off main
road through Drayton.* **Sun 28 Feb,
Sun 15 May (2-5.30). Adm £5, chd
free. Cream teas. Visits also by
arrangement Feb to June for
groups of 10+.** *Donation to CLIC
Sargent Care for Children.*
3 acre mature plantsman's garden
with rare trees, shrubs, perennials
and bulbs. Mixed borders, raised
beds, pergola, unusual topiary and
shade borders. Herb garden
designed by Rosemary Verey. Listed
C16 house (not open). Cottage
garden designed by MCL Garden
Design, focusing on colour
combinations and an iris garden with
over 100 varieties of tall bearded
irises. Many winter bulbs, hellebores
and shrubs. Garden featured in
Wedding magazine (Aug-Sept 2015).

44 MAGDALEN COLLEGE
Oxford OX1 4AU. Magdalen
College, www.magd.ox.ac.uk.
Entrance in High St. **Sun 10 Apr
(1-6). Adm £5, chd £4. Light
refreshments in the Old Kitchen.**
60 acres incl deer park, college
lawns, numerous trees 150-200 yrs
old; notable herbaceous and shrub
plantings. Magdalen meadow where
purple and white snake's head
fritillaries can be found is surrounded
by Addison's Walk, a tree lined circuit
by the R Cherwell developed since
the late C18. Ancient herd of 60 deer.
Press bell at the lodge for porter to
provide wheelchair access.

45 MANOR HOUSE
Manor Farm Road, Dorchester-on-
Thames OX10 7HZ. Mr & Mrs S H
Broadbent, 01865 340101,
manor@dotoxon.uk. *8m SSE of
Oxford. Off A4074, signs from village
centre. Parking at Bridge Meadow
400 metres. Disabled parking at
house.* **Sun 21 Aug (2-5). Adm £4,
chd free. Tea in Dorchester Abbey
Guesthouse (90 metres). Visits
also by arrangement June to Aug
for groups of 10-40.**
2 acre garden in beautiful setting
around Georgian house (not open)
and Medieval abbey. Spacious lawn
leading to riverside copse of towering
poplars with fine views of Dorchester
Abbey. Terrace with rose and vine

covered pergola around lily pond.
Colourful herbaceous borders, small
orchard and vegetable garden. Gravel
paths.

46 NEW MAPLE TREES
3 Vicarage Lane, Shrivenham,
Swindon SN6 8DT. Hazel Gregory.
*5m NE of Swindon. 9m from M4 J14.
From M4 J14 take the A419 toward
Cirencester for 4¹/₂ m. Take A420 R
toward Oxford for 3m. Take R turn
signed Shrivenham. At the end of the
High St turn L & then L again.* **Sat 16
Apr, Sat 16 July (10.30-4). Adm £3,
chd free. Light refreshments. Also
open Allsorts.**
We have a moderately sized garden
on the edge of Shrivenham with
views of the Berkshire Downs. A
wildlife friendly garden, full of colour,
with plenty of interest throughout the
seasons. At the front there are flower
and shrub borders and at the back
there are vegetables, fruit, borders
and a pond with planting designed to
attract insect life. We grow many of
our own plants.

47 MEADOW COTTAGE
Christmas Common, Watlington
OX49 5HR. Mrs Zelda Kent-Lemon,
01491 613779,
zelda_kl@hotmail.com. *1m from
Watlington. Coming from Oxford M40
to J6. Turn R & go to Watlington. Turn
L up Hill Rd to top. Turn L, then
immed R, down gravel track.* **Mon 30
May (11-5). Adm £5, chd free.
Home-made teas. Visits also by
arrangement in May.**
1³/₄ acre garden adjoining ancient
bluebell woods created by the owner
from 1995 onwards, with many areas
to explore. A professionally designed
vegetable garden, large composting
areas, wild flower garden and pond,
old and new fruit trees, many shrubs,
much varied hedging and large areas
of lawn. Shrubs, indigenous trees,
copious hedges, C17 barn. Tennis
court and swimming pool. During the
month of May, bluebell woodland.
Partial wheelchair access as gravel
driveway and lawns.

**48 MERTON COLLEGE
OXFORD FELLOWS' GARDEN**
Merton Street, Oxford OX1 4JD.
Merton College, 01865 276310.
Merton St runs parallel to High St.
**Sun 24 July (2-5). Adm £4.50, chd
free.**

Ancient mulberry, said to have
associations with James I. Specimen
trees, long mixed border, recently
established herbaceous bed. View of
Christ Church meadow.

Planting designed to attract insect life . . .

GROUP OPENING

**49 MIDDLETON CHENEY
GARDENS**
Middleton Cheney, Banbury
OX17 2ST. *3m E of Banbury. From
M40 J11 follow A422 signed
Middleton Cheney. Map available at
all gardens.* **Sun 19 June (1-6).
Combined adm £5, chd free.
Home-made teas at Peartree
House.**

CHURCH COTTAGE
David & Sue Thompson

8 CHURCH LANE
Mr & Mrs Style

CROFT HOUSE
Mr & Mrs Richard Walmsley

19 GLOVERS LANE
Michael Donohoe & Jane Rixon

38 MIDWAY
Margaret & David Finch

PEARTREE HOUSE
Roger & Barbara Charlesworth

14 QUEEN STREET
Brian & Kathy Goodey

NEW SPRINGFIELD HOUSE
Lynn & Paul Taylor

1 THE MOORS DRIVE
Charles & Anne Woolland

Large village with C13 church with
renowned William Morris stained
glass. 9 open gardens, some small,
some relatively large. You will see 2
modern gardens, one restrained, yet
elegant and serene, and one with an
interesting contrast of formal features
and herbaceous planting. Many
incorporate cottage garden style
planting, but with very different

South Newington House

© Andrew Lawson

effects. You will see a densely planted front and back garden which creates a sense of a private haven, and another where the owners have made many small areas of interest that is still a harmonious whole. One garden has a pergola to hide away under, and another has a summerhouse with statuary and objects not evident at first sight. One of the larger gardens has fine examples of mature trees and shrubs, another a feel of mystery with hidden corners and an extensive water feature weaving its way throughout the garden. A new large garden is a work in progress to retrieve a long lost garden of Middleton.

50 NEW MIDSUMMER HOUSE
Woolstone, Faringdon SN7 7QL. Anthony & Penny Spink. *7m W & 7m S of Faringdon. Woolstone is a small village off B4507, below Uffington White Horse Hill.* **Sun 11 Sept (2-5.30). Adm £2, chd free. Also open Woolstone Mill House.**
On moving to Midsummer House a year ago, new owners created the garden using herbaceous plants brought with them from their previous home at Mill House. Herbaceous border and espaliered Malus Everest.

Opening with Mill House which is now owned by their son, renowned landscape architect Justin Spink.

51 MILL BARN
25 Mill Lane, Chalgrove OX44 7SL. Pat Hougham, 01865 890020, pat@gmec.co.uk. *12m E of Oxford. Chalgrove is 4m from Watlington off B480. Mill Barn is in Mill Lane on the W of Chalgrove, 300yds S of Lamb PH. Parking in lane or gravel entrance yard.* **Visits by arrangement May to Oct. Adm £4, chd free. Light refreshments.**
Mill Barn has an informal cottage garden with a variety of flowers, shrubs and fruit trees including medlar, mulberry and quince in sunny and shaded beds. Wheelchair friendly brick paths with rose arches and a pergola leading to a vegetable plot surrounded by a cordon of fruit trees all set in a mill stream landscape.

52 MONKS HEAD
Weston Road, Bletchingdon OX5 3DH. Sue Bedwell, 01869 350155, bedwell615@btinternet.com. *Approx 4m N of Kidlington. From A34 take B4027 to Bletchingdon, turn R at Xrds into Weston Rd.*

Sun 6 Mar (2-5). Adm £3, chd free. Sun 3 Apr (2-6). Combined adm with Hollyhocks £5, chd free. Home-made teas. Visits also by arrangement.
Plantaholics' garden for all year interest. Bulb frame and alpine area, greenhouse. Changes evolving all the time.

53 32 NEW YATT ROAD
Witney OX28 1NZ. Montserrat & Nigel Holmes. *1/2 m NE of Witney town centre. Turn off A4095 towards Wood Green. Follow New Yatt Rd in NE direction. Garden is close to District Council offices (Elmfield).* **Sat 18, Sun 19 June, Sat 23, Sun 24 July (2-6). Adm £3, chd free.**
An exuberant, plantswoman's suburban oasis, brimming with traditional and unusual plants in a small, but long, rear garden to an Edwardian house. Features a 70 metre mixed herbaceous border noted for the quality and condition of planting including over 60 old fashioned roses, plus a patio crammed with exotic and tender container plants. Short but flat shingle driveway to access garden.

Share your day out on 🔵 and 🔵

GROUP OPENING

54 NORTH MORETON GARDENS

Nr Didcot OX11 9AT. *3m SE of Didcot. Off A4130 (Didcot-Wallingford Rd). Follow signs for car park.* **Sun 10 July (2-5). Combined adm £5, chd free. Home-made teas in C17 barn at North Moreton House.** *Donation to All Saints Church.*

THE FILBERTS
Mr & Mrs Prescott

LITTLE ORCHARD
Patrick & Mary Greene

NEW MOUNT PLEASANT
Roger & Liz Elliot

NEW QUEENS YARD
Steve & Sarah Rudge

Charming small village with many listed buildings and an interesting Grade I Medieval church with C13 stained glass window. Four gardens opening for the NGS this yr. Filberts a 1 acre garden demonstrating many different styles incl formal colour-themed garden with lily and fish ponds, island beds for old roses, architectural foliage, and grasses. Large informal pond, colourful mixed borders, secluded Japanese area and over 100 varieties of clematis. Formal parterre with roses and herbs, vegetable garden, fruit cage and orchard. Little Orchard has a long interesting garden with mixed orchard. The rear garden planted in three sections with a mixture of shrubs, roses and perennials with feature fish pond and waterfall. Mount Pleasant has a garden on two levels with a rockery in between. The lower level incl gravel garden and parterre and the higher level is grassed, interspersed with flower beds, fruit area and trees. Queens Yard also on two levels with the lower garden laid out for perennials, grasses and trees and the upper garden laid similarly, but incl an orchard and meadow. Some gardens have gravel, slopes and narrow paths.

55 ◆ NUFFIELD PLACE

Huntercombe, Henley-on-Thames RG9 5RX. National Trust, 01491 641224, louise.walker@nationaltrust.org.uk, www.nationaltrust.org.uk/nuffield-place. *On the A4130 between Henley & Wallingford. There is a brown NT road sign opp Bradley Rd, off which Nuffield Place is situated.* **For NGS: Thur 16 June (11-5). Adm £4, chd £3. For other opening times and information, please phone, email or visit garden website.**

9¼ acres laid out during the Arts and Crafts period and just after WWI. This is a garden restoration in action where you can see mature specimen trees, yew hedges, a pergola, herbaceous borders, a rock garden and hidden pathways in various states of repair. A croquet lawn for a challenging game and a genuine wildlife rich meadow to meander through. Pathways around garden are gravel or Yorkstone. There are some small steps in the garden, but can be avoided by going over grass.

56 NEW THE OLD BAKEHOUSE

South Newington, Banbury OX15 4JF. Peter & Jane Perry. *6m NE of Chipping Norton, 5m SW of Banbury situated just off A361. Main parking in South Newington House field (signed). Disabled parking opp church.* **Wed 17 Aug (1-5). Adm £3, chd free.**

½ acre garden, described as a 'hidden gem', in the grounds of a Horton Ironstone house dating back to 1600 (not open). Giant pines and mature trees provide a back drop to the garden which is bounded on three sides by stone walls. Late summer colour and interest is provided by plantings of fuchsias, hydrangeas, persicarias, phlox and sedums. Herbaceous borders, vegetable garden and ornamental pond.

GROUP OPENING

57 OLD BOARS HILL GARDENS

Jarn Way, Boars Hill, Oxford OX1 5JF. Charles & Lyn Sanders. *3m S of Oxford. From S ring road towards A34 at r'about follow signs to Wootton & Boars Hill. Up Hinksey Hill take R fork. 1m R into Berkley Rd to Old Boars Hill.* **Sun 1 May (2-5.30). Combined adm £4, chd free. Sun 10 July (2-6). Combined adm £5, chd free. Home-made teas at Tall Trees & Uplands.**

BLACKTHORN
Louise Edwards.
Open on Sun 10 July

HEDDERLY HOUSE
Mrs Julia Bennett.
Open on Sun 1 May

TALL TREES
Suzanne & David Clark.
Open on all dates
(See separate entry)

UPLANDS
Charles & Lyn Sanders.
Open on all dates
Visits also by arrangement Mar to Oct.
sandersc4@hotmail.com
01865 739486

YEW COTTAGE
John Hewitt.
Open on Sun 10 July

Five lightful gardens in a semi rural conservation area with views over Oxford. Each garden has a different setting. Hedderly House a terraced hillside garden with wooded walks and ponds with extensive views over the Vale of the White Horse. Yew Cottage, a thatched cottage nestled into its new redesigned plot as well as the treat of seeing the owner's veteran cars. Blackthorn an 8 acre parkland garden with woodland walks, floral herbaceous borders and ponds. Uplands a southerly facing garden full of colour and an extensive range of plants for all seasons and Tall Trees a cottage garden full of scents, roses and other floral treats.

NGS supports nursing and caring charities . . .

58 OLD RECTORY

Salford, nr Chipping Norton OX7 5YL. Mr & Mrs N M Chambers, 01608 643969. *Small village on A44, approx 3m W of Chipping Norton.* **Tue 16 Feb (10-1); Sun 29 May (2-6). Adm £4, chd free. Teas (Feb) & light refreshments in village hall (May). Visits also by arrangement Feb to Oct for groups of 20 max.**

1½ acres mainly enclosed by walls. Early spring garden with early flowering shrubs and many snowdrops. Some unusual plants in mixed borders, many old roses, small orchard and vegetable garden for yr-round interest. Bantams. Partial wheelchair access. No dogs.

59 OLD SWAN & MINSTER MILL

Old Minster, Minster Lovell, Witney OX29 0RN. Patrick Jones, 01993 774441, enquiries@oldswanandminstermill.com, www.oldswanandminstermill.com. *5 min drive from Witney. Approx 14m after Oxford take the sliproad signed Carterton, Minster Lovell. Turn R at the junction & travel through Minster Lovell.* **Fri 27 May, Fri 24 June (2-5). Adm £5, chd free. Light refreshments.**
The hotel is set in 65 acres of picturesque gardens, located beside the majestic R Windrush. The grounds comprise of formal gardens, a kitchen garden that supplies the inn, and 40 acres of wild flower meadows which were created in 2011. The apiary sits amongst the wild flowers supplying the hotels honey. There are a few steps along garden paths and gravelled areas where help may be required.

60 THE OLD VICARAGE

Aston Rowant, Watlington OX49 5ST. Julian & Rona Knight, 01844 351315, jknight652@aol.com. *Between Chinnor & Watlington, off B4009. From M40 J6, take B4009 towards Chinnor & Princes Risborough. After 1m, turn L signed Aston Rowant Village only.* **Visits by arrangement for groups of 10-30. Adm £4, chd free. Tea & home-made cake, or wine & snacks.**
Romantic, 1¾ acre vicarage garden lovingly rejuvenated and enjoyed by the present family. Centered around a croquet lawn surrounded by beds brimming with shrubs and herbaceous plants, hot bed and roses. Lushly planted pond leading through a pergola overflowing with roses and clematis to a tranquil green garden. Small vegetable and cutting garden.

61 THE OLD VICARAGE, BLEDINGTON

Main Road, Bledington, Chipping Norton OX7 6UX. Sue & Tony Windsor, 01608 658525, tony.g.windsor@gmail.com. *6m SW of Chipping Norton. 4m SE of Stow-on-the-Wold. On the main street B4450 through Bledington. Not next to church.* **Sun 19 June (2-6). Adm £4, chd free. Home-made teas.**

Visits also by arrangement May to July. Wine & canapés for evening visits on request.
1½ acre garden around a late Georgian vicarage (1843) not open. Borders and beds filled with hardy perennials, shrubs and trees. Informal rose garden with over 300 David Austin roses. Small pond and vegetable patch. Paddock with trees, shrubs and herbaceous border. Planted for yr-round interest. Gravel driveway and gentle sloped garden can be hard work.

62 NEW OLD WHITE BARN

Old Whitehill, Tackley, Kidlington OX5 3AB. Gill Withers. *10m N of Oxford. 3m from Woodstock. Hamlet ¾ m S of Tackley. Signed from A4260 & A4095.* **Sun 29 May (2-5.30). Adm £4, chd free. Home-made teas.**
1 acre country garden on a sloping site around a stone barn conversion. Created by the owners from a farmyard and surrounding field over last 15 yrs. Sunny walled courtyard. Colour themed borders. Field of formal and informal areas, mature hedging, orchard, meadow grass and enclosed vegetable garden.

Terrace with rose and vine covered pergola around lily pond . . .

63 50 PLANTATION ROAD

Oxford OX2 6JE. Philippa Scoones. *Central Oxford. N on Woodstock Rd take 2nd L. Coming into Oxford on Woodstock Rd turn R after Leckford Rd. No disabled parking nr house.* **Sat 7, Sun 8, Sat 14, Sun 15 May (2-6). Adm £3.50, chd free.**
Surprisingly spacious small city garden. North facing front garden, side alley filled with shade loving climbers, mature and unusual plants incl Mount Etna Broom, conservatory, terraced area and secluded water garden with rill, woodland plants and alpines.

64 THE PRIORY GARDEN

Charlbury OX7 3PX. Dr D El Kabir & Colleagues. *6m SE of Chipping Norton. Large Cotswold village on B4022 Witney-Enstone Rd, near St Mary's Church.* **Sun 22 May (2-5). Adm £3, chd free.**
1½ acre of formal terraced topiary gardens with Italianate features. Foliage colour schemes, shrubs, parterres with fragrant plants, old roses, water features, sculpture and inscriptions aim to produce a poetic, wistful atmosphere. Formal vegetable and herb garden. Arboretum of over 3 acres borders the R Evenlode and incl wildlife garden and pond. Partial wheelchair access.

65 RADCOT HOUSE

Radcot OX18 2SX. Robin & Jeanne Stainer, www.radcothouse.com. *1¼ m S of Clanfield. On A4095 between Witney & Faringdon, 300yds N of Radcot bridge.* **Sun 21 Aug, Sun 2 Oct (2-6). Adm £5, chd free. Home-made teas.**
Approx 3 acres of dramatic yet harmonious planting in light and shade, formal pond, fruit and vegetable cages. Convenient seating at key points enables relaxed observation and reflection. Extensive use of grasses and unusual perennials and interesting sculptural surprises. Spectacular autumn display. 'An exuberant new garden...' Financial Times. 'The best gardens must offer drama, surprise and contrast and you can find all three here...', 'Radcot House is a gem...' Oxford Times.

66 RIDGEWAY

Lincombe Lane, Boars Hill, Oxford OX1 5DZ. John & Viccy Fleming, garden@octon.eu. *Between Oxford & Abingdon. Off Foxcombe Rd & Fox Lane between A34 Hinksey Hill r'about & B4017 Wootton to Abingdon road. Nearly opp Fox PH.* **Sun 11 Sept (2-5.30). Combined adm with Whitsun Meadows £6, chd free. Visits also by arrangement Apr to Oct for groups of 10-25.**
Exceptional ¾ acre garden on sandy soil with some rare shrubs and plants. Developed over the last 10 yrs to provide yr-round interest. The intricate design incl 2 alpine beds, a fruit garden, a vegetable garden and multiple borders with varied planting.

© Ellen Rooney

Asthall Manor

67 NEW RIVERMEAD
Manor Road, Goring, Reading
RG8 9ED. Rob Jones,
07973 261852,
rob@gardendesignco.co.uk,
www.gardendesignco.co.uk. *5 mins
walk from Goring & Streatley train
station & 30 mins drive from M4 J12
& J13. NGS signs will be located at
top of Streatley High St, Goring, on
Thames High St & by station.* **Sat 10
Sept (2-5). Adm £4, chd £2. Home-
made teas. Visits also by
arrangement Mar to Nov.**
The 220ft long garden features a
north facing parterre, a formal water
feature and a terrace which leads to
an oval lawn surrounded by a striking
mixed herbaceous border, with
clipped yew dividing the garden from
the brick paved cut flower and
vegetable garden. The green oak
raised beds, a bespoke greenhouse,
a wild flower meadow and an orchard
all lead the eye to Streatley Hill
beyond. Petting Zoo, featuring a wide
range of furry friends in the garden.
There are 1-2 steps to access WC.

♿ 🐕 ❀ ☕

GROUP OPENING

68 SIBFORD GOWER
GARDENS
Sibford Gower OX15 5RX. *7m W of
Banbury. Nr the Warwickshire border,
S of B4035, in centre of village nr
Wykham Arms PH.* **Sun 26 June
(2-6). Combined adm £5, chd free.**

CARTER'S YARD
Sue & Malcolm Bannister
Visits also by arrangement May
to Oct for groups of 8+, guided
by the owner.
sebannister@gmail.com
01295 780365

GOWERS CLOSE 🖛
Judith Hitching & John Marshall
Visits also by arrangement May
to Oct for groups of 8+,
occasionally with Carters Yard.
j.hitching@virgin.net
01295 780348

Charming small village off the beaten
track with thatched stone cottages.
Two different and interesting cottage
gardens which complement the
ancient houses they surround.
Masses of roses, wisteria and
clematis clamber over walls and
pergolas. Box parterres, clipped yew
hedges, herb gardens, bosky borders
in pinks and purples, plus productive
kitchen gardens. Some new and
innovative planting with unusual
plants.

❀

---

69 SOMERVILLE COLLEGE
GARDENS
Woodstock Road, Oxford
OX2 6HD. Somerville College.
*1/2 m E of Carfax Tower. Enter from
Woodstock Rd, S of Radcliffe
Infirmary.* **Sun 26 June (1-6). Adm
£2.50, chd free. Tea.** *Donation to
Friends of Oxford Botanic Garden.*
Approx 2 acres, robust college
garden planted for yr-round interest.
Formal bedding, colour themed and
extensive vibrant old fashioned mixed
herbaceous borders.

♿ 🐕 ☕

70 SOUTH NEWINGTON
HOUSE
South Newington OX15 4JW. Mr &
Mrs David Swan, 01295 721866,
claire_ainley@hotmail.com. *6m SW
of Banbury. South Newington is
between Banbury & Chipping Norton.
Take Barford Rd off A361, 1st L after
100yds in between oak bollards. For
SatNav use OX15 4JL.* **Visits by
arrangement Feb to July for
groups. Adm £5, chd free. Light
refreshments.**
Meandering tree lined drive leads to
2 acre garden. Herbaceous borders
designed for yr-round colour. Organic
garden with established beds and
rotation planting scheme. Orchard full
of fruit trees with pond encouraging
wildlife. Walled parterre planted for
seasonal colour. A family garden with
a small menagerie, all beautifully
designed to blend seamlessly into the
environment; a haven for all. Some
gravel paths, otherwise full access for
wheelchair users.

♿ 🚐 ☕

71 SPARSHOLT MANOR
Wantage OX12 9PT. Sir Adrian &
Lady Judith Swire. *3½ m W of
Wantage. Off B4507 Ashbury Rd.*
**Mon 2 May (2-6). Adm £3, chd
free.**
Lakes and wildfowl; ancient
boxwood, wilderness with walkways
and summer borders. Wheelchair
access to most of the garden.

♿ 🐕 ☕

72 **64 SPRING ROAD**
Abingdon OX14 1AN. Mrs Janet
Boulton, 01235 524514,
j.boulton89@btinternet.com,
www.janetboulton.co.uk.
*S Abingdon from A34 take L turn
after police station into Spring Rd.
Minute's drive to number 64 on L.*
Visits by arrangement June to
Sept for limited numbers only.
Adm £5, chd free.
An artist's garden (4¹/₂ x 30¹/₂ metres)
behind a Victorian terrace house,
narrow with steps. Predominantly
green it contains numerous
sculptures with inscriptions relating to
art, history and the human spirit.

GROUP OPENING

73 **STEEPLE ASTON
GARDENS**
Steeple Aston OX25 4SP. *14m N of
Oxford, 9m S of Banbury. ¹/₂ m E of
A4260.* Sun 5 June (1-6).
Combined adm £6, chd free.
Home-made teas in village hall.

ACACIA COTTAGE
Jane & David Stewart

COMBE PYNE
Chris & Sally Cooper

GRANGE COTTAGE
Caroline & Christopher
Compston

KRALINGEN
Mr & Mrs Roderick Nicholson

THE LONGBYRE
Mr Vaughan Billings

PAYNE'S HILL HOUSE
Tim & Caroline Edwards

PRIMROSE GARDENS
Richard & Daphne Preston
Visits also by arrangement Apr
to Aug with refreshments on
request.
richard.preston5@btopenworld.
com
01869 340512

TOUCHWOOD
Gary Norris

Steeple Aston, often considered the
most easterly of the Cotswold
villages, is a beautiful stone built
village with gardens that provide a
huge range of interest. A stream
meanders down the hill as the
landscape changes from sand to clay.
The 8 open gardens incl; small
floriferous cottage gardens, large
landscaped gardens, natural
woodland areas, ponds and bog
gardens, themed borders. No
wheelchair access at Primrose
Gardens or Touchwood.

74 **TALL TREES**
Jarn Way, Boars Hill, Oxford
OX1 5JF. Suzanne & David Clark.
*At junction up Hinksey Hill turn R.
After 1m turn R into Berkley Rd &
next L into Jarn Way.* Sun 26 June
(2-5.30). Combined adm with
Tanglewood £5, chd free. Home-
made teas. Opening with Old
Boars Hill Gardens on Sun 1 May,
Sun 10 July.
A plantswoman's mature ¹/₂ acre
cottage garden adjoining Sir Arthur
Evans wild garden. Camellias,
clematis, rhododendrons, climbing
and shrub roses, flowering cherry and
crab apple trees, shrubs, spring bulbs
and perennials. All year interest with
colour coordination. Delicious home-
made teas and plant stall of donated
plants. Level access, but small
motorised wheelchairs may have
some difficulty.

Award-winning lavender garden . . .

75 **TANGLEWOOD**
Jarn Way, Boars Hill, Oxford
OX1 5JF. Wendy Becker. *Hinksey
r'about, uphill. Turn R to Wootton &
Boars Hill, after 1m turn R into
Berkley Rd & next L into Jarn Way.
Property on L framed by a drystone
wall.* Sun 26 June (2-5.30).
Combined adm with Tall Trees £5,
chd free. Home-made teas at Tall
Trees.
Splendid 2 acre garden with a wide
variety of flowering plants in borders
and beds, especially roses. Features
incl a croquet lawn, an avenue of
Robinia, a sculptural area made from
fallen trees and drystone walling, a
small stumpery area, a multilevel
pond feature, a large vegetable
garden and greenhouse. Wide
entrances available but mainly gravel
drives, pathways and steps which
limits wheelchair access.

GROUP OPENING

76 **THAME GARDENS**
Thame OX9 3TE. *From M40 J7/8
follow signs to Thame midway
between Oxford & Aylesbury on
A418.* Sun 3 July (2-5.30).
Combined adm £5, chd free.
Home-made teas.

NEW **BURGAGE HOUSE,
BULL LANE**
Mal & Michael Dolan

10 HAMILTON ROAD
Lesley Winward & Wendy Reid

33 LUDSDEN GROVE
Sandra & Graham Matthews

**4 AND 6 PARLIAMENT
ROAD**
Shirley Denny & Peter
Lawrence

NEW **STRIBLEHILLS,
15 PRIEST END**
Rachel & Shaun Moore

Five gardens set in the historic market
town of Thame. A C17 house with a
walled garden with views over St
Mary's church; a small cottage style
garden filled with pots, pools and
perennials; a hidden 35 x 8 metre
burgage plot in historic Bull Lane; a
colourful corner plot of beds,
borders and containers and
neighbours combining two gardens
with tropical plants, water features
and sculptures.

77 **TRINITY COLLEGE**
Broad Street, Oxford OX1 3BH.
Paul Lawrence, Head Gardener,
www.trinity.ox.ac.uk. *Central
Oxford. Entrance in Broad St.*
Sun 20 Mar, Sun 31 July (1-5).
Adm £2.50, chd free. Home-made
teas in dining hall.
Historic main College Gardens with
specimen trees incl aged forked
catalpa, spring bulbs, fine long
herbaceous border and handsome
garden quad originally designed by
Wren. President's Garden surrounded
by high old stone walls, mixed
borders of herbaceous, shrubs and
statuary. Fellows' Garden: small
walled terrace, herbaceous borders;
water feature formed by Jacobean
stone heraldic beasts. Award-winning
lavender garden and walk-through
rose arbour.

78 ◆ **UNIVERSITY OF OXFORD BOTANIC GARDEN**
Rose Lane, Oxford OX1 4AZ. University of Oxford, 01865 286690, www.botanic-garden.ox.ac.uk. *1m E of Oxford city centre. Bottom of High St in central Oxford, on banks of the R Cherwell by Magdalen Bridge & opp Magdalen College Tower.* **For opening times and information, please phone or visit garden website.**
The Botanic Garden contains plants that originate from all over the world. It is one of the most biodiverse collections of plants per acre globally. These plants are grown in 7 glasshouses, water and rock gardens, large herbaceous border, walled garden and every available space. In total there are around 5,000 different plants to see. Features incl glasshouses, systematic beds, National Collection of hardy Euphorbia species, herbaceous border, the Merton borders, biodiversity hotspot collections, fruit and vegetable collection. Gravel paths.

NGS & Perennial; giving support where it is needed

79 **UPPER CHALFORD FARM**
between Sydenham & Postcombe, Chinnor OX39 4NH. Mr & Mrs Paul Rooksby, 01844 351320, paulrooksby@talktalk.net. *4½ m SE of Thame. M40 exit J6. A40 to Postcombe turn R to Chalford (L if on A40 from Oxford). After 1m L at 1st telegraph pole (between Sydenham & Postcombe).* **Evening opening Wed 25 May, Thur 23 June, Thur 7 July (4-7.30). Adm £4, chd free. Wine or Pimms. Visits also by arrangement Feb to Sept for groups of up to 45. Refreshments on request.**
Jacobean farmhouse garden surrounded by fields, old roses, shrubs and perennials. Unusual trees, an ancient black pine, and Caucasian

wingnut tree. Hidden gardens with different plantings and peaceful places to sit. Spring fed ponds and stream with damp planted banks leading to reclaimed woodland with treehouse, bog garden and wild flower meadow. Features incl topiary, wildlife ponds, conservatory sundials and donkeys. Short gravel drive from car park. A closer drop-off point is possible.
  ♿ ❀ 🚐 ☕

80 **UPPER GREEN**
Brill Road, Horton cum Studley, Oxford OX33 1BU. Susan & Peter Burge, 01865 351310, sue.burge@ndm.ox.ac.uk. *6½ m NE of Oxford. Enter village, turn R up Horton Hill. At T-junction turn L into Brill Rd. Upper Green 250yds on R, 2 gates before pillar box. Roadside parking.* **Sun 17 Apr (2-5). Combined adm with Hilltop Cottage £4, chd free. Home-made teas at Studley Barn. Visits also by arrangement Jan to Oct for groups of up to 20.**
Mature ½ acre garden, a plantsman's paradise. Includes gravel area, mixed borders, potager, bog area and pond. Snowdrops start the year, and then spring colour comes, with marsh marigolds, hellebores, euphorbias, fritillaries and other bulbs. Perennials, ferns, grasses, and shrubs provide yr-round interest. Old apple trees support climbing roses. Plant lists for each bed. Metal sculptures by Sophie Thompson. Gravel drive limits wheelchair access.
☕

81 **WADHAM COLLEGE**
Parks Road, Oxford OX1 3PN. The Warden & Fellows. *Central Oxford. Wadham College gardens are accessed through the main entrance of the College on Parks Rd.* **Sun 10 Apr (2-5); Sun 10 July (2-5.30). Adm £2, chd free.**
5 acres, best known for trees, spring bulbs and mixed borders. In Fellows' main garden, fine ginkgo and *Magnolia acuminata*; bamboo plantation; in Back Quadrangle very large *Tilia tomentosa* 'Petiolaris'; in Mallam Court white scented garden est 1994; in Warden's garden an ancient tulip tree; in Fellows' private garden, Civil War embankment with period fruit tree cultivars, recently established shrubbery with unusual trees and ground cover amongst older plantings.

WARMINGTON VILLAGE GARDENS
See Warwickshire

82 ◆ **WATERPERRY GARDENS**
Waterperry, Wheatley OX33 1JZ. School of Economic Science, 01844 339226, office@waterperrygardens.co.uk, www.waterperrygardens.co.uk. *8m E of Oxford. For SatNavs please use OX33 1LA.* **For NGS: Sun 17 Apr, Sun 18 Sept (10-5.30). Adm £7.20, chd free. Home-made teas in the teashop (10-5). For other opening times and information, please phone, email or visit garden website.**
Waterperry Gardens are an inspiration. 8 acres of landscaped gardens incl rose and formal knot garden, water lily canal, riverside walk and one of the country's finest purely herbaceous borders. There is also a plant centre, garden shop, teashop, art gallery, museum and Saxon church. National Collection of Kabschia and Silver Saxifrages. Fritillaries looking fantastic for April opening. Michaelmas weekend coincides with Sept opening. Riverside Walk may be inaccessible to wheelchair users if very wet.
  ♿ ❀ 🚐 **NPC** ☕

83 **WAYSIDE**
82 Banbury Road, Kidlington OX5 2BX. Margaret & Alistair Urquhart, 01865 460180, alistairurquhart@ntlworld.com. *5m N of Oxford. On R of A4260 travelling N through Kidlington.* **Sun 5 June (2-6). Adm £3, chd free. Tea. Visits also by arrangement May & June.**
¼ acre garden shaded by mature trees. Mixed border with some rare and unusual plants and shrubs. A climber clothed pergola leads past a dry gravel garden to the woodland garden with an extensive collection of hardy ferns. Conservatory and large fern house with a collection of unusual species of tree ferns and tender exotics. Important garden fern collection. Featured in the Oxford Times. Partial wheelchair access.
  ♿ ❀ ☕

84 **WESTWELL MANOR**
Westwell, Nr Burford OX18 4JT. Mr Thomas Gibson. *2m SW of Burford. From A40 Burford-Cheltenham, turn L 1½ m after Burford r'about signed Westwell. After 1½ m at T-junction, turn R & Manor is 2nd house on L.* **Wed 25 May (2.30-6). Adm £5, chd**

free. *Donation to St Marys Church, Westwell.*

6 acres surrounding old Cotswold manor house (not open), with knot garden, potager, shrub roses, herbaceous borders, topiary, earth works, moonlight garden, auricula ladder, rills and water garden.

GROUP OPENING

85 WHEATLEY GARDENS
High Street, Wheatley OX33 1XX, 01865 875022, echess@hotmail.co.uk. *5m E of Oxford. Leave A40 at Wheatley, turn into High St. Gardens at W end of High St, S side.* **Sun 19 June (2-6).** Combined adm £4, chd free. Cream teas at The Manor House. Visits also by arrangement Apr to July.

BREACH HOUSE GARDEN
Liz Parry

THE MANOR HOUSE
Mrs Edward Hess

THE STUDIO
S & A Buckingham

Three adjoining gardens in the historic coaching village of Wheatley. Breach House Garden has an established main area with extensive shrubs and perennials, also a more contemporary reflective space with a wild pond. The Manor House is a 1½ acre garden surrounding an Elizabethan manor house (not open). Formal box walk, herb garden, cottage garden with rose arches and a shrubbery with old roses. The Studio is a cottage style walled garden developed from what was once a farmyard. Herbaceous borders, climbing roses and clematis, shrubs, vegetable plot and fruit trees. In all a lovely little collection of gardens set in the busy village of Wheatley. Various musical events. The Manor House was featured in the Country Life (June 2015). Wheelchair accessible with assistance, although there are gravel paths, 2 shallow steps and grass.

86 WHITEHILL FARM
Widford, Burford OX18 4DT. Mr & Mrs Paul Youngson, 01993 822894, anneyoungson@btinternet.com. *1m E of Burford. From A40 take road signed Widford. Turn R at the bottom of the hill.* **Sun 5 June (2-6).** Adm

£3.50, chd free. Home-made teas. Visits also by arrangement May to Sept for groups of 10+ only.
2 acres of hillside gardens and woodland with spectacular views overlooking Burford and Windrush valley. Informal plantsman's garden being continuously developed in various areas. Herbaceous and shrub borders, ponds and bog area, old fashioned roses, ground cover, ornamental grasses, bamboos and hardy geraniums. Large cascade water feature, pretty tea patio and wonderful Cotswold views.

Spectacular views overlooking Burford and Windrush valley . . .

87 WHITSUN MEADOWS
Berkeley Road, Oxford OX1 5ET. Jane & Nigel Jones. *3m SW of Oxford. From S ring road towards A34 at r'about follow signs to Wootton & Boars Hill. Up Hinksey Hill take R fork. 1m R into Berkley Rd to Old Boars Hill.* **Sun 26 June (2-5.30). Adm £4, chd free, also open Tall Trees. Sun 11 Sept (2-5.30). Combined adm with Ridgeway £6, chd free. Home-made teas at Tall Trees on Sun 26 June.**
The garden at Whitsun Meadows has a magical backdrop with a mixture of mature Scots pine, English oak, Acer and Cherry. Against this the owners have developed an interesting mixture of herbaceous borders, hosta beds, gravel gardens and a wild flower meadow defined by a curving cleft chestnut post and rail fencing. All on a pleasingly level site of 2 acres. The site is level and pathways have been designed to be wheelchair friendly.

88 WOOLSTONE MILL HOUSE
Woolstone, Faringdon SN7 7QL. Mr & Mrs Justin Spink. *7m W of Wantage. 7m S of Faringdon. Woolstone is a small village off B4507, below Uffington White Horse Hill.* **Sun 11 Sept (2-5.30). Adm £5, chd free. Home-made teas. Also open Midsummer House.**
Redesigned by new owner, garden designer Justin Spink in 2015, this 1½ acre garden has large mixed perennial beds, and small gravel,

cutting, kitchen and bog gardens. Topiary, medlars and old fashioned roses. Treehouse with spectacular views to Uffington White Horse and White Horse Hill. C18 millhouse and barn (not open). Partial wheelchair access.

GROUP OPENING

89 WOOTTON GARDENS
Wootton OX13 6DP. *Wootton is 3m SW of Oxford. From the Oxford ring road S, take the turning signed Wootton. Parking for 142 Cumnor Rd at Bystander PH only, then walk 10 mins following the NGS signs.* **Wed 15 June (1.30-6). Combined adm £5, chd free. Tea.**

NEW▶ **13 AMEY CRESCENT**
Mr & Mrs Gleed

60 BESSELSLEIGH ROAD
Mrs Freda East

142 CUMNOR ROAD
Mr & Mrs Ersin & Kate Aydin

8 MANOR ROAD
Mr & Mrs Dave & Gill Richards

22 SANDLEIGH ROAD
Mr & Mrs Peter & Jennie Debenham

35 SANDLEIGH ROAD
Mrs Hilal Baylav Inkersole

6 inspirational small gardens, all with very different ways of providing a personal joy. 13 Amey Cresent has a gravel garden with grasses and prairie plants. Small wildlife pond, alpine house and troughs. 60 Besselsleigh Road has 'The Deadwood Stage' with toadstools and a secret garden with many creatures to find. 142 Cumnor Road a sustainable wildlife garden with raised beds for vegetables, fences covered in espaliered fruit and a small wildlife pond. 8 Manor Road is an impeccable garden with brilliantly colourful planting as well as an area of shade loving plants. 22 Sandleigh Road is a wildlife friendly garden packed with cottage garden favourites beside brick paths. A kitchen garden is complete with chickens and a beach hut! 35 Sandleigh Road is a mature garden, laid to lawn on two levels. Grown mostly from cuttings the garden is brimming with vibrant flowers, pond side planting and mature shrubs. Partial wheelchair access.

SHROPSHIRE

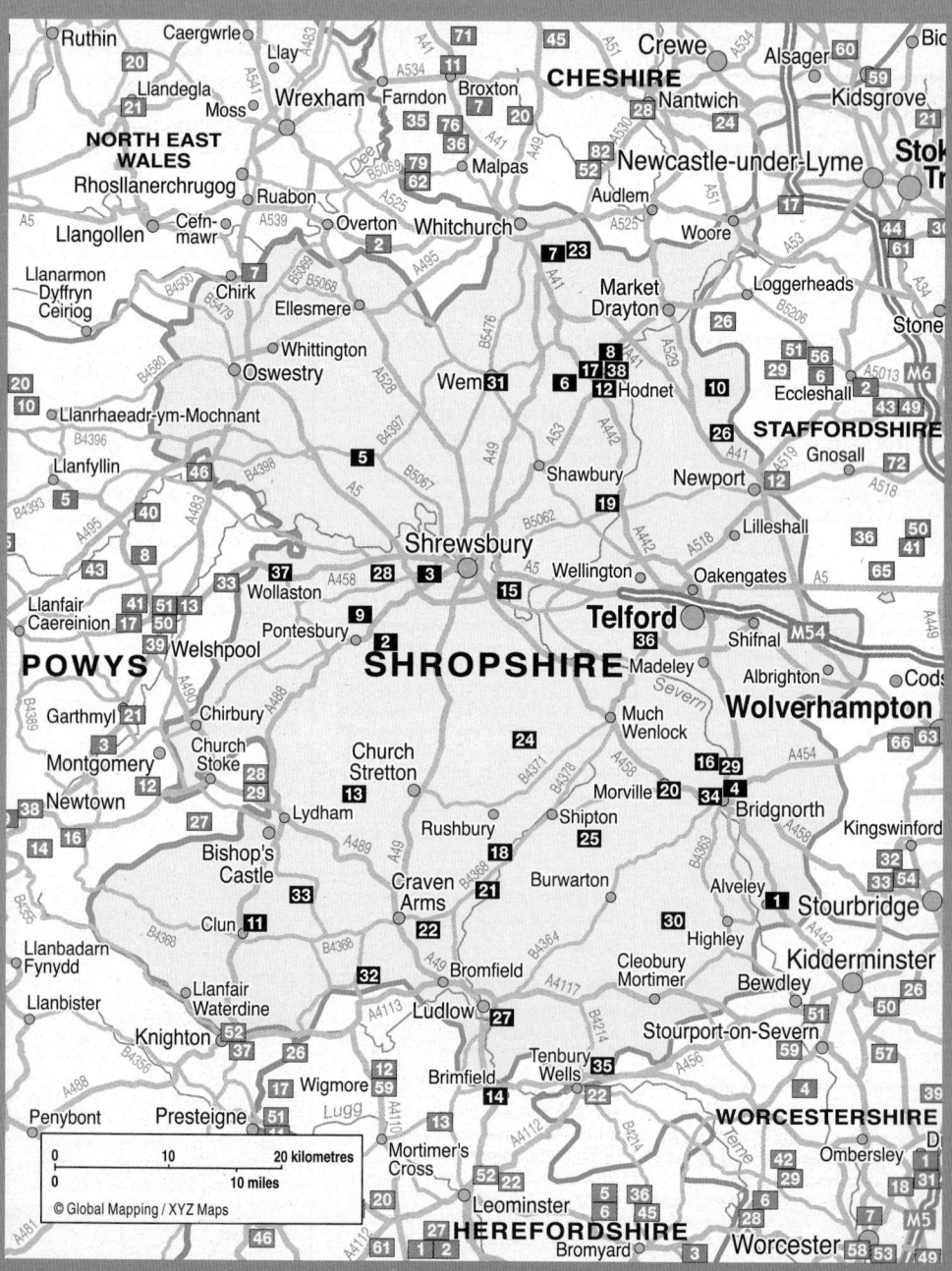

Shropshire

One of England's best kept secrets and one of the least populated areas in the country, Shropshire has a lot to offer visitors.

Our county has stunning gardens, majestic estates, interesting towns, history both modern and new (Shropshire was home to the ancient tribes of Mercia and also the birthplace of modern industry at Ironbridge), wonderful natural beauties such as the 'Blue Remembered Hills' that the poet A. E. Housman epitomised, and Shropshire is the self-proclaimed 'foodie' capital of Britain.

Above all, Shropshire's gardens are a must for the visitor. Generous garden owners and volunteers across the county have many open gardens, ranging from large estates to small, beautifully designed town gardens.

We are sure that 2016 will be another outstanding year for the NGS, so come to lovely Shropshire and enjoy our beautiful gardens, and raise money for the very important charities that we support.

Below: 8 Westgate Villas

Shropshire Volunteers

County Organiser
Chris Neil
01743 821651
bill@billfneil.fsnet.co.uk

County Treasurer
Suzanne Stevens
01588 660314
harrystevens@btconnect.com

Publicity
Allison Walter
01588 620055
allison.walter2@btinternet.com

Booklet Co-ordinator
Fiona Chancellor
01952 507675
fionachancellor@btinternet.com

Assistant County Organisers
Bill Neil
01743 821651
bill@billfneil.fsnet.co.uk

Penny Tryhorn
01746 783931
pennypottingshed@hotmail.co.uk

Opening Dates

All entries subject to change.
For latest information check www.ngs.org.uk
Extended openings are shown at the begining of the month

February

Snowdrop Festival

Sunday 21
18 Millichope Park

April

Sunday 10
9 Edge Villa

Friday 22
34 8 Westgate Villas (Evening)

Sunday 24
34 8 Westgate Villas

Tuesday 26
5 Brownhill House

May

Sunday 1
18 Millichope Park

Sunday 8
16 Lyndale House

Thursday 12
2 Avocet

Sunday 15
11 NEW Guilden Down Cottage

Friday 20
38 Wollerton Old Hall

Sunday 22
1 Ancoireán
6 The Citadel
21 Mynd Hardy Plants
29 Stanley Hall

Wednesday 25
9 Edge Villa
10 Goldstone Hall Gardens

Sunday 29
15 Longner Hall
32 Upper Shelderton House
33 Walcot Hall

Monday 30
32 Upper Shelderton House
33 Walcot Hall

Tuesday 31
5 Brownhill House

June

7 **The Croft (every Tuesday)**

Wednesday 1
10 Goldstone Hall Gardens

Friday 3
25 Ruthall Manor

Festival Weekend

Saturday 4
7 The Croft

Sunday 5
28 Shoothill House
36 Windy Ridge

Sunday 12
12 Hodnet Hall Gardens
20 Morville Hall Gardens
37 Wollaston Lodge

Wednesday 15
10 Goldstone Hall Gardens

Friday 17
25 Ruthall Manor

Saturday 18
27 Secret Garden

Sunday 19
8 Drayton Fields
18 Millichope Park
23 NEW The Old Vicarage
35 NEW Whistlewood

Thursday 23
2 Avocet

Friday 24
22 Norton Farm

Saturday 25
19 Moortown
25 Ruthall Manor

Sunday 26
14 Holmcroft
19 Moortown
21 Mynd Hardy Plants
25 Ruthall Manor

140 year old orchard with paths for those interested in wild flowers and bird life . . .

Monday 27
25 Ruthall Manor

Tuesday 28
5 Brownhill House

July

7 **The Croft (every Tuesday)**

Friday 1
22 Norton Farm

Saturday 2
30 Stottesdon & District Open Gardens

Sunday 3
3 Bowbrook Allotment Community
11 NEW Guilden Down Cottage
17 Marchamley House Garden
30 Stottesdon & District Open Gardens

Wednesday 6
10 Goldstone Hall Gardens

Friday 8
25 Ruthall Manor

Sunday 17
4 48 Bramble Ridge
26 Sambrook Manor
36 Windy Ridge

Wednesday 20
10 Goldstone Hall Gardens

Sunday 24
21 Mynd Hardy Plants
31 NEW Sunningdale

Wednesday 27
10 Goldstone Hall Gardens

Friday 29
25 Ruthall Manor

August

7 **The Croft (every Tuesday until 23 August)**

Thursday 4
2 Avocet

Wednesday 10
10 Goldstone Hall Gardens

Sunday 14
26 Sambrook Manor
36 Windy Ridge

Wednesday 17
10 Goldstone Hall Gardens

Sunday 21
21 Mynd Hardy Plants

Sunday 28
32 Upper Shelderton House

Monday 29
32 Upper Shelderton House

Wednesday 31
10 Goldstone Hall Gardens

September

Sunday 4
36 Windy Ridge

Wednesday 7
10 Goldstone Hall Gardens

Sunday 11
9 Edge Villa

Wednesday 14
10 Goldstone Hall Gardens

Wednesday 21
10 Goldstone Hall Gardens

October

Sunday 9
18 Millichope Park

Gardens open to the public

38 Wollerton Old Hall

By arrangement only

13 Holly Cottage
24 Preen Manor

Also open by arrangement

1 Ancoireán
2 Avocet
3 Bowbrook Allotment Community
4 48 Bramble Ridge
5 Brownhill House
7 The Croft
9 Edge Villa
10 Goldstone Hall Gardens
11 NEW Guilden Down Cottage
12 Hodnet Hall Gardens
23 NEW The Old Vicarage
25 Ruthall Manor
27 Secret Garden
28 Shoothill House
32 Upper Shelderton House
36 Windy Ridge

Ruthall Manor

The Gardens

❶ ANCOIREÁN
24 Romsley View, Alveley
WV15 6PJ. Judy & Peter Creed,
01746 780504, pdjc@me.com. *6m
S Bridgnorth off A442 Bridgnorth to
Kidderminster rd. N from
Kidderminster turn L just after Royal
Oak PH. S from Bridgnorth turn R
after Squirrel PH. Take 3rd turning on
R & follow NGS signs.* Sun 22 May
(1-5). Adm £3.50, chd free. Home-
made teas. **Visits also by
arrangement May to July 20+.**
Natural garden layout on several
levels, developed over 30yrs, with a
large variety of herbaceous plants
and shrubs, water features, wooded
area with bog garden containing
numerous varieties of ferns and
hostas, and colourful alpine scree.
Features incl chickens in wooded
area, stumpery, ornamental grass
border and Spring bulb collection,
clematis collection, acer and azalea
beds. Selection of plants and bird
and insect boxes for sale. Close to
Severn Valley Railway and Country
Park and Dudmaston Hall NT.

❷ AVOCET
3 Main Road, Plealey, Shrewsbury
SY5 0UZ. Malc & Jude Mollart,
01743 791743,
malcandjude@btinternet.com. *6m
SW of Shrewsbury. From A5 take
A488 signed Bishops Castle, approx
¹/₂ m past Lea Cross Tavern turn L
signed Plealey. In ³/₄ m turn L, garden
on R.* Thur 12 May, Thur 23 June,
Thur 4 Aug (2-5). Adm £3.50, chd
free. Home-made teas. **Visits also
by arrangement Apr to Aug,
groups of 10+.**
Cottage style garden with modern
twists owned by plantaholics and
shared with wildlife. Designed around
a series of garden compartments and
for year round interest. Features incl a
wildlife pool, mixed borders, seaside
garden, gravel garden, trained fruit
trees, chickens and sculpture.
Children are welcome. Countryside
views and walks from the garden.
Featured in Shropshire Star.

ALLOTMENTS

❸ BOWBROOK ALLOTMENT
COMMUNITY
Mytton Oak Road, Shrewsbury
SY3 5BT, 01743 791743,
malcandjude@btinternet.com,
www.bowbrookallotments.co.uk.
*¹/₂ m from Royal Shrewsbury
Hospital. From A5 Shrewsbury
bypass take B4386 following signs for
hospital. Allotments situated ¹/₂ m
along B4386. (Mytton Oak Rd) on R.*
Sun 3 July (2-6). Combined adm
£3.50, chd free. Home-made teas.
**Visits also by arrangement May to
Sept groups of 10+.**
Recipient of RHS National Certificate
of Distinction, this 5 acre site,
comprising 93 plots, displays wide
ranging cultivation methods. The site
has featured on BBC TV, local radio
programmes and in several
magazines. Members cultivate
organically with nature in mind using
companion planting and attracting
natural predators. Green spaces
flourish throughout and include
Gardens of the 4 Seasons, orchards,
and many wildlife features including
wild flower meadows and pond.. The
gardens provide a peaceful haven for
members and visitors. Children are
encouraged to be part of the
community and have their own
special places such as a story telling
willow dome, willow tunnel, sensory
garden and turf spiral. See how the
Contemplation Garden and the Prairie
Garden have developed. Visitors can
participate in voting for Favourite Plot
and follow the interest trail. Children
are particularly welcome and can
enjoy their own quizzes. The site was
featured in BBC2's Great British
Garden Revival and on BBC1's
'Breakfast' programme. In both the
site's wildlife features and community
atmosphere were highlighted.
Wheelchair access, flat wide grass
paths allow access to the main
features of the site and to the interest
trail.

4 48 BRAMBLE RIDGE

Bridgnorth WV16 4SQ. Chris & Heather, 07572 702702, quendalebears1@btinternet.com. *From Bridgnorth N on B4373 signed Broseley. 1st on R Stanley Lane, 1st R Bramble Ridge. From Broseley S on B4373, nr Bridgnorth turn L into Stanley Lane, 1st R Bramble Ridge.* Sun 17 July (12.30-6). Adm £4, chd free. Home-made teas. **Visits also by arrangement Apr to Oct, please specify group numbers.**
Steep garden with many steps, part wild, part cultivated, terraced in places and overlooking the Severn valley with views to High Rock and Queens Parlour. Described by some as fascinating and full of interest; the garden incl shrubs, perennials, small vegetable plot, herbs, wildlife pond and summerhouse. Full of interesting plants.

5 BROWNHILL HOUSE

Ruyton XI Towns, Shrewsbury SY4 1LR. Roger & Yoland Brown, 01939 261121, brownhill@eleventowns.co.uk, www.eleventowns.co.uk. *9m NW of Shrewsbury on B4397. On the B4397 in the village of Ruyton XI Towns.* Tue 26 Apr, Tue 31 May, Tue 28 June (1.30-5). Adm £3.50, chd free. Home-made teas. **Visits also by arrangement May to July individuals or groups.**
"Has to be seen to be believed,". A unique hillside garden (over 700 steps) bordering R Perry. Wide variety of styles and plants from formal terraces to woodland paths, plus large kitchen garden. Kit cars on show. Featured in Shropshire Review.

6 THE CITADEL

Weston-under-Redcastle SY4 5JY. Mr Beverley & Mrs Sylvia Griffiths, 01630 685204, griffiths@thecitadelweston.co.uk, www.thecitadelweston.co.uk. *12m N of Shrewsbury on A49. At Xrds turn for Hawkstone Park, through village of Weston-under-Redcastle, ¼ m on R beyond village.* Sun 22 May (2-5.30). Adm £4, chd free. Home-made teas.
Imposing castellated house (not open) stands in 4 acres. Mature garden, with fine trees, rhododendrons, azaleas, acers and camellias. Herbaceous borders; walled potager and Victorian thatched summerhouse provide added interest. Paths meander around and over sandstone outcrop at centre.

7 THE CROFT

Ash Magna, Whitchurch SY13 4DR. Peter & Shiela Martinson, 01948 663248, smartinson@ashbounty.co.uk. *2m S of Whitchurch. From Whitchurch bypass take A525 Newcastle (A530 Nantwich). 'Ash' signed at r'about. Village centre 2m. Please use Village Hall car park. Follow signs to garden.* Sat 4 June (1-5). Every Tue 7 June to 23 Aug (1-5). Adm £3, chd free. Home-made teas. **Visits also by arrangement June to Aug need at least a week's notice.**
As we enjoy all types of garden, we have incorporated many styles to create an interesting whole. The areas include herbaceous borders, banks of thyme, meandering paths, sunken hot spots, fruit terraces, bee and butterfly borders, shrubberies, woodland walks, poly-tunnel produce and a pond with a surprise. A little bit of everything, including contented chickens and four legged lawnmowers!.

8 DRAYTON FIELDS

Wollerton, Market Drayton TF9 3LU. Mr & Mrs Roberts. *Northern edge of Wollerton Village, Drayton Rd. Garden is set back with white railings.* Sun 19 June (1.30-5). Adm £4, chd free. Home-made teas.
3½ acres of interesting trees, incl Wellingtonias, herbaceous borders, lawns, box hedging, lavender parterre, rose garden. Vegetable garden and greenhouse, small pond, flowers abound and combining into partly organised floral, scented chaos.

9 EDGE VILLA

Edge, nr Yockleton SY5 9PY. Mr & Mrs W F Neil, 01743 821651, bill@billfneil.fsnet.co.uk. *6m SW of Shrewsbury. From A5 take either A488 signed to Bishops Castle or B4386 to Montgomery for approx 6m then follow NGS signs.* Sun 10 Apr (2-5). Home-made teas. Wed 25 May (9.30-1). Light refreshments. Sun 11 Sept (2-5). Home-made teas. Adm £4, chd free. **Visits also by arrangement Apr to Sept, groups 10+.**
Two acres nestling in South Shropshire hills. Self-sufficient vegetable plot. Chickens in orchard, foxes permitting. Large herbaceous borders. Dewpond surrounded by purple elder, irises, candelabra primulas and dieramas. Large selection of fragrant roses. Teas in sheltered courtyard. Wed 25th May is an a.m opening with plant sale. Wendy House and Teepee for children. Some gravel paths.

10 GOLDSTONE HALL GARDENS

Goldstone, Market Drayton TF9 2NA. Miss Victoria Cushing, 01630 661202, enquiries@goldstonehall.com, www.goldstonehall.com. *5m N of Newport on A41. Follow brown signs from Hinstock. From Shrewsbury A53, R for A41 Hinstock & follow brown signs.* Wed 25 May, 1, 15 June, Wed 6, 20, 27 July, Wed 10, 17, 31 Aug, Wed 7, 14, 21 Sept (2-5). Adm £4.50, chd free. Home-made teas. **Visits also by arrangement May to Dec for groups of 10+.**
Mature 5acre setting of Goldstone Hall Hotel/Restaurant with well-ordered kitchen garden(surplus available August/September) raised beds and herbal walkway of an acre. The herbs attract large numbers of butterflies and bees. Award winning oak pavilion perfect for afternoon teas. Unusual combination of roses with box hedging at best in June and double tiered colourful herbaceous borders June, July, Aug. Good Food Guide listed restaurant. Majority of garden can be accessed on gravel and lawns.

11 NEW GUILDEN DOWN COTTAGE

Guilden Down, Clun, Craven Arms SY7 8NZ. Mike Black & Sue Wilson, 01588 640124, sue.guilden@gmail.com. *Clun. In Clun Signs for YHA. Continue 1m up hill. Past cottages on L. At farm bear R through farm buildings. 100 yds at end of road. Garden on L.* Sun 15 May, Sun 3 July (2-6). Adm £4, chd free. Home-made teas. Visits also by arrangement Apr to Oct refreshments on request.

With spectacular views, this one acre organic garden has been developed over the past 12 years to be in harmony with its surroundings. Divided into many rooms, there are vibrant herbaceous borders and terraces, rose trellises and a large vegetable plot. Our wild garden includes a natural pond, living willow structures, wild flower orchard, trees, shrubs and planted borders. Partial wheelchair access, front garden only.

12 HODNET HALL GARDENS

Hodnet, Market Drayton TF9 3NN. Sir Algernon & The Hon Lady Heber-Percy, www.hodnethallgardens.org. *5½ m SW of Market Drayton. 12m NE Shrewsbury. At junction of A53 & A442.* Sun 12 June (12-5). Adm £6.50, chd £3. Light refreshments. Visits also by arrangement.

60-acre landscaped garden with series of lakes and pools; magnificent forest trees, great variety of flowers, shrubs providing colour throughout season. Unique collection of big-game trophies in C17 tearooms. Kitchen garden. For details please see website and Facebook page. Maps are available to show access for our less mobile visitors.

 NPC

13 HOLLY COTTAGE

Prolley Moor, Wentnor SY9 5EH. Julian French & Heather Williams, 01588 650610, heatherannw56@yahoo.co.uk. *7m NE of Bishop's Castle. From A489 take rd signed Wentnor. In Wentnor pass The Crown on R. Take next R signed Prolley Moor, then 1st L, signed Adstone.* Visits by arrangement Apr to Aug any number of visitors. Adm £3, chd free. Light refreshments.

Organic garden of 2½ acres set in beautiful countryside under the Long Mynd. Areas incl 1 acre of 12yr old native woodland, wild flower meadow with willow circle and allotment area. Nearer the house the flower garden is stocked with herbaceous plants, trees and shrubs with pond, trellis and improved layout in old orchard. New layout by pond. Refreshments Tea/coffee/soft drinks and biscuits/cakes. Gravel and grass paths.

> Our wild garden includes a natural pond, living willow structures, wild flower orchard . . .

14 HOLMCROFT

Wyson Lane, Brimfield, nr Ludlow SY8 4NW. Mr & Mrs Michael Dowding. *4m S of Ludlow & 6m N of Leominster. From Ludlow or Leominster leave the A49 at the Salway Arms PH, turn into lane signed Wyson only. From Tenbury Wells cross the A49 into Wyson Lane.* Sun 26 June (2-5.30). Adm £4, chd free. Home-made teas.

C17 thatched cottage set in terraced gardens of ³/₄ acre. Quintessential English cottage garden planting. Roses, which has been extended for this year to over 80, climbers, ramblers and rose bushes. Herbaceous borders, kitchen, gravel and woodland gardens all with spectacular views of surrounding countryside. Only the woodland walk is inaccessible for wheelchairs.

15 LONGNER HALL

Atcham, Shrewsbury SY4 4TG. Mr & Mrs R L Burton. *4m SE of Shrewsbury. From M54 follow A5 to Shrewsbury, then B4380 to Atcham. From Atcham take Uffington rd, entrance ¹/₄ m on L.* Sun 29 May (2-5). Adm £4, chd free. Home-made teas.

A long drive approach through parkland designed by Humphry Repton. Walks lined with golden yew through extensive lawns, with views over Severn Valley. Borders containing roses, herbaceous and shrubs, also ancient yew wood. Enclosed walled garden containing mixed planting, garden buildings, tower and game larder. Short woodland walk around old moat pond. 1-acre walled garden currently being restored now open to visitors. Woodland walk not suitable for wheelchairs.

16 LYNDALE HOUSE

Astley Abbotts, Bridgnorth WV16 4SW. Bob & Mary Saunders. *2m out of Bridnorth off B4373. From High Town Bridgnorth take B4373 Broseley Rd for 1¹/₂ m, then take lane signed Astley Abbotts & Colemore Green.* Sun 8 May (2-5). Adm £3.50, chd free. Light refreshments.

Large 1¹/₂ acre garden which has evolved over 20yrs. Terrace with roses, alliums and iris surrounded by box hedging. Specimen trees planted in large lawn. Hundreds of tulips for spring colour. Clematis and allium walk to pool and waterfall. Vegetable garden and working greenhouses. Densely planted borders. Wealth of peonies, viburnums and acers. Stumpery with late spring bulbs. New scree bed in progress. Courtyard garden with topiary, pool with waterfall and 'pebble beach'. Masses of blossom in spring. Birds in abundance. Featured in local press and county magazine. Please ask owner about wheelchair friendly access.

17 MARCHAMLEY HOUSE GARDEN

Marchamley, Hodnet SY4 5LE. Mr & Mrs A Davies. *6m SW of Market Drayton. At Hodnet on A53 between Market Drayton & Shrewsbury take road opposite the Bear Hotel to Marchamley & follow NGS signs for parking.* Sun 3 July (12.30-5). Adm £4, chd free. Home-made teas.

2-acre garden set in the Shropshire countryside with stunning views. Mixed perennial borders, lily pond and herb garden, fruit trees and vegetable garden. Sloping lawn leads to mature trees, ponds and stumpery and beyond is a meadow walk. Exhibition and sale of pictures by Botanical Artist Mary Morton.

Millichope Park

18 MILLICHOPE PARK
Munslow, Craven Arms SY7 9HA.
Mr & Mrs Frank Bury,
www.boutsviolas.co.uk. *8m NE of Craven Arms. off B4368 Craven Arms to Bridgnorth Rd. Nr Munslow then follow yellow signs.* Sun 21 Feb (2-5); Sun 1 May, Sun 19 June (2-6); Sun 9 Oct (2-5). Adm £5, chd free. Home-made teas.
Historic landscape gardens covering 14 acres with lakes, cascades dating from C18, woodland walks and wildflowers. Snowdrops in February, Bluebells and Violas in May, Roses and wild flower meadows in June and Autumn colour in October. Also open the Walled Garden at Millichope, an exciting restoration project bringing the walled gardens and C19 glasshouses back to life due to be completed in 2016. Rare opportunity to see the Bouts Viola collection. UK's largest collection of hardy, perennial, scented violas. Many varieties for sale during the May opening. The glasshouses and walled garden are due for completion in 2016. Walled garden and Viola collection featured on BBC Chelsea 2015, The Sunday Times and NFU Countryside magazine. Partial wheelchair access, incl WC.

19 MOORTOWN
nr Wellington TF6 6JE. Mr David Bromley. *8m N of Telford. 5m N of Wellington. Take B5062 signed Moortown 1m between High Ercall & Crudgington.* Sat 25, Sun 26 June (2-5.30). Adm £5, chd free. Home-made teas.
Approx 1-acre plantsman's garden. Here may be found the old-fashioned, the unusual and even the oddities of plant life, in mixed borders of 'controlled' confusion. **This year is a celebration of 50 years in the garden and 30 years opening for the NGS.**

GROUP OPENING

20 MORVILLE HALL GARDENS
Bridgnorth WV16 5NB. *3m W of Bridgnorth. On A458 at junction with B4368.* Sun 12 June (2-5). Combined adm £5, chd free. Home-made teas in Morville Church. *Donation to Morville Church.*

THE COTTAGE
Mrs J Bolton

THE DOWER HOUSE
Dr Katherine Swift

1 THE GATE HOUSE
Mr & Mrs Rowe

2 THE GATE HOUSE
Mrs G Medland

MORVILLE HALL
Mr & Mrs M Irving

SOUTH PAVILION
Mr & Mrs B Jenkinson

An interesting group of gardens that surround a beautiful Grade I listed mansion (not open). The Cottage has a pretty walled cottage garden with plenty of colour. The Dower House is a horticultural history lesson about Morville Hall which incl a turf maze, cloister garden, Elizabethan knot garden, C18 canal garden, Edwardian kitchen garden and more. It is the setting of Katherine Swift's bestselling book 'The Morville Hours', and the sequel 'The Morville Year'. 1 & 2 The Gate House are cottage-style gardens with colourful borders, formal areas, lawns and wooded glades. The 4-acre Morville Hall (NT) garden has a parterre, medieval stew pond, shrub borders and large lawns, all offering glorious views across the Mor Valley. South Pavilion features new thoughts and new designs in a small courtyard garden. Featured in Shropshire Magazine. Mostly level ground, but plenty of gravel to negotiate.

21 MYND HARDY PLANTS

Delbury Hall Estate, Mill Lane, Diddlebury, Craven Arms SY7 9DH. Mr & Mrs Rallings, www.myndhardyplants.co.uk. *8m W of Craven Arms. 1m off B4368, Craven Arms to Bridgnorth, through village of Diddlebury, turn R at Mynd Hardy Plants sign.* **Sun 22 May, Sun 26 June, Sun 24 July, Sun 21 Aug (11-5). Adm £4, chd free. Home-made teas.**
Commercial nursery within old walled garden, offering and selling more than 800 varieties of herbaceous perennials. Collections include hemerocallis and penstemon and a growing range of late summer flowering plants. The garden is undergoing a major restoration programme. Featured on BBC Gardeners World. Gravel and grass paths.

22 NORTON FARM

Norton, Craven Arms SY7 9LT. Holiday Property Bond, 01588 674050, nhmanager@hpb.co.uk, www.hpb-uppernorton.co.uk. *8m N of Ludlow. From A49 turn L on B4368 signed Much Wenlock & Bridgnorth 1 1/2 m turn R for Norton, Burley & Bache. From Bridgnorth take A458 W. At Morville L B4368 signed Craven Arms, L for Bache & Norton.* **Fri 24 June, Fri 1 July (11-3). Adm £4, chd free. Tea and cold drinks for children.**
Holiday cottages tastefully developed from old farm and buildings overlooking Clee Hills. Mediterranean style planting covering old walls and maturing herbaceous borders. Emphasis on low maintenance garden but with seasonal changes, scent and bee friendly plants. Reed bed, eco filtration system. New heritage orchard, herb garden and small ornamental pond with water lilies. The paths around the main garden are accessible.

23 NEW THE OLD VICARAGE

Church Lane, Ash Magna, Whitchurch SY13 4EA. Martin & Sandra Stone, 01948 663220, sandra@halestones.myzen.co.uk. *Ash Magna Whitchurch. 2 1/2 m SE of Whitchurch. From Whitchurch bypass take A525 Nantwich rd. Ash signed at r'about. After 2m turn L at White Lion PH. Signed for Ash Church/ Nantwich. House 1/2 m on R.* **Sun 19 June (1-5). Adm £3, chd free.**

Home-made teas. **Visits also by arrangement in June (Mons and Tues only).**
Renovation in this 2 acre Victorian vicarage garden began in 2011 and there are many plans for the future. The garden now has a terrace with a large formal rose garden, herbaceous and shrub borders, walled kitchen garden, greenhouses, woodlands, an orchard, wild flower meadow and wildlife pond. The large front lawn once hosted village fetes and is now used as a croquet lawn by the village. To most areas.Gravel paths + lawn.

24 PREEN MANOR

Church Preen SY6 7LQ. Mrs Ann Trevor-Jones, 01694 771207. *6m W of Much Wenlock. Signed from B4371.* **Visits by arrangement May to July for groups of 10+. Not evenings or weekends. Adm £6, chd free. Tea and biscuits.**
6-acre garden on site of Cluniac monastery and Norman Shaw mansion. Kitchen, chess, water and wild gardens. Fine trees in park; woodland walks. Developed for over 30yrs with changes always in progress. Refreshments coffee/tea & biscuits £1.

25 RUTHALL MANOR

Ditton Priors, Bridgnorth WV16 6TN. Mr & Mrs G T Clarke, 01746 712608, clrk608@btinternet.com. *7m SW of Bridgnorth. Ruthall Rd signed nr garage in Ditton Priors. See yellow arrows.* **Fri 3, Fri 17 June (2-6); Sat 25, Sun 26, Mon 27 June (12.30-6); Fri 8, Fri 29 July (2-6). Adm £4, chd free. Home-made teas. Light meals by arrangement. Visits also by arrangement May to Oct, refreshments on request.**
Offset by a mature collection of specimen trees, the garden is divided into intimate sections, carefully linked by winding paths. The front lawn flanked by striking borders, extends to a gravel, art garden and ha-ha. Clematis and roses scramble through an eclectic collection of wrought-iron work, unique pottery and secluded seating. A stunning horse pond features primulas, iris and bog plants. Jigsaws for sale Bring and Buy. Some paths too narrow.

26 SAMBROOK MANOR

Sambrook, Newport TF10 8AL. Mrs E Mitchell, 01952 550256, sambrookmanor@btconnect.com. *Between Newport & Ternhill. 1m off A41 in the village of Sambrook.* **Sun 17 July, Sun 14 Aug (12.30-5). Adm £4, chd free. Home-made teas.**
The garden surrounds the early C18 manor house (not open) and contains a wide selection of herbaceous plants and roses. Features incl a waterfall down to a pond and various acers. A new development leading to the river along the edge of the garden is filled with a variety of shrubs and trees. Plants on sale from Barlow Nurseries.

> Large front lawn once hosted village fetes and is now used as a croquet lawn by the village . . .

27 SECRET GARDEN

21 Steventon Terrace, Steventon New Road, Ludlow SY8 1JZ. Mr & Mrs Wood, 01584 876037, carolynwood2152@yahoo.co.uk. *Park & Ride if needed, stops outside garden.* **Sat 18 June (1-5). Adm £3.50, chd free. Home-made teas and cakes. Visits also by arrangement Feb to Sept, refreshments if requested.**
1/2 -acre of very secret S-facing garden, divided into different sections, roses, herbaceous borders, lawn and summer house. Developed over 30yrs by present owners. Terraced vegetable garden and greenhouses. 1/4 -acre project incl poly tunnel, vegetable plot, chickens, completed in 2011. Mediterranean style terrace garden. 3 times winners of Ludlow in Bloom.

28 SHOOTHILL HOUSE

Ford, Shrewsbury SY5 9NR. Colin & Jane Lloyd, 01743 850795, jane@lloydmasters.com. *5m W of Shrewsbury. From A458 turn L towards Shoothill (signed).* Sun 5 June (1.30-5). Adm £4.50, chd £1.50. Home-made teas. **Visits also by arrangement May to Sept, groups 10+.**

6-acre garden, incl small wood with swamp garden, wild flower meadows, tree house and several lawned areas surrounded by mixed borders. Large well maintained Victorian greenhouse in renovated walled kitchen garden. New areas of garden created in 2012. Mature wildlife pond surrounded by species trees and shrubs with extensive views over Welsh hills. Victorian manor house vintage tea stall walled garden. Wheelchair access is extremely difficult as the ground is uneven and there are also large areas of gravel.

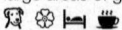

29 STANLEY HALL

Bridgnorth WV16 4SP. Mr & Mrs M J Thompson. *¹/₂ m N of Bridgnorth. Leave Bridgnorth by N gate; B4373; turn R at Stanley Lane. Pass Golf Course Club House on L & turn L at Lodge.* Sun 22 May (2-6). Combined adm £4, chd free. Home-made teas.

Drive ¹/₂ m with rhododendrons, fine trees and pools. Restored ice-house. Woodland walks. Also open Dower House (Mr & Mrs Colin Wells) 4 acre woodland and shrub garden with contemporary sculpture and walled vegetable garden. The Granary (Mr & Mrs Jack Major) Small trellis garden with flowers in hanging baskets and herbaceous borders and South Lodge (Mr Tim Warren) Cottage hillside garden.

GROUP OPENING

30 STOTTESDON & DISTRICT OPEN GARDENS

Stottesdon, Kidderminster DY14 8TZ. Stottesdon Garden Committee. *Between Bridgnorth & Cleobury Mortimer. Stottesdon is signposted on the B4364 between Bridgnorth and Ludlow and the B4363 between Bridgnorth and Cleobury Mortimer. The B4194 from Bewdley joins the B4363 4m from Stottesdon.* Sat 2, Sun 3 July (11-5). Combined adm £5, chd free.

Light refreshments in the garden of the Old Fox and Hounds. Located in unspoilt Shropshire countryside near the Clee Hills, up to 15 village gardens are open to the visitor offering a diverse and wonderful range of garden experiences to enjoy. There are traditional cottage gardens of different sizes which vary in content from the classic to the quirky; the grounds of an old manor house [not open]; two ' leisure spaces'- gardens that have been developed for outside entertaining; and two interesting vegetable gardens, one devoted to the principals of permaculture and the other the home of championship class produce. It is hoped there will be at least 3 new gardens this year, including one which has been designed specifically for people with mobility issues. Most of the gardens are in walking distance but allow plenty of time if you wish to visit all the gardens. Tickets are valid for both days. Most gardens have access for wheelchairs and suitable gardens will be clearly marked for visitors. Plant and produce stall. A competition, called NOTAPOT, will be held and will be judged by garden visitors. We are looking for unusual containers for plants. Coaches by prior arrangement. Light refreshments, tea, coffee, soft drinks and cakes. Most gardens have some wheelchair access. Suitable gardens will be listed.

Climbers and roses around a magnificent summer house used for serving homemade refreshments . . .

31 NEW SUNNINGDALE

9 Mill Street, Wem, Shropshire SY4 5ED. Mrs Susan Griffiths. *Town centre Wem. Wem is on B5476. Parking in public car park Barnard St. The property is opp the purple house below the church.* Sun 24 July (11-4). Adm £3, chd free. Light refreshments.

A developing half acre town garden. Incorporating sculptural elements, koi pond with natural stone rockery waterfall, solar panelled greenhouse and borehole irrigation system. 8ft x 60ft Lawson Cypress trees, large borders filled with perennials, climbers and roses around a magnificent summer house used for serving homemade refreshments. Antique and modern sculpture. Sound break yew walkway. Although the garden is on the level, there are a number of steps especially around the pond area. Paths are on the main thick gravel.

32 UPPER SHELDERTON HOUSE

Shelderton, Clungunford, Craven Arms SY7 0PE. Andrew Benton & Tricia McHaffie, 01547 540525. *Between Ludlow & Craven Arms. Heading from Shrewsbury to Ludlow on A49, take 1st R after Onibury railway crossing. Take 3rd R signed Shelderton. After approx 1m the house is last property on L. Garden will be signed.* Sun 29, Mon 30 May, Sun 28, Mon 29 Aug (2-5). Adm £4, chd free. Home-made teas. **Visits also by arrangement Apr to Aug for groups of 10+.**

Set in a stunning tranquil position, our naturalistic and evolving 6¹/₂ acre garden was originally landscaped in 1962. Most of the trees, azaleas and rhododendrons were planted then. There is a wonderful new kitchen garden designed and planted by Jayne and Norman Grove. Ponds and woodland walk encourage wildlife. A large sweeping lawn leads in various directions revealing a multitude of colourful rhododendron and azaelea beds ponds a varied collection of trees and a very productive kitchen garden. There are plenty of tranquil seating areas from which to enjoy a moment in our garden.

33 WALCOT HALL

Lydbury North SY7 8AZ. Mr & Mrs C R W Parish, 01588 680570, caitlin@walcothall.com, www.walcothall.com. *4m SE of Bishop's Castle. B4385 Craven Arms to Bishop's Castle, turn L by Powis Arms, in Lydbury North.* Sun 29, Mon 30 May (1.30-5.30). Adm £4, chd free. Home-made teas. Arboretum planted by Lord Clive of India's son, Edward. Cascades of rhododendrons, azaleas amongst specimen trees and pools. Fine views of Sir William Chambers' Clock Towers, with lake and hills beyond. Walled kitchen garden; dovecote; meat safe; ice house and mile-long lakes. Outstanding ballroom where excellent teas are served. Russian wooden church, grotto and fountain now complete and working; tin chapel. Relaxed borders and rare shrubs. Lakeside replanted, and water garden at western end re-established. The garden adjacent to the ballroom is accessible via a sloping bank, as is the walled garden and arboretum.

34 8 WESTGATE VILLAS

Salop Street, Bridgnorth WV16 4QX. Bill & Marilyn Hammerton. *From A458 Bridgnorth bypass, at Ludlow Rd r'about take rd into Bridgnorth signed town centre. At T-junction (?parking at council offices here) turn R, garden is 100yds on L past Victoria Road.* **Evening opening Fri 22 Apr (7-9.30). Adm £5, chd free. Wine & canapés. Sun 24 Apr (2-5.30). Adm £4, chd free. Tea & cake.**

Town garden having formal Victorian front garden with box hedging and water feature. Back garden has a shade border, lawn, small knot garden and orchard, together with a strong oriental influence incl Japanese style teahouse, Zen garden, Chinese style pebble path, moongate sculpture and new basalt sett and gravel hard landscaping. Wine, canapes, music and garden lighting incl at evening opening. Partial wheelchair access.

35 NEW WHISTLEWOOD

Boraston, Tenbury Wells WR15 8LH. Nick & Ali Bews. *Whistlewood lies 1m northeast of Tenbury on Burford to Cleobury Mortimer rd.* **Sun 19 June (2-5). Adm £4, chd free. Home-made teas.**

3/4 acre garden in a traditional orchard setting with emphasis on wildlife. Natural ponds, meadow, fruit trees with many rambling roses, as well as herbaceous borders, kitchen and cutting garden. Also an additional 4 acres of 140 year old mature orchard with paths for those interested in wild flowers and bird life. A relaxed blend of the natural world and gardening ambition.

36 WINDY RIDGE

Church Lane, Little Wenlock, Telford TF6 5BB. George & Fiona Chancellor, 01952 507675, fionachancellor@btinternet.com. *2m S of Wellington. Follow signs for Little Wenlock from N (J7, M54) or E (off A5223 at Horsehay). Parking signed. Do not rely on SatNav.* **Sun 5 June, Sun 17 July, Sun 14 Aug, Sun 4 Sept (12-5). Adm £5, chd free. Home-made teas. Visits also by arrangement May to Sept suitable for coaches.**

'Stunning' and 'inspirational' are how visitors frequently describe this multi-award-winning 2/3 acre village garden. The strong design and exuberant colour-themed planting (over 1000 species, mostly labelled) offer a picture around every corner. The grass and perennial gravel garden has created a lot of interest and versions are now appearing in gardens all over the country!. Featured in Period Living. Some gravel paths but help available.

37 WOLLASTON LODGE

Wollaston, Halfway House, Shrewsbury SY5 9DN. Sandy & Grant Williams, 01743 884831, enjoylife@wollastonlodge.co.uk, www.wollastonlodge.co.uk. *From A458, Shrewsbury - Welshpool Rd. 8m from Shrewsbury ringroad, 8m from Welshpool. Signed Wollaston.* **Sun 12 June (11.30-5). Adm £4, chd free. Cream teas in the orangery, home made cakes.**

Classic Italianate style gardens borrowing the views. Formal terraces, ornamental pool. Compact, plenty of places to sit and take in the views. Gardens surround award winning B&B.

38 ◆ WOLLERTON OLD HALL

Wollerton, Market Drayton TF9 3NA. Lesley & John Jenkins, 01630 685760, info@wollertonoldhallgarden.com, www.wollertonoldhallgarden.com. *4m SW of Market Drayton. On A53 between Hodnet & A53-A41 junction. Follow brown signs.* **For NGS: Fri 20 May (12-5). Adm £6.50, chd £1. Light refreshments. For other opening times and information, please phone, email or visit garden website.**

4-acre garden created around C16 house (not open). Formal structure creates variety of gardens each with own colour theme and character. Planting is mainly of perennials, the large range of which results in significant collections of salvias, clematis, crocosmias and roses. Ongoing lectures by Gardening Celebrities including Chris Beardshaw, Jules Hudson and Sir Roy Strong. Refreshments, food is freshly prepared in the Tea Room for each open day. Home-cooked, hot & cold lunches which have a reputation for excellent quality. Partial wheelchair access.

48 Bramble Ridge

SOMERSET, BRISTOL AREA & SOUTH GLOUCESTERSHIRE incl Bath

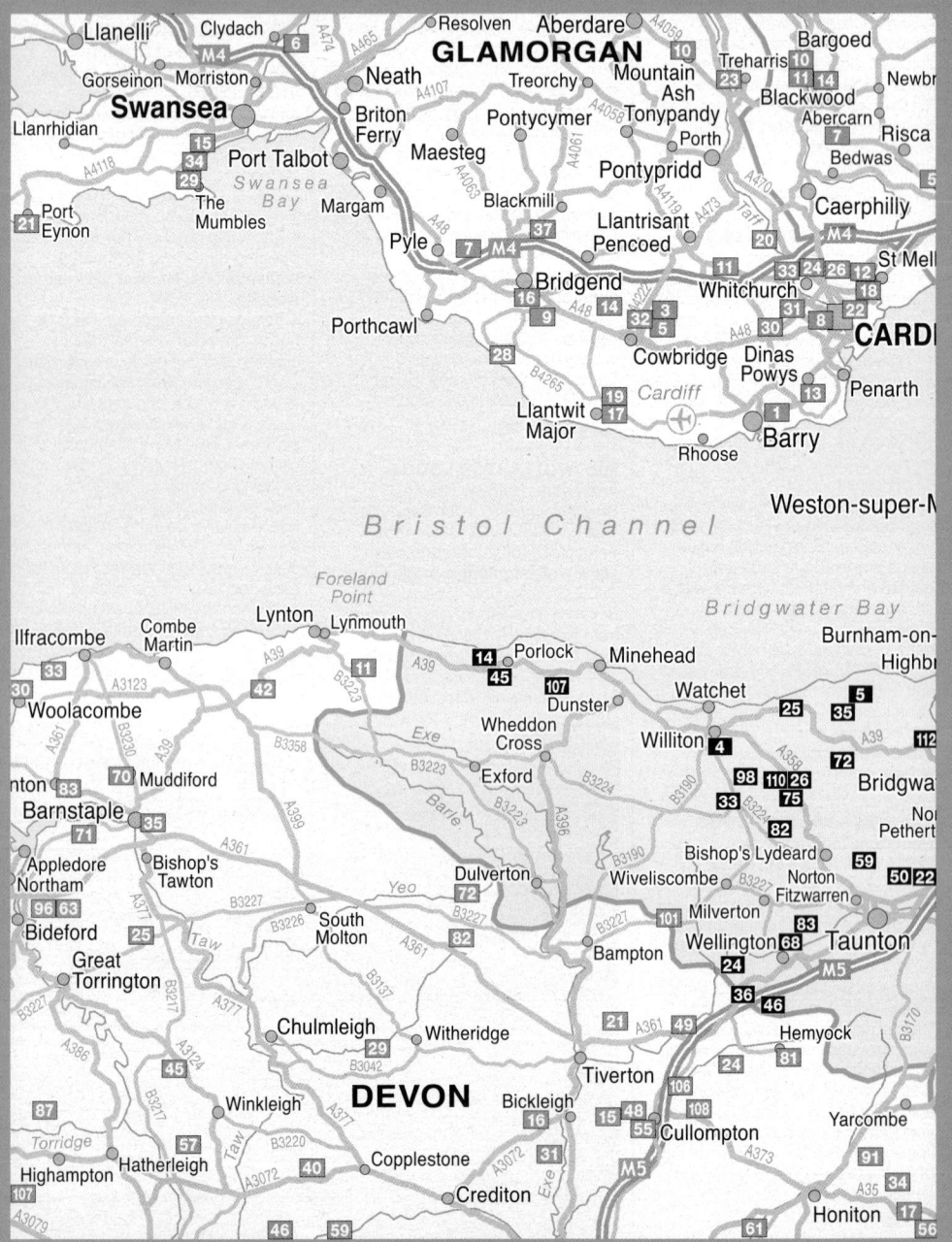

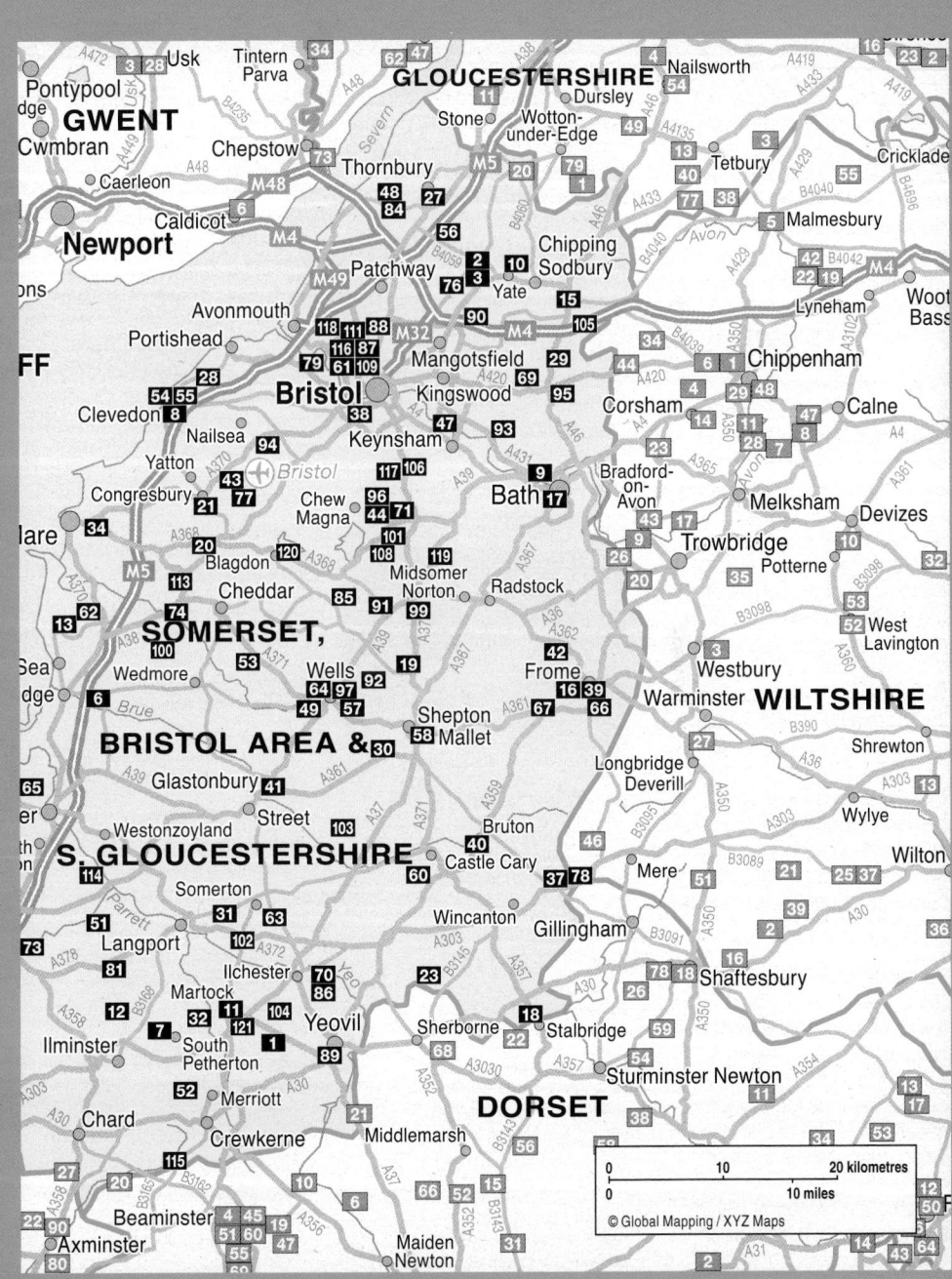

Somerset, Bristol Area & South Gloucestershire

Somerset, Bristol, Bath and South Gloucestershire make up an NGS 'county' of captivating contrasts, with castles and countryside and wildlife and wetlands, from amazing cities to bustling market towns, coastal resorts and picturesque villages.

Bristol's stunning location and famous landmarks offer a wonderful backdrop to our creative and inspiring garden owners who have made tranquil havens and tropical back gardens in urban surroundings. The rolling estates of our National Trust properties offer the visitor an experience on a different scale.

Bath is a world heritage site for its Georgian architecture and renowned for its Roman Baths. Our garden visitors can enjoy the quintessentially English garden of Bath Priory Hotel with its billowing borders and croquet lawn, or explore the hidden gem behind the house at 25 Chaucer Road.

Somerset is a rural county of rolling hills such as the Mendips, the Quantocks and Exmoor National Park contrasted with the low-lying Somerset Levels. Famous for cheddar cheese, strawberries and cider; agriculture is a major occupation. It is home to Wells, the smallest cathedral city in England, and the lively county town of Taunton.

Visitors can explore more than 150 diverse gardens, mostly privately owned and not normally open to the public ranging from small urban plots to country estates.

Gardens on windswept hilltops, by the seaside, hidden in lush green countryside, in idyllic villages as well as communal town allotments are all to be visited, as well as historic gardens designed by Gertrude Jekyll, Margery Fish and Harold Peto.

Below: The Dairy

Somerset Volunteers

County Organiser
Laura Howard 01460 282911
laura.howard@ngs.org.uk

County Treasurer
David Bull 01934 712609
d.bull08@btinternet.com

Publicity
Roger Peacock 01275 341584
barum@blueyonder.co.uk

Photographers
Sue Sayer & Joy Carter 07773 181891
suesayer58@hotmail.com

Presentations
Dave & Pru Moon 01373 473381
davidmoon202@btinternet.com

Booklet Distributor
Ash Warne 07548 889705
ashwarne@btinternet.com

Somerset Assistant County Organisers
Patricia Davies-Gilbert
01823 412187
pdaviesgilbert@btinternet.com

Alison Highnam 01747 838133
allies1@btinternet.com

Judith Stanford 01761 233045
judithstanford.ngs@hotmail.co.uk

Bristol Area Volunteers

County Organiser
Su Mills 01454 615438
susanlmills@gmail.com

County Treasurer
Ken Payne 01275 333146
kg.payne@yahoo.co.uk

Publicity
Jean Damey 01179 775587
jeandamey@gmail.com

Pat Davie 01275 790919
pattidavie@hotmail.com

Booklet Distributor
Graham Guest 01275 472393
gandsguest@btinternet.com

Assistant County Organisers
Angela Conibere 01454 413828
aeconibere@hotmail.com

Pat Davie (as above)

Christine Healey 01454 612795
christine.healey@uwclub.net

Margaret Jones 01225 891229
ian@weircott.plus.com

Jeanette Parker 01454 299699
jeanette_parker@hotmail.co.uk

Jane Perkins 01454 414570
janekperkins@gmail.com

Irene Randow 01275 857208
irene.randow@sky.com

Somerset, Bristol & South Gloucestershire

Booklet Advertising & Co-ordinator
Jean Damey (as above)

Opening Dates

All entries subject to change.
For latest information check www.ngs.org.uk

February

Snowdrop Festival

Saturday 6
47 Hanham Court

Sunday 7
32 East Lambrook Manor Gardens
33 Elworthy Cottage
47 Hanham Court
84 Rock House
108 Truffles

Monday 8
33 Elworthy Cottage

Sunday 14
84 Rock House
91 Sherborne Garden
108 Truffles

Monday 15
91 Sherborne Garden

Sunday 21
111 NEW Vine House

Sunday 28
2 Algars Manor
3 Algars Mill
68 Nynehead Court

March

Thursday 10
50 Hestercombe Gardens

Monday 28
33 Elworthy Cottage

Wednesday 30
99 Ston Easton Park

April

Sunday 3
84 Rock House

Thursday 7
37 Forest Lodge

Friday 8
105 Tormarton Court

Sunday 10
46 Hangeridge Farmhouse
96 Stanton Court Nursing Home

Tuesday 12
33 Elworthy Cottage

Thursday 14
9 Bath Priory Hotel

Saturday 16
7 Barrington Court
112 The Walled Gardens of Cannington

Sunday 17
26 Crowcombe Court
35 Fairfield
85 Rose Cottage
112 The Walled Gardens of Cannington

Tuesday 19
58 Kilver Court Secret Gardens

Sunday 24
2 Algars Manor
3 Algars Mill
55 NEW Jasmine House
113 Watcombe

May

Saturday 7
4 Aller Farmhouse
51 Hillcrest

Sunday 8
4 Aller Farmhouse
51 Hillcrest
120 The Yeo Valley Organic Garden at Holt Farm

Wednesday 11
43 Goblin Combe House

Saturday 14
32 East Lambrook Manor Gardens

Sunday 15
25 Court House
44 Greystones
61 Lucombe House
63 Midney Gardens
64 Milton Lodge

Wednesday 18
58 Kilver Court Secret Gardens

Friday 20
59 Little Yarford Farmhouse

Saturday 21
59 Little Yarford Farmhouse

Sunday 22
59 Little Yarford Farmhouse
75 NEW Orchard View
89 NEW 103 Seaton Road
113 Watcombe

Monday 23
59 Little Yarford Farmhouse

Tuesday 24
33 Elworthy Cottage

Thursday 26
37 Forest Lodge

Saturday 28
6 Babbs Farm
8 Barum
17 NEW 25 Chaucer Road
47 Hanham Court
82 NEW Reeds Court
119 Woodlea Bottom

Sunday 29
6 Babbs Farm
8 Barum
17 NEW 25 Chaucer Road
19 Church Farm House
47 Hanham Court
52 Hinton St George Gardens
82 NEW Reeds Court
83 Rendy Farm
87 NEW St Monica Trust
115 Wayford Manor
116 West Bristol Gardens
119 Woodlea Bottom

Monday 30
33 Elworthy Cottage
47 Hanham Court
52 Hinton St George Gardens

June

Wednesday 1
19 Church Farm House

Festival Weekend

Saturday 4
29 Dyrham Park
70 The Old Rectory, Limington
103 NEW Tilham Farm
118 18 Woodgrove Road

Sunday 5
29 Dyrham Park
30 East Burford House
32 East Lambrook Manor Gardens
64 Milton Lodge
65 NEW Model Farm
70 The Old Rectory, Limington
73 NEW The Old Vicarage, Ruishton
103 NEW Tilham Farm
104 Tintinhull
106 Tranby House

Monday 6
30 East Burford House
73 NEW The Old Vicarage, Ruishton

Tuesday 7
33 Elworthy Cottage
50 Hestercombe Gardens

Thursday 9
113 Watcombe

Saturday 11
14 Broomclose
45 NEW Halsecombe House
60 NEW Lower Cockhill Farmhouse
69 The Old Rectory, Doynton
100 Stone Allerton Gardens
118 18 Woodgrove Road

Sunday 12
14 Broomclose
21 Congresbury Gardens
39 Frome Gardens
45 NEW Halsecombe House
60 NEW Lower Cockhill Farmhouse
100 Stone Allerton Gardens

Tuesday 14
33 Elworthy Cottage
97 Stoberry Garden

Wednesday 15
16 9 Catherston Close
43 Goblin Combe House
97 Stoberry Garden

Thursday 16
95 Special Plants

Friday 17
105 Tormarton Court

Saturday 18
62 Lympsham Gardens

Sunday 19
22 Coombe Gardens at Thurloxton
39 Frome Gardens
62 Lympsham Gardens
89 NEW 103 Seaton Road
98 Stogumber Gardens
111 NEW Vine House
121 Yews Farm

A courtyard of potted plants surrounded by attractive colour co-ordinated herbaceous borders . . .

Gants Mill and Garden

October

Thursday 20
95 Special Plants

February 2017

Sunday 5
84 Rock House
Sunday 12
84 Rock House
91 Sherborne Garden
Monday 13
91 Sherborne Garden
Sunday 19
32 East Lambrook Manor Gardens

Gardens open to the public

7 Barrington Court
24 Cothay Manor & Gardens
25 Court House
29 Dyrham Park
32 East Lambrook Manor Gardens
33 Elworthy Cottage
50 Hestercombe Gardens
56 Jekka's Herbetum

58 Kilver Court Secret Gardens
63 Midney Gardens
64 Milton Lodge
91 Sherborne Garden
95 Special Plants
97 Stoberry Garden
99 Ston Easton Park
104 Tintinhull
109 University of Bristol Botanic Garden
112 The Walled Gardens of Cannington
120 The Yeo Valley Organic Garden at Holt Farm

By arrangement only

1 Abbey Farm
5 Ash Cottage
12 Bradon Farm
18 Cherry Bolberry Farm
23 NEW Corton Denham House
27 Daggs Allotments
31 East End Farm
34 14 Eskdale Close
49 Henley Mill
57 NEW 1 Kennion Road
71 2 Old Tarnwell
90 Serridge House

92 Sole Retreat
93 South Kelding
107 Troytes Farmstead
114 Waverley

Also open by arrangement

4 Aller Farmhouse
6 Babbs Farm
11 NEW 24 Birch Road
13 Ball Copse Hall, Brent Knoll Gardens
14 Broomclose
15 Camers
19 Church Farm House
20 NEW Laurel Cottage, Churchill Gardens
28 The Dairy
36 Fernhill
37 Forest Lodge
43 Goblin Combe House
46 Hangeridge Farmhouse
52 Hinton St George Gardens
52 Hooper's Holding, Hinton St George Gardens
52 The Olive Garden, Hinton St George Gardens

52 South Street Allotment, Hinton St George Gardens
53 Honeyhurst Farm
59 Little Yarford Farmhouse
61 Lucombe House
68 Nynehead Court
70 The Old Rectory, Limington
84 Rock House
85 Rose Cottage
86 Rugg Farm
88 St Peter's Hospice
97 Stoberry Garden
98 Knoll Cottage, Stogumber Gardens
100 Badgers Acre, Stone Allerton Gardens
102 Sutton Hosey Manor
105 Tormarton Court
108 Truffles
110 Vellacott
113 Watcombe
116 4 Haytor Park, West Bristol Gardens
116 West Bristol Gardens
116 159 Westbury Lane, West Bristol Gardens
117 NEW Whitewood Lodge

The Gardens

1 ABBEY FARM

Montacute TA15 6UA. Alisdair & Elizabeth McFarlane, 01935 823556, ct.fm@btopenworld.com. *4m from Yeovil. Follow A3088, take slip rd to Montacute, turn L at T-junction into village. Turn R between Church & King's Arms (no through rd).* Visits by arrangement May & June. Groups of 5+. Adm £5.50, chd free. Refreshments may be arranged for small groups at the garden or for larger parties at Montacute village hall if pre-booked.

2½ acres of mainly walled gardens on sloping site provide the setting for Cluniac Medieval Priory gatehouse. Interesting plants incl roses, shrubs, grasses, clematis. Herbaceous borders, white garden, gravel garden. Small arboretum. Pond for wildlife - frogs, newts, dragonflies. Fine mulberry, walnut and monkey puzzle trees. Seats for resting. Restored Grade 2 listed dovecote. Gravel area and one steep slope.

&. ⊗ ☕

This elegant garden shows how much can be created in a relatively small space . . .

2 ALGARS MANOR

Station Rd, Iron Acton BS37 9TB. Mrs B Naish. *9m N of Bristol, 3m W of Yate/Chipping Sodbury. Turn S off Iron Acton bypass B4059, past village green, 200yds, then over level crossing. NO access from Frampton Cotterell via lane; ignore Sat Nav.*

Parking at Algars Manor. Sun 28 Feb (2-5). Sun 24 Apr (2-5). Tea. Combined adm with Algars Mill £5, chd free.

2 acres of woodland garden beside R Frome, mill stream, native plants mixed with collections of 60 magnolias and 70 camellias, rhododendrons, azaleas, eucalyptus and other unusual trees and shrubs. Partial wheelchair access only, gravel paths, some steep slopes.

&. ☕

3 ALGARS MILL

Frampton End Rd, Iron Acton, Bristol BS37 9TD. Mr & Mrs John Wright. *9m N of Bristol, 3m W of Yate/Chipping Sodbury. (For directions see Algars Manor).* Sun 28 Feb (2-5). Sun 24 Apr (2-5). Tea. Combined adm with Algars Manor £5, chd free.

2-acre woodland garden bisected by R Frome; spring bulbs, shrubs; very early spring feature (Feb-Mar) of wild Newent daffodils. 300-400yr-old mill house (not open) through which millrace still runs.

&. 🪑 ☕

4 ALLER FARMHOUSE
Williton, nr Taunton TA4 4LY.
Mr & Mrs Richard Chandler,
01984 633702,
sylvana.chandler@gmail.com. *7m E of Minehead, 1m S of Williton. From A358 Taunton turn L into Sampford Brett. Follow signs to Capton. Follow lane downhill to Aller Farm. Car park in field beyond house. Sat 7, Sun 8 May (2-5). Adm £4, chd free.* **Cream teas. Visits also by arrangement Apr to Oct excluding Aug and first fortnight of Sept, for groups of 10+.**
2-3 acres. Hot, dry, sunny, S-facing, surrounded by pink stone walls and sub-divided into 5 separate compartments by same. Cliff Garden is old 3-sided quarry. Old magnolias, figs and Judas tree; many unusual and/or tender plants incl Beschorneria yuccoides, echium vars, buddleia colvilei Kewensis, carpenteria, Eupatorium ligustrinum, Caesalpinia gilliesi, feijoa, kiwi fruit. Partial wheelchair access.

♿ ✻ ☕

5 ASH COTTAGE
Shurton, Stogursey, Bridgwater TA5 1QF. Barbara & Peter Oates, 01278 732258,
oatespeter@gmail.com. *8m W of Bridgwater. From A39 nr Holford, follow signs to Stogursey then to Shurton. From A39 at Cannington follow signs to Hinkley Point then Shurton. Map supplied when appointment is made.* **Visits by arrangement May & June for groups of 10+. Light refreshments by prior arrangement. Adm £4, chd free.**
Tranquil cottage garden in rural area, approx ⅔ acre, wrapping around 3 sides of early C16 cottage (not open). Colour-themed borders and flowerbeds incl island bed, and raised 40ft border reached by steps from either end. Admire our amazing S-facing wall! Natural stream with planted banks runs through garden. Children must be supervised at all times. Some gravel paths and shallow steps.

♿ ☕

6 BABBS FARM
Westhill Lane, Bason Bridge, Highbridge TA9 4RF. Sue & Richard O'Brien, 01278 793244. *1½ m E of Highbridge, 1½ m SSE of M5 exit 22. Turn into Westhill Lane off B3141 (Church Rd), 100yds S of where it joins B3139 (Wells-Highbridge rd).*
Sat 28, Sun 29 May, Sun 28, Mon 29 Aug (2-5). Adm £4, chd free. Tea. Visits also by arrangement May to Sept.
¾ acre plantsman's garden in Somerset Levels, gradually created out of fields surrounding old farmhouse over last 20 yrs and still being developed. Trees, shrubs and herbaceous perennials planted with an eye for form and shape in big flowing borders. Various ponds (formal and informal), box garden, patio area and conservatory.

🐎 ✻ ☕

Colour and interest from spring to autumn . . .

7 ◆ BARRINGTON COURT
Barrington, Ilminster TA19 0NQ.
National Trust, 01460 241938,
barringtoncourt@nationaltrust.org.uk, www.nationaltrust.org.uk. *5m NE of Ilminster. In Barrington village on B3168. Follow brown NT signs.* **For NGS: Sat 16 Apr, Sat 16 July (10.30-5). Adm £12, chd £6. Tea/coffee, cake, lunches, cream teas, etc. For other opening times and information, please phone, email or visit garden website.**
Well known garden constructed in 1920 by Col Arthur Lyle from derelict farmland (C19 cattle stalls still exist). Gertrude Jekyll suggested planting schemes for the layout. Paved paths with walled rose and iris, white and lily gardens, large kitchen garden. The kitchen garden has been in continuous production for over 90yrs. Some paths a little uneven.

♿ ✻ 🚌 ☕

8 BARUM
50 Edward Road, Clevedon BS21 7DT. Marian & Roger Peacock,
www.barum.pwp.blueyonder.co.uk. *12m W of Bristol. M5 J20, follow signs to pier, continue N, past Walton Park Hotel, turn R at St Mary's Church. Up Channel Rd, over Xrds, turn L into Edward Rd at top. Sat 28, Sun 29 May (1-4.30). Adm £3, chd free.*
Informal ⅓ acre plantsman's garden, reclaimed by the owners from years of neglect. Now crammed with shrubs and perennials from around

the world, incl tender and exotic species using the clement coastal climate and well-drained soil. The vegetable patch uses a no-tread bedding system.

✻

9 BATH PRIORY HOTEL
Weston Rd, Bath BA1 2XT. Jane Moore, Head Gardener, 01225 331922, info@thebathpriory.co.uk, www.thebathpriory.co.uk. *Close to centre of Bath. From Bath centre take Upper Bristol Rd, turn R at end of Victoria Park and L into Weston Rd. Please note No Parking. Drop off and parking for disabled only. Meter parking available in Victoria Park. Thur 14 Apr, Thur 8 Sept (2-5). Adm £3, chd free. Home-made teas.*
Discover 3 acres of mature walled gardens. Quintessentially English, the garden has billowing borders, croquet lawn, wild flower meadow and ancient specimen trees. Spring is bright with tulips and flowering cherries; autumn alive with colour. Perennials and tender plants provide summer highlights while the kitchen garden supplies herbs, fruit and vegetables to the restaurant. Gravel paths and some steps.

♿ ✻ **NPC** 🛏 ☕

10 BEECHWELL HOUSE
51 Goose Green, Yate BS37 5BL.
Tim Wilmot, www.beechwell.com. *10m NE of Bristol. From Yate centre, go N onto Church Ln. After ½ m turn L onto Greenways Rd then R onto Church Ln. After 300yds take R fork, garden 100yds on L. Sun 11 Sept (1-5). Adm £3.50, chd free. Home-made teas.*
Enclosed, level, subtropical garden created over last 27 yrs and filled with exotic planting, incl palms (over 6 varieties), tree ferns, yuccas, agaves and succulent bed, rare shrubs, bamboos, bananas, aroids and other architectural planting. Wildlife pond and koi pond. C16 40ft deep well. Rare plant raffle every hour. Some narrow pathways.

♿ ☕

11 NEW 24 BIRCH ROAD
Martock TA12 6DR. Brenda Ellis, 01935 826624, b.ellis212@sky.com. *1m from A303 Martock turnoff. A303 into Martock, past church on L, Beech Rd 1st L before pedestrian crossing, opp shopping car park. Birch Rd is 1st R. Parking in shopping centre car park only. Disabled parking*

at house. Sat 30, Sun 31 July (1-4). Adm £3, chd free. Cream teas. **Visits also by arrangement June to Aug.**
Level walled cottage garden with border perennials, shrubs, fruit trees, raised vegetable beds, roses, pots of herbs and flowers, unusual plants, wildlife pond. Colour and interest from spring to autumn. Assistance dogs allowed on lead.

&. ⊗ ☕

BRADON FARM
Isle Abbotts, Taunton TA3 6RX. Mr & Mrs Thomas Jones, deborahjstanley@hotmail.com. *Take turning to Ilton off A358. Bradon Farm is 1 1/2 m out of Ilton on Bradon Lane. Visits by arrangement May to Sept for groups of 6 - 40. Adm £5, chd free. Home-made teas.*
A classic formal garden created in recent years, demonstrating the effective use of structure. There is much to see incl parterre, knot garden, pleached lime walk, formal pond, herbaceous borders, orchard and wildflower planting. Featured in Somerset County Gazette, Western Gazette.

&. 🚌 ☕

GROUP OPENING

BRENT KNOLL GARDENS
Highbridge TA9 4DF. *2m N of Highbridge. Off A38 & M5 J22. From M5 take A38 N (Cheddar etc) first L into Brent Knoll. Sun 24 July (11-5). Combined adm £7, chd free. Light refreshments and cream teas at Ball Copse Hall.*

BALL COPSE HALL
Mrs S Boss & Mr A J Hill
Visits also by arrangement Mar to Oct
susan.boss@gmail.com
01278 760301

ORCHARD
Roger & Lyn Brafield

PEN ORCHARD
John & Wiet Harper

The distinctive hill of Brent Knoll, an iron age hill fort, is well worth climbing 449ft for the 360 degree view of surrounding hills incl Glastonbury Tor and the Somerset Levels. Lovely C13 church renowned for its bench ends. Ball Copse Hall: S-facing Edwardian house (not open) on lower slopes of Knoll. Front garden maturing well with curving slopes and paths. Ha-ha, wild

area and kitchen garden. Views to Quantock and Polden Hills. Kitchen garden enclosed by crinkle crankle wall. Flock of Soay sheep. Working beehive on show with honey for sale. Pen Orchard is a lovely garden with several developements since last open. A busy person's garden to relax in. Orchard last opened 20yrs ago so a lot of maturing has happened! Wheelchair access in all gardens, some restricted.

&. 🐕 ⊗ ☕

BROOMCLOSE
Porlock, Minehead TA24 8NU. David & Nicky Ramsay, 01643 862078, davidjamesramsay@gmail.com. *Off A39 on Porlock Weir Rd, between Porlock and West Porlock. From Porlock take rd signed to Porlock Weir. Leave houses of Porlock behind, park in 2nd field on R (75m walk to property). NB Some SatNavs direct wrongly from Porlock - beware! Sat 11, Sun 12 June (2-6). Combined adm with Halsecombe House £5, chd free. Home-made teas at Broomclose only.* **Visits also by arrangement Mar to Oct.**
Large varied garden set around turn of century Arts and Crafts house overlooking the sea. Original stone terraces, Mediterranean garden, long borders, copse, camellia walk, wild flower meadow and vegetable garden. Maritime climate favours unusual sub-tropical trees, shrubs and herbaceous plants.

⊗ ☕

CAMERS
Old Sodbury BS37 6RG. Mr & Mrs A G Denman, 01454 322430, dorothydenman@camers.org, www.camers.org. *2m E of Chipping Sodbury. Entrance in Chapel Lane off A432 at Dog Inn. Sun 31 July (2-5). Adm £5, chd free. Home-made teas.* **Visits also by arrangement Feb to Sept for groups of 20+.**
Elizabethan farmhouse (not open) set in 4 acres of constantly developing garden and woodland with spectacular views over Severn Vale. Garden full of surprises, formal and informal areas planted with very wide range of species to provide yr-round interest. Parterre, topiary, Japanese garden, bog and prairie areas, waterfalls, white and hot gardens, woodland walks. Some steep slopes.

&. 🐕 ⊗ ☕

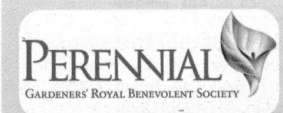 9 CATHERSTON CLOSE
Frome, Somerset BA11 4HR. Dave & Prue Moon. *15m S of Bath. Town centre W towards Shepton Mallet (A361). R at Sainsbury's r'about, follow lane for 1/2 m. L into Critchill Rd. Over Xrds, 1st L Catherston Close. Wed 15 June, Wed 6 July (12-5). Adm £3.50, chd free. Opening with Frome Gardens on Sun 12 June, Sun 19 June.*
A town garden which has grown over the years to 1/3 acre! Colour-themed shrub and herbaceous borders, pond, patios, pergolas and wild meadow areas lead to wonderful far reaching views. Productive vegetable and fruit garden with greenhouse. Exhibition of garden photography by the garden owner, from near and far, is displayed in the summerhouse. Gold winner in Frome-in-Bloom Competition. A surprise in waiting. Featured in The Visitor, regional press with Radio Bristol, Somerset and Glastonbury fm. Several shallow steps, gravel paths.

&. ⊗

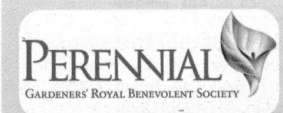

NEW 25 CHAUCER ROAD
Bath BA2 4QX. Tina Payne. *From centre of Bath follow signs to Radstock (A367) along Wellsway to Bear Flat. At T-lights by The Bear PH take any road to L and these will take you to junction with Chaucer Road. Sat 28, Sun 29 May (1.30-5). Adm £3, chd free. Home-made teas.*
Compact town garden designed by present owners which has achieved Bath In Bloom gold and silver gilt awards. A courtyard of potted plants surrounded by attractive colour co-ordinated herbaceous borders leads to the next levels which include small fish pond, resident tortoise and vegetable section. Garden is open to coincide with the Bear Flat Artists weekend.

⊗ ☕

18 CHERRY BOLBERRY FARM
Furge Lane, Henstridge BA8 0RN.
Mrs Jenny Raymond, 01963
362177,
cherrybolberryfarm@tiscali.co.uk.
*6m E of Sherborne. In centre of
Henstridge, R at small Xrds signed
Furge Lane. Continue straight up
lane, over 2 cattle grids, garden at
top of lane on R.* Visits by
arrangement May & June for
groups of 10+. Adm £5, chd free.
Home-made teas.

40 yr-old award winning, owner
designed and maintained 1 acre
garden planted for yr round interest
with wildlife in mind. Colour themed
island beds, shrub and herbaceous
borders, unusual perennials and
shrubs, old roses and an area of
specimen trees. Lots of hidden areas,
brilliant for hide and seek! Vegetable
and flower cutting garden,
greenhouses, nature ponds.
Wonderful extensive views. Garden
surrounded by our dairy farm which
has been in the family for nearly 100
years. You will see Jersey cows,
sheep, horses and hens!

19 CHURCH FARM HOUSE
Turners Court Lane, Binegar, nr
Wells BA3 4UA. Susan & Tony
Griffin, 01749 841628,
smgriffin@beanacrebarn.co.uk,
www.beanacrebarn.co.uk. *5m NE
of Wells. From Wells B3139 NE for
4¹/₂ m, turn R signed Binegar, yellow
NGS sign at Xrds. From A37 in
Gurney Slade at George Inn follow
sign to Binegar, past church, at Xrds
NGS sign turn R into Turners Court
Lane.* Sun 29 May, Wed 1, Sun 26,
Wed 29 June, Sun 24, Wed 27 July
(11-4.30). Adm £4, chd free. Visits
also by arrangement June to Aug,
adm £4.50.

Wrapped around an old farmhouse
are two walled gardens planted in
contemporary cottage style, roses
and clematis on walls and unusual
perennials in deep borders give
interest all seasons. South garden
has progressive colourist design. The
ever expanding insect friendly
planting in the gravel of the old
farmyard creates an interesting
display of form and colour often with
self-seeded surprises! Featured in
regional press and radio, Western
Morning News and Mendip Times.
Gravel forecourt, 2 shallow steps.

GROUP OPENING

20 NEW CHURCHILL GARDENS
Churchill, nr Winscombe
BS25 5NB. *14m S of Bristol. Turn off
A38 onto A371 at Churchill T-lights.
All 3 gardens are in older part of
village.* Sat 16, Sun 17 July (2-5).
Combined adm £5, chd free. Light
refreshments at Bay Tree House.

NEW BAY TREE HOUSE
Paul & Pam Millward

NEW CHURCH VIEW
John Simmons & Jill Maycock

NEW LAUREL COTTAGE
Colin Riddington & Alyson
Holland
Visits also by arrangement
June to Aug for individuals or
small groups
c.riddington@btinternet.com
01934 852093

Bay Tree House: 2¹/₂ acres with partly
walled vegetable and fruit garden,
formal lawn with seasonally planted
beds and rose garden. Victorian
rockery, courtyard with camellias and
fig tree, thatched summerhouse, tree
house, laburnum arch, ponds, and
mature Araucaria, Wellingtonia and
beech trees. The layout is essentially
unchanged from when the house was
built, c1830. Church View: mature
and overgrown 4 years ago, now
includes fruit and vegetable beds and
borders of shrubs and perennials. A
wildflower area and shade garden are
still emerging. Recent landscaping
incl themed planting, pond, patio
and, hopefully, a few exotics!
Secluded Laurel Cottage garden has
views to surrounding hills. A
plantaholics garden with all the right
plants but not necessarily in the right
order, developed to encourage wildlife
incl birds, butterflies, bees and frogs.
Features incl pond, greenhouse,
mature trees and shrubs, mixed
borders, thriving fruit and vegetable
plot (badger permitting!).

Thriving fruit and
vegetable plot
(badger
permitting!). . .

GROUP OPENING

21 CONGRESBURY GARDENS
Congresbury, Bristol BS49 5DN.
*Approx halfway between Bristol and
Weston-super-Mare. 13m S of Bristol
on A370. As you enter Congresbury
look for signs. Parking in village
centre at Ship & Castle PH and N of
bridge. Street parking available at
outlying gardens.* Sun 12 June
(10.30-4). Combined adm £5, chd
free. Home-made teas at
Fernbank and Middlecombe
Nursery.

CHURCH HOUSE
Mrs Lorraine Coles

FERNBANK
Julia Thyer
http://:juliathyer.blogspot.co.uk

LABURNUM COTTAGE
Mrs Mary Gilbert

MIDDLECOMBE NURSERY
Nigel J North
www.middlecombenursery.co.u
k

NEW 8 PAULS CAUSEWAY
Mr David Anderson

29 STONEWELL LANE
Mike & Janet Sweeting

YEO MEADS
Debbie Fortune & Mark
Hayward

Village group of 7 strikingly
contrasting gardens. Fernbank:
romantic haven for wildlife. Follow
paths to surprises, explore the
potager and picturesque greenhouse,
potter in the potting shed, lily ponds
with trickling water and more. Yeo
Meads: formally laid out in C17 incl
350yr-old Cedar of Lebanon tree
which fell in 2007 but survives as a
feature, Atlas Blue cedar, 150 yr-old
lime. Church House: courtyard
garden that shows what you can do
with an enclosed space within the
confines of the village. Laburnham
Cottage: Informal S-facing tranquil
rear garden. 8 Pauls Causeway:
Extensive traditional village garden
with many established rose beds
shrub and tree borders and
herbaceous beds. Middlecombe
Nursery: 3 acre nursery site in
country setting with series
of different gardens, owned by
Nigel North, a regular contributor to
BBC Radio Bristol. 29 Stonewell
Lane: garden to encourage wildlife
with a cottage garden feel with

borders, mature trees, pond and herbaceous perennials. No wheelchair access at Church House.

GROUP OPENING

22 COOMBE GARDENS AT THURLOXTON
Taunton TA2 8RE. *6m S of Bridgwater, 4m N of Taunton. Signed off A38 between Taunton and Bridgwater.* Sun 19 June (2-5.30). Combined adm £5, chd free. Cream teas at Coombe Quarry.

COOMBE QUARRY
Miss Patricia Davies-Gilbert

COOMBE WATER
Mr & Mrs M K Paul

THE COTTAGE
Jane Stott

DINGLEBROOK
Paul Wills & Penny Sharp

Delightful medium-sized gardens in hamlet between West Monkton & Thurloxton. Coombe Quarry: cottage garden with quarry walk. Roses, shrubs, vegetables, fruit and animals. Partial wheelchair access, quarry walk inaccessable. Coombe Water: cottage garden in secluded valley, stream and pond. Wide variety of trees, plants and roses. Dinglebrook: divided garden with much colour next to Coombe Water.The Cottage: tiered borders. Adjacent Thurloxton Church worth a visit with the two Jubilee windows, Victoria and ER. Wheelchair access in 3 gardens.

23 NEW CORTON DENHAM HOUSE
Corton Denham, Sherborne DT9 4LR. Dr & Mrs Robin Odgers, 01963 220205, odgers@cortondenhamhouse.co.uk, www.cortondenhamhouse.co.uk. *3m S of A303 at South Cadbury junction (signed Corton Denham) and 3m N of Sherborne. Situated in centre of the village.* Visits by arrangement May & June for groups of 10+, weekdays and weekday evenings only. Adm £7.50.
5 acre garden and 3 acre arboretum, surrounding fine Grade II Georgian rectory, wonderfully situated beneath the backdrop of Corton Hill. Extensively redesigned and replanted

9 Catherston Close, Frome Gardens

over past 15yrs, featuring majestic mature trees, mixed borders, lawns, formal walled kitchen garden, lake, stream garden and arboretum. In excess of 150 varieties of tree and 150 varieties of rose. Good wheelchair access throughout (on grass) but some steep slopes.

24 COTHAY MANOR & GARDENS
Greenham, Wellington TA21 0JR. Mr & Mrs Alastair Robb, 01823 672283, cothaymanor@btinternet.com, www.cothaymanor.co.uk. *5m SW of Wellington. 7m off M5 via A38, signed Greenham, follow brown signs for Cothay Manor & Gardens. See website for more detailed directions.* For NGS: Sun 31 July (1.30-4.30). Adm £7.50, chd £3.75. Home-made teas. For other opening times and information, please phone, email or visit garden website.
Few gardens are as evocatively romantic as Cothay. Laid out in 1920s and replanted in 1990s within the original framework, Cothay encompasses a rare blend of old and new. Plantsman's paradise set in 12 acres of magical gardens. Antiques, garden shop, tea room. Sorry no dogs or picnicing in gardens. Sunday house tours 11:45 and 2:15. £14.25 (ticket price incl garden entrance), advance booking recommended. Partial wheelchair access, gravel paths.

25 COURT HOUSE
East Quantoxhead TA5 1EJ. East Quantoxhead Estate (Hugh Luttrell Esq), 01278 741271, hugh_luttrell@yahoo.co.uk. *12m W of Bridgwater. Off A39, house at end of village past duck pond. Enter by Frog Lane (Bridgwater/Kilve side from A39). Car park 50p in aid of church.* For NGS: Sun 15 May, Sun 17 July (2-5). Adm £4, chd free. Teas. For other opening times and information, please phone or email.
Lovely 5 acre garden, trees, shrubs (many rare and tender), herbaceous and 3 acre woodland garden with spring interest and late summer borders. Traditional kitchen garden (chemical free). Views to sea and Quantocks. Gravel, stone and some mown grass paths.

26 CROWCOMBE COURT
Crowcombe, Taunton TA4 4AD. Mr & Mrs David Kenyon. *11m NW of Taunton. On A358.* Sun 17 Apr, Sun 3 July (2-5). Adm by donation. Teas.
Magnificent Grade 1 listed house (partly open to serve teas) which has benefitted from extensive refurbishment. The 10 acres of gardens, previously sadly neglected, are now being rejuvenated under new ownership. Woodland garden, lake, walled garden, all undergoing a rescue mission! Wheelchair access through most of garden.

ALLOTMENTS

27 DAGGS ALLOTMENTS
High Street, Thornbury BS35 2AW, 01454 415019, alison_makepeace@hotmail.com, www.thornburyallotments.com. Park in free car park off Chapel St. Visits by arrangement June to Aug for groups of 8 - 20. Adm £4, chd free. Coffee shops, cafes and PHs are available nearby in Thornbury High St.
Thornbury is a historic market town and has been a regular winner of awards in the RHS Britain in Bloom competition. 120 plots, all in cultivation, many organic, incl vegetables, soft fruit, herbs and flowers for cutting. Narrow, steep, grass paths between plots. A plot holder will be available to answer any questions you may have about the plots, cultivation techniques and varieties grown. Short talk on the history of Daggs since 1546.

28 THE DAIRY
Clevedon Road, Weston-in-Gordano, Bristol BS20 8PZ. Mrs Christine Lewis, 01275 849214, chris@dairy.me.uk. Weston in Gordano is on B3124 Portishead to Clevedon road. Find Parish Church on main road and take lane down side of churchyard for 200m. Sat 13, Sun 14 Aug (2-5). Adm £4, chd free. Home-made teas. Visits also by arrangement May to Sept, narrow access - small coaches only.
1 acre garden surrounded by wildlife reserve, with extensive views over the Gordano Valley. Developed over 12 years from concrete cattle yards and tipped land, and not yet complete. North and south courtyards planted for winter and summer interest. Lower garden has large pond and is planted to peak from midsummer to autumn. Separate fruit and vegetable garden. Changes of level, with steps and gravel paths, make wheelchair access difficult.

29 ◆ DYRHAM PARK
Bath SN14 8ER. National Trust, 01179 371331, dale.dennehy@nationaltrust.org.uk, www.nationaltrust.org.uk/dyrham-park. 8m N of Bath, 12m E of Bristol. On Bath to Stroud rd (A46), 2m S of Tomarton interchange with M4, J18.

SatNav use SN14 8HY. For NGS: Sat 4, Sun 5 June (10-5). Adm £5.20, chd £2.60. For other opening times and information, please phone, email or visit garden website.
C17 mansion with formal gardens on west side, lawns, herbaceous borders, fine yew hedges, ponds and cascade. Nichols orchard with perry pear trees, wild flower meadow. On E side of house is C17 orangery traditionally used for citrus plants. Garden tours, including a look at the historic pear orchard, at various times during both days. Please see NT website for times. Special tours for NGS opening, ask at Visitor Reception on the day. Steep slopes in park, cobbles in courtyard. Disabled WC.

30 EAST BURFORD HOUSE
Summer Hill Lane, West Compton, Pilton BA4 4PA. Christopher & Lindsay Bond. 3m W of Shepton Mallet. Xrds at bottom of hill in Pilton on A361 go uphill between PH and former shop for 1/2 m into bottom of valley, black gates on L beyond turn to farm. Sun 5, Mon 6 June (10.30-5). Adm £4.50, chd free. Home-made teas.
Set in isolated Mendip valley. 3 acre garden full of surprises surrounds a fine country house (not open). Formal walled and wild gardens, different areas incl herbaceous, bog, woodland, gravel, wisteria, pergola, desert, raised strawberry beds, lake with shell beach, rills, pagoda, pavilion, sculptures and children's playground. Hillside woodland walk, bring own picnic, dogs welcome. Stout shoes advised. Many garden sculptures and water features. Allow 1 hour to tour gardens and 30 minutes for woods. Please see http://thebristolmag.co.uk/explore-east-burford-house/. Wheelchair access limited to formal garden.

31 EAST END FARM
Pitney, Langport TA10 9AL. Mrs A M Wray, 01458 250598. 2m E of Langport. Please telephone for directions. Visits by arrangement in June. Adm £3, chd free.
Approx 1/3 acre. Timeless small garden of many old-fashioned roses in beautiful herbaceous borders set amongst ancient listed farm buildings. Mostly wheelchair access.

32 ◆ EAST LAMBROOK MANOR GARDENS
Silver Street, East Lambrook TA13 5HH. Mike & Gail Werkmeister, 01460 240328, enquiries@eastlambrook.com, www.eastlambrook.com. 2m N of South Petherton. Follow brown tourist signs from A303 South Petherton r'about or B3165 Xrd with lights N of Martock. For NGS: Sun 7 Feb, Sat 14 May, Sun 5 June (10-5). Adm £5.75, chd free. Tea. 2017: Sun 19 Feb. For other opening times please see below.
The quintessential English cottage garden created by C20 gardening legend Margery Fish. Plantsman's paradise with old-fashioned and contemporary plants grown in a relaxed and informal manner to create an extraordinary garden of great beauty and charm. With noted collections of snowdrops, hellebores and geraniums and the excellent specialist Margery Fish Plant Nursery. Plant Fair Easter Sat. Moish Sokal watercolour exhibition June. Also open Feb and May to July Tues to Sun & BH Mons; Mar, Apr and Aug to Oct Tues to Sat and BH Mons; (10-5). Featured in Daily Mail Weekend magazine, Somerset Life, The Guardian Weekend magazine, Country Life. Partial wheelchair access only due to narrow gravel paths and steps.

In excess of 150 varieties of tree and 150 varieties of rose . . .

33 ◆ ELWORTHY COTTAGE
Elworthy, Taunton TA4 3PX. Mike & Jenny Spiller, 01984 656427, mike@elworthy-cottage.co.uk, www.elworthy-cottage.co.uk. 12m NW of Taunton. On B3188 between Wiveliscombe and Watchet. For NGS: Sun 7, Mon 8 Feb, Mon 28 Mar, Tue 12 Apr, Tue 24, Mon 30 May, Tue 7, Tue 14 June, Tue 23, Mon 29 Aug, Tue 13 Sept (11-5). Adm £3, chd free. 2017: Feb openings to be announced on NGS website and in local press. Visitors also welcome by arrangement April to September and in February for Snowdrops.

1 acre plantsman's garden in tranquil setting. Island beds, scented plants, clematis, unusual perennials and ornamental trees and shrubs to provide yr round interest. In spring pulmonarias, hellebores and more than 250 varieties of snowdrops. Planted to encourage birds, bees and butterflies, lots of birdsong. Wild flower areas, decorative vegetable garden, living willow screen. Stone ex privy and pigsty feature. Adjoining nursery. Also open Thurs Apr - Aug incl (10-5).

34 14 ESKDALE CLOSE
Weston-super-Mare BS22 8QG. Janet & Adrian Smith, 01934 414543, ajs43jes46@yahoo.co.uk. *1½ m E of WsM town centre. From M5 J21, take B3440 to town centre, L at Corondale Rd, R into Garsdale Rd. Take footpath next to number 37.* Visits by arrangement Apr to Aug, groups of 25 max. Adm £3, chd free. Home-made teas.
Cottage style garden containing over 250 different plants. Pond and Mediterranean area with seating. 50 different conifers showing contrast of colour and form on raised rockery. Wisteria archway leads to productive area of fruit trees, herb garden and vegetable plot. Voted best large garden in Weston Horticultural Society's Weston in Bloom 2015. No wheelchair access to vegetable patch.

35 FAIRFIELD
Stogursey, Bridgwater TA5 1PU. Lady Acland Hood Gass. *7m E of Williton. 11m W of Bridgwater. From A39 Bridgwater to Minehead rd turn N. Garden 1½ m W of Stogursey on Stringston rd. No coaches.* Sun 17 Apr (2-5). Adm £4, chd free. Home-made teas.
Woodland garden with bulbs, shrubs and fine trees. Paved maze. Views of Quantocks and sea.

36 FERNHILL
Whiteball, Wellington TA21 0LU. Peter & Audrey Bowler, 01823 672423, muldoni@hotmail.co.uk, www.sampfordarundel.org.uk/fernhill/. *3m W of Wellington. At top of Whiteball hill on A38 on L going W just before dual carriageway, parking on site.* Sun 26 June, Sun 31 July, Sun 21 Aug (2-5). Adm £3.50, chd free. Tea. Visits also by

arrangement June to Aug for groups of 10+.
In approx 2 acres, a delightful garden to stir your senses, with a myriad of unusual plants and features. Intriguing almost hidden paths leading through English roses and banks of hydrangeas. Scenic views stretching up to the Blackdowns and its famous monument. Truly a Hide and Seek garden..... for all ages. Well stocked herbaceous borders, octagonal pergola and water garden with slightly wild boggy area. Wheelchair access to terrace and other parts of garden from drive.

The NGS: Marie Curie's largest ever benefactor . . .

37 FOREST LODGE
Pen Selwood BA9 8LL. Mr & Mrs James Nelson, 07974 701427, lucillanelson@gmail.com. *1½ m N of A303, 3m E of Wincanton. Leave A303 at B3081 (Wincanton to Gillingham rd), up hill to Pen Selwood, L towards church. ½ m, garden on L.* Thur 7 Apr, Thur 26 May, Thur 23 June (2.30-4.30). Adm £5, chd free. Home-made teas. Visits also by arrangement Apr to Oct for groups of 5+.
Donation to Heads Up Wells.
3 acre mature garden with many camellias and rhododendrons in May. Lovely views towards Blackmore Vale. Part formal with pleached hornbeam allée and rill, part water garden with lake. Wonderful roses in June. Unusual spring flowering trees such as Davidia Involucrata, many beautiful cornus. Interesting garden sculpture. Featured on BBC Open Gardens and in Country Homes and Interiors. Wheelchairs can access front garden only however much of garden viewable from there.

38 1 FROBISHER ROAD
Ashton Gate, Bristol BS3 2AU. Karen Thomas. *2m SW of city centre. Bristol City FC on R, next R Duckmoor Rd, 5th turning L before bollards.* Sun 10 July, Sun 21 Aug (2-5). Adm £3, chd free. Home-made teas in conservatory.
Compact city garden. Comments from visitors: 'Breathtaking amount of

plants you have, fantastic, a haven, magical, like in a wood, amazing so many different plants, it's a Tardis'. One 6 inch step in back garden.

GROUP OPENING

39 FROME GARDENS
Frome BA11 4HR. *15m S of Bath. 9 Catherson Close signed from Sainsbury r'about, W side of town, towards Shepton Mallet A361. Mercers Cottage no 41 from either end of Robins Lane, half way along. Signed on A362 Frome to Radstock rd.* Sun 12, Sun 19 June (12-5). Combined adm £4.50, chd free.

9 CATHERSTON CLOSE
Dave & Prue Moon
(See separate entry)

NEW MERCERS COTTAGE
Ms Sally Ferrers

2 varied gardens. 9 Catherston Close: (see separate entry). Mercers Cottage has been a work in progress for 4 yrs, with ongoing changes. From being uninteresting and non productive, the garden is being transformed with a wealth of plants and shrubs, unique art works, statuary and a small wildlife pond. Featured in regional press and radio, The Visitor and Western Morning News. Catherston Close has some gravel paths, slopes and shallow steps. Mercers Cottage not suitable for wheelchair users.

40 GANTS MILL & GARDEN
Gants Mill Lane, Bruton BA10 0DB. Elaine & Greg Beedle, www.gantsmill.co.uk. *½ m SW of Bruton. From Bruton centre take Yeovil rd, A359, under railway bridge, 100yds uphill, fork R down Gants Mill Lane. Parking for wheelchair users.* Sun 10 July (2-5). Adm £6, chd free. Home-made teas.
¾ acre garden. Clematis, rose arches and pergolas, streams, ponds, waterfalls. Riverside walk to top weir, delphiniums, day lilies, 100+ dahlia varieties, vegetable, soft fruit and cutting flower garden. Garden is overlooked by the historic watermill, open on NGS day. Firm wide paths round the garden. Narrow entrance to mill not accessible to wheelchairs. WC.

Fernbank, Congresbury Gardens

GROUP OPENING

41 GLASTONBURY SECRET GARDENS

Glastonbury BA6 9JJ. *100yds from Glastonbury Mkt Cross in Northload St (pedestrian area). Off A39 at Beckery r'about into Sedgemoor Way then take 2nd R into Northload West meter C/P. Garden entrances clearly signed.* Sun 17 July (1-4). Combined adm £4, chd free. Light refreshments at Jacob's Loft.

JACOB'S LOFT
William Knight
01458 835144
info@glastonburyholidayhomes.com
www.glastonburyholidayhomes.com

SAINT MARGARET'S CHAPEL GARDEN
Ms Sandra Booth
www.stmargaretschapel.org.uk

Jacob's Loft: 100 yds from Glastonbury Market Cross in Northload St. Inner town courtyard garden, example of what can be achieved in urban environment. Formerly rear gardens of inner town commercial properties and a Victorian/Georgian Terrace. Collection of agricultural and horticultural tools and artefacts. St Margaret's Chapel garden is accessed down a rather small alleyway, but in turning the corner everyone, without exception, gasps at the calm splendour of the garden, the peace of the C11 chapel and the ancient almshouses. Whether you are a pilgrim or a garden lover or both, we welcome you to these havens of peace, beauty, and tranquility. While in bohemian Glastonbury visit our curious/quirky range of shops, our famous Abbey and if you feel energetic climb Glastonbury Tor. Glastonbury in Bloom Gold Award and RHS 'It's Your Neighbourhood' Outstanding Award.

42 GLEBE FARMHOUSE

Lower Street, Buckland Dinham, Frome BA11 2QN. Marie & Andrew Gilchrist. *1m NE of Frome on A362. On A362, from Frome 1st L into Lower St; from Radstock last R at bottom of hill. Parking, centre of village close church, disabled & limited mobility drop off at farmhouse prior to parking near church.* Sat 16, Sun 24 July (10-5). Adm £4, chd free. Home-made teas.
At edge of village with extensive views of surrounding countryside lies this ½ acre garden surrounding a Georgian farmhouse (not open). Landscaped by present owners into separate planting areas consisting of terrace garden, parterre with charming cottage, shade walk and 2 further traditional gardens of attractive mixed and herbaceous colour themed borders. Featured in regional press/radio.

43 GOBLIN COMBE HOUSE

Plunder Street, Cleeve, Bristol BS49 4PQ. Mrs H R Burn, 01934 838599, hilaryburn@live.co.uk. *10m S of Bristol. A370, turn L onto Cleeve Hill Rd before Lord Nelson Inn; 300m L onto Plunder St, 1st drive on R. Parking just beyond Plunder St turning. On main bus route.* Wed 11 May, Wed 15, Wed 22, Wed 29 June (2-5). Adm £4, chd free. Home-made teas. **Visits also by arrangement May & June, groups of 8+.**
2 acre terraced garden with lovely views. Interesting collection of trees, mixed shrubs and herbaceous borders, surrounded by orchards, fields and woodlands. Home to the rare plant purple gromwell found on woodland edges with alkaline soils. Highly recommended by Trevor Fry from Radio Bristol. Uneven and steep paths, very slippery when wet.

44 GREYSTONES

Hollybush Lane, Bristol BS9 1JB. Mr & Mrs P Townsend. *2m N of Bristol city centre, close to Durdham Down in Bristol, backing onto the Botanic Garden. A4018 Westbury Rd, L at White Tree r'about, L into Saville Rd, Hollybush Lane 2nd on R. Narrow lane, parking limited, recommended to park in Saville Rd.* Sun 15 May (2-5). Adm £3, chd free. Also open Lucombe House, teas at Lucombe House.
Peaceful garden with places to sit and enjoy a quiet corner of Bristol. Interesting courtyard with raised beds and large variety of conifers and shrubs leads to secluded garden of contrasts - from sun drenched beds with olive tree and brightly coloured flowers to shady spots, with acers, hostas and a fern walk. Small apple orchard, espaliered pears and koi pond. Paved footpath provides level access to all areas.

45 NEW HALSECOMBE HOUSE
Parsons Hill, Porlock, Minehead TA24 8QP. Dr Judy Baxter. *On top of Porlock Hill. Follow A39 through Porlock and up Porlock Hill to top of tree line. When road bends sharply R, take L farm track, follow to end. For SatNav, use postcode TA24 8QH.* Sat 11, Sun 12 June (2-6). Combined adm with Broomclose £5, chd free.
Set on top of Porlock Hill with outstanding views of Welsh coast, the Bristol Channel and surrounding Exmoor hills, this garden has a breathtaking location. Comprises a mixture of lawns on different levels all with sweeping views of surrounding countryside. Of special interest are the series of ponds and 3 state-of-the-art, kidney-shaped reed beds, richly stocked with bulrushes, reeds, irises, kingcups and home to herons, ducks, butterflies and dragonflies. Fine examples of Exmoor drystone walls throughout garden. House is circled by generously sized beds featuring roses, agapanthus, heathers, hebe, irises, poppy, camellias and rhododendrons. Woodland walks for the more adventurous visitors!

46 HANGERIDGE FARMHOUSE
Wrangway, Wellington TA21 9QG. Mrs J M Chave, 01823 662339, hangeridge@hotmail.co.uk. *2m S of Wellington. 1m off A38 bypass signed Wrangway. 1st L towards Wellington Monument, over M'way bridge 1st R.* Sun 10 Apr, Sun 10, Sun 24 July (2-5). Adm £3, chd free. Home-made teas. Visits also by arrangement Apr to Aug for groups of 10+.
Rural fields and mature trees surround this 1 acre informal garden offering views of the Blackdown and Quantock Hills. Magnificent hostas and heathers, colourful flower beds, cascading wisteria and roses and a trickling stream are features on offer. Relax with homemade refreshments on sunny or shaded seating admiring the views and birdsong.

47 HANHAM COURT
Ferry Road, Hanham Abbots BS15 3NT. Hanham Court Gardens, www.hanhamcourtgardens.co.uk. *5m E of Bristol centre. Old Bristol Rd A431 from Bath, through Willsbridge (past Queen's Head), L at mini r'about, down Court Farm Rd for 1m.* Drive entrance on sharp L bend between signs on Court Farm Rd. For NGS: Sat 6, Sun 7 Feb (11-4); Sat 28, Sun 29, Mon 30 May, Sat 25, Sun 26 June (12-5). Adm £5, chd free. Tea.
Hanham Court Gardens develop this rich mix of bold formality, water, woodland, orchard, meadow and kitchen garden with emphasis on scent, structure and romance, set amid a remarkable cluster of manorial buildings between Bath and Bristol. Exclusively open to the NGS. Partial wheelchair access via slopes, caution dense gravel paths throughout.

48 HAYWOOD HOUSE
Littleton-upon-Severn, Bristol BS35 1NT. Andrew & Kath Bealing. *3½ m SW of Thornbury. Located between Elberton & Littleton on Severn, R from Elberton just after Bristol Water.* Sun 24 July (1-5.30). Adm £3.50, chd free. Home-made teas.
Approx 1½ acres with panoramic views over the Severn Estuary. Lawns, mixed borders, koi pond, small arboretum, rockeries. Gravel paths.

Home to herons, ducks, butterflies and dragonflies . . .

49 HENLEY MILL
Henley Lane, Wookey BA5 1AW. Peter & Sally Gregson, 01749 676966, millcottageplants@gmail.com, www.millcottageplants.co.uk. *2m W of Wells, off A371 towards Cheddar. Turn L into Henley Lane, driveway 50yds on L through stone pillars to end of drive.* Visits by arrangement Apr to Oct. Teas/home-made cake by arrangement. Adm £4.50, chd free.
2½ acres beside R Axe. Scented garden with roses, hydrangea borders, shady folly garden and late summer borders with grasses and perennials. Zig-zag boardwalk at river level. Kitchen and cutting garden. Rare Japanese hydrangeas and new Chinese epimediums. Garden is on one level but paths can get a bit muddy after heavy rain.

50 ♦ HESTERCOMBE GARDENS
Cheddon Fitzpaine, Taunton TA2 8LG. Hestercombe Gardens Trust, 01823 413923, info@hestercombe.com, www.hestercombe.com. *4m N of Taunton, less than 6m from J25 of M5. Follow brown tourist signs rather than SatNav.* For NGS: Thur 10 Mar, Tue 7 June (10-5). Adm £10.50, chd £4. For other opening times and information please phone, email or visit garden website.
Georgian landscape garden designed by Coplestone Warre Bampfylde, Victorian terrace and shrubbery and stunning Edwardian Lutyens/Jekyll partnership formal gardens. These together make up 50 acres of woodland walks, temples, terraces, pergolas, lakes and cascades. Hestercombe House is also now open comprising a contemporary art gallery and a second-hand book shop. Special features: restored watermill and barn, lesser horseshoe bats, historic house and family garden trails. Gravel paths, steep slopes, steps. All abilities route marked. A Tramper mobility scooter is available - booking required.

51 HILLCREST
Curload, Stoke St. Gregory, Taunton TA3 6JA. Charles & Charlotte Sundquist. *At top of Curload. From A358 turn L along A378, then branch L to North Curry and Stoke St. Gregory. L ½ m after Willows & Wetlands centre. Hillcrest is 1st on R with parking directions.* Sat 7, Sun 8 May (2-5). Adm £4, chd free. Home-made teas.
The garden boasts stunning views of the Somerset Levels, Burrow Mump and Glastonbury Tor, but even on a hazy day this 5 acre garden offers plenty of interest. Woodland walks, varied borders, flowering meadow and several ponds; also kitchen garden, greenhouses, orchards and unique standing stone as focal point. Most of garden is level. Path through flower meadow to lower pond and wood has gentle but quite long slope.

Share your day out on 🇫 and 🇩

GROUP OPENING

52 HINTON ST GEORGE GARDENS

High Street, Crewkerne TA17 8SE, 01460 76389, kenlyn@devonrex.demon.co.uk. *3m N of Crewkerne. N of A30 Crewkerne-Chard; S of A303 Ilminster Town Rd, at r'about signed Lopen & Merriott, then R to Hinton St George. Coaches must park on High St.* Sun 29, Mon 30 May (2-5.30). Combined adm £5, chd free. Home-made teas at Hooper's Holding. **Visits also by arrangement May to Aug, tea & cakes by prior arrangement.**

HOOPER'S HOLDING
Ken & Lyn Spencer-Mills
Visits also by arrangement May to Aug, tea and cakes by prior arrangement
kenlyn@devonrex.demon.co.uk
01460 76389

THE OLIVE GARDEN
Pat Read
Visits also by arrangement May to Aug.
01460 74043

SOUTH STREET ALLOTMENT
Mr John Studley
Visits also by arrangement May to Sept.
johnstudley12@talktalk.net
07831 489391

Gardens varying in size and style in beautiful hamstone village. C15 church. Country seat of the Earls of Poullett for 600yrs until 1973. Hooper's Holding has a ⅓ acre garden in colour compartments. Rare plants, many exotics, garden mosaics and sculptures. The Olive Garden is a loving restoration of a site which had been neglected for decades, maturing well. The South Street Allotment is a miracle of productivity with ingenious methods of providing water and heating. Sale of art work by Karen Dupe at Hooper's Holding. Hooper's Holding featured in The Bristol & The Bath Magazines. Wheelchair access to Hooper's Holding only.

53 HONEYHURST FARM

Honeyhurst Lane, Rodney Stoke, Cheddar BS27 3UJ. Don & Kathy Longhurst, 01749 870322, donlonghurst@btinternet.com,

www.ciderbarrelcottage.co.uk. *4m E of Cheddar. From A371 between Wells and Cheddar, turn into Rodney Stoke signed Wedmore. Pass church on L and continue for almost 1m.* Sun 24 July (2-5). Adm £3.50, chd free. Home-made teas. **Visits also by arrangement Apr to Sept for groups of 10 to 40.**
²/₃ acre part walled rural garden with babbling brook and 4 acre traditional cider orchard, with views. Specimen hollies, copper beech, paulownia, yew and poplar. Pergolas, arbour and numerous seats. Mixed informal shrub and perennial beds with many unusual plants. Many pots planted with shrubs, hardy and half-hardy perennials. Featured in Bristol Magazine (online). Level, grass and some shingle.

54 JASMINE COTTAGE

26 Channel Road, Clevedon BS21 7BY. Margaret & Michael Redgrave, http://jasminecottage.bologrew.net. *12m W of Bristol. M5 J20, signs to Clevedon seafront, travel N (0.8m), via Wellington Terrace, follow winding rd to St Mary's Church, R into Channel Rd. Half way up on L.* Sun 10 July (2-5.30). Combined adm with Jasmine House £5, chd free. Thur 18 Aug (2-5.30). Adm £3, chd free.
Mature peaceful ⅓ acre cottage style with plants chosen for form, scent and colour. 60ft pergola is covered in various climbing plants including Schisandra sphenanthera. Low maintenance gravel garden with grasses and Geranium sanguineum is decorative for months. Huge Araucaria araucana towers over island bed planted with herbaceous perennials and many salvias.

55 NEW JASMINE HOUSE

17 The Avenue, Clevedon BS21 7DZ. The Poulters. *12m W of Bristol. M5 J20, signs to Clevedon seafront, travel N (0.8m), via Wellington Terrace, follow winding rd. to St Mary's Church, R into Channel Rd. At top Xrds L into The Avenue, entrance 50yds on L.* Sun 24 Apr (2-5.30). Adm £3.50, chd free. Sun 10 July (2-5.30). Combined adm with Jasmine Cottage £5, chd free. Home-made teas. No teas on 24 April.
An acre of mature trees and shrubs surround a beautiful Queen Anne

style house decorated with climbing plants. The garden features rhododendrons, azaleas, camellias, spring-flowering trees, numerous bulbs and a raised pond. Summer colour is provided by varieties of roses, herbaceous perennials and lilies. A Bronze Age Burial Cist (circa 2500 BC) can be viewed.

56 ◆ JEKKA'S HERBETUM

Shellards Lane, Alveston, Bristol BS35 3SY. Mrs Jekka McVicar, 01454 418878, sales@jekkasherbfarm.com, www.jekkasherbfarm.com. *7m N of M5 J16 or 6m S from J14 of M5. 1m off A38 signed Itchington. From M5 J16, A38 to Alveston, past church turn R at junction signed Itchington. M5 J14 on A38 turn L after T-lights to Itchington.* For NGS: Sat 25 June, Sun 7 Aug (10-4). Adm £5, chd free. Home-made teas. **For other opening times and information, please phone, email or visit garden website.**
Jekka's Herbetum is a living herb encyclopaedia displaying the largest collection of culinary herbs in the UK. A wonderful resource for plant identification for the gardener and a gastronomic experience for chefs and cooks. Featured in Delicious Magazine, Financial Times, Sunday Times, Telegraph, Cotswold Style. Wheelchair access possible however terrain is rough from car park to Herbetum.

The QNI founded the NGS

57 NEW 1 KENNION ROAD

Wells BA5 2NP. John & Jean King, 01749 670671, john-king6@sky.com. *From Bristol down Pen Hill, turn 1st R after 30m sign then 3rd L to bottom of Kennion Rd. From Wells take Wookey Hole Rd, R fork 200yds after T-lights into Kennion Rd, garden 2nd on L.* **Visits by arrangement June to Aug, max 30. Refreshments and numbers to be confirmed 2 weeks prior to** visit. Adm £3.50, chd free. Tea. Garden planned for owners' pleasure and leisure. Enter under rose arch across crazy paving path to raised patio, small vegetable area and greenhouse. Well maintained plentiful garden, level lawn bordered by flower beds, productive fruit trees, vines trailing along their host. Summerhouse near covered deck area. Views of the cathedral, quiet and shady areas to sit and enjoy a cup of tea. One small step to access garden.

58 ◆ KILVER COURT SECRET GARDENS
Kilver Street, Shepton Mallet BA4 5NF. 01749 340417, info@kilvercourt.com, www.kilvercourt.com. *Directly off A37 rd to Bath, opp cider factory in Shepton Mallet.* For NGS: Tue 19 Apr, Wed 18 May, Thur 15 Sept (10-5, last entry 4). Adm £5, chd £2.50. Light refreshments in the Sharpham Pantry Restaurant and Harlequin Cafe. For other opening times and information, please phone, email or visit garden website.
Created in 1800s and restored in the early1960's, by the Showering family who commissioned George Whiteleg to recreate his gold medal winning Chelsea garden. The garden, which has recently been featured on BBC, showcases a millpond, herbaceous borders and formal parterre with the most stunning backdrop, the Grade II listed viaduct built for the historical Somerset and Dorset railway. Featured in The Bristol Magazine, Homes and Gardens, Bath, Wells & Frome Life, You, various food magazines, Somerset Life, regional press and radio. Some slopes and rockery not accessible for wheelchairs but can be viewed. Disabled parking in lower car park.

59 LITTLE YARFORD FARMHOUSE
Kingston St Mary, Taunton TA2 8AN. Brian Bradley, 01823 451350, yarford@ic24.net. *3¹/₂ m N of Taunton. From Taunton on Kingston St Mary rd. At 30mph sign turn L at Parsonage Lane. Continue 1¹/₄ m W, to Yarford sign. Continue 400yds. Turn R up concrete rd.* Fri 20 May (11-5). Light refreshments. Sat 21, Sun 22 May (2-5.30). Cream teas. Mon 23 May (11-5). Light refreshments. Adm £4.50,

chd free. Visits also by arrangement May to Oct day or eve.
This unusual garden embraces a C17 house (not open) overgrown with a tapestry of climbing plants. The 3 ponds exhibit a wide range of aquatic gems. Of special interest is the collection of 300 trees, of rare and unusual cultivars, both broad leaf and conifer, all differing in form and colour incl weeping and fastigiate: a tree for every place and occasion. Trees listed on NGS website. Guided tours of trees at 2 & 3.30. The 5 acres are a delight to both artist and plantsman. 'An inspirational, magical experience'. It is an exercise in landscaping and creating views both within the garden and without to the vale and the Quantock Hills. Art Nature Trail with GoCreate. Featured in The Daily Telegraph 'Gardens to Visit'. Mostly wheelchair access.

60 NEW LOWER COCKHILL FARMHOUSE
Cockhill, Castle Cary BA7 7NZ. David Curtis & Biddy Peppin. *1m SW of Castle Cary. From Station Rd Castle Cary turn down Torbay Rd, at bend take rd signed North Barrow for 1m. From Galhampton B3152 look for Cockhill signpost, down steep hill; 2 sharp bends, at fork turn R.* Sat 11, Sun 12 June (2-5.30). Adm £4, chd free. Tea.
Artist's small semi-walled garden concealed in farm setting; narrow paths, no grass, overflowing borders planted for colour with self-seeding welcomed. Pyramidal yews, box-edging and espaliered fruit trees for structure. Artists' studios open. Medieval painted room next door courtesy of Will Vaughan & Pek Peppin (see Pevsner guide; conducted tours only at 2.30 & 3.30, limited numbers). Some narrow paths in garden, one step up into studios; Medieval painted room inaccessible to the less able.

61 LUCOMBE HOUSE
12 Druid Stoke Ave, Stoke Bishop, Bristol BS9 1DD. Malcolm Ravenscroft, 01179 682494, famrave@gmail.com. *4m NW of Bristol centre. On L at top of Druid Hill. Garden on R 200m from junction.* Sun 15 May (2-5). Adm £3, chd free. Home-made teas. Also open Greystones. Visits also by arrangement May to Sept.

Woodland area with over 30 mature trees planted in last 5 yrs underplanted with ferns, bluebells and white foxgloves. Front garden to be redesigned in 2016 to include formal parterre. Separate semi-formal area and untouched wild area under 220yr-old Lucombe oak. Landscape gardener will be on site and happy to answer questions. Rough paths in woodland area, 2 steps to patio.

Artist's small semi-walled garden in farm setting . . .

GROUP OPENING

62 LYMPSHAM GARDENS
Church Road, Lympsham, Weston-super-Mare BS24 0DT. *5m S of Weston-super-Mare and 5m N of Burnham on Sea. 2m M5 J22. Entrance to both gardens from main gates of Manor at junction of Church Rd and Lympsham Rd.* Sat 18, Sun 19 June (2-5). Combined adm £5, chd free. Cream teas.

CHURCH FARM
Andy & Rosemary Carr

LYMPSHAM MANOR
James & Lisa Counsell

At heart of stunning village of Lympsham is C15 church of St Christopher. The Manor, built as the rectory exactly 200 years ago, and C17 Church Farm are by the church and connected to each other by side gate. The Manor is a Gothic pinnacled, castellated rectory manor house with 2 octagonal towers (not open), set in 10 acres of formal and semi-formal garden, surrounded by paddocks and farmland. Main features are its carefully preserved, fully working Victorian kitchen garden and greenhouse, arboretum of trees from all parts of the world, large stocked fish pond and beautiful old rose garden. Old outside Victorian privy. Church Farm: ³/₄ acre informal country garden surrounding farmhouse. Well-stocked herbaceous border, shrub lined paths, raised vegetable beds and small courtyard herb garden. Featured in Mendip Times and local press.

63 ◆ MIDNEY GARDENS
Mill Lane, Midney, Somerton
TA11 7HR. David Chase & Alison
Hoghton, 01458 274250,
www.midneygardens.co.uk. *1m SE
of Somerton. 100yds off B3151.
From Podimore r'about on A303 take
A372. After 1m R on B3151 towards
Street. After 2m L on bend into Mill
Lane.* For NGS: Sun 15 May, Fri 16
Sept (11-5). Adm £4.50, chd free.
Home-made teas/cream teas. For
other opening times and
information, please phone or visit
garden website.
1 acre plantsman's garden, where
unusual planting combinations,
interesting use of colour, subtle
themes and a natural flowing style
create a garden full of variety and
inspiring ideas. Increasingly known for
it's wildlife friendly planting it includes
a seaside garden, Clarice Cliff
inspired garden, white garden,
kitchen garden, woodland walk and
wildlife pond. Garden features a small
undercover area with planting from
around the world. Nursery offers
herbaceous perennials, alpines, herbs
and grasses.

64 ◆ MILTON LODGE
Old Bristol Road, Wells BA5 3AQ.
Simon Tudway Quilter, 01749
672168,
www.miltonlodgegardens.co.uk.
*½ m N of Wells. From A39 Bristol-
Wells, turn N up Old Bristol Rd; car
park 1st gate on L signed.* For NGS:
Sun 15 May, Sun 5 June, Sun 3
July (2-5). Adm £5, chd under 14
free. Tea. Please note Groupon
vouchers are not valid on NGS
open days. For other opening
times and information, please
phone or visit garden website.
Mature Grade II, terraced garden
conceived c1900. Sloping ground
transformed into architectural terraces
with profusion of plants, capitalising on

views of Wells Cathedral and Vale of
Avalon. 1960, garden lovingly restored
to former glory, orchard replaced with
raised collection of ornamental trees.
Cross Old Bristol Rd to 7 acre
woodland garden, the Combe, natural
peaceful contrast to formal garden at
Milton Lodge. First opened for NGS
1962. Also open Tues, Weds, Suns,
BHs, Easter - 31 Oct (2-5). Featured in
regional press, radio and Country
Gardener magazine. Unsuitable for
wheelchairs or those with limited
mobility due to slopes and differing
levels.

65 NEW MODEL FARM
Perry Green, Wembdon,
Bridgwater TA5 2BA. Mr & Mrs
Dave & Roz Young, 01278 429953,
daveandrozontour@hotmail.com,
www.modelfarm.com. *4m from J23
of M5. Follow Brown signs from
r'about on A39 2m W of Bridgwater.*
Sun 5 June (12-5). Adm £4, chd
free. Light refreshments.
4 acres of flat gardens to south of
Victorian country house. Created
from a field in last 6 years and still
being developed. A dozen large
mixed flower beds planted in cottage
garden style with wildlife in mind.
Wooded areas, lawns, wildflower
meadows and wildlife pond. Plenty of
seating throughout the gardens.
Lawn games including croquet.

ALLOTMENTS

**66 NEW MURIEL JONES
FIELD ALLOTMENTS**
Birchill Lane, Feltham, Frome
BA11 5ND. Frome Allotment
Association,
http://fromeallotments.co.uk. *15m
S of Bath. On Frome by-pass (take
A361). At r'about exit B3092 signed
Blatchbridge. Drive approx ½ m
towards Frome, turn R into Birchill
Lane. Continue to allotments, parking
on R.* Tue 5 July (10-5). Adm £4.50,
chd free. Home-made teas.
'The prettiest allotments I've ever
seen' said Penny Snell, ex-Chair of
the NGS. A little piece of heaven
down an overgrown lane, these
allotments are an unexpected
discovery. From no dig to well dug,
the allotments offer a tapestry of
gardening styles. The 98 plots are on
a gently sloping 5-acre site, leading to
the River Frome, with views of Cley
Hill and Longleat forest. Flowers, fruit

and vegetables in abundance. Visitors
are welcome to bring a picnic.
Featured in Kitchen Garden Magazine
and Somerset Standard. Viewing area
over allotments designated for
wheelchair users. Accessible WC.

GROUP OPENING

67 NUNNEY GARDENS
Nunney, nr Frome BA11 4NP. *3m S
of Frome. Nunney Catch, A361
between Frome and Shepton Mallet,
follow signs to Nunney (1m). In
market sq, follow car park signs then
NGS arrows.* Sat 25 June (11-4).
Combined adm £6, chd free. Teas
and plants at Sunny Bank. Home
made cakes.

THE MILLER'S HOUSE
Caroline Toll

SOMERSET LODGE GARDEN
Lord and Lady Watson

SUNNY BANK
Mr & Mrs S Thomas

3 contrasting gardens: Miller's House,
garden of person who considers
herself to be an untidy planter! Mostly
perennial garden, terraced borders,
rockeries, large romantic mill pond
and wild area designed for butterfly
attraction and perfume, areas to sit
and enjoy views of garden. Don't
miss the terraced veg patch and
small modern sculptures. Caution
needed around mill pond steps and
paths. Somerset Lodge, a garden
with many aspects including
topiaries, tall yew pyramids, lavender,
small, tucked away secret garden
leading to a glorious meadow with
many varieties of Rugosa Roses, an
orchard of rare hawthorns with large
wine coloured berries and grey
leaves. Old farmyard developed into a
Mediterranean Courtyard. Sunny
Bank transformed from a former
vegetable plot into intriguing ½ acre
garden providing variety and interest
in numerous sections. 2 subtropical
houses containing cacti and
succulents interspersed with fossils
and unusual natural objects. A garden
with surprises in store! Featured in
regional press, radio, The Visitor and
Western Morning News. Miller's Hse,
2 steps to top lawn for those with ltd
mobility, view of garden & millpond.
Sunny Bnk, incline to garden, outside
view of tropical house.

68 NYNEHEAD COURT

Nynehead, Wellington TA21 0BN. Nynehead Care Ltd, 01823 662481, nyneheadcare@aol.com. *2m N of Wellington. M5 J26 B3187 towards Wellington. R on r'about marked Nynehead & Poole, follow lane for 1m, take Milverton turning at fork.* Sun 28 Feb, Sun 26 June (2-4.30). Adm £4, chd free. Home-made teas in The Orangery. **Visits also by arrangement please telephone for details.**

Nynehead Court Gardens are on English Heritage's list of gardens of historic interest. Once the ancestral home of the Sanford family. Gardens laid out during the Victorian period, points of interest - pinetum, ice house, parterre and extended walks within parkland of old estate. A garden tour, approx 1 hr, will be conducted by Head Gardener, Justin Cole, at 2pm. Visitors can also explore freely using literature available. After 3pm, Justin will be on hand in the garden. Magnificent snowdrops to be seen at our February opening. Limited wheelchair access, cobbled yards/gentle slopes.

69 THE OLD RECTORY, DOYNTON

18 Toghill Lane, Doynton, Bristol BS30 5SY. Edwina & Clive Humby, www.doyntongardens.tumblr.com. *At heart of village of Doynton, between Bath and Bristol. Follow Toghill Lane up from The Holy Trinity Church about 500 metres, around cricket field to car park field. Signs to garden.* Sat 11 June (11-4). Adm £4, chd free. Cream teas.

Doynton's Grade II-listed Georgian Rectory's walled garden and extended 15 acre estate. Renovated over 12 yrs, it sits within AONB. Garden has diversity of modern and traditional elements, fused to create an atmospheric series of garden rooms. It is both a landscaped and large kitchen garden, featuring a canal, vegetable plots, fruit cages and tree house. Partial wheelchair access, some narrow gates and uneven surfaces.

70 THE OLD RECTORY, LIMINGTON

Church St, Limington, Yeovil BA22 8EQ. John Langdon & Paul Vintner, 01935 840127, jdlpv@aol.com. *2m E of Ilchester. From A303 exit on A37 to Yeovil/Ilchester. At 1st r'about L to Ilchester/Limington. 2nd R to Limington. Continue 1½ m.* Sat 4, Sun 5 June (1.30-6). Adm £4, chd free. Cream teas, tea & coffee, cold drinks. **Visits also by arrangement May to July daytime or evening for groups, wine available for evening group visits by prior arrangement.**

Romantic walled gardens of 1½ acres. Formal parterres, herbaceous borders. Many unusual shrubs and trees incl 200 yr-old lucombe oak, liriodendron, laburnocytisus, trochdendron, leycesteria and poncirus. Extensive planting of bulbs incl galanthus, anemone blanda, winter aconites, tulips and alliums. A variety of peaceful seating areas. Gravel drive, one gentle slope only.

71 2 OLD TARNWELL

Stanton Drew, Bristol BS39 4EA. Mrs Mary Payne, 01275 333146, maryjpayne@yahoo.co.uk. *6m S of Bristol. Between B3130 & A368 just W of Pensford. Detailed directions will be given when appt is made.* Visits by arrangement June to Aug for groups 8 -10.

A quart of good plants poured into a quarter-pint sized plot. Front garden planted in contemporary 'steppe' style in shades of yellow and orange. Back garden more traditional cottage style with cool shades. Small greenhouse. Interesting design details and plant selection offer plenty of ideas for small gardeners! Regret not suitable for children. Not suitable for wheelchairs.

72 NEW THE OLD VICARAGE, OVER STOWEY

Over Stowey, Bridgwater TA5 1HA. Mrs Sally Jago. *10m W of Bridgwater. A39 from Bridgwater, L fork at Cottage Inn to Over Stowey. Over Xrds, opp church, car park in field.* Sun 26 June (2-6). Adm £5, chd free. Home-made teas in village hall, opp The Old Vicarage.

Located in the beautiful Quantock Hills and developed from an original 1 acre garden to nearly 3 acres - converting a 3 acre field into an arboretum, large pond, willow arbour, sub-tropical palms and phormiums. The present owner discovered the original dry stone ha-ha built in 1780 by Rev William Holland - the book Paupers and Pig Killers depicts his life at the Old Vicarage - when taking down a cypressus hedge. Quirky garden with a huge eclectic variety of shrubs, trees, grass and agapanthus collection and exotic ornaments from far off lands, 16 raised beds for vegetables. A truly loved space. 'A garden is never finished' is the owner's mantra and each year new projects are in hand. Due to steep slopes, partial wheelchair access only to upper part of garden.

14 Eskdale Close

73 NEW THE OLD VICARAGE, RUISHTON

Church Lane, Ruishton, Taunton TA3 5LL. Mr & Mrs Xanthe & Andrew Lukes. *Opp church through white gates.* **Sun 5, Mon 6 June (2-5). Adm £3, chd free. Cream teas.** This is the 1st year for NGS of a new garden in progress. Much of the 1 acre plot was field but is now laid out and brimming with potential. Traces of the old garden are still in evidence. A lovely terrace overlooks compact formal lawns and pretty walled garden with attractive rope roses and herbaceous beds. Sweeping lawns lead to a wildlife area with pond.

74 NEW THE OLD VICARAGE, WEARE

Sparrow Hill Way, Weare, Axbridge BS26 2LE. Trish & Jeremy Gibson. *2.8m SW of Axbridge. Turn off A38 in Lower Weare, signed Wedmore, Weare. Turn L opp school into Sparrow Hill Way. Continue 0.3m. Garden on R on corner of Coombe Lane.* **Sat 6, Sun 7 Aug (2-5.30). Adm £3.50, chd free. Home-made teas.**

Behind tall hedges, discover a garden in transition - old Victorian shrubberies and a hard tennis court have made way for a relaxed country style of planting. Around charming Georgian outbuildings lie terraces and courtyards, stream garden and vegetable plot in 1½ acres of undulating lawns. Mature trees include ancient yew, giant sequoia. Mendip views. Partial wheelchair access. Some gravel/lawn paths and steep slopes. No disabled WC.

75 NEW ORCHARD VIEW

Flaxpool, Crowcombe, Taunton TA4 4AW. Briar & Roger Norton-Harding. *On A358, 9m SW of Taunton. Approx 5m E of Williton. Garden is at bungalow to rear of Flaxpool Garage forecourt. Parking available at garage.* **Sun 22 May, Sun 7 Aug (10-4). Adm £3, chd free. Cream teas. Selection of beverages. Gluten and dairy free cake alternative.**

Quaint medium sized cottage garden, lined with art pieces and containing diverse features. Attached to this beautiful garden is an artist's ceramics studio. A hidden gem of tranquility.

76 ORGANIC BLOOMS

Latteridge Road (Latteridge Hill), Latteridge, Bristol BS37 9TS. Jo Wright, www.organicblooms.co.uk. *5m W of Yate. On B4059, approx 150m from Latteridge Green. Entrance is at end of green steel corrugated fence that runs along site boundary.* **Sun 3 July (12-4). Adm £4, chd free. Light refreshments.** Working cut flower nursery run as social enterprise. We specialise in growing traditional cut flower crops from sweet williams and anemone to zinnias, dahlias and sweetpeas. We are under conversion to organic status with the Soil Association. We offer supported work experience and training to people with learning difficulties and mental health support needs. Hand-tied bouquet demonstration. Tour and talk on organic cut flower production and the social enterprise. Paths are woodchip, so wheelchair access may be more difficult in very wet conditions.

77 NEW PARK COTTAGE

Wrington Hill, Wrington, Bristol BS40 5PL. Mr & Mrs J Shepherd. *Halfway between Bristol & Weston S Mare. 10m S of Bristol on A370 turn L onto Cleeve Hill Rd before Lord Nelson PH; continue 1½ miles; car park in field on R approx 60yds from garden on L.* **Wed 13, Sat 23 July (11-5). Adm £4, chd free. Home-made teas provided by Wrington Pop-Up Vintage Cafe, proceeds to Weston Hospicecare.**

Follow every path! Take a colourful journey through 1¼ acres of this established, herbaceous perennial garden. The potager, jungle, rainbow border, white garden and 90ft double herbaceous borders are some of the compartments in this 'Alice in Wonderland' garden divided by high hedges. Large Victorian-style greenhouse displays tender plants. Countryside views and plenty of seating. Sorry no dogs. Mostly good wheelchair access, some narrow bark chip paths. Narrow flagstone bridge with steps.

78 PEN MILL FARM

Pen Selwood, Wincanton BA9 8NF. Mr & Mrs Peter FitzGerald, 01 747 840 895, fitzgeraldatpen@aol.com, www.penmillcottage.co.uk. *1m from Stourhead, off A303 between Mere and Wincanton. Leave A303 on A3081 (Bruton exit). Turn off old A303 to Penselwood. 2nd L fork up narrow unsigned lane. R at grass triangle to Zeals down steep hill. Pen Mill Farm is on the R.* **Sat 10 Sept (2-5). Sun 11 Sept (12-5). Adm £4, chd free. Home-made teas. Ploughmans lunches available Sun.**

Romantic garden with acid-loving mature trees and shrubs in secluded valley on Dorset, Somerset and Wiltshire border where tributary of R Stour cascades into the lake. Late summer herbaceous borders with abundant colour and over 40 salvias. Enjoy the peace and quiet of this lovely setting. Plant stall incl unusual salvias. Flock of Castle Milk Sheep. Featured in Garden Answers, Dorset Country Gardener and Dorset Gardens Trust Journal. Mostly wheelchair access. No dogs in garden but car park has shade and dogs can run in the fields.

79 PENNY BROHN CANCER CARE

Chapel Pill Lane, Pill, North Somerset BS20 0HH. Penny Brohn Cancer Care, 01275 370150, andrew.hufford@pennybrohn.org, www.pennybrohncancercare.org. *4m W of Bristol. Off A369 Clifton Suspension Bridge to M5 (J19 Gordano Services). Follow signs to Penny Brohn Cancer Care and to Pill/Ham Green (5 minutes).* **Sun 26 June (10.30-4). Adm £4, chd free. Light refreshments. Bed and breakfast bookings available.**

3½ acre tranquil garden surrounds Georgian mansion with many mature trees, wild flower meadow, flower garden, cedar summerhouse, fine views from historic gazebo overlooking R Avon, courtyard gardens with water features. Garden is maintained by volunteers and plays an active role in the Charity's Living Well with Cancer approach. Plants, teas, music and plenty of space to enjoy a picnic. Gift shop. Tours of centre to find out more about the work of Penny Brohn Cancer Care. Some gravel and grass paths.

81 NEW THE RED POST HOUSE
Fivehead, Taunton TA3 6PX. The Rev Mervyn & Mrs Margaret Wilson. *3m E of Taunton. On the corner of A378 and Butcher's Hill, opp garage. From M5 J26, take A358 towards Langport, turn R at T-lights at top of hill onto A378. Garden is at Langport end of Fivehead.* Sun 18 Sept (2-5). Adm £3, chd free. Home-made teas.
¹/₃ acre walled garden with shrubs, borders, trees, circular potager. We combine beauty and utility. Further 1¹/₂ acres with various planting, orchard and vineyard. 40 apple and 20 pear, plus plums. Mown paths, longer grass, many roses. Views aligned on Ham Hill. Summerhouse with sedum roof, belvedere. Garden in its present form developed over last 12yrs. Paths are gravel and grass, belvedere is not wheelchair accessible.

82 NEW REEDS COURT
Lydeard St. Lawrence, Taunton TA4 3RX. Ben Mack. *12m NW of Taunton. From Taunton take A358 towards Minehead, 4m outside Taunton take L turn signed B3224 Lydeard St. Lawrence. After 2m turn R into lane signed Lydeard St Lawrence.* Sat 28, Sun 29 May (11-5). Adm £3.50, chd free. Teas.
Structured but wild, with striking yet subtle planting, from desert to bog. About half the garden is accessible by wheelchair, though some quite steep slopes so you need a strong assistant!

83 RENDY FARM
Oake, Taunton TA4 1BB. Mr & Mrs N Popplewell. *1m from Oake PO and shop on rd from Oake to Nynehead.* Sun 29 May (2-5). Adm £4, chd free. Home-made teas.
3 acre garden with formal walled front garden, raised vegetable beds, greenhouse and polytunnel enclosed by hornbeam, box and yew hedging. Decorative fruit and cut flower beds, meadow with large wild pond and orchard with stream running through, marked by pollarded willows. New Shepherds Hut Garden.

84 ROCK HOUSE
Elberton BS35 4AQ. Mr & Mrs John Gunnery, 01454 413225. *10m N of Bristol. 3¹/₂ m SW Thornbury. From Old Severn Bridge on M48 take B4461 to Alveston. In Elberton, take 1st turning L to Littleton-on-Severn and turn immed R.* Sun 7, Sun 14 Feb, Sun 3 Apr (11-4). Adm £3.50, chd free. 2017: Sun 5, Sun 12 Feb. **Visits also by arrangement for small groups.**
2 acre garden. Pretty woodland with snowdrops, hellebores and spring bulbs. Cottage garden plants, roses, iris and many interesting varieties of trees. Limited wheelchair access.

85 ROSE COTTAGE
Smithams Hill, East Harptree, Bristol BS40 6BY. Bev & Jenny Cruse, 01761 221627, bandjcruse@gmail.com. *5m N of Wells, 15m S of Bristol. From B3114 turn into High St in EH. L at Clock Tower and immed R into Middle St, up hill for 1m. From B3134 take EH rd opp Castle of Comfort, continue 1¹/₂ m. Car parking in field opp cottage.* Sun 17 Apr (2-5). Adm £4.50, chd free. Home-made teas. **Visits also by arrangement Apr to July.**
1-acre hillside cottage garden with panoramic views over Chew Valley. Garden carpeted with primroses, spring bulbs and hellebores, in the summer with roses and hardy geraniums. Bordered by stream and established mixed hedges. Scented arbour and plenty of seating areas to enjoy the views and teas, as well as the music of the Congresbury Brass Band. Wildlife area and pond in corner of car park field. Regional press and radio. Featured in Your County, Wells Life and Western Morning News. Limited wheelchair access.

86 RUGG FARM
Church Street, Limington, nr Yeovil BA22 8EQ. Morene Griggs, Peter Thomas & Christine Sullivan, 01935 840503, griggsandthomas@btinternet.com. *2m E of Ilchester. From A303 exit on A37 to Yeovil/ Ilchester. At 1st r'about L to Ilchester/Limington, 2nd R to Limington, continue 1¹/₂ m.* Sun 17 July (11-5). Adm £4, chd free. Cream teas. **Visits also by arrangement mid June to early Aug, groups of 8+ welcome.**
2 acre garden created since 2007 around former farmhouse and farm buildings. Diverse areas of interest. Ornamental, kitchen and cottage gardens, lawn and borders, courtyard container planting, orchard, wildlife meadows and pond, developing shrubberies, woodland plantings and walk (unsuitable for wheelchairs). Exuberant annuals and perennials throughout. Metalwork designs by Andy Stevenson Garden Sculptures. Compost Champion in residence. Featured in Somerset Life, The County Magazine and The Langport Leveller. Some gravel paths.

Lympsham Manor

87 NEW ST MONICA TRUST
Cote Lane, Westbury on Trym,
Bristol BS9 3UN. Steve Llewellin.
*A4018 towards Bristol from
M5/Cribbs Causeway, St Monica
Trust is on R, just before start of
Durdham Downs.* Sun 29 May, Sun
31 July (10.30-3). Adm £5, chd
free. Light refreshments. Teas,
cold drinks and cakes.
St Monica Trust is a retirement
community which has extensive
gardens containing formal lawns and
bedding, herbaceous borders, many
trees, pond and wildlife areas,
woodland gardens and shrub
borders.
& 🐕 ⊗ ☕

88 ST PETER'S HOSPICE
Charlton Road, Brentry, Bristol
BS10 6NL. St Peter's Hospice,
01179 159429. *4m N of Bristol. From
Durdham Downs follow A4018 N
towards M5, follow signs for St
Peter's Hospice onto Charlton Rd,
car park, cycle parking also available,
ask at Reception.* Sat 25, Sun 26
June (10.30-4). Adm £4, chd free.
Home-made teas. Salads, soup,
sandwiches and cakes all made
by St Peter's Hospice chefs and
ice creams are available. Visits
also by arrangement June & July,
groups of 10 or less are welcome.
Spacious, tranquil garden for patients
and visitors. Historically a remnant of
nearby Repton House grounds.
Distant view across Severn Estuary.
Lawns with mature and maturing
trees, wild flower area and fruit trees,
gravel garden, herbaceous borders,
sensory labyrinth, formal bedding
display, tubs and baskets. Plenty of
seating for resting and picnics, and
room to run around. The garden has
consistently won awards from Bristol
in Bloom over the last 7 years and
also won a special award in 2015 in
recognition of 'particular effort and
achievement'. Snail racing is available
for light entertainment. Most of the
garden is accessible by wheelchair.
& 🐕 ⊗ 🚐 ☕

89 NEW 103 SEATON ROAD
Yeovil BA20 2AP. Ed & Tracey
Ramsbottom. *off West Hendford,
not far from AgustaWestland. From
B&M Home Stores T-lights on A3088
take exit rd (West Hendford); 4th
turning L (Seaton Road), go over T-
junction, follow cul de sac, garden
200 yards on L.* Sun 22 May, Sun 19
June, Sun 3 July (10-4). Adm
£3.50, chd free. Tea.

Small but perfectly formed, this
elegant garden shows how much can
be created in a relatively small space
with clever design. Inspired by Arts
and Crafts, there are two gardens in
one; with small parterre; patte d'oie,
ornamental pond, pergola, patio, rose
arch, corner arbour and stunning
herbaceous borders. 4 steps up to
garden.
☕

90 SERRIDGE HOUSE
Henfield Rd, Coalpit Heath
BS36 2UY. Mrs J Manning, 01454
773188. *9m N of Bristol. On A432 at
Coalpit Heath T-lights (opp church),
turn into Henfield Rd. R at PH, ½ m
small Xrds, garden on corner with
Ruffet Rd, park on Henfield Rd.* Visits
by arrangement July & Aug for
groups of 12 - 70. Adm £4.50, chd
free. Home-made teas/wine by
arrangement.
2½ acre garden with mature trees,
heather and conifer beds, island beds
mostly of perennials, woodland area
with pond. Colourful courtyard with
old farm implements. Lake views and
lakeside walks. Unique tree carvings.
Mostly flat grass and driveway.
Wheelchair access to lake difficult.
& ☕

Follow every path!
Take a colourful
journey through
1¼ acre . . .

91 ◆ SHERBORNE GARDEN
Litton, Radstock BA3 4PP. Mr &
Mrs John Southwell, 01761
241220. *15m S of Bristol. 15m W of
Bath, 7m N of Wells. On B3114
Chewton Mendip to Harptree rd, ½ m
past The Kings Arms.* For NGS: Sun
14, Mon 15 Feb (11-4). Adm £4,
chd free. Tea. 2017: Sun 12, Mon
13 Feb. For other opening times
and information, please phone.
4½ acre gently sloping garden with

small pinetum, holly wood and many
unusual trees and shrubs. Cottage
garden leading to privy. 3 ponds
linked by wadi and rills with stone and
wooden bridges. Snowdrops and
hellibores. Hosta walk leading to pear
and nut wood. Rondel and gravel
gardens with grasses and
phormiums. Collections of day lilies,
rambling and rose species. Good
labelling. Plenty of seats. Garden
open for private visits and parties.
Featured on BBC Radio Bristol.
Grass and gentle slopes.
& 🐕 🚐 ☕ ⊗

92 SOLE RETREAT
Haydon Drove, Haydon, nr West
Horrington, Wells BA5 3EH. Jane
Clisby, 01749 672648/07790
602906, janeclisby@aol.com,
www.soleretreat.co.uk. *3m NE of
Wells. From Wells take B3139
towards the Horringtons and keep on
main road for 3m. L into Haydon
Drove and Sole Retreat Reflexology,
signed, garden 50yds on L.* Visits by
arrangement in Aug for groups of
10+, please book teas in advance,
car sharing advised. Adm £4, chd
free. Home-made teas.
It is a challenge to garden at almost
1000ft on the Mendip Hills AONB but
this has been described as 'stepping
into a piece of paradise'. Laid out
with tranquility and healing in mind,
the garden is full of old garden
favourites set in ⅓ acre. Within dry
stone walls and raw face bedrock are
9 differing areas incl herbaceous
borders, labyrinth, water feature,
pool, fernery, vegetable plot and
contemplation garden. Featured in
Somerset Life, The Country Gardener,
regional press and radio. Some
gravel, narrow paths.
& 🐕 🛏 ☕

93 SOUTH KELDING
Brewery Hill, Upton Cheyney,
Bristol BS30 6LY. Barry & Wendy
Smale, 0117 9325145,
wendy.smale@yahoo.com. *Halfway
between Bristol and Bath off A431.
Upton Cheyney lies ½ m up Brewery
Hill off A431 just outside Bitton.
Detailed directions and parking
arrangements given when appt
made. Restricted access means pre-
booking essential.* Visits by
arrangement May to Sept, max
30. Adm £4, chd free. Home-made
teas.
This new 7 acre hillside garden offers
panoramic views from its upper
levels, with herbaceous and shrub

beds, prairie-style scree beds, orchard, native copses and small arboretum grouped by continents. Beyond this lie a large wildlife pond, boundary stream and wooded area featuring shade and moisture-loving plants. In view of slopes and uneven terrain this garden is unsuitable for disabled access.

94 SOUTHFIELD FARM
Farleigh Rd, Backwell, Bristol BS48 3PE. Pamela & Alan Lewis. *6m S of Bristol. On A370, 500yds after George Inn towards WsM. Farm directly off main rd on R with parking. Large car park.* Sun 3 July (2-5). Adm £4, chd free. Home-made teas.
2 acre owner-designed garden of rooms with views. Mixed shrub and herbaceous borders, perennials, bulbs and blossom. Roses, climbers, pergolas and seating. Formal ponds. Orchard, vegetable garden, herb garden, summerhouse, terracing and courtyards. Path through native meadow to woodland garden and to large wildlife pond with paths, seating and bird hide. Tearooms in old stable courtyard. Wheelchair access to most areas. Some gravel. Small courtyard and terrace only accessible by steps.

95 ◆ SPECIAL PLANTS
Greenway Lane, Cold Ashton SN14 8LA. Derry Watkins, 01225 891686, derry@specialplants.net, www.specialplants.net. *6m N of Bath. From Bath on A46, turn L into Greenways Lane just before r'about with A420.* For NGS: Thurs 16 June, 21 July, 18 Aug, 15 Sept, 20 Oct (11-5). Adm £5, chd free. Home-made teas. **For other opening times and information, please phone, email or visit garden website.**
Architect-designed ³/₄ acre hillside garden with stunning views. Started autumn 1996. Exotic plants. Gravel gardens for borderline hardy plants. Black and white (purple and silver) garden. Vegetable garden and orchard. Hot border. Lemon and lime bank. Annual, biennial and tender plants for late summer colour. Spring fed ponds. Bog garden. Woodland walk. Allium alley. Free list of plants in garden. New wavy bridge linking field and woods. Featured on BBC2 Gardener's World and in Saturday Telegraph.

96 STANTON COURT NURSING HOME
Stanton Drew BS39 4ER. Pam Townsend, www.stantoncourtnh.net. *5m S of Bristol. From Bristol on A37, R onto B3130 signed Chew Magna. Approx 1¹/₂ m, L at old thatched toll house into Stanton Drew, 1st property on L.* Sun 10 Apr, Sun 18 Sept (1-4). Adm £3, chd free. Light refreshments. Delicious light lunches and cream teas.
2 acres of tranquil gardens around gracious Georgian House (grade II listed). Mature trees, extensive herbaceous borders with many interesting plants and spring bulbs. Large vegetable garden, fruit trees and soft fruit bushes. Gardener Judith Chubb Whittle keeps this lovely garden interesting in all seasons. Set in beautiful countryside. Stanton Drew's Ancient Stone Circle can be seen from the end of the garden - just a short walk from Stanton Court. Paved, level footpaths allow access to all parts of the garden.

> 2 acre owner-designed garden of rooms with views . . .

97 ◆ STOBERRY GARDEN
Stoberry Park, Wells BA5 3LD. Frances & Tim Young, 01749 672906, stay@stoberry-park.co.uk, www.stoberryhouse.co.uk. *¹/₂ m N of Wells. From Bristol - Wells on A39, L into College Rd and immed L through Stoberry Park, signed.* For NGS: Tue 14, Wed 15 June (11.30-5). Adm £5, chd free. Light lunches, home-made teas. Visits also by arrangement Apr to Sept, please mention NGS when booking. **For other opening times and information, please phone, email or visit garden website.**
With breathtaking views over Wells Cathedral, this 6 acre family garden planted sympathetically within its landscape provides a stunning

combination of vistas accented with wildlife ponds, water features, sculpture, 1¹/₂ acre walled garden, gazebo, lime walk. Colour and interest in every season; spring bulbs, irises, acer glade, salvias; wild flower circles, a new meadow walk, and fernery. Featured on BBC TV and in national garden magazines, Gardens of Somerset, Somerset Life, regional press and radio. Gravel paths, steep slopes.

GROUP OPENING

98 STOGUMBER GARDENS
Station Road, Stogumber TA4 3TQ. *11m NW of Taunton. 3m W of A358. Signed to Stogumber, W of Crowcombe. Village maps given to all visitors.* Sun 19 June (2-6). Combined adm £5, chd free. Home-made teas in Village Hall.

BRAGLANDS BARN
Simon & Sue Youell
www.braglandsbarn.com

BROOK HOUSE
Jan & Jonathan Secker-Walker

CRIDLANDS STEEP
Audrey Leitch

HIGHER KINGSWOOD
Fran & Tom Vesey

KNOLL COTTAGE
Elaine & John Leech
Visits also by arrangement May to Oct
john@knoll-cottage.co.uk
01984 656689

POUND HOUSE
Barry & Jenny Hibbert

6 delightful and very varied gardens in picturesque village at edge of Quantocks. 2 surprisingly large gardens in village centre, one semi-wild garden, and 3 very large gardens on outskirts of village, with many rare and unusual plants. Conditions range from waterlogged clay to well-drained sand. Features include a walled garden, ponds, bog gardens, rockery, vegetable and fruit gardens, a collection of over 80 different roses, even a cider-apple orchard. Fine views of surrounding countryside. Dogs on leads allowed in 5 gardens. Wheelchair access to main features of all gardens.

99 ◆ STON EASTON PARK
Ston Easton, Radstock BA3 4DF.
Ston Easton Ltd, 01761 241631,
reception@stoneaston.co.uk,
www.stoneaston.co.uk. *On A37
between Bath & Wells. Entrance to
Park through high metal gates set
back from main road, A37, in centre
of village, opp bus shelter.* For NGS:
Wed 30 Mar, Wed 29 June, Wed 28
Sept (10.30-4). Adm £4.50, chd
free. Tea in the hotel as signed,
light refreshments of tea/coffee
and cake. Booking essential for
lunch and full afternoon tea,
please phone 01761 241631 to
make reservation. For other
opening times and information,
please phone, email or visit garden
website.
A hidden treasure in the heart of the
Mendips. Do come and see for
yourself, walk through the glorious
parkland of the historic Repton
landscape, along the quietly
cascading River Norr. Productive
walled Victorian Kitchen Garden,
octagonal rose garden, stunning
herbaceous border, fruit cage and
orchard. Snowdrops and Hellebores
in abundance during early spring;
June brings clematis, magnolias and
early roses with the start of planting
unusual vegetable seed, not
forgetting the famous loofahs.
September a very productive month,
brings autumnal colours, cyclamen in
flower, harvesting of apples from long
gone varieties, the loofah harvest and
the biggest root vegetables grown for
miles around. Featured in Bath
Magazine, Your County, Somerset
Life & Bath Life. Deep gravel paths,
steep slopes, shallow steps.
🏵 🚐 🛏 ☕

GROUP OPENING

100 STONE ALLERTON GARDENS
Stone Allerton BS26 2NW. *Near
Wedmore. 2m from A38, signed from
Lower Weare.* Sat 11, Sun 12 June
(2-5.30). Combined adm £7, chd
free. Home-made teas at
Greenfield House.

BADGERS ACRE
Lucy Hetherington & Jim
Mathers
Visits also by arrangement Apr
to July please request home-
made teas when booking.
Admission £4
lucy.hetherington@ngs.org.uk

GREENFIELD HOUSE
Mr & Mrs Bull

NEW MYRTLE COTTAGE
Mr Grahame Fry

OLD CHAPEL HOUSE
Pat & George Hacker

NEW OSBORNE HOUSE
Lester & Kate Durston

5 beautiful gardens. Badgers Acre:
1-acre. Colour themed borders.
Secret walk, pond and rockery.
Vegetable potager with pergola
draped in rambling roses and
clematis. Greenfield House:
4 gardens. Grass and shrub border,
colour and cottage gardens. Many
unusual shrubs, perennials, bulbs.
How to make a garden using garden
centre bargains. Ponds for fish and
wildlife. Myrtle Cottage: Over 1 acre,
tranquil garden, recently redesigned,
colourful planting with restored
Victorian gazebo in newly planted
arboretum. Old Chapel House: 1
acre. To front is pergola with wisteria
and climbing roses. Enter through
Prunus Pissardi Nigra avenue to
lawns, island beds, shrubs,
ornamental trees, vegetable patch
and orchard. Osborne House:
¹/₃ acre developed from old orchard.
2 fine Scots pines in front with
gravel planting. At rear patio
container planting of Japanese
maples, hostas and fuchsias,
herbaceous plants, specimen trees,
bog garden, vegetable patch and
pergolas with vine, clematis and
honeysuckle. Featured in Mendip
Times, local press and BBC Radio
Bristol.
🛝 🚐 ☕

STOURHEAD GARDEN
See Wiltshire

GROUP OPENING

101 STOWEY GARDENS
Stowey, Bishop Sutton, Bristol
BS39 5TL. *10m W of Bath. Stowey
Village A368 between Bishop Sutton
and Chelwood. From Chelwood
r'about take Weston-s-Mare rd A368.
At Stowey Xrds turn R to car park,
150 yards down lane, ample off road
parking opp Dormers.* Sun 17 July
(2-6). Combined adm £5, chd free.
Home-made teas at Stowey Mead.

DORMERS
Mr & Mrs G Nicol

2 STOWEY CROSS COTTAGE
Viv & Roger Hodge

STOWEY MEAD
Mr Victor Pritchard

The opening this year in late July
affords an opportunity to see some
very interesting and varied gardens at
a different time of year, to allow the
visitor an insight into their
development through the season.
The gardens cover a broad spectrum
of interest and include flower packed
beds and borders, roses in variety,
topiary, gravel gardens, exotic
garden, ponds and water features,
vegetables, shrubs, trees, orchards,
some serious sweet peas and lots of
seating with wonderful views. There is
something of interest for everyone, all
within a few minutes' walk of the car
park and with natural progression
from one to another. Featured in
Somerset Life, regional press and on
local radio. Wheelchair access quite
limited in places.
♿ ❀ ☕

102 SUTTON HOSEY MANOR
Long Sutton TA10 9NA. Roger
Bramble, 0207 3906700,
rbramble@bdbltd.co.uk. *2m E of
Langport, on A372. Gates N of A372
at E end of Long Sutton.* Sun 24 July
(2.30-6). Adm £4, chd £2. Home-
made teas. Visits also by
arrangement Aug & Sept.
3 acres, of which 2 walled. Lily canal
through pleached limes leading to
amelanchier walk past duck pond;
rose and juniper walk from Italian
Terrace; judas tree avenue; ptelea
walk. Ornamental potager. Drive-side
shrubbery. Music by Young Musicians
Symphony Orchestra.
♿ ❀ ☕

103 NEW ▶ TILHAM FARM
Baltonsborough, Glastonbury
BA6 8QA. Robert & Sue Peto,
www.tilhamfarm.com. *6m E of
Glastonbury. 6m N from A303 up
A37. 7m S of Shepton Mallet. Centre
of Baltonsborough turn up Ham
Street, past school, after 1m L down
Tilham Lane. N up A37. L at Fourfoot
Xrds signed Baltonsborough. After
1m L to Baltonsborough.* Sat 4, Sun
5 June (2-6). Adm £4, chd free.
Home-made teas. Indoor space
with tables and chairs.
Tilham Farm is situated on a hill with
spectacular views of the Mendips to
the North. South facing garden
extends to approx ½ acre, designed
to offer a number of separate seating
areas and vistas. Colour themed
herbaceous borders, wide variety of
roses and rose arch walkway.
Vegetable garden, natural pond and
woodland walk. Wheelchair access
with help to the wooded walkway.
Accessible WC.

104 ◆ TINTINHULL
Tintinhull, Yeovil BA22 8PZ.
National Trust, 01935 823289,
www.nationaltrust.org.uk/tintinhull-
garden. *5m NW of Yeovil. Tintinhull
village. Signs on A303, W of Ilchester.*
For NGS: Sun 5 June (11-5). Adm
£7.60, chd £3.80. Light
refreshments. For other opening
times and information, please
phone or visit garden website.
Famous 2-acre garden in
compartments developed 1900 to
present day, partly influenced by
Hidcote, many interesting plants.
Wheelchair access with care to most
of garden, uneven paths.

105 ▶ TORMARTON COURT
Church Road, Tormarton GL9 1HT.
Noreen & Bruce Finnamore, 01454
218236,
home@thefinnamores.com. *3m E of
Chipping Sodbury, off A46 J to M4.
Follow signs to Tormarton from A46
then follow signs for car parking.* Fri 8
Apr, Fri 17 June (10-3). Adm £5,
chd free. Home-made teas. Visits
also by arrangement Mar to July
weekdays 10am-3pm for groups
of 12+, refreshments by prior
arrangement.
11 acres of formal and natural
gardens in stunning Cotswold setting.
Features incl roses, herbaceous,
kitchen garden, Mediterranean
garden, mound and natural pond.

Extensive walled garden, spring glade
and meadows with young and mature
trees.

106 ▶ TRANBY HOUSE
Norton Lane, Whitchurch, Bristol
BS14 0BT. Jan Barkworth. *5m S of
Bristol. ½ m S of Whitchurch. Leave
Bristol on A37 Wells Rd, through
Whitchurch village, over old railway
bridge and take 1st turning on R.*
Suns 5 June, 17 July, 14 Aug, 4
Sept (2-5). Adm £3.50, chd free.
Tea.
1¼ -acre well-established informal
garden, designed and planted to
encourage wildlife. Wide variety of
trees, shrubs and cottage garden
plants; pond and wild flower
meadow. Garden is divided into
smaller areas, each with its own
characteristics. Continually evolving
to provide colour and interest from
spring to autumn. Plants for sale in
aid of Wildlife Trust.

*Spring opening
features a beautiful
naturalised bulb
display . . .*

107 ▶ TROYTES FARMSTEAD
Tivington, Minehead TA24 8SU. Mr
Theodore Stone,
info@mineheadcottage.com. *Take
A39 from Minehead to Porlock. L at
1st Xrds for Wooton Courteney,
garden ½ m on R.* Visits by
arrangement, refreshments by
prior arrangement. Adm by
donation.
Garden now 23yrs old. 2 acres
originally neglected farmland has 2
small water courses incl ancient C12
sheep wash. Main feature some very
fine trees well placed to view and
photograph.

108 ▶ TRUFFLES
Church Lane, Bishop Sutton,
Bristol BS39 5UP. Sally
Monkhouse, 01275 333665,
sallymonkhouse961@btinternet.co
m. *10m W of Bath. On A368 Bath to*

*Weston-super-Mare rd. Take rd opp
PO/stores uphill towards Hinton
Blewett. 1st R into Church Lane.* Sun
7, Sun 14 Feb (11-3.30). Adm £2,
chd free. Light refreshments. Sat
2, Sun 3 July (1-5.30). Adm £4, chd
free. Home-made teas. In
February: homemade soup and a
roll and/or homemade teas. Visits
also by arrangement for groups of
10+ on 4th, 5th, 6th, 7th July.
2 acres, a surprising, relaxing large
garden, views, new developments
2016. Formal and wildlife planting
linked with meandering paths, lots of
seating. Magical hidden wooded
valley, small stream, naturalised
snowdrops. Wildlife pond, flower
meadows, varied flower beds, some
sculpture. Unique ¼ acre kitchen
garden with several 21ft long x 4ft
wide large waist high raised beds.
Featured on ITV. Grass and gravel
paths, partial wheelchair access.
Sturdy seating throughout garden for
resting en route.

**109 ◆ UNIVERSITY OF BRISTOL
BOTANIC GARDEN**
Stoke Park Road, Stoke Bishop,
Bristol BS9 1JG. University of
Bristol Botanic Garden, 01173
314906, botanic-
gardens@bristol.ac.uk,
www.bristol.ac.uk/Botanic-Garden.
*¼ m W of Durdham Downs. Located
in Stoke Bishop next to Durdham
Downs 1m from city centre. After
crossing the Downs to Stoke Hill,
Stoke Park Rd is first on R.* For NGS:
Sun 3 July (10-5). Adm £4.50, chd
free. Tea. For other opening times
and information, please phone,
email or visit garden website.
Exciting contemporary botanic
garden with organic flowing network
of paths which lead visitors through
collections of Mediterranean flora,
rare native, useful plants (incl
European and Chinese herbs) and
those that illustrate plant evolution.
Large floral displays illustrating
pollination/flowering plant evolution.
Glasshouses, home to giant Amazon
waterlily, tropical fruit and medicine
plants, orchids, cacti and unique
sacred lotus collection. Open at other
times by arrangement. Special tours
of garden throughout day. Wheelchair
available to borrow from Welcome
Lodge. Wheelchair friendly route
through garden available upon
request, also accessible WC.

110 VELLACOTT

Lawford, Crowcombe TA4 4AL.
Kevin & Pat Chittenden, 01984
618249. *9m NW of Taunton. Off
A358, signed Lawford. For directions
please phone.* Sun 3, Mon 4, Sun
10, Mon 11 July (1-5). Adm £3, chd
free. Home-made teas. **Visits also
by arrangement May to Sept, 30
max.**
1-acre informal garden on S-facing
slope with lovely views of the
Quantock and Brendon Hills.
Profusely stocked with wide selection
of herbaceous plants, shrubs and
trees. Other features include ponds,
ruin and potager. Plenty of places to
sit and enjoy the surroundings.

VENN CROSS RAILWAY GARDENS

See Devon

111 NEW VINE HOUSE

Henbury Road, Henbury, Bristol
BS10 7AD. Pippa Atkinson. *2m
from M5 J17. From M5 J17 head to
Bristol Centre. At 3rd r'about, R to
Blaise. L at end of Crow Lane. 1st
house on R.* Sun 21 Feb (2-5); Sun
19 June (1.30-5.30). Adm £4, chd
free. Tea, coffee, cakes, biscuits.
1½ acres of garden behind listed
Georgian house. Mature trees,
shrubs, herbaceous borders, rock
stream and gunnera. Garden
originally planted in 1940's for yr
round interest by the Hewer family,
and features many unusual plants
and trees. Spring opening features a
beautiful naturalised bulb display.
Limited wheelchair access. Some
paths around upper area of garden.

112 ◆ THE WALLED GARDENS OF CANNINGTON

Church Street, Cannington
TA5 2HA. Bridgwater College,
01278 655042,
walledgardens@bridgwater.ac.uk,
www.canningtonwalledgardens.co.
uk. *3m NW of Bridgwater. On A39
Bridgwater-Minehead rd - at 1st
r'about in Cannington 2nd exit,
through village. War memorial, 1st L
into Church Street then 1st L. For
NGS:* Sat 16, Sun 17 Apr, Sat 24,
Sun 25 Sept (10-4). Adm £4, chd
free. **For other opening times and
information, please phone, email or
visit garden website.**
Within the grounds of a medieval
Priory, the Gardens have undergone
extensive redevelopment over the last
few years. Classic and contemporary
features include a National Collection
of Deschampsia with two further
collections in progress, stunning blue
garden, sub-tropical walk, Victorian-
style fernery, large botanical
glasshouse. Gravel paths. A
motorised scooter can be borrowed
free of charge (only one available).

NPC

113 WATCOMBE

92 Church Road, Winscombe
BS25 1BP. Peter & Ann Owen,
01934 842666, peter.o@which.net.
*12m SW of Bristol, 3m N of Axbridge.
100 yds after signs on A38 turn L
(from S), R (from N) into Winscombe
Hill. After 1m reach The Square. Pink
house on L after further 150yds.*
Sun 24 Apr, Sun 22 May, Thur 9
June (2-5.30). Adm £3.50, chd
free. Home-made cakes & cream
teas, some gluten free. **Visits also
by arrangement Apr to July, any
size of group welcome.**
¾-acre mature Edwardian garden
with colour-themed, informally
planted herbaceous borders. Strong
framework separating several
different areas of the garden; pergola
with varied wisteria, unusual topiary,
box hedging, lime walk, pleached
hornbeams, cordon fruit trees, 2
small formal ponds and growing
collection of approx 80 clematis.
Many unusual trees and shrubs.
Small vegetable plot. Featured in
Somerset Gardens Trust publication.
Some steps but most areas
accessible by wheelchair with minimal
assistance.

114 WAVERLEY

Moorland, Bridgwater TA7 0AT. Ash
& Alison Warne, 01278 691058,
ashwarne@btinternet.com. *3m from
J24 M5. Please phone for directions.*
Visits by arrangement Mar to Aug
for groups from 1 - 25, day or
evening. Phone to discuss
catering. Adm £3.50, chd free.
Started in 2010, this ⅓ acre garden is
packed with informal arrangements of
shrubs, trees and perennials. Flooded
to a depth of 1 mtr for 3 weeks in Feb
2014, this garden demonstrates the
resilience of nature. Over 50 roses
and 20 clematis vie for space
amongst 20 different young trees. 12
different species of bamboo thrive.
Paths allow access to all areas.
Featured in Amateur Gardening
magazine. No steps but gravel drive.
Paths level, most paved but some
woodchip.

115 WAYFORD MANOR

Wayford, Crewkerne TA18 8QG. *3m
SW of Crewkerne. Turn N off B3165
at Clapton or S off A30 Chard to
Crewkerne rd.* Sun 29 May (2-5).
Adm £5, chd £2.50. Light
refreshments.
The mainly Elizabethan manor (not
open) mentioned in C17 for its 'fair
and pleasant' garden was redesigned
by Harold Peto in 1902. Formal
terraces with yew hedges and topiary
have fine views over W Dorset. Steps
down between spring-fed ponds past
mature and new plantings of
magnolia, rhododendron, maples,
cornus and, in season, spring bulbs,
cyclamen, giant echium. Primula
candelabra, arum lily, gunnera around
lower ponds.

GROUP OPENING

116 WEST BRISTOL GARDENS

Bristol BS9 2LR, 07779 203626,
p.l.prior@gmail.com. *3m NW of
Bristol city centre. Please see below
for directions.* Sun 29 May (2-5.30).
Combined adm £5, chd free.
Home-made teas at 159 Westbury
Lane. **Visits also by arrangement
Apr to Aug for groups 10-25.**

4 HAYTOR PARK

Mr & Mrs C J Prior
Visits also by arrangement Apr
to Aug for groups 10 to 30
p.l.prior@gmail.com
07779 203626

159 WESTBURY LANE

Maureen Dickens
Visits also by arrangement Apr
to Aug for groups 10 to 30
159jmd@gmail.com
01179 043008

Pair of interesting and contrasting gardens. 4 Haytor Park, BS9 2LR: From A4162 Inner Ring Rd take turning into Coombe Bridge Ave, garden 1st on L. Please no parking in Haytor Park. Amble through this peaceful, secluded and surprisingly long suburban haven. If you dare to explore, discover amazing plants at every level, a green-roofed hideaway, a fern-filled sanctuary, mysterious pond and maybe a dragon or two! Linger a while on benches hidden under arches and in secret spaces. 159 Westbury Lane, BS9 2PY: L A4162/Sylvan Way, B4054/Shirehampton Rd. R to Westbury Lane, 1st House on R. Lovely quiet garden, barely overlooked on edge of city. Planted to owners' design from scratch in cottage garden style. Full of interesting and many unusual plants bought from specialist nurseries. Primarily an early summer garden but being developed to show flowers all yr. Quirky touch with garden artifacts in many places. Many interesting visiting birds. A garden full of interesting plants full of colour and leaf structure with lots of hidden artifacts to find.

---

117 **NEW** **WHITEWOOD LODGE**
Norton Lane, Whitchurch, Bristol BS14 0BU. Guy and Selena Norfolk, 07753 322318, selena.gray@btopenworld.com. *S of Bristol off A37 Wells Rd. Leave Bristol on A37 Wells rd. Pass Whitchurch Village into green belt, R down Norton Lane for approx 1m, garden on R. Parking in field behind house.* Sun 21 Aug (2-5). Adm £4, chd free. Home-made teas. Music by Pizzazz www.pizzazz.org.uk.
Visits also by arrangement Mar to Nov for groups of 6-10 weekends or evenings.
³/₄ acre garden developed over 30yrs from field. Pond, orchard, vegetable potager, mature trees and beds. Minimal use of chemicals in the garden, which aims to provide an ecologically friendly and sustainable environment. Many seats in different parts of garden from which to enjoy the wonderful views of Maes Knoll, an ancient hill fort. Partial wheelchair access, gravel paths and some steps.

118 **18 WOODGROVE ROAD**
Henbury, Bristol BS10 7RE. Peter & Ruth Whitby. *4m N of Bristol. M5 J17, follow B4018, R at 3rd r'about signed Blaise Castle. R opp Blaise Castle car park - rd next to Avon riding centre.* Sat 4, Sat 11 June (2-6). Adm £3, chd free. Home-made teas.
Medium-sized garden divided into 3 sections. Traditional flower garden with Bonsai display and small wildlife pond. Cottage garden with greenhouse and plant sale area. Small orchard with dwarf fruit trees and small vegetable garden. Peter's art studio open for sale of watercolour and oil paintings, 10% to NGS. Gravel path from patio, or grass access for wheelchairs.

119 **WOODLEA BOTTOM**
Greyfield Road, High Littleton, Bristol BS39 6YA. Adrian & Jane Neech. *Follow A39 to High Littleton. Turn into Greyfield Rd, opp Dando's Stores. Garden 400 yds on L. Limited parking available on Greyfield Rd.* Sat 28, Sun 29 May (10-4). Adm £3, chd free.
A garden of rooms, each with a different theme. A balance of naturalised planting and herbaceous borders alongside productive greenhouses and fruit and vegetable areas. Interesting specimen trees and roses, don't forget to look up and through the hedge windows! Summerhouse and attractive garden pots. No dogs please. Featured in regional press and radio, Western Morning News and Mendip Times.

120 ◆ **THE YEO VALLEY ORGANIC GARDEN AT HOLT FARM**
Bath Road, Blagdon BS40 7SQ. Mr & Mrs Tim Mead, 01761 461650, gardens@yeovalley.co.uk, www.theyeovalleyorganicgarden.co.uk. *12m S of Bristol. Off A368. Entrance is approx ¹/₂ m outside Blagdon towards Bath, on L, then follow garden signs past dairy.* For NGS: Sun 8 May (2-5). Adm £5, chd free. Home-made teas. For other opening times and information, please phone, email or visit garden website.
One of only a handful of ornamental gardens that is Soil Association accredited, 6.5 acres of contemporary planting, quirky sculptures, bulbs in their thousands,

purple palace, glorious meadow and posh vegetable patch. Great views, green ideas. Garden lectures, events, workshops and exhibitions held throughout the year - see website for further details. Featured in The Garden and Gardens Illustrated. Level access to the cafe, around the garden some grass paths, some uneven bark and gravel paths. Accessibility map available at ticket office.

> Many seats in different parts of the garden from which to enjoy the wonderful views of Maes Knoll . . .

121 **YEWS FARM**
East Street, Martock TA12 6NF. Louise & Fergus Dowding, www.louisedowding.co.uk. *Turn off main road through village at Market House, onto East St, past PO, garden 150 yards on R, 50 yards before Nag's Head.* Sun 19, Mon 20 June (2-6). Adm £4.50, chd free. Tea. Glass of fine home-made cider to all with a healthy constitution and aged over 18.
1 acre theatrical planting in large walled garden. Outsized plants in jungle garden. Sculptural planting for height, shape, leaf and texture. Self-seeded gravel garden, box and bay ball border, espalier apples, eclectic cloud pruning, much block planting. Working organic kitchen garden. Hens, pigs, orchard and active cider barn - the full monty! We grow the Martock broad bean, the only known survivor of a mediaeval variety of broad bean. Visitors may throw Beauty of Bath apples to the pigs. Child friendly garden, with hammocks, swing etc. Mostly wheelchair access.

STAFFORDSHIRE

Birmingham & West Midlands

Staffordshire, Birmingham & West Midlands

Staffordshire, Birmingham and part of the West Midlands is a landlocked 'county', one of the furthest from the sea in England and Wales.

It is an NGS 'county' of surprising contrasts, from the 'Moorlands' in the North East, the 'Woodland Quarter' in the North West, the 'Staffordshire Potteries' and England's 'Second City' in the South East, with much of the rest of the land devoted to agriculture, both dairy and arable.

The garden owners enthusiastically embraced the NGS from the very beginning, with seven gardens opening in the inaugural year of 1927, and a further thirteen the following year.

The county is the home of the National Memorial Arboretum, the Cannock Chase Area of Outstanding Natural Beauty and part of the new National Forest.

There are many large country houses and gardens throughout the county with a long history of garden-making and with the input of many of the well known landscape architects.

Today, the majority of NGS gardens are privately owned and of modest size. However, a few of the large country house gardens still open their gates for NGS visitors.

Below: 'John's Garden' at Ashwood Nurseries

Staffordshire, Birmingham & West Midlands Volunteers

County Organiser
John & Susan Weston
01785 850448
john.weston@ngs.org.uk

County Treasurer
John Weston
(as above)

Publicity
Graham & Judy White
01889 563930
graham&judy.white@ngs.org.uk

Booklet Co-ordinator
Peter Longstaff
01785 282582
peter.longstaff@ngs.org.uk

Assistant County Organisers
Jane Cerone
01827 873205
janecerone@btinternet.com

Ken & Joy Sutton
01889 590631
suttonjoy2@gmail.com

Sheila Thacker
01782 791244
metbowers@gmail.com

Opening Dates

All entries subject to change.
For latest information check www.ngs.org.uk

January

Wednesday 27
61 The Trentham Estate

February

Snowdrop Festival

Wednesday 24
61 The Trentham Estate

March

Wednesday 23
61 The Trentham Estate

April

Sunday 3
40 Millennium Garden
52 St John's Gardens
Sunday 24
48 50 Pereira Road

May

Sunday 1
27 Hall Green Gardens
72 Yew Tree Cottage
Monday 2
68 Wits End
Thursday 5
72 Yew Tree Cottage
Sunday 8
33 NEW Keeper's Cottage; Bluebell Wood
42 Moseley Corner, The Art of Gardens
53 The Secret Garden
Wednesday 11
7 Birmingham Botanical Gardens
Saturday 14
33 NEW Keeper's Cottage; Bluebell Wood
Wednesday 18
30 High Trees
Friday 20
52 St John's Gardens (Evening)
Saturday 21
22 Four Seasons

Sunday 22
4 The Beeches
14 Castle Bromwich Hall Gardens Trust
17 Courtwood House
20 Dorset House
22 Four Seasons
28 Hamilton House
58 Tanglewood Cottage
Wednesday 25
30 High Trees
Thursday 26
25 NEW 22 Greenfield Road
Friday 27
25 NEW 22 Greenfield Road (Evening)
Saturday 28
12 NEW Brook House
Sunday 29
44 The Old Dairy House
55 190 Station Road
68 Wits End
Monday 30
11 Bridge House
44 The Old Dairy House

June

Thursday 2
72 Yew Tree Cottage
Friday 3
15 Coley Cottage
53 The Secret Garden

Festival Weekend

Sunday 5
23 The Garth
38 89 Marsh Lane
43 The Mount, Great Bridgeford
49 The Pintles
60 91 Tower Road
62 41 Twentylands
63 19 Waterdale
Tuesday 7
63 19 Waterdale
66 NEW Wightwick Manor

Enjoy tea and cake in the potting shed . . .

Thursday 9
72 Yew Tree Cottage
Saturday 11
5 Biddulph Grange Garden
45 The Old Vicarage
Sunday 12
2 Ashcroft and Claremont
5 Biddulph Grange Garden
45 The Old Vicarage
67 Wild Wood Lodge
Monday 13
1 Alton Towers Gardens
Sunday 19
4 The Beeches
15 Coley Cottage
34 13 Lansdowne Road
36 NEW Little Onn Hall
37 3 Marlows Cottages
39 Middleton Hall
53 The Secret Garden
54 NEW 9 Station Road
69 Woodland Grange Gardens
Wednesday 22
3 Bankcroft Farm
Thursday 23
37 3 Marlows Cottages
Saturday 25
16 Colour Mill
Sunday 26
10 Breakmills
13 Brooklyn
21 NEW 304 Ford Green Road
23 The Garth
52 St John's Gardens
Wednesday 29
3 Bankcroft Farm

July

Friday 1
70 Woodleighton Grove Gardens (Evening)
71 Yarlet House
Sunday 3
24 Grafton Cottage
40 Millennium Garden
41 Mitton Manor
43 The Mount, Great Bridgeford
47 Pereira Road Gardens
49 The Pintles
57 NEW 32 Tamar Drive
63 19 Waterdale
64 NEW The Wentlows
Wednesday 6
56 Sugnall Walled Garden
61 The Trentham Estate (Evening)

Thursday 7
72 Yew Tree Cottage
Saturday 9
70 Woodleighton Grove Gardens
Sunday 10
9 NEW Bournville Village
59 Tilewright Close
70 Woodleighton Grove Gardens
Sunday 17
4 The Beeches
20 Dorset House
24 Grafton Cottage
26 NEW Hales Hall
27 Hall Green Gardens
34 13 Lansdowne Road
55 190 Station Road
65 The Wickets
Thursday 21
65 The Wickets
Sunday 24
6 Birch Trees
35 Little Indonesia
72 Yew Tree Cottage
Thursday 28
72 Yew Tree Cottage

August

Wednesday 3
56 Sugnall Walled Garden
Thursday 4
16 Colour Mill
Saturday 6
8 Blore Hall
Sunday 7
24 Grafton Cottage
68 Wits End
Wednesday 10
15 Coley Cottage
53 The Secret Garden
Sunday 14
4 The Beeches
24 Grafton Cottage
67 Wild Wood Lodge
Sunday 21
31 Idlerocks Farm
32 'John's Garden' at Ashwood Nurseries
Sunday 28
6 Birch Trees
65 The Wickets
Monday 29
6 Birch Trees
11 Bridge House

September

Sunday 11
51 Rowley House Farm

October

Saturday 22
22 Four Seasons

Sunday 23
22 Four Seasons

Gardens open to the public

1 Alton Towers Gardens
5 Biddulph Grange Garden
7 Birmingham Botanical Gardens
14 Castle Bromwich Hall Gardens Trust
39 Middleton Hall
56 Sugnall Walled Garden

61 The Trentham Estate
66 NEW Wightwick Manor

By arrangement only

18 12 Darges Lane
19 4 Dene Close
29 Heath House
46 Paul's Oasis of Calm
50 Priory Farm

Also open by arrangement

4 The Beeches
6 Birch Trees
11 Bridge House
15 Coley Cottage

16 Colour Mill
20 Dorset House
23 The Garth
24 Grafton Cottage
25 NEW 22 Greenfield Road
27 16 Burnaston Road, Hall Green Gardens
27 37 Burnaston Road, Hall Green Gardens
27 36 Ferndale Road, Hall Green Gardens
27 120 Russell Road, Hall Green Gardens
31 Idlerocks Farm
34 13 Lansdowne Road
35 Little Indonesia
41 Mitton Manor
49 The Pintles
51 Rowley House Farm

52 St John's Gardens
52 29 St John's Road, St John's Gardens
55 190 Station Road
58 Tanglewood Cottage
62 41 Twentylands
63 19 Waterdale
65 The Wickets
67 Wild Wood Lodge
68 Wits End
70 Woodleighton Grove Gardens
72 Yew Tree Cottage

The Gardens

1 ◆ ALTON TOWERS GARDENS
Alton, Stoke on Trent ST10 4DB. Alton Towers Resort, 01538 703344, www.altontowers.com. *6m N of Uttoxeter. From A50, follow 'brown signs' for Alton Towers. At the theme park follow signs for Alton Towers Hotel. Enter garden through the Alton Towers Hotel.* **For NGS: Mon 13 June (3-6). Adm £4, chd free. For other opening times and information, please phone or visit garden website.**
Alton Tower's magnificent early C19 gardens, designed by the flamboyant 15th Earl of Shrewsbury, feature pools, pagoda fountain, statues, mature trees, shrubs, rhododendrons and azaleas set in a steep sided valley with steep walks and viewing terraces. Access via the 1m long 'woodland walk' from the Alton Towers Hotel. Refreshments in hotel. One of the first gardens in Staffordshire to 'Open' for the NGS in 1932. Unfortunately the historic nature of the gardens makes them unsuitable for wheelchair users or those with limited mobility.

GROUP OPENING

2 ASHCROFT AND CLAREMONT
Eccleshall ST21 6JP. *7m W of Stafford. J14 M6. At Eccleshall end of A5013 the garden is 100 metres before junction with A518. On street parking nearby.* **Note: Some Satnavs** give wrong directions. **Sun 12 June (2-5). Combined adm £4, chd free. Home-made teas at Ashcroft.**

ASHCROFT
Peter & Gillian Bertram

26 CLAREMONT ROAD
Maria Edwards

Two gardens as different as Monet's soft pastel colours are to Vincent's bright sunflowers. Ashcroft is a 1-acre wildlife-friendly garden, pond and covered courtyard. Rooms flow seamlessly around the Edwardian house. Herb bed, treillage, greenhouse with raised beds. Find the topiary peacock that struts in the gravel bed. In the woodland area Gollum lurks in the steps of the ruin. Claremont is a small town garden its design based on feng shui principles. Manicured lawns, herbaceous borders, shrubs, perennials and annuals. Constantly evolving with colour and new features, maintaining interest throughout the year. Come and be inspired! Maria is happy to explain the principles of feng shui in garden layout. Tickets, teas & plants available at Ashcroft. Wheelchair access at Ashcroft only.

Keeper's Cottage, Bluebell Wood

3 BANKCROFT FARM

Tatenhill, Burton-on-Trent
DE13 9SA. Mrs Penelope Adkins.
2m SW of Burton-on-Trent. Take Tatenhill Rd off A38 Burton-Branston flyover. 1m, 1st house on L approaching village. Parking on farm. **Wed 22, Wed 29 June (2-5). Adm £3, chd free.**
Lose yourself for an afternoon in our 1½-acre organic country garden. Arbour, gazebo and many other seating areas to view ponds and herbaceous borders, backed with shrubs and trees with emphasis on structure, foliage and colour. Productive fruit and vegetable gardens, wildlife areas and adjoining 12-acre native woodland walk. Picnics welcome. Many gravel paths.
&

4 THE BEECHES

Mill Street, Rocester ST14 5JX.
Ken & Joy Sutton, 01889 590631,
suttonjoy2@gmail.com. *5m N of Uttoxeter. On B5030 from Uttoxeter turn R at 2nd r'about into village by JCB factory. At Red Lion PH & mini r'about take rd signed Mill Street. Garden 250 yds on R. Parking at JCB Academy Sunday's only.* **Sun 22 May, Sun 19 June, Sun 17 July, Sun 14 Aug (1.30-5). Adm £4, chd free. Home-made teas. Visits also by arrangement May to Aug min charge £80 if less than 20 people. Teas.**
Stroll along the driveway containing island beds planted with mixed shrubs and perennials, and enter a stunning plant lover's garden of approx ⅔ acre, enjoying views of surrounding countryside. Box garden, mixed shrubs incl rhododendrons and azaleas, vibrant colour-themed herbaceous borders, roses, clematis and climbing plants, fruit trees, pools and late flowering perennials also raised vegetable and soft fruit garden, yr-round garden. Featured in Garden News Magazine. Garden of the week. Partial wheelchair access.
& ❀ 🚐 ☕

5 ◆ BIDDULPH GRANGE GARDEN

Grange Road, Biddulph ST8 7SD.
National Trust, 01782 375 533,
biddulphgrange@nationaltrust.org.uk, www.nationaltrust.org.uk.
3½ m SE of Congleton. 7m N of Stoke-on-Trent off A527, Congleton to Biddulph rd. **For NGS: Sat 11, Sun 12 June (11-5.30). Adm £8.25, chd £4.05. For other opening times**
and information, please phone, email or visit garden website.
Amazing Victorian garden created by Darwin contemporary and correspondent James Bateman as an extension of his beliefs, scientific interests and collection of plants. Visit the Italian terrace, Chinese inspired garden, dahlia walk and the oldest surviving golden larch in Britain brought from China by the great plant hunter Robert Fortune.
❀ 🚐 ☕

WE ARE
MACMILLAN.
CANCER SUPPORT

The NGS is
Macmillan's largest
single donor

6 BIRCH TREES

Copmere End, Eccleshall
ST21 6HH. Susan & John Weston,
01785 850448,
johnweston123@btinternet.com.
1½ m W of Eccleshall. On B5026, turn at junction signed Copmere End. After ½ m straight across Xrds by Star Inn. **Sun 24 July, Sun 28, Mon 29 Aug (1.30-5.30). Adm £3, chd free. Home-made teas. Visits also by arrangement June to Aug, groups of 10 - 30.**
Surprising ½ acre SW-facing sun trap which takes advantage of the 'borrowed landscape' of the surrounding countryside. Take time to explore the pathways between the island beds which contain many unusual herbaceous plants, grasses and shrubs; also vegetable patch, stump bed, alpine house, orchard and water features.
& ❀ ☕

7 ◆ BIRMINGHAM BOTANICAL GARDENS

Westbourne Road, Edgbaston
B15 3TR. Birmingham Botanical & Horticultural Society,
0121 454 1860,
www.birminghambotanicalgardens.org.uk. *1½ m SW of the centre of Birmingham. From J6 M6 take A38(M) to city centre. Follow underpasses signed Birmingham West to A456. At Fiveways island turn L onto B4217 (Calthorpe Rd) signed Botanical Gardens.* **For NGS: Wed 11 May (10-6). Adm £7, chd free. Light snacks & refreshments in Terrace Pavilion tearoom. For other opening times and information, please phone or visit garden website.**
Extensive botanical garden set in a green urban environment with a comprehensive collection of plants from throughout the world growing in the glasshouses and outside. Four stunning glasshouses take you from tropical rainforest to arid desert. Fifteen acres of beautiful landscaped gardens. Roses, alpines, perennials, rare trees and shrubs. Playground, Children's Discovery Garden, Gallery, Gift Shop. Birmingham Botanical Gardens are open every day of the year except Christmas Day and Boxing Day.
& ❀ 🚐 ☕

8 BLORE HALL

Blore, Ashbourne DE6 2BS. Mr Chris Green. *Leaving Ashbourne head towards Leek on the A52. Take 1st turn on your R to Mappleton/Okeover & continue to the end of rd, then turn L heading towards Blore.* **Sat 6 Aug (10.30-3). Adm £5, chd free. Light refreshments.**
Set just outside the peak district Blore Hall dates back to the 1400. Take a walk around our koi carp ponds while taking in the glorious views over Dove Dale or just enjoy the densely planted borders which surround our old hall and converted outbuildings. The gardens also attract a wide range of wildlife, and birds has certainly been encouraged. Refreshments includ<ed in the entry fee. All of the gardens can be accessed with a wheelchair, disabled WC facilities located at the swimming pool.
& 🐕 ☕

GROUP OPENING

9 NEW BOURNVILLE VILLAGE

Birmingham B30 1QY,
www.bvt.org.uk. *Follow brown signs to Cadbury World in Bournville. Nearest garden to Cadbury World, Selly Manor, B30 2AE. Park in Sycamore Road car park and local roads. Park at Rowheath Pavilion for Oak Farm Road.* **Sun 10 July (11-5). Combined adm £5, chd free. Light refreshments at Selly Manor Museum (Sycamore Road); 32**

Knighton Road and 63 Witherford Way. Rowheath Pavilion (Heath Road) and Wyevale Garden Centre (Maple Road).

NEW 39 HAWTHORNE ROAD
Mrs Harriet Martin

NEW 32 KNIGHTON ROAD
Mrs Anne Ellis and
Mr Lawrence Newman

NEW 143 OAK FARM ROAD
Sue Harris

NEW SELLY MANOR MUSEUM
Ms Gillian Ellis
www.sellymanormuseum.org.uk

NEW 8 SYCAMORE ROAD
Mrs Sue Adams

NEW 63 WITHERFORD WAY
Mr Nigel Wood
www.youtube.com/
watch?v=vY8iFGVdBFo

Bournville Village is showcasing 6 very different gardens across the 1,000 acre estate. They include: a plant collector's garden, where jungle meets cottage style; a Mediterranean inspired garden with plenty of seating, statuary and curios; an overgrown and now restored urban cottage garden; a super-home, eco and wildlife friendly garden; a traditional Tudor garden surrounding a timber-framed house and a garden with fruit trees old and new with a small organic vegetable plot, inspired by the vision of Bournville Village Trust founder, George Cadbury. Bournville is famous for its large gardens, open spaces and parks. The gardens reflect its diverse community and the unique architecture of the garden village. A walking trail between the gardens will be available for visitors. Not all gardens have full access to wheelchairs, so please check listings for individual gardens.

10 BREAKMILLS
Hames Lane, Newton Regis, Tamworth B79 0NH. Mr Paul Horobin. *Approx 5m N of Tamworth & 3m S of M42 J11. Signed from B5493, Hames Lane is a single track lane near the Queens Head PH. Disabled parking at the house, other visitors please follow parking signs or park in village centre.* **Sun 26 June (11.30-5). Adm £3.50, chd free. Home-made teas and cakes.**
Just under 2 acres of low

maintenance garden featuring small tropical area, island beds, shale area for grasses. Pond, man made stream, vegetable patch and mature trees. Originally a paddock area, trees planted some 15-20 yrs ago but garden really developed over the last 5yrs and still a work in progress. Lots of seating areas to enjoy both the fun aspects of our garden and the surrounding countryside. Larger grassed area may be difficult for wheelchairs on very wet days but access to long drive and eating area in all conditions.

11 BRIDGE HOUSE
Dog Lane, Bodymoor Heath B76 9JF. Mr & Mrs J Cerone, 01827 873205, janecerone@btinternet.com. *5m S of Tamworth. From A446 at Belfry Island take A4091 after 1m turn R onto Bodymoor Heath Lane & continue 1m into village, parking in field opp garden.* **Mon 30 May, Mon 29 Aug (2-5). Adm £3.50, chd free. Home-made teas. Visits also by arrangement May to Sept for groups 5-30.**
1-acre garden surrounding converted public house. Divided into smaller areas with a mix of shrub borders, azalea and fuchsia, herbaceous and bedding, orchard, kitchen garden with large greenhouse and wild flower meadow. Pergola walk, formal fish pool, pond, bog garden and lawns. Kingsbury Water Park and RSPB Middleton Lakes Reserve located within a mile.

12 NEW BROOK HOUSE
Meretown, Newport TF10 8BX. Mr S O'Donovan. *1m NE of Newport. From A41 Take A519 to Eccleshall. In ½ m turn R at Forton to Meretown.* **Sat 28 May (2-5). Adm £4, chd free. Home-made teas.**
The 2 acre garden surrounds a C15 house (not open) bordered by a stream and the R Meese. Large lawn with herbaceous borders, many acers and unusual trees and shrubs, bog garden, vegetable plot, 4 greenhouses and chickens. An orchard with several heritage apple trees. There is also the remains of a Saxon mill mentioned in the Doomsday Book, and a skew bridge by Thomas Telford on garden boundary. Featured in local press. Beware some gravel paths and steps.

13 BROOKLYN
Gratton Lane, Endon, Stoke-on-Trent ST9 9AA. Janet & Steve Howell. *4m W of Leek. 6m from Stoke-on-Trent on A53 turn at Black Horse PH into centre of village, R into Gratton Lane 1st house on R. Parking signed in village.* **Sun 26 June (12-5). Adm £3, chd free. Cream teas.**
Cottage garden in heart of the old village of Endon. Pretty front garden overflowing with roses geraniums and astrantias. Pots house scented geraniums, annuals and houseleeks. Rear garden features shady area with hostas and ferns, small waterfall and pond. Steps to lawn surrounded by well stocked borders, summerhouse, seating areas with village and rural views. Enjoy tea and cake in the potting shed.

Mediterranean inspired garden with plenty of seating, statuary and curios . . .

14 ◆ CASTLE BROMWICH HALL GARDENS TRUST
Chester Road, Castle Bromwich, Birmingham B36 9BT. Castle Bromwich Hall & Gardens Trust, 0121 749 4100, admin@cbhgt.org.uk, www.cbhgt.org.uk. *4m E of Birmingham. 1m J5 M6 (exit N only).* **For NGS: Sun 22 May (12.30-4.30). Adm £4.50, chd £1. Light refreshments. For other opening times and information, please phone, email or visit garden website.**
10 acres of restored C17/18 walled gardens attached to a Jacobean manor (now a hotel) just minutes from J5 of M6. Formal yew parterres, wilderness walks, summerhouses, holly maze, espaliered fruit and wild areas.

Witherford Way, Bournville Village

15 COLEY COTTAGE

Coley Lane, Little Haywood ST18 0UU. Yvonne Branson, 01889 882715, yvonnebranson0uu@btinternet.com. *5m SE of Stafford. A51 from Rugeley or Weston signed Little Haywood. 1/2 m from Seven Springs. A513 Coley Lane from Red Lion PH past Back Lane, 100yds on L opp red post box.* **Fri 3, Sun 19 June, Wed 10 Aug (11-4). Adm £2.50. Home-made teas in the garden. Visits also by arrangement June to Aug pre bookings 10+.**

A plant lover's cottage garden, full of subtle colours and perfume, every inch packed with plants. Clematis and old roses covering arches, many hostas and agapanthus, a wildlife pool, all designed to attract birds and butterflies. This garden is now 8yrs old, trees, roses and herbaceous planting has become well established.

16 COLOUR MILL

Winkhill, Leek, Staffs ST13 7PR. Bob & Jackie Pakes, 01538 308680, jackie.pakes@icloud.com, www.colourmill.webplus.net. *7m E of Leek. Follow A523 from either Leek or Ashbourne, look for NGS signs on the side of the main rd which will direct you down to Colour Mill.* **Sat 25 June, Thur 4 Aug (1.30-5). Adm £3.50, chd free. Visits also by arrangement June to Aug. Home-made teas.**

3/4 -acre S-facing garden, created in the shadow of a former iron foundry, set beside the delightful R Hamps frequented by kingfisher and dipper. Informal planting in a variety of rooms surrounded by beautiful 7ft beech hedges. Large organic vegetable patch complete with greenhouse. Maturing trees provide shade for the interesting seating areas.

17 COURTWOOD HOUSE

3 Court Walk, Betley CW3 9DP. Mike Reeves. *6m S of Crewe. On A531 toward Keele & Newcastle under Lyme or from J16 off M6, pickup A531 off A500 on Nantwich rd, into village by Betley Court.* **Sun 22 May (12.30-5.30). Adm £3, chd free. Light refreshments.**

Small L-shaped, walled garden, which is designed as a walk-through sculpture. Mainly shrubs with structures and water features, hidden spaces and seating areas, with strong shapes and effects utilising a wide range of materials, incl. a synthetic lawn. Small art gallery with acrylic paintings by owner for sale.

18 12 DARGES LANE

Great Wyrley WS6 6LE. Mrs A Hackett, 01922 415064, annofdarges@orange.net. *2m SE of Cannock. From A5 take A34 towards Walsall. Darges Lane is 1st turning on R (over brow of hill). House on R on corner of Cherrington Drive.* **Visits by arrangement May to Sept. Adm £3, chd free.**

1/4 -acre well-stocked enthusiastic plantsman's garden on two levels. Foliage plants are a special feature, together with shrubaceous borders containing rare and unusual plants, divided into areas that link with each other. The use of an extensive collection of clematis gives height in small spaces. Objects of art are eased into every corner, and the owner's own artwork is available to view. Constant updating gives fresh interest to both owner and visitors.

19 4 DENE CLOSE

Penkridge ST19 5HL. David & Anne Smith, 01785 712580. *6m S of Stafford. On A449 from Stafford. At far end of Penkridge turn L into Boscomoor Lane, 2nd L into Filance Lane, 3rd R into Dene Close. Please park with consideration in Filance Lane. Disabled only in Dene Close.* **Visits by arrangement June & July individuals and larger groups welcome. Coaches permitted. Adm £3, chd free. Home-made teas.**

A medium-sized garden of many surprises. Vibrant colour-themed herbaceous areas including a long 'rainbow border'. Many different grasses and bamboos creating texture and interest in the garden. Attractive display of many unusual hostas shown for great effect 'theatre style'. Shady area for ferns etc. Water feature. Summerhouse and quiet seating areas within the garden. Featured in local press.

20 DORSET HOUSE
68 Station Street, Cheslyn Hay WS6 7EE. Mary & David Blundell, 01922 419437, david.blundell@talktalk.net. *2m SE of Cannock J11 M6 A462 towards Willenhall. L at island. At next island R into 1-way system (Low St), at T junction L into Station St. A5 Bridgetown L to island, L Coppice St. R into Station St.* **Sun 22 May, Sun 17 July (11-5). Adm £3, chd free. Home-made teas. Visits also by arrangement May to July, groups of 10+.**
Step back in time with a visit to this inspirational ¹/₂ -acre garden which incorporates country cottage planting at its very best. Unusual rhododendrons, acers, shrubs and perennials planted in mixed borders. Clematis-covered arches and hidden corners with water features including stream and wildlife pool all come together to create a haven of peace and tranquillity. Featured in local press.

21 NEW 304 FORD GREEN ROAD
Norton Le Moors, Stoke-On-Trent ST6 8LS. Janet Machin. *Leave A500 onto A5271 Tunstall/Burslem follow signs for Ford Green Hall continue past the Hall garden approx 400yds on R. Parking at front & rear of St Mary's church/school.* **Sun 26 June (12.30-5). Adm £3, chd free. Home-made teas.**
A semi detached townhouse garden with my dream 11 year old large surprise attached. Many many areas of interest approx. ¹/₃ acre. Sorry... Not suitable for wheelchair access.

22 FOUR SEASONS
26 Buchanan Road, Walsall WS4 2EN. Marie & Tony Newton, www.fourseasonsgarden.co.uk. *Adjacent to Walsall Arboretum. From Ring Rd A4148 near Walsall town centre. At large junction take A461 to Lichfield. At 1st island 3rd exit Buchanan Ave, fork R into Buchanan Rd.* **Sat 21, Sun 22 May, Sat 22, Sun 23 Oct (10-5). Adm £3.50, chd free. Tea.**

Stunning in all seasons. Suburban, s-facing ¹/₄ acre, gently sloping to arboretum. 150 acers, 350 azaleas, bulbs, hellebores, camellias, perennials, begonias, bright conifers, topiary and shrubs. Autumn colours, bark and berries. Semi-formal, oriental and woodland-like areas. Themes include contrast of red, blue and yellow. Pagoda, bridges, water features, stone ornaments. Some steps. WC. Awarded first place in ITV 'Britain's Best Back Gardens' for achieving the impossible, Featured on BBC1 Weather, BT Homepage, and in Radio Times, Daily Mail, Mail Online, Times, Guardian, Aesculapius, Romania 'Home & Garden'.

23 THE GARTH
2 Broc Hill Way, Milford, Stafford ST17 0UB. Mr & Mrs David Wright, 01785 661182, anitawright1@yahoo.co.uk, www.anitawright.co.uk. *4¹/₂ m SE of Stafford. A513 Stafford to Rugeley rd; at Barley Mow turn R (S) to Brocton; L after ¹/₂ m.* **Sun 5, Sun 26 June (2-6). Adm £3, chd free. Cream teas. Visits also by arrangement.**
¹/₂ -acre garden of many levels on Cannock Chase AONB. Acid soil loving plants. Series of small gardens, water features, raised beds. Rare trees, island beds of unusual shrubs and perennials, many varieties of hosta and ferns. Varied and colourful foliage, summerhouse, arbours and quiet seating to enjoy the garden. Ancient sandstone caves. Featured on Radio Stoke.

24 GRAFTON COTTAGE
Barton-under-Needwood DE13 8AL. Margaret & Peter Hargreaves, 01283 713639, marpeter1@btinternet.com. *6m N of Lichfield. Leave A38 for Catholme S of Barton, follow sign to Barton Green, L at Royal Oak, ¹/₄ m.* **Sun 3, Sun 17 July, Sun 7, Sun 14 Aug (11.30-5). Adm £4, chd free. Home-made teas. Visits also by arrangement June to Aug min admission £80 if less than 20 people.** *Donation to Alzheimer's Research Trust.*
A visitor commented 'worth coming all the way from Cornwall, a real feast for the eyes' where the bees and owners work overtime producing a traditional cottage garden, admired over the years. Coloured themed

borders with unusual herbaceous plants and perfume from old fashioned roses, sweet peas, violas, dianthus, phlox and lilies. Particular interests are viticella clematis, salvia penstemon, cottage garden annuals and use of foliage plants. Brook, small vegetable plot and more. Garden design-a book of ideas Die Geheimen Garten Von England Both by Heidi Howcroft and Marianne Materus. Featured in English Garden.

25 NEW 22 GREENFIELD ROAD
Stafford ST17 0PU. Alison & Peter Jordan, 01785 660819, alison.jordan2@btinternet.com. *3m S of Stafford. Follow the A34 out of Stafford towards Cannock. 2nd L onto Overhill Rd.1st R into Greenfield Rd.* **Thur 26 May (2-5). Adm £2.50, chd free. Home-made teas. Evening opening Fri 27 May (6.30-9). Adm £4, chd free. Wine. Visits also by arrangement Apr to Aug for groups 10 - 30. Home-made teas.**
Small suburban garden created in the last 4 years. Stunning azaleas and rhododendrons, interesting perennials and grasses. A peaceful haven to sit and enjoy.

A peaceful haven to sit and enjoy . . . .

26 NEW HALES HALL
Market Drayton TF9 2PP. Mr & Mrs A R C Hall. *3m E of Market Drayton (off A53). Signed from A53 between Loggerheads & Market Drayton to Hales. Close to Shropshire/Staffordshire border.* **Sun 17 July (2-5). Adm £5, chd free. Home-made teas.**
C18 house (not open) in wonderful setting. 11 acres of garden. Woodland walks, bog garden, borders, Victorian yew garden, Edwardian walled garden undergoing development. Many unusual plants and trees. All-yr-round interest.

GROUP OPENING

27 HALL GREEN GARDENS
Hall Green, Birmingham B28 8SQ. *Off A34, 3m city centre, 6m from M42 J4. From City Centre start at Russell Rd B28 8SQ & and from M42 start at Boden Rd B28 9DL, Hall Green.* **Sun 1 May, Sun 17 July (1.30-5.30). Combined adm £4, chd free. Home-made teas at 16 Burnaston Rd & 120 Russell Road.**

42 BODEN ROAD
Mrs Helen Lycett

16 BURNASTON ROAD
Howard Hemmings & Sandra Hateley
Visits also by arrangement May to July no min, 30 max. Adm incl drink and cake.
howard.hemmings@blueyonder
.co.uk
0121 624 1488

37 BURNASTON ROAD
Mrs Carolyn Wynne-Jones
Visits also by arrangement May to July.
markwynne-
jones@blueyonder.co.uk
0121 608 2397

36 FERNDALE ROAD
Mrs E A Nicholson
0121 777 4921
Visits also by arrangement Mar to Sept, no min, 30 max.

120 RUSSELL ROAD
Mr David Worthington
Visits also by arrangement May to Sept, groups up to 30 max.
Teas incl in adm.
hildave@hotmail.com
0121 624 7906

19 STAPLEHURST ROAD
Mrs Sheena Terrace

A group of 6 suburban gardens, each unique in style. A large restful garden with mature trees, 2 lawns, cottage style borders, seating areas and small vegetable area. S-facing lawned and border garden with interesting features incl a log display, conifers, water feature and various artefacts. 'Find it' quiz for children. A tranquil garden with curving borders containing different perennials, shade areas, soft fruit and vegetables. A florist's large suburban garden with many unusual plants giving year round interest, the garden is divided into distinct areas, large ornamental garden with ponds and waterfalls,

fruit garden.Plantsman's garden featuring formal raised pond and hosta collection with unusual perennials and container planting. A shady garden with mature trees, pond, cottage style borders. Steps, narrow side access Staplehurst Rd, 16 Burnaston Rd 1 step, ramp available, Boden Rd & 37 Burnaston patio viewing only, Russell Rd door sill.

  ✤

Stunning bluebell wood adorns the banks of a river deep in the South Staffordshire countryside . . .

28 HAMILTON HOUSE
Roman Grange, Roman Road, Little Aston Park, Sutton Coldfield B74 3GA. Philip & Diana Berry, www.hamiltonhousegarden.co.uk. *3m N of Sutton Coldfield. Follow A454 (Walsall Rd) & enter Roman Rd, Little Aston Park. Roman Grange is 1st L after church but enter rd via pedestrian gate.* **Sun 22 May (2-5). Adm £5, chd free. Home-made teas.**
¹/₂-acre n-facing English woodland garden in tranquil setting, making the most of challenging shade, providing haven for birds and other wildlife. Large pond with stone bridge, pergolas, water features, box garden with a variety of roses and herbs. Interesting collection of rhododendrons, clematis, hostas, ferns and old English roses. Join us for afternoon tea, listening to live music and admire the art of our garden. Featured on BBC 2 'The Great British Garden Revival', The Big TV Company Freeview Channel 8, and in The Sutton Coldfield Observer, The Journal, Birmingham Mail.

✤

29 HEATH HOUSE
Offley Brook, Eccleshall ST21 6HA. Dr D W Eyre-Walker, 01785 280318, neyrewalker@btinternet.com. *3m W of Eccleshall. From Eccleshall take B5026 towards Woore. At Sugnall turn L, after 1¹/₂ m turn R immed by stone garden wall. After 1m straight

across Xrds. Use Satnav, mobile phones do not work locally.* **Visits by arrangement Apr to Sept. Adm £5, chd free. Refreshments available for small numbers.**
1¹/₂-acre country garden of C18 miller's house in lovely valley setting, overlooking mill pool. Plantsman's garden containing many rare and unusual plants in borders, bog garden, woodland, alpine house, raised bed and shrubberies and incl slowly expanding collection of hardy terrestrial orchids.Vegetable garden now converted to wild flower meadow. Wheel chair access difficult with only partial access.

30 HIGH TREES
18 Drubbery Lane, nr Longton Park ST3 4BA. Peter & Pat Teggin. *5m S of Stoke-on-Trent. Off A5035, midway between Trentham Gardens & Longton. Opp Longton Park.* **Wed 18, Wed 25 May (1-4). Adm £3, chd free. Cream teas.**
Garden designer's pretty, perfumed hidden garden. Colourful herbaceous plants juxtapose to create a rich woven tapestry of spires, flats and fluffs interwoven with structure planting and focal points. An ideas garden continuing to inspire, evoking orderly diversity. All within two minutes walk of a Victorian park. Featured in the local press.

☕

31 IDLEROCKS FARM
Hilderstone Road, Spot Acre, nr Stone ST15 8RP. Barbara Dixon, 01889 505450. *3m E of Stone. From Stone take A520 to Meir Heath, turn R onto B5066 towards Hilderstone, farm 1¹/₂ m on R. ¹/₂ m drive with parking in the field by house.* **Sun 21 Aug (1.30-4.30). Adm £3, chd free. Home-made teas. Coffee. Visits also by arrangement also Feb for snowdrops.**
Medium sized garden set in farmland and woodland, 800ft above sea level. Long herbaceous border, wildlife pond, views across the Trent Valley to the Wrekin and Clee Hills.

☕

32 'JOHN'S GARDEN' AT ASHWOOD NURSERIES
Ashwood Lower Lane, Ashwood, nr Kingswinford DY6 0AE. John Massey, www.ashwoodnurseries.com. *5m S of Wolverhampton. 1m past Wall Heath on A449 turn R to Ashwood

along Doctor's Lane. At T-junction turn L. Park at Ashwood Nurseries. **Sun 21 Aug (10-4). Adm £5, chd free. Home-made teas at adjacent Tea Room at Ashwood Nurseries.** A stunning private garden adjacent to Ashwood Nurseries, it has a huge plant collection and many innovative design features in a beautiful canalside setting. There are informal beds, woodland dells, a South African border, a rock garden, a unique succulent garden and a wildlife meadow. Fine displays of grasses, herbaceous perennials and clematis together with a notable collection of hydrangeas. Tea Room, Garden Centre and Gift Shop at adjacent Ashwood Nurseries. Coaches are by appointment only. Disabled access difficult if very wet.

 🚗 ❀ 🚌 **NPC** ☕

33 NEW KEEPER'S COTTAGE; BLUEBELL WOOD
24 Greensforge Lane, Stourton, Stourbridge DY7 5BB. Peter & Jenny Brookes, 07974 454503, peter@brookesmedia.com. *2m NW of Stourbridge. At junction of A449 & A458 at Stourton, take Bridgenorth Rd (A458) westward, after ¹/₂ m turn R into Greensforge Lane. Keeper's Cottage ¹/₂ m on R.* **Sun 8, Sat 14 May (12-4). Adm £3, chd free. Home-made teas. Gluten free & diabetic cakes also available.** This stunning bluebell wood adorns the banks of a river deep in the South Staffordshire countryside, yet only a few miles from the conurbation. In May, the bluebells form a beautiful carpet, sweeping through the natural woodland and down to the river, the site of ancient nail making. It is a quintessentially English landscape which can only be glimpsed for a few short weeks of the year.

☕

34 13 LANSDOWNE ROAD
Hurst Green, Halesowen B62 9QT. Mr Peter Bridgens & Mr Michael King, 0121 421 7796. *7m W of Birmingham. A458 Hagley Rd out of Birmingham, towards Stourbridge. From M5 J2 take 1st exit A4123 towards Birmingham.* **Sun 19 June, Sun 17 July (2.30-5.30). Adm £3.50, chd free. Home-made teas. Visits also by arrangement May to Oct groups of between 4 and 20.** A plantsman's suburban garden designed to ensure maximum use of space. The garden features rare and unusual plants, incl Meconopsis,

Buddleia agathosma, Stewartia, Billadera, and Sinocallicanthus. Water features and area. The mixed borders are planted giving a long season of interest. Attention paid to plant association and colour themes. The garden presents a softly planted look and tropical feel. The entrance to the 'Secret' garden, and 36ft colour themed mixed border The use of exotic and architectural plants in a different way. The use of ornamentation within the garden. Featured in our local paper.

❀ ☕

Marie Curie

Patients and families can enjoy beautiful gardens at our hospices

35 LITTLE INDONESIA
20 Poston Croft, Birmingham B14 5AB. Dave & Pat McKenna, 0121 628 1397, patanddave76@yahoo.co.uk, www.littleindonesia.wordpress. com. *1¹/₂ m from Kings Heath High St. Poston Croft is 6th L off Broad Lane, off A435 Alcester Rd, parking limited in the cul-de-sac but more parking available on service rd on Broad Lane opp Poston Croft.* **Sun 24 July (11-4.30). Adm £3.50, chd free. Home-made teas. Visits also by arrangement June to Sept. Mon, Tue & Sun afternoons only.** A garden that is the realisation of my dreams. An amazing plant paradise with the feel of entering a jungle, even though we are in the heart of Birmingham. Planted so that it seems to go on for ever. Plants of unusual leaf shapes and textures. Bananas, cannas and grasses jostle with one another for space. A plantaholic's paradise. Steps down to garden, stepping stone pathways leading to lawns.

☕

36 NEW LITTLE ONN HALL
Little Onn, Church Eaton ST20 0AU. David & Caroline Bradshaw. *6m SW of Stafford. A449 Wolverhampton to Stafford; at Gailey r'about turn W onto A5 for 1¹/₄ m; turn R to Stretton, 200 yds turn L for Church Eaton. Follow signs.* **Sun 19 June (10-4). Adm £5, chd free. Light refreshments.** 6-acre garden; herbaceous lined drive, terraces, Summer House and some woodland planting by old Saxon moat. The gates and gardens were designed by Thomas Mawson who in 1870 was a leading designer of the period. Present owners are working to restore the gardens to their former glory. Area for picnics.

🚗 🚌 ☕

MARLBROOK GARDENS
See Worcestershire

37 3 MARLOWS COTTAGES
Little Hay Lane, Little Hay WS14 0QD. Phyllis Davies. *4m S of Lichfield. Take A5127, Birmingham Rd. Turn L at Park Lane (opp Tesco Express) then R at T junction into Little Hay Lane, ¹/₂ m on L.* **Sun 19, Thur 23 June (11-4). Adm £3, chd free. Home-made teas.** Long, narrow, gently sloping cottage style garden with borders and beds containing abundant herbaceous perennials and shrubs leading to vegetable patch.

❀ ☕

38 89 MARSH LANE
Solihull B91 2PE. Mrs Gail Wyldes. *¹/₂ m from Solihull town centre. A41 from M42 J5. Turn sharp L at first T-lights. Garden on R. Parking 400 metres further along Marsh Lane at Solihull Cricket Club by mini r'about.* **Sun 5 June (2-5). Adm £3.50, chd free. Home-made teas.** Suburban Oasis. Trees, shrubs and herbaceous planting for all year interest with emphasis on leaf shape and structure. Wildlife pond, bog garden, water features, african style gazebo, gravel gardens, shady places and sunny seating areas. Patio with pergola and raised beds. Hostas and ferns abound. The garden is continually evolving with new plants and features. Small step from patio to the main back garden and paths may be a little narrow.

♿ ❀ ☕

39 ◆ MIDDLETON HALL
Tamworth B78 2AE. Middleton Hall Trust, www.middleton-hall.co.uk. *4m S of Tamworth, 2m N J9 M42. On A4091 between The Belfry & Drayton Manor.* **For NGS: Sun 19 June (11-4). Adm £4, chd free. Light refreshments. For other opening times and information, please visit garden website.**
Two walled gardens set in 40 acres of grounds surrounding Grade 2 Middleton Hall, the C17 home of naturalists Sir Francis Willoughby and John Ray. Large colour-themed herbaceous borders radiating from a central pond, restored gazebo, pergola planted with roses, clematis and wisteria. Courtyard garden with raised beds. Entertainment in the Hall. House and Grounds featured on Countryfile.

40 MILLENNIUM GARDEN
London Road, Lichfield WS14 9RB. Carol Cooper. *1m S of Lichfield. Off A38 along A5206 towards Lichfield 1/4 m past A38 island towards Lichfield. Park in field on L. Yellow signs on field gate.* **Sun 3 Apr, Sun 3 July (1-5). Adm £3.50, chd free. Tea.**
2-acre garden with mixed spring bulbs in the woodland garden and host of golden daffodils fade slowly into the summer borders in this English country garden. Designed with a naturalistic edge and with the environment in mind. A relaxed approach creates a garden of quiet sanctuary with the millennium bridge sitting comfortably, with its surroundings of lush planting and mature trees. Well stocked summer borders give shots of colour to lift the spirit and the air fills with the scent of wisterias and climbing roses. A stress free environment awaits you at the Millennium Garden.

41 MITTON MANOR
Mitton, Penkridge, Stafford ST19 5QW. Mrs E A Gooch, 07970 457457, eag@egsplc.com. *2m W of Penkridge. Property is on Whiston Rd. Parking in field before house. No parking for coaches.* **Sun 3 July (11.30-4.30). Adm £5, chd free. Cream teas. Visits also by arrangement May to Sept.**
This 7-acre country garden was started in 2001 and has been developed from an overgrown wilderness. The garden surrounds a

Victorian manor (not open) and contains rooms of different styles, formal box/topiary, prairie planting and natural woodland bordered by a stream. Stunning vistas, water features and sculpture. Live music. Many levels, narrow and gravel paths. Wheelchair users will need assistance.

Summer House and some woodland planting by old Saxon moat . . .

GROUP OPENING

42 MOSELEY CORNER, THE ART OF GARDENS
Birmingham B13 9PN. *3m S of city centre. From Moseley take St Mary's Row which becomes Wake Green Rd. After 1/2 m turn R into St Agnes Rd & L at the church, park here for both gardens.* **Sun 8 May (1-5.30). Combined adm £3, chd free. Home-made teas at 56 St Agnes Road.**

> **56 ST AGNES ROAD**
> Michael & Alison Cullen
>
> **48 ST AGNES ROAD**
> Mrs Judy Wenban-Smith

Both gardens are on St Agnes Road in Moseley. They demonstrate unique design, each expressing the garden owners' creative vision and endeavour. 56 St Agnes Rd is immaculately maintained with curving borders around a formal lawn with delicate acers and contemporary sculpture. The tranquillity of this elegant garden is enhanced by a Victorian style fish pond with fountain and waterfall. 48 St Agnes Road has a courtyard leading to a pond with frogs, newts and water lilies. There are mature herbaceous borders with perennial and annual planting and poles for climbing roses and clematis, some unusual plants as well as fruit trees, currant bushes and vegetables.

43 THE MOUNT, GREAT BRIDGEFORD
33 Newport Road, Great Bridgeford, Stafford ST18 9PR. Adrian Hubble. *2m NW of Stafford. From J14 M6 take A5013 to Great Bridgeford. Turn L on to B5405. Park at village hall on L, or with consideration in Jasmine Rd on R. Short walk along B5405 to last house on R.* **Sun 5 June, Sun 3 July (1-5). Adm £3, chd free. Also open The Pintles.**
The garden consists of distinct areas each with beds and borders with their own colour schemes planted with rare and choice plants spread over 1/3 acre. Raised beds, alpine garden, water feature and a Roman style feature. A garden of harmonies and contrasts guaranteed to provoke planting ideas. Refreshments will be available at 'The Pintles'.

44 THE OLD DAIRY HOUSE
Trentham Park, Stoke-on-Trent ST4 8AE. Philip & Michelle Moore. *S edge of Stoke-on-Trent. Next to Trentham Gardens. Off Whitmore Rd. Please follow NGS signs or signs for Trentham Park Golf Club. Parking in church car park.* **Sun 29, Mon 30 May (1-5). Adm £3, chd free. Tea.**
Grade 2 listed house (not open) designed by Sir Charles Barry forms backdrop to this 2-acre garden in parkland setting. Shaded area for rhododendrons, azaleas plus expanding hosta and fern collection. Mature trees, 'cottage garden' and long borders. Narrow brick paths in vegetable plot. Large courtyard area for teas. Some gravel paths but lawns are an option.

45 THE OLD VICARAGE
Fulford, nr Stone ST11 9QS. Mike & Cherry Dodson. *4m N of Stone. From Stone A520 (Leek). 1m R turn to Spot Acre & Fulford, turn L down Post Office Terrace, past village green/PH towards church. Parking in signed field on L.* **Sat 11, Sun 12 June (2-5). Adm £3.50, chd free. Home-made teas.**
On edge of attractive village, 1 1/2 acres of formal sloping garden around Victorian house. Sit on the back terrace or in the summerhouse and enjoy homemade cakes and tea amongst mature trees, relaxed herbaceous borders, roses and a small pond. Move onto the organic vegetable garden with raised beds,

fruit cage and very big compost heaps! In complete contrast, walk around the natural setting of a two-acre reclaimed lake planted with native species designed to attract wildlife. Waterfall, jetty, fishing hut, acer and fern glade plus young arboretum provide more interest. Children will enjoy meeting the chickens and horses. Featured in Saturday Telegraph. Wheelchair access to most areas.

46 PAUL'S OASIS OF CALM
18 Kings Close, Kings Heath, Birmingham B14 6TP. Mr Paul Doogan, 0121 444 6943, gardengreen18@hotmail.co.uk. *4m from city centre. 5m from the M42 J4. Take A345 to Kings Heath High St then B4122 Vicarage Rd. Turn L onto Kings Rd then R to Kings Close.* **Visits by arrangement May to Aug groups up to 15. Adm £2.50, chd free. Cream teas.**
Garden cultivated from nothing into a little oasis. Measuring 18ft x 70ft. It's small but packed with interesting and unusual plants, water features and 7 seating areas. It's my piece of heaven.

GROUP OPENING

47 PEREIRA ROAD GARDENS
Harborne, Birmingham B17 9JN. *Between Gillhurst Rd & Margaret Grove, ¼ m from Hagley Rd or ½ m from Harborne High St.* **Sun 3 July (2-5). Combined adm £4, chd free. Home-made teas at Pereira Road allotments, accessed via driveway between 31 and 33 Pereira Road or through 55 Pereira Road. Drinks and homemade cakes plus jams and vegetables on sale.**

14 PEREIRA ROAD
Mike Foster

50 PEREIRA ROAD
Peg Peil
(See separate entry)

55 PEREIRA ROAD
Emma Davies & Martin Commander

Group of 3 different urban gardens. No.14 a well established suburban garden with mixed herbaceous and shrub borders. Wildlife-friendly with 2 ponds and wild flower area. Ongoing alterations provide new areas of interest each year. No. 50 is a

Wild Wood Lodge

plantaholic's paradise with over 1000 varieties, many rare, incl fruits, vegetables, herbs, grasses and large bed of plants with African connections. Over 100 varieties on sale - see how they grow. No. 55 is a sloping garden, incl gravelled beds with mixed planting, grasses and small pond. All gardens have steps. In July, free admission to Harborne Nature Reserve and Pereira Road allotments incl.

48 50 PEREIRA ROAD
Harborne, Birmingham B17 9JN. Peg Peil. *Between Gillhurst Rd & Margaret Grove, ¼ m from Hagley Rd or ½ m from Harborne High St.* **Sun 24 Apr (2-5). Adm £2.50, chd free. Opening with Pereira Road Gardens on Sun 3 July.**
Plantaholic's garden with over 1000 varieties, many rare. Large bed of plants with African connections. Fruits, vegetables, herbs, grasses. Over 100 varieties available for sale. This garden slopes steeply and access to some areas may be difficult for less mobile visitors.

49 THE PINTLES
18 Newport Road, Great Bridgeford, Stafford ST18 9PR. Peter & Leslie Longstaff, 01785 828582, peter.longstaff@ngs.org.uk. *J14 M6 take A5013 towards Eccleshall. In Great Bridgeford turn L onto B5405. Car park on L after ½ m in Village Hall car park.* **Sun 5 June, Sun 3 July (1-5). Adm £3, chd free. Home-**

made teas. Also open The Mount, Great Bridgeford. **Visits also by arrangement June & July for groups of 10 - 30.**
Located in the village of Great Bridgeford this traditional semi-detached house has a medium sized wildlife friendly garden designed to appeal to many interests. There are two greenhouses, over 200 cacti and succulents, vegetable and fruit plot, wildlife pond, weather station, and hidden woodland shady garden. Plenty of outside seating to enjoy the home made cakes and refreshments. Featured in Amateur Gardening. Steps or small ramp into main garden.

50 PRIORY FARM
Mitton Road, Bradley, Stafford ST18 9ED. Debbie Farmer, 07817 669700, debbie_farmer@live.co.uk. *3½ m W Penkridge. At Texaco island on A449 in Penridge take Bungham Lane. Cont for 2½ m past Swan & Whiston Hall to Mitton. Turn R to Bradley, cont 1m to Priory Farm on L.* **Visits by arrangement June & July for groups of 10+. Adm £4, chd free. Home-made teas.**
Delightful gardens and a warm welcome awaits you at Priory Farm. Stroll around the picturesque grounds and lake. Check out the wildlife. New projects for 2016 planned. Scrumptious refreshments available. Delicious home made cakes. BBQ subject to availability. Featured in the Express & Star Newspaper. Limited wheelchair access.

51 ROWLEY HOUSE FARM
Croxton, Stafford ST21 6PJ. Tony & Beryl Roe, 01630 620248. *4m W of Eccleshall. Between Eccleshall & Loggerheads on B5026. At Wetwood Xrds turn for Fairoak. Take 1st L turn & continue for 3/4 m.* **Sun 11 Sept (2-5). Adm £3.50, chd free. Home-made teas. Visits also by arrangement June & July.**
Quiet country garden, part reclaimed from farm rick-yard. Shrub roses in orchard, soft fruits, vegetables and water feature incl. Extensive views towards the Wrekin and Welsh hills from adjacent land at 570ft, with plantings of 95 varieties of 7 species of ilex, various corylus and specimen trees. Small water feature. Gravel paths.

GROUP OPENING

52 ST JOHN'S GARDENS
23 & 29 St Johns Road, Rowley Park, Stafford ST17 9AS. Fiona Horwath, 01785 258923, fiona_horwath@yahoo.co.uk. *1/2 m S of Stafford town centre. Just a few mins from J13 M6 off A449 just after Rising Brook. Through entrance to private park. Please park considerately.* **Sun 3 Apr (2-5). Combined adm £4, chd free. Home-made teas at No 29. Evening opening Fri 20 May (6.30-9). Combined adm £5, chd free. Wine at No 29. Sun 26 June (2-5). Combined adm £4, chd free. Home-made teas at No 29. Visits also by arrangement Mar to Oct no maximum group size - the more the merrier!**

23 ST JOHNS ROAD
Fiona Horwath

29 ST JOHN'S ROAD
Mrs Carol Shanahan

Two near neighbours who share a passion for all things horticultural - we are lucky that our respective gardens enjoy a southerly aspect which we use to its full advantage. However, you will also find plenty of ideas for dry shade and challenging areas. You are most welcome to sit and relax with home-made tea and cake whilst being inspired by the well-stocked beds that surround you. No.23 is a Victorian house (not open) and as you pass through the black and white gate you enter a part-walled plant lover's haven. There are bulbs and

shady woodlanders in spring and a plethora of herbaceous plants and climbers. At no.29, against a backdrop of mature Hornbeams there are 2 acres of informal garden made up of many complementary areas. View the wooded 'dingly dell', colourful terraces, abundant kitchen garden, bronze armillary, water features, circular lawns plus the roses and clematis that scramble through the trees. As both gardeners are keen hardy planters and sow far too many seeds there is always something good for sale. Covered conservatory for taking tea on wet days.
Wheelchair access only at no 29.

Scrumptious refreshments available. Delicious home made cakes. BBQ . . .

53 THE SECRET GARDEN
3 Banktop Cottages, Little Haywood ST18 0UL. Derek Higgott & David Aston, 01889 883473, poshanddeks@gmail.com. *5m SE of Stafford. A51 from Rugeley or Weston signed Little Haywood A513 Stafford Coley Lane, Back Lane R into Coley Grove. Entrance 50 metres on L.* **Sun 8 May (11-4). Fri 3, Sun 19 June, Wed 10 Aug (11-4). Also open Coley Cottage. Adm £3, chd free. Home-made teas.**
Wander past the other cottage gardens and through the evergreen arch and there before you a fantasy for the eyes and soul. Stunning garden approx 1/2 acre, created over the last 30yrs. Strong colour theme of trees and shrubs, underplanted with perennials, 1000 bulbs and laced with clematis; other features incl water, laburnum and rose tunnel and unique buildings. Is this the jewel in the crown? Raised gazebo with wonderful views over untouched meadows and Cannock Chase. Some slopes.

54 NEW 9 STATION ROAD
Great Wyrley, Walsall WS6 6LH. Mrs Elaine Thurston. *Great Wyrley. J12 of M6 take A5 to Cannock, in 4m at bridge over M6 Toll take A34 to Walsall, take 1st turn R into Darges Lane. Turn R into Station Rd.* **Sun 19 June (11-4). Adm £2.50, chd free. Home-made teas.**
A small, wildlife friendly, plantsman's garden, measuring 80 x 30 ft. Designed as a romantic, cottage style featuring herbaceous perennials, English shrub roses and climbers. Although planted in an informal style, the garden offers some formality in its overall design with the use of clipped box and bay trees.

55 190 STATION ROAD
Boldmere, Sutton Coldfield B73 5LH. Jenny & Bill Baker, 0121 244 2916 evening, furfuls2000@yahoo.co.uk. *Leave M6 at J6 following signs for Birmingham NE A38. Then take A5127 signed to Sutton Coldfield. Turn L into Station Rd after 3m.* **Sun 29 May, Sun 17 July (11-5). Adm £3, chd free. Home-made teas in adjoining garden. Visits also by arrangement May to Sept, groups 12 max welcomed at the weekends.**
Medium-sized suburban garden designed for visual impact with colour and interest provided predominantly by foliage. Many different acers, ferns and hostas grown in containers. Mints, herbs, shrubs, trees and bedding also grown in pots. Greenhouse, pond, rockery and tortoise enclosure. Home made teas and plant sale in adjoining garden.

56 ◆ SUGNALL WALLED GARDEN
Sugnall, Eccleshall, Stafford ST21 6NF. Dr David Jacques, 01785 850820, info@sugnallwalledgarden.co.uk, www.sugnall.co.uk. *2 1/2 m NW of Eccleshall. Just off B5026 Eccleshall to Loggerheads Rd. Turn at the Sugnall Xrds & use the Sugnall Business Centre car park.* **For NGS: Wed 6 July, Wed 3 Aug (12-4). Adm £3, chd free. Home-made teas. For other opening times and information, please phone, email or visit garden website.**
Historic walled kitchen garden of 1737, renovated for today. Work in progress, e.g. glass houses still to be

repaired, but most of the 2 acres is under cultivation with 200 apple and pear dwarf pyramids, 50 fan-trained wall fruit and a wide variety of produce within the quarters. Flower borders around marquee and events area. Tearoom serving light lunches made from produce in the garden, wine and beer also available. Garden shop.

57 NEW 32 TAMAR DRIVE
Sutton Coldfield B76 1YT. Mr A Green. *3m from J9 M42. J9 M42 follow signs to Minworth A4097 Kingsbury Rd. At island follow sign to Walmley, Walmley Ash Rd, R at 2nd island Webster Way 1st L Calder Drive, Tamar Drive is 2nd L.* **Sun 3 July (1-5). Adm £3, chd free. Home-made teas.**
Tony and Wendy welcome you to their small suburban garden, which over many years with Tony's passion for Rare and Unusual plants has developed into the garden it is today. Lots of Quirky !!! and Interesting features. A Japanese style area and Wildlife Pond, mature trees and shrubs.

58 TANGLEWOOD COTTAGE
Crossheads, Colwich, Stafford ST18 0UG. Dennis & Helen Wood, 01889 882857, shuvitdog@hotmail.com. *5m SE of Stafford. A51 Rugeley/Weston R into Colwich. Church on L school on R, under bridge R into Crossheads Lane follow railway approx ¹/₄ m (it does lead somewhere). Parking signed on grass opp brick kiln cottage.* **Sun 22 May (10-4). Adm £3, chd free. Home-made teas. Visits also by arrangement May to Sept for groups 15+. Catering requirements on request.**
A tranquil country cottage with koi carp pool, vegetables and fruit, chickens, aviary and an array of wonderful perennials. A garden of peace and tranquillity, different rooms and variety. Sit in the courtyard and enjoy Helen's homemade Fayre. Year on year people spend many hours relaxing with us. and don't forget Lucky the parrot he can be naughty! Art/jewellery/crafts/book sales. HPS Plant Fair in village hall Sun 22nd May. Lots of gravel paths, people with walking sticks seem to manage quite well. Wheelchairs would have difficulty.

59 TILEWRIGHT CLOSE
7 Tilewright Close, Kidsgrove, Stoke-on-Trent ST7 4TR. Karon Hackney-Bourne. *Travelling N, leave A500 at exit signed Kidsgrove A50. At Xrds in Kidsgrove turn R into Mount Rd, 3rd L into Whiteridge Rd, 2nd R into Tilewright Close.* **Sun 10 July (12-4). Adm £2.50, chd free. Light refreshments. Squash, quiche with side salad and cakes.**
An unexpected, highly maintained suburban garden, containing over 20 clematis, alongside honeysuckle and climbing roses with garden rooms, each designed with a specific purpose in mind.This is a family garden on different levels,on a difficult landscape and includes three seating areas, a fire pit, various trees, formal lawn and deep herbaceous borders. An interesting plot which will inspire you. Gold award for Residential Garden from Newcastle in Bloom.

60 91 TOWER ROAD
Four Oaks, Sutton Coldfield B75 5EQ. Heather & Gary Hawkins. *3m N Sutton Coldfield. From A5127 at Mere Green island, turn onto Mere Green Rd, L at St James Church, L again onto Tower Road.* **Sun 5 June (1.30-5.30). Adm £3, chd free. Cream teas.**
163ft S-facing garden with sweeping borders and island beds planted with an eclectic mix of shrubs and perennials. A well stocked fishpond, imposing cast iron water feature and a hiding griffin enhance your journey around the garden. A vast array of home made cakes to tempt you during your visit. The ideal setting for sunbathing, children's hide and seek and lively garden parties. Amazing selection of home-made cream teas to eat in the garden or take away. More than just an Open Garden, we like to think of it as a garden party! Featured in Sutton Coldfield Observer.

61 ◆ THE TRENTHAM ESTATE
Stone Road, Stoke-on-Trent ST4 8JG. Michael Walker, 01782 646646, enquiry@trentham.co.uk. www.trentham.co.uk. *M6 J15. Well signed on r'about, A34 with A5035.* **For NGS: Wed 27 Jan, Wed 24 Feb, Wed 23 Mar (12-1). Adm £7.75, chd free. Evening opening Wed 6 July (5-8). Adm £5.25, chd free. Light refreshments in the gardens. For other opening times**

and information, please phone, email or visit garden website.
In 2016 Trentham will be an Urban Hub for the Capability BBC Countryfile Garden of the Year 2015, has undergone a major programme of restoration which has both revealed the historic landscape designed by Capability Brown and is replenishing this with vast new contemporary plantings of annuals, perennials, trees and shrubs. NGS Special Openings with Trenthams' Head of Garden and Estate, Michael Walker, will provide a complimentary tour of the recently revealed areas around Browns mile long lake. Refreshments throughout the shopping village.

62 41 TWENTYLANDS
Rolleston-on-Dove, Burton-on-Trent DE13 9AJ. Maureen & Joe Martin, 01283 520208, joe.martin11@btinternet.com. *3m E of Tutbury. At r'about on Tutbury by-pass A511 take Rolleston Lane continue through Rolleston-on-Dove, past Scout HQ. Twentylands on R, opp the Jinny Inn. From A38 take turn off to Stretton continue to Rolleston.* **Sun 5 June (12-5). Adm £3, chd free. Home-made teas. Visits also by arrangement May to Sept 6 min 20 max. Teas.**
Small back garden. Every corner used and packed with plants. Herbaceous borders with fruit trees and shrubs. Herb corner, fernery, bog garden with many candelabra primula, in Spring, and other bog plants. Chinese garden with chess pavilion and bonsai, water features, small pond with lilys, wood carvings, greenhouses, Water harvesting and composting systems. Many plants raised from seed. Tutbury Castle, Blue Cross Horse Sanctuary and Jinny Nature Trail nearby.

Waterdale

63 19 WATERDALE

Compton, Wolverhampton
WV3 9DY. Anne & Brian Bailey,
01902 424867,
m.bailey1234@btinternet.com,
www.facebook.com/pages/Garden
-of-Surprises/165745816926408.
*1½ m W of Wolverhampton city
centre. From Wolverhampton Ring Rd
take A454 towards Bridgnorth for 1m.
Waterdale is on L off A454 Compton
Rd West.* **Sun 5 June (12.30-5).
Home-made teas. Tue 7 June (11-
5). Also open Wightwick Manor.
Sun 3 July (12.30-5). Home-made
teas. Adm £3.50, chd free. Visits
also by arrangement June & July
for groups of 10-35.**
A romantic garden, full of surprises,
which gradually reveals itself on a
journey through deep, lush planting,
full of unusual plants. From the sunny,
flower filled terrace, a ruined folly
emerges from a luxuriant fernery and
leads into an oriental garden,
complete with teahouse. Towering
bamboos hide the way to the gothic
summerhouse and mysterious shell
grotto. Tues 7 June - Refreshments
available at Wightwick Manor and
map of 2m canal-side walk to
Waterdale. Winner of the Daily Mail
National Garden Competition 2015
and featured in local press.

64 NEW THE WENTLOWS

64 Cheadle Road, Tean, Stoke-On-
Trent ST10 4DN. Peter & Catherine
Wright. *Approx 8m NW of Uttoxeter.
Located in Tean on A522 between
Tean & Cheadle. Free public car park
located in Tean village centre ~300
yds from Garden.* **Sun 3 July (1.30-
5). Adm £3, chd free. Light
refreshments.**
Project rejuvenation, integrating the
new with the old in a wrap around
garden of varying rooms situated on
terraced layers and slopping lawns
against a backdrop of open fields. A
living garden with something for all; a
herb checker board, miniature
orchard with pocket size vegetable
patch, wooded haven, parterre, a
taste of the orient, traditional rose
terrace, waterfall and marginal
garden. As the garden is made up of
gentle slopes, steps and terraces it
has very limited access for wheelchair
users.

WESTACRES

See Worcestershire

65 THE WICKETS

47 Long Street, Wheaton Aston
ST19 9NF. Tony & Kate Bennett,
01785 840233,
ajtonyb@talktalk.net. *8m W of
Cannock, 10m N of Wolverhampton,
10m E of Telford. M6 J12 W towards
Telford on A5; 3m R signed Stretton;
150yds L signed Wheaton Aston; 2m
L; over canal, garden on R or at
Bradford Arms on A5 follow signs.*
**Sun 17, Thur 21 July, Sun 28 Aug
(1.30-5). Adm £3, chd free. Tea.
Visits also by arrangement June
to Aug.**
There's a surprise around every
corner and lots of quirky delights in
this most original garden. Its themed
areas incl '50 Shades of Green' (the
fernery), station platform, oriental dry
stream, succulent theatre and even a
cricket match! It will ignite your
imagination and give you ideas for
your own garden as you sit and enjoy
our acclaimed tea and cake. Two
steps in garden.

66 NEW ◆ WIGHTWICK MANOR

Wightwick Bank, Wolverhampton
WV6 8EE. National Trust,
01902 764100,
wightwickmanor@nationaltrust.org.
uk, www.nationaltrust.org.uk.
*Entrance off Bridgnorth road, A454.
Sat Nav WV6 8BN. Brown signs from
Wolverhampton city centre.* **For
NGS: Tue 7 June (11-5). Adm
£5.75, chd £2.85. Light
refreshments. Also open 19
Waterdale.** For other opening
times and information, please
phone, email or visit garden
website.
17 acre Arts & Crafts garden
designed in 1905 and 1910 by
Thomas Mawson. Formal gardens set
off late Victorian house (not open Tue)
with wisteria, vine and Banksia Rose
on south front. Formal lawns with
beds of roses, herbaceous planting
surrounded by yew hedges. Orchards
leading to lakes surrounded by
rhododendron, with woodland
beyond. Tea-room and shop which
specialises in William Morris related
products open daily. Access around
most of garden by certain routes.
Largely over grass paths and lawns.

67 WILD WOOD LODGE

Bushton Lane, Anslow, Burton-On-
Trent DE13 9QL. Mr & Mrs Richard
& Dorothy Ward, 01283 812100.
*Bushton Lane is signed in centre of
village. Wild Wood Lodge is ¼ m
down Bushton Lane.* **Sun 12 June,
Sun 14 Aug (1.30-5). Adm £3, chd
free. Home-made teas. Visits also
by arrangement May to Aug.**
The garden established over the last
few years much of which was a
former farm yard and buildings with
extensive views of the Staffordshire
countryside towards Needwood
Forest. Covering approx 2 acre it
consists of a productive orchard,
raised vegetable beds, colourful
herbaceous borders, shrubs,
ornamental trees, wild life pond and
fishing lake. Level garden, wide
paths.

68 WITS END

59 Tanworth Lane, Shirley, Solihull
B90 4DQ. Sue Mansell, 0121 744
4337, wits-end@hotmail.co.uk. *2m
SW of Solihull. Take B4102 from
Solihull for 2m. R at island onto A34.
After next island (Sainsbury's)
Tanworth Lane 1st L off A34.*

Mon 2 May (11.30-4); Sun 29 May, Sun 7 Aug (12.30-4). Adm £3, chd free. Home-made teas. **Visits also by arrangement May to Aug, groups 10+.**
Interesting all-yr-round plantaholic's cottage-style garden. Perennials and shrubs, many unusual in various shaped beds (some colour co-ordinated) plus spectacular late summer border. Various containers displaying an array of sempervivum and jovibarba. Various water features, scree and planting changes planned for 2016.

GROUP OPENING

69 WOODLAND GRANGE GARDENS
Rowley Hall Drive, Stafford ST17 9FF. *1m SW of Stafford town centre. Off A518 Newport Rd. Turn into Rowley Ave, signed Rowley Hall Hospital. Continue through the white gates following the lane straight on. Park in the hospital car park. No access from A449.* **Sun 19 June (1-5). Combined adm £4, chd free. Home-made teas.**

7 ROWLEY HALL DRIVE
Mr Paul Brett & Mr John McEvoy
https://mallardscottage.wordpress.com

10 ROWLEY HALL DRIVE
Mr & Mrs Wootton

12 ROWLEY HALL DRIVE
Jane & Chris Whitney-Cooper

A trio of smaller-scale suburban 'real-life' gardens to spark the imagination. Three suburban gardens established over the past 20 years on a site that was once part of the grounds of Rowley Hall. They are planted in contrasting styles, but all draw on features of the parkland that still surrounds these modern houses. No. 10 is a villa-style garden, open and spacious, with formal lawns surrounded by professionally laid-out borders for year-round colour and interest. No.12 is a country/cottage style garden, combining productive vegetable areas as well as attractive borders and mixed planting. The owners use organic principles and have completed their country-style 'Good Life' with a brood of hens. No.7 is an edge of woodland style garden with a feel of peace, calm and tranquility. It uses focal points and

perspective principles to enhance this effect. Shrubs and foliage plants, rather than flowers are used to create a naturalistic setting attractive to wildlife. Pimms will be available at No.10, tea and cakes at No.12 and plants from the gardens will be on sale at No.7 for you to take home to your own 'earthly paradise'. Parking at Rowley Hall Hospital, short walk down drive to Rowley Hall Drive. Gardens will be signed. Tickets available at 10 Rowley Hall Drive.

Lots of Quirky !!! and Interesting features . . .

GROUP OPENING

70 WOODLEIGHTON GROVE GARDENS
Woodleighton Grove, Uttoxeter ST14 8BX, 01889 563930, graham&judy.white@ngs.org.uk. *SE of Uttoxeter. From Uttoxeter take B5017 (Marchington). Go over Town Bridge, 1st exit at r'about, then 3rd exit at r'about into Highwood Rd, After 1/4 m turn R.* **Evening opening Fri 1 July (6-10). Combined adm £6. Sat 9 July (11-5); Sun 10 July (1-5). Combined adm £3.50, chd free. Home-made teas. Visits also by arrangement June & July min 12, adm £6 per head, incl home-made teas. WC available.**

APOLLONIA
Helen & David Loughton

KARIBU
Graham & Judy White

At the end of a quiet cul-de-sac in Woodleighton Grove, Uttoxeter, you will receive a warm welcome to the gardens of two next door neighbours who will be really pleased to discuss with visitors, any aspects of their gardens. The gardens are varied and fascinating, and include numerous features, such as a Fruit Arch, Natural Stream, Summerhouses, Greenhouses, Alpine House on wheels; a Folly, Gazebo, Stumpery, Arbour, Insect Hotel and Wormery,

together with many archways, bridges, steps, pagoda's and a boardwalk, all leading to a selection of tranquil resting places. The gardens display many unusual and interesting plants, and discreetly house many fascinating artefacts, antiques, collections and other items of interest. For the 1st time this year, in addition to the Open Weekend, the gardens will also be having an Evening Opening on Fri 1 July. Adm £6 per head, which will incl admission to both gardens. plus tea, coffee, soft drink or wine and canapés.

71 YARLET HOUSE
Yarlet, Stafford ST18 9SD. Mr & Mrs Nikolas Tarling. *2m S of Stone. Take A34 from Stone towards Stafford, turn L into Yarlet School & L again into car park.* **Fri 1 July (10-2). Adm £4, chd free. Home-made teas.** *Donation to Staffordshire Wildlife Trust.*
4 acre garden with extensive lawns, walks, lengthy herbaceous borders and traditional Victorian box hedge. Water gardens with fountain and rare lilies. Sweeping views across Trent Valley to Sandon. Victorian School Chapel. 9 hole putting course. Boules pitch. Yarlet School Art Display. Gravel paths.

72 YEW TREE COTTAGE
Podmores Corner, Long Lane, White Cross, Haughton ST18 9JR. Clive & Ruth Plant, 01785 282516, pottyplantz@aol.com. *4m W of Stafford. Take A518 W Haughton, turn R Station Rd (signed Ranton) 1m, then turn R at Xrds 1/4 m on R.* **Sun 1 May (2-5); Thur 5 May, Thur 2, Thur 9 June, Thur 7 July (11-5); Sun 24 July (2-5); Thur 28 July (11-5). Adm £3, chd free. Home-made teas. Visits also by arrangement May to July.**
Hardy Plant Society member's garden brimming with unusual plants. All-yr-round interest incl Meconopsis, Trillium, and Arisaema. Large collection of Dierama, National Collection status applied for. 1/2 -acre incl gravel, borders, vegetables and plant sales area. Covered courtyard with oak-timbered vinery to take tea in if the weather is unkind, and seats in the garden for lingering on sunny days. Level access, grass and paved paths, some narrow.

SUFFOLK

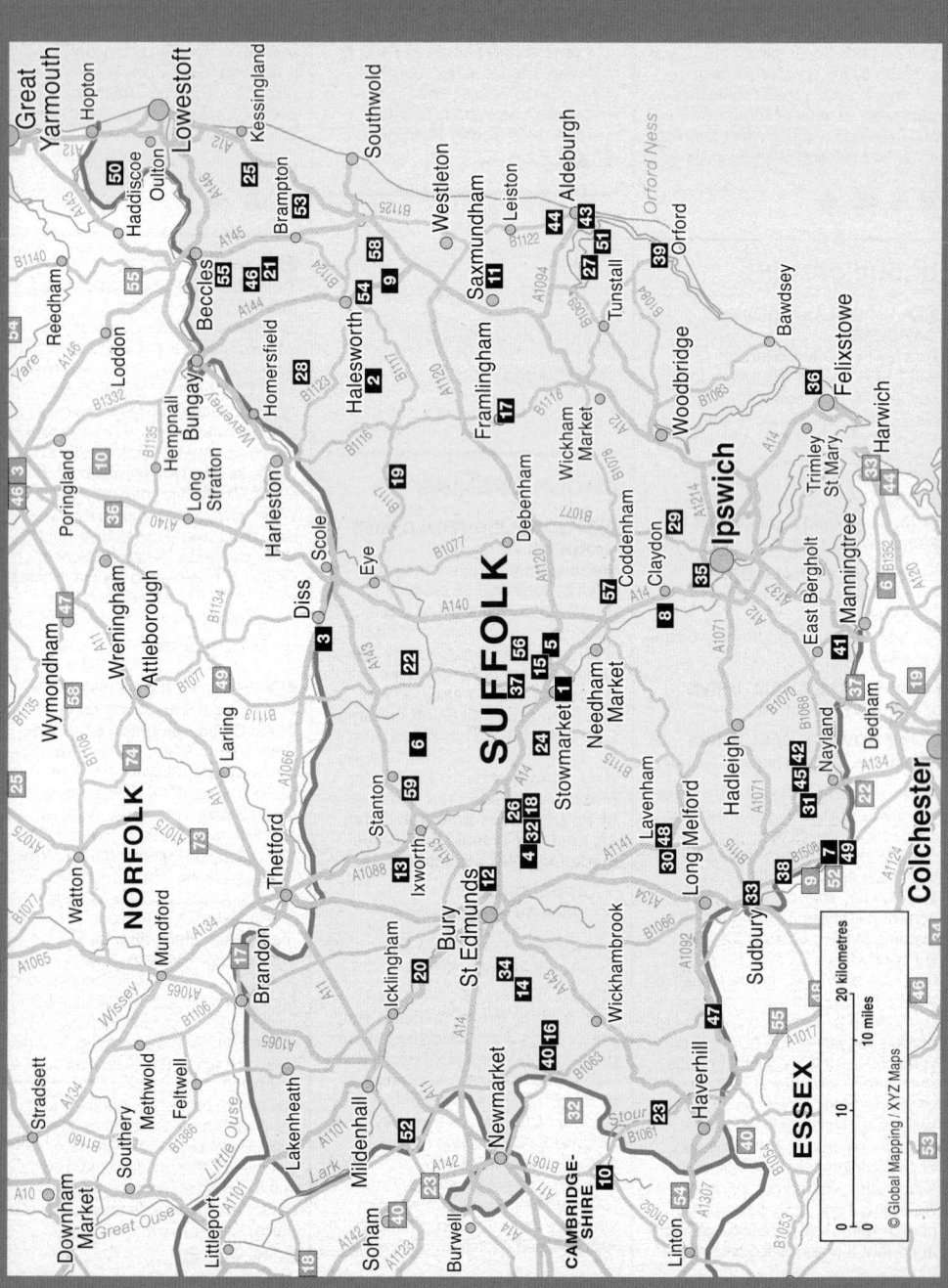

Suffolk

Suffolk has so much to offer – from charming coastal villages, ancient woodlands and picturesque valleys – there is a landscape to suit all tastes.

Keen walkers and cyclists will enjoy Suffolk's low-lying, gentle countryside, where fields of farm animals and crops reflect the county's agricultural roots.

Stretching north from Felixstowe, the county has miles of Heritage Coast set in an Area of Outstanding Natural Beauty. The Suffolk coast was the inspiration for composer Benjamin Britten's celebrated work, and it is easy to see why.

To the west and north of the county are The Brecks, a striking canvas of pine forest and open heathland, famous for its chalky and sandy soils – and one of the most important wildlife areas in Britain.

A variety of gardens to please everyone open for Suffolk NGS, so come along on an open day and enjoy the double benefit of a beautiful setting and supporting wonderful charities.

Suffolk Volunteers

County Organiser
Jenny Reeve
01638 715289
j.reeve05@tiscali.co.uk

County Treasurer
David Reeve
01638 715289
dreeve43@gmail.com

Publicity
Jenny Reeve
(as above)

Booklet Co-ordinator
Adrian Simpson-James
01502 710555
sjs@megenna.freeserve.co.uk

Assistant County Organisers
Gilly Beddard
01394 450468
gbedd@btinternet.com

Frances Boscawen
01728 638768
francesboscawen@gmail.com

Catherine Horwood Barwise
01787 279315
catherine@richmondhouse-clare.com

David & Yvonne Leonard
01638 712742
yj.leonard@btinternet.com

Marie-Anne Mackenzie
01728 831155
marieanne_mackenzie@yahoo.co.uk

Barbara Segall
01787 312046
barbara@bsegall.plus.com

Adrian Simpson-James
(as above)

Left: Bay Tree House

Opening Dates

All entries subject to change.
For latest information check www.ngs.org.uk

February

Snowdrop Festival

Sunday 14
21 Gable House
Sunday 21
8 Blakenham Woodland Garden

March

Sunday 27
57 Woodwards
Monday 28
28 The Laburnums

April

Sunday 3
23 Great Thurlow Hall
41 The Place for Plants, East Bergholt Place Garden
Sunday 10
5 Bays Farm
6 The Beeches
Sunday 17
40 Ousden House

River Cottage

Sunday 24
37 Old Newton Gardens
Saturday 30
10 Brinkley Gardens

May

Sunday 1
8 Blakenham Woodland Garden
10 Brinkley Gardens
19 Frythe Barn
38 Old Rectory House
Monday 2
7 Bevills
Sunday 8
34 Moat House
57 Woodwards
Sunday 15
3 Batteleys Cottage
5 Bays Farm
20 Fullers Mill Garden
27 Iken Gardens
41 The Place for Plants, East Bergholt Place Garden
47 Richmond House
49 Rosedale
52 Street Farm
Sunday 22
15 Columbine Hall
30 Lavenham Hall
36 Old Felixstowe Gardens
45 The Priory
Saturday 28
4 NEW Bay Tree House
Sunday 29
2 Appleacre
51 NEW Stanny House Farm
54 NEW Wenhaston Grange
Monday 30
18 Drinkstone Park

June

Festival Weekend

Saturday 4
33 22 Melford Road
57 Woodwards
59 Wyken Hall
Sunday 5
21 Gable House
31 NEW Leaven Hall
33 22 Melford Road
35 428 Norwich Road
39 Orford Gardens
56 Wood Farm, Gipping
59 Wyken Hall

Wednesday 8
50 Somerleyton Hall Gardens
Saturday 11
29 Larks' Hill
Sunday 12
18 Drinkstone Park
32 NEW Malting Farm
Sunday 19
1 Abbot's Hall Walled Garden
26 Hessett House
Sunday 26
13 Church Cottage
44 Priors Oak
53 Uggeshall Hall

July

Saturday 2
55 White House Farm
Sunday 3
18 Drinkstone Park
24 Green Farmhouse
Tuesday 5
57 Woodwards
Sunday 10
12 Cattishall Farmhouse
46 Redisham Hall
Sunday 17
18 Drinkstone Park
Sunday 24
57 Woodwards

August

Saturday 6
22 Gislingham Gardens
Sunday 7
22 Gislingham Gardens
49 Rosedale
Tuesday 9
57 Woodwards
Sunday 14
5 Bays Farm
48 NEW River Cottage
Sunday 21
25 Henstead Exotic Garden
Sunday 28
57 Woodwards

September

Sunday 4
9 Bramfield Hall
19 Frythe Barn
Sunday 11
5 Bays Farm
11 By the Crossways
Sunday 18
43 Priors Hill, Aldeburgh

October

Sunday 9
41 The Place for Plants, East Bergholt Place Garden

Gardens open to the public

8 Blakenham Woodland Garden
20 Fullers Mill Garden
41 The Place for Plants, East Bergholt Place Garden
50 Somerleyton Hall Gardens
58 Woottens of Wenhaston
59 Wyken Hall

By arrangement only

14 Cobbs Hall
16 Dip-on-the-Hill
17 28 Double Street
42 Polstead Mill

Also open by arrangement

3 Batteleys Cottage
5 Bays Farm
13 Church Cottage
18 Drinkstone Park
19 Frythe Barn
21 Gable House
24 Green Farmhouse
25 Henstead Exotic Garden
29 Larks' Hill
33 22 Melford Road
34 Moat House
36 41 Westmorland Road, Old Felixstowe Gardens
43 Heron House, Priors Hill, Aldeburgh
43 Priors Hill, Aldeburgh
43 Stanny, Priors Hill, Aldeburgh
44 Priors Oak
46 Redisham Hall
47 Richmond House
48 NEW River Cottage
49 Rosedale
53 Uggeshall Hall
55 White House Farm
57 Woodwards

Wenhaston Grange

The Gardens

1 ABBOT'S HALL WALLED GARDEN

Iliffe Way, Stowmarket IP14 1DL. Museum of East Anglian Life, www.eastanglianlife.org.uk. *The Museum of East Anglian Life is adjacent to ASDA supermarket in Stowmarket. The Museum is signed from the main A14 trunk rd & B1115 to Great Finborough. For SatNav users please search for 'Iliffe Way' or IP14 1DE.* **Adm £2.50, chd free. Home-made teas.**

An oasis in the heart of Stowmarket this ½ acre walled Victorian kitchen garden has been restored and replanted since 2012. Showcasing many heritage vegetable varieties as well as trained fruit trees, herb bed, cut flower border, old roses and apple tunnel. It also boasts a renovated greenhouse, potting shed and conservatory. Good wheelchair access, gravel paths. A small car park is located in the grounds of Abbot's Hall for visitors with access needs only.

2 APPLEACRE

Bell Green, Cratfield, Halesworth IP19 0DH. Mr & Mrs Tim & Naomi Shaw. *7m W of Halesworth. B1123 to Harleston. At Linstead Parva, turn L up Godfrey's Hill. After approx 1m turn R onto Mary's Lane & follow NGS signs. 50 metres W of the Poacher PH.* **Sun 29 May (11-5). Adm £3.50, chd free. Home-made teas.**

A country garden covering an acre that has evolved over forty years. A garden full of secrets waiting to be revealed, with open vistas over the Suffolk countryside. Explore a variety of large herbaceous borders, box topiary, mature trees, lily pond, greenhouse, lawns, vegetable garden and wildlife area. Partial wheelchair access, but caution needed in some areas.

3 BATTELEYS COTTAGE

The Ling, Wortham, Diss IP22 1ST. Mr & Mrs Andy & Linda Simpson, 07949 204820, lindaruth11@gmail.com. *3m W of Diss. Turn signed from A143 Diss/Bury Rd at Wortham. By church turn R at T-junction. At top of hill turn L. Go down hill & round sharp L corner.* **Sun 15 May (1-5.30). Adm £4, chd free. Home-made teas. Visits also by arrangement May to Sept, refreshments available for groups on request.**

A varied one acre garden planted for abundance in all seasons. Formality and informality, a mix of winding bark paths, light and shade, secluded spots to sit, new vistas at every turn. Fitting into its rural setting, it supports a wealth of bird life. There is a diversity of planting in densely planted borders as well as pots, sculptures, meadow, ponds, stream and vegetable areas to inspire you. Featured in EDP Suffolk Magazine. Wheelchair access to most parts of the garden, gravel, grass and bark paths.

4 NEW BAY TREE HOUSE

The Green, Rougham, Bury St. Edmunds IP30 9JP. Mrs Claire Farthing. *Rougham Green. Come off A14 at J45 & head for Rougham at T-Junction, turn L follow road for approx 1½ m, past Rougham Sports Hall. Go round 90 degree bend to R. Take 2nd L gravel driveway.* **Sat 28 May (10.30-5.30). Adm £4.50, chd free. Home-made teas.**

Nearly 2 acres of garden with a wildlife pond, mature trees, long border, rose arbour, parterre garden. Green oak arches with wisteria and Italian pots. Lollipop hornbeams with curved yew hedging. Patio with wisteria draped pergola. Lovely country views. The garden is mainly flat with only one small gravel path which can be avoided.

5 BAYS FARM

Forward Green, Earl Stonham, Stowmarket IP14 5HU. Richard & Stephanie Challinor, 01449 711286, stephanie@baysfarmsuffolk.co.uk, www.baysfarmgardens.co.uk. *3½ m E of Stowmarket. J50 A14, take A1120 direction Stowupland. Proceed through Stowupland on A1120 for 1m, at sharp L bend turn R signed Broad Green. 1st house on R.* **Sun 10 Apr, Sun 15 May, Sun 14 Aug, Sun 11 Sept (2-5.30). Adm £3.50, chd free. Home-made teas. Visits also by arrangement Mar to Oct, refreshments on request for groups - please see website for details.**

New 2016 opening dates show the year-round colour at Bays Farm. The Xa Tollemache designed borders form the backdrop of this true plantsman's garden. New borders, hard landscaping and heated greenhouse, redeveloped moat and the recently planted Shepherds Hut cottage garden all display the ever changing interest at Bays Farm. Not opening in June/July so check our website for private visits info. Formal gardens designed by Chelsea Gold Medal winner, Xa Tollemache of Helmingham Hall and recently redesigned moat. Featured in The Suffolk Magazine, East Anglian Daily Times, The English Garden and Homes and Gardens. Gravel paths.

6 THE BEECHES

Grove Road, Walsham-le-Willows IP31 3AD. Dr A J Russell. *11m E of Bury St Edmunds. A143 to Diss. Turn R to Walsham-le-Willows. 1st Xrds in village turn R. Church on L. After 100yds turn L. Beeches on L.* **Sun 10 Apr (2-5). Adm £4, chd free. Tea.** *Donation to St Marys Church, Walsham-le-Willows.*

150yr-old, 3-acre garden, which incl specimen trees, pond, stream, potager, memorial garden, lawns and a variety of beds. Stream area landscaped. Mediterranean bed and camellia bed. Gravel paths.

7 BEVILLS

Sudbury Road, Bures CO8 5JW. Mr & Mrs G T C Probert. *4m S of Sudbury. Just N of Bures on the Sudbury rd B1508.* **Mon 2 May (2-5.30). Adm £4, chd free. Home-made teas.**

A beautiful house (not open) overlooking the Stour Valley with parkland trees, hills and woodland. The gardens are formal and Italianate in style with hedges and lawns flanked by Irish yews and mature specimen trees. Terraces, borders, ponds, vistas and woodland walks. Spring bulbs and bluebell wood. Gravel paths.

The Queen's Nursing Institute

QNI

The NGS is The QNI's largest single donor

8 ◆ BLAKENHAM WOODLAND GARDEN

Little Blakenham, Ipswich IP8 4LZ. M & M Blakenham, 07760 342131, www.blakenhamwoodlandgarden.org.uk. *4m NW of Ipswich. Follow signs at Little Blakenham, 1m off B1113 or go to Blakenham Woodland Garden web-site.* **For NGS: Sun 21 Feb, Sun 1 May (10-5). Adm £3, chd £1.50. Home-made teas. For other opening times and information, please phone or visit garden website.**

Beautiful 6-acre woodland garden with variety of rare trees and shrubs, Chinese rocks and a landscape sculpture. Lovely in spring with snowdrops, daffodils, camellias, magnolias and bluebells followed by roses in early summer. Partial wheelchair access.

9 BRAMFIELD HALL

Bramfield, Halesworth IP19 9HX. Mr Simon Robey. *3m S of Halesworth on A144. From Halesworth drive through Bramfield & once out of village entrance on R. From A12 entrance is past rd to Sibton Green.* **Sun 4 Sept (2-5). Adm £3, chd free. Home-made teas.**

Garden consists of formal and informal areas. Within the garden there is yew topiarys a parterre rose garden, herbaceous borders, ponds, vegetable garden and greenhouses; and has been extensively renovated in the last 10yrs by the current owner.

The garden is reached from a drive through parkland containing some fine trees. This garden was one of the first to open when the NGS was formed in 1927. Gravel paths and some slopes.

GROUP OPENING

10 BRINKLEY GARDENS

Newmarket CB8 0SB. *6m S of Newmarket. Enter village and follow yellow signs.* **Sat 30 Apr, Sun 1 May (11.30-4.30). Combined adm £4, chd free. Light refreshments at Brinkley Village Hall.**

THE GROVE
Dr & Mrs Alexander Gimson

THE OLD RECTORY
Mr & Mrs Mark Coley

Two lovely gardens, one of one acre and one of two acres in the attractive village of Brinkley. The Grove 1-acre garden surrounding C19 house (not open), with mature yew trees and beech hedges. Walled garden area has established shrubs and wisteria, with new beds and planting created over the last 8yrs. This incls a dry bed with irises, terrace beds with tulips and a mixed herbaceous border along the curved wall. The Old Rectory two acre garden was started in 1973. Interesting trees planted to supplement beech, yew and chestnut already there. Mixed Herbaceous borders. Traditional potager with box hedges planted in 1993. Small woodland area still being developed. 1st May food available at local village PH.

11 BY THE CROSSWAYS

Kelsale, Saxmundham IP17 2PL. Mr & Mrs William Kendall. *2m NE of Saxmundham, just off Clayhills Rd. ½ m N of town centre, turn R to Theberton on Clayhills Rd. After 1½ m, 1st L to Kelsale, then turn L immed after white cottage.* **Sun 11 Sept (11-4). Adm £4, chd free. Home-made teas.**

3-acre wildlife garden designed as a garden within an organic farm, where wilderness areas lie next to productive beds. Large semi-walled vegetable and cutting garden, a spectacular crinkle-crankle wall. Extensive perennial planting, grasses and wild areas. Set around the owner's Edwardian family home built by suffragist ancestor. The garden is mostly flat, with paved or gravel pathways around the main house, a few low steps and extensive grass paths and lawns.

12 CATTISHALL FARMHOUSE
Cattishall, Great Barton, Bury St. Edmunds IP31 2QT. Mrs J Mayer, 01284 787340, joannamayer42@googlemail.com. *3m NE of Bury St Edmunds. Approaching Great Barton from Bury on A143 take 1st R turn to church. If travelling towards Bury take last L turn to church as you leave the village. At church bear R and follow lane to Farmhouse on R.* **Sun 10 July (1-5). Adm £4, chd free. Home-made teas.**
Approx 2 acre farmhouse garden enclosed by a flint wall and mature beech hedge laid mainly to lawns with both formal and informal planting and a large herbaceous border. There is an abundance of roses and a recently developed kitchen garden incl a wild flower area and fruit cages. Chickens, bees and a boisterous Labrador also live here. Generally flat with some gravel paths. The occasional small step.

Lollipop hornbeams with curved yew hedging. Patio with wisteria draped pergola . . .

13 CHURCH COTTAGE
Church Lane, Troston, Bury St Edmunds IP31 1EX. Graeme & Marysa Norris, 07855 284816, marysa.i@lmrinternational.co.uk. *5 m NE of Bury St Edmunds. From the A143 turn at the Bunbury Arms, signed Troston & Gt Livermere. Follow the road through Gt Livermere, signed to Troston.* **Sun 26 June (2-5). Adm £3.50, chd free. Home-made teas. Visits also by arrangement June to Sept.**
³/₄ acre garden, of several different areas and still developing. A yew allee gives a view over open fields. There are mixed borders, an area to

encourage wildlife with an informal pond and mini meadow, an area of woodland plants, young trees and shrubs, a gravel garden and a productive kitchen garden with raised beds and a greenhouse. Church Cottage is opposite St Mary's Church, famous for its medieval wall painting and graffiti and which will be open on the same day.

14 COBBS HALL
Great Saxham IP29 5JN. Dick & Sue Soper, 01284 850678, soperdoc@gmail.com. *4¹/₂ m W of Bury St Edmunds. A14 exit to Westley. R at Westley Xrds. L fork at Lt.Saxham towards Chevington. 1.4m to R turn marked 'Gt Saxham'. Mustard coloured house 300yds on L.* **Visits by arrangement June to Sept, adm includes refreshments £7, chd free.** *Donation to St Andrews Church, Gt Saxham.*
2 acres of lawns and borders, ornamental trees, large fish and lily pond. Parterre, folly, walled kitchen garden, fernery/stumpery, grass tennis court and pretty courtyard. Cascade water feature. Generally flat with a few gentle slopes and some gravel paths.

15 COLUMBINE HALL
Gipping Road, Stowupland, Stowmarket IP14 4AT. Hew Stevenson & Leslie Geddes-Brown, www.columbinehall.co.uk. *1¹/₂ m NE of Stowmarket. Turn N off A1120 opp petrol station across village green, then R at T-junction into Gipping Rd. Garden on L just beyond derestriction sign.* **Sun 22 May (2-6). Adm £4, chd free. Home-made teas.**
George Carter's formal garden and herb garden surround moated medieval manor (not open). Outside the moat, vistas, stream, ponds and bog garden, Mediterranean garden, colour-themed vegetable garden, orchards and parkland. Gardens developed since 1994 with constant work-in-progress, incl transformed farm buildings and eyecatchers. Disabled WC.

16 DIP-ON-THE-HILL
Ousden, Newmarket CB8 8TW. Dr & Mrs Geoffrey Ingham, 01638 500329, gki1000@cam.ac.uk. *5m E of Newmarket; 7m W of Bury St Edmunds. From Newmarket: 1m from*

junction of B1063 & B1085. From Bury St Edmunds follow signs for Hargrave. Parking at village hall. **Visits by arrangement June to Sept, 20 max. Adm £4, chd free. Tea.**
Approx one acre in a dip on a S-facing hill based on a wide range of architectural/sculptural evergreen trees, shrubs and groundcover: pines; grove of Phillyrea latifolia; 'cloud pruned' hedges; palms; large bamboo; ferns; range of kniphofia and croscosmia. Featured in Country Living and The English Garden. Visitors may wish to make an appointment when visiting gardens nearby.

17 28 DOUBLE STREET
Framlingham IP13 9BN. Mr & Mrs David Clark, clarkdn@btinternet.com. *250yrds from Market Hill (main square) Framlingham opp Church. Leave square from top L into Church St. Double St is 100yds on R. Car parking in main square & near to Framlingham Castle.* **Visits by arrangement June & July, groups of 10+. Adm £3, chd free. Tea.**
A recently developed town garden featuring roses together with a wide range of perennials and shrubs. Conservatory, greenhouse, gazebo, summerhouse and terrace full of containers all add interest to the garden. Good views of Framlingham's roofscape. Fine shingle access drive with two ramps.

18 DRINKSTONE PARK
Park Road, Drinkstone, Bury St. Edmunds IP30 9ST. Michael & Christine Lambert, 01359 272513, chris@drinkstonepark.co.uk, www.drinkstonepark.co.uk. *6m from Bury St Edmunds. E on A14 J46 turn R & head for Drinkstone. W on A14 J46 take R next junction turn L and immed R to Drinkstone.* **Mon 30 May, Sun 12 June, Sun 3, Sun 17 July (1-5.30). Adm £3.50, chd free. Home-made teas. Visits also by arrangement June & July, refreshments on request to suit group.**
Three acre garden with wildlife pond formal Koi pond, herbaceous borders, orchard, woodland and wildlife area, large productive vegetable plot with poly tunnel and greenhouses. Some gravel paths.

Malting Farm

19 FRYTHE BARN

Wilby Road, Stradbroke, Eye
IP21 5JP. Don & Carol Darling,
01379 388098,
caroldon01@gmail.com. *11m SE of
Diss, 10m N of Framlingham. From
Framlingham B1118 to Stradbroke.
Through Wilby past Neaves Lane on
R 2nd driveway on R. From Diss
B1118 to Stradbroke, R church,
immed L, follow signs.* **Sun 1 May,
Sun 4 Sept (11-5). Adm £4, chd
free. Home-made teas. Savoury,
Gluten and Dairy free options
available. Visits also by
arrangement Apr to Sept, groups
of 10 - 30.**
A maze of concrete and brick
buildings transformed in 9 yrs into a
delightfully relaxing 2 acre garden.
Take a stroll via a willow tunnel,
spinney with bee hives and bog
garden through the orchard to a leafy
arbour, surrounded by flowing
grasses.View from here the large
pond and stream to the left,
sensitively planted borders to the
right and Italian style patio in front of
the renovated barn. Wildlife area,
large grass beds, pond, mixed
borders, roses. No wheelchair access
to spinney/wild flower meadow.

20 ◆ FULLERS MILL GARDEN

West Stow IP28 6HD. Perennial,
01284 728888,
fullersmillgarden@perennial.org.uk,
www.fullersmillgarden.org.uk. *6m
NW of Bury St Edmunds. Turn off
A1101 Bury to Mildenhall Rd, signed
West Stow Country Park, go past
Country Park continue for 1/4 m,
garden entrance on R. Sign at
entrance.* **For NGS: Sun 15 May
(2-5). Adm £4, chd free. Home-
made teas. For other opening
times and information, please
phone, email or visit garden
website.**
An enchanting 7 acre garden on the
banks of R Lark. A beautiful site of
light, dappled woodland with a
plantsman's paradise of rare and
unusual shrubs, perennials and
marginals planted with great natural
charm. Euphorbias and lilies are a
particular feature. A garden with
interest in every season. In late
Sept colchicums in flower incl
outstanding white variety. Tea/Coffee
and soft drinks. Homemade cakes.
Partial wheelchair access around
garden.

21 GABLE HOUSE

Halesworth Road, Redisham,
Beccles NR34 8NE. John & Brenda
Foster, 01502 575298,
gablehouse@btinternet.com. *5m
S of Beccles. A144 S from Bungay, L
at St Lawrence School, 2m to Gable
House. Or A12 Blythburgh, A145 to
Beccles, Brampton Xrd L to Station
Rd. 3m on is garden.* **Sun 14 Feb
(11-4); Sun 5 June (11-5). Adm £4,
chd free. Home-made teas.
Warming soups available in
February. Salad lunches in June.
Visits also by arrangement Feb to
Sept, 50 max.** *Donation to St
Peter's Church, Redisham.*
One acre mature Plantsman's garden
of all year interest. Vast collection of
snowdrops, cyclamen, hellebores etc
for the Snowdrop day in February.
The June open day brings colour and
variety from roses, perennials and
shrubs. Greenhouses contain rare
bulbs and tender plants. Featured in
Suffolk magazine and East Anglian
Daily Times.

GROUP OPENING

22 GISLINGHAM GARDENS

Mill Street, Gislingham IP23 8JT.
*4m W of Eye. Gislingham 2 1/2 m W of
A140. 9m N of Stowmarket, 8m S of
Diss. Disabled parking at Ivy
Chimneys.* **Sat 6, Sun 7 Aug
(11-4.30). Combined adm £3.50,
chd free. Home-made teas at Ivy
Chimneys. Teas cakes and soft
drinks if hot.**

HAREBELLS
Jenny & Darrel Charles

IVY CHIMNEYS
Iris & Alan Stanley

2 varied gardens in a picturesque
village with a number of Suffolk
timbered houses. Ivy Chimneys is
planted for yr round interest with
ornamental trees, some topiary,
exotic borders and fishpond set in an
area of Japanese style. Wisteria
draped pergola supports a productive
vine. Also a separate ornamental
vegetable garden. New for 2014 fruit
trees in the front garden. Harebells,
150 yards further down Mill Street
from Ivy Chimneys, was a new build
property in 2013 and the garden has
since been developed from scratch.
The garden has a feature round lawn
edged by colour themed borders. A
walk through pergola leads to a

productive area incl a greenhouse and raised vegetables beds, a wildlife pond and views over open countryside. Featured in Bury & West Suffolk magazine.

23 GREAT THURLOW HALL

Great Thurlow, Haverhill CB9 7LF. Mr & Mrs George Vestey. *12m S of Bury St Edmunds, 4m N of Haverhill. Great Thurlow village on B1061 from Newmarket; 3½ m N of junction with A143 Haverhill/Bury St Edmunds rd.* **Sun 3 Apr (2-5). Adm £4, chd free. Home-made teas are available in the church.**

13 acres of beautiful gardens set around the R Stour, the banks of which are adorned with stunning displays of daffodil and narcissi together with blossoming trees in spring. Herbaceous borders, rose garden and extensive shrub borders come alive with colour from late spring onwards, there is also a large walled kitchen garden and arboretum.

24 GREEN FARMHOUSE

The Green, Shelland, Stowmarket IP14 3JE. Miss Rosemary Roe, 01449 736591. *4m NW of Stowmarket, 10m SE of Bury St Edmunds. A14 W-bound. A1308-signed Wetherden, L to Harleston, follow NGS signs. A14 E-bound take Wetherden/Haughley Park turn, then R signed Buxhall. Follow NGS signs.* **Sun 3 July (2-5). Adm £3.50, chd free. Home-made teas. Visits also by arrangement June to Sept, groups of up to 40. Adm £5 to incl tea and cake.**

2 acre garden created around a thatched cottage commanding wonderful views of Mid-Suffolk countryside. A garden with all-year interest and wide variety of plants. Easy walks through garden rooms with shrubs, herbaceous borders, lawns and vistas, courtyard and gravel gardens, stumpery, natural pond and developing wild flower meadow. Garden would be a good subject for photographic/art groups. Featured in Peggy Cole's column in East Anglian Daily Times. Partial wheelchair access.

25 HENSTEAD EXOTIC GARDEN

Church Road, Henstead, Beccles NR34 7LD. Andrew Brogan, www.hensteadexoticgarden.co.uk. *Equal distance between Beccles, Southwold & Lowestoft approx 5m. 1m from A12 turning after Wrentham (signed Henstead) very close to B1127.* **Sun 21 Aug (11-4). Adm £4, chd £1. Home-made teas. Visits also by arrangement May to Sept.**

2-acre exotic garden featuring 100 large palms, 20+ bananas and 200 bamboo plants. 2 streams, 20ft tiered walkway leading to Thai style wooden covered pavilion. Mediterranean and jungle plants around 3 large ponds with fish. Suffolk's most exotic garden. Newly extended this year.

26 HESSETT HOUSE

Drinkstone Road, Beyton, Bury St Edmunds IP30 9AH. Mr & Mrs Richard Holt. *5m E of Bury St Edmunds. 1m up Drinkstone Rd, from Beyton on R.* **Sun 19 June (2-6). Adm £4, chd free. Home-made teas.**

Large country garden with S-facing lawns, looking over the ha ha to parkland planted with native mature trees and a young copse. The rose garden is set in 16 formal beds of mature old fashioned roses backed by a pergola of roses and clematis. Shrub beds border the lawns. Swimming pool and tennis court gardens with hedges of yew and viburnum and beech hedge of impressive size. A gate leads through to young arboretum and beds of hydrangea. Gravel paths.

GROUP OPENING

27 IKEN GARDENS

Tunstall Road, Iken, Woodbridge IP12 2ER. *3m from Tunstall & Snape. From A12 take A1094 towards Aldeburgh. At Snape Church turn R to Snape. Past Snape Maltings turn L signed Orford. At next Xrds turn L signed Iken. After 1m Church Farm & Decoy Cottage on R.* **Sun 15 May (2-5). Combined adm £3.50, chd free. Home-made teas at Church Farm.**

CHURCH FARM
Mrs Caroline Erskine

DECOY COTTAGE
Sir Thomas Hughes-Hallett

Two adjoining gardens in a charming Suffolk village. Decoy Cottage is a twenty acre country garden with woods, orchard, lake and highland cattle on show. Church Farm is a two acre area surrounded by mature alders and pines. Many young specimen trees and shrubs planted over the last six years. Mixed planting of perennials, grasses and smaller shrubs. Wheelchair access is fine for garden but not for woods etc. No access for wheelchairs through Church Farm garden.

> Natural pond and developing wild flower meadow . . .

28 THE LABURNUMS

The Street, St. James Sth. Elmham, Halesworth IP19 0HN. Mrs Jane Bastow, 01986 782413. *6m W of Halesworth, 7m E of Harleston & 6m S of Bungay. Parking at nearby village hall. For disabled parking please phone to arrange.* **Mon 28 Mar (11-5). Adm £4, chd free. Home-made teas. Hot/Cold drinks, cakes and hot soup.**

1-acre garden is 20+ years old and is packed with annuals, perennials, flowering shrubs and trees and areas dedicated to wild flowers. The spring garden is awash with colour-snowdrops, aconites, hellebores, daffodils and much more. There are three ponds, a sunken garden and two glasshouses 2015 sees the new larger conservatory where the refreshments will be served surrounded by citrus plants etc. Plant stall with a variety of plants and bulbs. Featured in The Garden News and The East Anglian Daily Times and Jane holds a Chelsea Gold Medal. Gravel drive. Partial access to front garden. Steps to sunken garden. Concrete path in back garden.

29 LARKS' HILL
Clopton Road, Tuddenham St Martin IP6 9BY. Mr John Lambert, 01473 785248, jrlambert@talktalk.net. *3m NE of Ipswich. From Ipswich take B1077, go through village, take the Clopton Rd.* Sat 11 June (1.30-5). Adm £5, chd free. Home-made teas. Visits also by arrangement May to Aug, groups of 15+.
The gardens of eight acres comprise woodland, field and formal areas, and fall away from the house to the valley floor. A hill within a garden and in Suffolk at that! Hilly garden with a modern castle keep with an interesting and beautiful site overlooking the gentle Fynn valley and the village beyond. A garden worthy of supporting the House, its family members and its visitors. A fossil of a limb bone from a Pliosaur that lived at least sixty million years ago was found in the garden in 2013. The discovery was reported in the national press but its importance has been recognised world-wide. A booklet is available to purchase giving all the details.

Peach, nectarine and apricots by the pool . . .

30 LAVENHAM HALL
Hall Road, Lavenham, Sudbury CO10 9QX. Mr & Mrs Anthony Faulkner. *Next to Lavenham's iconic church & close to High St. From church turn off the main rd down the side of church (Potland Rd). Go down hill. Car Park on R after 100 metres.* Sun 22 May (11-5). Adm £4, chd free.
5-acre garden built around the ruins of the original ecclesiastical buildings on the site and the village's 1-acre fishpond. The garden incl deep borders of herbaceous planting with sweeping vistas and provides the perfect setting for the sculptures

which Kate makes in her studio at the Hall and exhibits both nationally and internationally. 40 garden sculptures on display. There is a gallery in the grounds which displays a similar number of indoor sculptures and working drawings. Note large number of gravel paths and slopes within the garden.

31 NEW LEAVEN HALL
Nayland Road, Leavenheath, Colchester CO6 4PU. Mr & Mrs Mark Ellis, 01787 210579, www.leavenhall.com. *6m W of Colchester, Essex. Off A134 in Leavenheath between church & Hare and Hounds PH.* Sun 5 June (2-6). Adm £4, chd free. Home-made teas.
A long gravel drive leads to the wisteria and rose clad C17 house set amid 15 acres of meadows and gardens. Walled garden and a huge pond/bog garden/woodland with lawns and mature trees. There is a working vegetable/cut flower garden and peach, nectarine and apricots by the pool. Chickens, horses and pigs live here too! Featured in The Garden Magazine and Suffolk Magazine. B&B. Gravel paths, some steps by the pond and woodchips in veg/woodland areas. Grass fairly flat and can be used to reach all areas.

32 NEW MALTING FARM
Heath Road, Hessett, Bury St. Edmunds IP30 9BJ. Mrs Klair Bauly. *In the village of Hessett. 5m E of Bury St Edmunds, A14 exit 46, at Beyton Green take Church Road up the side of the White Horse PH, at Hessett Green turn R into Heath Road. We are located opposite Hessett Green.* Sun 12 June (2-6). Adm £3.50, chd free. Home-made teas.
This new garden is now in its fourth year designed and maintained by the owner to sit with the surrounding landscape using formal and natural planting combined. A natural pond, aquatic and marginal planting, woodland walk, meadow with countryside views. 100ft border with repeat planting and sculptural forms. Wooded area with grass beds. Fruit and vegetable garden. Some gravel paths, NB pond is unfenced. Some gravel paths, woodland walk is unsuitable.

33 22 MELFORD ROAD
Sudbury CO10 1LS. Mr & Mrs C Bentley, 01787 374249, colette@ceebees.demon.co.uk. *Outskirts of town - 500 metres from town centre. Located on A134 Sudbury to Long Melford rd opp the Bay Horse PH. Parking is possible at the rear of the garden in Queens Rd. Town centre car park (free) 300 metres from the garden.* Sat 4, Sun 5 June (11-5). Adm £3.50, chd free. Light refreshments. Visits also by arrangement Apr to Sept.
An unusual compact Victorian town garden with large fish pond and waterfall. It has been divided into several areas to create the illusion of space and individuality. Mature shrubs provide the perfect backdrop for the various colourful seating areas to enjoy light refreshments. Partial wheelchair access as majority of garden is viewed by ascending steps.

34 MOAT HOUSE
Little Saxham, Bury St. Edmunds IP29 5LE. Mr & Mrs Richard Mason, 01284 810941, rnm333@live.com. *2m SW of Bury St Edmunds. Leave A14 at J42, through Westley Village, at Xrds R towards Barrow/Saxham 1.3m L (follow signs).* Sun 8 May (2-6). Adm £4.50, chd free. Home-made teas. Visits also by arrangement May to July, groups between 20 min 40 max.
Set in a 2 acre historic and partially moated site. This tranquil mature garden has been developed by the present owners over 20yrs. Bordered by mature trees the garden is in various sections incl a sunken garden, rose and clematis arbours, herbaceous borders surrounded by box hedging, small arboretum. Featured in Suffolk Magazine, Homes and Gardens,.

35 428 NORWICH ROAD
Ipswich IP1 5DU. Robert & Gloria Lawrence. *1 1/2 m W of Ipswich town centre. On A1156 Norwich Rd garden is 200yds W of railway bridge.* Sun 5 June (2-5). Adm £2.50, chd free. Strawberry Cream Teas.
Front garden of roses and large tubs of bedding plants. Rear 1/3 acre garden with sunken terrace leading up to lawn with rose beds, herbaceous border and dry stone garden. Lawn leads to bog garden,

island mixed bed and on to orchard (17 fruit trees), asparagus bed, small vegetable plot with composting area and greenhouse. Strawberry Cream Teas. Wheelchair access is limited to the front and terrace area because of steps leading to lawn area and orchard.

GROUP OPENING

36 OLD FELIXSTOWE GARDENS
Felixstowe IP11 9TJ. *Corner of Wrens Park & Westmoreland Road. Enter Felixstowe on A154. At r'about take 1st exit then turn R - into Beatrice Av. L to High Road East. Proceed to Clifflands Car Park. Follow signs.* **Sun 22 May (11-5). Combined adm £4, chd free. Home-made teas. Savouries will be available during the day.**

NEW 43 ST. GEORGE'S ROAD
Marion Isaacs

41 WESTMORLAND ROAD
Mrs Diane Elmes
Visits also by arrangement Apr to Sept for groups up to 10. dianeelmes@talktalk.net 01394 284647

Two very different gardens quite close to the sea. Open for the first time, 43 St. George's Road is a good example of a town garden with terraces, water features and good planting. It benefits from having a backdrop to an historical Church. The owners of 41 Westmorland Road

moved into their house seven years ago, since when they have recovered the garden by taking down 21 leylandii trees and various other dead trees. It is now full of perennials and has interesting and eclectic features. Featured in East Anglian Daily Times Felixstowe Society Newsletter and on Felixstowe Television.

GROUP OPENING

37 OLD NEWTON GARDENS
Church Road, Old Newton, Stowmarket IP14 4ED. *2½ m N of Stowmarket. From B1113 R at Shoulder of Mutton in Old Newton. Parking 150yds on L at village hall.* **Sun 24 Apr (1-5). Combined adm £4, chd free. Light refreshments, home-made teas and savouries at Hill House.**

HILL HOUSE
Sue and Phill Bowler

THE OLD VICARAGE
Mr & Mrs R M Brooks

Hill House is a thatched cottage with a 1½ acre garden. Lots of flowers and flowering shrubs, much appreciated by bees and butterflies. Also roses, a natural pond, mature trees, an orchard (about 36 trees) which should have spring blossom, soft fruit and vegetable garden. Some of the ground can be uneven, especially in the orchard. The Old Vicarage's small garden is for plant enthusiasts. It has been extensively developed since 2006. There are many interesting ornamental trees, shrubs and bulbs. The informal beds are packed with herbaceous perennials. Clematis and roses scramble through trees and pergola. Not suitable for wheelchairs at the Old Vicarage: partially suitable at Hill House.

38 OLD RECTORY HOUSE
Kedington Hill, Little Cornard, Sudbury CO10 0PD. Jane & David Mann. *2½ m outside Sudbury off B1508 Bures Rd. From Bures Rd follow signs to Little Cornard Parish Church. Garden is approx ½ m up the lane on L. Parking opp.* **Sun 1 May (2-5). Adm £4, chd free. Home-made teas.**
Large country garden with

established specimen trees and some interesting more recent plantings. Small woodland with ponds and stream. Cottage garden, roses, walled fruit and vegetable garden, greenhouse, parterre with tulips in late spring. Extensive bank with mixed planting including irises, grasses, herbaceous and shrubs. Surrounding meadows managed for native floral diversity. Some slopes and uneven ground. Loose gravel in places.

GROUP OPENING

39 ORFORD GARDENS
High Street, Orford, Woodbridge IP12 2NW. *8m from Woodbridge. In Orford, follow main road down to the Quay. Turn L into Daphne Rd at Xrds & start tour at Bell House. Tickets for all 3 houses will be on sale here.* **Sun 5 June (2-5). Combined adm £5, chd free. Home-made teas at Brundish Lodge.**

BELL HOUSE
Tim Allen

BRUNDISH LODGE D
Mrs Elizabeth Spinney

WAYSIDE
Geoffrey & Anne Smeed

Three very different gardens with varied planting situated in the picturesque village of Orford. Bell House: a small, sheltered, cottage garden with a rill, planned to give year-round interest. approx one third newly planted following building work in 2013. No lawn so as to give maximum room for plants. Wheelchair accessible. Brundish Lodge: is a garden of approx one third of an acre. It was completely redesigned, reconstructed and replanted in 2005. It has beds which are a mixture of shrubs, herbaceous plants and grasses grouped around a central lawn. Wayside: a village garden of approx ¼ acre, comprising a series of 'rooms' surrounding the house (not open). A mixture of shrubs and perennials, chosen to suit the light, dry soil, and to cope with the cold easterly winds. Orford is a very attractive village with an historic castle and church. It also has excellent PHs and restaurants.

40 OUSDEN HOUSE
Ousden, Newmarket CB8 8TN.
Mr & Mrs Alastair Robinson.
Newmarket 6m, Bury St Edmunds 8m. Ousden House stands at the west end of the village next to the Church. **Sun 17 Apr (2-5.30). Adm £5, chd free. Home-made teas.**
All of this spectacular garden will be open but the focus at this time of year is on the spring gardens, incl the lake and spring wood with daffodils, narcissi and flowering shrubs, sheltered mown grass pathways, primrose banks and viewing mound. A long moat garden with hellebores and two fountains leads to the courtyard with eight formal tulip beds. Teas will be in the house with log fires. Featured in Country Life, The English Garden, Telegraph, East Anglian Times, Suffolk & Cambridgeshire Magazines. Not suitable for wheelchairs.

41 ◆ THE PLACE FOR PLANTS, EAST BERGHOLT PLACE GARDEN
East Bergholt CO7 6UP. Mr & Mrs Rupert Eley, 01206 299224, sales@placeforplants.co.uk, www.placeforplants.co.uk. *2m E of A12, 7m S of Ipswich. On B1070 towards Manningtree, 2m E of A12. Situated on the edge of East Bergholt.* **For NGS: Sun 3 Apr, Sun 15 May (2-5); Sun 9 Oct (1-5). Adm £6, chd free. Home-made teas.**
For other opening times and information, please phone, email or visit garden website.
20-acre garden originally laid out at the turn of the last century by the present owner's great grandfather. Full of many fine trees and shrubs, many seldom seen in East Anglia. A fine collection of camellias, magnolias and rhododendrons, topiary, and the National Collection of deciduous Euonymus. Partial Wheelchair access in dry conditions - it is advisable to telephone before visiting.

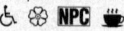

42 POLSTEAD MILL
Mill Lane, Polstead, Colchester CO6 5AB. Mrs Lucinda Bartlett, 01206 265969, lucyofleisure@hotmail.com. *Between Stoke by Nayland & Polstead on the R Box. From Stoke by Nayland take rd to Polstead - Mill Lane is 1st on L & Polstead Mill is 1st house on R.* **Visits by arrangement May to Sept for groups of 10+.**

Adm £6, chd free. Home-made teas.
The garden has formal and informal areas, a wild flower meadow and a large kitchen garden. The R Box runs through the garden and there is a mill pond, which gives opportunity for damp gardening, while much of the rest of the garden is arid and is planted to minimise the need for watering. Featured in Gardens Illustrated. Partial wheelchair access.

> Look out for a Spotty Dotty and a giant Amorphophallus . . .

GROUP OPENING

43 PRIORS HILL, ALDEBURGH
Priors Hill Road, Aldeburgh IP15 5EP. *Turn R off A1094 into Park Rd 100yds after r'about with B1122. After 400yds, turn R into Priors Hill Rd.* **Sun 18 Sept (2-5). Combined adm £5, chd free. Tea. Visits also by arrangement May to Sept.**

HERON HOUSE
Mr & Mrs Jonathan Hale
Visits also by arrangement
May to Oct.
jonathanrhhale@aol.com
01728 452200

STANNY
Kimberley & Angus Robertson
Visits also by arrangement May to Sept, painting groups welcome.
stannyhouse@live.com

Two gardens, both south-facing, situated in Priors Hill Road with enviable views over the R Alde and the sea. Both gardens are on a slope which gives the opportunity for terracing and associated planting. Heron House consists of two acres with views over coastline, river and marshes. Unusual trees, herbaceous beds, shrubs and ponds with waterfall in large rock garden, stream and bog garden. Stanny is terraced

over three levels. There are many established camellias, hydrangea, grasses and mature trees, which include Holm Oaks, Scots Pine, Japanese Maples and Strawberry Trees. There is a waterfall, a large natural pond and a wild flower meadow along with some exotic planting. Please note both gardens have ponds and children must be supervised. Lovely views. Wheelchair access with difficulty in some instances.

44 PRIORS OAK
Leiston Road, Aldeburgh IP15 5QE. Mrs Trudie Willis, 01728 452580, trudie.willis@dinkum.free-online.co.uk, https://sites.google.com/site/priorsoakbutterflygarden. *1m N of Aldeburgh on B1122. Garden on L opp RSPB Reserve.* **Sun 26 June (2-6). Adm £5, chd free. Tea. Visits also by arrangement May to Sept.**
10-acre wildlife and butterfly garden. Ornamental salad and vegetable gardens with companion planting. Herbaceous borders, ferns and Mediterranean plants. Pond and wild flower acid grassland with a small wood. Skirting the wood are 100 buddleia in excess of 30 varieties forming a perfumed tunnel. Very tranquil and fragrant garden with grass paths and yearly interest. Rich in animal and bird life. Specialist butterfly garden, as seen in SAGA magazine, renovated railway carriages, tortoise breeding, wildlife walks. Coaches or private visits by appointment only.

45 THE PRIORY
Stoke by Nayland, Colchester CO6 4RL. Mr & Mrs H F A Engleheart. *5m SW of Hadleigh. Entrance on B1068 to Sudbury (NW of Stoke by Nayland).* **Sun 22 May (2-5). Adm £5, chd free. Home-made teas.**
Interesting 9-acre garden with fine views over Constable countryside; lawns sloping down to small lakes and water garden; fine trees, rhododendrons and azaleas; walled garden; mixed borders and ornamental greenhouse. Wide variety of plants. Access over most of garden. Some steps.

Stanny House Farm

 REDISHAM HALL

Redisham, nr Beccles NR34 8LZ.
The Palgrave Brown Family,
01502 575894,
sarah.hammond7@hotmail.co.uk.
5m S of Beccles. From A145, turn W
on to Ringsfield-Bungay rd. Beccles,
Halesworth or Bungay, all within 5m.
Sun 10 July (2-6). Adm £4, chd
free. Home-made teas. Visits also
by arrangement July to Sept,
groups 10 min.
C18 Georgian house (not open). 5-
acre garden set in 400 acres parkland
and woods. Incl 2-acre walled kitchen
garden (in full production) with peach
house, vinery and glasshouses.
Lawns, herbaceous borders,
shrubberies, ponds and mature trees.
Sorry No Dogs. We have been open
for the NGS for over 50 yrs, during
this time we have only been closed
once due to an outbreak of foot and
mouth. The garden has lots of gravel
paths and there are lawned slopes.
Wheelchair access is possible with
assistance. Parking is on uneven
parkland.
&. ✿ ☕

47 RICHMOND HOUSE

20 Nethergate Street, Clare
CO10 8NP. Dr Catherine
Horwood Barwise,
catherine@richmondhouse-
clare.com,
www.facebook.com/richmondhous
egarden. *100 metres from centre of*
Clare. On L of Nethergate St (A1092)

from direction of Stoke-by-Clare.
Limited on-street parking. Please use
Country Park car park off Well Lane.
Sun 15 May (2-5). Adm £3.50, chd
free. Home-made teas. Visits also
by arrangement May to Sept for
groups of 10+. Refreshments
available for groups of 10-20.
Romantic walled garden: pleached-
tree-framed steps lead to formal 'new
perennial' parterre, grasses, growing
collection of Cedric Morris/Benton
End irises; Med. terrace by swimming
pool; informal garden with species
roses, peonies and spring bulbs; mini
meadow; vegetable/cutting garden,
trained fruit trees, greenhouse; tulips;
hellebore/fern path, hostas. Over 40
small-flowered clematis. Featured in
'The English Garden' and 'Suffolk'
magazine.
✿ ☕

48 NEW RIVER COTTAGE

Lower Road, Lavenham, Sudbury
CO10 9QJ. Mr & Mrs Geoff Heald,
07747 827605,
geoff@artmarketing.co.uk. *It is best*
to park your car in the Village Square
& walk down Prentice St which can
be found by walking past The Angel
proceed to the bottom then turn R on
Lower Rd. **Sun 14 Aug (11-5). Adm**
£4, chd free. Home-made teas. A
selection of home made cakes,
teas and coffees. Visits also by
arrangement Apr to Sept for
groups of 2 to 10.
A tranquil plantsman's garden with a

400ft river frontage ending with a
hydrangea walk with many newly
planted hostas, dahlias, lilies, roses,
clematis ivies and grasses. The newly
created woodland garden has many
rare plants including Paris Arisaemas.
Look out for a Spotty Dotty and a
giant Amorphophallus. The new
owners are constantly looking for new
and unusual plants to delight visitors.
There will be a wheel chair route
clearly signed for use in dry weather.
✿ ☕

49 ROSEDALE

40 Colchester Road, Bures
CO8 5AE. Mr & Mrs Colin Lorking,
01787 227619,
rosedale40@btinternet.com. *6m SE*
of Sudbury. From Colchester take
B1508. After 10m garden on L as you
enter the village, from Sudbury
B1508 after 5m garden on R. **Sun 15**
May, Sun 7 Aug (12-5). Adm £3,
chd free. Home-made teas. Visits
also by arrangement May to Aug,
evenings and weekends.
Approx one-third of an acre
plantsman's garden developed over
the last 22 years, containing many
unusual plants, herbaceous borders
and pond. For the May opening see a
super collection of peonies and for
the July opening a stunning collection
of approx 60 Agapanthus in full
flower. Featured in Suffolk Magazine,
Garden Answers Magazine and East
Anglian Daily Times.
✿ ☕

50 ◆ SOMERLEYTON HALL GARDENS

Somerleyton NR32 5QQ. Lord Somerleyton, 01502 734901, www.somerleyton.co.uk. *5m NW of Lowestoft. From Norwich (30mins) - on the B1074, 7m SE of Great Yarmouth (A143). Coaches should follow signs to the rear west gate entrance.* **For NGS: Wed 8 June (10-3). Adm £6.45, chd free. Light refreshments in Cafe. For other opening times and information, please phone or visit garden website.**

12½ acres of beautiful gardens contain a wide variety of magnificent specimen trees, shrubs, borders and plants providing colour and interest throughout the yr. Sweeping lawns and formal gardens combine with majestic statuary and original Victorian ornamentation. Highlights incl the Paxton glasshouses, pergola, walled garden and famous yew hedge maze. House and gardens remodelled in 1840s by Sir Morton Peto. House created in Anglo-Italian style with lavish architectural features and fine state rooms. All areas of the gardens are accessible, path surfaces are gravel and can be a little difficult after heavy rain. Wheelchairs available on request.

51 NEW STANNY HOUSE FARM

High Street, Iken, Woodbridge IP12 2EY. Mr & Mrs Paul Cooke. *Take Aldeburgh turning off the A12 (A1094). Turn R into Snape (B1069) opp Snape church, pass Snape Maltings on your L take 1st L signed to Orford then next L signed Iken.* **Sun 29 May (12-5). Adm £4, chd free. Home-made teas.**

Farmhouse garden with walled potager, pool garden, mediterranean borders, herbaceous border, quarry garden and extensive clipped yew hedges. There is a conservatory/orangery containing tender plants. Partial wheelchair access, some gravel paths.

52 STREET FARM

North Street, Freckenham IP28 8HY. David & Clodagh Dugdale. *3m W of Mildenhall. From Newmarket, follow signs to Snailwell, & Chippenham & then onto Freckenham.* **Sun 15 May (11-5). Adm £4, chd free. Home-made teas.**

Approx 1 acre of landscaped garden, with several mature trees. The garden includes a water cascade, pond with island and a number of bridges. Formal rose garden, rose pergola, herbaceous borders and hornbeam walk. Gravel paths with steps and slopes.

Wildlife is very much encouraged in all parts of the garden (particularly bees and butterflies) . . .

53 UGGESHALL HALL

Uggeshall, Beccles NR34 8BG. Stevie & Bob Nicholson, 01502 578695, uggeshall@clara.co.uk. *6m W of Southwold, 6.8m S of Beccles. A12 from S, turn L at Wangford bypass to Uggeshall, take 1st R then R again, garden 250 metres on L. A12 from N turn R at Frostenden (signed Clay Common) garden on R after Z bend.* **Sun 26 June (1-5). Adm £4, chd free. Home-made teas. Visits also by arrangement June to Aug for groups of 10+ Wednesday afternoons.**

2 acre, relaxed style, country garden of contrasting areas, curved paths and circular lawn lead to a gravel garden at the front of the house, to the side a large pond with walkways and platform, walled garden with beds and trees, an orchard, avenue of lime trees, vegetable garden and formal area with box hedging and pergola covered in old fashioned roses. Featured in Suffolk Magazine. Wheelchair access possible but limited. There are changes of level and some of the lawn areas are uneven.

54 NEW WENHASTON GRANGE

Wenhaston, Halesworth IP19 9HJ. Mr & Mrs Bill Barlow. *Turn SW from A144 between Bramfield & Halesworth. Take the single track rd (signed Walpole) & Wenhaston Grange is approx ½ m, at the bottom of the hill on the L.* **Sun 29 May (11-5). Adm £5, chd free. Home-made teas.**

Over 3 acres of varied gardens on a long established site which has been extensively landscaped and enhanced over the last 15 yrs. Long herbaceous borders, old established trees and a series of garden rooms created by beech hedges. Levels and sight lines have been carefully planned. The garden is on a number of levels, with steps so wheelchair access would be difficult.

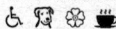

55 WHITE HOUSE FARM

Ringsfield, Beccles NR34 8JU. James & Jan Barlow, (gardener) 07780 901233, coppertops707@aol.com. *2m SW of Beccles. From Beccles take B1062 to Bungay, after 1¼ turn L signed Ringsfield. Continue for approx 1m. Parking near church. Garden 300yds on L.* **Sat 2 July (10.30-4.30). Adm £4, chd free. Home-made teas. Cakes and savoury flans. Visits also by arrangement May to Aug, Tuesday - Friday, daytime or evening, not wk/ends.**

Tranquil park-type garden approx 30 acres, bordered by farmland and with fine views. Comprising formal areas, copses, natural pond, ornamental pond, woodland walk, vegetable garden and orchard. Picnickers welcome. NB The pond and beck are unfenced. Partial wheelchair access to the areas around the house.

56 WOOD FARM, GIPPING

Back Lane, Gipping, Stowmarket IP14 4RN. Mr & Mrs R Shelley. *From A14 take A1120 to Stowupland, Turn L opp Petrol Station., Turn R at T- junction, follow for approx 1m turn L at Allards Farm Shop, then imm R & follow for 1m along country lane. Wood Farm is on L.* **Sun 5 June (1-5). Adm £3.50, chd free. Home-made teas. Large Party Barn with Facilities.**

Wood Farm is an old farm with ponds, orchards and a magnificent 8 acre wild flower meadow (with mown paths) bordered with traditional hedging, trees and woodland. The large cottage garden was created in 2011 with a number of beds planted with flowers, vegetables and topiary. Wildlife is very much encouraged in all parts of the garden (particularly bees and butterflies). Partial wheelchair access.

57 WOODWARDS

Blacksmiths Lane, Coddenham, Ipswich IP6 9TX. Marion & Richard Kenward, 01449 760639, richardwoodwards@btinternet.com. *7m N of Ipswich. From A14 turn onto A140, after ¼ m take B1078 towards Wickham Market, Coddenham is on route. Coaches please use postcode IP6 9PS. Ample parking for coaches.* **Sun 27 Mar, Sun 8 May, Sat 4 June, Tue 5, Sun 24 July, Tue 9, Sun 28 Aug (10.30-5.30). Adm £2.50, chd free. Home-made teas. Visits also by arrangement Mar to Sept, groups 2-100+.**
Award winning S-facing gently sloping garden of 1½ acres, overlooking the rolling Suffolk countryside. Designed and maintained by owners for yr-round

colour and interest, lots of island beds, well stocked with 1000s of bulbs, shrubs and perennials, vegetable plot, display of 100+ hanging baskets for spring and summer. Well kept lawns, with large mature trees. More than 25000 bulbs have been planted over the last 3yrs for our spring display. Featured in W.I. Magazine, East Anglian Magazine, Suffolk Magazine and on Radio Suffolk.

58 ◆ WOOTTENS OF WENHASTON

Blackheath Road, Wenhaston IP19 9HD. Mrs E Loftus, 01502 478258, info@woottensplants.co.uk, www.woottensplants.com. *18m S of Lowestoft. On A12 & B1123, follow signs to Wenhaston.* **For opening times and information, please phone, email or visit garden website.**
Woottens Display Garden was redesigned in 2003 and consists of 27 raised display areas overflowing with hardy perennials to admire and inspire. The garden is inhabited with

many rare and unusual cultivars and some of our traditional favourites. Spring Fair Early May. Collections of auriculas, irises, pelargoniums, and hemerocallis to view. Courses and Open Days run throughout the year.

59 ◆ WYKEN HALL

Stanton IP31 2DW. Sir Kenneth & Lady Carlisle, 01359 250287, www.wykenvineyards.co.uk. *9m NE of Bury St Edmunds. Along A143. Follow signs to Wyken Vineyards on A143 between Ixworth & Stanton.* **For NGS: Sat 4, Sun 5 June (10-6). Adm £4, chd free. For other opening times and information, please phone or visit garden website.**
4-acre garden much developed recently; knot and herb garden; old-fashioned rose garden, wild garden, nuttery, pond, gazebo and maze; herbaceous borders and old orchard. Woodland walk, vineyard. Restaurant and shop. Vineyard. Farmers' Market on Saturdays 9-1.

Church Cottage

© Rosalind Simon

SURREY

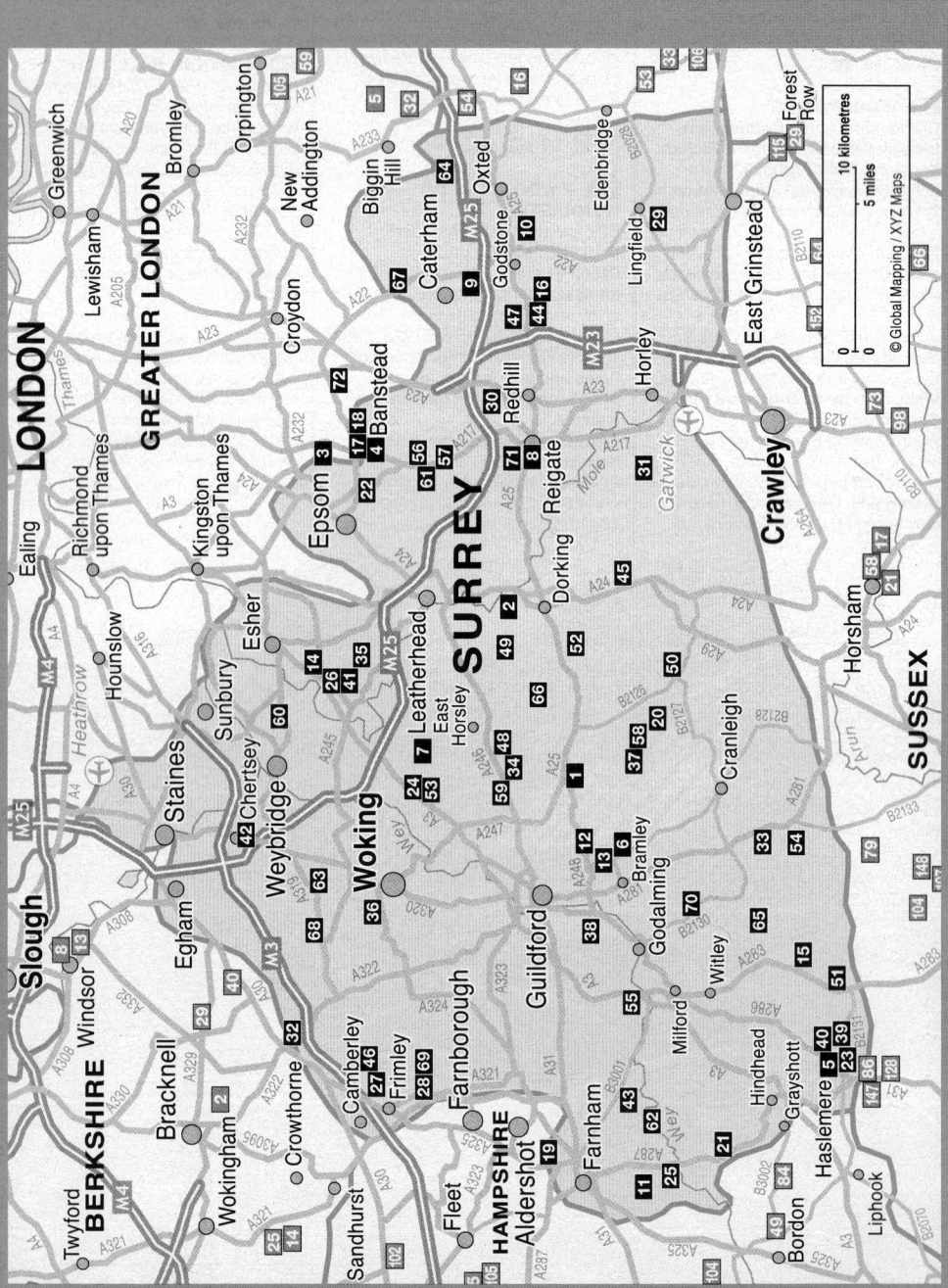

Surrey

As a designated Area of Outstanding Natural Beauty, it's no surprise that Surrey has a wealth of gardens on offer.

With its historic market towns, lush meadows and scenic rivers, Surrey provides the ideal escape from the bustle of nearby London.

Set against the rolling chalk uplands of the unspoilt North Downs, the county prides itself on extensive country estates with historic houses and ancient manors. Visitors are inspired by the breathtaking panorama from Polesden Lacey, lakeside views at The Old Croft or timeless terraces at Albury Park.

Surrey is the heartland of the NGS at Hatchlands Park and the RHS at Wisley, both promoting a precious interest in horticulture. Surrey celebrates a landscape coaxed into wonderful vistas by great gardeners such as John Evelyn, Capability Brown and Gertrude Jekyll.

With many eclectic gardens to visit, there's certainly plenty to treasure in Surrey.

Surrey Volunteers

County Organiser
Maggie Boyd
01428 652283
maggie.boyd@ngs.org.uk

County Treasurer
David Boyd
01428 652283
david.boyd@ngs.org.uk

Publicity
Annie Keighley
01252 838660
annie.keighley12@btinternet.com

Booklet Co-ordinator
Keith Lewis
01737 210707
kandelewis@ntlworld.com

**Booklet Production
& Group Tours**
David Boyd
(as above)

Assistant County Organisers
Margaret Arnott
01372 842459
m.a.arnott@btinternet.com

Anne Barnes
01306 730196
spurfold@btinternet.com

Di Grose
01883 742983
di.grose@godstone.net

Annie Keighley
(as above)

Keith Lewis
(as above)

Caroline Shuldham
01932 596960
cshuldham@yahoo.co.uk

Shirley Stoneley
01737 244235
woodburycottage@gmail.com

Jean Thompson
01483 425633
norney.wood@btinternet.com

Left: The Old Rectory © Nicola Stocken

Opening Dates

All entries subject to change.
For latest information check www.ngs.org.uk

February

Snowdrop Festival

Sunday 14
- **30** Gatton Park
- **63** Timber Hill

March

Sunday 20
- **1** Albury Park

Sunday 27
- **8** Caxton House

Monday 28
- **63** Timber Hill
- **65** Vann

Tuesday 29
- **65** Vann

Wednesday 30
- **65** Vann

Thursday 31
- **65** Vann

Cake made
with eggs
supplied
by our
chickens . . .

April

Friday 1
- **65** Vann

Saturday 2
- **65** Vann

Sunday 3
- **9** The Chalet
- **65** Vann

Sunday 10
- **9** The Chalet
- **20** Coverwood Lakes
- **54** Saffron Gate

Sunday 17
- **20** Coverwood Lakes
- **56** 41 Shelvers Way

Sunday 24
- **20** Coverwood Lakes

Saturday 30
- **24** Dunsborough Park

May

Sunday 1
- **11** Chestnut Cottage
- **21** Crosswater Farm
- **54** Saffron Gate
- **60** Stuartfield

Monday 2
- **20** Coverwood Lakes
- **21** Crosswater Farm
- **54** Saffron Gate
- **57** Shieling
- **65** Vann
- **66** Walton Poor House

Tuesday 3
- **65** Vann

Wednesday 4
- **65** Vann

Thursday 5
- **65** Vann

Friday 6
- **65** Vann

Saturday 7
- **29** The Garth Pleasure Grounds
- **65** Vann
- **68** Westways Farm

Sunday 8
- **6** Barnett Hill
- **20** Coverwood Lakes
- **29** The Garth Pleasure Grounds
- **63** Timber Hill
- **65** Vann
- **68** Westways Farm

Saturday 14
- **32** Hall Grove School

Sunday 15
- **20** Coverwood Lakes
- **27** 26 The Fairway
- **34** Hatchlands Park
- **39** NEW Malabar
- **64** Titsey Place Gardens
- **66** Walton Poor House

Friday 20
- **51** Ramster

Sunday 22
- **12** Chilworth Manor
- **22** Culverkeys
- **37** Knowle Grange
- **40** The Manor House

Monday 23
- **10** Chauffeur's Flat

Tuesday 24
- **10** Chauffeur's Flat

Wednesday 25
- **10** Chauffeur's Flat

Thursday 26
- **10** Chauffeur's Flat

Friday 27
- **10** Chauffeur's Flat

Saturday 28
- **3** 15 The Avenue (Evening)
- **10** Chauffeur's Flat

Sunday 29
- **10** Chauffeur's Flat
- **11** Chestnut Cottage
- **45** The Old Croft
- **46** NEW Old Knowles
- **58** Spurfold
- **67** 57 Westhall Road

Monday 30
- **3** 15 The Avenue
- **27** 26 The Fairway
- **45** The Old Croft
- **46** NEW Old Knowles
- **67** 57 Westhall Road

June

Festival Weekend

Sunday 5
- **14** Claremont Landscape Garden
- **17** NEW 53 Commonfield Road
- **18** 29 Commonfield Road
- **54** Saffron Gate
- **65** Vann
- **70** Winkworth Arboretum

Monday 6
- **65** Vann

Tuesday 7
- **65** Vann

Wednesday 8
- **28** Frimley Green Gardens
- **65** Vann

Thursday 9
- **65** Vann

Friday 10
- **65** Vann

Saturday 11
- **28** Frimley Green Gardens
- **31** Ghassan's Farm
- **48** NEW Old Tunmore Farm
- **57** Shieling (Evening)
- **65** Vann

Sunday 12
- **24** Dunsborough Park
- **31** Ghassan's Farm
- **38** Loseley Park
- **55** NEW Shackleford Garden Safari
- **57** Shieling
- **64** Titsey Place Gardens

Friday 17
- **2** Ashleigh Grange (Evening)

Saturday 18
- **15** NEW The Coach House
- **52** NEW Rookery Farm

Sunday 19
- **2** Ashleigh Grange
- **4** NEW Banstead Community Junior School
- **13** Chinthurst Lodge
- **15** NEW The Coach House
- **48** NEW Old Tunmore Farm
- **52** NEW Rookery Farm

Monday 20
- **10** Chauffeur's Flat

Tuesday 21
- **10** Chauffeur's Flat

Wednesday 22
- **2** Ashleigh Grange
- **10** Chauffeur's Flat
- **13** Chinthurst Lodge

Thursday 23
- **10** Chauffeur's Flat

Friday 24
- **10** Chauffeur's Flat
- **49** Polesden Lacey
- **59** Stuart Cottage (Evening)

Saturday 25
- **10** Chauffeur's Flat
- **23** NEW Down Court

Sunday 26
- **10** Chauffeur's Flat
- **23** NEW Down Court
- **26** Fairmile Lea
- **36** Horsell Group Gardens
- **41** Moleshill House
- **47** The Old Rectory

July

Saturday 2
- **5** Bardsey
- **43** Monksfield

Sunday 3
- **5** Bardsey
- **22** Culverkeys
- **42** NEW Monks Lantern
- **50** Pratsham Grange

Saturday 9
- **53** 7 Rose Lane
- **71** Woodbury Cottage

Sunday 10
- **71** Woodbury Cottage

Saturday 16
- **33** NEW Hall Place Farm
- **45** The Old Croft

Sunday 17
- **45** The Old Croft
- **64** Titsey Place Gardens

Saturday 23
5 Bardsey
25 NEW Earleywood
72 48 Woodmansterne Lane

Sunday 24
5 Bardsey
25 NEW Earleywood
56 41 Shelvers Way

Saturday 30
61 35 Tadorne Road

Sunday 31
61 35 Tadorne Road

August

Saturday 13
50 Pratsham Grange

Sunday 14
50 Pratsham Grange
64 Titsey Place Gardens

September

Saturday 3
16 Coldharbour House
71 Woodbury Cottage

Sunday 4
16 Coldharbour House

17 NEW 53 Commonfield Road
18 29 Commonfield Road
71 Woodbury Cottage

Wednesday 7
71 Woodbury Cottage

Sunday 11
37 Knowle Grange

Sunday 18
24 Dunsborough Park

October

Sunday 2
1 Albury Park
70 Winkworth Arboretum

Sunday 9
14 Claremont Landscape Garden

Saturday 15
66 Walton Poor House

Sunday 16
20 Coverwood Lakes
66 Walton Poor House

February 2017

Sunday 12
30 Gatton Park

Gardens open to the public

14 Claremont Landscape Garden
21 Crosswater Farm
24 Dunsborough Park
30 Gatton Park
34 Hatchlands Park
38 Loseley Park
49 Polesden Lacey
51 Ramster
64 Titsey Place Gardens
65 Vann
70 Winkworth Arboretum

By arrangement only

7 Bridge End Cottage
19 56 Copse Avenue
35 Heathside
44 Odstock
62 Tilford Cottage
69 Wildwood

Also open by arrangement

2 Ashleigh Grange
3 15 The Avenue

5 Bardsey
8 Caxton House
13 Chinthurst Lodge
15 NEW The Coach House
16 Coldharbour House
17 NEW 53 Commonfield Road
18 29 Commonfield Road
22 Culverkeys
28 Oakleigh, Frimley Green Gardens
28 Tabor, Frimley Green Gardens
29 The Garth Pleasure Grounds
37 Knowle Grange
41 Moleshill House
47 The Old Rectory
54 Saffron Gate
56 41 Shelvers Way
58 Spurfold
59 Stuart Cottage
66 Walton Poor House
68 Westways Farm

The Gardens

 ALBURY PARK
Albury GU5 9BH. **Trustees of Albury Estate.** *5m SE of Guildford. From A25 take A248 towards Albury for ¹/₄ m, then up New Rd, entrance to Albury Park immed on L.* **Sun 20 Mar, Sun 2 Oct (2-5). Adm £4.50, chd free. Home-made teas.**
14 acre pleasure grounds laid out in 1670s by John Evelyn for Henry Howard, later 6th Duke of Norfolk. ¹/₄ mile terraces, fine collection of trees, lake and river. Gravel path and slight slope.

 **ASHLEIGH GRANGE**
Off Chapel Lane, Westhumble RH5 6AY. **Clive & Angela Gilchrist, 01306 884613, ar.gilchrist@btinternet.com.** *2m N of Dorking. From A24 at Boxhill/Burford Bridge follow signs to Westhumble. Through village & L up drive by ruined chapel (1m from A24).* **Evening opening Fri 17 June (6-8). Adm £6, chd free. Wine. Sun 19, Wed 22 June (2-5.30). Adm £4, chd free. Home-made teas. Visits also by arrangement May to July.**

Donation to Barnardo's.
Plant lover's chalk garden on 3¹/₂ acre sloping site in charming rural setting with delightful views. Many areas of interest incl rockery and water feature, raised ericaceous bed, prairie style bank, foliage plants, woodland walk, fernery and folly. Large mixed herbaceous and shrub borders planted for dry alkaline soil and widespread interest.

15 The Avenue

Follow NGS Twitter 📧 @NGSOpenGardens

3 15 THE AVENUE

Cheam, Sutton SM2 7QA. Jan & Nigel Brandon, 02086 438686. *1m SW of Sutton. By car; exit A217 onto Northey Av, 2nd R into The Avenue. By train; 10 mins walk from Cheam station. By bus; use 470.* **Evening opening Sat 28 May (6-9). Adm £7, chd £2. Wine. Mon 30 May (1-5). Adm £4, chd free. Home-made teas. Visits also by arrangement May to July for groups min 10, max 20.**

A contemporary garden designed by RHS Chelsea Gold Medal Winner, Marcus Barnett. Four levels with steps and gravel paths. Divided into rooms by beech hedging and columns; formal entertaining area, lawn and wildflower meadow. Over 100 hostas hug the house. Silver birch, cloud pruned box, ferns, grasses, tall bearded irises, contemporary sculptures. Partial wheelchair access, terraced with steps; sloping path provides view of whole garden but not all accessible.

♿ ☕

4 NEW BANSTEAD COMMUNITY JUNIOR SCHOOL

The Horseshoe, Banstead SM7 2BQ. Banstead Community Junior School. *3m S of Sutton heading S on A217 turn L at Banstead T-lights into Winkworth Rd. Turn R at mini r'about - Bolters Lane. 3rd turning on R - The Horseshoe. School car park is on L at 1st bend.* **Sun 19 June (1.30-4.30). Adm £3, chd free. Home-made teas.**

The rear of our award winning school, opens up into a variety of gardening areas maintained by our Gardening Club. Please visit us and see our Greek Garden (it won silver gilt at Hampton Court Flower Show and donated by designer Tony Smith). bottle greenhouse, raised vegetable beds, poly tunnel, wildlife area, living wall (planted in pallets), fruit bushes, outdoor classroom, multi sensory bed and more! Recycling is encouraged at school so lots of recycled items used throughout the school grounds incl water recycling. Crowned overall winner of South & South East in Bloom schools' competition.

♿ ☸ ☕

5 BARDSEY

11 Derby Road, Haslemere GU27 1BS. Maggie & David Boyd, 01428 652283, maggie.boyd@live.co.uk,

www.bardseygarden.co.uk. *¼ m N of Haslemere station. Turn off B2131 (which links A287 to A286 through town) 400yds W of station into Weydown Rd, 3rd R into Derby Rd, garden 400yds on R.* **Sat 2, Sun 3, Sat 23, Sun 24 July (11-5). Adm £5, chd free. Home-made teas. Visits also by arrangement June & July for groups 10+.**

Unexpected 2 acre garden in the heart of Haslemere. Several distinct areas containing scent, colour, texture and movement. Stunning pictorial meadow within a parterre. Prairie planted border provides a modern twist. Large productive fruit and vegetable garden. Natural ponds and bog gardens. Several unusual sculptures. Ducks and chickens supply the eggs for cakes. Classic MGs on parade. Featured in Surrey Life. First third of garden level, other two thirds sloping.

♿ ☸ ★ 🚌 ☕

PERENNIAL
GARDENERS' ROYAL BENEVOLENT SOCIETY

NGS & Perennial; over 30 years of caring for horticulturists

6 BARNETT HILL

Blackheath Lane, Wonersh, Guildford GU5 0RF. The Sundial Group, 01483 893361, barnett@sundialgroup.com, www.sundialgroup.com. *Between Guildford & Cranleigh. From Guildford take A281 Shalford. At r'about 1st exit A248 Dorking. After 1m, just past 30mph & Wonersh signs go L into Blackheath Lane. Cont up narrow lane, turn R at top of hill.* **Sun 8 May (11.30-4.30). Adm £5, chd free. Cream teas.**

First time opening in May for the NGS, this 26 acre hill top estate is combining it with its ever so popular spring plant sale. Known for its eclectic plantings and tranquil setting it is filled with spring colour. Paths

wind down to the bluebell woods with views over the surrounding countryside. Wendy house and Edwardian greenhouses. Teas served on the terrace or in the Queen Anne style house. Good wheelchair access but some steps and steep pathways in places off main lawns.

♿ ☸ ★ 🚌 🛏 ☕

7 BRIDGE END COTTAGE

Ockham Lane, Ockham GU23 6NR. Clare & Peter Bevan, 01483 479963, c.fowler@ucl.ac.uk. *Nr RHS Gardens, Wisley. At Wisley r'about turn L onto B2039 to Ockham/Horsley. After ½ m turn L into Ockham Lane. House ½ m on R. From Cobham go to Blackswan Xrds.* **Visits by arrangement May to July groups 30 max. Adm £4.50, chd free. Light refreshments.**

A 2 acre country garden with different areas of interest, incl perennial borders, mature trees, pond and streams, small herb parterre, fruit trees and a vegetable patch. An adjacent 2 acre field was sown with perennial wildflower seed in May 2013 and has flowered well in June ever since. Large perennial wildflower meadow. Partial wheelchair access.

♿ ☸ ★ 🚌 ☕

8 CAXTON HOUSE

67 West Street, Reigate RH2 9DA. Bob Bushby, 01737 243158, Bob.bushby@sky.com. *On A25 towards Dorking, approx ¼ m W of Reigate on L. Parking on rd or past Black Horse PH on Flanchford Rd.* **Sun 27 Mar (2-5). Adm £5, chd free. Cream teas. Visits also by arrangement Mar to Sept for groups 10+.**

Lovely large spring garden with Arboretum, 2 well stocked ponds, large collection of hellebores and spring flowers. Pots planted with colourful displays. Interesting plants. Small Gothic folly built by owner. Herbaceous borders with grasses, perennials, spring bulbs, and parterre. New bed with wild daffodils, and prairie style planting in summer. Antique dog cart completes the picture in all about.

♿ ☸ ★ 🚌 ☕

9 THE CHALET

Tupwood Lane, Caterham CR3 6ET. Miss Lesley Manning & Mr David Gold. *½ m N of M25 J6. Exit J6 off M25 onto A22 to N. After ½ m take sharp 1st L, or follow signs from Caterham. Ample free parking.*

Disabled access via top gate. Sun 3, Sun 10 Apr (11-4.30). Adm £5, chd free. Home-made teas. Donation to St Catherine's Hospice.
55 acres. Carpets of tens of thousands of daffodils; lakes, ornamental ponds, koi pond and waterfall. Ancient woodlands, grasslands and formal garden. Large planted terraces. Beautiful Victorian mansion (not open). Woodland and garden trail. On view, a limited edition Blue Train Bentley, a Silver Phantom Rolls Royce and a helicopter. Partial wheelchair access; some steep slopes. 3 large unfenced ponds.

10 CHAUFFEUR'S FLAT
Tandridge Lane, Tandridge RH8 9NJ. Mr & Mrs Richins. *2m E of Godstone. 2m W of Oxted. Turn off A25 for Tandridge. Take drive on L past church. Follow arrows to circular courtyard.* Daily Mon 23 to Sun 29 May and Mon 20 to Sun 26 June (10-5). Adm £4, chd free. Home-made teas (Sats & Suns only). *Donation to Sutton & Croydon MS Therapy Centre.*
Enter a 1 acre tapestry of magical secret gardens with magnificent views. Touching the senses, all sure footed visitors may explore the many surprises on this constantly evolving exuberant escape from reality. Imaginative use of recycled materials creates an inspired variety of ideas, while wild and specimen plants reveal an ecological haven.

11 CHESTNUT COTTAGE
15 Jubilee Lane, Boundstone, Farnham GU10 4SZ. Mr & Mrs David Wingent. *2½ m SW of Farnham. At A31 r'about take A325 - Petersfield, ½ m bear L. At r'about into School Hill, ½ m over staggered Xrds into Sandrock Hill Rd, 4th turn R after PH.* Sun 1, Sun 29 May (2-5.30). Adm £3.50, chd free. Home-made teas.
½ acre secret garden created on different levels, with mature rhododendrons, azaleas, acers, herbaceous border all set in a sylvan setting. A particular feature of the garden is a pergola supporting a 24ft long wisteria. Attractive gazebo copied from the original National Trust's Hunting Lodge in Odiham. Visitors say wherever you sit there is a completely different vista. Plant expert John Negus will be in attendance.

12 CHILWORTH MANOR
Halfpenny Lane, Chilworth, Guildford GU4 8NN. Mia & Graham Wrigley. *3½ m SE of Guildford. From centre of Chilworth village turn into Blacksmith Lane. 1st drive on R on Halfpenny Lane.* Sun 22 May (11-5). Adm £6, chd free. Home-made teas.
Extensive grounds of lawns and mature trees around C17/C18 manor on C11 monastic site. Substantial C18 terraced walled garden laid out by Sarah, Duchess of Marlborough, with herbaceous borders, topiary and fruit trees. Original stewponds integrated with new Japanese themed garden and woodland garden and walk. Paddock home to alpacas. Ongoing restoration project aims to create a contemporary and practical garden sensitive to its historic context. Garden and tree walks at 12 noon, 1.30pm, 2.30pm and 4pm.

13 CHINTHURST LODGE
Wonersh Common, Wonersh, Guildford GU5 0PR. Mr & Mrs M R Goodridge, 01483 535108, michaelgoodridge@ymail.com. *4m S of Guildford. From A281 at Shalford turn E onto B2128 towards Wonersh. Just after Waverley sign, before village, garden on R.* Sun 19, Wed 22 June (11-5.30). Adm £5, chd free. Home-made teas. **Visits also by arrangement May to July for groups 10+.**
1 acre yr-round enthusiast's atmospheric garden, divided into rooms. Herbaceous borders, dramatic white garden, specimen trees and shrubs, gravel garden with water feature, fruit cage, 2 wells, ornamental ponds, herb parterre and millennium parterre garden, as featured in the May edition of Period Homes and Interiors. Some gravel paths, which can be avoided.

14 ◆ CLAREMONT LANDSCAPE GARDEN
Portsmouth Road, Esher KT10 9JG. National Trust, 01372 467806, claremont@nationaltrust.org.uk, www.nationaltrust.org.uk. *1m SW of Esher. On E side of A307 (no access from A3 bypass).* For NGS: Sun 5 June, Sun 9 Oct (10-6). Adm £8.50, chd £4.25. Light refreshments. For other opening times and information, please phone, email or visit garden website.
One of the earliest surviving English landscape gardens, begun by Vanbrugh and Bridgeman before 1720 and extended and naturalised by Kent and Capability Brown. Lake, island with pavilion; grotto and turf amphitheatre; viewpoints and avenues. Free guided walk at 2pm both NGS days with member of the gardening team. Cafe serving home-made cakes, light lunches and afternoon teas. Access maps available with recommended route.

Recycled materials create an inspired variety of ideas . . .

15 NEW THE COACH HOUSE
The Green, Chiddingfold, Godalming GU8 4TU. Mr & Mrs S Brooks, 01428 687767, barbarabrooks@btinternet.com. *7m S of Godalming. Eastern corner of village green. Parking around village green or along Pickhurst Rd.* Sat 18, Sun 19 June (11-5). Adm £4, chd free. Home-made teas. **Visits also by arrangement Apr to Sept for groups 8+.**
Plant enthusiast's garden comprising one acre walled garden and additional courtyards, designed by the owners and created since 2013. Lawns divided into areas by trees and borders filled with perennials, shrubs and roses. A courtyard rose garden, wildflower meadow, white garden and kitchen garden provide varied interest. A secluded courtyard filled with garden pots of exotic ferns and hostas. Mostly accessible by wheelchair but paths are grass so care needed if wet.

The Coach House

with the garden. Refreshments provided by The Inner Wheel Club of Banstead.

19 ▶ 56 COPSE AVENUE

Farnham GU9 9EA. Lyn & Jimmy James, 01252 323473, lynandjimmy@virginmedia.com. *Approx 1¹/₂ m N of Farnham. At Shepherd & Flock r'about take A325 to Farnborough. At 2nd r'about take Weybourne exit. At 2nd turn L. Take 2nd R at end of rd L.* **Visits by arrangement May & June for groups 10+. Adm £4.00, chd free. Tea.**

A fascinating and unusual 1 acre garden in a residential area. The garden was originally landscaped in the late 1960s following the plans of a Chelsea Flower Show garden, but was subsequently allowed to become very overgrown. The present owners have restored many of the original features and are adding innovative areas of planting and interest. Accessible for wheelchairs but some steep steps and uneven paths.

&. ⊗ ☕

20 ▶ COVERWOOD LAKES

Peaslake Road, Ewhurst GU6 7NT. The Metson Family, 01306 731101, coverwoodfarm@coverwoodlakes. co.uk, www.coverwoodlakes.co.uk. *7m SW of Dorking. From A25 follow signs for Peaslake; garden ¹/₂ m beyond Peaslake on Ewhurst rd.* **Sun 10, Sun 17, Sun 24 Apr, Mon 2, Sun 8, Sun 15 May, Sun 16 Oct (11-5). Adm £5, chd free. Light refreshments.**

14 acre landscaped garden in stunning position high in the Surrey Hills with 4 lakes and bog garden. Extensive rhododendrons, azaleas and fine trees. 3¹/₂ acre lakeside arboretum. Marked trail through the 180 acre working farm with Hereford cows and calves, sheep and horses, extensive views of the surrounding hills. Light refreshments incl home produced Hereford burgers, cakes, etc.

&. 🚐 ☕

21 ▶ ◆ CROSSWATER FARM

Crosswater Lane, Churt, Farnham GU10 2JN. The Millais family, 01252 792698, sales@rhododendrons.co.uk, www.rhododendrons.co.uk. *6m S of Farnham, 6m NW of Haslemere. From A287 turn E into Jumps Rd ¹/₂ m N of Churt village centre. After*

16 ▶ COLDHARBOUR HOUSE

Coldharbour Lane, Bletchingley, Redhill RH1 4NA. Mr Tony Elias, 01883 742685, eliastony@hotmail.com. *Coldharbour Lane off Rabies Heath Rd ¹/₂ m from A25 at Bletchingley & 0.9m from Tilburstow Hill Rd. Park in field & walk down to house.* **Sat 3, Sun 4 Sept (1-5). Adm £4.50, chd free. Home-made teas. Visits also by arrangement Apr to Oct for groups 10+.**

This 1¹/₂ acre garden offers breathtaking views to the South Downs. Originally planted in the 1920's, it has since been adapted and enhanced. Several mature trees and shrubs incl a copper beech, a Canadian maple, magnolias, azaleas, rhododendrons, camellias, wisterias, fuschias, hibiscus, potentillas, mahonias, a fig tree and a walnut tree.

☕

17 ▶ NEW 53 COMMONFIELD ROAD

Banstead SM7 2JR. Jennifer Russell, 01737 379510, jenniferlindarussell@hotmail.co.uk. *From A217 turn into Winkworth Rd, then 1st turning on L after mini r'about. Parking on rd, please do not block neighbours drives.* **Sun 5 June, Sun 4 Sept (11-4). Combined adm with 29 Commonfield Road £5, chd free. Home-made teas. Visits also by arrangement May to Sept for groups 10+.**

A small colourful garden designed and created by the present owner in late 2012, to incorporate her two passions, interesting plants and nature. Enter through a side gate through a rose and clematis arch into a packed and interesting garden, a small wildlife pond with beach, next to a bog garden. An alpine bed, large rose arch, woodland and a screened working area with plenty more to discover. Small wheelchair available.

&. ⊗ ☕

18 ▶ 29 COMMONFIELD ROAD

Banstead SM7 2JR. Lynne Quick, 01737 357617, lynne.quick@virginmedia.com. *A217 from Reigate to Sutton. Turn on to Winkworth Rd A2022 at T-lights at Banstead Xrds towards Purley. Commonfield Rd 1st L.* **Sun 5 June, Sun 4 Sept (11-4). Combined adm with 53 Commonfield Road £5, chd free. Home-made teas. Visits also by arrangement May to Sept for groups 10+.**

A plantswoman's small garden with a rich diversity of colourful shrubs, herbaceous perennials, roses, clematis and wisteria providing all round seasonal interest. A meandering garden providing vistas for acers, tree peonies, specimen trees and hosta beds with a clever use of foliage shape and colour. A magnificent display of unusual plants in containers cleverly link the patio

¼ m turn acute L into Crosswater Lane & follow signs for Millais Nurseries. For NGS: Sun 1, Mon 2 May (10-5). Adm £4, chd free. Home-made teas. For other opening times and information, please phone, email or visit garden website.

Idyllic 6 acre woodland garden. Plantsman's collection of rhododendrons and azaleas, incl rare species collected in the Himalayas, hybrids raised by the owners. Everything from alpine dwarfs to architectural large leaved trees. Ponds, stream and companion plantings incl sorbus, magnolias and Japanese acers. Trial gardens of new varieties. Woodland garden and specialist plant centre. Featured on BBC TV, The Garden and feature on Gold award winning display of new late flowering Azaleas at RHS Hampton Court Flower Show. Grass paths may be difficult for wheelchairs after rain.

22 CULVERKEYS

20A Longdown Lane North, Ewell, Epsom KT17 3JQ. Anne Salt, 020 8393 6861. 1m E of Epsom, 1m S of Ewell Village. Leave Ewell bypass (A24) by Reigate Rd (A240) to pass Nescot on L. Turn R in ¼ m. Sun 22 May, Sun 3 July (2-5). Adm £3, chd free. Home-made teas. Visits also by arrangement May to Sept, groups min 10, max 20.

A romantic somewhat secret garden on the edge of Epsom Downs. Meandering paths pass borders planted to capacity with interesting and unusual plants. Arches smothered in climbers reveal secluded corners and running water soothes the spirit. Designed for yr-round interest, shrubs and trees play host to many clematis.

23 NEW DOWN COURT

12 Courts Hill Road, Haslemere GU27 2NG. Beryl & Peter Bailey. Take A286 to Midhurst out of Haslemere centre. At Xrds (300 yrds) turn R. Property on R. NB: House numbering sequence is 8-12-9. Entrance under large oak tree behind cottage. Sat 25, Sun 26 June (11-5.30). Adm £4, chd free. Tea. Part of an old garden landscaped for an Arts and Crafts property. Long views from it's terrace to the Surrey Hills over what was once it's parkland. Small but with many interesting

features: azalea border; pond; greenhouse with nectarine and citrus; pottager; herb border; courtyard garden; conservatory with Mediterranean and tropical zones. Irrigated from its own rainwater cisterns. Access via sloping pea shingle drive, slopes within the garden.

24 ◆ DUNSBOROUGH PARK

Ripley GU23 6AL. Baron & Baroness Sweerts de Landas Wyborgh, 01483 225366, office@sweerts.com, www.dunsboroughpark.com. 6m NE of Guildford. Entrance across Ripley Green via The Milkway past cricket green on R & playground on L, round corner to double brown wooden gates. For NGS: Sat 30 Apr, Sun 12 June, Sun 18 Sept (12-4.30). Adm £6, chd free. Tea. For other opening times and information, please phone, email or visit garden website.

6 acres of walled gardens redesigned by Penelope Hobhouse and Rupert Golby - a box hedged parterre showcasing spectacular tulip displays in April; different garden rooms; lush herbaceous borders with standard wisterias; 70ft Ginkgo hedge; Rose Walk; ancient mulberry tree; Italian Garden; potager; water garden and folly bridge. Enjoy Roses and Peonies in June and Dahlias in September. Produce for sale. Festival of Tulips 20,000 new bulbs/20,000 1yr old bulbs planted in wild meadow. NGS: Sat, 30 Apr 12-4.30pm. Not for NGS: Sun 17 and Sun 24 Apr 12-4.30pm; Thurs 21 Apr 2-7pm.

25 NEW EARLEYWOOD

Hamlash Lane, Frensham, Farnham GU10 3AT. Mrs Penny Drew, 01252 792909. 3m S of Farnham just off A287. From A31 Farnham take A287 towards Frensham. R 1st turn passed Edgeborough School into Kennel Lane. Cross into Hamlash Lane. From A3, N on A287 to Frensham, L into Shortfield Common Rd. Roadside parking in lower half of Hamlash Lane & in Shortfield Common Rd - 5-10 mins walk. Sat 23, Sun 24 July (11-5). Adm £4, chd free. Home-made teas.

Award winning, ½ acre garden with colourful shrubberies, unusual trees and mixed borders throughout. Wide variety of summer flowering shrubs, particularly hydrangeas, colour

themed borders - vibrant reds and yellows and cool pinks and blues - also shady areas with groundcover and shade loving plants. Productive greenhouse. Awarded Best Large Garden in Farnham area. Disabled drop off at front gate, short gravel drive then level lawns throughout.

Meandering paths pass borders planted to capacity . . .

26 FAIRMILE LEA

Portsmouth Road, Cobham KT11 1BG. Steven Kay. 2m NE of Cobham. On Cobham to Esher rd. Access by lane adjacent to Moleshill House & car park for Fairmile Common woods. Sun 26 June (2-5). Combined adm with Moleshill House £6, chd free. Home-made teas.

Large Victorian sunken garden fringed by rose beds and lavender with a pond in the centre. An old acacia tree stands in the midst of the lawn. Interesting planting on a large mound camouflages an old underground air raid shelter. Caged vegetable garden. Formality adjacent to wilderness.

27 26 THE FAIRWAY

Camberley GU15 1EF. Jacky Sheppard. 1½ m from M3 J4. Follow signs to Frimley Pk Hosp. At r'about take 3rd exit B311 Chobham Rd. Cont on B311 L at 2nd r'about. 1st L into Fairway. Sun 15 May (11-4). Mon 30 May (11-4), also open 150 Upper Chobham Road. Adm £3.50, chd free. Tea.

Spring and summer is the ideal time to see the azaleas, rhododendrons and heathers that surround the house. Bulbs, primroses and winter anemones give ground cover beneath the shrubs. Climbers and a variety of plants continue a theme to make way for summer flowering. A new water feature has been added, with other additions to the garden. Small area at back of garden not easily accessed by wheelchair.

GROUP OPENING

28 **FRIMLEY GREEN GARDENS**
Frimley Green GU16 6HE. *3m S of Camberley. M3 J4 follow A325 to Frimley Green for 1m. Turn R by the green, R into The Hatches for on street parking. Some parking also opp Elmcroft at Recreation Ground on B3411. Tickets & maps available at all gardens.* **Wed 8, Sat 11 June (2-5). Combined adm £5, chd free.**

ELMCROFT
Mrs Geraldine Huggon

OAKLEIGH
Mrs Angela O'Connell
Visits also by arrangement in June for groups 6+
01252 668645
angela.oconnell@icloud.com

TABOR
Susan Filbin
Visits also by arrangement Apr to Sept for groups of 4+

Enjoy the personal touch at three very popular gardens in Frimley Green. Be inspired by immaculate designer chic in a very individual space at Tabor. Here you can admire a riot of hostas, colourful pots and soothing water features. At Elmcroft a huge *Buddleia alternifolia* forms a stunning backdrop for cottage classics in this propagator's paradise. Look for surprises at winding Oakleigh, with a variety of plants creating a bright palette of colour. Elmcroft will have some old favourites and unusual plants for sale. Tabor and Oakleigh featured in Surrey Life. Gravel paths and steps may limit access at Elmcroft and Tabor.

29 **THE GARTH PLEASURE GROUNDS**
Newchapel Road, Lingfield RH7 6BJ. Mr Sherlock & Mrs Stanley, ab_post@yahoo.com, www.oldworkhouse.webs.com. *From A22 take B2028 by Mormon Temple to Lingfield. The Garth is on L after 1 1/2 m, opp Barge Tiles. Parking: Barge Tiles or Gunpit Rd.* **Sat 7, Sun 8 May (2-5.30). Adm £5, chd free. Home-made teas. Visits also by arrangement June to Aug, please email 2 weeks in advance.**
Mature 9 acre Pleasure Grounds created by Walter Godfrey in 1919 present an idyllic setting surrounding the former parish workhouse

refurbished in Edwardian style. The formal gardens, enchanting nuttery, a spinney with many mature trees and a pond attract wildlife. Wonderful bluebells in spring. The woodland gardens and beautiful borders full of colour and fragrance for yr-round pleasure. Many areas of interest incl pond, woodland garden, formal gardens, spinney with large specimen plants incl 500yr old oak and many architectural features designed by Walter H Godfrey. Partial wheelchair access in woodland, iris and secret gardens.

Large Victorian sunken garden fringed by rose beds and lavender . . .

30 ◆ **GATTON PARK**
Rocky Lane, Merstham RH2 0TW. Royal Alexandra & Albert School, 01737 649068, www.gattonpark.com. *3m NE of Reigate. 5 mins from M25 J8 (A217) or from top of Reigate Hill, over M25 then follow sign to Merstham. Entrance off Rocky Lane accessible from Gatton Bottom or A23 Merstham.* **For NGS: Sun 14 Feb (11-4). Adm £4, chd free. Light refreshments at Gatton Hall. 2017: Sun 12 Feb. For other opening times and information, please phone or visit garden website.**
Gatton Park is the core 250 acres of the estate originally laid out by Capability Brown. Gatton also boasts a Japanese garden, rock and water garden and Victorian parterre nestled within the sweeping parkland. Stunning displays of snowdrops and aconites in February and March. Free activities for children. Tea, cake, soup and rolls available on the day. Partial wheelchair access.

31 ▶ **GHASSAN'S FARM**
Norwood Hill, Nr Horley RH6 0HR. Mr Ghasan Al Nemar. *4m SW of Reigate. Take A217 towards Horley; after 2m turn R down Irons Bottom Lane (just after Sidlow Bridge). 1st R Dean Oak Lane, then L at T-junction. Disabled drop off & parking.* **Sat 11, Sun 12 June (12-5). Adm £5, chd free. Tea.**
The house where Lord Baden-Powell lived. 12 acre garden in lake setting around old farmhouse (not open). Walled garden, old fashioned roses, shrubs, herbaceous. Tudor courtyard and orchard. Bird and butterfly garden. Kitchen garden with large greenhouses. Secret garden, parterre with box hedging. Many areas of the garden are easily accessible for wheelchair users.

32 ▶ **HALL GROVE SCHOOL**
London Road (A30), Bagshot GU19 5HZ. Mr & Mrs A R Graham. *6m SW of Egham. M3 J3, follow A322 1m until sign for Sunningdale A30, 1m E of Bagshot, opp Long Acres garden centre, entrance at footbridge. Ample car park.* **Sat 14 May (2-5). Adm £5, chd free. Home-made teas.**
Formerly a small Georgian country estate, now a co-educational preparatory school. Grade II listed house (not open). Mature parkland with specimen trees. Historical features incl ice house, old walled garden, heated peach wall. Lake, woodland walks, rhododendrons and azaleas. Live music at 3pm.

33 ▶ **NEW HALL PLACE FARM**
Hall Place, Cranleigh GU6 8LD. Mr & Mrs C Britton. *2m W of Cranleigh. From A281 take B2130 Dunsfold Rd; after 3/4 m turn L into Stovolds Hill at tight bend. After 1/2 m take gravel track on L, sp 'Hall Place'. Follow signs to parking in field after 200yds.* **Sat 16 July (11-5). Adm £4, chd free. Light refreshments.**
Work-in-progress restoration of 2 1/4 acre gardens centred on 550yr old house. Elements of Victorian gardens created for Hall Place Estate in 1865 and parts created by present owners since 2010. A wide variety of character and planting; walled garden, wooded sunken dell, orchard, greenhouse, vegetable garden, walled cottage garden,

formal courtyard with fountain, lawns with mixed borders and views. Wheelchair access to main parts of the garden.

♿ 🚾 ☕

34 ◆ HATCHLANDS PARK
East Clandon, Guildford GU4 7RT. National Trust, 01483 222482, hatchlands@nationaltrust.org.uk, www.nationaltrust.org.uk. *4m E of Guildford. Follow brown signs to Hatchlands Park (NT).* **For NGS: Sun 15 May (10.30-6). Adm £6, chd £3.** **For other opening times and information, please phone, email or visit garden website.**
Garden and park designed by Repton in 1800. Follow one of the park walks to the stunning bluebell wood in spring (2.5km/1.7m round walk over rough and sometimes muddy ground). In autumn enjoy the changing colours on the long walk. Partial wheelchair access to parkland, rough, undulating terrain, grass and gravel paths, dirt tracks, cobbled courtyard. Tramper booking essential.

♿ 🚾 🐕 🚐 ☕

35 HEATHSIDE
10 Links Green Way, Cobham KT11 2QH. Miss Margaret Arnott & Mr Terry Bartholomew, 01372 842459, m.a.arnott@btinternet.com. *1½ m E of Cobham. Through Cobham A245, 4th L after Esso garage into Fairmile Lane. Straight on into Water Lane. Links Green Way 3rd turning on L.* **Visits by arrangement. Home-made teas.**
⅓ acre terraced, plantsman's garden, designed for yr-round interest. A sumptuous collection of wonderful plants, all set off by harmonious landscaping. Urns and obelisks aid the display. Two ponds and two water features add tranquil sound. A contemporary parterre and various topiary shapes add formality. Stunning colour combinations excite. Many inspirational ideas. 5m from RHS Wisley.

🚐 ☕

GROUP OPENING

36 HORSELL GROUP GARDENS
Horsell, Woking GU21 4XA. *1½ m W of Woking in Village of Horsell. Leave M25 at junction 11. Take A320 signed Woking then A3046 signed*

Chobham after approx 1m at r'about turn L signed Horsell, with parking on Village Green outside Cricketers PH. **Sun 26 June (11-5). Combined adm £5, chd free. Home-made teas.**

BIRCH COTTAGE
Celia & Mel Keenan

3-4 BIRCH COTTAGES
Mr & Mrs Freeman

115 HIGH STREET
Mr & Mrs Barden

HORSELL ALLOTMENTS
Horsell Allotments Association www.horsellalots.wordpress.com

3 gardens and an award winning allotment in the village of Horsell which is on the edge of the Common, famously mentioned in HG Wells's, War of the Worlds. 3-4 Birch Cottages is full of charm with an interesting courtyard with rill. Walk down this long garden through into a series of rooms with topiary and attractive planting and many specimen roses. Birch Cottage is a grade II listed cottage with a box hedge style knot garden, a chinese slate courtyard with planted pots and hanging baskets, a canal water feature and an active white dove dovecote, surrounded with an abundance of planting. Horsell Allotments have over 100 individual plots growing a variety of unusual flowers and vegetables, many not seen in supermarkets, 2 working beehives with informative talks from their owners. 115 High Street is a plant lover's garden designed and created by owners for yr-round interest, with ideas for planting woodland dry shade and many rare and unusual plants. Allotments and 3-4 Birch Cottage are flat, Birch Cottage, has gravel and steps but wheelchair visitors can see main garden. None at 115 High Street.

♿ 🚾 🐕 ☕

37 KNOWLE GRANGE
Hound House Road, Shere, Guildford GU5 9JH. Mr P R & Mrs M E Wood, 01483 202108, prmewood@hotmail.com. *8m S of Guildford. From Shere (off A25), through village for ¾ m. After railway bridge, cont 1½ m past Hound House on R (stone dogs on gatepost). After 100yds turn R at Knowle Grange sign, go to end of lane.* **Sun 22 May, Sun 11 Sept**

(11-4.30). Adm £6.50, chd free. Home-made teas. **Visits also by arrangement May to Sept groups of 20+. Mini buses only.**
80 acre idyllic hilltop position. Extraordinary and exciting 7 acre gardens, created from scratch since 1990 by Marie-Elisabeth Wood, blend the free romantic style with the strong architectural frame of the classical tradition. Walk the rural 1 mile Bluebell Valley Unicursal Path of Life and discover its secret allegory. Deep unfenced pools, high unfenced drops.

☕

38 ◆ LOSELEY PARK
Guildford GU3 1HS. Mr & Mrs M G More-Molyneux, 01483 304440/405112, pa@loseleypark.co.uk, www.loseleypark.com. *4m SW of Guildford. For SatNav please use GU3 1HS Stakescorner Lane.* **For NGS: Sun 12 June (11-5). Adm £5, chd £2.50. Tea. For other opening times and information, please phone, email or visit garden website.**
Delightful 2½ acre walled garden. Award winning rose garden (over 1,000 bushes, mainly old fashioned varieties), extensive herb garden, fruit/flower garden, white garden with fountains, and spectacular organic vegetable garden. Magnificent vine walk, herbaceous borders, moat walk, ancient wisteria and mulberry trees. Refreshments available in our newly refurbished tea room. Featured in Country Living Magazine.

♿ 🐕 🚐 ☕

39 NEW MALABAR

**Holdfast Lane, Haslemere
GU27 2EY. Beryl & Tony Bishop.** *Off B2136 Petworth Rd from Haslemere High St. Turn L in to Holdfast Lane, well before Lythe Hill Hotel. Parking in field opp or neighbours drives. Please drop off passengers before parking.* Sun 15 May (1-5). Adm £4.50, chd free. **Home-made teas.**
2¹/₂ acre country garden bounded by mature oaks with climbing hydrangeas, clematis and roses. Undulating lawns bordered by imaginative colourful planting of unusual shrubs, rhododendrons, and azaleas. Bluebells, hellebores, primulas, lily of the valley and wood anemones throughout. Tranquil bark chipped level woodland walks with natural archways give a host of different vistas. How many owls can you find? Paths are wide and firm.

40 THE MANOR HOUSE

**Three Gates Lane, Haslemere
GU27 2ES. Mr & Mrs Gerard Ralfe.** *1m NE of Haslemere. From Haslemere centre take A286 towards Milford. Turn R after Museum into Three Gates Lane. At T-Junction turn R into Holdfast Lane. Car park on R.* Sun 22 May (12-5). Adm £5, chd free. **Home-made teas.**
Described by Country Life as 'The hanging gardens of Haslemere', The Manor House gardens are in a valley of the Surrey Hills. One of Surrey's inaugural NGS gardens, fine views, 6 acres, water gardens.

41 MOLESHILL HOUSE

The Fairmile, Cobham KT11 1BG. Penny Snell, pennysnellflowers@btinternet.com, www.pennysnellflowers.co.uk. *2m NE of Cobham. On A307 Esher to Cobham Rd next to free car park by A3 bridge, at entrance to Waterford Close.* Sun 26 June (2-5). Combined adm with Fairmile Lea £6, chd free. **Visits also by arrangement May to Sept for groups 15+.**
Romantic garden. Short woodland path leads from dovecote to beehives. Informal planting contrasts with formal topiary box and garlanded cisterns. Colourful courtyard and pots, conservatory, fountains, bog garden. Pleached avenue, circular gravel garden replacing most of the lawn. Gypsy caravan garden, new green wall and stumpery. Chickens.

Music at Moleshill House, teas at Fairmile Lea. Garden 5 mins from Claremont Landscape Garden, Painshill Park and Wisley, also adjacent excellent dog walking woods. Featured in Period Homes and Interiors.

> Weeping silver birch leads to the oranges and yellows of a tropical bed . . .

42 NEW MONKS LANTERN

**Ruxbury Road, Chertsey
KT16 9NH. Janice Granell,** 01932 569578, janicegranell@hotmail.com. *1m NW from Chertsey. M25 J11, signed A320/Woking. R'about 2nd exit A320/Staines, straight over next r'about. L onto Holloway Hill, R Hardwick Lane.* ¹/₂ m, R over motorway bridge, on Almners then Ruxbury Rd. Sun 3 July (1-5). Adm £3.50, chd free. **Light refreshments.**
A delightful garden with borders arranged with colour in mind: silvers and white, olive trees, nicotiana and senecio blend together. Large rockery and an informal pond. A weeping silver birch leads to the oranges and yellows of a tropical bed, with large bottle brush, hardy palms, and fatsia japonica. There is a display of hostas, cytisus battandieri and a selection of grasses in an island bed. Aviary with small finches. Winner Runnymede Gardens in Bloom. Featured in Surrey Herald. For wheelchair access, park on gravel drive to front of house, side access to garden, no steps, flat lawn.

43 MONKSFIELD

Charles Hill (B3001), Tilford, Farnham GU10 2AL. Mr & Mrs Mark Reynolds, 07734 155298, Monksfieldhouse@gmail.com. *On B3001 Farnham to Elstead Rd, approx 800 metres S of junction with Crooksbury Rd. Car parking opp house in field.* Sat 2 July (10.30-5.30). Adm £5, chd free. **Home-made teas.**
10¹/₂ acre varied family garden. With Hampton Court show garden, orchard/walled garden, formal garden to the south of the house, incl large sculptures, cottage garden, ¹/₂ acre wildlife pond, wildlife garden, greenhouse with vegetable plot and large selection of mature and newly planted specimen trees. Internal road allowing wheelchair access to many parts of grounds.

44 ODSTOCK

**Castle Square, Bletchingley
RH1 4LB. Averil & John Trott,** 01883 743100. *3m W of Godstone. Castle Square. Just off A25 in Bletchingley. At top of village nr Red Lion PH.* Visits by arrangement Apr to Sept for groups 10+. Adm £4.00, chd free. **Home-made teas.**
²/₃ acre plantsman's garden maintained by owners and developed for yr-round interest. Special interest in grasses, climbers and dahlias. A no dig, low maintenance vegetable garden. Short gravel drive. Main lawn suitable for wheelchairs but some paths maybe too narrow.

45 THE OLD CROFT

**South Holmwood, Dorking
RH5 4NT. David & Virginia Lardner-Burke,** www.lardner-burke.org.uk. *2m S of Dorking. From Dorking A24 S for 2m, L to Leigh/Brockham into Mill Rd.* ¹/₂ m on L, 2 free NT car parks on Holmwood Com. Access 500yds along woodland walk. Sun 29, Mon 30 May, Sat 16, Sun 17 July (2-6). Adm £5, chd free. **Home-made teas.**
Beautiful 5 acre garden with many diverse areas of natural beauty, giving a sense of peace and tranquillity. Stunning vistas incl lake, bridge, pond fed by natural stream running over rocky weirs, bog gardens, roses, perennial borders, elevated viewing hide, tropical bamboo maze, curved pergola of rambling roses, unique topiary buttress hedge, many specimen trees and shrubs. Visitors return again and again. Featured in Period Living and Surrey Life. **For direct access for disabled and elderly visitors please phone 01306 888224.**

46 NEW OLD KNOWLES

150 Upper Chobham Road, Camberley GU15 1ET. The Hobbs Family, hobbsgreta@btinternet.com. *2¹/₂ m from M3 J4. Follow signs to Frimley Pk Hosp. At r'about take 3rd exit*

B311 Chobham Rd. Cont on. Please park on Upper Chobham Rd (B311) nr Prior Rd, outside drive to Old Knowles. **Sun 29 May (11-5). Mon 30 May (11-5), also open 26 The Fairway. Adm £3.50, chd free. Coffee, tea and cakes.**
Take tea on the broad terrace and enjoy a stunning panorama of Douglas pines, bright azaleas, mature rhododendrons and an oriental surprise. Period sunken rose garden and birch copse offer space to wander or sit in shade. Children are welcome to tumble on our family friendly lawn. Care must be taken on paths and near the poolside.

♿ ❀ ☕

47 THE OLD RECTORY
Sandy Lane, Brewer Street, Bletchingley RH1 4QW. Mr & Mrs A Procter, 01883 743388 or 07515 394506, trudie.y.procter@googlemail.com. *Top of village nr Red Lion PH, turn R into Little Common Lane then R Cross Rd into Sandy Lane. Parking nr house, disabled parking in courtyard.* **Sun 26 June (11-4). Adm £5, chd free. Home-made teas. Visits also by arrangement Apr to Sept please phone/email for bookings.**
Georgian Manor House (not open). Quintessential Italianate topiary garden, statuary, box parterres, courtyard with columns, water features, antique terracotta pots. Much of the 4 acre garden is the subject of ongoing reclamation. This incl the ancient moat, woodland with fine specimen trees, rill, sunken and exotic garden under construction. Featured in Surrey Life, UK Vogue and Grazia magazine. Gravel paths.

♿ 🐕 ❀ ☕

48 NEW OLD TUNMORE FARM
Butlers Hill (off The Street), West Horsley, Leatherhead KT24 6AZ. Mr & Mrs J Kopij, 01483 285888, johnkopij@hotmail.com. *5m E of Guildford. Off A246, take The Street, W Horsley at Bell & Colville Garage r'about. 1st L in 200m. From A3 (M25), E Horsley B2309. R to E Lane, then The Street. Pass PH & Ripley Lane: Butlers Hill on R.* **Sat 11, Sun 19 June (2-5.30). Adm £4, chd free. Home-made teas.**
Quintessential English cottage and rose garden covering 3½ acres in idyllic setting with Grade II farmhouse (c1420). There is a circular walk taking in woodlands, natural areas

Caxton House

and the ancient village pond with views over rolling Surrey countryside. Around the house are terraces teaming with old English roses, various mixed borders, courtyards and cottage paths that delight at every turn. Partial wheelchair access. Garden set on hill with many steps and terraces.

♿ 🐕 ☕

49 ◆ POLESDEN LACEY
Great Bookham, Dorking RH5 6BD. National Trust, 01372 452048, camilla.morgan@nationaltrust.org. uk, www.nationaltrust.org.uk. *Nr Dorking, off A246 Leatherhead to Guildford rd. 1½ m S of Great Bookham, well signed.* **For NGS: Fri 24 June (10-5). Adm £9.40, chd £4.75. Cream teas in the Granary Cafe and Cowshed Coffee Shop. For other opening times and information, please phone, email or visit garden website.**
Designed as the perfect setting for social climber, Mrs Greville, to entertain royalty and the best of Edwardian society. Polesden Lacey has beautiful formal gardens with something to offer for every season, as well as glorious views over the rolling Surrey Hills in an Area of Outstanding Natural Beauty. There

are coffee outlets throughout the grounds, as well as Pimms tents and ice-cream stalls throughout the summer months. Wheelchairs and battery cars are available from visitor reception. There is also a courtesy shuttle. It is advisable to pre-book wheelchairs.

♿ 🐕 ❀ 🚐 ☕

50 PRATSHAM GRANGE
Tanhurst Lane, Holmbury St Mary RH5 6LZ. Alan & Felicity Comber, 01306 621116, alancomber@aol.com. *12m SE of Guildford, 8m SW of Dorking. From A25 take B2126. After 4m turn L into Tanhurst Lane. From A29 take B2126. Before Forest Green turn R on B2126 then 1st R to Tanhurst Lane.* **Sun 3 July, Sat 13, Sun 14 Aug (1-5). Adm £5, chd free. Home-made teas.**
5 acre garden overlooked by Holmbury Hill and Leith Hill. Features incl 2 ponds joined by cascading stream, extensive scented rose and blue hydrangea beds. Also herbaceous borders, cutting flower garden, white, yellow and dahlia beds. Some slopes and gravel paths. Deep ponds.

♿ ❀ ☕

51 ◆ **RAMSTER**
Chiddingfold, Surrey GU8 4SN. Mr & Mrs Paul Gunn, 01428 654167, office@ramsterhall.com, www.ramsterevents.com. *On A283 1½ m S of Chiddingfold; large iron gates on R, signed from rd.* **For NGS: Fri 20 May (10-5). Adm £7, chd free. Light refreshments. For other opening times and information, please phone, email or visit garden website.**
A stunning, mature woodland garden set in over 20 acres, famous for its rhododendron and azalea collection and its carpets of bluebells in Spring. Enjoy a peaceful wander down the woodland walk, explore the bog garden with its stepping stones, or relax in the tranquil enclosed Tennis Court Garden. Tea house open every day while the garden is open, serving delicious cakes and sandwiches. Teahouse and WC wheelchair accessible, some paths in garden suitable for wheelchairs.

 ♿ 🐕 ❀ 🚐 ☕

52 NEW **ROOKERY FARM**
Balchins Lane, Westcott, Dorking RH4 3LL. Mrs Tanya Demaine. *Off A25. From Dorking, go through Westcott, at bottom of Coast Hill turn R onto Balchins Lane. Parking past garden in field on R. Please turn R when exiting field as rd is single track.* **Sat 18, Sun 19 June (2-5). Adm £5, chd free. Home-made teas.**
This Queen Anne house is set in 3 acres of formal and informal gardens. A white circular garden, roses, old brick paths and scented arbour. Cutting and vegetable garden, with apiary. Herbaceous borders with rose walk. Garden becomes less formal as it radiates from house. The topiary and box hedging of the patio and courtyard, lead to wildflower meadow, mown paths, small orchard, wild pond and views to Ranmore.

☕

53 **7 ROSE LANE**
Ripley, Woking GU23 6NE. Mindi McLean, 01483 223200, info@broadwaybarn.com, www.broadwaybarn.com. *Just off Ripley High St on Rose Lane, 3rd house on L next to show repair shop.* **Sat 9 July (10-4). Adm £3, chd free. Home-made teas.**
7 Rose Lane is a small but perfectly formed village centre garden behind an historic listed cottage. It has 3 rooms - a traditional perennial flower garden laid to lawn; a vegetable and

fruit garden with Agriframe orchard and a working garden with greenhouse, compost bins and shed. It is a perfect example of how to make the most of a cottage garden. Monthly Ripley Farmers Market held on 9 July (9-1).

🛏 ☕

Enjoy home-made teas worthy of a royal celebration . . .

54 **SAFFRON GATE**
Tickners Heath, Alfold, Cranleigh GU6 8HU. Mr & Mrs D Gibbison, 01483 200219, clematis@talk21.com. *Between Alfold & Dunsfold. A281 between Guildford & Horsham approx 8m turn at Alfold crossways follow signs for Dunsfold. Do not turn at A281 T-lights for Dunsfold (wrong road).* **Sun 10 Apr, Sun 1, Mon 2 May, Sun 5 June (11-4). Adm £3.50, chd free. Home-made teas. Visits also by arrangement Feb to July, evening visits possible during summer months.**
April is for snowdrops, helebores and tulips. May starts with many rare trees and early flowering clematis. June is all about lots of clematis as some of the several hundred varieties will be in flower along with the first of the herbaceous plantings. An arbor with wisteria. Akebia, vitis, roses, underplanted with geranium gives height and shade. Vegetables hopefully all yr-round. Disabled drop off point.

 ♿ 🐕 ❀ 🚐 ☕

GROUP OPENING

55 NEW **SHACKLEFORD GARDEN SAFARI**
Godalming GU8 6AY. *5m SW of Guildford. Go to centre of Shackleford Village which is ½ m towards Elstead from A3 Hurtmore/Shackleford junction.*

Follow signs for parking. **Sun 12 June (11-6). Combined adm £10, chd free. Home-made teas at Norney Wood.**

> **DOLPHIN HOUSE**
> Mr & Mrs C Bell

> NEW **HEADLANDS**
> David & Jackie Sowerbutts

> **NORNEY WOOD** Ⓓ
> Mr & Mrs R Thompson
> www.norneywood.co.uk

> NEW **NORTH BARN** Ⓓ
> David & Anna Morgan

> NEW **THE TIMBER BARN**
> Gavin & Trish Bell

Enjoy a leisurely Sunday visiting five inspirational gardens in the village of Shackleford in the Surrey Hills, ending with a royal tea party at Norney Wood. Three of the gardens are opening for the first time. Meet the garden owners and hear what inspired them, challenged them and gives them great pleasure. Experience the charming courtyard garden at The Timber Barn, brimming with plants for yr-round colour. Meander through the naturalistic planting, meadow and woodland of Headlands. See the historical walls and the sophisticated and richly planted borders of Dolphin House. Share in the pleasure of the developing garden at The North Barn, designed by Acres Wild and in its 3rd year of planting. And finally, relax in the gardens of Norney Wood amidst the heavenly scented Gertrude Jekyll roses to enjoy home-made teas worthy of a royal celebration. Follow signs for parking and start your visit at either Headlands or Dolphin House. Surrey Hills village, historic buildings and structures, courtyard gardens, country gardens, contemporary landscaping, woodland, ancient trees, formal and informal water features, Society of Garden Designer gardens. Partial wheelchair access available at most gardens. Gravel paths, steps and slopes.

 ♿ ❀ ☕

56 **41 SHELVERS WAY**
Tadworth KT20 5QJ. Keith & Elizabeth Lewis, 01737 210707, kandelewis@ntlworld.com. *6m S of Sutton off A217. 1st turning on R after Burgh Heath T-lights heading S on A217. 400yds down Shelvers Way on L.* **Sun 17 Apr, Sun 24 July**

(2-5.30). Adm £4, chd free. Home-made teas. **Visits also by arrangement Apr to Aug for groups 10+.**

Visitors say 'one of the most colourful back gardens in Surrey'. In spring, a myriad of small bulbs with specialist daffodils and many pots of colourful tulips. Choice perennials follow, with rhododendrons and azaleas. Cobbles and shingle support grasses and self sown plants with a bubble fountain. Annuals, phlox and herbaceous plants ensure colour well into September. A garden for all seasons.

57 SHIELING

The Warren, Kingswood, Tadworth KT20 6PQ. Dr Sarah Wilson, 01737 833370, sarahwilson@doctors.org.uk. *Kingswood Warren Estate. Off A217, gated entrance just before church on southbound side of dual carriageway after Tadworth r'about. ³/₄ m walk from Station. Parking on The Warren or by church on A217.* Mon 2 May (2-4). Adm £5, chd free. Home-made teas. Evening opening Sat 11 June (6-8). Adm £7, chd free. Wine. Sun 12 June (2-4). Adm £5, chd free. Home-made teas.

1 acre garden restored to its original 1920s design. Formal front garden with island beds and shrub border. Unusual large rock garden and mixed borders with collection of beautiful slug free hostas and uncommon perennials. The rest is a woodland garden with acid loving plants and some old and interesting trees and shrubs. Plant list provided for visitors. Gravel drive and some narrow paths in back garden. Otherwise grass and paths easy for wheelchairs.

58 SPURFOLD

Radnor Road, Peaslake, Guildford GU5 9SZ. Mr & Mrs A Barnes, 01306 730196, spurfold@btinternet.com. *8m SE of Guildford. A25 to Shere then through to Peaslake. Pass Village stores & L up Radnor Rd.* Sun 29 May (11-5). Adm £5, chd free. Home-made teas. Visits also by arrangement May to Aug, home-made teas (day), wine (eve).

4 acres, large herbaceous and shrub borders, formal pond with Cambodian Buddha head, sunken gravel garden with topiary box and water feature, terraces, beautiful lawns, mature rhododendrons and azaleas, woodland paths, and gazebos. Garden contains a collection of Indian elephants and other objets d'art. Topiary garden created 2010 and new formal lawn area created in 2012.

The NGS is Marie Curie's largest single donor

59 STUART COTTAGE

Ripley Road, East Clandon GU4 7SF. John & Gayle Leader, 01483 222689, gayle@stuartcottage.com, www.stuartcottage.com. *4m E of Guildford. Off A246 or from A3 through Ripley until r'about, turn L & cont through West Clandon until T-lights, then L onto A246. East Clandon 1st L.* Evening opening Fri 24 June (6-9). Adm £7.50, chd free. Wine and nibbles. **Visits also by arrangement May to Sept for groups 15+ (no upper limit).**

This much visited ¹/₂ acre garden seems to please many, being planted to offer floral continuity through the seasons. In June, the romance of the rose walk combines with the sound of water, in July, flowerbeds are floriferous with soft coordinated colours and scented plants, in August, vibrant colours will lift the spirits and in September, tender perennials reach their zenith. Music from The John Sargeant Band. Visitors are welcome to picnic in the paddock. Wheelchair access to all of garden.

60 STUARTFIELD

113 Silverdale Avenue, Walton-on-Thames KT12 1EQ. Caroline Ingram MBE & Kevin Ingram. *1.3m S of Walton-on-Thames. From A3, A245 to Walton. R B365 Seven Hills Rd. At 2nd r'about A317 to Walton. L next r'about B365 Ashley Rd.*

Silverdale Av 2nd on L. Sun 1 May (11-5). Adm £4, chd free. Home-made teas.

An inspiring garden that takes you to different parts of the world, whether through New Zealand tree ferns, Japanese acers, or Moroccan inspired summerhouse. A mature garden with beautiful rhododendrons, extensively redesigned 15yrs ago by Joe Swift of Gardener's World fame. There is also a pond and many sculptural features to enjoy.

61 35 TADORNE ROAD

Tadworth KT20 5TF. Rod & Thelma Lay. *6m S of Sutton, 3m N of M25 J8. On A217 to large r'about. Take B2220 signed Tadworth. Tadorne Rd 2nd on R.* Sat 30, Sun 31 July (1.30-5.30). Adm £3.50, chd free. Home-made teas.

Colourful, curvaceous garden with lots of variety and hidden corners. We have bright herbaceous borders, shrubby island beds, flower covered pergolas, secluded seating areas, potager style vegetable plot, pebble patch, wild woodland corner and varied patio display - all in ¹/₃ acre! Delicious home-made teas served in plant filled conservatory. Gravel drive at entrance.

62 TILFORD COTTAGE

Tilford Road, Tilford GU10 2BX. Mr & Mrs R Burn, 01252 795423, rodburn@tiscali.co.uk, www.tilfordcottagegarden.co.uk. *3m SE of Farnham. From Farnham station along Tilford Rd. Tilford Cottage opp Tilford House. Parking by village green.* Visits by arrangement Mar to Aug for groups 6+. Refreshments available on request. Adm £6, chd free.

Artist's garden designed to surprise, delight and amuse. Formal planting, herb and knot garden. Numerous examples of topiary combine beautifully with the wild flower river walk. Japanese and water gardens, hosta beds, rose, apple and willow arches, treehouse and fairy grotto all continue the playful quality especially enjoyed by children. Dogs on lead please! Holistic centre open for taster sessions. Art studio open for viewing. Featured on Great British Garden Revival BBC4 Series 3. Partial wheelchair access. Some gravel paths and steep slopes.

Old Tunmore Farm

Jubilee rose garden. Etruscan summer house adjoining picturesque lakes and fountains. 15 acres of formal and informal gardens in idyllic setting within the M25. Tearooms with delicious home-made teas served between 12:30-5 on open days. Last admissions to gardens at 4pm, gardens close at 5pm. Dogs allowed in picnic area, car park and woodland walks. Good wheelchair access and disabled car park alongside tearooms.

65 ◆ **VANN**
Hambledon GU8 4EF.
Mrs M Caroe, 01428 683413,
www.vanngarden.co.uk. *6m S of Godalming. A283 to Wormley. Turn L at Hambledon. On NGS days only, follow yellow Vann signs for 2m. Please park in field, not in rd or see website instructions.* **For NGS: Mon 28 Mar (2-6). Daily Tue 29 Mar to Sun 3 Apr (10-6). Mon 2 May (2-6). Daily Tue 3 May to Sun 8 May (10-6). Daily Sun 5 June to Sat 11 June (10-6). Home-made teas Mon 2 May only. Adm £6, chd free.** For other opening times and information, please phone or visit garden website.
5 acre English Heritage registered garden surrounding Tudor and William and Mary house (not open) with Arts and Crafts additions by W D Caröe incl a Bargate stone pergola. At the front, brick paved original cottage garden; to the rear, $^{1}/_{4}$ acre pond, yew walk with rill and Gertrude Jekyll water garden. Snowdrops and hellebores, spring bulbs, spectacular Fritillaria in Feb/March. Island beds, crinkle crankle wall, orchard with wild flowers. Vegetable garden. Centenary Garden. Gertrude Jekyll water garden. Featured in Country Life, Daily Telegraph Magazine, Groei & Bloei (Belgium) and Period Homes and Interiors. Deep water. Water garden paths not suitable for wheelchairs, but many others are. Please ring prior to visit to request disabled parking.

63 ► **TIMBER HILL**
Chertsey Road, Chobham
GU24 8JF. Mr & Mrs Nick Sealy,
01932 873875,
nicksealy@chobham.net,
www.timberhillgarden.co.uk. *4m N of Woking. 2¹/₂ m E of Chobham & ¹/₃ m E of Fairoaks aerodrome on A319 (N side). 1¹/₄ m W of Ottershaw, J11 M25.* **Sun 14 Feb (11-4); Mon 28 Mar, Sun 8 May (11-4.30). Adm £5, chd free. Home-made light lunches and teas.**
Beautifully kept 15 acre park like garden and woodland with views to N Downs. Fine oaks, liquidambar and liriodendron. Early witch hazel walk, a sea of snowdrops and species crocus; beech, cherry, maples, acers, over 200 camellias and magnolias. Drifts of spring narcissi, daffodils and stunning camassias, tulips in borders; bluebells/azaleas in May; early roses in June. Fine autumn colour. A garden for all seasons! Nature and wildlife trails for children. Refreshments

served in beautiful old Surrey barn. Preferably book for lunch or take pot luck! **For alternative non NGS openings, please phone or see garden website.** Excellent help available for disabled.

64 ◆ **TITSEY PLACE GARDENS**
Titsey Hill, Titsey, Oxted RH8 0SD.
The Trustees of the Titsey Foundation, 01273 715356,
www.titsey.org. *3m N of Oxted. A25 between Oxted & Westerham. Follow brown signs to Titsey Estate from A25 at Limpsfield or see website directions.* **For NGS: Suns 15 May, 12 June, 17 July, 14 Aug (1-5). Adm £4.50, chd £1. Cream teas. For other opening times and information, please phone or visit garden website.**
One of the largest surviving historic estates in Surrey. Magnificent ancestral home and gardens of the Gresham family since 1534. Walled kitchen garden restored early 1990s. Golden

66 ► **WALTON POOR HOUSE**
Ranmore RH5 6SX. Prue Calvert,
01483 282273 or 07889 651316,
wnscalvert@btinternet.com. *6m NW of Dorking. From Dorking take rd to Ranmore, cont for approx 4m, after Xrds 1m on L. From A246 at E Horsley go S into Greendene, 1st L Crocknorth Rd, 1m on R.* **Mon 2, Sun 15 May (12-5). Home-made**

teas. **Sat 15, Sun 16 Oct (11-5). Adm £3.50, chd free. Visits also by arrangement May to Oct for groups 10+.**
Tranquil, almost secretive, 4 acre mostly wooded garden in North Downs AONB, planted to show contrast between colourful shrubs and mature trees. Paths wind through garden to pond, hideaway dell and herb garden, planted to show the use of aromatic plants and shrubs. Specialist nursery with wide variety of herbs, shrubs and aromatic plants. Herb talks, recipe leaflets and refreshments available for groups by appt. Grass paths.

Relax on the pond's deck amongst darting dragonflies and enjoy tea by the chicken run . . .

67 ▶ 57 WESTHALL ROAD
Warlingham CR6 9BG. Robert & Wendy Baston. *3m N of M25. M25, J6, A22 London, at Whyteleafe r'about, take 3rd R, under railway bridge, turn immed R into Westhall Rd.* **Sun 29, Mon 30 May (1-5). Adm £3.50, chd free. Home-made teas.** *Donation to Warlingham Methodist Church.*
Reward for the sure footed - many steep steps to 3 levels! Swathes of tulips and alliums. Mature kiwi and grape vines. Mixed borders. Raised vegetable beds. Box, bay, cork oak and yew topiaries. Amphitheatre of potted plants on lower steps. Stunning views of Caterham and Whyteleafe from top garden. Featured in Surrey Life.

68 ▶ WESTWAYS FARM
Gracious Pond Road, Chobham GU24 8HH. Paul & Nicky Biddle, 01276 856163, nicolabiddle@rocketmail.com. *4m N of Woking. From Chobham Church proceed over r'about towards Sunningdale, 1st Xrds R into Red*

Lion Rd to junction with Mincing Lane. **Sat 7 May (2-5); Sun 8 May (11-5). Adm £4, chd free. Home-made teas. Visits also by arrangement Apr to June for groups min 10, max 50.**
Open 6 acre garden surrounded by woodlands planted in 1930s with mature and some rare rhododendrons, azaleas, camellias and magnolias, underplanted with bluebells, lilies and dogwood; extensive lawns and sunken pond garden. Working stables and sandschool. Lovely Queen Anne House (not open) covered with listed *Magnolia grandiflora*. Victorian design glasshouse. New planting round garden room.

69 ▶ WILDWOOD
34 The Hatches, Frimley Green, Camberley GU16 6HE. Annie Keighley, 01252 838660, annie.keighley@ngs.org.uk. *3m S of Camberley. M3 J4 follow A325 to Frimley Centre, towards Frimley Green for 1m. Turn R by the green, R into The Hatches for on street parking.* **Visits by arrangement May to July. Adm £4, chd free. Home-made teas. Also open by arrangement with Oakleigh & Tabor (June only). Combined adm £5.**
Visitors love the hidden surprises in this romantic cottage garden with tumbling roses, topiary and towering magnolia. Holly hedges hide a secret haven with wildlife pond, dell, fernery and shaded loggia. Quirky organic potager with raised beds, fruit trees, tadpole nursery, greenhouses and composting areas. Wildlife gardening groups. Featured in Surrey Life. Gravel drive and paths. Care needed by pond.

70 ▶ ◆ WINKWORTH ARBORETUM
Hascombe Road, Godalming GU8 4AD. National Trust, 01483 208477, www.nationaltrust.org.uk. *2m SE of Godalming on B2130. Car: nr Hascombe, 2m SE of Godalming on E side of B2130. Bus: 42/44 Guildford to Cranleigh (stops at Arboretum).* **For NGS: Sun 5 June, Sun 2 Oct (10-5.30). Adm £8, chd £4. Home-made teas. For other opening times and information, please phone or visit garden website.**
This dramatic hillside Arboretum

perfectly demonstrates what Dr Fox, the Arboretum's creator, described as 'using trees and shrubs to paint a picture'. Impressive displays of daffodils, bluebells and azaleas await in spring. Picnic by the lake in summer. Don't miss the stunning autumnal display created by maples, cherries and tupelos. Guided walk with member of the garden team. Steep slopes.

71 ▶ WOODBURY COTTAGE
Colley Lane, Reigate RH2 9JJ. Shirley & Bob Stoneley, 01737 244235. *1m W of Reigate. M25 J8, A217 (Reigate). Immed before level Xing turn R into Somers Rd, cont as Manor Rd. At end turn R into Coppice Lane & follow signs to car park.* **Sat 9, Sun 10 July, Sat 3, Sun 4, Wed 7 Sept (1-5). Adm £4, chd free. Home-made teas.**
Cottage garden just under ¼ acre. It is stepped on a slope, enhanced by its setting under Colley Hill and the North Downs. We grow a colourful diversity of plants incl perennials, annuals and tender ones. A particular feature throughout the garden is the use of groups of pots containing unusual and interesting plants. The garden is colour themed and is still rich and vibrant in September.

72 ▶ 48 WOODMANSTERNE LANE
Wallington SM6 0SW. Joanne & Graham Winn, www.joannewinngardendesign.co.uk. *2.6m NE of Banstead. From A217 E on A2022 for 2½ m, turn L onto Woodmansterne Lane. Park at Flitton's nursery or on rd. DO NOT park on grass verges (Traffic wardens).* **Sat 23 July (1-5). Adm £4, chd free. Home-made teas.**
Approx ⅓ acre. Part of former smallholding, converted by garden designer Joanne Winn and husband Graham. Built around the original orchard's remaining fruit trees, the bold, curvy design is softened by a sumptuous palette of perennials and grasses. Pop into the secluded kitchen garden, relax on the pond's deck amongst darting dragonflies and enjoy tea by the chicken run. Partial wheelchair access, some gravel and narrow paths, raised deck and boardwalk.

SUSSEX

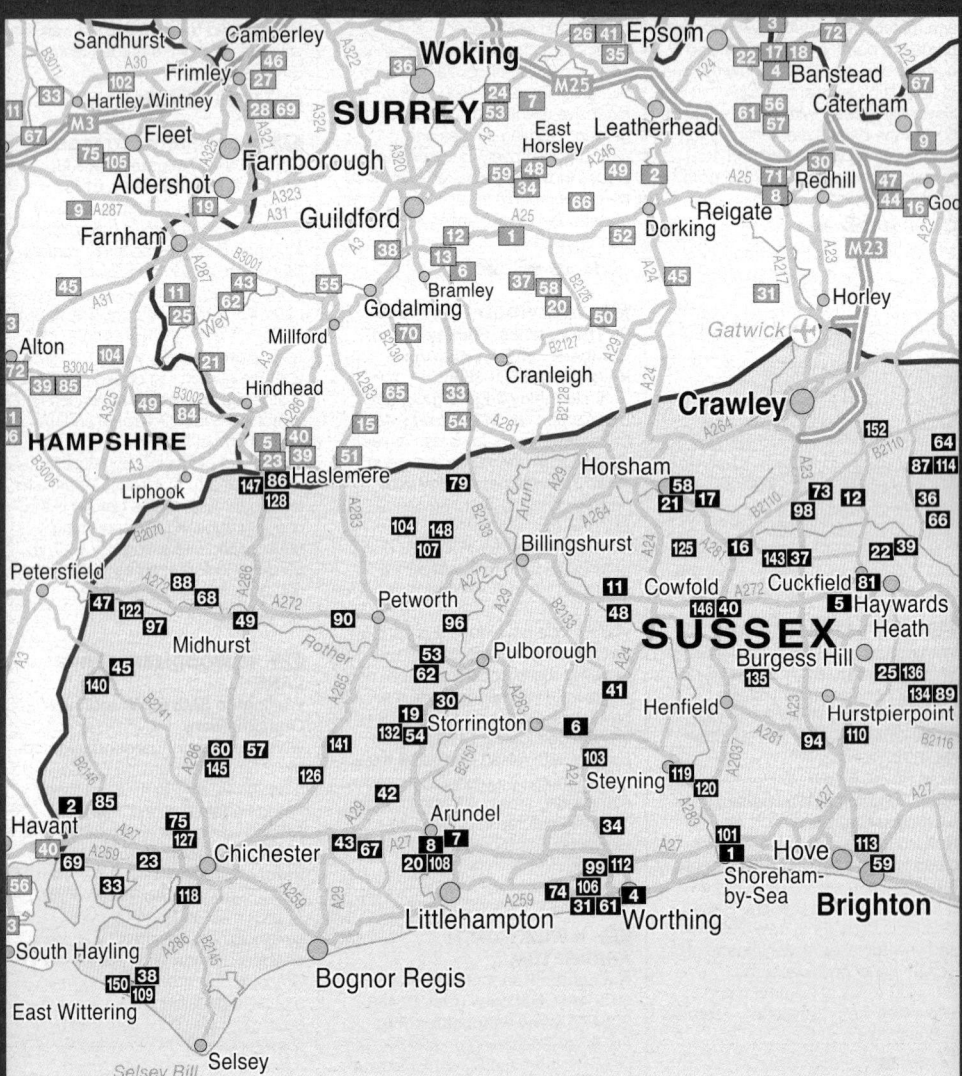

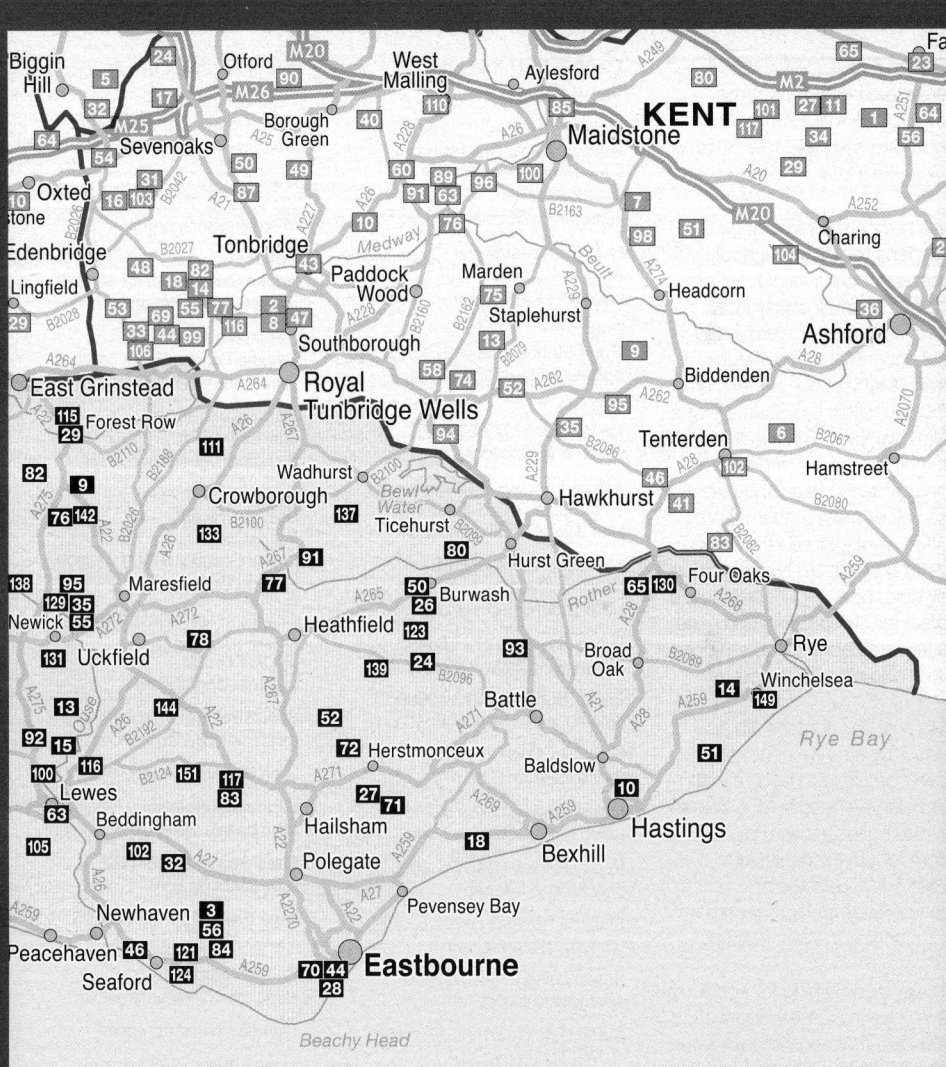

Sussex

Sussex is a vast county with two county teams, one covering East and Mid Sussex and the other covering West Sussex.

We have a stunning range of gardens to visit throughout the year, from rolling acres of parkland, small courtyards, country and town gardens to school gardens and village trails. Many of our gardens are located within the South Downs National Park. There is also the added bonus of delicious home-made cakes and tea served at most of them, and often plants for sale that have been propagated by the garden owners. Lots of our gardens are great for children too, and quite a few are happy for you to bring your dog along with you.

Many of our gardens are also open 'by arrangement', so don't be afraid to book a visit! Should you need advice, please e-mail ngseastsussex@gmail. com for anything related to East & Mid Sussex, or sussexwestngs@gmail.com for anything in West Sussex.

There is something for absolutely everyone in Sussex, and we feel sure that you will enjoy your garden-visiting experience.

Left: Rymans © Judi Lion

East & Mid Sussex Volunteers

County Organiser, Booklet & Advertising Co-ordinator
Irene Eltringham-Willson
01323 833770
irene.willson@btinternet.com

County Treasurer
Andrew Ratcliffe 01435 873310
anratcliffe@gmail.com

Publicity
Geoff Stonebanks 01323 899296
ngseastsussex@gmail.com

Twitter
Liz Warner 01273 586050
lizwarner69@outlook.com

Assistant County Organisers
Jane Baker 01273 842805
jane.baker47@btinternet.com

Michael & Linda Belton
01797 252984
belton.northiam@virgin.net

Lynne Brown 01273 556439
brown.lynne@ntlworld.com

Emma Burnett 01273 400606
emmaburnett16@btinternet.com

Linda Field 01323 720179
lindafield3@gmail.com

Diane Gould 01825 732253
heron.brook@btinternet.com

Peggy Harvey 01424 532093
chantry@talktalk.net

Philippa Hopkins 01342 822090
piphop@btinternet.com

Susan Laing 01444 892500
splaing@btinternet.com

Sarah Ratcliffe 01435 873310
sallyrat@btinternet.com

Geoff Stonebanks (as above)

Liz Warner (as above)

West Sussex Volunteers

County Organiser
Patty Christie 01730 813323
sussexwestngs@gmail.com

County Treasurer
Liz Collison 01903 719245
liz.collison@ngs.org.uk

Publicity
Adrian Skeates 07743 505392
as13cs@btinternet.com

Social Media
Claudia Pearce 07985 648216
claudiapearce17@gmail.com

Photographer
Judi Lion 07810 317057
dumpford1-jlp@yahoo.co.uk

Booklet Advertising
Position Vacant
For details please contact
Louise Grainger 01483 213909
lgrainger@ngs.org.uk

Assistant County Organisers
Teresa Barttelot
01798 865690
tbarttelot@gmail.com

Sanda Belcher 01428 723259
sandambelcher@gmail.com

Jane Burton 01243 527822

Lesley Chamberlain 07950 105966
chamberlain_lesley@hotmail.com

Sue Foley 01243 814452
suefoley@mac.com

Jane Lywood 01403 820225
jmlywood@aol.com

Carrie McArdle 01403 820272
carrie.mcardle@btinternet.com

Claudia Pearce (as above)

Fiona Phillips 01273 462285
fiona.h.phillips@btinternet.com

Susan Pinder 01403 820430
nasus.rednip@gmail.com

Caroline & Adrian Skeates
07743 505392
as13cs@btinternet.com

Opening Dates

All entries subject to change.
For latest information check www.ngs.org.uk
Extended openings are shown at the begining of the month.

February

Snowdrop Festival

Sunday 14
90 Manor of Dean
145 West Dean Gardens

Saturday 20
146 NEW Westlands Court

Thursday 25
92 McBean's Orchids

Friday 26
92 McBean's Orchids

Saturday 27
34 NEW Cissbury

Sunday 28
103 The Old Vicarage

March

Thursday 3
34 NEW Cissbury

Sunday 6
2 Aldsworth House
80 King John's Lodge

Tuesday 8
2 Aldsworth House

Sunday 13
90 Manor of Dean

Saturday 26
85 Lordington House

Sunday 27
106 Palatine School Gardens

Monday 28
85 Lordington House
103 The Old Vicarage

April

Friday 1
83 Limekiln Farm

Saturday 2
27 Butlers Farmhouse
83 Limekiln Farm

Sunday 3
27 Butlers Farmhouse
41 Dachs

Saturday 9
62 The Grange

Sunday 10
41 Dachs
62 The Grange
128 Shalford House

Thursday 14
39 Copyhold Hollow
152 NEW Worth Abbey & Grounds

Saturday 16
23 NEW Bosham Art In The Garden Trail
59 The Garden House
118 Rymans

Sunday 17
23 NEW Bosham Art In The Garden Trail
59 The Garden House
90 Manor of Dean
94 Newtimber Place
111 NEW Penns in the Rocks
118 Rymans
152 NEW Worth Abbey & Grounds

Saturday 23
45 Down Place
122 Sandhill Farm House
149 Winchelsea's Secret Gardens

Sunday 24
19 Bignor Park
35 Clinton Lodge
45 Down Place
100 Offham House
103 The Old Vicarage
122 Sandhill Farm House

Thursday 28
39 Copyhold Hollow
144 NEW Weavers House

Friday 29
13 NEW Banks Farm

Saturday 30
13 NEW Banks Farm
52 Fineoaks

May

53 Fittleworth House (every Wednesday)

Sunday 1
20 4 Birch Close
38 Cookscroft
52 Fineoaks
74 Highdown Gardens
88 Malt House

Monday 2
20 4 Birch Close
88 Malt House

Thursday 5
140 Uppark

Saturday 7
133 Stone Cross House

Sunday 8
68 Hammerwood House
88 Malt House
93 Mountfield Court
108 Peelers Retreat
133 Stone Cross House

Thursday 12
39 Copyhold Hollow

Friday 13
29 Caxton Manor
115 2 Quarry Cottages

Saturday 14
21 Blue Jays
29 Caxton Manor
76 Holly House
80 King John's Lodge
115 2 Quarry Cottages

Currently the NGS donates around £2.5 million every year . . .

Sunday 15
5 Ansty Gardens
21 Blue Jays
68 Hammerwood House
76 Holly House
80 King John's Lodge
111 NEW Penns in the Rocks
125 Sedgwick Park House
128 Shalford House

Wednesday 18
12 Balcombe Gardens
125 Sedgwick Park House

Saturday 21
10 96 Ashford Road

Sunday 22
9 Ashdown Park Hotel
11 Bakers House
16 Beedinglee
60 Gardeners' Cottage
82 Legsheath Farm

Thursday 26
39 Copyhold Hollow

Saturday 28
10 96 Ashford Road
114 The Priest House

Sunday 29
2 Aldsworth House
8 Arundel Gardens
141 Upwaltham Barns

Monday 30
8 Arundel Gardens
66 Great Lywood Farmhouse
141 Upwaltham Barns

Tuesday 31
2 Aldsworth House

June

53 Fittleworth House (every Wednesday)

Wednesday 1
131 Sparrow Hatch

Thursday 2
39 Copyhold Hollow
81 NEW Ladywell
131 Sparrow Hatch
140 Uppark

Friday 3
66 Great Lywood Farmhouse

Festival Weekend

Saturday 4
86 Lowder Mill

Sunday 5
14 Beauchamps
18 Bexhill Gardens
66 Great Lywood Farmhouse
67 Halfpenny Cottage
86 Lowder Mill
100 Offham House

Wednesday 8
129 Sheffield Park and Garden

Thursday 9
46 Driftwood
74 Highdown Gardens
137 Tidebrook Manor

Friday 10
113 NEW Preston Park Gardens

Saturday 11
28 51 Carlisle Road
49 54 Elmleigh
91 Mayfield Gardens
97 Nyewood House
113 NEW Preston Park Gardens
118 Rymans
122 Sandhill Farm House

Sunday 12
16 Beedinglee
28 51 Carlisle Road
42 Dale Park House
44 NEW Dittons End
49 54 Elmleigh
70 Hardwycke
73 High Beeches Woodland and Water Garden
90 Manor of Dean
91 Mayfield Gardens
97 Nyewood House
103 The Old Vicarage
118 Rymans
122 Sandhill Farm House
138 Town Place

Share your day out on 📘 and 🐦

53 **Fittleworth House (every Wednesday)**

Monday 13
35 Clinton Lodge

Tuesday 14
3 Alfriston Clergy House

Thursday 16
50 Elphicks Cottage
138 Town Place

Friday 17
50 Elphicks Cottage
107 Parsonage Farm

Saturday 18
12 Balcombe Gardens
31 Channel View
45 Down Place
49 54 Elmleigh
61 Goring Folly
102 Old Vicarage
116 Ringmer Park
117 1 Rose Cottage
132 Stane House
149 Winchelsea's Secret Gardens
151 2 Woodside

Sunday 19
11 Bakers House
31 Channel View
45 Down Place
49 54 Elmleigh
61 Goring Folly
116 Ringmer Park
126 Selhurst Park
132 Stane House

Monday 20
127 Sennicotts

Tuesday 21
127 Sennicotts

Wednesday 22
127 Sennicotts

Friday 24
120 St Mary's House Gardens

Saturday 25
47 Durford Mill House
51 Fairlight End
80 King John's Lodge
95 North Hall
114 The Priest House
120 St Mary's House Gardens

Sunday 26
1 Adur Lodge
4 Ambrose Place Back Gardens
5 Ansty Gardens
38 Cookscroft (Evening)
47 Durford Mill House
51 Fairlight End
58 NEW Foxglove Cottage
63 6 Grange Road
80 King John's Lodge

87 Luctons
95 North Hall
99 Oak Grove College Grounds
124 Seaford Gardens
138 Town Place
143 Warninglid Gardens

Monday 27
35 Clinton Lodge

Tuesday 28
46 Driftwood
87 Luctons

Thursday 30
39 Copyhold Hollow

Marie Curie

Our nurses care for people at home across the UK

July

53 **Fittleworth House (every Wednesday)**

Saturday 2
17 4 Ben's Acre
26 NEW Burwash Gardens
49 54 Elmleigh
52 Fineoaks
56 Follers Manor
72 Herstmonceux Parish Trail
104 NEW Orchard House

Sunday 3
49 54 Elmleigh
52 Fineoaks
56 Follers Manor
57 NEW The Folly
72 Herstmonceux Parish Trail
96 North Springs
108 Peelers Retreat
109 33 Peerley Road
128 Shalford House
138 Town Place

Thursday 7
84 The Long House

Saturday 9
36 Cobb Cottage North
49 54 Elmleigh
76 Holly House

Sunday 10
19 Bignor Park
49 54 Elmleigh
58 NEW Foxglove Cottage
76 Holly House
106 Palatine School Gardens

Tuesday 12
77 NEW The Homegrown Flower Company

Wednesday 13
77 NEW The Homegrown Flower Company
130 South Grange

Thursday 14
39 Copyhold Hollow
71 Gardens & Grounds of Herstmonceux Castle

Saturday 16
62 The Grange
105 NEW Ouse Valley To The Coast Trail

Sunday 17
36 Cobb Cottage North
62 The Grange
105 NEW Ouse Valley To The Coast Trail

Tuesday 19
46 Driftwood

Saturday 23
55 NEW Fletching Secret Gardens and Glasshouses

Sunday 24
15 NEW The Beeches
25 Burgess Hill NGS Gardens
75 4 Hillside Cottages
119 Saffrons

Monday 25
25 Burgess Hill NGS Gardens

Tuesday 26
150 Windhaven

Wednesday 27
119 Saffrons

Thursday 28
15 NEW The Beeches
39 Copyhold Hollow

Sunday 31
15 NEW The Beeches
40 NEW Cowfold Gardens
46 Driftwood
148 Whithurst Park

August

Thursday 4
39 Copyhold Hollow
78 The Hundred House

123 Sarah Raven's Cutting Garden
147 Whitehanger (Evening)

Friday 5
146 NEW Westlands Court

Sunday 7
78 The Hundred House

Monday 8
35 Clinton Lodge

Friday 12
32 NEW Charleston (Evening)

Saturday 13
27 Butlers Farmhouse
30 Champs Hill
64 Gravetye Manor

Sunday 14
27 Butlers Farmhouse
30 Champs Hill
57 NEW The Folly
108 Peelers Retreat

Thursday 18
39 Copyhold Hollow

Saturday 20
76 Holly House
104 NEW Orchard House

Sunday 21
25 Burgess Hill NGS Gardens
76 Holly House
89 Malthouse Farm
90 Manor of Dean
103 The Old Vicarage

Wednesday 24
89 Malthouse Farm

Saturday 27
17 4 Ben's Acre

Sunday 28
44 NEW Dittons End
70 Hardwycke

Monday 29
48 Durrance Manor
135 Sussex Prairies

September

Thursday 1
147 Whitehanger (Evening)

Sunday 4
79 Jacaranda
108 Peelers Retreat
128 Shalford House

Saturday 10
130 South Grange
136 30 Sycamore Drive (Evening)

Sunday 11
80 King John's Lodge
107 Parsonage Farm
130 South Grange
136 30 Sycamore Drive (Evening)

Tuesday 13
142 Vachery Forest Garden

Thursday 15
137 Tidebrook Manor

Saturday 17
118 Rymans
122 Sandhill Farm House

Sunday 18
118 Rymans
122 Sandhill Farm House

Sunday 25
73 High Beeches Woodland and Water Garden
98 Nymans

October

Tuesday 4
22 Borde Hill Garden

Sunday 9
19 Bignor Park

Sunday 16
103 The Old Vicarage

November

Wednesday 16
65 Great Dixter House, Gardens & Nurseries

Gardens open to the public

3 Alfriston Clergy House
7 Arundel Castle & Gardens - The Collector Earl's Garden
22 Borde Hill Garden
32 NEW Charleston
35 Clinton Lodge
43 Denmans Garden
65 Great Dixter House, Gardens & Nurseries
71 Gardens & Grounds of Herstmonceux Castle
73 High Beeches Woodland and Water Garden
74 Highdown Gardens
80 King John's Lodge
92 McBean's Orchids
98 Nymans
114 The Priest House
120 St Mary's House Gardens
123 Sarah Raven's Cutting Garden
129 Sheffield Park and Garden
135 Sussex Prairies
140 Uppark
145 West Dean Gardens

By arrangement only

6 Arborgarth
24 Brightling Down Farm
33 Chidmere Gardens
37 Colwood House
54 Five Oaks Cottage
69 Harbourside
101 Old Erringham Cottage
110 Pembury House
112 6 Plantation Rise
121 8 Sandgate Close
134 Stonehealed Farm
139 Turners House

Also open by arrangement

11 Bakers House
12 46 Westup Farm Cottages, Balcombe Gardens
12 Winterfield, Balcombe Gardens
15 NEW The Beeches
16 Beedinglee
17 4 Ben's Acre
18 14 Chantry Avenue, Bexhill Gardens
20 4 Birch Close

21 Blue Jays
25 47 Leylands Road, Burgess Hill NGS Gardens
27 Butlers Farmhouse
28 51 Carlisle Road
30 Champs Hill
31 Channel View
38 Cookscroft
39 Copyhold Hollow
41 Dachs
42 Dale Park House
45 Down Place
46 Driftwood
47 Durford Mill House
48 Durrance Manor
49 54 Elmleigh
51 Fairlight End
52 Fineoaks
53 Fittleworth House
57 NEW The Folly
58 NEW Foxglove Cottage
59 The Garden House
66 Great Lywood Farmhouse
68 Hammerwood House
70 Hardwycke
75 4 Hillside Cottages
76 Holly House
79 Jacaranda

84 The Long House
85 Lordington House
86 Lowder Mill
87 Luctons
88 Malt House
89 Malthouse Farm
90 Manor of Dean
95 North Hall
97 Nyewood House
103 The Old Vicarage
105 NEW 144 Rodmell Avenue, Ouse Valley To The Coast Trail
108 Peelers Retreat
109 33 Peerley Road
111 NEW Penns in the Rocks
117 1 Rose Cottage
118 Rymans
122 Sandhill Farm House
125 Sedgwick Park House
130 South Grange
136 30 Sycamore Drive
138 Town Place
141 Upwaltham Barns
147 Whitehanger
150 Windhaven
151 2 Woodside

Ringmer Park

© Leigh Capp

The Gardens

ADUR LODGE
The Street, Shoreham-by-Sea BN43 5NJ. Jeremy & Gilda Buckwell. *2m W of Southwick. From A27 on Shoreham bypass take A283 exit signed Shoreham. 1st L to Upper Shoreham Rd, immed L into St Nicholas Lane, then R into The Street.* **Sun 26 June (2-5). Adm £3.50, chd free. Tea, coffee, soft drinks & cakes.**
Walled garden with herbaceous bed, conifer bed, shrubs, vegetables and conservatory. Climbing and shrub roses.
&. ❀ ☕

② ALDSWORTH HOUSE
Emsworth Common Road, Aldsworth PO10 8QT. Tom & Sarah Williams. *6m W of Chichester. From Havant follow signs to Stansted House until Emsworth Common Rd, stay on this road until Aldsworth. From Chichester B2178 follow road through Funtington to Aldsworth.* **Sun 6, Tue 8 Mar, Sun 29, Tue 31 May (11-5). Adm £4, chd free. Home-made teas.**
Sheets of crocus and daffodils under

a 200 yr old plane tree herald spring. This 6 acre garden contains walled and gravel gardens, numerous borders and 2 mini arboretums packed full of a wide variety of unusual trees, shrubs and perennials. Particular specialities are hellebores, peonies, roses, epimediums, hostas, magnolias, clematis and very old fruit trees. Children's quiz. Short film of the garden in the 1930s. Some gravel areas and gentle slopes. Good access if ground not too wet.
&. ❀ ☕

③ ◆ ALFRISTON CLERGY HOUSE
Alfriston BN26 5TL. National Trust, 01323 871961, alfriston@nationaltrust.org.uk, www.nationaltrust.org.uk/alfriston. *4m NE of Seaford. Just E of B2108, in Alfriston Village, adjoining The Tye & St Andrew's Church. Bus: RDH 125 from Lewes, Autopoint 126 from Eastbourne & Seaford.* **For NGS: Tue 14 June (10.30-4.30). Adm £5.20, chd £2.60. For other opening times and information, please phone, email or visit garden website.**
Enjoy the scent of roses; admire the vegetable garden and orchard in a

tranquil setting with views across the R Cuckmere. Visit this C14 thatched Wealden hall house, the first building to be acquired by the NT in 1896. Our gardener will be available to talk to you about the garden. Partial wheelchair access.
&. ❀

GROUP OPENING

④ AMBROSE PLACE BACK GARDENS
Richmond Road, Worthing BN11 1PZ. *Worthing Town Centre. Entry points: Ambrose Villa, corner Portland Rd & Richmond Rd; No 1, next to St Paul's Church; No 10, opp Worthing Library.* **Sun 26 June (11-5), all gardens closed from 1pm-2pm. Combined adm £5, chd free. Light refreshments available at some gardens.**

> **1 AMBROSE PLACE**
> Tom Watson
>
> **3 AMBROSE PLACE**
> Paul & Denise Boyes
>
> **4 AMBROSE PLACE**
> Graham & Terri Heald
>
> **5 AMBROSE PLACE**
> Pat & Sue Owen
>
> **6 AMBROSE PLACE**
> Sue Swanborough
>
> **7 AMBROSE PLACE**
> Mark & Susan Frost
>
> **8 AMBROSE PLACE**
> Steve & Claire Hughes
>
> **9 AMBROSE PLACE**
> Derek & Anna Irvine
>
> **10 AMBROSE PLACE**
> Alan & Marie Pringle
>
> **11 AMBROSE PLACE**
> Steve & Carolyn Bailey
>
> **12 AMBROSE PLACE**
> Peter & Nina May
>
> **13 AMBROSE PLACE**
> Malcolm & Hilary Leeves
>
> **14 AMBROSE PLACE**
> Mr & Mrs A Marks
>
> **AMBROSE VILLA**
> Mark & Christine Potter

The highly acclaimed back gardens of Ambrose Place have been described as a 'horticultural phenomenon', and have a rich panoply of styles, plantings and layouts. Behind a classic Regency terrace, itself the architectural jewel of Worthing, the

Colwood House

gardens draw inspiration from such exotic diversity as Morocco, Provence and the Alhambra to the more traditional sources of the English cottage and Victorian gardens. All within the typically limited space of a terrace (seriously restricted disabled access), a variety of imaginative water features add to the charm and attraction for all gardeners and prove that small can be beautiful. Do come and enjoy our special spaces, we have 14 gardens open this year. Featured on BBC Sussex Radio Dig-it programme, and in the Worthing Herald, West Sussex Gazette, The Scotsman (4 Apr 2015) and other local media.

Come, enjoy and take home some ideas for your garden . . .

GROUP OPENING

5 **ANSTY GARDENS**
Bolney Road, Ansty, Haywards Heath RH17 5AW. *3m W of Haywards Heath on A272. 1m E of A23. Park on L of A272, 300yds W of r'about at junction of A272 & B2036, or if too wet try Council car park at Ansty end of Deaks Lane, just W of r'about (RH17 5AS). Not suitable for coaches.* **Sun 15 May, Sun 26 June (1.30-6). Combined adm £5, chd free. Home-made teas at Whydown (May) & Appletree Cottage (June).**

APPLETREE COTTAGE
Mr & Mrs G J Longfield.
Open on all dates

3 LAVENDER COTTAGES
Derry Baillieux.
Open on all dates

SPRINGFIELD
David Pyrah.
Open on all dates

WHYDOWN COTTAGE
Mrs M Gibson & Lance Gibson.
Open on Sun 15 May

Ansty's gardens offer interesting contrast. Whydown Cottage covers an acre with water features and an atmospheric woodland incl an

Embothrium. 3 Lavender Cottages has an attractive garden to the front and pretty brick courtyard to the rear with cottage flowers. Close by is picturesque C16 Appletree Cottage set in 2 acres with herbaceous beds, vegetable garden and fruit cage with wonderful views. Springfield's 1 acre offers mature trees and large pond, also camellias, azaleas, rhododendrons, and herbaceous border. Wheelchair access at Whydown Cottage unless very wet, partial access at 3 Lavender Cottages and no access at Springfield.

6 **ARBORGARTH**
Bracken Lane, Storrington, Pulborough RH20 3HS. Ted & Syb Hickford, syb.hickford@sky.com. *1½ m from centre of Storrington Village. Travel N from S coast on A24. After Washington r'about, L into Rock Rd signed Thakeham & West Chiltington. Bracken Lane is 5th turning on L, drive on R just past Bunbury Close.* **Visits by arrangement Mar to Sept for groups of 10-24 max. Home-made teas on request. Adm £5, chd free.** 1 acre terraced garden designed, developed and maintained over 30 yrs by current owners giving three seasons of colour and interest from mid Mar to end of Sept. The garden incl spring bulbs, camellias, azaleas, bluebells, unusual trees, large thyme bed in June, herbaceous borders, box hedging, stream, pond, waterfall, bog garden, and some topiary, all surrounded by high yew and beech hedging. Wheelchair access to two levels only, giving good views over the garden. Wide steps and sloping grass paths give access to lower levels.

7 **♦ ARUNDEL CASTLE & GARDENS - THE COLLECTOR EARL'S GARDEN**
Arundel BN18 9AB. Arundel Castle Trustees Ltd, 01903 882173, visits@arundelcastle.org, www.arundelcastle.org. *In the centre of Arundel, N of A27.* **For opening times and information, please phone, email or visit garden website.**
Ancient castle. Family home of the Duke of Norfolk. 40 acres of grounds and gardens. The Collector Earl's Garden with hot subtropical borders and wild flowers. English herbaceous borders. Stumpery. Wild flower

garden, 2 restored Victorian glasshouses with exotic fruit and vegetables. Walled flower and organic kitchen gardens. C14 Fitzalan Chapel white garden.

GROUP OPENING

8 **ARUNDEL GARDENS**
Arundel BN18 9HL. *¼ m W of Arundel town centre. Take Ford Rd exit off main A27 r'about by river, then 1st L Torton Hill Rd. Both locations well signed & within easy walking distance.* **Sun 29, Mon 30 May (2-5). Combined adm £4, chd free. Home-made teas at Torton Top.**

20 DALLOWAY ROAD
Mr Geoff Allen

TORTON TOP
Barry & Lucy Hopkins

Two gardens situated in Torton Hill, a residential area. Torton Top, 36 Torton Hill Road, has mature gardens of ½ acre with ancient oak trees and large lawn areas, interspersed with well stocked beds and borders full of specimen shrubs, acers, clematis, roses and annuals. Delightful natural pond feature with waterfall. 20 Dalloway Road is a charming split level woodland garden designed 16 yrs ago in a peaceful setting with many specimen shrubs and trees. Lovely summerhouse in the woodland corner with garden seating. Partial wheelchair access.

9 **ASHDOWN PARK HOTEL**
Wych Cross, East Grinstead RH18 5JR. Mr Kevin Sweet, 01342 824988, reservations@ashdownpark.co.uk, www.elitehotels.co.uk. *6m S of East Grinstead. Turn off A22 at Wych Cross T-lights.* **Sun 22 May (1-5). Adm £5, chd free. Light refreshments.**
186 acres of parkland, grounds and gardens surrounding Ashdown Park Hotel. Our Secret Garden is well worth a visit with many new plantings. Large number of deer roam the estate and can often be seen during the day. Enjoy and explore the woodland paths, quiet areas and views. Featured in Sussex Life and local press. Some gravel paths and uneven ground with steps.

10 96 ASHFORD ROAD

Hastings TN34 2HZ. Lynda & Andrew Hayler. *From A21 (Sedlescombe Rd N) towards Hastings take 1st exit on r'about A2101, then 3rd on L.* **Sat 21, Sat 28 May (1-5). Adm £3, chd free.** Small (100ft x 52ft) Japanese inspired front and back garden. Full of interesting planting, with many acers, azaleas and bamboos. Over 100 different hostas, many miniature. Lower garden with greenhouse and raised beds. Also an attractive Japanese Tea House.

11 BAKERS HOUSE

Bakers Lane, Shipley RH13 8GJ. Mr & Mrs Mark Burrell, 01403 741215, margot@dragons.me.uk. *5m S of Horsham. Take A24 to Worthing, then A272 W, 2nd turn to Dragon's Green. L at George & Dragon PH, Bakers Lane then 300yds on L.* **Sun 22 May (2-6); Sun 19 June (2-5.30). Adm £5, chd free. Home-made teas. Visits also by arrangement May & June.** There is so much to see in this large parkland garden incl great oaks, lake, laburnum tunnel, rose walks with old fashioned roses, scented knot garden, woodland hosta walk, bog gardens and a big kitchen garden with potager. Partial wheelchair access, garden has gravel paths.

GROUP OPENING

12 BALCOMBE GARDENS

Balcombe. *3m N of Cuckfield on B2036. From J10A on M23, follow B2036 S for 2½ m. ¼ m N of station, turn L off B2036 immed before Balcombe Primary School (signed) for ¾ m.* **Wed 18 May, Sat 18 June (12-5). Combined adm £5, chd free. Light refreshments at Krawden.**

KRAWDEN D
Victoria Road, RH17 6LJ.
Ann & Eddie Bryant

46 WESTUP FARM COTTAGES
London Road, RH17 6JJ.
Chris Cornwell
Visits also by arrangement Apr to Sept for groups of 4+.
chris.westup@btinternet.com
01444 811891

WINTERFIELD
Oldlands Avenue, RH17 6LP.
Sue & Sarah Howe
Visits also by arrangement Apr to Sept for groups of 4+.
sarahjhowe_uk@yahoo.co.uk
01444 811380

Balcombe is in a designated AONB. Traceable back to the Saxons, the village contains 55 listed buildings incl C15 parish church of St Mary's. Nearby is the famous Ouse Valley Viaduct, ancient woodlands, lake, millpond and reservoir. The three gardens opening for the NGS will especially appeal to plant lovers and are full of variety and interest. Hidden in the countryside of the High Weald, 46 Westup Farm Cottages' garden contains unique and traditional features linked by intimate paths through lush and subtle planting. Winterfield contains as many trees and shrubs as can be crammed into ½ acre with wild flowers, gravelled areas, alpine troughs, a secret garden, pond and borders. Krawden offers roses, herbaceous borders, fruit and vegetables, a Mediterranean area with gravel and water feature and provides the venue for teas. Wheelchair access at Winterfield and Krawden only.

13 NEW BANKS FARM

Boast Lane, Barcombe, Lewes BN8 5DY. Nick & Lucy Addyman. *From Barcombe Cross follow signs to Spithurst & Newick. 1st road on R into Boast Lane towards the Anchor PH. At sharp bend carry on into Banks Farm.* **Fri 29, Sat 30 Apr (11-4). Adm £4, chd free. Home-made teas.** 9 acre garden set in rural countryside, extensive lawns and shrub beds merge with the more naturalistic woodland garden set around the lake. An orchard, vegetable garden, ponds and a wide variety of plant species add to an interesting and very tranquil garden.

14 BEAUCHAMPS

Float Lane, Udimore, Rye TN31 6BY. Matty & Richard Holmes. *3m W of Rye. 3m E of Broad Oak Xrds. Turn S off B2089 down Float Lane ½ m.* **Sun 5 June (2-5). Adm £4.50, chd free. Home-made teas.** With fine views of the beautiful Brede Valley, this lovely informal garden, maintained by its owners, displays a wide range of unusual herbaceous plants, shrubs and trees incl fine specimens of *Cornus controversa* 'Variegata', *Crinodendron hookerianum*, and *Baptisia australis*. Small orchard, kitchen garden and copse. Many home propagated herbaceous plants for sale. Full wheelchair access, but difficult after any recent rainfall.

Constantly revised planting to maintain the magical and secluded atmosphere . . .

15 NEW THE BEECHES

Church Road, Barcombe, Lewes BN8 5TS. Sandy Coppen, 01273 401339, sand@passionforplants.net. *From Lewes, A26 towards Uckfield for 3m, turn L signed Barcombe. Follow road for 1½ m, then turn L signed Hamsey & Church. Follow road for approx ½ m. Parking on RH-side in field.* **Sun 24, Thur 28, Sun 31 July (2-5). Adm £5, chd free. Home-made teas. Visits also by arrangement July to Sept for groups of 12 max. Teas & wine for early eve visits.** C18 walled garden with cut flowers, vegetables, salads and fruit. Separate orchard and rose garden. Herbaceous borders and hot border. There are two ponds, one with a willow house. Extensive lawns and an C18 barn. Some of the ground is a little bumpy but everything is accessible without steps.

16 BEEDINGLEE

Brighton Road, Lower Beeding, Horsham RH13 6NQ. Mrs Jo Longley, 01403 891251, joslongley@gmail.com. *4m SE of Horsham on A281 to Cowfold. Approx ½ m N of South Lodge Hotel on A281 from Cowfold to Horsham.*

The entrance is almost opp a red post box on a stalk. **Sun 22 May, Sun 12 June (1-5). Adm £4, chd free. Home-made teas. Visits also by arrangement May to Oct for groups of 25 max.**
Originally part of the Leonardslee Estate, the 1987 hurricane brought down much of the Victorian/Edwardian planting. The present 6 acre garden has evolved since then with many interesting and unusual trees and shrubs, and a longer flowering season. Still an informal garden, there are hidden paths, a secret garden, lawns and a wild flower garden.

NGS donations help support over 200 hospices across the country

17 4 BEN'S ACRE
Horsham RH13 6LW. Pauline Clark, 01403 266912, brian.clark8850@yahoo.co.uk. *NE of Horsham. From A281 via Cowfold after Hilliers Garden Centre, take 2nd R by Tesco, St Leonards Rd, then into Comptons Lane. 5th R Heron Way after mini r'about, 2nd L Glebe Cres, 1st L Ben's Acre.* **Sat 2 July, Sat 27 Aug (1-5). Adm £4, chd free. Home-made teas. Visits also by arrangement late June to early Sept for groups of 15-35. Refreshments on request.**
A keen Hardy Plant Society member's garden, that is said to have the wow effect, with surprises and delights for the visitor. On the edge of St Leonards Forest and riverside walk, 100ft x 45ft using steps and terraces to take you to borders planted to capacity with interesting potpourri of colour, texture and form. Featuring arbours, summerhouse, ponds with waterfall, topiary and pots of succulents. Many seats around the garden while having one of our delicious teas. Come, enjoy and take home some ideas for your garden. You can also see our garden on www.youtube.com, search pauline&brian@sussexgarden. Featured in Daily Mail Weekend magazine and short listed in the Daily Mail National Garden competition 2015.

GROUP OPENING

18 BEXHILL GARDENS
Bexhill. *Bexhill & Little Common. Proceed to Little Common r'about on A259, then see individual addresses below. Follow NGS signs or SatNav & yellow balloons will be displayed outside each garden. Tickets & maps available at each garden.* **Sun 5 June (11-5). Combined adm £6, chd free. Light refreshments at Clare Cottage.**

NEW 61 BARNHORN ROAD
Little Common, TN39 4QB. Barbara Harris

14 CHANTRY AVENUE
TN40 2EA. Peggy Harvey
Visits also by arrangement May to Oct for groups of 8+.
chantry@talktalk.net
07989 245423

CLARE COTTAGE
Collington Lane East, TN39 3RG. Mr Terry Johns

ERANSLEA
17 Collington Lane East, TN39 3RG. Eric & Sue Fasey

GARDEN FLAT 1, ELM TREE HOUSE
5 Hastings Road, TN40 2HJ. Linda Exley

NEW GREEN HEDGES
Birchington Close, TN39 3TF. Sara & Paul Barker

6 KINGSWOOD AVENUE
TN39 4EJ. Mr & Mrs Lal & Gloria Ratnayake

ORCHARD COTTAGE
22 Gatelands Drive, TN39 4DP. Pat McCarthy

NEW ORCHARD LEIGH HOUSE
19 Collington Lane East, TN39 3RG. Leigh Thompson

26 WINSTON DRIVE
TN39 3RP. Ron & Clare Brazier

An attractive Edwardian residential seaside town famous for its De la Warr Pavilion Arts Centre. Gardens incl: 14 Chantry Avenue, an unusual Chinese inspired garden. 6 Kingswood Avenue has mature trees, shrubs, herbaceous borders, bonsai plants, fuschias and pelargoniums and small pond, with plants for sale. Clare Cottage has a restful atmosphere with herbaceous borders and a log cabin. Orchard Cottage is a plantswoman's recently designed small garden with a wonderful variety of plants for sale. 61 Barnhorn Road, owned by flower arranger/ plantswoman is a colourful ¹/₂ acre garden developed over the past 25 yrs. Elm Tree House is a pretty cottage style garden with interesting mixed planting, pergola and wildlife ponds. Green Hedges has an extensive mix of planting incl tropical plants, wildlife pond and greenhouse. 26 Winston Drive has been established over the past 10 yrs with 275 different plants. Orchard Leigh House is an attractively laid out plant persons garden with feature sundial. Eranslea a garden with views and lots of seating, mixture of planting using evergreens, shrubs, perennials and bulbs. Wheelchair access to some gardens.

19 BIGNOR PARK
Pulborough RH20 1HG. The Mersey Family, www.bignorpark.co.uk. *5m S of Petworth & Pulborough. Well signed from B2138. Nearest villages Sutton, Bignor & West Burton. Approach from the E, directions & map available on website.* **Sun 24 Apr, Sun 10 July, Sun 9 Oct (2-5). Adm £5, chd free. Home-made teas.**
11 acres of peaceful garden to explore with magnificent views of the South Downs. Interesting trees, shrubs, wild flower areas, with swathes of daffodils in spring. The walled flower garden has been replanted with herbaceous borders. Temple, Greek loggia, Zen pond and unusual sculptures. Former home of romantic poet Charlotte Smith, whose sonnets were inspired by Bignor Park. Spectacular Cedars of Lebanon and rare Holm Oak. Wheelchair access to shrubbery and croquet lawn, gravel paths in rest of garden and steps in stables quadrangle.

20 4 BIRCH CLOSE
Arundel BN18 9HN. Elizabeth & Mike Gammon, 01903 882722, e.gammon@talktalk.net. *1m S of Arundel. From A27 & A284 r'about at W end of Arundel take Ford Rd. After ¹/₂ m turn R into Maxwell Rd & follow signs.* **Sun 1, Mon 2 May (2-5). Adm £3, chd free. Home-made teas. Visits also by arrangement May & June for groups of 10+.**
¹/₃ acre of woodland garden on edge of Arundel. Wide range of mature trees and shrubs with many hardy perennials. Emphasis on extensive selection of spring flowers and clematis with over 100 incl 11 montana. All in a tranquil setting with secluded corners, meandering paths and plenty of seating. Partial wheelchair access to approx half of garden.

21 BLUE JAYS
Chesworth Close, Horsham RH13 5AL. Stella & Mike Schofield, 01403 251065. *5 mins walk SE of St Mary's Church Horsham. From A281 (East St) L down Denne Rd, L to Chesworth Lane, R to Chesworth Close. Garden at end of close. 4 disabled spaces, other parking in local streets & Denne Rd car park (free on Suns).* **Sat 14, Sun 15 May (12.30-5). Adm £3.50, chd free. Home-made teas. Visits also by arrangement Apr to July for groups of 15+.** *Donation to The Badger Trust.*
Wooded 1 acre garden with rhododendrons, camellias and azaleas. Candelabra primulas and ferns edge the R Arun. Primroses and spring bulbs border woodland path and stream. Cordylines, gunneras, flower beds, a pond, a fountain and new formal rose garden set in open lawns. Arch leads to a vegetable plot and orchard bounded by the river. Large WW2 pill box in the orchard; visits inside with short talk are available. Wheelchair access to most areas.

22 ◆ BORDE HILL GARDEN
Borde Hill Lane, Haywards Heath RH16 1XP. Borde Hill Garden Ltd, 01444 450326, www.bordehill.co.uk. *1¹/₂ m N of Haywards Heath. 20 mins N of Brighton, or S of Gatwick on A23 taking exit 10a via Balcombe.* **For NGS: Tue 4 Oct (10-6). Adm £8.20, chd £5.50. For other opening times**

and information, please phone or visit garden website.
Great English garden with rare plants and stunning landscapes make Borde Hill the perfect day out for horticulture enthusiasts, country lovers and families. 17 acres of formal outdoor rooms, magical woodland walks, strolls by the lakes, adventure playground and events throughout the season. Nationally important collection of rare shrubs and champion trees, outdoor rooms including the Rose and Italian gardens, makes Borde Hill the perfect day out destination. Shop, plant sales, cafe, tea house and restaurant. Wheelchair access to formal garden (17 acres). Dogs welcome on leads.

Quirky celebration of community spirit featuring over 20 back gardens in one road . . .

GROUP OPENING

23 NEW ▶ BOSHAM ART IN THE GARDEN TRAIL
North Road, Bosham, Chichester PO18 8NL. Karen Ongley-Snook. *Bosham approx 2m S of Chichester, at E end of Chichester Harbour. From A27 at Fishbourne r'about take A259 exit (Fishbourne Rd W) signed Bosham, after 2¹/₄ m at r'about take 5th exit (Penwarden Way) for ¹/₄ m, then turn L onto North Rd. Park in surrounding roads. Trail starts at No 38.* **Sat 16, Sun 17 Apr (11-4). Combined adm £3.50, chd free. Weekend Pass £5.00. Lunches, tea, coffee & home-made cakes.**
Visit a wonderful event in the Bohemian quarter of the picturesque village of Bosham. This is a quirky celebration of community spirit featuring over 20 back gardens in one road. Behind the terraced houses there are many surprises, from totally naturalised gardens to a tiny courtyard. One of the gardens even has 'The Bikers Shed' as featured on Channel 4's Shed of the Year 2015. Each garden showcases work by artists who specialise in items suitable for the outdoors, many of whom are

residents of the road. Original garden art works for sale. Wheelchair access is available, but a number of gardens have uneven surfaces.

24 BRIGHTLING DOWN FARM
Observatory Road, Dallington TN21 9LN. Mr & Mrs P Stephens, 07770 807060 / 01435 831118, valstephens@icloud.com. *1m from Woods Corner. At Swan PH at Woods Corner, take road opp signed Brightling. Take 1st L, signed Burwash. Almost immed turn into 1st driveway on L.* **Visits by arrangement May to Oct for groups of 10-30. Adm £7.50, chd free. Home-made teas.**
The garden has several different areas incl a Zen garden, water garden, walled vegetable garden with 2 large greenhouses, herb garden and herbaceous borders. The garden makes clever use of grasses and is set amongst woodland with stunning countryside views. Winner of the Society of Garden Designers award.

GROUP OPENING

25 BURGESS HILL NGS GARDENS
Burgess Hill. *10m N of Brighton. Tickets & maps from any garden.* **Sun 24, Mon 25 July (1-5). Combined adm £5, chd free. Sun 21 Aug (1-5). Combined adm £4, chd free. Home-made teas at 47 Leylands Road (July) & 30 Sycamore Drive (Aug).**

14 BARNSIDE AVENUE
RH15 0JU. Brian & Sue Knight.
Open on Sun 24, Mon 25 July

47 LEYLANDS ROAD
RH15 8AF. Diane & Stephen Rabson.
Open on Sun 24, Mon 25 July
Visits also by arrangement in July for groups of up to 10.
dianerabson@btinternet.com
01444 247937

9 SYCAMORE DRIVE
RH15 0GG. Peter Machin & Martin Savage.
Open on all dates

30 SYCAMORE DRIVE
RH15 0GH. John Smith & Kieran O'Regan.
Open on all dates
(See separate entry)

59 SYCAMORE DRIVE

RH15 0GG. Steve & Debby Gill.
Open on all dates

This diverse group of five gardens is a mixture of established and small new gardens. Three of the group are a great example of what can be achieved over a 7 yr period from a blank canvas in a new development (Sycamore Drive) while close by is 14 Barnside Avenue, a wisteria clad house (pruning advice given) with a family lawn and borders. 47 Leylands Road is a garden packed with an array of plants and a wildlife pond. Teas will be served here in July. Many useful ideas for people living in new build properties with small gardens and heavy clay soil. Partial wheelchair access to some gardens.

GROUP OPENING

26 NEW BURWASH GARDENS
Burwash TN19 7EN,
www.burwashopengardens.org.uk.
Burwash is on the A265, 3m E of junction with A21 at Hurst Green; 6m W of Heathfield. Parking in village. Tickets & detailed map at entry points: Longstaffes, High St, adjacent to The Bear PH; Mandalay, entrance off Ham Lane opp Rose & Crown PH. **Sat 2 July (2-5.30). Combined adm £5, chd free. Home-made teas, cakes & refreshments in Burwash Village Hall, High Street.**

NEW BOWZELL
Shirley Viney

NEW FARLEY HOUSE
Ian & Nancy Craston

NEW LIME COTTAGE
Shelagh Bedford-Turner

NEW LINDEN COTTAGE
Philip & Anne Cutler

NEW LONGSTAFFES
Dorothy & Paul Bysouth

NEW MANDALAY
David & Vivienne Wright

Burwash is a small village of 2,600 inhabitants located in the High Weald AONB. Once a centre for iron smelting and smuggling it's now much quieter! Rudyard Kipling's former home at Bateman's (NT) is just ¹/₂ m away and the C11 parish church is worth visiting and has beautiful views over the Dudwell Valley. Gardens are situated on or close to the High Street, a conservation area

Bowzell, Burwash Gardens

with numerous listed buildings dating back to the C16. The six gardens vary in size, design and planting, and are within a very short, level walk of each other. Being mainly terraced properties wheelchair access to rear gardens is restricted. Partial access possible in three gardens.

27 BUTLERS FARMHOUSE
Butlers Lane, Herstmonceux BN27 1QH. Irene Eltringham-Willson, 01323 833770, irene.willson@btinternet.com. *3m E of Hailsham. Take A271 from Hailsham, go through village of Herstmonceux, turn R signed Church Rd then approx 1m turn R. Do not use SatNav!* **Sat 2, Sun 3 Apr (2-5). Adm £3.50, chd free. Sat 13, Sun 14 Aug (2-5). Adm £5, chd free. Home-made teas. Jazz in the garden in Aug. Visits also by arrangement Mar to Oct with refreshments provided.**
Lovely rural setting for 1 acre garden surrounding C16 farmhouse (not open) with views of South Downs. Pretty in spring with primroses and hellebores. Mainly herbaceous with rainbow border, small pond with dribbling frogs and Cornish inspired beach corners. Restored to former

glory, as shown in old photographs, but with a few quirky twists such as a poison garden and a secret jungle garden. Relax and listen to live jazz in the garden in August. Featured in Sussex Life (April & May 2015), a book entitled 'Coastal and Country Gardens', and a TV programme for USA TV. Most of garden accessible by wheelchair.

28 51 CARLISLE ROAD
Eastbourne BN21 4JR. Mr & Mrs N Fraser-Gausden, 01323 722545, n.fg@sky.com. *200yds inland from seafront (Wish Tower), close to Congress Theatre.* **Sat 11, Sun 12 June (2-5). Adm £3, chd free. Home-made teas. Visits also by arrangement May & June.**
Walled, s-facing garden (82ft x 80ft) with mixed beds intersected by stone paths and incl small pool. Profuse and diverse planting. Wide selection of shrubs, old roses, herbaceous plants and perennials mingle with specimen trees and climbers. Constantly revised planting to maintain the magical and secluded atmosphere. Featured in many gardening magazines over the yrs and won a number of awards.

29 CAXTON MANOR

Wall Hill, Forest Row RH18 5EG.
Adele & Jules Speelman. *1m N of Forest Row, 2m S of E Grinstead. From A22 take turning to Ashurstwood, entrance on L after ⅓ m, or 1m on R from N.* **Fri 13, Sat 14 May (2-5). Adm £5, chd free. Home-made teas.** *Donation to St Catherine's Hospice, Crawley.*
Delightful 5 acre Japanese inspired gardens planted with mature rhododendrons, azaleas and acers surrounding large pond with boathouse, massive rockery and waterfall, beneath the home of the late Sir Archibald McIndoe (house not open). Japanese tea house and Japanese style courtyard. **Also open 2 Quarry Cottages (separate admission).**

30 CHAMPS HILL

Waltham Park Road, Coldwaltham, Pulborough RH20 1LY. Mr & Mrs David Bowerman, 01798 831205, mary@thebct.org.uk. *3m S of Pulborough. On A29 turn R to Fittleworth into Waltham Park Rd, garden 400 metres on R.* **Sat 13, Sun 14 Aug (11-5). Adm £5, chd free. Home-made teas. Visits also by arrangement Mar to Sept for groups of 10+.**
Re-opening after a break of over 5 yrs. Champs Hill has been developed around three disused sand quarries since 1960. The woodlands are full of beautiful rhododendrons and azaleas, but the most striking feature is the collection of heathers, over 300 cultivars. The garden also has some interesting sculptures, and stupendous views.

31 CHANNEL VIEW

52 Brook Barn Way, Goring-by-Sea, Worthing BN12 4DW. Jennie & Trevor Rollings, 01903 242431, tjrollings@gmail.com. *1m W of Worthing near seafront. Turn S off A259 into Parklands Ave, L at T-junction into Alinora Crescent. Brook Barn Way is immed on L.* **Sat 18, Sun 19 June (1-5). Combined adm with Goring Folly £5, chd free. Home-made teas. Visits also by arrangement May to Sept for groups of 10+ only.**
A seaside Tudor cottage garden blending traditional and subtropical plants. Dense planting, secret rooms and intriguing sight-lines, with brick paths radiating from a wildlife pond.

Shady viewpoints, sunny patios, insect friendly flowers and unusual structures supporting over a hundred roses, clematis and other climbers. Many unusual home grown plants for sale. Featured in Worthing Herald, West Sussex Gazette, Goring Guide and Worthing Journal 2015. Partial wheelchair access.

32 NEW ♦ CHARLESTON

Firle, Lewes BN8 6LL. The Charleston Trust, 01323 811626, www.charleston.org.uk. *Charleston is on the A27 signed halfway between Brighton & Eastbourne.* **Evening opening Fri 12 Aug (7-9). Adm £25. Pre-booking essential, please visit www.ngs.org.uk or phone 01483 211535 for information & booking. Cocktail on arrival & canapés with pay bar available. For other opening times and information, please phone or visit garden website.**
The Bloomsbury artists Vanessa Bell and Duncan Grant moved to Charleston in 1916. They transformed the walled vegetable plot into a quintessential painters' garden mixing Mediterranean influences with cottage garden planting. The garden is full of surprises including a variety of sculpture, from classical forms to works by Quentin Bell, mosaics and tiled pools, an orchard and tranquil pond. Gravel pathways with partial wheelchair access.

33 CHIDMERE GARDENS

Chidham Lane, Chidham, Chichester PO18 8TD. Jackie & David Russell, janetetk68@gmail.com, www.chidmerefarm.com. *6m W of Chichester at SE end of Chidham Lane by pond in village.* **Visits by arrangement Apr to Sept for groups of 10-20, incl a cup of tea or coffee. Adm £5, chd free. Home-made teas.**
Wisteria clad C15 house (not open) surrounded by yew and hornbeam hedges situated next to Chidmere pond; a natural wildlife preserve approx 5 acres. Garden incl formal rose garden, well stocked herbaceous borders and springtime woods. 8 acres of orchards with wide selection of heritage and modern varieties of apples, pears and plums incl 200 yr old varieties of Blenheim Orange and Bramley Seedling. Partial wheelchair access.

34 NEW CISSBURY

Nepcote Lane, Findon, Worthing BN14 0SR. Geoffrey & Etta Wyatt, www.cissbury.com. *5m N of Worthing in the hamlet of Nepcote, Findon. From A24 S follow signs to Worthing. Only turn L at the sign for Nepcote. After about 100 metres at the sharp LH-corner, turn R into Cissbury's driveway.* **Sat 27 Feb, Thur 3 Mar (10-4). Adm £4, chd free. Home-made teas.**
Set in its own parkland and grounds in the SDNP with views towards Cissbury Ring and the sea. Spectacular drifts of snowdrops and daffodils. Cedar trees and a holm oak hedge line the drive; by the pond is a metasequoia glyptostroboides. Walled kitchen garden with plots let out to Findon Gardening Club. Original L-shaped greenhouse featuring cork screw winding gear, still in partial working order. Wheelchair access is available from the car park, around the house and walled garden.

35 ♦ CLINTON LODGE

Fletching, Uckfield TN22 3ST. Lady Collum, 01825 722952, garden@clintonlodge.com, www.clintonlodgegardens.co.uk. *4m NW of Uckfield. Clinton Lodge is situated in Fletching High St, N of Rose & Crown PH. Off road parking provided. It is important visitors do not park in street. Parking available from 1pm.* **For NGS: Sun 24 Apr, Mon 13, Mon 27 June, Mon 8 Aug (2-5.30). Adm £5, chd free. Home-made teas. For other opening times and information, please phone, email or visit garden website.** *Donation to local charities.*
6 acre formal and romantic garden overlooking parkland with old roses, William Pye water feature, double white and blue herbaceous borders, yew hedges, pleached lime walks, copy of C17 scented herb garden, Medieval style potager, vine and rose allée, wild flower garden. Canal garden, small knot garden, shady glade and orchard. Caroline and Georgian house (not open).

36 COBB COTTAGE NORTH

Selsfield Rd, Ardingly, Haywards Heath RH17 6TH. Peter & Marlene Holter. *B2028 N of village. Opp S gate of South of England showground, 1m S of Wakehurst Place (National Trust). Gravel car park*. **Sat 9, Sun 17 July (11-5). Adm £4, chd free. Home-made teas.**

½ acre edge of village garden with shrubs, perennials and annuals set off by lawns, several interesting trees, 3 wildlife ponds with cascades, patio with seating, terracotta pots and hanging baskets. Marvel at Peter's giant show onions in raised beds along with an extensive range of other vegetables, soft fruit, and full greenhouse. Plants and soft fruit for sale. Public WC 150yds away in village. Featured in Sussex Living (July 2015). The garden is mostly accessible by wheelchair, but sloping site and grass paths.

37 COLWOOD HOUSE
Cuckfield Lane, Warninglid RH17 5SP. Mr & Mrs Patrick Brenan, 01444 461831, rbrenan@me.com. *6m W of Haywards Heath, 6m SE of Horsham. Entrance on B2115 (Cuckfield Lane). From E, N & S, turn W off A23 towards Warninglid for ¾ m. From W come through Warninglid Village.* **Visits by arrangement Apr to Sept for groups of 10+. Tea.** *Donation to Seaforth Hall.*

12 acres of garden with mature and specimen trees from the late 1800s, lawns and woodland edge. Formal parterre, rose and herb gardens. 100ft terrace and herbaceous border overlooking flower rimmed croquet lawn. Cut turf labyrinth and forsythia tunnel. Water features, statues and gazebos. Pets' cemetery. Giant chessboard. Lake with island and temple. The garden has gravel paths and some slopes.

38 COOKSCROFT
Bookers Lane, Earnley, Chichester PO20 7JG. Mr & Mrs J Williams, 01243 513671, williams.cookscroft330@btinternet.com, www.cookscroft.co.uk. *6m S of Chichester. At end of Birdham Straight A286 from Chichester, take L fork to E Wittering B2198. 1m on before sharp bend, turn L into Bookers Lane, 2nd house on L. Parking available.* **Sun 1 May (1-5). Light refreshments. Evening opening Sun 26 June (5-9). Wine. Adm £4, chd free. Visits also by arrangement Mar to Sept, groups welcome, ample parking.**

This is a garden for all seasons which delights the visitor. Started in 1988, it features cottage, woodland cottage and Japanese style gardens, water features and borders of perennials with a particular emphasis on S Hemisphere plants. Unusual plants for the plantsman to enjoy, many grown from seed. Extensive open borders with correas, corokias, leptospermum, prostatheras and trees from down under. Featured in the Chichester Observer. The garden has grass paths and unfenced ponds.

NGS support helps us improve patient care in the community

39 COPYHOLD HOLLOW
Copyhold Lane, Borde Hill, Haywards Heath RH16 1XU. Frances Druce, 01444 413265, ngs@copyholdhollow.co.uk, www.copyholdhollow.co.uk. *2m N of Haywards Heath. Follow signs for Borde Hill Gardens on L over brow of hill, take 1st R signed Ardingly. Garden ½ m. Please phone or email to book time slot as parking is limited.* **Thurs 14, 28 Apr, 12, 26 May, 2, 30 June, 14, 28 July, 4, 18 Aug (12-3). Adm £4, chd free. Home-made teas. Visits also by arrangement Apr to Aug for groups of 4+.**

Cottage garden in a hollow with woodland garden above. Spring fed pond with dam and waterfall edged with damp loving perennials including species primulas. The oak stumpery gives way to a rock garden on the way to the crow's nest and the whole garden is planted for yr-round interest. Crow's nest viewing platform slung between two oak trees affording far reaching views of garden and countryside. Featured in a German magazine, Living at Home (Spring 2015). Wheelchair access for the cottage garden immediately surrounding the cottage.

GROUP OPENING

40 NEW COWFOLD GARDENS
Cowfold, Horsham RH13 8QZ. *Cowfold on A272, 7m S of Horsham. Park at St Peters School Car Park, Potters Green, Station Rd RH13 8QZ where entry ticket can be purchased & map provided. For Coopers Cottage, RH13 8AZ, please drive on A272 ½ m E of Cowfold towards Bolney on L. Parking in field at King Henry's Barn.* **Sun 31 July (2-5). Combined adm £4, chd free. Home-made teas at St Peter's Church.**

NEW **5 ALLEY GROVES**
Mr Don Fuller

NEW **COOPERS COTTAGE**
Mrs Judy Penhaligon

NEW **8 THORNDEN**
Mrs Eileen Precious

An opportunity to visit 3 gardens all planted in different styles and to explore St Peter's Church at Cowfold founded in 1232. 5 Alley Groves is a compact 3 yr old garden, completely designed and replanted by the current owner who has spent many yrs working in horticulture. It is packed with hardy plants, interesting shrubs and statuary. Coopers Cottage is a ⅓ acre garden on the outskirts of the village, developed over the last 5 yrs by the present owners. It is a well stocked garden for all seasons, encouraging wildlife and working with its own rabbit population. 8 Thornden has a formal front garden with well established topiary and relaxed planting in the back garden for yr-round interest. There is a productive greenhouse and newly installed chickens. This group opening visit will require some walking on pavements alongside busy main roads. There is an opportunity to enjoy home-made teas in the picturesque village churchyard. Of interest in the church is a life-size brass of Thomas Nelond, Prior of the great monastery at Lewes in the C15 (which came to St. Peter's following the dissolution of the monasteries), and an impressive array of stained glass in the windows dating from the 1860s onwards. Wheelchair access at Coopers Cottage only, please telephone 07973 954970 in advance for parking details.

![Preston Manor Walled Garden, Preston Park Gardens]

Preston Manor Walled Garden, Preston Park Gardens

41▶ DACHS

Spear Hill, Ashington RH20 3BA. Bruce Wallace, 01903 892466, wallacebuk@aol.com. *Approx 6m N of Worthing. From A24 at Ashington onto B2133 Billingshurst Rd, R into Spear Hill. We are the 1st house, garden runs along Billingshurst Rd.* **Sun 3, Sun 10 Apr (2.30-5.30). Adm £4, chd free. Home-made teas. Visits also by arrangement Mar to Sept for day or eve visits.** A waterlogged field turned into a beautiful garden of about 2 acres incl white garden, bog area and stream. Several other themed beds with perennials of different textures and colours. Over 200 varieties of daffodils (some new this year) and narcissi, some snowdrops, fritillaria and iris in spring. Free gifts for children to encourage them to grow things. Featured in Sussex Life.

42▶ DALE PARK HOUSE

Madehurst, Arundel BN18 0NP. Robert & Jane Green, 01243 814260, robertgreen@farming.co.uk. *4m W of Arundel. Take A27 E from Chichester or W from Arundel, then A29 (London) for 2m, turn L to Madehurst & follow red arrows.* **Sun 12 June (2-5). Adm £4, chd free. Home-made teas. Visits also by**

arrangement May to Aug for any size group.
Set in parkland within the South Downs National Park, enjoying magnificent views to the sea. Come and relax in the large walled garden which features an impressive 200ft herbaceous border. There is also a sunken gravel garden, mixed borders, a small rose garden, dreamy rose and clematis arches, interesting collection of hostas, foliage plants and shrubs, an orchard and kitchen garden.

43▶ ◆ DENMANS GARDEN

Denmans Lane, Fontwell BN18 0SU. Michael Neve & John Brookes, 01243 542808, denmans@denmans-garden.co.uk, www.denmans-garden.co.uk. *5m from Chichester & Arundel. Off A27, ¹/₂ m W of Fontwell r'about.* **For opening times and information, please phone, email or visit garden website.**
Denmans is a unique 4 acre garden designed for yr-round interest through use of form, colour and texture. Owned by Michael Neve and John Brookes MBE, renowned garden designer and writer. It is a garden full of ideas to be interpreted within smaller home spaces. Award-winning café and plant centre.

44▶ NEW▶ DITTONS END

Southfields Road, Eastbourne BN21 1BZ. Mrs Frances Hodkinson, 01323 647163. *Town centre 500 metres from train station. Off A259 in Southfields Rd. House directly opp Dittons Rd. 3 doors from NGS open garden Hardwycke.* **Sun 12 June, Sun 28 Aug (11-5). Combined adm with Hardwycke £4, chd free. Home-made teas at Hardwycke.**
Lovely well maintained, small town garden. At the back, a very pretty garden (35ft x 20ft) with small lawn area, patio surrounded by a selection of pots and packed borders with lots of colour. In the front a compact lawn with colourful borders (25ft x 18ft). No steps.

45▶ DOWN PLACE

South Harting, Petersfield GU31 5PN. Mr & Mrs D M Thistleton-Smith, 01730 825374, selina@downplace.co.uk. *1m SE of South Harting. B2141 to Chichester, turn L down unmarked lane below top of hill.* **Sat 23, Sun 24 Apr, Sat 18, Sun 19 June (2-6). Adm £4, chd free. Cream teas. Visits also by arrangement Apr to July for groups of 15+.** *Donation to Friends of Harting Church.*
7 acre hillside, chalk garden on the

north side of South Downs with fine views of surrounding countryside. Extensive herbaceous, shrub and rose borders on different levels merging into natural wild flower meadow renowned for its collection of native orchids. Fully stocked vegetable garden and greenhouses. Spring flowers and blossom. Substantial top terrace and borders accessible to wheelchairs.

46 DRIFTWOOD

4 Marine Drive, Bishopstone, Seaford BN25 2RS. Geoff Stonebanks & Mark Glassman, 01323 899296, geoffstonebanks@gmail.com, www.driftwoodbysea.co.uk. *A259 between Seaford & Newhaven. Turn L into Marine Drive from Bishopstone Rd, 2nd on R. Please park carefully in road, but not on bend beyond house.* Thur 9, Tue 28 June, Tue 19, Sun 31 July (11-5). Adm £4, chd free. Light refreshments. Visits also by arrangement June & July for groups of 4-20. Combined visit with 8 Sandgate Close for larger groups.

After visiting in 2015, Francine Raymond wrote in her feature in The Sunday Telegraph 'I was overwhelmed and charmed, and wondered how so many plants have fitted into such a perfectly formed space (112ft x 48ft)? Geoff's enthusiasm is catching and he and his amazing garden deserve every visitor that makes their way up his enchanting garden path'. It is an exuberant yet immaculate seaside garden. Celebrated 5 yrs of opening in 2015, this is a real must see garden! Large selection of home-made cakes and savoury items available, all served on vintage china on trays in the garden. Featured in The Sunday Telegraph Living Magazine (Aug), Daily Mail Weekend Magazine (June) and Garden News (June) in 2015. Steep drive, narrow paths and many levels, but help readily available on-site or call ahead before visit.

47 DURFORD MILL HOUSE

West Harting, Petersfield GU31 5AZ. Mrs Sue Jones, 01730 821125, sdurford@btinternet.com. *3m E of Petersfield. Just off A272 between Petersfield & Rogate, signed Durford Mill & the Hartings. From S Harting past village shop, 1st L to West Harting.* Sat 25, Sun 26 June (2-5.30). Adm £4, chd free. Home-

made teas. Visits also by arrangement May & June.

Come and relax in our peaceful mill garden with its meandering stream and quiet places to sit. Wander along the paths and over the bridges among the flowers, shrubs and beautiful trees. Finishing up with delicious home-made cakes and tea. Wheelchair access to main garden and tea area.

48 DURRANCE MANOR

Smithers Hill Lane, Shipley RH13 8PE. Gordon & Joan Lindsay, 01403 741577, galindsay@gmail.com. *7m SW of Horsham. A24 to A272 (S from Horsham, N from Worthing), turn W towards Billingshurst. Approx 1³/4 m, 2nd L Smithers Hill Lane signed to Countryman PH. Garden 2nd on L.* Mon 29 Aug (2-6). Adm £4.50, chd free. Home-made teas. Visits also by arrangement Apr to Oct.

This 2 acre garden surrounding a Medieval hall house (not open) with Horsham stone roof, enjoys uninterrupted views over a ha-ha of the South Downs and Chanctonbury Ring. There are many different gardens here incl colourful long borders, Japanese inspired gardens, a large pond, wild flower meadow and orchard, shade gardens, greenhouse and vegetable garden.

49 54 ELMLEIGH

Midhurst GU29 9HA. Wendy Liddle, 07796 562275, wendyliddle@btconnect.com. *¹/4 m W of Midhurst off A272. Wheelchair users please use designated parking spaces at top of drive, phone on arrival for assistance.* Sats & Suns 11, 12, 18, 19 June, 2, 3, 9, 10 July (10-5). Adm £3, chd free. Home-made teas. Visits also by arrangement June to Sept. Coaches please drop off visitors, then park in Midhurst Coach Park.

Come and walk around this beautiful, award-winning garden on the edge of Midhurst. Planted with majestic Scots pines, shrubs, perennials and annuals, packed with interest, a tapestry of unusual plants giving all season colour. Many raised beds and numerous statues. A child-friendly garden. New wildlife pond, bog garden and stumpery.

50 ELPHICKS COTTAGE

Spring Lane, Burwash TN19 7HU. Lorna Chernajosvky. *200yds L down Spring Lane from Burwash High St. 6m E of Heathfield on A265, Spring Lane L after petrol station. From Hurst Green take A265, 4m W through Burwash passing shops & PH. Turn R 200yds after car sales room into Spring Lane.* Thur 16, Fri 17 June (1-4). Adm £4, chd free. Home-made teas.

2 acre site surrounding 300 yr old cottage (not open). Formal front garden with knot garden contrasts with areas of naturalistic planting. On different levels with steep paths in places. A tranquil unfenced ¹/4 acre lake with island is stocked with carp and rudd. Woodland was cleared of 200 Scots pine trees in 2013 and replanting is currently underway.

A magical space in the midst of bustling urban life . . .

51 FAIRLIGHT END

Pett Road, Pett, Hastings TN35 4HB. Chris & Robin Hutt, 07774 863750, chrishutt@btopenworld.com. *4m E of Hastings. From Hastings take A259 to Rye. At White Hart Beefeater turn R into Friars Hill. Descend into Pett Village. Park in village hall car park, opp house.* Sat 25, Sun 26 June (11-5). Adm £4.50, chd free. Home-made teas & Pimms. Visits also by arrangement May to Sept for groups of 10+. *Donation to Pett Village Hall.*

3 acre sloping garden with lovely views. Model kitchen garden with 30 raised beds. Wild flower meadow with mown paths, large orchard, and two natural ponds. Meadows exhibition in studio. Ian Kitson designed split level garden in front of house with corten steel wall and plant supports, herbaceous planting, topiary, and decking, all around ancient cherry tree. Featured in Homes & Gardens (Sept 2015). Awarded Sussex Heritage Trust Award 2015. Steep paths, gravelled areas, unfenced ponds.

52 FINEOAKS

Hammer Lane, Cowbeech, Nr Hailsham TN21 9HF. Brian & Brenda Taylor, 01435 812762, thecontehs@yahoo.co.uk. *5m S of Heathfield, 5m N of Hailsham. From A22 Boship r'about take A271 Bexhill Rd for 5 mins, then follow signs for Cowbeech. From Cowbeech 1m on LH-side.* **Sat 30 Apr, Sun 1 May, Sat 2, Sun 3 July (1-5.30). Adm £5, chd free. Home-made teas. Visits also by arrangement Mar to Sept.** An immaculate 3¹/₂ acre garden in idyllic countryside. A rural farming setting with a trout stream that flows in spring, trickling in summer. The lawns are punctuated with island beds planted idiosyncratically with a mix of shrubs, herbaceous and bedding plants. Further afield an orchard, large vegetable and fruit garden, greenhouse and ancient woodland. Nearer the house a pond, fountain and pretty rockery. Ancient woodland with bluebells in early May, ideal for little explorers! Home-made organic jams and marmalades for sale. Wheelchair access to all gardens with flat lawns and slight incline. No WC.

♿ ⚙ 🚐 ☕

53 FITTLEWORTH HOUSE

Bedham Lane, Fittleworth, Pulborough RH20 1JH. Edward & Isabel Braham, 01798 865074, marksaunders66.com@gmail.com, www.marksaunders66.com. *2m E, SE of Petworth. Midway between Petworth & Pulborough on the A283 in Fittleworth, turn into lane by sharp bend signed Bedham. Garden is 50yds along on the L.* **Every Wed 4 May to 27 July (2-5). Adm £5, chd free. Home-made teas. Visits also by arrangement Apr to July for groups of 5+.** 3 acre tranquil country garden featuring working walled kitchen garden with long herbaceous borders and a wide range of fruit and vegetables. Large glasshouse and old potting shed, mixed flower borders, rose beds, rhododendrons and lawns. Magnificent 112ft tall cedar overlooks wisteria covered Grade II listed Georgian house (not open). Wildlife pond, wild garden, long grass areas and spring bulbs. Head gardener with 30 yrs experience on hand to answer questions. The garden sits on a gentle slope but is accessible for wheelchairs and buggies.

♿ 🐕 ⚙ 🚐 ☕

54 FIVE OAKS COTTAGE

Petworth RH20 1HD. Jean & Steve Jackman, 07939 272443, jeanjackman@hotmail.com. *5m S of Pulborough. SatNav does not work! To ensure best route, please ring or email & printed directions will be provided.* **Visits by arrangement in July for individuals or groups of 20 max. Adm £5, chd free.** An acre of delicate jungle surrounding Arts and Crafts style cottage, owned by artists and founders of The Floral Fringe Wildlife Fair. Award-winning wildlife garden with stunning views of the South Downs, quirky garden artefacts, creative clashes of colour and use of shrubs. Knapweed meadow attracting clouds of butterflies in July, two small ponds and lots of seating areas.

GROUP OPENING

55 NEW FLETCHING SECRET GARDENS AND GLASSHOUSES

Fletching, Uckfield TN22 3SS. *4m NW of Uckfield. Follow sign from r'about on A272 onto the A275. Turn E into Mill Lane to Fletching Glasshouses: proceed to High St. Parking signed. Tickets at each venue.* **Sat 23 July (12-5). Combined adm £5, chd free. Home-made teas at 4 Corner Cottages.**

> **NEW 4 CORNER COTTAGES**
> Mrs Jackie Pateman
>
> **NEW FLETCHING GLASSHOUSES**
> The Rae Family
> www.fletchingglasshouses.co.uk/NGS.htm
>
> **NEW STONES**
> Belinda & David Croft

A trio with a difference in and around picturesque Fletching village. This opening gives an opportunity to visit 2 gardens and commercial glasshouses, plus a historic church in a village setting. Near the church are 2 welcoming, cottage style gardens, each with their own character. 4 Corner Cottages where home-made teas will be served, has a small restful garden, tucked behind the High Street. Stunning views across farmland to Sheffield Park with pond, water feature, small white border, plus more. Stones is packed with interest in a relatively small space. Colourful hanging baskets and pots, vegetable plot, a kiwi fruiting climber, cardoon

bed, and mistletoe. The edge of the garden is wild to provide habitat for birds and wildlife. Castle for children to climb into under supervision. Rarely offered conducted 1 hr tours of the organic nursery at Fletching Glasshouses. Discover the challenges of large scale salad, vegetable and flower growing. Eco initiatives. First tour 12pm, then as numbers warrant, last tour 4pm. No dogs, supervised children only. Please phone Fletching Glasshouses 01825 721162 to check wheelchair access.

♿ 🐕 ⚙ ☕

56 FOLLERS MANOR

Seaford Road, Alfriston BN26 5TT. Geoff & Anne Shaw, anne.shaw1@hotmail.com, www.follersmanor.co.uk. *¹/₂ m S of Alfriston. From Alfriston uphill towards Seaford. Park on L in paddock before garden. Garden next door to the old Alfriston Youth Hostel immed before road narrows.* **Sat 2, Sun 3 July (1-5). Adm £5, chd free. Home-made teas & light refreshments.** Contemporary garden designed by Ian Kitson attached to C17 listed historic farmhouse. Entrance courtyard, sunken garden, herbaceous displays, wildlife pond, wild flower meadows, woodland area and beautiful views of the South Downs. Winner of Sussex Heritage Trust Award and three awards from the Society of Garden Designers; Best Medium Residential Garden, Hard Landscaping and, most prestigious, the Judges Award. Featured in the RHS magazine (July 2015) and numerous magazines as far afield as Shanghai. Also appeared on Channel 4's Landscape Man, Gardeners World and ITV's Britain's Best Back Gardens.

⚙ 🛏 D ☕
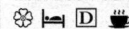

57 NEW THE FOLLY

Charlton, Chichester PO18 0HU.
Joan Burnett & David Ward, 07711
080851, jkburnett@hotmail.co.uk,
www.thefollycharlton.com. *7m N of
Chichester & S of Midhurst off A286
at Singleton, follow signs to Charlton.
Follow NGS parking signs. No parking
in lane, drop off only.* **Sun 3 July,
Sun 14 Aug (2-5.30). Adm £4, chd
free. Home-made teas. Visits also
by arrangement June to Sept for
groups of 10-30, for afternoon or
eve visits.**
Colourful cottage garden surrounding
a C16 period house (not open), set in
pretty downland village of Charlton
close to Levin Down Nature Reserve.
Herbaceous borders well stocked
with a wide range of plants. Variety of
perennials, grasses, annuals and
shrubs to provide long season of
colour and interest. Old well. Busy
bees and chickens. Partial wheelchair
access. Steps from patio to lawn. No
dogs.
& ❀ ⊨ ☕

58 NEW FOXGLOVE COTTAGE

29 Orchard Road, Horsham
RH13 5NF. Peter & Terri Lefevre,
01403 256002,
teresalefevre@outlook.com.
*Horsham Station. Over bridge signed
Crawley, 1st r'about 4th exit, 1st L
Station Rd signed Brighton, 1st L
Depot Rd, 3rd R Orchard Rd. From
A281 Clarance Rd B2180 to 5th R
Depot Rd. Street parking.* **Sun 26
June, Sun 10 July (1-5). Adm £4,
chd free. Cream teas. Visits also
by arrangement May to July for
groups of 10+.**
Unusual 150ft x 50ft plantaholic's
garden with a plethora of planted
containers, quirky vintage finds and
gardenalia. Gravel and bark paths are
interspersed by planting areas
encompassing sun drenched and
shady borders, with plenty of seating
dotted about. A beach inspired
summerhouse and decking at the end of
the garden is dedicated to
propagation, cut flowers and fruit
growing.
❀ ☕

59 THE GARDEN HOUSE

5 Warleigh Road, Brighton
BN1 4NT. Bridgette Saunders &
Graham Lee, 07729 037182 or
01273 702840,
contact@gardenhousebrighton.co.
uk,

www.gardenhousebrighton.co.uk.
*1½ m N of Brighton Pier. The Garden
House can be found 1½ m N of
seafront, 1st L off Ditching Rd, past
T-lights. Street paid parking available.*
**Sat 16, Sun 17 Apr (11-4.30). Adm
£3.50, chd free. Home-made teas.
Visits also by arrangement for
groups of 10+.**
Tucked away in the heart of the city
this really is a secret garden, in
Victorian times a market garden. The
garden is organic and gives interest
all yr, supporting cut flowers,
vegetables, fruit, old climbing roses
and a pond. Many of the plants have
been propagated by the garden
owner, and the garden has unique
features using many recycled
materials. Garden produce and plants
for sale.
❀ ☕

> Small, serene and
> secluded theatrical
> retreat with strong
> emphasis on
> texture, foliage and
> good structure . . .

60 GARDENERS' COTTAGE

West Dean, Chichester PO18 0RX.
Jim Buckland & Sarah Wain. *6m N
of Chichester. Off A286 follow signs
to West Dean Gardens & park in car
park. Follow signs to cottage.* **Sun 22
May (11-5). Adm £3.50, chd free.
Cream teas.**
The home garden of the husband and
wife Head Gardener team at the
neighbouring West Dean Gardens.
Small, serene and secluded theatrical
retreat with strong emphasis on
texture, foliage and good structure
created by trees, topiary, labyrinthine
paths, interesting spaces. Separate
courtyard garden with pond and
extensive pot grown succulent, hosta
and fern collections. Delicious range
of home-made cakes and good tea
and coffee.
☕

61 GORING FOLLY

29 Harvey Road, Goring-by-Sea,
Worthing BN12 4DS. Tim & Jean
Blewitt. *Just W of Worthing, nr to
coast. Turn S off A259 into Parklands*

Ave. Harvey Rd is 3rd on L. **Sat 18,
Sun 19 June (1-5). Combined adm
with Channel View £5, chd free.
Home-made teas & plant sale at
Channel View only.**
An artist's s-facing garden designed
by the owner to have something of
interest throughout the yr. This incl
'Goring Folly' which was featured on
Channel 4's Shed of the Year 2015.
Lots of ideas for the smaller garden,
plus a sempervivum house, bonsai
collection, koi pond, children's trail
and some impressive cacti. Featured
in The Argus and West Sussex
Gazette. Wheelchairs may have to go
around the other side of the house,
please ask.
& 🐱 ☕

62 THE GRANGE

Hesworth Lane, Fittleworth,
Pulborough RH20 1EW. Mr & Mrs
W Caldwell. *3m W of Pulborough.
From Pulborough or Petworth on
reaching Fittleworth turn S onto
B2138, then W at Swan PH. From
the S, turn L off A29 onto B2138 at
Bury Gate, then L again at Swan PH.
Please do not use SatNav.* **Sat 9,
Sun 10 Apr, Sat 16, Sun 17 July
(2-5.30). Adm £4.50, chd free.
Home-made teas.**
3 acre garden gently sloping to R
Rother. Formal areas enclosed by
yew hedges comprising colour
themed beds and herbaceous
borders around pretty C18 house (not
open). Small potager and orchard.
Tulips and other spring flowering
bulbs and snakeshead fritillaries a
feature in April. The garden has gravel
paths.
& 🐱 ☕

63 6 GRANGE ROAD

Lewes BN7 1TR. Bridget Millmore.
*Gate between 2 & 3 Grange Rd. 350
metres W of Southover Grange
Gardens & the historic cobbled Keere
St.* **Sun 26 June (2-5.30). Adm
£3.50, chd free. Home-made teas.**
Hidden historic town garden
established in the 1930s by the
Martin sisters and developed since
the 1980s by the late Paul Millmore.
Accessed via steps to a narrow
cobbled passageway which opens
out to reveal a truly secret garden.
½ acre in size, laid out formally with
brick paviour paths, perennial
borders, pond, mature trees and
topiary. A magical space in the midst
of bustling urban life.
☕

64 ▶ GRAVETYE MANOR
West Hoathly RH19 4LJ. Jeremy & Elizabeth Hosking, 01342 810567, info@gravetyemanor.co.uk, www.gravetyemanor.co.uk. *From M23, J10 E Grinstead, A264 Dukes Head, B2028 Turner's Hill. After Turner's Hill take L fork for Sharpthorne, then take first L into Vowels Lane.* **Sat 13 Aug (2-5). Adm £20, chd free. Pre-booking essential, please visit www.ngs.org.uk or phone 01483 211535 for information & booking. Adm incl tea & home-made cake.**
The gardens at Gravetye Manor can be considered amongst the most influential in English gardening history. The manor was the home of revolutionary gardener, William Robinson from 1884-1935. Thanks to the backing of new owners, a major restoration project is under way. Overseeing the project is head gardener, Tom Coward, who has come from working 3 years alongside Fergus Garrett at Great Dixter. Parts of the garden are accessible via ramps.

& ❀ ⊨ ☕

Views and cameos of plants and trees round every corner . . .

65 ▶ ◆ GREAT DIXTER HOUSE, GARDENS & NURSERIES
Northiam TN31 6PH. Great Dixter Charitable Trust, 01797 254048, friends@greatdixter.co.uk, www.greatdixter.co.uk/whats-on. *8m N of Rye. ¹/₂ m NW of Northiam off A28.* **For NGS: Wed 16 Nov (12-3). Adm £50. Light refreshments in the Great Hall. Special event with Fergus Garrett talk on the 10th anniversary of Christopher Lloyd's death. Pre-booking essential. Donation to NGS (50%). For other opening times and information, please phone, email or visit garden website.**
Designed by Edwin Lutyens and Nathaniel Lloyd. Christopher Lloyd officiated over these gardens for 50 years creating one of the most experimental and constantly changing gardens of our time, a tradition now being carried on by Fergus Garrett. Clipped topiary, wild flower meadows, pot displays and the famous Long Border and Exotic Garden.

❀ 🚐 ☕

66 ▶ GREAT LYWOOD FARMHOUSE
Lindfield Road, Ardingly RH17 6SW. Richard & Susan Laing, 01444 892500, splaing@btinternet.com. *2¹/₂ m N of Haywards Heath. Between Lindfield & Ardingly on B2028. 2m N of Lindfield, turn L (W) down paved track. 1st house on R, car park beyond house.* **Mon 30 May, Fri 3, Sun 5 June (2-6). Adm £5, chd free. Home-made teas. Visits also by arrangement May & June for groups of 10+, no coaches.**
Approx 1¹/₂ acre garden surrounding C17 Sussex farmhouse (not open). The extensive but accessible and gentle terracing provides immediate views of many different aspects of the garden and distant views towards the South Downs. There are garden seats on every level making this a garden in which to rest and enjoy the countryside. Featured in Sussex Life (June 2015). Wheelchair access possible, some slopes and short grass.

& 🏚 ❀ ☕

67 ▶ HALFPENNY COTTAGE
Copse Lane, Walberton BN18 0QH. Sue & Dave Settle. *5m from Chichester & Arundel. Off A27 at Fontwell r'about, past petrol station to end of village. At last mini-r'about turn R onto West Walberton Lane, Copse Lane next L.* **Sun 5 June (1.30-5.30). Adm £4, chd free. Home-made teas.**
Delightful ¹/₂ acre garden designed and planted by the present owners in a romantic cottage style, with different colour themed borders using a palette of soft colours, winding brick paths and rose pergola. Mediterranean garden, green oak gazebo and enclosed kitchen garden. Lots of interesting perennial planting combinations.

🏚 ❀ ☕

68 ▶ HAMMERWOOD HOUSE
Iping, Midhurst GU29 0PF. Mr & Mrs M Lakin, 07785 776222, amandalakin@me.com. *3m W of Midhurst. Take A272 from Midhurst, approx 2m outside Midhurst turn R for Iping. From A3 leave for Liphook, follow B2070, turn L for Iping.* **Sun 8, Sun 15 May (1.30-5). Adm £5, chd free. Home-made teas. Visits also by arrangement in May for groups of 10+. Donation to Iping Church.**
Large s-facing garden with lots of mature shrubs incl camellias, rhododendrons and azaleas. An arboretum with a variety of flowering and fruit trees. The old yew and beech hedges give a certain amount of formality to this traditional English garden. Tea on the terrace is a must with the most beautiful view of the South Downs. For the more energetic there is a woodland walk. Partial wheelchair access as garden is set on a slope.

& 🏚 ❀ ☕

69 ▶ HARBOURSIDE
Prinsted Lane, Prinsted, Emsworth PO10 8HS. Ann Moss, 01243 370048, ann.moss8@btinternet.com. *6m E of Chichester. Turn off A27 Tesco r'about onto A259 W, after 2nd r'about take 2nd turning on L. Chinese takeaway on corner, follow road until forced to turn R at Scout Hut. House next door with boat in front garden.* **Visits by arrangement for groups of 12-24. Various refreshment options available, please call and ask. Adm £4.50, chd free.**
Award-winning coastal garden takes you on a journey through garden styles from around the world. Visit France, Holland, Spain, New Zealand and Japan. View and enjoy tree ferns, topiary, shady area, secret woodland parlor, potager, containers, unusual shrubs, silver birch walk and herbaceous borders for yr-round interest. Wide variety of plants, music, seating, art and crafts. Winner of Chichester District Council, The News, Hampshire Federation of Horticultural Societies, Emsworth Horticultural Society competitions. Wheelchair access to most of the garden, after 10ft of gravel at the garden entrance.

& ❀ ☕

70 ▶ HARDWYCKE
Southfields Road, Eastbourne BN21 1BZ. Lois Machin, 01323 729391, loisandpeter@yahoo.co.uk. *Centre of Eastbourne, Upperton. A259 towards Eastbourne, Southfields Rd on R just before junction with A2270 (Upperton Rd). Limited parking,*

public car park (pay) in Southfields Rd. **Sun 12 June, Sun 28 Aug (11-5). Combined adm with Dittons End £4, chd free. Home-made teas. Visits also by arrangement May to Sept for groups of 10-25. Refreshments on request.**
Delightful s-facing town garden mainly of chalky soil, with many usual and unusual plants. Separate vegetable garden with restored 1920s summerhouse. Wide selection of shrubs incl 50 types of clematis. L-shaped garden that has 2 spaces 70ft x 50ft and 18ft x 50ft. 2 slight steps to rear garden area, wheelchair accessible with care.

71 ◆ GARDENS & GROUNDS OF HERSTMONCEUX CASTLE
Herstmonceux, Hailsham BN27 1RN. Bader International Study Centre, Queen's University (Canada), 01323 833816, c_harber@bisc.queensu.ac.uk, www.herstmonceux-castle.com. *Located between Herstmonceux & Pevensey on the Wartling Rd. From Herstmonceux take A271 to Bexhill, 2nd R signed Castle. Do not use SatNav.* **For NGS: Thur 14 July (10-5). Adm £6, chd free. Cream teas & light lunches in Chestnuts Tearoom. For other opening times and information, please phone, email or visit garden website.**
Herstmonceux is renowned for its magnificent moated castle set in beautiful parkland and superb Elizabethan walled gardens, leading to delightful discoveries such as our rhododendron, rose and herb gardens and onto our woodland trails. Take a slow stroll past the lily covered lakes to the 1930s folly and admire the sheer magnificence of the castle. The Gardens & Grounds first opened for the NGS in 1927. Partial wheelchair access to formal gardens.

GROUP OPENING

72 HERSTMONCEUX PARISH TRAIL
Hailsham BN27 4JF. *4m NE of Hailsham. 5m S of Heathfield. Herstmonceux Parish Trail starts at Cowbeech House in the centre of Cowbeech village, opp the Merrie Harriers PH. Follow NGS signs.* **Sat 2, Sun 3 July (10-5). Combined adm £4, chd free.**

Whithurst Park
© Judi Lion

THE ALLOTMENTS, STUNTS GREEN
George Taylor

COWBEECH HOUSE
Mr Anthony Hepburn

NEW ▶ 1 ELM COTTAGES
Audrey Jarrett

LIME CROSS NURSERY PINETUM
Vicky and Helen Tate
www.limecross.co.uk

Herstmonceux Parish Trail starts at Cowbeech House in Cowbeech village with its tranquil setting, relaxing water features and maybe a few stunning surprises. The next part of the trail is the 54 allotments set in a picturesque fruit farm at Stunts Green showing community spirit aplenty. The final part of the trail takes you to Herstmonceux village where you will find Lime Cross Nursery, where delicious refreshments and cream teas are available in the cafe. This will give you a chance to sit down, relax and take in the beauty of the gardens especially overlooking the Pinetum. A short stroll or drive into Windmill Hill brings you to 1 Elm Cottages, a stunning cottage garden packed full of edible and flowering plants you can't afford to miss; particularly impressive as this space was

transformed from wasteland into the garden that it is today. This small gem of a garden is really inspirational, especially given the owner's physical handicaps, her long-handled fork is her best friend! Partial wheelchair access to some gardens.

73 ◆ HIGH BEECHES WOODLAND AND WATER GARDEN
High Beeches Lane, Handcross, Haywards Heath RH17 6HQ. High Beeches Gardens Conservation Trust, 01444 400589, gardens@highbeeches.com, www.highbeeches.com. *5m NW of Cuckfield. On B2110, 1m E of A23 at Handcross.* **For NGS: Sun 12 June, Sun 25 Sept (1-4). Adm £7.50, chd free. Cream teas. For other opening times and information, please phone, email or visit garden website.**
25 acres of enchanting landscaped woodland and water gardens with spring daffodils, bluebells and azalea walks, many rare and beautiful plants, an ancient wild flower meadow and glorious autumn colours. Picnic area. National Collection of Stewartias.

 NPC

74 ◆ HIGHDOWN GARDENS

33 Highdown Rise, Littlehampton Road, Goring-by-Sea, Worthing BN12 6FB. Worthing Borough Council, 01903 501054, www.highdowngardens.co.uk. *3m W of Worthing. Off A259 approx 1m from Goring-by-Sea Train Station.* **For NGS: Sun 1 May, Thur 9 June (10-6). Adm by donation. For other opening times and information, please phone or visit garden website.**
Famous garden created by Sir Frederick Stern situated on downland countryside in a chalk pit. The garden contains a wide collection of plants; many were raised from seed brought from China by great collectors like Wilson, Farrer and Kingdon-Ward. Winner of Silver Gilt South East in Bloom Heritage Section 2015 and Green Flag Award 2015. Partial wheelchair access to hillside garden with mainly grass paths.

 NPC ☕

75 4 HILLSIDE COTTAGES

Downs Road, West Stoke, Chichester PO18 9BL. Heather & Chris Lock, 01243 574802, chlock@btinternet.com. *3m NW of Chichester. From A286 at Lavant head W for 1½ m, nr Kingley Vale.* **Sun 24 July (2-5). Adm £3, chd free. Tea. Visits also by arrangement June to Aug.**
Garden 120ft x 27ft in a rural setting, densely planted with mixed borders and shrubs. Large collection of roses, mainly New English shrub roses; walls, fences and arches covered with mid and late season clematis; baskets overflowing with fuchsias. A profusion of colour and scent in a well maintained small garden.
☕

76 HOLLY HOUSE

Beaconsfield Road, Chelwood Gate, Haywards Heath RH17 7LF. Mrs Deirdre Birchell, 01825 740484, db@hollyhousebnb.demon.co.uk, www.hollyhousebnb.demon.co.uk. *7m E of Haywards Heath. From Nutley Village on A22 turn off at RajRani signed Chelwood Gate 2m. Chelwood Gate Village Hall on R, Holly House is opp.* **Sat 14, Sun 15 May, Sat 9, Sun 10 July, Sat 20, Sun 21 Aug (2-5). Adm £3.50, chd free. Home-made teas. Visits also by arrangement May to Sept.**
An acre of English garden providing views and cameos of plants and trees round every corner with many different areas giving constant interest. A fish pond and a wildlife pond beside a grassy area with many shrubs and flower beds. Among the trees and winding paths there is a cottage garden which is a profusion of colour and peace. Exhibition of paintings and cards by owner. Garden accessible by wheelchair in good weather, but it is not easy.
♿ 🌸 🚐 🛏 ☕

NGS & Perennial; giving support where it is needed

77 NEW THE HOMEGROWN FLOWER COMPANY

The Old Forge, Butchers Cross, Five Ashes, Mayfield TN20 6JN. Zelie Billins, www.thehomegrownflowercompany. co.uk. *¼ m NE of Five Ashes. From Five Ashes village proceed N on A267 towards Mayfield. Turn L on Skippers Hill for parking on lane.* **Tue 12, Wed 13 July (12-5). Adm £4, chd free. Home-made teas.**
A densely planted country garden with views over the High Weald AONB. Large cut flower plot in field supplying an abundance of flowers and foliages for floristry business. Ornamental garden surrounding house includes a decorative cutting garden, topiary, greenhouse and small vegetable plot with raised beds. Cut flowers for sale.
🌸 ☕

78 THE HUNDRED HOUSE

Pound Lane, Framfield TN22 5RU. Dr & Mrs Michael Gurney. *4m E of Uckfield. From Uckfield take B2102 through Framfield. 1m from centre of village turn L into Pound Lane, then ¾ m on R. Disabled parking is close by the entrance gate.* **Thur 4, Sun 7 Aug (2-5.30). Adm £4, chd free. Home-made teas.**
Delightful garden with panoramic views set in the grounds of the historic The Hundred House. Fine stone ha-ha. 1½ acre garden with mixed herbaceous borders, productive vegetable garden, greenhouse, ancient yew tree, pond area with some subtropical plants, secret woodland copse and orchard. Beech hedge, field and butterfly walk, Silver Birch (jacquemontii) grove under development. Home grown plants, vegetables and fruit for sale.
♿ 🌸 🐾 ☕

79 JACARANDA

Chalk Road, Ifold RH14 0UE. Brian & Barbara McNulty, 01403 751532, bam101@btinternet.com. *1m S of Loxwood. From A272/A281 take B2133 (Loxwood). ½ m S of Loxwood take Plaistow Rd, then 3rd R into Chalk Rd. Follow signs for parking & garden. Wheelchair users can park in driveway.* **Sun 4 Sept (2-5). Adm £3, chd free. Home-made teas. Visits by arrangement Apr to Oct for groups of 30 max.**
A plant lover's garden of ¼ acre created from scratch over past 17 yrs. Gracefully curving borders contain trees, shrubs, perennials, roses, bulbs and climbers, with a hosta theatre beneath an old walnut tree. The kitchen garden has a large raised bed, a greenhouse, a herb garden in pots and a potting bench and compost area. A truly delightful and tranquil garden.
♿ 🐾 ☕

80 ◆ KING JOHN'S LODGE

Sheepstreet Lane, Etchingham TN19 7AZ. Jill Cunningham, 01580 819220, harry@kingjohnsnursery.co.uk, www.kingjohnsnursery.co.uk. *2m W of Hurst Green. A265 Burwash to Etchingham. Turn L before Etchingham Church into Church Lane which leads into Sheepstreet Lane after ½ m. Turn L after 1m.* **For NGS: Sun 6 Mar (1-4); Sat 14, Sun 15 May, Sat 25, Sun 26 June (10-5); Sun 11 Sept (1-5). Adm £5, chd free. Home-made teas & lunches in the tearoom of King John's Nursery. For other opening times and information, please phone, email or visit garden website.**
4 acre romantic garden for all seasons surrounding an historic listed house (not open). Formal garden with water features, rose walk and wild garden and pond. Rustic bridge to

shaded ivy garden, large herbaceous borders, old shrub roses and secret garden. Further 4 acres of meadows, fine trees and grazing sheep. Nursery and shop. Featured in the book Wild Garden Weekends, and an article in Period Living magazine (March 2015). Garden is mainly flat. Stepped areas can usually be accessed from other areas. No disabled WC.

  [icons]

81 **NEW** **LADYWELL**
Courtmead Road, Cuckfield, Haywards Heath RH17 5LP. **Robert & Sarah Salisbury.** *On S side of Cuckfield. From A272 between Ansty & Haywards Heath at r'about take the B2184 (Broad St), turn 3rd L (passing school) into Courtmead Rd. Park as directed. Public transport to Broad St.* **Thur 2 June (2-5.30). Adm £4, chd free. Home-made teas.**
Shrubs, trees and herbaceous planting, plus vegetable garden and winding paths entice you to explore this evolving ½ acre country garden. Grassy slopes sculpted in the 30s and a spring have been creatively used; further plans for a waterfall. Interest for much of the year in this s-facing garden on clay/sandstone. Peach tree growing on outside s-facing wall. Fine view of nearby church. Please be aware of deep water.

  [icons]

82 **LEGSHEATH FARM**
Legsheath Lane, nr Forest Row RH19 4JN. **Mr & Mrs M Neal.** *4m S of East Grinstead. 2m W of Forest Row, 1m S of Weirwood Reservoir.* **Sun 22 May (2-5). Adm £5, chd free. Home-made teas.** *Donation to Holy Trinity Church, Forest Row.*
Panoramic views over Weirwood Reservoir. Exciting 10 acre garden with woodland walks, water gardens and formal borders. Of particular interest, clumps of wild orchids, fine davidia, acers, eucryphia and rhododendrons. Mass planting of different species of meconopsis on the way to ponds.

  [icons]

83 **LIMEKILN FARM**
Chalvington Road, Chalvington, Hailsham BN27 3TA. **Dr J Hester and Mr M Royle.** *10m N of Eastbourne. Nr Hailsham. Turn S off A22 at Golden Cross & follow the Chalvington road for 1m. The entrance has white gates on the LH-side of the road, car parking 100*

metres further on. **Fri 1, Sat 2 Apr (2-5). Adm £4, chd free. Home-made teas in the Oast House.**
The garden was designed in the 1930s when the house was owned by Charles Stewart Taylor, MP for Eastbourne. It has not changed in basic layout since then. The planting aims to reflect the age of the C17 property and original garden design. The house and garden are mentioned in Virginia Woolf's diaries of 1929, depicting a dilapidated charm that still exists today. Flint walls enclose the main lawn, herbaceous borders and rose garden. There is a vegetable garden, informal pond, secret garden, mature and newly planted specimen trees and many spring bulbs. Disabled parking space close to the house.

  [icons]

84 **THE LONG HOUSE**
The Lane, Westdean, Nr Seaford BN25 4AL. **Robin & Rosie Lloyd,** 01323 870432, rosiemlloyd@gmail.com. *3m E of Seaford, 6m W of Eastbourne. From A27 follow signs to Alfriston then Litlington, Westdean 1m on L. From A259 at Exceat, L on Litlington Rd, ¼ m on R. Free parking in the village.* **Thur 7 July (2-5). Adm £5, chd free. Home-made teas. Visits also by arrangement May to July for groups of 10+.**
An Austrian garden tour group voted The Long House and Sissinghurst the two most enjoyable that they had visited and they said we 'serve the best cakes in the whole of Sussex!' A great compliment but not hard to see why. Westdean is an idyllic South Downs hamlet, the C17 flint Long House has a romantic, peaceful, interesting 1 acre garden with wild flowers, lavenders, hollyhocks, roses and a folly. Situated on The South Downs Way. Gravel forecourt at entrance, some slopes and steps.

  [icons]

85 **LORDINGTON HOUSE**
Lordington, Chichester PO18 9DX. **Mr & Mrs John Hamilton,** 01243 375862. *7m W of Chichester. On W side of B2146, ½ m S of Walderton, 6m S of South Harting. Enter through white railings.* **Sat 26, Mon 28 Mar (1.30-4.30). Adm £4, chd free. Home-made teas. Visits also by arrangement June & July, regret no coaches.**
Early C17 house (not open) and walled gardens in South Downs

National Park. Clipped yew and box, lawns, borders and fine views. Vegetables, fruit and poultry in old kitchen garden. Carpet of daffodils in spring. Nearly 100 roses planted since 2008. Various trees both mature and young. Lime avenue planted in 1973 to replace elms. Overlooks farmland, Ems Valley and wooded slopes of South Downs, all in AONB. Gravel paths, some uneven paving and slopes.

  [icons]

Stunning cottage garden packed full of edible and flowering plants you can't afford to miss . . .

---

86 **LOWDER MILL**
Bell Vale Lane, Fernhurst, Haslemere GU27 3DJ. **Anne & John Denning,** 01428 644822, anne@denningconsultancy.co.uk, www.lowdermill.com. *1½ m S of Haslemere. Follow A286 out of Midhurst towards Haslemere, through Fernhurst & take 2nd R after Kingsley Green into Bell Vale Lane. Lowder Mill is approx ½ m on R.* **Sat 4 June (11-5.30); Sun 5 June (10.30-5.30). Adm £4.50, chd £2. Home-made teas. Visits also by arrangement close to garden open days.**
C17 mill house and former mill set in 3 acre garden. The garden has been restored with the help of Bunny Guinness. Interesting assortment of container planting forming a stunning courtyard between house and mill. Streams, waterfalls, innovative and quirky container planting around the potting shed and restored greenhouse. Raised vegetable garden. Rare breed chicken and ducks, as well as resident kingfishers. Renowned for superb home-made teas, served overlooking the mill lake. Extensive plant stall, mainly home propagated. Choir singing on Sunday. Featured in Country Life, Country Living, and many national and regional publications.

  [icons]

Charleston

87 LUCTONS

North Lane, West Hoathly, East Grinstead RH19 4PP. Drs Hans & Ingrid Sethi, 01342 810085, ingrid@sethis.co.uk. *4m SW of East Grinstead, 6m E of Crawley. Off minor road between Turners Hill & Forest Row. Nr Church, Cat Inn & Priest House. Car parks in village.* **Sun 26, Tue 28 June (1.30-5.30). Adm £5, chd free. Home-made teas. Visits also by arrangement May to July for groups of 10-20.**

A 2 acre garden in Gertrude Jekyll style, with small box parterre, lawns, yew topiary, shrubberies, pond, much loved mixed borders, large fruit and vegetable garden, many culinary, medicinal and other herbs, chickens, vine, peach and greenhouses, and wild flower orchard with meadow flowers and spotted orchids in June.

88 MALT HOUSE

Chithurst Lane, Rogate, Petersfield GU31 5EZ. Mr & Mrs G Ferguson, 01730 821433, g.ferguson34@btinternet.com. *3m W of Midhurst. On A272 turn N signed Chithurst for 1½ m, narrow lane; or off A3 at Liphook to old A3 (B2070) for 2m, L to Milland following signs to Chithurst for 1½ m. Narrow lanes not suitable for large coaches.* **Sun 1, Mon 2, Sun 8 May (2-6). Adm £5, chd free. Home-made teas. Visits also by arrangement Apr to June.**

6 acres; flowering shrubs incl exceptional rhododendrons and azaleas, leading to 50 acres of arboretum and lovely woodland walks, plus many rare plants and trees. On the South Downs. Partial wheelchair access only.

89 MALTHOUSE FARM

Street Lane, Streat, Hassocks BN6 8SA. Richard & Helen Keys, 01273 890356, helen.k.keys@btinternet.com. *2m SE of Burgess Hill. From r'about between B2113 & B2112 take Folders Lane & Middleton Common Lane E; after 1m, R into Street Lane, garden is ½ m on R. Ample parking on grass verge.* **Sun 21, Wed 24 Aug (2-5.30). Adm £5, chd free. Home-made teas. Visits also by arrangement Apr to Sept for groups of 10+.**

Rural 5 acre garden with stunning views to South Downs. Garden divided into separate rooms, box parterre and borders with glass sculpture, herbaceous and shrub borders, newly planted mixed border for seasonal colour, and kitchen garden. Orchard leading to partitioned areas with grass walks, snail mound, birch maze and willow tunnel. Wildlife farm pond with planted surround. Featured in Period Living and Sussex Life 2015. Wheelchair access possible although some steps. Caution if wet as much access is across grass.

90 MANOR OF DEAN

Tillington, Petworth GU28 9AP. Mr & Mrs James Mitford, 07887 992349, emma@mitford.uk.com. *3m W of Petworth. From Petworth towards Midhurst on A272, go through Tillington & turn R onto Dean Lane following NGS signs. From Midhurst on A272 towards Petworth past Halfway Bridge, turn L following NGS signs.* **Sun 14 Feb (2-4); Suns 13 Mar, 17 Apr, 12 June, 21 Aug (2-5). Adm £4, chd free. Home-made teas. Visits also by arrangement Feb to Sept for groups of 10+, regret no coaches.**

Traditional English garden, approx 3 acres with herbaceous borders, a variety of early flowering bulbs, snowdrops, spring bulbs, grass walks and grass steps. Walled kitchen garden with fruit, vegetables and cutting flowers. Lawns, rose garden and informal areas with views of the South Downs. Garden under a long-term programme of improvements. Come along to one of our themed open days: Rhubarb Sunday (17 Apr), Asparagus Sunday (12 Jun) and Dahlia Sunday (21 Aug) when you can see how they are grown, buy some to take home and enjoy the productive walled garden. Come early to avoid disappointment. Garden on many levels with old steps and paths.

GROUP OPENING

91 MAYFIELD GARDENS
Mayfield TN20 6AB. *10m S of Tunbridge Wells. Turn off A267 into Mayfield. Parking is available in the village & a detailed map will be available at each of the gardens.* **Sat 11, Sun 12 June (2-5). Combined adm £5, chd free. Home-made teas at Hoopers Farm & The Oast.**

HOOPERS FARM
Andrew & Sarah Ratcliffe

MAY COTTAGE
M Prall

MEADOW COTTAGE
Adrian & Mo Hope

THE MIDDLE HOUSE
Johnny Marsh
01435 872146
info@themiddlehousemayfield.
co.uk

MULBERRY
M Vernon

THE OAST
Mike & Tessa Crowe

SOUTH STREET PLOTS
Val Buddle

Mayfield is a beautiful Wealden village with tearooms, an old PH and many interesting historical connections. The gardens to visit are all within walking distance of the village centre. They vary in size and style, including colour themed and cottage style planting, a wild flower meadow, and vegetables. There are far reaching, panoramic views over the beautiful High Weald. There is partial access to some gardens; see leaflet for details.

92 ◆ MCBEAN'S ORCHIDS
Resting Oak Hill, Cooksbridge, Lewes BN8 4PR. Mr Jim Durrant, 01273 400228, www.mcbeansorchids.co.uk. *A275 1m N of Cooksbridge Station, 4m N of Lewes. Follow yellow signs on A275.* **For NGS: Thur 25, Fri 26 Feb (10-4). Adm £4, chd free. For other opening times and information, please phone or visit garden website.**
A selection of orchids bred by McBeans since 1879 on this site. Includes tropical plants, award winning cymbidium and oncidium orchids, plus other plants of interest from around the world. Working

nursery tour throughout the day, plus exotic growing house display with shop full of plants to buy. Wheelchair access to shop and display house. Flight of 4 steps for nursery tour.

93 MOUNTFIELD COURT
Robertsbridge TN32 5JP. Mr & Mrs Simon Fraser. *3m N of Battle. On A21 London-Hastings; ¹/₂ m NW from Johns Cross.* **Sun 8 May (2-5). Adm £4, chd free. Home-made teas.**
3 acre wild woodland garden; bluebell lined walkways through exceptional rhododendrons, azaleas, camellias, and other flowering shrubs; fine trees and outstanding views. Beautiful paved herb garden.

94 NEWTIMBER PLACE
Newtimber BN6 9BU. Mr & Mrs Andrew Clay, 01273 833104, andy@newtimberholidaycottages.co.uk, www.newtimberplace.co.uk. *7m N of Brighton. From A23 take A281 towards Henfield. Turn R at small Xrds signed Newtimber in approx ¹/₂ m. Go down Church Lane, garden is at end of lane on L.* **Sun 17 Apr (2-5.30). Adm £4, chd free. Home-made teas.**
Beautiful C17 moated house (not open). Gardens and woods full of bulbs and wild flowers in spring. Herbaceous border and lawns. Moat flanked by water plants. Mature trees, wild garden, ducks, chickens and fish. Wheelchair access across lawn to some of garden, tearoom and WC.

95 NORTH HALL
North Hall Lane, Sheffield Green, Uckfield TN22 3SA. Celia & Les Everard, 01825 791103, indigodogs@yahoo.co.uk. *1¹/₂ m NW of Fletching Village. 6m N Uckfield. From A272 turn N at Piltdown or N Chailey. From A275 turn E at Sheffield Green into North Hall Lane.* **Sat 25, Sun 26 June (2-5.30). Adm £4, chd free. Home-made teas. Visits also by arrangement June & July for groups of 10+.**
This quintessential cottage garden surrounding a C16 house (not open) is planted to please the senses. Roses tumble, clematis scramble and the dense and varied planting needs little support, a palette of soft colours and heady scent. Themed island beds and a moated terrace add to the many other cottage garden

features. Wildlife and self seeding encouraged. Home grown plants and scrumptious teas.

New for 2016 there is the Japanese Zen garden complete with waterfall and pond . . .

96 NORTH SPRINGS
Bedham, nr Fittleworth RH20 1JP. Mr & Mrs R Haythornthwaite. *Between Fittleworth & Wisborough Green. From Wisborough Green take A272 towards Petworth. Turn L into Fittleworth Rd signed Coldharbour & proceed 1¹/₂ m. From Fittleworth take Bedham Lane off A283 & proceed for approx 3m NE. Limited parking.* **Sun 3 July (1-6). Adm £4, chd free. Home-made teas.**
Hillside garden with beautiful views surrounded by mixed woodland. Focus on structure with a wide range of mature trees and shrubs. Stream, pond and bog area. Abundance of roses, clematis, hostas, rhododendrons and azaleas.

97 NYEWOOD HOUSE
Nyewood, Rogate GU31 5JL. Mr & Mrs C J Wright, 01730 821563, s.warren.wright@gmail.com. *4m E of Petersfield. From A272 at Rogate take South Harting Rd for 1¹/₂ m. Turn L at pylon towards South Downs Manor. Nyewood House 2nd on R over cattle grid.* **Sat 11, Sun 12 June (2-5.30). Adm £4, chd free. Home-made & cream teas. Visits also by arrangement May & June for groups of 15+.**
Victorian country house garden with stunning uninterrupted views of South Downs. 3 acres comprising formal gardens with rose walk and arbours, pleached hornbeam, colour themed herbaceous borders, shrub borders, lily pond and fully stocked kitchen garden with greenhouse. Wooded area featuring spring flowers followed by wild orchids and wild flowers. Gravel drive.

98 ◆ NYMANS
Handcross RH17 6EB. National Trust, 01444 405250, nymans@nationaltrust.org.uk, www.nationaltrust.org.uk/nymans. *4m S of Crawley. On B2114 at Handcross signed off M23/A23 London-Brighton road. Metrobus 271 & 273 stop nearby.* **For NGS: Sun 25 Sept (10-5). Adm £11.50, chd £6.20. For other opening times and information, please phone, email or visit garden website.**
One of the National Trust's premier gardens, Nymans was a country retreat for the creative Messel family, and has views stretching out across the Sussex Weald. Today it's still a place to recharge the batteries where you can glimpse hidden corners through stone archways, walk along tree lined avenues and be surrounded by lush green countryside.

   NPC

99 OAK GROVE COLLEGE GROUNDS
The Boulevard, Worthing BN13 1JX, oakgrovecollege.org.uk. *1m W of Worthing. When driving W on A2032 dual carriageway, turn into Oak Grove College car park immed on L before r'about, The Boulevard turn off.* **Sun 26 June (11-5). Adm £4, chd free. Light refreshments, lunches & wine.**
An inspiring example of how special needs children have transformed their school grounds into a green oasis. Extensive and unusual planting, polytunnels, vegetable growing area, herb garden, sculptures and mosaics. Small reclaimed woodland, camera obscura, outdoor performance and cooking areas.

100 OFFHAM HOUSE
The Street, Offham, Lewes BN7 3QE. Mr S Goodman and Mr & Mrs P Carminger. *2m N of Lewes on A275. Offham House is on the main road (A275) through Offham between the filling station & the Blacksmiths Arms.* **Sun 24 Apr, Sun 5 June (1-5). Adm £5, chd free. Home-made teas.**
Romantic garden with fountains, flowering trees, arboretum, double herbaceous border, long peony bed. 1676 Queen Anne house (not open) with well knapped flint facade. Herb garden and walled kitchen garden with glasshouses, coldframes, chickens, guinea fowl, sheep and friendly pig. Tea and home-made cake on the lawn, or in the conservatory.

101 OLD ERRINGHAM COTTAGE
Steyning Road, Shoreham-By-Sea BN43 5FD. Fiona & Martin Phillips, 01273 462285, fiona.h.phillips@btinternet.com. *2m N of Shoreham by Sea. From A27 Shoreham flyover take A283 towards Steyning. Take 2nd R into private lane. Follow sharp LH-bend at top, house on L.* **Visits by arrangement from mid May to early July for groups of 10+. Adm £4.50, chd free. Home-made teas.**
In South Downs National Park 1 acre plantsman's garden with mixed borders, pond, meadow and panoramic views. At back divided by yew hedging with stream, parterre and paths leading through wide variety of perennials. Many plants grown from seed and coastal climate allows for success with unusual tender plants. Greenhouses for melon, peach, fig, persimmon and highly productive fruit and vegetable area.

103 THE OLD VICARAGE
The Street, Washington RH20 4AS. Sir Peter & Lady Walters, 07766 761926, meryl.walters@me.com. *2¹/₂ m E of Storrington, 4m W of Steyning. From Washington r'about on A24 take A283 to Steyning. 500yds R to Washington. Pass Frankland Arms, R to St Mary's Church.* **Sun 28 Feb (11-3.30); Mon 28 Mar (10.30-4); Sun 24 Apr, Sun 12 June, Sun 21 Aug (10.30-4.30); Sun 16 Oct (11-3.30). Adm £4.50, chd free. Home-made teas. Gluten free cakes & biscuits available. Visits also by arrangement Apr to Oct for groups of 10+.**

3¹/₂ acre garden set around 1832 Regency style house (not open). Front is formally laid out with topiary, a large lawn and mixed border. To the rear some mature trees dating back to C19, herbaceous border, new large pond and stunning uninterrupted 20m view to the North Downs. Stream and copse area with log cabin. New for 2016 there is the Japanese Zen garden complete with waterfall and pond. As featured in The Daily Telegraph, Period Living magazine and also listed as one of the 25 great gardens to visit in Sussex by Sussex Life magazine.

102 OLD VICARAGE
The Street, Firle, Lewes BN8 6NR. Mr & Mrs Charlie Bridge. *Off A27 5m E of Lewes. Signed from main road.* **Sat 18 June (2-5). Adm £4, chd free. Cream teas.**
Garden originally designed by Lanning Roper in the 1960s. 4 acre garden set around a Regency vicarage (not open) with wonderful Downland views. Features a walled garden with vegetable parterre and flower borders, wild flower meadow, pond, pleached limes and over 100 roses. Partial wheelchair access as some areas may be difficult.

104 NEW ORCHARD HOUSE
Pipers Lane, Ebernoe, Nr Petworth GU28 9JY. Sue Nyfield. *Ebernoe, nr Petworth. SatNav has variable results! Orchard House is just near the corner of Piper's Lane & Scratchings Lane & can be accessed from either Northchapel (A283) or Balls Cross.* **Sat 2 July, Sat 20 Aug (2-6). Adm £6, chd free. Home-made teas.**
A tranquil garden of several acres set on the edge of the South Down National Park with far-reaching fine views. Well managed meadows, lake, woodland area, conservation planting of new native trees and fabulous newly planted herbaceous borders ranging from gentle pastels to vibrant hot colours. Relaxing with tea and cake on the raised decking is a must to take in the view. Wheelchair accessible except for raised decking.

GROUP OPENING

105 NEW OUSE VALLEY TO THE COAST TRAIL

Visitors can start at any of the 3 gardens listed. **Sat 16, Sun 17 July (2-5). Combined adm £5, chd free. Home-made teas.**

NEW CATTLEGATE
Swanborough, BN7 3PE. Caroline Courtauld

NEW 28 GRAND CRESCENT
Rottingdean, BN2 7GL. Angie Hart & Scott Dennis

NEW 144 RODMELL AVENUE
Saltdean, BN2 8PJ. Sue & Ray Warner
Visits also by arrangement July & Aug.
suwarner@xeonflux.com
01273 305137

3 brand new and uniquely different Sussex gardens flowing from the Ouse Valley down to the coast! Cattlegate in Swanborough has a small garden surrounding a white modernist house, with a spectacular view as painted by the artist Eric Ravilious and stunning views of the South Downs. It's full of architectural interest and thoughtful planting. Down on the coast there is 144 Rodmell Avenue in Saltdean, a fun jungle garden, 65ft x 36ft, but appearing larger with winding paths meandering through lush jungle and insect friendly planting, listen out for the parrots squawking in the trees! Finally, 28 Grand Crescent in Rottingdean, 49ft x 39ft, is a quirky, open plan coastal garden with lovely sea views, but fierce salt winds to combat. It's filled with brightly coloured mixed borders flowering right through until late summer. Marvel at the fabulous swing seat and hot composter. Full of attractive paving, pots and pond. No wheelchair access at 144 Rodmell Avenue and partial access at other gardens.

106 PALATINE SCHOOL GARDENS
Palatine Road, Worthing BN12 6JP. Mrs N Hawkins,
www.palatineschool.org. *Turn S off A2032 at r'about onto The Boulevard signed Goring. Take R at next r'about into Palatine Rd. School approx 100yds on R.* **Sun 27 Mar, Sun 10 July (2-5). Adm £4, chd free. Cream teas.**

This is a many roomed mature garden with varied planting. Constructed by teachers, volunteers and children with special needs, it never ceases to surprise visitors. Wildlife corner, large and small ponds, themed gardens and children's outdoor art features, along with rockeries, living willow, labyrinth, mosaics and interesting tree collection.

107 PARSONAGE FARM
Kirdford RH14 0NH. David & Victoria Thomas,
davidandvictoria.thomas@gmail.com. *5m NE of Petworth. From centre of Kirdford (before church) turn R through village towards Balls Cross, past Foresters PH on R. Entrance on L, just past R turn to Plaistow. For SatNav use RH14 0NG.* **Fri 17 June, Sun 11 Sept (2-6). Adm £6, chd free. Home-made teas.** *Donation to Churchers College - Sudden Death in Epilepsy (SUDEP).*

Major garden in beautiful setting developed over 20 yrs with fruit theme and many unusual plants. Formally laid out on grand scale with long vistas; C18 walled garden with borders in apricot, orange, scarlet and crimson; topiary walk; pleached lime allée; tulip tree avenue; rose borders; large vegetable garden with trained fruit; turf amphitheatre; lake; informal autumn shrubbery and jungle walk. Featured in Country Life (26 Aug 2015).

108 PEELERS RETREAT
70 Ford Road, Arundel BN18 9EX. Tony & Lizzie Gilks, 01903 884981, timespan70@tiscali.co.uk, www.peelersretreat.co.uk. *1m S of Arundel. At Chichester r'about take exit to Ford & Bognor Regis onto Ford Rd. We are situated close to Maxwell Rd, Arundel.* **Suns 8 May, 3 July, 14 Aug, 4 Sept (2-5). Adm £3.50, chd free. Home-made teas. Visits also by arrangement Apr to Sept for groups of 2-30.**

An immaculate and stunningly laid out town garden with ingenious ideas of how to incorporate well stocked flower beds with yr-round colour and texture, herbs, fruit and vegetable beds. In all, a wonderfully lush sanctuary in which to relax in. Exhibition of historical artefacts (weather dependent). Restricted wheelchair access due to our narrow side entrance, regret no motorised wheelchairs.

109 33 PEERLEY ROAD
East Wittering PO20 8PD. Paul & Trudi Harrison, 01243 673215, stixandme@aol.com. *7m S of Chichester. From A286 take B2198 to Bracklesham. Turn R into Stocks Lane, L at Royal British Legion into Legion Way. Follow road round to Peerley Rd halfway along.* **Sun 3 July (12-4). Adm £2.50, chd free. Visits also by arrangement May to Sept for groups of up to 20 max.**

Small seaside garden 65ft x 32ft, 110yds from the sea. Packed full of ideas and interesting plants using every inch of space to create rooms and places for adults and children to play. A must for any suburban gardener. Specialising in unusual plants that grow well in seaside conditions with advice on coastal gardening. Featured in Gardeners World (March 2015).

> Winding paths meandering through lush jungle and insect friendly planting . . .

110 PEMBURY HOUSE
Ditchling Road (New Road), Clayton, Hassocks BN6 9PH. Nick & Jane Baker, 01273 842805, jane.baker47@btinternet.com, www.pemburyhouse.co.uk. *6m N of Brighton, off A23. On B2112, 110 yds from A273. Limited parking at village green (BN6 9PJ) clearly signed. Good public transport service. Entry from Cinder Track public footpath only, not front gate.* **Visits by arrangement May & June for groups of 10-20. Adm £5.00, chd free. Home-made teas.**

Winding paths give a choice of walks through 2 acres of owner maintained garden, which is in, and enjoys views of the SDNP. In summer the garden comes to life again; the snowdrops and hellebores give way to an abundance of ferns, shrubberies and herbaceous plants. It is a country garden, tidy but not manicured, welcoming and relaxed. Look at the NGS website for pop-up public openings in late May/early June. Featured on Sky 1 TV garden series, in Rustica a French magazine and many others.

111 NEW PENNS IN THE ROCKS

Groombridge, nr Tunbridge Wells, East Sussex TN3 9PA. Mr & Mrs Hugh Gibson, 01892 864244, hmtgibson@pennsintherocks.co.uk, www.pennsintherocks.co.uk. *7m SW of Tunbridge Wells. On B2188 Groombridge to Crowborough road, just S of Xrd to Withyham. For SatNav users use TN6 1UX which takes you to the white drive gates, through which the visitor should enter the property.* **Sun 17 Apr, Sun 15 May (2-6). Adm £5, chd free. Home-made teas. Visits also by arrangement.**

Large garden with spectacular outcrop of rocks, lake, C18 temple and woods. Daffodils, bluebells, azaleas, magnolias and tulips. Old walled garden with herbaceous borders, roses and shrubs. House (not open) part C18. Walls recently restored by Richard and Columba Strachey. Restricted wheelchair access. No disabled WC. Dogs on lead in park only.

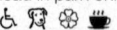

An artist's working garden, unusually growing plants for their dyeing properties . . .

112 6 PLANTATION RISE

Worthing BN13 2AH. Nigel & Trixie Hall, 01903 262206, trixiehall@btinternet.com. *2m from seafront on outskirts of Worthing. A24 meets A27 at Offington r'about. Turn into Offington Lane, 1st R into The Plantation, 1st R again into Plantation Rise.* **Visits by arrangement Mar to Sept for groups of 4-20, incl home-made teas. Adm £5, chd free.**

Our garden is 70ft x 80ft with pond, summerhouse, folly, flower decked pergolas over patios, 9 silver birches, plus evergreen shrubs, azaleas, rhododendrons and acers. Heathers in spring, and a profusion of roses, clematis and perennials in August, all to ensure yr-round colour and interest. The garden has some steps. WC available on request.

GROUP OPENING

113 NEW PRESTON PARK GARDENS

Preston Park Avenue, Brighton BN1 6HG. *Preston Park is 1½ m N of Brighton centre on the A23. Entry points: 31 Preston Park Ave, BN1 6HG (Preston Park Ave runs E of the park) & 32 Clermont Terrace, BN1 6SJ (Clermont Terrace is 2 mins W, off Cumberland Rd).* **Fri 10, Sat 11 June (11-5). Combined adm £5, chd free. Light refreshments & home-made cakes at 32 Claremont Terrace & 31 Preston Park Avenue.**

> **NEW 24 CLERMONT TERRACE**
> Sue Shepherd

> **NEW 32 CLERMONT TERRACE**
> Sue Fletcher

> **NEW PRESTON MANOR WALLED GARDEN**
> George Harris

> **NEW 30 PRESTON PARK AVENUE**
> Jo Brook

> **NEW 31 PRESTON PARK AVENUE**
> Lindy Craig-Hall

> **NEW 32 PRESTON PARK AVENUE**
> Anastasia Broome

A group of 5 urban gardens with the same challenges of chalk soil, varying slopes and levels, all tackled in individual ways. 32 Preston Park Avenue has had a large amount of hard landscaping creating areas from formal to a wild area. 31 Preston Park Avenue, created 11 yrs ago, incorporating natural and cultivated planting with new pink steps! 30 Preston Park Avenue, an artist's working garden, unusually growing plants for their dyeing properties; the studio at the top of the garden will be open. 32 Clermont Terrace, sympathetically landscaped for this romantic and lovely garden with fascinating echos of its past history. 24 Clermont Terrace, approached from within the house the garden has impact and draws you upward into its exotic secrets. These gardens lie either side of the beautiful Preston Manor walled garden where the Head Gardener will be conducting tours.

114 ♦ THE PRIEST HOUSE

North Lane, West Hoathly RH19 4PP. Sussex Archaeological Society, 01342 810479, priest@sussexpast.co.uk, www.sussexpast.co.uk. *4m SW of East Grinstead. Turn E to West Hoathly, 1m S of Turners Hill at Selsfield Common junction on B2028. 2m S turn R into North Lane, garden ¼ m.* **For NGS: Sat 28 May, Sat 25 June (10.30-5.30). Adm £2, chd free. For other opening times and information, please phone, email or visit garden website.**

C15 timber framed farmhouse with cottage garden on acid clay. Large collection of culinary and medicinal herbs in a small formal garden and mixed with perennials and shrubs in exuberant borders. Long established yew topiary, box hedges and espalier apple trees provide structural elements. Traditional fernery and stumpery, recently enlarged with a small secluded shrubbery and gravel garden. Adm to Priest House Museum £1 for NGS visitors.

115 2 QUARRY COTTAGES

Wall Hill Road, Ashurst Wood, East Grinstead RH19 3TQ. Mrs Hazel Anne Archibald. *1m S of East Grinstead. From N turn L off A22 from East Grinstead, garden adjoining John Pears Memorial Ground. From S turn R off A22 from Forest Row, garden on R at top of hill.* **Fri 13, Sat 14 May (2-5). Adm £3, chd free. Home-made teas.**

Peaceful little garden that has evolved over 40 yrs in the present ownership. A natural sandstone outcrop hangs over an ornamental pond; mixed borders of perennials and shrubs with specimen trees. Many seating areas tucked into corners. Highly productive vegetable plot. Terrace round house revamped in 2013. Florist and gift shop in barn. Feature article in Landscape (March/April 2015). **Also open Caxton Manor (separate admission).**

116 RINGMER PARK

Ringmer, Lewes BN8 5RW. Deborah & Michael Bedford, www.ringmerpark.com. *On A26 Lewes to Uckfield road. 1½ m NE of Lewes, 5m S of Uckfield.* **Sat 18, Sun 19 June (2-5). Adm £5, chd free. Home-made teas.**

Ringmer Park is a classic English country house with a garden appropriately scaled to the proportions of the house, and optimising the glorious views of the neighbouring South Downs. 2016 will see it open in June specifically for its first ever Rose Festival, celebrating Michael Bedford's pride and joy, the 650 plus spectacular roses throughout the various garden rooms.

117 1 ROSE COTTAGE

Chalvington Road, Golden Cross, Nr Hailsham BN27 3SS. Chris & Jackie Burgess, 01825 872753. *Approx 11m N of Eastbourne, just off A22, turn into Chalvington Road immed S of Golden Cross PH.* **Sat 18 June (11-5). Combined adm with 2 Woodside £5, chd free. Home-made teas. Visits also by arrangement May to Aug.**

A cottage garden created by enthusiastic owners passionate about plants. Narrow paths lead through densely planted colour themed borders and some unusual plants. Other areas incl raised vegetable beds with polytunnel, a small cutting garden, a fruit cage and a summerhouse. The garden has evolved and increased in size over 26 yrs as small pieces of land have been added. Home-made teas served on vintage china. Plants propagated by owners will be on sale.

118 RYMANS

Apuldram, Chichester PO20 7EG. Mrs Michael Gayford, 01243 783147, suzanna.gayford@btinternet.com. *1m S of Chichester. Take Witterings Rd, at 1½ m SW turn R signed Dell Quay. Turn 1st R, garden ½ m on L.* **Sat 16, Sun 17 Apr, Sat 11, Sun 12 June, Sat 17, Sun 18 Sept (2-5). Adm £5, chd free. Home-made teas. Visits also by arrangement Apr to Sept for groups of 10+.**

Walled and other gardens surrounding lovely C15 stone house (not open); bulbs, flowering shrubs, roses, ponds, potager. Many unusual and rare trees and shrubs. In late spring the wisterias are spectacular. The heady scent of hybrid musk roses fills the walled garden in June. In late summer the garden is ablaze with dahlias, sedums, late roses, sages and Japanese anemones. Featured in The English Garden magazine (June 2015).

119 SAFFRONS

Holland Road, Steyning BN44 3GJ. Tim Melton & Bernardean Carey, 01903 810082, tim.melton@btinternet.com. *6m NE of Worthing. Exit r'about on A283 at S-end of Steyning bypass into Clays Hill Rd. 1st R into Goring Rd, 4th L into Holland Rd. Park in Goring Rd & Holland Rd.* **Sun 24, Wed 27 July (2-5.30). Adm £4.50, chd free. Home-made teas. Visits also by arrangement in July for groups of 10+.**

A stylish garden of textural contrasts and rich colour. The herbaceous beds are filled with agapanthus, spiky eryngium and fragrant lilies, alliums and salvias. A broad lawn is surrounded by borders of Japanese maples, rhododendrons, hydrangeas and specimen trees interspersed with ferns and grasses. Fruit cage, vegetable beds and fruit trees. Wheelchair access difficult in very wet conditions.

120 ◆ ST MARY'S HOUSE GARDENS

Bramber BN44 3WE. Peter Thorogood & Roger Linton, 01903 816205, info@stmarysbramber.co.uk, www.stmarysbramber.co.uk. *1m E of Steyning. 10m NW of Brighton in Bramber Village off A283.* **For NGS: Fri 24, Sat 25 June (2-5.30). Adm £5, chd free. Home-made teas. For other opening times and information, please phone, email or visit garden website.**

5 acres incl formal topiary, large prehistoric *Ginkgo biloba*, and magnificent *Magnolia grandiflora* around enchanting timber-framed Medieval house (not open). Victorian 'Secret Gardens' incl splendid 140ft fruit wall with pineapple pits, Rural Museum, Terracotta Garden, Jubilee Rose Garden, King's Garden and unusual circular Poetry Garden. Woodland walk and Landscape Water Garden. In the heart of the South Downs National Park.

Driftwood

© Vanessa C Clark

See more images at nationalgardensscheme.com

121 ▸ 8 SANDGATE CLOSE
Seaford BN25 3LL. Mr & Mrs
Jones, 01323 899452,
sweetpeasa52@gmail.com,
www.sandgateclosegarden.co.uk.
*From A259 follow signs to Alfriston, E
of Seaford. Turn R into Hillside Ave, L
into Hastings Ave, R into Deal Close
& R into Sandgate Close.* **Visits by
arrangement June to Aug for
groups of 2-20. Combined visit
with Driftwood for larger groups.
Light refreshments.**
8 Sandgate Close is a green and
tranquil haven with a delightful mix of
trees, shrubs and perennial borders in
different themed beds. Courtyard
garden, gazebo, summerhouse,
water features, sweet pea arches,
huge range of plants in all seasons.
Plenty of places to sit and enjoy,
either in the shade or under cover.
Our lunches have proved to be
popular in 2015. We also provide
delicious afternoon tea. If given notice
we can accommodate many dietary
requirements. Plants, jams and books
for sale. Mostly flat but with a small
number of steps into the courtyard
and WC.

122 ▸ SANDHILL FARM HOUSE
Nyewood Road, Rogate,
Petersfield GU31 5HU. Rosemary
Alexander, 07551 777873,
r.a.alexander@talk21.com,
www.rosemaryalexander.co.uk. *4m
SE of Petersfield. From A272 Xrds in
Rogate take road S signed Nyewood
& Harting. Follow road for approx 1m
over small bridge. Sandhill Farm
House on R, over cattle grid.* **Sat 23,
Sun 24 Apr, Sat 11, Sun 12 June,
Sat 17, Sun 18 Sept (2-5). Adm £4,
chd free. Home-made teas. Visits
also by arrangement Mar to Oct
for groups of 10+. Gardening Club
bookings welcome.**
Front and rear gardens broken up
into garden rooms incl small kitchen
garden. Front garden incl small
woodland area planted with early
spring flowering shrubs, ferns and
bulbs; topiary and white garden, large
leaf border and terraced area. Rear
garden has mirror borders, small
decorative vegetable garden, red
border, grasses border garden. Home
of author and Principal of The English
Gardening School. The garden has
been featured in most gardening
magazines. The garden has gravel
paths and a few steps not easy to
negotiate in a wheelchair.

123 ▸ ◆ SARAH RAVEN'S CUTTING GARDEN
Perch Hill Farm, Willingford Lane,
Robertsbridge, Brightling
TN32 5HP. Sarah Raven, 01424
838000, www.sarahraven.com. *7m
SW of Hurst Green. From Burwash
turn off A265 by church & memorial,
follow road for 3m. From Woods
Corner take road opp Swan Inn, take
1st L, go uphill & take 1st L again.
Parking is in a field (uneven ground
possible).* **For NGS: Thur 4 Aug
(9.30-4). Adm £5, chd free. Tea,
coffee & cake served all day.
Lunch available from 12.15. For
other opening times and
information, please phone or visit
garden website.**
Sarah's inspirational, productive 2
acre working garden with different
garden rooms incl large cut flower
garden, vegetable and fruit garden,
salads and herbs area, plus two
ornamental gardens. We have some
steps and gravel paths so wheelchair
access is difficult in these areas.

GROUP OPENING

124 ▸ SEAFORD GARDENS
Seaford. *Start at 1 of the 3 gardens
& you will be given a map to direct
you to the next garden. All properties
are within a 5 /15 mins walk of
coastal bus route. NGS signs placed
on the A259 from east & west.*
**Sun 26 June (11-5). Combined
adm £5, chd free. Home-made
teas.**

> NEW **34 CHYNGTON ROAD**
> BN25 4HP. Dr Maggie
> Wearmouth & Richard Morland
>
> **HIGH TREES**
> 83 Firle Road, BN25 2JA. Tony
> & Sue Luckin
>
> NEW **LAVENDER COTTAGE**
> Steyne Road, BN25 1QH.
> Christina & Steve Machan

3 unique gardens are opening for
Seaford Gardens group this year.
High Trees, is a beautiful garden with
numerous interesting plants, ferns
and grasses. Woodland garden
accessed through a beautiful pergola.
Lavender Cottage is a flinted walled
garden with a coastal and kitchen
garden, terraced bank, and views of
Seaford Head from the balcony.
34 Chyngton Road is divided into
garden rooms with pastels, hot beds,
a small meadow, Japanese inspired

courtyard and a prairie under
construction. Level wheelchair access
to part of the garden at 34 Chyngton
Road & Lavender Cottage.

125 ▸ SEDGWICK PARK HOUSE
Sedgwick Park, Horsham
RH13 6QQ. John & Clare Davison,
01403 734930,
clare@sedgwickpark.com,
www.sedgwickpark.co.uk. *1m S of
Horsham off A281. A281 towards
Cowfold, Hillier Garden Center on R,
then 1st R into Sedgwick Lane. At
end of lane enter N gates of
Sedgwick Park or W gate via
Broadwater Lane, from Copsale or
Southwater off A24.* **Sun 15 May
(1-5); Wed 18 May (2-6.30). Adm
£5, chd free. Home-made teas.
Visits also by arrangement May to
Sept for tours of house and
gardens.**
Parkland, meadows and woodland.
Formal gardens by Harold Peto
featuring 20 interlinking ponds,
impressive water garden known as
The White Sea. Large Horsham stone
terraces and lawns look out onto
clipped yew hedging and specimen
trees. Well stocked herbaceous
borders, set in the grounds of Grade
II listed Ernest George Mansion. One
of the finest views of South Downs,
Chanctonbury Ring and Lancing
Chapel. Turf labyrinth and organic
vegetable garden with chickens.
Featured in The English Garden
magazine (Nov 2015). Garden has
uneven paving, slippery when wet;
unfenced ponds and swimming
pool.

126 SELHURST PARK

Selhurst Park, Halnaker, Chichester PO18 0LZ. Richard & Sarah Green. *8m S of Petworth. 4m N of Chichester on A285.* **Sun 19 June (2-5). Adm £4, chd free. Home-made teas.**
Large flint walled garden with interesting planting in 160ft south and east facing herbaceous border. Rose, hellebore and hydrangea borders overlooked by a conservatory at one end. Knot and herb garden. Pool border with exotic palms and grasses. Vegetable and cutting garden with rose arches. Fruit garden with fan trained trees. Wheelchair access to walled garden, partial access to other areas.

127 SENNICOTTS

West Broyle, Chichester PO18 9AJ. Mr & Mrs James Rank, www.sennicotts.com. *2m NW of Chichester. White gates diagonally opp & W of the junction between Salthill Rd & the B2178.* **Mon 20, Tue 21, Wed 22 June (9.30-4). Adm £4, chd free. Home-made teas in the walled garden.**
Historic gardens set around a Regency villa (not open) with views across mature Sussex parkland to South Downs. Working walled kitchen and cutting garden. Lots of space for children and a warm welcome for all. For this year restricted access to the main lawn area.

128 SHALFORD HOUSE

Square Drive, Kingsley Green GU27 3LW. Sir Vernon & Lady Ellis. *2m S of Haslemere. Just S of border with Surrey on A286. Square Drive is at brow of hill to the E. Turn L after approx 1/4 m & follow road to R at bottom of hill.* **Sun 10 Apr (2-5); Sun 15 May, Sun 3 July, Sun 4 Sept (2-5.30). Adm £5, chd free. Home-made teas.**
Highly regarded 10 acre garden designed and created from scratch over last 24 yrs. Beautiful hilly setting with streams, ponds, waterfall, sunken garden, good late borders, azaleas and walled kitchen garden. Wild flower meadow with orchids, prairie style plantation and stumpery merging into further 7 acre woodland. Additional 30 acre arboretum with beech, rhododendrons, bluebells, ponds and specimen trees.

D

129 ◆ SHEFFIELD PARK AND GARDEN

Uckfield TN22 3QX. National Trust, 01825 790231, sheffieldpark@nationaltrust.org.uk, www.nationaltrust.org.uk. *10m S of East Grinstead. 5m NW of Uckfield; E of A275.* **For NGS: Wed 8 June (10-5). Adm £9.50, chd £4.75. Light refreshments in Coach House Tearoom. For other opening times and information, please phone, email or visit garden website.**
Magnificent 120 acres (40 hectares) landscaped garden laid out in C18 by Capability Brown and Humphry Repton. Further development in early yrs of this century by its owner Arthur G Soames. Centrepiece is original lakes with many rare trees and shrubs. Beautiful at all times of the yr, but noted for its spring and autumn colours. National Collection of Ghent azaleas. Natural play trail for families on South Park. Large number of Champion Trees, 87 in total. Garden largely accessible for wheelchairs, please call for information.

NPC

This year we are participating in the Snowdrop Festival. Over 500,000 bulbs have been planted in recent years . . .

130 SOUTH GRANGE

Quickbourne Lane, Northiam, Rye TN31 6QY. Linda & Michael Belton, 01797 252984, belton.northiam@virgin.net. *Between A268 & A28, approx 1/2 m E of Northiam. From Northiam centre follow Beales Lane into Quickbourne Lane, or Quickbourne Lane leaves A286 approx 1/2 m S of A28/A286 junction.* **Wed 13 July (2-5); Sat 10, Sun 11 Sept (11-5). Adm £4, chd free. Home-made teas. Sandwiches made to order at Sept openings only. Visits also by arrangement Apr to Oct for groups of 20 max.**
Hardy Plant Society members' garden for all yr interest combining grasses, herbaceous perennials, shrubs, trees, raised beds, wildlife pond, and vegetable plot. Orchard incl meadow flowers, fruit cage with willow windbreak, rose arbour and polytunnel. Woodland is left wild. House roof runoff diverted to pond and bulk storage. We try to maintain varied habitats for most of the creatures that we share the garden with, hoping that this variety will keep the garden in good heart. Home propagated plants for sale.

131 SPARROW HATCH

Tilehouse Lane, Newick BN8 4RD. Tony & Jane Welfare. *5m E of Haywards Heath. From A272 turn R into Oxbottom Lane (signed Barcombe), 1/2 m fork L into Tilehouse Lane, continue to T-junction & park in Cornwells Bank (no parking at house).* **Wed 1, Thur 2 June (2-5). Adm £3, chd free.**
Delightful 1/3 acre plantsman's cottage garden, wholly designed, made and maintained by owners. Many features incl 2 ponds, formal and wildlife, herbaceous borders, shady dell, vegetables, herbs, alpines. Planned for owners' enjoyment and love of growing plants, both usual and unusual. Plants for sale, propagated and grown by garden owner. Cold drinks will be available. Featured in Garden News and Garden Answers magazines. Dogs on leads only.

132 STANE HOUSE

Bignor RH20 1PQ. Mr & Mrs Nicholas Symes, 01798 869454, angie@stanehouse.co.uk, www.stanehouse.co.uk. *Equidistant Arundel, Petworth & Pulborough, each approx 6m. Follow signs for Roman Villa off A29 at Bury or A285 4m S of Petworth. Garden next to Bignor Roman Villa.* **Sat 18, Sun 19 June (11-5). Adm £4.50, chd free. Cream teas.** *Donation to Sussex Air Ambulance.*
Beautiful country location overlooking South Downs with tremendous views. Classic English 1 acre garden with water features, herbaceous borders, kitchen and herb garden, vintage machinery and sculpture. Flowing structure in the romantic style. Garden orientated poetry. The garden has some gentle slopes, gravel and grass paths.

Newtimber Place

© David Gadsby

133 STONE CROSS HOUSE

Alice Bright Lane, Crowborough TN6 3SH. Mr & Mrs D A Tate. *1¹/₂ m S of Crowborough Cross. At Crowborough T-lights (A26) turn S in to High St & shortly R on to Croft Rd. Over 3 mini-r'abouts to Alice Bright Lane. Garden on L at next Xrds.* **Sat 7, Sun 8 May (2-5). Adm £5, chd free. Home-made teas.**
Beautiful 9 acre country property with gardens containing a delightful array of azaleas, acers, rhododendrons and camellias, interplanted with an abundance of spring bulbs. The very pretty cottage garden has interesting examples of topiary and unusual plants. Jacob sheep graze the surrounding pastures. Mainly flat and no steps. Gravel drive.

134 STONEHEALED FARM

Streat Lane, Streat BN6 8SA. Lance & Fiona Smith, 01273 891145, afionasmith@hotmail.com. *2m SE of Burgess Hill. From Ditchling B2116, 1m E of Westmeston, turn L (N) signed Streat, 2m on R immed after railway bridge.* **Visits by arrangement Apr to Oct for groups of 10+. Adm £5, chd free. Home-made teas.** *Donation to St Peter & St James Hospice.*
C17 house (not open) in beautiful rural setting. Sheltered garden rooms link with areas open to views of the South Downs. Paths wind through relaxed informal plantings of trees, shrubs, climbers and unusual perennials, around ponds, through a vegetable garden and extending out into surrounding fields. Wonderful overview from a raised platform in an ancient oak tree. Delicious home-made teas served under cover. Some gravel paths and steps not suitable for wheelchairs.

135 ◆ SUSSEX PRAIRIES

Morlands Farm, Wheatsheaf Road (B2116), Henfield BN5 9AT. Paul & Pauline McBride, 01273 495902, morlandsfarm@btinternet.com, www.sussexprairies.co.uk. *2m NE of Henfield on B2116 Wheatsheaf Rd (also known as Albourne Rd). Follow Brown Tourist signs indicating Sussex Prairie Garden.* **For NGS: Mon 29 Aug (11-5). Adm £7, chd free. Home-made teas. For other opening times and information, please phone, email or visit garden website.**
Exciting prairie garden of approx 8 acres planted in the naturalistic style using 30,000 plants and over 1000 different varieties. A colourful garden featuring a huge variety of unusual ornamental grasses. Expect layers of colour, texture and architectural splendour. Surrounded by mature oak trees with views of Chanctonbury Ring and Devil's Dyke on the South Downs. Permanent sculpture collection and exhibited sculpture throughout the season. Rare breed sheep and pigs. Persicaria feature in The Garden magazine by Paul McBride (Oct 2015) and German magazine Garten Design Exklusiv. Woodchip paths in borders not accessible, but plenty of flat garden for both wheelchairs and mobility scooters. Disabled WC.

136 30 SYCAMORE DRIVE

RH15 0GH. John Smith & Kieran O'Regan, 01444 871888, jsarastroo@aol.com. *8m N of Brighton. Sycamore Drive is off Folders Lane (B2113) in Burgess Hill at Ditchling Common end.* **Evening openings Sat 10, Sun 11 Sept (7-9.30). Adm £5. Wine. Opening with Burgess Hill NGS Gardens on Sun 24, Mon 25 July, Sun 21 Aug. Visits also by arrangement June to Oct for 10 max. Home-made teas.**
See this garden transform at night into a candlelit calm oasis with summerhouse, gravel garden and grasses. Have a glass of wine and canapés as you enjoy this magical space. Adm includes wine & canapés, no concessions. Licenced bar available. Ticket only event, please phone or email for information and booking. Regret no children. Featured in the Saturday Daily Mail, Sussex Living, Amateur Gardener and on ITV Good Morning Britain.

137 TIDEBROOK MANOR
Tidebrook, Wadhurst TN5 6PD.
Edward Flint, Head Gardener.
Between Wadhurst & Mayfield. From Wadhurst take B2100 towards Mark Cross, L at Best Beech PH, downhill 200 metres past church on R, then a drive on L. **Thur 9 June, Thur 15 Sept (10-4). Adm £5, chd free.**
4 acre garden developed over the last decade with outstanding views of the Sussex countryside. In the Arts and Crafts tradition the garden features large mixed borders, intimate courtyards, meadows, hydrangea walk, kitchen garden with raised beds, a willow platt and a wild woodland of particular interest in the spring. A lively and stimulating garden throughout the yr. There will be tours with Edward Flint, Head Gardener at 1pm (£2.50 additional charge), and plants for sale. Refreshments available in nearby Mayfield. No wheelchair access to woodland area.

138 TOWN PLACE
Ketches Lane, Freshfield, Sheffield Park RH17 7NR. Anthony & Maggie McGrath, 01825 790221, mcgrathsussex@hotmail.com, www.townplacegarden.org.uk. *5m E of Haywards Heath. From A275 turn W at Sheffield Green into Ketches Lane for Lindfield. 1³/₄ m on L.* **Sun 12, Thur 16, Sun 26 June, Sun 3 July (2-6). Adm £5, chd free. Cream teas. Visits also by arrangement June & July for groups of 20+.**
A stunning 3 acre garden with a growing international reputation for the quality of its design, planting and gardening. Set round a C17 Sussex farmhouse (not open), the garden has over 600 roses, herbaceous borders, herb garden, topiary inspired by the sculptures of Henry Moore, ornamental grasses, an ancient hollow oak, potager, and a unique 'ruined' Priory Church and Cloisters, in hornbeam. Featured in Sussex Life and Rustica, No 2379 (July 2015).

139 TURNERS HOUSE
Turners Green, Heathfield TN21 9RB. Christopher Miscampbell & Julia Padbury, 01435 831191, chris-joolz@zen.co.uk. *4m E of Heathfield. S off B2096 at Middle Lane, 3 Cups Corner signed Rushlake Green, Hailsham, for ¹/₃ m. Look for big clock face on L. Park on green, not roads.*

Visits by arrangement May to July for individuals and groups with advanced notice. Home-made teas on request. Adm £4, chd free.
²/₃ acre country garden of lush, densely planted, colour themed shrubaceous borders, developed and maintained by owners battling against the combined challenges of exposure and drought. Catenary rose walk leading to summerhouse, displaying photos showing the development of the garden. Scrubbed birch grove, small underplanted orchard. Partial wheelchair access following wet weather. Grass, old brick paths, stepping stones, and some gravel. WC on request (not disabled WC).

140 ◆ UPPARK
South Harting, Petersfield GU31 5QR. National Trust, 01730 825415, uppark@nationaltrust.org.uk, www.nationaltrust.org.uk/uppark. *1¹/₂ m S of South Harting. 5m SE of Petersfield on B2146.* **For NGS: Thur 5 May, Thur 2 June (10-5). Adm £10, chd £5. For other opening times and information, please phone, email or visit garden website.**
A late C18 garden, initially shaped by Lancelot Capability Brown, well maintained garden with fine lawns and a number of specimen trees. Island beds stocked with herbaceous plants and many fragrant shrubs are the key feature of the main garden. Humphry Repton's architectural features of the game larder and dairy create some interesting focal points. The recently restored Gothic seat is a great place to relax and take in the views of the south meadow and South Downs National Park beyond. Refreshments can be enjoyed on the lawn outside the Orangery café. Wheelchair access to the formal garden except in very wet weather.

141 UPWALTHAM BARNS
Upwaltham GU28 0LX. Roger & Sue Kearsey, 01798 343145, suekearsey39@gmail.com. *6m S of Petworth. 6m N of Chichester on A285.* **Sun 29, Mon 30 May (1.30-5). Adm £4.50, chd free. Home-made teas & wine. Visits also by arrangement May to July for groups of 12+.** *Donation to St Mary's Church.*
Unique farm setting transformed into a garden of many rooms. Entrance is

a tapestry of perennial planting to set off C17 flint barns. At the rear is a walled, terraced garden redeveloped and planted with an abundance of unusual plants. Extensive vegetable garden. Beautiful inner courtyard and sitting area. Roam at leisure, relax and enjoy in all seasons. Features incl lovely views of the South Downs and a C12 Shepherds Church (open to visitors). The grounds have some gravel paths.

A rill along the base of a sloping bank of seasonal snowdrops, daffodils and primroses . . .

---

142 VACHERY FOREST GARDEN
Wych Cross TN22 3HR. Conservators of Ashdown Forest, 01342 823583, conservators@ashdownforest.org, www.ashdownforest.org. *²/₃ m W of A22 between Wych Cross & Nutley. Park 1¹/₂ m S of Wych Cross on A22 at Trees Car Park. Access along rides, across heath & down steepish bridleway. Round trip 2¹/₂ m, no facilities.* **Tue 13 Sept (10-4.30). Adm £5, chd free.**
The Vachery Garden, a hidden gem of Ashdown Forest is being part restored. It comprises a string of lakes, sluices and weirs with a Folly Bridge; a gorge of Cheddar Gorge limestone landscaped by Gavin Jones in 1925; and fine stands of rhododendrons and native and introduced trees. Guided tours at 10.30am and 2pm, starting from the Trees Car Park on A22. The circular walk is approx 2 hrs, over steep and rugged terrain and will only take place weather permitting, please phone on the day by 9am for confirmation or check our website. Pre-booking for tours is essential, please phone or email by 9 Sept.

GROUP OPENING

143 WARNINGLID GARDENS
Warninglid, Haywards Heath RH17 5TR. *Midway between Haywards Heath & Horsham, both 6m. From A23 W towards Warninglid for ³/₄ m. S at B2115 Xrds (Cuckfield/Warninglid Lane). From W through Warninglid. Park at recreation ground. Road parking limited for disabled access, drop off for elderly.* **Sun 26 June (2-5). Combined adm £5, chd free. Cream teas in Cricket Pavilion adjoining parking.**

BEECHES
Mr & Mrs C Steel

HAY HOUSE
David Brewerton

1 HERRINGS COTTAGES
Mr A L Brown

OLD BARN COTTAGE
Alison & David Livesley

OLD POST
Mariola & Bob Clark

7 THE STREET
Mrs Angela Buckton

Warninglid is a pretty Medieval village set in a conservation area of outstanding natural beauty. The village architecture provides a perfect back drop to the gardens on view. Several of the gardens are sited in The Street and on Spronketts Lane; part of the old coach and horses smuggling route along the south coast towards Shoreham, through Wineham. The gardens are of remarkable variety and in different ways reflect the distinctive approach of each gardener. Terraces, shrubs and water features are used to enhance the natural landscapes and offer variety and contrast, stimulating thoughts and ideas for you as the visitor. We have many gardening ideas to take away for everyone! Partial wheelchair access.

144 NEW WEAVERS HOUSE
Knowle Lane, Halland, Lewes BN8 6PR. Mrs Miranda Gibb. *3m S of Uckfield. From Uckfield A22, turn R before Halland, 1st house on R. From Lewes go N on A26, through Ringmer Village onto Broyle, continue 3¹/₄ m. Turn L onto Knowle Lane & continue ³/₄ m. House on L.* **Thur 28 Apr (2-5.30). Adm £4, chd free. Home-made teas.**

Sloping south and west facing garden, stocked with fragrant flowers, shrubs and trees. There is an attractive rill along the base of a sloping bank of seasonal snowdrops, daffodils and primroses. From the garden two sets of steep steps take you to the ancient bluebell wood with seasonal ponds and mature broad leaf trees. The woodland is approximately 3¹/₂ acres and is covered in swathes of English bluebells in April and early May. There is a developing bog garden and choice of walks around wood. Wellies recommended.

145 ◆ WEST DEAN GARDENS
West Dean PO18 0QZ. Edward James Foundation, 01243 818221, www.westdean.org.uk. *5m N of Chichester. On A286 midway between Chichester & Midhurst.* **For NGS: Sun 14 Feb (10.30-4). Adm TBC. Light refreshments. For other opening times and information, please phone or visit garden website.**

35 acre historic garden in downland setting. This year we are participating in the Snowdrop Festival. Over 500,000 bulbs have been planted in recent years throughout the gardens; every year the display is more impressive. 300ft Harold Peto pergola, 2¹/₂ acre walled garden with fruit collection, specimen trees, 13 Victorian glasshouses, large working kitchen garden and extensive plant collection. Circuit walk (2¹/₄m) climbs through parkland to 45 acre St Roche's Arboretum. Most areas of the walled garden and grounds are accessible.

146 NEW WESTLANDS COURT
Cowfold Road, West Grinstead, Horsham RH13 8LZ. Mrs Jane Gates. *Off the A272 between Buck Barn Services & Cowfold. From A24 Buck Barn, A272 E towards*

Haywards Heath for 2m, take 3rd L drive after Kennel Lane. Or from M23, A272 W through Cowfold towards Billingshurst for 1¹/₄ m, drive 1st R after Burnthouse Lane. **Sat 20 Feb (11-4); Fri 5 Aug (11-5). Adm £4, chd free. Hot beverages (Feb) & light refreshments (Aug).**

Owned by a garden designer, the garden is 1 acre with 2 acres of meadow with unusual mature trees and a lake. Laid out in organically shaped beds the planting is mainly prairie style with grasses, structural plants, shrubs and herbaceous plants. In early spring masses of snowdrops and hellebores bring welcome interest followed by narcissus Thalia, naturalised narcissus, tulips and alliums.

147 WHITEHANGER
Marley Lane, Haslemere GU27 3PY. David & Lynn Paynter, 01428 653273, l.paynter@btopenworld.com. *3m S of Haslemere. Take the A286 Midhurst road from Haslemere & after approx 2m turn R into Marley Lane (opp Hatch Lane). After 1m turn into drive shared with Rosemary Park Nursing Home.* **Evening openings Thur 4 Aug, Thur 1 Sept (5-8). Adm £6, chd £3. Wine. Visits also by arrangement July to Sept for groups of 10+.**

Set in 6 acres on the edge of the South Downs National Park surrounded by NT woodland, this rural garden was started in 2012 when a new Huf house was built on a derelict site. Now there are lawned areas with beds of perennials, a serenity pool with Koi carp, a wild flower meadow, a Japanese garden, a sculpture garden and a woodland walk.

148 WHITHURST PARK
Plaistow Road, Kirdford, Billingshurst RH14 0JW. Mr Richard Taylor & Mr Rick Englert, www.whithurst.com. *7m NW of Billingshurst. A272 to Wisborough Green, follow signs to Kirdford village, turn R at 1st T-junction through village, then R onto Plaistow Rd, 1m to Whithurst Park sign, then L uphill to garden.* **Sun 31 July (1.30-5.30). Adm £5, chd free. Home-made teas.**

5 yr old walled kitchen garden with many espaliered fruit trees within and without. Herb beds, vegetable beds,

flower borders and cutting beds. Central greenhouse and potting shed with interesting behind the wall support buildings, incl extensive compost area close to beehives and the bee border and bee wildflower meadow. Sustainability through permaculture principles. Ramp up 3 inch step onto garden paths.

&♿ ⊛ ☕

GROUP OPENING

149► WINCHELSEA'S SECRET GARDENS
Winchelsea TN36 4EJ. *2m W of Rye, 8m E of Hastings. Purchase ticket for all gardens at first garden visited; a map will be provided showing gardens & location of teas.* **Sat 23 Apr, Sat 18 June (1-5.30). Combined adm £6, chd free. Home-made teas.**

  ALARDS
  Vicky Jessup.
  Open on all dates

  THE ARMOURY
  Mr & Mrs A Jasper.
  Open on all dates

  BACKFIELDS END
  Sandra & Peter Mackenzie Smith.
  Open on Sat 18 June

  NEW CHESTNUT COTTAGE
  Yvette Allen.
  Open on Sat 18 June

  CLEVELAND HOUSE
  Mr & Mrs J Jempson.
  Open on all dates

  CLEVELAND PLACE
  Sally & Graham Rhodda.
  Open on all dates

  NEW THE ORCHARDS
  Brenda & Ralph Courtenay.
  Open on Sat 18 June

  PERITEAU HOUSE
  Dr & Mrs Lawrence Youlten.
  Open on all dates

  THE WELL HOUSE
  Alice Kenyon.
  Open on all dates

Six spring gardens and nine summer gardens in the beautiful Cinque Port town of Winchelsea. Many styles, large and small, secret walled gardens, spring bulbs, herbaceous borders and more. See the gardens and explore the town with its magnificent church and famous Medieval merchants' cellars. Town

information at winchelsea.com and winchelseachurch.co.uk. Enquiries to david@ryeview.net 01797 226524. If you are bringing a coach, please let us know. Guided tours of cellars both dates at 11am, see winchelseacellars.com, booking essential 01797 222629. Wheelchair access to four April and five June gardens; see map for details.

&♿ ⊛ 🚐 ☕

150► WINDHAVEN
Longlands Road, East Wittering, Chichester PO20 8DD. Mr & Mrs Cedric Marshall, 07971 833218. *Please do not use Satnav! Enter East Wittering village & turn L at the end of Shore Rd (if you don't, you're in the sea), 150yds on L.* **Tue 26 July (1-4). Adm £3, chd free. Visits also by arrangement May to Sept.**
Retired garden designer downsized to 600 metre square garden, 100 metres from the sea, quite a different ball game coping with salt wind without tree protection! Size and layout relevant to most suburban gardens; low maintenance seaside gravel to front, two compartments to rear and a courtyard. On the menu: garden redesign incl mixed salt resistant planting, compatible seasonal and colour groupings, contextual contrast, agapanthus collection and effective use of weed suppressing ground cover.

&♿ 🐕 ⊛

151► 2 WOODSIDE
Lewes Road, Laughton, Lewes BN8 6BL. Dick & Kathy Boland, 01323 811507, kathy.boland01@btinternet.com. *Approx 6m E of Lewes on B2124. In Laughton village 300yds E of Roebuck PH.* **Sat 18 June (11-5). Combined adm with 1 Rose Cottage £5, chd free. Home-made teas at 1 Rose Cottage. Visits also by arrangement June to Aug.**
The garden was designed for summer living by its retired owners. The garden of approx $1/3$ acre comprises a herb garden, a rockery and pond with fish, lawn and herbaceous borders, a small stream and wildlife pond, fruit trees, rose garden and vegetables in raised beds. A shaded area is being developed in a less formal setting among trees, planted with hellebores, pulmonarias and heucheras.

🐕 ⊛ ☕

152► NEW WORTH ABBEY & GROUNDS
Paddockhurst Road, Turners Hill, Crawley RH10 4SB. Worth Abbey, www.worth.org.uk. *On the B2110, Paddockhurst Rd, $1^1/4$ m W of Turners Hill. SE of Crawley, $1^1/4$ m from J10A of the M23, S on the Balcombe Road (B2036). Follow signs for Worth Abbey.* **Thur 14, Sun 17 Apr (2-5). Adm £4.50, chd free. Cream teas.**
Visit the gardens of the iconic Worth Abbey Church, set in 500 acres on a ridge of the High Weald with views towards the South Downs. Pleasant walks around the monastery/school grounds including a bijou Pinetum, the Quiet Garden, pond and wildlife rich woodland. Livery stables and sheep. Tea and cake served in the Cowdray Room, a Victorian room with a frieze depicting the history of travel. Active English Benedictine monastery and Abbey Church. Clock Tower and Model Farm built by Robert Whitehead, inventor of the Torpedo. For wheelchair users, designated route includes access to the Abbey Church and Cowdray Room.

&♿ 🐕 🚐 🛏 ☕

Foxglove Cottage
© Judi Lion

WARWICKSHIRE

(for Birmingham & West Midlands see Staffordshire

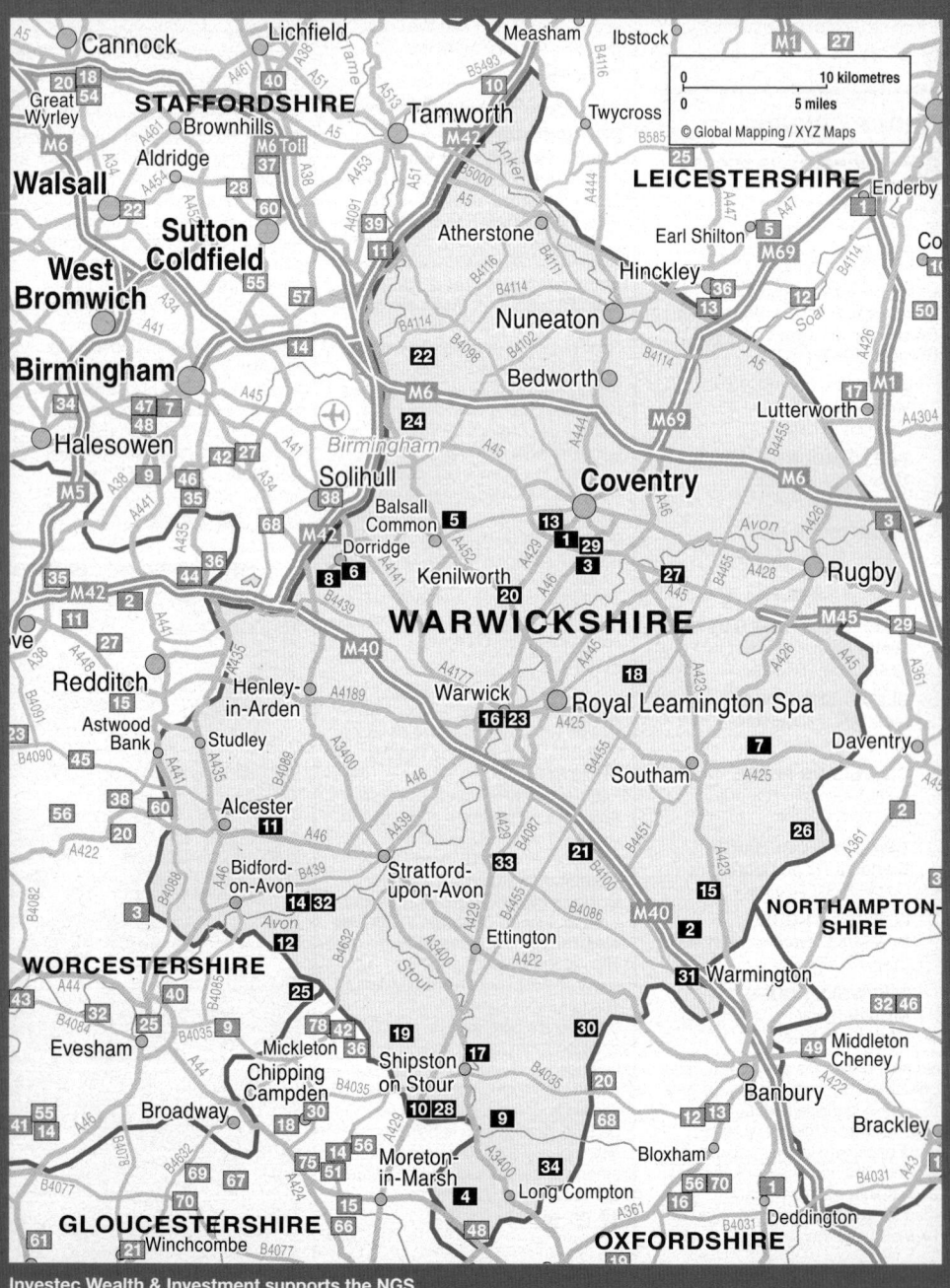

Warwickshire

This county – say it 'Worrick-sher' – is a landlocked county, with a small capital town, a fashionable spa and plenty of quintessentially English villages.

There are also many welcoming Tudor beam and pretty stone 'foodie' pubs, and many varieties of plants and trees, depending on the soil type, all year round. Undulating countryside takes you from the edge of the Cotswolds in the south to the Evesham Vale in the west, up to the hillside of Atherstone in the north and on to Rugby and the farming land of the east. The gardens of Warwickshire are as varied as its landscape; gardens of every shape and size welcome visitors in aid of the National Gardens Scheme.

Today, Warwickshire has a new theme for a new century – Tourism. Inspired by our old poacher William Shakespeare at Stratford-upon-Avon, the Bard's fans flock to Warwickshire from all over the world to delight in theatre, history and castles. But Warwickshire's gardens are also well worth a visit, being wonderfully varied in size and style, and all lovingly-looked after by very generous owners.

So next time you are visiting Warwickshire be sure to bring your Yellow Book with you, and enjoy the wonderful gardens our county has to offer!

Warwickshire Volunteers

County Organiser
Julia Sewell
01295 680234
sewelljulia@btinternet.com

County Treasurer
Eleni Tovey
02476 419049
elenitovey@aol.com

Publicity
Lily Farrah
01789 204858
lily.farrah@ngs.org.uk

Elspeth Napier
01608 666278
elspeth@cherryvilla.demon.co.uk

Peter Pashley
01789 294932
peter@peterpash.mail1.co.uk

Booklet Co-ordinators
Janet Neale
01295 690515
janetneale5@gmail.com

Hugh Thomas
01926 423063
hugh@charityview.co.uk

Assistant County Organisers
Sal Renwick
01564 770215
sal.renwick@blueyonder.co.uk

David Ruffell
01926 316456
de.ruffell@btinternet.com

Left: Maxstoke Castle

Opening Dates

All entries subject to change.
For latest information check www.ngs.org.uk
Extended openings are shown at the begining of the month.

February

Snowdrop Festival

Saturday 20
16 Hill Close Gardens
Sunday 21
14 Elm Close
Sunday 28
10 Court House

April

5 **Bridge Nursery**
(every Thursday to Sunday from Apr 14)
Sunday 10
28 Stretton-on-Fosse Gardens
Sunday 17
8 Broadacre

May

5 **Bridge Nursery (every Thursday to Sunday, plus Bank Hols)**
Monday 2
13 Earlsdon Gardens
Sunday 15
24 Packington Hall
Sunday 29
4 Barton House
15 The Granary
25 Pebworth Gardens
Monday 30
15 The Granary
25 Pebworth Gardens

June

5 **Bridge Nursery (every Thursday to Sunday)**

Festival Weekend

Saturday 4
30 NEW Tysoe Gardens
Sunday 5
11 The Croft House
30 NEW Tysoe Gardens

Saturday 11
18 Hunningham Village Gardens
Sunday 12
12 Dorsington Gardens
18 Hunningham Village Gardens
22 Maxstoke Castle
Sunday 19
17 Honington Village Gardens
20 Kenilworth Gardens
31 Warmington Village Gardens
34 Whichford & Ascott Gardens
Saturday 25
19 Ilmington Gardens
32 Welford-on-Avon & District Gardens
Sunday 26
5 Berkswell Gardens
19 Ilmington Gardens
21 Lighthorne Gardens
29 Styvechale Gardens
32 Welford-on-Avon & District Gardens

July

5 **Bridge Nursery (every Thursday to Sunday)**

Sunday 3
2 Avon Dassett Gardens
33 Wellesbourne Allotments
Saturday 9
27 Ryton Organic Gardens
Sunday 10
27 Ryton Organic Gardens
Sunday 24
3 Avondale Nursery
28 Stretton-on-Fosse Gardens
Sunday 31
6 NEW 75 Blue Lake Road

August

5 **Bridge Nursery (every Thursday to Sunday, plus Bank Hols)**
Sunday 21
3 Avondale Nursery
Sunday 28
15 The Granary
Monday 29
15 The Granary

Knight's Place, Whichford & Ascott Gardens

September

5 **Bridge Nursery (every Thursday to Sunday until Sept 18)**

Saturday 10
27 Ryton Organic Gardens

Sunday 11
9 Burmington Grange

27 Ryton Organic Gardens

Saturday 24
16 Hill Close Gardens

Gardens open to the public

3 Avondale Nursery
7 Bridge Nursery
16 Hill Close Gardens
23 The Mill Garden
27 Ryton Organic Gardens

By arrangement only

26 Priors Marston Manor

Also open by arrangement

1 43 Armorial Road
4 Barton House
8 Broadacre
10 Court House

11 The Croft House
14 Elm Close
15 The Granary
19 Ilmington Manor, Ilmington Gardens
20 Fieldgate, Kenilworth Gardens
29 16 Delaware Road, Styvechale Gardens
29 2 The Hiron, Styvechale Gardens

The Gardens

1 **43 ARMORIAL ROAD**
Coventry CV3 6GH. Gary & Jane Flanagan, 07860 154638, garyflanagan@hotmail.co.uk. Sun 26 June (11-5). Combined adm with Styvechale Gardens £3.50, chd free. Opening with Earlsdon Gardens on Mon 2 May. Visits also by arrangement May to Sept. A mature garden featuring deep, full borders bursting with colour from spring flowering shrubs, herbaceous plants and bulbs. To the rear are hidden spaces for quiet reflection and the smallest allotment space where fruits and vegetables (sometimes) prosper.

GROUP OPENING

2 **AVON DASSETT GARDENS**
Southam CV47 2AE. *7m N of Banbury. From M40 J12 turn L & L again B4100. 2nd L into village. Park in village & at top of hill.* Sun 3 July (2-6). Combined adm £5, chd free. Home-made teas at The Limes.

10 AVON CARROW
Anna Prosser

11 AVON CARROW
Mick & Avis Forbes

THE COACH HOUSE
Diana & Peter Biddlestone

THE EAST WING, AVON CARROW
Christine Fisher & Terry Gladwin

HILL TOP FARM
Mrs N & Mr D Hicks

THE LIMES
John & Diane Anderson

THE OLD NEW HOUSE
Mr & Mrs W Allan

THE OLD RECTORY
Lily Hope-Frost

POPPY COTTAGE
Bob & Audrey Butler

THE THATCHES
Trevor & Michele Gill

Pretty Hornton stone village sheltering in the lee of the Burton Dassett hills, well wooded with parkland setting and The Old Rectory mentioned in Domesday Book. Wide variety of gardens incl kitchen gardens, gravel and tropical gardens. Range of plants incl alpines, herbaceous, perennials, roses, climbers and shrubs. Features incl book sale, plant sales, tombola and two churches open. Wheelchair access to most properties.

Relax in the gardens and enjoy the warm, friendly welcome . . .

3 **◆ AVONDALE NURSERY**
at Russell's Nursery, Mill Hill, Baginton CV8 3AG. Mr Brian Ellis, 02476 673662, enquiries@avondale nursery.co.uk, www.avondalenursery.co.uk. *3m S Coventry. At junction of A45 & A46 take slip road to Baginton, 1st L to Mill Hill, opp Old Mill Inn.* For NGS: Sun 24 July, Sun 21 Aug (11-4). Adm £3, chd free. Light refreshments in Potting Shed Cafe at Russell's Nursery. For other opening times and information, please phone, email or visit garden website.

Vast array of flowers and ornamental grasses, incl National Collections of *Anemone nemorosa*, *Sanguisorba* and *Aster novae-angliae*. Choc-a-bloc with plants, our Library Garden is a well labelled reference book illustrating the unusual, exciting and even some long-lost treasures. Adjacent nursery is a plantaholic's delight! Big collections of *Helenium*, *Crocosmia*, *Sanguisorba* and ornamental grasses, and the garden will be looking at its best in July and August! Featured on Gardener's World, and in the House & Garden, The English Garden, and RHS Garden magazines.

NPC

4 **BARTON HOUSE**
Barton-on-the-Heath GL56 0PJ. Mr & Mrs I H B Cathie, 01608 674303, hamish.cathie@thebartonfarms. com. *2m W of Long Compton. 2m W off A3400 Stratford-upon-Avon to Oxford road; 1¼ m N off A44 Chipping Norton to Moreton-in-Marsh road.* Sun 29 May (2-6). Adm £5, chd free. Home-made teas. Visits also by arrangement spring to autumn.
6½ acres with mature trees, azaleas, species and hybrid rhododendrons, magnolias, moutan tree peonies. National collections of *Arbutus* and *Catalpa*. Japanese garden, rose garden, secret garden and many rare and exotic plants. Victorian kitchen garden. Exotic garden with palms, cypresses and olive trees established 2002. Vineyard planted in 2000, free wine tasting. Manor house by Inigo Jones (not open). Some gravel paths and steps. Can be slippery but generally wheelchair friendly. Dogs strictly on leads only.

NPC

GROUP OPENING

5 ▶ BERKSWELL GARDENS
Berkswell, Coventry CV7 7BB.
*7m W of Coventry. A452 to Balsall
Common & follow signs to Berkswell.
Tickets & maps available at the village
Reading Room (CV7 7BB) & also at
each garden. Car necessary to visit
all gardens.* Sun 26 June
(11-6). Combined adm £5, chd
free. Light refreshments at Yew
Tree Barn, Eardley Cottage & 248
Station Road.

BROOKSIDE HOUSE
Truggist Lane, CV7 7BX.
Shirley & Frank Rounthwaite

145 DUGGINS LANE
CV4 9GP. Mary & Edward
Cotterrell

EARDLEY COTTAGE
Meriden Road, CV7 7BG.
June & Bob Smitten

FAIRWAYS
Waste Lane, CV7 7GG. Tom
Bunt & Janet Lloyd-Bunt

FIRS FARM
Windmill Lane, CV7 7GY.
Mr & Mrs C Ellis

NEW ▶ HOLLY LODGE
Spencers Lane, CV7 7BZ.
Anne & Alastair Dymond

HOLLY OAK
Shirley Lane, Meriden, CV7
7LE. Jane Bostock

THE PINES
Hodgetts Lane, CV7 7DG.
Mr & Mrs C Davis

SQUIRRELS JUMP
Waste Lane, CV7 7GG.
Brian & Jenny Harris

NEW ▶ 248 STATION ROAD
CV7 7EE. Caroline & Paul
Joyner

YEW TREE BARN
Baulk Lane, CV7 7BD. Angela &
Ken Shaw

Berkswell is a beautiful village dating
back to Saxon times with a C12
Norman church and has several C16
and C17 buildings incl the village PH
and Museum. In 2014 and 2015 the
village was awarded Gold in the RHS
Britain in Bloom campaign, plus a
special RHS award in 2014 for the
Best Large Village in the Heart of
England. The gardens provide great
variety with fine examples of small
and large, formal and informal, wild,
imaginatively planted herbaceous
borders and productive vegetable
gardens. Something for everyone and
plenty of ideas to take home. Plants
for sale at some gardens. Also open
to visitors is the C12 Norman church
with a garden, and the village
Museum. Wheelchair access to some
gardens.

🏵 ❀ ☕

**6 NEW ▶ 75 BLUE LAKE
ROAD**
Dorridge, Solihull B93 8BH. Sal &
Peter Renwick. *S side of Dorridge,
nr the station. Close to the junction of
Darley Green Rd & Norton Green
Lane.* Sun 31 July (11.30-5.30).
Adm £3.50, chd free. Home-made
teas.
A lovely ¹⁄₂ acre garden. Redesigned
12 yrs ago and laid out with lawns,
hedges, topiary and deep
herbaceous borders, bursting with
perennials. Some areas are left more
natural to encourage wildlife. Paths
lead to secret corners and sitting
areas, including a gazebo by a large
pond, a wonderful spot to sit quietly
and look out for newts, butterflies,
dragonflies and the occasional toad!
Wheelchair access through side gate
onto main patio area, but possibly
difficult through the rest of the
garden, due to narrow paths and
slightly sloping site.

❀ ☕

7 ◆ BRIDGE NURSERY
Tomlow Road, Napton, Southam
CV47 8HX. Christine Dakin &
Philip Martino, 01926 812737,
www.bridge-nursery.co.uk.
*3m E of Southam. Brown tourist
sign at Napton Xrds on A425
Southam to Daventry road.* For NGS:
Every Thur to Sun 14 Apr to 18
Sept (10-4). Adm £2.50, chd free.
Mon 2, Mon 30 May, Mon 29 Aug
(10-4). Adm £2.50. Tea. For other
opening times and information,
please phone or visit garden
website.
Clay soil? Don't despair. Here is a
garden full of an exciting range of
plants which thrive in hostile
conditions. Grass paths lead you
round borders filled with many
unusual plants. Features incl a pond
and a bamboo grove complete with
panda! A peaceful haven for wildlife
and visitors.

♿ 🏵 ❀ 🚐 ☕

8 ▶ BROADACRE
Grange Road, Dorridge, Solihull
B93 8QA. John Woolman, 07818
082885, jw234567@gmail.com,
www.broadacregarden.org. *Approx
3m SE of Solihull. On B4101 opp
Railway PH. Plenty of parking
available.* Sun 17 Apr (2-6). Adm £5,
chd free. Home-made teas. Visits
also by arrangement for most
group sizes.
Broadacre is a semi-wild garden
attractively landscaped with pools,
lawns and trees, and with adjoining
stream and wild flower meadows.
There are 5 beehives and it is
managed organically. Bring stout
footwear to follow the nature trail.
Dorridge Cricket Club is on-site.
Lovely venue for a picnic. Dogs and
children are welcome.

♿ 🏵 ❀ 🚐 ☕

BROUGHTON GRANGE
See Oxfordshire

9 ▶ BURMINGTON GRANGE
Cherington, Shipston on Stour
CV36 5HZ. Mr & Mrs Patrick
Ramsay. *2m E of Shipston-on-Stour.
Take Oxford Rd (A3400) from
Shipston-on-Stour, after 2m turn L to
Burmington, go through village &
continue for 1m, turn L to Willington &
Barcheston, on sharp L bend turn R
over cattle grid.* Sun 11 Sept (2-6).
Adm £5, chd free. Home-made
teas.
Interesting plantsman's garden
extending to about 1¹⁄₂ acres, set in
the rolling hills of the North Cotswolds
with wonderful views over unspoilt
countryside. The garden is well
developed considering it was planted
13 yrs ago. Small vegetable garden,
beautiful sunken rose garden with
herbaceous and shrub borders.
Orchard and tree walk with unusual
trees.

10 ▸ COURT HOUSE
GL56 9SD. **Christopher White,
01608 663811, mum@star.co.uk.**
*Off A429 between Moreton-in-Marsh
& Shipston-on-Stour.* **Sun 28 Feb
(11-3). Adm £5, chd free. Opening
with Stretton-on-Fosse Gardens
on Sun 10 Apr, Sun 24 July.
Visits also by arrangement Feb to
Sept.**
4 acre garden with yr-round interest
and colour. Extensive and varied
spring bulbs, and garden of winter
interest. Herbaceous borders, spring
beds, fernery, recently redesigned
and restored walled kitchen garden.
Rose garden, pond area and
paddocks established with wild
flowers. Featured in Cotswold Life.
Wheelchair access is not impossible
but difficult with a gravel drive.

Organically
grown walled
garden with
a living
shed roof . . .

11 ▸ THE CROFT HOUSE
Haselor, Alcester B49 6LU.
**Isobel & Patrick Somers, 01789
488881, ifas1010@aol.com.** *6m W
of Stratford-upon-Avon, 2m E of
Alcester, off A46. From A46 take
Haselor turn. From Alcester take old
Stratford Rd, turn L signed Haselor,
then R at Xrds. Garden in centre of
village. Please park considerately.*
**Sun 5 June (12-5). Adm £3, chd
free. Tea. Visits also by
arrangement May & June for
individuals or groups of 35 max.**
Wander through an acre of trees,
shrubs and herbaceous borders
densely planted with a designer's
passion for colour and texture.
Hidden areas invite you to linger.
Gorgeous scented wisteria on two
sides of the house. Organically
managed, providing a haven for birds
and other wildlife. Frog pond,
treehouse, small vegetable plot and a
few venerable old fruit trees from its
days as a market garden. Art and
Crafts Exhibition in the garden studio,
donating to NGS. Featured on BBC
Coventry and Warwickshire Radio.
Garden is on a gentle slope. Step free
access available but too narrow for
most wheelchairs.

6 DINGLE END
See Worcestershire

GROUP OPENING

12 ▸ DORSINGTON GARDENS
Dorsington CV37 8AR. *6m SW of
Stratford-upon-Avon. On B439 from
Stratford turn L to Welford-on-Avon,
then R to Dorsington. Disabled
parking available, please follow
signs.* **Sun 12 June (1-5).
Combined adm £5, chd free.
Home-made teas in the village
(signed on the day).**

THE BARN
Mr & Mrs P Reeve

CEDAR BARN
Pat & Derek Hudson

**CRABTREE FARM
COTTAGE**
Mr & Mrs David Boulton

CRABTREE FARM HOUSE
Nigel & Jane Davies

2 DORSINGTON MANOR
Mr & Mrs C James

**NEW ▸ 10 DORSINGTON
MANOR**
Mr & Mrs Mansford

**THE GARDEN OF HEROES
AND VILLAINS**
The Heart of England Forest

1 GLEBE COTTAGES
Mr & Mrs A Brough

THE OLD RECTORY
Mr & Mrs Nigel Phillips

2016 will mark the 40th anniversary
of gardens being opened for charity in
Dorsington, come and enjoy our
celebrations! Dorsington is a tranquil
hamlet mentioned in the Domesday
book with a conservation area at the
heart of the village. You can visit a
varied selection of country gardens,
ranging from small cottage gardens
to extensive mature gardens with
abundant herbaceous borders,
alongside fruit and vegetables.
Splendid teas served in the marquee.
Additional village gardens will open on
the day.

GROUP OPENING

13 ▸ EARLSDON GARDENS
Coventry CV5 6FS. *Turn towards
Coventry at A45 & A429 T-lights.
Take 3rd L into Beechwood Ave,
continue ¹/₂ m to St Barbara's Church
at Xrds with Rochester Rd. Maps &
tickets at St Barbara's Church Hall.*
**Mon 2 May (11-4). Combined adm
£3.50, chd free. Light
refreshments at St Barbara's
Church Hall.**

43 ARMORIAL ROAD
Gary & Jane Flanagan
(See separate entry)

3 BATES ROAD
Victor Keene MBE

40 HARTINGTON CRESCENT
Viv & George Buss

**114 HARTINGTON
CRESCENT**
Liz Campbell & Denis Crowley

NEW 40 RANULF CROFT
Mr & Mrs Spencer & Sue Swain

54 SALISBURY AVENUE
Pam Moffit

2 SHAFTESBURY ROAD
Ann Thomson & Bruce Walker

23 SPENCER AVENUE
Susan & Keith Darwood

Varied selection of town gardens from
small to more formal with interest for
all tastes incl a mature garden with
deep borders bursting with spring
colour, a large garden with extensive
lawns and an array of
rhododendrons, azaleas and large
mature trees; densely planted town
garden with sheltered patio area and
wilder woodland and surprisingly
large garden offering interest to all
ages! There is also a pretty garden
set on several levels with hidden
aspects, large peaceful garden with
water features and vegetable plot and
a large mature garden in peaceful
surroundings. Plantaholic's garden
with a large variety of plants, clematis
and small trees.

14 ELM CLOSE

Welford on Avon CV37 8PT. Eric & Glenis Dyer, 01789 750793, glenisdyer@gmail.com. *5m SW of Stratford, off B4390. Elm Close is between Welford Garage & The Bell Inn.* **Sun 21 Feb (11-4). Adm £3, chd free. Home-made teas. Opening with Welford-on-Avon & District Gardens on Sat 25, Sun 26 June. Visits also by arrangement Feb to Sept for groups of 10-50. Adm £3 per head or min £30. Refreshments by prior request.** Drifts of snowdrops, aconites, erythroniums and hellebores in spring are followed by species peonies, sumptuous tree peonies, herbaceous peonies and delphiniums. Colourful Japanese maples, daphnes and cornus are underplanted with hostas, heucheras, and brunneras. Then agapanthus, salvias and hydrangeas extend the seasons, with hundreds of clematis providing yr-round colour. Gravel front drive slightly sloping. Garden mainly flat.

Art and Crafts Exhibition in the garden studio . . .

15 THE GRANARY

Fenny Compton Wharf, Fenny Compton, Southam CV47 2FE. Lucy & Mike Davies, 01295 770033, bookings@the-granary.co.uk, www.the-granary.co.uk. *7m S of Southam. On A423 Southam to Banbury road. 200yds S of turning to Fenny Compton, turn R into service road signed Fenny Compton Wharf. Follow NGS signs.* **Sun 29, Mon 30 May, Sun 28, Mon 29 Aug (11-4.30). Adm £4, chd free. Light lunches & home-made teas. Visits also by arrangement May to Sept for groups of 10-30.** Attractive 1 acre canal-side garden with views of the Oxford canal and Dassett Hills. Recent additions incl herbaceous beds, water feature, a cutting garden and herb garden. Beyond is a kitchen plot comprising a vegetable area (grown on organic principles), a polytunnel for propagation and salad crops, fruit cage and orchard. There is also a copse of native British trees in the 3 acre paddock. Refreshments incl teas with home-made cakes, light lunches, quiches and produce from the garden. Gravel paths with steps down to the herb garden and up to the vegetable area.

16 ◆ HILL CLOSE GARDENS

Bread and Meat Close, Warwick CV34 6HF. Hill Close Gardens Trust, 01926 493339, centremanager@hcgt.org.uk, www.hillclosegardens.com. *Town centre. Entry from Friars St on Bread & Meat Close. Car park by entrance next to racecourse. 2hrs free parking. Disabled parking outside the gates.* **For NGS: Sat 20 Feb (11-4); Sat 24 Sept (11-5). Adm £4, chd £1. Light refreshments in Visitor Centre. For other opening times and information, please phone, email or visit garden website.** Restored Grade II* Victorian leisure gardens comprising 16 individual hedged gardens, 8 brick summerhouses. Herbaceous borders, heritage apple and pear trees, C19 daffodils, over 100 varieties of snowdrops, many varieties of asters and chrysanthemums. Heritage vegetables. Plant Heritage border, auricula theatre, and Victorian style glasshouse. Children's garden. Wheelchair available which can be booked in advance by phone. Access route indicated on plan of the gardens.

GROUP OPENING

17 HONINGTON VILLAGE GARDENS

Shipston-on-Stour CV36 5AA. *1½ m N of Shipston-on-Stour. Take A3400 towards Stratford-upon-Avon then turn R signed Honington.* **Sun 19 June (2-6). Combined adm £5, chd free. Home-made teas.**

HONINGTON GLEBE
Mr & Mrs J C Orchard

HONINGTON HALL
B H E Wiggin

MALT HOUSE RISE
Mr & Mrs M Underhill

NEW▶ THE MALTHOUSE
Mr & Mrs R Hunt

THE OLD COTTAGE
Liz Davenport

THE OLD HOUSE
Mr & Mrs I F Beaumont

ORCHARD HOUSE
Mr & Mrs Monnington

SHOEMAKERS COTTAGE
Christopher & Anne Jordan

C17 village, recorded in Domesday, entered by old toll gate. Ornamental stone bridge over the R Stour and interesting church with C13 tower and late C17 nave after Wren. Eight super gardens. 2 acre plantsman's garden consisting of rooms planted informally with yr-round interest in contrasting foliage, texture, lily pool and parterre. Extensive lawns and fine mature trees with river and garden monuments. Small garden that is well stocked with interesting established shrubs and container plants, and a structured cottage garden formally laid out with box hedging and small fountain. Small, developing garden created by the owners with informal mixed beds and borders. Wheelchair access to most gardens.

GROUP OPENING

18 HUNNINGHAM VILLAGE GARDENS

Hunningham, Leamington Spa CV33 9DS. *6m NE of Leamington Spa, 8m SW of Rugby, 7m S of Coventry. Just off the Fosseway (B4455), or take B4453 from Leamington through Weston-under-Wetherley, then turn R to Hunningham, signed car park in village.* **Sat 11, Sun 12 June (12.30-5.30). Combined adm £4.50, chd free. Home-made teas.**

BIRKDALE COTTAGE
Dean & Rose Woodford

THE DORMERS
Irene & Oliver Ryan

GLENCOVE
Mr & Mrs S Shackleton

NEW▶ HALL FARM
Crick & Maggie Ellis

THE MOTTE
Margaret & Peter Green

THE OLD HALL
Nicholas & Rona Horler

NEW▶ SANDY ACRE
David & Janis Tait

Fieldgate, Kenilworth Gardens

Hunningham, a hamlet nestling in the countryside close to the R Leam with St Margaret's church dating in part to the C13. Seven gardens in varied styles with more open on the day. Two plant lover's gardens brimming with woodland plants, tender perennials, unusual shrubs and trees and with plant filled conservatories. Redesigned garden with herbaceous borders, wildlife friendly pond and hard landscaping. Newly formed garden with pleached Hornbeam avenue, parterre with feature sculpture, panoramic views, wooded areas, cut flower garden and new Holm Oak circle. Large partly walled garden with mature shrubs and trees surrounding the Old Hall. Walled farmhouse cottage garden, with herbaceous borders and newly planted orchard. Hedged cottage garden with herbaceous perennials, fruit and vegetable areas and chickens. Views across the R Leam from some of the gardens. Good plant sale and tea, coffee and home-made cakes in the Parish Room from 1.30pm. Visit Hill Top Farm Shop and café or the Red Lion PH. One garden without wheelchair access.

GROUP OPENING

19 ILMINGTON GARDENS
Ilmington CV36 4LA, 01608 682230. *8m S of Stratford-upon-Avon. 8m N of Moreton in Marsh. 4m NW of Shipston-on-Stour off A3400. 3m NE of Chipping Campden.* **Sat 25, Sun 26 June (2-6). Combined adm £6, chd free. Cream teas at Ilmington Village Hall.** *Donation to Shipston Home Nursing.*

CHERRY ORCHARD
Mr Angus Chambers

COMPTON SCORPION FARM
Mrs Karlsen

CRAB MILL
Mr & Mrs D Brown

THE DOWER HOUSE
Mr & Mrs M Tremellen

FROG ORCHARD
Mr & Mrs Jeremy Snowden

GRUMP COTTAGE
Mr & Mrs Martin Underwood

ILMINGTON MANOR
Mr Martin Taylor
Visits also by arrangement.
mtilmington@btinternet.com
01608 682230

PARK FARM HOUSE
Mike & Lesley Lane

NEW PUDDOCKS
Bill Buckley

RAVENSCROFT
Mr & Mrs Clasper

Ilmington is an ancient hillside Cotswold village 2m from the Fosse Way with two good PHs and splendid teas at the village hall. Buy your ticket at Ilmington Manor (next to the Red Lion PH); wander the 3 acre gardens with fish pond. Then walk to the upper green behind the village hall to tiny Grump Cottage's small stone terraced suntrap. Up Grump Street to Crab Mill's hillside gardens, then up to Ravenscroft's large sculpture filled sloping vistas commanding the hilltop. Walk to nearby Frog Lane, view cottage gardens at Park Farm House, Cherry Orchard, Frog Orchard and Puddocks. Cross the village to The Dower House, a delightful garden overlooking the Manor ponds and the Norman church. Drive 2m to isolated bliss at beautiful Compton Scorpion Farm. Ilmington Morris Men performing round the village on Sunday only.

GROUP OPENING

20 KENILWORTH GARDENS
Kenilworth CV8 1BT. *Fieldgate Lane off A452. Tickets & maps available at all gardens. Parking available at Abbey Fields. Street parking at Fieldgate Lane (limited), Malthouse Lane, Beehive Hill & Forest Road.* **Sun 19 June (1-5). Combined adm £5, chd free. Home-made teas at St Nicholas Parochial Hall.**

> **BEEHIVE HILL ALLOTMENTS**
> Mr Keith Rocket
>
> **FIELDGATE**
> Liz & Bob Watson
> Visits also by arrangement Apr to Sept for groups of 5-25.
> bob.watson@lineone.net
> 01926 512307
>
> **7 FIELDGATE LAWN**
> Mr Simon Cockell
>
> **25 MALTHOUSE LANE**
> David & Linda Pettifor
>
> **NEW PRIORSFIELD**
> Mr Phil Pegler
>
> **ST NICHOLAS PAROCHIAL HALL**
> St Nicholas Church
>
> **NEW SOUTH BRENT**
> Mrs Vera Ainsworth

Kenilworth was historically a very important town in Warwickshire, which now has one of England's best castle ruins and plenty of PHs and good restaurants. This year we welcome two new gardens, Priorsfield and South Brent to the group. This makes seven in all, providing great variety; the group includes small and large gardens, formal and informal, and floral and vegetable gardening. Many of the gardens have won Gold in the Kenilworth in Bloom garden competition.

GROUP OPENING

21 LIGHTHORNE GARDENS
Lighthorne, Warwick CV35 0AR. *10m S of Warwick. Lighthorne will be signed from the Fosse Way & B4100.* **Sun 26 June (2-5.30). Combined adm £6, chd free. Home-made teas at the village hall.**

> **1 CHURCH HILL COURT**
> Irene Proudman

> **4 CHURCH HILL COURT**
> Carol Schofield
>
> **THE OLD RECTORY**
> The Hon Lady Butler
>
> **THE PADDOCK**
> Martin & Lesley Thornton
>
> **ROSEMARY COTTAGE**
> Jane & Edward Stroud
>
> **SMITHY COTTAGE**
> Paul & Josette Tait
>
> **TAWTON**
> David Copson & Maureen Thomson

Lighthorne is a compact, pretty village between the Fosse Way and the B4100, with a charming church (open), PH and village hall. The seven gardens opening are within easy reach on foot. At The Old Rectory the garden is sheltered by old stone walls clothed with roses and dominated by two magnificent copper beeches. Some gardens are very small, particularly the tiny one beside the village green 12ft x 6ft, but all are interesting and different. Partial wheelchair access.

THE MANOR
See Gloucestershire

Currently the NGS donates around £2.5 million every year . . .

22 MAXSTOKE CASTLE
Coleshill B46 2RD. Mr & Mrs M C Fetherston-Dilke. *2½ m E of Coleshill. E of Birmingham, on B4114. Take R turn down Castle Lane, Castle Drive 1¼ m on R.* **Sun 12 June (11-5). Adm £7.50. Home-made teas.** Approx 5 acres of garden and grounds with herbaceous, shrubs and trees in the immediate surroundings of this C14 moated castle. No wheelchair access to house.

74 MEADOW ROAD
See Worcestershire

23 ◆ THE MILL GARDEN
55 Mill Street, Warwick CV34 4HB. Julia (née Measures) Russell & David Russell. *Off A425 beside old castle gate, at the bottom of Mill St. Use St Nicholas car park.* This garden lies in a magical setting on the banks of the R Avon beneath the walls of Warwick Castle. Winding paths lead round every corner to dramatic views of the castle and ruined Medieval bridge. This informal cottage garden is a profusion of plants, shrubs and trees. Beautiful all year. **Open daily from 1st Apr to 31st Oct (9-6). Partial wheelchair access. Unsuitable for electric wheelchairs.**
❀

MORTON HALL
See Worcestershire

24 PACKINGTON HALL
Meriden, nr Coventry CV7 7HF. Lord & Lady Aylesford. *Midway between Coventry & Birmingham on A45. Entrance 400yds from Stonebridge island towards Coventry. For SatNav please use CV7 7HE.* **Sun 15 May (2-5). Adm £5, chd free. Home-made teas in the Pompeiian Room.** Packington is the setting for an elegant Capability Brown landscape. Designed from 1750 in 100 acres of parkland which sweeps down to a lake incl 1762 Japanese bridge. Delicious WI teas on the terrace. Wheelchair access to gardens, but all areas are grass, so difficult in wet conditions.

GROUP OPENING

25 PEBWORTH GARDENS
Stratford-upon-Avon CV37 8XZ. *9m SW of Stratford-upon-Avon. On B439 at Bidford turn S towards Honeybourne, after 3m turn L at Xrds signed Pebworth.* **Sun 29, Mon 30 May (2-6). Combined adm £6, chd free. Home-made teas at Pebworth Village Hall.**

> **1 ELM CLOSE**
> Mr & Mrs G Keyte
>
> **FELLY LODGE**
> Maz & Barrie Clatworthy
>
> **IVYBANK** NPC
> Mr & Mrs R Davis
>
> **JASMINE COTTAGE**
> Ted & Veronica Watson

THE KNOLL
Mr & Mrs K Wood

NEW ▶ **MAPLE BARN**
Mr & Mrs Richard & Wendi Weller

NEW ▶ **MEON COTTAGE**
David & Sally Donnison

THE MOUNT
Mr & Mrs J Ilott

ORCHARD HOUSE
David & Susan Lees

PRIMROSE HILL
Richard & Margaret Holland

NEW ▶ **4 WESLEY GARDENS**
Anne & Mike Johnson

Pebworth received a Gold award in 2015 RHS Britain in Bloom Heart of England campaign. The gardens in Pebworth are topped by St. Peter's church (open) that came 4th in 2015 Worcestershire Best Kept Churchyard and has large ring of ten bells, which is unusual for a small rural church. This is a delightful village with old thatched cottages, and properties of various ages. There are a variety of garden styles to be seen from cottage gardens to modern, walled and terraced gardens. This year we have 11 gardens opening and yummy tea and cakes at the village hall. No wheelchair access to The Knoll, Maple Barn, 4 Wesley Gardens, The Mount, Meon Cottage & Jasmine Cottage.

---

26 ▶ **PRIORS MARSTON MANOR**
The Green, Priors Marston CV47 7RH. Dr & Mrs Mark Cecil, 07477 600887, damianholst@icloud.com. *8m SW of Daventry. Off A361 between Daventry & Banbury at Charwelton. Follow sign to Priors Marston approx 2m. Arrive at T-junction with war memorial on R. Manor on L.* **Visits by arrangement Apr to Oct, weekdays only. Adm £4.50, chd free. Home-made teas.**
Arrive through the woodland rotunda garden and explore the manor gardens. Greatly enhanced by present owners to relate back to a Georgian manor garden and pleasure grounds. Wonderful walled kitchen garden provides seasonal produce and cut flowers for the house. Herbaceous flower beds and a sunken terrace with water feature by William Pye. Lawns lead down to the lake around which you can walk

amongst the trees and wildlife with stunning views up to the house and garden aviary. Sculptures. Partial wheelchair access.

PUMP COTTAGE
See Worcestershire

27 ▶ ◆ **RYTON ORGANIC GARDENS**
Wolston Lane, Ryton on Dunsmore, Coventry CV8 3LG. Garden Organic, 02476 303517, enquiries@gardenorganic.org.uk, www.gardenorganic.org.uk/ryton. *5m SE of Coventry. From A45 take N exit signed Wolston with brown tourist signs for Ryton Gardens.* **For NGS: Sat 9, Sun 10 July, Sat 10, Sun 11 Sept (10-4). Adm £5.50, chd £3.50 (5-16yrs). Vegetarian, vegan & exciting street food. For other opening times and information, please phone, email or visit garden website.**
The UK's national centre for organic gardening offers visitors acres of beautiful organic demonstration gardens from modest to expansive, showcasing a range of organic best practice. The Organic Way is an introduction to the history and practice of organic growing, leading to a series of demonstration areas highlighting soil management, composting and natural feeds. Guided tours each Saturday at 11am and 2pm in the summer months from our experienced volunteer organic growers highlighting the seasonal aspects of the organic gardens.

Please phone for a detailed wheelchair access report.

GROUP OPENING

28 ▶ **STRETTON-ON-FOSSE GARDENS**
Stretton on Fosse, Moreton-in-Marsh GL56 9SD. *Off A429 between Moreton-in-Marsh & Shipston-on-Stour. Two gardens in the centre of the village. Court House is next to the church, Old Beams a few doors away.* **Sun 10 Apr, Sun 24 July (2-6). Combined adm £6, chd free. Home-made teas at Court House.**

    COURT HOUSE
    Christopher White
    (See separate entry)

    OLD BEAMS
    Mrs Hilary Fossey

Court House is a continually evolving, 4 acre garden with yr-round interest and colour. Extensive and varied spring bulbs. Herbaceous borders, fernery, recently redesigned and restored walled kitchen garden. Rose garden, newly planted winter garden, pond area and paddocks which are gradually being established with wild flowers. Old Beams is a walled cottage garden on a slope with traditional cottage garden plants, small lawn, rockery, fruit cage and vegetable garden.

Illmington Manor, Illmington Gardens
© James Kerr

GROUP OPENING

29 STYVECHALE GARDENS
Baginton Road, Coventry CV3 6FP.
The gardens are located on the S-side of Coventry close to A45. Tickets & map available on the day from West Orchard United Reformed Church, The Chesils, CV3 6FP. Advance tickets available from suepountney@btinternet.com. **Sun 26 June (11-5). Combined adm with 43 Armorial Road £3.50, chd free. Home-made teas.** *Donation to Warwickshire & Northamptonshire Air Ambulance Service.*

NEW 11 BAGINTON ROAD
Ken & Pauline Bond

164 BAGINTON ROAD
Fran & Jeff Gaught

166 BAGINTON ROAD
Wilf & Ann Hawes

59 THE CHESILS
John Marron & Richard Bantock

16 DELAWARE ROAD
Val & Roy Howells
Visits also by arrangement June to Sept with other Styvechale gardens.
valshouse@hotmail.co.uk
02476 419485

2 THE HIRON
Sue & Graham Pountney
Visits also by arrangement May to Sept with other Styvechale gardens.
suepountney@btinternet.com
02476 502044

NEW 177 LEAMINGTON ROAD
Barry & Ann Suddens

8 THE SPINNEY
Professor Michael & Eleni Tovey

A collection of lovely, mature, suburban gardens, each one different in style and size. Come and enjoy the imaginatively planted herbaceous borders, spectacular roses, water features, fruit and vegetable patches, cottage garden planting and shady areas, something for everyone and plenty of ideas for you to take home. Relax in the gardens and enjoy the warm, friendly welcome you will receive from us all. There will be refreshments available and plants for sale in some of the gardens. Other gardens will be open on the day. A vehicle will be required to visit 8 The Spinney, but a garden well worth the trip; an easy 10 min drive from the ticket office.

GROUP OPENING

30 NEW TYSOE GARDENS
Middle and Upper Tysoe, Warwick CV35 0SE. *W of A422, N of Banbury (9m). E of A3400 & Shipston-on-Stour (4m). N of A4035 & Brailes (3m). Parking on the recreation ground. Entrance tickets & maps to gardens at the village hall.* **Sat 4, Sun 5 June (2-6). Combined adm £5, chd free. Home-made teas in Tysoe Village Hall & cold drinks at Garden Cottage.**

NEW CHURCH FARM HOUSE
Sylvia & Charles Davies

NEW DINSDALE HOUSE
Julia & David Sewell

NEW GARDEN COTTAGE
Sue & Mike Sanderson

NEW IVYDALE
Sam & Malcolm Littlewood

NEW 7 JEFFS CLOSE
Emma & Tom Moffatt

NEW KERNEL COTTAGE
Christine Duke

NEW LAUREL HOUSE
Damaris & Michael Appleton

NEW THE OLD BUTCHER'S HOUSE
Sue & Gerald Hart

NEW THE OLD POLICE HOUSE
Bridget & Digby Norton

NEW SMARTSWELL COTTAGE
Jan & Colin Lumley

Tysoe, set in the foothills at the north-eastern edge of the Cotswolds is an ancient Hornton stone village with C11 church. There are ten gardens opening around the centre of the village, all in easy and flat walking distance of each other and of the home-made teas in the village hall. An organically grown walled garden with a living shed roof, one courtyard garden, two cottage gardens, two gardens with surprising plants, one garden with a goldfish pond, another garden with unusual variegated leaf plants and the Old Policeman's garden as well as the Old Butcher's garden. You can walk up the nearby hill to Tysoe Windmill with its recently added sails and gaze down at the Elizabethan manor house, Compton Wynyates, below. A warm welcome awaits you in this buzzy, energetic, friendly village and gardening community. Partial wheelchair access.

GROUP OPENING

31 WARMINGTON VILLAGE GARDENS
Banbury OX17 1BU. *5m NW of Banbury. Take B4100 N from Banbury, after 5m turn R across short dual carriageway into Warmington. From N take J12 off M40 onto B4100.* **Sun 19 June (2-5.30). Combined adm £5, chd free. Home-made teas at village hall.**

THE MANOR COTTAGE
Mr & Mrs T Hall

THE MANOR HOUSE
Mr & Mrs G Lewis

OLD RECTORY FARMHOUSE
Dr & Mrs J Deakin

SPRINGFIELD HOUSE
Jenny & Roger Handscombe
01295 690286
jenny.handscombe@virgin.net

WESTERING
Mr & Mrs R Neale

1 THE WHEELWRIGHTS
Ms E Bunn

2 THE WHEELWRIGHTS
Mrs C Hunter

WOODCOTE
Ruth Warrior

Warmington, at the edge of the Cotswolds is an exceptionally attractive village with its C17 Hornton stone houses set around the village green. In front of the pond is The Manor House with its Elizabethan knot garden, and topiary. 1 and 2 The Wheelwrights are adjacent courtyard gardens with very different and attractive characters. Springfield House with its gravel garden is terraced and informal. A garden of many parts is to be found at Old Rectory Farmhouse, incl a slate and heather garden and a wooded area. Manor Cottage is conspicuous on The Green for its beautiful lavender border. Westering and Woodcote have colourful herbaceous beds with many unusual plants. Do visit St Michael's Church at the top of the village containing the Millennium Tapestry. Warmington is on a hill with many steps and gravel driveways which could be difficult for wheelchairs.

GROUP OPENING

32 **WELFORD-ON-AVON & DISTRICT GARDENS**
Welford-on-Avon CV37 8PT. *5m SW of Stratford-upon-Avon. Off B4390.* **Sat 25, Sun 26 June (2-6).** **Combined adm £5, chd free. Home-made teas in the village hall.**

ARDENCOTE
Mike & Sally Luntley

ASH COTTAGE
Mr & Mrs Peter & Sue Hook

NEW **AVON HOUSE**
Mr & Mrs Richard & Lucia Ham

NEW **BADSEY COTTAGE**
Mr & Mrs Janice & Noel Kirkwood

ELM CLOSE
Eric & Glenis Dyer
(See separate entry)

THE HOLLIES
Mr & Mrs Brad Plimmer

SOUTHLAWNS
Dr & Mrs Guy & Amanda Kitteringham

In addition to its superb position on the river, with serene swans, dabbling ducks and resident herons, Welford-on-Avon has a beautiful church, an excellent family butcher's shop, a very convenient general store and selection of PHs serving great food. Just down the road is a highly popular farm shop where seasonal fruit and vegetables are much in demand. With its great variety of house styles, including an abundance of beautiful cottages with thatched roofs and chocolate-box charisma, Welford also has an army of keen gardeners. The gardens open for the NGS range from small to large, from established to newly designed and planted, from a plot with fantastic topiary, herb knot and live willow weaving, to those with wild areas and croquet lawns. Fruit and vegetable areas are also integral to these gardens for all seasons.

Paths lead to secret corners and sitting areas . . .

ALLOTMENTS

33 **WELLESBOURNE ALLOTMENTS**
Kineton Road, Wellesbourne, Warwick CV35 9NE. *5m E of Stratford-upon-Avon. On Kineton Rd (B4086) E side of Wellesbourne.* **Sun 3 July (2-5). Adm £4, chd free. Afternoon teas.**
The 7¼ acre Wellesbourne allotment site with 96 members is one of the oldest in the country. Its impressive range of vegetables from ridiculously large to miniscule, delicious fruits and beautiful flowers offers much of interest to novice, experienced gardeners and young enthusiasts. It's amazing to see how much produce can be grown in the heart of England! Plants and produce for sale. Master gardener, scarecrows, children's questionnaire, beekeepers tent and a band. Level site with hard surface entrance and roadway.

GROUP OPENING

34 **WHICHFORD & ASCOTT GARDENS**
Whichford & Ascott, Shipston-on-Stour CV36 5PP. *6m SE of Shipston-on-Stour. Taking the A3400, the road to Whichford & Ascott is equidistant between Chipping Norton & Shipston-on-Stour. From Banbury & villages to the NE, take the Hook Norton/Whichford road from Bloxham.* **Sun 19 June (2-5.30). Combined adm £6, chd free. Home-made teas at Whichford House, with jazz entertainment.**

ASCOTT LODGE
Charlotte Copley

KNIGHT'S PLACE
Mr & Mrs Derek Atkins

THE OLD RECTORY
Peter & Caroline O'Kane

PLUM TREE COTTAGE
Janet Knight

WHICHFORD HILL HOUSE
Mr & Mrs John Melvin

WHICHFORD HOUSE
Bridget & Simon Herrtage

THE WHICHFORD POTTERY
Jim & Dominique Keeling
www.whichfordpottery.com

This group of gardens reflects a range of several garden types and sizes. The two villages are in an area of outstanding natural beauty. They nestle in a dramatic landscape of hills, pasture and woodland, which is used to picturesque effect by the garden owners. Fine lawns, mature shrub planting and much interest to plantsmen provide a peaceful visit to a series of beautiful gardens. Many incorporate the inventive use of natural springs, forming ponds, pools and other water features. Classic cottage gardens contrast with other larger gardens which adopt variations on the traditional English garden of herbaceous borders, climbing roses, yew hedges and walled enclosures. Other amenities are the C12 church, the internationally renowned pottery, and a PH serving meals. Free car parking opposite the church, and some in Ascott. This group of gardens receives press notice in local newspapers and journals covering the North Cotswolds. Partial wheelchair access as some gardens are on sloping sites.

WILTSHIRE

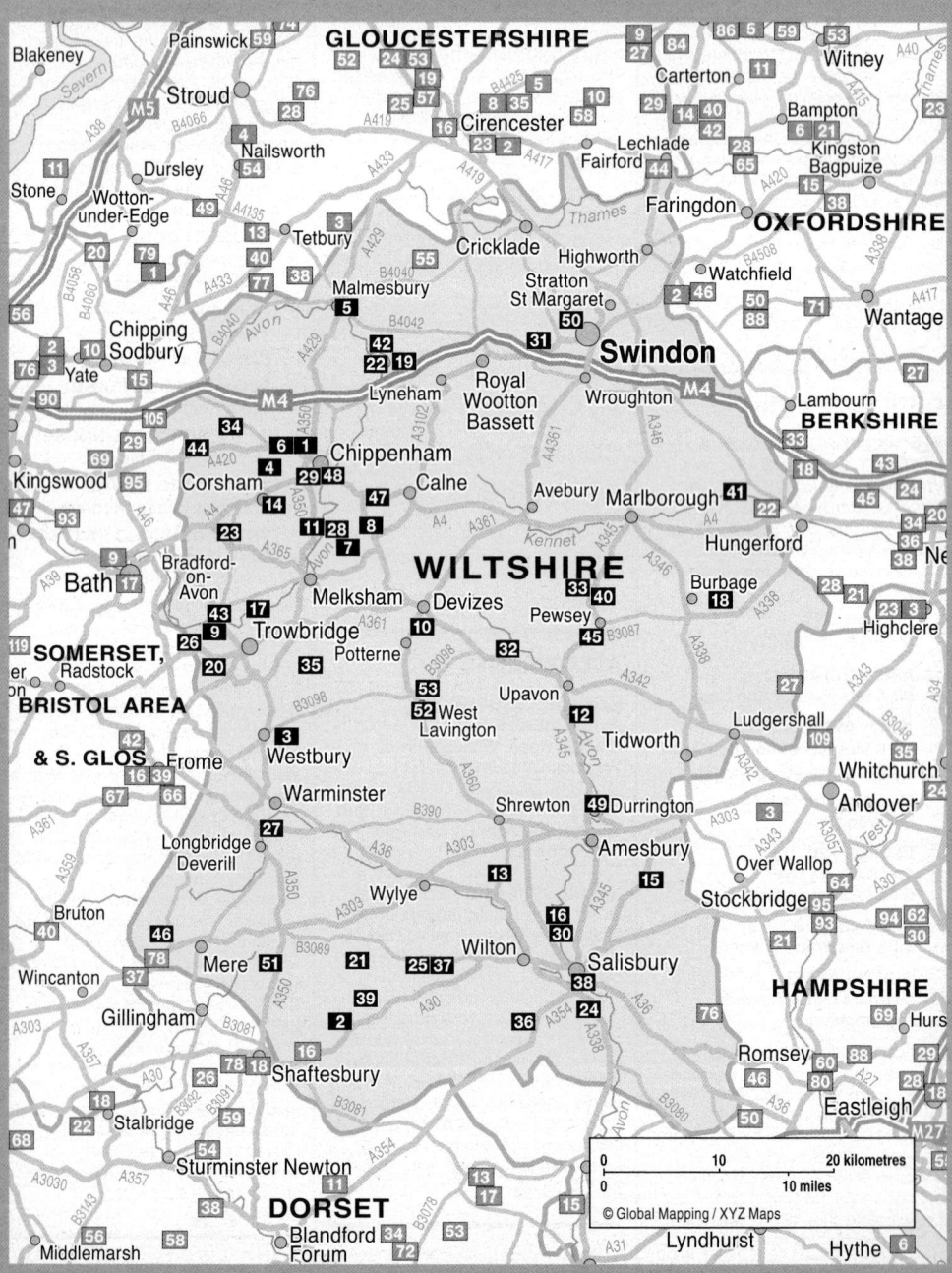

Wiltshire

Wiltshire, a predominantly rural county, covers 1346 square miles and has a rich diversity of landscapes, including downland, wooded river valleys and Salisbury Plain.

Chalk lies under two-thirds of the county, with limestone to the north, which includes part of the Cotswolds Area of Outstanding Natural Beauty.

The county's gardens reflect its rich history and wide variety of environments. Gardens opening for the NGS include the celebrated landscape garden of Stourhead and other National Trust properties, large privately owned gems such as Broadleas, Little Durnford Manor and Iford Manor, and more modest properties lovingly maintained by the owners such as Ridleys Cheer and Priory House.

The season opens with the snowdrops at Lacock Abbey and continues with fine spring gardens like Fonthill House, Corsham Court and Allington Grange. A wide selection of gardens, large and small, are at their peak in the summer; gardens like Sharcott Manor open throughout the season until September. There are also town gardens, village openings, allotments and a Chinese garden at Beggars Knoll. Some gardens open 'by arrangement' and there is something to delight the senses from February to September.

Wiltshire Volunteers

County Organisers
Sean & Kena Magee
01666 880009
spbmagee@googlemail.com

County Treasurers
Sean & Kena Magee
(as above)

**Publicity
& Booklet Co-ordinator**
Tricia Duncan
01672 810443
tricia@windward.biz

Social Media
Marian Jones
01249 657400
marian.jones@ngs.org.uk

Assistant County Organiser
Suzie Breakwell
01985 850297
suzievb@me.com

Sarah Coate
01722 782365
sarah.coate@woodfordvalley.net

Jo Hankey
01722 742472
rbhankey@gmail.com

Shirley Heywood
01985 844486
shirleyheywood@btinternet.com

Diana Robertson
01672 810515
diana@broomsgrovelodge.co.uk

Left: Little Durnford Manor

Opening Dates

All entries subject to change.
For latest information check www.ngs.org.uk

February

Snowdrop Festival

Wednesday 24
28 Lacock Abbey Gardens

Saturday 27
28 Lacock Abbey Gardens

March

Sunday 20
21 Fonthill House

April

Sunday 3
14 Corsham Court

Wednesday 6
45 Sharcott Manor

Sunday 10
10 Broadleas House Gardens

Thursday 14
32 Mallards

Sunday 17
30 Little Durnford Manor

Wednesday 20
23 Hazelbury Manor Gardens

Saturday 23
27 Job's Mill

Sunday 24
15 Cottage in the Trees
26 Iford Manor
40 Oare House
46 Stourhead Garden

May

Sunday 1
1 Allington Grange
51 Waterdale House

Monday 2
1 Allington Grange

Wednesday 4
45 Sharcott Manor

Sunday 8
4 Biddestone Manor

Thursday 12
32 Mallards

Friday 13
38 Mompesson House

Sunday 15
2 Ark Farm
10 Broadleas House Gardens
14 Corsham Court
44 Ridleys Cheer

Wednesday 18
7 Bowden Park
23 Hazelbury Manor Gardens

Sunday 22
9 Bradford on Avon Gardens
15 Cottage in the Trees
35 **NEW** The Manor House, Steeple Ashton
39 North Cottage
50 Twigs Community Garden

Friday 27
53 Windmill Cottage

Sunday 29
25 Hyde's House

June

Wednesday 1
45 Sharcott Manor

Festival Weekend

Saturday 4
27 Job's Mill
49 Trantor House

Sunday 5
15 Cottage in the Trees
18 Crofton Lock House
30 Little Durnford Manor
33 Manor Farm
49 Trantor House

Thursday 9
53 Windmill Cottage

Friday 10
53 Windmill Cottage

Saturday 11
52 West Lavington Manor

Sunday 12
11 Cantax House
12 Chisenbury Priory
23 Hazelbury Manor Gardens
35 **NEW** The Manor House, Steeple Ashton
39 North Cottage
49 Trantor House

Tuesday 14
17 The Courts Garden

Thursday 16
32 Mallards
34 **NEW** The Manor House, Castle Combe

Sunday 19
6 Bolehyde Manor
10 Broadleas House Gardens
19 Dauntsey Gardens

Thursday 23
53 Windmill Cottage

Friday 24
53 Windmill Cottage

Saturday 25
20 **NEW** Duck Pond Barn
22 Great Somerford Gardens

Sunday 26
22 Great Somerford Gardens
40 Oare House

July

Sunday 3
5 Blicks Hill House

37 Mitre Cottage
39 North Cottage
41 The Old Mill
43 Priory House

Wednesday 6
45 Sharcott Manor

Sunday 10
47 **NEW** 84 Studley Lane

Thursday 14
53 Windmill Cottage

Friday 15
53 Windmill Cottage

Sunday 17
10 Broadleas House Gardens
31 Lydiard Park Walled Garden
50 Twigs Community Garden

Wednesday 20
36 Manor House, Stratford Tony

Sunday 24
29 130 Ladyfield Road and Allotments
48 Sweet Briar Cottage

Sunday 31
18 Crofton Lock House

August

Wednesday 3
45 Sharcott Manor

Saturday 6
20 **NEW** Duck Pond Barn

Sunday 7
43 Priory House

Sunday 14
41 The Old Mill

September

Wednesday 7
36 Manor House, Stratford Tony
45 Sharcott Manor

Sunday 11
24 Horatio's Garden

Wednesday 14
23 Hazelbury Manor Gardens

Sunday 18
11 Cantax House

February 2017

Saturday 25
28 Lacock Abbey Gardens

Broadleas House Gardens

Gardens open to the public

- **8** Bowood Woodland Gardens
- **14** Corsham Court
- **17** The Courts Garden
- **26** Iford Manor
- **28** Lacock Abbey Gardens
- **31** Lydiard Park Walled Garden
- **38** Mompesson House
- **46** Stourhead Garden
- **50** Twigs Community Garden
- **51** Waterdale House

By arrangement only

- **3** Beggars Knoll Chinese Garden
- **13** NEW Cockspur Thorns
- **16** The Court House
- **42** The Pound House

Also open by arrangement

- **1** Allington Grange
- **4** Biddestone Manor
- **5** Blicks Hill House
- **6** Bolehyde Manor
- **11** Cantax House
- **15** Cottage in the Trees
- **18** Crofton Lock House
- **20** NEW Duck Pond Barn
- **32** Mallards
- **35** NEW The Manor House, Steeple Ashton
- **36** Manor House, Stratford Tony
- **39** North Cottage
- **43** Priory House
- **47** NEW 84 Studley Lane
- **48** Sweet Briar Cottage
- **49** Trantor House
- **52** West Lavington Manor
- **53** Windmill Cottage

The Gardens

1 ALLINGTON GRANGE
Allington, Chippenham SN14 6LW. Mrs Rhyddian Roper, 01249 447436, rhyddianroper@hotmail.co.uk, www.allingtongrange.com. *2m W of Chippenham. Take A420 W from Chippenham. 1st R signed Allington Village, entrance 1m up lane on L.* Sun 1, Mon 2 May (2-5). Adm £4, chd free. Home-made teas. **Visits also by arrangement Feb to June for groups.**
Informal country garden of approx 1½ acres, around C17 farmhouse (not open) with a diverse range of plants. Mixed and herbaceous borders, colour themed; white garden with water fountain. Pergola lined with clematis and roses. Walled potager. Small orchard with chickens. Wildlife pond with natural planting. Many spring bulbs. Featured in the English Garden and Wiltshire Life magazine. Mainly level with ramp into potager. Dogs on leads.
 ♿ 🐕 🌐 ☕

2 ARK FARM
Old Wardour, Tisbury, Salisbury SP3 6RP. Mrs Miranda Thomas. *Old Wardour is 2m from Tisbury. Drive down High Street and on, past station, take 1st R. Follow signs to Old Wardour Castle.* Sun 15 May (2-5). Adm £4, chd free. Home-made teas.
Informal hidden gardens in beautiful setting with small wooded area, pond, water plants, lakeside walk, views of Old Wardour castle. This is a very difficult garden for wheelchairs. Not advised!
☕

3 BEGGARS KNOLL CHINESE GARDEN
Newtown, Westbury BA13 3ED. Colin Little & Penny Stirling, 01373 823383, silkendalliance@talktalk.net. *1m SE of Westbury. Turn off B3098 at White Horse Pottery, up hill towards the White Horse for ¾ m. Parking at end of drive for 10 -12 cars.* Visits by arrangement June & July, max 24. Visits incl guided tour. Adm £4.50, chd free. Home-made teas. We already have quite a reputation for the homemade cakes served at Beggars Knoll - especially the walnut and coffee cake!
This inspirational 1-acre garden is filled with colourful plantings set against a backdrop of Chinese pavilions, gateways, statues and dragons. Intricate Chinese mosaic pavements wind around ponds and rocks. Rare Chinese shrubs, mature trees and flower filled borders form a haven of serenity. Large potager houses chickens, pigs live in the woods. Spectacular views too!
🌐 ☕

4 BIDDESTONE MANOR
Chippenham Lane, Biddestone SN14 7DJ. Rosie Harris, Head Gardener, 01249 713211. *5m W of Chippenham. On A4 between Chippenham & Corsham turn N. From A420, 5m W of Chippenham, turn S. Use car park.* Sun 8 May (2-5). Adm £5, chd free. Home-made teas. **Visits also by arrangement weekday evenings only mid May to mid June, groups of 10+ and coaches welcome.**
Stroll through our 8 peaceful acres of wide lawns, lake and ponds, arboretum and roses. Kitchen cutting gardens and orchard. Then join us for tea in the formal front garden and see the magnificent wisteria dripping with flowers, perfume and beauty. C17 Manor House (not open) with ancient dovecote. Wheelchair access to most parts, a few steps, help always available.
 ♿ 🐕 🌐 ☕

5 BLICKS HILL HOUSE
Blicks Hill, Malmesbury SN16 9HZ. Alan & Valerie Trotman, 01666 829669, vat@timberwright.co.uk. *½ m E of Malmesbury. On A429 Malmesbury bypass, turn off halfway between r'abouts.* Sun 3 July (11-5.30). Adm £4, chd free. Home-made teas. **Visits also by arrangement May to July for groups of 10+.**
Stunning, and having the wow factor is how visitors describe this garden situated on a 1 acre stepped and sloping site. Mature trees give a backdrop to the colourful beds and borders which have all been created since 2004 for yr-round interest. Unique pergola leading to a woodland glade, water feature and stream constructed in green slate, hanging baskets, tubs and bedding plants add extra impact. Very much a plantsman's garden containing many unusual and special plants. Large slate sculpture. Gradual slope.
 ♿ 🌐 🚐 ☕

Pigs live in the woods . . .

6 BOLEHYDE MANOR
Allington SN14 6LW. The Earl & Countess Cairns, 01249 443056, amandamcairns@gmail.com. *1½ m W of Chippenham. On Bristol Rd (A420). Turn N at Allington Xrds. ½ m on R. Parking in field.* Sun 19 June (2.30-5.30). Adm £5, chd free. Tea. **Visits also by arrangement May & June, groups on weekdays preferred.**
Series of gardens around C16 manor house (not open), enclosed by walls and topiary. Formal framework densely planted with many interesting shrubs and climbers, especially roses. Mixed borders. Blue walk of alliums and agapanthus. Inner courtyard with troughs full of tender plants. Collection of tender pelargoniums. Vegetable/fruit garden and greenhouse.

7 BOWDEN PARK
Lacock, Chippenham SN15 2PP. Bowden Park Estate. *10 mins from Chippenham. Entrance via Top Lodge at top of Bowden Hill, between A342 at Sandy Lane and A350 in Lacock.* Wed 18 May (10.30-4). Adm £5, chd free. Home-made teas.
22 acre private garden within surrounding parkland. Pleasure garden, water garden, working kitchen garden with formal lawns and grotto. Rhododendrons and azaleas in flower.

Hospice care is there for 1 in 3 people in the UK

8 ◆ BOWOOD WOODLAND GARDENS
Calne SN11 9PG. The Marquis of Lansdowne, 01249 812102, reception@bowood.org, www.bowood.org. *3½ m SE of Chippenham. Located off J17 M4 nr Bath & Chippenham. Entrance off A342 between Sandy Lane & Derry Hill Villages. Follow brown signs.* **For opening times and information, please phone, email or visit garden website.**

This 60 acre woodland garden of azaleas, magnolias, rhododendrons and bluebells is one of the most exciting of its type in the country. From the individual flowers to the breathtaking sweep of colour formed by hundreds of shrubs, this is a garden not to be missed. Planting began in 1850 and some of the earliest known hybrids feature among the collection. The Woodland Gardens are located 2m from Bowood House and Gardens.

GROUP OPENING

9 BRADFORD ON AVON GARDENS
Bradford on Avon BA15 1LF, 01225 865042, annette.seekings@gmail.com. *nr centre of Bradford on Avon. Car parking for all gardens except 13 Woolley Green on one of three nearby pay & display public parking. Many nearby inns and restaurants for lunch.* Sun 22 May (2-6). Combined adm £5, chd free. Home-made teas at Horton's House.

NEW 34 BUDBURY CLOSE
Mr & Mrs E Tate

HORTON'S HOUSE
Annette Seekings

LYNCHETTS
Professor & Mrs George Lunt
lynchetts@hotmail.com

1 ROSEMARY WALK
Penny Hopwood & Sally Wilson

13 WOOLLEY GREEN
Mr A Dark & Mrs S Dark

34 Budbury Close: Steeply sloping, now terraced. Series of varied small gardens, incl vegetable garden on garage roof, linked by paths and steps. Views of Westbury White Horse, Tithe Barn and Avon Valley. Horton's House: the steeply sloping land of approx 1 acre is now terraced and planted by owners with orchard and fig trees, roses and plants that love sunny S-facing aspect. 1 Rosemary Walk: Walled, terraced garden, landscaped and planted in 2008. Colour themed beds with a variety of plants and shrubs. Lynchetts garden extends to almost 2 acres and slopes up hillside. An old tennis court provides a large central level lawn. Few of the original fruit trees remain but many new plantings of old varieties of apples have been

made. Among the older trees are mulberry and medlar and more recently quince and figs have been established. Nearer house is herbaceous border and small terraced beds. 13 Woolley Green: C18 converted coach house with impressive gothic entrance arch in ²/₃ acre of gardens. Cottage garden with mixed herbaceous borders, shrubs, roses, set around independent terraced lawns. Mature trees, paddock and free range chickens and ducks. Also studio barn and vegetable garden with half standard fruit trees. Except for 13 Woolley Green none of the gardens are suitable for wheelchairs, too many steep steps.

10 BROADLEAS HOUSE GARDENS
Devizes SN10 5JQ. Mr & Mrs Cardiff. *1m S of Devizes. From Hartmoor Rd turn into Broadleas Park, follow road for 350 metres then turn R into estate. Please note, there is no access from A360 Potterne Rd.* Suns 10 Apr, 15 May, 19 June, 17 July (2-5.30). Adm £5, chd free. Home-made teas.
6 acre garden of hedges, herbaceous borders, rose arches, bee garden and orchard stuffed with good plants. It is overlooked by the house and arranged above the small valley garden which is crowded with magnolias and rhododendrons, cornus and hydrangeas.

11 CANTAX HOUSE
Lacock SN15 2JZ. Andrew & Deborah van der Beek, dvdb@deborahvanderbeek.com, www.deborahvanderbeek.com. *3m S of Chippenham. Off A350 between Chippenham & Melksham. Please use signed public car park if possible (except disabled). Entrance to garden in Cantax Hill.* Sun 12 June (2-6); Sun 18 Sept (2-5.30). Adm £5, chd free. Cream teas. **Visits also by arrangement Apr to Oct, 10+ preferred.** *Donation to Amnesty International.*
Queen Anne former vicarage (not open). Medium-sized garden of colour, pattern and scent straddling the Bide Brook. Designed and maintained by sculptor owner for 28yrs; both common and unusual plants incl wild flower sports; hornbeam spire, yew castle and other

topiary; old orchard wildflower garden; sculpture by owner and friends. In lovely old village featured in many films. House front featured in Cranford, BBC Emma and Harry Potter. Featured in many publications and magazines incl RHS The Garden (cover feature).

12 CHISENBURY PRIORY
East Chisenbury SN9 6AQ. Mr & Mrs John Manser,
john.peter.manser@live.com. *3m SW of Pewsey. Turn E from A345 at Enford then N to E Chisenbury, main gates 1m on R.* Sun 12 June (2-6). Adm £5, chd free. Home-made teas.
Medieval Priory with Queen Anne face and early C17 rear (not open) in middle of 5 acre garden on chalk. Mature garden with fine trees within clump and flint walls, herbaceous borders, shrubs, roses. Moisture loving plants along mill leat, carp pond, orchard and wild garden, many unusual plants. Front borders redesigned in 2009 by Tom Stuart-Smith.

13 NEW COCKSPUR THORNS
Berwick St James, Salisbury SP3 4TS. Stephen & Ailsa Bush, 01722 790445, stephenjdbush@gmail.com. *8m NW of Salisbury. 1m S of A303, on B3083 at S end of village of Berwick St James.* Visits by arrangement May to Aug for groups of 10+, weekdays preferred. Adm £4.00, chd free. Home-made teas.
2¼ acre garden, completely redesigned 15yrs ago and developments since, featuring roses (particularly colourful in June), herbaceous border, shrubbery, small walled kitchen garden, secret pond garden, mature and new trees, fruit trees and areas of wild flowers. Beech, yew and thuja hedgings planted to divide the garden. Small number of vines planted during winter of 2015.

14 ◆ CORSHAM COURT
Corsham SN13 0BZ. Lord Methuen, 01249 701610, staterooms@corsham-court.co.uk, www.corsham-court.co.uk. *4m W of Chippenham. Signed off A4 at Corsham.* For NGS: Sun 3 Apr, Sun 15 May (2-5.30). Adm £5, chd £2.50. For other opening times and information, please phone, email or visit garden website.
Park and gardens laid out by Capability Brown and Repton. Large lawns with fine specimens of ornamental trees surround the Elizabethan mansion. C18 bath house hidden in the grounds. Spring bulbs, beautiful lily pond with Indian bean trees, young arboretum and stunning collection of magnolias. Wheelchair (not motorised) access to house, gravel paths in garden.

Enchanting ¹/₂ acre cottage garden . . .

15 COTTAGE IN THE TREES
Tidworth Rd, Boscombe Village, nr Salisbury SP4 0AD. Karen & Richard Robertson, 01980 610921, robertson909@btinternet.com. *7m N of Salisbury. Turn L of A338 just before Social Club. Continue past church, turn R after bridge to Queen Manor, cottage 150yds on R.* Sun 24 Apr, Sun 22 May (2-5). Sun 5 June (2-5), also open Trantor House. Adm £2.50, chd free. Home-made teas. Visits also by arrangement Mar to June for groups of 10+.
Enchanting ¹/₂ acre cottage garden, immaculately planted with water feature, raised vegetable beds, small wildlife pond and gravel garden. Spring bulbs, hellebores and pulmonarias give a welcome start to the season, with pots and baskets, roses and clematis. Mixed borders of herbaceous plants, dahlias, grasses and shrubs giving all-yr interest.

16 THE COURT HOUSE
Lower Woodford SP4 6NQ. Mr & Mrs J G Studholme, 01722 782237, joestudholme@icloud.com. *3m N of Salisbury. On Woodford Valley rd, parallel to A360 & A345. Driving S, The Court House is 2nd house on L after Lower Woodford village sign.* Visits by arrangement May to July for groups of 10+. Adm £5.00, chd free.
3¹/₂ -acre garden on banks of R Avon. Herbaceous borders, waterside planting, yew hedges, rambler roses and wild flowers. Unusual trees.

Ancient site of Bishop's Palace when the cathedral was at Old Sarum. Tree house. Garden developed by present owners over past 25 years.

17 ◆ THE COURTS GARDEN
Holt, Trowbridge BA14 6RR. National Trust, 01225 782875, courtsgarden@nationaltrust.org.uk, www.nationaltrust.org.uk/courts-garden/. *2m E of Bradford-on-Avon. S of B3107 to Melksham. In Holt follow NT signs, park at village hall and at orchard car park when signed.* For NGS: Tue 14 June (11-5.30). Adm £7.80, chd £3.90. Light refreshments & hot & cold lunches in The Rose Garden tea-room. For other opening times and information, please phone, email or visit garden website.
Beautifully kept but eclectic garden. Yew hedges divide garden compartments with colour themed borders and organically shaped topiary. Water garden with 2 pools, temple, conservatory and small kitchen garden split by an apple allée, all surrounded by 3¹/₂ acres of arboretum with specimen trees. Wheelchair access map available.

18 CROFTON LOCK HOUSE
Crofton, Great Bedwyn, Marlborough SN8 3DW. Michael & Jenny Trussell, 01672 870674, jennytrussell@hotmail.com. *Lock 62, K&A Canal, Crofton, 1m W of Great Bedwyn. 4m W of Hungerford. Signs from A4 at Great Bedwyn turning, and from A338 at East Grafton. Limited parking. Garden 8 - 10 mins walk along towpath.* Sun 5 June, Sun 31 July (1.30-5.30). Adm £3, chd free. Home-made teas. Visits also by arrangement May to Aug incl for groups of 20 max. Donation to Wiltshire Air Ambulance.
³/₄ acre garden in idyllic setting around 200 yr old lock keeper's cottage. Garden comprises herbaceous beds designed with a painter's eye to provide riotous colour, sculptural form, and an abundance of wildlife from spring to autumn; at rear a small orchard, collection of apple and soft fruit trees and raised vegetable beds and chickens. Artist's studio open. Off grid house relying on sun and wind for electricity, own water supply. Crofton steam pumping station and Wilton Windmill close by.

GROUP OPENING

19 DAUNTSEY GARDENS
Church Lane, Dauntsey, Chippenham SN15 4HW. *5m SE of Malmesbury. Approach via Dauntsey Rd from Gt Somerford, 1¼ m from Volunteer Inn Great Somerford.* Sun 19 June (1.30-5). Combined adm £6, chd free. Home-made teas at Idover House.

THE COACH HOUSE
Col & Mrs J Seddon-Brown

DAUNTSEY PARK
Mr & Mrs Giovanni Amati
enquiries@daunseyparkhouse.co.uk
01249 721777

THE GARDEN COTTAGE
Miss Ann Sturgis

IDOVER HOUSE
Mr & Mrs Christopher Jerram

THE OLD POND HOUSE
Mr & Mrs Stephen Love

This group of 5 gardens, centred around the historic Dauntsey Park Estate, ranges from the Classical C18 country house setting of Dauntsey Park, with spacious lawns, old trees and views over the R Avon, to mature country house gardens and traditional walled gardens. Enjoy the formal rose garden in pink and white, old fashioned borders and duck ponds at Idover House, and the quiet seclusion of The Coach House with its thyme terrace and gazebos, climbing roses and clematis. Here, mop-headed pruned crataegus prunifolia line the drive. The Garden Cottage has a traditional walled kitchen garden with organic vegetables, apple orchard, woodland walk and yew topiary. Meanwhile the 2 acres at The Old Pond House are both clipped and unclipped! Large pond with lilies and fat carp, and look out for the giraffe and turtle.

20 NEW DUCK POND BARN
Church Lane, Wingfield, Trowbridge BA14 9LW. Janet & Marc Berlin, 01225 777764, janet@berlinfamily.co.uk. *On B3109 from Frome to Bradford on Avon, turn R opp Poplars PH into Church Lane.* Duck Pond Barn is at end of lane. Sat 25 June, Sat 6 Aug (2-5). Adm £4, chd free. Visits also by arrangement Apr to Oct.

Garden of 1.6 acres with large duck pond, flower garden, orchard, vegetable garden, spinney and wild area of grass and trees. Set in farmland and mainly flat. For Janet and Marc it is a new garden, having moved from South London in 2015.

21 FONTHILL HOUSE
Tisbury SP3 5SA. The Lord Margadale of Islay, www.fonthill.co.uk/gardens. *13m W of Salisbury. Via B3089 in Fonthill Bishop. 3m N of Tisbury.* Sun 20 Mar (12-5). Adm £6, chd free. Light refreshments. Sandwiches and cakes, all proceeds to NGS. Large woodland garden. Daffodils, rhododendrons, azaleas, shrubs, bulbs; magnificent views; formal gardens. The gardens have been extensively redeveloped recently under the direction of Tania Compton and Marie-Louise Agius. The formal gardens are being continuously improved with new designs, exciting trees, shrubs and plants. Partial wheelchair access.

Wild flower drive from butterfly rich common . . .

GROUP OPENING

22 GREAT SOMERFORD GARDENS
Great Somerford, Chippenham SN15 5JB. Doreen Jevons. *4m SE of Malmesbury. 4m N of M4 between J16 & J17. 2m S of B4042 Malmesbury to Royal Wootton Basset. 3m E of A4209 Cirencester to Chippenham road. Cross river bridge in Great Somerford. Park opp The Mount, additional parking on Dauntsey Road opp allotments and West St opp Manor House.* Sat 25, Sun 26 June (1.30-5). Combined adm £5, chd free. Home-made teas at The Mount. Ice creams.

GREAT SOMERFORD'S FREE GARDENS & ALLOTMENTS
In trust to Great Somerford Parish Council.
Open on all dates

MANOR HOUSE
Mr & Mrs Davies.
Open on all dates

THE MOUNT
Mr & Mrs McGrath.
Open on all dates

THE OLD POLICE HOUSE
Steve & Diane Hunt.
Open on all dates

SOMERFORD HOUSE
Dr & Mrs Hyde.
Open on Sat 25 June

Great Somerford is a medium-sized village, with a lovely walk by R Avon. Maintained by very active gardeners, there are three well-established large gardens and a charming smaller one and Gt Somerford's Free Gardens and Allotments. Partial wheelchair access.

23 HAZELBURY MANOR GARDENS
Wadswick, Box SN13 8HX. Mr L Lacroix. *5m SW of Chippenham, 5m NE of Bath. From A4 at Box, A365 to Melksham, at Five Ways junction L onto B3109 toward Corsham, 1st L at top of hill, drive immed on R.* Wed 20 Apr, Wed 18 May (11-3); Sun 12 June (2-5.30); Wed 14 Sept (11-3). Adm £5, chd free. Teas on Sunday opening only.
8 Acres of Grade II landscaped organic gardens around C15 fortified manor (not open). Edwardian garden with yew hedges and topiary, beech stilt hedges, laburnum tunnel and pleached lime avenue. Large variety of plants, shrubs fill 5000 sq metres of planting, many herbal and native species. Productive vegetable gardens, orchards and a circle of megaliths. Wild flower drive from butterfly rich common.

24 HORATIO'S GARDEN
Duke of Cornwall Spinal Treatment Centre, Salisbury Hospital NHS Foundation Trust, Odstock Road, Salisbury SP2 8BJ. Horatio's Garden Charity, www.horatiosgarden.org.uk. *1m from centre of Salisbury. Please park in car park 8 or 10.* Sun 11 Sept (2-5). Adm £5, chd free. Teas, served

in Horatio's Garden mugs made by Emma Bridgewater, and delicious cakes made by Horatio's Garden volunteers. *Donation to Horatio's Garden.*

Award winning hospital garden which opened in Sept 2012 and was designed by Cleve West for patients with spinal cord injury at the Duke of Cornwall Spinal Treatment Centre. Built from donations given in memory of Horatio Chapple who was a volunteer at the centre in his school holidays. Low limestone walls, which represent the form of the spine, divide densely planted beds and double as seating. Everything in the garden has been designed to benefit patients during their long stays in hospital. Garden is run by Head Gardener Tina Crossley and team of volunteers. At 3pm there will be a talk about therapeutic gardens by Charity Chair Dr Olivia Chapple & Head Gardener Tina Crossley. 3 Society of Garden Designers Awards 2015 and Bali Award 2014. Cleve West has 8 RHS gold medals, incl Best in Show at Chelsea Flower Show in 2011 and 2012. Featured in Telegraph Weekend, Mail on Sunday & Weekend Times magazines. Fully accessible to wheelchairs.

25 HYDE'S HOUSE
Dinton SP3 5HH. Mr George Cruddas. *9m W of Salisbury. Off B3089 nr Dinton Church on St Mary's Rd.* **Sun 29 May (2-5). Adm £5, chd free. Home-made teas at Thatched Old School Room with outside tea tables.**
3 acres of wild and formal garden in beautiful situation with series of hedged garden rooms. Numerous shrubs, flowers and borders, all allowing tolerated wild flowers and preferred weeds. Large walled kitchen garden, herb garden and C13 dovecote (open). Charming C16/18 Grade I listed house (not open), with lovely courtyard. Every year varies. Free walks around park and lake. Steps, slopes and gravel paths.

26 ◆ IFORD MANOR
Lower Westwood, Bradford-on-Avon BA15 2BA. Mrs Cartwright-Hignett, 01225 863146, info@ifordmanor.co.uk, www.ifordmanor.co.uk. *7m S of Bath. Off A36, brown tourist sign to Iford 1m. Or from Bradford-on-Avon or Trowbridge via Lower Westwood*

Cantax House

Village (brown signs). **For NGS: Sun 24 Apr (2-5.30). Adm £5.50, chd £5. Cream teas. Tea room also serves home made cakes, ice cream, fresh coffee and selection of specialist teas. For other opening times and information, please phone, email or visit garden website.**
Very romantic award-winning, Grade I listed Italianate garden famous for its tranquil beauty. Home to Edwardian architect and designer Harold Peto 1899-1933. Garden is characterised by steps, terraces, sculpture and magnificent rural views. (House not open). 2016 is yr 4 of a 5 yr historic replant of Great Terrace and rose garden. Housekeeper's cream teas and home made cakes at weekends. Light refreshments in Loggia at other times. World famous Summer Arts festival June to Aug, www.ifordarts.org.uk. Please see website for wheelchair access details.

27 JOB'S MILL
Five Ash Lane, Crockerton, Warminster BA12 8BB. Lady Silvy McQuiston. *1½ m S of Warminster. Down lane E of A350, S of A36 r'about.* **Sat 23 Apr (2-5); Sat 4 June (2-6). Adm £4, chd free. Home-made teas.**

Delightful 5 acre garden through which R Wylye flows. Laid out on many levels surrounding an old converted water mill. Water garden, herbaceous border, vegetable garden, orchard, riverside and woodland walks and secret garden. Grass terraces designed by Russell Page. Bulbs and erythronium in the spring and perhaps the tallest growing wisteria?

28 ◆ LACOCK ABBEY GARDENS
High Street, Lacock, Chippenham SN15 2LG. National Trust, 01249 730459, www.nationaltrust.org.uk/lacock. *3m S of Chippenham. Off A350. Follow NT signs. Use public car park (parking fee).* **For NGS: Wed 24, Sat 27 Feb (10.30-5.30). Adm £5.50, chd £2.75. 2017: Sat 25 Feb. For other opening times and information, please phone or visit garden website.**
Woodland garden with carpets of aconites, snowdrops, crocuses and daffodils. Botanic garden with greenhouse, medieval cloisters and magnificent trees. Mostly level site, some gravel paths.

29 130 LADYFIELD ROAD AND ALLOTMENTS

Ladyfield Road, Chippenham SN14 0AP. Philip & Pat Canter and Chippenham Town Council. *1m SW of Chippenham. Between A4 Bath and A420 Bristol rds. Signed off B4528 Hungerdown Lane which runs between A4 & A420.* Sun 24 July (1.30-5.30). Adm £3.50, chd free. Home-made teas.

Very pretty small garden with more than 30 clematis, climbing roses and small fish pond. Curved neat edges packed with colourful herbaceous plants and small trees. 2 patio areas with lush lawn, pagoda and garden arbour. Also Hungerdown Allotments, 15 allotments owned by Chippenham Town Council. Wheelchair access to garden and to allotments on main drive only.

30 LITTLE DURNFORD MANOR

Little Durnford, Salisbury SP4 6AH. The Earl & Countess of Chichester. *3m N of Salisbury. Just N beyond Stratford-sub-Castle. Remain to E of R Avon at road junction at Stratford Bridge and continue towards Salterton for 1/2 m heading N. Entrance on L just past 'Little Durnford' sign.* Sun 17 Apr, Sun 5 June (2-5). Adm £4, chd free. Home-made teas in cricket pavilion.

Extensive lawns with cedars, walled gardens, fruit trees, large vegetable garden, small knot and herb gardens. Terraces, borders, sunken garden, water garden, lake with islands, river walks, labyrinth walk. Little Durnford Manor is a substantial grade II listed, C18 private country residence (not open) built of an attractive mix of Chilmark stone and flint. Camels, alpacas, llama, pigs, pygmy goats, donkeys and sheep are all grazing next to the gardens. Gravel paths, some narrow. Steep slope and some steps.

31 ◆ LYDIARD PARK WALLED GARDEN

Lydiard Tregoze, Swindon SN5 3PA. Swindon Borough Council, 01793 466664, www.lydiardpark.org.uk. *3m W Swindon, 1m from J16 M4. Follow brown signs from W Swindon. Light refreshments in tearooms by walled garden.* For NGS: Sun 17 July (11-5). Adm £2.50, chd £1.50. Also open Twigs Community Garden.

For other opening times and information, please phone or visit garden website.

Beautiful ornamental C18 walled garden. Trimmed shrubs alternating with individually planted flowers and bulbs incl rare daffodils and tulips, sweet peas, annuals and wall-trained fruit trees. Park and children's playground. Unique features incl well and sundial. Wide level paths, no steps.

32 MALLARDS

Chirton SN10 3QX. Tim & Jenny Papé, 01380 840593, jennypape@tiscali.co.uk. *4 1/2 m SE of Devizes. 1m N of A342 at Chirton on road to Patney.* Thur 14 Apr, Thur 12 May, Thur 16 June (11-5). Adm £3, chd free. Light refreshments. Visits also by arrangement Apr to July.

1 acre hidden garden sloping gently down to woodland beside the upper R Avon. Colourful sunny gravel bed, mixed borders, woodland glade, miniature dell and waterside, all informally planted for yr-round interest. Vegetable garden and woodland walk. Most of garden and some of wood wheelchair accessible. No disabled WC.

200 year old Italian garden design . . .

33 MANOR FARM

Huish, Marlborough SN8 4JN. Lygo & James Roberts. *3m NW of Pewsey. Huish is signed from A345 by White Hart PH in Oare. Follow lane for 1m into Huish, turn R immed after row of thatched cottages on L.* Sun 5 June (2-5.30). Adm £4.50, chd free. Home-made teas.

After a 2 year break for new projects, we are ready to open again. The stunning downland setting has inspired this intriguing garden which offers a stone circle, Bannerman grotto, spiral maze, pleached lime walk, gravel garden, wildlife ponds and extensive herbaceous borders. A surprise around every corner makes this a garden to be enjoyed by all ages. Some paths too narrow for wheelchairs.

34 NEW THE MANOR HOUSE, CASTLE COMBE

Castle Combe, Chippenham SN14 7HR. The Manor House, Castle Combe, 01249 782206, enquiries@manorhouse.co.uk, www.exclusive.co.uk. *15 mins from J17 of M4. Follow signs for Castle Combe race circuit, continue past circuit, follow road round to R, take 3rd L into village. Hotel immediately R after hump back bridge.* Thur 16 June (11-4). Adm £5, chd free. Light refreshments. Tea and cake incl in entry fee.

200 yr old Italian garden design with kitchen garden supplying our Michelin starred restaurant. Mature wild flower orchard with bee hives and livestock area with rare breed pigs and various birds and fowl. The garden also boasts intricate rock gardens, mature Japanese magnolias, stunning walks and over 2000 years of fascinating history linked to the estate and village of Castle Combe. Garden is in grounds of C14, 5 star Manor House Hotel and is also a fantastic wildlife area, abundant in flora and fauna.

35 NEW THE MANOR HOUSE, STEEPLE ASHTON

Church Street, Steeple Ashton, Trowbridge BA14 6EW. John & Penny Aeberhard, 01380 870602, Aeberhard@btinternet.com. *7m east of Trowbridge. In Church St, continue past church to private driveway.* Sun 22 May, Sun 12 June (2-6). Adm £5, chd £1. Home-made teas. Visits also by arrangement Mar to Sept for groups of 10+.

2 acres surrounding Jacobean Manor (1647) with detached non-Conformist meeting house. Gardens featured in Wiltshire Life magazine. Late Perpendicular church of St Mary's (C15) provides exceptionally picturesque backdrop to gardens. Limited wheelchair access to rear gardens.

36 MANOR HOUSE, STRATFORD TONY

Stratford Tony, Salisbury SP5 4AT. Mr & Mrs Hugh Cookson, 01722 718496, lucindacookson@stratfordtony.co.uk, www.stratfordtony.co.uk. *4m SW of Salisbury. Take minor rd W off A354 at Coombe Bissett. Garden on S after 1m. Or take minor rd off*

A3094 from Wilton signed Stratford Tony and racecourse. Wed 20 July, Wed 7 Sept (2-5). Adm £4, chd free. Home-made teas. **Visits also by arrangement Mar to Oct for groups of 5+, refreshments by arrangement.**
Varied 4 acre garden with all yr interest. Formal and informal areas. Small lake fed from R Ebble, waterside planting, herbaceous borders with colour from spring to late autumn. Pergola-covered vegetable garden, formal parterre garden, orchard, shrubberies, roses, specimen trees, winter colour and structure, many original contemporary features and places to sit and enjoy the downland views. Some gravel.

37 MITRE COTTAGE
Snow Hill, Dinton SP3 5HN. Mrs Beck. *9m W of Salisbury. From B3089 turn up Snowhill by shop. From Wylye bear L at fork by church.* Sun 3 July (2-6). Adm £3.50, chd free.
Cottage style garden of ³/₄ acre with a wide variety of plants and shrubs and winding paths down a slight slope. Many hellebores and bulbs in spring and old fashioned roses. Mature garden with a wide variety of bulbs, shrubs and trees for yr-round interest. Paths wander down slight hillside from one part to another. It could be called a plantsman's garden I am told.

38 ◆ MOMPESSON HOUSE
The Close, Salisbury SP1 2EL. National Trust, 01722 335659, www.nationaltrust.org.uk. *Central Salisbury. Enter Cathedral Close via High St Gate, Mompesson House on R.* For NGS: Fri 13 May (11-4). Adm £1, chd free. Light refreshments. **For other opening times and information, please**

phone or visit garden website.
The appeal of this comparatively small but attractive garden is the lovely setting in Salisbury Cathedral Close, with a well known Queen Anne house (not open). Planting as for an old English garden with raised rose and herbaceous beds around the lawn. Climbers on pergola and walls, shrubs and small lavender walk. Cake stall.

39 NORTH COTTAGE
Tisbury Row, Tisbury SP3 6RZ. Jacqueline & Robert Baker, 01747 870019, robert.baker@pearceseeds.co.uk. *12m W of Salisbury. From A30 turn N through Ansty, L at T-junction, towards Tisbury. From Tisbury take Ansty road. Car park entrance nr junction signed Tisbury Row.* Sun 22 May, Sun 12 June, Sun 3 July (11.30-5). Adm £3, chd free. Scrumptious home-made light lunches and teas. **Visits also by arrangement June & July for groups of 10+.**
Cottage garden and smallholding set in quiet vale in a beautiful part of S Wiltshire. Though small, there is room for all to explore the divided areas, each differs in style and feel. Orchard, wild flowers and coppice wood. In 2016 we are thrilled to host an exhibition of metal sculpture made from recycled tools by Amy Lancaster (Metal Menagerie), featured in many publications. It will be a memorable visit. Ceramics and handicrafts all made by garden owners, many made from their own sheep's wool.

40 OARE HOUSE
Rudge Lane, Oare, nr Pewsey SN8 4JQ. Sir Henry Keswick. *2m N of Pewsey. On Marlborough Rd (A345).* Sun 24 Apr, Sun 26 June (2-6). Adm £5, chd free. Home-made teas. Coffee, soft drinks. *Donation to The Order of St John.*
1740s mansion house later extended by Clough Williams Ellis in 1920s (not open). The formal gardens originally created around the house have been developed over the years to create a wonderful garden full of many unusual plants. Current owner is very passionate and has developed a fine collection of rarities. Garden is undergoing a renaissance but still maintains split compartments each with its own individual charm; traditional walled garden with fine

herbaceous borders, vegetable areas, trained fruit, roses and grand mixed borders surrounding formal lawns. The Magnolia garden is wonderful in spring with some trees dating from 1920s, together with strong bulb plantings. Large arboretum and woodland with many unusual and champion trees. In spring and summer there is always something of interest, with the glorious Pewsey Vale as a backdrop. Partial wheelchair access.

41 THE OLD MILL
Ramsbury SN8 2PN. Annabel & James Dallas. *8m NE of Marlborough. From Marlborough head to Ramsbury. At The Bell PH follow sign to Hungerford. Garden behind yew hedge on R 100yds beyond The Bell.* Sun 3 July, Sun 14 Aug (2-6). Adm £5, chd free. Tea.
Water running through multitude of channels no longer drives the mill but provides backdrop for whimsical garden of pollarded limes and naturalistic planting. Paths meander by streams and over small bridges. Vistas give dramatic views of downs beyond. Potager style kitchen garden and separate cutting garden provide a more formal contrast to the relaxed style elsewhere. Limited wheelchair access as gravel paths and bridges.

PEN MILL FARM
See Somerset, Bristol & South Gloucestershire

42 THE POUND HOUSE
Little Somerford, Chippenham SN15 5JW. Mr & Mrs Michael Baines, 01666 823212, squeezebaines@yahoo.com. *2m E of Malmesbury on B4024. In village turn S, leave church on R. Car park on R before railway bridge.* Visits by arrangement Apr to Sept. Adm £5.00, chd free. Home-made teas.
Large well planted garden surrounding former rectory attached to C17 house. Mature trees, hedges and spacious lawns. Well stocked herbaceous borders, roses, shrubs, pergola, parterre, swimming pool garden, water, ducks, chickens, alpacas and horses. Raised vegetable garden and lots of places to sit. A very beautiful English garden! Featured in Wiltshire Life.

43 PRIORY HOUSE

Market Street, Bradford-on-Avon BA15 1LH. Mr & Mrs Tim Woodall, trwwoodall@yahoo.com. *Town centre. Park in town centre. Take A363 signed Bath up Market St. House 500yds.* Sun 3 July, Sun 7 Aug (2-5.30). Adm £4, chd free. Home-made teas. **Visits also by arrangement June to Aug, conducted tours for 10+.**
³/₄ -acre town garden, mostly formal. Late summer borders planted in traditional manner using asters, heleniums, dahlias, daylilies and others, but with a modern twist using grasses. Knot garden in front of part Georgian house is an interpretation of the sash windows. Featured in The English Garden and Gardens Illustrated. Steep slopes and steps at bottom of garden.
♿ 🛈 ♲ ☕

44 RIDLEYS CHEER

Mountain Bower, N Wraxall, Chippenham SN14 7AJ.
Mr & Mrs A J Young,
www.ridleyscheer.co.uk. *9m WNW of Chippenham. At The Shoe, on A420 8m W of Chippenham, turn N (signed Grittleton) then take 2nd L & 1st R.* Sun 15 May (2-5). Adm £4, chd free. Home-made teas.
Largely informal garden; mixed borders, lawns, extensive collection of shrubs and trees incl acers, magnolias, liriodendrons, tree peonies, deutzias, daphnes, oaks, beech, birch and hollies. Some 130 rose varieties; old-fashioned and modern shrub roses, and magnificent tree ramblers. Potager, miniature box garden, arboretum, 3 acre wild flower meadow, plus new ¹/₂ acre flower meadow. Dew pond. One of the main features of the garden in May is the collection of magnolias, deutzias and daphnes. Early shrub roses and Banksian roses in full bloom as well as Abutilon vitifolium and tulip trees. Oxeye daisies in the wild flower meadows. Wheelchair access from car park in meadow.
♿ ♲ ☕

45 SHARCOTT MANOR

Pewsey SN9 5PA. Mrs D Armytage, 01672 563485. *1m SW of Pewsey. Via A345 from Pewsey towards Salisbury. Turn R signed Sharcott at grass triangle. 400yds up lane, garden on L over cattle-grid.* Weds 6 Apr, 4 May, 1 June, 6 July, 3 Aug, 7 Sept (11-5). Adm £5, chd free. Home-made teas.

6 acre plantsman's garden on greensand, planted for yr-round interest. Wide range of trees and shrubs, densely planted mixed borders with many unusual plants and climbers. Magnificent tree ramblers. Woodland walk carpeted with spring bulbs around ¹/₂ acre lake. Good autumn colour. Private arrangement visits also welcome April to September. Gravel and narrow grass paths, grass slope.
♿ ♲ 🚶 ☕

Relax in 12 seating areas . . .

46 ◆ STOURHEAD GARDEN

Stourton, Warminster BA12 6QD. National Trust, 01747 841152, www.nationaltrust.org.uk/ stourhead. *3m NW of Mere on B3092. Follow NT signs, the property is very well signed from all main roads incl A303.* For NGS: Sun 24 Apr (9-6). Adm £9.20, chd £5. **For other opening times and information, please phone or visit garden website.**
One of the earliest and greatest landscape gardens in the world, creation of banker Henry Hoare in 1740s on his return from the Grand Tour, inspired by paintings of Claude and Poussin. Planted with rare trees, rhododendrons and azaleas over last 250yrs. Wheelchair access and buggy available.
♿ ♲ 🚶 🛏 ☕

47 NEW 84 STUDLEY LANE

Studley, Calne SN11 9NH. Stephen Cox, 01249 812968, stephen.b.cox@ntlworld.com. *Studley Lane: just off A4 between Chippenham & Calne. At A4 Studley Xrds take turning opp the one for Derry Hill village & Bowood. 1st house down the lane. Purple fence & gates. High Buddleia hedging. Parking in field. SatNav poor.* Sun 10 July (2-6). Adm £3, chd free. Tea & coffee by local voluntary group.
Visits also by arrangement May to Sept for groups, max 10. Student groups for art & nature studies also welcome.
Small garden with series of rooms created from field divided by lawns, paths, arches. Fish pond/fountains;

stone statues; 30 plaques of garden wisdom. Relax in 12 seating areas. Stephen is a tenant of the Bowood Estate (the entrance to Bowood House & Gardens is less than 200 metres away). Private conducted tours are also available.
♲ ☕

48 SWEET BRIAR COTTAGE

19 Gladstone Road, Chippenham SN15 3BW. Paul & Joy Gough, 01249 656005, paulgough@btopenworld.com. *Chippenham town centre. In town centre, turn off A4 Ave La Fleche into Gladstone Rd. Park in Borough Parade car parks. Garden just above car park opp Angel Hotel.* Sun 24 July (1-5). Adm £3.50, chd free. Home-made teas. **Visits also by arrangement June to Aug.**
Town centre oasis of nearly 1 acre of wildlife friendly planted beds, still wowing our visitors. Low Box edged borders full of succession flowering plants has the garden buzzing throughout the year. Large collection of roses, ornamental and fruit trees, the garden can be accessed by slate paths. Two small ponds, 4ft beds, gravel beds, crisp edged lawns. Large patio and seating throughout.
♲ ☕

49 TRANTOR HOUSE

Hackthorne Road, Durrington SP4 8AS. Mrs Jane Turner, 01980 655101. *10m N of Salisbury. Turn off A345 (signed Village Centre) onto Hackthorne Rd. Approx 200 yds on L.* Sat 4 June (2-5). Sun 5 June (2-5), also open Cottage in the Trees. Sun 12 June (2-5). Adm £3, chd free. **Visits also by arrangement May to Aug.**
Border Oak timber framed house on country lane surrounded by approx ²/₃ acre of both formal and informal gardens. Attractive mixed and herbaceous colour themed borders, rose garden, wildlife pond and stream. Summerhouse, raised vegetable beds and wildflower meadow. Chickens. Sloping garden with steps.

50 ◆ TWIGS COMMUNITY GARDEN

Manor Garden Centre, Cheney Manor, Swindon SN2 2QJ. TWIGS, 01793 523294, twigs.reception@gmail.com, www.twigscommunitygardens.org. uk. *From Gt Western Way, under*

Bruce St Bridges onto Rodbourne Rd. 1st L at r'about, Cheney Manor Industrial Est. Through estate, 2nd exit at r'about. Opp Pitch & Putt. Signs on R to Manor Garden Centre. For NGS: Sun 22 May (1-5). Sun 17 July (1-5), also open Lydiard Park Walled Garden. Adm £3, chd free. Home-made teas. Excellent hot and cold lunches available at Olive Tree café within Manor Garden centre adj to Twigs. **For other opening times and information, please phone, email or visit garden website.**
Delightful 2 acre community garden, created and maintained by volunteers. Features incl 7 individual display gardens, ornamental pond, plant nursery, Iron Age round house, artwork, fitness trail, separate kitchen garden site, Swindon beekeepers and the haven, overflowing with wild flowers. Featured in Garden Answers. Most areas wheelchair accessible. Disabled WC.

51 ◆ WATERDALE HOUSE
East Knoyle SP3 6BL. Mr & Mrs Julian Seymour, 01747 830262. *8m S of Warminster. N of East Knoyle, garden signed from A350. Do not use SatNav.* For NGS: Sun 1 May (2-6). Adm £5, chd free. Home-made teas. **For other opening times and information, please phone.**
4 acre mature woodland garden with rhododendrons, azaleas, camellias, maples, magnolias, ornamental water, bog garden, herbaceous borders. Bluebell walk. Shrub border created by storm damage mixed with agapanthus and half hardy salvias. Sensible footwear is essential due to difficult surfaces, parts of the garden are very wet. Limited wheelchair access.

52 WEST LAVINGTON MANOR
1 Church Street, West Lavington SN10 4LA. Andrew Doman, andrewdoman01@gmail.com. *6m S of Devizes, on A360. House opp White St, where parking available.* Sat 11 June (9-6). Adm £7, chd free. Home-made teas provided by West Lavington Youth Club. **Visits also by arrangement for groups of 10+ any weekday.** *Donation to West Lavington Youth Club.*
5 acre walled garden first established in C17 by John Danvers who brought Italianate gardens to the UK. Herbaceous border, redeveloped Japanese garden, new rose garden, orchard and arboretum with some outstanding specimen trees all centred around a trout stream and duck pond. This year the opening coincides with our biennial sculpture exhibition - see www.friendsofthegarden.org.uk for details.

53 WINDMILL COTTAGE
Kings Road, Market Lavington SN10 4QB. Rupert & Gill Wade, 01380 813527. *5m S of Devizes. Turn E off A360 1m N of West Lavington, 2m S of Potterne. At top* of hill turn L into Kings Rd, L into Windmill Lane after 200yds. Limited parking. Fri 27 May, Thur 9, Fri 10, Thur 23, Fri 24 June, Thur 14, Fri 15 July (2-5). Adm £3, chd free. Home-made teas. **Visits also by arrangement May to July for groups of 4+.**
1 acre cottage style, wildlife friendly garden on greensand. Mixed beds and borders with long season of interest. Roses on pagoda, large vegetable patch for kitchen and exhibition at local shows, polytunnel and greenhouse. Whole garden virtually pesticide free for last 19yrs. Small bog garden by wildlife pond. Secret glade with prairie.

Manor Farm

WORCESTERSHIRE

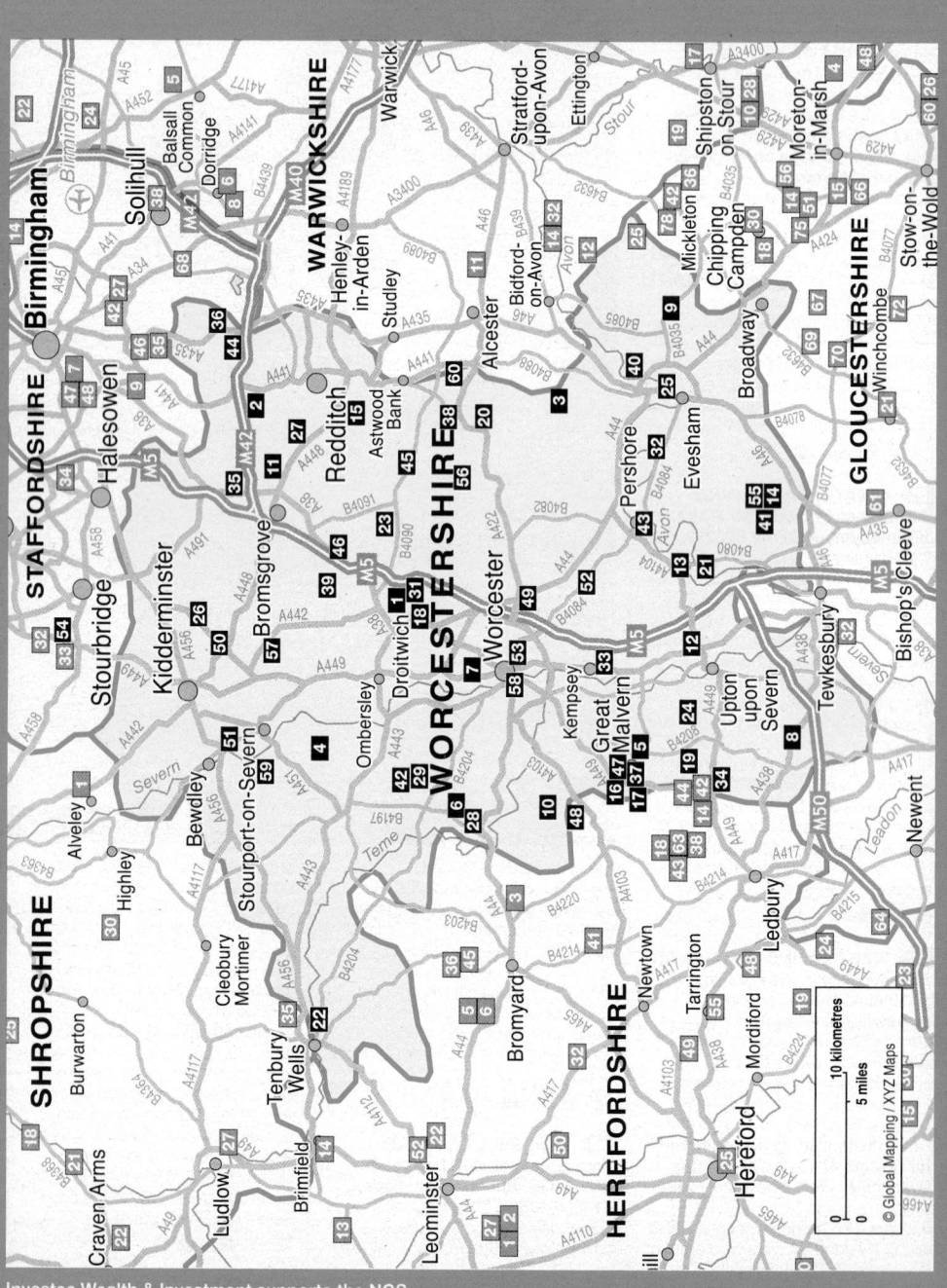

© Global Mapping / XYZ Maps

Worcestershire

Worcestershire has something to suit every taste, and the same applies to its gardens.

From the magnificent Malvern Hills, the inspiration for Edward Elgar, to the fruit orchards of Evesham which produce wonderful blossom trails in the spring, and from the historic city of Worcester, with its 11th century cathedral and links to the Civil War, to the numerous villages and hamlets that are scattered throughout the county, there is so much to enjoy in this historic county.

Worcestershire is blessed with gardens created by celebrated gardeners such as Capability Brown to ordinary amateur gardeners, and the county can boast properties with grounds of over one hundred acres to small back gardens of less than half an acre, but all have something special to offer.

Visitors to Worcestershire's NGS gardens will find some with wonderful arrays of plants, trees and vegetables, while others show the owners' creativity or sense of fun. There are gardens with significant historical interest and some with magnificent views. We also have a number of budding artists involved with the Scheme, and a few display their works of art on garden open days.

Worcestershire's garden owners guarantee visitors beautiful gardens, some real surprises and a warm welcome.

Below: Worralls Mill

Worcestershire Volunteers

County Organiser
David Morgan
01214 453595
meandi@btinternet.com

County Treasurer
Cliff Woodward
01562 886349

Publicity
Pamela Thompson
01886 888295
peartree.pam@gmail.com

Booklet Advertising & Co-ordinator
Alan Nokes
01214 455520
alan.nokes@ngs.org.uk

Assistant County Organisers
Mike George
01905 427567
mikeatthemansion@aol.com

Lynn Glaze
01386 751924
lynnglaze@cmail.co.uk

Brian Bradford
07816 867137
brianbradford101@outlook.com

Opening Dates

All entries subject to change.
For latest information check www.ngs.org.uk

February

Snowdrop Festival

Saturday 13
- **57** Whitlenge Gardens

Sunday 14
- **57** Whitlenge Gardens

March

Thursday 3
- **45** Red House Farm

Sunday 20
- **34** Little Malvern Court

Friday 25
- **49** Spetchley Park Gardens

April

Saturday 2
- **57** Whitlenge Gardens

Sunday 3
- **57** Whitlenge Gardens

Thursday 7
- **45** Red House Farm

Sunday 10
- **1** 24 Alexander Avenue
- **56** White Cottage & Nursery

Saturday 16
- **9** Bretforton Manor

Sunday 17
- **12** Bylane

Saturday 30
- **48** Shuttifield Cottage

May

Sunday 1
- **3** Ashley
- **13** 1 Church Cottage
- **42** Pear Tree Cottage
- **56** White Cottage & Nursery

Monday 2
- **13** 1 Church Cottage
- **34** Little Malvern Court
- **42** Pear Tree Cottage
- **56** White Cottage & Nursery

Thursday 5
- **45** Red House Farm

Saturday 7
- **27** Hewell Grange
- **39** New House Farm, Elmbridge
- **48** Shuttifield Cottage
- **53** The Walled Garden

Sunday 8
- **27** Hewell Grange
- **39** New House Farm, Elmbridge
- **48** Shuttifield Cottage

Wednesday 11
- **31** Hiraeth
- **53** The Walled Garden

Sunday 15
- **5** Barnard's Green House
- **37** Model Farm

Sunday 22
- **3** Ashley
- **12** Bylane
- **25** Harrells Hardy Plants Nursery Garden
- **51** Toll House Cottage
- **55** Whitcombe House

Monday 23
- **32** NEW Holland House

Wednesday 25
- **7** 5 Beckett Drive

Saturday 28
- **48** Shuttifield Cottage
- **58** 68 Windsor Avenue

Sunday 29
- **13** 1 Church Cottage
- **35** Marlbrook Gardens
- **58** 68 Windsor Avenue

Monday 30
- **13** 1 Church Cottage

June

Thursday 2
- **45** Red House Farm

Festival Weekend

Saturday 4
- **6** The Barton
- **11** Burcot Gardens
- **21** Eckington Gardens
- **57** Whitlenge Gardens

Sunday 5
- **6** The Barton
- **21** Eckington Gardens
- **25** Harrells Hardy Plants Nursery Garden
- **29** Highfield Cottage
- **57** Whitlenge Gardens
- **60** NEW Zinnia

Monday 6
- **25** Harrells Hardy Plants Nursery Garden

Saturday 11
- **24** Hanley Swan NGS Gardens
- **53** The Walled Garden

Sunday 12
- **5** Barnard's Green House
- **8** Birtsmorton Court
- **24** Hanley Swan NGS Gardens
- **42** Pear Tree Cottage
- **56** White Cottage & Nursery

Wednesday 15
- **53** The Walled Garden

Saturday 18
- **9** Bretforton Manor
- **43** Pershore Gardens
- **47** Rothbury

Sunday 19
- **22** NEW Farlands
- **25** Harrells Hardy Plants Nursery Garden
- **31** Hiraeth
- **43** Pershore Gardens

Monday 20
- **25** Harrells Hardy Plants Nursery Garden

Saturday 25
- **2** Alvechurch Gardens
- **7** 5 Beckett Drive
- **18** NEW David's Garden
- **32** NEW Holland House
- **48** Shuttifield Cottage

Sunday 26
- **2** Alvechurch Gardens
- **4** Astley Towne House
- **7** 5 Beckett Drive
- **16** Cowleigh Lodge
- **17** NEW 24 Croft Bank
- **18** NEW David's Garden
- **29** Highfield Cottage

Secluded fairy garden and romantic folly garden . . .

July

Saturday 2
- **26** Harvington Hall

Sunday 3
- **26** Harvington Hall
- **49** Spetchley Park Gardens

Thursday 7
- **25** Harrells Hardy Plants Nursery Garden
- **45** Red House Farm

Saturday 9
- **23** Hanbury Hall & Gardens

Sunday 10
- **23** Hanbury Hall & Gardens
- **25** Harrells Hardy Plants Nursery Garden
- **56** White Cottage & Nursery

Saturday 16
- **15** The Cottage, 3 Crumpfields Lane
- **18** NEW David's Garden
- **48** Shuttifield Cottage
- **54** Westacres

Sunday 17
- **15** The Cottage, 3 Crumpfields Lane
- **18** NEW David's Garden
- **54** Westacres

Thursday 21
- **25** Harrells Hardy Plants Nursery Garden

Saturday 23
- **47** Rothbury

Sunday 24
- **1** 24 Alexander Avenue
- **25** Harrells Hardy Plants Nursery Garden
- **31** Hiraeth
- **47** Rothbury
- **51** Toll House Cottage
- **60** NEW Zinnia

Friday 29
- **33** Kempsey NGS Gardens

Saturday 30
- **33** Kempsey NGS Gardens

Sunday 31
- **4** Astley Towne House
- **33** Kempsey NGS Gardens

August

Wednesday 3
- **7** 5 Beckett Drive (Evening)

Thursday 4
- **45** Red House Farm

Saturday 6
- **59** Worralls Mill

Sunday 7
- **16** Cowleigh Lodge
- **59** Worralls Mill

Saturday 13
- **40** Offenham Gardens

Sunday 14
10 Bridges Stone Mill
22 **NEW** Farlands
40 Offenham Gardens

Sunday 21
35 Marlbrook Gardens

Saturday 27
11 Burcot Gardens
48 Shuttifield Cottage

Sunday 28
4 Astley Towne House

Monday 29
4 Astley Towne House
42 Pear Tree Cottage (Evening)

Sunday 4
12 Bylane
39 New House Farm, Elmbridge
57 Whitlenge Gardens

Sunday 11
56 White Cottage & Nursery

Sunday 18
5 Barnard's Green House

Gardens open to the public
23 Hanbury Hall & Gardens
25 Harrells Hardy Plants Nursery Garden
26 Harvington Hall
34 Little Malvern Court
45 Red House Farm
46 Riverside Gardens at Webbs
49 Spetchley Park Gardens

50 Stone House Cottage Gardens
57 Whitlenge Gardens

By arrangement only
14 Conderton Manor
19 **NEW** The Dell House
20 6 Dingle End
28 High View
36 74 Meadow Road
38 Morton Hall
41 Overbury Court
44 Pump Cottage
52 The Tynings

Also open by arrangement
1 24 Alexander Avenue
5 Barnard's Green House
6 The Barton
7 5 Beckett Drive
8 Birtsmorton Court

12 Bylane
13 1 Church Cottage
15 The Cottage, 3 Crumpfields Lane
17 **NEW** 24 Croft Bank
18 **NEW** David's Garden
21 Eckington Gardens
24 Blackmore Grange, Hanley Swan NGS Gardens
31 Hiraeth
35 Marlbrook Gardens
35 Oak Tree House, Marlbrook Gardens
35 Round Hill Garden, Marlbrook Gardens
39 New House Farm, Elmbridge
42 Pear Tree Cottage
48 Shuttifield Cottage
51 Toll House Cottage
54 Westacres
55 Whitcombe House
56 White Cottage & Nursery

The Gardens

1 **24 ALEXANDER AVENUE**
Droitwich Spa WR9 8NH. Malley & David Terry, 01905 774907, terrydroit@aol.com. *1m S of Droitwich. Droitwich Spa towards Worcester A38. Or from M5 J6 to Droitwich Town centre.* **Sun 10 Apr, Sun 24 July (2-5.30). Adm £3.50, chd free. Visits also by arrangement Apr to Aug.**
Beautifully designed giving feeling of space and tranquillity. 100+ clematis varieties interlacing high hedges. Borders with rare plants and shrubs. Sweeping curves of lawns and paths to woodland area with shade-loving plants. Drought-tolerant plants in S-facing gravel front garden. Alpine filled troughs. April spring bulbs, July clematis. Shortlisted in a national garden competition 2015. Partial wheelchair access.

GROUP OPENING

2 **ALVECHURCH GARDENS**
Alvechurch B48 7LP. Group Co-ordinator Philip Aubury, 0121 445 3895. *3m N of Redditch, 3m NE of Bromsgrove. NGS Gardens are signed from all roads into Alvechurch village. Pick up your map when you*

pay at your first garden. **Sat 25, Sun 26 June (1-6). Combined adm £6, chd free. Teas at Rectory Cottage and The Lounge in village square.**

THE ALLOTMENTS
Tony Ellis.
Open on Sun 26 June

28 CALLOW HILL ROAD
Martin & Janet Wright.
Open on all dates

NEW **CORNER COTTAGE**
Janice Wiltshire.
Open on all dates

HILL COTTAGE
Philip & Elisabeth Aubury.
Open on all dates

THE OLD SWAN
Ray & Norma Yarnell.
Open on all dates

RECTORY COTTAGE
Celia Hitch.
Open on all dates
0121 445 4824
celia@rectorycottage-alvechurch.co.uk

THE SHRUBBERY
Chris & Stephanie Miall.
Open on all dates

NEW **4 SNAKE LANE**
Jason & Paul Emery.
Open on all dates

SUNNYMEAD
Anne & Andy Humphries.

Open on all dates

76 TANYARD LANE
Dianne & Barry Court.
Open on all dates

8 TRANTER AVENUE
Kevin Baker.
Open on all dates

TUDOR COTTAGE
Jill Green.
Open on all dates

Large village - much new development but interesting core - buildings spanning medieval to Edwardian church on hill with a selection of lovely gardens ranging from a riverside rectory with waterfall to a corner plot 'gardened' for wildlife. There's a professionally landscaped terraced garden and a cottage garden with lots of colour in pots and a wrap-around informal garden. Sloped garden with potted plants and shrubs, and a garden with wooden bridge, decking and pebbled areas. Around the dozen gardens there are rose beds, shrubberies, herbaceous beds, a meadow and fruit and vegetable gardens. Last but not least many gardens include sculptures. Not all gardens are wheelchair accessible.

© Nicola Stocken

Bretforton Manor

3 ASHLEY

Low Road, Church Lench, Evesham WR11 4UH. Roy & Betty Bowron, 01386 871347, bettybowz@gmail.com. *6m N of Evesham. In centre of Church Lench take Low Rd N at junction with Main Street. Ashley is 4th property on R.* **Sun 1, Sun 22 May (2-6). Adm £3, chd free. Home-made teas. Gluten free cake available.** Sloping garden with steps down to lawn, garden pond with plants and fish. Mixed flower beds, greenhouse and vegetable garden. Large pergola with climbing roses, and shaded section with semi-exotic plants which incl tree ferns, other ferns, banana plants, etc. Plants on the large patio incl sago palms, bird of paradise (strelitzia), Hawaiian Palm, agaves and various other plants.

4 ASTLEY TOWNE HOUSE

Astley DY13 0RH. Tim & Lesley Smith, www.astleytownehousesubtropical garden.co.uk. *3m W of Stourport-on-Severn. On B4196 Worcester to Bewdley Road.* **Sun 26 June, Sun 31 July, Sun 28, Mon 29 Aug (1-5).**

Adm £4, chd free. Home-made teas. 2¹/₂ acres garden of a Grade II listed timber building (not open) incl sub-tropical planting. Stumpery garden with tree ferns and woodland temple. Mediterranean garden, tree house, revolving summerhouse and underground grotto with shell mosaics and water features. A recent addition is 'Mr McGregor's' vegetable garden. Teas/cakes and plant stall within the garden. Partial wheelchair access.

5 BARNARD'S GREEN HOUSE

Hastings Pool, Poolbrook Road, Malvern WR14 3NQ. Mrs Sue Nicholls, 01684 574446. *1m E of Malvern. At junction of B4211 & B4208.* **Sun 15 May, Sun 12 June, Sun 18 Sept (2-6). Adm £4, chd free. Home-made teas. Visits also by arrangement Mar to Sept.** With a magnificent backdrop of the Malvern Hills, this 1¹/₂ acre old-fashioned garden is a plantsman's paradise. The main feature is a magnificent cedar. 3 herbaceous and 2 shrub borders, rose garden, red

and white and yellow borders, an evergreen and hydrangea bed, 2 rockeries, pond, sculptures and vegetable garden. Good garden colour throughout the year. Was the home of Charles Hastings - founder of the British Medical Association (1794-1866). Dogs on leads.

6 THE BARTON

Berrow Green, Martley WR6 6PL. David & Vanessa Piggott, 01886 822148, v.piggott@btinternet.com. *1m S of Martley. On B4197 between Martley & A44 at Knightwick, corner of lane to Broadheath. Parking & lunches (12.30 to 2.30) at Admiral Rodney PH opp.* **Sat 4, Sun 5 June (1-5). Adm £4, chd free. Home-made teas. Visits also by arrangement June & July.** This ¹/₂ acre cottagey garden full of colour and texture contains unusual shrubs and billowing herbaceous planting. Paths wind through colour-themed gardens, gravel and grass beds. Roses, clematis and unusual climbers decorate pergolas and trellises. Terracotta-decorated walls enclose a vegetable plot and new tender bed. Visitors comments 'Best private garden I've seen.' ' So unusual and beautiful.' Book sale.

7 5 BECKETT DRIVE

Northwick, Worcester WR3 7BZ. Jacki & Pete Ager, 01905 451108, agers@outlook.com. *1¹/₂ m N of Worcester city centre. Cul-de-sac off A449 Ombersley Rd directly opp Grantham's garage, 1m S of Claines r'about on A449.* **Wed 25 May, Sat 25, Sun 26 June (2-5). Adm £3, chd free. Home-made teas. Evening opening Wed 3 Aug (6-9). Adm £4, chd free. Wine. Visits also by arrangement May to July groups or societies between 10 & 30 people.** An extraordinary town garden on the northern edge of Worcester packed with different plants and year-round interest guaranteed to give visitors ideas and inspiration for their own gardens. Over the past 12 years visitors have enjoyed the unique and surprising features of this garden which has many planting schemes for a variety of situations. Plants at bargain prices and delicious home-made teas.

8 BIRTSMORTON COURT

Birtsmorton, nr Malvern WR13 6JS. Mr & Mrs N G K Dawes, rosaliedawes@btinternet.com. *7m E of Ledbury. Off A438 Ledbury/Tewkesbury rd.* **Sun 12 June (2-5.30). Adm £6, chd free. Teas. Visits also by arrangement May to Sept groups and societies welcome by appointment.**

10 acre garden surrounding beautiful medieval moated manor house (not open). White garden, built and planted in 1997 surrounded on all sides by old topiary. Potager, vegetable garden and working greenhouses, all beautifully maintained. Rare double working moat and waterways including Westminster Pool laid down in Henry VII's reign to mark the consecration of the nave of Westminster Abbey. Ancient yew tree under which Cardinal Wolsey reputedly slept in the legend of the Shadow of the Ragged Stone. No dogs. Teas, plants.

♿ ❀ ☕

Look out for the watcher of the lower garden and scourge of the bind weed . . .

9 BRETFORTON MANOR

Main Street, Bretforton, Evesham WR11 7JH. Mr & Mrs M L Chambers. *4m E of Evesham, 6½ m N of Broadway. Centre of Bretforton village, next to the church.* **Sat 16 Apr (11-4); Sat 18 June (11-5). Adm £6, chd free.**

An outstanding garden of 5 acres recently redesigned and replanted. The immaculately maintained garden contains mixed and herbaceous borders, an exotic border, scented walk and many tender and unusual plants. Hedges and topiary both old and new, several water features and many listed buildings and structures. The orchard has been extended and now contains a wide variety of fruit and specimen trees. The dovecote, aviary, apiary, cider barn and old village stocks are all listed. Beautiful walled garden, waterfall and ponds.

Glasshouses and small kitchen garden with cut flower borders. Featured in Cotswold Life, 'Maintaining Standards'; The English Garden, 'Beauty reborn'; Landscape, 'Late Colour Spectacle'; Countryside, 'Autumnal charm'; Period Living, 'Keeping with tradition'. Gravel paths, unfenced ponds.

♿ ❀

10 BRIDGES STONE MILL

Alfrick Pound WR6 5HR. Sir Michael & Lady Perry. *6m NW of Malvern. A4103 from Worcester to Bransford r'about, then Suckley Rd for 3m to Alfrick Pound.* **Sun 14 Aug (2-5.30). Adm £5, chd free. Home-made teas.**

Formerly a cherry orchard adjoining the mainly C19 water mill, this is now a 2½ -acre garden laid out with trees, shrubs, mixed beds and borders. Small lake, stream and brook. The garden is bounded by 200yd stretch of Leigh Brook (an SSSI), and a mill stream from the mill's own weir. Extensive all-yr round planting. Ornamental vegetable parterre completes the picture. Wheelchair access by car to courtyard.

♿ ❀ ☕

GROUP OPENING

11 BURCOT GARDENS

Bromsgrove B60 1LJ. *2m N from Bromsgrove, 1m W from Tardebigge, 1m SE from J1 of M42, 2m SE from J4 of M5. On B4096 approx 1m S of J1 of M42 towards Burcot. Park at Fresh@ Burcot Garden Centre, Alcester Rd just past 1st r'about on R. Both gardens a short walk away & signed. For SatNav - B60 1PW.* **Sat 4 June, Sat 27 Aug (12-5). Combined adm £3.50, chd free. Fresh will be donating profits from refreshment sales to NGS - please show your NGS ticket to ensure this happens.**

APPLETREEWICK
Mrs Ruth Edwards

16 GREEN HILL
Mr Chris Franklin

Two contrasting gardens in the small village of Burcot near Bromsgrove. 16 Green Hill, A small garden created by owner over last 3yrs. Designed for minimum maintenance and all year round colour mainly with trees and shrubs. A good example of what can be achieved with a small garden.

Appletreewick is a long, sloping, natural garden recently redesigned and still developing to encourage local wildlife. Small natural swimming pond (not for public use), sculptures, artefacts, seating and with a view of the Clent Hills from the top orchard. Plants and refreshments at Fresh@Burcot Garden Centre (where you park the car) who are offering a special deal - buy 1 outdoor plant and get 1 free when you show your NGS admission ticket (limited to one per ticket holder) a donation to the NGS for all plants sold to NGS visitors.

🚐 ☕

12 BYLANE

Worcester Road, Earls Croome WR8 9DA. Shirley & Fred Bloxsome, 01684 592489, shirleymay70@hotmail.co.uk. *1m N of Upton on Severn turning. On main A38 directly past Earls Croome Garden Centre, signed Bridle Way. Directly behind Earls Croome Garden Centre, turn down bridle way to park.* **Sun 17 Apr, Sun 22 May, Sun 4 Sept (1-5). Adm £3, chd free. Home-made teas. Visits also by arrangement Apr to Sept please give one months notice. Adm £5 to include tea.**

Herbaceous garden, paddock with wildlife pond, vegetable garden, and chickens, wood with mature trees and bluebells. Approximately 2 acres in all, Private parties welcome. Plenty of seating areas and shelter if needed, very quiet and secluded.

🐔 ❀ ☕

13 1 CHURCH COTTAGE

Church Road, Defford WR8 9BJ. John Taylor & Ann Sheppard, 01386 750863, ann98sheppard@btinternet.com. *3m SW of Pershore. A4104 Pershore to Upton rd, turn into Harpley Rd, Defford, black & white cottage at side of church. Parking in village hall car park.* **Sun 1, Mon 2, Sun 29, Mon 30 May (11-5). Adm £3, chd free. Home-made teas. Visits also by arrangement May to Sept groups of 10 - 30.**

True countryman's ⅓ -acre garden. Interesting layout. Japanese - style feature with 'dragons den'. Specimen trees; water features; vegetable garden; poultry and cider making. Perennial garden being developed. Wheelchair access to most areas.

♿ 🐔 ❀ ☕

14 ▶ **CONDERTON MANOR**
Conderton, nr Tewkesbury
GL20 7PR. Mr & Mrs W Carr, 01386
725389, carrs@conderton.com.
*5¹/₂ m NE of Tewkesbury. From M5 -
A46 to Beckford - L for Overbury/
Conderton. From Tewkesbury B4079
to Bredon - then follow signs to
Overbury. Conderton from B4077
follow A46 directions from Teddington
r'about.* **Visits by arrangement Apr
to Nov individuals and groups
welcome. 30 max. Teas.**
7-acre garden, recently replanted in a
contemporary style with magnificent
views of Cotswolds. Flowering
cherries and bulbs in spring. Formal
terrace with clipped box parterre;
huge rose and clematis arches, mixed
borders of roses and herbaceous
plants, bog bank and quarry garden.
Many unusual trees and shrubs make
this a garden to visit at all seasons.
Visitors are particularly encouraged to
come in spring and autumn. This is a
garden/small arboretum of particular
interest for tree lovers. The views
towards the Cotswolds are
spectacular. Some gravel paths and
steps - no disabled WC.

15 ▶ **THE COTTAGE,
3 CRUMPFIELDS LANE**
Webheath, Redditch B97 5PN.
Victor Johnson,
pjohnson889@btinternet.com.
*From A448 through Redditch take
slip rds signed to Headless Cross,
at r'about take 3rd exit then follow
NGS signs.* **Sat 16, Sun 17 July
(11-4.30). Adm £5, chd free. Tea
and cakes, soft drinks. Visits also
by arrangement June & July for
groups from 2 to 20.**
Recently established 1¹/₂ - acre
garden landscaped to provide
5 rooms on 4 levels stepped into a
hillside. From the 2nd level are
stunning views over Vale of Evesham.
2 water features, (1 in a cave) and
places to sit and enjoy the wildlife.

Wonderland can be found in meadow
area of wild flowers. Partial wheelchair
access to levels 2 and 3 are
accessible with able body escort
(help available).
&♿ ✿ ☕

16 ▶ **COWLEIGH LODGE**
16 Cowleigh Bank, Malvern
WR14 1QP. Jane & Mic Schuster,
01684 439054,
dalyan@hotmail.co.uk. *7m SW from
Worcester, on the slopes of the
Malvern Hills. From Worcester or
Ledbury follow the A449 to Link Top.
Take North Malvern Rd (behind Holy
Trinity church), follow yellow signs.
From Hereford take B4219 after
Storridge church, follow yellow signs.*
**Sun 26 June, Sun 7 Aug (11-5).
Adm £3.50, chd free. Home-made
teas.**
Just under an acre this is the second
year of opening with new features to
see. Original well, formal rose garden,
grass beds, colour themed beds and
wildlife path leading to a pond.
Wander up through the wooded area
to the veggie garden, pumpkin patch
and up to the new raised area with
wonderful views. Look in the
polytunnel and greenhouses and then
relax with a cuppa and slice of
homemade cake. This year we shall
be taking part in the 'well dressing'
festival that takes place in Malvern.
Slopes and steps throughout the
garden. WC and refreshments.
✿ ☕

17 ▶ **NEW** ▶ **24 CROFT BANK**
Malvern WR14 4DU. Andy & Cathy
Adams, 01684 899405. *From
Worcester on A449 to Gt Malvern. R
onto B4232 signed Bromyard + West
Malvern. Continue approx 1¹/₂ m.
Turn R at Elim College Conference
centre onto Croft Bank. No 24 is on
the R.* **Sun 26 June (1-5). Adm
£3.50, chd free. Home-made teas.
Visits also by arrangement May to
Aug, groups of 10+.**
The garden enjoys wonderful far
reaching south and westerly views
from high on the Malvern Hills. This
half acre garden has undergone
extensive landscaping and rebuilding
and now contains flower borders for
all seasons, trained fruit trees,
vegetable beds, some specimen
trees and small woodland area.
Garden Studio has a display of
paintings and cards inspired by the
garden. Sloping areas and woodland
walk not suitable for wheelchairs.
&♿ ✿ ☕

18 ▶ **NEW** ▶ **DAVID'S GARDEN**
Badgers Way, Ash Lane, Martin
Hussingtree, Worcester WR3 8TB.
Sarah & David Beauchamp,
01905 340104,
davidsnurseries0@tiscali.co.uk.
*Parking at David's Nurseries, Martin
Hussingtree and follow yellow signs
from car park.* **Sat 25 June (2-5);
Sun 26 June (12-4); Sat 16 July
(2-5); Sun 17 July (12-4). Adm £4,
chd free. Home-made teas. Visits
also by arrangement June to
Sept.**
A new garden created from scratch
over the last 12 months. After retiring
from running the Garden Centre,
David and Sarah were able to follow
their passion for plants. The 1¹/₂ acre
garden has been divided into areas
each with it's own unique style and
planting, which include secluded fairy
garden, romantic folly garden, beach
garden, herbaceous borders,
vegetable patch and green houses.
&♿ 🐕 ✿ 🚐 ☕

19 ▶ **NEW** ▶ **THE DELL HOUSE**
2 Green Lane, Malvern Wells
WR14 4HU. Kevin & Elizabeth
Rolph, 01684 564448,
stay@thedellhouse.co.uk,
www.thedellhouse.co.uk. *2m S of
Great Malvern. Behind former church
on corner of Wells Rd & Green Lane
just N of petrol station on A449 Wells
Rd.* **Visits by arrangement Apr to
Nov for groups of 8 to 20. Adm
£3.50, chd free. Light
refreshments.**
Two acre wooded hillside garden of
the 1820 Dell House; a former rectory
now a B&B. Currently undergoing
recovery and development by new
owners. Peaceful and natural, the
garden contains many magnificent
specimen trees. Informal in style with
wild flower areas, sculptures, tree
carving and Victorian garden
structures. Garden spaces linked by
meandering bark paths. Look out for
the watcher of the lower garden and
scourge of the bind weed. Views over
the Severn valley. Wheelchair access
limited. Parking is on gravel. Sloping
bark paths, some quite steep.
🐕 🛏 ☕

20 ▶ **6 DINGLE END**
Inkberrow, Worcester WR7 4EY.
Mr & Mrs Glenn & Gabriel Allison,
01386 792039. *12m E of Worcester.
A422 from Worcester. At the 30 sign
in Inkberrow turn R down Appletree
Lane then 1st L up Pepper St. Dingle
End is 4th on R of Pepper St. Limited*

parking in Dingle End but street parking on Pepper St. **Visits by arrangement Apr to Sept groups 6 min, 26 max. Adm £3, chd free. Light refreshments.** Over 1 acre garden with formal area close to the house opening into a flat area featuring a large pond, stream and weir with apple orchard and woodland area. Large vegetable garden incl an interesting variety of fruits. Garden designed for wildlife. Pond, stream and weir. Refreshments for pre arranged groups can be tailored to requirements e.g. light lunches/supper (soup & sandwiches/tea & cakes) - mainly home grown food. Slopes beside every terrace.

GROUP OPENING

21 ECKINGTON GARDENS
Eckington WR10 4DQ. Group Coordinator Lynn Glaze, 01386 751924, lynnglaze@cmail.co.uk. *3 gardens - 2 in or close New Rd/Nafford Rd, 3rd is 1m out on Nafford Rd. A4104 Pershore to Upton & Defford, L turn B4080 to Eckington. In centre, by war memorial turn L for gardens.* **Sat 4, Sun 5 June (11-5). Combined adm £4, chd free. Home-made teas at Mantoft on Saturday & at Nafford House on Sunday. Visits also by arrangement May to Sept.**

HILLTOP
Richard & Margaret Bateman.

MANTOFT
Mr & Mrs M J Tupper.

NAFFORD HOUSE
Janet & John Wheatley.
01386 750233

3 very diverse gardens; formal walled garden, hilltop garden with' windows' in formal hedging and sunken garden and natural wooded garden sloping down to the riverside. Set in/close to lovely village of Eckington with riverside parking and picnic site. Mantoft - formal walled garden with fish pond, topiary and dew pond, with ducks and geese. Hedges and stone paths, gazebo overlooking garden and new dovecote. Hilltop - 1 acre with sunken garden/pond, rose garden, herbaceous borders and formal hedging with 'windows' and views over extensive countryside. Nafford House - 2 acre mature natural garden/wood with slopes to R Avon,

Whitcombe House

formal gardens, magnificent wisteria. Partial wheelchair access at Nafford House to wooded area and slopes to river.

22 NEW FARLANDS
Kyrewood, Tenbury Wells WR15 8SG. Alan & Frances Eachus. *1/2 m E of Tenbury Wells on the B4204. Approaching from Tenbury slow down when you reach the 40mph sign at Kyrewood & proceed with care around the sharp L turn. Parking available behind the green barn on the L - follow signs.* **Sun 19 June, Sun 14 Aug (2-6). Adm £4, chd free. Home-made teas.**
Beech and hornbeam hedges divide the one acre garden into separate compartments all linked by a central hedged pathway. There is a mature Atlantic cedar at the centre of the garden but the most striking features are the extensive drifts of herbaceous perennials planted around a naturalised pond and through the kitchen garden. There is also a vegetable garden in a series of raised beds.

23 ◆ HANBURY HALL & GARDENS
School Road, Hanbury, Droitwich WR9 7EA. National Trust, 01527 821214, hanburyhall@nationaltrust.org.uk, www.nationaltrust.org.uk/ hanburyhall. *4m E of Droitwich. From M5 exit 5 follow A38 to Droitwich; from Droitwich 4m along B4090.* **For NGS: Sat 9, Sun 10 July (10.30-5). Adm £11.50, chd £5.70. Light refreshments. For other opening times and information, please phone, email or visit garden website.**
Visit Hanbury Hall in the year the garden restoration comes of age, turning 21. The early C18 gardens and park are a rare example of the work of Royal Designer, George London, pre-eminent Gardener of his time, whose creations provided order in a chaotic world before the later loosening of garden design in the Landscape Movement. Servants Hall Tea-Room - catering hot lunches, tea and cake. Stableyard cafe catering for take away snacks and drinks. Chambers Tea-Room. Buggy available to bring visitors from the car park to the front of the property and wheelchairs are available from the Hall.

GROUP OPENING

24 ◆ HANLEY SWAN NGS GARDENS

Hanley Swan, Worcester WR8 0DJ. Group Co-ordinator Brian Skeys, 01684 311297, brimfields@icloud.com. *5m E of Malvern, 3m NW of Upton upon Severn, 9m S of Worcester. From Worcester/Callow End take B4424 to Hanley Castle then turn R. From Upton upon Severn B4211 to Hanley Castle turn L. From Malvern/Ledbury from A449 take B4209. Gardens signed from village.* **Sat 11, Sun 12 June (1-5). Combined adm £5, chd free. Cream teas at 19 Winnington Gardens.**

BLACKMORE GRANGE
Mr & Mrs D Robertson
Visits also by arrangement June to Aug for groups of 10+ annerobertson54@btinternet.com
01684 311446

CHASEWOOD
Mrs Sydney Harrison
01684 310527
sydney.harrison@cmail.co.uk

NEW MEADOW BANK
Mrs Lesley Stroud & Mr Dave Horrobin
01684 310917
Dave@meadowbankhs.freeserve.co.uk

NEW THE PADDOCKS
Mr & Mrs N. Fowler

19 WINNINGTON GARDENS
Brian & Irene Skeys

5 gardens different in size and style in Hanley Swan. Blackmore Grange, a two acre informal garden packed with plants, shrubs and trees. A swimming pool has been transformed into the stable yard garden, with traditional cottage-style planting. There's a woodland walk, wild area, orchard, kitchen garden and mixed borders. Chasewood has lavender and old fashioned roses. A gravel garden with an Iris and Thyme walk. A collection of Bonsai and Coach Built Prams. Meadow Bank is a modern interpretation of a cottage garden, with a hot border, Dahlias grown for show and collections of Iris and Auriculas. The Paddocks is a wildlife garden with ponds, a tadpole nursery, mixed borders, and a collection of cacti and succulents. 19 Winnington Gardens is a garden of rooms. Mixed borders for all seasons enclosed with climbing roses, a small oriental garden, trained fruit trees, raised herb bed with a special standard gooseberry bush. Entrance tickets from either Blackmore Grange or Chasewood.

❀ ☕

25 ◆ HARRELLS HARDY PLANTS NURSERY GARDEN

Rudge Road, Evesham WR11 4JR. Liz Nicklin & Kate Phillips, 01386 443077, mail@harrellshardyplants.co.uk, www.harrellshardyplants.co.uk. *¼ m from centre of Evesham. From A4184 turn into Queens Rd R at end, then L, Rudge Rd. 150 yds on R down lane. SatNav WR11 4LA.* **For NGS: Sun 22 May, Sun 5 June (2-5); Mon 6 June (10.30-12.30); Sun 19 June (2-5); Mon 20 June (10.30-12.30); Thur 7, Sun 10, Thur 21, Sun 24 July (2-5). Adm £3, chd free. Home-made teas. For other opening times and information, please phone, email or visit garden website.**

This garden is naturalistic in style and informally planted with a glorious array of hardy perennials, grasses and a large range of hemerocallis. The 1-acre site consists of beds and borders accessed by bark paths, with several seating areas giving views over the garden. 'Harrell's Hardy Plants is an absolute gem! The garden is absolutely breathtaking- the web site gives you a hint, you really do need to visit to appreciate the wonderful planting scheme, and learn the story behind the garden'. Featured in Gloucester Echo & Gloucester Citizen Weekend supplement.

❀ 🚐 ☕

Extensive drifts of herbaceous perennials planted around a naturalised pond . . .

26 ◆ HARVINGTON HALL

Harvington, Kidderminster DY10 4LR. The Roman Catholic Archdiocese of Birmingham, 01562 777846, www.harvingtonhall.com. *3m SE of Kidderminster. ½ m E of A450 Birmingham to Worcester Rd & approx ½ m N of A448 from Kidderminster to Bromsgrove.* **For NGS: Sat 2, Sun 3 July (11.30-4). Adm £3.50, chd £1.50. Light refreshments. For other opening times and information, please phone or visit garden website.**

Romantic Elizabethan moated manor house with island gardens, small Elizabethan-style herb garden, all tended by volunteers. Tours of the Hall, which contains secret hiding places and rare wall paintings, are also available. Tea Room serves morning coffee, light lunches and afternoon teas. Access to gardens, Malt House Visitor Centre, tea room, shop and WC.

♿ ❀ 🚐 ☕

27 HEWELL GRANGE

Hewell Lane, Tardebigge, Redditch B97 6QS. HMP Hewell, 01527 783017, roy.jones01@hmps.gsi.gov.uk. *2m NW of Redditch. HMP Hewell is situated on B4096. For SatNav use B97 6QQ. Follow signs to Grange Resettlement Unit. Visitors must book in advance via email (address above). This is a prison and there are booking and security procedures to be followed.* **Sat 7, Sun 8 May (10-3.30). Adm £5, chd free. Home-made teas. All visitors must be pre booked by email (see above) before arriving.**

Hewell Grange is an C18 landscape park and lake laid out by Lancelot Brown and modified around 1812 by Humphery Repton. The grounds of this prison feature rhododendrons and azaleas, Lake and Repton bridge, formal garden, water tower, and rock garden. Grounds have mature woodland. Not a flower garden. Please note - Visitors to the garden will be shown the garden features in escorted small groups. The garden tour may be over 60 minutes. Therefore, visitors must be physically able to walk for this length of time. There are uneven surfaces in the grounds so sensible walking footwear is essential. Lakeside walk and bluebell walk a chance to see a historic garden not normally open to the public. Please

Note - All visits have to have been booked prior to date for security reasons. There is no wheelchair access to the Gardens.

28 HIGH VIEW

Martley WR6 6PW. Mike & Carole Dunnett, 01886 821559, mike.dunnett@btinternet.com. *1m S of Martley. On B4197 between Martley & A44 at Knightwick. Visits by arrangement June to Aug group of 10+. Adm £4.50, chd free. Home-made teas.*

Intriguing and mature 2½ acre garden developed over 40yrs. Visitors have described the garden as magical, inspirational and one of the best kept horticultural secrets of Worcestershire! With superb views over the Teme valley, vast range of plants and many interesting features, it's a garden not to be missed. Steps and steep slopes so appropriate foot wear needed. Other local attractions available.

29 HIGHFIELD COTTAGE

Kings Green, Wichenford, Worcester WR6 6YG. Valerie Mills. *7m from Worcester. Take B4204 from Worcester to Martley turn R at the Masons Arms PH. Follow yellow NGS signs from here. Parking available. Sun 5, Sun 26 June (2-6). Adm £3.50, chd free. Home-made teas.*

A real picture book cottage garden with roses and clematis in abundance clambering over rustic arches. Traditional borders overflowing with delphiniums, lupins, geraniums, campanulas and many others. A lovely cool, shady area with mature trees and shrubs and a large water garden area. Small woodland with a live variety of ornamental pheasants. Exhibition and sale of local art.

31 HIRAETH

30 Showell Road, Droitwich WR9 8UY. Sue & John Fletcher, 07752 717243/01905 778390, jfletcher@inductotherm.co.uk. *1m S of Droitwich. On The Ridings estate. Turn off A38 r'about into Addyes Way, 2nd R into Showell Rd, 500yds on R. Follow the yellow signs! Wed 11 May (1.30-5); Sun 19 June, Sun 24 July (2-5.30). Adm £3, chd free. Home-made teas. Visits also by arrangement June to Aug for groups of 10-30.*

'A haven on the way to heaven' - description in Visitors Book. Front,

rear gardens contain unusual plants, traditional cottage garden, herbaceous, hostas, ferns, 300yr-old Olive Tree, arches, pool, waterfall, 200yr-old stile, oak sculptures, metal animals, birds etc incl, giraffes, elephant. An oasis of colours in a garden not to be missed. Tea, coffee, cold drinks, home-made cakes and scones served with china cups, saucers, plates, tea-pots and coffee-pots! Partial wheelchair access.

32 NEW HOLLAND HOUSE

Main Street, Cropthorne WR10 3NB. Holland House Charitable Trust, 01386 860330, reservations@hollandhouse.org, www.hollandhouse.org. *5m W of Evesham. The village of Cropthorne is situated between Pershore and Evesham.* **Mon 23 May (10-4); Sat 25 June (2-6). Adm £4, chd free. Cream teas.** *Donation to USPG.*

Formal gardens laid out by Lutyens in 1904 with rose garden; thatched house dating back to C16 (not open). Lovely riverside setting with roses in June. Sunken garden, with steps at each angle and a central sundial. Large vegetable garden. Holland House kitchens will be open to serve cream tea and full afternoon tea.

GROUP OPENING

33 KEMPSEY NGS GARDENS

Kempsey, Worcester WR5 3NG. Group Co-ordinator Gail Brookes, 01905 821823. *4M SW M5 J7; 4M S Worcester City Centre, in Kempsey village off opp. sides of A38. For 35 Bannut Hill take Plovers Rise opp. Lawns Nursing Home. 9 Old Road South is directly off A38 or via Squires Walk. This garden is situated in narrow lane with restricted parking, please leave small layby opp. for Blue Badge holders. Both gardens will be signed from A38 in village.* **Fri 29, Sat 30, Sun 31 July (10.30-4.30). Combined adm £3.50, chd free. Home-made teas at 9 Old Road South.**

35 BANNUT HILL
Gail Brookes

9 OLD ROAD SOUTH
Anne Potter

There are two gardens on show, one situated at 35 Bannut Hill (last year

part of Bannut Hill Gardens) and the other at 9 Old Road South (last year open as a sole garden). 35 Bannut Hill is a small garden with many interesting and quirky ideas including wildlife pond, hexagonally style greenhouse, 7 fruit trees, pixie house and lots of homes for wildlife, also look out for the giant ants!! An unusual water feature and a new 8'5 x 8'5 Cedar gazebo summer house. 9 Old Road South is a third of an acre garden with expansive views of the Malvern Hills and open countryside. Established during the last 6yrs it is a rustic/country garden with some modern sculpture and has been described as quirky! Seating area within young mixed orchard. Flat but somewhat even paths.

34 ◆ LITTLE MALVERN COURT

Little Malvern WR14 4JN. Mrs T M Berington, 01684 892988, littlemalverncourt@hotmail.com, www.littlemalverncourt.co.uk. *3m S of Malvern. On A4104 S of junction with A449.* **For NGS: Sun 20 Mar, Mon 2 May (2-5). Adm £7, chd £1. Home-made teas. For other opening times and information, please phone, email or visit garden website.**

10 acres attached to former Benedictine Priory, magnificent views over Severn valley. Garden rooms and terrace around house designed and planted in early 1980s; chain of lakes; wide variety of spring bulbs, flowering trees and shrubs. Notable collection of old-fashioned roses. Topiary hedge and fine trees. The May Bank Holiday - Flower Festival in the Priory Church. Partial wheelchair access.

Whitlenge Gardens

GROUP OPENING

35 ▸ MARLBROOK GARDENS
Braces Lane, Marlbrook,
Bromsgrove B60 1DY. Group Co-
ordinator Alan Nokes, 0121 445
5520, alyn.nokes@btinternet.com.
*2m N of Bromsgrove. 1m N of M42
J1, follow B4096 signed Rednal, turn
L at Xrds into Braces Lane. 1m S of
M5 J4, follow A38 signed
Bromsgrove, turn L at T-lights into
Braces Lane. Parking available.*
Sun 29 May, Sun 21 Aug (1.30-
5.30). Combined adm £5, chd free.
Home-made teas. **Visits also by
arrangement June to Aug for
groups of 10+ Viewing for one or
both gardens.**

OAK TREE HOUSE
Di & Dave Morgan
Visits also by arrangement
June to Aug groups of 10+
meandi@btinternet.com
0121 445 3595

ROUND HILL GARDEN
Lynn & Alan Nokes
Visits also by arrangement
June to Aug groups of 10+
alyn.nokes@btinternet.com
0121 445 5520

Two unique and stunning gardens,
each have opened individually in their
own right. Experience the contrasting
styles, Round Hill Garden an ideal
garden for art groups. A traditional
garden with a twist into the exotic
and unusual. Rear garden divided into
four distinct areas, Mediterranean,
Patio/pond, Lawn with borders and
islands and vegetable garden with
raised beds and greenhouses. Oak

Tree House a plantswoman's cottage
garden with views over open fields.
Past the twisted rail, through the arch
leads to a garden packed full of
shrubs and herbaceous planting with
grass paths weaving in and out. Both
gardens overflowing with plants for
sun and shade, also ponds, water
features, patios, artifacts and
sculptures. Recognised for
excellence, with many articles over
the years published in national
papers/gardening magazines.
Continually evolving, many repeat
visitors enjoy sharing with us their
new discoveries. Art displays at both
gardens by garden owners. Garden
Quiz for children. Round Hill Garden
will be featured in Garden News late
summer.

❀ ☕

36 74 MEADOW ROAD

Wythall B47 6EQ. Joe Manchester, 01564 829589, joe@cogentscreenprint.co.uk. *4m E of Alvechurch. 2m N from J3 M42. On A435 at Becketts Farm r'about take rd signed Earlswood/Solihull. Approx 250 metres turn L into School Drive, then L into Meadow Rd.* **Visits by arrangement May to Sept. Adm £3, chd free. Home-made teas.** Has been described one of the most unusual urban garden dedicated to woodland, shade-loving plants. 'Expect the unexpected' in a few tropical and foreign species. Meander through the garden under the majestic pine, eucalyptus and silver birch. Sit and enjoy the peaceful surroundings and see how many different ferns and hostas you can find.

37 MODEL FARM

Montpelier Road, West Malvern WR14 4BP. Deirdre & Phil Drake, phil@modelfarm2.plus.com. *W side of Malvern Hills. B4232 at Elim Pentecostal HQ (Stately stone building). Turn down Croft Bank 200yds & park. Walk L down Montpelier Rd to Model Farm.* **Sun 15 May (1.30-5.30). Adm £5, chd free. Home-made teas, cakes and cream teas.** Stunning 2-acre tranquil garden in the Malvern Hills. Victorian tudor-style house (not open) surrounded by well-stocked borders, patio and courtyard. Picturesque contours of garden complemented by natural stream, ponds, mixed borders, orchard, bog garden, meadow. Ancient oaks, specimen trees, acers, panoramic views to Hay Bluff. Steep in some areas. Wonderful spring bulbs, wisteria and clematis. New for 2016 a high level circular folly and a 60x10ft new border now blooming. Some of the main features of the garden afford assisted wheelchair access including the 'welcome bed', the new 60ft border, courtyard, orchard,etc.

38 MORTON HALL

Morton Hall Lane, Holberrow Green, Redditch B96 6SJ. Mrs A Olivieri, 01386 791820, morton.garden@mhcom.co.uk, www.mortonhallgardens.co.uk. *In the centre of Holberrow Green, at a wooden bench around a tree, turn up Morton Hall Lane. You will reach the main gates to Morton Hall on your R.*

Press intercom to be admitted. **Visits by arrangement Apr to Sept for groups of 10-20. Adm £8, chd free incl refreshments.** An elegant stroll garden around a late Georgian house (not open), with potager, hot coloured borders, formalised flower garden, wisteria arbour, large rock garden leading to soft plantings around pools and teahouse, into fritillary meadows with wild roses and towering redwoods. Living roof, Mediterranean plantings, and Ha-Ha with views over vale of Evesham'. Refreshments tea/coffee and savoury snack for morning appointments, tea/coffee and cake for afternoon visits. Unable to cater for special dietary requirements. Featured in Country Life.

39 NEW HOUSE FARM, ELMBRIDGE

Elmbridge Lane, Elmbridge WR9 0DA. Charles & Carlo Caddick, 01299 851249, Carlocaddick@hotmail.com. *2¹⁄₂ m N of Droitwich Spa. A442 from Droitwich to Cutnall Green. Take lane opp Chequers PH. Go 1m to T-junction. Turn L towards Elmbridge Green/Elmbridge (past church & hall). At T-junction go R into Elmbridge Lane, garden on L.* **Sat 7, Sun 8 May, Sat 3, Sun 4 Sept (2-4.30). Adm £4, chd free. Home-made teas. Visits also by arrangement May to Sept.** This charming garden surrounding an early C19 red brick house (not open) has a wealth of rare trees and shrubs under planted with unusual bulbs and herbaceous plants. Special features are the 'perry wheel', ornamental vegetable gardens. Water garden, dry garden, rose garden, mews, the

retreat, potager and greenhouse. Topiary and tropical plants complete the effect. Plant nursery with many exotics for sun and shade. Plant clearance sale. Mews garden not accessible to wheelchairs.

GROUP OPENING

40 OFFENHAM GARDENS

Main Street, Offenham WR11 8QD. *Approaching Offenham on B4510 from Evesham, L into village signed Offenham & ferry ³⁄₄ m. Follow road round into village. Park in Village Hall car park opp Church. Garden 5 mins walk from car park, follow signs, R out of car park down to Maypole, L at Maypole into Church St, gardens next to each other on R & opposite. No parking in Church St..* **Sat 13, Sun 14 Aug (11-5). Combined adm £4, chd free. Home-made teas.**

> **DECHMONT**
> Angela & Paul Gash
>
> **LANGDALE**
> Sheila & Adrian James
> www.adrianjames.org.uk
>
> **WILLOWAY**
> Stephen & Linda Pitts

Offenham is a picturesque village in the heart of the Vale of Evesham, with thatched cottages and traditional maypole. Three gardens of diverse interests from woodland and wildlife to topiary, herbaceous and exotic. Langdale is a plant lovers garden designed for all year round interest. Surrounding a formal rill are relaxed borders in a variety of styles leading down to a productive vegetable garden and experimental naturalistic planting of mainly southern Africa plants. Willoway, an oasis of sound and colour, is initially hidden by the traditional front garden. A corridor of Hostas leads the visitor to the patio, a lush carpet of lawn, and then, via the bamboo curtain, to the oriental area. A streptocarpus collection contains varieties from Eastern Europe and Japan. With a mature walnut tree Dechmont features box topiary, patio areas, year round interest from conifers, shrubs and acers, colour from bulbs, perennials, annuals, clematis and roses set within curved borders. Langdale was featured in Cotswold Life.

41 OVERBURY COURT
Overbury, Tewkesbury GL20 7NP.
Mr & Mrs Bruce Bossom,
01386 725111(office),
gardens@overburyestate.co.uk. *5m
NE of Tewkesbury. Village signed off
A46, Turn off village rd beside the
church. Park by gates & walk up
drive.* **Visits by arrangement Mar
to Aug for groups of 10+. Adm £4,
chd free.**
Georgian house 1740 (not open);
landscape garden of same date with
stream and pools; daffodil bank and
grotto. Plane trees; yew hedges;
shrubs; cut flowers; coloured foliage;
gold and silver, shrub rose borders.
Norman church adjoins garden. Close
to Whitcombe and Conderton Manor.
Some slopes, while all the garden can
be viewed, parts are not accessible to
wheelchairs.

42 PEAR TREE COTTAGE
Witton Hill, Wichenford, Worcester
WR6 6YX. Pamela & Alistair
Thompson, 01886 888295,
peartree.pam@gmail.com,
www.peartreecottage.me. *13m NW
of Worcester & 2m NE of Martley.
From Martley, take B4197. Turn R into
Horn Lane then take 2nd L signed
Witton Hill. Keep L & Pear Tree
Cottage is on R at top of hill.* **Sun 1
May (2-6); Mon 2 May (2-10) after
6 adm £4.50 glass of wine, coffee
and cakes available; Sun 12 June
(2-6). Adm £4. Home-made teas.
Evening opening Mon 29 Aug
(6-10). Adm £4.50 glass of wine,
coffee and cakes available. Visits
also by arrangement May to Aug
all visitors very welcome but
please telephone first!**
A Grade II listed black and white
cottage (not open) with SW-facing
gardens and far reaching views
across orchards to Abberley clock
tower. The gardens extend to approx
³/₄ acre and comprise of gently
sloping lawns with mixed and
woodland borders, shade and plenty
of strategically placed seating. The
garden exudes a quirky and
humorous character with the odd
surprise! 'Garden by Twilight'
evenings are very popular. Trees,
shrubs and sculptures are softly uplit
and the garden is filled with candles
and nightlights (weather permitting!)
Visitors are invited to listen to the
owls and watch the bats whilst
enjoying a glass of wine. ('Gardeners'
Loo' available to visitors). Silver medal
winner in Britain's Best Gardeners'

Garden. Featured in 'The English
Garden' magazine and
Worcestershire Life & Worcester
News. Partial wheelchair access.

> Garden exudes
> a quirky and
> humorous character
> with the odd
> surprise . . . !

GROUP OPENING

43 PERSHORE GARDENS
Pershore WR10 1BG. Group Co-
ordinator Jan Garratt, 01386
553197, jangarratt@btinternet.com,
www.visitpershore.co.uk. *On
B4084 between Worcester &
Evesham, & 6m from exit 7 on M5.
There is also a train station to the
north of the town.* **Sat 18, Sun 19
June (1-5). Combined adm £5, chd
free. Home-made teas at Primary
School, Broad Street, No. 8
Community Arts Centre, High
Street.**
Each year about twenty gardens
open in Pershore. This small
Georgian market town has been
opening gardens as part of the NGS
for 50 years, almost continuously. In
those days the open gardens were in
the Georgian heart of the town but
now, gardens open from all over the
town, including the Community
Orchard in the Abbey Park. Some
gardens are surprisingly large, well
over an acre, while others are little
more than courtyard gardens. All
have their individual appeal and
present great variety. Some gardens
are open every year, some on
alternate years and every year there
are at least two new gardens. This
keeps it fresh and interesting for
returning visitors. The wealth of pubs
and cafes offer ample opportunities
for refreshment and teas are served
at one of the gardens in Broad Street.
Tickets are valid for both days and
are available in advance from the

Tourist Information and 'Blue' in
Broad Street and on the day at
Number 8 Community Arts Centre in
the High Street or any open garden.
Refreshments available in PHs and
cafes in the town. Wheelchair access
to some gardens.

44 PUMP COTTAGE
Hill Lane, Weatheroak, nr
Alvechurch B48 7EQ. Barry Knee &
Sue Hunstone, 01564 826250,
barryknee.1947@btinternet.com,
www.pumpcottage.org.uk. *3m E of
Alvechurch. 1¹/₂ m from J3 M42 off
N-bound c'way of A435 (signed
Alvechurch). Parking in adjacent field.*
**Visits by arrangement May to July
individuals and/or groups are
most welcome. Adm £6, chd free.
Home-made teas, incl gluten free.**
Described by visitors as 'A secret
wonderland, surprises at every turn'.
C19 cottage, rural setting.
Enchanting, romantic 1 acre
plantaholic's garden with yr-round
interest. Colourful borders, roses,
rockery, fernery, water features,
natural pond, and wildlife area. Many
unusual plants. Creative features,
artefacts and ornaments which
provide inspirational ideas. Partial
wheelchair access due to slopes and
narrow gravelled paths.

45 ◆ RED HOUSE FARM
Flying Horse Lane, Bradley Green,
Redditch B96 6QT. Mrs M M
Weaver, 01527 821269,
www.redhousefarmgardenandnurs
ery.co.uk. *7m W of Redditch, 7m E
of Droitwich. On B4090 Alcester to
Droitwich Spa. Ignore sign to Bradley
Green. Turn opp The Red Lion PH.*
**For NGS: Thur 3 Mar, 7 Apr, 5 May,
2 June, 7 July, 4 Aug, 1 Sept (12-
5). Adm £2.50, chd free. For other
opening times and information,
please phone or visit garden
website.**
Created as a peaceful haven from its
working farm environment, this
mature ¹/₂ acre country garden offers
yr-round interest. In densely planted
borders accessed by winding paths a
wide range of traditional favourites
rub shoulders with the newest of
introductions and make each visit a
pleasurable and rewarding
experience. Adjacent nursery open
daily 10-5.

46 ◆ RIVERSIDE GARDENS AT WEBBS

Wychbold, Droitwich WR9 0DG. Webbs of Wychbold, 01527 860000, www.webbsdirect.co.uk. *2m N of Droitwich Spa. 1m N of M5 J5 on A38. Follow tourism signs from M5.* **For opening times and information, please phone or visit garden website.**

2½ acres. Themed gardens incl Colour spectrum, tropical and dry garden, New David Austin Rose collection, vegetable garden area, new seaside garden, bamboozelum, Contemplation and self sufficient Garden. New Wave gardens opened 2004, designer Noel Kingsbury, to create natural seasonal interest with grasses and perennials.This area is now home to beehives which produce honey for our own food hall. The New Wave Garden was slightly changed over 2014 to become more of a natural wildlife area. There are willow wigwams made for children to play in. This area now incl a bird hide. Open all yr except Christmas, Boxing Day and Easter Sun. Our New Wave Gardens area has grass paths which are underlaid with mesh so people with heavy duty wheelchairs can be taken around.

47 ROTHBURY

5 St Peters Road, North Malvern, WR14 1QS. John Bryson, Philippa Lowe & David. *7m W of M5 J7 (Worcester). Turn off A449 Worcester to Ledbury Rd at B4503, signed Leigh Sinton. Almost immed take the middle rd (Hornyold Rd). St Peter's Rd is ¼ m uphill, 2nd R.* **Sat 18 June, Sat 23, Sun 24 July (11-5.30). Adm £3, chd free. Homemade light lunches, cakes and teas.**

Set on slopes of Malvern Hills, ⅓ acre plant-lovers' garden surrounding Arts and Crafts house (not open), created by owners since 1999. Herbaceous borders, rockery with thyme walk, wildlife pond, vegetable patch, small orchard, containers. A series of hand-excavated terraces accessed by sloping paths and steps. Views to Lickey Hills and Worcester and of the Malverns. Seats. Partial wheelchair access. One very low step at entry, one standard step to main lawn and one to WC. Decking slope to top lawn.

48 SHUTTIFIELD COTTAGE

Birchwood, Storridge WR13 5HA. Mr & Mrs David Judge, 01886 884243, judge.shutti@btinternet.com. *8m W of Worcester. Turn R off A4103 opp Storridge Church to Birchwood. After 1¼ m L down steep tarmac drive. Please park on roadside but drive down if walking is difficult (150 yards).* **Sat 30 Apr, Sat 7, Sun 8, Sat 28 May, Sat 25 June, Sat 16 July, Sat 27 Aug (1.30-5). Adm £5, chd free. Home-made teas. Visits also by arrangement Apr to Aug groups of 10 or more.**

Superb position and views. Unexpected 3-acre plantsman's garden, extensive herbaceous borders, primula and stump bed, many unusual trees, shrubs, perennials, colour-themed for all-yr interest. Walks in 20-acre wood with ponds, natural wild areas, anemones, bluebells, rhododendrons, azaleas are a particular spring feature. Large old rose garden with many spectacular mature climbers. Good garden colour throughout the yr. Small deer park, vegetable garden. Wildlife ponds, wild flowers and walks in 20 acres of ancient woodland. Featured in local and county papers. Some sloping lawns and steep paths in wooded area.

WE ARE MACMILLAN. CANCER SUPPORT

In 2016 the Chesterfield Royal NGS Macmillan Cancer Unit will open

49 ◆ SPETCHLEY PARK GARDENS

Spetchley, Worcester WR5 1RS. Mr John Berkeley, 01905 345106, enquiries@spetchleygardens.co.uk, www.spetchleygardens.co.uk. *2m E of Worcester. On A44, follow brown signs.* **For NGS: Fri 25 Mar, Sun 3 July (11-6). Adm £6.50, chd £2. Light refreshments. For other opening times and information, please phone, email or visit garden website.**

Surrounded by glorious countryside lays one of Britain's best-kept secrets. Spetchley is a garden for all tastes containing one of the biggest private collections of plant varieties outside the major botanical gardens. Spetchley is not a formal paradise of neatly manicured lawns or beds but rather a wondrous display of plants, shrubs and trees woven into a garden of many rooms and vistas. Spetchley hosts a Specialist plant fair on 24 April. Gravel paths.

50 ◆ STONE HOUSE COTTAGE GARDENS

Church Lane, Stone DY10 4BG. James & Louisa Arbuthnott, 07817 921114, www.shcn.co.uk. *2m SE of Kidderminster. Via A448 towards Bromsgrove, next to church, turn up drive.* **For opening times and information, please phone or visit garden website.**

A beautiful and romantic walled garden adorned with unusual brick follies. This acclaimed garden is exuberantly planted and holds one of the largest collections of rare plants in the country. It acts as a shop window for the adjoining nursery. Open Wed to Sat late March to early Sept 10-5. Partial wheelchair access.

51 TOLL HOUSE COTTAGE

Stourport Road, Bewdley DY12 1PU. Joan & Rob Roberts, 01299 402331, joanroberts7@live.co.uk. *1m S of Bewdley, 2m N of Stourport, 3m W of Kidderminster. On A456 between Bewdley & Stourport, Opp Blackstone car park & picnic site (free parking). Disabled parking on drive.* **Sun 22 May, Sun 24 July (10-5). Adm £3.50, chd free. Home-made teas. Visits also by arrangement May to Aug 10 min, 30 max.**

Developing ½ acre garden started in 2008 in 2 sections. Cottage garden with a collection of bulbs, herbaceous and shrubs for year round colour incl lawn. A small arboretum with grass walkways and summerhouse and arbour. A large pool with waterfall and beach for wildlife. Vegetable garden with raised beds in large fruit cage. A painters garden. Gallery for Woodturning and Paintings also open.

52 THE TYNINGS

Church Lane, Stoulton, Worcester WR7 4RE. John & Leslie Bryant, 01905 840189, johnlesbryant@btinternet.com. *5m S of Worcester; 3m N of Pershore. On the B4084 (formerly A44) between M5 J7 & Pershore. The Tynings lies beyond the church at the extreme end of Church Lane. Ample parking.* Visits by arrangement July to Sept. Adm £3.50, chd free. Light refreshments.

Acclaimed plantsman's ½ -acre garden, generously planted with a large selection of rare trees and shrubs. Features incl specialist collection of lilies, many unusual climbers and rare ferns. The colour continues into late summer with dahlia, berberis, euonymus and tree colour. Surprises around every corner. You will not be disappointed. Lovely views of adjacent Norman Church and surrounding countryside. Plants labelled and plant lists available. Further info and photos on NGS website.

Rose arch leading to paddock with arbour and long border . . .

53 THE WALLED GARDEN

6 Rose Terrace, off Fort Royal Hill, Worcester WR5 1BU. William & Julia Scott, 01905 354629. *Close to the City centre. ½ m from Cathedral. Via Fort Royal Hill, off London Rd (A44). Park on 1st section of Rose Terrace & walk the last 20yds down track.* Sat 7, Wed 11 May, Sat 11, Wed 15 June (1-5). Adm £3.50, chd free. Teas.

In this peaceful oasis of scent and colour, a tapestry of culinary and medicinal herbs, vegetables, flowers and fruit grow organically. History, symmetry and historic references are the foundation of this C19 walled kitchen garden which is seasonally evolving with new projects and planting schemes. Common and rare herbs, maturing fruit trees incl Mulberry, Medlar and Quince.

54 WESTACRES

Wolverhampton Road, Prestwood, Stourbridge DY7 5AN. Mrs Joyce Williams, 01384 877496. *3m W of Stourbridge. A449 in between Wall Heath (2m) & Kidderminster (6m). Ample parking Prestwood Nurseries (next door).* Sat 16, Sun 17 July (11-4). Adm £4, chd free. Light refreshments. Visits also by arrangement June to Aug 15 min, 30 max.

³/₄ -acre plant collector's garden with unusual plants and many different varieties of acers, hostas, shrubs. Woodland walk, large koi pool. Covered tea area with home-made cakes. Come and see for yourselves, you won't be disappointed. Described by a visitor in the visitors book as 'A garden which we all wished we could have, at least once in our lifetime'. Plants for Sale. Koi Pool, Woodland walk, Tea area. Garden is flat. Disabled parking.

55 WHITCOMBE HOUSE

Overbury, Tewkesbury GL20 7NZ. Faith & Anthony Hallett, 01386 725206, faith.hallett1@gmail.com. *9m S of Evesham, 5m NE Tewkesbury. Leave A46 at Beckford to Overbury (2m). Or B4080 from Tewkesbury through Bredon/Kemerton (5m). Or small lane signed Overbury at r'about junction A46, A435 & B4077. Approx 5m from J9 M5.* Sun 22 May (2-5). Adm £3.50, chd free. Teas. Visits also by arrangement May to Aug and evening visits (with wine) also possible.

1 acre planted for every season in an idyllic Cotswold stone setting. Spring bulbs give way to cool blue and white, allium and flowering shrubs are followed by cascading roses, summer pastels and fiery oranges, red and yellows. The spring-fed stream flows through colourful moisture loving plants. Asters, cosmos and yet more roses provide late summer colour. Lots of seats for relaxation. For easiest wheelchair access please contact us in advance for details.

56 WHITE COTTAGE & NURSERY

Earls Common Road, Stock Green, Inkberrow B96 6SZ. Mr & Mrs S M Bates, 01386 792414, smandjbates@aol.com. *2m W of Inkberrow, 2m E of Upton Snodsbury. A422 Worcester to Alcester, turn at sign for Stock Green by Red Hart PH, 1½ m to T- junction, turn L 500 yds on the L.* Sun 10 Apr, Sun 1, Mon 2 May, Sun 12 June, Sun 10 July, Sun 11 Sept (11-4.30). Adm £3, chd free. Visits also by arrangement Apr to Oct groups up to 10+. Nursery open on request.

2 acre garden with large herbaceous and shrub borders, island beds, stream and bog area. Spring meadow with 100's of snakes head fritillaries. Formal area with lily pond and circular rose garden. Alpine rockery and new fern area. Large collection of interesting trees incl Nyssa Sylvatica, Parrotia persica, and Acer 'October Glory' for magnificent Autumn colour and many others. Gravel drive to the gate but it is manageable.

57 ◆ WHITLENGE GARDENS

Whitlenge Lane, Hartlebury DY10 4HD. Mr & Mrs K J Southall, 01299 250720, keith.southall@creativelandscapes.co.uk, www.whitlenge.co.uk. *5m S of Kidderminster, on A442. A449 Kidderminster to Worcester L at T-lights, A442 signed Droitwich, over island, ¼ m, 1st R into Whitlenge Lane. Follow brown signs.* For NGS: Sat 13, Sun 14 Feb, Sat 2, Sun 3 Apr, Sat 4, Sun 5 June, Sat 3, Sun 4 Sept (10-5). Adm £4, chd free. Light refreshments in the adacent Tea rooms. For other opening times and information, please phone, email or visit garden website.

3 acre show garden of professional designer with over 800 varieties of trees, shrubs etc. Twisted pillar pergola, Moongate, waterfalls, ponds and streams. Mystic features of the Green Man, 'Sword in the Stone' and cave fernery. Walk the turf labyrinth and take refreshments in The Garden 'Design Studio' tearoom. 2½ metre high brick and oak Moongate with 4 cascading waterfalls, deck walk through giant Gunnera leaves, Camomile paths through herb gardens, 400 sq metre grass labyrinth, play and pet corner. Locally sourced homemade food in tearoom, plant nursery. Showcased on ITV with Alan Titchmarsh's ' Love your Gardens' featuring the unique Moongate and waterfalls.

58 68 WINDSOR AVENUE
St Johns, Worcester WR2 5NB.
Roger & Barbara Parker, 01905
428723. *W area of Worcester, W side of R Severn. Off the A44 to Bromyard. Into Comer Rd, 3rd L into Laugherne Rd, 3rd L into Windsor Ave, at bottom in Cul-de-sac. Limited parking, please park courteously on road sides, car share if possible.* **Sat 28, Sun 29 May (11-4). Adm £4, chd free. Teas. Soft drinks also available.**
Almost one acre garden divided into three areas, situated behind a 1930's semi detached house in a cul-de-sac, visitors are amazed and often comment on size of garden. Garden includes a bog garden, flower beds, 'oriental' area, vegetable patch, four greenhouses and four ponds each in very different styles. If that is not enough we have Chickens, Quail, Ornamental Pheasants and Finches. Gravel paths are everywhere.

59 WORRALLS MILL
Netherton Lane, Abberley
DY13 0UL. Mr & Mrs B J Merriman.
3m SW of Stourport-on-Severn. From Stourport on Severn take Gt Witley rd over R Severn. Continue to sign for Dunley on L, take 2nd turn on R Heightington tel box on corner, top of lane, turn L. **Sat 6, Sun 7 Aug (11-5). Adm £5, chd free. Home-made teas.**
Old water mill, brook runs through garden. Large trees, oak, ash, shrubs and red bridge at front of house. Back of house, terracing, hot bed, mixed borders, pergola to 'jungle', bamboo, fatsia etc. Fish pond; large pool (wildlife) in what was once mill race bog; garden stream; old woodland. Approx 1/4 m long, 2 acres. Partial wheelchair access, gravel paths and some steps.

60 NEW ZINNIA
41 Lower Cladswell Lane, Cookhill,
Worcestershire B49 5JY. Stuart & Kate Clowes. *7m S of Redditch on A441. From M42 J2 follow A441 Evesham. After 10m pass Nevill Arms PH on R, 800yds turn R into Church Lane. Follow NGS signs. Park in local rds but please observe private reserved parking signs opp garden.* **Sun 5 June, Sun 24 July (1.30-5.30). Adm £3.50, chd free. Light refreshments.**
Half-acre garden divided into 5 sections. Patio with raised beds leading to lawn with mixed borders. Pond garden with rockery, varied beds and 'bandstand' seating area. Rose arch leading to paddock with arbour and long border. Small orchard and a birch grove.

White Cottage & Nursery

0   10   20 kilometres
0   10 miles
© Global Mapping / XYZ Maps

Bank   Saltburn-by-the-Sea
Middlesbrough   Hinderwell
Guisborough **32**   Sandsend
Great Ayton   **44** Whitby
Stokesley   Danby   Sleights   Robin Hood's Bay
Goathland
Burniston
104   **33**   Scalby
Kirkbymoorside   **89**   West Ayton   Scarborough
35   Pickering   **4**   Eastfield
Helmsley   **3**   Snainton   Filey
Oswaldkirk   **47** **41**   Hunmanby   Filey Bay
100   Hovingham   **98**   **54**   **53** **123**
Brandsby   **97** **95**   Flamborough Head
93   Malton   **128**   Norton   **70**   Flamborough
Easingwold   North Grimston
YORKSHIRE   Sledmere   Langtoft   Bridlington
Shipton   **66**   Burton Agnes   **14**   Bridlington Bay
Stamford Bridge   **51**   Driffield
Haxby   **13**   **39** Fridaythorpe   **43**   **73**   Skipsea
York   **105**   Bainton
81   **58** Pocklington   Hutton Cranswick
68   Fulford   **25**   Brandesburton   Hornsea
110   Hayton   Market Weighton   **87**   **82**
106   **9** **120** **29**   **101**   **77** **2** **114**   Aldbrough
Cawood   **103**   Holme-on-Spalding-Moor   Beverley   **92** **117**   **28**
15   Barlby   Bubwith   **52**   Cottingham   Bilton
Selby   North Cave   **31** **107**   South Cave   **11**
71   Howden   M62   **30**   Hessle   **Kingston upon Hull**
ottingley   Snaith   Goole   North Ferriby   **21** **5**   **85** Hedon   **16** Withernsea
fract **10**   Barton-upon-Humber   **125**   **50** **67**
Askern   Thorne   Crowle   **30**   Patrington   Easington
Hatfield   Scunthorpe   **4** **52**   Spurn Head
Bentley   M180   M181   Winterton   **53**   Immingham   Humberside
M18   Epworth   Bottesford   **38**   Grimsby
Doncaster   Brigg   Laceby   Cleethorpes
A1(M)   **112**   **116**   Caistor   **35**   Humberston
49   Robin Hood   Blyton   **26**   Waltham
Bawtry   Kirton in Lindsey   Binbrook   Ludborough   North Somercotes
Maltby   **12** **20**   **23**   Market Rasen   **16** **57**
19   Gainsborough   **LINCOLNSHIRE**   **54** Louth   Mablethorpe
Retford   **3** **14**   **22**   **34**   **50**
Worksop   **25**   Dunholme   **48** **44**   Maltby le Marsh   **33**
8   Newton on Trent   Milton   **4**   Saxilby   **11** **43** **49**   **17**   Wragby   Alford
Nettleham

Yorkshire

Yorkshire, England's largest county, stretches from the Pennines in the west to the rugged coast and sandy beaches of the east: a rural landscape of moors, dales, vales and rolling wolds.

Nestling on riverbanks lie many historic market towns, and in the deep valleys of the west and south others retain their 19th century industrial heritage of coal, steel and textiles. The wealth generated by these industries supported the many great estates, houses and gardens throughout the county. From Hull in the east, a complex network of canals weaves its way across the county, connecting cities to the sea and beyond.

The Victorian spa town of Harrogate with the RHS garden at Harlow Carr, or the historic city of York with a minster encircled by Roman walls, are both ideal centres from which to explore the gardens and cultural heritage of the county.

There are many NGS gardens to choose from, the majority of which enjoy visits from groups – Parcevall Hall in the west, Newby Hall near Ripon, Scampston Hall with a Piet Oudolf designed walled garden, and Burton Agnes Hall in the east are gardens for all seasons and are among the finest of all English gardens.

Right: The Court © Lee Beel

Yorkshire Volunteers

County Organisers

East Yorks
Helen Marsden
01430 860222
jerryhelen@btinternet.com

North Yorks – Cleveland, Hambleton, Richmond, Rydale & Scarborough
Josephine Marks
01845 501626
jlmarks60@gmail.com

South & West Yorks & North Yorks - Craven, Harrogate, Selby & York
Bridget Marshall BEM
01423 330474
biddymarshall@btinternet.com

County Treasurer
Angela Pugh
01423 330456
amjopugh@clannet.co.uk

Publicity
Jane Cooper 01484 604232
jane.cooper@ngs.org.uk

Booklet Advertising
John Plant
01347 888125
plantjohnsgarden@btinternet.com

By Arrangement Visits
Penny Phillips
01937 834970
hornington@btinternet.com

Assistant County Organisers
East Yorks
Ian & Linda McGowan 01482 896492
adnil_magoo@yahoo.com

Natalie Verow 01759 368444
natalieverow@aol.com

Kate Willans 01964 534502
kwkatewillans32@gmail.com

North Yorks
Gillian Mellor 01723 891636
gill.mellor@btconnect.com

Hugh Norton 01653 628604
hughnorton0@gmail.com

Judi Smith 01765 688565
lowsutton@hotmail.co.uk

West & South Yorks
Deborah Bigley 01609 748915
debsandbobbigley@btinternet.com

Felicity Bowring 01729 823551
diss@austwick.org

Veronica Brook 01423 340875
veronicabowring@me.com

Rosie Hamlin 01302 535135
rosiehamlin@aol.com

Jane Hudson 01924 840980
janehudson42@btinternet.com

Opening Dates

All entries subject to change.
For latest information check www.ngs.org.uk
Extended openings are shown at the begining of the month

February

Snowdrop Festival

127 **3 Bainton Close (from Sunday 14 to Sunday 21)**

Friday 19
31 Fawley House

Sunday 21
25 Devonshire Mill

Wednesday 24
1 Austwick Hall

Sunday 28
109 NEW Sutton Gardens

March

Sunday 20
84 The Old Vicarage

Thursday 31
52 Hotham Hall

April

Sunday 3
3 NEW Barnville
18 Clifton Castle

Thursday 7
52 Hotham Hall

Sunday 10
29 Ellerker House
36 Goldsborough Hall

Sunday 17
45 Highfields

Wednesday 20
19 Cold Cotes

Sunday 24
17 The Circles Garden

May

Sunday 1
5 Beacon Garth
71 Maspin House
93 Rewela Cottage
120 Weathervane House

Wednesday 4
71 Maspin House

Friday 6
100 Shandy Hall Gardens (Evening)

Sunday 8
94 RHS Garden Harlow Carr
106 Stillingfleet Lodge
118 Warley House Garden

Tuesday 10
48 NEW The Himalayan Gardens

Wednesday 11
88 Parcevall Hall Gardens
118 Warley House Garden

Saturday 14
108 NEW Sunny Mount

Sunday 15
21 The Court
45 Highfields
46 Hillbark
62 Low Hall
108 NEW Sunny Mount
124 Woodlands Cottage

Wednesday 18
6 Beacon Hill House

Sunday 22
43 NEW Highfield Cottage
54 Jackson's Wold
95 The Ridings
122 Whixley Gardens

Sunday 29
23 Creskeld Hall
30 NEW Ellerker Manor
43 NEW Highfield Cottage

Monday 30
10 Bridge Farm House

June

26 **Dove Cottage (every Friday from 3 June)**

Festival Weekend

Saturday 4
53 Hunmanby Grange
83 Old Sleningford Hall
101 Shiptonthorpe Gardens

Sunday 5
18 Clifton Castle
40 16 Hallam Grange Croft
53 Hunmanby Grange
76 Millrace Garden
77 23 Molescroft Road
82 Nutkins
83 Old Sleningford Hall
101 Shiptonthorpe Gardens
128 The Yorkshire Arboretum

Wednesday 8
104 Sleightholmedale Lodge

Saturday 11
14 Burton Agnes Hall & Gardens
57 Langton Hall

Sunday 12
14 Burton Agnes Hall & Gardens
86 The Orchard
89 Penny Piece Cottages

Wednesday 15
91 Pilmoor Cottages

Thursday 16
103 Skipwith Hall

Friday 17
114 Tickton CE Primary

Saturday 18
51 Holmfield
108 NEW Sunny Mount

Sunday 19
42 High Hall
51 Holmfield
68 The Manor House
74 Millgate House
108 NEW Sunny Mount
111 Swale Cottage

Wednesday 22
122 Whixley Gardens

Saturday 25
85 Omega
102 Sion Hill Hall

Sunday 26
8 Birstwith Hall
27 34 Dover Road
28 Dowthorpe Hall & Horse Pasture Cottage
32 Fernleigh
119 Green Hill House
49 2 Hollin Close
54 Jackson's Wold
65 Maidens Folly
67 Manor Farm
73 NEW 4 Mill Lane
85 Omega
96 NEW Rivelin Cottage
102 Sion Hill Hall
127 Yorke House

Wednesday 29
7 Beechcroft Farmhouse

Autumn brings a blaze of coloured foliage, berries and late flowers . . .

July

26 **Dove Cottage (every Friday)**

Friday 1
100 Shandy Hall Gardens (Evening)

Sunday 3
33 Fernwood
46 Hillbark
75 NEW 115 Millhouses Lane
80 Norton Conyers
95 The Ridings
97 Rustic Cottage
125 NEW Wyedale

Friday 8
90 Pictorial Meadows

Saturday 9
15 Cawood Gardens
90 Pictorial Meadows
123 Whyncrest

Sunday 10
15 Cawood Gardens
24 Dacre Banks & Summerbridge Gardens
41 Havoc Hall
58 Linden Lodge
74 Millgate House
110 Sutton upon Derwent School
117 NEW Walled Gardens of Beverley
123 Whyncrest

Wednesday 13
37 The Grange

Saturday 16
58 Linden Lodge

Sunday 17
44 20 Highfield Road
58 Linden Lodge
59 Little Eden
81 The Nursery
109 NEW Sutton Gardens

Wednesday 20
19 Cold Cotes (Evening)
81 The Nursery

Friday 22
31 Fawley House
107 NEW Stonefield Cottage

Saturday 23
31 Fawley House
107 NEW Stonefield Cottage

Sunday 24
16 NEW 14 Chellsway
22 Cow Close Cottage
31 Fawley House
36 Goldsborough Hall
42 High Hall

Share your day out on **f** and **t**

26 Dove Cottage
(every Friday)
50 54 Hollym Road
92 Queensgate & Kitchen
Lane Allotments
104 Sleightholmedale
Lodge
107 NEW Stonefield
Cottage

Wednesday 27
99 Serenity

Thursday 28
76 Millrace Garden

Friday 29
72 Mere'stead (Evening)

Sunday 31
32 Fernleigh
38 NEW Grasmere
93 Rewela Cottage
99 Serenity
105 Stamford Bridge
Gardens
113 Thornycroft

August

26 Dove Cottage
(every Friday until
26 Aug)

Wednesday 3
129 Butterfield Heights

Saturday 6
63 NEW Low Westwood
Garden
70 Mansion Cottage
112 Tamarind

Sunday 7
60 Littlethorpe Gardens
70 Mansion Cottage

112 Tamarind

Wednesday 10
37 The Grange
79 2 Newlay Grove

Sunday 14
7 Beechcroft Farmhouse

Sunday 21
39 Greenwick Farm
59 Little Eden
76 Millrace Garden

Wednesday 24
116 NEW Walker's
Nursery (Evening)

Sunday 28
32 Fernleigh
91 Pilmoor Cottages

September

Sunday 4
66 Manor Farm

Sunday 11
3 NEW Barnville
9 Boundary Cottage
47 NEW Hillside
61 Littlethorpe Manor
106 Stillingfleet Lodge

Sunday 18
19 Cold Cotes

February 2017

Sunday 19
25 Devonshire Mill

Wednesday 22
1 Austwick Hall

Gardens open to the public

14 Burton Agnes Hall &
Gardens
20 Constable Burton Hall
Gardens
54 Jackson's Wold
55 Land Farm
78 Newby Hall & Gardens
80 Norton Conyers
88 Parcevall Hall Gardens
90 Pictorial Meadows
94 RHS Garden Harlow
Carr
98 Scampston Walled
Garden
100 Shandy Hall Gardens
106 Stillingfleet Lodge
113 Thornycroft
126 York Gate
128 The Yorkshire
Arboretum

By arrangement only

2 3 Bainton Close
4 Basin Howe Farm
11 Brook Farm
12 Brookfield
13 Bugthorpe Gardens
34 Firvale Allotment
Garden
35 Friars Hill
56 Langton Farm
64 Lower Crawshaw
69 NEW The Manor
House
87 Orchard House

115 Vicarage House
121 The White House

Also open by arrangement

3 NEW Barnville
5 Beacon Garth
8 Birstwith Hall
129 Butterfield Heights
15 9 Anson Grove,
Cawood Gardens
15 21 Great Close,
Cawood Gardens
15 The Pigeoncote,
Cawood Gardens
19 Cold Cotes
21 The Court
22 Cow Close Cottage
24 Dacre Banks &
Summerbridge
Gardens
27 34 Dover Road
28 Dowthorpe Hall &
Horse Pasture Cottage
30 NEW Ellerker Manor
32 Fernleigh
33 Fernwood
37 The Grange
39 Greenwick Farm
40 16 Hallam Grange
Croft
47 NEW Hillside
51 Holmfield
52 Hotham Hall
58 Linden Lodge
59 Little Eden
60 Greencroft, Littlethorpe
Gardens
62 Low Hall
70 Mansion Cottage
76 Millrace Garden
81 The Nursery
82 Nutkins
84 The Old Vicarage
85 Omega
86 The Orchard
89 Penny Piece Cottages
91 Pilmoor Cottages
93 Rewela Cottage
95 The Ridings
97 Rustic Cottage
99 Serenity
103 Skipwith Hall
105 NEW Newstead,
Stamford Bridge
Gardens
105 Stamford Bridge
Gardens
111 Swale Cottage
118 Warley House Garden
122 Cobble Cottage,
Whixley Gardens
122 Lydiate House,
Whixley Gardens
123 Whyncrest
124 Woodlands Cottage
127 Yorke House

Langton Hall

The Gardens

1 AUSTWICK HALL

Town Head Lane, Austwick, Settle LA2 8BS. James E Culley & Michael Pearson, 015242 51794, austwickhall@austwick. org, www.austwickhall.co.uk. *5m W of Settle. Leave the A65 to Austwick. Pass the PO on R, Gamecock Inn on L. Take first L onto Town Head Lane. Parking on Town Head Lane.* **Wed 24 Feb (12-4). Adm £4, chd free. Home-made teas. 2017: Wed 22 Feb.**

Set in the dramatic limestone scenery of the Dales the garden nestles into a steeply wooded hillside. Extensive drifts of common single and double snowdrops are an impressive sight with examples of over 50 other varieties. Sculptures along the trail add further interest. Woodland paths may be slippery in wet weather so sensible footwear is recommended.

2 3 BAINTON CLOSE

Beverley HU17 7DL. Mrs Elaine Thornton, 01482 861643. *Located off New Walk opp Police Station. Please use address at 'final destination', as Sat Nav takes you to next lane.* **Visits by arrangement in Feb 14 to 21 Feb 10.30-3 for groups of 1-10. Adm £3, chd free.**

Small town garden with a variety of spring flowers incl hellebores and a collection of approx 150 varieties of snowdrop which will be of particular interest to 'Galanthophiles'.

3 NEW BARNVILLE

Wilton, Pickering YO18 7LE. Bill & Liz Craven, lizcraven40@gmail.com. *4m E of Pickering. On main A170, travelling from Pickering towards Scarborough, enter village of Wilton. Turn R. House on L in 200yrds.* **Sun 3 Apr (12-5). Sun 11 Sept (12-5). Home-made teas. Adm £3, chd free. Visits also by arrangement Feb to Oct 10+.**

Over an acre of hidden gardens on the edge of the North York Moors. Unusual plants make a garden for all seasons: Winter is coloured by cyclamen, snowdrop, hellebore and witch hazel. Spring, magnolia and azalea shelter naturalised bulbs, trillium and erythronium. Summer's cool green foliage highlights allium, agapanthus and foxtail lilies. Autumn brings a blaze of coloured foliage,

berries and late flowers. Lower garden unsuitable for wheelchairs in wet, but level stone paths in upper gardens. Access to sunken garden via steps - can be viewed from above.

Amongst old orchard trees is hidden a restful family suburban garden of $^{1}/_{3}$ acre . . .

4 BASIN HOWE FARM

Cockmoor Road, Sawdon, Scarborough YO13 9EG. Mr & Mrs Richard & Heather Mullin, 01723 850180, info@basinhowefarm.co.uk, www.basinhowefarm.co.uk. *Turn off A170 between Scarborough & Pickering at Brompton by Sawdon follow sign to Sawdon. Basin Howe Farm 1½ m above Sawdon village on the L.* **Visits by arrangement May to Aug (not Sats), groups and couples welcome. Adm £5, chd free. Refreshments by arrangement (small charge).**

These gardens have a lovely atmosphere. 3 acres of garden with rose garden, box parterre with seasonal planting and koi pond, herbaceous borders, wildlife pond and elevated viewing deck with Pod summer house. Orchard and woodland shelter belt, ferns, lawns and shrubs. Paved seating areas but gravel paths. Basin Howe is high above the Wolds and has a Bronze Age Burial Mound. Maintained by owners. Winners of Yorkshire in Bloom Gold Award and Category winner and Gold Award Scaborough in Bloom. Wheelchair Access is possible to most areas but a helper is required. Paths are gravel and grass.

5 BEACON GARTH

Redcliff Road, Hessle, Hull HU13 0HA. Ivor & June Innes, 01482 646140, ivorinnes@mac.com. *4½ m W of Hull. Follow signs for Hessle*

Foreshore. **Sun 1 May (12-5). Adm £4, chd free. Home-made teas. Visits also by arrangement Apr to July.**

Edwardian, Arts and Crafts House (mentioned in Peysner's Guide to Hull) and S-facing garden set in 3½ acres, in an elevated position overlooking the Humber. Stunning sunken rock garden with bulbs and specimen trees, hostas and ferns. Mature trees, large lawns and herbaceous borders. Gravel paths, haha, box hedges and topiary. Child friendly; children's play area. Teas served in main hallway of house. Partial wheelchair access.

6 BEACON HILL HOUSE

Langbar, Ilkley LS29 0EU. Mr & Mrs H Boyle. *4m NW of Ilkley. 1¼ m SE of A59 at Bolton Bridge.* **Wed 18 May (1.30-5). Adm £4, chd free. Home-made teas.** *Donation to Riding for the Disabled.*

Look over the garden wall onto a grouse moor. This 7-acre 'intake', steeply sloping but gardened since 1848, is a spring paradise with early rhododendrons, magnolias and bulbs. Roses, large scented rhododendrons and borders take over, some unusual trees, an established liriodendron, pterostyrax, hoherias and several species of eucryphia. Small kitchen garden, orchard, pond, C19 fernery and C19 hotwall. Featured in Ilkley Gazette and Craven Herald.

7 BEECHCROFT FARMHOUSE

Aldwark, nr Alne, York YO61 1UB. Alison Pollock. *14m NW of York, 17m E of Harrogate, 7m SW of Easingwold. Follow signs for Aldwark Manor hotel & golf course for village. Approach from A1(M) and W is via Aldwark Toll Bridge (40p toll for cars).* **Wed 29 June, Sun 14 Aug (1-5). Adm £3.50, chd free. Home-made teas.**

Country garden surrounding Georgian farmhouse (not open). All yr interest starts with rare snowdrops, hellebores and borders for winter colour. Winding paths lead through series of smaller gardens with different planting themes. Cottage borders with old roses, tulips, clematis. Hidden areas with seating give a secluded feel. Gravel courtyard with small formal pool, late and unusual perennials and grasses.

8 BIRSTWITH HALL
High Birstwith, Harrogate HG3 2JW. Sir James & Lady Aykroyd, 01423 770250, ladya@birstwithhall.co.uk. *5m NW of Harrogate. Between Hampsthwaite & Birstwith villages, close to A59 Harrogate/Skipton Rd.* **Sun 26 June (2-5). Adm £4, chd free. Home-made teas. Visits also by arrangement groups and coaches welcome.**
Large 8 acre garden nestling in secluded Yorkshire dale with formal garden and ornamental orchard, extensive lawns, picturesque stream, large pond and Victorian greenhouse.

 ♿ 🚉 ⊗ 🚐 ☕

9 BOUNDARY COTTAGE
Seaton Ross, York YO42 4NF. Roger Brook, www.nodiggardener.co.uk. *5m SW of Pocklington. From A64 York take Hull exit and immed. B1228. Approx 10m to Seaton Ross. From M62 Howden N on B1228. From A1079 follow Seaton Ross.* **Sun 11 Sept (11-4.30). Adm £4, chd free. Light refreshments in the conservatory.**
Lecturer and creator of Bolton Percy churchyard garden, Roger Brook's own no-dig garden. 1500 different plant varieties, many rare, provide colour all yr round. The acre garden has numerous and varied intimate features, visually connected in sweeping views. Horticulturally unorthodox, especially the fruit and vegetables, the overall effect is dramatic. The garden holds the National Collection of Dicentra. Very friendly rheas in the field next door! Artist in the garden. Access to all parts of the garden. Some pushing required on fescue lawns. WC access up a step.

 ♿ 🚉 ⊗ **NPC** ☕

10 BRIDGE FARM HOUSE
Long Lane, Great Heck, Selby DN14 0BE. Barbara & Richard Ferrari, 01977 661277, barbaraferrari@mypostoffice.co.uk. *6m S of Selby, 3m E M62 J34. At M62 J34 take A19 to Selby, at r'about turn E to Snaith on A645. R at T-lights, L at T-junction onto Main St, past Church, turn L at T-junction, cross to car park.* **Mon 30 May (12-4.30). Adm £3, chd free. Tea in church (opp).**
2-acre garden on sandy soil, designed and planted by owners since 2002. Divided by hedges to house a varied collection of plants:

many unusual and rarely seen elsewhere, providing year round colour and interest. Including mature trees, bog, gravel, ponds, long double mixed borders, hens, compost heaps and wildlife.

 ♿ 🚉 ⊗ ☕

11 BROOK FARM
Elstronwick, Hull HU12 9BP. Mrs Janet Dolling, 01964 670191. *10m E of Hull city centre. Go N on Hedon to Withernsea Rd. Turn off L before Burton Pidsea. Go down Back Lane. Garden at junction of Elstronwick & Danthorpe, next to beck bridge.* **Visits by arrangement Feb to Sept for groups of 2 - 25. Adm £3, chd free.**
Plantsman's garden with large collection of Hellebores. ³/₄ acre with borders, gravel and formal areas. Many species of snowdrops, hellebores and narcissus, tulips and peonies. Large vegetable and fruit garden. Wooded area with large collection of woodland plants. Flowering and ornamental trees. Spring and late summer good for viewing.

 ⊗

12 BROOKFIELD
Jew Lane, Oxenhope, Keighley BD22 9HS. Mrs R L Belsey, 01535 643070. *5m SW of Keighley. From Keighley take A629 (Halifax) Fork R A6033 towards Haworth & Oxenhope turn L at Xrds into village. Turn R (Jew Lane) at bottom of hill.* **Visits by arrangement, May to end July, 30 max. Refreshments available by arrangement. Adm £4, chd free.**
1-acre, intimate garden, incl large pond with an island, mallards and wild geese also greylags. Many

varieties of primula, candelabra and florindae; azaleas and rhododendrons. Unusual trees and shrubs, screes, greenhouses and conservatory. Series of island beds. Children's quiz and garden notes. Partial wheelchair access - steep slope and steps.

 ♿ 🚉 ⊗ 🚐 ☕

GROUP OPENING

13 BUGTHORPE GARDENS
York YO41 1QG, 01759 368444 or 01759 368152, natalieverow@aol.com, barriecreaser@gmail.com. *4m E of Stamford Bridge, A166, village of Bugthorpe.* **Visits by arrangement June & July, adm to both gardens, incl refreshments. Combined adm £6, chd free. Light refreshments at The Old Rectory.**
Two contrasting gardens situated in the small village of Bugthorpe. Barrie Creaser & David Fielding, 3 Church Walk: a garden created from scratch 14 years ago, surprisingly mature, with mixed borders and trees, water feature and pond. Raised vegetable garden and greenhouse. The lawn leads onto a paddock with views of open countryside. Dr & Mrs P W Verow, The Old Rectory: ³/₄ acre country garden with views of the Yorkshire Wolds. Mixed borders, ponds, stumpery, terrace, summerhouse, courtyard and many mature trees. Raised vegetable beds.

 🚐 ☕

14 ◆ BURTON AGNES HALL & GARDENS
Burton Agnes, Driffield YO25 4NB. Mrs S Cunliffe-Lister, 01262 490324, www.burtonagnes.com. *Between Driffield & Bridlington on A614 in village of Burton Agnes. Parking signed.* **For NGS: Sat 11, Sun 12 June (11-5) Gardeners Fair. Adm to Gardeners Fair incls entry to gardens, from which a donation will be made to NGS. For other opening times and information, please phone or visit garden website.**
Beautiful award-winning gardens of Burton Agnes Hall are home to 3,000 different plant species, herbaceous borders, jungle garden, potager, coloured gardens, giant games, maze and collection of campanulas. Surrounded by lawns, topiary yews,

fountains and woodland walk. Collections of hardy geraniums, clematis, penstemons and unusual perennials.

129 BUTTERFIELD HEIGHTS
4 Park Crescent, Guiseley, Leeds LS20 8EL. Vicky & Trevor Harris 078521 63733
vicky.harris2@btinternet.com *11m NW of Leeds. From Guiseley A65 (Otley-Leeds) A6038 towards Shipley (Bradford Rd). Park Crescent 1/2m on L. Park on Bradford Rd or surrounding streets.* **Wed 3 Aug (11-5). Adm £3, chd free.**
Hardy plantswoman's garden with view towards Otley Chevin. Restoration of this dark, damp plot since 1998 revealed 1930s landscape on 3 levels linked by steps. Sumptuous planting for late summer colour, unusual herbaceous plants, shrubs and trees. Winding gravel paths and tall perennials, secluded Japanese corner. Small pond, box parterre, new thugs border and steep steps to paved area

GROUP OPENING

15 CAWOOD GARDENS
Cawood, nr Selby YO8 3UG. *On B1223 5m N of Selby & 7m SE of Tadcaster. Between York & A1 on B1222. Village maps given at all gardens.* **Sat 9, Sun 10 July (12-5). Combined adm £5, chd free. Home-made teas at 9 Anson Grove & 21 Great Close. Visits also by arrangement May to Aug.**

9 ANSON GROVE
Tony & Brenda Finnigan
beeart@ansongrove.co.uk
01757 268888

21 GREAT CLOSE
David & Judy Jones
dave-judyjones@hotmail.co.uk
01757 268571

THE PIGEONCOTE
Maria Parks & Angela Darlington
mariaparks@gmail.com
01757 268661

These three contrasting gardens in an attractive historic village are linked by a pretty riverside walk to the C11 church and Memorial garden and across the Castle Garth to the remains of Cawood Castle.

9 Anson Grove is a small garden with tranquil pools and secluded sitting places. Narrow winding paths and raised areas give views over oriental-style pagoda, bridge and Zen garden. 21 Great Close is a flower arranger's garden, designed and built by the owners. Interesting trees and shrubs combine with herbaceous borders incl many grasses. Two ponds are joined by a stream, winding paths take you to the vegetable garden and summerhouse, then back to the colourful terrace for views across the garden and countryside beyond. The small walled garden, Pigeoncote at 2 Wistowgate is surrounded by historic C17 buildings. A balanced design of formal box hedging, cottage garden planting and creative use of grasses. Angled brick pathways lead to shaded seating areas with all day sunny views. Crafts and paintings on sale at 9 Anson Grove. Wheelchair access limited at 9 Anson Grove and 21 Great Close.

16 NEW 14 CHELLSWAY
Chellsway, Withernsea HU19 2EN. Neil & Caroline Ziemski. *Chellsway is located on the Beaconsfield estate to the W of the town.* **Sun 24 July (12-6). Combined adm with 54 Hollym Road £5, chd free. Light refreshments and home-made cakes.**
Jungle garden with grass and gravel paths surrounded by hardy and tender plants. Collection of bamboo, bananas, gingers, palms, succulents and other exotic plants, combine to create a tropical effect rarely seen on the Yorkshire coast. An authentic jungle hut and various seating areas allow the visitor to see different aspects of the garden. Small pond and rockery area to see.

17 THE CIRCLES GARDEN
8 Stocksmoor Road, Midgley, nr Wakefield WF4 4JQ. Joan Gaunt. *Equidistant from Huddersfield, Wakefield & Barnsley, W of M1. Turn off A637 in Midgley at the Black Bull PH (sharp bend) onto B6117 (Stocksmoor Rd). Please park on L adjacent to houses.* **Sun 24 Apr (1.30-5). Adm £3.50, chd free. Home-made teas.**
An organic and self-sustaining plantswoman's 1/2 -acre garden on gently sloping site overlooking fields, woods and nature reserve opposite. Designed and maintained by owner.

Interesting herbaceous, bulb and shrub plantings linked by grass and gravel paths, a woodland area with mature trees, spring and summer meadows, fernery, greenhouse, fruit trees, viewing terrace with pots. Also, around 100 hellebores grown from my seed. South African plants, hollies, small bulbs are particular interests.

18 CLIFTON CASTLE
Ripon HG4 4AB. Lord & Lady Downshire. *2m N of Masham. On rd to Newton-le-Willows & Richmond. Gates on L next to red telephone box.* **Sun 3 Apr, Sun 5 June (2-5). Adm £4, chd free. Home-made teas.**
Fine views, river walks, wooded pleasure grounds with bridges and follies. Cascades, wild flower meadow and C19 walled kitchen garden. Gravel paths and steep slopes to river.

19 COLD COTES
Cold Cotes Road, nr Kettlesing, Harrogate HG3 2LW. Susan Bailey, 01423 770937,
info@coldcotes.com, www.coldcotes.com. *7m W of Harrogate off A59. From Skipton turn L after Menwith Hill before Black Bull PH. From Harrogate turn R for Menwith Hill/Cold Cotes.* **Wed 20 Apr (1-5). Home-made teas. Evening opening Wed 20 July (5-9). Wine. Sun 18 Sept (1-5). Home-made teas. Adm £3.50, chd free. Visits also by arrangement Apr to Sept for groups of 10+.**
This large peaceful garden with expansive views under new ownership is at ease in its rural setting. Year round interest moves through a series of discrete gardens incl formal areas, stream-side walk, sweeping herbaceous borders inspired by the designer Piet Oudolf peak in late summer. Chatto-influenced woodland garden underplanted with masses of bulbs and perennials for spring to autumn interest. Nursery open Wednesdays by appointment and on NGS days. Full afternoon teas and formal hot lunches by arrangement. Fully licensed. Local cheeses and pork pie available on wine evening. Wheelchair accessible WC.

20 ◆ CONSTABLE BURTON HALL GARDENS

Constable Burton, Leyburn DL8 5LJ. Mr Charles Wyvill, 01677 450428, gardens@constableburton.com, www.constableburton.com. *3m E of Leyburn. Constable Burton Village. On A684, 6m W of A1.* **For opening times and information, please phone, email or visit garden website.**
Large romantic garden with terraced woodland walks. Garden trails, shrubs, roses and water garden. Display of daffodils and over 6,500 tulips planted annually amongst extensive borders. Fine John Carr house (not open) set in splendour of Wensleydale countryside. Constable Burton Hall Gardens plays host to a magnificent Tulip Festival, on the first May Bank Holiday weekend. Sponsored by Chelsea award winning nursery Bloms Bulbs, over 6,500 traditional and new variant tulips are planted throughout the gardens. BBC Gardeners World. Featured in several local and national publications.

21 THE COURT

Humber Road, North Ferriby HU14 3DW. Guy & Liz Slater, 01482 633609, liz@guyslater.karoo.co.uk. *7m W of Hull. Travelling E on A63 to Hull, follow sign for N Ferriby. Through village to Xrds with war memorial, turn R & follow rd to T-junction with Humber Rd. Turn L & immed R into cul-de-sac, last house on L.* **Sun 15 May (1-5). Adm £3, chd free. Home-made teas. Visits also by arrangement Feb to Aug, groups of 10+.**
Romantic and restful, with hidden seating areas offering different vistas. Roses and clematis scrambling up walls and trees. 2 summerhouses, small pond and waterfall with secluded arbours and historical items. A long tunnel of wisteria, clematis and laburnum leads to a little path with Betula jacquemontii, small stumpery, and grown up swing. Featured in Yorkshire Post Magazine. Profile by David Overend.

22 COW CLOSE COTTAGE

Stripe Lane, Hartwith, Harrogate HG3 3EY. William Moore & John Wilson, 01423 779813, cowclose1@btinternet.com. *8m NW of Harrogate. From A61(Harrogate-Ripon) at Ripley take B6165 to Pateley Bridge. 1m beyond Burnt Yates turn R signed Hartwith onto Stripe Lane. Parking available.* **Sun 24 July (10.30-4.30). Adm £4, chd free. Home-made teas. Visits also by arrangement June to Aug, 8 min for group visits. Teas by prior arrangement.**
²/₃ -acre recently redeveloped country garden on sloping site with stream and far reaching views. Large borders with drifts of interesting, well-chosen, later flowering summer perennials and some grasses contrasting with woodland shade and streamside plantings. Gravel path leading to vegetable area. Terrace and seating with views of the garden. Orchard and ha-ha with steps leading to meadow. Featured in Gardens Illustrated.

23 CRESKELD HALL

Arthington, nr Leeds LS21 1NT. J & C Stoddart-Scott. *5m E of Otley. On A659 between Pool & Harewood.* **Sun 29 May (12-5). Adm £4, chd free. Home-made teas.**
Historic picturesque 3¹/₂ -acre Wharfedale garden with beech avenue, mature rhododendrons and azaleas. Gravel path from terrace leads to attractive water garden with canals set amongst woodland plantings. Walled kitchen garden and flower garden. Specialist nurseries.

Informal planting and a wildlife friendly approach . . .

GROUP OPENING

24 DACRE BANKS & SUMMERBRIDGE GARDENS

Nidderdale HG3 4EW. *4m SE of Pateley Bridge, 10m NW of Harrogate, 10m SW of Ripon, 10m N of Otley on B6451 & B6165. Parking at each garden. For Riverside House please park at sawmill, no vehicle access to Riverside Lane. Maps available to show garden locations.* **Sun 10 July (11-5). Combined adm £8, chd free. Cream teas at Yorke House, Low Hall and Woodlands Cottage. Visits also by arrangement June & July for groups of 12+.**

LOW HALL
Mrs P A Holliday
(See separate entry)
Visits also by arrangement May to Sept small groups of 3 or 4 and large groups up to 50. Teas by prior arrangement
pamela@pamelaholliday.co.uk
01423 780230

RIVERSIDE HOUSE
Joy Stanton

WOODLANDS COTTAGE
Mr & Mrs Stark
(See separate entry)
Visits also by arrangement May to Aug
01423 780765

YORKE HOUSE
Tony & Pat Hutchinson
(See separate entry)
Visits also by arrangement June to Aug for groups of 10+
pat@yorkehouse.co.uk
01423 780456

Dacre Banks and Summerbridge Gardens are situated in the beautiful countryside of Nidderdale and designed to take advantage of the scenic Dales landscape. The gardens are linked by an attractive walk along the valley and may be accessed individually by car. Low Hall has a romantic walled garden set on different levels around the historic C17 family home (not open) with extensive herbaceous borders, shrubs, climbing roses and tranquil water garden. Riverside House is a mysterious waterside garden on many levels, supporting shade-loving plants and incorporates a Victorian folly, fernery, courtyard and naturalistic riverside plantings. Woodlands Cottage is designed to harmonise with boulder-strewn woodland whilst also having varied areas of formal and informal planting, a wild flower meadow and productive fruit and vegetable garden. Yorke House has extensive colour-themed borders, attractive waterside plantings and secluded millennium garden full of fragrant plants and rambling roses. Visitors welcome to use orchard picnic area at Yorke House. Featured in Harrogate Advertiser. Partial wheelchair access at some gardens.

25 **DEVONSHIRE MILL**
Canal Lane, Pocklington, York
YO42 1NN. Sue & Chris Bond,
01759 302147,
chris.bond.dm@btinternet.com,
www.devonshiremill.co.uk. *1m S of
Pocklington. Situated on Canal Lane,
Pocklington off A1079 at The
Wellington Oak PH.* **Sun 21 Feb (11-
5). Adm £3.50, chd free. Home-
made teas. 2017: Sun 19 Feb.**
Organic two acre garden surrounding
an old watermill. Early spring flowers
with double snowdrops (galanthus
flore pleno), hellebores and ferns in
old orchards and a woodland setting.
Different areas with a mill stream.
Raised beds, polytunnel,
greenhouses, hen run and well-
stocked herbaceous borders.

26 **DOVE COTTAGE NURSERY
GARDEN**
Shibden Hall Road, nr Halifax
HX3 9XA. Kim & Stephen Rogers,
www.dovecottagenursery.co.uk.
*1m E Halifax. From Halifax take A58
turn L signed Claremount, cont over
bridge, cont 1/2 m. J26 M62- A58
Halifax. Drive 4m. L turn at Paw Prints
pet store down Tanhouse Hill, cont 1/2
m.* **Every Fri 3 June to 26 Aug (10-
5). Adm £3, chd free. Tea.**
Hedges and green oak gates enclose
1/3 -acre sloping garden, generously
planted by nursery owners over
18yrs. A beautiful mix of late summer
perennials and grasses. Winding
paths and plenty of seats incl a
romantic tulip arbour. Plants for sale
in nursery. Wildlife friendly.
'Considered good example of cottage
garden' (Carole Klein thought so!).
Featured in The English Garden,
House & Garden. 'Garden Design A
Book of Ideas'. The Garden-Nurseries
by Roy Lancaster.

27 **34 DOVER ROAD**
Hunters Bar, Sheffield S11 8RH.
Marian Simpson, 079575 36248,
marian@mjsimpson.plus.com.
*11/2 m SW of city centre. From A61
(ring rd) A625 Moore St/Eccleshall Rd
for approx 1m. Dover Rd on R.* **Sun
26 June (10-4). Adm £3.50, chd
free. Wide range of home made
drinks and cakes. Visits also by
arrangement May to Aug for
groups of 10 to 30.**
Colourful, small town garden packed
with interest and drama, combining
formality with exotic exuberance.
Attractive alpine area replacing old

Barnville

driveway, many interesting containers
and well-stocked borders.
Conservatory, seating areas and
lawns complement unusual plants
and planting combinations. Featured
in Daily Mail, Yorkshire Post, Sheffield
Telegraph and on BBC Radio
Sheffield.

28 **DOWTHORPE HALL &
HORSE PASTURE COTTAGE**
Skirlaugh, Hull HU11 5AE. Mr &
Mrs J Holtby, 01964 562235,
john.holtby@farming.co.uk,
www.dowthorpehall.com. *6m N of
Hull, 8m E of Beverley. From Hull
A165 towards Bridlington. Through
Ganstead & Coniston. 1m S of
Skirlaugh on R, (long drive white
railings & sign at drive end).* **Sun 26
June (11-5). Adm £5, chd free.
Visits also by arrangement Apr to
July. Lunch or afternoon tea for
groups on request.**
Dowthorpe Hall: 31/2 acres, large
herbaceous borders, lawns, shady
area, pond with bridge, scree garden,
hardy garden, orchards and
vegetable potager. Horse Pasture
Cottage: small cottage garden,
herbaceous border and woodland
water feature. New sundial border
with roses and catmint. 'The sundial

was a gift from our daughter and son
in law. In the spring 200 pink and blue
Hyacinths were planted. This border
now forms a link with the other
borders, and forms a central feature'.
Gravel, lawns, no steps.

29 **ELLERKER HOUSE**
Everingham, York YO42 4JA.
Mrs R Los & Mr M Wright,
www.ellerkerhouse.weebly.com.
*15m SE of York. 51/2 m from
Pocklington. Just out of the village
heading towards Harswell.* **Sun 10
Apr (10-5). Adm £4.50, chd free.
Home-made teas. Savouries
served over lunch time.**
5 acres of garden on sandy soil. Lots
of spring bulbs and plants. Many
unusual mature trees in a parkland
setting, formal lawns, woodland
walkway and stumpery around lake.
11 acres of bluebell woods to stroll
around. Traditional oak and thatched
breeze hut. Several seating areas
around the garden. Rose archway,
colour themed herbaceous borders
planted with many unusual plants for
all year colour. RARE PLANT FAIR
(Many different stalls selling a variety
of unusual plants).

30 NEW **ELLERKER MANOR**
Cave Lane, Ellerker, Brough
HU15 2DX. Philip & Sally, 01430
423035, Pmegabean@aol.com.
*From the S Cave exit on the A63 turn
towards West end S Cave and the
lorry sign to Ellerker. At the T junction,
turn L. Garden is on L after the
Ellerker Village sign.* **Sun 29 May
(11-5). Adm £4, chd free. Home-
made teas. Visits also by
arrangement.**
A village garden belonging to the
previous owners of Saltmarshe Hall.
The garden has good trees and
shrubs, borders packed with
herbaceous plants and bulbs.
Climbers grow on trellis. The pretty
potager has vegetables and flowers.
A less structured part of the garden
has ponds and wild flower area.

The pretty potager has vegetables and flowers . . .

31 **FAWLEY HOUSE**
7 Nordham, North Cave, Brough
HU15 2LT. Mr & Mrs T Martin,
01430 422266,
louisem200@hotmail.co.uk,
www.nordhamcottages.co.uk. *15m
W of Hull. M62 E, J38. L towards N
Cave Wetlands, then R to Nordham,
where rd bends to L. 'Fawley' is tall
house on R, 1/2 m. Carpark beyond
house, just through gates to Hotham
Hall. NO cars on st please, only
disabled.* **Fri 19 Feb (11-3). Adm £4,
chd free. Teas. Fri 22, Sat 23, Sun
24 July (12-5). Combined adm
with 27 Nordham £6, chd free.**
Tiered, 2¹/₂ -acre garden with lawns,
mature trees, formal hedging and
gravel pathways. Lavender beds,
mixed shrub/herbaceous borders,
and hot double herbaceous borders.
Apple espaliers, pears, soft fruit,
produce and herb gardens. Terrace
with pergola and vines. Sunken
garden with white border. Woodland
with naturalistic planting and spring
bulbs. Quaker well, stream and spring
area with 3 bridges, Ferns and
Hellebores near mill stream. Beautiful

snowdrops and aconites early in year.
Exhibition of art from East Riding
Artists in July, with art displayed from
many NGS East Yorkshire gardens
from 2015. For accommodation,
please see website/phone. Treasure
Hunt for children in Feb and July.
Teas in Feb. Ices in July. Partial
wheelchair access to top of garden
and terrace on pea gravel.

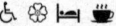

32 **FERNLEIGH**
9 Meadowhead Avenue,
Meadowhead, Sheffield S8 7RT. Mr
& Mrs C Littlewood, 01142 747234,
littlewoodchristine@gmail.com. *4m
S of Sheffield city centre. From
Sheffield city centre. A61, A6102,
B6054 r'about, exit B6054. 1st R
Greenhill Ave, 2nd R. From M1 J33,
A630 to A6102, then as above.* **Sun
26 June, Sun 31 July, Sun 28 Aug
(11-5). Adm £3, chd free. Home-
made teas. Visits also by
arrangement Apr to Aug groups
of 10 to 30.**
Plantswoman's 1/3 acre cottage style
garden. Large variety of unusual
plants set in differently planted
sections to provide all-yr interest.
Seating areas to view different
aspects of garden. Auricula theatre,
patio, gazebo and greenhouse.
Miniature log cabin with living roof
and cobbled area with unusual plants
in pots. Sempervivum, alpine displays
and wildlife 'hotel'. Wide selection of
home grown plants for sale. Featured
in Yorkshire Post. Active 8 & Bradway
Bugle Magazines.

33 **FERNWOOD**
Cropton YO18 8HL. Dick & Jean
Feaster, 01751 417692,
adrian.feaster@btinternet.com.
*4m NW of Pickering. From A170 turn
at Wrelton signed Cropton.*
**Sun 3 July (1-5). Adm £3.50, chd
free. Visits also by arrangement
May to Aug groups of 10+. Light
refreshments.**
A hidden one acre garden
overlooking the North Yorkshire
Moors will delight visitors with the
scale and variety of planting in mixed
and herbaceous borders, island beds
and theme areas. Cottage garden
favourites including old, shrub and
climbing roses, delphiniums, peonies
and phlox abound together with
newer introductions. Tropaeolum
speciosum is well established in
several areas. Gravel paths.

34 **FIRVALE ALLOTMENT
GARDEN**
Winney Hill, Harthill, nr Worksop
S26 7YN. Don & Dot Witton,
01909 771366,
donshardyeuphorbias@btopenworl
d.com, www.euphorbias.co.uk.
*12m SE of Sheffield, 6m W of
Worksop. M1 J31 A57 to Worksop.
Turn R to Harthill. Allotments at S end
of village, 26 Casson Drive at N end
on Northlands Estate.* **Visits by
arrangement Apr to July.
Adm £3, chd free. Home-made
teas at 26 Casson Drive Harthill
(S26 7WA).**
Large allotment containing 13 island
beds displaying 500+ herbaceous
perennials incl the National Collection
of hardy Euphorbias with over 100
varieties flowering between March
and October. Organic vegetable
garden. Refreshments, WC, plant
sales at 26 Casson Drive - small
garden with mixed borders, shade
and seaside garden.

 NPC

35 **FRIARS HILL**
Sinnington YO62 6SL. Mr & Mrs C
J Baldwin, 01751 432179,
friars.hill@abelgratis.co.uk. *4m W of
Pickering. On A170.* **Visits by
arrangement Mar to July, quite
happy with groups of 10+. Adm
£4, chd free.**
Plantswoman's 1³/₄ -acre garden
containing over 2500 varieties of
perennials and bulbs, with yr-round
colour. Early interest with hellebores,
bulbs and woodland plants.
Herbaceous beds. Hostas,
delphiniums, old roses and stone
troughs. Excellent Autumn colour.

36 **GOLDSBOROUGH HALL**
Church Street, Goldsborough
HG5 8NR. Mr & Mrs M Oglesby,
01423 867321,
info@goldsboroughhall.com,
www.goldsboroughhall.com. *2m
SE of Knaresborough. 3m W of A1M.
Off A59 (York-Harrogate) carpark
300yds past PH on R.* **Sun 10 Apr
(12-4); Sun 24 July (12-5). Adm £5,
chd free. Cream teas. Light
lunches, sandwiches and cakes.**
*Donation to St Mary's Church,
Goldsborough.*
Previously opened for NGS from
1928-30 and now beautifully restored
by present owners (re-opened in
2010). 12-acre garden and formal
landscaped grounds in parkland
setting and Grade II*, C17 house,

former residence of the late HRH Princess Mary, daughter of George V and Queen Mary. Gertrude Jekyll inspired replanted 120ft double herbaceous borders and rose garden. Quarter-mile Lime Tree Walk planted by royalty in the 1920s and a flower border featuring 'Yorkshire Princess' rose, named after Princess Mary. Featured in Yorkshire Post and other local magazines and newspapers. Gravel paths and some steep slopes.

37 THE GRANGE
Carla Beck Lane, Carleton in Craven, Skipton BD23 3BU. Mr & Mrs R N Wooler, 07740 639135, margaret.wooler@hotmail.com. *1¹/₂ m SW of Skipton. Turn off A56 (Skipton-Clitheroe) into Carleton. Keep L at Swan PH, continue to end of village then turn R into Carla Beck Lane.* **Wed 13 July, Wed 10 Aug (12-4.30). Adm £5, chd free. Cream teas. Visits also by arrangement July & Aug, groups of 30+.** *Donation to Sue Ryder Care Manorlands Hospice.*
Over 4 acres set in the grounds of Victorian house (not open) with mature trees and panoramic views towards The Gateway to the Dales. The garden has been restored by the owners over the last 2 decades with many areas of interest being added to the original footprint. Bountiful herbaceous borders with many unusual species, rose walk, parterre, mini-meadows and water features. Large greenhouse and raised vegetable beds. Oak seating placed throughout the garden invites quiet contemplation, a place to 'lift the spirit'. Gravel paths and steps.

38 NEW GRASMERE
48 Royds Lane, Rothwell LS26 0BH. Terry & Tina Cook. *5m S of Leeds, 6¹/₂ m N of Wakefield. M62 J30 follow A642 towards Leeds. Turn L after 200yds (Royds School) Pennington Lane follow rd for 1m. Car parking at school opp or in rd nr Squash Club.* **Sun 31 July (1-5). Adm £3.50, chd free. Home-made teas.**
Amongst old orchard trees is hidden a restful family suburban garden of ¹/₃ acre. Wildlife encouraged by many nesting boxes, ponds, wild flower area, log piles for hedgehogs and flowers to attract butterflies. Secluded summerhouse enclosed by colourful tapestry hedge and architectural

planting. Pergola walkway leads to hidden vegetable garden.

119 GREEN HILL HOUSE
Water Hill Lane HX2 7SG. Mrs Pamela Berry. *2m W of Halifax. From Halifax take A58 (Rochdale/Burnley). At A58/A646 Junction proceed onto A646. After 1m turn R (Windle Royd Lane) Turn L, park on Stock Lane prior to Village, 5 min (signed) walk to garden.* **Sun 26 June (11-5). Adm £3, chd free. Home-made teas.**
Situated in the historic village of Warley this continually evolving ¹/₄ acre family garden has a woodland glade, formal lawn, topiary, clipped yew, herbaceous borders and courtyard garden. Plenty of places to sit and admire the contrasting colours, shapes and textures of the plants, shrubs as well as views of the Pennine hills. I-Spy trail for children. Fused glass for garden and home by local artist Genevieve Thompson. WC. Village has 2 hostelries, unique allotments, cemetery with outstanding views of the countryside. Plenty to see on your walk. Garden photographed for feature article for Amateur Gardening magazine.

39 GREENWICK FARM
Huggate, York, East Yorkshire YO42 1YR. Fran & Owen Pearson, 01377 288122, greenwickfarm@hotmail.com. *2m W of Huggate. From York on A166, turn R 1m after Garrowby Hill, at brown sign for picnic area & scenic route. White wind turbine on drive.* **Sun 21 Aug (1-5). Adm £3.50, chd free. Home-made teas. Visits also by arrangement July to Sept, adm incl refreshments.**
1 acre woodland garden created 6yrs ago from disused area of the farm. Set in a large dell with many mature

trees incl Elm. Interesting planting of shrubs, unusual trees, herbaceous/mixed borders and island beds. Paths lead up through planting to give spectacular views across wooded valley and the Wolds. Tea tables in conservatory and outside. Access for wheelchairs difficult, but good view of garden from hard standing outside house/tea area.

40 16 HALLAM GRANGE CROFT
Fulwood, Sheffield S10 4BP. Tricia & Alistair Fraser, 0114 230 6508, tricia.fraser@talktalk.net. *Approx 4m SW of Sheffield city centre. Follow A57 (Glossop). 1¹/₂ m after University turn L at Crosspool shops. After 1m turn L at top of hill & follow signs.* **Sun 5 June (12.30-4.30). Adm £3, chd free. Light refreshments. Visits also by arrangement May to Aug min entry charge for 10 people applies.**
Developed over 20yrs, a plantswoman's SE-facing sloping wildlife-friendly garden. Backed by mature trees with established perennial and shrub planting incl many unusual hardy geraniums. Shady areas, pond, summerhouse, greenhouse and vegetable plots. Raised bed, rockery and decking area feature alpines and sun-loving perennials. Plants propagated by the owners on sale.

41 HAVOC HALL
York Rd, Oswaldkirk, York YO62 5XY. David & Maggie Lis, 01439 788846, maggielis@me.com, www.havochall.co.uk. *21m N of York. On B1363, 1st house on R as you enter Oswaldkirk from S & last house on L as you leave village from N.* **Sun 10 July (1-5.30). Adm £5, chd free. Home-made teas.**
Started in 2009, comprising 8 areas incl knot, herbaceous, mixed shrub and flower gardens, courtyard, vegetable area and orchard, woodland walk and large lawned area with hornbeam trees and hedging. To the S is a 2-acre wild flower meadow and small lake. Extensive collection of roses, herbaceous perennials and grasses. See website for other opening times. Featured on Radio York. Participant garden in The English Garden magazine Yorkshire Gardens tour. Some steps but these can be avoided.

Skipwith Hall

42 HIGH HALL

St Stephen's Road, Steeton, Keighley BD20 6SB. **Roger & Christine Lambert.** *3m W of Keighley. Enter Steeton from A629. Turn R at lights & R after 100yds & down St St Rd. No parking at house except disabled. Follow signs for parking in village.* **Sun 19 June, Sun 24 July (11-5). Adm £4, chd free. Home-made teas.**
2-acre surprising suburban Arts and Crafts garden and historic house (not open) adjacent to St Stephen's Church. Formal walled garden with pond, belvedere, pergola, dovecote, summerhouse and ancient yew, herbaceous planting in formal beds connected by gravel paths. Walled kitchen garden with vegetable beds and fruit trees. Natural woodland area, bog garden and small croquet lawn. Historical notes available. Exhibition of Alexander Keighley photographs and pottery display by Barbara Miskin. Child-friendly activities. Some steps and gravelled paths may make access difficult in places.

43 NEW HIGHFIELD COTTAGE

North Street, Driffield YO25 6AS. **Debbie Simpson.** *30m E of York, 29m E of M62. Exit at A614/A166 r'about onto York Rd into Driffield. Carry straight until you reach the park with the Rose & Crown PH opp. Highfield Cottage is the white detached house next to PH.*

Sun 22, Sun 29 May (10.30-3.30). Adm £3.50, chd free. Cream teas.
A ¾ acre suburban garden bordered by mature trees and stream. Numerous yew and box topiary, and summerhouse delivering year round interest and structure. Pergola and sculptures made by owner. Lawns with island beds, mixed shrubs, fruit trees and herbaceous borders add interest and colour. A natural and evolving garden, designed and maintained by the owner.

44 20 HIGHFIELD ROAD

Whitby YO21 3LW. **Mr & Mrs Les & Ann Spedding.** *From York/Middlesbrough at r'about adjacent to park & ride take 1st exit onto B1460 after garage turn L onto Love Lane B1416 turn L onto Highfield Road.* **Sun 17 July (12-4). Adm £3, chd free. Home-made teas. Sweet & savoury homemade refreshments.**
Situated 5mins from cliff top and beach, a garden with variety of plants. Gravel paths lead to herbaceous borders some shady with mature trees contrasting to sun loving plants. 2 raised timber framed ponds with running water largest formal containing water lilies. Many pots some with specimen plants and tropical. Collection of succulents, perennial pelargoniums and dahlias. Greenhouse and seating areas. Winner of a gold award and best in category Whitby in Bloom 'Practically Paradise Garden'.

45 HIGHFIELDS

Manorstead, Skelmanthorpe, Huddersfield HD8 9DW. **Julie & Tony Peckham.** *8m SE of Huddersfield. M1 (J39) A636 towards Denby Dale. Turn R in Scissett village (B6116). Turn L (Barrowstead) just before zebra crossing.* **Sun 17 Apr, Sun 15 May (1-4). Adm £2.50, chd free. Tea.**
Small garden which shows creativity within metres rather than acres. Focuses on early spring/summer plants. Incl two ponds, rock gardens, alpine beds, woodland plants and small alpine display in greenhouse. New this year grass bed and vegetable bed. Summerhouse and lots of intimate seating areas. Featured in Real Homes Magazine.

46 HILLBARK

Church Lane, Bardsey, Leeds LS17 9DH. **Tim Gittins & Malcolm Simm,** www.hillbark.co.uk. *4m SW of Wetherby. Turn W off A58 into Church Lane, garden on L before church.* **Sun 15 May, Sun 3 July (11-4.30). Adm £4, chd free. Tea.**
Award-winning 1-acre country garden. 3 S-facing levels, hidden corners and surprise views. Formal topiary, relaxed perennial planting. Dramatic specimen yew. Ornamental ponds, summerhouse overlooking gravel, rock and stream gardens, large natural pond with ducks. Marginal planting incl bamboo. Woodland area. Large rambling roses. Unusual ceramics.

47 NEW HILLSIDE

West End, Ampleforth, York YO62 4DY. **Sue Shepherd & Jon Borgia,** 01439 788993. *4m S of Helmsley. At W end of village, half way up hill in direction of Wass. From A19, follow brown signs to Byland Abbey & continue to Ampleforth. From A170 take B1257 to Malton, after 1m turn R to Ampleforth. Roadside parking only. Please be considerate.* **Sun 11 Sept (1-5). Adm £4, chd free. Home-made teas. Visits also by arrangement June to Sept, groups of 10+.**
Half acre garden on a south facing slope. The design is evolving, based on informal planting and a wildlife friendly approach. Woodland and meadow areas. 2 ponds and drainage ditch with bog garden. Lawn rising up to summer house and deck with fine views of the Coxwold -

Gilling Gap. Fruit trees and kitchen garden. All year round interest with an emphasis on autumn colour.

❀ ⊨ ☕

48 NEW THE HIMALAYAN GARDENS
Hutts Lane, Grewelthorpe, Ripon, North Yorkshire HG4 3DA. Mr & Mrs Peter Roberts, www.himlayangarden.com. *From the N A1(M) J51 A684 to Bedale then B6268 to Masham - follow signs to Grewelthorpe from town centre. From the S A1M J50 to Ripon then A6108 (Masham) after North Stainley turn L to Mickley and Grewelthorpe. In Grewelthorpe turn up steep hill adjacent to Crown Inn PH then R following signs to The Hutts approx. 1m.* **Tue 10 May (10-4). Adm £7.50, chd free. Light refreshments.**
A stunning hidden gem 20 acre woodland garden. It is home to an extensive collection of rare Rhododendrons, Azaleas and Himalayan plants, set amongst plantings of showy hybrids. A rich tapestry of spring colour with streams meandering through valleys teaming with arrays of plants and Sculptures leading down to peaceful lakes.Tearoom and Garden Nursery available. Group Tours and Talks also available. Wheelchair Access to Garden Nursery only.

🐕 ❀ 🚐 ☕

A rich tapestry of spring colour with streams meandering through valleys . . .

49 2 HOLLIN CLOSE
Rossington, nr Doncaster DN11 0XX. Mr & Mrs Hann. *5m S of Doncaster. on A638 after Hare & Tortoise PH turn R (Littleworth Lane) 5m N of Bawtry after T-lights signed Airport take next L (Littleworth Lane). Hollin Close is 2nd R.* **Sun 26 June (11-5). Adm £3, chd free. Home-made teas.**
¹/₃ acre terraced garden designed and

maintained by owners with four themes on three levels. Cottage style herbaceous planting surrounds a circular lawn alongside a tranquil oriental garden. Steps lead to the greenhouse and Mediterranean gravel garden with sun-loving plants for bees and butterflies. Below lies a wildlife friendly small woodland glade with bug hotel, stumpery, fruit and ferns. Winner Doncaster in Bloom Best Private residents Garden.

❀ ☕

50 54 HOLLYM ROAD
Withernsea HU19 2PJ. Mr Matthew Pottage. *23m E of Hull, 16m S of Hornsea. Enter Withernsea from A1033 onto Hollym Rd. From Hornsea, B1242 through town onto Hollym Rd.* **Sun 24 July (12-6). Combined adm with 14 Chellsway £5, chd free. Cream teas. Gluten free cake available.**
A beautifully presented garden with a little bit of everything for the plant lover. Tapestries of foliage plants thrive in the shade of trees complimenting creative combinations of herbaceous plants, bulbs and shrubs. A meadow area of grasses and perennials gives contrast to a manicured lawn and finely clipped topiary hedge. A secret garden tucked away behind the conservatory showcases exotics. Excellent plantsman's display of plants. Online blog by renowned plantsman Dr John Grimshaw http://johngrimshawsgardendiary.blog spot.co.uk/2013/07/a-gardeners-garden.html. Unsuitable for wheelchairs after very wet weather as most of the garden is accessed via the lawn.

♿ 🐕 ❀ ☕

51 HOLMFIELD
Fridaythorpe YO25 9RZ. Susan & Robert Nichols, 01377 236627, susan.nichols@which.net. *9m W of Driffield. From York A166 through Fridaythorpe. 1m turn R signed Holmfield. 1st house on the left.* **Sat 18, Sun 19 June (12-5). Adm £4, chd free. Home-made teas. Visits also by arrangement May to July, groups of 10+.**
Informal 2-acre country garden on gentle S-facing slope. Developed from a field over last 25yrs. Large mixed borders, octagonal gazebo. Vegetable, orchard and fruit areas. Cut flower garden. Collection of phlomis. Family friendly garden with sunken trampoline, large lawn, tennis

court and hidden paths for hide and seek. Display of wire sculptures. Bee friendly planting. Some gravel areas, sloping lawns.

♿ ❀ ☕

52 HOTHAM HALL
Hotham YO43 4UA. Stephen & Carolyn Martin, 01430 422054, carolynandstephenmartin@btintern et.com. *15m W of Hull. J38 of M62 turn towards North Cave Wetlands, & at sharp corner go straight on to Hotham. Turn R & R again through Hall gates.* **Thur 31 Mar, Thur 7 Apr (11-3). Adm £5, chd £2.50 (under 3 free). Light refreshments incl in adm. Visits also by arrangement Mar to June.**
C18 Grade II house (not open), stable block and clock tower in mature parkland setting with established gardens. Bridge over lake to island walk/arboretum. Garden with Victorian pond and mixed borders. Many spring flowering bulbs. CHILD ticket gives access to children's play area, games, treasure hunt with Easter Egg prize, Easter craft and incl picnic basket. ADULT ticket also incl refreshments. Pea gravel pathways.

♿ 🐕 ☕

53 HUNMANBY GRANGE
Wold Newton, Driffield YO25 3HS. Tom & Gill Mellor, 01723 891636, gill.mellor@btconnect.com. *12¹/₂ m SE of Scarborough. Hunmanby Grange home of Wold Top Brewery, between Wold Newton & Hunmanby on rd from Burton Fleming to Fordon.* **Sat 4, Sun 5 June (11-5). Adm £4, chd free. Home-made teas in Wold Top Brewery bar area.**
3-acre garden created over the last 30 yrs from exposed open field, on top of Yorkshire Wolds nr coast. Hedges and fences now provide shelter from wind, making series of gardens with yr-round interest and seasonal highlights. New for 2016, in the courtyard, the water feature from The Welcome to Yorkshire Chelsea Garden - The Brewers Yard. Field and Forage will also be catering in the courtyard with Cream of the Wold Ice creams. Wold Top Brewery open with garden. Picnics welcome so bring your Teddy Bears down to our woodland area. Steps can be avoided by using grass paths and lawns. Pond garden not completely accessible to wheelchairs but can be viewed from gateway.

♿ 🚐 ☕

54 ◆ JACKSON'S WOLD
Sherburn, Malton YO17 8QJ.
Mr & Mrs Richard Cundall,
07966 531995,
info@jacksonswoldgarden.com,
www.jacksonswoldgarden.com.
*11m E of Malton, 10m SW of
Scarborough. A64 Eastbound to
Scarborough.R at T-lights in Sherburn
take the Weaverthorpe rd after 100
metres R fork to Helperthorpe &
Luttons. 1m to top of hill, turn L at
garden sign.* **For NGS: Sun 22 May,
Sun 26 June (1-5). Adm £3, chd
free. Home-made teas. For other
opening times and information,
please phone, email or visit garden
website.**
2-acre garden with stunning views of
the Vale of Pickering. Walled garden
with mixed borders, numerous old
shrub roses underplanted with
unusual perennials. Woodland paths
lead to further shrub and perennial
borders. Lime avenue with wild flower
meadow. Traditional vegetable garden
with roses, flowers and box edging
framed by Victorian greenhouse.
Adjoining nursery. Tours by
appointment.
&♿ 🌼 🚐 ☕

Enjoy views
of open fields
under a rose
arch, and
the scent of
the wisteria
sitting in
the pergola . . .

55 ◆ LAND FARM
Edge Lane, Colden, Hebden
Bridge HX7 7PJ. Mr J Williams,
01422 842260,
www.landfarmgardens.co.uk. *8m
W of Halifax. At Hebden Bridge
(A646) after 2 sets of T-lights take
turning circle to Heptonstall & Colden.
After 2³/₄ m in Colden village turn R at
Edge Lane 'no through rd'.* **For
opening times and information,
please phone or visit garden
website.**
An intriguing 6 acre upland garden
within a sheltered valley, created
entirely by the present owner over a
period of 40 years. In that time the
valley has been planted with 20,000
trees by friends, neighbours and
myself, which has encouraged a
habitat rich in bird and wildlife. Within
the garden, vistas have been created
around thought provoking sculpture.
Meconopsis and cardiocrimum lilies.
Latest addition is a half-acre highly
individual moss garden. Open
weekends and Bank Hol Mons May
to end Aug. Partial wheelchair
access, please telephone.
♿ 🦮 ☕

56 ▶ LANGTON FARM
Great Langton, Northallerton
DL7 0TA. Richard & Annabel Fife,
01609 748446,
annabelfife@fsmail.net. *5m W of
Northallerton. B6271 in Great
Langton between Northallerton &
Scotch Corner.* **Visits by
arrangement Apr to Aug for
groups of 10+. Light
refreshments.**
Designers garden created since
2000. Comprising formal and informal
gravel areas, nuttery, romantic flower
garden with mixed borders and
pebble pool. Double helix of
Narcissus Actea through Pear Walk to
River Swale. Many other bulbs and
much blossom. Organic. Featured in
The English Garden and Gardens
Illustrated.
♿ 🚐 ☕

57 ▶ LANGTON HALL
Little Langton, Northallerton
DL7 0PX. Mr & Mrs J A Fife. *NB
SatNav not reliable. B6271 to Great
Langton between A1 & Northallerton.
In village from W take R turn, or E
take L turn & continue for 1m.
Entrance gates on R topped by stone
balls.* **Sat 11 June (2-4.30). Adm £5,
chd free. Cream teas.**
Set in stunning rural surroundings
perched above the R Swale and
surrounded by wonderful old
parkland. Large lawned garden with
wonderful trees, colourful borders
and rose beds with beautiful views
over the parkland down to the river.
The wild flowers on the drive are
spectacular in early summer. Access
through green garden door off main
drive.
♿ 🌼 ☕

58 ▶ LINDEN LODGE
Newbridge Lane, nr Wilberfoss,
York YO41 5RB. Robert Scott &
Jarrod Marsden, 07900 003538,
rdsjsm@gmail.com. *10m E of York.
Do not enter the village of Wilberfoss
from the A1079, take the turning
signed Bolton village.* **Sun 10, Sat
16, Sun 17 July (1-5). Adm £4, chd
free. Cream teas in the Bothy.
Visits also by arrangement in July
15 min.**
6 acres in all. 1 acre garden owner
designed and constructed since
2000. Gravel paths edged with brick
or lavender, many borders with
unusual mixed herbaceous
perennials, shrubs and feature trees.
A wild life pond, summer house,
kitchen garden, glasshouse. Orchard
and woodland area. Formal garden
with pond and water feature. 5 acres
of developing meadow, trees,
pathways, hens and Shetland sheep.
Plants and local craft stalls. Featured
in 100 Inspirational Gardens of
England, The Yorkshire Post, Amateur
Gardening, Yorkshire Life and Kitchen
Garden. Gravel paths and shallow
steps.
♿ 🦮 🌼 🚐 ☕

59 ▶ LITTLE EDEN
Lancaster Street, Castleford
WF10 2NP. Melvyn & Linda Moran,
01977 514275,
melvynmoran609@btinternet.com.
*2¹/₂ m NW of M62 J32. A639
(Castleford) 1st r'about 2nd exit
B6136. At hill top turn L at T-lights,
next r'about straight on, then 3rd R
(Elizabeth Drive) then 2nd L, then 3rd
L.* **Sun 17 July, Sun 21 Aug
(10-4.30). Adm £3, chd free.
Home-made teas. Visits also by
arrangement July & Aug, groups
7 min.**
Plant lovers' small hidden oasis of
unusual, tender, exotic and tropical
plants in the midst of large housing
estate. Trellis and archway festooned
with climbers, colourful pots and
hanging baskets. Herbaceous
perennials, succulents, tree ferns,
palms, bananas, pond and a
decorative summerhouse.
♿ 🦮 🌼 🚐 ☕

GROUP OPENING

60 LITTLETHORPE GARDENS
Ripon HG4 3LS. 1½ m SE of Ripon. Off A61 bypass follow signs to Littlethorpe. Turn R at church. From Bishop Monkton follow signs to Ripon (Knaresborough Rd), turn R to Littlethorpe. The gardens are at least ¾ m apart. **Sun 7 Aug (12-5). Combined adm £5, chd free. Home-made teas at Greencroft.**

GREENCROFT
David & Sally Walden
Visits also by arrangement, July to mid Aug. Refreshments available
s.walden@talk21.com
01765 602487

KIRKELLA
Jacky Barber

Littlethorpe is a small village characterised by houses interspersed with fields. Greencroft is a ½ acre informal garden made by the owners. Special ornamental features incl gazebo, temple pavilions, formal pool, stone wall with mullions, and gate to rose pergola leading to a cascade water feature. Long herbaceous borders packed with colourful late flowering perennials, annuals and exotics culminate in circular garden with views through to large wildlife pond and surrounding countryside. Kirkella is a small garden recently created by plantswoman and flower arranger to give constant interest. Gravel garden to the front with Mediterranean feel. Densely planted hidden paved rear garden with decorative summerhouse; hostas, half-hardy perennials, salvias, succulents, desirable small shrubs, many in pots and containers. A willow hedge conceals a small productive vegetable plot.

61 LITTLETHORPE MANOR
Littlethorpe Road, Littlethorpe, Ripon HG4 3LG.
Mr & Mrs J P Thackray, www.littlethorpemanor.com. *Outskirts of Ripon nr racecourse. Ripon bypass A61. Follow Littlethorpe Rd from Dallamires Lane r'about to stable block with clock tower. Map supplied on application.* **Sun 11 Sept (1.30-5). Adm £6, chd free. Home-made teas served in marquee.**
11 acres. Walled garden based on cycle of seasons with box,
herbaceous, roses, gazebo. Sunken garden with white rose parterre and herbs. Brick pergola with white wisteria, blue and yellow borders. Terraces with ornamental pots. Formal lawns with fountain pool, hornbeam towers and yew hedging. Box headed hornbeam drive with Aqualens water feature. Extensive perennial borders. Parkland with lake, late summer plantings and classical pavilion. Cut flower garden. Spring bulbs and winter garden. Gravel paths, some steep steps.

62 LOW HALL
Dacre Banks, Nidderdale HG3 4AA.
Mrs P A Holliday, 01423 780230, pamela@pamelaholliday.co.uk. *10m NW of Harrogate. On B6451 between Dacre Banks & Darley.* **Sun 15 May (1-5). Adm £4, chd free. Home-made teas. Opening with Dacre Banks & Summerbridge Gardens on Sun 10 July. Visits also by arrangement May to Sept small groups of 3 or 4 and large groups up to 50. Teas by prior arrangement.**
Romantic walled garden set on differing levels designed to complement historic C17 family home (not open). Spring bulbs, rhododendrons; azaleas round tranquil water garden. Asymmetric rose pergola underplanted with auriculas and lithodora links orchard to the garden. Extensive herbaceous borders, shrubs and climbing roses give later interest. Bluebell woods and lovely countryside of the farm all round overlooking the R Nidd. 80% of garden can be seen from a wheelchair but access involves three stone steps.

63 NEW LOW WESTWOOD GARDEN
Golcar, West Yorkshire, Huddersfield HD7 4ER. Craig Limbert. *3½ m W of Huddersfield off A62. R at T-lights in Linthwaite signed 'Titanic Spa'. Park on road by Spa. Garden is over canal bridge.* **Sat 6 Aug (10.30-5.30). Adm £3, chd free. Home-made teas.**
With 110yds of canal frontage and recently landscaped, this garden of 1½ acres has both flat and steep sloping aspects with views across the Colne Valley. The mature lime tree walk, terraced herbacious beds, pond and vegetable plot contrast plantings in deep shade and open sunny sites. These incl
rhododendron, kniphofia, astrantia and hydrangea. Late summer colour is plentiful. Partial wheelchair access into lower garden only.

64 LOWER CRAWSHAW
off Stringer House Lane, Emley, nr Huddersfield HD8 9SU. Mr & Mrs Neil Hudson, 01924 840980, janehudson42@btinternet.com. *8m E of Huddersfield. Close to Emley Moor TV mast.* **Visits by arrangement July & Aug groups of 15+. Home-made teas.**
2 acre country garden with extensive open views developed by the owners over the past 20 years. At over 600 feet on the east facing slopes of the Pennines the garden surrounds a 1690's farmhouse. A natural stream runs through the garden which is dammed on several levels and leads into 2 ponds. Partial wheelchair access.

65 MAIDENS FOLLY
Youlton, nr Tollerton, York YO61 1QL. Mr Henry Dean. *11m NW of York. From A1(M) and W, 2m NE of Aldwark toll bridge (40p). 4m SW of Easingwold. Off A19 follow signs to Tollerton then take Helperby Rd, turn L at Alne Xrds. Car parking in adjacent paddock.* **Sun 26 June (1-5). Adm £3.50, chd free. Home-made teas.**
Large cottage garden comprising 4 different themes: double herbaceous borders bounded by beech hedges and divided by stone pathway; enclosed white garden with central feature inspired by Gertrude Jekyll surrounded by flower beds, arches and trellis festooned with climbers; walled area with lavender walk, rose and penstemon border; attractive courtyard garden. Level access to all parts of the garden.

66 **MANOR FARM**
Thixendale, Malton YO17 9TG.
Charles & Gilda Brader,
01377 288315,
manorfarmthixendale@hotmail.
com,
www.manorfarmthixendale.co.uk.
*10m SE of Malton. Unclassified rd
through Birdsall, ¹/₂ m up hill, turn L at
Xrds for Thixendale - 3m, 1st farm on
R. 17m E of York, turn off A166 rd at
top of Garrowby Hill, follow signs for
Thixendale, 4m turn into village, drive
through to end, farm on L. Yellow
signs will be on route.* **Sun 4 Sept
(12-5). Adm £4, chd free. Home-
made teas.**
Main lawn surrounded by shrub and
herbaceous borders. Ruined shed,
small knot garden, little arbour,
running water and rocks. Topiary and
pots throughout garden. Central
pergola to bespoke summerhouse,
formal pool with sphere, set in stone
flagged trellised area. Through curved
pergola to alpines planted among
farm stones, small courtyard, into
garden room overflowing with plants.
🌼 🚐 🛏 ☕

Marie Curie

Patients and
families can
enjoy beautiful
gardens at our
hospices

67 **MANOR FARM**
North Leys Road, Hollym,
Withernsea HU19 2QN. David &
Trish Smith. *2m S of Withernsea.
Enter Hollym on A1033 Hull to
Withernsea Rd. Turn E at Xrds.
Garden on R after double bend.
Strictly no roadside parking, please
park in grounds.* **Sun 26 June (11-5).
Adm £3, chd free. Home-made
teas.**
Quiet country garden near sea.
Borders generously planted with
choice perennials, roses, shrubs,
trees and exotics. Log arch to shady

hosta walk, emerging through rose
arch to large wildlife pond. Specimen
evergreens complement box topiary
and hedging. Gravel garden with
ornamental pond and summerhouse.
Through folly wall clothed with
clematis, to orchard and bee/butterfly
border. Plenty of seating. Hosta walk
too narrow for wheelchairs but can be
viewed from entrance.
♿ 🚗 🌼 ☕

68 **THE MANOR HOUSE**
Main Street, Heslington, York
YO10 5EA. George Smith &
Brian Withill,
www.georgesmithflowers.com. *2m
S York City Centre.* **Sun 19 June
(2-5). Pre-booking essential adm
£15, chd free, please visit
www.ngs.org.uk or phone 01483
211535 for information & tickets.
Adm incl homemade teas.**
Home of the world renowned flower
arranger George Smith, this 3 acre
garden reflects his painterly style of
planting. Sub-divided by mellow walls
it abounds with many surprises as
each area is colour themed featuring
herbaceous perennials, especially
hostas and ferns. Exotic sheltered
corners, ponds and a shaded
woodland create a wildlife haven. The
eye of the artist abounds and the
effect is of a living flower arrangement
with careful attention to plant
associations. Refreshments with
George Smith will be served in the
tiled rustic loggia beneath his Old
Granary Studio. House not open.
Featured in Britains's Best Gardens
with Alan Titchmarsh and numerous
national and international
publications.
🌼 ☕

69 **NEW** **THE MANOR HOUSE**
Main Street, Tollerton, York
YO61 1QQ. Dr Weland & Audrey
Stone, 01347 838454. *10m N of
York off A19. Turn up Main Street
from village green. House is 200
yards on R.* **Visits by arrangement
May to July can provide teas for
10 max, wine for 20.**
An acre in village centre, developed
over 45 years. Outbuildings and barn
of old brick are covered with
climbers. Various mixed borders,
shrub rose and geranium bed, smaller
areas of Hostas and Heathers.
Vegetable bed behind yew hedge.
Shaded front garden mainly for
spring, Rear lawn dominated by fine
Genista aetnensis in July.
♿ 🏵 ☕

70 **MANSION COTTAGE**
8 Gillus Lane, Bempton,
Bridlington YO15 1HW. Polly &
Chris Myers, 01262 851404,
chrismyers0807@gmail.com. *2m
NE of Bridlington. From Bridlington
take B1255 to Flamborough. 1st L at
T lights - Bempton Lane, turn 1st R
into Short Lane then L at end.
Continue - L fork at Church.* **Sat 6,
Sun 7 Aug (10-4). Adm £3.50, chd
free. Light refreshments. Visits
also by arrangement June to Aug,
groups of 10+.**
Exuberant, lush, vibrant perennial
planting highlighted with grasses in
this hidden, peaceful and surprising
garden offering many views and
features. Visitors book comments 'A
truly lovely garden and a great lunch',
'The garden is inspirational, a
veritable oasis!' Delicious home made
lunches, produce stalls and hand
made soaps. Areas include a globe
garden, mini hosta walk, 100 ft
border, summerhouse, vegetable
plot, cuttery, late summer hot border,
bee and butterfly border, bog garden
and ponds, decking areas and lawns.
Access into the house involves steep
steps.
🏵 🌼 ☕

71 **MASPIN HOUSE**
Hillam Common Lane, Hillam,
Monk Fryston, nr Leeds LS25 5HU.
Howard & Susan Ferguson,
www.maspin-house.co.uk. *7m W of
Selby. 4m E of A1 on A63. Turn R
after leaving Monk Fryston signed
Birkin & Beal, L at T-junction. House
1m on L.* **Sun 1, Wed 4 May (1-5).
Adm £4, chd free. Home-made
teas.**
2 acres of unusual and interesting
plants in this lovely country garden.
From crab apples, Judas tree and
wisteria to dicentra, epimediums,
primula and tulips. Two ponds and a
rill; 10 different areas, each with
appropriate planting and seating; plus
woodland, orchard with meadow and
summerhouse. Gravel drive.
♿ 🌼 🚐 ☕

72 **MERE'STEAD**
28 Kelmscott Garth, Manston
Crossgates, Leeds LS15 8LB. Mr
Roberto Renzi. *6m E of Leeds. 1m
from M1 J46 follow A63 towards
Leeds.Take ring rd A6120 then follow
signs to Barwick-in-Elmet. At 2nd T-
lights turn R to Pendas Way, then 1st
L. No parking in cul-de-sac. Car park
signed.* **Evening opening Fri 29
July (5-8.30). Adm £3, chd free.**

Light refreshments and pizza.
A small enclosed English town garden with an Italian twist lovingly developed and cared for by owners. Mature trees, magnolia and cedar deodara, underplanted with interesting perennials and bulbs giving colour and foliage interest throughout the year. Arches festooned with climbers, small wildlife pond, pots with succulents, colourful summer bulbs and alpine troughs. Winner of Leeds in Bloom for past 10yrs.

73 NEW 4 MILL LANE
Foston-On-The-Wolds, Driffield YO25 8BW. Linda Lawson. *6m ESE of Driffield. Take B1249 through Wansford. At Brigham Xrds turn L to Foston. Over bridge, past '30'. 1st R. Mill Lane isn't named but shows a dead end sign - No.4 is on L. White gates & hedge.* **Sun 26 June (1-5). Adm £3, chd free. Cream teas at Foston on the Wolds Village Hall, 15 minutes walk from garden or 5 minute drive.**
Small cottage garden with lawns and lavender lined drive. Cottage front has Rosa Rambling Rector and to rear, the paved courtyard has trellis covered with Clematis armandii and climbing roses. Centred by a mill stone water feature, four brick edge beds are filled with roses, aquilegia and cottage favourites. Enjoy views of open fields under a rose arch, and the scent of the wisteria sitting in the pergola. Bantams to see. Gravel drive (mid size stones), narrow paved paths, and lawn.

74 MILLGATE HOUSE
Millgate, Richmond DL10 4JN. Tim Culkin & Austin Lynch, 01748 823571, oztim@millgatehouse.demon.co.uk, www.millgatehouse.com. *Centre of Richmond. House located at bottom of Market Place opp Barclays Bank. Just off corner of Market Place. Park in the Market Place no restrictions on Sunday.* **Sun 19 June (8-8). Also open Swale Cottage. Sun 10 July (8-8). Adm £3.50, chd free.**
SE walled town garden overlooking R Swale. Although small, the garden is full of character, enchantingly secluded with plants and shrubs. Foliage plants incl ferns and hostas. Old roses, interesting selection of clematis, small trees and shrubs. RHS associate garden. Immensely

stylish, national award-winning garden. Featured in GGG and on BBC Gardeners' World. Specialist collections of ferns, hostas and roses. MANY STEPS AND STEEP SLOPES.

75 NEW 115 MILLHOUSES LANE
Sheffield S7 2HD. Sue & Phil Stockdale. *Approx 4m SW of Sheffield City Centre. Follow A625 Castleton/Dore rd, 4th L after Prince of Wales PH, 2nd L. OR take A621 Baslow Rd; after Tesco garage take 2nd R, then 1st L.* **Sun 3 July (12.30-4.30). Adm £3.50, chd free. Home-made teas.**
Plantswoman's ⅓ acre south facing level cottage style garden, containing many choice and unusual perennials and bulbs, providing year round colour and interest. There is also a large collection of hostas, roses, peonies and clematis, together with unusual tender perennials - aeoniums, echeverias etc. Range of seating areas throughout the garden. Plants propagated by the owners for sale.

76 MILLRACE GARDEN
84 Selby Road, Garforth, Leeds LS25 1LP. Mr & Mrs Carthy, 0113 286 9233, carol@millrace-plants.co.uk, www.millrace-plants.co.uk. *5m E of Leeds. On A63 in Garforth. 1m from M1 J46, 3m from A1.* **Sun 5 June (1-5). Adm £4, chd free. Thur 28 July (1-5). Adm £4, chd £2. Sun 21 Aug (1-5). Adm £4, chd free. Home-made teas. Visits also by arrangement Apr to Aug.**
Overlooking a secluded valley, garden incl large herbaceous borders containing over 3000 varieties of perennials, shrubs and trees, many of which are unusual and drought tolerant. Ornamental pond, vegetable garden and walled terraces leading to wild flower meadow, small woodland, bog garden and wildlife lakes. 5 June cutting collecting opportunity. 28 July Family Day with activities including giant games and treasure hunt in the wood - weather dependent so please ring to check. 21 Aug seed/cutting collecting opportunity. Art exhibition.

Sion Hill
© Marcus Harpur

77▶ 23 MOLESCROFT ROAD
Beverley HU17 7DX. Mr & Mrs D Bowden. *Located ½ m N of the North Bar, Beverley.* **Sun 5 June (12-5). Adm £3, chd free. Home-made teas.**
A suburban garden facing SW, bordered by mature trees. Mixed borders and old herbaceous favourites. Several climbers, incl roses. The garden is terraced, on three different levels with lawns and seating areas providing different aspects of the garden. A paved patio area with three steps leads up to the lawn. The attractive summer house in one corner, enjoys views of the garden. A small productive area with fruit cage and greenhouse is screened from the rest of the garden. The lower area around the house has a paved area with rhododendrons and camellias. Sorry there is no wheelchair access, also note that the garden has steps which some visitors may find difficult.

78▶ ◆ NEWBY HALL & GARDENS
Ripon HG4 5AE. Mr R C Compton, 01423 322583, info@newbyhall.com, www.newbyhall.com. *4m SE of Ripon. (HG4 5AJ for Sat Nav).* Follow brown tourist signs from A1 & Ripon town centre. **For opening times and information, please phone, email or visit garden website.**
40 acres of extensive gardens and woodland laid out in 1920s. Full of rare and beautiful plants. Formal seasonal gardens, stunning double herbaceous borders to R Ure and National Collection of Cornus. Miniature railway and adventure gardens for children. Contemporary sculpture exhibition (open June - Sept). Wheelchair map available.

79▶ 2 NEWLAY GROVE
Horsforth, Leeds LS18 4LH. Kate & Chris van Heel. *4m NW Leeds city centre. From A65 turn down Newlay Lane then 2nd R onto Newlay Grove. House is 25 metres on L, limited parking near house.* **Wed 10 Aug (1-5). Adm £3, chd free. Light refreshments.**
Large, rear family garden within a third of an acre plot in quiet conservation area close to R. Aire. Landscaped over past 20 years, featuring late summer perennials, shrubs, pond and shade loving plants. Steps and slopes link lawns and paved terracing. Various seating areas allow viewing from different perspectives. Featured on BBC The Instant Gardener. Leeds in Bloom Gold Award.

> Emphasis throughout on strong, dramatic colours and sweeping vistas . . .

80▶ ◆ NORTON CONYERS
Wath, Ripon HG4 5EQ. Sir James & Lady Graham, 01765 640333, info@nortonconyers.org.uk, www.weddingsatnortonconyers.co.uk. *4m NW of Ripon.* Take Melmerby & Wath sign off A61 Ripon-Thirsk. Go through both villages to boundary wall. Signed entry 300 metres on R. **For NGS: Sun 3 July (2-5). Adm £6, chd free. Home-made teas. For other opening times and information, please phone, email or visit garden website.**
Outstanding mid C18 walled garden of interest to garden historians. Lawns, herbaceous borders, yew hedges, and central Orangery with attractive pond. Small sales area specialising in unusual hardy plants. House, long closed for major repairs. For its 2016 opening dates and times see website www.nortonconyers.org.uk. The garden retains the essential features of its original 18th century design, combined with sympathetic replanting in the English style. There are borders of gold and silver plants, of old-fashioned peonies, and irises in season. Visitors frequently comment on its tranquil atmosphere. Winner of the HHA/ Sotheby's annual restoration award with extensive press coverage, owners interviewed for BBC (Leeds)TV News. Most areas wheelchair accessible, gravel paths.

81▶ THE NURSERY
15 Knapton Lane, Acomb, York YO26 5PX. Tony Chalcraft & Jane Thurlow, 01904 781691. *2½ m W of York.* From A1237 take B1224 direction Acomb. At r'about turn L (Beckfield Ln.), after 150 metres Turn L. **Sun 17 July (1-5); Wed 20 July (2-7). Adm £3, chd free. Home-made teas. Visits also by arrangement Apr to Nov for groups 10+.**
Hidden, attractive and productive 1-acre organic garden behind suburban house (not open). Wide range of top and soft fruit with over 100 fruit trees, many in trained form. Many different vegetables grown both outside and under cover incl. a large 20m greenhouse. Productive areas interspersed with informal ornamental plantings providing colour and habitat for wildlife.

82▶ NUTKINS
72 Rolston Road, Hornsea HU18 1UR. Alan & Janet Stirling, 01964 533721, ashornsea@aol.com. *12 NE of Beverley.* On B1242 S-side of Hornsea between Freeport & golf course. **Sun 5 June (11-4). Adm £3.50, chd free. Tea. Visits also by arrangement for groups.**
The garden covers over ¾ acre with herbaceous borders, bog garden, streamside walk and woodland garden with features to bring a smile to your face. Pergolas, gazebo and plenty of seating to linger and enjoy different views of the garden and see light play on the many pieces of stained glass. Gravel and wood chip paths.

83▶ OLD SLENINGFORD HALL
Mickley, nr Ripon HG4 3JD. Jane & Tom Ramsden. *5m NW of Ripon.* Off A6108. After N Stainley turn L, follow signs to Mickley. Gates on R after 1½ m opp cottage. **Sat 4, Sun 5 June (12-4). Adm £5, chd free. Home-made teas.**
A large English country garden and developing 'Forest Garden'. Early C19 house (not open) and garden with original layout; wonderful mature trees, woodland walk and Victorian fernery; romantic lake with islands, watermill, walled kitchen garden; beautiful long herbaceous border, yew and huge beech hedges. Award winning permaculture forest garden. Several plant and other stalls. Picnics

very welcome. Reasonable wheelchair access to most parts of garden. Disabled WC at Old Sleningford Farm next to the garden.

84 THE OLD VICARAGE
Church Street. YO26 8AR. Mr & Mrs Roger Marshall, biddymarshall@btinternet.com. *8m W of York, 8m E of Harrogate, 6m N of Wetherby. off A59 3m E of A1M Junction 47.* **Sun 20 Mar (11-4). Adm £4, chd free. Light refreshments. Opening with Whixley Gardens on Sun 22 May, Wed 22 June. Visits also by arrangement Mar to June groups of 10+.**
This delightful ³/₄ acre walled flower garden overlooks the old deer park. The walls, house and various structures within the garden are festooned with climbers. Mixed borders, old roses, hardy and half-hardy perennials, topiary, bulbs and many hellebores give interest all year. Gravel and old brick paths lead to hidden seating areas creating the atmosphere of a romantic English garden. Partial wheelchair access due to gravelled surfaces and some steps.

85 OMEGA
79 Magdalen Lane, Hedon HU12 8LA. Mr & Mrs D Rosindale, 01482 897370, mavirosi@hotmail.co.uk. *6m E of Hull. Through to E Hull onto A1033. L into St Augustine's Gate through Market Place, immed R to Magdalen Gate, ahead to Magdalen Lane.* **Sat 25, Sun 26 June (12.30-5.30). Adm £3, chd free. Cream teas. Visits also by arrangement June & July 20+ incl cream teas.**
Front garden has box hedging and densely planted borders. Small side garden with acers, ferns and planted troughs. The patio has planted containers. The back has herbaceous borders and a shady area. An arch leads to a small border, greenhouses and, the wild garden, the mini-meadow is a work-in-progress. A small garden nursery offers lots of plants for sale. Cream Teas, beverages and cakes available. Afternoon Tea can be booked in advance by telephone. Large range of perennial plants for sale incl hostas, succulents and some bedding plants.

86 THE ORCHARD
4a Blackwood Rise, Cookridge, Leeds LS16 7BG. Carol & Michael Abbott, 0113 2676764, michael.john.abbott@hotmail.co.uk. *5m N of Leeds centre. Off A660 (Leeds-Otley) N of A6120 Ring Rd. Turn L up Otley Old Rd. At top of hill turn L at T-lights (Tinshill Lane). Please park in Tinshill Lane.* **Sun 12 June (12.30-5.30). Adm £3, chd free. Home-made teas. Pop up cafe and cover for inclement weather. Visits also by arrangement June & July, groups of 10+.**
³/₄ acre plantswoman's hidden oasis of peace and tranquillity. A wrap around garden of differing levels made by owners using stone, found on site, planted for yr-round interest. Extensive rockery, unusual fruit tree arbour, oriental style seated area linked by grass paths, lawns and steps. Mixed perennials, shrubs, bulbs and pots amongst paved and pebbled areas. Best in area award Leeds in Bloom.

An English Country garden, ³/₄ acre with far reaching views to Lincolnshire Wolds . . .

87 ORCHARD HOUSE
Sandholme Lane, Leven, Beverley HU17 5LW. Mrs Frances Cooper, 01964 542359, francescooper1@gmail.com. *On outskirts of Leven village. In Leven turn between Hare & Hounds PH & PO. Continue for 400yds then onto Carr Lane picking up yellow signs to Orchard House.* **Visits by arrangement Mar to Sept for groups of 2-30, adm incl refreshments. Adm £5, chd free. Light refreshments.**
A peaceful leafy, woodland garden.

Amongst the many trees, there are several different areas which have been created including a new English rose garden. Hidden paths to tucked away spaces. Greenhouse. Bulging borders are a haven for the abundant wildlife. Tea, fresh coffee or cold drinks and cake. Some parts of the garden are accessible.

88 ◆ PARCEVALL HALL GARDENS
Skyreholme, Skipton BD23 6DE. Walsingham College, 01756 720311, parcevallhall@btconnect.com, www.parcevallhallgardens.co.uk. *9m N of Skipton. Signs from B6160 Bolton Abbey-Burnsall rd or off B6265 Grassington-Pateley Bridge & at A59 Bolton Abbey r'about.* **For NGS: Wed 11 May (10-5). Adm £7, chd free. Light refreshments. For other opening times and information, please phone, email or visit garden website.**
The only garden open daily in the Yorkshire Dales National Park. 24 acres in Wharfedale sheltered by mixed woodland; terrace garden, rose garden, rock garden, ponds. Mixed borders, spring bulbs, tender shrubs and autumn colour. Tea rooms (contact no. 01756 720630) at the foot of the gardens. There is no wheelchair access in the garden as it is set on a steep hillside with uneven paths.

89 PENNY PIECE COTTAGES
41/43 Piercy End, Kirkbymoorside, York YO62 6DQ. Mick & Ann Potter, 07890 870551, skimmers@gmail.com. *Follow A170 to Kirkbymoorside at r'about turn up into Kirkby Main St approx 300yds on R. Some street parking plus council car park at top of Main St.* **Sun 12 June (12-5). Adm £4, chd free. Home-made teas. Visits also by arrangement Apr to Sept, groups 10+.**
Hidden away off the main street in Kirkbymoorside is a romantic cottage garden. Now fully matured it offers a sunny circular gravel garden incl lawns with island beds and mixed shrub and herbaceous borders. Gravel pathway leads to a brick garden, informal pond, bog garden and colourful herbaceous border. A rose arbour leads through to a wildlife pond and flower meadow.

90 ◆ PICTORIAL MEADOWS
Sheffield Manor Lodge, 389 Manor Lane, Sheffield S2 1UL. Green Estate Ltd, 0114 2762828, info@pictorialmeadows.co.uk, www.pictorialmeadows.co.uk. *1m Sheffield City Centre. M1 J33/34 Sheffield Parkway A57 to city centre. Follow B6070 from Park Square. Manor Oaks Entrance of Sheffield Manor Lodge.* **For NGS: Fri 8, Sat 9 July (10-4.30). Adm £3, chd free. Light refreshments in Rhubarb Shed Café. For other opening times and information, please phone, email or visit garden website.**
A chance to get 'behind the scenes' of Pictorial Meadows. Public access to the research beds and seed production nursery. 12pm on both days there will be a 30 minute introduction to the science and botany of meadows and staff and volunteers will be on hand to answer questions. Lots more to see and do on site as part of the general garden offer incl the fabulous Lavender Labyrinth. Disabled WC. Paths mostly grass and land is sloping but access to most areas with a helper is possible.

🚻 ⛔ ⊛ 🚐 ☕

Inspirational use of space and wide variety of plant interest . . .

91 ▸ PILMOOR COTTAGES
Pilmoor, nr Helperby YO61 2QQ. Wendy & Chris Jakeman, 01845 501848, cnjakeman@aol.com. *20m N of York. From A1M J48. N end B'bridge follow rd towards Easingwold. From A19 follow signs to Hutton Sessay then Helperby. Garden next to mainline railway.* **Wed 15 June, Sun 28 Aug (12-5). Adm £3.50, chd free. Light refreshments. Visits also by arrangement May to Sept.**
2-acre garden round C19 cottages. Developed by 2 avid garden visitors unable to visit a garden without buying a new plant, leading to an informal cottage style, but always with something to look at from bulbs in spring to colchicum and cyclamen in autumn. New 1½ acre wild flower meadow with pond. Clock-golf putting green. 7¼' Gauge railway around the garden, ponds and rockery.

⛔ 🚻 ⊛ ☕

ALLOTMENTS

92 ▸ QUEENSGATE & KITCHEN LANE ALLOTMENTS
Beverley HU17 8NN. Beverley Town Council. *Outskirts of Beverley Town Centre. On A164 towards Cottingham, allotment site is before Victoria Rd, after double mini r'about & opp Beverley Grammar School.* **Sun 24 July (12-4). Adm £2.50, chd free. Tea.**
Varied allotment site of 85 plots, plus another 35 on Kitchen Lane, growing a wide variety of fruit, vegetables and flowers. Some allotment holders will be present to discuss their plots. Wide grass path for easy viewing and plots either side. Dogs on leads.

🚻 ☕

---

93 ▸ REWELA COTTAGE
Skewsby YO61 4SG. John Plant & Daphne Ellis, 01347 888125, plantjohnsgarden@btinternet.com. *4m N of Sheriff Hutton, 15m N of York. After Sheriff Hutton, towards Terrington, turn L towards Whenby & Brandsby. Turn R just past Whenby to Skewsby. Turn L into village. 400yds on R.* **Sun 1 May, Sun 31 July (11-5). Adm £4, chd free. Home-made teas. Visits also by arrangement May to July excl June, min group 15.**
³⁄₄-acre ornamental garden, designed by current owner, featuring unusual trees, shrubs, and architectural plants. Pond, pergola, natural stone sunken garden, breeze house, vegetable garden/nursery and new outdoor kitchen. Specialist grower of heuchera, hosta and penstemon. Many varieties also for sale. A very friendly welcome. Lovely surroundings for lunch, great cakes and scones, teas and coffees, soft drinks. Plus BBQ serving Burgers and Sausages. WC. All unusual trees and shrubs have labels giving full descriptions, picture, and any cultivation notes incl propagation. Plant sales are specimens from garden. Many varieties of Heuchera, Heucherella and Tiarellas,

Penstemon, Hostas and herbs for sale. Some gravel paths may be an effort for a wheelchair. Plenty of seats.

⛔ 🚻 ⊛ 🚐 ☕

94 ▸ ◆ RHS GARDEN HARLOW CARR
Crag Lane, Harrogate HG3 1QB. Royal Horticultural Society, 01423 565418, harlowcarr@rhs.org.uk, www.rhs.org.uk/harlowcarr. *1½ m W of Harrogate town centre. On B6162 (Harrogate - Otley).* **For NGS: Sun 8 May (9.30-5). For other opening times, admission and information, please phone, email or visit garden website.**
One of Yorkshire's most relaxing yet inspiring locations! Highlights incl spectacular herbaceous borders, streamside garden, alpines, scented and kitchen gardens. Lakeside Gardens, woodland and wild flower meadows. Betty's Cafe Tearooms, gift shop, plant centre and childrens play area incl tree house and log ness monster. Wheelchairs and mobility scooters available, advanced booking recommended.

⛔ ⊛ 🚐 ☕

95 ▸ THE RIDINGS
South Street, Burton Fleming, Driffield YO25 3PE. Roy & Ruth Allerston, 01262 470489. *11m NE of Driffield. 11m SW of Scarborough. 7m NW of Bridlington. From Driffield B1249, before Foxholes turn R to Burton Fleming. From Scarborough A165 turn R to Burton Fleming.* **Sun 22 May (1-5). Adm £3, chd free. Sun 3 July (1-5). Combined adm with Rustic Cottage £5, chd free. Home-made teas. Visits also by arrangement.**
Tranquil cottage garden designed by owners in 2001 on reclaimed site. Brick pergola and arches covered with climbers lead to secret garden with box edged beds. Colour-themed mixed borders with old English roses. Paved terrace with water feature and farming bygones, small potager; summerhouse and greenhouse. N B On 3rd July Rustic cottage is open 12-4 and Ridings 1-5. Wheelchair access limited to terrace and tea area.

🚻 ⊛ 🚐 ☕

96 NEW ▸ RIVELIN COTTAGE
1 Green Lane, Aston, Sheffield S26 2BD. Mr & Mrs S Pashley. *S26 2BD. J31 M1, Take A57 exit to Sheffield (SE), 1st exit onto A57, travel approx 700 yds on Worksop Rd. Turn L onto*

Beechcroft Farmhouse

© Marcus Harpur

Green Lane, Parking at Yellow Lion PH, Worksop Rd, Aston,. **Sun 26 June (12-5). Adm £3.50, chd free. Home-made teas.**

An English cottage garden with long flowing borders filled with trees, shrubs and perennials. Roses are a passion for the owner and feature throughout the garden. Pergolas, arbour, water feature, box hedging and box balls. Shabby chic shed. Ornamental vegetable garden. Inspirational use of space and wide variety of plant interest. Wheelchair access to main garden but steps to house and patio.

97 ▶ RUSTIC COTTAGE
Front Street, Wold Newton, nr Driffield YO25 3YQ. Jan Joyce, 01262 470710. 13m N of Driffield. From Driffield take B1249 to Foxholes (12m), take R turning signed Wold Newton. Turn L onto Front St, opp village pond, continue up hill, garden on L. **Sun 3 July (12-4). Single adm £3. Combined adm with The Ridings £5, chd free. Home-made teas at The Ridings. Visits also by arrangement Apr to Sept 20 max. Adm £5 if combined with Ridings. Refreshments at Ridings.**

Plantswoman's cottage garden of much interest with many choice and unusual plants. Hellebores and bulbs are treats for colder months. Old-fashioned roses, fragrant perennials, herbs and wild flowers, all grown together provide habitat for birds, bees, butterflies and small mammals. It has been described as 'organised chaos'! The owner's 2nd NGS garden. Small dogs only. NB Gardens are open at different times.

98 ◆ SCAMPSTON WALLED GARDEN
Scampston Hall, Scampston, Malton YO17 8NG. The Legard Family, 01944 759111, info@scampston.co.uk, www.scampston.co.uk/gardens. 5m E of Malton. 1/2 m N of A64, nr the village of Rillington & signed Scampston only. **For opening times and information, please phone, email or visit garden website.**

An exciting modern garden designed by Piet Oudolf. The 4-acre walled garden contains a series of hedged enclosures designed to look good throughout the year. The garden contains many unusual species and is a must for any keen plantsman. The Walled Garden is set within the grounds and parkland surrounding Scampston Hall. The Hall opens to visitors for a short period during the summer months. A newly restored Richardson conservatory at the heart of the Walled Garden re-opened as a Heritage and Learning Centre in 2015.

99 ▶ SERENITY
Arkendale Road, Ferrensby, nr Knaresborough HG5 0QA. Mr & Mrs Smith, 01423 340062, geoffsmith269@gmail.com. 3m NE of Knaresborough, 4m SW of Boroughbridge. On A6055 between Boroughbridge & Knaresborough. A1M J47 follow A168 N, after 3m turn L to Arkendale & Ferrensby. **Wed 27, Sun 31 July (12-5). Adm £3, chd free. Home-made teas. Visits also by arrangement July to Sept, groups of 20+, tours and coaches.**

After the complete renovation of a 1/4 acre garden by removal of all conifers and large overgrown evergreens in 2013 the garden is now full of colour with wide borders and circular lawn feature, over 100 clematis and many thousand herbaceous perennials and annuals propagated by enthusiastic knowledgeable owners. Vegetable garden, patio, terrace, garden structures, greenhouse and seating areas.

© Lee Beel

Beacon Garth

2. A NEW larger garden, with different areas, each planted accordingly; 3. A traditional garden with mixed and evergreen planting; and lastly 4. A narrow cottage garden, tucked out of sight..... 6 All Saints is 'maze-like' with a mix of contemporary and cottage garden features; hidden corners, water features and pond. Wayside is NEW and inspirational. A stunning addition to the group, showing gardening skill, and interesting planting in the several different areas of the garden. Vegetable and fruit growing areas with greenhouse and poly tunnel. Cairngorm has gravelled paths, conifers, ferns, hostas, vegetable plot, a relaxing log cabin, and greenhouse. East View, is a peaceful haven, hidden away - a long narrow garden with cottage herbaceous planting. Hostas and ferns set off a water feature near the cottage and a wildlife pond is peacefully tucked away at the end of the garden. Wheelchairs possible with help at 6 All Saints also at Wayside (narrow access and large gravel). Not at other gardens: steep drives/difficult access.

100 ◆ SHANDY HALL GARDENS
Coxwold YO61 4AD. The Laurence Sterne Trust, 01347 868465, www.laurencesternetrust.org.uk/shandy-hall-garden.php. *N of York. From A19, 7m from both Easingwold & Thirsk, turn E signed Coxwold.* **For NGS: Evening opening Fri 6 May, Fri 1 July (6.30-8). Adm £3, chd free. For other opening times and information, please phone or visit garden website.**
Home of C18 author Laurence Sterne. 2 walled gardens, 1 acre of unusual perennials interplanted with tulips and old roses in low walled beds. In old quarry, another acre of trees, shrubs, bulbs, climbers and wild flowers encouraging wildlife, incl. over 370 recorded species of moths. Moth trap, identification and release. Wildlife garden. Wheelchair access to wild garden by arrangement.

GROUP OPENING

101 SHIPTONTHORPE GARDENS
York YO43 3PQ. *2m NW of Market Weighton. From Market Weighton on A1079, take 2nd turn off to Shiptonthorpe Cairngorm on R is start point with car parking opp.* **Sat 4, Sun 5 June (11-5). Combined adm £6, chd free.**

6 ALL SAINTS
Di Thompson.

CAIRNGORM
Peter & Ann Almond.
EAST VIEW
Maureen Almond.

NEW WAYSIDE
Susan Sellars.

Four contrasting gardens offering different approaches to gardening style - 1. A contemporary garden;

102 SION HILL HALL
Kirby Wiske, Thirsk YO7 4EU. H W Mawer Trust, sionhill@btconnect.com, www.sionhillhall.co.uk. *6m S of Northallerton off A167 4m W of Thirsk, 6m E of A1 via A61.* **Sat 25, Sun 26 June (11-4.30). Adm £5, chd free. Home-made teas.**
The extensive gardens surround an Arts and Crafts Neo-Georgian house built in 1913, designed by Walter Brierley, York (house not open). The beautiful grounds have been designed and restored by Michael Mallaby, to include a formal parterre with Baroque statuary, clipped box and hornbeam, a Long Walk with yews, shrubs and herbaceous planting, a traditional Kitchen garden, and Centenary rose garden. Mostly level gravelled paths surround the parterre.

103 SKIPWITH HALL
Skipwith, Selby YO8 5SQ. Mr & Mrs C D Forbes Adam, www.escrick.com/hall-gardens. *9m S of York, 6m N of Selby. From York A19 Selby, L in Escrick, 4m to Skipwith. From Selby A19 York, R onto A163 to Market Weighton, then L after 2m to Skipwith.*

Thur 16 June (1-4). Adm £5, chd free. Tea. Visits also by arrangement May & June, groups of 10+.
4-acre walled garden of Queen Anne house (not open). Extensive mixed borders and lawns, walled areas by renowned designer Cecil Pinsent. Recreated working kitchen garden with 15' beech hedge, pleached fruit walks, herb maze and pool. Woodland with specimen trees and shell house. Decorative orchard with espaliered and fan-trained fruit on walls. Italian Garden recently restored. Gravel paths.

104 SLEIGHTHOLMEDALE LODGE
Fadmoor YO62 7JG. Patrick & Natasha James, 01751 430955, patrick.james@landscapeagency. co.uk. *6m NE of Helmsley. Parking can be limited in wet weather. Garden is the first property in Sleightholmedale, 1m from Fadmoor.* **Wed 8 June (2-6). Sun 24 July (2-6). Tea. Adm £3.50, chd free.** Hillside garden, walled rose garden and herbaceous borders with delphiniums, roses, verbascums in July. Species tulips and meconopsis in early June. Views over peaceful valley in N.Yorks Moors.

GROUP OPENING

105 STAMFORD BRIDGE GARDENS
Grove Lodge, Butts Close, Stamford Bridge YO41 1PD. G & D Tattersall, 01759 373838, dmt9245@hotmail.co.uk. *Stamford Bridge. Approx 7m E of York on the A166 to Bridlington. Please use main car park in village or station car park on Church Rd.* **Sun 31 July (12-5). Combined adm £5, chd free. Tea at Daneswell House. Visits also by arrangement July & Aug groups of 10+.**

DANESWELL HOUSE
Brian & Pauline Clayton

GROVE LODGE
Mr & Mrs G Tattersall

MILL TIMBER
Mr & Mrs K Chapman

NEW NEWSTEAD
Jayne Chomyn
01759 371492

Four interesting and contrasting gardens situated in the historic village of Stamford Bridge. Grove Lodge has a large collection of plants grown from seed or propagated from cuttings by the owner. There are small number of vegetables grown in planters, fruit trees and greenhouse containing a variety of salad vegetables. Mill Timber has a good collection of perennials in a large, eye catching and sloping border. The garden is sheltered on one side by mature trees. Patio planters with summer flowers and hanging baskets displaying a kaleidoscope of colour. Daneswell House is a ³/₄ -acre terraced garden that sweeps down to the R Derwent. Pond and water feature with walk over bridge. Large lawned area with mixed borders and shrubs. Attracts wildlife. The 4th garden is NEW: Newstead has some interesting herbaceous perennials and shrubs, and the planting shows a passion for gardening, a good addition to the group. The gardens are not next door to each other, so a ¹/₂ m walk should be anticipated.

106 ◆ STILLINGFLEET LODGE
Stewart Lane, Stillingfleet, York YO19 6HP. Mr & Mrs J Cook, 01904 728506, vanessa.cook@stillingfleetlodgenur series.co.uk, www.stillingfleetlodgenurseries.co. uk. *6m S of York. From A19 York-Selby take B1222 towards Sherburn in Elmet. In village turn opp church.* **For NGS: Sun 8 May, Sun 11 Sept (1-5). Adm £5, chd £1. Home-made teas. For other opening times and information, please phone, email or visit garden website.**
Organic, wildlife garden subdivided into smaller gardens, each based on colour theme with emphasis on use of foliage plants. Wild flower meadow

and natural pond. 55yd double herbaceous borders. Modern rill garden. Rare breeds of poultry wander freely in garden. Adjacent nursery. Wildlife Day in June. Garden Courses run all summer see website. Featured on Living North, Garden Answers, BBC York. Gravel paths and lawn. Ramp to cafe if needed. No disabled wc.

107 NEW STONEFIELD COTTAGE
27 Nordham, North Cave, Brough HU15 2LT. Nicola Lyte. *15m W of Hull. M62 E, J38 towards N Cave. Turn L towards N Cave Wetlands, then R at LH bend. Stonefield Cottage is on R, ¹/₄ m along Nordham.* **Fri 22, Sat 23, Sun 24 July (12-5). Combined adm with Fawley House £6, chd free. Home-made teas at Stonefield Cottage. Ices at Fawley House.**
A hidden and surprising 1-acre garden, with an emphasis throughout on strong, dramatic colours and sweeping vistas. Rose beds, mixed borders, vegetables, a riotous hot bed, boggy woodland, jacquemontii under-planted with red hydrangeas and a Portmeirion garden. Collections of Hellebores, Primulas, Astilbes, Hostas, Heucheras, Dahlias, Thyme and Hemerocallis are planted *en masse* in their own areas. Art exhibition and Treasure Hunt for children at Fawley House.

108 NEW SUNNY MOUNT
Well Hill, Honley, Holmfirth HD9 6JF. Barry & Jenny Kellington. *3m S of Huddersfield, 3m N of Holmfirth. Turn to Honley off A616 (New Mill Rd), drive through village, turn R at r'about. Garden entrance 100 metres on L. Please park in village.* **Sat 14, Sun 15 May, Sat 18, Sun 19 June (10-6). Adm £3, chd free. Cream teas.**
The garden, designed by present owner around Georgian cottage (not open), contains an interesting range of planting, stone and mosaic paving, sheltered courtyard and summerhouse. Attractive kitchen garden, with raised vegetable beds, divided by gravel paths, central pergola, potting shed, fruit garden and pond. Art, craft and garden design exhibition. Featured in Huddersfield Examiner. Society of Garden Designers website.

Landscaped sunken garden with pool and Japanese styled pagoda . . .

GROUP OPENING

109 NEW **SUTTON GARDENS**
Sutton Lane, Masham HG4 4PB.
1¹/₂ m W of Masham. From Masham towards Leyburn (A6108) L into Sutton Lane, single track tarmac rd Low Sutton ¹/₄ m on L for parking & entry tickets. **Sun 28 Feb (12-4). Light refreshments. Sun 17 July (12-5). Home-made teas. Combined adm £5, chd free. at Low Sutton, home made soup and rolls, hot beverages for Snowdrop Festival. Home made teas in July.**

> **LOW SUTTON** |🛌|
> Steve & Judi Smith
> 01765 688565
> info@lowsutton.co.uk
> www.lowsutton.co.uk

> **SUTTON GRANGE** |🛌|
> Mr & Mrs Robert Jameson
> 01765 689068
> jameson3@btinternet.com
> www.themews-masham.com

Set down a peaceful country lane outside Masham, two contrasting styles of gardens. Low Sutton set within 6 acre smallholding, has a circular colour wheel cottage garden surrounded with scented roses and clematis. Wide variety of fruit and vegetables decoratively grown in raised beds, fruit cage, greenhouse and coldframe. Perennial border, grasses, fernery and courtyard with hostas surround the house. Old orchard that is newly planted with fruit trees has a rill and seasonal pond, and a walk on the wildside. Sutton Grange, 1¹/₂ acre established garden and orchard with woodland walk. Greenhouse with tomatoes and fig tree. Walled vegetable garden with cutting flower bed, gazebo, summerhouse, lawns surrounded by herbaceous borders with iris, roses, peonies, wisteria and clematis. Laburnum and honeysuckle arches and water features. Many places to sit and enjoy the views, or have a game of croquet or boules. Snowdrop Festival. An abundance of naturalised snowdrops carpet the old orchard and hillside at Low Sutton and throughout the garden at Sutton Grange. Warming winter refreshments.

🏵 ⊛ ☕

110 **SUTTON UPON DERWENT SCHOOL**
Main Street, Sutton On Derwent, York YO41 4BN. Head - Angela Ekers. Garden - Annette Atkin.
From M Weighton on A1079, pass Pocklington. At Jet garage on R, go L into Sutton Lane. Follow rd to village, L at tennis courts. Blind corner, school on R. **Sun 10 July (11-4). Adm £2.50, chd free. Tea.**
Sutton upon Derwent school is an RHS level 5 school garden. Grounds developed over the past 7yrs, have become the gardens which are now an integral part of school life; encouraging outdoor lessons in all areas of the curriculum. Outdoor learning spaces incl, a sensory garden, wildlife area, extensive vegetable growing areas, greenhouse and poly tunnel. Children's wildlife activities.

♿ ⊛ 🚌 ☕

111 **SWALE COTTAGE**
Station Road, Richmond DL10 4LU. Julie Martin & Dave Dalton, 01748 829452. *Richmond town centre. On foot, facing bottom of Market Place, turn L onto Frenchgate, then R onto Station Rd. House 1st on R.* **Sun 19 June (1-5). Adm £3, chd free. Home-made teas. Also open Millgate House. Visits also by arrangement May to Sept for groups of 10+.**
¹/₂ -acre urban oasis on steep site, with sweeping views and hidden corners. Several enclosed garden rooms on different levels. Mature herbaceous, rose and shrub garden with some areas of recent improvement. Magnificent yew and cedar. Organic vegetables and soft fruit and pond. Adjacent orchard and paddock with sheep and hens.

⊛ ☕

112 **TAMARIND**
2 Whin Hill Road, Bessacarr, Doncaster DN4 7AE. Ken & Carol Kilvington. *2m S of Doncaster. A638 S Doncaster-Bawtry. After Lakeside, straight on at T-lights then 1st L. A638 N turn R signed Cantley-Branton (B1396).* **Sat 6, Sun 7 Aug (1-5). Adm £3.50, chd free. Light refreshments.**
A ²/₃ acre garden is level at the front with acers and interesting varied planting. Round lawn leads to a steeply terraced rear garden full of colour and differing styles. White border with dovecote and doves; hot border, rose garden, herbaceous, embankment and newly developed rhododendron garden. Stream with waterfalls, ponds, rockery and bog garden, thatched summerhouse, patio. Steep steps. Featured in Amateur Gardening. The front garden and rear lower patio is accessible to wheelchairs, from which most of the rear garden can be viewed. Steps to the rest of the garden.

🏵 ⊛ ☕

113 ♦ **THORNYCROFT**
Rainton, nr Thirsk YO7 3PH. Martin & Jill Fish, 01845 577157, martin@martinfish.com, www.martinfish.com. *1m E of A1(M) between Ripon & Thirsk. Approx 6m N of Boroughbridge, Access to Rainton is from J48 or 50 of A1(M) or from A168 dual carriageway at Asenby or Topcliffe.* **For NGS: Sun 31 July (11-4.30). Adm £4, chd free. Home-made teas. For other opening times and information, please phone, email or visit garden website.**
A ³/₄ acre country garden created since 2009 comprising lawn areas, trees, shrubs and perennials and featuring some unusual plant specimens. Pergola, summerhouse and paved courtyard garden with container plants and raised beds. Orchard with mixture of heritage and modern varieties and an ornamental kitchen garden. Wooden greenhouse with decorative plants and productive poly-tunnel. BBC Radio York and BBC Radio Nottingham gardening expert Martin Fish will be on hand during the day to answer your gardening questions. Features regularly in Garden News, Kitchen Garden magazine and the Harrogate Advertiser/Ripon Gazette series of newspapers. Gravel drive leading to main garden and gravel paths in kitchen garden.

♿ ⊛ 🚌 |🛌| ☕

114 TICKTON CE PRIMARY

Main Street, Tickton, Beverley HU17 9RZ. Head Teacher - Miss C Brown. Garden - Sue McCallum. *E of Beverley. Tickton is signed from A1035.* **Fri 17 June (10-3). Adm £2.50, chd free. Light refreshments.**

At Tickton school we actively encourage outdoor learning incl gardening. The aim is to provide a stimulating environment for play and educational activities whilst creating habitats for wildlife. Children will be involved in a variety of activities to demonstrate the use of the grounds. Many of the refreshments will have been prepared by the children. Featured in Beverley Guardian. Wheelchair access to most of the garden incl the refreshment area.

115 VICARAGE HOUSE

Kirkby Wharfe, Tadcaster LS24 9DE. Mr & Mrs R S A Hall, 01937 835458. *1m S of Tadcaster. (A162) turn L (B1223) after 1m turn L to Kirkby Wharfe Vicarage House is the 1st house on the L as you enter the village.* **Visits by arrangement May & June, groups of 10 to 30. Adm incl refreshments. Adm £5, chd free.**

Secluded 1-acre country garden surrounded by mature trees, colour-themed border, extensive herbaceous borders, raised beds. Species primulae and aquilegias, 'jewel bed', productive vegetable plot, asparagus bed, vine shaded terrace, gravel pathways.

116 NEW WALKER'S NURSERY

Mosham Road, Blaxton, Doncaster DN9 3BA. Mr Graham Bodle, www.walkersnurseries.tv. *7m S of Doncaster on the B1396.* **Evening opening Wed 24 Aug (5.30-9). Adm £7, chd free. Wine and canapes.**

Refreshments will be served from the small private family garden designed by Chelsea Gold Medal winner, which leads to 8 acres of gardens where paths meander through a box parterre, mature conifers, deciduous shrubs and trees to open grassland with specimen trees, standing stones and recently landscaped sunken garden with pool and Japanese styled pagoda. The RHS Chelsea Flower Show Gold Medal and Best

Artisan Garden 2015 have been rebuilt in the garden. Suitable for wheelchairs.

GROUP OPENING

117 NEW WALLED GARDENS OF BEVERLEY

Beverley HU17 7AG. *On L of North Bar Without as approached through the Bar & on York Rd. Gardens are within a short walking distance of each other, with parking on the street 'North Bar Without'. 5 minute walk from Beverley town centre parking. No parking on York Rd.* **Sun 10 July (12-4.30). Combined adm £6, chd free. Tea at 39 North Bar Without.**

NEW THE ELMS
Mr & Mrs R Hudson

NEW 45 NORTH BAR WITHOUT
Mrs Gill Morrison

NEW 39 NORTH BAR WITHOUT
Mr & Mrs C Ryan

NEW 6 YORK ROAD
Pamela Hopkins

These walled gardens have all been in existence for over a hundred years. They are now home to diverse styles of gardening with herbaceous borders, mature trees and a variety of fruit and vegetables. They can each be enjoyed for their seclusion and tranquillity; a haven from the noise and bustle of the town. Wheelchair access The Elms No. 29 is easily accessible. Nos 39 & 45 have limited access but are still able to be seen. No 6 York Rd has no access for wheelchairs.

118 WARLEY HOUSE GARDEN

Stock Lane, Warley, Halifax HX2 7RU. Dr & Mrs P J Hinton, 01422 831431, warleyhousegardens@outlook.com, www.warleyhousegardens.com. *2m W of Halifax. Take A646 (Burnley) from Halifax. Go through large intersection after approx 1m. 1m further take R turn up Windle Royd Lane. Signs will direct you from here. Disabled parking adjacent to the house limited to 4/5 vehicles.* **Sun 8, Wed 11 May (1-5). Adm £4, chd free. Home-made teas. Visits also by arrangement May to July refreshments by arrangement with individual groups. 4 weeks notice please.**

Partly walled 2½ acre garden of demolished C18 House, renovated by the present owners. Rocky paths and Japanese style planting lead to lawns and lovely S-facing views. Alpine ravine planted with ferns and fine trees give structure to the developing woodland area. Drifts of shrubs, herbaceous plantings, wild flowers and heathers maintain constant seasonal interest. Featured in the Halifax Courier. Partial wheelchair access to Japanese garden. Disabled access to WCs.

120 WEATHERVANE HOUSE

Mill Lane, Seaton Ross YO42 4NE. Peter & Julie Williams, 01759 318663. *6m S of Pocklington. 15m SE of York & 12m N of Howden Tel: 01759 318663.* **Sun 1 May (11-4). Adm £4, chd free. Home-made teas.**

Two-acre woodland garden with magnolias, rhododendrons, azaleas, flowering trees and shrubs. A wide range of spring bulbs incl erythroniums and trilliums together with mixed herbaceous borders, lawns and circular meadow. Fruit garden, glasshouse with wide range of hardy and tender plants and large polytunnel with specimen rhododendrons and many other plants. A wide range of interesting and uncommon shrubs and herbaceous perennials for sale that reflect the plants growing in the garden. Examples of plants propagated by cuttings, grafting and raised from seed are available. Artist in the garden. Gravel drive and paths but wheelchair passage possible.

121 THE WHITE HOUSE

Husthwaite YO61 4QA.
Mrs A Raper, 01347 868688,
audrey.husthwaite@btinternet.com.
5m S of Thirsk. Turn R off A19 signed Husthwaite. 1¹/₂ m to centre of village opp village parish church. **Visits by arrangement any size group. Adm £6, chd free.**
Meet an enthusiastic plantswoman. Exchange ideas and visit a 1-acre country garden. Walled garden, conservatory, herbaceous borders, fresh lavender and purple palette in late spring and hot summer border. Unusual plants and shrubs. Collections of peonies, clematis and hemerocallis (in season), landscaping, planting and bed of English and shrub roses in the old orchard. A garden for all seasons.

GROUP OPENING

122 WHIXLEY GARDENS

York YO26 8AR, 01423 330474. *8m W of York, 8m E of Harrogate, 6m N of Wetherby. 3m E of A1(M) off A59 York-Harrogate. Signed Whixley.* **Sun 22 May, Wed 22 June (12-5). Combined adm £6, chd free. Home-made teas at The Old Vicarage.**

ASH TREE HOUSE
Mr & Mrs E P Moffitt

COBBLE COTTAGE
John Hawkridge & Barry Atkinson
Visits also by arrangement May to July only groups of 10+
johnbarry44@talktalk.net
01423 331419

LYDIATE HOUSE
Roger & Sheila Lythe
Visits also by arrangement May to July groups of 10+ with other Whixley gardens
sheila.lythe@hotmail.co.uk
01423 330178

THE OLD VICARAGE
Mr & Mrs Roger Marshall
(See separate entry)
Visits also by arrangement Mar to June groups of 10+
biddymarshall@btinternet.com

Attractive rural yet accessible village nestling on the edge of the York Plain with beautiful historic church and Queen Anne Hall (not open). The gardens are spread throughout the village with good footpaths. A plantsman's and flower arranger's garden at Cobble Cottage has views to the Hambleton Hills. Further towards the village centre are two small well designed gardens on sloping sites. Ash Tree House with extensive rock garden and borders full of established herbaceous plants, shrubs and roses creating a tapestry of soft colour and textures achieving a cottage garden effect and Lydiate House, recently redesigned, with sloping alpine rockeries, naturalistic borders, foliage plants and unusual perennials. Close to the church, The Old Vicarage, with a ³/₄-acre walled flower garden, overlooks the old deer park. The walls, house and various structures are festooned with climbers. Gravel and old brick paths lead to hidden seating areas creating the atmosphere of a romantic English garden.

123 WHYNCREST

Bridlington Road, Hunmanby, Filey YO14 9RS. Mrs Lieke Swann, 01723 890923,
lieke@whyncrest.wanadoo.co.uk.
Between Hunmanby & Reighton Nursery off A165 between Hunmanby Gap & Reighton. Exit A165, junction signed Reigthon Nurseries & Hunmanby, follow this rd for 200 yds, Whyncrest is on R. Parking on grass verge outside. **Sat 9, Sun 10 July (11-4). Adm £4, chd free. Tea. Visits also by arrangement May to Sept, groups of 10+.**
Elevated garden with fabulous views across Filey Bay and beyond. The garden has been carefully designed, creating micro climate 'rooms' taking you from jungle garden to a pond garden with tropical planting and a huge waterfall, herbaceous borders and topiary shrubs. The collection of plants is varied, giving an all year interest from early spring with all its bulbs all the way into late autumn. All proceeds from tea, coffee and cakes are for the benefit of a local charity of our choice. in 2015 this was the Sue Ryder Care charity.

124 WOODLANDS COTTAGE

Summerbridge, Nidderdale HG3 4BT. Mr & Mrs Stark, 01423 780765,
www.woodlandscottagegarden.co.uk. *10m NW of Harrogate. On the B6165 W of Summerbridge.* **Sun 15 May (2-5). Adm £3.50, chd free.**

Tea. **Opening with Dacre Banks & Summerbridge Gardens on Sun 10 July. Visits also by arrangement May to Aug.**
A one-acre country garden created by its owners and making full use of its setting, which includes natural woodland with wild bluebells and gritstone boulders. There are several gardens within the garden, from a wild flower meadow and woodland rock-garden to a formal herb garden and herbaceous areas; also a productive fruit and vegetable garden. Gravel paths with some slopes.

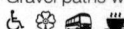

A haven from the noise and bustle of the town . . .

125 NEW WYEDALE

Ottringham Road, Keyingham, Hull HU12 9RX. Mrs Angie Woodmancy & Mr J Woodmancy. *10m E of Hull. Enter Keyingham on A1033 Hull to Withernsea rd, continue through village, garage on R, head towards mill. Parking on L at Eastend Nurseries, garden approx 70 yds on R.* **Sun 3 July (11-5). Adm £3, chd free. Home-made teas.**
An English Country garden, ³/₄ acre with far reaching views to Lincolnshire Wolds. Curved borders of herbaceous perennials, scented seating area with pinks, jasmin, philadelphus and herbs, wildlife pond. Gravel garden with grasses leading to pergola clothed in roses and clematis followed by cutting garden with interesting 'folly wall'. Vegetable garden. Wild life area with hedgehog houses leads to orchard. All areas have wheelchair access.

126 ◆ YORK GATE

Back Church Lane, Adel, Leeds LS16 8DW. Perennial, 0113 267 8240, yorkgate@perennial.org.uk, www.yorkgate.org.uk. *5m N of Leeds. N of Leeds 2¹/₄ m SE of Bramhope, signed from A660. Park in Church Lane in lay-by opp church & take public footpath through churchyard to garden.* **For opening times and information, please phone, email or visit garden website.**

One-acre masterpiece and outstanding example of late C20 garden design. A series of smaller gardens with different themes and in contrasting styles are linked by a succession of delightful vistas. Striking architectural features found throughout the garden. White and Silver Borders, Pinetum and Arbour, Woodland Dell, Kitchen and Cutting Gardens, Herb Garden and Summerhouse, Paved Garden, Nut Walk, Potting Shed, Pavement Maze, the Old Orchard, Alley and Sundial, Fern Border, Sybil's Garden, Scree Garden and Canal Garden. As seen on TV's 'Glorious Gardens from Above' with Christine Walkden and winner of Yorkshire in Bloom. Steps and gravel paths make the garden unsuitable for wheelchairs.

127 YORKE HOUSE
Dacre Banks, Nidderdale
HG3 4EW. Tony & Pat Hutchinson,
01423 780456,
pat@yorkehouse.co.uk,
www.yorkehouse.co.uk. *4m SE of Pateley Bridge, 10m NW of Harrogate, 10m N of Otley. On B6451 near centre of Dacre Banks.*

Car park. **Sun 26 June (11-5). Adm £5, chd free. Cream teas. Opening with Dacre Banks & Summerbridge Gardens on Sun 10 July. Visits also by arrangement June to Aug for groups of 10+.**
Award-winning flower arranger's 2-acre garden with colour-themed borders full of flowering & foliage plants. Water feature incl ornamental ponds and stream with attractive waterside plantings. Other features incl nut walk, rose walk, gazebo, millennium garden, woodland sanctuary & wildlife areas. Large collection of hostas. The garden enjoys beautiful views across Nidderdale. Orchard picnic area. Winner Harrogate's Glorious Gardens. Featured in Harrogate Advertiser, Daily Telegraph. All main features accessible to wheelchair users.

128 ◆ THE YORKSHIRE ARBORETUM
Castle Howard, York YO60 7BY.
The Castle Howard Arboretum Trust, 01653 648598,
visit@yorkshirearboretum.org,
www.yorkshirearboretum.org. *15m*

NE of York. Off A64. Follow signs to Castle Howard then look for Yorkshire Arboretum signs at the obelisk r'about. **For NGS: Sun 5 June (10-4). Adm £6, chd free. Light refreshments. For other opening times and information, please phone, email or visit garden website.**
A glorious, 120 acre garden of trees from around the world set in a stunning landscape of parkland, lakes and ponds. With walks and lakeside trails, tours, family activities, a woodland playground, café and gift shop we welcome visitors of all ages wanting to enjoy the space, serenity and beauty of this sheltered valley as well as those interested in our extensive collection of trees and shrubs. Internationally renowned collection of trees in a beautiful setting, accompanied by a diversity of wild flowers, birds, insects and other wildlife. The Arboretum Café enjoys an enviable reputation for its delicious food and drink, prepared on-site using the very best in seasonal, local produce. Not suitable for wheelchairs. Motorised buggies available on loan, please book 24hrs in advance.

Manor Farm

Stable Cottage, Carmarthenshire & Pembrokeshire

WALES

Cheshire & Wirral

North East Wales

Gwynedd & Anglesey

WALES

Shropshire

Ceredigion

Powys

Herefordshire

Carmarthenshire & Pembrokeshire

Gwent

Glamorgan

The areas shown on this map are specific to the organisation of The National Gardens Scheme. The Gardens of England, listed by area, precede the Gardens of Wales.

Somerset, Bristol Area & S. Glos

CARMARTHENSHIRE & PEMBROKESHIRE

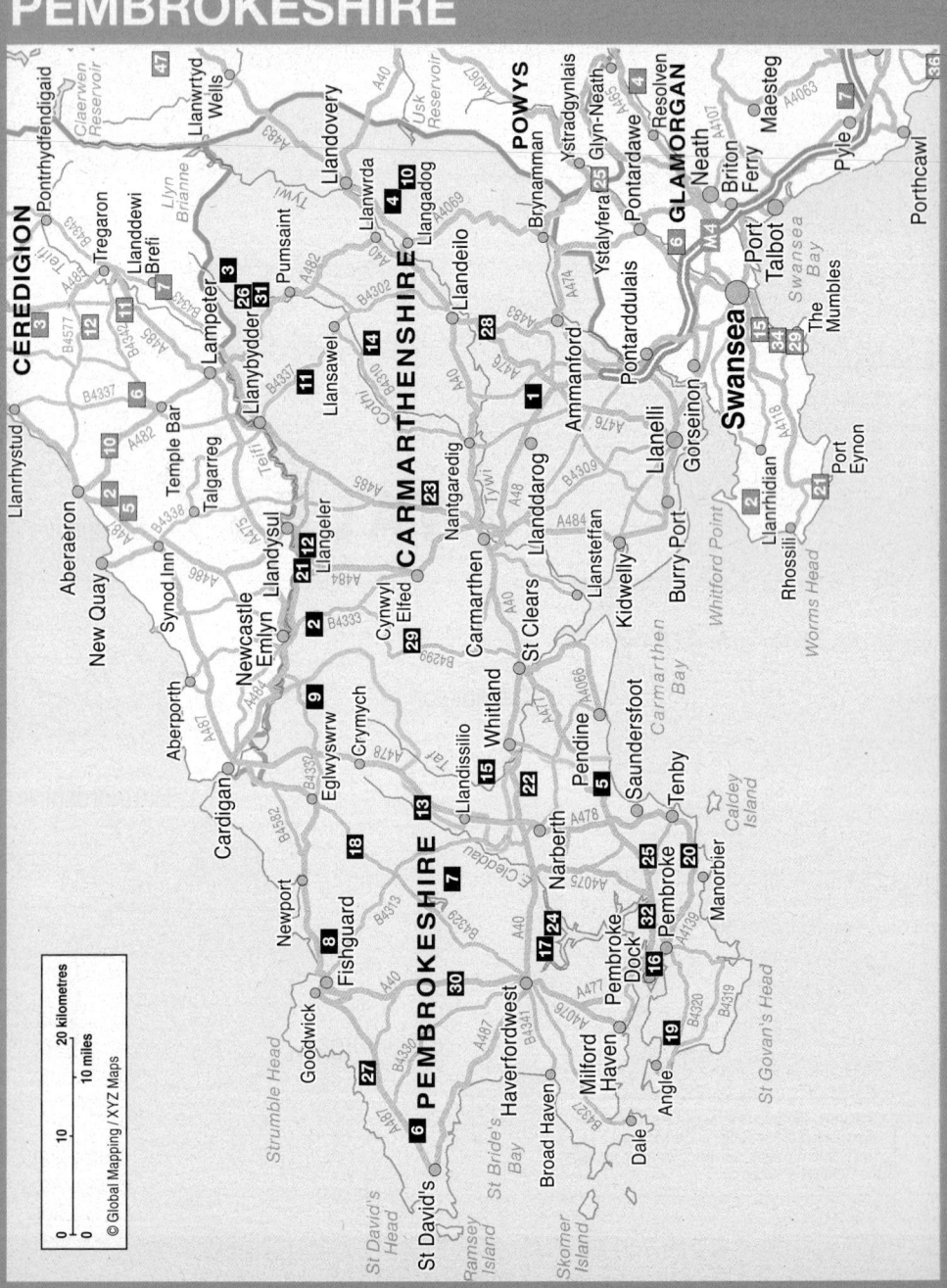

Carmarthenshire
& Pembrokeshire

From the rugged western coast, bathed in mild weather thanks to the Gulf Stream, to the foothills of the Black Mountains, Carmarthenshire and Pembrokeshire offer a wide range of gardens to enjoy in countryside untroubled by the traffic jams of more populated areas.

A special feature of many of our gardens is the benefit of superb borrowed landscapes, where the extensive rural views emphasise the overall effect of an uncluttered environment.

Visitors to the area will know the delightful seaside town of Tenby, but may not be acquainted with the opportunities to visit the less well-known gems to be found in The Yellow Book. Even if you do not manage to reach a garden on its specific open day, garden owners who open 'by arrangement' are genuinely delighted to welcome you: just ring to arrange when to visit.

Gardeners in Wales are often also known for their tempting home-baking, which visitors can enjoy as a finale to a stroll in a beautiful garden.

Carmarthenshire & Pembrokeshire Volunteers

County Organiser
Jane Stokes
01558 823233
jane.h.stokes@btinternet.com

County Treasurer
Christine Blower
01267 253334
cheahnwood@toucansurf.com

Publicity
Liz & Paul O'Neill
01994 240717
lizpaulfarm@yahoo.co.uk

Jane Stokes
(as above)

Booklet Co-ordinator
Jane Stokes
(as above)

Assistant County Organisers
Jackie Batty
01437 741115
bathole2000@aol.com

Liz & Paul O'Neill
(as above)

Ivor Stokes
01558 823233
ivor.t.stokes@btopenworld.com

Left: Rosewood

Opening Dates

All entries subject to change.
For latest information check www.ngs.org.uk
Extended openings are shown at the begining of the month

April

6 **The Crystal Garden** (every day from 23 April)

May

6 **The Crystal Garden** (every day until 15 May)
18 **Moorland Cottage Plants** (every day except Wednesday from 7 May)

Sunday 1
9 Ffynone Mansion
30 Treffgarne Hall

Monday 2
15 Llwyngarreg

Sunday 8
8 Dyffryn Fernant

Saturday 14
5 Colby Woodland Garden

Sunday 15
5 Colby Woodland Garden

Sunday 22
24 Picton Castle & Gardens

June

6 **The Crystal Garden** (every day until 14 June)

18 **Moorland Cottage Plants** (every day except Wednesday)

Friday 3
12 Glandwr

Festival Weekend

Saturday 4
9 Ffynone Mansion
12 Glandwr

Sunday 5
2 Blaenfforest
9 Ffynone Mansion
10 NEW Gelli Mydog
12 Glandwr

Monday 6
12 Glandwr

Sunday 12
24 Picton Castle & Gardens

Saturday 18
13 Glyn Bach Gardens

Sunday 19
13 Glyn Bach Gardens
32 Upton Castle Gardens

Sunday 26
3 Bwlchau Duon
15 Llwyngarreg
19 NEW Neath Farm
26 Sculptors Garden, The Old Post Office

July

6 **The Crystal Garden** open every day until 14 July
18 **Moorland Cottage Plants** (every day except Wednesday)

Sunday 3
23 Pentresite
29 Tradewinds

Saturday 9
13 Glyn Bach Gardens

Sunday 10
13 Glyn Bach Gardens
30 Treffgarne Hall

Sunday 17
25 Rosewood

Sunday 24
10 NEW Gelli Mydog
28 Talardd

Saturday 30
13 Glyn Bach Gardens

Sunday 31
13 Glyn Bach Gardens

August

6 **The Crystal Garden** open every day until 14 August
18 **Moorland Cottage Plants** (every day except Wednesday)

Sunday 7
8 Dyffryn Fernant
31 Ty'r Maes

Sunday 14
13 Glyn Bach Gardens

Monday 15
13 Glyn Bach Gardens

Sunday 21
29 Tradewinds

Sunday 28
13 Glyn Bach Gardens
15 Llwyngarreg

Monday 29
13 Glyn Bach Gardens
15 Llwyngarreg

September

6 **The Crystal Garden** open every day from 4 to 14 September

18 **Moorland Cottage Plants** (every day except Wednesday)

Sunday 4
8 Dyffryn Fernant

Gardens open to the public

5 Colby Woodland Garden
8 Dyffryn Fernant
24 Picton Castle & Gardens
32 Upton Castle Gardens

By arrangement only

1 NEW Blaencwm Cottage
4 Cilgwyn Lodge
7 Cwm Pibau
11 Gelli Uchaf
14 NEW Lan Farm
16 Mead Lodge
17 Millinford
20 Norchard
21 The Old Vicarage
22 Panteg
27 Stable Cottage

Also open by arrangement

2 Blaenfforest
6 The Crystal Garden
12 Glandwr
15 Llwyngarreg
18 Moorland Cottage Plants
25 Rosewood
28 Talardd
30 Treffgarne Hall
31 Ty'r Maes

The Gardens

1 NEW ▶ **BLAENCWM COTTAGE**
Foelgastell, Cefneithin, Llanelli, Carmarthenshire SA14 7HL. Pat & Robin Fisher, 01269 832678, robpat.4@btopenworld.com, www.reginascottage.com. *From E, 2nd R on A48 after Cross Hands r'about toward Carmarthen, from W 1st L after National Botanic Garden signs on A48 toward Swansea,* *downhill, 1st cottage on R.* Visits by arrangement Apr to Aug weekdays only, groups 10+. Adm £3.00, chd free. Home-made teas. A His & Hers potager cottage garden where the plants do the planning. Displays of auriculas mid April to late May. Through summer, fruit, vegetables and herbaceous borders full of colour and variety, perfumed wisteria tunnel. Relax at the bird hide edged by woodland and stream. National Plant Collection Open Day Sun 24 April. Day will incl short talks on auricula care - booking essential. Partial wheelchair access.
🐾 ❀ NPC ☕

Magic around every corner; truly wonderful . . .

Picton Castle & Gardens

2 BLAENFFOREST

Newcastle Emlyn, Carmarthenshire SA38 9JD. Sally & Russell Jones, 01559 371264, enquiries@blaenfforest.co.uk, www.cottageholidayswales.com. *2m S of Newcastle Emlyn. From Newcastlle Emlyn take A484 to Carmarthen turn R on B4333. From Carmarthen take A484 to Cardigan, L on B4333 at Cynwyl Elfed. Follow brown tourist signs to Blaenfforest Cottages.* Sun 5 June (11.30-4.30). Adm £3.50, chd free. Light refreshments. **Visits also by arrangement, please arrange refreshments when booking.**
Relaxed and tranquil gardens incl stunning views from the patio, lush planting by the wildlife ponds, interesting, tucked away corners, bees in the orchard and Woodland Walk, deep in the valley of the R Arad. Peacocks roam freely. Children to be supervised. A place to write poetry! Partial wheelchair access to some parts of gardens.

  ♿ 🎧 ❀ 🛏 ☕

3 BWLCHAU DUON

Ffarmers, Llanwrda, Carmarthenshire SA19 8JJ. Brenda & Allan Timms, http://bwlchauduon.blogspot.co.uk. *7m SE Lampeter, 8m NW Llanwrda. From the A482 turn to Ffarmers. In Ffarmers, take lane opp. Drovers Arms PH. Shortly after caravan site on L there is a very small Xrds, turn L*

into single track lane & follow NGS arrows. Sun 26 June (2-6). Combined adm with Sculptors Garden, The Old Post Office £4, chd free. Home-made teas.
A 1 acre, ever evolving garden challenge, set in the foothills of the Cambrian Mountains at 1100ft. This is a plantaholics haven where borders are full of many unusual plants and lots of old favourites. There are raised vegetable gardens, a 100ft herbaceous border, recently planted natural bog areas, winding pathways through semi woodland and magnificent views over the Cothi valley. Rare breed turkeys,chickens, geese and rabbits!

  ❀ ☕

4 CILGWYN LODGE

Llangadog, Carmarthenshire SA19 9LH. Keith Brown & Moira Thomas, 01550 777452, keith@cilgwynlodge.co.uk, www.cilgwynlodge.co.uk. *3m NE of Llangadog village. Turn off A40 into Llangadog. Bear L in front of village shop then 1st R to Myddfai. After 2¹/₂ m pass Cilgwyn Manor on L then 1st L. Garden ¹/₄ m on L.* Visits by arrangement June to Aug. Teas on request 12 max. Adm £4.00, chd free.
A well established and much admired 1 acre garden with something for everyone. Wide variety of plants displayed in extensive colour themed borders, large collection of hostas, many herbaceous perennials, hardy

and tender, common, rare or unusual. Traditional vegetable and fruit garden and large waterlily pond and Koi Pond. A Welsh wonderland. Partial wheelchair access.

  ♿ ❀ 🚐 ☕

5 ♦ COLBY WOODLAND GARDEN

Amroth, Narberth, Pembrokeshire SA67 8PP. National Trust, 01834 811885, www.nationaltrust.org.uk. *6m N of Tenby. 5m SE of Narberth. Follow brown tourist signs on coast rd & A477.* For NGS: Sat 14, Sun 15 May (10-5). Adm £6.60, chd £3.30. Cream teas in the Bothy Tearoom. **For other opening times and information, please phone or visit garden website.**
8 acre woodland garden in a secluded valley with fine collection of rhododendrons and azaleas. Wildflower meadow and stream with rope swings and stepping stones for children to explore and play. Ornamental walled garden incl unusual gazebo, designed by Wyn Jones, incl in the *Register of Historic Parks and Gardens: Pembrokeshire.* Extensive play area for children incl den building and log climbing. Free family activities incl duck racing, pond dipping, campfire lighting etc. Children under 5, free entry. Full range of refreshments incl lunches. Partial access for wheelchair users.

  ♿ 🎧 ❀ 🚐 ☕

6 THE CRYSTAL GARDEN

Golwg yr Ynys, Carnhedryn, St Davids, Pembrokeshire SA62 6XT. Mrs Sue Clark, 01437 721082, sueclark132@gmail.com, www.thecrystalgarden.org.uk. *4m E of St Davids, 11m SW of Fishguard, 2m N of Solva. Village of Carnhedryn, off A487 between Fishguard & St Davids. Daily Sat 23 Apr to Sun 15 May (1-5). Daily Wed 1 June to Tue 14 June (1-5). Daily Fri 1 July to Thur 14 July (1-5). Daily Mon 1 Aug to Sun 14 Aug (1-5). Daily Sun 4 Sept to Wed 14 Sept (1-5). Adm £3, chd free. Tea.* **Visits also by arrangement May to Oct.**

A ¾ acre garden for plantaholics with yr-round floral colour and foliage interest. Intriguing layout of sheltered rooms full of surprises packed with unusual shrubs, perennials and garden favourites. Ever changing outer garden. The garden never stands still. Specialities incl hebes and hydrangeas. A warm welcome awaits. Art wall, glazed visitor room.

7 CWM PIBAU

New Moat, Haverfordwest, Pembrokeshire SA63 4RE. Mrs Duncan Drew, 01437 532454. *10m NE of Haverfordwest. 3m SW of Maenclochog. Off A40, take B4313 to Maenclochog, follow signs to New Moat, pass church, then 2nd concealed drive on L, ½ m rural drive.* **Visits by arrangement, please telephone first to ensure a welcome. Adm £3.00, chd free.**

5 acre woodland garden surrounded by old deciduous woodland and streams. Created in 1978, contains many mature, unusual shrubs and trees from Chile, New Zealand and Europe, set on S facing hill. More conventional planting nearer house.

8 ◆ DYFFRYN FERNANT

Llanychaer, Fishguard, Pembrokeshire SA65 9SP. Christina Shand & David Allum, 01348 811282, www.dyffrynfernant.co.uk. *3m E of Fishguard, ½ m inland. Off A487 towards Llanychaer.* **For NGS: Sun 8 May, Sun 7 Aug, Sun 4 Sept (11-6). Adm £6, chd free. Home-made teas. For other opening times and information, please phone or visit garden website.**

'The gardens ambitions are many: to be colourful at all seasons, to provide a fascinating journey through a score of different spaces and atmospheres, to create some rich and surprising planting' Stephen Anderton. 6 acres incl ornamental grasses, marsh packed with wild flowers, wide views of the Preseli landscape, many highly cultivated areas. 'With a drama and flair rarely seen' Noel Kingsbury. Workshops and Guided Talks. A Library for garden visitors incl a wide selection of books on gardening and art. Occasional art exhibitions and poetry readings. Home-made teas on NGS days and for pre booked groups. Featured on BBC Gardeners World and in Weekend Mail, Gardens Illustrated, Member Great Gardens of West Wales.

> Intriguing layout of sheltered rooms full of surprises - the garden never stands still . . .

9 FFYNONE MANSION

Newchapel, Boncath, Pembrokeshire SA37 0HQ. The Hon Robert Lloyd George, 01239 841610, contact@ffynone.com, www.ffynone.org. *9m SE of Cardigan. 7m W of Newcastle Emlyn. From Newcastle Emlyn take A484 to Cenarth, turn L on B4332, turn L again at Xrds just before Newchapel. On site parking.* **Sun 1 May, Sat 4, Sun 5 June (11-4.30). Adm £3.50, chd free. Home-made teas in the Old Kitchen Tea Rooms.**

Large woodland garden designated Grade I on Cadw Register of Historic Parks and Gardens in Wales. Lovely views, fine mature specimen trees; formal garden nr house with massive yew topiary; rhododendrons, azaleas, woodland walks and bluebells. House (also Grade I) by John Nash (1793). Later additions and garden terraces by F Inigo Thomas c1904. House (with garden) open for guided tours on other days. Please see website for details and booking. Partial wheelchair access. Some steep paths and steps.

10 NEW GELLI MYDOG

Myddfai, Llandovery, Carmarthenshire SA20 0JQ. Robert Lee & Barry Williams. *1.4m S of Myddfai. From Llandovery follow signs to Myddfai, approx 3m then follow yellow NGS signs. From Llangadog follow signs to Myddfai, approx 5m.* **Sun 5 June, Sun 24 July (12-5). Adm £3.50, chd free. Home-made teas.**

Approx 2 acre garden set in 9 acre grounds. Garden incl immaculate sweeping lawns, formal and informal herbaceous and shrub borders containing wide variety of plants. Recently completed stream side and pond gardens adjacent to restored wildlife meadows. Extensive views across the upland landscape.

11 GELLI UCHAF

Rhydcymerau, Llandeilo, Carmarthenshire SA19 7PY. Julian & Fiona Wormald, 01558 685119, thegardenimpressionists@gmail.com, www.thegardenimpressionists.com. *5m SE of Llanybydder. 1m NW of Rhydcymerau. In Rhydcymerau on B4337 turn up Mountain Rd for Llanllwni (by BT phone box). After about 300yds turn R up farm track, cont ½ m bearing R up hill.* **Visits by arrangement Feb to May (19 Feb to 21 May, Fris & Sats only). Groups 6+. Adm £4.00, chd free. Home-made teas.**

Complementing a C17 Longhouse and 11 acre smallholding. Beautiful 1 acre garden. Stunning views, meadow walks and flowers from Feb, 50+ fruit trees. Snowdrop and Heritage daffodil collections. Comments from visitors: Magic around every corner; Truly wonderful. Gardens within a garden and amazing plants and natural effects. For photos through the yr see website. Spring bulb collections incl snowdrops. Stunning location. Listed in 2014 by Wales on Line as one of 10 secret gardens in Wales to visit.

12 GLANDWR

Pentrecwrt, Llandysul, Carmarthenshire SA44 5DA. Mrs Jo Hicks, 01559 363729, leehicks@btinternet.com. *15m N of Carmarthen, 2m S of Llandysul, 7m E of Newcastle Emlyn. On A486. At Pentrecwrt village, take minor rd opp Black Horse PH. After bridge keep L for ¼ m. Glandwr is on R.* **Fri 3, Sat 4, Sun 5, Mon 6 June (11-5). Adm £3, chd free. Visits also by arrangement, please telephone first.**
Delightful easily accessed 1 acre cottage garden, bordered by a natural stream. Incl a rockery and colour themed beds. Enter the mature woodland, now transformed into an adventurous wander with plenty of shade loving plants, ground covers, interesting trees, shrubs and many surprises.

13 GLYN BACH GARDENS

Pont Hywel, Efailwen, Pembrokeshire SA66 7JP. Peter & Carole Whittaker, 01994 419104, carole.whittaker7@btinternet.com, www.glynbachgardens.co.uk. *Efailwen 8m N of Narberth, 15m S of Cardigan. About 1m N of Efailwen turn W off A478 at Glandy Cross garage, follow signs for 1m towards Llangolman & Pont Hywel Bridge.* **Sat 18, Sun 19 June, Sat 9, Sun 10, Sat 30, Sun 31 July, Sun 14, Mon 15, Sun 28, Mon 29 Aug (11-5). Adm £3, chd free. Home-made teas.**
2 acres of garden with numerous perennial borders, alpine walls, tropical beds, large pond, bog garden, rose garden, grass beds, raised vegetable beds, cottage garden, polytunnel, greenhouse and succulents, with emphasis on nectar rich plants for pollinators. Surrounded by 4 acres of mixed woodland and grassland; woodland walk with bluebells and wildflowers in Spring. Activities for children. Holders of a National Collection of Monarda. Wheelchair access on grass pathways.

  ♿ 🐕 ❀ 🚐 **NPC** ☕

14 NEW LAN FARM

Talley, Llandeilo, Carmarthenshire SA19 7BQ. Karen & David Thomas, 07950 178333, davidhuw@gmail.com. *10m N of Llandeilo. Talley is on B4302 between Llandeilo & Crugybar. In Talley follow signs to Abbey, passing it on R. Cont*

on single track lane for 2m. Drive to Lan, ¼ m, on L. **Visits by arrangement June to Aug, light refreshments available on request. Adm £3.50, chd free.**
Extremely rural 2 acre SW facing garden oasis 900ft above sea level that has been sympathetically developed to augment the countryside. There are spectacular borrowed views in all directions. Interesting planting with plenty of surprises incl a wildflower meadow, utilisation of old farm buildings, bog and Mediterranean areas. There is also a small lake that attracts a variety of wildlife.

WE ARE MACMILLAN. CANCER SUPPORT

In 2016 the Chesterfield Royal NGS Macmillan Cancer Unit will open

15 LLWYNGARREG

Llanfallteg, Whitland, Carmarthenshire SA34 0XH. Paul & Liz O'Neill, 01994 240717, lizpaulfarm@yahoo.co.uk, www.llwyngarreg.co.uk. *19m W of Carmarthen. A40 W from Carmarthen, turn R at Llandewi Velfrey, 2½ m to Llanfallteg. Go through village, garden ½ m further on: 2nd farm on R. Disabled car park in bottom yard on R.* **Mon 2 May, Sun 26 June, Sun 28, Mon 29 Aug (1.30-6). Adm £4, chd free. Home-made teas. Visits also by arrangement. For other opening times please check our website.**
3 acre plantaholic's haven with yr-round impact, from spring bulbs through to glorious autumn colour; tapestries of colour and texture in the many trees, interspersed with unusual shrubs and perennial underplantings. Willow tunnel welcomes visitors into a maturing shelter belt, beyond which

lies the main garden with wide mixed borders. Closely planted areas in front of the house, gravel gardens behind. Woodland garden leads down to the potager. Plantsmen will linger to find many gems. Several deep ponds. Children to be closely supervised. Wildlife ponds, twig piles for overwintering insects, composting, numerous living willow structures. Featured in Whitland and Tenby Journal. Partial wheelchair access.

♿ 🐕 ❀ 🚐 ☕

16 MEAD LODGE

Imble Lane, Pembroke Dock, Pembrokeshire SA72 6PN. John & Eileen Seal, 01646 682504, eileenseal@aol.com. *From A4139 between Pembroke & Pembroke Dock take B4322 signed Pennar & Leisure Centre. After ½ m turn L into Imble Lane. Mead Lodge at end.* **Visits by arrangement Mar to Oct, individuals or groups very welcome. Adm £3.00, chd free. Home-made teas.**
Unexpected, secluded country garden, a relaxing oasis on S facing slope overlooking the Pembroke River estuary. Varied ¾ acre garden reflects the owners' keen interest in ferns, grasses and herbs. Incl terraces with Chinese and Mediterranean influences, colour themed beds, small arboretum underplanted for spring colour, fernery, vegetable garden, pond and bog garden. Wheelchair access limited to path around house and across lawn.

♿ 🐕 ❀ 🚐 ☕

17 MILLINFORD

The Rhos, Haverfordwest, Pembrokeshire SA62 4AL. Drs B & A Barton, 01437 762394. *3m E of Haverfordwest. From Haverfordwest on A40 to Carmarthen, turn R signed The Rhos, take turning to Millin. Turn R at Millin Chapel then immed L over river bridge.* **Visits by arrangement throughout the year, please arrange teas when booking. Adm £3.00, chd free. Tea.**
Beautiful, spacious, and peaceful garden of 5 acres on bank of Millin Creek. Varied collection of over 125 trees; horse chestnuts, rowans, catalpas, many unusual conifers, plus shrubs, herbaceous plants and bulbs. Impressive terracing and water features. Visit in spring, summer and early autumn; you will be most welcome!

Blaencwm Cottage

18 MOORLAND COTTAGE PLANTS

Rhyd-y-Groes, Brynberian, Pembrokeshire SA41 3TT. Jennifer & Kevin Matthews, 01239 891363, jenny@moorlandcottageplants.co.uk, www.moorlandcottageplants.co.uk. *12m SW of Cardigan. 16m NE of Haverfordwest, on B4329, 3/4 m downhill from cattlegrid (from Haverfordwest) & 1m uphill from signpost to Brynberian (from Cardigan).* **Every Thur to Tue 7 May to 30 Sept** (10.30-4.30). Adm £3, chd £1. **Visits also by arrangement May to Sept (Weds & evenings). Refreshments by prior arrangement for groups 20+.** *Donation to Paul Sartori Foundation.* 1½ acres at 700ft on NE hillside overlooking a vast wilderness. Exuberant and diverse plantings provide propagating material for the adjacent nursery. Secretive, enclosed areas where carpets of spring flowers give way to jungly perennials, grasses, bamboos and ferns contrast with formal herbaceous borders and extensive shrubberies. Stunning mountain and moorland vistas. Garden entirely organic. Mollusc proof plantings. Adjoining nursery of hardy perennials.

19 NEW NEATH FARM

Rhoscrowther, Pembroke, Pembrokeshire SA71 5AB. Howell & Mary Woods. *6½ m W of Pembroke. B4320 from Pembroke towards Angle for 6½ m. Ignore 1st R turn signed Valero, Rhoscrowther but turn R at next junction signed Rhoscrowther. Neath Farm ½ m on L.* **Sun 26 June** (1-5). Adm £3, chd free. **Home-made teas.** 1½ acre garden situated on coastal peninsula. Salt laden winds determine planting. Lawn and raised beds around house. Herbaceous borders, grass beds overlooking small lake which attracts wildlife; bordered by arum lilies and gunnera. Lavender edged path meanders around lake to secluded area with willows. Newly planted orchard. Children to be closely supervised please. Partial wheelchair access around house.

20 NORCHARD

The Ridgeway, Manorbier, Tenby, Pembrokeshire SA70 8LD. Ms H E Davies, 07790 040278, h.norchard@hotmail.co.uk. *4m W of Tenby. From Tenby, take A4139 for Pembroke. ½ m after Lydstep, take R at Xrds. Proceed down lane for 3/4 m. Norchard on R.* **Visits by arrangement Apr to June and September, groups 10+. Teas on request when booking.** Adm £4.00, chd free. Historic gardens at medieval residence. Nestled in tranquil and sheltered location with ancient oak woodland backdrop. Strong structure with formal and informal areas incl early walled gardens with restored Elizabethan parterre and potager. 1½ acre orchard with old (many local) apple varieties. Mill and millpond. Extensive collections of roses, daffodils and tulips. Partial wheelchair access due to gravel paths. Access to potager via steps only.

21 THE OLD VICARAGE
Llangeler, Llandysul, Carmarthenshire SA44 5EU. Mr & Mrs J C Harcourt, 01559 371168. *4m E of Newcastle Emlyn. 15m N of Carmarthen on A484. From N Emlyn turn down lane on L in Llangeler before church.* Visits by arrangement May to Sept, please request teas when booking. Adm £2.50, chd free.
A garden gem created since 1993. Less than 1 acre divided into 3 areas. Rose and shrub borders, semi formal pool with adjacent rose and clematis covered loggia. Extensive rose covered pergola leads onto lawn area. Interesting collection of unusual herbaceous plants. Ever changing scene. Optimum colour, mid June onwards. Gravel yard, temporary ramp available for wheelchair users.

22 PANTEG
Llanddewi Velfrey, Narberth, Pembrokeshire SA67 8UU. Mr & Mrs D Pryse Lloyd, 01834 860081, d.pryselloyd@btinternet.com. *Situated off main A40 in village of Llanddewi Velfrey. A40 from Carmarthen, after garage take 1st L. At next T-junction turn L. On R gateway with stone gate pillars which is ½ m drive to Panteg.* Visits by arrangement Mar to Sept, groups 6+. Adm £3.00, chd free.
Approached down a woodland drive, this tranquil, S facing, large garden, surrounding a Georgian house (not open), has been developed since early 1990s. A Plantsman's garden set off by lawns on different levels. Walled garden, wisteria covered pergola. Vegetable garden, camellia and azalea bank, wild flower woodland. Many rare shrubs and plants incl, *Embothrium*, *Eucryphia* and *Hoheria*.

23 PENTRESITE
Rhydargaeau Road, Carmarthen, Carmarthenshire SA32 7AJ. Gayle & Ron Mounsey, 01267 253928, gayle.mounsey@gmail.com. *4m N of Carmarthen. Take A485 heading N out of Carmarthen, once out of village of Peniel take 1st R to Horeb & cont for 1m. Turn R at NGS sign, 2nd house down lane.* Sun 3 July (2-5). Adm £3.50, chd free. Light refreshments.
1¼ acre garden developed over the last 7yrs with extensive lawns, herbaceous and mixed borders, on several levels. A bog garden and magnificent views of the surrounding countryside. South facing, catching the south westerly winds. Steep in places but possible for wheelchairs.

Since our foundation we have donated more than £45 million to charity . . .

24 ◆ PICTON CASTLE & GARDENS
The Rhos, Haverfordwest, Pembrokeshire SA62 4AS. Picton Castle Trust, 01437 751326, info@pictoncastle.co.uk, www.pictoncastle.co.uk. *3m E of Haverfordwest. On A40 to Carmarthen, signed off main rd.* For NGS: Sun 22 May, Sun 12 June (10-5). Adm £7, chd £4. For other opening times and information, please phone, email or visit garden website.
Mature 40 acre woodland garden with unique collection of rhododendrons and azaleas, many bred over 42yrs, producing hybrids of great merit and beauty; rare and tender shrubs and trees incl *Magnolia*, myrtle, *Embothrium* and *Eucryphia*. Wild flowers abound. Walled garden with roses; fernery; herbaceous and climbing plants and large clearly labelled collection of herbs. Exciting art exhibitions and a wide range of seasonal events. Visit Maria's@Picton - our famous Spanish influenced restaurant. Some woodland walks unsuitable for wheelchair users.

25 ROSEWOOD
Redberth, Nr Tenby, Pembrokeshire SA70 8SA. Jan & Keith Treadaway, 01646 651405, janatredberth@btinternet.com. *3m WSW of Kilgetty. On W side of village on old A477, now bypassed. Parking in field opp if dry, or on verge by side of rd if wet.* Sun 17 July (12-5). Adm £3.50, chd free. Home-made teas. Visits also by arrangement Apr to Sept groups 10+. Please request refeshments when booking.
Intimate well maintained ¼ acre garden, cleverly designed in different areas with long season of interest. Abundant colourful mixed plantings with many exotic species and a collection of clematis in bloom all yr, but especially in summer. There is a pergola with clematis and other climbers, as well as a good collection of Hemerocallis, grasses and ferns. A pond and bog garden is new for 2016. Partial wheelchair access.

26 SCULPTORS GARDEN, THE OLD POST OFFICE
Ffarmers, Llanwrda, Carmarthenshire SA19 8LQ. Mr Martin & Mrs Angela Farquharson-Duffy, www.farquharsonduffysculpture. com. *7m SE of Lampeter, 8m NW of Llanwrda,. Turning to Ffarmers village off A482, garden in centre of village opp Drovers Arms PH.* Sun 26 June (2-6). Combined adm with Bwlchau Duon £4, chd free. Home-made teas.
A compact courtyard garden with formal and informal planting on different levels, which has been created to form a backdrop for the garden sculptures created by the owners. Formal structured planting; herbaceous borders and water features, subtly blending into an informal shaded, damp area with a wide variety of ferns, hostas, acers, bamboo and gunnera. Figurative sculpture by international artists for sale with 10% of proceeds to NGS on open day.

27 ▶ STABLE COTTAGE
Rhoslanog Fawr, Mathry,
Haverfordwest, Pembrokeshire
SA62 5HG. Mr Michael &
Mrs Jane Bayliss, 01348 837712,
michaelandjane1954@
michaelandjane.plus.com.
*Rhoslanog, nr Mathry. Between
Fishguard & St David's. Head W on
A487 turn R at Square & Compass
sign. ¹/₂ m, past Chris Neale gallery, at
hairpin take track L. Stable Cottage
on L with block paved drive.* Visits by
arrangement May to Sept very
limited parking, max 5 cars.
Refreshments available with prior
notice. Adm £2.50, chd free.
Garden extends to approx ¹/₃ of an
acre. It is divided into several smaller
garden types, with a seaside garden,
small orchard and wildlife area,
scented garden, small
vegetable/kitchen garden, and two
Japanese areas.

28 ▶ TALARDD
Golden Grove, Carmarthen
SA32 8NN. Mr Steve Bryan, 01558
822418, steve@stevebryan.org.uk,
www.talardd-cottages.co.uk. *Off
A476 between Crosshands &
Llandeilo. R 6m N of Crosshands, L
1¹/₂ m S of Llandeilo on A476 nr Z
bends. Lane marked by small Garage
sign. Turn L at T junction follow signs
to Talardd.* Sun 24 July (2-6). Adm
£4, chd free. Tea. Visits also by
arrangement Mar to Oct, groups
min 6, max 16. Please request
teas when booking. *Donation to
Robert Dickie Charitable Trust.*
The historic house is set above the
stream with its banks of primulas,
astilbes, *Gunnera* and diverse bog
garden plants. Nearby is the
productive walled kitchen garden,
surrounded by beds of herbaceous
plants and grasses. Elsewhere,
extensive grassed areas are planted
with unusual trees, shrubs and spring
bulbs. There is also a riverside walk
and boules court! The garden covers
some 5 acres. Guided tours on
request. Wheelchair access to
kitchen garden and part of woodland
areas on bound gravel paths.

29 ▶ TRADEWINDS
Ffynnonwen, Pen-y-Bont, nr
Trelech, Carmarthenshire
SA33 6PX. Stuart & Eve Kemp-
Gee, 01994 484744. *10m NW of
Carmarthen. From A40 W of
Carmarthen, take B4298 to Meidrim,*
then R onto B4299 towards Trelech.
After 5m turn R at Tradewinds sign.
Sun 3 July, Sun 21 Aug (11-5.30).
Adm £3.50, chd free. Home-made
teas.
2¹/₂ acre plantsman's garden with
abundance of herbaceous perennials,
shrubs and trees giving yr-round
interest. Mixed borders, natural
streams and pond. Picturesque
garden in tranquil setting. 100ft grass,
100ft herbaceous and 80ft conifer
borders. The arboretum incl *Quercus
cerris* 'Argenteovariegata', *Salix
fargesii, Catalpa, Decaisnea* plus
numerous rhododendrons, azaleas
and hydrangeas. Stream banks
planted with many moisture loving
plants. Many rare and unusual plants
to be seen.

30 ▶ TREFFGARNE HALL
Treffgarne, Haverfordwest,
Pembrokeshire SA62 5PJ.
Martin & Jackie Batty, 01437
741115, bathole2000@aol.com.
*7m N of Haverfordwest, signed
off A40. Proceed up through village
& follow rd round sharply to L, Hall
¹/₄ m further on L.* Sun 1 May,
Sun 10 July (1-5). Adm £3.50,
chd free. Home-made teas. Visits
also by arrangement, teas on
request.
Stunning hilltop location with
panoramic views: handsome Grade II
listed Georgian house (not open)
provides formal backdrop to garden
of four acres with wide lawns and
themed beds. A walled garden, with
double rill and pergolas, is planted
with a multitude of borderline hardy
exotics. Also large scale sculptures,
summer broadwalk, meadow patch,
gravel garden, heather bed and
stumpery. Planted for yr-round
interest. The planting schemes are
the owner's, and seek to challenge
the boundaries of what can be grown
in Pembrokeshire!

31 ▶ TY'R MAES
Ffarmers, Carmarthenshire
SA19 8JP. John & Helen Brooks,
01558 650541,
johnhelen@greystones140.
freeserve.co.uk. *7m SE of Lampeter.
8m NW of Llanwrda. 1¹/₂ m N of
Pumsaint on A482, opp turn to
Ffarmers.* Sun 7 Aug (1-5). Adm
£3.50, chd free. Home-made teas.
Visits also by arrangement Apr to
Sept please request teas when
booking.
4 acre garden with splendid views.
Herbaceous and shrub beds - formal
design, exuberantly informal planting,
full of cottage garden favourites and
many unusual plants. Burgeoning
arboretum (200+ types of tree);
wildlife and lily ponds, pergola,
gazebos, post and rope arcade
covered in climbers. Gloriously
colourful; spring (rhododendrons,
azaleas, primulas, 1000's bulbs); late
summer (tapestry of annuals/
perennials). Craft, produce, books
and jewellery stalls! Some gravel
paths.

**32 ▶ ♦ UPTON CASTLE
GARDENS**
Cosheston, Pembroke Dock,
Pembrokeshire SA72 4SE. Prue &
Stephen Barlow, 01646 689996,
info@uptoncastle.com,
www.uptoncastlegardens.com. *4m
E of Pembroke Dock. 2m N of A477
between Carew & Pembroke Dock.
Follow brown signs to Upton Castle
Gardens through Cosheston.* For
NGS: Sun 19 June (10-4.30). Adm
£4, chd free. Light refreshments.
For other opening times and
information, please phone, email or
visit garden website.
Lovely location in a tranquil valley
leading to the upper reaches of the
Cleddau estuary. 35 acres of mature
gardens and arboretum; many rare
trees and shrubs surrounding the
C13 castle (not open) and C12
chapel. Formal rose gardens,
herbaceous borders, productive
walled kitchen garden, wildflower
meadow, woodland walks to estuary.
Walk on the Wild Side: Woodland
walks funded by C. C. W. and Welsh
Assembly Government. Partial
wheelchair access.

*Since our
foundation we
have donated
more than
£45 million to
charity . . .*

Norchard

CEREDIGION

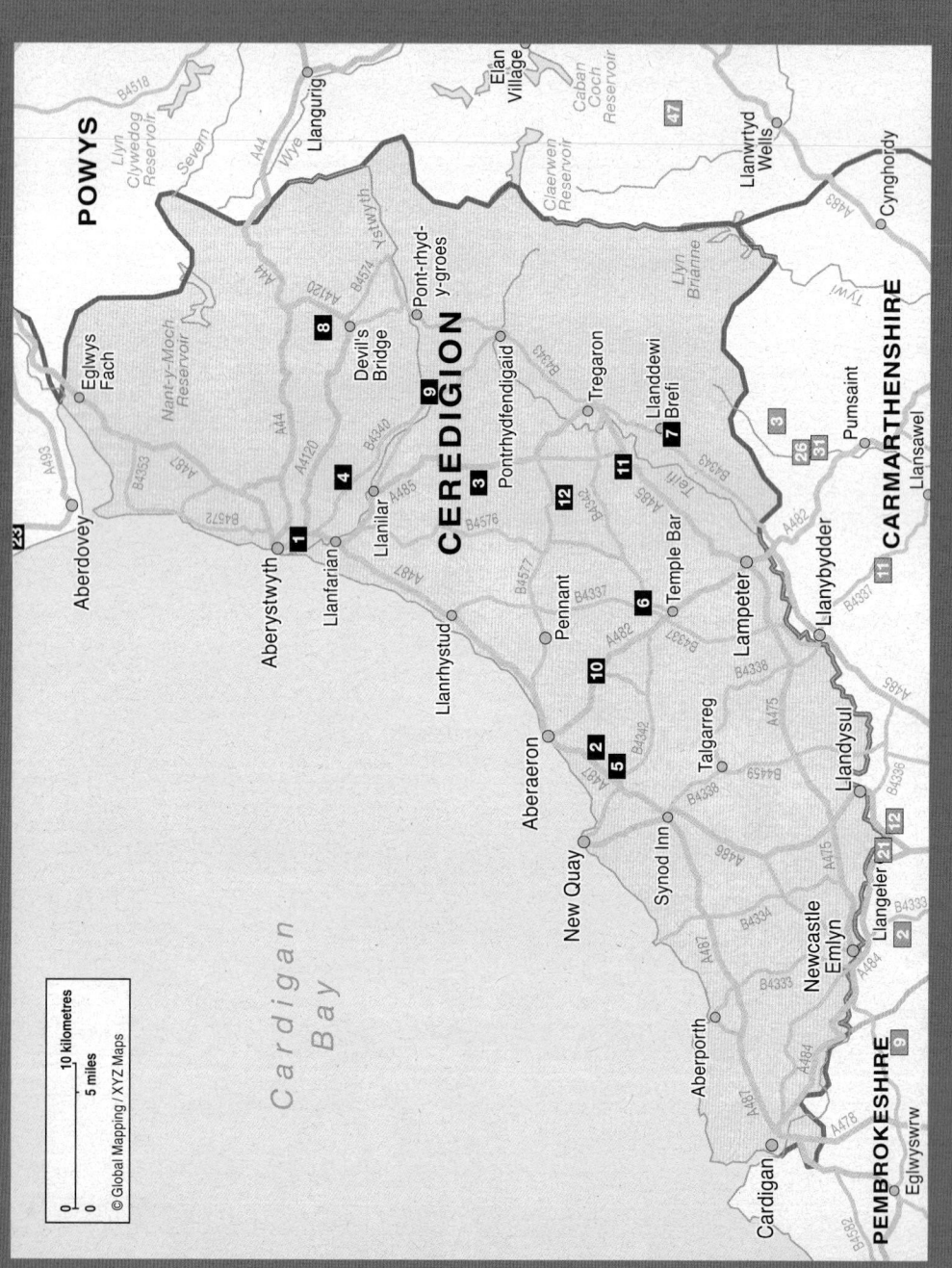

Ceredigion

Ceredigion is essentially a rural county, and is the second most sparsely populated in Wales.

There are steep-sided wooded valleys, fast-flowing rivers and streams, acres of moorland and sandy beaches on the coast. Everywhere in the county offers breathtaking views of the Cambrian Mountains, and there are often glimpses of the sea in Cardigan Bay.

The gardens in Ceredigion sit comfortably in the dramatic scenery. There are gardens that have been created with great imagination and enterprise from the barren water-soaked moorland; others have sensitively enhanced and embellished stony hillsides. Rhododendrons and azaleas thrive in the acid soil, and from April until June the gardens are awash with their bright jewel-like blossoms.

One of our gardens is of particular historic interest: Llanllyr, which sits on the site of a medieval nunnery. Both Bwlch y Geuffordd and Ty Glyn Walled Garden provide children with hours of fun and adventure.

In one small, hilly, rock-strewn county, it is surprising how different the gardens are from each other, yet one thing they have in common: they are all created and tended with love, care and imagination.

Ceredigion Volunteers

County Organiser
Pat Causton
01974 272619
pat.causton@ngs.org.uk

County Treasurer
Steve Yeomans
01974 299370
s.j.yeomans@btinternet.com

Assistant County Organisers
Gay Acres
01974 251559
gayacres@aol.com

Lisa Raw-Rees
01545 570107
hywelrawrees@hotmail.com

Below: Bwlch y Geuffordd, New Cross

Opening Dates

All entries subject to change.
For latest information check www.ngs.org.uk

February

Snowdrop Festival

Sunday 14
10 Ty Glyn Walled Garden

May

Sunday 22
4 Bwlch y Geuffordd

Sunday 29
2 Arnant House

June

Festival Weekend

Sunday 5
7 Pantyfod

Sunday 19
8 Pantygorlan

Sunday 26
6 Llanllyr

July

Sunday 3
7 Pantyfod
12 Ysgoldy'r Cwrt

Sunday 10
1 Aberystwyth Allotments

Saturday 16
11 Yr Efail

Sunday 17
10 Ty Glyn Walled Garden
11 Yr Efail

Sunday 31
9 Penybont

Gardens open to the public

10 Ty Glyn Walled Garden

By arrangement only

3 Bwlch y Geuffordd Gardens

---

5 Castell Pigyn

Also open by arrangement

2 Arnant House
6 Llanllyr
9 Penybont
12 Ysgoldy'r Cwrt

NGS supports nursing and caring charities

The Gardens

ALLOTMENTS

1 ABERYSTWYTH ALLOTMENTS

Caeffynnon, Penparcau, Aberystwyth SY23 1RE. Ceredigion County Council. *On S side of R. Rheidol on Aberystwyth by-pass. From N or E, take A4120 between Llanbadarn & Penparcau. Cross bridge then take 1st R into Minyddol. Allotments 1/4 m on R.* **Sun 10 July (1-5). Adm £3.50, chd free. Home-made teas.**
Group of 27 plots in lovely setting alongside R Rheidol close to Aberystwyth. Wide variety of produce grown, vegetables, soft fruit, top fruit, flowers. Sample tastings from allotment produce. Grass and gravel paths.

2 ARNANT HOUSE

Llwyncelyn, Aberaeron SA46 0HF. Pam & Ron Maddox, 01545 580083. *On A487, 2m S of Aberaeron. Next to Llwyncelyn Village Hall. Parking in lay-by opp house.* **Sun 29 May (12-5). Adm £3.50, chd free. Light refreshments.**
Visits also by arrangement Apr to Aug.
Garden created 14yrs ago from derelict ground. 1 acre, in Victorian style and divided into rooms and themes. Laburnum arch, wildlife ponds, rotunda and tea house. Wide, long borders full of perennial planting with a good variety of species, numerous statues and oddities to be discovered. Many attractive ornamental shrubs incl acers, magnolias and rhododendrons in May, plus about 50 different types of clematis. Also a good selection of hellebores, primulas and fritillaries. Garden is level, but help may be needed on gravel paths.

3 BWLCH Y GEUFFORDD GARDENS

Bronant, Aberystwyth SY23 4JD. Mr & Mrs J Acres, 01974 251559, gayacres@aol.com, www.facebook.com/BwlchyGeuffordGarden. *12m SE of Aberystwyth, 6m NW of Tregaron off A485. Take turning opp Bronant school for 1 1/2 m then L up 1/2 m track.* **Visits by arrangement any time but advisable to phone first. 24hrs notice required for home-made teas. Adm £3.50, chd 50p.**
1000ft high, 3 acre, constantly evolving wildlife garden featuring a lake and several pools. There are a number of themed gardens, incl Mediterranean, cottage garden, woodland, oriental, memorial and jungle, an adventure garden for children. Plenty of seating. Unique garden sculptures and buildings, incl a cave, gazebo and jungle hut. Also a tranquil healing garden for those dealing with cancer. Pond dipping, treasure hunt and play areas available for children. Unique garden art and buildings. Please contact for information on wheelchair access.

4 BWLCH Y GEUFFORDD

New Cross, Aberystwyth SY23 4LY. Manuel & Elaine Grande. *4 1/2 m SE of Aberystwyth. Off A487, take B4340 to New Cross. Garden 3m on R at bottom of small dip. Park in lay-bys.* **Sun 22 May (10.30-5). Adm £3.50, chd free. Home-made teas.**
An ever evolving 1 acre country garden set on a steep slope with views of the Cambrian mountains. Banks of rhododendrons, azaleas and bluebells. Unusual shade loving perennials, acers and ferns merging into carefully managed informal areas. Areas on different levels with mature trees, shrubs, ponds, climbing roses, hardy geraniums and many cacti. Plenty of seating.

The NGS: Marie Curie's largest ever benefactor . . .

![Pantyfod garden photograph]

Pantyfod

5 ▶ CASTELL PIGYN
Llanarth SA47 0PT. Wendy & Steve Thacker, 01545 580014. *1m N of Llanarth, 3m S of Aberaeron. On A487 midway Cardigan-Aberystwyth. White cottage close to rd, on L when travelling N. Parking for max 4 vehicles on hard standing & drive.* **Visits by arrangement Apr to Aug, 11am - 7pm most days, groups 16 max. Please ring first. Adm £3.50, chd free. Light refreshments.**
Knowledgable plantswoman's garden developed from old orchard. Paths wind through herbaceous borders full of hardy geraniums, roses, shrubs and trees. Many varieties of clematis and hellebores. Bog garden, incl gunnera. Fernery, dry river bed, grasses, hostas. 4 wildlife ponds with frogs, newts and dragonflies. Old apple varieties. Seating.

❀ ☕

6 ▶ LLANLLYR
Talsarn, Lampeter SA48 8QB. Mr & Mrs Robert Gee, 01570 470900, lgllanllyr@aol.com. *6m NW of Lampeter. On B4337 to Llanrhystud.* **Sun 26 June (2-6). Adm £4, chd free. Home-made teas. Visits also by arrangement Apr to Oct.**
Large early C19 garden on site of medieval nunnery, renovated and replanted since 1989. Large pool, bog garden, formal water garden, rose and shrub borders, gravel gardens, laburnum arbour, allegorical labyrinth and mount, all exhibiting fine plantsmanship. Yr-round appeal, interesting and unusual plants. Specialist plant fair by Ceredigion Growers Association.

♿ ❀ 🚐 ☕

Share your day out on and

7 PANTYFOD

Llanddewi Brefi, Tregaron SY25 6PE. David & Susan Rowe, www.pantyfodgarden.co.uk. *About 3m S of Tregaron. From Llanddewi Brefi village square, take R fork past Community Centre. Go up hill, past Ffarmers turning, cont for approx ³/₄ m. Pantyfod is on R.* **Sun 5 June (12-6). Sun 3 July (12-6). Also open Ysgoldy'r Cwrt. Adm £3.50, chd free. Home-made teas. Authentic Italian pizzas cooked to order in woodfired oven (July only).**

Peaceful well established 3¹/₂ acre garden with lots of pathways through a wide variety of perennials, trees and shrubs, many unusual. Varying habitats incl terraces, woodland, mature trees, natural ponds. Hardy geraniums, candelabra primulas, Iris sibirica, grasses, rugosa roses. Wildlife friendly. Stunning, panoramic views of the Teifi Valley and mountains beyond. Unusual and rare plants in a variety of habitats. Wheelchair access limited due to gravel paths, slopes and steps.

8 PANTYGORLAN

Ystumtuen, Aberystwyth SY23 3AE. Mr & Mrs Winter, 01970 890244. *12m E of Aberystwyth. On A44, 1m W of Ponterwyd, turn L for Ystumtuen. At top of hill turn R by parking areas. Disabled parking close to house; phone ahead to secure a space.* **Sun 19 June (10-5). Adm £3.50, chd free. Light refreshments.**

3¹/₂ acre garden high in Cambrian mountains, comprising small formal garden with pond, rockery, vegetable plot and shrubbery, encompassed by large mixed woodland with walks, carefully sited sculptures and seating. 2 established lakes with waterfalls accommodating a variety of water plants. Steep slopes make part of the garden unsuitable for those with mobility issues.

9 PENYBONT

Llanafan, Aberystwyth SY23 4BJ. Norman & Brenda Jones, 01974 261737, blakeley@graphics.wanadoo.co.uk. *9m SW of Aberystwyth. In Ystwyth valley off B4340. From Aberystwyth, stay on B4340 for 9m via Trawscoed. R over stone bridge. ¹/₄ m up hill, turn R past row of cream houses.*

Sun 31 July (11-5). Adm £3.50, chd free. Light refreshments. Visits also by arrangement May to Aug. Starting with a clean sheet and maturing fast. Penybont shows what can be achieved from a green field sloping site in just a few yrs. This exciting and beautifully planted garden has been designed to compliment the modern building, its forest backdrop and panoramic views. Country location with stunning views of the Ystwyth valley. Level around house, but sloping ground, gravel paths and lawn make much of garden difficult for wheelchairs.

Pond dipping, treasure hunt and play areas available for children . . .

10 ◆ TY GLYN WALLED GARDEN

Ciliau Aeron, Lampeter SA48 8DE. Ty Glyn Davis Trust, 07977 342836, tyglyngardener@yahoo.co.uk, www.tyglyndavistrust.co.uk. *3m SE of Aberaeron. Turn off A482 Aberaeron to Lampeter at Ciliau Aeron signed to Pennant. Entrance 700 metres on L.* **For NGS: Sun 14 Feb (12-3). Home-made teas. Sun 17 July (1-5). Light refreshments. Also open Yr Efail. Adm £3.50, chd free. For other opening times and information, please phone, email or visit garden website.**

Secluded walled garden in beautiful woodland setting alongside R Aeron, developed specifically for special needs children. Terraced kitchen garden overlooks herbaceous borders, orchard and ponds with child orientated features and surprises amidst unusual shrubs and perennials. Planted fruit trees selected from former gardener's notebook of C19. Children's play area. Access paths and lower garden accessible to wheelchairs.

11 YR EFAIL

Llanio Road, Tregaron SY25 6PU. Mrs Shelagh Yeomans, 01974 299370, shelaghyeo@hotmail.com. *3m SW of Tregaron. From Lampeter: A485 towards Tregaron. L at Llanio to B4578. From Aberystwyth: A487, L at Llanfarian (A485) towards Tregaron. At Tyncelyn B4578, 4m on R.* **Sat 16, Sun 17 July (11-5). Adm £3.50, chd free. Home-made teas.** A vegetable growers' paradise, with newly developed beds growing a wide variety of hardy vegetables in addition to glasshouse and poly tunnels full of tender crops and fruit garden. Established ornamental area with wildlife pond, herbaceous borders, bog and gravel gardens and shaded areas. Quiz sheet for children. Garden vegetables for sale and local plant nursery stall. Home grown vegetables and fruit used in sweet and savoury refreshments. Gravel and grass paths accessible to wheelchairs with pneumatic wheels.

12 YSGOLDY'R CWRT

Llangeitho, Tregaron SY25 6QJ. Mrs Brenda Woodley, 01974 821542. *1¹/₂ m N of Llangeitho. Llangeitho, turn L at school signed Penuwch. Garden 1¹/₂ m on R. From Cross Inn take B4577 past Penuwch Inn, R after brown sculptures in field. Garden ³/₄ m on L.* **Sun 3 July (11-5). Adm £3.50, chd free. Home-made teas. Visits also by arrangement Apr to Aug (no visitor WC available).**

1 acre hillside garden, with 4 natural ponds which are a magnet for wildlife. Areas of wildflower meadow, bog, dry and woodland gardens. Newly established rose walk. Rare trees, large herbaceous beds, acer collection, bounded by a mountain stream, with 2 natural cascades, and magnificent views. New shade bed with acers and azaleas. Children must be supervised because of steeply sloping ground. Large Iris ensata and Iris laevigata collections in a variety of colours.

Yr Efail

GLAMORGAN

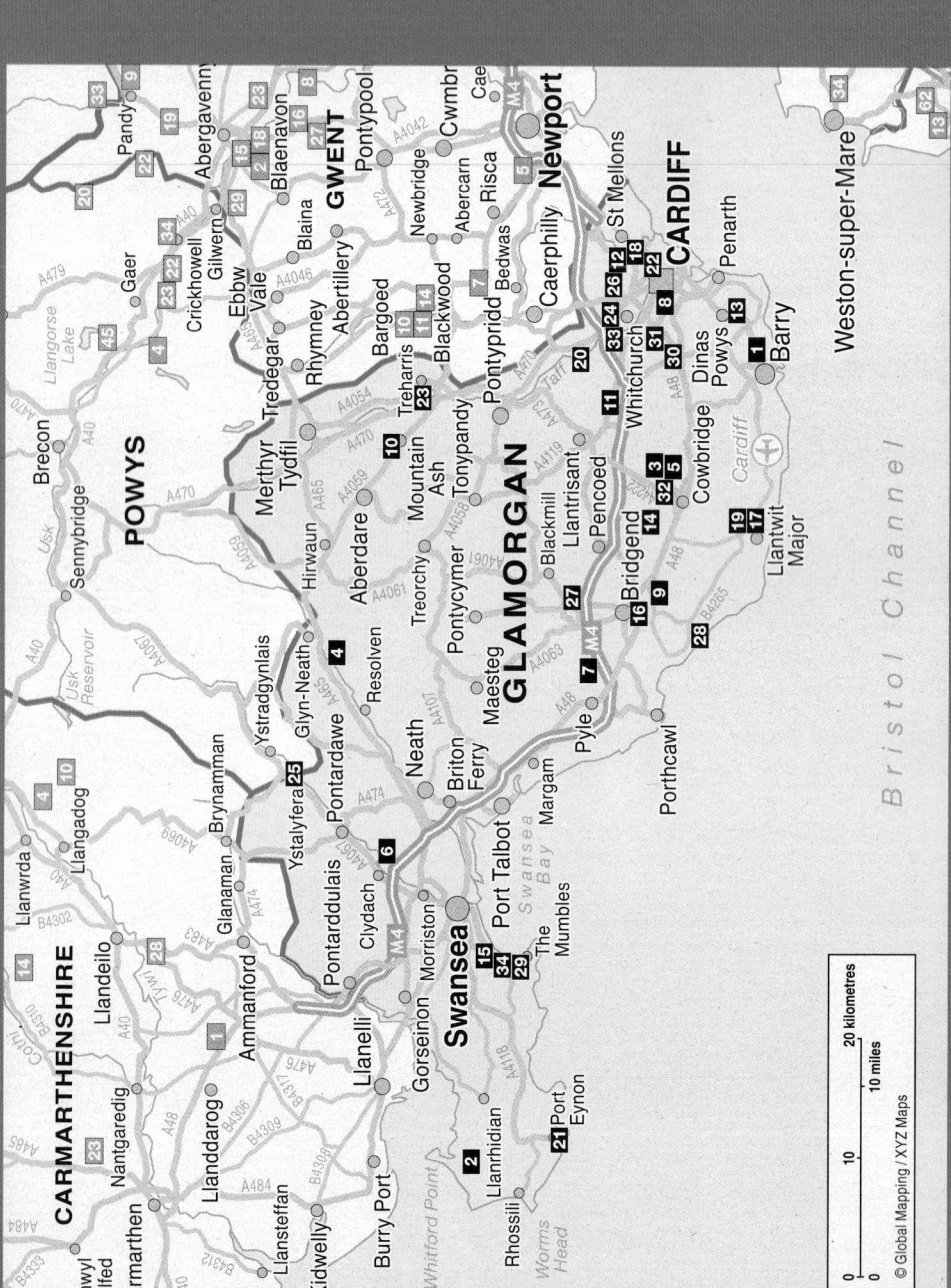

© Global Mapping / XYZ Maps

Glamorgan

Glamorgan is a large county stretching from the Brecon Beacons in the north to the Bristol Channel in the south, and from the city of Cardiff in the east to the Gower Peninsula in the west. The area has a natural divide where the hills rise from the vale in a clear line of demarcation.

There are gardens opening for the NGS throughout the county, and in recent years the number of community openings has greatly increased and have been very successful.

A number of gardens open in villages or suburbs; often within walking distance of each other, providing a very pleasant afternoon for the visitors. Each garden has its own distinct character and the locality is full of hospitality and friendliness.

Gardens range from Mediterranean-style to gardens designed to encourage wildlife. Views from our coastal gardens are truly spectacular.

Our openings start around Easter with a woodland and spring bulbs garden and continue through to mid-September.

So just jump in the car – Yellow Book in hand – and head west on the M4. The gardens in Wales are waiting for you!

Glamorgan Volunteers

County Organiser
Rosamund Davies
01656 880048
ros@sladewoodgarden.plus.com

County Treasurer
Trevor Humby
02920 512709
humbyt@cardiff.ac.uk

Publicity
Sara Bentley
02920 512709
sarajanebentley@googlemail.com

Booklet Co-ordinator
Lesley Sherwood
02920 890055
lesleywheeler@btinternet.com

Assistant County Organisers
Sol Blytt Jordens
01792 391676
solinge22@yahoo.co.uk

Frances Bowyer
02920 892264
frances5860@icloud.com

Melanie Hurst
01446 773659
melanie@hurstcreative.co.uk

Ceri Macfarlane
01792 404906
ceri@mikegravenor.plus.com

Left: Knightsbridge

Opening Dates

All entries subject to change.
For latest information check www.ngs.org.uk

April

Saturday 23
28 Slade

Sunday 24
28 Slade

May

Sunday 8
34 9 Willowbrook Gardens

Sunday 15
17 Knightsbridge

Tuesday 24
3 Bordervale Plants

Sunday 29
19 Llanmaes Gardens
29 19 Slade Gardens
32 Trerhyngyll Gardens

June

Festival Weekend

Saturday 4
20 The Old Post Office
23 Pontygwaith Farm

Sunday 5
20 The Old Post Office
23 Pontygwaith Farm
33 **NEW** Ty George Thomas

Sunday 12
9 Corntown Gardens

Tuesday 14
3 Bordervale Plants

Sunday 19
2 Big House Farm
7 Cefn Cribwr Garden Club

Saturday 25
24 Rhiwbina Open Gardens
25 Rhos y Bedw

Sunday 26
16 Heronsbridge School
18 Llanedeyrn Primary School
21 Overton and Port Eynon Gardens
24 Rhiwbina Open Gardens
25 Rhos y Bedw
30 St Fagans Church Primary School

July

Saturday 2
13 Dinas Powys

Sunday 3
13 Dinas Powys
33 **NEW** Ty George Thomas

Sunday 10
1 Barry Gardens

---

12 Cyncoed Gardens

Saturday 16
31 St Peter's Community Garden

Sunday 17
11 Creigiau Village Gardens
26 Rhydypenau Allotments
31 St Peter's Community Garden

Tuesday 19
3 Bordervale Plants

Sunday 24
6 Brynyrenfys
22 Penylan Gardens

August

Saturday 13
15 16 Hendy Close

Tuesday 16
3 Bordervale Plants

September

Saturday 3
8 Chapter Community Garden

Sunday 4
27 Rose Cottage

Tuesday 6
3 Bordervale Plants

Gardens open to the public

3 Bordervale Plants

By arrangement only

4 Brynheulog
5 Bryn-y-Ddafad
10 The Cottage
14 Ham Farmhouse

Also open by arrangement

1 47 Aneurin Road, Barry Gardens
2 Big House Farm
6 Brynyrenfys
16 Heronsbridge School
17 Knightsbridge
22 7 Cressy Road, Penylan Gardens
23 Pontygwaith Farm
25 Rhos y Bedw
34 9 Willowbrook Gardens

Lots of scent and colour with roses and lilies . . .

The Gardens

GROUP OPENING

1 BARRY GARDENS
Barry CF63 4PP. *Barry Town. 47 Aneurin Rd - head for Police Station on Gladstone rd then follow yellow signs. 11 Arno Rd - head to Waitrose on Palmerston Rd then follow yellow signs.* **Sun 10 July (12-5.30). Combined adm £3.50, chd free. Light refreshments.**

47 ANEURIN ROAD
Dave Bryant
Visits also by arrangement May to Aug
bryantdj@outlook.com
07894 339821

11 ARNO ROAD
Debbie Palmer

2 town gardens. 47 Aneurin Rd is an ever changing small vertical garden with a collection of over 30 clematis, fuchsias and Cranesbill Geraniums. 11 Arno Rd is a redesigned plant lover's small garden with a new front garden with unusual shrubs and shade loving plants.

2 BIG HOUSE FARM
Llanmadoc, Gower, Swansea SA3 1DE. Mark & Sheryl Mead, 07831 725753, sherylandmark@tiscali.co.uk. *15m W of Swansea. M4 J47, L A483 for Swansea, 2nd r'about R, A484 Llanelli 3rd r'about L, B4296*

Gowerton T-lights, R B4295, pass Bury Green R to Llanmadoc. **Sun 19 June (1-6). Adm £4, chd free. Home-made teas. Visits also by arrangement June to Aug for groups 10+.**
Award winning inspirational garden of just under an acre combines colour form and texture in this beautiful much loved Gower village, described by one visitor as 'the best I've seen this season'. Large variety of interesting plants and shrubs, with ambient cottage garden feel, Mediterranean garden, kitchen garden, beautiful views. Located on the Gower Peninsular, Britain's first designated Area of Outstanding Natural Beauty. Majority of garden accessible to wheelchairs.

3 ◆ **BORDERVALE PLANTS**
Sandy Lane, Ystradowen,
Cowbridge CF71 7SX. Mrs Claire
Jenkins, 01446 774036,
bordervaleplants@gmail.com,
www.bordervale.co.uk. *8m W of
Cardiff. 10 mins from M4 or take
A4222 from Cowbridge. Turn at
Ystradowen postbox, then 3rd L &
proceed ¹/₂ m, follow brown signs.
Garden on R. Parking in rd.* **For NGS:
Tues 24 May, 14 June, 19 July, 16
Aug, 6 Sept (10-5). Adm £3, chd
free. For other opening times and
information, please phone, email or
visit garden website.**
Within mature woodland valley (semi
tamed), with stream and bog garden,
extensive mixed borders; mini
wildflower meadow, providing diverse
wildlife habitats. Children must be
supervised. The Nursery specialises
in unusual perennials and cottage
garden plants. Nursery open: Fri -
Sun (10-5), (and often open Mon -
Thurs) Mar - Sept, when garden is
also open mid May - Sept. Not for
NGS. Awarded Silver Gilt Medal (for
category) RHS Flower Show Cardiff.
Featured in Garden Answers - A
hidden gem near Cardiff. Wheelchair
access to top third of garden as well
as Nursery.

4 **BRYNHEULOG**
45 Heol y Graig, Cwmgwrach,
Neath SA11 5TW. Lorraine Rudd,
01639 722593,
lorrainejrudd@sky.com. *8m W of
Neath. Turn off A465 at McDonalds
r'about & take exit for Cwmgwrach.
(Yellow NGS sign visible on main
r'about). Turn R at mini r'about.* **Visits
by arrangement June to Aug,
garden clubs welcome - no min
admissions. Adm £4, chd free.
Home-made teas.**
This keen plantswoman's hillside
garden perfectly reflects the dramatic
setting and surrounding natural
beauty. ³/₄ acre plot on many levels
with cottage style planting, tropical
greenhouse, 2 other greenhouses
showing begonias and carnations,
wildflower areas, large rockery and
ponds. Polytunnel houses all yr-round
vegetables. Lots of scent and colour
with roses and lilies.

5 **BRYN-Y-DDAFAD**
Welsh St Donats, Cowbridge
CF71 7ST. Glyn & June Jenkins,
01446 774451,
junejenkins@bydd.co.uk,

www.bydd.co.uk. *10m W of Cardiff.
3m E of Cowbridge. From A48 follow
signs to Welsh St Donats village (for
SatNav use CF71 7SS). Follow brown
tourist signs from Xrds, Bryn-y-
Ddafad is approx 1m from here.*
**Visits by arrangement June to
Sept, groups 10+. Adm £4, chd
free. Home-made teas.**
This plant woman's garden has areas
of unusual plantings giving interest
through the seasons. Terraced rear
garden, mature trees, flowering
shrubs, Lily pond, pergola of clematis
and wisteria, rose garden leading to a
bridge crossing the natural stream
and bog garden, areas of grasses,
candelabra primulas, rhododendrons
and azaleas. Attractive raised
courtyard garden planted in pastel
shades. Most of garden accessible by
wheelchair.

6 **BRYNYRENFYS**
30 Cefn Road, Glais, Swansea
SA7 9EZ. Edith & Roy Morgan,
01792 842777,
edith.morgan@tiscali.co.uk. *8m N
of Swansea. M4 J45, take A4067 R
at 2nd r'about, then 1st R & follow
yellow signs.* **Sun 24 July (12-4.30).
Adm £3.50, chd free. Home-made
teas. Visits also by arrangement
May to Aug for groups 10+.**
If you love plants you'll be at home
here. A small surprising garden full of
interest. Unusual trees, shrubs and
perennials vie for attention with the
panoramic view. Wildlife and weed
friendly with no bedding! Seating on
different levels, so stay a while,
unwind and be welcome. Croeso i
bawb. Rare and unusual plants for
sale. Featured on S4C Life in the
Garden.

Pontygwaith Farm

GROUP OPENING

7 CEFN CRIBWR GARDEN CLUB

Cefn Cribwr, Bridgend CF32 0AP. *5m W of Bridgend on B4281.* Sun 19 June (11-5). Combined adm £4, chd free. Tea.

13 BEDFORD ROAD
Mr John Loveluck

6 BEDFORD ROAD
Carole & John Mason

2 BRYN TERRACE
Alan & Tracy Birch

CEFN CRIBWR GARDEN CLUB ALLOTMENTS
Cefn Cribwr Gardening Club

CEFN METHODIST CHURCH

77 CEFN ROAD
Peter & Veronica Davies & Mr Fai Lee

25 EAST AVENUE
Mr & Mrs D Colbridge

15 GREEN MEADOW
Tom & Helen

6 TAI THORN
Mr Kevin Burnell

Cefn Cribwr is an old mining village atop a ridge with views to Swansea in the west, Somerset to the south and home to Bedford Park and the Cefn Cribwr Iron Works. The village hall is at the centre with teas, cakes and plants for sale. The allotments are to be found behind the hall. Children, art and relaxation are just some of the themes to be found in the gardens besides the flower beds and vegetables. There are also water features, fish ponds, wildlife ponds, summerhouses and hens adding to the diverse mix. Themed colour borders, roses, greenhouses, recycling, composting and much more. The chapel grounds are peaceful with a woodland trail meandering off. There will also be craft stalls, games, raffles and a table top sale in the hall.

8 CHAPTER COMMUNITY GARDEN

Market Road, Canton, Cardiff CF5 1QE. Mr Roger Phillips (Coordinator), www.cantoncommunitygardens.co.uk. *At front of Chapter Arts Centre. Garden situated in Canton, behind Cowbridge Rd East (A4161), between Llandaff Rd (B4267) & Market Rd.* Sat 3 Sept (11.30-3). Adm £3, chd free. Home-made teas. Adm incl tea/coffee and a cake.

Canton Community Gardens was established in July 2009, with the intention of bringing local people together for a range of gardening, recycling and environmental projects in the area. The Chapter Community Garden is an ongoing project involving members and volunteers of Canton Community Gardens. This is a predominantly edible garden based on permaculture principles. There are tours to see Chapters bee hives and a chance to buy Chapter honey. Flat site with excellent wheelchair access.

NGS support helps us to champion community nurses

GROUP OPENING

9 CORNTOWN GARDENS

Corntown, Bridgend CF35 5BB. *Take B4265 from Bridgend to Ewenny. Take L in Ewenny on B4525 to Corntown follow yellow NGS signs. From A48 take B4525 to Corntown.* Sun 12 June (11-4). Combined adm £3.50, chd free. Home-made teas.

RHOS GELER
Bob Priddle & Marie D Robson

Y BWTHYN
Mrs Joyce Pegg

Y Bwythyn has had over 30yrs of hard labour, some guesswork and considerable good luck resulting in a delightful garden. The area at the front of the house is a mixture of hot colour combinations whilst at the rear of this modest sized garden the themes are of a more traditional cottage garden style which incl colour themed borders as well as soft fruit, herbs and vegetables. Rhos Geler's garden has a lavender hedge at the front and subjects to attract butterflies. The main garden area at the back of the house is a long narrow garden that is in a series of themed areas. These incl an herbaceous border, shade loving plants, an Elizabethan style knot garden and a Japanese influenced area. Containers hold a range of subjects incl a collection of sempervivums.

10 THE COTTAGE

Cwmpennar, Mountain Ash CF45 4DB. Helen & Hugh Jones, 01443 472784, hhjones1966@yahoo.co.uk. *18m N of Cardiff. A470 from N or S. Then follow B4059 to Mountain Ash. Follow signs for Cefnpennar then turn R before bus shelter into village of Cwmpennar.* Visits by arrangement Apr to July, groups 15 max. Adm £3.50, chd free. Home-made teas. 4 acres and 40yrs of amateur muddling have produced what it is hoped is an interesting garden incl bluebell wood, rhododendron and camellia shrubbery, herbaceous borders, rose garden, small arboretum, many uncommon trees and shrubs. Garden slopes NE/SW.

GROUP OPENING

11 CREIGIAU VILLAGE GARDENS

Maes Y Nant, Creigiau CF15 9EJ. *W of Cardiff (J34 M4). From M4 J34 follow A4119 to T-lights, turn R by Castell Mynach PH, pass through Groes Faen & turn L to Creigiau. Follow NGS signs.* Sun 17 July (11-5). Combined adm £5, chd free. Home-made teas at 28 Maes-y-Nant.

28 MAES Y NANT
Mike & Lesley Sherwood

31 MAES Y NANT
Frances Bowyer

WAUNWYLLT
John Hughes & Richard Shaw

On the NW side of Cardiff and with easy access from the M3 J34, the village of Creigiau conceals a wonderful surprise in this trio of vibrant and innovative small gardens. Each quite different, they combine some of the best characteristics of design and planting for modern town gardens with the naturalism of old fashioned cottage gardens. Each has its own forte; at Waunwyllt it is what has been achieved over 4yrs and the coloured themed rooms. At 28 Maes y Nant, cottage garden pastoralism reigns. This is in complete contrast to the strong architecture of 31 Maes y Nant, where the design coordinates water, the garden room and planting, incl a small scale prairie. Anyone looking for ideas for a garden in an urban setting will not go away disappointed; enjoy a warm welcome, home-made teas and plant sales.

 ❀ ☕

> Lovely
> home-made teas
> will be served
> and there are
> many restful and
> beautiful areas to
> sit and relax. . . .

GROUP OPENING

12 CYNCOED GARDENS
Cyncoed, Cardiff CF23 6SW. *From Hollybush Rd follow yellow NGS signs to Cyncoed Crescent & Danycoed Rd.* **Sun 10 July (2-6). Combined adm £3, chd free. Home-made teas.**

8 CYNCOED CRESCENT
Alistair & Teresa Pattillo

22 DAN Y COED ROAD
Alan & Miranda Workman

KINSLEY
Ms Jill Davey

This is a group of three, 1930's suburban gardens. Each one has its own individual style. They have been designed by the owner and are continually evolving to create an eclectic collection of climber, perennials and shrubs that reflect the interests of these gardeners. Garden structures and summerhouses are used to add interest and to create different viewpoints over the gardens. All are within walking distance from each other. Partial wheelchair access only.

 ♿ ❀ ☕

GROUP OPENING

13 DINAS POWYS
Dinas Powys CF64 4TL. *Approx 6m SW of Cardiff. Exit M4 at J33, follow A4232 to Leckwith, onto B4267 & follow to Merry Harrier T-lights. Turn R & enter Dinas Powys. Follow yellow NGS signs.* **Sat 2, Sun 3 July (11-6). Combined adm £5, chd free. Home-made teas. Gluten free options available.** *Donation to Dinas Powys Voluntary Concern.*

1 ASHGROVE
Sara Bentley.
Open on all dates
02920 512709
sarajanebentley@gmail.com

BROOKLEIGH
Mr Duncan & Melanie Syme.
Open on all dates

THE HUNTSMAN RESTAURANT
Hilary & Peter Rice.
Open on Sun 3 July

30 MILLBROOK ROAD
Mr & Mrs R Golding.
Open on all dates

32 MILLBROOK ROAD
Mrs G Marsh.
Open on all dates

NEW NIGHTINGALE COMMUNITY GARDENS
Mr Keith Hatton.
Open on all dates

THE POUND
Helen & David Parsons.
Open on all dates

WEST CLIFF
Jackie Hurley & Alan Blakoe.
Open on all dates

An inspiring and eclectic group of 8 gardens in this small friendly village, all with something different to offer. Attractions incl a garden based on permaculture principles, using perennials, shrubs and edibles together. There are ponds of all sizes and styles, planting in shade and sun, boggy areas, pergolas, child friendly attractions, a caravan and summerhouse, mature shrubs and trees, vegetables and fruit, challenging terraced designs and wild areas. Plus we have our community gardens opening for the first time. Lovely home-made teas will be served and there are many restful and beautiful areas to sit and relax. Plants sales are also an attraction. Good wheelchair access at 30 and 32 Millbrook Rd and the community gardens. Partial access elsewhere.

 ♿ ❀ ☕

14 HAM FARMHOUSE
Graig Penllyn, Cowbridge CF71 7RT. Steve Barasi & Debbie Wilson, deborahwilson865@gmail.com. *4m NW of Cowbridge. From A48, take B4268 at Pentre Meyrick N to Pencoed/M4 1m. Take 3rd R ¾ m to Craig Penllyne. Parking on R before tennis courts/playground. On foot, R at T-junction, L down unmade track.* **Visits by arrangement May to Aug. Adm £3, chd free.**
Approx 4 acres with herbaceous borders, alpine bed and sinks, vegetable garden, orchard with lime walk, ponds, wildflower areas, 15yr old native woodland and new arboretum area with specialist oaks and other specimen trees. Many changes made quite recently with new planting - a garden in transition.

15 16 HENDY CLOSE
Derwen Fawr, Swansea SA2 8BB. Peter & Wendy Robinson. *Approx 3m W of Swansea. A4067 Mumbles Rd follow sign for Singleton Hospital. Then R onto Sketty Lane at mini r'about, turn L then 2nd R onto Saunders Way. Follow yellow signs. Please park on Saunders Way if possible.* **Sat 13 Aug (2-5). Adm £3.50, chd free. Home-made teas.**
Originally the garden was covered with 40ft conifers. Cottage style, some unusual and mainly perennial plants which provide colour in Spring, Summer and Autumn. Hopefully the garden is an example of how to plan for all seasons. Visitors say it is like a secret garden because there are a number of hidden places. Plants to encourage all types of wildlife in to the garden.

 ☕

31 Maes y Nant, Creigiau Village Gardens

---

16 ▶ HERONSBRIDGE SCHOOL
Ewenny Road, Bridgend CF31 3HT.
Heronsbridge School,
01446 710423,
broadclose1@btinternet.com. *In
Bridgend, from A48 turn R onto
B4265 Ewenny Rd. School on R.*
Sun 26 June (1-4). Adm £3, chd
free. Home-made teas. **Visits also
by arrangement Apr to July for
any size group.**
RHS gold winners, a centre for
excellence, 3 acres of gardens with
different areas - a grass maze, bee
garden, kitchen garden, herb garden,
heritage orchard, formal rose garden,
and new for this year an inter school
scarecrow competition! Everywhere is
child and wheelchair friendly as
almost all our gardens are purpose
built for the disabled. Plenty of play
spaces for kids. Free gardening
advice from 6 times gold medallist.
Home grown plants for sale.
Playground with swings. Beehives,
chickens, wild areas, willow tunnel to
play in. Disability friendly with full
access to our afternoon teas and
WC.

17 ▶ KNIGHTSBRIDGE
21 Monmouth Way, Boverton,
Llantwit Major CF61 2GT. Don &
Ann Knight, 01446 794529,
anncknight@hotmail.co.uk. *At*
Llanmaes rd T-lights turn onto
Eagleswell Rd, next L into Monmouth
Way, garden halfway down on R. **Sun
15 May (11-5). Adm £3, chd free.
Home-made teas. Visits also by
arrangement Mar to Sept, groups
10+.**
National Trust Wales Garden proud
winners. This is a Japanese garden
with a Zen gate, Torri gate and
Japanese lanterns featuring a large
collection of Japanese style trees,
which incl an English elm, oak, larch
etc., a pagoda and 3 water features
which incl the great Amazon
waterfall. Wheelchair access via rear
garden.

**18 ▶ LLANEDEYRN PRIMARY
SCHOOL**
Wellwood, Llanedeyrn, Cardiff
CF23 9JN. Mr I James
(Headteacher). *Follow directions to
Llanedeyrn from A48M. From Circle
Way take 2nd turning off r'about onto
Llanedeyrn Drive & take 1st R. School
on the R.* **Sun 26 June (2-4). Adm
£3, chd free. Home-made teas.**
Our school garden has developed
recently and we were delighted to win
1st prize in Cardiff in Bloom in 2014
and 2015. Features incl vegetable
and flower beds, a pond, a bumble
bee garden, forest school and a
chicken run. Come and listen to our
range of experts who will give talks

and advice on the above. There will
be lots of activities for young and old
to do.

GROUP OPENING

19 ▶ LLANMAES GARDENS
Llanmaes, Llantwit Major
CF61 2XR. *5m S of Cowbridge.
From Mehefin & West Winds travel to
Church via Gadlys Farm House & on
to Brown Lion House, cont down lane
for 1m to Old Froglands.* **Sun 29 May
(12-5). Combined adm £5, chd
free. Light refreshments at Old
Froglands & Mehefin.**

BROWN LION HOUSE D
Mrs Wendy Hewitt-Sayer

GADLYS FARM HOUSE
Dot Williams

MEHEFIN
Mrs Alison Morgan
01446 793427
bb@mehefin.com
www.mehefin.com

OLD FROGLANDS
Dorne & David Harris

Llanmaes, 1m from Llantwit Major, is
a pretty village with attractive village
green, stream running through and
C13 church. Old Froglands is an
historic farmhouse with streams and

woodland areas linked by bridges. Ducks swim and chickens roam free. The vegetable plot is now productive. Plantings are varied with interesting foliage. Brown Lion House is a newly renovated garden around mature trees and shrubs with patios and pathways. Gadlys Farm House is 1 acre of informal family garden surrounding a C17 farmhouse. Various sitting areas to relax amongst mature trees, herbaceous borders, summerhouse water feature and courtyard with planters. Mehefin is an enchanting garden with bursts of colour.

♿ ⊛ ☕

20 ▶ THE OLD POST OFFICE
Main Road, Gwaelod-Y-Garth,
Cardiff CF15 9HJ. Ms Christine
Myant. *N of Cardiff nr Radyr &
Pentyrch. Garden on L of rd, 4
houses pass PH. Parking in school
car park further down hill.* **Sat 4, Sun
5 June (11.30-5). Adm £3, chd
free. Home-made teas.**
Situated in the popular village of
Gwaelod-y-Garth on the northern
edge of Cardiff this informal terraced
garden provides some splendid views
of the green valley and hills opposite.

♿ ☕

GROUP OPENING

**21 ▶ OVERTON AND PORT
EYNON GARDENS**
Overton Lane, Port Eynon,
Swansea SA3 1NR. *16.8m W of
Swansea on Gower Peninsula. From
Swansea follow A 4118 to Port
Eynon. Parking in public car park in
Port Eynon. Yellow signs showing
gardens. Maps of gardens locations
available at all gardens on entry.* **Sun
26 June (2-5.30). Combined adm
£4.50, chd free. Home-made teas
at Westcliffe House.**

6 THE BOARLANDS
Robert & Annette Dyer

BOX BOAT COTTAGE
Ms Christine Williams

WESTCLIFFE HOUSE
David Carlsen-Browne

Overton offers breathtaking views of the Gower Peninsula. There you will find Westcliffe House which has brought a flavour of Italy to The Gower. The garden is divided into many rooms each one different bringing excitement and surprise.

Created from a windswept cliff top site 40yrs ago. Port Eynon is the most southerly point on the Gower. Set in the heart of Port Eynon, Box Boat Cottage is a delight set with pretty borders and a riot of colour. 6 The Boarlands is a plantman's paradise! A gently sloping garden designed for yr-round interest lots of shrubs bulbs and perennials.

♿ ☕

Visitors say it is like a secret garden because there are a number of hidden places . . .

GROUP OPENING

22 ▶ PENYLAN GARDENS
Penylan, Cardiff CF23 5BY. *1¹/₂ m
NE of Cardiff city centre. M4 J29,
Cardiff E A48, then Llanedeyrn/Docks
junction, towards Cyncoed. L down
Penylan Rd. Marlborough is L at T-
lights at bottom of hill. 10 mins walk
between gardens.* **Sun 24 July (2-6).
Combined adm £3, chd free.
Delicious home-made teas.**

7 CRESSY ROAD
Victoria Thornton
**Visits also by arrangement July
& Aug for individuals or groups
10 max**
thornton.victoria@me.com
02920 311215

5 SOUTHCOURT ROAD
Pat & Mel Griffiths

Set in the Victorian suburb of Penylan, 2 gardens that demonstrate in a variety of ways how to add interest and individuality to a small space. 5 Southcourt Road. Enjoy the fragrance and colour of this pretty garden. Follow the path under clematis laden arches to the summerhouse. Plentiful seating away from the elements. Awarded Gold Best Senior Citizen Gardener (Penylan area) and second place in same category for Cardiff as a whole. 7 Cressy Road. Small subtropical garden, creating an illusion of a much

larger space. Lush tropical planting, alive with colour and texture. Nectar rich planting, barrel frog pond. Side return planted with a collection of ferns and arisaema. Shady conservatory housing ferns, bromeliads, Hoya and orchids. Terrariums on display.

♿ ☕

23 ▶ PONTYGWAITH FARM
Edwardsville, nr Treharris
CF46 5PD. Mrs D Cann, 07511
744976. *2m NW of Treharris. N from
Cardiff on A470. At r'about take
A4054 N towards Aberfan. 1m after
Edwardsville turn sharp L by black
bus shelter. Garden at bottom of hill.*
**Sat 4, Sun 5 June (10-5). Adm
£3.50, chd free. Light
refreshments. Visits also by
arrangement May to Aug, groups
10 max.**
4¹/₂ acre garden surrounding C17 farmhouse adjacent to Trevithick's Tramway. Situated in picturesque wooded valley. Fish pond, lawns, perennial borders, vegetable patch, lakeside walk, rose garden, Japanese garden. Grade II listed humpback packhorse bridge in garden, spanning R Taff. Welcome to visitors on the Taff Trail (April - Sept, 10am - 5pm). Partial wheelchair access due to steep slope to river, gravel paths.

♿ ⚏ ♿ ☕

GROUP OPENING

24 ▶ RHIWBINA OPEN GARDENS
Rhiwbina CF14 6EL. *N Cardiff. M4
J32. 1st L to mini r'about, turn R into
village at T-lights, turn R to Pen Y Dre.*
**Sat 25, Sun 26 June (11-4.30).
Combined adm £5, chd free.
Home-made teas.**

9 GERNANT
Pat Morrey

7 PEN Y DRE
Christine Lewis

89 PEN Y DRE
Lorraine & Emil Nelz

7 Pen y Dre is a charming garden approached from a bridge over a babbling brook. 9 Gernant is an 10yr old garden, 89 Pen y Dre is a small but interesting garden with palms, ferns and so much more that definately must be seen to be believed!

♿ ♿ ☕

25 RHOS Y BEDW

4 Pen y Wern Rd, Ystalyfera, Swansea SA9 2NH. Robert & Helen Davies, 01639 843306, helendyer@btinternet.com. *13m N of Swansea. M4 J45 take A4067. Follow signs for Dan yr Ogof caves across 5 r'abouts. After T-lights follow yellow NGS signs. Parking above house on rd off to R.* **Sat 25, Sun 26 June (12-5). Adm £2.50, chd free. Home-made teas incl gluten free. Visits also by arrangement June to Aug groups of 6+.**

A haven of peace and tranquility with spectacular views, this glorious compact garden with its amazing array of planting areas is constantly evolving. Our diverse planting areas incl cottage, herb, and bog gardens also an array of roses and a knot garden are sure to provide inspiration. A garden with something different around every corner to be savored slowly, relax and enjoy.

> Designed with patient enjoyment and relaxation in mind . . .

ALLOTMENTS

26 RHYDYPENAU ALLOTMENTS

Heath Halt Road, Cyncoed, Cardiff CF23 5QF. City of Cardiff Council. *Behind Heath Halt Rd & Lake Rd N. From M4 J32 go towards City Centre. After 1m look out for Xrds with T-lights & turn L. Cont straight through 2 junctions then turn L.* **Sun 17 July (1-6). Adm £4, chd free. Home-made teas.**

This group of over 100 allotments is a hidden oasis within a Cardiff suburb, with mature trees and bright communal areas and a variety of allotments, growing vegetables, fruit and flowers, one of which was winner of Cardiff in Bloom best allotment in 2014. Plants and some produce available for sale. Most of the site is suitable for wheelchairs. However, entrance from rd is steep. Limited parking within gates.

27 ROSE COTTAGE

32 Blackmill Road, Bryncethin, Bridgend CF32 9YN. Maria & Anne Lalic, www.marialalic.co.uk. *1m N of M4 J36 on A4061. Follow A4061 to Bryncethin. Straight on at mini r'about for approx 400 metres. Just past Used Car Garage, turn R onto side rd at grassed area.* **Sun 4 Sept (12-5). Adm £3.50, chd free. Home-made teas.**

If you want a proper garden with manicured borders and Latin plant names, Rose Cottage isn't the place for you. If you want to see how jumbled flower beds, a herb yard, seasonal growing of fruit and vegetables, ideas borrowed from Permaculture, NoDig, Companion Planting and old fashioned cottage gardening helps us with our simple, self reliant lifestyle, join us as we celebrate our Harvest. A raised terrace area alongside the conservatory allows viewing of the field where the goats, chickens and ducks graze. Rock Bottom Cottage will be creating a vintage tea room for afternoon refreshments incl lovely home-made cakes served on china. Maria leads tours around the garden every 30 mins. Main paths and gateways suitable for wheelchairs. Narrower, bark chip paths around vegetable beds and polytunnel interior are not.

28 SLADE

Southerndown CF32 0RP. Rosamund & Peter Davies, 01656 880048, ros@sladewoodgarden.plus.com, www.sladeholidaycottages.co.uk. *5m S of Bridgend. M4 J35 Follow A473 to Bridgend. Take B4265 to St. Brides Major. Turn R in St. Brides Major for Southerndown, then follow yellow NGS signs.* **Sat 23, Sun 24 Apr (2-5). Adm £4, chd free. Home-made teas.**

Set in 8 acres, Slade garden is an unexpected gem with established drifts of spring bulbs and a woodland plant collection. Ponds attract wildlife. The terraced lawns, mature specimen trees, living willow arbours, rose and clematis pergola, orchard and herbaceous borders, create a very natural garden. Extensive views over the Bristol Channel. Heritage Coast wardens will give guided tours of adjacent Dunraven Gardens with slide shows every hour from 2pm. Partial wheelchair access.

29 19 SLADE GARDENS

West Cross, Swansea SA3 5QP. Norma & Peter Stephen. *5m SW of Swansea. At mini r'about on Mumbles Rd A4067 take 2nd exit (Fairwood Rd), 1st L onto West Cross Lane & follow yellow NGS signs.* **Sun 29 May (2-5). Adm £3, chd free. Light refreshments.**

A small enclosed front and rear garden designed to lead you around its informal planting of over 200 species. A garden to sit in. Narrow paths and steps make access difficult for less mobile visitors.

30 ST FAGANS CHURCH PRIMARY SCHOOL

Drope Road, Cardiff CF5 4SZ. Alison Price, www.stfaganscwprimary.com. *1m from A4232 at Culverhouse Cross r'about, West Cardiff. At r'about, take A48 towards Cardiff & Ely. Turn L at T-lights into Michaelston Rd & L at PH into Drope Rd. Parking available on site.* **Sun 26 June (1-5). Adm £3, chd free. Home-made teas.**

Pupils, parents and staff have worked together to develop The Secret Garden from a piece of wasteland to a stimulating learning environment and beautiful garden. Features incl vegetable beds, a wildlife pond, log circle, woodland area and a fruit forest garden. Tours of the garden by the children will be on offer. The School has received a special award from Cardiff Healthy Schools for the development of the garden.

31 ST PETER'S COMMUNITY GARDEN

St Fagans Road, Cardiff CF5 3DW. Father Colin Sutton, www.stpeterschurchfairwater.org.uk. *Next door to church, set back from St Fagans Rd. A48 to Culverhousecross r'bout take A48 Cowbridge Rd West to Ely r'bout 1st L. At T-lights go L B4488 to Fairwater Green, follow yellow NGS signs.* **Sat 16, Sun 17 July (10-6). Adm £3, chd free. Light refreshments.**

Secret garden in city suburb. Unusual combination of flower beds, raised vegetable beds and nature reserve, all created by volunteers. Features incl a large natural pond surrounded by wild plants, Welsh heritage apple trees, long herb border and wildflower meadow. Planted to encourage birds, butterflies and bees. Latest edition is our Quiet Garden with water feature and planned planting. Home-made refreshments available all day. Also Fairtrade food and wine tastings. Featured in South Wales Echo and on a Diocesan Film. Full wheelchair access and disabled WC.

GROUP OPENING

32 TRERHYNGYLL GARDENS
Trerhyngyll, Cowbridge CF71 7TN. *2m N of Cowbridge on A4222. 15m W of Cardiff via A48 turn L to Cowbridge. Take R turn at next T-lights & cont 2m along A4222 to Trerhyngyll, signed on L.* **Sun 29 May (1-5). Combined adm £5, chd free. Home-made teas.**

BIRCHBROOK
Mrs Janice Whiteley

WHISPERING WINDS
Mrs Philippa Walsh

Trerhyngyll is a quiet rural village off the beaten track in the gently folding hills of the Vale of Glamorgan. Both gardens have wonderful views over the surrounding countryside and are opening later in 2016 than previous years so that returning visitors will have an opportunity to see how different the gardens look as the season progresses. Birchbrook is an excellent example of how to bring together perennials and an extensive range of fruit and veg together to create both a beautiful and productive garden. Whispering Winds is a mix of shrubs and perennials surrounding a large pond, it is stuffed with many unusual varieties of plants grown from seed which provide colour, shape and form all year round.

33 NEW TY GEORGE THOMAS
Whitchurch Hospital Grounds, Park Road, Whitchurch, Cardiff CF14 7BF. George Thomas Memorial Trust Ltd, www.gthc.org.uk. *Follow M4 to J32. Take A4054 signed Whitchurch. After 1m turn R through gates into Whitchurch Hospital, follow directions to George Thomas Hospice Care.* **Sun 5 June, Sun 3 July (2-5). Adm £4, chd free. Cream teas.**
Hospice garden of some 0.8 acres, designed with patient enjoyment and relaxation in mind. Hosts established trees, shrubs, and planting providing yr-round colour. Wildlife pond stocked with fish and aquatic plants and rock waterfall feature providing comforting sounds with natural woodland as a backcloth. Tended by volunteers, the paths and seating allow easy access for all.

34 9 WILLOWBROOK GARDENS
Mayals, Swansea SA3 5EB. Gislinde Macphereson, 01792 403268, gislinde@willowgardens.idps.co.uk. *Nr Clyne Gardens. Go along Mumbles Rd to Blackpill. Turn R at Texaco garage up Mayals Rd. 1st R along top of Clyne Park, at mini r'about into Westport Ave. 1st L into Willowbrook gardens.* **Sun 8 May (12.30-5). Adm £5, chd free. Home-made teas. Visits also by arrangement Apr to Sept.**
Informal ½ acre mature garden on acid soil, designed to give natural effect with balance of form and colour between various areas linked by lawns; unusual trees suited to small suburban garden, especially conifers and maples; rock and water garden.

[image: garden with flowering tree and lawn]

9 Willowbrook Gardens

GWENT

Gwent

Gwent is a county of contrasts with the lush agricultural valley of the River Usk, a handful of stunning border castles, the wild Black Mountains and some of the old industrial heartlands of the South Wales Valleys.

The small town of Usk sits on either side of the river overlooked by the ruins of Usk Castle. The gardens of the castle gatehouse are partly in these romantic ruins opening with the Usk Open Gardens weekend and 'by arrangement'. Occasionally a cannon is discharged from the ramparts by the owners.

The Black Mountains are wild, sheep farming country with mountain ponies grazing on the tops and small stone farmhouses nestling in the shelter of the valleys.

The landscape of the South Wales Valleys has abundant evidence of the industrial past, and Big Pit National Coal Museum and ironworks in Blaenavon are working examples of this.

History, beauty, wilderness and water are all alive in Gwent.

Gwent Volunteers

County Organiser
Joanna Kerr
01873 840422
Joanna@amknet.com

County Treasurer
Ian Mabberley
01873 890219
ian.mabberley@ngs.org.uk

Publicity
Ian Mabberley
(as above)

Joanna Kerr
(as above)

Assistant County Organiser
Sue Torkington
01873 890045
sue@torkington.myzen.co.uk

Below: Rockfield Park

Opening Dates

All entries subject to change.
For latest information check www.ngs.org.uk

March

Sunday 20
6 Dewstow Gardens & Grottoes

April

Sunday 3
16 Llanover
Saturday 23
8 Glebe House
Sunday 24
8 Glebe House

May

Sunday 1
12 High Glanau Manor
Monday 2
9 NEW Great Campston
Saturday 7
23 Penpergwm Lodge
Sunday 8
23 Penpergwm Lodge
Saturday 14
20 Nant y Bedd
Sunday 15
20 Nant y Bedd

Sunday 22
2 Castell Cwrt
18 Middle Ninfa Farm & Bunkhouse
Saturday 28
14 Hillcrest
25 Rockfield Park
Sunday 29
14 Hillcrest
25 Rockfield Park
29 Wenallt Isaf
Monday 30
14 Hillcrest

June

Festival Weekend

Sunday 5
13 High House
15 Llanfoist Village Gardens
21 The Old Vicarage
Saturday 11
17 Longhouse Farm
Sunday 12
17 Longhouse Farm
Saturday 18
22 The Pant
27 Ty Boda
Sunday 19
22 The Pant
24 Pentwyn Farm
27 Ty Boda
Friday 24
19 Mione

Saturday 25
28 Usk Open Gardens
Sunday 26
28 Usk Open Gardens

July

Friday 1
19 Mione
Sunday 3
19 Mione
Friday 8
19 Mione
Saturday 9
10 10 Gwerthonor Lane
11 14 Gwerthonor Lane
Sunday 10
10 10 Gwerthonor Lane
11 14 Gwerthonor Lane
Friday 15
19 Mione
Sunday 17
1 Birch Tree Well
Saturday 30
11 14 Gwerthonor Lane
Sunday 31
4 Clytha Park
11 14 Gwerthonor Lane

August

Saturday 6
14 Hillcrest
Sunday 7
14 Hillcrest
Sunday 21
5 Croesllanfro Farm

September

Sunday 11
6 Dewstow Gardens & Grottoes

October

Sunday 2
2 Castell Cwrt

Gardens open to the public

6 Dewstow Gardens & Grottoes
20 Nant y Bedd

By arrangement only

3 Castle House
7 Forest House
26 Sunnyside

Also open by arrangement

1 Birch Tree Well
5 Croesllanfro Farm
8 Glebe House
14 Hillcrest
16 Llanover
17 Longhouse Farm
23 Penpergwm Lodge
25 Rockfield Park
28 Usk Open Gardens

The Gardens

1 BIRCH TREE WELL
Upper Ferry Road, Penallt, Monmouth NP25 4AN.
Jill Bourchier,
gillian.bourchier@btinternet.com.
4m SW of Monmouth. Approx 1m from Monmouth on B4293, turn L for Penallt & Trelleck. After 2m turn L to Penallt. On entering village turn L at Xrds & follow yellow signs. Sun 17 July (2-6). Adm £3.50, chd free. Home-made teas. **Visits also by arrangement May to Sept, groups welcome but restricted parking.**
Situated in the heart of the Lower Wye Valley, amongst the ancient habitat of woodland, rocks and streams. These 3 acres are shared with deer, badger and fox. A woodland setting with streams and boulders which can be viewed from a lookout tower and a Butterfly garden planted with specialist hydrangeas incl many plants to also attract bees and insects. Live music will be played (harp and cello). Children are very welcome (under supervision) with plenty of activities in the form of treasure hunts. Not all areas of garden suitable for wheelchairs but refreshments certainly are!

 ♿ ✿ ☕

Espaliered cherries, pears and scented evergreens in courtyard . . .

2 CASTELL CWRT
Llanelen, Abergavenny NP7 9LE.
Lorna & John McGlynn. *1m S of Abergavenny. From Llanfoist B4629 signed Llanelen. ½ m R up single track rd. Approx 500yds past canal, garden entrance 2nd on L. Disabled parking. On combined opening day (May) main parking at Castell Cwrt.* Sun 22 May (1-6). Combined adm with Middle Ninfa Farm & Bunkhouse £4, chd free. Sun 2 Oct (2-5). Adm £3, chd free. Home-made teas.
Large informal wildlife friendly, family garden on 10 acre small holding with fine views overlooking Abergavenny. Lawns with established trees, shrubs and perennial borders. Organic soft fruit and vegetable gardens. Woodland and hay meadow walks, chickens and geese, livestock in fields and family pets. Children very

The Pant

welcome, animals to see and space to let off steam. Woodland walk to Middle Ninfa. Hay meadow in bloom in May. Visitors welcome to picnic in field. Some gravel paths.

 ♿ ✺ ☕

3 CASTLE HOUSE

Castle Parade, Usk NP15 1SD. Mr & Mrs J H L Humphreys, 01291 672563, www.uskcastle.com. *200yds NE from Usk centre. Footpath access signed to Usk Castle 300yds E from town square. Vehicles 400yds (next L) on Castle Parade in Usk.* Visits by arrangement all year. Refreshments for groups on request. Adm £4.00, chd free. Overlooked by the romantic ruins of Usk Castle, the gardens date from early C20, with yew hedges and topiary, long herbaceous border, croquet lawn and pond. The herb garden has plants that would have been used when the castle was last lived in c.1469. Most areas easily accessible to wheelchair users.

♿ ⛳ 🛌 ☕

4 CLYTHA PARK

Abergavenny NP7 9BW. Sir Richard Hanbury-Tenison. *Between Abergavenny (5m) & Raglan (3m). On old A40 signed Clytha at r'abouts either end.* Sun 31 July (2-5). Adm £5, chd free. Home-made teas.

Large C18/19 garden around lake with wide lawns and specimen trees, original layout by John Davenport, with C19 arboretum, and H. Avray Tipping influence. Visit the 1790 walled garden, the newly restored greenhouses, and the Growing Space charity gardening project (linked to that at the National Trust's Tredegar House). Gravel and grass paths.

♿ ⛳ ✺ ☕

5 CROESLLANFRO FARM

Groes Road, Rogerstone, Newport NP10 9GP. Barry & Liz Davies, 01633 894057, lizplants@gmail.com. *3m W of Newport. From M4 J27 take B4591 towards Risca. Take 3rd R, Cefn Walk (also signed 14 Locks Canal Centre). Proceed over bridge, cont ¹/₂ m to island in middle of rd.* Sun 21 Aug (1.30-5). Adm £4.50, chd free. Home-made teas. **Visits also by arrangement May to Sept for any size group.**

Surrounding a Welsh long house (not open) this 2 acre garden is full of surprises around every corner. Informal, mass planted, perennial borders concentrating on late summer colour incl many unusual plants. The site is dominated by the tithe barn (open) standing in a large, formal courtyard, designed on 6 different levels. A garden for all moods. Let the children try the quiz!

Owner co-author of Designing Gardens on Slopes. Some gravel paths and shallow steps to main area of garden.

♿ ✺ 🚐 ☕

6 ♦ DEWSTOW GARDENS & GROTTOES

Caerwent, Caldicot NP26 5AH. John Harris, 01291 431020, www.dewstowgardens.co.uk. *Dewstow House, 6m W of Chepstow. 8m E of Newport. A48 Newport to Chepstow rd, drive into village of Caerwent. Follow brown tourist daisy signs to Gardens. (1¹/₂ m from Caerwent Village).* For NGS: Sun 20 Mar, Sun 11 Sept (10-4). Adm £6, chd free. Light refreshments. **For other opening times and information, please phone or visit garden website.**

5 acre Grade I listed unique garden which was buried and forgotten after World War II and rediscovered in 2000. Created around 1895 by James Pulham & Sons, the garden contains underground grottoes, tunnels and ferneries and above ground stunning water features. You will not be disappointed. Various events throughout the season. Featured on Britain's Best Back Garden with Alan Titchmarsh. No wheelchair access to underground areas. Partial access elsewhere.

♿ ✺ 🚐 ☕

7 FOREST HOUSE

Commercial Street, Ynysddu, Newport NP11 7JN. Mrs Joy Beacham, 01495 200333, clivebeacham315@btinternet.com. *9m N of J28, M4. At J28 follow A467 for Brynmawr, then B4251 via Wattsville. At Xrds in Ynysddu turn R then R again. 2m S of Blackwood on B4251, L at Xrds then R.* Visits by arrangement Apr to July, groups 10 max. Adm £3.50, chd free. Home-made teas.

Informal, pretty country garden, with borders overflowing with colour. Gravel garden and mixed borders to the front. Sloping back garden with terraces leading to small waterfall, shady areas and wildlife pond. Small lawn and borders with seating to rest awhile. Productive vegetable plot, fruit cage and cold frames.

8 GLEBE HOUSE

Llanvair Kilgeddin, Abergavenny NP7 9BE. Mr & Mrs Murray Kerr, 01873 840422, joanna@amknet.com. *Midway between Abergavenny (5m) & Usk (5m) on B4598.* Sat 23, Sun 24 Apr (2-6). Adm £4, chd free. Home-made teas. Visits also by arrangement Apr to July.

Spring garden bursting with tulips, bulb filled borders and orchard, some topiary and formal hedging in 1½ acre garden in picturesque Usk Valley. S facing terrace and productive vegetable garden. Old Rectory of St Mary's Llanvair Kilgeddin with famous Victorian Scraffito Murals which will also be open. Some gravel and gently sloping lawns.

9 NEW GREAT CAMPSTON

Campston Hill, Pandy, Abergavenny NP7 8EE. Mr & Mrs C Dunn, ccdunn@greatcampston.com. *7m NE of Abergavenny. 13m SW of Hereford. 2½ m towards Grosmont off A465 at Pandy. Drive on R just before brow of hill. 10m SW of Hereford on A465. Over bridge into Wales, L in Llangua follow rd for 4m. Drive on L.* Mon 2 May (2-6). Adm £4.50, chd free. Home-made teas.

Pretty 3 acres set in wonderful surroundings with far reaching views, on the edge of the Breacon Beacons National Park. Lots of beautiful spring bulbs, wide variety of interesting plants and trees, a woodland walk with magnolias, rhododendrons and

camellias, stone walls and summerhouse. Set 750ft above sea level on S facing hillside with spring fed stream feeding 2 ponds. Wheelchair access to lower section of garden only.

WE ARE MACMILLAN. CANCER SUPPORT

The NGS is Macmillan's largest single donor

10 10 GWERTHONOR LANE

Gilfach, Bargoed CF81 8JT. Mr Paul Spearman. *8m N of Caerphilly. A469 to Bargoed. Through T-lights next to school, then L filter lane at next T-lights to turn onto Cardiff Rd. Follow yellow NGS signs.* Sat 9, Sun 10 July (11-6). Combined adm with 14 Gwerthonor Lane £4, chd free. Light refreshments.

A Japanese garden with over 80 mature bonsai trees, alpines and stone garden features.

11 14 GWERTHONOR LANE

Gilfach, Bargoed CF81 8JT. Suzanne & Philip George. *8m N of Caerphilly. A469 to Bargoed. Through T-lights next to School, then L filter lane at next T-lights to turn onto Cardiff Rd. Follow yellow NGS signs.* Sat 9, Sun 10 July (11-6). Combined adm with 10 Gwerthonor Lane £4, chd free. Sat 30, Sun 31 July (11-6). Adm £3, chd free. Light refreshments.

The garden has a beautiful panoramic view of the Rhymney Valley and is in a semi rural setting. A real plantswoman's garden with over 600 varieties of perennials, annuals, bulbs, shrubs and trees. There are numerous rare and unusual plants combined with traditional and well loved favourites (many available for sale). A pond with a small waterfall adds to the tranquil feel of the garden. Featured in Amateur Gardening magazine.

12 HIGH GLANAU MANOR

Lydart, Monmouth NP25 4AD. Mr & Mrs Hilary Gerrish. *4m SW of Monmouth. Situated on B4293 between Monmouth & Chepstow. Turn R into Private Rd, ¼ m after Craig-y-Dorth turn on B4293.* Sun 1 May (2-5.30). Adm £5, chd free. Home-made teas.

Listed Arts and Crafts garden laid out by H Avray Tipping in 1922. Original features incl impressive stone terraces with far reaching views over the Vale of Usk to Blorenge, Skirrid, Sugar Loaf and Brecon Beacons. Pergola, herbaceous borders, Edwardian glasshouse, rhododendrons, azaleas, tulips, orchard with wild flowers and woodland walks. Garden guide by owner, Helena Gerrish, available to purchase.

13 HIGH HOUSE

Penrhos NP15 2DJ. Mr & Mrs R Cleeve. *4m N of Raglan. From r'about on A40 at Raglan take exit to Clytha. After 50yds turn R at Llantilio Crossenny. Follow NGS signs, 10mins through lanes.* Sun 5 June (2-6). Combined adm with The Old Vicarage £6.50, chd free. Home-made teas.

3 acres of spacious lawns and trees surrounding C16 house (not open) in a beautiful, hidden part of Monmouthshire. S facing terrace and extensive bed of old roses. Swathes of grass with tulips, camassias, wild flowers and far reaching views. Espaliered cherries, pears and scented evergreens in courtyard. Large extended pond, orchard with chickens and ducks. Partial wheelchair access, some shallow steps, sloping lawn, gravel courtyard.

14 HILLCREST

Waunborfa Road, Cefn Fforest, Blackwood NP12 3LB. Mr M O'Leary & Mr B Price, 01443 837029, bev.price@mclweb.net. *3m W of Newbridge.* Follow A4048 to Blackwood town centre or A469 to Pengam (Glan-y-Nant) T-lights, then NGS signs. Sat 28, Sun 29, Mon 30 May, Sat 6, Sun 7 Aug (11-8). Adm £4, chd free. Cream teas. Visits also by arrangement Apr to Sept for groups 30 max. Refreshments on request.

A cascade of secluded gardens of distinct character, all within 1½ acres. Magnificent, unusual trees with interesting shrubs and perennials. With choices at every turn, visitors exploring the gardens are well rewarded as hidden delights and surprises are revealed. Well placed seats encourage a relaxed pace to fully appreciate the garden's treasures. Delicious cream teas to be enjoyed. Parts of lower garden not accessible to wheelchairs.

GROUP OPENING

LLANFOIST VILLAGE GARDENS

Llanfoist, Abergavenny NP7 9NF. *1m SW of Abergavenny on B4246. Map provided with ticket. Most gardens within easy walking distance of village centre. Minibus to others.* Sun 5 June (10.30-5.30). Combined adm £5, chd free. Home-made teas in village hall. Make this a great day out. Visit around 15 exciting and contrasting village gardens, both large and small, set just below the Blorenge Mountain on the edge of the Black Mountains. A number of new gardens opening along with many regulars. This is our 14th annual event. Fantastic lunches and home-made cakes not to be missed. Canal boat trips. Wheelchair access not available at all gardens.

LLANOVER

nr Abergavenny NP7 9EF. Mr & Mrs M R Murray, 07753 423635, www.llanovergarden.co.uk. *4m S of Abergavenny, 15m N of Newport, 20m SW Hereford. On A4042 Abergavenny - Pontypool rd, in village of Llanover.* Sun 3 Apr (2-5). Adm £5, chd free. Really delicious home-made cakes and sandwiches available. Visits also by arrangement Mar to Oct, groups min 15 for conducted tours.
15 acre listed garden and arboretum with lovely water features and a circular walled garden. The Rhyd-y-Meirch stream tumbles into ponds, down cascades and beneath flagstone bridges suitable for playing pooh sticks. Lawns for children to run on or play hide and seek. Given a fine spring, many of the spring bulbs and 30+ magnolias will be in flower. Home of the Llanover Garden School. The House (not open) is the birthplace of Augusta Waddington, Lady Llanover,

C19 patriot and supporter of the Welsh Language Descendants. The flock of Welsh Black Mountain Sheep which she introduced, can be seen grazing in the park. Gravel and grass paths and lawns.

LONGHOUSE FARM

Penrhos, Raglan NP15 2DE. Mr & Mrs M H C Anderson, 01600 780389, m.anderson666@btinternet.com. *Midway between Monmouth & Abergavenny. 4m from Raglan. Off Old Raglan/Abergavenny rd signed Clytha. At Bryngwyn/Great Oak Xrds turn towards Great Oak - follow yellow NGS signs from red phone box down narrow lane.* Sat 11, Sun 12 June (2-6). Adm £4.50, chd free. Home-made teas. Visits also by arrangement May to Oct.
Hidden 2 acre garden with S facing terrace, collection of pelargoniums, millrace wall, pond and spacious lawns with extensive views. Colourful and unusual plants in the borders, a malus avenue and a recently revamped productive vegetable garden. A woodland walk is being created with a stream, hidden ponds and massed bluebells in Spring. Possible to push wheelchairs around garden and into barn for tea.

ᴬ MIDDLE NINFA FARM & BUNKHOUSE

Llanelen, Abergavenny NP7 9LE. Richard Lewis, 01873 854662, bookings@middleninfa.co.uk, www.middleninfa.co.uk. *2¹/₂ m SSW Abergavenny. At A465/ B4246 Junction, S for Llanfoist, L at mini r'about, B4269 towards Llanelen, ¹/₂ m R turn up steep lane, over canal. ³/₄ m to Middle Ninfa on R. Main parking at Castell Cwrt.* Sun 22 May (1-6). Combined adm with Castell Cwrt £4, chd free.
Large terraced eco-garden on east slopes of the Blorenge mountain. Vegetable beds, polytunnel, 3 greenhouses, orchard, flower borders, wild flowers. Great views, woodland walks, cascading water and ponds. Paths steep in places, unsuitable for less able. Campsite and small bunkhouse on farm. 5 mins walk uphill to scenic Punchbowl Lake and walks on the Blorenge. Gardens steep and unsuited to all but the most determined visitor using a wheelchair.

ᴬ MIONE

Old Hereford Road, Llanvihangel Crucorney, Abergavenny NP7 7LB. Yvonne & John O'Neil. *5m N of Abergavenny. From Abergavenny take A465 to Hereford. After 4.8m turn L - signed Pantygrli. Mione is ¹/₂ m on L.* Every Fri 24 June to 15 July (10.30-6). Home-made teas. Sun 3 July (10.30-6). Adm £3, chd free.
Beautiful garden with a wide variety of established plants, many rare and unusual. Pergola with climbing roses and clematis. Wildlife pond with many newts, insects and frogs. Numerous containers with diverse range of planting. Several seating areas, each with a different atmosphere. Summerhouse. Featured Gardeners World magazine.

> This gem is not to be rushed. It gets better each year . . .

ᴬ ◆ NANT Y BEDD

Grwyne Fawr, Fforest Coal Pit, Abergavenny NP7 7LY. Sue & Ian Mabberley, 01873 890219, garden@nantybedd.com, www.nantybedd.com. *In Grwyne Fawr valley. From A465 Llanv Crucorney, direction Llanthony, then L to Fforest Coal Pit. At grey telephone box cont for 4¹/₂ m towards Grwyne Fawr Reservoir.* For NGS: Sat 14, Sun 15 May (11-5). Adm £5, chd free. Tea. For other opening times and information, please phone, email or visit garden website.
A blend of the wild and the tame, this 6¹/₂ acre garden has been described as 'Absolutely enchanting. Of the place and so imaginative'. Set in the Grwyne Fawr valley in the Black Mountains, it features lots of places to sit and soak up the tranquility. Wander through this inspiring mix of productive organic vegetable and fruit gardens, stream, forest and river walks, wildflowers and natural swimming pond. Plants and garden accessories available for sale. Shepherd's Hut and eco-features. See garden website for details. Featured in Gardens Illustrated (Sarah Price articles).

21 THE OLD VICARAGE
Penrhos, Raglan, Usk NP15 2LE.
Professor & Mrs Luke Herrmann.
*3m N of Raglan. From A449 take
Raglan exit, join A40 & move immed
into R lane & turn R across dual
carriageway. Follow yellow NGS
signs.* **Sun 5 June (2-6). Combined
adm with High House £6.50, chd
free. Home-made teas.**
The Old Vicarage has a series of
skillfully crafted gardens surrounding
a beautiful Victorian Gothic house
which invite you to explore as the eye
is drawn from one garden into the
next. With sweeping lawns, a
summer house and formal garden,
two charming ponds and immaculate
kitchen garden all enhanced by
imaginatively placed pots, this gem is
not one to be rushed. It gets better
each yr. Plant stall.

A nature reserve
with meadows as
beautiful as
anything under
cultivation . . .

22 THE PANT
Fforest Coal Pit, Abergavenny
NP7 7LT. Dr & Mrs Jeremy Swift &
Mr & Mrs Andrew Bruce. *5m N of
Abergavenny. From A465 Llanv
Crucorney, direction Llanthony,
then L to Fforest Coal Pit. At five
ways Xrd turn 1st R before grey
telephone box.* **Sat 18, Sun 19 June
(2-6). Adm £6, chd free. Home-
made teas.**
2 adjoining and contrasting gardens
set in secluded, spectacular Black
Mountains scenery with 25 acres of
landscaped woodland, orchard, knot
garden, walled garden, Islamic
garden and green theatre. Large dry
stone turtle, ruined village, curious
whale shaped lake, all with wonderful
views. Wheelchair users welcome but
access to lower gardens only.

23 PENPERGWM LODGE
Nr Abergavenny NP7 9AS. Mr &
Mrs Simon Boyle, 01873 840208,
boyle@penpergwm.co.uk,
www.penplants.com. *3m SE of
Abergavenny, 5m W of Raglan. On
B4598. Turn opp King of Prussia Inn.
Entrance 150yds on L.* **Sat 7, Sun 8
May (2-6). Adm £4.50, chd free.
Home-made teas. Visits also by
arrangement Apr to Sept.**
3 acre garden with Jubilee tower
overlooking terraced ornamental
garden containing canal, cascading
water and loggia at head of canal.
South facing terraces planted with
rich profusion and vibrant colours all
surrounded by spacious lawns and
mature trees. Brick waisted tower
built 2011. Some gravel paths.

24 PENTWYN FARM
Penallt, Monmouth NP25 4SE.
Gwent Wildlife Trust,
www.gwentwildlife.org/reserves.
*3m SW of Monmouth. From
Monmouth take B4233 towards
Trellech, at top of hill turn L towards
Penallt & follow yellow NGS signs.*
**Sun 19 June (10-3.30). Adm £3,
chd free. Home-made teas.**
Donation to Gwent Wildlife Trust.
A nature reserve with meadows as
beautiful as anything under
cultivation. Gwent Wildlife Trust
invites you to view the wildflowers
of Pentwyn Farm, famous for
orchids, teeming with butterflies
and with spectacular views over
the Wye Valley. Guests can also
visit Wyeswood Common, a 100 acre
grassland and woodland restoration
project home to the Trust's flock of
Hebridean and Hill Radnor sheep and
lambs. Guided walks through the
meadows at 11am and 1:30pm.

25 ROCKFIELD PARK
Rockfield, Monmouth NP25 5QB.
Mark & Melanie Molyneux, 07803
952027. *On arriving in Rockfield
village from Monmouth, turn R by
phone box. After approx 400yds,
church on L. Entrance to Rockfield
Park on R, opp church, via private
bridge over river.* **Sat 28, Sun 29
May (12-5.30). Adm £5, chd free.
Home-made teas. Visits also by
arrangement May & June, 20 max
for conducted tour.**
Rockfield Park dates from C17 and is
situated in the heart of the
Monmouthshire countryside on the
banks of the R Monnow. The

extensive grounds comprise formal
gardens, meadows and orchard,
complemented by riverside and
woodland walks. Possible to picnic
on riverside walks. Main part of
gardens can be accessed by
wheelchair but not steep garden
leading down to river.

26 SUNNYSIDE
The Hendre, Monmouth NP25 5HQ.
Helen & Ralph Fergusson-Kelly,
01600 714928,
helen_fk@hotmail.com. *4m W of
Monmouth. On B4233 Monmouth to
Abergavenny rd.* **Visits by
arrangement May to Sept single
visitors or groups 25 max.
Evenings and weekends. Adm
£4.00, chd free. Home-made teas.**
There is much to be enjoyed
throughout the yr with formal plant
structure. The season is extended
with a Chelsea chop to delay some
flowers - these then meet up with
those plants which have a main later
flowering to create a peak in the
Autumn with the biscuit and russet
tones of grasses then bold injections
of scarlet, cerise, violet and gold from
bulbs, perennials and trees. Some
gravel paths.

27 TY BODA
Upper Llanover, Abergavenny
NP7 9EP. Mike & Mary Shooter. *Off
A4042. Follow directions to Upper
Llanover (coming from Abergavenny)
or Pencroesoped (coming from
Cwmbran), narrow lanes. Watch out
for signs to Goose & Cuckoo PH. If
you get there, you've past us!* **Sat 18,
Sun 19 June (10-5). Adm £5, chd
free. Home-made teas.**
A 4 acre hillside garden with stunning
views out over the Vale of Usk.
Wildlife pond, stream and winding
paths through a meadow newly
planted with fifteen hundred native
trees. Medieval style medicinal herb
garden, potager, fernery, orchard,
rope swing, stone circle and roses,
roses everywhere. Steep slopes and
slippery steps, so come prepared!
Scrumptious home-made cakes and
tea.

28 USK OPEN GARDENS
Twyn Square, Usk NP15 1BH,
www.uskopengardens.com. *From
M4 J24 take A449, proceed 8m N to
Usk exit. Good free parking in town.
Blue badge car parking in main car*

parks & at Usk Castle. Map of gardens provided with ticket. Sat 25, Sun 26 June (10-5). Combined adm £7.50, chd free. **Visits also by arrangement in June.**

Winner of Wales in Bloom for over 30yrs, Usk is full of hanging baskets and boxes and a wonderful backdrop to around 20 gardens from small cottages packed with colourful and unusual plants to large gardens with brimming herbaceous borders. Romantic garden around the ramparts of Usk Castle. Gardeners' Market with wide selection of interesting plants. Great day out for all the family with lots of places to eat and drink incl places to picnic by the R Usk. Various cafes, PH and restaurants available for refreshments, and many volunteer groups offering teas and cakes. Not all gardens are wheelchair accessible.

29 WENALLT ISAF
Twyn Wenallt, Gilwern, Abergavenny NP7 0HP. Tim & Debbie Field. *3m W of Abergavenny.*

From Gilwern r'about follow A465 towards Merthyr Tydfil take 1st L & follow signs. Sun 29 May (2-6). Adm £4, chd free. Home-made teas. 2¹/₂ acre garden 650ft up on a N facing hillside with magnificent views of the Black Mountains. Mature trees, flowering shrubs, borders, productive vegetable garden, small polytunnel, orchard, pigs, chickens, and plenty of space to run about.

The Old Vicarage

GWYNEDD & ANGLESEY

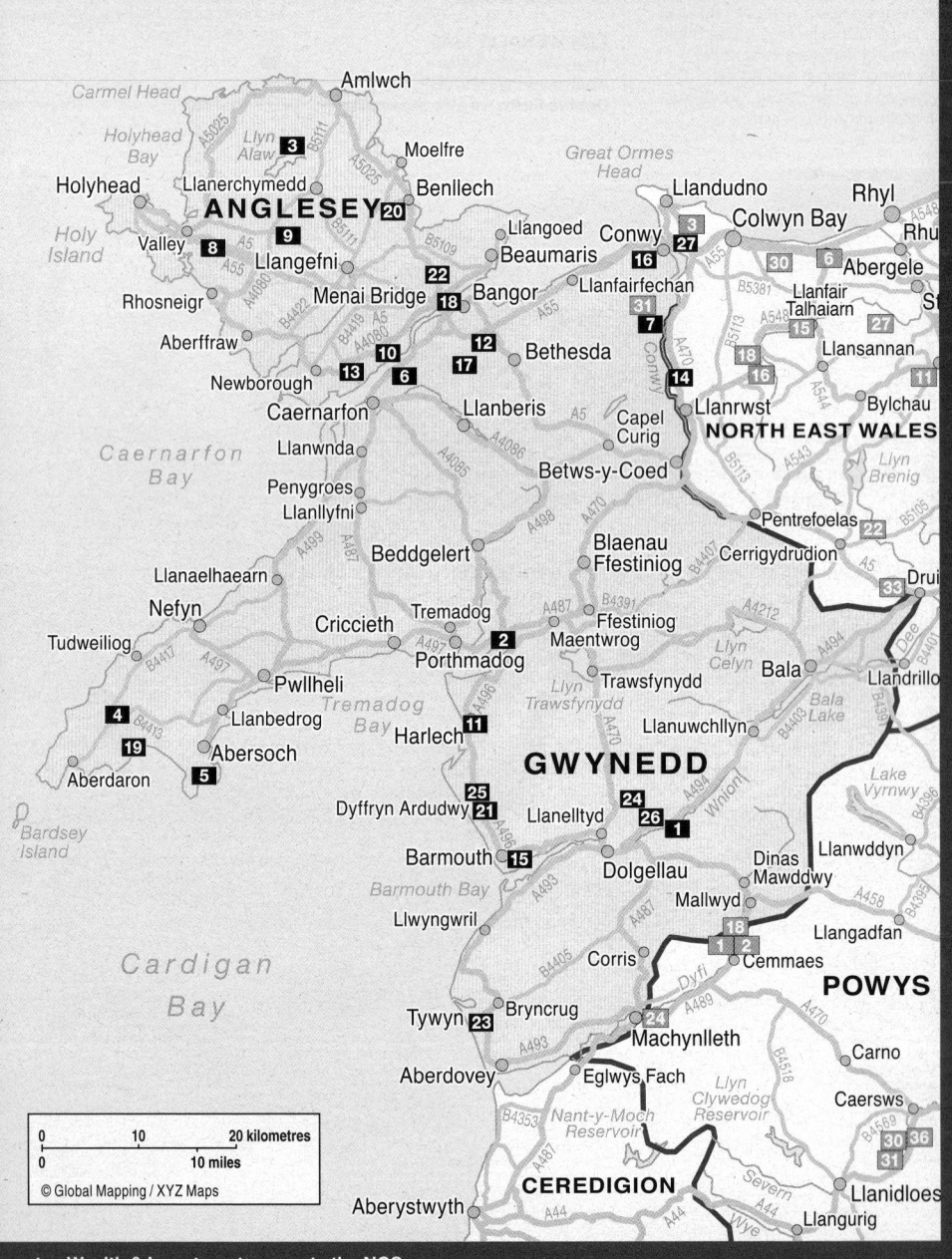

Gwynedd & Anglesey

Gwynedd is a county rich in history and outstanding natural beauty. Bordered by the Irish Sea and home to Snowdonia National Park, Gwynedd can boast some of the most impressive landscapes in the UK.

The mountains in Gwynedd are world famous, and have attracted visitors for hundreds of years – the most famous perhaps, was Charles Darwin in 1831. As well as enjoying the tallest peaks in the UK, Gwynedd has fine woodland – from hanging oak forests in the mountains to lush, riverside woods.

Holiday-makers flock to Gwynedd and Anglesey to take advantage of the sandy beaches, and many can enjoy sightings of dolphins and porpoises off the coast.

The gardens of Gwynedd and Anglesey are just as appealing an attraction for visitors. A variety of gardens open for Gwynedd NGS, ranging from the harmonious two-acre garden of Llys-y-Gwynt with magnificent views of Snowdonia, to the glorious hillside garden of Pen y Bryn with panoramic views of the Mawddach Estuary.

So why not escape from the hustle and bustle of everyday life and relax in a beautiful Gwynedd garden? You will be assured of a warm welcome at every garden gate.

Below: Rhosbach Cottage

Gwynedd & Anglesey Volunteers

North Gwynedd & Anglesey

County Organiser
Grace Meirion-Jones
01286 831195

County Treasurer
Nigel Bond
01407 831354
nigel.bond@ngs.org.uk

Assistant County Organisers
Hazel Bond
01407 831354
nigel@cae-newydd.co.uk

Janet Jones
01758 740296
janetcoron@hotmail.co.uk

South Gwynedd

County Organiser
Hilary Nurse
01341 450255
antique_pete@btinternet.com

County Treasurer
Michael Bishton
01654 710882
m.bishton@btopenworld.com

Opening Dates

All entries subject to change.
For latest information check www.ngs.org.uk

February

Snowdrop Festival

Sunday 7
19 Plas Yn Rhiw

March

Saturday 26
11 Llyn Rhaeadr
Sunday 27
11 Llyn Rhaeadr
Monday 28
11 Llyn Rhaeadr

April

Sunday 10
2 Bwlch y Fedwen
Monday 18
21 **NEW** Selwyn Lodge
Saturday 23
10 Llanidan Hall
Sunday 24
14 Maenan Hall
Wednesday 27
18 Plas Cadnant Hidden Gardens

May

Sunday 1
7 Gilfach
11 Llyn Rhaeadr
15 Pen y Bryn
Monday 2
11 Llyn Rhaeadr
Sunday 15
1 Bryn Gwern
Sunday 22
12 Llys-y-Gwynt
Saturday 28
6 Crûg Farm
Sunday 29
3 Cae Newydd
11 Llyn Rhaeadr
Monday 30
11 Llyn Rhaeadr

June

Festival Weekend

Saturday 4
8 Gwaelod Mawr
Sunday 5
2 Bwlch y Fedwen
8 Gwaelod Mawr
16 Pensychnant
24 Ty Capel Ffrwd
Sunday 12
22 Treffos School
23 Ty Cadfan Sant
Saturday 18
5 Crowrach Isaf

Sunday 19
5 Crowrach Isaf
20 Rhosbach Cottage
Saturday 25
10 Llanidan Hall
17 Pentir Gardens
Sunday 26
3 Cae Newydd

July

Sunday 3
7 Gilfach
9 Gwyndy Bach
12 Llys-y-Gwynt
Saturday 9
10 Llanidan Hall
16 Pensychnant
Sunday 10
27 41 Victoria Drive
Sunday 24
1 Bryn Gwern
3 Cae Newydd
Saturday 30
4 Coed Ty Mawr
Sunday 31
4 Coed Ty Mawr

August

Sunday 14
14 Maenan Hall
Saturday 27
26 Tyn-Twll
Sunday 28
11 Llyn Rhaeadr

Monday 29
11 Llyn Rhaeadr

Gardens open to the public

6 Crûg Farm
16 Pensychnant
19 Plas Yn Rhiw

By arrangement only

25 Ty Newydd

Also open by arrangement

1 Bryn Gwern
4 Coed Ty Mawr
7 Gilfach
8 Gwaelod Mawr
9 Gwyndy Bach
10 Llanidan Hall
11 Llyn Rhaeadr
12 Llys-y-Gwynt
14 Maenan Hall
20 Rhosbach Cottage
23 Ty Cadfan Sant
24 Ty Capel Ffrwd
26 Tyn-Twll

The garden is now a haven for wildlife . . .

The Gardens

1 **BRYN GWERN**
Llanfachreth, Dolgellau, Gwynedd LL40 2DH. H O & P D Nurse, 01341 450 255, antique_pete@btinternet.com. *5m NE of Dolgellau. Do not go to Llanfachreth village, stay on A494 Bala-Dolgellau rd: 13m from Bala. Take 1st R Llanfachreth. From Dolgellau 4m Llanfachreth turn L, follow signs. No coach parking.* **Sun 15 May, Sun 24 July (10-5). Adm £3.50, chd free. Cream teas. Visits also by arrangement Mar to Oct, parking for mini bus, coaches to park in lay-by on main rd.**
Sloping 2 acre garden in the hills overlooking Dolgellau with views to Cader Idris, originally wooded but redesigned to enhance its natural features with streams, ponds and imaginative and extensive planting and vibrant colour. The garden is now a haven for wildlife with hedgehogs and 27 species of birds feeding last winter as well as being home to ducks, dogs and cats. Wheelchair access to main area of garden but only when dry.

2 **BWLCH Y FEDWEN**
Penrhyndeudraeth LL48 6BT. David & Gillian Surman. *22m N of Dolgellau, 3m E of Porthmadog, 2m E of Portmeirion. Opp Griffin PH, take A4085 along High St to village car park. Walking from there, follow signs to garden approx 150yds.* **Sun 10 Apr, Sun 5 June (1-4.30). Adm £3.50, chd free. Home-made teas.**
With views towards the Rhinogs, Moelwyns and the Dwyryd estuary ³/₄ acre of neglected, rocky hillside has been transformed, providing terraced gardens with inter twining paths, many steps with handrails, seating, planted pots, baskets and alpine sinks. Spring bulbs, hellebores, roses, clematis and trees incl embothrium, halesia, koelreuteria, camellias, azaleas, magnolias provide yr-round interest. The owners have a passion for terracotta pots of all shapes and sizes and quirky structures.

3 **CAE NEWYDD**
Rhosgoch, Anglesey LL66 0BG. Hazel & Nigel Bond, 01407 831354, nigel@cae-newydd.co.uk. *3m SW of Amlwch. A5025 from Benllech to Amlwch, follow signs for leisure centre & Lastra Farm. Follow yellow NGS signs (approx 3m), car park on L.* **Sun 29 May, Sun 26 June, Sun**

24 July (11-4). Adm £4, chd free. **Light refreshments.**
A maturing country garden of $2^1/2$ acres which blends seamlessly into the open landscape with stunning views of Snowdonia and Llyn Alaw. Variety of shrubs, trees and herbaceous areas, large wildlife pond, meadow, polytunnel, greenhouse, vegetable garden and chicken run. Adjacent sheltered paddock garden. Formal pond and patio area. Rose garden with aquilegias, dianthus and lavender. Hay meadow best seen in June. Lots of seating throughout the garden, visitors are welcome to bring a picnic. Garden area closest to house suitable for wheelchairs.

4 ► COED TY MAWR
Ty Mawr, Bryncroes, Pwllheli LL53 8EH. Nonni & David Goadby, 01758 730359, nonni@goadby.net, www.coed-tymawr.co.uk. *12m W of Pwllheli. Take B4413 Llanbedrog to Aberdaron. $1^3/4$ m past Sarn Meyllteyrn. Turn R at Penygroeslon sign. From Nefyn take B4417, at Xrds with B4413 turn L.* **Sat 30, Sun 31 July (10.30-5). Adm £4, chd free. Home-made teas. Visits also by arrangement Apr to Sept.**
Outstanding 5 acre woodland garden created from wilderness and situated among some of the most beautiful scenery of Wales. Over 3,000 trees and shrubs incl growing collections of magnolia, rhododendron, hydrangea and cornus. Also large pond, orchard, fernery, vegetable, oriental and sea view gardens. Plenty of seating. Sit on the raised deck, take in the sea views and enjoy a home-made tea. Grass paths.

5 ► CROWRACH ISAF
Bwlchtocyn LL53 7BY. Margaret & Graham Cook. *$1^1/2$ m SW of Abersoch. Follow rd through Abersoch & Sarn Bach, L at sign for Bwlchtocyn for $1/2$ m until junction & no-through rd - TG Holiday Complex. Turn R, parking 50 metres on R.* **Sat 18, Sun 19 June (1-5). Adm £3.50, chd free. Cream teas.**
2 acre plot incl 1 acre fenced against rabbits, developed from 2000, incl island beds, windbreak hedges, vegetable garden, wild flower area and wide range of geraniums, shrubs and herbaceous perennials. Views over Cardigan Bay and Snowdonia. Grass and gravel paths, some gentle slopes.

Pensychnant

6 ► ◆ CRÛG FARM
Griffiths Crossing, Caernarfon LL55 1TU. Mr & Mrs B Wynn-Jones, 01248 670232, sue@crug-farm.co.uk, www.crug-farm.co.uk. *2m NE of Caernarfon. $1/4$ m off main A487 Caernarfon to Bangor rd. Follow signs from r'about.* **For NGS: Sat 28 May (10-4.30). Adm £3.50, chd free. Home-made teas. For other opening times and information, please phone, email or visit garden website.**
3 acres; grounds to old country house (not open). Gardens filled with choice, unusual plants collected by the Wynn-Jones. Woodland garden with shade loving plants, many not seen in cultivation before. Walled garden with more wonderful collections growing. Chelsea Gold Medallists and winners of the President's Award among other many prestigious awards. Partial wheelchair access.

NPC

7 ► GILFACH
Rowen, Conwy LL32 8TS. James & Isoline Greenhalgh, 01492 650216, isolinegreenhalgh@btinternet.com. *4m S of Conwy. At Xrds 100yds E of Rowen S towards Llanrwst, past Rowen School on L, turn up 2nd drive on L.* **Sun 1 May, Sun 3 July (2-5.30). Adm £3, chd free. Home-made teas. Visits also by arrangement May to Aug, coffee/biscuits (am), tea/cake (pm). Groups 45 max.**
1 acre country garden on S facing slope with magnificent views of the R Conwy and mountains; set in 35 acres of farm and woodland. Collection of mature shrubs is added to yearly; woodland garden, herbaceous border and small pool. Spectacular panoramic view of the Conwy Valley and the mountain range of the Carneddau. Classic cars. Large coaches can park at bottom of steep drive, disabled visitors can be driven to garden by the owner.

© Fiona Lea

Gwyndy Bach

8 ▶ GWAELOD MAWR
Caergeiliog, Anglesey LL65 3YL.
John & Tricia Coates,
01407 740080,
patriciacoates36@gmail.com.
*6m E of Holyhead. ¹/₂ m E of
Caergeiliog. From A55 J4. r'about
2nd exit signed Caergeiliog. 300yds,
Gwaelod Mawr is 1st house on L.*
**Sat 4, Sun 5 June (11-5). Adm
£3.50, chd free. Home-made teas.
Visits also by arrangement May
to Aug.**
2½ acre garden created by owners
over 20yrs with lake, large rock
outcrops and palm tree area. Spanish
style patio and laburnum arch lead to
sunken garden and wooden bridge
over lily pond with fountain and
waterfall. Peaceful Chinese orientated
garden offering contemplation.
Separate Koi carp pond. Abundant
seating throughout. Mainly flat, with
gravel and stone paths, no wheelchair
access to sunken lily pond area.
  ♿ 🐕 ❀ ☕

9 ▶ GWYNDY BACH
Tynlon, Llandrygarn LL65 3AJ.
Keith & Rosa Andrew,
01407 720651,
keithandrew.art@gmail.com. *5m W
of Llangefni. From Llangefni take
B5109 towards Bodedern, cottage
exactly 5m out on L. Postcode good
for SatNav.* **Sun 3 July (11-4.30).
Adm £3, chd free. Home-made
teas. Visits also by arrangement
May to July.**
³/₄ acre artist's garden, set amidst
rugged Anglesey landscape.
Romantically planted in informal
intimate rooms with interesting rare
plants and shrubs, box and yew
topiary, old roses and Japanese
garden with large Koi pond (deep
water, children must be supervised).
National Collection of Rhapis
miniature Japanese palms. Gravel
entrance to garden.
  ♿ ❀ 🚐 **NPC** ☕

10 ▶ LLANIDAN HALL
Brynsiencyn LL61 6HJ.
Mr J W Beverley (Head Gardener),
07759 305085,
beverley.family@btinternet.com.
*5m E of Llanfair PwII. From Llanfair
PG follow A4080 towards
Brynsiencyn for 4m. After Hooton's
farm shop on R take next L, follow
lane to gardens.* **Sat 23 Apr, Sat 25
June, Sat 9 July (10-4). Adm £3.50,
chd free. Tea. Visits also by
arrangement Apr to Aug (daytime
visits only).** *Donation to CAFOD.*
Walled garden of 1³/₄ acres. Physic
and herb gardens, ornamental
vegetable garden, herbaceous
borders, water features and many
varieties of old roses. Sheep, rabbits
and hens to see. Children must be
kept under supervision. Well behaved
dogs on leads welcome. Llanidan
Church will be open for viewing. The
walled garden will be open early in
the season for viewing of the spring
bulbs. Hard gravel paths, gentle
slopes.
  ♿ 🐕 ❀ ☕

11 ▶ LLYN RHAEADR
Parc Bron-y-Graig, Centre of
Harlech LL46 2SR. Mr D R Hewitt &
Miss J Sharp, 01766 780224.
*Centre of Harlech. From A496 take
B4573 into Harlech, take turning to
main car parks S of town, L past
overspill car park, garden 75yds on R.*
**Sat 26, Sun 27, Mon 28 Mar, Sun
1, Mon 2, Sun 29, Mon 30 May,
Sun 28, Mon 29 Aug (2-5). Adm £3,
chd free. Visits also by
arrangement Mar to Oct most
days (2-5). Groups of 1-20.**
Donation to WWF UK.

GWYNEDD & ANGLESEY 689

Hillside garden blending natural wildlife areas with garden plants, shrubs, vegetables and fruit. Small lake with 20 species of waterfowl, fish and wildlife ponds, waterfalls, woodland, rockeries, lawns, borders, snowdrops, daffodils, heathers, bluebells, ferns, camellias, azaleas, rhododendrons, wild flowers, views of Tremadog Bay, Lleyn Peninsula. Good paths and seating with gazebos. Waterfowl collection.

12 ► LLYS-Y-GWYNT
Pentir Road, Llandygai, Bangor LL57 4BG. Jennifer Rickards & John Evans, 01248 353863. *3m S of Bangor..300yds from Llandygai r'about at J11, A5 & A55, just off A4244. Follow signs for services (Gwasanaethau). No through rd sign, 50yds beyond. Do not use SatNav.* **Sun 22 May, Sun 3 July (11-4). Adm £3.50, chd free. Cream teas. Visits also by arrangement.**
Interesting, harmonious and very varied 2 acre garden incl magnificent views of Snowdonia. An exposed site incl Bronze Age burial cairn. Winding paths and varied levels planted to create shelter, yr-round interest, microclimates and varied rooms. Ponds, waterfall, bridge and other features use local materials and craftspeople. Wildlife encouraged, well organised compost. Good family garden.

14 ► MAENAN HALL
Maenan, Llanrwst LL26 0UL. The Hon Mr & Mrs Christopher Mclaren, 01492 640441, cmmclaren@gmail.com. *2m N of Llanrwst. On E side of A470, ¼ m S of Maenan Abbey Hotel.* **Sun 24 Apr, Sun 14 Aug (10.30-5.30). Adm £4, chd free. Home-made teas. Visits also by arrangement Apr to Sept for groups 8+.** *Donation to Wales Air Ambulance.*
A superbly beautiful 4 hectares on the slopes of the Conwy Valley, with dramatic views of Snowdonia, set amongst mature hardwoods. Both the upper part, with sweeping lawns, ornamental ponds and retaining walls, and the bluebell carpeted woodland dell contain copious specimen shrubs and trees, many originating at Bodnant. Magnolias, rhododendrons, camellias, pieris, cherries and hydrangeas, amongst many others, make a breathtaking display. Treasure Hunt (£1) on both

open days. Upper part of garden accessible but with fairly steep slopes.

15 ► PEN Y BRYN
Glandwr, Barmouth LL42 1TG. Phil & Jenny Martin. *2m E of Barmouth. On A496 7m W of Dolgellau, 2m E of Barmouth, situated on N side of Mawddach Estuary. Park in or nr layby & walk L up narrow lane.* **Sun 1 May (11-5). Adm £3.50, chd free. Cream teas.** *Donation to Gwynedd Hospice at Home.*
A glorious hillside garden with panoramic views of The Mawddoch Estuary. Woodland walks awash with Bluebells in the spring. Lawns on different levels with vibrant rhododendrons and azaleas, arches of clematis, honeysuckle and roses. Heather filled natural rocks, unusual conifer feature, a rock cannon and a pond for wildlife.

Home-made jams and chutneys for sale as well as cakes and Barabrith scones . . .

16 ► ◆ PENSYCHNANT
Sychnant Pass, Conwy LL32 8BJ. Pensychnant Foundation; Wardens Julian Thompson & Anne Mynott, 01492 592595, jpt.pensychnant@btinternet.com, www.pensychnant.co.uk. *2½ m W of Conwy at top of Sychnant Pass. From Conwy: L into Upper Gate St; after 2½ m Pensychnant's drive signed on R. From Penmaenmawr: fork R, up pass, after walls U turn L into drive.* **For NGS: Sun 5 June, Sat 9 July (10-5). Adm £3.50, chd free. Home-made teas. For other opening times and information, please phone, email or visit garden website.**
Wildlife Garden. Diverse herbaceous cottage garden borders surrounded by mature shrubs, banks of

rhododendrons, ancient and Victorian woodlands. 12 acre woodland walks with views of Conwy Mountain and Sychnant. Woodland birds. Picnic tables, archaeological trail on mountain. A peaceful little gem. Large Victorian Arts and Crafts house (open) with art exhibition. Partial wheelchair access, please phone for advice.

GROUP OPENING

17 ► PENTIR GARDENS
Pentir, Bangor LL57 4YA. *Take A4244 from J11 of A55/A5, cont for 3m to Pentir. Turn R signed Caerhun/Vaynol PH, into Pentir Sq.* **Sat 25 June (12-5). Combined adm £5, chd free. Home-made teas at Bryn Meddyg.**

2 RHYD Y GROES
Mr & Mrs IwanThomas

TAN RALLT
John Lewis & Gary Carvalho

TAN Y BRYN
Mrs Eliz Battle

TY UCHAF
Sian Lewis

Ty Uchaf is a small densely packed garden with a wide variety of cottage favourites, plus unusual planting schemes, surrounding an attractive summerhouse. It enjoys a romantic feel, prioritizing colour and texture. A secret gate takes visitors to neighbouring Bryn Meddyg, serving refreshments. 10 mins walk takes you to Tan y Bryn, a garden with mature shrubs, a lawned area with herbaceous planting. There is also a paddock with stunning views, a pond and a dwarf conifer collection. Continue along to the secluded garden, 2 Rhyd y Groes, through No 1's garden, to enjoy views of Moel y Ci and the Menai Strait. This former quarryman's allotment has a variety of planted areas, seating, pond, summerhouse and sculptures. Further along the lane, a 5 mins walk to Tan Rallt, backing onto Moel y Ci, the 0.8 acre garden incl a range of mature trees and shrubs, vegetable and soft fruit, herbaceous borders and areas of lawn. A diversely planted pond with tree ferns, bog plants and giant gunnera.

18 PLAS CADNANT HIDDEN GARDENS

Cadnant Road, Menai Bridge LL59 5NH. Mr Anthony Tavernor, 01248 717174, plascadnantgardens@gmail.com, www.plascadnantgardens.co.uk. *1/2 m E of Menai Bridge. Take A545 & leave Menai Bridge heading for Beaumaris, then follow brown tourist information signs.* **Wed 27 Apr (12-5). Adm £6.50, chd free. Home-made teas in traditional Tea Room.** *Donation to Wales Air Ambulance; Anglesey Red Squirrel Trust; Menai Bridge Community Heritage Trust.*

Early C19 picturesque garden undergoing restoration since 1996. Valley gardens with waterfalls, large ornamental walled garden, woodland and early pit house. Recently created Alpheus water feature and Ceunant (Ravine) which gives visitors a more interesting walk featuring unusual moisture loving Alpines. Tea room serving home-made light lunches, delicious home-made scones and cakes. Visitor centre open. Partial wheelchair access to parts of gardens. Some steps, gravel paths, slopes. Access statement available. Accessible Tea Room and WC.

19 ◆ PLAS YN RHIW

Rhiw, Pwllheli LL53 8AB. National Trust, 01758 780219, plasynrhiw@nationaltrust.org.uk, www.nationaltrust.org.uk. *4m E of Aberdaron. 12m from Pwllheli, signed from B4413 to Aberdaron.* **For NGS: Sun 7 Feb (11-3). Adm £3, chd free. Light refreshments. For other opening times and information, please phone, email or visit garden website.**

Essentially a cottage garden of *3/4* acre laid out around C17 manor house (not open) overlooking Porth Neigwl. Flowering shrubs and trees flourish in compartments framed by formal box hedges and paths. On summer days, scented plants infuse the air. A place of romance and charm. Snowdrops in spring.

20 RHOSBACH COTTAGE

Brynteg LL78 8JY. Ena Green, 01248 853625, ena.bryan1@sky.com. *Brynteg, Anglesey. 1.4m W of Benllech. Take B5108 to Brynteg. Follow NGS signs to limited parking on lane on L, extra parking approx 50 metres further* along rd on R at Storws Wen Golf Club. **Sun 19 June (1-4.30). Adm £3.50, chd free. Home-made teas incl gluten free option. Visits also by arrangement May to July, groups 8+.**

Situated close to Cors Goch Nature Reserve, a recently rejuvenated garden full of country charm, a blend of mature trees, shrubs and wide, mixed borders planted to attract wildlife. The garden gently slopes with some steps, seating areas, and a small pond.

21 NEW SELWYN LODGE

Talybont LL43 2AU. Val Smedley. *Talybont, Nr Barmouth. Take 1st R turn after 30 mph sign entering Talybont from Barmouth. 1/2 m up lane on R.* **Mon 18 Apr (1-4.30). Adm £3, chd free. Tea.**

Selwyn Lodge has a Bijou garden that is set in a quiet rural location, offering excellent views of the sea and surrounding countryside. planted with a vast array of plants and shrubs providing colour and flowers throughout the yr, and is a haven for the wildlife which frequents the garden. Home-made jams and chutneys for sale as well as cakes and Barabrith scones.

22 TREFFOS SCHOOL

Llansadwrn, Anglesey LL59 5SD. Stuart & Joyce Humphreys. *2 1/2 m N of Menai Bridge. A5025 Amlwch/Benllech exit from Britannia Bridge onto Anglesey. Approx 3m turn R towards Llansadwrn. Entrance to Treffos School 200yds on L.* **Sun 12 June (12-3.30). Adm £3, chd free. Home-made teas.**

7 acres, child friendly garden, in rural location, surrounding C17 house now run as school. Garden consists of mature woodland, underplanted with spring flowering bulbs and rhododendrons, ancient beech avenue leading down to rockery, herbaceous borders and courtyards. Art and Craft activities for children. Also face painting. Partial wheelchair access.

23 TY CADFAN SANT

National Street, Tywyn LL36 9DD. Mrs Katie Pearce, 01654 712188, Katie@tycadfansant.co.uk. *A493 going S & W. L into one way, garden ahead. Bear R, parking 2nd L. A493 going N, 1st R in 30mph zone, L at bottom by garden, parking 2nd L.* **Sun 12 June (10-4). Adm £3.50, chd free. Cream teas and home baked cakes, special diets also catered for. Visits also by arrangement May to Sept, refreshments available on request.**

Large eco friendly garden. In the front, shrubbery, mixed flower beds and roses surround a mature copper beech. Up six steps the largely productive back garden has chickens in the orchard, fruit, vegetables, flowers and a poly tunnel. Seasonal produce, crafts. Partial wheelchair access due to steps to rear garden.

24 TY CAPEL FFRWD

Llanfachreth, Dolgellau LL40 2NR. Revs Mary & George Bolt, 01341 422006, georgebolt34@gmail.com. *4m NE of Dolgellau, 18m SW of Bala. From Dolgellau 4m up hill to Llanfachreth. Turn L at War Memorial. Follow lane 1/2 m to chapel on R. Park & walk down lane past chapel to cottage.* **Sun 5 June (11-5). Adm £3.50, chd free. Cream teas. Visits also by arrangement May to Aug, groups 10 max. Art groups and gardening clubs welcome.**

True cottage garden in Welsh mountains. Azaleas, rhododendrons, acers; large collection of aquilegia. Many different hostas give added strength to spring bulbs and corms. Stream flowing through the garden, 10ft waterfall and on through a small woodland bluebell carpet. For summer visitor's there is a continuous show of colour with herbaceous plants, roses, clematis and lilies, incl cardiocrinum giganteum.

25 ▸ TY NEWYDD

Ffordd Clwt Glas, Dyffryn Ardudwy LL44 2DB. Guy & Margaret Lloyd, 01341 247357, guylloyd@btinternet.com. *5¹/₂ m N of Barmouth, 4¹/₂ m S of Harlech. Situated just off A496 Barmouth to Harlech rd ¹/₂ m N of Dyffryn village centre. Ample parking for cars. Coaches may need to use nearby lay-by.* **Visits by arrangement. Adm £3.50, chd free. Home-made teas.**

3¹/₂ acre maritime garden diversley planted with trees and shrubs to provide yr-round interest through contrasting foliage colours and forms as well as floral displays. Plants incl a number of more tender subjects such as echium, grevillea and pittosporum. Areas devoted to fruit and vegetable growing and the so called Diamond apple tree. Partial wheelchair access, uneven surfaces, granite chip driveway.

26 ▸ TYN-TWLL

Llanfachreth, Dolgellau LL40 2DP. Sue & Pete Nicholls, 01341450673, sue-nicholls@hotmail.com. *1¹/₂ m NE of Llanfachreth. From Dolgellau on Bala rd (A494), 1st L to Llanfachreth opp Brithdir sign. Continue up hill, 1st R then 1st L & follow signs to Tyn Twll.* **Sat 27 Aug (10-4). Adm £3, chd free. Cream teas. Visits also by arrangement Apr to Sept, groups please email.**

Created by 2 artists. A garden of over an acre incl ancient woodland with imaginative architectural features using local materials. Traditional planting, rockeries, small walled fruit and rose garden, short woodland walk and pond area in sheltered setting, providing a haven for wildlife. A sculpture of a 35ft sleeping giant nestled in the woodland inspired by Welsh legends. Large variety of plants for sale. Cream teas, variety of cakes available as well as cold drinks.

Wildlife and nature cards also available by illustrator Sue Nicholls. Featured on Byw Yn Ardd S4C and various local newspaper coverage. Some challenging areas for wheelchair users.

27 ▸ 41 VICTORIA DRIVE

Llandudno Junction LL31 9PF. Allan Evans. *Llandudno Junction. A55 J18. From Bangor 1st exit, from Colwyn Bay 2nd exit, A546 to Conwy. Next r'about 3rd exit then 1st L.* **Sun 10 July (1-4). Adm £3, chd free. Light refreshments.**

A very interesting small urban garden, offering so much in creative ideas incl growing exhibition sweet peas and dahlias and colourful bedding and other shrubs and herbaceous plants. Winner for Display Class Sweet Peas at the Royal Welsh Show.

Pen y Bryn

Find a garden near you – download our free iOS **APP**

NORTH EAST WALES

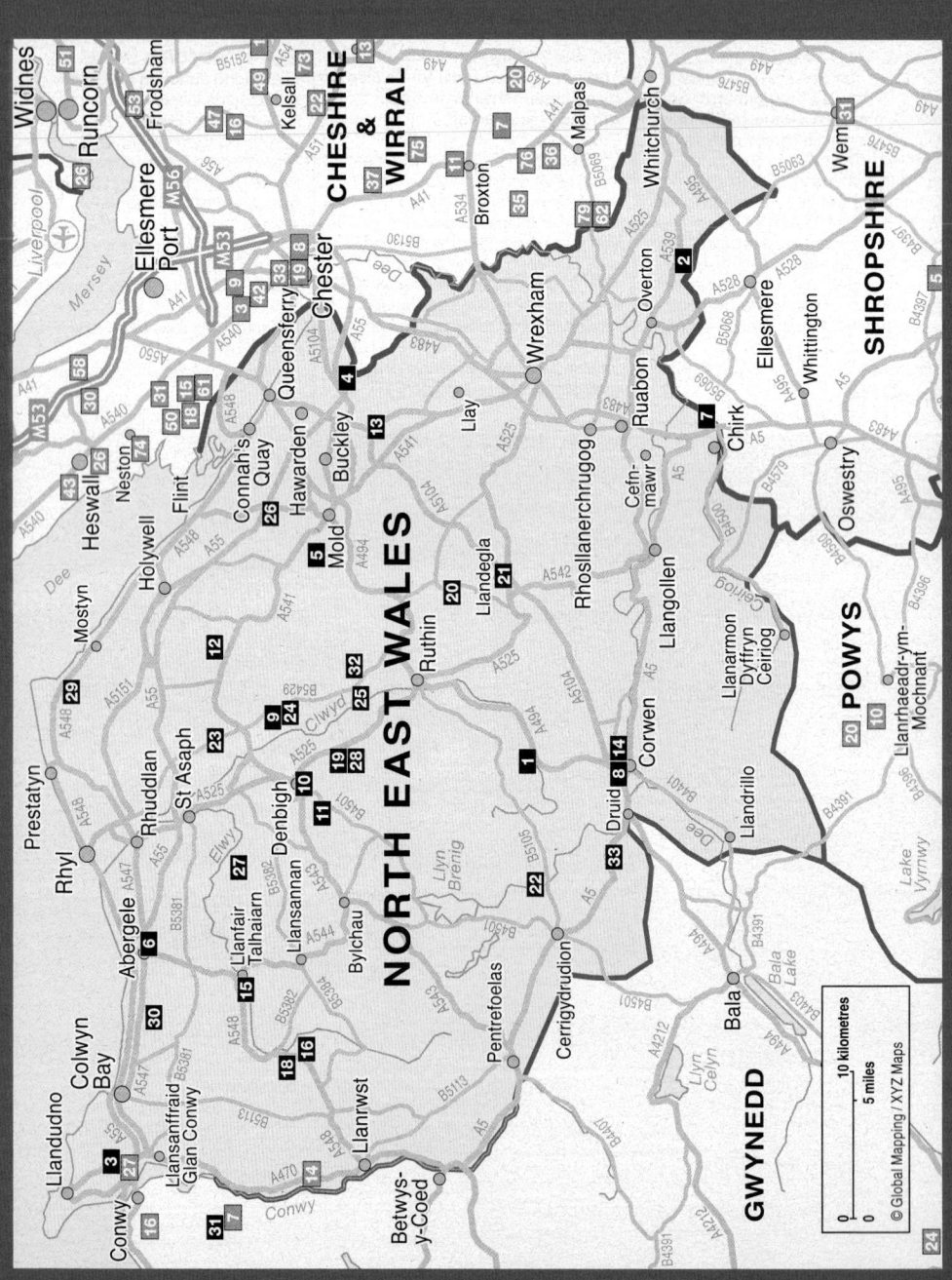

North East Wales

With its diversity of countryside from magnificent hills, seaside vistas and rolling farmland, North East Wales offers a wide range of gardening experiences.

North East Wales Volunteers

County Organiser
Jane Moore
07769 046317
jemoore01@live.com

County Treasurer
Elizabeth Sasse
01745 710174
elizabeth.sasse246@btinternet.com

Publicity
Jane Moore
(as above)

Booklet Co-ordinator
Roy Hambleton
01352 740206
royhambleton@btinternet.com

Assistant County Organisers
Fiona Bell
07813 087797
bell_fab@hotmail.com

Ruth Davies
01978 790475
arfrynpentrecelyn@btinternet.com

Ann Knowlson
01745 832002
apk@slaters.com

Ann Rathbone
01244 532948
rathbone.ann@gmail.com

Anne Saxon
01352 771222
annemsaxon@yahoo.co.uk

Our gardens offer a wealth of designs and come in all shapes and sizes, ranging from abundant plantsmen's gardens to informal natural hillside planting. Visitors will have something to see from the frost-filled days of February through till the magnificent colourful days of autumn.

The majority of our gardens are within easy reach of North West England, and being a popular tourist destination make an excellent day out for all the family.

Come and enjoy the beauty and the variety of the gardens of North East Wales with the added bonus of a delicious cup of tea and a slice of cake. Our garden owners await your visit.

Above: 33 Bryn Twr and Lynton

Opening Dates

All entries subject to change.
For latest information check www.ngs.org.uk

February

Snowdrop Festival

Wednesday 10
9 Clwydfryn
Thursday 18
16 Glog Ddu
Thursday 25
16 Glog Ddu
Sunday 28
1 Aberclwyd Manor
22 The Old Rectory

March

Wednesday 9
9 Clwydfryn

April

Wednesday 6
1 Aberclwyd Manor
Wednesday 13
9 Clwydfryn
Wednesday 20
1 Aberclwyd Manor
Sunday 24
31 NEW Ty Hwnt Yr Afon

May

Wednesday 4
1 Aberclwyd Manor

Wednesday 11
9 Clwydfryn
Sunday 15
10 NEW Denbigh Town Gardens
Wednesday 18
1 Aberclwyd Manor
Sunday 22
33 Maesmor Hall
Thursday 26
7 Brynkinalt Hall
Saturday 28
12 Donadea Lodge
26 90 St Peters Park
Sunday 29
8 Caereuni
12 Donadea Lodge
19 The Laundry
28 Tan-y-Parc
Monday 30
8 Caereuni
19 The Laundry
28 Tan-y-Parc

June

Wednesday 1
1 Aberclwyd Manor

Festival Weekend

Saturday 4
24 Plas Ashpool
Sunday 5
24 Plas Ashpool
31 NEW Ty Hwnt Yr Afon
Wednesday 8
9 Clwydfryn
Saturday 11
8 Caereuni
14 Ffridd-y-Gog
25 NEW Plas Coch

Sunday 12
8 Caereuni
14 Ffridd-y-Gog
25 NEW Plas Coch
Wednesday 15
1 Aberclwyd Manor
Saturday 25
2 The Beeches
Sunday 26
27 Tal-y-Bryn Farm
Tuesday 28
3 Bodysgallen Hall & Spa
Wednesday 29
1 Aberclwyd Manor

July

Friday 1
29 Tree Tops Caravan Park
Saturday 2
29 Tree Tops Caravan Park
Sunday 3
24 Plas Ashpool
Wednesday 6
1 Aberclwyd Manor
Saturday 9
20 NEW Llanarmon-yn-Ial Village Gardens
Wednesday 13
9 Clwydfryn
Sunday 17
4 Broughton & Bretton Allotments
Wednesday 20
1 Aberclwyd Manor
Saturday 23
30 Tudor Cottage
Sunday 24
21 Llandegla Village Gardens
30 Tudor Cottage

Sunday 31
8 Caereuni

August

Wednesday 3
1 Aberclwyd Manor
Sunday 7
13 Dove Cottage
Wednesday 10
9 Clwydfryn
Sunday 14
16 Glog Ddu
18 NEW Hafodunos Hall
Wednesday 17
1 Aberclwyd Manor
Sunday 21
21 Llandegla Village Gardens
Sunday 28
8 Caereuni
Monday 29
8 Caereuni
Wednesday 31
1 Aberclwyd Manor

September

Friday 2
5 Bryn Bellan (Evening)
Wednesday 14
1 Aberclwyd Manor
Wednesday 28
1 Aberclwyd Manor

By arrangement only

6 33 Bryn Twr and Lynton
11 Dolhyfryd
15 Garthewin
23 Pen Y Graig Bach
32 Wylan

Also open by arrangement

1 Aberclwyd Manor
5 Bryn Bellan
13 Dove Cottage
14 Ffridd-y-Gog
19 The Laundry
21 Plas Yn Coed, Llandegla Village Gardens
24 Plas Ashpool
29 Tree Tops Caravan Park
30 Tudor Cottage
31 NEW Ty Hwnt Yr Afon

Brynkinalt Hall

The Gardens

1 ABERCLWYD MANOR
Derwen, Corwen LL21 9SF. Miss Irene Brown & Mr G Sparvoli, 01824 750431, irene662010@live.com. *7m from Ruthin. Travelling on A494 from Ruthin to Corwen. At Bryn S.M service station turn R, follow sign to Derwen. Aberclwyd gates on L before Derwen.* **Sun 28 Feb (11-3). Combined adm with The Old Rectory, Llanfihangel Glyn Myfyr £5, chd free. Weds 6, 20 Apr, 4, 18 May, 1, 15, 29 June, 6, 20 July, 3, 17, 31 Aug, 14, 28 Sept (11-4). Adm £3.50, chd free. Tea. Visits also by arrangement Feb to Sept for groups 10+, daytime or evenings.**
A 4 acre garden on a sloping hillside overlooking the Upper Clwyd Valley. The garden has many mature trees underplanted with snowdrops, fritillaries and cyclamen. An Italianate garden of box hedging lies below the house and shrubs, ponds, perennials, roses and an orchard are also to be enjoyed within this cleverly structured area. Mass of cyclamen in Sept. Snowdrops and many spring flowering bulbs. Mostly flat with some steps and slopes.
♿ 🐕 ✿ 🛏 ☕

2 THE BEECHES
Vicarage Lane, Penley, Wrexham LL13 0NH. Stuart & Sue Hamon. *Western edge of village. From Overton turn 1st L after 30mph sign. From Whitchurch go along A539 through village & turn R just after church, signed to Adrefelyn. N.B. SatNavs may show Vicarage Lane as Hollybush Lane.* **Sat 25 June (1-5). Adm £3.50, chd free. Home-made teas.**
The garden surrounds an 1841 former vicarage and extends to 3¹⁄₂ acres. It has been redesigned to create an attractive open garden laid mainly to lawn with a mixture of mature and younger specimen trees and shrubs. There are two to four yr old shrub, rose and herbaceous beds together with a productive vegetable and fruit area. The walled courtyard garden has tender plants incl many agapanthus. A mostly flat garden with gravelled paths. Grass is usually firm so allowing ease of movement. The courtyard has three very shallow steps.
♿ 🐕 ✿ ☕

3 BODYSGALLEN HALL & SPA
The Royal Welsh Way, Llandudno LL30 1RS. The National Trust, 01492 584466, info@bodysgallen.com, www.bodysgallen.com. *2m from Llandudno. Take A55 to intersection with A470 (The Royal Welsh Way) towards Llandudno. Proceed 1m, hotel is 1m on R.* **Tue 28 June (1-4.30). Adm £4.95, chd £3.75. Home-made teas in The Wynn Rooms.**
Garden is well known for C17 box hedged parterre. Stone walls surround lower gardens with rose gardens and herbaceous borders. Outside walled garden is cascade over rocks. Enclosed working fruit and vegetable garden with espalier trained fruit trees, hedging area for cut flowers with walls covered in wineberry and Chinese gooseberry. Restored Victorian woodland, walks with stunning views of Conwy and Snowdonia. Luncheon available in the Main Hall. Booking in advance recommended. Feature on BBC Glorious Gardens from Above. Gravel paths in places and steep slopes.
♿ ✿ 🛏 ☕

A chance to see a new garden evolving within an old setting . . .

ALLOTMENTS

4 BROUGHTON & BRETTON ALLOTMENTS
Main Road, Broughton CH4 0NT. Broughton & Bretton Allotments Association, www.broughtonandbretton allotments.co.uk. *5m W of Chester. On A5104 (signed Penyffordd) in village of Broughton.* **Sun 17 July (1-5). Adm £3, chd free. Home-made teas at War Memorial Institute.**

56 half sized allotment plots used by the local community to grow a mix of vegetables, flowers and soft fruit. Seasonal produce and plants for sale.
🐕 ✿ ☕

5 BRYN BELLAN
Bryn Road, Gwernaffield CH7 5DE. Gabrielle Armstrong & Trevor Ruddle, 01352 741806, trevor@indigoawnings.co.uk. *2m W of Mold. Leave A541 at Mold on Gwernaffield rd (Dreflan), ¹⁄₂ m after Mold derestriction signs turn R to Rhydymwyn & Llynypandy. After 200 yds park in field on R.* **Evening opening Fri 2 Sept (5-8). Adm £6, chd free. Wine and nibbles available. Visits also by arrangement May to Sept for groups 10+.**
A late summer tranquil and elegant garden which is perfect for a relaxing evening visit. The garden has been designed on two levels, a partly walled upper garden with circular sunken lawn, featuring a Wellingtonia and structured borders of a green and white colour scheme with striking hydrangeas and cyclamen. Lower garden, mainly lawn, has an ornamental cutting and vegetable garden with bijou potting shed. Some gravel paths.
♿ ✿ ☕

6 33 BRYN TWR AND LYNTON
Lynton, Highfield Park, Abergele LL22 7AU. Mr & Mrs Colin Knowlson and Bryn Roberts & Emma Knowlson-Roberts, 01745 832002 or 07712 623836, apk@slaters.com. *From A55 heading W take slip rd into Abergele town centre. Turn L at 2nd set of T-lights signed Llanfair TH, 3rd rd on L. For SatNav use LL22 8DD.* **Visits by arrangement May to Aug for any size group. Adm £4, chd free. Home-made teas.**
More changes have been made to the gardens for 2016, mixed herbaceous and shrub borders, some trees plus many unusual plants. Lawn at Lynton replaced with slate chips and more planting. Garage with interesting fire engine; cars and memorabilia; greenhouse over water capture system; surrounding planting coming along nicely. Featured in Garden News. Partial wheelchair access.
🐕 ✿ 🚌 ☕

7 BRYNKINALT HALL
Brynkinalt, Chirk, Wrexham LL14 5NS. Iain & Kate Hill-Trevor, 01691 773425, info@brynkinalt.co.uk, www.brynkinalt.co.uk. *6m N of Oswestry, 10m S of Wrexham. Turn into Trevor Rd (beside St Mary's Church). Cont past houses on R. Turn R on bend into Estate Gates. Over 2 bridges. Straight on at fork. N.B. Do not use postcode for SatNav (uses tiny lane).* **Thur 26 May (2-5). Adm £4, chd free. Tea, coffee and home-made cakes.**
5 acre ornamental woodland shrubbery, overgrown until recently, now cleared and replanted, rhododendron walk, historic ponds, well, grottos, ha-ha and battlements, new stumpery, ancient redwoods and yews. Also 2 acre garden beside Grade II* house (see website for opening), with modern rose and formal beds, deep herbaceous borders, pond with shrub/mixed beds, pleached limes and hedge patterns. Home of the first Duke of Wellington's grandmother. Partial wheelchair access. Gravel paths in West Garden and grass paths and slopes in shrubbery.

8 CAEREUNI
Ffordd Ty Cerrig, Godre'r Gaer, Corwen LL21 9YA. Mr S Williams, www.plantationcaereunigarden.co.uk. *1m N of Corwen. A5 Corwen to Bala rd, turn R at T-lights onto A494 to Chester. 1st R after lay by. House ¹/₄ m on L.* **Sun 29, Mon 30 May (2-5). Adm £3.50, chd free. Sat 11, Sun 12 June (2-5). Combined adm with Ffridd-y-Gog £5, chd free. Sun 31 July, Sun 28, Mon 29 Aug (2-5). Adm £3.50, chd free.**
Plantsman's collection of rare trees, shrubs, plants, containers of tender plants and topiary set in a quirky themed garden. This approx ¹/₃ acre garden incls Japanese smoke water garden, old ruin, Spanish courtyard, Welsh gold mine, Chinese peace garden, Mexican chapel, 1950s petrol garage, woodman's lodge and jungle. Featured in Amateur Gardening Magazine - Garden of the week.

9 CLWYDFRYN
Bodfari LL16 4HU. Keith & Susan Watson, 01745 710232, clwydfryn@btinternet.com. *5m outside Denbigh. Halfway between Bodfari & Llandyrnog on B5429.* **Weds 10 Feb, 9 Mar, 13 Apr,**

11 May, 8 June, 13 July, 10 Aug (11-4). Adm £3.50, chd free. Home-made teas.
³/₄ acre plantswoman's garden, well worth a visit any time of the yr. Collection of epimediums, hellebores and daffodils in spring. Many unusual spring shade loving plants and perennial borders in summer. Grass border, orchard and colourful cottage garden potager. Garden access up a slope from parking area to main garden.

GROUP OPENING

10 NEW DENBIGH TOWN GARDENS
Denbigh LL16 3DE. *Many car parks in town. Tickets & disabled parking at 21 Park St located to the side of The Infirmary on A543.* **Sun 15 May (12.30-5.30). Combined adm £6, chd free. Tea at 21 Park St.**

NEW THE COURTS
Mr & Mrs Richard Lake

NEW FROGAIN, 23 PARK ST
Mr & Mrs Jim Van den Akker

NEW GARREG LWYD
Mrs Mary Jones

NEW NONESUCH, 25 PARK ST
Dr & Mrs Tim Webb

NEW 21 PARK STREET
Mrs Jane Moore

NEW PEACOCK HOUSE
Mr & Mrs Peter Ellis

Overlooking the stunning Vale of Clwyd is the historic market town of Denbigh with more listed buildings than any other town in Wales. The Castle with its ancient town walls sits on top of the hill and our 6 gardens are all in a conservation area not too far from the town centre, 4 of the gardens are next door to each other at the bottom of Park St, one is on the way up and one sits within the ancient town walls. The Courts has the largest garden with well tended lawns, mixed borders and trees, both ornamental and fruit. The next two gardens are behind a pair of Victorian semis. No 25 is a much loved cottage garden with wall trained fruit trees, vegetable, top fruit and flowers all in a rampant free for all! No 23 has old espalier fruit trees, trees, lawns and borders, stone terrace, veranda and raised pond. No 21 was bought 2yrs ago and is developing well. Gareg

Lwyd has a lawn and borders with wonderful views up the valley and Peacock House has a listed gazebo, old box hedges, borders, many acers. Steep slope to terrace at Peacock House and then steps to main garden. No access to Nonesuch vegetable garden. Disabled parking at 21 Park St.

11 DOLHYFRYD
Lawnt, Denbigh LL16 4SU. Captain & Mrs Michael Cunningham, 01745 814805, virginia@dolhyfryd.com. *1m SW of Denbigh. On B4501 to Nantglyn, from Denbigh - 1m from town centre.* **Visits by arrangement Feb to Oct. Adm £4, chd free. Light refreshments.**
Established garden set in small valley of R Ystrad. Acres of crocuses in late Feb/early Mar. Paths through wildflower meadows and woodland of magnificent trees, shade loving plants and azaleas; mixed borders; walled kitchen garden - recently redesigned. Many woodland and riverside birds, incl dippers, kingfishers, grey wagtails. Many species of butterfly encouraged by new planting. Much winter interest, exceptional display of crocuses. Gravel paths, some steep slopes.

12 DONADEA LODGE
Mynydd Llan, Babell, Holywell CH8 8QD. Tony & Wendy Lander. *7m NE of Denbigh. Turn off A541 Mold to Denbigh at Afonwen signed Babell. At T-junction turn L. Garden approx 500 meters on R. A55 towards Conwy take B5122 to Caerwys J31, 3rd turn on L. Garden 1m on L.* **Sat 28, Sun 29 May (12-4). Adm £4, chd free. Tea, coffee and home-made cakes.**
1 acre shady country garden showing 25yrs of imaginative planting to

Bodysgallen Hall and Spa

enhance the magic of dappled shade, moving through different colour schemes, with each plant complementing its neighbour. Productive kitchen garden and young orchard with a variety of heritage fruit trees. Rescue chickens on site and small picnic area. Wheelchair access on large lawned area.

13 ▶ DOVE COTTAGE
Rhos Road, Penyffordd, Chester CH4 0JR. Chris & Denise Wallis, 01244 547539, dovecottage@supanet.com. *6m SW of Chester. Leave A55 at J35 take A550 to Wrexham. Drive 2m, turn R onto A5104. From A541 Wrexham/Mold Rd in Pontblyddyn take A5104 to Chester. Garden opp train stn.* **Sun 7 Aug (2-5). Adm**

£3.50, chd free. Home-made teas. **Visits also by arrangement July & Aug for groups 10+.**
Approx 1½ acre garden, shrubs and herbaceous plants set informally around lawns. Established vegetable area, 2 ponds (1 wildlife), summerhouse and woodland planted area. Featured in Garden News - Garden of the Week. Gravel paths.

Follow NGS Twitter 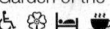 @NGSOpenGardens

14 FFRIDD-Y-GOG
Ffordd Ty Cerrig, Corwen
LL21 9YE. Mr & Mrs D Watkins,
ffriddygog@hotmail.com. *1m out of
Corwen. From A5 to Bala rd turn R at
T-lights onto A494 to Chester, 1st R
after lay-by. Ist L into Ffridd-y-Gog.
Park on Est Rd except for disabled.
Turn L then R into drive.* Sat 11, Sun
12 June (2-5). Combined adm with
Caereuni £5, chd free. Home-
made teas. Visits also by
arrangement June to Sept.
Old Welsh farmhouse set in ³/₄ acre of
grounds. Organic kitchen garden
growing fruit, vegetables and herbs.
Greenhouse and polytunnel.
Ornamental gardens with particular
emphasis on perennials and alpines.
Many container grown plants, mostly
propagated and grown by the
owners. A haven for wildlife and a
peaceful and tranquil space to just sit
and enjoy. All of garden accessible by
wheelchair.

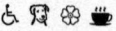

15 GARTHEWIN
Llanfairtalhaiarn LL22 8YR. Mr
Michael Grime, 01745 720288,
michaelgrime12@btinternet.com.
*6m S of Abergele & A55. From
Abergele take A548 to Llanfair TH &
Llanrwst. Entrance to Garthewin
300yds W of Llanfair TH on A548 to
Llanrwst. SatNav misleading.* Visits
by arrangement Apr to July,
groups 40 max. Regret, no
coaches. Adm £4, chd free.
Valley garden with ponds and
woodland areas. Much of the 8 acres
have been reclaimed and redesigned
providing a younger garden with a
great variety of azaleas,
rhododendrons and young trees, all
within a framework of mature shrubs
and trees.

16 GLOG DDU
Llangernyw, Abergele LL22 8PS.
Pamela & Anthony Harris, 01745
860611. *1m S of Llangernyw.
Llangernyw is halfway between
Abergele & Llanrwst on A548. SatNav
misleading. Feb visits - turn up Uwch
Afon Rd on Llanrwst side of village. At
grass triangle follow yellow sign. No
parking in summer.* Thur 18, Thur 25
Feb (12-3). Adm £5, chd free. Sun
14 Aug (11-5). Combined adm
with Hafodunos Hall £6, chd free.
Soup and roll incl (Feb).
Refreshments at Hafodunus Hall
(Aug).

Approx 2 acres consisting of
snowdrops, rhododendrons,
herbaceous borders, rare trees and
shrubs many grown from seed,
vegetables, wildlife and ornamental
ponds. Over 300 different varieties of
snowdrops, many hard to find, can
be seen in February. In summer
colourful borders and the prairie style
borders are spectacular. Good views
across the valley.

18 NEW HAFODUNOS HALL
Llangernyw, Abergele, Conwy
LL22 8TY. Dr Richard Wood,
www.hafodunoshall.co.uk. *1m W of
Llangernyw. Halfway between
Abergele & Llanrwst on A548. Turn W
at Old Stag PH drive ¹/₂ m to
Gatehouse. Turn L up drive. Park
here. Bus to Glog Ddu. NO parking at
Glog Ddu.* Sun 14 Aug (11-5).
Combined adm with Glog Ddu £6,
chd free. Light refreshments.
Historic garden undergoing
restoration after 30yrs of neglect
surrounds a Sir G G Scott Grade1
Hall derelict after an arson attack.
¹/₂ m treelined drive, formal terraces,
woodland walks with ancient
redwoods, laurels, yews, lake,
streams, waterfalls and a gorge.
Unique setting. Some uneven paths
and steep steps. Children must be
supervised by an adult at all times.
Most areas around the hall accessible
to wheelchairs by gravel pathways.
Some gardens are set on slopes.

19 THE LAUNDRY
Llanrhaeadr, Denbigh LL16 4NL. Mr
& Mrs T Williams, 01745 890515,
tomjenny@btinternet.com. *3m SE
of Denbigh. Entrance off A525
Denbigh to Ruthin Rd.* Sun 29, Mon
30 May (11.30-5.30). Combined
adm with Tan-y-Parc £5, chd free.
Home-made teas. Visits also by
arrangement Feb to Sept, groups
strictly 10+.
Terraced courtyard garden developed
since 2009 surrounded by old stone
walls enclosing cottage style planting
and formal hedging. 3yrs ago work
started on the old kitchen walled
garden with a view to incorporating it
within the whole garden plan. A
chance to see a new garden evolving
within an old setting. Woodland walk,
roses, pleached limes, peonies and
herbaceous planting. Some gravel
areas.

GROUP OPENING

20 NEW LLANARMON-YN-IAL VILLAGE GARDENS
Mold CH7 4PZ, 01824 780833,
ravenmad@raveninn.co.uk. *6m S of
Mold. From Mold to Ruthin Rd turn S
to B5430. Or 3m from A525 & A5104
rds.* Sat 9 July (11-4). Combined
adm £6, chd free. Light
refreshments at The Old
Schoolroom.

> NEW **12A MAES IAL**
> Beryl Campbell

> NEW **ARDWYN**
> Mrs Gillian Hodson

> NEW **BRONALLT**
> Brenda & Tony Rigby

> NEW **BRYDAL COTTAGE**
> Jill Finlow

> NEW **CALON-Y-PENTRE**
> Jo Tobler

> NEW **CRUD-Y-GWYNT**
> Elaine & Gareth Jones

> NEW **FERN COTTAGE**
> Pat Fuld

> NEW **7 MAES IAL**
> Viv & Don Bennion

> NEW **THE MEADOWS**
> Wendy & David Steele

> NEW **RAVEN INN**
> Sue Willis

> NEW **TREFALYN**
> Alma Gaffney

> NEW **TY ERW**
> Liz & Meirion Jones

Entering Llanarmon-yn-Ial from the B5430 you will drive over the ancient stone bridge and up the hill to The Old Schoolroom - Yr Hen Ysgoldy. Here you can buy your entrance ticket to all the gardens and refresh yourself with tea/coffee and cakes. Maps of the village showing the gardens will be incl with your ticket. There is limited parking here. The gardens are all close to the heart of the village and Ty Erw, which is a gentle 5 min stroll along the lane has some disabled parking available. The people of Llanarmon-yn-Ial have been successfully running the Raven Inn and Village Shop as community ventures for many yrs now. These efforts were rewarded in July 2015 by a visit from Prince Charles and the Duchess of Cornwall. This was followed by BBC Breakfast Time broadcasting live from the Village and using it as an example of how rural communities can survive.

GROUP OPENING

21 LLANDEGLA VILLAGE GARDENS
Llandegla LL11 3AP. *10m W of Wrexham. Park in NGS car park in Llandegla village. Minibus available from car park to take visitors to out lying gardens as parking at some not possible.* **Sun 24 July (2-6). Combined adm £6, chd free. Sun 21 Aug (2-6). Combined adm £5, chd free. Home-made teas at Plas yn Coed & The Gate House (July), Plas yn Coed (Aug).**

THE GATE HOUSE, RUTHIN ROAD
Rod & Shelagh Williams.
Open on Sun 24 July

11 MAES TEG
Mr & Mrs L Evans.
Open on Sun 24 July

PLAS YN COED
Fraser & Helen Robertson.
Open on all dates
Visits also by arrangement in Aug for groups 10+
helen@plasyncoed.me
01978 790666

THE RECTORY
The Ven & Mrs R H Griffiths.
Open on Sun 24 July

SWN Y GWYNT
Phil Clark.
Open on all dates

TY PENDLE
Matt Ellis & Sandra Rogers.
Open on Sun 24 July

Llandegla Village offers the visitor a truly old fashioned village welcome in the most picturesque area of the county. Every part of the community appears to enjoy the busy atmosphere of the day when the gardens attract so many visitors to raise funds for the NGS charity. The garden owners work hard to get their gardens looking their best, the bakers of the village supply tasty cakes for visitors to buy and enjoy in various venues and there are plenty of plants for sale. Perfect! Not all gardens accessible for wheelchair users. WC in Memorial Hall.

Wild flowers, hens, bees and the odd pig complete this rural picture . . .

---

33 MAESMOR HALL
Maerdy, Corwen LL21 0NS.
Dr & Mrs G M Jackson 01490 460411 www.maesmor.com. *5m W of Corwen. Take A5 from Corwen, through 2 sets of T-lights. In Maerdy take 1st L after church & opp The Goat PH.* **Sun 22 May (10-6). Adm £4, chd free. Home-made teas. Donation to St Dunstans (charity for injured soldiers)**
Garden with riverside and estate walks featuring a water and white plant garden. The rhododendrons are extensive and provide a fitting backdrop to the parkland. New and large azalea beds are a mixture of colour. Wooded walks around the hall go towards a new folly amongst the bluebells in the arboretum. A 100yr old Fig and Vine House has been

restored and incl exotic plants, flowers, pomegranates, lemons, oranges, and bananas. Also many patios and front of hall rose displays. A nut arch sits by a soft fruit wall and there is an enormous stone table which has been brought down from the surrounding mountain - it could have been King Arthur's. Gravel paths.

22 THE OLD RECTORY
Llanfihangel Glyn Myfyr, Corwen LL21 9UN. Mr & Mrs E T Hughes. *2¹/₂ m NE of Cerrigydrudion. From Ruthin take B5105 SW for 12m. From Cerrigydrudion take B5105 for 3m.* **Sun 28 Feb (11-3). Combined adm with Aberclwyd Manor £5, chd free. Tea.** *Donation to Cancer Research U.K.*
Garden of approx 1 acre set in beautiful, tranquil, sheltered valley alongside the R Alwen. Opening for the first time in early spring when a variety of snowdrops, beautiful hellebores, crocus and abundance of spring flowers may be seen. Together with Aberclwyd Manor they offer a welcome start to the gardening year. Partial wheelchair access.

23 PEN Y GRAIG BACH
Tremeirchion, St Asaph LL17 0UR. Roger Pawling & Christine Hoyle, 07875 642270, christinehoyle@gmail.com. *4m SE of St Asaph. Off A55 take J28/29/30 to Tremeirchion, then B5429 to Bodfari, go 0.7m (wide verge), turn L up hill, L at fork, cont to rd end. From Bodfari take B5429 take 2nd R (after 1¹/₄ m).* **Visits by arrangement Apr to Sept. Adm £3, chd free. Tea/coffee with biscuits or cake (depending on numbers). Wine on request.**
¹/₂ acre wildlife friendly rural cottage garden. Box hedges and fruit trees enclose 5 plots of herbaceous perennials, unusual climbers, flowering shrubs, soft fruit and vegetables. Over 200 native and ornamental trees. Succession of colour throughout the yr. 4 ponds and 2 acres of paddocks which are managed organically for wild flowers and hay. Beehives. Stunning views from sea to mountains. Partial wheelchair access, gravel paths between box hedges and grass paths.

24 ▶ PLAS ASHPOOL
Llandyrnog LL16 4HP. Fiona Bell,
07813 087797. *5m outside Denbigh.
Halfway between Bodfari &
Llandyrnog on B5429.* **Sat 4, Sun 5
June, Sun 3 July (2-5.30). Adm
£3.50, chd free. Home-made teas.
Visits also by arrangement June
to Aug.**
This country house garden with views
of the Clwydian hills and Vale of
Clwyd was developed over 40yrs ago
by present owner's family and is now
undergoing restoration. The
herbaceous and shrub borders,
orchard, vegetable garden and

sunken rose garden are surrounded
by historic farm buildings, now being
rescued from disrepair. Wild flowers,
hens, bees and the odd pig complete
this rural picture. Partial wheelchair
access.

25 ▶ NEW ▶ PLAS COCH
Llanychan, Ruthin LL15 1UF. Sir
David & Lady Henshaw, 01824
790972, Enquiries@annedd.com.
*Llanychan. Situated on B5429
between villages of Llandyrnog &
Llanbedr.* **Sat 11, Sun 12 June

(10-4.30). Adm £3.50, chd free.
Morning coffee, cakes, afternoon
teas.**
Well established country garden with
deep and varied herbaceous borders,
vegetable garden and fruit trees with
recently planted heritage variety small
orchard. Other sections incl small
yard garden, pond areas, three seater
tybach (outside privy) MG TC 1949,
all in the centre of the vale of Clwyd
with extensive views towards the
Clwydian Hills. Wheelchair access but
gravel paths.

Ty Hwnt Yr Afon

26 90 ST PETERS PARK

Northop CH7 6YU. Mr P Hunt, 01352 840758, philipbhunt@hotmail.co.uk. *3m N of Mold, 3m S of Flint. Leave A55 at Northop exit J33. Opp cricket ground, turn R. Take 5th turning on R. Garden on R.* **Sat 28 May (2-5). Adm £3, chd free. Light refreshments.**

Garden planted by professional botanist and horticulturalist, Custos Hortorum at Chester Cathedral and creator of Cloister Garth, Cheshire a Garden of Distinction. A plantsman's garden with exotic and rare species of trees and ornamental plants. Unique garden cruck house with sedum roof, beamed ceilings, stained glass windows and inglenook fireplace. Other interesting timber framed structures.

27 TAL-Y-BRYN FARM

Llannefydd, Denbigh LL16 5DR. Mr & Mrs Gareth Roberts, 01745 540256, llaeth@villagedairy.co.uk, www.villagedairy.co.uk. *3m W of Henllan. From Henllan take rd signed Llannefydd. After 2¹/₂ m turn R signed Bont Newydd. Garden ¹/₂ m on L.* **Sun 26 June (2-5.30). Adm £4, chd free. Vintage home-made teas.** *Donation to Elderly Committee of Llannefydd.*

Medium sized working farmhouse cottage garden. Ancient farm machinery. Incorporating ancient privy festooned with honeysuckle, clematis and roses. Terraced arches, sunken garden pool and bog garden, fountains and old water pumps. Herb wheels, shrubs and other interesting features. Lovely views of the Clwydian range. Water feature, new rose tunnel, vegetable tunnel and small garden summer house.

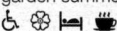

28 TAN-Y-PARC

Llanrhaeadr, Denbigh LL16 4NL. Mrs Sandra Edwards. *3m S of Denbigh. 5m N of Ruthin. Take A525 from Denbigh or Ruthin. Follow signs at Llanrhaeadr.* **Sun 29, Mon 30 May (11.30-5.30). Combined adm with The Laundry £5, chd free. Cream teas.**

Small cottage garden, new planted borders in paddock area, greenhouse and raised vegetable plots, fruit bushes. Rear garden enclosed with beech hedges, 2 large raised beds. Pergola with grape vine. New features in paddock, pond and wild flower area, new planted beds in front areas. Level grass areas suitable for wheelchairs.

29 TREE TOPS CARAVAN PARK

Tanlan Hill, Tanlan, Ffynnongroyw, Holywell CH8 9JP. Andrew Walker, 01745 560279, www.treetopscaravanpark.co.uk. *300yds off A548 main coast rd between Flint & Prestatyn.* **Fri 1 July (2-7.30); Sat 2 July (11-6). Adm £5, chd free. Tea. Visits also by arrangement Mar to Sept.**

We have 11 acres of manicured gardens, each yr we plant around 15,000 bedding plants, many of which we grow in our own greenhouses. In addition to the bedding plants we have tens of thousands of trees and shrubs. Our gardens have won Wales in Bloom for the last 21yrs. We're not the average caravan park and we are sure you will be pleasantly surprised. We are on a sloping site, but much of the park is accessible to wheelchairs.

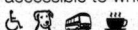

Marie Curie

Last year, NGS funded 25,000 hours of our nursing care

30 TUDOR COTTAGE

Isallt Road, Llysfaen, Colwyn Bay LL29 8LJ. Mr & Mrs C Manifold, 01492 518510, andrina50@outlook.com. *1¹/₂ m SE of Old Colwyn. Turn S off A547 between Llandulas & Old Colwyn. Up Highlands Rd for ¹/₂ m, R onto Tan-y-Graig, ignore SatNav, ³/₄ m to swings. Take Isallt Rd on far R.* **Sat 23, Sun 24 July (2-5). Adm £4, chd free. Home-made teas. Visits also by arrangement July & Aug.**

³/₄ acre garden on different levels set amongst natural rock faces. Unusual and varied planting featuring cottage, scree, Japanese, shade and bog gardens. Display bedding, an abundance of colourful pots and baskets, together with quirky statues, ponds, bridges and a folly. Lovely views from upper level. Some uneven paths and steep steps. Care required. Children must be supervised by an adult at all times please. Featured in Garden News.

31 NEW TY HWNT YR AFON

Rowen, Conwy LL32 8YT. Ian & Margaret Trevette, 01492 650871, ian.trevette@btinternet.com. *Take B5106 from Conwy, R at Groes Inn. Follow signs. Park on rd below Ty Gwyn Hotel, garden 500yds thru village on L fork in rd. Disabled parking on drive.* **Sun 24 Apr, Sun 5 June (1-5). Adm £3, chd free. Home-made teas. Visits also by arrangement Apr to Aug.**

³/₄ acre garden relandscaped by owners over last 5yrs. With the backdrop of R Ro and preserved woodland beyond have used the gardens natural features of glacial stone, stream and springs to create an amphitheatre of garden shrubs and plants incl acers, azaleas, camellias, rhododendrons and a multitude of other favourite perennials. Wheelchair access to view most of garden and for home-made teas on the sun terrace. Some steps.

32 WYLAN

Llangynhafal, Ruthin LL15 1RU. John & Carol Perkins, 07713 163652, carolperkins24@yahoo.co.uk. *3m N of Ruthin. Take A494 from Ruthin to Llanbedr then B5429. After ¹/₂ m turn R signed Llangynhafal 1¹/₂ m. Entrance on R.* **Visits by arrangement May to July, groups 25 max. Adm £3, chd free.**

1 acre garden designed by owners for all parts to be easily accessible. Magnificent panoramic views. Mature shrubs, mixed borders and water features. Pergola leading into sunken patio with colourful summer planted containers. Winner of Best Kept Country Garden in Ruthin Flower Show (6th consecutive yr). Gradual grass slope at end of front garden to access back garden.

POWYS

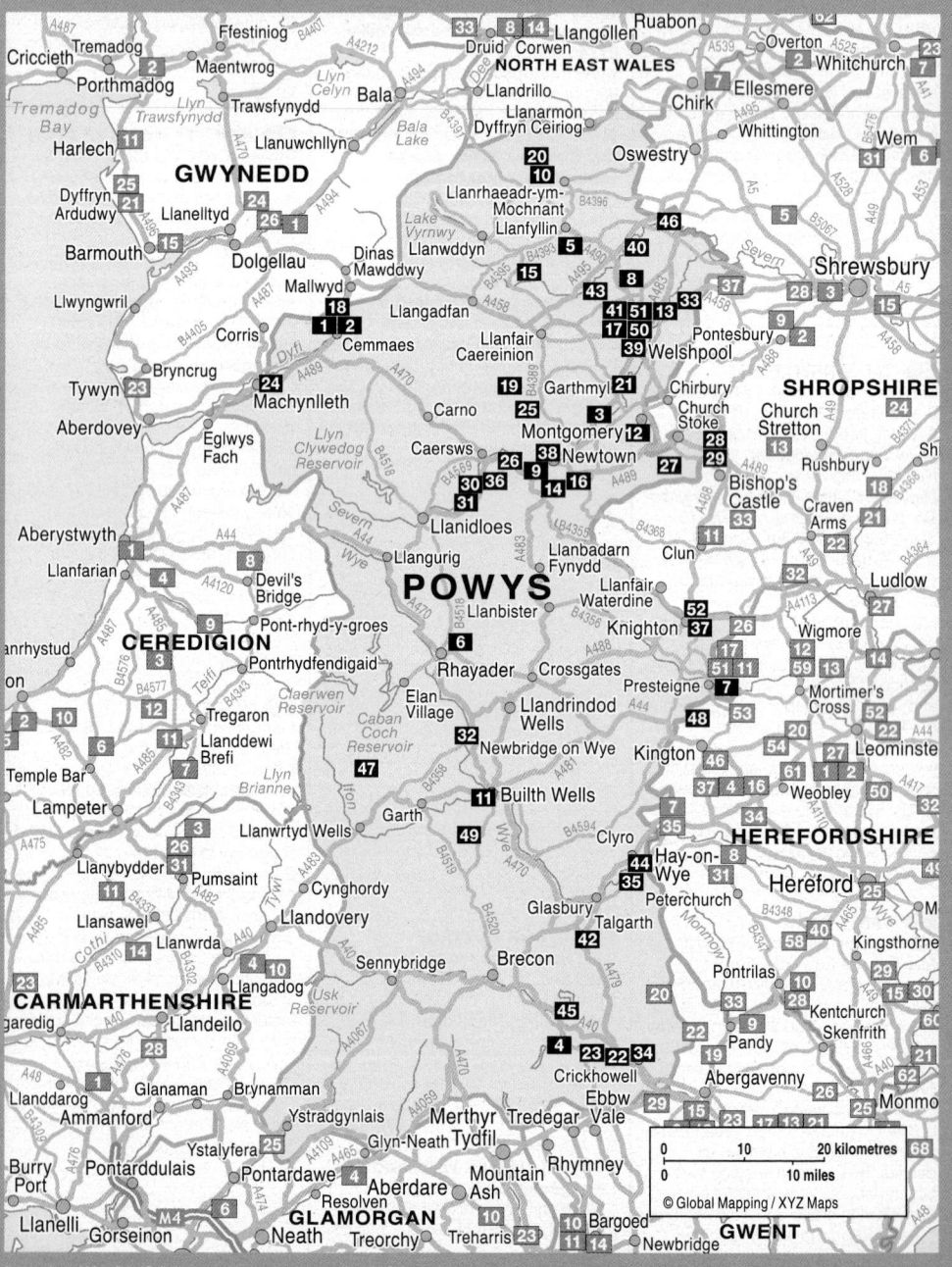

Powys

A three hour drive through Powys takes you through the spectacular and unspoilt landscape of Mid Wales, from the Berwyn Hills in the north to south of the Brecon Beacons.

Through the valleys and over the hills, beside rippling rivers and wooded ravines, you will see a lot of sheep, pretty market towns, half timbered buildings and houses of stone hewn from the land.

The stunning landscape is home to many of the beautiful NGS gardens of Powys. Some are clustered around the eastern side of the county, where Wales meets the Marches. There are a few in town centres, and the rest, both large and small, are scattered throughout this agricultural paradise.

Powis Castle, whose 18th century Italian terraces set the gold standard for the other gardens, owes much of its wealth to the farming and mining in the area. The Dingle is world-renowned for the dark, still lake at the centre of fantastic planting.

Here in Powys is the spectacular, the unusual, the peaceful and the enchanting, all opened by generous and welcoming garden owners.

Powys Volunteers

North Powys

County Organiser
Susan Paynton
01686 650531
susan.paynton@ngs.org.uk

County Treasurer
Gwyneth Jackson-Jones
01691 648578
gjacksonjones@icloud.com

Publicity
Group Captain Neil Bale
01691 648451
info@cyfiefarm.co.uk

Booklet Co-ordinator
Susan Paynton
(as above)

Assistant County Organisers
Penny Davies
01691 828373
digbydavies@aol.com

Christine Scott
01691 780080
christinemargaretscott@yahoo.com

South Powys

County Organiser
Katharine Smith
01982 551308
katharinejsmith@hotmail.co.uk

County Treasurer
Steve Carrow
01591 620461
stevetynycwm@hotmail.co.uk

Assistant County Organisers
Christine Carrow
01591 620461
stevetynycwm@hotmail.co.uk

Left: Plas Dinam

Opening Dates

All entries subject to change.
For latest information check www.ngs.org.uk

Extended openings are shown at the begining of the month

March

Sunday 27
51 Welshpool, Oak Cottage
Monday 28
51 Welshpool, Oak Cottage

April

4 Ashford House (every Tuesday)
Sunday 3
25 Gregynog Hall & Garden
Sunday 10
33 Maesfron Hall and Gardens

May

4 Ashford House (every Tuesday)
Sunday 1
51 Welshpool, Oak Cottage
Monday 2
51 Welshpool, Oak Cottage

Saturday 7
17 Dingle Nurseries & Garden
Sunday 8
17 Dingle Nurseries & Garden
Saturday 14
13 1 Church Bank
19 Fraithwen
Sunday 15
13 1 Church Bank
19 Fraithwen
Sunday 22
7 Broadheath House
22 Glanusk Estate Garden
Sunday 29
7 Broadheath House
11 Caer Beris Manor Hotel
Monday 30
32 Llysdinam

June

4 Ashford House (every Tuesday)

Festival Weekend

Saturday 4
7 Broadheath House
28 NEW Hyssington, Gorsty House
29 NEW Hyssington, The Old Barn
52 1 Ystrad House
Sunday 5
7 Broadheath House

23 Gliffaes Country House Hotel
25 Gregynog Hall & Garden
28 NEW Hyssington, Gorsty House
29 NEW Hyssington, The Old Barn
34 The Neuadd
47 Tyn y Cwm
52 1 Ystrad House
Saturday 11
10 Bryn y Llidiart
Sunday 12
10 Bryn y Llidiart
Wednesday 15
21 Glansevern Hall Gardens
Saturday 18
46 Tremynfa
Sunday 19
14 Cwm-Weeg
35 Pen-y-Maes
46 Tremynfa
Tuesday 21
39 Powis Castle Garden
Saturday 25
5 Bachie Uchaf
13 1 Church Bank
28 NEW Hyssington, Gorsty House
29 NEW Hyssington, The Old Barn
37 Pont Faen House
44 Tinto House
Sunday 26
5 Bachie Uchaf
13 1 Church Bank
28 NEW Hyssington, Gorsty House

29 NEW Hyssington, The Old Barn
37 Pont Faen House
40 Rhosddu House
44 Tinto House

July

4 Ashford House (every Tuesday)
Saturday 2
30 NEW Llandinam, Little House
31 NEW Llandinam, Neuaddllwyd
42 Talgarth Mill
Sunday 3
14 Cwm-Weeg
30 NEW Llandinam, Little House
31 NEW Llandinam, Neuaddllwyd
42 Talgarth Mill
45 Treberfydd House
Saturday 9
38 NEW Ponthafren
Saturday 16
50 NEW Welshpool, Elmhurst
51 Welshpool, Oak Cottage
Sunday 17
49 Welsh Lavender
50 NEW Welshpool, Elmhurst
51 Welshpool, Oak Cottage
Saturday 23
8 Broniarth Hall

Broadheath House

Sunday 24
- **6** Beili Neuadd
- **8** Broniarth Hall

Saturday 30
- **9** Bryn Teg

Sunday 31
- **14** Cwm-Weeg
- **16** NEW Delfryn

August

- **4** Ashford House (every Tuesday)

Saturday 6
- **19** Fraithwen
- **49** Welsh Lavender

Sunday 7
- **1** NEW Aberangell, The Old Coach House
- **2** NEW Aberangell, Pen Pentre
- **19** Fraithwen
- **47** Tyn y Cwm
- **49** Welsh Lavender

Saturday 13
- **38** NEW Ponthafren
- **52** 1 Ystrad House

Sunday 14
- **41** Rose Cottage
- **52** 1 Ystrad House

Wednesday 24
- **24** Grandma's Garden

Sunday 28
- **7** Broadheath House
- **14** Cwm-Weeg

September

- **4** Ashford House (every Tuesday)

Sunday 4
- **37** Pont Faen House

Sunday 11
- **33** Maesfron Hall and Gardens

October

Saturday 15
- **17** Dingle Nurseries & Garden

Sunday 16
- **11** Caer Beris Manor Hotel
- **17** Dingle Nurseries & Garden

Gardens open to the public

- **4** Ashford House
- **17** Dingle Nurseries & Garden
- **21** Glansevern Hall Gardens
- **24** Grandma's Garden
- **25** Gregynog Hall & Garden
- **39** Powis Castle Garden
- **49** Welsh Lavender

By arrangement only

- **3** Abernant
- **12** Castell y Gwynt
- **15** Cyfie Farm
- **18** Esgair Angell

- **20** NEW Glan yr Afon
- **26** NEW Holly Bush
- **27** Holly Cottage
- **36** Plas Dinam
- **43** Tan-y-Llyn
- **48** The Walled Garden

Also open by arrangement

- **6** Beili Neuadd
- **7** Broadheath House
- **10** Bryn y Llidiart
- **13** 1 Church Bank
- **14** Cwm-Weeg
- **19** Fraithwen
- **30** NEW Llandinam, Little House
- **32** Llysdinam
- **34** The Neuadd
- **41** Rose Cottage
- **44** Tinto House
- **52** 1 Ystrad House

The Gardens

1 NEW **ABERANGELL, THE OLD COACH HOUSE**
Aberangell, Machynlleth SY20 9AB. Sue McKillop, 01650 511333, paddy5130@gmail.com, www.theoldcoachhousecottage.co.uk. *On A470 midway beween Dolgellau & Machynlleth. From Mallwyd r'about to Cemmaes Rd, turn R after 3m just after turn for Aberangell village.* Sun 7 Aug (11-4.30). Adm £2.50, chd free. Home-made teas. Also open Aberangell Pen Pentre.
Nestled in the heart of the Dyfi Valley this small, cottage style garden is a haven for birds and pollinating insects. Narrow paths take you around the flower beds some raised, a mini meadow and little pond. Planting is informal with mostly perennials and shrubs. Secluded sitting areas allow the visitor to relax and enjoy different aspects of the garden with views down to the R Dyfi. A gravel drive and cobbled area in front of the house leads to a grassy slope into the garden. There are a few low steps within the garden.
♿ ✿ ▭ ☕

2 NEW **ABERANGELL, PEN PENTRE**
Aberangell, Machynlleth SY20 9ND. Jacqueline Parsons. *From A470, follow signs for Aberangell. Past caravan park to Xrds. Turn R, Pen Pentre is 2nd house on R.* Sun 7 Aug (11-4.30). Adm £2.50, chd free. Home-made teas. Also open Aberangell The Old Coach House.
Situated on the very southern tip of the Snowdonia National Park, this delightful cottage garden is built up around the old disused Aberangell railway station. Contains many historical artefacts from the station and the neighbouring slate tramway. The garden is on various levels, using the old station platform and railway line and also has the mighty R Dovey as one of its borders. Garden not suitable for the less mobile.
☕

3 **ABERNANT**
Garthmyl SY15 6RZ. Mrs B M Gleave, 01686 640494, john.gleave@mac.com. *On A483 midway between Welshpool & Newtown (both 8m). 1½ m S of Garthmyl. Approached over steep humpback bridge, then straight ahead through gate. No parking for coaches.* Visits by arrangement Apr to July. Adm £3.50, chd free. Light refreshments.
Approx 3 acres incl cherry orchard, roses, knot garden, lavender, box hedging, rockery, pond, shrubs, ornamental trees, raised specimen fern beds in natural setting. Examples of archaic sundials, fossilized wood and stone heads. Additional woodland of 9 acres, pond and stream with borrowed views of the Severn Valley. Late April - 90 cherry trees blossom: late June - roses. Picnics welcome.
✿ ☕

4 ◆ **ASHFORD HOUSE**
Talybont-on-Usk LD3 7YR. Mrs E Anderson, 01874 676271. *6½ m SE of Brecon. Off A40 on B4558. 1m SE of Talybont-on-Usk.* For NGS: Every Tue 5 Apr to 27 Sept (2-5). Adm £3, chd free. Tea. For other opening times and information, please phone.
1 acre walled garden surrounded by woodland and wild garden approx 4 acres altogether. Mixed shrub and herbaceous borders; meadow garden and pond; alpine house and beds; vegetables. A relaxed plantsman's garden. Weekly openings mean visitors may enjoy a peaceful garden in its everyday state. Wheelchair access to main garden only.
♿ ✿ ✿ 🚐 ☕

5 ▶ BACHIE UCHAF

**Bachie Road, Llanfyllin SY22 5NF.
Glyn & Glenys Lloyd.** *S of Llanfyllin.
Going towards Welshpool on A490
turn R onto Bachie Rd after Llanfyllin
primary school. Keep straight for
0.8m. Take drive R uphill at cottage
on L.* Sat 25, Sun 26 June (1.30-5).
Adm £4, chd free. Home-made
teas.
Inspiring, colourful hillside country
garden. Gravel paths meander around
extensive planting and over streams
cascading down into ponds.
Specimen trees, shrubs and vegetable
garden. Enjoy the wonderful views
from one of the many seats; your
senses will be rewarded.

6 ▶ BEILI NEUADD

**St Harmon, Rhayader LD6 5NS.
Alison Parker, 01597 810211,
info@beilineuadd.co.uk,
www.beilineuadd.co.uk.** *2m from
Rhayader. Take A44 E from clock
tower. Leaving Rhayader fork L
(Abbey-Cwm-Hir, Brown sign Beili
Neuadd). After 1m turn L (brown
sign). Beili Neuadd 2nd property on
R.* Sun 24 July (2-5). Adm £3, chd
free. Home-made teas. **Visits also
by arrangement June to Sept.**
2 acre garden set within a 6 acre
small holding. Established ponds,
trees and stunning landscape, set in
the foothills of the Cambrian
Mountains, provides the framework
for an exciting, evolving garden with
herbaceous borders, ponds, streams
and wooded areas. A haven for birds
and wildlife along with our flock of
Shetland sheep, rare breed pigs and
hens.

7 ▶ BROADHEATH HOUSE

**Broadheath, Presteigne LD8 2HG.
Andrea Jude, 07887 556419,
apange@aol.com,
broadheathhousegardens.co.uk.**
*2m E of Presteigne, 4m W of
Shobdon on B4362. From W turn R
into drive opp middle of common.
From E, 30 seconds after sign for
Wales turn L into drive.* Sun 22, Sun
29 May, Sat 4, Sun 5 June, Sun 28
Aug (10-6). Adm £5, chd free.
Home-made teas. **Visits also by
arrangement Apr to Oct,
individuals/groups any size
welcome, day/eve visits.**
Two acres of formal landscaped
gardens, originally designed by Sir
Clough Williams Ellis in 1925. Garden
divided into distinct rooms: the
italianate sunken garden with loggia,
rose beds and lily ponds; the secret
garden with magnolia tree and yew
hedging; yew tree walkway with
summerhouse and formal kitchen
garden with orchard and peach
house, the Nuttery and walkway to
the Hindwell Brook. Views of ancient
monument Wapley Hill Fort. Easy
access apart from some steps into
sunken garden. However, sunken
Italianate garden can be fully enjoyed
from the loggia.

8 ▶ BRONIARTH HALL

**Pentrebeirdd, Guilsfield, Welshpool
SY21 9DW. Mrs Janet Powell.** *From
Londis petrol station, Guilsfield, take
A490 towards Llanfyllin for just over
2m. Take R towards Sarnau. After 1m
turn R for Broniarth Hall.* Sat 23 July
(2-6); Sun 24 July (2.30-5). Adm
£3.50, chd free. Home-made teas.
Broniarth Hall is a C17 farm house
(not open) SE facing cottage style
garden with 2 small ponds, aviary and
perennial filled beds. Unique and
quirky features and containers incl a
collection of approx 70 heucheras.
Stunning views to be appreciated
from patio areas with summer
bedding and foliage plants.

9 ▶ BRYN TEG

**Bryn Lane, Newtown SY16 2DD.
Dolly Childs.** *N side of Newtown.
Lane on L before hospital on Llanfair
rd towards Bettws Cedewain.* Sat 30
July (11-5). Adm £3, chd free.
Home-made teas.
An exciting walk through the jungle in
Newtown! High above the head are
banana leaves and colourful climbers.
An exotic Caribbean garden planted
to remind me of my childhood. A
winding path from the front door
around the side of the house to the
back door takes you on a journey
through another land. Featured in
County Times.

10 ▶ BRYN Y LLIDIART

**Cefn Coch, Llanrhaeadr ym
Mochnant, Oswestry SY10 0BP.
Dr John & Mrs Christine Scott,
01691 780080,
christinemargaretscott@yahoo.com.**
*2m W of Llanrhaeadr ym Mochnant.
On rd between Llanrhaeadr village &
Penybontfawr. Follow yellow NGS
signs up hill on single track rd for 1m.*
Sat 11, Sun 12 June (2-5). Adm
£4.50, chd free. Home-made teas.
**Visits also by arrangement May to
Sept.**
Up the airy mountain you are in for a
big surprise! On S facing lee of
Berwyns at 1100ft with spectacular
views, meander mown paths through
8 acres of wildflower meadows to
discover lush planting around house.
Stone walls, boulders, slate and shale
reflect the landscape. Extensive green
roof, sitouterie in Welsh orchard, bog
garden, wildlife pond and vegetables.
Good footwear required. Partial
wheelchair access, shale and rough
grass paths, some steps.

11 ▶ CAER BERIS MANOR HOTEL

**Builth Wells LD2 3NP. Mr Peter &
Mrs Katharine Smith, 01982
552601, caerberis@btconnect.com,
www.caerberis.com.** *W edge Builth
Wells. From Builth Wells town centre
take A483 signed Llandovery. Caer
Beris Manor is on L as you leave
Builth.* Sun 29 May (11-5.30); Sun
16 Oct (11-4). Adm £4, chd free.
Home-made teas.
An original 1927 NGS pioneer
garden. 27 acres of mature
parklands, with the R Irfon bordering
the property. The grounds were
planted early C20 by the Vivien family
who were plant hunters. Many varied
specimen trees form an Arboretum.
Large displays of rhododendrons at
time of opening. An Edwardian Rose
archway has been recently replanted
with David Austin roses. Concert by
Builth Wells Ladies Voice Choir.
Sunday lunches and afternoon teas
available. Lower parkland can be
accessed by car or wheelchair.

12 ▶ CASTELL Y GWYNT

**Llandyssil, Montgomery SY15 6HR.
John & Jacqui Wynn-Jones, 01686
668569, jacquiwj@btinternet.com.**
*2m out of Montgomery on the Sarn
Rd, 1st R, 1st R.* **Visits by
arrangement May to July, prior
booking necessary as parking**

limited. **Adm £5, chd free.**
1½ acre garden at 900ft, set within 6 acres of land managed for wildlife. Native woodland corridors with mown rides surround hayfield/wildflower meadow and pool with turf roofed summerhouse. Enclosed kitchen garden with boxed beds of vegetables, fruit and cutting flowers, greenhouse and orchard. Shrubberies, deep mixed borders and more formal areas close to house. Outstanding views of Welsh mountains. Circular path around the whole property which gives unique views of the house, garden and surrounding countryside. Bring good footwear and enjoy the walk.

13 1 CHURCH BANK
Welshpool SY21 7DR. Mel & Heather Parkes, 01938 559112, melandheather@live.co.uk. *Centre of Welshpool. Church Bank leads onto Salop Rd from Church St. Follow one way system, use main car park then short walk. Follow yellow NGS signs.* **Sat 14, Sun 15 May, Sat 25, Sun 26 June (12-5). Adm £3.50, chd free. Home-made teas. Visits also by arrangement Apr to Sept, groups 6+.**
A jewel in the town. Walk through the ground floor of this C17 town house into a large garden room which also houses a museum of tools from different trades. Mystic pool of smoke and sounds. Outside a Gothic arch and zig zag path leads to a shell grotto and bonzai garden, fernery and many unusual features. Sounds of water fill the air and interesting plants fill the intimate space. Children's garden quiz. Featured in Garden News.

14 CWM-WEEG
Dolfor, Newtown SY16 4AT. Dr W Schaefer & Mr K D George, 01686 628992, wolfgang@cwmweeg.co.uk, www.cwmweeg.co.uk. *4½ m SE of Newtown. Take A489 E from Newtown for 1½ m, turn R towards Dolfor. After 2m turn L down farm track, signed at entrance. N.B. Do not rely on SatNav. Also signed from Dolfor village. Coaches (max 33 seater).* **Suns 19 June, 3, 31 July, Sun 28 Aug (2-5). Adm £4, chd free. Home-made teas. Visits also by arrangement June to Aug.**
2½ acre garden set within 24 acres of wildflower meadows and bluebell

woodland with stream centred around C15 farmhouse (open by prior arrangement). Formal garden in English landscape tradition with vistas, grottos, sculptures, lawns and extensive borders terraced with stone walls. Translates older garden vocabulary into an innovative C21 concept. Under cover area for refreshments if wet. House open by arrangement. Featured in a number of TV programmes. Partial wheelchair access.

Linger on a seat and enjoy the garden with views and sounds of the church . . .

15 CYFIE FARM
Llanfihangel, Llanfyllin SY22 5JE. Group Captain Neil & Mrs Claire Bale, 01691 648451, info@cyfiefarm.co.uk, www.cyfiefarm.co.uk. *6m SE of Lake Vyrnwy. ½ m N Llanfyllin on B490 turn L B4393 towards L Vrynwy. 4m turn L B4382 signed Llanfihangel go straight through, 1½ m, 1st L, 3rd on L.* **Visits by arrangement Apr to Oct. Adm £4, chd free. Cheese and nibbles or teas.**
Beautiful 1 acre hillside garden with spectacular views of Vyrnwy valley and Welsh hills. Linger over the roses or wander through the woodland garden with rhododendrons and bluebell banks. Many places to sit and contemplate the stunning views. Wildflower meadow and garden sculptures. Unusual garden statues. Spectacular views, peaceful setting. Partial wheelchair access.

16 NEW DELFRYN
5 Chestnut View, Kerry, Newtown SY16 4PR. John & Stella Roberts. *Newtown 3m. A489 from Newtown to Kerry. Turn R at The Herbert Arms. Chestnut View is 2nd L after zebra crossing, then follow yellow NGS signs.* **Sun 31 July (1-6). Adm £3, chd free. Home-made teas.**
Small intricate garden with bountiful brightly coloured borders. Quirky

features, sink gardens, lots of plant variety incl perennials, shrubs and bulbs. Large collection of Sempervivums, miniature stumpery/fernery. Linger on a seat and enjoy the garden with views and sounds of the church. Additional parking in Village Hall car park behind Herbert Arms. Flat garden, with lawn and stepping stones. Disabled parking outside house.

17 ◆ DINGLE NURSERIES & GARDEN
Welshpool SY21 9JD. Mr & Mrs D Hamer, 01938 555145, www.dinglenurseries.co.uk. *2m NW of Welshpool. Take A490 towards Llanfyllin & Guilsfield. After 1m turn L at sign for Dingle Nurseries & Garden.* **For NGS: Sat 7, Sun 8 May, Sat 15, Sun 16 Oct (9-5). Adm £3.50, chd free. For other opening times and information, please phone or visit garden website.**
RHS recommended 4½ acre garden on S facing site, sloping down to lakes surrounded by yr-round interest. Beds mostly colour themed with a huge variety of rare and unusual trees, ornamental shrubs and herbaceous plants. Set in hills of mid Wales this beautiful and well known garden attracts visitors from Britain and abroad. Open all yr except 24 Dec - 2 Jan.

18 ESGAIR ANGELL
Aberangell, Machynlleth SY20 9QJ. Carole Jones, 01650 511176, jonesey200@gmail.com, www.upperbarncottage.co.uk. *Midway between Dogellau & Machynlleth. Turn off A470 towards village of Aberangell, then signed.* **Visits by arrangement May to July for groups 10+. Adm £4.50, chd free. Home-made teas.**
The garden extends to over 2 acres just above the R Angell, within the Dovey Forest and Snowdonia National Park. Around the central lake, which supports an abundance of plant and animal life, is a small wood, a wildlife meadow, vegetable garden and the aviaries that house our families of owls. New for 2016 - a second lake and a circular walk through the neighbouring fields with spectacular views. Partial wheelchair access, mainly laid to lawn. Access on gravelled area above lake affording excellent views.

Holly Cottage

lavenders, salvias, roses and peonies, a gazebo by the river, rose swags, Sunray pergola, woodland path, riverside walk. Shelter available if wet. Gravel footpath on riverside walk.

19 ▶ FRAITHWEN
Tregynon SY16 3EW. Sydney Thomas, 01686 650307. *6m N of Newtown. On B4389 midway between villages of Bettws Cedewain & Tregynon.* Sat 14, Sun 15 May, Sat 6, Sun 7 Aug (2-5). Adm £3.50, chd free. **Visits also by arrangement Feb to Oct.**

1½ acre established garden with herbaceous borders, rockeries and ponds. Planted with rare plants for yr-round interest. Plants in flower every day of the year: spring bulbs and alpines, alstroemeria collection, lilies in garden not pots, vegetable plot and newly refurbished pool. Partial wheelchair access. Some steps, gravel and slopes.

53 NEW ▶ GARTHMYL HALL
Garthmyl, Montgomery SY15 6RS. Julie Pugh www.garthmylhall.co.uk. *On A483 midway between Welshpool & Newtown (both 8m). Turn R 200yrds S of Nag's Head PH.* Sun 31 July, Mon 1 Aug (11-4.30). Adm £3.50, chd free. Cream teas.

Grade II listed Georgian manor house (partially open) surrounded by 5 acres of grounds currently under

restoration. Over 100 metres newly planted herbaceous borders, 1 acre walled garden, fountain, 3 magnificent Cedar of Lebanon, giant redwood. Teas served in drawing room if wet. Partial wheelchair access. Accessible WC.

20 NEW ▶ GLAN YR AFON
Commins, Llanrhaeadr Ym Mochnant, Oswestry SY10 0BZ. Brian & Marian Jones, 01691 780479, jones.brian.c@btinternet.com, www.pistyllrhaeadrholidays.com. *15m NW Welshpool, 15m W of Oswestry. From Greatorex corner store 1.6m along Waterfall Rd. Single track rd take 1st L turn at white cottage. Sign at top of drive Riverside Retreat.* Visits by arrangement June to Sept (Mons and Weds only) (2-5). Cars 10 max. Parking very limited. Adm £4, chd free. Home-made teas.

Situated in the valley stretching from the famous 240ft Pistyll Rhaeadr Waterfall to Llanrhaeadr Village. A tranquil, romantic location with the R Rhaeadr flowing through the length of the 2 acre garden. Lawn surrounded by cottage garden planting, with

21 ◆ GLANSEVERN HALL GARDENS
Berriew, Welshpool SY21 8AH. The Owen Family, 01686 640644, www.glansevern.co.uk. *5m SW of Welshpool. On A483 between Newtown & Welshpool, clearly marked on brown tourist signs.* For NGS: Wed 15 June (10.30-5). Adm £7, chd £3.50. Home-made teas. **For other opening times and information, please phone or visit garden website.**

Beautiful Greek revival house (not open) set in mature parkland with rare and ancient trees. 25 acres of gardens incl walled garden of rooms, vegetable garden, original potting shed, Victorian grotto and orangery. Wysteria scented fountain walk, 4 acre lake with shady seating areas, folly island and wildfowl. Birdhide on banks of R Severn and R Rhiw. Featured in Shropshire Star and County Times as RHS Partner garden. Some parts of the garden will be difficult for wheelchairs.

22 ▶ GLANUSK ESTATE GARDEN
The Glanusk Estate, Crickhowell NP8 1LP. Mrs Harry Legge-Bourke, 01873 810414, Robyn@glanuskestate.com, www.glanuskestate.com. *2m NW of Crickhowell. Please access open garden via main estate entrance off A40 & follow signs to car park.* Sun 22 May (11-4). Adm £6.50, chd free. Light refreshments.

The garden is adorned with many established plant species such as rhododendrons, azaleas, acers, amelia, magnolia, prunus and dogwood giving a vast array of colour in the spring and summer months. The Glanusk Estate Garden Fayre will feature exhibits of works for sale from over 25 craftsmen and artists such as traditional quilts, botanical prints, handmade gifts, bespoke furniture, slate ware and wood turning, and a selection of gardening books. There will be a presentation of slides from the private archives in the family Rod Room throughout the day, delicious food for sale, and the private Penmyarth church will be open. Updates about the Glanusk Estate

Garden Fayre and NGS Open Gardens will be posted on our website, facebook and twitter pages.

23 GLIFFAES COUNTRY HOUSE HOTEL

Gliffaes Rd, Crickhowell NP8 1RH. Mrs N Brabner & Mr & Mrs J C Suter, 01874 730 371, calls@gliffaeshotel.com, www.gliffaes.com. *3½ m W of Crickhowell. 1m off A40, 2½ m W of Crickhowell.* Sun 5 June (2-5). Adm £4.50, chd free. Cream teas.

The Gliffaes gardens lie in a dream position on a plateau 120ft above the spectacular fast flowing R Usk. As well as breath taking views of the Brecon Beacons and 33 acres of parkland and lawns there are ancient and ornamental trees, fine maples, new tree plantings, spring bulbs, rhododendrons, azaleas, many shrubs and an ornamental pond. Gliffaes is a country house hotel and is open for lunch, bar snacks, afternoon tea and dinner to non residents and garden visitors. Wheelchair ramp to the west side of the hotel. In dry weather main lawns accessible, but more difficult if wet.

24 ◆ GRANDMA'S GARDEN

Dolguog Estates, Felingerrig, Machynlleth SY20 8UJ. Richard Rhodes, 01654 702244, info@plasdolguog.co.uk, www.plasdolguog.co.uk. *1½ m E of Machynlleth. Turn L off A489 Machynlleth to Newtown rd. Follow brown tourist signs to Plas Dolguog Hotel.* For NGS: Wed 24 Aug (10.30-4.30). Adm £4, chd free. Light refreshments. For other opening times and information, please phone, email or visit garden website.

Inspiration for the senses, unique, fascinating, educational and fun. Strategic seating, continuous new attractions, wildlife abundant, 9 acres of peace. Sculptures, poetry arboretum. Seven sensory gardens, wildlife pond, riverside boardwalk, stone circle, labyrinth. Azaleas and bluebells in May. Children welcome. Open every Sun and Wed (10.30-4.30). Cream teas. Plas Dolguog Hotel open their café in the conservatory - the hotel is the admission point - serving inside and out on patio overlooking gardens.

25 ◆ GREGYNOG HALL & GARDEN

Tregynon, Newtown SY16 3PW. Gregynog, 01686 650224, enquiries@gregynog.org, www.gregynog.org. *5m N of Newtown. From main A483, take turning for Berriew. In Berriew follow sign for Bettws then for Tregynon (£2.50 car parking charge applies).* For NGS: Sun 3 Apr, Sun 5 June (11-4). Adm £3, chd £1. For other opening times and information, please phone, email or visit garden website.

Grade I listed garden set within 750 acres of Gregynog Estate which was designated a National Nature Reserve in 2013. Fountains, lily lake and water garden. A mass display of rhododendrons and yew hedge create a spectacular backdrop to the sunken lawns. Thousands of daffodils in Spring. Courtyard café serving morning coffee, light lunches and Welsh afternoon teas. Some gravel paths.

Inspiration for the senses, unique, fascinating, educational and fun . . .

26 NEW HOLLY BUSH

Mochdre, Newtown SY16 4LB. Douglas & Jane Wood, 01686 623154, douglas_jane_wood@yahoo.co.uk. *3m out of Newtown on A470 for Llanidloes, over College r'about for 1m turn L into narrow lane by letterbox, NGS sign on post, house at top of steep lane.* Visits by arrangement in June, very limited parking, max 6 cars. Adm £3, chd free. Light refreshments.

A garden in the making, lawn and flower beds surround the house, with views NE over the R Severn valley, Steps to lower lawn, rose bed, and day lilies. Field with young specimen trees and pond: wet area with mown path and wild orchids. Fields with orchard and daffodils in spring followed by bluebells. Good footwear required.

27 HOLLY COTTAGE

Great Argoed, Mellington, Nr Churchstoke SY15 6TH. Martin & Allison Walter, 01588 620055, allison.walter2@btinternet.com. *On Powys/Shropshire border, 5m from Bishops Castle & Montgomery, 1m off B4385 at Mellington. B4385 runs between Bishops Castle & Brompton Xrds with A489 Churchstoke to Newtown rd. Take minor rd off B4385 at Courthouse Farm at Mellington. Follow yellow NGS signs to Great Argoed, approx 1m.* Visits by arrangement Apr to Aug, single visitors/small groups (25 max) welcome. Adm £4, chd free. Home-made teas or wine and nibbles available.

Started from scratch in 2007, this naturalistic garden at 800ft has spectacular views; 80m long perennial/wildflower border; Tree Bank with 30+ fruit and ornamental trees, 2000+ spring bulbs and further developing wildflower/perennial planting. Colourful planting around house: walled terrace cascading with flowers, alpine bank, fruit and flower garden; Welsh slate garden; spring wildflower bank. Many levels and steps with places to sit and enjoy the views which are from every direction, including a sunken seating area. A still developing garden. Not suitable for the less mobile.

28 NEW HYSSINGTON, GORSTY HOUSE

Hyssington, Montgomery SY15 6AT. Gary & Annie Frost. *A488 N from Bishop's Castle. Approx 3½ m, turn L (signed Churchstoke & Hyssington), then follow yellow NGS signs. Also signed A489 E from Churchstoke. Please park at Village Hall.* Sat 4, Sun 5, Sat 25, Sun 26 June (1-5). Combined adm with Hyssington Old Barn £5, chd free. Home-made teas.

A new renovation, started late in 2014, of a neglected garden. Just over 2 acres, an acre of which is wildflower meadow. We are planting to attract wildlife, with wooded and shady areas, herbaceous borders, new orchard, wildlife pond, and a secret garden, planted to encourage pollinators. Lovely views. This is a new garden, so planting is still immature, but it still offers plenty to see!

29 NEW▶ HYSSINGTON, THE OLD BARN

Hyssington, Montgomery SY15 6AT. Avril & Stuart Dickinson. *A488 N from Bishop's Castle. Approx 3½ m, turn L (signed Churchstoke & Hyssington), then follow yellow NGS signs. Also signed A489 E from Churchstoke. Please park at Village Hall.* Sat 4, Sun 5, Sat 25, Sun 26 June (1-5). Combined adm with Hyssington Gorsty House £5, chd free.

A peaceful ½ acre hideaway with winding paths and archways leading to colourful mixed borders with evergreens and mature trees, incl a handkerchief tree. There is a wildlife pond, summerhouse and vegetable and soft fruit areas. ☕

30 NEW▶ LLANDINAM, LITTLE HOUSE

Llandinam SY17 5BH. Peter & Pat Ashcroft, 07443 524128, littlehouse1692@gmail.com. *1m from Llandinam Lion Hotel. Cross river at statue of David Davies on A470 in Llandinam. Follow rd for just under 1m, Little House is black & white cottage on roadside. Limited parking.* Sat 2, Sun 3 July (1-5). Combined adm with Llandinam Neuaddllwyd £5, chd free. Visits also by arrangement June & July (Tues only). Donation to Montgomery Wildlife Trust. Tea/coffee by request.

Little House is on a quiet lane surrounded by fields and woodland, bordered by a stream. The ⅓ acre garden has evolved over 6yrs. Planting incl shrubs, grasses, conifers, azaleas, herbaceous perennials, ferns, bulbs and self sown seedlings vying for space. Varied habitats incl fish and wildlife ponds, bog, woodland, damp shade and mini meadow areas plus a vegetable garden with raised beds. ❀ ☕

31 NEW▶ LLANDINAM, NEUADDLLWYD

Llandinam SY17 5AU. Roger & Pat Scull. *Take A470 to Llandinam, turn off main rd over bridge by statue. Take 1st lane on L, follow track for ¾ m. Garden on L. Do not use SatNav.* Sat 2, Sun 3 July (1-5). Combined adm with Llandinam Little House £5, chd free. Light refreshments.

1 acre garden set within 4 acres of wildlife meadows around C19 Grade II listed farmhouse (not open). Shrub and herbaceous borders, lawn leading down to R Severn with magnificent views to hills beyond. Garden in process of renovation. Recently reclaimed cottage garden, old orchard, pond, a wooded area and a small allotment used by Llandinam Village. Species Habitat Group will be in attendance to explain their work. ☕

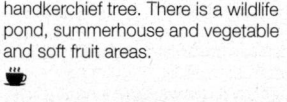

Sensory garden with long grasses, herbs, scented plants and shrubs. . . .

32▶ LLYSDINAM

Newbridge-on-Wye LD1 6NB. Sir John & Lady Venables-Llewelyn & Llysdinam Charitable Trust, 01597 860190, llethr@outlook.com, llysdinamgardens.co.uk. *5m SW of Llandrindod Wells. Turn W off A470 at Newbridge-on-Wye; turn R immed after crossing R Wye; entrance up hill.* Mon 30 May (2-5). Adm £4, chd free. Cream teas. Visits also by arrangement, conducted tours/refreshments for groups 15+.

Llysdinam Gardens are among the loveliest in Mid Wales, especially noted for a magnificent display of rhododendrons and azaleas in May. Covering some 6 acres in all, they command sweeping views down the Wye Valley. Successive family members have developed the gardens over the last 150yrs to incl woodland with specimen trees, large herbaceous and shrub borders and a water garden, all of which provide varied and colourful planting throughout the yr. The Victorian walled kitchen garden and extensive greenhouses grow a wide variety of vegetables, hothouse fruit, and exotic plants. Gravel paths. ♿ 🏠 ❀ 🚐 ☕

33▶ MAESFRON HALL AND GARDENS

Trewern, Welshpool SY21 8EA. Dr & Mrs TD Owen, www.maesfron.co.uk. *4m E of Welshpool. On N side of A458 Welshpool to Shrewsbury Rd.* Sun 10 Apr, Sun 11 Sept (2-5). Adm £4, chd free. Home-made teas.

Georgian house (partly open) built in Italian villa style set in 4 acres of S facing gardens on lower slopes of Moel-y-Golfa with panoramic views of The Long Mountain. Terraces, walled kitchen garden, tropical garden, restored Victorian conservatories, tower and shell grotto. Newly restored hanging gardens down rock face below tower. Woodland and parkland walks with a wide variety of trees. Some gravel, steps and slopes. ♿ 🏠 ☕

34▶ THE NEUADD

Llanbedr, Crickhowell NP8 1SP. Robin & Philippa Herbert, 01873 812164, philippahherbert@gmail.com. *1m NE of Crickhowell. Leave Crickhowell by Llanbedr Rd. At junction with Great Oak Rd bear L, cont up hill for approx 1m, garden on L. Ample parking.* Sun 5 June (2-6). Adm £4.50, chd free. Home-made teas. Visits by arrangement May to Aug. Adm £4.50, chd free. Light refreshments.

Robin and Philippa Herbert have worked on the restoration of the garden at The Neuadd since 1999 and have planted a wide range of unusual trees and shrubs in the dramatic setting of the Brecon Beacons National Park. One of the major features is the walled garden, which has both traditional and decorative planting of fruit, vegetables and flowers. There is also a woodland walk with ponds, streams and a formal garden with flowering terraces. Water and spectacular views. The owner uses a wheelchair and most of the garden is accessible, but some steep paths. ♿ 🏠 ❀ ☕

35▶ PEN-Y-MAES

Hay-on-Wye HR3 5PP. Shân Egerton. *1m SW of Hay-on-Wye. On B4350 towards Hay from Brecon. 2½ m from Glasbury.* Sun 19 June (2-5). Adm £5, chd free. Home-made teas.

2 acre garden incl mixed and herbaceous borders; topiary; walled formal kitchen garden; shrub, modern and climbing roses, peony borders, espaliered pears. Fine mulberry. Beautiful dry stone walling and mature trees. Great double view of Black Mountains and the Brecon Beacons. Emphasis on foliage and shape. Artist's garden. ♿ 🏠 ❀ 🚐 ☕

36 PLAS DINAM

Llandinam SY17 5DQ. Eldrydd Lamp, 07415 503554, eldrydd@plasdinam.co.uk, www.plasdinamcountryhouse. co.uk. *7¹/₂ m SW Newtown. on A470 Visits by arrangement Mar to Nov for groups 10+ (weekdays only, excl school holidays). Home-made teas.*
12 acres of fabulous gardens, lawns and woodland set at the foot of glorious rolling hills with spectacular views across the Severn Valley. Parkland setting. Spring: hundreds of daffodils; May to July: wildflower meadows with wild orchids; Autumn: glorious colour. From 1884 until recently the home of Lord Davies and his family (house not open).

37 PONT FAEN HOUSE

Farrington Lane, Knighton LD7 1LA. Mr John & Mrs Brenda Morgan. *S of Knighton off Ludlow Rd. W from Ludlow on A4113 into Knighton. 1st L after 20mph sign before school. Sat 25, Sun 26 June, Sun 4 Sept (1-4.30). Adm £3.50, chd free. Home-made teas.*
Colourful ¹/₂ acre garden, full of flowers, surrounds house on edge of town. Paths through floriferous arches and gazebos lead from shady, ferny corners to deep borders filled with a large range of colourful perennials, annuals, 40 varieties of roses, rhododendrons, azaleas and hydrangeas. Water features and a fish pond. Enjoy the views of the hills beyond from many seats in this flat garden. Sept; full of colourful flowers, alstroemerias, rudbeckias, inulas. Featured in local publications. disabled parking in garden.

38 NEW PONTHAFREN

Long Bridge Street, Newtown SY16 2DY. Janet Rogers (volunteer gardener), 01686 621586, www.ponthafren.org. *Park in main car park in town centre, 5 mins walk. Turn L out of car park, turn L over bridge, garden on L. Limited disabled parking, please phone for details. Sat 9 July, Sat 13 Aug (10-4). Adm by donation. Light refreshments.*
Ponthafren is a registered charity for people with mental health issues or those that feel lonely or isolated. We have an open door policy so everyone is welcome. Our beautiful, community garden is on the banks of the R Severn. Sensory garden with long grasses, herbs, scented plants and shrubs. Productive vegetable plot. Our gardens are run and maintained totally by volunteers. Seating areas positioned around the garden so you can sit and enjoy the views. Featured on BBC Glorious Gardens from Above and visited by Nick Clegg and Jane Dodd. Some of the garden is accessible to wheelchairs.

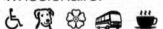

39 ◆ POWIS CASTLE GARDEN

Welshpool SY21 8RF. National Trust, 01938 551929, www.nationaltrust.org.uk. *1m S of Welshpool. From Welshpool take A490 S towards Newtown. After ³/₄ m turn R into Red Lane. Cont up lane for ¹/₄ m & turn R into property. For NGS: Tue 21 June (10-5). Adm £8.96, chd £4.48. Light refreshments. For other opening times and information, please phone or visit garden website.*
Laid out in early C18 the garden features the finest remaining examples of Italian terraces in Britain. Richly planted herbaceous borders; enormous yew hedges; lead statuary, orangery and large wild flower areas. One of the NT's finest gardens. National Collection of *Laburnum*. Short introductory talks about the castle and garden run throughout the day. Refreshments served in Courtyard Restaurant and Garden Coffee Shop. Featured on Countryfile. Step free route around the garden, gravel paths, due to steep slopes only 4 wheeled PMV's permitted.

 **NPC**

40 RHOSDDU HOUSE

Llansantffraid SY22 6TH. Margaret Clennett & Peter Stokes. *3m SSW of Llansantffraid. From Welshpool on A490 after 7m turn R (signed Trefnannau) at L bend. After ¹/₂ m take 1st L & cont on winding lane for 1¹/₂ m. Sun 26 June (2.30-5.30). Adm £3.50, chd free. Tea.*
1 acre informal rural garden with views of the Vrynwy valley. Wildlife pond, mixed island beds, extensive vegetable plot, orchard, young and mature ornamental trees. Exhibition of paintings by Penrhos Art Group. No hard paths, grass throughout.

41 ROSE COTTAGE

Cloddiau, Welshpool SY21 9JE. Peter & Frances Grassi, 01938 553723, effgrassi@gmail.com. *3m N of Welshpool. Take A490 towards Guilsfield & Llanfyllin. After 1m turn L at sign for Dingle Nurseries & follow yellow NGS signs. Sun 14 Aug (2-5.30). Adm £4, chd free. Home-made teas.* **Visits also by arrangement in Aug.**
S facing 1 acre garden set in wooded valley and bordered by farmland. Small stream meanders through site, dammed to form pools teeming with wildlife. Stylish summerhouse at pool edge, elegant fruit cage, rustic archways, bespoke chicken hut all add extra interest to informal ribbon borders, raised beds, vegetable plots and cutting garden. Wheelchair access to most of garden with help. No access to WC.

42 TALGARTH MILL

The Square, Talgarth, Brecon LD3 0BW. Talgarth Mill, www.talgarthmill.com. *In centre of Talgarth. Park in free car park opp rugby club, turn L out of car park entrance, follow high st to end, cross bridge, the Mill is on your R. Sat 2, Sun 3 July (10-4). Adm £5, chd free. Light refreshments.*
A pretty riverside garden, maintained by volunteers. Along the riverside there is mixed herbaceous planting, a shady area, and steps up to a productive garden with espalier fruit trees, vegetables, soft fruits and a wildlife area. Places to sit and watch the river and its bird life (dippers, wagtails, kingfishers, herons) and the mill wheel turning. Garden is part of a working water mill. Tour explaining how we use water power to mill our wide range of flours. Award winning cafe and bakery which champions local, seasonal produce, gourmet coffee and tea. Open 10-4pm. Garden can be accessed by lift. Wide, flat paths for wheelchair access.

43 TAN-Y-LLYN

Meiod SY22 6YB. Callum Johnston & Brenda Moor, 01938 500370, admin@tanyllyn-nurseries.co.uk, www.tanyllyn-nursery.co.uk. *1m SE of Meifod. From Oswestry on A495 turn L in village, cross R Vyrnwy & climb hill for ¹/₂ m. From Welshpool on A490 look for Meifod sign on L just past Groesllwyd.* **Visits by arrangement Jan - Dec. Adm by donation.**
The garden sits on the side of Broniarth Hill above the Vyrnwy Valley. Shrubs and perennials border the grass paths running along the contours: wild hedges are punctuated with porthole views before merging into the surrounding woodland. The garden hovers between clipped control and barely tamed nature. It is 550ft up, S facing and sheltered; the soil is well drained, slightly acid clay loam.

44 TINTO HOUSE

13 Broad Street, Hay-on-Wye HR3 5DB. Karen & John Clare, 01497 821556, tintohouse13@gmail.com, www.tinto-house.co.uk. *Tinto House faces the clocktower in the centre of Hay-on-Wye. Entrance to garden is through the coach arch.* Sat 25, Sun 26 June (2-5). Adm £3.50, chd free. Home-made teas. **Visits also by arrangement Apr to Sept.**
Tinto House is a hidden treasure in Hay. Beyond the Georgian townhouse lies an extensive traditional English garden overlooking the R Wye. It is divided into different rooms, each with its own character, featuring a wide range of plants incl climbing and shrub roses, clematis, hardy perennials and annuals. The vegetable garden is stocked with a wide range of soft fruit and vegetables. Art gallery. Home-made afternoon tea served in the garden. Wheelchair users may require some assistance as entrance is via a cobble courtyard.

45 TREBERFYDD HOUSE

Llangasty, Bwlch, Brecon LD3 7PX. David Raikes & Carla Rapoport, www.treberfydd.com. *6m E of Brecon. From Abergavenny on A40, turn R in Bwlch on B5460. Take 1st turning L towards Pennorth & cont 2m along lane. From Brecon, turn L off A40 towards Pennorth in*

Llanhamlach. Sun 3 July (1-5.30). Adm £3.50, chd free. Home-made teas.
Grade 1 listed Victorian Gothic house with 10 acres of grounds designed by W A Nesfield. Magnificent Cedar of Lebanon, avenue of mature Beech, towering Atlantic Cedars, Victorian rockery, herbaceous border and manicured lawns ideal for a picnic. Wonderful views of the Black Mountains. Plants available from Commercial Nursery in grounds - Walled Garden Treberfydd. House tours every half hour (additional £2), last tour 4pm.

Spectacular views in all directions . . . .

46 TREMYNFA

Carreghofa Lane, Llanymynech SY22 6LA. Jon & Gillian Fynes. *Edge of Llanymynech village. From N leave Oswestry on A483 to Welshpool. In Llanymynech turn R at Xrds (car wash on corner). Take 2nd R then follow yellow NGS signs. 300 yds park signed field, limited disabled parking nr garden.* Sat 18, Sun 19 June (1-5). Adm £4, chd free. Light refreshments.
S facing 1 acre garden developed over 8yrs. Old railway cottage set in herbaceous and raised borders, patio with many pots of colourful and unusual plants. Garden slopes down to productive fruit and vegetable area, ponds, spinney, wild areas and peat bog. Patio and seats to enjoy extensive views incl Llanymynech rocks and surrounding farmland. Pet ducks on site. Montgomery canal close by. 100s of home grown plants for sale. Featured in Amateur Gardening Magazine.

47 TYN Y CWM

Beulah, Llanwrtyd Wells LD5 4TS. Steve & Christine Carrow, 01591 620461, stevetynycwm@hotmail.co.uk. *10m W of Builth Wells. On A483 at Beulah take rd towards Abergwesyn for 2m. Drive drops down to L.* Sun 5 June,

Sun 7 Aug (2-5.30). Adm £3.50, chd free. Home-made teas.
Garden mainly started 14yrs ago, lower garden has spring/woodland area, raised beds mixed with vegetables, fruit trees, fruit and flowers. Perennial borders, summer house gravel paths through rose and clematis pergola. Upper garden, partly sloped, incl bog, winter, water gardens and perennial beds with unusual slate steps. Beautiful views. Property bounded by small river. Craft Stall. Lower garden has wide gravel mainly level paths. Upper garden is grassed with slopes and not suitable for wheelchairs.

48 THE WALLED GARDEN

Knill, nr Presteigne LD8 2PR. Dame Margaret Anstee, 01544 267411, agapanthus1@btinternet.com. *3m SW of Presteigne. B4362 Walton-Presteigne rd. In Knill village turn R over cattle grid, keep R down drive. SatNav stops short of property. Coaches park up hill by church.* **Visits by arrangement. Adm £4, chd free.**
4 acres: walled garden; river, bog garden and small grotto; primulas; over 100 varieties of roses, shrub, modern and climbing; peonies; mixed and herbaceous borders; many varieties of shrubs and mature trees; lovely spring garden. Nr C13 church in beautiful valley. The Walled Garden figures in the Macmillan Calendar for 2016. Most of main garden accessible to wheelchairs.

49 ◆ WELSH LAVENDER

Cefnperfedd Uchaf, Maesmynis, Builth Wells LD2 3HU. Nancy Durham & Bill Newton-Smith, 01982 552467, farmers@welshlavender.com, www.welshlavender.com. *Approx 4¹/₂ m S of Builth Wells & 12m from Brecon Cathedral off B4520.* For NGS: Sun 17 July, Sat 6, Sun 7 Aug (11.30-6). Adm £3.50, chd free. Tea. **For other opening times and information, please phone, email or visit garden website.**
Our 10,000 lavenders grow high in the hills of mid-Wales. We distil the Grosso variety to produce essential oil. At 1100 feet our growing season is short and challenging. Flower beds around the house are colourful and unpredictable. Spectacular views in all directions. Visitors are welcome to roam the lavender fields, see how the

Llandinam, Little House

distillation process works, and visit the farm shop to try body creams and other potions made with lavender oil distilled on the farm. 10% of sales go to the NGS. Coffee, tea, wine and light refreshments available. Talked about in Tatler, Country Living, House and Garden, Sunday Times Style Magazine and featured in BBC, S4C, ITV and Monocle Films. Partial wheelchair access. Large paved area adjacent to tea and shop area easy to negotiate.

50 NEW WELSHPOOL, ELMHURST

Severn Road, Welshpool SY21 7AR. Tony Solomon. *On Severn Rd, drive up to property between fire & police station.* Sat 16, Sun 17 July (2-5). Adm £4, chd free. Cream teas. Also open Welshpool Oak Cottage.
The garden must have been created when the house was built in 1841 and consists of a drive from the road, lawns and flower beds, many replanted and a large vegetable

garden and orchard. Small woodland planted 35yrs ago, adjacent area planted with native trees 2yrs ago. 3 greenhouses. Refreshments served on the lawn or in the old scullery. Flat gravel paths.

51 WELSHPOOL, OAK COTTAGE

23 High Street, Welshpool SY21 7JP. Tony Harvey. *Entered from Bowling Green Lane which runs parallel to the High St in centre of Welshpool.* Sun 27, Mon 28 Mar, Sun 1, Mon 2 May (2-5). Tea. Sat 16, Sun 17 July (2-5). Also open Welshpool Elmhurst. Adm £3, chd free.
Revamped during the last 2yrs this is a plantsman's small and hidden garden providing an oasis of green in the town centre. Gravel paths and stepping stones meander through a wide variety of plants, incl unusual species. Alpines are a favourite (more enthusiasm than knowledge!) Gravel paths and steep slope at entrance.

52 1 YSTRAD HOUSE

1 Church Road, Knighton LD7 1EB. John & Margaret Davis, 01547 528 154, jamdavis@ystradhouse.plus.com. *At junction of Church Rd & Station Rd. 225yds along Station Rd (488 Clun) opp Knighton Hotel. Yellow House at junction with Church Rd.* Sat 4, Sun 5 June, Sat 13, Sun 14 Aug (2-5.30). Adm £3.50, chd free. Home-made teas. **Visits also by arrangement May to Sept.**
An unsuspected town garden hidden behind Ystrad House, a Regency villa of earlier origins. Developed over the last 10yrs with an emphasis on tranquility and timelessness: having broad lawns and wide borders, mature trees and more intimate features adding interest and surprise. The formal areas merge with wooded glades leading to a riverside walk alongside the Teme. Featured in Mid Wales Journal, Hereford Times and Ludlow Advertiser. Lawns and gravelled paths mostly flat except access to riverside walk.

Early Openings 2017
Plan your garden visiting well ahead – put these dates in your 2017 diary!

Gardens across the country open from early January onwards – before the next year's guide is published – with glorious displays of colour including hellebores, aconites, snowdrops and carpets of spring bulbs.

Berkshire
Sun 19 February (2-4.30)
Oak Cottage

Cheshire & Wirral
Sun 26 February (1-3)
Bucklow Farm

Cumbria
Sun 19 February (11-4.30)
Summerdale House

Derbyshire
By arrangement in February
Highfield House

Devon
Sun 26 February (2-5)
Higher Cherubeer

Gloucestershire
Sun 29 January, Sun 12 February (11-4)
Home Farm
Sun 12, Sun 19 February (11-5)
Trench Hill

Hampshire
Sun 19, Mon 20, Tue 21 February (2-5)
Little Court

Herefordshire
Thurs 2, 9, 16, 23 February (9-4)
Ivy Croft

Kent
Sun 12 February (12-4)
Copton Ash
Sat 4, Sun 5 February (11-3)
Knowle Hill Farm
Sun 19, Sun 26 February (2-5)
Mere House
By arrangement in February
The Old Rectory
By arrangement in February
Spring Platt

Lancashire, Merseyside & Greater Manchester
Sun 12, 19, 26 February (12-4)
Weeping Ash Garden

Lincolnshire
Sat 25, Sun 26 February (11-4)
21 Chapel Street

Northamptonshire
Sun 26 February (12-4)
Jericho

Oxfordshire
Sun 19 February (1.30-4)
Hollyhocks

Somerset, Bristol & South Gloucestershire
Sun 19 February (10-5)
East Lambrook Manor Gardens
Sun 5, Sun 12 February (11-4)
Rock House
Sun 12, Mon 13 February (11-4)
Sherborne Garden

Surrey
Sun 12 February (11-4)
Gatton Park

Wiltshire
Sat 25 February (10.30-5.30)
Lacock Abbey Gardens

Yorkshire
Wed 22 February (12-4)
Austwick Hall
By arrangement 14 to 21 February
3 Bainton Close
Sun 19 February (11-5)
Devonshire Mill

Gatton Park, Surrey

© Leigh Clapp

Garden Index

This index lists gardens alphabetically and gives the page number on which they are to be found.

Accommodation available at NGS Gardens

We feature here a list of NGS gardens offering accommodation, listed by county. You will find contact details in the garden listing.

We are happy to provide this list to help you find accommodation, however please note:

The NGS has no statutory control over the establishments or their methods of operating. The NGS cannot become involved in legal or contractual matters and cannot get involved in seeking financial recompense. All liability for loss, disappointment, negligence or other damage is hereby excluded.

Bedfordshire
Luton Hoo Hotel Golf & Spa

Berkshire
Field Farm Cottage
Littlecote House Hotel
Rookwood Farm House
Sunningdale Park

Buckinghamshire
9 Brookside, Lillingstone Lovell Gardens
Danesfield House
Glebe Farm, Lillingstone Lovell Gardens
Magnolia House, Grange Drive Wooburn
Nether Winchendon House
Westend House

Cambridgeshire
57 Cakebreade Cottage, Orwell Gardens
Chequer Cottage, Streetly End Gardens
Ferrar House
39 Foster Road
Madingley Hall

Carmarthenshire & Pembrokeshire
Blaenfforest
Dyffryn Fernant
Ffynone Mansion
The Old Vicarage
Picton Castle & Gardens
Talardd
Upton Castle Gardens

Cheshire & Wirral
Tatton Park

Cornwall
Boconnoc
Bonython Manor
Carminowe Valley Garden
Cosawes Barton
Creed House & Creed Lodge
Eden Project
Hidden Valley Gardens
The Homestead Woodland Garden & Tearoom
Meudon Hotel
Tregoose
Trelissick
Trereife Park
Trerice

Cumbria
Askham Hall
Braeside
Broom Cottage
Eller How House
Lakeside Hotel & Rocky Bank
Matson Ground
Rydal Hall
Swarthmoor Hall
Windy Hall

Derbyshire
Cascades Gardens
Tissington Hall

Devon
Avenue Cottage
Fursdon
Higher Ash Farm, Ash Gardens
Hotel Endsleigh
Lake Farmhouse, Sheepwash Gardens
Regency House
Shapcott Barton Estate
Southcombe Gardens
West Down House
Whitstone Bluebells
Whitstone Farm

Dorset
Deans Court
Domineys Yard
Farrs
Marren
Old Down House
The Secret Garden

Essex
Horkesley Hall
Rookwoods

Glamorgan
1 Ashgrove, Dinas Powys
Bryn-y-Ddafad
Mehefin, Llanmaes Gardens
Slade

Gloucestershire
Barnsley House
Berrys Place Farm
Matara Gardens of Wellbeing
Oakwood Farm Plant Fair and Garden
Snugborough Mill, Blockley Gardens
Wells Cottage

Gwent
Castle House
Middle Ninfa Farm & Bunkhouse
Penpergwm Lodge
Usk Open Gardens

Gwynedd & Anglesey
Plas Cadnant Hidden Gardens

Hampshire
12 Christchurch Road
Durmast House
Tylney Hall Hotel

Herefordshire

Brobury House Gardens
Caves Folly Nurseries
Coddington Vineyard
Kentchurch Court, Kentchurch
  Gardens
Lawless Hill
Little Llanavon
Midland Farm
Montpelier Cottage
The Old Rectory, Thruxton
Perrycroft
Rhodds Farm

Isle of Wight

Clatterford House
The Clifton
The Havelock
Northcourt Manor Gardens

Kent

Boldshaves
Canterbury Cathedral Gardens
Port Lympne, The Aspinall
  Foundation
Rock Farm
The Secret Gardens of Sandwich
  at The Salutation
Sissinghurst Castle Garden

Lancashire, Merseyside & Greater Manchester

Mill Barn
Milntown
The Ridges
The Secret Valley
Sefton Villa, Sefton Park Gardens

Leicestershire & Rutland

Hill Top Farm, Braunston Gardens
Tresillian House

Lincolnshire

Doddington Hall Gardens
Goltho House
Gunby Hall & Gardens
Hall Farm
Hope House
Manor House
Marigold Cottage

London

28 Old Devonshire Road
West Lodge Park

Norfolk

Bagthorpe Hall
Chapel Cottage
Chaucer Barn
Hindringham Hall
Narborough Hall
Oxnead Hall
Severals Grange

North East

Bichfield Tower
Broaches Farm
Cotherstone Village Gardens
Crook Hall & Gardens
Fallodon Hall
Gibside
Ingram House
Loughbrow House
Mindrum Garden
Romaldkirk Gardens
Whalton Manor Gardens

North East Wales

Aberclwyd Manor
Bodysgallen Hall & Spa
Dove Cottage
Plas Coch
Tal-y-Bryn Farm

Northamptonshire

Dale House, Spratton Gardens
Hodsock Priory Gardens
Patchings Art Centre

Oxfordshire

Gowers Close, Sibford Gower
  Gardens
Old Swan & Minster Mill
Ruskin College, Headington
  Gardens

Powys

Aberangell, The Old Coach House
Beili Neuadd
Broadheath House
Caer Beris Manor Hotel
Cyfie Farm
Esgair Angell
Glan yr Afon
Glanusk Estate Garden
Gliffaes Country House Hotel
Grandma's Garden
Gregynog Hall & Garden
Powis Castle Garden
Tinto House
Tyn y Cwm
1 Ystrad House

Shropshire

Brownhill House
The Citadel
Edge Villa
Goldstone Hall Gardens
Sambrook Manor
Shoothill House
Upper Shelderton House
Walcot Hall
Wollaston Lodge

Somerset, Bristol & South Gloucestershire

Bath Priory Hotel
Cherry Bolberry Farm
Church Farm House
Goblin Combe House
Honeyhurst Farm
Jacob's Loft, Glastonbury Secret
  Gardens
Model Farm
Penny Brohn Cancer Care
Sole Retreat
Stoberry Garden
Ston Easton Park

Staffordshire, Birmingham & West Midlands

Colour Mill
Grafton Cottage
The Trentham Estate

Suffolk

Bays Farm
Cattishall Farmhouse
Drinkstone Park
Leaven Hall

Surrey

Barnett Hill
7 Rose Lane

Sussex

Ashdown Park Hotel
The Beeches
Butlers Farmhouse
Copyhold Hollow
Dittons End
Follers Manor
The Folly
Gravetye Manor
Holly House
King John's Lodge
Lordington House
The Middle House, Mayfield
  Gardens
Newtimber Place
South Grange
Stane House
West Dean Gardens
Worth Abbey & Grounds

Warwickshire

The Granary
Springfield House, Warmington
  Village Gardens

Wiltshire

Dauntsey Park, Dauntsey Gardens
Lynchetts, Bradford on Avon
  Gardens
The Manor House, Castle Combe
North Cottage
The Pound House
Stourhead Garden

Worcestershire

Chasewood, Hanley Swan NGS
  Gardens
The Dell House
Holland House
Meadow Bank, Hanley Swan NGS
  Gardens
Nafford House, Eckington Gardens
Rectory Cottage, Alvechurch
  Gardens

Yorkshire

Austwick Hall
Basin Howe Farm
Cold Cotes

Devonshire Mill
Dowthorpe Hall & Horse Pasture
  Cottage
Fawley House
Goldsborough Hall
Greenwick Farm
Havoc Hall
Hillside
Low Hall, Dacre Banks &
  Summerbridge Gardens
Low Sutton, Sutton Gardens
Manor Farm
Millgate House
Shandy Hall Gardens
Sutton Grange, Sutton Gardens
Thornycroft

Askham Hall, Cumbria

Garden Visiting Around the World

The National Gardens Scheme is without doubt the largest and oldest of its type in the world but there are others in existence. So if you are heading off on holiday and a passionate garden visitor here are the details of other schemes that you can support.

America

GARDEN CONSERVANCY
W www.gardenconservancy.org
Saving and sharing outstanding America Gardens. Visit America's very best rarely seen private gardens. Open Days is a national program of The Garden Conservancy, a non-profit organisation that saves and shares outstanding American gardens for the education and inspiration of the public.

VIRGINIA'S HISTORIC GARDEN WEEK
April 23-30 2016
W www.vagardenweek.org
Each spring visitors are welcomed to over 250 of Virginia's most beautiful gardens, homes and historic landmarks during "America's Largest Open House." This 8-day state-wide event provides visitors a unique opportunity to see unforgettable gardens at the peak of Virginia's springtime colour, as well as beautiful houses sparkling with over 2,000 flower arrangements created by Garden Club of Virginia members. Tour proceeds fund the restoration and preservation of Virginia's historic gardens, and provide graduate level research fellowships for building comprehensive and ongoing records of historic gardens and landscapes in the Commonwealth, and support the mission of the Garden Club of Virginia.

Belgium

Publication Catalogue of private Belgian Open Gardens, published annually in March Contact Dominique Petit-Heymans
E info@jardinsouverts.be
W www.jardinsouverts.be
A non-profit organization founded in 1994. Over 200 remarkable private gardens throughout Belgium open to members. Membership (for two people) of €25 entitles you to the full colour yearly agenda, comprising photographs, descriptions, opening dates and access plans of the gardens. Most of the proceeds from the gardens. The philosophy of the gardens owners is to invite visitors to discover gardens of quality, of all kinds and sizes.

France

JARDINS ET SANTE
E contact@jardins-sante.org
W www.jardins-sante.org
Founded in 2004, Jardins et Santé is a charitable voluntary association with humanitarian aims. Increasing numbers of gardens open each year across many regions of France. Entry often includes guided tours, exhibitions and concerts. Funds raised from visitor entry fees help finance scientific research in the field of mental illness and also contribute to developing the therapeutic role of the garden, particularly in hospitals and care centres. Every two years the Charity receives appeals from establishments seeking assistance in the creation of their healing gardens.150 appeals were tendered in 201, and we are happy to be able to contribute towards many of these projects. Our role as information hub for the growing interest, research and activities in the field of hortitherapy is rapidly gaining momentum. Our 5th Symposium held under the patronage of the French Ministry of Environment, will take place in Paris in 2016. Further details can be found on our website.

Japan

THE N.G.S. JAPAN
Contact Tamie Taniguchi
E tamieta@syd.odn.ne.jp
W www.ngs-jp.org
The N.G.S. Japan was founded in 2001. Most of the proceeds from the entry fees support children's and welfare charities as nominated by owners and garden conservation with Japanese flowers. It has run a series of lectures entitled 'Lifestyle & Gardening with Charity with British life culture since 2004.

Netherlands

Publication Open Tuinen Gids, published annually in March
E info@tuinenstichting.nl
W www.tuinenstichting.nl
Over 300 selected private gardens from all over Holland open on behalf of the Dutch Garden Society. This is a not-for profit organisation which was founded in 1980 to protect and restore Dutch gardening heritage consisting of gardens, public parks, urban spaces and cemeteries . https://www.youtube.com/watch?v=q QqUeN4GcWc

New Zealand

E valeside@xtra.co.nz
W www.gardenstovisit.co.nz
Welcome to Gardens to Visit in New Zealand. A site that lists private/public and International Gardens along with garden events. If you have a garden or an event that you would like to list please contact me. This site lists formal gardens, tropical gardens, vegetable gardens, and 'many other garden designs and venues for Weddings, Accommodation, Plant sales, Other sales (gifts, garden art), Cafe/Restaurant and Functions.

Scotland

SCOTLAND'S GARDENS
Publication Scotland's Gardens Guide
T 0131 226 3714
E info@scotlandsgardens.org
W www.scotlandsgardens.org
Founded in 1931 Scotland's Gardens facilitates the opening of Scotland's finest gardens of all sizes and kinds to the public as a means of raising money for charity. 40% of the funds raised goes to charities nominated by each garden owner whilst 60% net goes to the Scotland's Gardens beneficiaries: Maggie's Cancer Caring Centres, The Queen's Nursing Institute Scotland, The Gardens Fund of The National Trust for Scotland and Perennial.

Plant Heritage
National Council for the Conservation of Plants & Gardens

NCCPG

Nearly 80 gardens that open for The National Gardens Scheme are guardians of a Plant Heritage National Plant Collection®, although this may not always be noted in the garden description. These gardens carry the **NPC** symbol.
The county that appears after the garden name indicates the section of the book where the entry can be found.

Plant Heritage 12 Home Farm, Loseley Park, Guildford, Surrey GU3 1HS. Tel: 01483 447540 Website: www.plantheritage.com

ACER (EXCL. PALMATUM CVS.)
Blagdon
North East

AGAPANTHUS - FAIRWEATHER NURSERY TRIALS COLLECTION (HORTICULTURAL)
Fairweather's Nursery
Hampshire

ALNUS
Blagdon
North East

ANEMONE NEMOROSA
Avondale Nursery
Warwickshire

Kingston Lacy
Dorset

ARALIACEAE
Meon Orchard
Hampshire

ARBUTUS
Barton House
Warwickshire

ARUNCUS
Windy Hall
Cumbria

ASPLENIUM SCOLOPENDRIUM
Sizergh Castle
Cumbria

ASTER & RELATED GENERA (AUTUMN FLOWERING)
The Picton Garden
Herefordshire

ASTER NOVAE-ANGLIAE
Avondale Nursery
Warwickshire

ASTILBE
Holehird Gardens
Cumbria

ASTILBE
Marwood Hill Garden
Devon

BRUNNERA
Hearns House
Oxfordshire

BUDDLEJA DAVIDII CVS. & HYBRIDS
Shapcott Barton Estate
Devon

CAMELLIAS & RHODODENDRONS INTRODUCED TO HELIGAN PRE-1920
The Lost Gardens of Heligan
Cornwall

CARPINUS
Sir Harold Hillier Gardens
Hampshire

CARPINUS BETULUS CVS.
West Lodge Park
London

CATALPA
Barton House
Warwickshire

CEANOTHUS
Eccleston Square
London

CERCIDIPHYLLUM
Hodnet Hall Gardens
Shropshire

Sir Harold Hillier Gardens
Hampshire

CHRYSANTHEMUM (KOREAN, RUBELLUM & HARDY SPRAY)
Hill Close Gardens
Warwickshire

CLEMATIS VITICELLA CVS.
Roseland House
Cornwall

CONVALLARIA
Kingston Lacy
Dorset

CORIARIA
Crûg Farm
Gwynedd & Anglesey

CORNUS
Sir Harold Hillier Gardens
Hampshire

CORNUS (EXCL. C. FLORIDA CVS.)
Newby Hall & Gardens
Yorkshire

CORYLUS
Sir Harold Hillier Gardens
Hampshire

COTINUS
Bath Priory Hotel
Somerset, Bristol & South Gloucestershire

COTONEASTER
Sir Harold Hillier Gardens
Hampshire

CYCLAMEN (EXCL. PERSICUM CVS.)
Higher Cherubeer
Devon

CYDONIA OBLONGA
Norton Priory Museum & Gardens
Cheshire & Wirral

CYSTOPTERIS
Sizergh Castle
Cumbria

DABOECIA
Holehird Gardens
Cumbria

DAHLIA
Varfell Farm
Cornwall

DESCHAMPSIA
The Walled Gardens of Cannington
Somerset, Bristol & South Gloucestershire

DICENTRA
Boundary Cottage
Yorkshire

DIGITALIS
The Harris Garden
Berkshire

DRYOPTERIS
Sizergh Castle
Cumbria

**ERICA & CALLUNA –
SUSSEX HEATHER CVS.**
Nymans
Sussex

EUCALYPTUS
Meon Orchard
Hampshire

EUCALYPTUS SPP.
The World Garden at Lullingstone
Castle
Kent

EUCRYPHIA
Whitstone Farm
Devon

EUONYMUS (DECIDUOUS)
The Place for Plants, East Bergholt
Place Garden
Suffolk

EUPHORBIA
University of Oxford Botanic Garden
Oxfordshire

EUPHORBIA (HARDY)
Firvale Allotment Garden
Yorkshire

FRAXINUS
The Lovell Quinta Arboretum
Cheshire & Wirral

**GERANIUM SYLVATICUM &
RENARDII - FORMS, CVS. &
HYBRIDS**
Wren's Nest
Cheshire & Wirral

GEUM
1 Brickwall Cottages
Kent

GUNNERA
The Mowle
Norfolk

HAMAMELIS
Sir Harold Hillier Gardens
Hampshire

HEDERA
Ivybank, Pebworth Gardens
Warwickshire

HELIOTROPIUM
Hampton Court Palace
London

**HELIOTROPIUM
ARBORESCENS CVS.**
The Homestead
Leicestershire & Rutland

HEMEROCALLIS
Antony
Cornwall

**HEPATICA SPP. & CVS.
(EXCL. H NOBILIS VAR.
JAPONICA CVS.)**
Hazelwood Farm
Cumbria

**HILLIERS (PLANTS RAISED
BY)**
Sir Harold Hillier Gardens
Hampshire

HOHERIA
Abbotsbury Gardens
Dorset

HOSTA
Cleave House
Devon

**HOSTA (EUROPEAN AND
ASIATIC)**
Hanging Hosta Garden
Hampshire

HYPERICUM
Sir Harold Hillier Gardens
Hampshire

**IRIS TALL BEARDED
RAISED BY BRYAN
DODSWORTH**
Marshgate House
Norfolk

JUGLANS
Upton Wold
Gloucestershire

LABURNUM
Powis Castle Garden
Powys

LANTANA
Hampton Court Palace
London

**LAPAGERIA ROSEA (&
NAMED CVS.)**
Roseland House
Cornwall

**LEUCANTHEMUM X
SUPERBUM
(CHRYSANTHEMUM
MAXIMUM)**
Shapcott Barton Estate
Devon

LEWISIA
'John's Garden' at Ashwood
Nurseries
Staffordshire, Birmingham & West
Midlands

LIGUSTRUM
Sir Harold Hillier Gardens
Hampshire

LITHOCARPUS
Sir Harold Hillier Gardens
Hampshire

**MALUS (CVS. FROM NOTTS
& DERBY, LINCS, LEICS &
YORKS)**
Clumber Park Walled Kitchen Garden
Nottinghamshire

MALUS (ORNAMENTAL)
Barnards Farm
Essex

**MECONOPSIS (LARGE
PERENNIAL SPP. &
HYBRIDS)**
Holehird Gardens
Cumbria

**MENTHA - UK CULTIVATED
MINTS IN POTS**
Canalia, Adderbury Gardens
Oxfordshire

METASEQUOIA
Sir Harold Hillier Gardens
Hampshire

MONARDA
Glyn Bach Gardens
Carmarthenshire & Pembrokeshire

Hole's Meadow
Devon

MUSCARI
16 Witton Lane
Norfolk

NEPETA
Hole's Meadow
Devon

**NERINE - HARDY SPP.,
CVS., & HYBRIDS**
Bickham Cottage
Devon

NERINE SARNIENSIS CVS.
Bickham Cottage
Devon

OMPHALODES
Hearns House
Oxfordshire

OSMUNDA
Sizergh Castle
Cumbria

PARIS
Crûg Farm
Gwynedd & Anglesey

PATRINIA
The Hyde
Hampshire

PELARGONIUM
Ivybank, Pebworth Gardens
Warwickshire

PENNISETUM
Knoll Gardens
Dorset

PENSTEMON
Froggery Cottage
Northamptonshire

Kingston Maurward Gardens and
Animal Park
Dorset

PHLOMIS
Foamlea
Devon

PHOTINIA
Sir Harold Hillier Gardens
Hampshire

PINUS (EXCL DWARF CVS.)
Sir Harold Hillier Gardens
Hampshire

PINUS SPP.
The Lovell Quinta Arboretum
Cheshire & Wirral

PLATANUS
Broadview Gardens
Kent

**PODOCARPUS & RELATED
PODOCARPACEAE**
Meon Orchard
Hampshire

POLYGONATUM
Crûg Farm
Gwynedd & Anglesey

POLYSTICHUM
Holehird Gardens
Cumbria

**PRIMULA AURICULA
(BORDER)**
Blaencwm Cottage
Carmarthenshire & Pembrokeshire

PTEROCARYA
Upton Wold
Gloucestershire

**QUEEN MARY II EXOTICKS
COLLECTION**
Hampton Court Palace
London

QUERCUS
Chevithorne Barton
Devon

Sir Harold Hillier Gardens
Hampshire

RHAPIS SPP. & CVS.
Gwyndy Bach
Gwynedd & Anglesey

RHEUM (CULINARY CVS.)
Clumber Park Walled Kitchen Garden
Nottinghamshire

**RHODODENDRON (GHENT
AZALEAS)**
Sheffield Park and Garden
Sussex

RODGERSIA
The Gate House
Devon

ROSA (RAMBLING)
Moor Wood
Gloucestershire

SALVIA (TENDER)
Kingston Maurward Gardens and
Animal Park
Dorset

SANGUISORBA
Avondale Nursery
Warwickshire

**SAXIFRAGA SECT.
LIGULATAE: SPP. & CVS.**
Waterperry Gardens
Oxfordshire

**SAXIFRAGA SUBSECT.
KABSCHIA & ENGLERIA**
Waterperry Gardens
Oxfordshire

**SIBERIAN IRIS CVS:
BRITISH, AWARD WINNERS
& HISTORICALLY
SIGNIFICANT**
Aulden Farm, Aulden Arts and
Gardens
Herefordshire

SORBUS
Blagdon
North East

Ness Botanic Gardens
Cheshire & Wirral

**STERN, SIR F (PLANTS
SELECTED BY)**
Highdown Gardens
Sussex

STEWARTIA - ASIAN SPP.
High Beeches Woodland and Water
Garden
Sussex

**STYRACACEAE (INCL
HALESIA, PTEROSTYRAX,
STYRAX, SINOJACKIA)**
Holker Hall Gardens
Cumbria

TAXODIUM SPP. & CVS.
West Lodge Park
London

YUCCA
Renishaw Hall & Gardens
Derbyshire

Waterperry Gardens, Oxfordshire

© Andrew Lawson

Acknowledgements

Each year the NGS receives fantastic support from the community of garden photographers who donate and make available images of gardens. The NGS would like to thank them for their generous donations.

We also thank the garden owners who have kindly submitted images of their gardens.

Unless otherwise stated, photographs are kindly supplied by permission of the garden owner.

The 2016 Production Team: Elna Broe, Linda Ellis, Rosalind Ellis, Louise Grainger, Rachel Hick, Kali Masure, Chris Morley, Azam Parkar, George Plumptre, Jane Sennett, Georgina Waters, Debbie Wilson. With special thanks to our NGS County Volunteers.

CONSTABLE
First published in Great Britain in 2016 by Constable
Copyright © The National Gardens Scheme 2016

A CIP catalogue record for this book is available from the British Library.
ISBN 9-781472-124234
ISSN 1365-0572
EAN 9 781905 942008

Designed by Level Partnership Ltd
Maps by Mary Spence © Global Mapping and XYZ Maps
Typeset in Helvetica Neue by Chat Noir Design
Printed and bound in Italy by Rotolito Lombarda

Constable
is an imprint of
Little, Brown Book Group
Carmelite House
50 Victoria Embankment
London EC4Y ODZ

An Hachette UK Company
www.hachette.co.uk
www.littlebrown.co.uk

If you require this information in alternative formats, please telephone 01483 211535 or email ngs@ngs.org.uk

The Society of Garden Designers

Members of The Society of Garden Designers participating in the NGS in 2016.

Fellow of the Society of Garden Designers (FSGD) is awarded to Members for exceptional contributions to the Society or to the profession

Rosemary Alexander FSGD
John Brookes MBE, FSGD
Sally Court FSGD
Andrew Fisher Tomlin FSGD
Roderick Griffin FSGD
Lucy Huntington FSGD
Ian Kitson FSGD
Robin Templar-Williams FSGD
Julie Toll FSGD

Member of the Society of Garden Designers (MSGD) is awarded after passing adjudication

Timothy Carless MSGD
Cheryl Cummings MSGD
Chris Eves MSGD
Jill Fenwick MSGD
Julia Fogg MSGD
Paul Hensey MSGD
Joanna Herald MSGD
Thomas Hoblyn MSGD
Barbara Hunt MSGD (retired)
Dawn Isaac MSGD
Barry Kellington MSGD
Arabella Lennox-Boyd MSGD
Chris Parsons MSGD
Dan Pearson MSGD
Emma Plunket MSGD
Debbie Roberts MSGD
Charles Rutherfoord MSGD
Ian Smith MSGD
Tom Stuart-Smith MSGD
Sue Townsend MSGD
Roger Webster MSGD
Cleve West MSGD

Pre-Registered Member is a member working towards gaining Registered Membership

Tamara Bridge
Fiona Cadwallader
Wendy Cartwright
Anna Dargavel
Anoushka Feiler
Sara Gadd
Fiona Green
Louise Hardwick
Darren Hawkes
Hilary May
Sarah Murch
Faith Ramsay
Virginia von Celsing
Jo Ward-Ellison
Alison Wear
Julia Whiteaway
Joanne Winn
Rebecca Winship
Susan Young

SCOTLAND'S GARDENS

GARDENS OPEN FOR CHARITY

Charity No SC011337

OPEN FOR DISCOVERY

T: 0131 226 3714
WWW.SCOTLANDSGARDENS.ORG

For the Love of Gardens

Have you enjoyed visiting our gardens? Or perhaps you have enjoyed opening your garden, welcoming visitors and raising money for the National Gardens Scheme? If you have, then it is likely you know that the money we raise goes to a group of nursing and caring charities. Alternatively, perhaps you are a garden lover who might like to support us.

We make the link between people's love of gardens and the vital work our beneficiaries do. We need all the help we can get to ensure we give them as much as possible.

If you would like to help us extend the support we give to our beneficiaries, you might consider making a gift in your will to the National Gardens Scheme. Any gift, large or small, is of great significance. To find out more please call Kali Masure on 01483 213907, or have a look at our website:
www.ngs.org.uk/leaveagift